A Powerful Learning Tool

You can use *Learning Biological Psychology* to enhance your understanding of this book in a variety of ways.

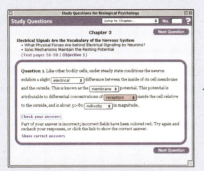

Reinforce your knowledge of the chapter material through a variety of targeted study questions.

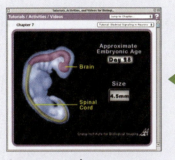

Learn complex concepts and processes through animated tutorials and videos.

LEARNING *Biological Psychology*

3 *Neurophysiology: Conduction, Transmission, and Integration of Neural Signals*

- Objectives
- Study Questions
- Tutorials/Activities
- Terminology Quiz
- Multiple Choice Quiz
- Glossary

Chapter Summary:
Electrical signals are the vocabulary of the nervous system. This chapter describes the basic mechanisms by which nerve cells conduct nerve impulses and how chemical signals move across the synaptic gaps between neurons. It then considers how neurons and synapses combine to make neural circuits.

Chapter Outline: Expand | Collapse

▶ **Electrical Signals Are the Vocabulary of the Nervous System**
Tutorial: Electrical Signaling in Neurons
- What Physical Forces Are behind Electrical Signaling by Neurons?
- Ionic Mechanisms Maintain the Resting Potential
  Objective 1 / Study questions: 1|2|3|4|5|6
- A Threshold Amount of Depolarization Triggers an Action Potential
- Ionic Mechanisms Underlie the Action Potential
  Objective 2 / Study questions: 7|8|9|10|11|12|13|14|15|16|17|18
- How Can We Study Ion Channels?
  Objective 3 / Study questions: 19|20|21|22
- Nerve Impulses Are Actively Propagated Down the Axon
  Objective 4 / Study questions: 23|24|25|26|27
- In Synaptic Transmission the Activity of Presynaptic Axon Terminals Elicits Postsynaptic Potentials
- Box 3.1 Electrical Synapses Work with No Time Delay
  Objective 5 / Study questions: 28|29|30|31|32|33
- Temporal Summation and Spatial Summation Integrate Synaptic Inputs.
  Objective 6 / Study questions: 34|35|36|37|38

▶ **The Sequence of Transmission Processes at Chemical Synapses**
Tutorial: Synaptic Transmission

Use the interactive terminology quiz to learn key terms from each chapter.

Test your grasp of the material with comprehensive self-quizzing.

Tutorials, Activities, and Videos for Biologi...

Tutorials / Activities / Videos   Jump to Chapter...

Chapter 3   Tutorial: Synaptic Transmission

INTRODUCTION | ANIMATION | CONCLUSION | QUIZ

Myelin
Axon terminal
Mitochondrion
Ca²⁺ channel
Ca²⁺ ions
Synaptic vesicle
Transmitter molecules
Synaptic cleft
Receptors
Postsynaptic cell

REWIND | STOP | PLAY | ◀ PREV | NEXT ▶   3 / 9

When the axon terminal is depolarized, voltage-gated calcium channels open, and calcium ions rush into the axon terminal. Some of the calcium ions bind to a protein on the synaptic vesicle membrane called synaptotagmin.

Link directly from the chapter outline to related tutorials and activities.

Biological Psychology

DON JUAN: . . . Will you not agree with me
. . . that it is inconceivable that Life,
having once produced [birds],
should, if love and beauty were her
object, start off on another line
and labor at the clumsy elephant
and hideous ape, whose grandchildren
we are?

THE DEVIL: You conclude then, that Life
was driving at clumsiness and
ugliness?

DON JUAN: No, perverse devil that you
are, a thousand times no. Life was
driving at brains—at its darling
object: an organ by which it can
attain not only self-consciousness
but self-understanding.

George Bernard Shaw
Man and Superman, Act III

The brain is wider than the sky,
   For, put them side by side,
The one the other will include
   With ease, and you beside.

The brain is deeper than the sea,
   For, hold them, blue to blue,
The one the other will absorb,
   As sponges, buckets do.

The brain is just the weight of God,
   For, lift them, pound for pound,
And they will differ, if they do,
   As syllable from sound.

Emily Dickinson

Biological Psychology

AN INTRODUCTION TO BEHAVIORAL, COGNITIVE, AND CLINICAL NEUROSCIENCE

Third Edition

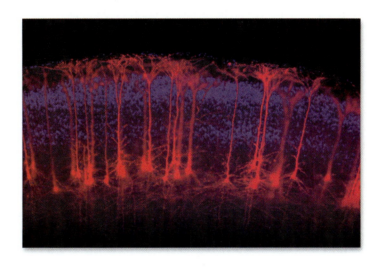

Mark R. Rosenzweig
UNIVERSITY OF CALIFORNIA, BERKELEY

S. Marc Breedlove
MICHIGAN STATE UNIVERSITY

Arnold L. Leiman
LATE, UNIVERSITY OF CALIFORNIA, BERKELEY

Sinauer Associates, Inc. • PUBLISHERS
SUNDERLAND, MASSACHUSETTS

About the Cover

Double-exposure micrograph of somatosensory cortex in a 6-day-old rat (see Chapters 7 and 8). Cortical tissue was stained with the fluorescent blue nuclear (DNA) stain bisBENZIMIDE and photographed with an ultraviolet filter (purple cells). Pyramidal cells with cell bodies in Layer V were labeled with the fluorescent neuronal tracer DiI and photographed with a Rhodamine filter (red cells). The pyramidal cells' apical dendrites (thick processes) span the thickness of the cortex and terminate in Layer I at the top of the image. At the bottom of the image, their axons (thin processes) are seen extending into the subcortical white matter, where they project to the thalamus. Courtesy of Brad Miller, Washington University School of Medicine, St. Louis, MO.

Biological Psychology, Third Edition

Copyright © 2002 by Sinauer Associates, Inc.
All rights reserved. This book may not be reproduced in whole or in part
without permission from the publisher.

For information, address Sinauer Associates, 23 Plumtree Road, Sunderland, MA 01375 U.S.A.
FAX: 413-549-1118
E-mail: publish@sinauer.com
Internet: www.sinauer.com

Library of Congress Cataloging-in-Publication Data

Rosenzweig, Mark R.
   Biological psychology : an introduction to behavioral, cognitive, and clinical
neuroscience / Mark R. Rosenzweig, S. Marc Breedlove, Arnold L. Leiman.--3rd ed.
     p. cm.
   Includes bibliographical references and index.
   ISBN 0-87893-709-9
   1. Psychobiology. I. Breedlove, S. Marc. II. Leiman, Arnold L. III. Title.

QP360 .R658 2001
612.8--dc21

                                           2001042684

5 4 3

We dedicate this book affectionately to our wives, children, and grandchildren.
We appreciate their support and patience over the years of this project.

M.R.R.			S.M.B.
Janine			*Cindy*
Anne *Jim*	*Suzanne* *Kent*	*Philip* *Laura*	*Ben Nick Tessa Kit*
	Lauren *David* *Gregory* *Elise*	*Thomas* *Caroline*	

Arnold L. Leiman
July 5, 1932–January 5, 2000

With fond memories and deep appreciation, we pay tribute to our friend and colleague Arnie Leiman. It was our privilege to collaborate with him over many years, including the initial planning of this edition of our textbook.

Arnie joined the faculty at the University of California at Berkeley in 1964 and served as Professor of Psychology for 36 years. During his wide-ranging scientific career, he studied the emergence of connections in the developing brain; sleeping and dreaming; memory; and the effects of brain damage on behavior in organisms ranging from crayfish to human beings. He was renowned for his encyclopedic knowledge of biological psychology and related fields.

Known as a kind and caring professor, Arnie developed popular undergraduate and graduate courses at Berkeley dealing with human brain disorders. He inspired countless undergraduate and graduate students, who recall Arnie's masterful lectures laced with his trademark Bronx-bred humor, his genuine concern for his students, and his encouragement to all to follow their dreams.

In addition to his contributions as a scientist and teacher, Arnie served in important administrative positions related to the improvement of higher education, including serving as Director of the Center for Studies in Higher Education at Berkeley.

Arnie's many contributions to the University were recognized in 1990 with the Berkeley Campus Distinguished Teaching Award, and in 1999 with the Berkeley Citation, the highest honor bestowed on faculty members.

Arnie's passion for life was nurtured and sustained by a loving partnership of 32 years with his wife Lannon and by the devotion of their children, Jessica and Timothy. Family, friends, colleagues, and generations of students deeply miss Arnie's zest for living, his sharp wit, his unfailing wisdom, and his enduring compassion.

MARK R. ROSENZWEIG
S. MARC BREEDLOVE

Brief Contents

Contents

PART 1: Biological Foundations of Behavior

PART 2: Evolution and Development of the Nervous System

PART 3: *Perception and Action*

Chapter 13 *Homeostasis: Active Regulation of Internal States* 399

Chapter 14 *Biological Rhythms, Sleep, and Dreaming* 433

PART 5: Emotions and Mental Disorders

PART 6: Cognitive Neuroscience

Chapter 18 Learning and Memory: Neural Mechanisms 571

Chapter 19 Language and Cognition 607

Preface

As we write, the cover story of a newsmagazine proclaims that stem-cell research offers hope for cures for neurological disorders such as Alzheimer's disease and Parkinson's disease. In a TV interview a neuroscientist says she has taken up jogging because her research with laboratory rodents shows that exercise increases the production of new brain cells. A newspaper story reports that many teenage Americans suffer hearing deficits caused by exposure to loud sounds such as rock music, lawn mowers, and fireworks. Other recent news articles have dealt with the following questions:

- Can genetic treatments improve memory?
- Does strong liking for sweet foods involve the same brain mechanisms as addiction to drugs?
- Do brain responses during emotions vary with personality?
- Does a gene that predisposes for Alzheimer's disease impair memory even in those who do not develop the disease?

These are important questions, but the basic issues they address and the research being conducted to answer them cannot be reduced to "sound bites." A meaningful approach to questions like these requires an understanding of the bodily systems that underlie behavior and experience. Our aim in *Biological Psychology* is to provide a foundation that places these and other important problems in a unified scientific context.

This book explores the biological bases of our experience and behavior: the ways in which bodily states and processes produce and control behavior and cognition, and—just as important—the ways in which behavior, cognition, and the environment exert their influence on bodily systems. We treat biology in a broad sense. As in most textbooks of this sort, there is substantial coverage of the proximate, physiological underpinnings of behavior, but we have also attempted to give due attention to ultimate causes by placing these discussions in an evolutionary framework whenever possible. The focus of the book is human behavior, but we include numerous discussions of other species' solutions to the problems of survival as well.

Many scientific disciplines contribute to these themes, so we draw upon the research of psychologists, anatomists, biochemists, endocrinologists, engineers, geneticists, immunologists, neurologists, physiologists, evolutionary biologists, and zoologists. In order to gain a panoramic view of the questions that concern biological psychologists, we have tried to rise above the limits of any single specialty.

Throughout, the text employs a five-fold approach to biological psychology—descriptive, comparative/evolutionary, developmental, mechanistic, and applied/clinical. We emphasize neuroscience research, whether conducted by psychologists or nonpsychologists, that aims to inform our understanding of behavior. Finally, we give special attention to work that explores the remarkable plasticity of the nervous system; a final chapter drives home the particular importance of plasticity in the psychological approach to neuroscience.

In our experience, students enrolled in biological psychology courses can be quite diverse in terms of their academic backgrounds and their personal interests, so we have taken pains to make the subject as accessible as possible to the widest spectrum of students by providing both the behavioral and biological foundations for each main topic. Some students will feel comfortable skipping or skimming some of this background material, but others will benefit from studying it carefully before moving on to the core of each chapter.

We have kept the ordering of the chapters found in the second edition because it has proved successful. However, we realize that some instructors may prefer to teach topics in a different order or to omit some chapters entirely, so we have written each chapter as a relatively self-contained unit. Recognizing that courses also vary in length from a single quarter or semester to two semesters, we wrote the text with the intent that it could be reasonably covered in a single quarter by omitting a few chapters, but the text provides enough material for a two-quarter or even a two-semester course. Specific suggestions for creating syllabi with different emphases can be found in the Instructor's Resource Manual. We have successfully taught the course using the book in each of these settings.

Many features of the text are designed to enhance students' mastery of the material:

- We have continued to refine what we believe is the finest full-color illustration program in any biological psychology text. The acclaimed art program from the second edition has undergone hundreds of additions and refinements, always with a clear pedagogical goal in mind. Data from original sources have been recast in ways that are designed to aid the student's understanding. All-new photographs and drawings of the human brain—clear, detailed, and consistent—are another feature of this edition.

- Each chapter opens by laying the groundwork for the content by placing it in a "real-world" context, and concludes with a concise Summary and list of Recommended Reading.

- Key terms are set in boldface type where first defined, and are also included in an improved, more comprehensive Glossary.

- "Boxes" describe interesting applications, important methods, sidelights, or refreshers on theoretical concepts relevant to biological psychology, or place the findings in the chapter in a historical perspective.

- Icons in the margins call attention to six special aspects of the text:

COMPETING HYPOTHESES

We frequently underscore the point that science is a process, and that it advances by continually testing competing hypotheses to account for observations. As examples in the text illustrate, sometimes further research indicates which of a group of hypotheses is correct; sometimes all the hypotheses are rejected for a new, more adequate hypothesis.

IMPORTANT METHOD

Many of the stunning advances in neuroscience in recent years are due to the introduction of powerful new methods that have made it possible to make progress on previously intractable problems. This icon highlights these new methods as well as more venerable research techniques. Important animal models used in research are also highlighted with this icon.

GENES AND BEHAVIOR

The revolution in molecular biology is clarifying many of the mechanisms involved in genetic influences on behavior, and this icon highlights important examples.

EVOLUTION AT WORK

Evolution is a major theme of current research on neuroscience and behavior, and we highlight many examples.

NEURAL PLASTICITY

As noted above, plasticity of the nervous system is a repeated theme in the text. This icon calls attention to particularly robust examples of plasticity.

CLINICAL ISSUE

Discussion of clinical issues occurs frequently in the text, and this icon points out discussions of important disorders of the nervous system.

Learning Biological Psychology, a new electronic study guide by Neil V. Watson of Simon Fraser University, is a powerful companion to the textbook that enhances the learning experience with a variety of multimedia resources. The CD icon appears wherever the student can make use of the interactive activities or animations included in *Learning Biological Psychology* to clarify important concepts.

Some of the most satisfying experiences in writing—and revising—this book have been the lively and creative discussions among the authors. We are fortunate that Arnold Leiman was able to participate in early discussions of this revision before his untimely death. Each of us has a different research focus, and each of us is involved in certain fields more fully than the others. Pooling our experiences and discussing the relevance of findings in one area to other aspects of biological psychology has been a rewarding experience, and we believe that this integration of knowledge from diverse but complementary fields has enriched the book.

Acknowledgments

In preparing this book we benefited from the help of many people. These include members of the staff of Sinauer Associates: Peter Farley, Editor; Kerry Falvey, Production Editor; Kathaleen Emerson, Ancillaries Editor; Christopher Small, Production Manager; Jefferson Johnson, Book Designer; Janice Holabird, Electronic Book Production. Copy editor Stephanie Hiebert once again skillfully edited the text. Patrick Lane, Mike Demaray, and colleagues at J/B Woolsey Associates transformed our rough sketches into the handsome and dynamic art program of this text.

Most of the renderings of the human nervous system seen in this edition (see the Illustration Credits) were adapted from drawings originally rendered for Hal Blumenfeld's forthcoming *Neuroanatomy through Clinical Cases* (Blumenfeld, in press). We are grateful to Dr. Blumenfeld for the hard work and expertise he brought to bear in making these illustrations aesthetically pleasing and neuroanatomically accurate.

We also want to thank our past undergraduate and graduate students ranging back to the 1950s for their helpful responses to our instruction, and the colleagues who provided information and critical comments about our manuscript: Brian Derrick, Karen De Valois, Russell De Valois, Jack Gallant, Ervin Hafter, Richard Ivry, Lucia Jacobs, Dacher Keltner, Raymond E. Kesner, Joe L. Martinez, Jr., James L. McGaugh, Frederick Seil, Arthur Shimamura, and Irving Zucker.

We remain grateful to the reviewers whose comments helped shape the first and second editions, including: Duane Albrecht, University of Texas; Anne E. Powell Anderson, Smith College; Mark S. Blumberg, University of Iowa; Eliot A. Brenowitz, The University of Washington; Catherine P. Cramer, Dartmouth College; Loretta M. Flanagan-Cato, University of Pennsylvania; Francis W. Flynn, University of Wyoming; Diane C. Gooding, University of Wisconsin; Janet M. Gray, Vassar College; James Gross, Stanford University; Mary E. Harrington, Smith

College; Wendy Heller, University of Illinois; Janice Juraska, University of Illinois; Joseph E. LeDoux, New York University; Michael A. Leon, University of California, Irvine; Stephen A. Maren, University of Michigan; Robert J. McDonald, University of Toronto; Robert L. Meisel, Purdue University; Jeffrey S. Mogil, University of Illinois; Randy J. Nelson, The Ohio State University; Lee Osterhout, The University of Washington; James Pfaus, Concordia University; Helene S. Porte, Cornell University; Scott R. Robinson, University of Iowa; David A. Rosenbaum, Pennsylvania State University; Martin F. Sarter, The Ohio State University; Jeffrey D. Schall, Vanderbilt University; Dale R. Sengelaub, Indiana University; Matthew Shapiro, McGill University; Cheryl L. Sisk, Michigan State University; Franco J. Vaccarino, University of Toronto; Cyma Van Petten, University of Arizona; Charles J. Vierck, University of Florida; Neil V. Watson, Simon Fraser University; Robert Wickesberg, University of Illinois; Walter Wilczynski, University of Texas; and Mark C. Zrull, Appalachian State University.

The following reviewers read and critiqued drafts of the third edition text, and we are grateful for their assistance:

Peter C. Brunjes, *University of Virginia*
Rebecca D. Burwell, *Brown University*
John D. E. Gabrieli, *Stanford University*
Mark Hollins, *University of North Carolina*
Keith R. Kluender, *University of Wisconsin*
Leah A. Krubitzer, *University of California-Davis*
Simon LeVay
Miguel Nicolelis, *Duke University*
Helene S. Porte, *Cornell University*
George V. Rebec, *Indiana University*
Stan Schein, *University of California-Los Angeles*
Rae Silver, *Columbia University*
Laura Smale, *Michigan State University*
Robert L. Spencer, *University of Colorado*
Steven K. Sutton, *University of Miami*
S. Mark Williams, *Duke University*

Finally, we would like to thank all our colleagues who contribute research in biological psychology and related fields.

Mark R. Rosenzweig
S. Marc Breedlove

1

Biological Psychology: Scope and Outlook

A legend from India (retold by Thomas Mann in *The Transposed Heads*) provides a colorful introduction to the main theme of this book. In this story the beautiful Sita marries a slender, intellectual merchant, but she is also attracted to his best friend, a spirited, brawny blacksmith. One day each young man beheads himself in a temple of the goddess Kali. Sita enters the temple, looking for them, and finds them lying in pools of blood in front of the statue of Kali. Horrified, Sita prays to Kali, begging the goddess to restore the men to life. Kali grants the wish and instructs Sita to place the heads carefully on the bodies.

Sita undertakes the task with feverish energy and soon sees the men come back to life. Only then does she realize that she has placed each head on the wrong body! Now the three young people are faced with a baffling problem: Which man is Sita's spouse? The one with the intellectual's head and the muscular body, or the one with the blacksmith's head and the intellectual's body? The legend explores the complexities of how each head affects the body that it now controls, and how each body influences the head. This old Hindu legend emphasizes that individual identity, personality, and talents are functions of brain–body interactions.

Gerry Bergstein, Illustrated Man #2, 1999, oil on canvas, 72" × 29"

What Is Biological Psychology?

In this book we explore the many ways in which the structures and actions of the brain produce mind and behavior. But that is only half of our task. We are also interested in the ways in which behavior in turn modifies the structures and actions of the brain. One of the most important lessons we hope to convey is that interactions between brain and behavior are reciprocal. The brain controls behavior, and in turn behavior alters the brain.

Our goal is to provide an interesting and coherent account of the main ideas and research in biological psychology, which is of great popular as well as scientific interest (Figure 1.1). Because there are so many pieces to tie together, we try to introduce a given piece of information when it makes a difference to the understanding of a subject—especially when it forms part of a story. Most importantly, we seek to communicate our own interest and excitement about the mysteries of mind and body.

Many Disciplines Contribute to Biological Psychology

No treaty or trade union agreement has ever defined the boundaries of biological psychology. It is a field that includes many players who come from quite different backgrounds—psychologists, biologists, physiologists, engineers, neurologists, psychiatrists, and many others. Further, it shares concepts and research approaches with many other disciplines. Figure 1.2 maps the relations of biological psychology to other disciplines. Clearly, the biological psychology umbrella is very wide.

1.1 Biological Psychology in the News Many newspaper and magazine articles feature topics in biological psychology.

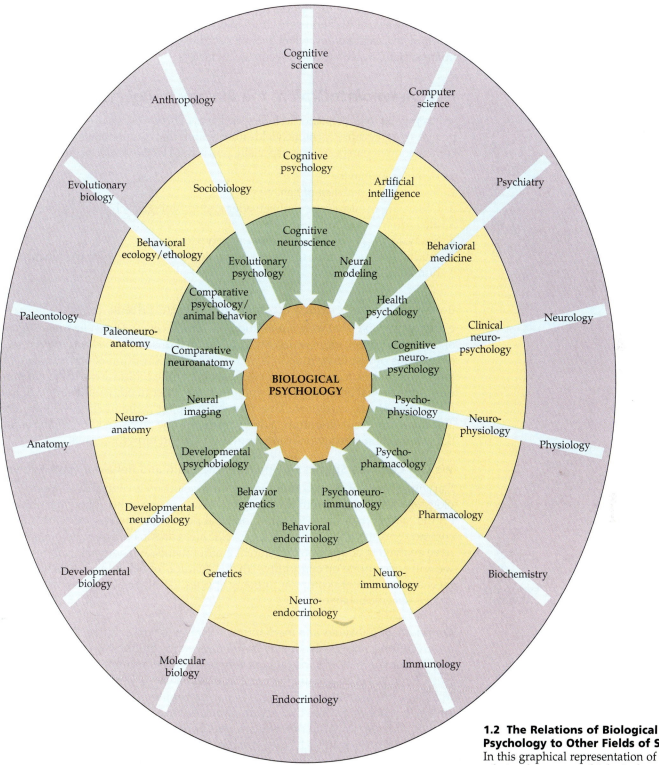

1.2 The Relations of Biological Psychology to Other Fields of Study In this graphical representation of the relationships among biological psychology and other scientific disciplines, fields toward the center of the map are closest to biological psychology in their history, outlook, aims, or methods.

Biological psychology is the field that relates behavior to bodily processes, especially the workings of the brain. The main goal of this area of study is to understand behavior and experience in terms of their biological substrates. Like other sciences, biological psychology is dedicated to improving the human condition. As Einstein once said in an address to students, concern for humanity and its fate must always form the chief interest of all scientific endeavor "in order that the creations of our minds shall be a blessing and not a curse."

Workers in the health sciences increasingly recognize the reciprocal interactions between behavior and body structure and function. For example, one new area is psychoneuroimmunology, which includes studies of relations among illness, the immune system, the brain, and psychological factors.

Five Viewpoints Explore the Biology of Behavior

In our pursuit to understand the biological bases of behavior, we use several different perspectives. Because each one yields information that complements the others, the combination of perspectives is especially powerful. The five major perspectives are:

1. *Describing* behavior
2. Studying the *evolution* of behavior
3. Observing the *development* of behavior and its biological characteristics over the life span
4. Studying the biological *mechanisms* of behavior
5. Studying *applications* of biological psychology—for example, to dysfunctions of human behavior

Behavior Can Be Described according to Different Criteria

Until we describe what we want to study, we cannot get far. Depending on the goals of our investigation, we may describe behavior in terms of detailed acts or processes, or in terms of results or functions. An analytical description of arm movements might record the successive positions of the limb or the contraction of different muscles. A functional behavioral description, on the other hand, would state whether the limb was being used in walking, running, hopping, swimming, or shooting dice. To be useful for scientific study, a description must be precise and reveal the essential features of the behavior, using accurately defined terms and units.

We Can Compare Species to Find How the Brain and Behavior Have Evolved

**EVOLUTION
AT WORK**

Darwin's theory of evolution through natural selection is central to all modern biology and psychology. From this perspective emerge two rather different emphases: (1) the *continuity* of behavior and biological processes among species because of common ancestry and (2) the species-specific *differences* in behavior and biology that have evolved in adaptation to different environments. At some points in this book we will concentrate on continuity—that is, features of behavior and its biological mechanisms that are common to many species. At other points, we will look at species-specific behaviors.*

Continuity of behaviors and mechanisms. Nature is conservative. Body or behavior inventions, once evolved, may be maintained for millions of years and may be seen in animals that otherwise appear very different. For example, the nerve impulse (see Chapter 3) is essentially the same in a jellyfish, a cockroach, and a human being. Some of the chemical compounds that transmit messages through the bloodstream (hormones) are also the same in diverse animals (although the same hormone may do different things in different species). Some of the sex hormones occur in all mammalian species. In such cases we share these characteristics with these species because the characteristics first arose in a shared ancestral species (Box 1.1). But similarity of a feature between species does not guarantee that it came from a common ancestor. Similar solutions to a problem may have evolved independently in different classes of animals.

Species-specific behaviors. Different species have evolved some specific ways of dealing with their environments. An earthworm's sensory endowments, for example, are quite different from those of a robin. Certain species of bats rely almost exclusively on hearing to navigate and find their prey; these species have become

---

*The icons that appear in the margins throughout the book are explained in the Preface.

BOX 1.1   *We Are All Alike and We Are All Different*

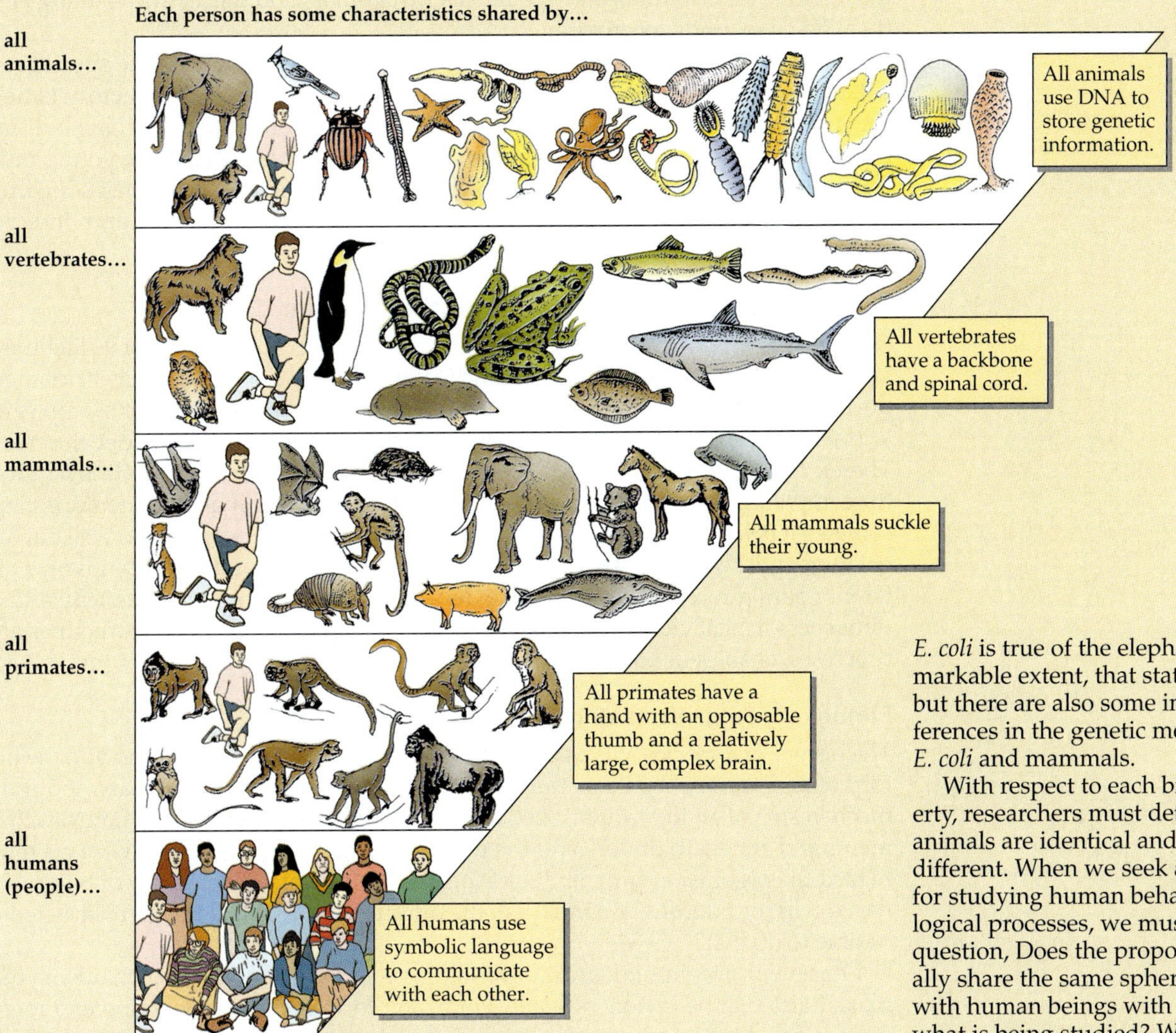

Each person has some characteristics shared by...

all animals...

All animals use DNA to store genetic information.

all vertebrates...

All vertebrates have a backbone and spinal cord.

all mammals...

All mammals suckle their young.

all primates...

All primates have a hand with an opposable thumb and a relatively large, complex brain.

all humans (people)...

All humans use symbolic language to communicate with each other.

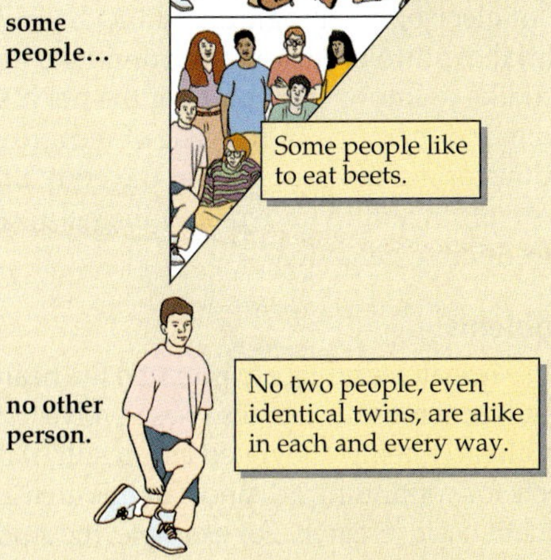

some people...

Some people like to eat beets.

no other person.

No two people, even identical twins, are alike in each and every way.

How do similarities and differences among people and animals fit into biological psychology? The anthropologist Clyde Kluckhohn (1949) observed that each person is in some ways like all other people, in some ways like some other people, and in some ways like no other person. As the figure shows, we can extend this observation to the much broader range of animal life. In some ways each person is like all other animals (e.g., needing to ingest complex organic nutrients), in some ways like all other vertebrates (e.g., having a spinal column), in some ways like all other mammals (e.g., nursing our young), and in some ways like all other primates (e.g., having a hand with an opposable thumb and a relatively large, complex brain).

Whether knowledge gained about a process in another species applies to humans depends on whether we are like that species in regard to that process. The fundamental research on the mechanisms of inheritance in the bacterium *Escherichia coli* proved so widely applicable that some molecular biologists proclaimed, "What is true of *E. coli* is true of the elephant." To a remarkable extent, that statement is true, but there are also some important differences in the genetic mechanisms of *E. coli* and mammals.

With respect to each biological property, researchers must determine how animals are identical and how they are different. When we seek animal models for studying human behavior or biological processes, we must ask the question, Does the proposed model really share the same sphere of identity with human beings with respect to what is being studied? We will see many cases in which it does.

Even within the same species, however, individuals differ from one another: cat from cat, blue jay from blue jay, and person from person. Biological psychology seeks to understand individual differences as well as similarities. This interest in the individual is one of the most important differences between psychology and other approaches to behavior. The lottery of heredity ensures that each individual has a unique genetic makeup (the only exception being identical twins). The way the individual's unique genetic composition is translated into body form and behavioral capacities is part of our story. Furthermore, each individual has a unique set of personal experiences. Therefore, the way in which each person is able to process information and store the memories of these experiences is another part of our story.

nearly blind. Other species of bats, however, are visually oriented, depending on their eyes to find their way around and to secure their food. Human beings use both vision and audition (hearing). However, we ignore electrical fields in the environment, while certain kinds of fish emit electrical pulses and detect the resulting electrical fields to guide locomotion.

Communicative behavior also differs greatly among species. Some species rely chiefly on visual signals, some on auditory signals, and some on olfactory (smell) signals. In many species the production of signals does not require learning but simply follows an inherited species-specific pattern. In other species, the young must learn behavior from adults. For example, some songbirds must learn their song from their parents, and even though there are many varieties of birdsong, each individual's song conforms fairly closely to the pattern of its species.

The Body and Behavior Develop over the Life Span

Ontogeny is the process by which an individual changes in the course of its lifetime—grows up and grows old. Observing the way in which a particular behavior changes during ontogeny may give us clues to its functions and mechanisms. For example, we know that learning ability in monkeys increases over several years of development. Therefore, we can speculate that prolonged maturation of neural circuits is required for complex learning tasks. In rodents the ability to form long-term memories lags somewhat behind the maturation of learning ability. Young rodents learn well but forget more quickly than older ones, suggesting that learning and memory involve different neural processes. Studying the development of reproductive capacity and of differences in behavior between the sexes, along with changes in body structures and processes, enables us to throw light on body mechanisms of sex behaviors.

Biological Mechanisms Underlie All Behavior

The history of a species tells us the evolutionary determinants of its behavior; the history of an individual tells us the developmental determinants. To learn about the mechanisms of an individual's behavior, we study his or her present body endowments and states. To understand the underlying mechanisms of behavior, we must regard the organism (with all due respect) as a "machine," made up of billions of nerve cells, or **neurons.** We must ask the question, How is this thing constructed to be able to do that?

Our major aim in biological psychology is to examine body mechanisms that make particular behaviors possible. For example, in the case of learning and memory, we would like to know the sequence of electrophysiological and biochemical processes that must occur between the initial capture of information and its eventual retrieval from memory. We would also like to know what parts of the nervous system are particularly involved in learning and memory. In the case of reproductive behavior, we would like to know the developmental processes in the body that produce the capacity for sexual behavior. We also want to understand the neuronal and hormonal processes that underlie reproductive behavior.

Research Can Be Applied to Human Problems

CLINICAL ISSUE

A major goal of biological psychology is to use research findings to improve the health and well-being of humans and other animals. Numerous human diseases involve malfunctioning of the brain. Many of these are already being alleviated as a result of research in the neurosciences, and the prospects for continuing advances in this area are good. Attempts to apply knowledge also benefit basic research. For example, the study of memory disorders in humans has pushed investigators to extend our knowledge of the brain regions involved in different kinds of memory (see Chapter 17). Table 1.1 shows how each of these perspectives can be applied to three kinds of behavior.

Three Approaches Relate Brain and Behavior

Biological psychologists use three approaches to understand the relationship between brain and behavior: somatic intervention, behavioral intervention, and cor-

TABLE 1.1 *Five Research Perspectives Applied to Three Kinds of Behavior*

Research perspective	Sexual behavior	Learning and memory	Language and communication
1. Description			
Structural description	What are the main patterns of reproductive behavior and sex differences in behavior?	In what main ways does behavior change as a consequence of experience—for example, conditioning?	How are the sounds of speech patterned?
Functional description	How do specialized patterns of behavior contribute to mating and to care of young?	How do certain behaviors lead to rewards or avoidance of punishment?	What behavior is involved in making statements or asking questions?
2. Comparative/ evolutionary	How does mating depend on hormones in different species?	How do different species compare in kinds and speed of learning?	How did the human speech apparatus evolve?
3. Development	How do reproductive and secondary sex characteristics develop over the life span?	How do learning and memory change over the life span?	How do language and communication develop over the life span?
4. Mechanisms	What neural circuits and hormones are involved in reproductive behavior?	What anatomical and chemical changes in the brain hold memories?	What brain regions are particularly involved in language?
5. Applications	Low doses of testosterone restore libido in some postmenopausal women.	Gene therapy and behavioral therapy improve memory in some senile patients.	Speech therapy, in conjunction with amphetamine treatment, speeds language recovery following stroke.

relation. In the most commonly employed approach, **somatic intervention** (Figure 1.3*a*), the investigator alters a structure or function of the brain or body to see how this change alters behavior. In this approach, somatic intervention is the independent variable, and the behavioral effect is the dependent variable; that is, the resulting behavior depends on how the brain has been altered. For example, in response to mild electrical stimulation of one part of her brain, one patient not only laughed, but she found whatever she happened to be looking at amusing (Fried et al., 1998).

In later chapters we will describe many kinds of somatic intervention with both humans and other animals—for example:

• A hormone is administered to some animals but not to others; various behaviors of the two groups are later compared.

• A part of the brain is stimulated electrically, and behavioral effects are observed.

• A connection between two parts of the nervous system is cut, and changes in behavior are measured.

The approach opposite to somatic intervention is psychological or **behavioral intervention** (Figure 1.3*b*). In this approach, the scientist intervenes in the behavior of an organism and looks for resultant changes in body structure or function. Here behavior is the independent variable, and change in the body is the dependent variable. Among the examples that we will consider in later chapters are the following:

• Putting two adults of opposite sex together may lead to increased secretion of certain hormones.

• Exposing a person or animal to a visual stimulus provokes changes in electrical activity and blood flow in parts of the brain.

• Training of animals in a maze is accompanied by electrophysiological, biochemical, and anatomical changes in parts of their brains.

(a) Manipulating the body may affect behavior

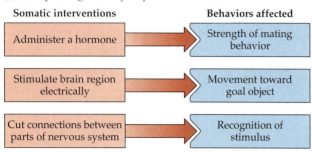

(b) Experience affects the body (including the brain)

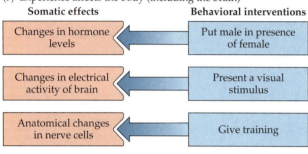

(c) Bodily and behavioral measures covary

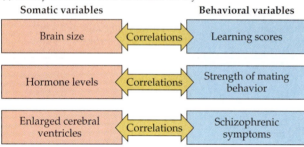

(d) Biological psychology seeks to understand all these relationships

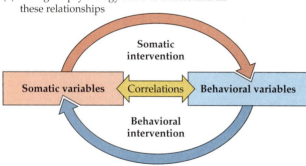

1.3 Three Main Approaches to Studying the Physiology of Behavior (a) In somatic intervention, investigators change the body structure or chemistry of an animal in some way and observe and measure any resulting behavioral effects. (b) Conversely, in behavioral intervention, researchers change an animal's behavior or its environment and try to ascertain whether the change results in physiological or anatomical changes. (c) Measurements of both kinds of variables allow researchers to arrive at correlations between somatic changes and behavioral changes. (d) Each approach enriches and informs the others.

The third approach to brain–behavior relations, **correlation** (Figure 1.3c), consists of finding the extent to which a given body measure varies with a given behavioral measure. Some questions we will examine later are as follows:

- Are people with large brains more intelligent than people with smaller brains?
- Are individual differences in sexual behavior correlated with levels of certain hormones in the individuals?
- Is the severity of schizophrenia correlated with the magnitude of changes in brain structure?

Such correlations should not be taken as proof of causal relationship. For one thing, even if a causal relation exists, the correlation does not reveal its direction—that is, which variable is independent and which is dependent. For another, two factors might be correlated only because a third factor determines the values of the two factors measured. What a correlation does indicate is that the two variables are linked in some way—directly or indirectly. Such a correlation often stimulates investigators to formulate hypotheses and to test them by somatic or behavioral intervention.

Combining these three approaches yields the circle diagram of Figure 1.3d. This diagram incorporates the basic approaches to studying relationships between bodily processes and behavior. It also emphasizes the theme (brought out in the myth of the transposed heads that was related at the beginning of this chapter) that the relations between brain and body are reciprocal: Each affects the other in an ongoing cycle of bodily and behavioral interactions. We will see examples of this reciprocal relationship throughout the book.

Neural Plasticity: Behavior Can Change the Brain

The idea that there is a reciprocal relationship between brain and behavior has embedded within it a concept that is, for most people, startling. When we say that behavior and experience affect the brain, we mean that they literally, physically alter the brain. The brain of a child growing up in a French-speaking household assembles itself into a configuration that is different from the brain of a child who hears only English. That's why the first child, as an adult, understands French effortlessly while the second does not. In this case we cannot tell you what the structural differences are exactly, but we do know one part of the brain that is being altered by these different experiences (see Chapter 19).

There are numerous examples, almost all in the animal literature, in which experience has been demonstrated to affect the number or size of neurons, or the number or size of connections between neurons. This ability of the brain, both in development and in adulthood, to be changed by the environment and by experience, is called **neural plasticity.**

Today when we hear the word *plastic*, we think of the class of materials found in so many modern products. But originally *plastic* meant "flexible, malleable" (from the Greek *plassein*, "to mold or form"), and the modern materials were named plastics because they can be molded into nearly any shape. William

James (1890) described plasticity as the possession of a structure weak enough to yield to an influence, but strong enough not to yield all at once

> .... Nervous tissue seems endowed with a very extraordinary degree of plasticity of this sort; so that we may without hesitation lay down as our first proposition the following, that the phenomena of habit in living beings are due to the plasticity of the organic materials of which their bodies are composed. (p. 110)

In the ensuing decades, research has shown that the brain is even more plastic than James suspected. For example, parts of neurons known as dendritic spines (see Chapter 2) appear to be in constant motion, changing shape in the course of seconds (M. Fischer et al., 1998). In this book we will see many examples in which experience alters the structure and/or function of the brain. In Chapter 5, hearing a baby cry will cause the mother's brain to secrete a hormone; in Chapter 7, visual experience in developing kittens will direct the formation of connections in the brain; in Chapter 12, a mother rat's grooming of her pups will affect the survival of spinal cord neurons; and in Chapter 18, a sea slug learning a task will strengthen the connections between two particular neurons.

NEURAL PLASTICITY

Biological and Social Psychology Are Related

This plasticity of the brain has a remarkable consequence: Other individuals can have an effect on the physical structure of your brain! Indeed, the whole point of coming to a lecture hall is to have the instructor use words and figures to alter your brain, so that you can retrieve that information in the future (in other words, she is teaching you something). Many of these alterations in your brain last only until you take an exam, but every once in a while the instructor may tell you something that you'll remember for the rest of your life. Most aspects of our social behavior are learned—from the language we speak to the clothes we wear and the kinds of food we eat—so our examination of the mechanisms of learning and memory (see Chapters 17 and 18) is important for understanding social behavior.

For an example from an animal model, consider the fact that rats spend a lot of time investigating the smells around them, including those coming from other rats. Cooke et al. (2000) took young rats, just weaned from their mother, and either raised each male in a cage alone, or raised them with other males to play with. Examination of these animals as adults found only one brain difference between the groups: A region of the brain known to process odors was smaller in the isolated males than in the males raised with playmates (Figure 1.4). Was it the lack of play, the lack of odors to investigate, or the stress of isolation that made the region smaller? Whatever the case, social experience affects this brain structure. In Chapter 18 we'll see that social experience also enhances effects of environmental enrichment on brain growth.

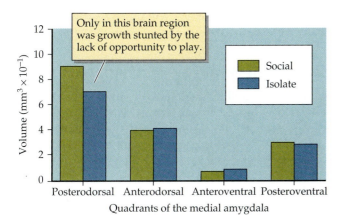

1.4 The Role of Play in Brain Development
A brain region involved in processing odors (the posterodorsal portion of the medial amygdala) was smaller in male rats housed individually compared to males housed together and allowed to play. Other nearby regions were identical in the two groups. (After Cooke et al., 2000.)

1.5 Pictures of Pain   Subjects told to expect only mild discomfort from putting a hand into 47°C water (*left*) showed less activation in a particular brain region (the anterior cingulate cortex) than subjects expecting more discomfort (*right*). Areas of high activation are indicated by orange, red, and white. (From Rainville et al., 1997; courtesy of Pierre Rainville.)

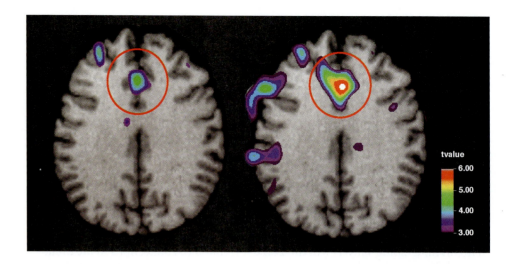

Here's an example of how social influences can affect the human brain. When people were asked to put a hand into moderately hot water (47°C), part of the brain became active, presumably because of the discomfort involved (Rainville et al., 1997). But subjects who were led to believe the water would be *very* hot had a more activated brain than subjects who were led to believe the discomfort would be minimal (Figure 1.5), even though the water was the same temperature for all subjects. The socially induced psychological expectation affected the magnitude of the brain response, even though the physical stimulus was exactly the same. (By the way, the people with the more activated brain also reported that their hand hurt more.)

In most cases, biological and social factors continuously interact and affect each other in an ongoing series of events as behavior unfolds. For example, the level of the hormone testosterone in a man's circulation affects his dominance behavior and aggression in social groups. The dominance may be exhibited in a great variety of social settings, ranging from playing chess to physical aggression. In humans and other primates, the level of testosterone correlates positively with the degree of dominance and with the amount of aggression exhibited. Winning a contest, whether a game of chess or a boxing match, raises the level of testosterone; losing a contest lowers the levels. Thus at any moment the level of testosterone is determined, in part, by recent dominance–submissive social experience, and the level of testosterone determines, in part, the degree of dominance and aggression. Of course, social and cultural factors also help determine the frequency of aggression; cross-cultural differences in rates of aggression exist that cannot be correlated with hormonal levels, and ways of expressing aggression and dominance are determined in part by sociocultural factors.

Perhaps nothing distinguishes biological psychology from other neurosciences more clearly than this fascination with neural plasticity and the role of experience. Biological psychologists have a pervasive interest in how experience physically alters the brain and therefore affects future behavior. We will touch on this theme in almost every chapter and review some of these examples again in the Afterword.

Biological Psychologists Use Several Levels of Analysis

Finding explanations for behavior often involves dealing with several levels of biological analysis. The units of each level of analysis are simpler in structure and organization than those of the level above. Figure 1.6 shows how the levels of analysis range from social interactions to the brain, continuing to successively less complex units until we arrive at single nerve cells and their even simpler, molecular constituents.

Scientific explanations usually involve analysis on a simpler or more basic level of organization than that of the structure or function to be explained. This approach is known as **reductionism.** In principle it is possible to reduce each explanatory se-

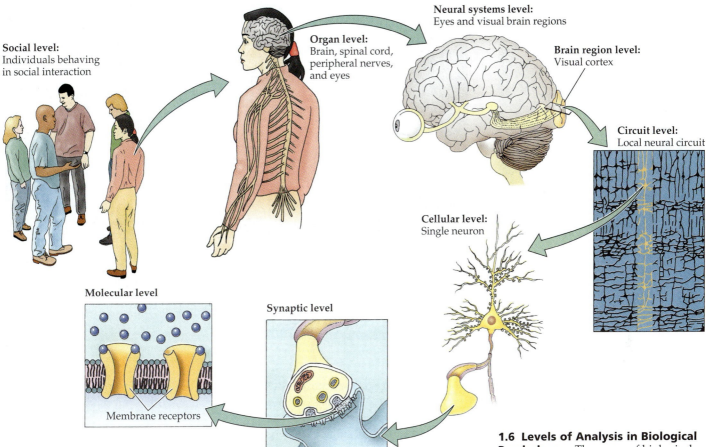

Social level:
Individuals behaving
in social interaction

Organ level:
Brain, spinal cord,
peripheral nerves,
and eyes

Neural systems level:
Eyes and visual brain regions

Brain region level:
Visual cortex

Circuit level:
Local neural circuit

Cellular level:
Single neuron

Molecular level

Synaptic level

Membrane receptors

1.6 Levels of Analysis in Biological Psychology The scope of biological psychology ranges from the level of the individual interacting with others, to the level of the molecule. Depending on the question at hand, investigators use different techniques to focus on these many levels, but always with an eye toward how their findings apply to behavior.

ries down to the molecular or atomic level, though for practical reasons this extent of reductionism is rare. For example, organic chemists and neurochemists usually deal with large complex molecules and the laws that govern them; seldom do they seek explanations in terms of atoms.

Naturally, in all fields different problems are carried to different levels of analysis, and fruitful work is often being done simultaneously by different workers at several levels. Thus in their research on visual perception, behavioral psychologists advance analytical descriptions of behavior. They try to determine how the eyes move while looking at a visual pattern, or how the contrast among parts of the pattern determines its visibility. Meanwhile, other psychologists and biologists study the differences in visual endowments among species and try to determine the adaptive significance of these differences. For example, how is the presence (or absence) of color vision related to the life of a species? At the same time, other investigators trace out brain structures and networks involved in different kinds of visual discrimination. Still other neuroscientists try to ascertain the electrical and chemical events that occur at synapses in the brain during vision.

A Preview of the Book: Fables and Facts about the Brain

Here are some examples of research topics that will be considered in this book:

- How does the brain grow, maintain, and repair itself over the life span, and how are these capacities related to the growth and development of the mind and behavior from the womb to the tomb?

- How does the nervous system capture, process, and represent information about the environment? For example, sometimes brain damage causes a person to no longer identify other people's faces; what does that tell us about how the brain recognizes faces?

(a)

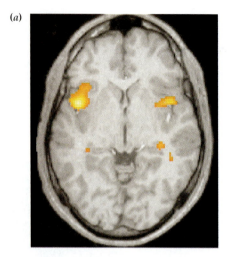

(b)

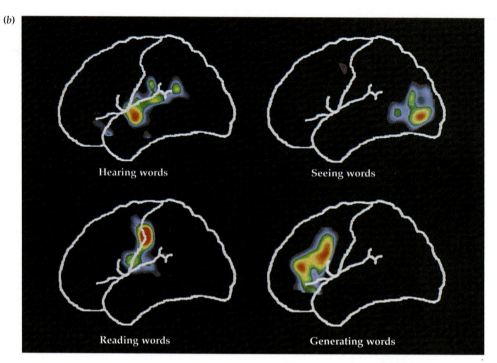

1.7 "Tell Me, Where Is Fancy Bred?" (*a*) The highlighted parts of the brain become especially active when a person thinks about his or her romantic partner. (*b*) Different brain regions are activated when people perform four different language tasks. The techniques used to generate such images are described in Chapter 2. (Part *a* from Bartels and Zeki, 2000; part *b* courtesy of Marcus Raichle.)

- How does sexual orientation develop? Some brain regions are different in heterosexual versus homosexual men; what do such studies tell us about the development of human sexual orientation?
- What brain sites and activities underlie feelings and emotional expression? Are particular parts of the brain active in romantic love, for example (Figure 1.7*a*)? In Chapter 15 we'll discuss finding regions for different emotions in the brain.
- Some people suffer damage to the brain and afterward seem alarmingly unconcerned about dangerous situations and unable to judge the emotions of other people; what parts of the brain are damaged to cause such changes?
- The ability to recollect and use the past is critical for the survival of any animal, from the most simple to the most complex. How does the brain manage to change during learning and how are memories retrieved?
- What are the neurobiological bases of language in humans?
- Why are different brain regions active during different language tasks (Figure 1.7*b*)?

The relationship between the brain and behavior is on the one hand very mysterious because it is difficult to understand how a physical device, the brain, could be responsible for our subjective experiences of fear, love, and awe. Yet despite this mystery, we all use our brains every day. Perhaps it is the "everyday miracle" aspect of the topic that has generated so much folk wisdom about the brain.

Sometimes these popular ideas about the brain are in line with our current knowledge, but in many cases we know they are false. For example, the notion that we normally use only a tenth (or a third, or a half, or some other fraction) of our brain is commonplace, but patent nonsense. Brain scans make it clear that the entire brain is activated by even fairly mundane tasks. Indeed, although the areas of activation shown in Figure 1.7 appear to be rather small and discrete, we will show in Box 2.3 that experimenters must work very hard to create images that separate activation related to a particular task from the background of widespread, ongoing brain activity.

In fact, it's fairly easy to reel off a host of commonly held beliefs about the relationships between the brain and behavior. Table 1.2 presents a list of such beliefs (many of which you may have heard) interspersed with some claims that may be new to you. Before you move on, you may wish to guess which items are true,

TABLE 1.2   *Facts or Fables of Biological Psychology?*

Statement	True/False/Unknown	Chapter Where Discussed
Some human nerve cells are three feet long.	T / F / U	3
More people die each year from the use of legal drugs than illegal ones.	T / F / U	4
Only humans ingest mind-altering substances.	T / F / U	4
Our bodies make chemicals that are similar in structure to heroin and marijuana and act on the same sites in the brain.	T / F / U	4
Testosterone is a male sex hormone, and estrogen is a female sex hormone.	T / F / U	5
Only humans have created cultures.	T / F / U	6
There are no anatomical differences between men's and women's brains.	T / F / U	7
Once our brains are developed, we can never grow new nerve cells.	T / F / U	7
People have five senses.	T / F / U	8
Some people are incapable of feeling pain.	T / F / U	8
Different parts of the tongue are specialized to recognize certain tastes.	T / F / U	9
The brightness and color of the objects we see are creations of our perceptual systems, not properties of the objects themselves.	T / F / U	10
Dogs are color-blind.	T / F / U	10
Each side of the brain controls the muscles on the opposite side of the body.	T / F / U	11
In some animal species every individual is female. In some other species, individuals can change sex during their lifetimes.	T / F / U	12
Some people are "born gay."	T / F / U	12
Most of our energy is expended just maintaining our body temperature.	T / F / U	13
We can lose weight permanently by surgically removing fat from our bodies.	T / F / U	13
During sleep the brain is relatively inactive.	T / F / U	14
Sleepwalkers are acting out dreams.	T / F / U	14
Prolonged sleep deprivation will make you temporarily crazy.	T / F / U	14
Some animals can have half their brain asleep and the other half awake.	T / F / U	14
The left side of the face is more emotionally expressive than the right side.	T / F / U	15
Prolonged stress can cause heart disease or cancer.	T / F / U	15
All cultural groups recognize the same facial expressions for various emotions.	T / F / U	15
It is possible to scientifically determine whether someone is lying.	T / F / U	15
Scientists are not sure why antidepressant drugs work.	T / F / U	16
People in Northern countries are more susceptible to seasonal depression.	T / F / U	16
Some people are incapable of producing any new memories.	T / F / U	17
We never really forget anything we have experienced.	T / F / U	17
Each memory is stored in its own brain cells.	T / F / U	18
We can change the structure of an animal's brain by raising it in a more stimulating environment.	T / F / U	18
People are "right-brained" or "left-brained": dominance of the left or right hemisphere of the brain accounts for major differences in people's cognitive styles or personalities.	T / F / U	19
Some brain disorders can cause people to no longer recognize their own face in the mirror. In other disorders, patients are unable to name only certain kinds of animals or certain kinds of food.	T / F / U	19
A child can have half of its brain removed and still develop normally.	T / F / U	19
Chimpanzees can use symbols to communicate.	T / F / U	19

which are false, and which are still unresolved, and then check your answers as you work your way through the text.

Neuroscience Contributes to Our Understanding of Psychiatric Disorders

One of the great promises of biological psychology is that it can contribute to the understanding and devising of treatment strategies of disorders that involve the brain. Like any other complex mechanism, the brain is subject to a variety of malfunctions and breakdowns. People afflicted by disorders of the brain are not an exotic few. At least one person in five around the world currently suffers from neurological and/or psychiatric disorders that vary in severity from complete disability to significant changes in quality of life.

Figure 1.8a shows the estimated numbers of U.S. residents afflicted by some of the main neurological disorders. Figure 1.8b gives estimates of the numbers of U.S. adults who suffer from certain major psychiatric disorders. The division of disorders in Figure 1.8 reflects the traditional distinctions between neurology and psychiatry, but both fields are becoming oriented more toward neuroscience.

The toll of these disorders is enormous, both in terms of individual suffering and in social costs. The National Foundation for Brain Research estimated that direct and indirect costs of behavioral and brain disorders amount to $400 billion a year in the United States. For example, $160 billion a year is spent on the treatment of alcohol and substance abuse, and the cost for treatment of dementia (severely disordered thinking) exceeds the costs of treating cancer and heart disease combined. The high cost in suffering and expense has impelled researchers to try to understand the mechanisms involved in these disorders and to try to alleviate or even to prevent them.

The following are examples of research that is providing relief from some of these grave disorders—examples that will be discussed in later chapters:

• The first generation of antipsychotic drugs, introduced in the 1950s, enabled many people suffering from schizophrenia to lead fuller lives, less haunted by crippling, intense symptoms. Differences in brain structure between patients with schizophrenia and other people (Figure 1.9) suggest certain mechanisms that might someday provide a new treatment approach.
• Discoveries that reveal the modes of action of habit-forming drugs and their effects on the nervous system give hope of effective cures for people addicted to drugs and of the ability to prevent lasting damage in infants born to mothers who take drugs.
• The fastest-growing affliction in industrialized societies is Alzheimer's disease, a profound loss of cognitive abilities that strikes especially older people. Current research is exploring some of the causes and brain mechanisms of this devastating condition.

Laboratory and Clinical Approaches Complement Each Other

Basic research and clinical practice influence each other. Basic research provides concepts and techniques that clinicians use to understand and help people with malfunctioning brains. At the same time, clinical observation of these patients provides data and stimulates the development of theories about brain mechanisms. This exchange is mutually beneficial, and the boundaries between laboratory and clinic are disappearing.

1.8 The Toll of Brain Disorders As these pie charts show, neurological (a) and psychiatric (b) disorders are quite common in the United States. As brain research progresses, many disorders previously characterized as psychiatric are thought to be neurological in origin.

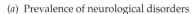

(a) Prevalence of neurological disorders

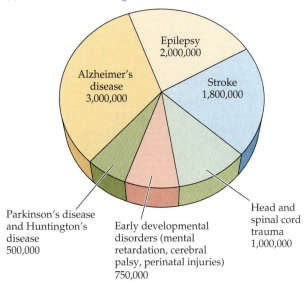

Epilepsy 2,000,000

Alzheimer's disease 3,000,000

Stroke 1,800,000

Parkinson's disease and Huntington's disease 500,000

Early developmental disorders (mental retardation, cerebral palsy, perinatal injuries) 750,000

Head and spinal cord trauma 1,000,000

(b) Incidence of psychiatric disorders

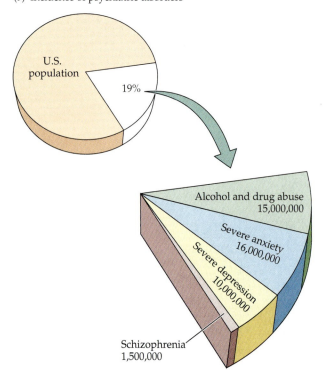

U.S. population

19%

Alcohol and drug abuse 15,000,000

Severe anxiety 16,000,000

Severe depression 10,000,000

Schizophrenia 1,500,000

(*a*) Normal

(*b*) Person with schizophrenia

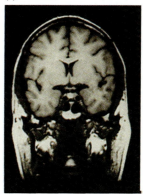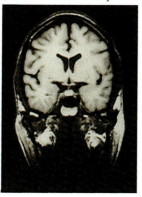

1.9 Identical Twins but Nonidentical Brains and Behavior
In these images of the brains of identical twins, the fluid-filled cerebral ventricles are prominent as dark "butterfly" shapes. The twin whose brain is imaged in part *b* suffers from schizophrenia and has the enlarged cerebral ventricles that some researchers believe are characteristic of this disorder. The other twin does not suffer from schizophrenia; his brain (*a*) clearly has smaller ventricles. (Courtesy of E. Fuller Torrey.)

Two Brains in One Head

Research on the functions of the two cerebral hemispheres illustrates the productive interplay between laboratory and clinic. Suppose that each time a right-handed person buttoned a shirt, the person's left hand sought to unbutton it. Two separate controllers would seem to be involved, but is this possible? Most of us are saved from such frustration because information from the right and left sides of the body is integrated by pathways that connect the two sides of the brain. But what happens when these connections are severed? Can we then observe two different types of consciousness?

Although the structures of the left and right sides of the brain seem very much alike, functional differences between the cerebral hemispheres of human brains become evident after brain damage such as that resulting from a stroke. For instance, injury to certain parts of the left cerebral hemisphere can produce striking changes in speech and language, whereas injury to the right hemisphere rarely affects speech. This situation used to be described as *cerebral dominance,* implying that a talkative left cerebral hemisphere dominated a mute right hemisphere.

New information about hemispheric specialization of function has come from studies of patients in whom the connections between the right and left cerebral hemispheres have been cut; these people are referred to as **split-brain individuals.** Early work with such patients in the 1930s did not reveal clear differences between the functions of the two hemispheres, because of a lack of appropriate methods of behavioral assessment.

Coming from a background of animal research, however, Roger Sperry (1974) and his collaborators (e.g., Gazzaniga, 1992) understood how to test separately the functioning of the two hemispheres, and they found remarkable differences in humans. These results prompted Sperry to speak of separate forms of consciousness in the two hemispheres of the brain. The patients seemed literally to be of two minds. Indeed, one of Sperry's patients was seen to button a shirt with one hand and try to unbutton it with the other. For his research with split-brain subjects and other contributions, Sperry was awarded the 1981 Nobel Prize in physiology or medicine.

Tests have indicated similar but much more subtle differences in cognitive style of the two hemispheres even in normal humans. Whereas the left is said to be analytical and verbal, the right has been characterized as spatial and holistic. However, most researchers emphasize the integrative functioning of the hemispheres in human cognitive activities.

Roger Sperry
(1913–1995)

Animal Research Makes Vital Contributions

Because we will draw on animal research throughout this book, we should comment on some of the ethical issues of experimentation on animals. Human beings' involvement and concern with other species pre-dates recorded history. Early humans had to study animal behavior and physiology in order to escape some species and hunt others. To study biological bases of behavior inevitably requires research on animals of other species as well as on human beings.

Because of the importance of carefully regulated animal research for both human and animal health and well-being, the National Research Council (NRC, Commission on Life Science 1988; NRC, Committee on Animals as Monitors of Environmental Hazards 1991) undertook a study on the many uses of animals in research. The study notes that 93% of the mammals used in research are laboratory-reared rodents. It also reports that most Americans agree that animal research should continue and that this conclusion is well founded.

**IMPORTANT
METHOD**

It makes no sense to sacrifice future human health and well-being by not using animals in research today. We owe our good health to past investigators and the animals they studied. As we decide on the future of animal research, we should keep in mind the generations who will look back at us and ask if we acted wisely.

Further improvements in human health and well-being and reduction of the disorders listed in Figure 1.8 depend on ongoing research, much of which requires animal subjects. Students of psychology usually underestimate the contributions of animal research to all the main fields of psychology because, as one study found (Domjan and Purdy, 1995, p. 501), the most widely used introductory psychology textbooks obscure the contributions of animal research, and they present major findings from animal research as if they had been obtained with human subjects.

The History of Research on the Brain and Behavior Begins in Antiquity

Although the brain has long been studied, only recently have scientists recognized the central role of the brain in controlling behavior. When Egyptian pharaoh Tutankhamen was mummified (around 1300 B.C.E.), four important organs were preserved in alabaster jars in his tomb: liver, lungs, stomach, and intestines. The heart was preserved in its place within the body. All these organs were considered necessary to ensure the pharaoh's continued existence in the afterlife. The brain, however, was removed from the skull and discarded. Although the Egyptian version of the afterlife entailed considerable struggle, the brain was not considered an asset.

Neither the Hebrew Bible (written from the twelfth to the second century B.C.E.) nor the New Testament ever mentions the brain. However, the Bible mentions the heart hundreds of times and makes several references each to the liver, the stomach, and the bowels as the seats of passion, courage, and pity, respectively. "Get thee a heart of wisdom," said the prophet.

**COMPETING
HYPOTHESES**

The heart is also where Aristotle (around 350 B.C.E.), the most prominent scientist of ancient Greece, located mental capacities. We still reflect this ancient notion when we call people *kind-hearted, open-hearted, hard-hearted, faint-hearted,* or *heartless,* and when we speak of learning *by heart.* Aristotle considered the brain to be only a cooling unit to lower the temperature of the hot blood from the heart. Other Greek thinkers, however, did consider the brain to be the seat of intellect and the organ that controls behavior. Thus around 400 B.C.E. Hippocrates, the great physician of Greek antiquity, wrote:

> Not only our pleasure, our joy and our laughter but also our sorrow, pain, grief, and tears rise from the brain, and the brain alone. With it we think and understand, see and hear, and we discriminate between the ugly and the beautiful, between what is pleasant and what is unpleasant and between good and evil. (Hippocrates, 1991)

The dispute between those who located intellect in the heart and those who located it in the brain still raged 2000 years later, in Shakespeare's time: "Tell me, where is fancy bred,/Or in the heart or in the head?" (*The Merchant of Venice,* Act III, Scene 2).

Around 350 B.C.E., the Greek physician Herophilus (called the "Father of Anatomy") advanced our knowledge of the nervous system by dissecting bodies of both people and animals. Among other investigations, he traced spinal nerves from

(*a*) Early drawing

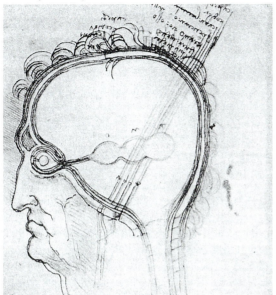

(*b*) Later drawing based on observation

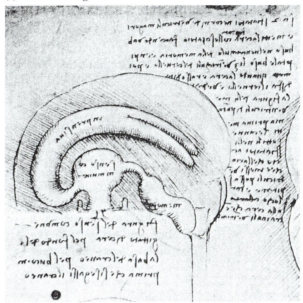

1.10 Leonardo da Vinci's Changing View of the Brain (*a*) In an early representation, Leonardo simply copied old schematic drawings that represented the cerebral ventricles as a linear series of chambers. (*b*) Later he made a drawing based on direct observation: After making a cast of the ventricles of an ox brain by pouring melted wax into the brain and letting it set, he cut away the tissue to reveal the ventricles' true shape.

muscles and skin into the spinal cord. He also noted that each region of the body is connected to separate nerves.

A second-century Greco-Roman physician, Galen (frequently described as the "Father of Medicine"), treated the injuries of gladiators and dissected some animals. He advanced the idea that animal spirits—a mysterious fluid—passed along nerves to all regions of the body. Although this concept did not advance our understanding of the nervous system, Galen provided interesting descriptions of the organization of the brain. His assessment of the behavioral changes produced by injuries to the heads of gladiators also drew attention to the brain as the controller of behavior.

Renaissance Scientists Began to Understand Brain Anatomy and Physiology

The eminent Renaissance painter and scientist Leonardo da Vinci (1452–1519) studied the workings of the human body and laid the foundations of anatomical drawing. He especially pioneered in providing views from different angles and cross-sectional representations. His artistic renditions of the body included portraits of the nerves in the arm and the fluid-filled ventricles of the brain (Figure 1.10).

Descriptions of the brain by Renaissance anatomists emphasized the shape and appearance of the external surfaces of the brain because these were the parts that were easiest to see when the skull was removed. It was immediately apparent to anyone who looked that the brain has an extraordinarily strange shape. The complexity of its visible form led to the use of an elaborate, precise vocabulary to label different regions.

In 1633, René Descartes (1596–1650) wrote an influential book (*De homine* [*On Man*]), in which he tried to explain how the behavior of animals, and to some extent of humans, could be like the workings of a machine. In addition to tackling other topics, Descartes proposed the concept of spinal reflexes and a neural pathway for them (Figure 1.11).

Attempting to relate the mind to the body, he suggested that the two come into contact in the pineal gland, located within the brain. His reasons for suggesting the

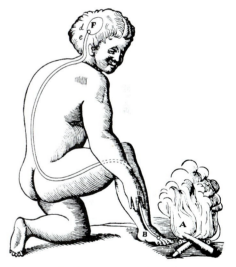

1.11 An Early Account of Reflexes In this depiction of an explanation by Descartes, when a person's toe touches fire, the heat causes nervous activity to flow up the nerve to the brain. There the nervous activity is "reflected" back down to the leg muscles, which contract, pulling the foot away from the fire; the idea of activity being reflected back is what gave rise to the word *reflex*. In Descartes's time, the difference between sensory and motor nerves had not yet been discovered, nor was it known that nerve fibers normally conduct in only one direction. Nevertheless, Descartes promoted thinking about bodily processes in scientific terms, and this focus led to steadily more accurate knowledge and concepts.

pineal gland were these: (1) Whereas most brain structures are double, located symmetrically in the two hemispheres, the pineal gland is single, like consciousness. (2) Descartes believed, erroneously, that the pineal gland exists only in humans and not in animals. Although the latter aspect of his reasoning did not hold up, Descartes did clearly pose problems of relations between mind and brain that later thinkers and investigators have continued to study.

As Descartes was preparing to publish his book, he learned that the Vatican had forced Galileo to renounce his teaching that Earth revolves around the sun, threatening to execute him if he did not recant. Fearful that his own speculations about mind and body could also incur the wrath of the church, Descartes withheld his book from publication, and it did not appear until 1662, after his death.

Descartes believed that if people were nothing more than intricate machines, they could have about as much free will as a pocket watch and no opportunity to make the moral choices that were so important to the church. He asserted that humans, at least, had a nonmaterial soul as well as a material body. This notion of **dualism** spread widely, and left other philosophers with the task of determining how a nonmaterial soul could exert influence over a material body and brain. Biological psychologists reject dualism and insist that all the workings of the mind can also, in theory, be understood as purely physical processes in the material world, specifically in the brain.

The Concept of Localization of Function Arose in the Nineteenth Century

Only in the nineteenth and twentieth centuries did educated people in the Western world finally accept the brain as the organ that coordinates and controls behavior. A popular notion of the nineteenth century, called *phrenology*, held that the cerebral cortex consisted of separate functional areas, or *organs*, and that each organ was respon-

(a)

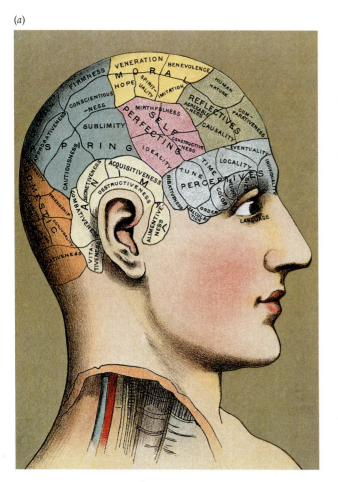

(b)

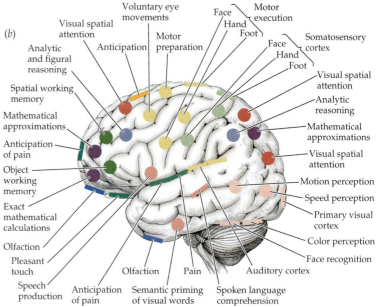

1.12 Old and New Phrenology (a) In the early nineteenth century, certain "faculties," such as skill at mathematics or a tendency toward aggression, were believed to be directly associated with particular brain regions. Phrenologists used diagrams like this one to measure bumps on the skull, which they took as an indication of how fully developed each brain region was in an individual, and hence how fully that person should display particular qualities. (b) Today technology allows us to roughly gauge how active different parts of the brain are when a person is performing various tasks (see Chapter 2). But virtually the entire brain is active during any task, so the localization of function that such studies provide is really a measure of where *peak* activity occurs, rather than a suggestion of a single region that is involved in a particular task. (Part b after Nichols and Newsome, 1999.)

sible for a behavioral faculty; *faculties* were qualities such as love of family, perception of color, or curiosity. Investigators assigned functions to brain regions anecdotally, by observing the behavior of individuals and noting, from the shape of the skull, which underlying regions of the brain were more or less developed (Figure 1.12*a*).

Many opponents of the idea rejected the entire concept of localization of brain function, insisting that the brain, like the mind, functions as a whole. Today we know that the whole brain is indeed active when we are doing almost any task. On the other hand, as we saw earlier in this chapter, when we are performing particular tasks, particular brain regions become even more activated. Different tasks activate different brain regions. Modern brain maps of these places where *peaks* of activation occur (Figure 1.12*b*) bear a passing resemblance to their phrenological predecessors, differing only in the specific location of functions. But unlike the phrenologists, we can find confirmation of these modern maps by other methods, such as examining what happens after brain damage.

Even as far back as the 1860s, the French surgeon Paul Broca (1824–1880) argued against formidable critics that language ability was not a property of the entire brain but rather was localized in a restricted brain region. Broca presented a postmortem analysis of a patient who had been unable to talk for several years. The only portion of the patient's brain that appeared damaged was a small region within the frontal portions of the brain on the left side—a region now known as *Broca's area* (labeled "Speech production" in Figure 1.12*b*). The study of additional patients further convinced Broca that language expression is mediated by this specific brain region rather than reflecting the activities of the entire brain.

These nineteenth-century observations form the background for a continuing theme of research in biological psychology—notably the search for distinguishing differences among brain regions on the basis of their structure, and the effort to relate different kinds of behavior to different brain regions (Kemp, 2001). An additional theme emerging from these studies is the relation of brain size to ability (Box 1.2). Nineteenth-century microscopic studies of sections of the brain revealed for the first time the shapes, sizes, and identity of nerve cells of the brain (Figure 1.13).

In 1890, William James's book *Principles of Psychology* signaled the beginnings of a modern approach to biological psychology. The strength of the ideas described in this book is evident by the continuing frequent citation of the work, especially by contemporary cognitive neuroscientists. In James's work, psychological ideas such as consciousness and other aspects of human experience came to be seen as properties of the nervous system, and a more complete understanding of psychological phenomena was to be achieved by the study of the nervous system. A true biological psychology began to emerge from this approach.

1.13 A Nineteenth-Century Anatomist's Look at Nerve Cells These drawings of brain cells, still cited today, were made by the great Spanish anatomist Santiago Ramón y Cajal (1852–1934) on the basis of his careful observations with the microscope.

Modern Biological Psychology Arose in the Twentieth Century

The end of the nineteenth century and the start of the twentieth brought many important developments for biological psychology. German psychologist Hermann Ebbinghaus had shown in 1885 how to measure learning and memory in humans. In 1898, American psychologist Edward L. Thorndike showed in his doctoral thesis how to measure learning and memory in animal subjects. Early in the twentieth century, Russian physiologist Ivan P. Pavlov announced research in his laboratory on the conditioned reflex in animals.

American psychologist Shepard I. Franz (1902) sought the site of learning and memory in the brain, combining Thorndike's training procedures with localized brain lesions in animal subjects. This work started a search for the traces of experience in the brain—a quest that Karl S. Lashley (1890–1958) referred to as the "search for the engram." Lashley studied with Franz and took over the problem of inves-

Karl S. Lashley (1890–1958)

BOX 1.2 *Is Bigger Better? The Case of the Brain and Intelligence*

Does a bigger brain indicate greater intelligence? This question has been the subject of lively controversy for at least two centuries. Sir Francis Galton (1822–1911), the scientist who invented the correlation coefficient, stated that the greatest disappointment in his life was his failure to find a significant relationship between head size and intelligence. But Galton didn't have the proper tools to conduct this investigation. He had to use head size when he really wanted to measure brain size. In addition, at the time he undertook this study, there were no good measures of intelligence. Galton had to rely on teachers' estimates of their students' intelligence, and every student knows that teachers can be quite wrong. Other investigators in the nineteenth century measured the volumes of skulls (Figure A) of various groups and estimated intelligence on the basis of occupations or other doubtful criteria.

The development and standardization of intelligence tests in the twentieth century provided invaluable help for one side of the question, but until recently, measures of head size still had to be used to estimate brain size for any sample of living subjects. Such studies usually showed positive but small correlations between brain size and intelligence. In one review of several such

(A) A nineteenth-century apparatus for head measurement

studies, the correlations ranged from +0.08 to +0.22 (van Valen, 1974).

The invention of noninvasive techniques to visualize and measure the brains of living subjects has made possible a direct approach to the question of relations between brain size and intelligence. A team of psychologists and other neuroscientists (Willerman et al., 1991) selected college students who

had no history of neurological problems and whose intelligence test scores were either high (IQ >130) or average (IQ <103). Excluding students with a middle range of IQ scores reflected the investigators' attempt to increase the possibility of finding a relationship between IQ and brain size.

Brain size was measured for each student by magnetic resonance imag-

tigating the locations and mechanisms of memory functions in the brain. His approach was primarily anatomical, and he focused on assessing the behavioral effects of brain lesions. In a long career, Lashley contributed many important findings and trained many students to study the biological mechanisms not only of learning and memory, but also of perception and motivation (R. F. Thompson, 1992).

Current biological psychology bears the strong imprint of Canadian psychologist Donald O. Hebb (1904–1985), a student of Lashley (P. M. Milner, 1993). By the 1940s, electrophysiological studies of the nervous system had begun to offer tantalizing pictures of an incessantly active brain. In his book *The Organization of Behavior* (1949), Hebb showed in principle how complex cognitive behavior could be accomplished by networks of active neurons. He suggested how brain cell connections that are initially more or less random could become organized by sensory input and stimulation into strongly interconnected groups that he called *cell assemblies*. His hypothesis about how neurons strengthen their connections through use became known as the *Hebbian synapse,* a topic much studied by current neuroscientists (see Chapters 17 and 18).

ing (MRI). (This technique is discussed in more detail in Chapter 2.) Any influence of body size on brain size was removed statistically so that it could not affect the final results. The overall result was a significant correlation coefficient, 0.51, with no significant difference between values for men and women. Because this correlation was probably increased by the selection for high or average IQ, the investigators estimated that the correlation would be about 0.35 for a more representative sample.

In a second study, 67 normal adult subjects were recruited through newspaper advertising and screened for neurological or psychiatric disorders, then given IQ tests. MRI scans such as those shown in Figure B were used for accurate measurement of the size of different brain regions. After correction for body size, the correlation between brain size and IQ scores was 0.38 (Andreasen et al., 1993). Thus on the basis of modern techniques, the long-standing controversy appears to have been settled in favor of a significant correlation between brain size and intelligence. Note, however, that the modest size of the correlation, while statistically significant, still allows for many additional important factors as determinants of intelligence. Plus there is still plenty of dispute

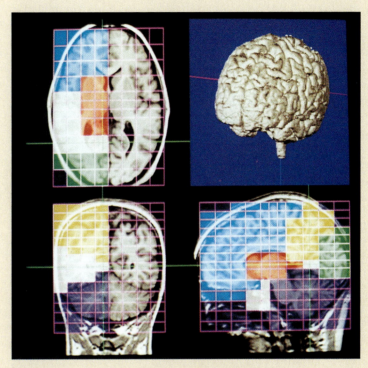

(B) Images from a modern brain measurement study

about whether IQ tests really measure a general property of intelligence (Sternberg, 2000).

Historically, scientists have often misused information about brain size in racially or ethnically prejudicial ways (S. J. Gould, 1981). In fact, however, all racial groups show overlapping and widely varying intelligence and brain size. (Figure A from the Bettmann Archive; Figure B courtesy of Nancy Andreasen.)

Recommended Reading

Finger, S. (1994). *Origins of neuroscience.* New York: Oxford University Press.

Howard, P. J. (2000). *Owner's manual for the brain: Everyday applications from mind-brain research* (2nd ed.). Austin, TX: Bard Press.

Pechura, C. M., and Martin, J. B. (Eds.). (1991). *Mapping the brain and its functions.* Washington, DC: National Academy Press.

Ratey, J. J. (2001). *User's guide to the brain: Perception, attention, and the four theaters of the brain.* New York: Pantheon.

To keep in touch with progress in this field, look for reviews and evaluations of research in the following publications:

Annual Review of Neuroscience. Palo Alto, CA: Annual Reviews.

Annual Review of Psychology. Palo Alto, CA: Annual Reviews.

Nature Neuroscience. New York: Nature America.

The Neuroscientist. Baltimore: Williams & Wilkins.

Trends in Neurosciences. Amsterdam: Elsevier.

Refer to the *Learning Biological Psychology* CD for the following study aids for this chapter:

7 Objectives

41 Study Questions

PART ONE

Biological Foundations of Behavior

Within your head is an information processing system, the brain, that contains at least 100 billion nerve cells, also known as neurons. These cells are connected to one another in extremely varied and elaborate patterns. A single neuron may receive connections from thousands of others. The essence of our identity is locked up in the character of these brain connections. An extensive web of nerve fibers connects the brain to every part of the body—monitoring, regulating, and modulating the functions of every body structure and system. The workings of this vast assembly make possible our perceptions, thoughts, movements, motives, and feelings.

Our first objective in this section is to describe the basic structures of the adult human brain—structures we share with all other humans (Chapter 2). Chapter 3 describes the electrical signals that a neuron uses to integrate information and the chemical signals that a neuron uses to transmit information to other cells, including other neurons. Chapter 4 offers a greater understanding of these chemical signals, explaining, among other things, how drugs affect behavior. Some chemical signals are released into the bloodstream to affect neurons and other cells, and therefore behavior; these chemical signals, called hormones, are the subject of Chapter 5.

2

Functional Neuroanatomy: The Nervous System and Behavior

Thoughts, feelings, perceptions, and acts—all are products of the workings of the human brain. These accomplishments depend on the architecture of the brain and the way it works. In this chapter we will discuss the structural character of the brain. The basic ways in which these structures work will be taken up in Chapters 3, 4, and 5, when we discuss electrical signals in neurons, chemical signals between neurons, and hormonal signals between the nervous system and the rest of the body.

To understand the structure of the brain we have to consider its components and the extensive network of linkages among them. These paths and circuits form the anatomical basis for information processing. This structure is a highly precise arrangement of parts. Our efforts to achieve a biological understanding of behavior must start with an appreciation of the basic units of the brain, including their connections and their arrangements into networks that process information.

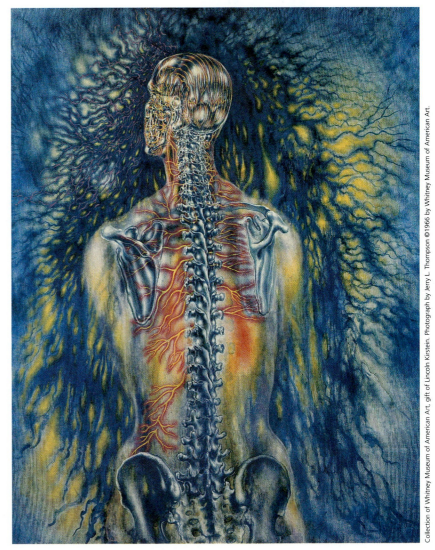

Pavel Tchelitchew, *Anatomical Painting*, 1946

On a Small Scale, the Nervous System Is Composed of Cells

In any animal the nervous system extends throughout the body; every organ is connected to the brain. The building blocks of the entire nervous system are cells, the most important of which are the **nerve cells**, or **neurons**. Each human being has about 100 billion to 150 billion neurons; the assemblies of these building blocks into circuits are what underlie the simplest and the most complex of our abilities and talents. Each neuron receives inputs from many other nerve cells and distributes information to many other nerve cells. The integration and analysis of information are primary operations of the brain. After discussing these operations at the cellular level, we will turn to a large-scale view.

The Neuron Doctrine Defines Neurons and Their Connections

In the late nineteenth century, anatomists sought to understand the differences between human and animal brains by using microscopes to study brain cells. They used distinctive dyes or stains that highlighted particular elements of the brain and showed that brains contain a large assembly of oddly shaped neurons. Unlike other organs, the brain exhibits an extraordinary range of variation in cell shape.

Some nineteenth-century anatomists thought that neurons were continuous with one another, forming a nearly endless series of interconnected tubes. According to this view, information in the nervous system was carried through continuous channels. However, the brilliant Spanish anatomist Santiago Ramón y Cajal offered a convincing alternative. He presented elegant studies of nerve cells and patiently drew portraits of neurons that continue to be cited today (see Figure 1.13). Ramón y Cajal was convinced that although neurons come very close to one another (i.e., they are contiguous), they are not quite continuous with one another. He insisted that at each point of contact between neurons is a tiny gap that keeps the cells separate.

From these studies emerged a new perspective—the **neuron doctrine.** According to this doctrine, (1) the brain is composed of separate neurons and other cells that are independent structurally, metabolically, and functionally; and (2) information is transmitted from cell to cell across tiny gaps, which were later named **synapses.** By the 1950s, the high-resolution abilities of the electron microscope had fully confirmed the neuron doctrine. Nerve cells are indeed separate from each other.

Another important class of cells in the nervous system consists of the **glial cells** (also sometimes called glia or neuroglia). We will discuss the main types of glial cells and their functions later, but because neurons are generally larger and produce readily measured electrical signals, we know much more about them than about glial cells. We know that neurons integrate information, so in this book we will be concerned mainly with neurons.

Neurons Have Three Principal Components

The typical neuron collects signals from several sources, integrates the information, transforms it, changes it into complex output signals, and distributes these signals to many other cells. The ways in which information is represented and processed in the nervous system are determined by the interactions of nerve cells.

Some features are common to all nerve cells. Most neurons have three distinct structural parts that are directly related to the functional properties of the cell: (1) a **cell body** region, which is defined by the presence of the nucleus; (2) extensions of the cell body called **dendrites** (from the Greek *dendron*, "tree"), which receive information; and (3) a single extension, the **axon,** for sending out information. These three parts are illustrated in Figure 2.1.

In many neurons the axon is only a few micrometers long, but in spinal sensory and motor neurons, it can reach more than a meter in length.* For example, the gi-

Santiago Ramón y Cajal
(1852–1934)

---

*The meter (m), the unit of length in the metric system, equals 39.37 inches. A centimeter (cm) is one-hundredth of a meter (10^{-2} m); a millimeter (mm) is one-thousandth of a meter (10^{-3} m); a micrometer, or micron (μm), is one-millionth of a meter (10^{-6} m); and a nanometer (nm) is one-billionth of a meter (10^{-9} m).

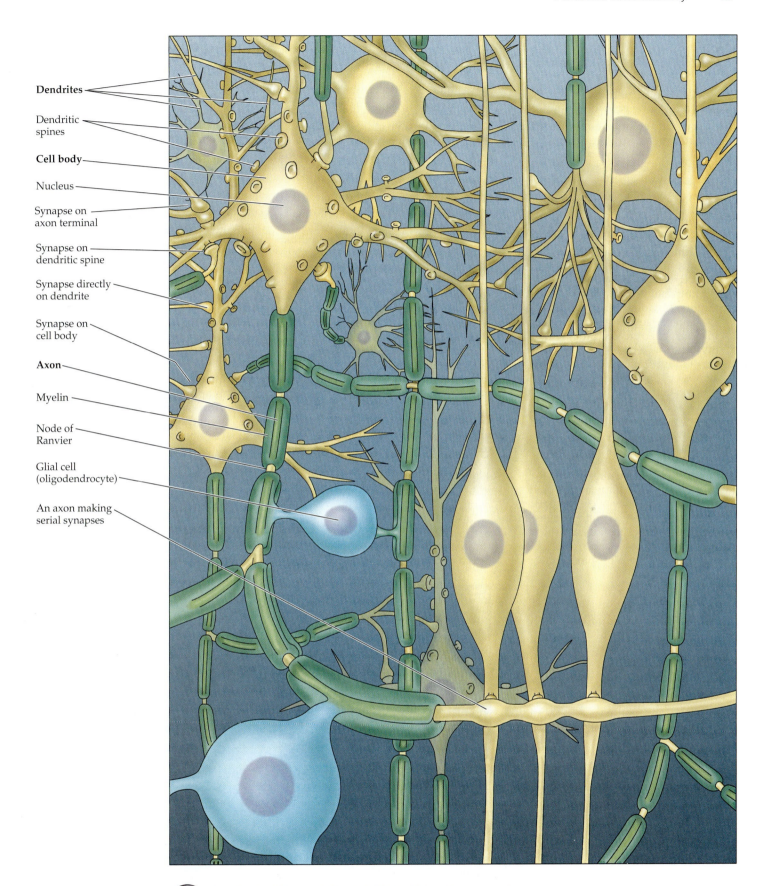

Dendrites

Dendritic spines

Cell body

Nucleus

Synapse on axon terminal

Synapse on dendritic spine

Synapse directly on dendrite

Synapse on cell body

Axon

Myelin

Node of Ranvier

Glial cell (oligodendrocyte)

An axon making serial synapses

2.1 Typical Nerve Cells with Their Major Components
Most neurons have three structurally distinct parts: cell body, dendrites, and axon. Many axon terminals contact dendritic spines; others contact dendrites directly. Note that the many dendritic spines shown would probably be occupied by an axon terminal, but for clarity here they have been left empty.

BOX 2.1   *Neuroanatomical Methods Provide Ways to Make Sense of the Brain*

Visualizing Structures in the Brain

In the middle of the nineteenth century, dyes used to color fabrics provided a breakthrough in anatomical analysis. Dead, preserved nerve cells treated with these dyes, known in histology (the study of tissue slices under the microscope) as *stains*, suddenly become vivid, and hidden parts become evident. Different dyes have special affinities for different parts of the cell, such as membranes, the cell body, or the sheaths surrounding axons.

Golgi stains outline the full cell, including details such as dendritic spines (Figure A). Golgi staining is often used to characterize the variety of cell types in a region. For reasons that remain a mystery, this technique stains only a small number of cells, each of which stands out in dramatic contrast to adjacent unstained cells. Injecting fluorescent molecules directly into a neuron provides a Golgi stain–like view of its dendrites (Figure B).

Nissl stains outline all cell bodies because the dyes are attracted to RNA, which encircles the nucleus. Nissl stains allow us to measure cell body size and the density of cells in particular regions (Figure C). Other stains are absorbed by myelin, the fatty sheaths that surround some axons (see, for example, the sections of spinal cord

shown in Figure 2.9). Improved microscopes have also broadened our understanding of the fine structure of cells. Observations using routine forms of light microscopy provide detailed resolution down to about 1 to 2 µm. Smaller objects fail to deflect light particles (photons), so they cannot be detected with light. But because electrons are deflected more readily than photons, electron microscopy extends a hundredfold the range of structures that can be visualized, making it possible to see some of the smallest details within cells (e.g., see Figures 2.4 and 2.6).

Some histological techniques can reveal aspects of the dynamic neurochemistry of nerve cells, particularly the metabolic processes of the cell. A cell can be manipulated into taking its own photograph—a method called **autoradiography**. For example, we might inject a living animal with radioactively labeled **2-deoxyglucose** (**2-DG**). 2-DG resembles glucose enough that active cells take it up more readily than inactive cells do. But once the 2-DG is inside, it cannot be broken down, so it just sits inside even the most active neurons.

To create an autoradiogram, the experimenter presents the animal with a stimulus condition that results in neural activity while the 2-DG is injected. The

neurons that are active during that stimulus take up more of the radioactive 2-DG than do the inactive neurons. The experimenters then sacrifice the animal, cut thin sections of brain tissue, and place the sections on slides, which they cover with photographic emulsion. Radioactivity emitted by the 2-DG in the cells causes silver to be deposited—the same effect that light has on film. The silver deposition produces fine, dark grains immediately above the active neurons that took up the radioactive substance (see Box 5.1 and Figure 14.3).

Another approach to marking cells of the brain is to apply immunological techniques. These techniques allow neuroanatomists to mark groups of cells that have an attribute in common, such as particular membrane components or particular proteins within a cell. This approach is known as **immunocytochemistry** (**ICC**) because it uses immune system molecules (antibodies) to label cells chemically (the Greek *kytos*, from which we get the prefix *cyto-*, means "hollow vessel"; *cyto-* is used to mean "cells"). We slice up the brain, expose the sections to the antibodies, allow time for them to find and attach to the target protein, rinse off unattached antibodies, and use chemical treatments to visualize the antibodies. Cells that were making the

(A) Golgi stain

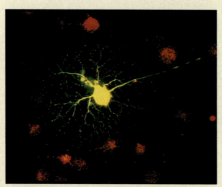

(B) Neuron injected with fluorescent dye

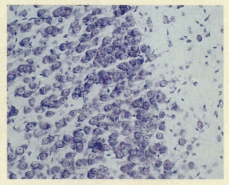

(C) Nissl stain

raffe has axons that are an incredible several meters long. In order for you to wiggle your toes, individual axons must carry the instructions from the spinal cord to muscles in your foot. Long fibers of sensory neurons then carry messages back to the spinal cord.

The ability to see and measure nerve cells and trace their connections is vital to solving many problems in biological psychology and neuroscience (Box 2.1). A few of these problems are: How do neurons grow and make connections during individual development? What differences in nerve cells and their connections characterize Alzheimer's disease? How do nerve cells change as a consequence of learn-

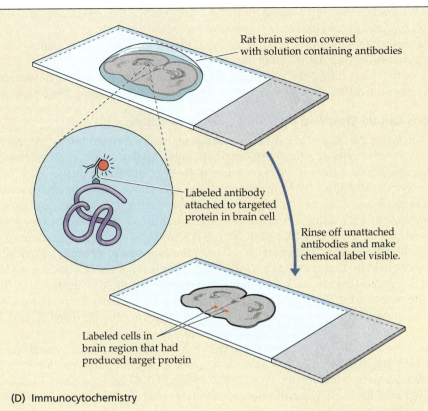

Rat brain section covered with solution containing antibodies

Labeled antibody attached to targeted protein in brain cell

Rinse off unattached antibodies and make chemical label visible.

Labeled cells in brain region that had produced target protein

(D) Immunocytochemistry

protein will be labeled from the chemical treatments (Figure D).

This technique can even tell us where, within the cell, the protein is found. For example, if the protein is a neurotransmitter, the antibodies will detect it in axon terminals. Because neurons often produce distinctive proteins (immediate early gene products) when active, ICC for those proteins is quickly replacing 2-DG as a means of determining which neurons are active during a particular behavior. For example, brain neurons involved in a particular process express immediate early gene products when a rat is performing a task related to that process, and ICC reveals those neurons.

Tracing Pathways in the Brain

The cells of the brain are interconnected through a complex web of pathways.

Gaining an understanding of the circuits formed by these cells and their extensions required the development of techniques that clearly outline the terminals of particular cell groups or show the cells of origin of particular axon tracts. Tracing pathways in the nervous system is difficult for several reasons: (1) Axons have an even smaller diameter than cell bodies; (2) axons from different sources look alike; and (3) fibers with different destinations often travel together over parts of their routes, making it hard to disentangle one set from the rest. Although at first glance this task of tracing neural pathways seems insurmountable—remember, our brain contains billions of neurons—anatomists were not daunted.

Classic anatomical techniques for tracing pathways rely on visualization of the products of degenerating axons.

Newer procedures accomplish the same goal by the injection of radioactively labeled amino acids into a collection of cell bodies. These radioactive molecules are taken up by the cell, incorporated into proteins, and transported to the tips of the axons. Brain sections are then coated with a sensitive emulsion as a film would be. After some time (which ranges from hours to weeks), the slides are developed and stained. If the pathway originates in the area of the injected cells, developed silver grains will be located in axons and their terminals, making the whole pathway visible.

A powerful technique for determining the cells of origin of a particular set of axons employs a tracer such as **horseradish peroxidase** (**HRP**), an enzyme found in the roots of horseradish. HRP catalyzes certain chemical reactions that leave a visible reaction product of dark granules. HRP acts as a tracer of pathways because it is taken up into the axon at the terminals and transported back to the cell body. After HRP is injected into one part of the nervous system, any neurons that have axon terminals there transport the HRP back to the cell body, which can be made visible with chemical reactions (Figure E). All along the way, visible reaction products are formed—akin to footprints along a pathway. (Figure A courtesy of Timothy DeVoogd; Figure B courtesy of Carla Shatz; Figure E courtesy of Dale Sengelaub and Cynthia Jordan.)

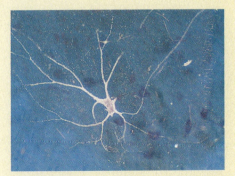

(E) HRP-filled motoneuron

ing? What changes in neurons and their connections permit recovery of function after damage to the nervous system?

Although answers to these questions depend on our ability to study nerve cells, neurons are difficult to examine and measure for several reasons. First, they are small, and their extensions (dendrites and axons) are even smaller (1 to 3 μm in diameter). Furthermore, if you cut a thin slice of brain tissue and look at it under a microscope, you will find it hard to see any brain cells because they don't contrast with surrounding areas. The ability to see details of cells requires special chemical agents to make cells or parts of cells stand out from the background. These various techniques for visualizing neurons and for tracing pathways in the nervous system will appear in almost every chapter in this book.

Neurons are remarkably diverse in shape; at least 200 geometrically distinguishable types of nerve cells are found in the brains of mammals. Figure 2.2 offers a small sample of the many different shapes neurons may take. These differences in size and shape reflect the different ways in which neurons process and transmit information.

Neurons Can Be Classified by Shape, Size, or Function

Anatomists use the shapes of cell bodies, dendrites, and axons to classify the many varieties of nerve cells into three principal types: multipolar, bipolar, and monopolar neurons. These different types of neurons are specialized for particular kinds of interactions. **Multipolar neurons** are nerve cells that have many dendrites and a single axon (Figure 2.3*a*). Most of the neurons of the vertebrate brain are multipolar. **Bipolar neurons** have a single dendrite at one end of the cell and a single axon at the other end (Figure 2.3*b*). This type of nerve cell is found in some sensory systems, including the retina and the olfactory (smell) system. **Monopolar neurons** have a single branch (usually thought of as an axon) that, after leaving the cell body, extends in two directions (Figure 2.3*c*). One end is the receptive pole (the input zone), the other the output zone. Such cells transmit touch information from the body into the spinal cord. In all three types of neurons, the dendrites are the input zone, and in multipolar cells, the cell body is part of the input zone.

Another common way of classifying nerve cells is by size. Examples of small nerve cells are the types called granule ("grain"), spindle, and stellate ("star-shaped"). Large cells include the types called pyramidal, Golgi type I, and Purkinje. Each region of the brain is a collection of both large and small neurons. Vertebrate nerve cell bodies range from as small as 10 μm to as large as 100 μm in diameter.

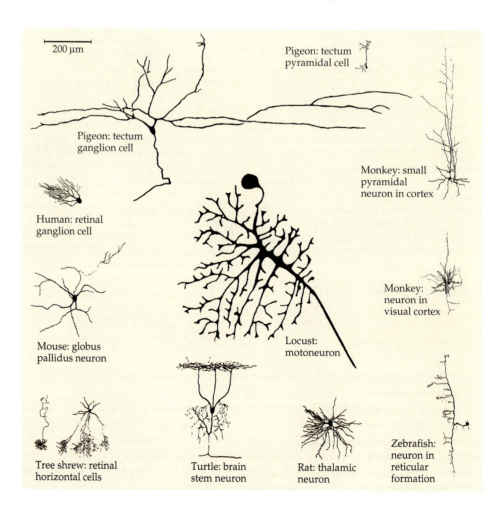

200 μm

Pigeon: tectum pyramidal cell

Pigeon: tectum ganglion cell

Human: retinal ganglion cell

Monkey: small pyramidal neuron in cortex

Mouse: globus pallidus neuron

Locust: motoneuron

Monkey: neuron in visual cortex

Tree shrew: retinal horizontal cells

Turtle: brain stem neuron

Rat: thalamic neuron

Zebrafish: neuron in reticular formation

2.2 Variety in the Form of Nerve Cells Note the considerable variety in the shape and size of these neurons (drawn to scale) from the brain or spinal cord of different animals.

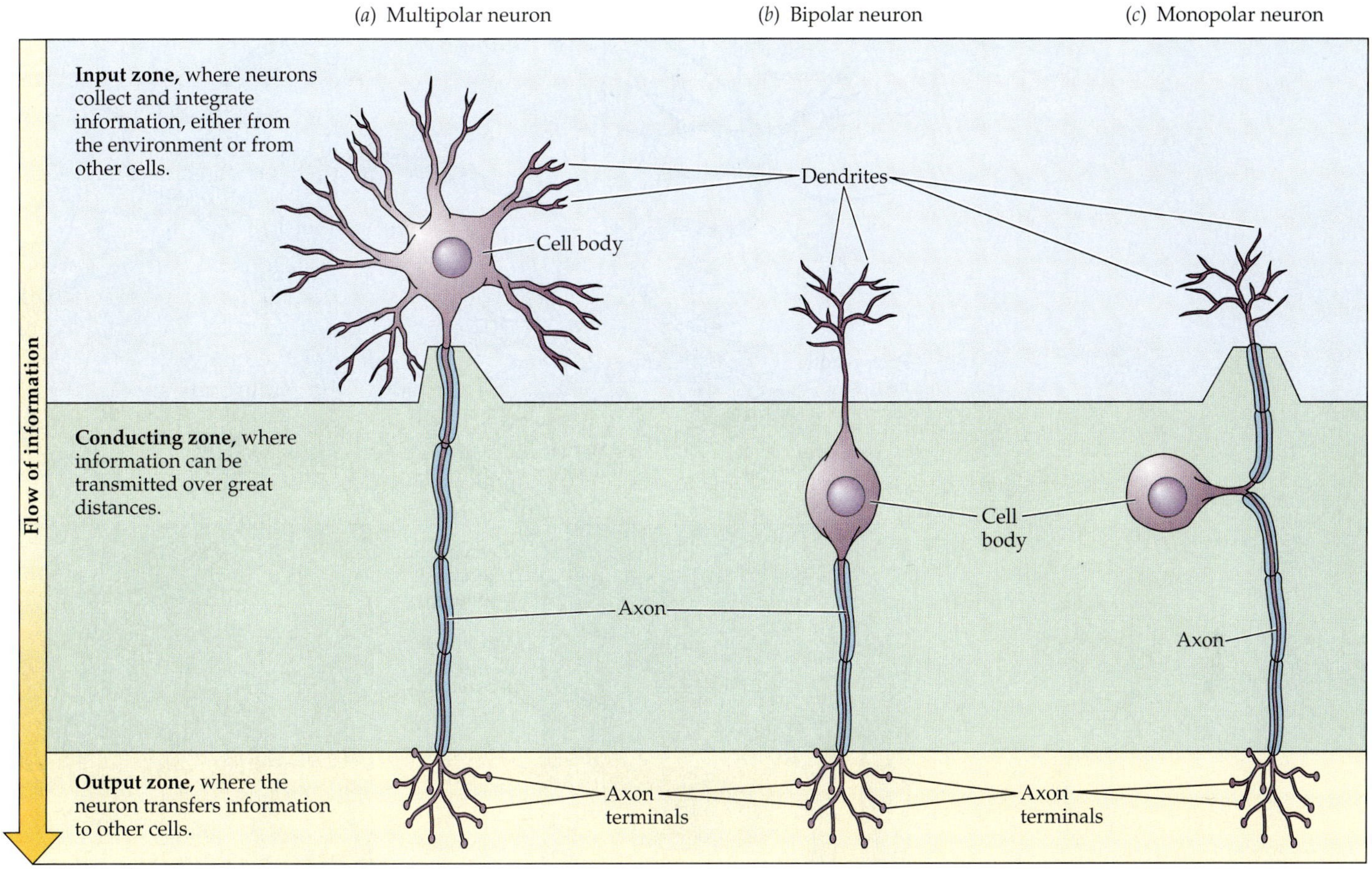

(a) Multipolar neuron (b) Bipolar neuron (c) Monopolar neuron

Flow of information

Input zone, where neurons collect and integrate information, either from the environment or from other cells.

Dendrites

Cell body

Conducting zone, where information can be transmitted over great distances.

Cell body

Axon

Axon

Output zone, where the neuron transfers information to other cells.

Axon terminals

Axon terminals

2.3 A Classification of Neurons into Three Principal Types (a) A multipolar neuron has many dendrites extending from the cell body, and a single axon. (b) A bipolar neuron has a single dendrite extending from the cell body, and a single axon. (c) A monopolar neuron has a single branch that emerges from the cell body and extends in two directions.

A third simple classification of neurons is by function. Some neurons send their axons to muscles or glands, and the job of these neurons is to make the muscle contract or to change the activity of the gland. Such neurons are called **motoneurons** (or motor neurons). Other neurons are directly affected by changes in the environment; they respond to light, a particular odor, or touch. These cells are **sensory neurons.** The remaining neurons, which constitute the vast majority, receive input from and send their output to other neurons. Thus they are called **interneurons.**

The Neuronal Cell Body and Dendrites Receive Information across Synapses

The diversity of neuronal shapes arises especially from the variation in the form and shape of dendrites, the extensions that arise from the nerve cell body and branch out in highly complex ways (see Figure 2.2). The shape of the dendritic tree—the full arrangement of dendrites of a single cell—provides clues about the information processing of a particular cell. All along the surface of the dendrite are many contacts, the synapses. Most neurons receive thousands of synapses. Through the synapses, information is transmitted from one neuron to the next. A synapse, or synaptic region, has three principal components (Figure 2.4):

1. the **presynaptic zone,** in many instances a swelling of the axon terminal called the **synaptic bouton** ("button")
2. a specialized **postsynaptic membrane** in the surface of the dendrite or cell body
3. a **synaptic cleft**—that is, a space between the presynaptic and postsynaptic elements—which measures about 20 to 40 nm

Detailed electron microscopic examination of the presynaptic terminal shows that it contains many small spheres, called **synaptic vesicles.** They range in size from 30 to 140 nm. These vesicles contain a chemical substance that can be released into the

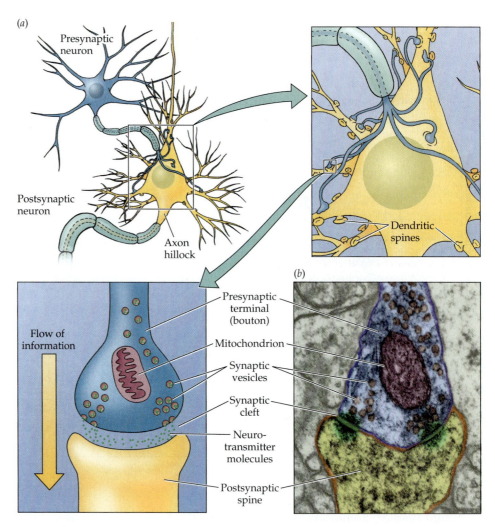

2.4 Synapses (*a*) Axons typically form a synapse on the cell body or dendrites of a neuron. On dendrites, synapses may form on dendritic spines or on the shaft of a dendrite. A transmission electron micrograph (*b*) provides a view of the fine structure of synapses.

synaptic cleft, and this release is triggered by electrical activity in the axon. The released chemical, called a **synaptic transmitter,** or **neurotransmitter,** flows across the cleft and produces electrical changes in the postsynaptic membrane. Many different transmitters have been identified in the brain, including acetylcholine, dopamine, and glutamate, but many more remain to be discovered.

The electrical changes in the postsynaptic membrane determine whether the postsynaptic cell will be excited or inhibited. The surface of the postsynaptic membrane is different from adjacent regions of the membrane. It contains special **receptor molecules** (often referred to simply as receptors) that capture and react to molecules of the transmitter agent (see Figure 1.6). Numerous synapses cover the surfaces of dendrites and of the cell body. This number is possible because these synaptic junctions are very small—less than 1 μm² each. Some individual cells of the brain have as many as 100,000 synapses, although the more common number for larger cells is about 5000 to 10,000. Synaptic contacts are particularly numerous in nerve cells that have elaborate dendrites.

Along the dendrites on many nerve cells of the brain are outgrowths called **dendritic spines** or thorns (see Figure 2.1). These spines give some dendrites a rough or corrugated surface. They have become the focus of considerable attention because their structural appearance and function may be modified by experience (see Chapter 18). In some cases they seem to change shape within seconds (M. Fischer et al.,

1998). Both the size and the number of dendritic spines are affected by various treatments of an animal, such as training or exposure to sensory stimuli.

The Axon Is a Specialized Output Zone

A typical axon has several regions that are structurally and functionally distinguishable (see Figure 2.3). In multipolar neurons the axon originates out of the cell body from a cone-shaped region called the **axon hillock** (see Figure 2.4*a*). The electrical impulse that carries the message of each neuron to other neurons begins in the axon hillock and travels down the axon (see Chapter 3). The axon beyond the hillock is tubular, with a diameter ranging from 0.5 to 20 µm in mammals and up to 500 µm in the "giant" axons of some invertebrates.

With very few exceptions, nerve cells have only one axon. But axons often divide into several branches, called **axon collaterals.** Because of this branching, a single nerve cell can exert influence over a wide array of other cells. Toward its ending, an axon or a collateral typically divides into numerous branches of fine diameter. At the ends of the branches (the **axon terminals;** see Figure 2.5*a*), specialized structures form the synapse, the connection to the next cell. By synapsing on this target, the axon terminals are said to **innervate** (or supply neural input to) the cell. Table 2.1 compares the main structural features of axons and dendrites.

A pair of terms are used to describe axons, always in relation to a particular brain region or structure under discussion. Axons carrying information into the region are said to be **afferents.** Axons carrying information away from the brain region are called **efferents.** Every axon can be described as either an efferent from the region containing its cell body, or an afferent to the target it innervates. Most often the structure under discussion is the brain, so if you read *afferents* without any qualification, you may assume that these are axons bringing information into the brain. Similarly, unless the context provides another structure as a reference point, *efferents* refers to axons carrying commands from the brain out to the body.

The cell body manufactures proteins under the guidance of DNA in the cell nucleus (see the Appendix). Therefore, proteins needed for growth and function must be transported from the cell body to distant regions in the axon. The movement of materials within the axon is referred to as **axonal transport** (Figure 2.5). Some molecules are transported along axons at a "slow" rate (1 to 3 mm per day); others are transported by a "fast" system (400 mm per day).

How do substances move in axons? Investigators have observed structures in axons referred to as **microtubules** (20 to 26 nm in diameter) that look like hollow cylinders (see Figure 2.5*b*). There are also systems of smaller rods (10 nm in diameter) that are called **neurofilaments** (found only in neurons). Smaller yet are **microfilaments** (7 nm in diameter), which are found in all cells. These three molecules determine the shape of a cell, but evidence suggests that they are also involved in

TABLE 2.1 *Distinctions between Axons and Dendrites*	
Axons	**Dendrites**
Usually one per neuron, with many terminal branches	Usually many per neuron
Diameter is uniform until start of terminal branching	Diameter tapers progressively toward its ending
Join cell body at a distinct region called the axon hillock	No hillocklike region
Usually covered with myelin	No myelin covering
Lengths from practically nonexistent to several meters	Usually much shorter than axons
Along length, branches tend to be perpendicular	Along lengths, branches occur over wide range of acute angles

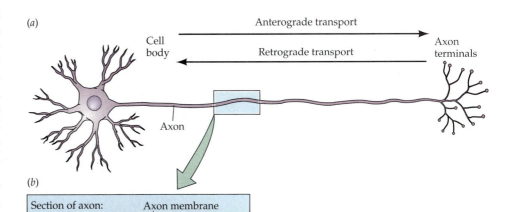

2.5 Axonal Transport (*a*) Axons transport proteins via microtubules and neurofilaments in both anterograde (from cell body to axon terminals) and retrograde (from axon terminals to cell body) directions. (*b*) A cross section of the cytoskeleton of an axon shows microtubules and neurofilaments with specialized "protein motors" moving material.

axonal transport. At least three types of proteins have been identified that are part of the "motor" mechanism that moves substances in conjunction with microtubules (Amos and Cross, 1997; Schnapp, 1997).

Glial Cells Support Neural Activity

Glial cells are named after the original conception of their function—that they serve as something like glue (the Greek *glia* means "glue"). Clearly, structural support—or some aspects of it—is one biological role of glial cells. Glial cells may also serve a nutritive role, providing a pathway from the vascular system to the nerve cells for delivering raw materials that neurons use to synthesize complex compounds. Unlike nerve cells, glial cells are produced throughout our lifetime. Although many aspects of the functional roles of glial cells remain a puzzle, we do know some things—and there are many other interesting ideas—about their function.

There are four classes of glial cells. One type, called an **astrocyte** (from the Greek *astron*, "star"), is a star-shaped cell with numerous extensions (or processes) in all directions (Figure 2.6*a*). Some astrocytes form end feet on the blood vessels of the brain. These end feet look as though they are attached to the vessels by suckerlike extensions. Extensions of astrocytes form the tough sheets that wrap around the outer surface of the brain, the dura mater. Bundles of astrocyte extensions interweave among nerve fibers, as though giving structural support. Astrocytes may also

(*a*) Astrocyte

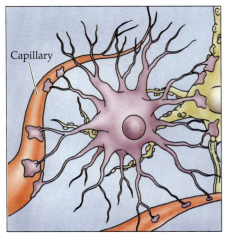

(*b*)

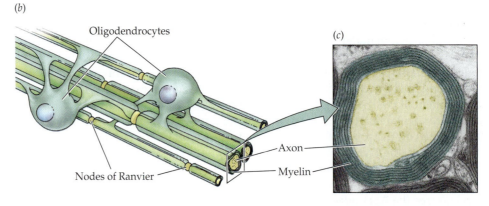

(*c*)

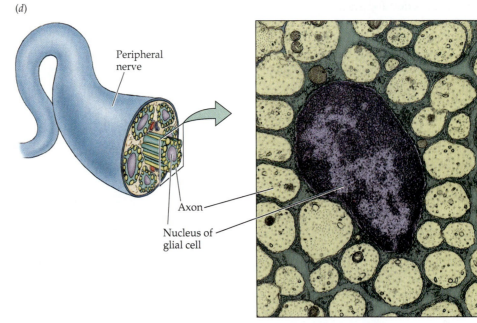

2.6 Types of Glial Cells (*a*) One type of astrocyte—the protoplasmic astrocyte—contacts capillaries and is adjacent to nerve cell membranes. (*b*) Extensions or arms of oligodendrocytes form myelin wrapping (blue) on axons (yellow); four axons are shown in this view. (*c*) This colorized electron micrograph of a myelinated axon shows the many layers of the myelin sheath. (*d*) Axons that lack this wrapping, called unmyelinated axons, are embedded in the troughs of glial cells. In the magnified cross section shown here, the light-colored circular shapes are unmyelinated axons. The large dark area in the center of the photograph is the nucleus of a glial cell, the cytoplasm of which surrounds the axons. (Micrographs from Peters et al., 1991.)

contribute to the metabolism of synaptic transmitters and may regulate the balance of ions. In addition, astrocytes release growth factors, proteins that are important in the growth and repair of nerve cells.

A second type of glial cell is the **microglial cell.** As the name suggests, microglial cells are very small. They migrate in large numbers to sites of injury or disease in the nervous system, apparently to remove debris from injured or dead cells.

The third and fourth types of glial cells—oligodendrocytes and Schwann cells—perform a vital function for nerve cells, as the next section describes.

Some Glial Cells Wrap around Axons, Forming Myelin Sheaths

Wrapped around most axons are sheaths consisting of a substance called **myelin** (Figure 2.6b), formed by nearby glial cells. The production of this wrapping is called **myelination.** This sheathing affects the speed of conduction of neural impulses. Anything that interferes with the myelin sheath can have catastrophic consequences for the individual, as is evident in various demyelinating diseases, such as multiple sclerosis, which is caused by loss of myelin on the axons of the brain.

Within the brain and spinal cord, the myelin sheath is formed by a type of glial cell called an **oligodendrocyte** (see Figure 2.6b). This cell is much smaller than an astrocyte and has fewer extensions (the Greek *oligos* means "few"). The myelination performed by oligodendrocytes continues for extended periods of time in human beings—in some brain regions up to 10 to 15 years after birth, and possibly throughout life. Oligodendrocytes are also commonly associated with nerve cell bodies, especially the bodies of larger neurons. Because of this association, they are frequently regarded as satellite cells of neurons.

For axons outside the brain and spinal cord, myelin is provided by another type of glial cell—the **Schwann cell.** A single Schwann cell produces the myelin coat for a very limited length of the axon, seldom extending more than 200 μm. Hence numerous Schwann cells are needed to myelinate the length of a single axon.

Between the segments of myelin are small gaps in the coating. Such a gap, where the axon membrane is exposed, is called a **node of Ranvier** (see Figure 2.6b). The regularity of the wrapping is nicely illustrated in cross sections of the axon (see Figure 2.6c).

Many axons of very thin diameter have no close wrapping of myelin; they are commonly referred to as unmyelinated fibers or axons. Although these fibers do not have an elaborate coating, they still have a relationship with glial cells. Several axons become embedded in troughs of the Schwann cell, but without elaborate wrapping (Figure 2.6d). The manner in which these glial cells surround neurons, especially the synaptic surfaces of neurons, suggests that one of their roles is to isolate receptive surfaces to prevent interactions among synapses by keeping various inputs segregated.

Glial cells are of clinical interest because they form many of the tumors that arise in the brain. Furthermore, some glial cells, especially astrocytes, respond to brain injury by changing in size—that is, by swelling. This **edema** damages neurons and is responsible for many symptoms of brain injuries.

CLINICAL ISSUE

On a Large Scale, the Nervous System Consists of Central and Peripheral Divisions

To this point we have described the basic building blocks of the nervous system: neurons and their synapses, and glial cells. Structural analysis in neuroscience research involves many different levels, from these basic building blocks to features of an entire brain. These levels are analogous to the different views of a scene that a zoom lens can provide, ranging from close-up, intimate views of fine detail to much broader views of interactions of different brain regions or the properties of the whole brain (see Figure 1.6).

In this section we will describe the human nervous system on a much larger scale, viewing the brain with the unaided eye. For this discussion you will need to understand the conventions that anatomists use for describing various viewpoints of the body and the brain. These conventions are described in Box 2.2.

Figure 2.7*a* presents a view of the entire human nervous system. Examining the nervous system from this viewpoint reveals a natural subdivision into a **central nervous system** (**CNS**), consisting of the brain and spinal cord (Figure 2.7*b*), and a **peripheral nervous system** (all nervous system parts that are outside the bony skull and spinal column). After discussing the peripheral nervous system, we will turn our attention to the control center of the entire nervous system, the brain.

The Peripheral Nervous System Consists of Three Components

The peripheral nervous system consists of nerves—collections of axons bundled together—that extend throughout the body. These nerves transmit information to muscles (motor pathways) or arise from sensory surfaces (sensory pathways). Three components make up the peripheral nervous system: (1) the cranial nerves, which are connected directly to the brain; (2) the spinal nerves, which are connected at regular intervals to the spinal cord; and (3) the autonomic nervous system, which originates from both the brain and the spinal cord. All three components inform the CNS about events in the environment and transmit commands from the CNS to the body.

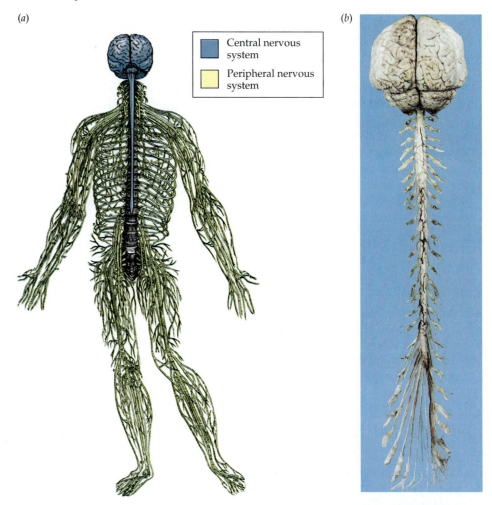

(a)

(b)

Central nervous system

Peripheral nervous system

2.7 The Central and Peripheral Nervous Systems   (*a*) This view of the nervous system is a composite of two drawings. A modern view of the central nervous system (the brain and spinal cord) is shown in blue and is superimposed on a rendering of the peripheral nervous system by the great sixteenth-century anatomist Andreas Vesalius. The peripheral nervous system, shown in yellow, courses through the body and connects all body organs and systems to the central nervous system. (*b*) The brain and spinal cord form the central nervous system.

BOX 2.2 *Three Customary Orientations for Viewing the Brain and Body*

Because the nervous system is a three-dimensional structure, two-dimensional illustrations and diagrams cannot represent it completely. The brain is usually cut in one of three main planes to obtain a two-dimensional section from this three-dimensional object. It is useful to know the terminology and conventions that apply to these sections, which are shown in the figure.

The plane that bisects the body into right and left halves is called the **sagittal plane** (from the Latin *sagitta*, "arrow"). The plane that divides the body into a front (anterior) and a back (posterior) part is called by several names: **coronal plane** (from the Latin *corona*, "crown"), frontal plane, or transverse plane. For clarity, we will view coronal sections from behind so that the right side of the figure represents the right side of the brain. (In medicine, coronal sections are viewed as if you were fac-

ing the patient, with the patient's left on your right.) The third main plane, which divides the brain into upper and lower parts, is called the **horizontal plane.**

In addition, several directional terms are used. **Medial** means "toward the middle" and is contrasted with **lateral,** "toward the side." The head end is referred to by any of several terms: **anterior, cephalic** (from the Greek *kephale*, "head"), or **rostral** (from the Latin *rostrum*, "prow of a ship"). The tail end is called **posterior** or **caudal** (from the Latin *cauda*, "tail"). **Proximal** (from the Latin *proximus*, "nearest") means "near the trunk or center," and **distal** means "toward the periphery" or "toward the end of a limb" (distant from the origin or point of attachment).

Dorsal means "toward or at the back," and **ventral** means "toward or at the belly or front." In four-legged animals, such as the cat or the rat, *dorsal*

refers to both the back of the body and the top of the head and brain. For consistency in comparing brains among species, this term is also used to refer to the top of the brain of a human or of a chimpanzee, even though in such two-legged animals the top of the brain is not at the back of the body. Similarly, *ventral* is understood to designate the bottom of the brain of a two-legged as well as of a four-legged animal.

Although these terms may seem strange at first, they provide a means of describing anatomy without ambiguity. If you want to become adept with these terms, you might find it helpful to get together with a friend and quiz each other about anatomical relations. "Where's the navel? In a medial position on the ventral surface, caudal to the rib cage, and rostral to the pelvis." (Photographs courtesy of S. Mark Williams and Dale Purves, Duke University Medical Center.)

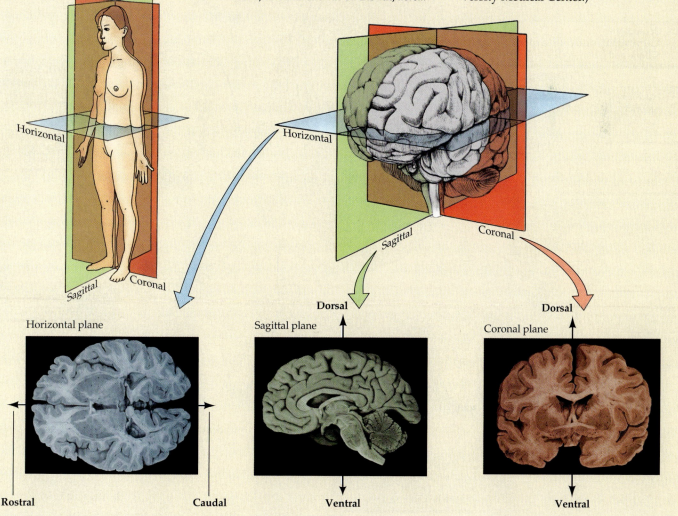

Horizontal

Sagittal   Coronal

Horizontal

Sagittal

Coronal

Dorsal

Dorsal

Horizontal plane

Sagittal plane

Coronal plane

Rostral   Caudal

Ventral

Ventral

2.8 The Cranial Nerves
Bundles of axons form the 12 pairs of cranial nerves, which are conventionally referred to by the Roman numerals I through XII. This basal view of the brain (see inset for orientation) shows the cranial nerves and their primary functions. Blue represents sensory nerves; red represents motor.

The cranial nerves. The 12 pairs of **cranial nerves** in the human brain are concerned mainly with sensory and motor systems associated with the head (Figure 2.8). These nerves pass through small openings in the skull to enter or leave the brain. The cranial nerves are known both by name and by Roman numeral. Three cranial nerves are exclusively sensory pathways to the brain: the olfactory (I), optic (II), and auditory (or vestibulocochlear; VIII) nerves. Five are exclusively motor pathways from the brain: The oculomotor (III), trochlear (IV), and abducens (VI) nerves innervate muscles to move the eye; the spinal accessory (XI) nerves control neck muscles; and the hypoglossal (XII) nerves control the tongue.

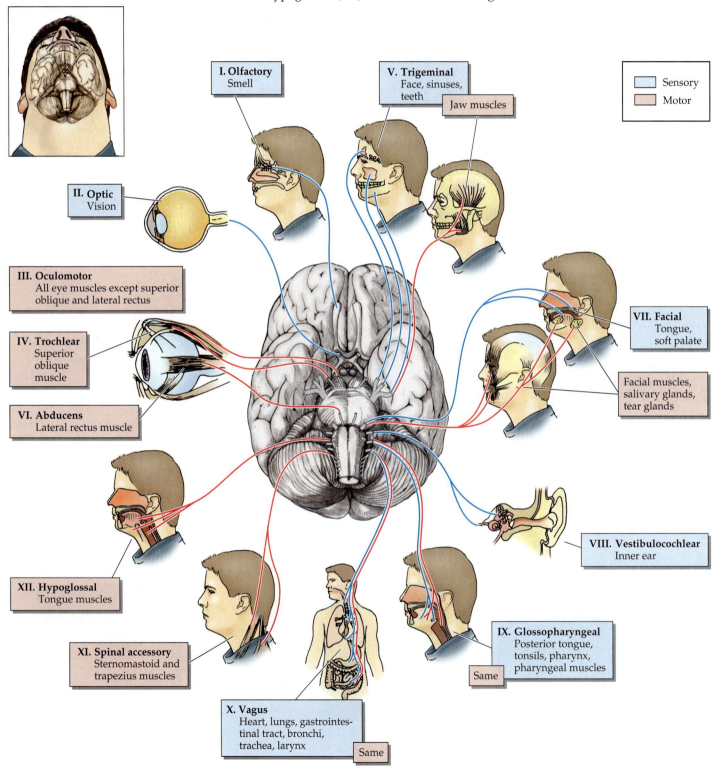

Sensory
Motor

I. Olfactory
Smell

V. Trigeminal
Face, sinuses, teeth
Jaw muscles

II. Optic
Vision

III. Oculomotor
All eye muscles except superior oblique and lateral rectus

IV. Trochlear
Superior oblique muscle

VI. Abducens
Lateral rectus muscle

VII. Facial
Tongue, soft palate

Facial muscles, salivary glands, tear glands

VIII. Vestibulocochlear
Inner ear

XII. Hypoglossal
Tongue muscles

XI. Spinal accessory
Sternomastoid and trapezius muscles

X. Vagus
Heart, lungs, gastrointestinal tract, bronchi, trachea, larynx
Same

IX. Glossopharyngeal
Posterior tongue, tonsils, pharynx, pharyngeal muscles
Same

The remaining cranial nerves have both sensory and motor functions. The trigeminal (V), for example, serves facial sensation through some axons and controls chewing movements through other axons. The facial (VII) nerves control facial muscles and receive taste sensation, while the glossopharyngeal (IX) nerves receive sensation from the throat and control muscles there. The vagus (X) nerve extends far from the head, running to the heart, liver, and intestines. Its long, convoluted route is the reason for its name, which is Latin for "wandering." The vagus and some other cranial nerves are also part of the parasympathetic nervous system, which we'll describe shortly.

The spinal nerves.   Along the length of the spinal cord are 31 pairs of **spinal nerves,** with one member of each pair for each side of the body (Figure 2.9). These nerves join the spinal cord at regularly spaced intervals through openings in the bony structures of the spinal column. Each spinal nerve consists of the fusion of two distinct branches, called roots, which are functionally different. The **dorsal** (back) **root** of each spinal nerve consists of sensory pathways from the body to the spinal cord. The **ventral** (front) **root** consists of motor pathways from the spinal cord to the muscles.

The name of a spinal nerve is the same as the segment of spinal cord to which it is connected: There are 8 **cervical** (neck), 12 **thoracic** (trunk), 5 **lumbar** (lower back), 5 **sacral** (pelvic), and 1 **coccygeal** (bottom) spinal segments. Thus, the T12 spinal nerve is the spinal nerve that is connected to the twelfth segment of the thoracic portion of the spinal cord (see Figure 2.7*b*). Fibers from different spinal nerves join to form peripheral nerves, usually at some distance from the spinal cord.

2.9 The Spinal Cord and Spinal Nerves   (*Middle*) The spinal column runs from the base of the brain to the sacrum; a pair of nerves emerges from each level (see Figure 2.7*b*). (*Bottom right*) The spinal cord is surrounded by bony vertebrae and is enclosed in three membrane layers (the meninges). Each vertebra has an opening on each side through which the spinal nerves pass. (*Top right*) The spinal cord gray matter is located in the center of the cord and is surrounded by white matter. In the gray matter are interneurons and the motoneurons that send axons to the muscles. The white matter consists of myelinated axons that run up and down the spinal column. (*Left*) Stained cross sections show the spinal cord at the cervical, thoracic, lumbar, and sacral levels. (Photographs from Hanaway et al, 1998.)

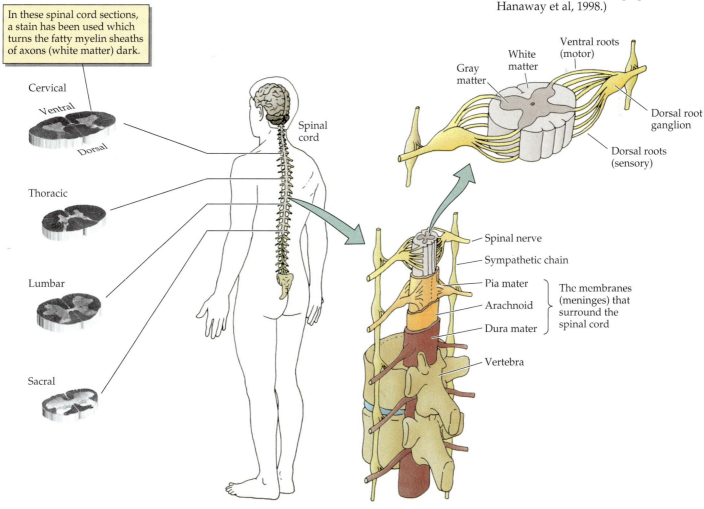

In these spinal cord sections, a stain has been used which turns the fatty myelin sheaths of axons (white matter) dark.

Cervical
Ventral
Dorsal

Thoracic

Lumbar

Sacral

Spinal cord

Gray matter
White matter
Ventral roots (motor)
Dorsal root ganglion
Dorsal roots (sensory)

Spinal nerve
Sympathetic chain
Pia mater
Arachnoid
Dura mater
} The membranes (meninges) that surround the spinal cord

Vertebra

The autonomic nervous system.   Ancient anatomists found collections of neurons outside the CNS, which we call **ganglia** (singular *ganglion*). Because they were outside the CNS, these neuron aggregates were named **autonomic** ("independent") **ganglia.** Today we know that the autonomic ganglia are controlled by neurons in the CNS; the autonomic nervous system actually spans both the central and the peripheral nervous systems. Autonomic neurons within the brain and spinal cord send out their axons to innervate neurons in the ganglia. These neurons, which have their cell bodies within the ganglia, in turn send their axons out to innervate all the major organs. The central neurons that innervate the ganglia are known as **preganglionic** autonomic cells; the ganglionic neurons that innervate the body are known as **postganglionic** autonomic cells.

The autonomic nervous system is divided into two components: the **sympathetic nervous system** and the **parasympathetic nervous system.** The preganglionic cells of the sympathetic nervous system are found exclusively in the spinal cord, specifically in the thoracic and lumbar regions. These cells send their axons a short distance to innervate a chain of ganglia running along each side of the spinal column; this chain is called the **sympathetic chain** (Figure 2.10 *left*). Cells of the sympathetic chain innervate smooth muscles in organs and in the walls of blood vessels. A convenient, if somewhat oversimplified, summary of the effects of sympathetic activation is that it prepares the body for action: Blood pressure increases, the pupils of the eyes widen, and the heart quickens.

The parasympathetic (from the Greek *para*, "around") nervous system gets its name because its preganglionic neurons are found above and below those of the sympathetic system—in the brain and the sacral spinal cord (Figure 2.10 *right*). These preganglionic cells also innervate ganglia, but parasympathetic ganglia are not collected in a chain as sympathetic ganglia are. Rather, parasympathetic ganglia are dispersed throughout the body, usually near the organ affected. For many body functions, the sympathetic and parasympathetic divisions act in opposite directions, and the result is very accurate control. For example, the heartbeat is quickened by the activity of sympathetic nerves during exercise, but it is slowed by the vagus nerve (part of the parasympathetic system) during rest. Sympathetic activation constricts blood vessels, raising blood pressure, while parasympathetic activation relaxes vessel walls; sympathetic activation inhibits digestion, while parasympathetic stimulates it. The functions of the autonomic nervous system are "independent" in another sense: We cannot voluntarily control the activity of this system in the same way that we can control our movements.

The Central Nervous System Consists of Brain and Spinal Cord

The spinal cord is a conduit that funnels sensory information from the body up to the brain and conveys brain motor commands out to the body. Thus we will discuss the spinal cord later when we are examining sensation (in Chapter 8) and movement (in Chapter 11). The remainder of this chapter will deal with the executive portion of the CNS: the brain.

Brain features that are visible to the naked eye.   Given the importance of the adult human brain, it is surprising that it weighs a mere 1400 g, just 2% of the average body weight. However, even gross inspection reveals that what the brain lacks in weight it makes up for in intricacy. Figure 2.11 offers three views of the human brain in standard orientations. These views will be helpful in our future discussions. Viewed from the side (see Figure 2.11*a*) or from the top, the human brain is dominated by the **cerebral hemispheres** (the telencephalon, also known as the cerebrum), which sit atop and surround the brainstem, which is continuous with the spinal cord.

The shape of the paired cerebral hemispheres is the result of elaborate folding together of tissue. The resulting ridges of tissue, called **gyri** (singular *gyrus*), are separated from each other by furrows called **sulci** (singular *sulcus*). Such folding enormously increases the cerebral surface area; about two-thirds of the cerebral surface is hidden in the depths of these folds.

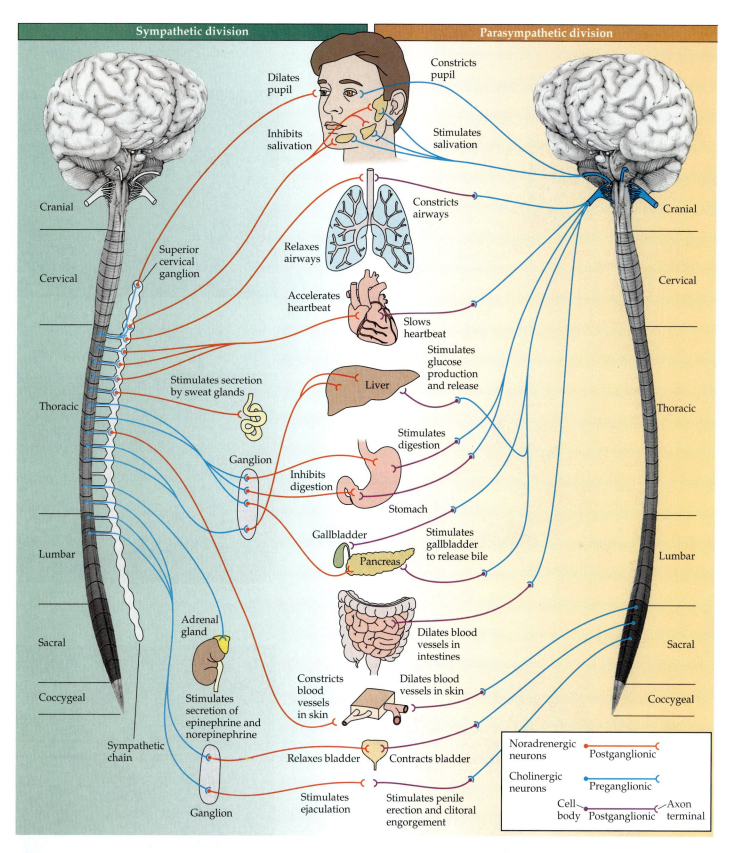

Sympathetic division

Parasympathetic division

Cranial

Cervical

Thoracic

Lumbar

Sacral

Coccygeal

Dilates pupil

Inhibits salivation

Superior cervical ganglion

Relaxes airways

Accelerates heartbeat

Stimulates secretion by sweat glands

Ganglion

Inhibits digestion

Adrenal gland

Stimulates secretion of epinephrine and norepinephrine

Sympathetic chain

Relaxes bladder

Stimulates ejaculation

Ganglion

Constricts pupil

Stimulates salivation

Constricts airways

Slows heartbeat

Stimulates glucose production and release

Liver

Stimulates digestion

Stomach

Gallbladder

Stimulates gallbladder to release bile

Pancreas

Dilates blood vessels in intestines

Constricts blood vessels in skin

Dilates blood vessels in skin

Contracts bladder

Stimulates penile erection and clitoral engorgement

Cranial

Cervical

Thoracic

Lumbar

Sacral

Coccygeal

Noradrenergic neurons — Postganglionic

Cholinergic neurons — Preganglionic

Cell body — Postganglionic — Axon terminal

2.10 The Autonomic Nervous System   (*Left*) The sympathetic division of the autonomic nervous system consists of the sympathetic chains and the nerve fibers that flow from them. (*Right*) The parasympathetic division arises from both the cranial and the sacral parts of the spinal cord. All preganglionic axons, whether sympathetic or parasympathetic, release acetylcholine as a neurotransmitter, as do parasympathetic postganglionic cells. Sympathetic postganglionic cells use norepinephrine (noradrenaline) as a neurotransmitter. The two different postganglionic transmitters are what allow the autonomic nervous system to have two opposing effects on target organs. These transmitters are discussed in more detail in Chapter 4.

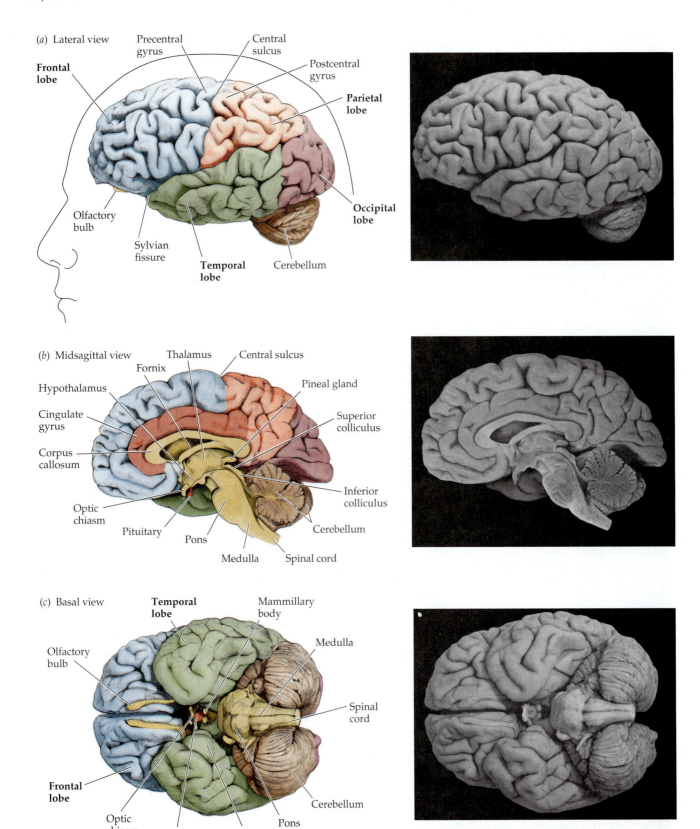

(*a*) Lateral view

Frontal lobe
Precentral gyrus
Central sulcus
Postcentral gyrus
Parietal lobe
Olfactory bulb
Sylvian fissure
Temporal lobe
Occipital lobe
Cerebellum

(*b*) Midsagittal view

Thalamus
Fornix
Central sulcus
Hypothalamus
Pineal gland
Cingulate gyrus
Superior colliculus
Corpus callosum
Optic chiasm
Inferior colliculus
Pituitary
Pons
Cerebellum
Medulla
Spinal cord

(*c*) Basal view

Temporal lobe
Mammillary body
Olfactory bulb
Medulla
Spinal cord
Frontal lobe
Optic chiasm
Pituitary
Uncus
Pons
Cerebellum

2.11 Three Views of the Human Brain   (*a*) Lateral view (from the side). (*b*) Midsagittal (midline) view. (*c*) Basal view (from below). On the right is a postmortem brain specimen seen from each view. (Photographs courtesy of S. Mark Williams and Dale Purves, Duke University Medical Center.)

Because the pattern of folding has many features that are common to all humans, the major divisions of the cerebral hemispheres can be labeled. The major sectors of the cerebral hemispheres are the **frontal, parietal, temporal,** and **occipital** regions, or lobes. These lobes, named after the bones of the skull that overlie them, are distinguished by colors in the left-hand column of Figure 2.11. Some of the boundaries defined by folds are clearly marked; for example, the lateral sulcus, or **Sylvian fissure** (which demarcates the temporal lobe), and the **central sulcus** (which divides frontal from parietal lobes) are quite prominent. Others (those dividing parietal from occipital and occipital from temporal lobes) are less well defined. The outer shell of the hemispheres is the **cerebral cortex** (the word *cortex,* Latin for "bark of a tree," refers to the outermost layers of a structure), sometimes referred to as simply the cortex.

Whereas the cerebral hemispheres seem to serve "higher," more abstract functions—damage to the cerebrum, for example, may deprive us of speech or sight—"lower" parts of the brain regulate respiration, heart rate, and other basic functions. The occipital cortex receives information from the eyes and analyzes that information to give us sight. Most auditory information reaches the temporal lobe, and damage there can impair hearing. Touch information is integrated in a strip of parietal cortex just behind the central sulcus (the **postcentral gyrus** of the parietal lobe), while in front of the central sulcus, the **precentral gyrus** of the frontal lobe is crucial for motor control. A view from a midline position (see Figure 2.11*b*) shows a large bundle of axons called the **corpus callosum,** which connects corresponding points of the right and left cerebral hemispheres.

No matter what plane is used to section the brain (see Box 2.2), two distinct shades of color are evident (Figure 2.12). The whitish areas contain tracts that appear relatively white because of the lipid (fat) content of myelin covering the axons. Darker gray areas are dominated more by cell bodies, which are devoid of myelin. Thus the term **white matter** refers to bundles of nerve fibers, and the term **gray matter** refers to areas that are rich in nerve cell bodies.

The importance of this distinction between gray and white matter is clear in the study by Andreasen et al. (1993) noted in Box 1.2. In that study, the correlation between intelligence and the volume of gray matter in the cerebral hemispheres was much higher than that between intelligence and the volume of white matter. Note that a given neuron may have its cell body in the gray matter but also extend a myelinated axon to the white matter.

2.12 Inside the Brain　(*a*) The colored lines indicate the planes of section shown in (*b*) and (*c*). The light color of the white matter is from the fatty myelin surrounding the axons in the major fiber tracts. Gray matter consists of cell bodies that form the outer layers of the brain and nuclei within the brain. (Photographs courtesy of S. Mark Williams and Dale Purves, Duke University Medical Center.)

(*a*) Lateral view showing planes of section

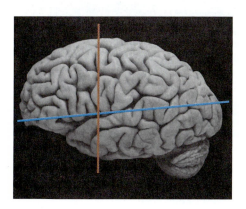

(*b*) Horizontal section

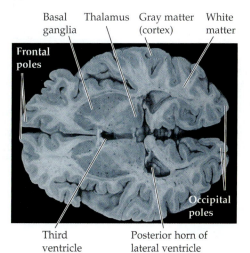

Basal ganglia　Thalamus　Gray matter (cortex)　White matter

Frontal poles

Occipital poles

Third ventricle　　Posterior horn of lateral ventricle

(*c*) Coronal or transverse section

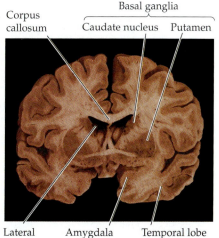

Basal ganglia

Corpus callosum　　Caudate nucleus　Putamen

Lateral ventricle　　Amygdala　　Temporal lobe

Developmental subdivisions of the brain. The complex form of the adult human brain makes it hard to understand why anatomists use terms the way they do. For example, the part of your brain closest to the back of your head is labeled as part of the forebrain. How can we make sense of this terminology? The clue to how the brain is subdivided lies in the way it develops early in life. In Chapter 7 we will consider brain development as a subject in its own right. For now we will discuss brain development in the context of categorizing brain structures.

In a very young embryo of any vertebrate, the CNS looks like a tube. The walls of this **neural tube** are made of cells, and the interior is filled with fluid. A few weeks after conception, the human neural tube begins to show three separate swellings at the head end (Figure 2.13a): the **forebrain** (or *prosencephalon*), the **midbrain** (or **mesencephalon**), and the **hindbrain** (or *rhombencephalon*). (The term *encephalon*, meaning "brain," comes from the Greek *en*, "in," and *kephale*, "head.")

About 50 days after conception, the forebrain and hindbrain have already developed clear subdivisions. At the very front of the developing brain is the **telencephalon**, which will become the cerebral hemispheres. The other part of the forebrain is the **diencephalon** (or "between brain"), which will include regions called the thalamus and the hypothalamus. The midbrain comes next. Behind it the hindbrain has two divisions: the **metencephalon**, which will develop into the **cerebellum** ("little brain") and the **pons** ("bridge"); and the **myelencephalon**, or **medulla**. The term **brainstem** usually refers to the midbrain, pons, and medulla combined. Figure 2.13c shows the positions of these main structures and their relative sizes in the adult human brain. Even when the brain achieves its adult form, it is still a fluid-filled tube, but one of very complicated shape.

2.13 Divisions of the Human Nervous System in the Embryo and the Adult

(a) A few weeks after conception, the head end of the neural tube shows three main divisions. About 50 days after conception, five main divisions of the brain are visible. Part *b* depicts the organization of these divisions schematically; part *c* shows their positions in the adult brain.

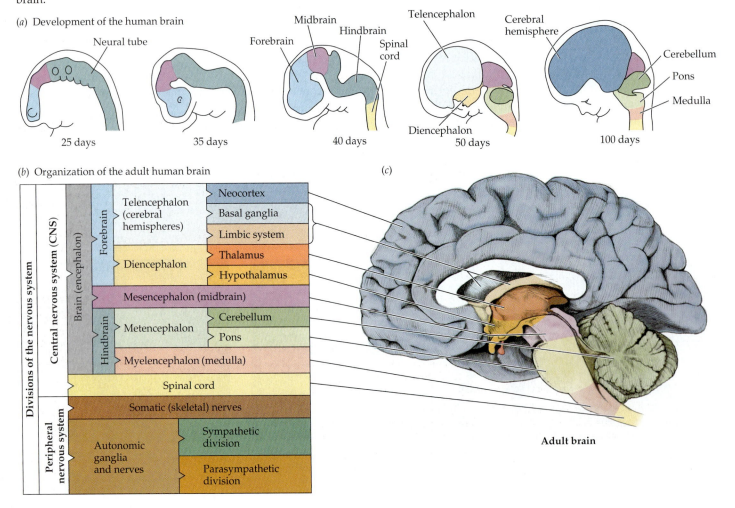

(a) Development of the human brain

Neural tube

25 days 35 days 40 days

Forebrain Midbrain Hindbrain Spinal cord

Telencephalon Cerebral hemisphere

Diencephalon 50 days

Cerebellum Pons Medulla

100 days

(b) Organization of the adult human brain

(c)

Adult brain

Each of these five main sections (telencephalon, diencephalon, mesencephalon, metencephalon, and myelencephalon) can be subdivided in turn. We can work our way from the largest, most general divisions of the nervous system at the left of the schematic in Figure 2.13*b* to more specific ones at the right. Within each region are aggregations of neurons called **nuclei** (singular *nucleus*) and bundles of axons called **tracts.** Recall that in the periphery, aggregations of neurons are called ganglia, and bundles of axons are called nerves. Unfortunately, the same word *nucleus* can mean either "a collection of nerve cell bodies" or "the spherical center of a single cell," so you must rely on the context to understand which meaning is intended. Because these nuclei and tracts are recognizable from individual to individual, and often from species to species, they have names too.

You are probably more interested in the functions of all these parts of the brain than in their names, but each region serves more than one function, most functions are spread out through several structures, and ideas about function are constantly being revised by new data. Having now oriented you to the general organization of the brain, we will embark on just a brief look at the functions of specific parts, leaving the detailed discussion for later chapters.

Now that you've seen both small- and large-scale views of the nervous system, you can refer to Figure 2.14 to compare the sizes of some important neural structures.

Brain Structures Can Be Described on the Basis of Function

Although we give simple, capsule statements about functions here, later chapters take them up more fully, so we concentrate now on understanding the physical layout of the parts rather than their functions. We'll look briefly at each of the five basic parts of the brain in turn and then examine the cerebral cortex in a little more detail. Although there are some single structures around the midline, such as the corpus callosum, pineal gland, and pituitary gland (see Figure 2.11*b*), each of the structures we'll describe next is found in both the right and the left sides of the brain.

Within the Cerebral Hemispheres Are the Basal Ganglia and the Limbic System

The **basal ganglia** include the **caudate nucleus, putamen,** and the **globus pallidus** in the telencephalon under the cerebral cortex, and the **substantia nigra** in the midbrain (Figure 2.15*a*; see also Figure 2.12*b* and *c*). These four nuclei (not really ganglia, despite the unfortunate name *basal ganglia*) send axons back and forth to innervate one another, forming a neural system. The basal ganglia are very important in motor control, as we will see in Chapter 11.

The **limbic system** is a loosely defined, widespread network of brain nuclei (Figure 2.15*b*) that are involved in mechanisms of emotion and learning. The **amygdala** (Latin for "almond," which it resembles in shape), which is also sometimes considered part of the basal ganglia, consists of several subdivisions with quite diverse functions, including emotional regulation (Chapter 15) and the perception of odor (Chapter 9). The **hippocampus** (from the Greek *hippokampos,* "sea horse," which it resembles in shape) and the **fornix** are important for learning (Chapter 17). Other components of the limbic system include a strip of cortex called the **cingulate gyrus** and the **olfactory bulb.** The rest of the limbic system is found in the diencephalon (see the next section), including the hypothalamus and the breast-shaped **mammillary bodies** (see Figure 2.11*c*).

The Diencephalon Is Divided into Thalamus and Hypothalamus

The uppermost portion of the diencephalon is the **thalamus,** seen in the center of the adult brain in Figures 2.11*b* and 2.12*b*. The thalamus is a complex cluster of nuclei that act as way stations to the cerebral cortex. Almost all sensory information enters the thalamus, where neurons send that information to the overlying cortex. The cortical cells in turn innervate the thalamus, perhaps to control which sensory information is transmitted.

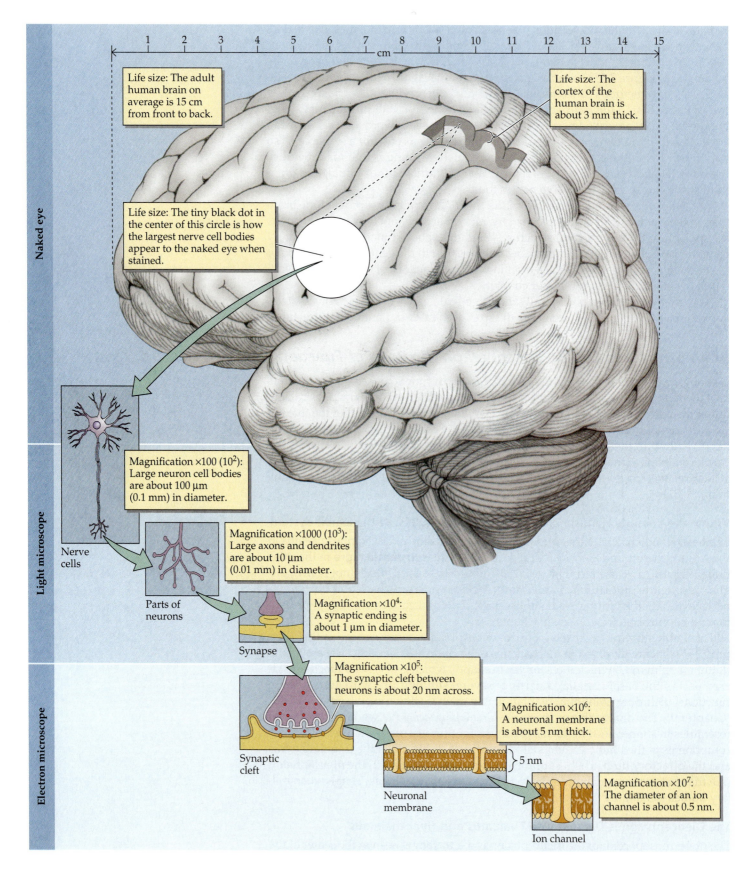

Naked eye

Light microscope

Electron microscope

Life size: The adult human brain on average is 15 cm from front to back.

Life size: The cortex of the human brain is about 3 mm thick.

Life size: The tiny black dot in the center of this circle is how the largest nerve cell bodies appear to the naked eye when stained.

Magnification ×100 (10^2): Large neuron cell bodies are about 100 μm (0.1 mm) in diameter.

Nerve cells

Magnification ×1000 (10^3): Large axons and dendrites are about 10 μm (0.01 mm) in diameter.

Parts of neurons

Magnification ×10^4: A synaptic ending is about 1 μm in diameter.

Synapse

Magnification ×10^5: The synaptic cleft between neurons is about 20 nm across.

Magnification ×10^6: A neuronal membrane is about 5 nm thick.

Synaptic cleft

5 nm

Neuronal membrane

Magnification ×10^7: The diameter of an ion channel is about 0.5 nm.

Ion channel

2.14   Sizes of Some Neural Structures and the Units of Measure and Magnification Used in Studying Them

(*a*) Basal ganglia

(*b*) Limbic system

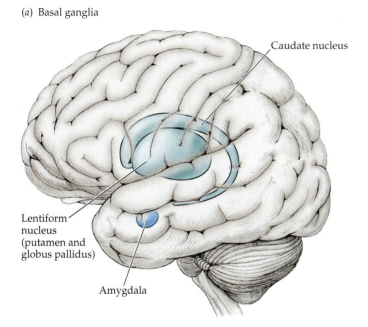

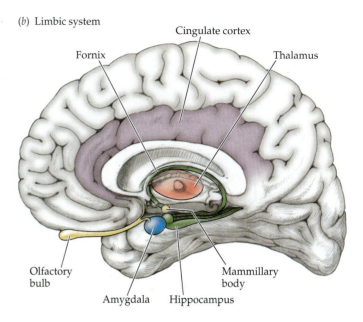

Because it is under the thalamus, the second part of the diencephalon is known as the **hypothalamus** (see Figure 2.11*b*). The hypothalamus is relatively small, but it is packed with many distinct nuclei that have vital functions. It has been implicated in hunger, thirst, temperature regulation, reproductive behaviors, and much more. The hypothalamus also controls the pituitary gland, which in turn controls almost all hormone secretion, as we'll learn in Chapter 5.

2.15 Two Important Brain Systems
(*a*) The basal ganglia—caudate nucleus, putamen, globus pallidus, substantia nigra, and amygdala—are important in movement. (The substantia nigra is not visible here because it is buried deep within the midbrain.) (*b*) The limbic system—hippocampus, thalamus, cingulate cortex, fornix, olfactory bulb, amygdala, and mammillary bodies—is important for emotion, learning, and memory.

The Midbrain Has Sensory and Motor Systems

The most prominent features of the midbrain are two pairs of bumps on the dorsal surface. The more rostral pair are the **superior colliculi** (singular *colliculus*), and the caudal pair are the **inferior colliculi** (see Figure 2.11*b*). The superior colliculi receive visual information; the inferior colliculi receive information about sound.

Two important motor centers are embedded within the midbrain. One is the substantia nigra, which we mentioned as part of the basal ganglia, containing neurons that release the transmitter dopamine into the caudate (loss of this dopamine leads to Parkinson's disease, discussed in Chapter 11). The other motor center is the **red nucleus** (because it looks red in freshly dissected tissue), which communicates with motoneurons in the spinal cord. The midbrain also contains several nuclei that send their axons out to form cranial nerves. Other such cranial nerve nuclei are found throughout the brainstem.

Also found in the midbrain is a distributed network of neurons collectively referred to as the **reticular formation** (from the Latin *reticulum,* "network"). The reticular formation stretches from the midbrain down to the medulla. Many varied functions have been attributed to different parts of this loose aggregation of neurons, including sleep and arousal, temperature regulation, and motor control.

The Cerebellum Is Attached to the Pons

The lateral, midline, and basal views of the brain in Figure 2.11 show the cerebellum. Like the cerebral hemispheres, the cerebellum includes an elaborately folded surface sheet; in this case the folds are very close together. The arrangement of cells within the sheet is relatively simple (Figure 2.16). A middle layer is composed of a single row of large, multipolar neurons called **Purkinje cells** after the anatomist who

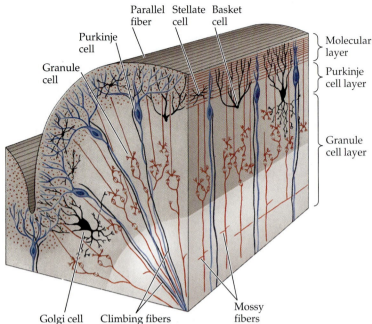

Parallel Stellate Basket
fiber   cell   cell

Purkinje
cell

Granule
cell

Molecular
layer

Purkinje
cell layer

Granule
cell layer

Golgi cell   Climbing fibers

Mossy
fibers

2.16 The Arrangement of Cells within the Cerebellum Large Purkinje cells dominate the cerebellum. Innervation between the various types of cells in the cerebellum forms a very consistent pattern. Cells depicted here in black inhibit the actions of other cells.

first described their elaborate fan-shaped dendritic patterns. All along the surface of these dendrites are numerous dendritic spines. In the depths beneath the Purkinje cells is a huge collection of small **granule cells,** whose axons form the **parallel fibers** of the surface.

Purkinje cell axons project to deep cerebellar nuclei at the base of the structure. These deep cerebellar nuclei in turn project out to brainstem centers that communicate with the spinal cord, and to thalamic centers that communicate with motor cortex. The cerebellum's role in motor coordination is also reflected in its inputs from the spinal cord and from brainstem centers for movement and body balance.

Immediately below (ventral to) the cerebellum, contributing to the brainstem, is the pons (see Figure 2.11*b* and *c*). The pons includes regions involved in motor control and sensory analysis, including several cranial nerve nuclei. Information from the ear first enters the brain in the pons. The pons also contains several groups of neurons that send their axons down to affect the spinal cord, primarily to regulate movement.

The Medulla Maintains Vital Body Functions

The medulla forms the bottom of the brainstem and marks the transition from brainstem to spinal cord. Within the medulla are the nuclei of cranial nerves XI and XII—cell bodies of neurons that control the neck and tongue muscles, respectively. The reticular formation, which we first saw in the midbrain, stretches through the pons and ends in the medulla. The medulla also contributes to the regulation of breathing and heart rate, so lesions (tissue damage) there are often fatal. Several groups of medullary neurons send their axons down the spinal cord to communicate with neurons there. Axons from the rest of the brain that reach down to affect the spinal cord must also pass through the medulla.

The Cerebral Cortex Serves Many Functions

Neuroscientists have long argued that understanding human cognition depends on unraveling the structure and fundamental functions of the cerebral cortex. In fact, by accepting electrical silence of the cortex as a criterion for defining death, many governments now define human life in terms of the workings of the cerebral cortex. The cerebral cortex is estimated to contain 50 billion to 100 billion neurons. If the cerebral cortex were unfolded, it would occupy an area of about 2000 cm^2 (315 square inches), or a square about 45 cm (18 inches) on a side. How are these cells arranged? How do the arrangements allow for particular feats of human information processing?

The neurons of the cerebral cortex are arranged in distinct layers—a laminar form of organization. Cell body and axon stains, such as those illustrated in Figure 2.17*a*, show six distinct layers in most of the cerebral cortex. (In Chapter 6 we'll discuss the three types of cerebral cortex.) Each cortical layer is distinct because it consists either of groups of cells of particular sizes, or of patterns of dendrites or axons. For example, the outermost layer, layer I, is distinct because it has few cell bodies, while layer III stands out because of its many neurons with large cell bodies.

The relative thickness of the layers varies across the cerebral cortex, suggesting a division of the cortex into subregions defined in terms of differences in the aggregation of nerve cells. Researchers have developed maps of these subregions of the cerebral cortex based on differences in cell density, in sizes and shapes of cortical neurons, and in intracortical connection patterns. The map in Figure 2.17*c* is based on these criteria. Divisions based on these structural criteria also seem to define func-

(*a*) Six layers of cortex

(*b*) A single pyramidal neuron

(*c*) Cytoarchitectonic map of regions of the cortex

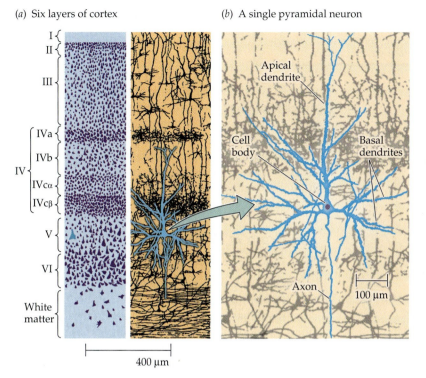

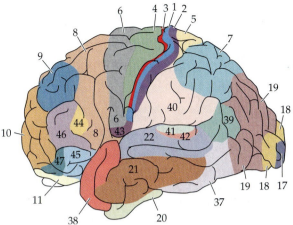

2.17 Layers of the Cerebral Cortex
(*a*) The six layers of cortex can be distinguished with stains that reveal all cell bodies (*left*), or with stains that reveal a few neurons in their entirety (*right*). (*b*) This pyramidal cell has been enlarged about 100 times. (c) Regions of the cortex are delineated here in a classic cytoarchitectonic map by Korbinian Brodmann (1909).

tional zones such as sensory and motor zones. The numbered cortical regions in Figure 2.17*c* are known as **Brodmann's areas;** sometimes we will refer to them by number in later chapters. For example, in Chapter 10 we will refer to area 17, the primary visual area at the occipital (posterior) pole of the brain.

The most prominent kind of neuron in the cerebral cortex—the **pyramidal cell** (Figure 2.17*b*)—usually has its cell bodies in layer III or V. One dendrite of each pyramidal cell (called the **apical dendrite**) usually extends to the outermost surface of the cortex. The pyramidal cell also has several dendrites (called **basal dendrites**) that spread out horizontally from the cell body. Frequently neurons of the cortex appear to be arranged in columns perpendicular to the layers, as we'll see shortly.

The variation in thickness of the different layers of cerebral cortex is related to differences in their functions. Incoming sensory fibers from the thalamus terminate especially in layer IV, so this layer is particularly prominent in regions that represent sensory functions. In fact, in part of the visual cortex in the occipital lobe, layer IV is so prominent that it appears to the naked eye as a stripe in sections cut through this area. For this reason part of the visual cortex is known as striate ("striped") cortex. Fibers that leave the cerebral cortex arise especially from layer III, which is particularly prominent in the main motor regions of the cortex. Layer III is also characterized by especially large pyramidal cells.

Cortical columns.   Some brain regions have distinctive geometric arrangements of cells that can function as information processing units. Visible in the cortex are columns of nerve cells that extend through the entire thickness of the cortex, from the white matter to the surface. In humans these **cortical columns** are about 3 mm deep and about 400 to 1000 µm in diameter (Mountcastle, 1979). Within such a column, the functional connections among cells (synaptic connections) are mainly in the vertical direction, but there are also some horizontal connections. The human cerebral cortex contains about a million cortical columns, which are thought to be the functional modules of cortical operations. In Chapter 10 we will discuss in some detail the cortical columns that analyze visual stimuli.

Vernon Mountcastle

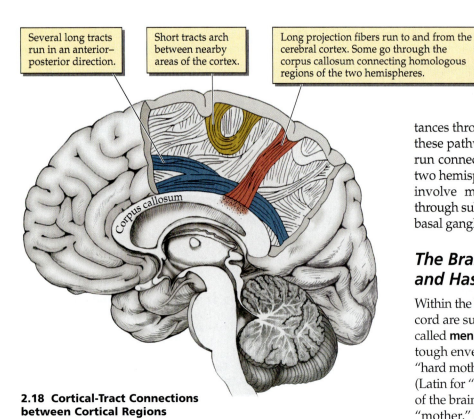

Several long tracts run in an anterior–posterior direction.

Short tracts arch between nearby areas of the cortex.

Long projection fibers run to and from the cerebral cortex. Some go through the corpus callosum connecting homologous regions of the two hemispheres.

Corpus callosum

2.18 Cortical-Tract Connections between Cortical Regions

Cortical regions communicate with one another via tracts of axons looping through the underlying white matter (Figure 2.18). Some of these connections are short pathways to nearby cortical regions; others travel longer distances through the cerebral hemispheres. The largest of these pathways is the corpus callosum, through which run connections between corresponding points on the two hemispheres. Longer links between cortical regions involve multisynaptic chains of neurons that loop through subcortical regions such as the thalamus and the basal ganglia.

The Brain Is Well Protected and Has an Abundant Blood Supply

Within the bony skull and vertebrae, the brain and spinal cord are surrounded by three protective sheets of tissue called **meninges** (see Figure 2.9). The outermost sheet is a tough envelope called the **dura mater** (in Latin, literally "hard mother"). The innermost layer, called the **pia mater** (Latin for "tender mother"), adheres tightly to the surface of the brain and follows all its contours. (The term *mater*, "mother," reflects the medieval belief that these tissues gave birth to the brain.) The delicate, weblike membrane between the dura mater and the pia mater is called the **arachnoid** (literally, "spiderweb-like"). Space within the arachnoid is filled with **cerebrospinal fluid** (**CSF**), a clear, colorless liquid.

The Cerebral Ventricles Are Chambers Filled with Fluid

Inside the brain is a series of chambers filled with CSF (Figure 2.19). These cavities form what is known as the **ventricular system.** A highly vascular (full of blood vessels) portion of the lining of the ventricles, called the **choroid plexus,** secretes cerebrospinal fluid, essentially by removing blood cells from plasma. CSF has at least two main functions:

1. It acts mechanically as a shock absorber for the brain. Because the brain floats in CSF as the head moves, movements of the head do not result in forceful shifting of the brain inside the skull cavity.
2. It mediates between blood vessels and brain tissue in the exchange of materials, including nutrients.

2.19 The Cerebral Ventricles These views of an adult human brain show the position of the cerebral ventricles within it. Cerebrospinal fluid is made in the lateral ventricles and exits from the fourth ventricle to surround the brain and spinal cord.

(*a*) Cerebral ventricles of the brain

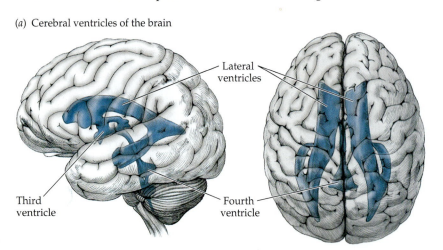

Lateral ventricles

Third ventricle

Fourth ventricle

(*b*) A closer view

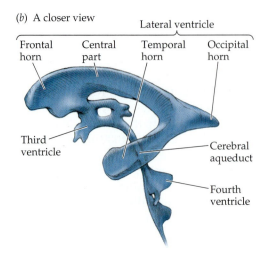

Lateral ventricle

Frontal horn

Central part

Temporal horn

Occipital horn

Third ventricle

Cerebral aqueduct

Fourth ventricle

Each hemisphere of the brain contains a **lateral ventricle** (ventricles 1 and 2) that has a complex shape. CSF forms in the lateral ventricles and flows from them into the **third ventricle,** which is located in the midline and continues down a narrow passage to the **fourth ventricle,** which lies anterior to the cerebellum. Just below the cerebellum is a small aperture, through which CSF leaves the ventricular system to circulate over the outer surface of the brain and spinal cord. CSF is absorbed back into the circulatory system through large veins beneath the top of the skull.

The Brain Has an Elaborate Vascular System

Because the brain works intensely, it has a strong metabolic demand for its fuels, oxygen and glucose. Having very little reserve of either fuel, the brain depends critically on its blood supply to provide them. Blood is delivered to the brain via two main channels: the carotid arteries and the vertebral arteries (Figure 2.20).

The common **carotid arteries** ascend the left and right sides of the neck. The internal carotid artery enters the skull and branches into anterior and middle cerebral arteries, which supply blood to large regions of the cerebral hemispheres. The **vertebral arteries** ascend along the bony vertebrae and enter the base of the skull. They join together to form the **basilar artery,** which runs along the ventral surface of the brainstem. Branches of the basilar artery supply blood to the brainstem and to posterior portions of the cerebral hemispheres.

At the base of the brain, the carotid and basilar arteries join to form a structure called the **circle of Willis.** This joining of vascular paths may provide some needed

(*a*) Basal view of brain

Circle of Willis

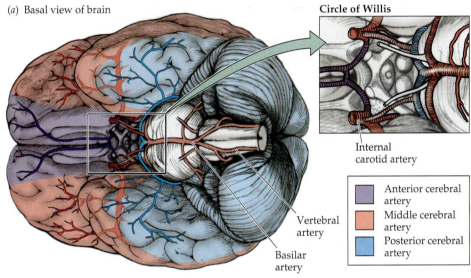

Internal carotid artery

Vertebral artery

Basilar artery

	Anterior cerebral artery
	Middle cerebral artery
	Posterior cerebral artery

2.20 The Blood Supply of the Human Brain The anterior (purple), middle (red), and posterior (blue) cerebral arteries—the three principal arteries that provide blood to the cerebral hemispheres—are depicted here in views of the basal (*a*), midsagittal (*b*), and lateral (*c*) surfaces of the brain. Each artery's "territory" is shaded in color, as shown in the key. The basilar and internal carotid arteries form a circle at the base of the brain known as the circle of Willis.

(*b*) Midsagittal view

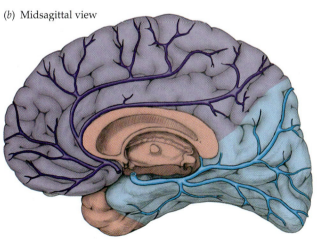

(*c*) Lateral view

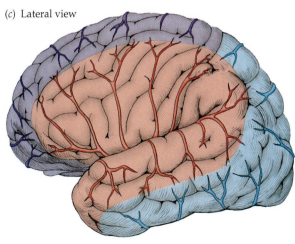

"backup" if any of the main arteries to the brain should be damaged or blocked by disease. The common term *stroke* refers to changes in the flow of blood in the brain produced by blockage or rupture of blood vessels, or by reduced flow due to heart impairment. Stroke is among the most common life-threatening disorders of humans.

The very fine capillaries that branch off from small arteries deliver nutrients and other substances to brain cells and remove waste products. This exchange in the brain is quite different from exchanges between blood vessels and cells in other body organs. Capillaries in the brain offer much greater resistance to the passage of molecules across their walls than do capillaries elsewhere. The brain is thus protected from exposure to some substances found in the blood. We refer to this protective mechanism as the **blood–brain barrier.** This barrier results from the tight fit between the cells that make up the walls of capillaries (endothelial cells) in the brain, which thus do not readily let through large molecules. The blood–brain barrier may have evolved to protect the brain from substances that other organs can tolerate.

Newer Imaging Techniques Allow Us to Look into the Living Human Brain

Xray images dense material of brain only.

Researchers have long sought ways to peer into the living human brain to see structures and how they work in different behavioral states. An ordinary X-ray of the head reveals an outline of the skull with little or no definition of brain tissue. Because the X-ray density of all parts of the brain is very similar, there is little contrast between regions of the brain. To provide contrast between brain tissue and blood vessels, investigators inject dyes into the vessels. The resultant X-ray pictures—called **angiograms** (from the Greek *angeion*, "blood vessel," and *gramma*, "record" or "picture")—provide an outline of the vascular paths of the brain and are useful in describing vascular disease, such as stroke.

Developments in computers and computer programs since the mid-1970s have enabled us to integrate many different X-ray views into a portrait that enhances small differences in density and resembles a cross section of the brain. These portraits are referred to as *tomograms* (from the Greek *tomos*, "cross-cut" or "section").

Xray → absorption shows density of skull.

Producing **computerized axial tomograms (CATs)**, or **CT** (computerized tomography) **scans,** involves moving an X-ray source in an arc around the head. The patient lies on a table, and the patient's head is then inserted into the middle of a doughnut-shaped ring (Figure 2.21*a*). An X-ray source is moved in a circular path around the head, at each position delivering a small amount of X-radiation, which passes through the head. The amount of this radiation that is absorbed within the head depends on the density of the tissue. A ring of detectors opposite the X-ray source analyzes the amount of X-radiation that has passed through the head. The X-ray tube and detectors are then moved to a new position, and the process is repeated until a composite picture can be constructed by a computer on the basis of the many X-ray views from different angles around the head.

2.21 Visualizing the Living Human Brain   The procedures of important brain imaging techniques (*left column*) and the images obtained from them (*middle and right columns*). (*a*) CT scans from a normal individual and from a patient who suffered a stroke; the stroke lesion is visible as a large yellow area. (*b*) Coronal and horizontal MRI images of a normal human brain. Note the clarity in the definition of gyri and sulci of the cerebral cortex. (*c*) PET scans show levels of metabolic activity in the brain, as in these images from a normal human and a patient with Alzheimer's; note the greater level of activity in the normal brain. (*d*) With fMRI, subjects can be presented with visual or auditory stimuli while changes in regional brain metabolism are recorded. The images are three-dimensional renderings showing areas where brain activity declined in subjects viewing images of their romantic partner (see Figure 1.7). (Images in *d* courtesy of Semir Zeki.)

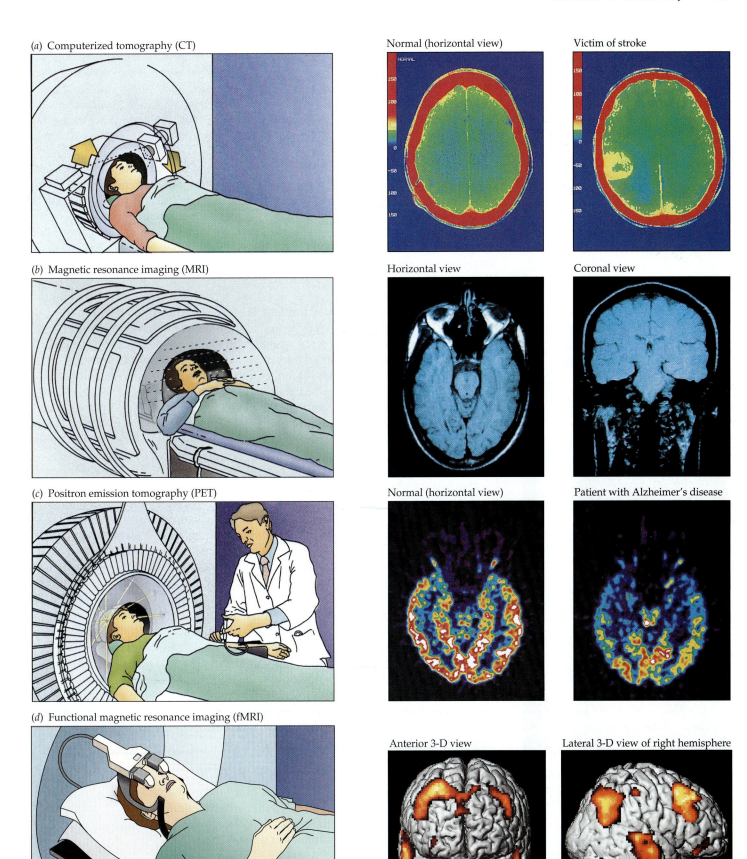

(*a*) Computerized tomography (CT)

Normal (horizontal view)

Victim of stroke

(*b*) Magnetic resonance imaging (MRI)

Horizontal view

Coronal view

(*c*) Positron emission tomography (PET)

Normal (horizontal view)

Patient with Alzheimer's disease

(*d*) Functional magnetic resonance imaging (fMRI)

Anterior 3-D view

Lateral 3-D view of right hemisphere

PET: radioisotopes injected into bloodstream. Detect emissions from brain.

Temporal & spatial resolutions - limited as well as time.

Figure 2.21*a* shows typical CT scans of one level of the brain. Each picture element (or pixel) in the final portrait is the result of a complex mathematical analysis of this small brain region viewed from many different angles. The spatial resolution of this technique has now been improved to the point where relatively small changes, such as shrinkage of a gyrus, can be visualized. Figure 2.21*a* illustrates the use of CT in the study of the behavioral effects of stroke. This technique has enabled observation of cerebral cortical changes or differences in Alzheimer's disease, schizophrenia, dyslexia, and many other disorders.

CT has been a very valuable tool, although a newer approach, **magnetic resonance imaging** (**MRI**), has become a robust competitor. MRI generates pictures that reveal some structural details in the living brain without exposing the patient to X-rays (Andreasen, 1989). MRI uses radio waves and other magnetic energy. The patient lies within a large magnet (Figure 2.21*b*), and the molecular effect of applied magnetic fields is registered by a coil detector, from which successive outputs are analyzed by computer. The resultant image can display extremely small changes in the brain, such as the loss of myelin around groups of axons, a symptom that is characteristic of demyelinating diseases. With this technique, structural abnormalities have been studied intensively in humans of all ages and conditions.

Images of the physiological functioning of the brain were first provided by a technique called **positron emission tomography** (**PET**) (Figure 2.21*c*). To obtain images of the functional state of the brain, radioactive chemicals are injected into the blood vessels. These radioisotopes travel to the brain, and their emission can be assessed by detectors outside the body. Computerized analysis of these data reveals the differential uptake and use of the chemicals in various brain regions. The most commonly used substance is a type of radioactive glucose that is taken up into different brain regions according to their levels of metabolic activity. A color transform of this information yields a striking picture that highlights areas of intense metabolic response (see Figure 2.21*c*) (Holcomb et al., 1989).

Using this technique, we can generate metabolic maps of the brain during states such as attention, movements, responses to sensory stimuli, and decision making. Special techniques, as outlined in Box 2.3, can identify brain regions that are especially activated by specific stimuli or tasks. In addition, we can identify regions that are abnormal in metabolic responses even if they are structurally intact.

Each of the methods we have described here has limitations in terms of speed (temporal resolution), sharpness (spatial resolution), or cost. Some of these limitations have been overcome by an expensive but very powerful technique called **functional MRI** (**fMRI**), which has gained enormous popularity during the past several years; most of the images of brain activity you may have seen in newspapers and magazines are created using this method (Figure 2.21*d*). This technique uses high-powered, rapidly oscillating magnetic-field gradients (the magnets in fMRI machines could lift an automobile) to detect small changes in brain metabolism. As with PET, scientists can use this data to create images that reflect the activity of different parts of the brain while subjects engage in various experimental tasks, but fMRI has several advantages over PET. First of all, fMRI does not require subjects to be injected with radioactive material. Also, fMRI has greater spatial and temporal resolution than PET.

As we will see in Chapter 10, much of what we know about visual perception and the brain has been learned in studies of monkeys. Recently, scientists used an extremely powerful, custom-built fMRI machine to monitor activity in a monkey's brain during visual tasks (Logothetis et al., 1999). The resulting images (Figure 2.22) were the sharpest functional images of primate brains (including human brains) ever created. Future monkey fMRI studies will allow scientists to draw on our extensive knowledge of the monkey brain when designing and interpreting human fMRI studies.

Other investigators are using light to make images of brain activity within the head (Gratton et al., 1998; Villringer and Chance, 1997). Near-infrared light (wavelengths of 700–1000 nm) passes through skin, scalp, and skull and penetrates into

(*a*)

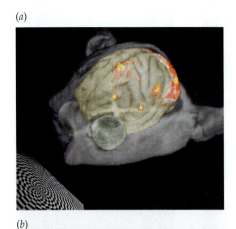

(*b*)

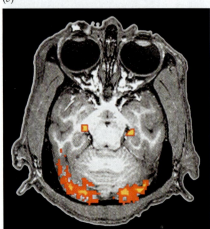

2.22 An fMRI Breakthrough (*Top*) Three-dimensional MRI/fMRI reconstruction showing active regions in a macaque monkey's brain while the monkey viewed a visual stimulus. (*Bottom*) Coronal fMRI section from the same experiment shows high activity in a part of the thalamus known as the lateral geniculate nucleus (middle of the image) and in a region of occipital cortex known as primary visual cortex, or V1 (bottom of the image). (Courtesy of Nikos Logothetis.)

BOX 2.3 *Isolating Specific Brain Activity*

Many illustrations in this and later chapters show scans of brain activity that are specifically related to brain disorders or cognitive processes. Usually most of the brain is active, so isolating specific activity requires special procedures. The PET scan shown in the figure beneath the box labeled "Visual stimulus" was made while a person looked at a fixation point surrounded by a flickering checkerboard ring. The scan next to it (beneath the box labeled "Control") was made while a person looked at a fixation point alone. In a comparison of the two, it is hard to see differences, but subtracting the control values from the stimulation values yields an image such as that shown at the upper right ("Difference image"); in this scan, it is easy to see that the main difference in activity is in the posterior part of the brain (the visual cortex).

The PET scans shown in the bottom row are difference images for five individuals who performed the same two stimulation and control tasks. Averaging these five scans results in the mean difference image for all five subjects that is shown at far right. Averaged images yield more reliable results than individual images, but they lack some of the specificity of the individual images.

Visual stimulus   Control

Brain scans are made while a subject is in a control condition, and while he or she is exposed to an experimental stimulus or performs a task. The difference in brain activity in the scans can be computed and represented as a color-coded "difference image" that shows the areas of the brain that were most active during the experimental condition.

Resulting brain activity   Difference image

Difference images from several subjects can be added together and averaged . . .

. . . to arrive at a "mean difference image" that shows the most active brain areas across subjects in an experiment.

Mean difference image

All the PET and fMRI images in this book are difference images, usually made from scans of a single individual's brain. When you see brain function images in this book or in the popular press, note whether they are direct scans or difference images; if the latter, note whether they show values for an individual or for the mean of a group. (PET scans courtesy of Marcus Raichle.)

---

the brain. When such light is transmitted into the brain and detectors pick up the reflections at various nearby sites, the responses reflect the activity of cortical regions. Some components of the optical responses reflect the electrical signals of neurons, and other components reflect blood flow. The relatively low expense and small size of the optical imaging apparatus may allow many more laboratories to use brain imaging in their research. Optical studies could be done with young children or children with attention deficits who will not lie still in an MRI magnet or a PET scanner. They could also be used to monitor patients at bedside.

To investigate many problems of biological psychology, imaging provides convergent evidence with studies of naturally occurring or experimental brain lesions. Each of these kinds of investigation helps to overcome limitations on the other sources of evidence. Furthermore, "remarkable progress in brain imaging techniques does not compete with the psychological analysis of behavior but instead places a new premium upon the thoughtfulness and accuracy of such analysis" (Gabrieli, 1998, p. 89). We will see many examples of brain imaging in later chapters.

Summary

1. The nervous system is extensive—monitoring, regulating, and modulating the activities of all parts and organs of the body.

Refer to the *Learning Biological Psychology* CD for the following study aids for this chapter:

9 Objectives

67 Study Questions

10 Activities

2. Nerve cells (neurons) are the basic units of the nervous system. The typical neuron of most vertebrate species has three main parts: (1) the cell body, which contains the nucleus; (2) dendrites, which receive information; and (3) an axon, which carries impulses from the neuron. Because of the variety of functions they serve, neurons are extremely varied in size, shape, and chemical activity.

3. Neurons make functional contacts with other neurons, or with muscles or glands, at specialized junctions called synapses. At most synapses a chemical transmitter liberated by the presynaptic terminal diffuses across the synaptic cleft and binds to special receptor molecules in the postsynaptic membrane.

4. The axon is the specialized output zone of the nerve cell and is generally tubular, branching at the end into many collaterals. Axonal transport is the movement of materials within the axon.

5. Glial cells serve many functions, including the breakdown of transmitters, the production of myelin sheaths around axons, the exchange of nutrients and other materials with neurons, and the removal of cellular debris.

6. The nervous system of vertebrates is divided into central and peripheral nervous systems.

7. The central nervous system (CNS) consists of the brain and spinal cord. The main divisions of the brain can be seen most clearly in the embryo. These divisions are the forebrain (telencephalon and diencephalon), the midbrain (mesencephalon), and the hindbrain (metencephalon and myelencephalon).

8. The peripheral nervous system includes the cranial nerves, spinal nerves, and autonomic ganglia. The autonomic nervous system consists of the sympathetic nervous system, which tends to ready the body for action, and the parasympathetic nervous system, which tends to have an effect opposite to that of the sympathetic system.

9. The human brain is dominated by the cerebral hemispheres, which include the cerebral cortex, an extensive sheet of folded tissue. The cerebral cortex is responsible for higher-order functions such as vision, language, and memory. Other neural systems include the basal ganglia, which regulate movement; the limbic system, which controls emotional behaviors; and the cerebellum, which aids coordination and some kinds of learning.

10. The brain and spinal cord are protected by coverings of tissue called meninges and by cerebrospinal fluid (CSF), which surrounds and infiltrates the brain (via cerebral ventricles) to act as a shock absorber.

11. The blood system of the brain is an elaborate array of blood vessels that deliver nutrients and other substances to the brain. The walls of the blood vessels in the brain provide a barrier to the flow of large, potentially harmful molecules into the brain.

12. Modern techniques make it possible to visualize the anatomy of the living human brain and regional metabolic differences through external monitoring devices. These techniques include computerized axial tomography (CT scans), positron emission tomography (PET scans), magnetic resonance imaging (MRI), and functional MRI (fMRI).

Recommended Reading

Blumenfeld, H. (In press). *Neuroanatomy through clinical cases.* Sunderland, MA: Sinauer Associates.

Brodal, P. (1992). *The central nervous system: Structure and function.* New York: Oxford University Press.

Hanaway, J., Woolsey, T. A., Gado, M. H., and Roberts, M. P. (1998). *The brain atlas.* Bethesda, MD: Fitzgerald Science.

Mai, J. K., Assheuer, J., and Paxinos, G. (1997). *Atlas of the human brain.* San Diego, CA: Academic Press.

Martin, J. H. (1996). *Neuroanatomy: Text and atlas* (2nd ed.). Stamford, CT: Appleton & Lange.

Posner, M. I., and Raichle, M. E. (1997). *Images of mind.* San Francisco: Freeman.

Posner, M. I., and Raichle, M. E. (Eds.). (1998). National Academy of Sciences Colloquium on Neuroimaging of Human Brain Function. *Proceedings of the National Academy of Sciences, USA, 95,* 736–939.

Stewart, M. G. (1992). *Quantitative methods in neuroanatomy.* New York: Wiley-Liss.

3

Neurophysiology: Conduction, Transmission, and Integration of Neural Signals

As you read this page, light stimulates your eye and starts a barrage of signals that travels along nerve cells to your brain. Soon you recall connections between what you are reading and memories and thoughts of related ideas. In both cases, circuits of neurons in the brain provide the biological substrates for these experiences. What are the elementary signals of nerve cells? How do these signals speed along axons and move across the synaptic gaps between neurons? How can neural circuits process information? In this chapter we describe the basic electrical signals of nervous systems and the physico-chemical basis of these electrical events. Understanding how nerve cells conduct signals prepares us to consider how information is transmitted from one neuron to another and how information is processed in different kinds of circuits.

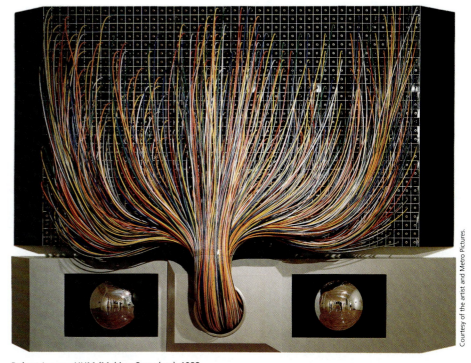

Robert Longo, *HUM (Making Ourselves)*, 1988

Courtesy of the artist and Metro Pictures.

Electrical Signals Are the Vocabulary of the Nervous System

The chemical machinery that evolved in the first, single-celled, organisms included a lot of molecules, such as proteins, that carry a negative electrical charge. Thus all living cells today are electrically polarized: Their interior is more negatively charged than the fluid surrounding them. Long ago nerve cells began to exploit this electrical polarity to communicate with one another. In this chapter we'll learn how hundreds of neurons each perturb the electrical charge of a particular target neuron, and how that neuron in turn may send a signal to affect the polarity of hundreds more.

This electrical communication system works in much the same way in animals as diverse as human beings, insects, and jellyfish. These neural signals underlie the whole range of thought and action, from composing music or solving a mathematical problem to feeling an itch on the skin and swatting a mosquito. To understand this system, we'll first review the physical forces at work, then discuss some details of why nerve cells are electrically polarized, how one neuron influences the polarity of others, and how a change of polarity in one part of a neuron can spread throughout that cell.

What Physical Forces Are behind Electrical Signaling by Neurons?

First let's review a few basics of electricity. Some molecules have a net negative charge because they have an abundance of electrons, while other molecules have a net positive charge because they have relatively few electrons. When such molecules are dissolved in fluid, we call them **ions.** Taken all together, the ions in the **intracellular fluid** found inside a cell have a negative charge compared to the **extracellular fluid** outside the cell, so we say there is an electrical *potential difference* between the inside and outside of the cell. Differences in electrical potential are measured in units called **volts.**

Most cells have a **membrane potential** (a potential difference across the membrane) of about 50 to 80 thousandths of a volt (50–80 millivolts, **mV**). If we put one electrode of a voltmeter inside a neuron and another electrode in the fluid around that neuron, the voltmeter will indicate a membrane potential of, say, –60 mV (the minus sign indicates that the inside of the cell is more negative than the outside). To get an electrode inside the tiny neuron, we use a fluid-filled, hollow glass tube with a small, sharp tip forming a **microelectrode,** as depicted in Figure 3.1.

A basic principle of charged particles is that they exert **electrical force** on one another: Like charges repel, and opposite charges attract (Figure 3.2a). So positively charged ions (called **cations**) are attracted to the intracellular fluid of the cell because it is more negative than the fluid outside the cell. Negatively charged ions (**anions**) are repelled by the cell interior and so tend to exit to the extracellular fluid. (To remember which type of ion is positively charged, note that the word cation has a *t* in it, which is similar to a plus sign.)

Another force that plays an important role in neuronal signaling is generated by **concentration gradients:**

3.1 Measuring the Resting Potential

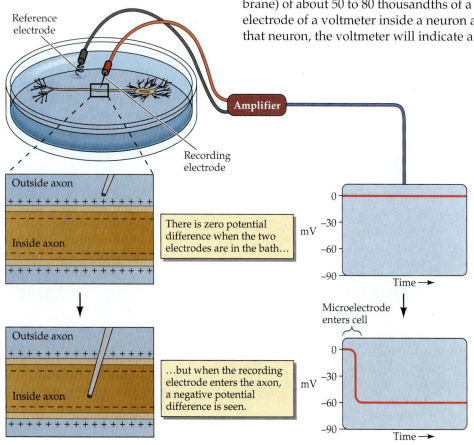

Reference electrode

Recording electrode

Amplifier

Outside axon

+ + + + + + + + + + + + + + +

Inside axon

+ + + + + + + + + + + + + + +

There is zero potential difference when the two electrodes are in the bath…

Outside axon

+ + + + + + + + + + + + + + +

Inside axon

+ + + + + + + + + + + + + + +

…but when the recording electrode enters the axon, a negative potential difference is seen.

mV
0
–30
–60
–90
Time →

Microelectrode enters cell

mV
0
–30
–60
–90
Time →

Ions move from regions of high concentration to regions of low concentration (Figure 3.2*b*). If you put a drop of food coloring in a glass of water, the molecules of dye move from the drop, where they are highly concentrated, to the rest of the glass, where they are less concentrated. In other words, molecules tend to move down their concentration gradient until they are evenly distributed.

Finally, neuronal signaling makes use of **selective permeability,** the property of cell membranes that allows some ions to cross much more readily than others. What accounts for selective permeability? Neuronal membranes contain **ion channels,** protein tubes that span the membrane. Some of these channels seem to stay open all the time, and only ions small enough to go through the tubes can cross the membrane (Figure 3.2*c*). As we'll see, if ion channels that are usually closed open rapidly, the permeability of a neuronal membrane can change suddenly.

Ionic Mechanisms Maintain the Resting Potential

Because the membrane potential of a neuron can be influenced by other cells, it is convenient to consider the neuron's membrane potential when it is not being perturbed, the so-called **resting potential** (or resting membrane potential). Nerve cells are special because changes in their resting potential are signals that can be transmitted and integrated in complex ways. To understand those changes in membrane potential, we have to learn more about why neurons have a resting potential somewhere between –50 mV and –80 mV.

To begin, imagine a single-celled organism in the sea. As we said before, the protein machinery inside the cell includes many large anions. The total negative charge of these anions makes the cell more negative than the sea around it, which means that surrounding cations are attracted to the cell's interior by electrical force (Figure 3.3*a*). Cell membranes are relatively permeable to potassium (K^+) ions, mainly because these ions are small. So K^+ ions are pulled into the cell until eventually the concentration of K^+ ions inside the cell is much greater than that in the sea. Indeed, the concentration of K^+ ions is about twenty times greater inside cells than outside (Figure 3.3*b*). Note that the influx of positively charged K^+ ions makes the cell a little less negatively polarized than it was initially. But the difference between intracellular and extracellular K^+ ions sets up a concentration gradient.

Now the concentration gradient of K^+ ions is pushing them out (from high concentration inside the cell to low concentration outside). So the electrical force, pulling K^+ ions into the cell, is being opposed by the concentration gradient pushing the K^+ ions out. Eventually the cell reaches a point at which the electrical force pulling K^+ ions in is exactly balanced by the concentration gradient pushing them out (see Figure 3.3*b*). At this point, every K^+ ion entering the cell is matched by one exiting the cell, and we say that the cell is at equilibrium.

Why do most cells have a membrane potential of –50 to –80 mV? Because this range marks the point at which the tendency of K^+ ions to flow out (from the regions of high concentration inside the cell) is exactly balanced by the negative charge that

(*a*) Electrostatic forces

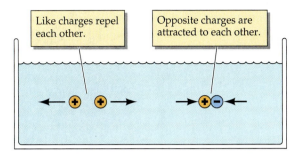

Like charges repel each other.

Opposite charges are attracted to each other.

(*b*) Diffusion

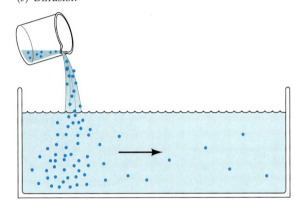

Particles move from areas of high concentration to areas of low concentration. They move down their concentration gradient.

(*c*) Diffusion through semipermeable membranes

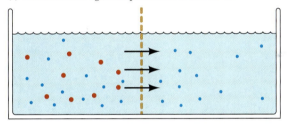

Certain membranes, including those found in cells, permit some substances to pass through, but not others.

3.2 Ionic Forces Underlying Electrical Signaling in Neurons

3.3 The Ionic Basis of the Resting Potential

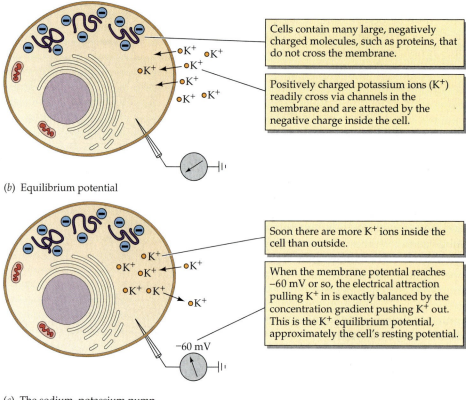

(a) Membrane permeability to ions

Cells contain many large, negatively charged molecules, such as proteins, that do not cross the membrane.

Positively charged potassium ions (K⁺) readily cross via channels in the membrane and are attracted by the negative charge inside the cell.

(b) Equilibrium potential

Soon there are more K⁺ ions inside the cell than outside.

When the membrane potential reaches −60 mV or so, the electrical attraction pulling K⁺ in is exactly balanced by the concentration gradient pushing K⁺ out. This is the K⁺ equilibrium potential, approximately the cell's resting potential.

−60 mV

(c) The sodium–potassium pump

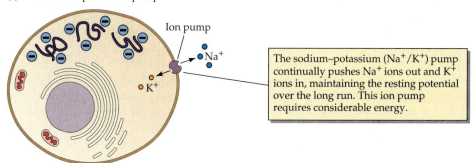

Ion pump

Na⁺

K⁺

The sodium–potassium (Na⁺/K⁺) pump continually pushes Na⁺ ions out and K⁺ ions in, maintaining the resting potential over the long run. This ion pump requires considerable energy.

attracts them in. This electrical potential is called the **potassium equilibrium potential** and is so predictable according to the laws of physical chemistry that it can be calculated by an equation, called the **Nernst equation.** The Nernst equation represents the voltage that develops when a semipermeable membrane separates different concentrations of ions. It predicts that the potential across an axon from a squid, for example, will be about –75 mV. The actual value is about –70 mV. So the resting potential of neurons is approximately the same as the potassium equilibrium potential.

The predicted value differs from the observed value because the membrane is not absolutely impermeable to sodium (Na⁺) ions. Small numbers of Na⁺ ions leak in. Later we'll see occasions when many Na⁺ ions enter the cell. Eventually such leakage would cause the concentrations inside and outside the cell to become the same, and the membrane potential would disappear. But the neuron prevents this with a mechanism, the **sodium–potassium pump,** that actively pumps Na⁺ out of the cell, and K⁺ in, just rapidly enough to counter the leakage (Figure 3.3c).

Maintaining the membrane potential, which is necessary for the neuron to be ready to conduct impulses, demands metabolic work by the cell. In fact, much of the energy expended by the brain—whether waking or sleeping—is used to maintain the ionic gradients across neuronal membranes. Thus there are always more K⁺ ions inside the neuron than outside, and more Na⁺ ions outside the neuron than inside (Figure 3.4).

The resting potential of a neuron provides a baseline level of polarization. What distinguishes neurons from most other cells is that they routinely undergo a brief but radical change in polarization, sending an electrical signal from one end of the neuron to the other, as we'll discuss next.

A Threshold Amount of Depolarization Triggers an Action Potential

Nerve impulses, or **action potentials,** are brief, propagated changes in neuronal polarization that travel rapidly along the axon. A major way for a neuron to send a message to other cells is by producing an action potential, so we need to describe what action potentials are and how they are made. Let's conduct some experiments in which we cause a neuron to produce an action potential.

To talk about these experiments, we must add two terms to our vocabulary: **Hyperpolarization** is an increase in membrane potential (even greater negativity inside the membrane in comparison with the outside). Because the neuron already has a negative membrane potential, of say, –60 mV (meaning that it is 60 mV more negative inside than outside), hyperpolarization makes it *even more* negative inside, maybe –70 mV. **Depolarization** is a reduction of the membrane potential (decreased negativity inside the neuron). Note that depolarization of a neuron from a resting potential of –60 mV to, say, –50 mV makes the inside of the neuron more like the outside. In other words, depolarization of a neuron brings its membrane potential *closer to zero.*

Later we'll talk about how other neurons hyperpolarize or depolarize a particular neuron, but for now it's simpler to see what happens when we impose these changes on a neuron by inserting a stimulating electrode into the axon, as in Figure 3.5a. We'll also place a recording electrode inside the axon to see how the neuron responds to the stimulating electrode. Applying a *hyperpolarizing* stimulus to the axonal membrane results in responses that almost mirror the *shape* of the stimulus pulse (Figure 3.5b). In several ways, these responses from the neuron seem to passively reflect the stimulus. For example, the greater the stimulus, the greater the response, so the neuron's response is **graded.**

Notice that there are distortions at the leading and trailing edges of the response—abrupt stimulations produce gradually rising responses—because of an electrical property of the membrane: its capacitance, or the ability to store electrical charges. But aside from the more gradual onset of the response, notice that the change in the neuron's membrane potential is nearly immediate: When the stimulation begins, the neuronal membrane response begins. Likewise, when the stimulation stops, the response begins fading immediately, which also suggests that the neuron is passively responding to these inputs.

If we placed several fine electrodes at successive positions along the axon and applied a hyperpolarizing pulse, we would see another way in which the neuron seems passive. The responses are progressively smaller at greater and greater distances from the stimulus site. A simple law of physics describes this relationship: In a conducting medium, the size of a potential decays as a function of the square of the distance. Because the amplitudes of these responses decline with distance, they are examples of **local potentials** that diminish progressively as you move away from the site of stimulation.

Key

		= Na⁺		= K⁺		= Cl⁻		= Ca²⁺		⁻ = Anion
Outside cell		440		20		560		10		few
Inside cell		50		400		40–150		0.0001		many

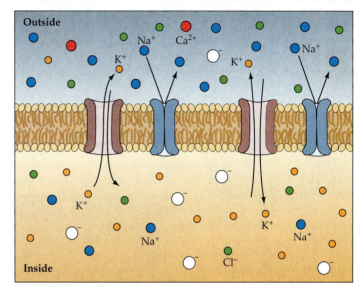

3.4 The Distribution of Ions inside and outside a Neuron Most potassium ions (K⁺) are found inside the neuron; most sodium (Na⁺) and chloride (Cl⁻) ions are in the extracellular space. These ions are exchanged through specialized channels in the cell membrane. The large, negatively charged protein molecules stay inside the neuron and account for much of the negative resting potential.

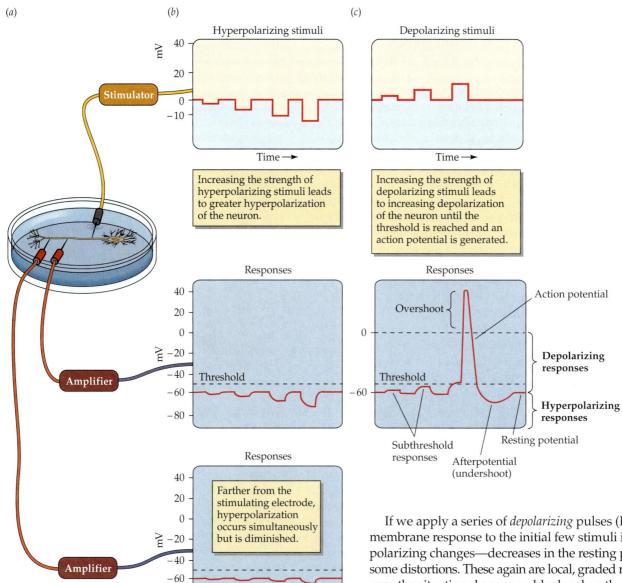

(a)

(b)

(c)

Hyperpolarizing stimuli

Depolarizing stimuli

Time →

Time →

Increasing the strength of hyperpolarizing stimuli leads to greater hyperpolarization of the neuron.

Increasing the strength of depolarizing stimuli leads to increasing depolarization of the neuron until the threshold is reached and an action potential is generated.

Responses

Responses

Threshold

Threshold

Overshoot

Action potential

Depolarizing responses

Hyperpolarizing responses

Subthreshold responses

Resting potential

Afterpotential (undershoot)

Responses

Farther from the stimulating electrode, hyperpolarization occurs simultaneously but is diminished.

Stimulator

Amplifier

Amplifier

3.5 The Effects of Hyperpolarizing and Depolarizing Stimuli on a Neuron (a) Experimental setup. (b) Effects of hyperpolarizing stimuli at two recording locations. (c) Generation of an action potential with depolarizing stimuli.

If we apply a series of *depolarizing* pulses (Figure 3.5c), the membrane response to the initial few stimuli is a series of depolarizing changes—decreases in the resting potential—with some distortions. These again are local, graded responses. However, the situation changes suddenly when the stimulus depolarizes the cell to –50 mV or so. At this potential, known as the **threshold,** a brief (0.5–2.0 ms) response is provoked: the action potential or nerve impulse. This response is a brief change in the membrane potential that momentarily makes the inside of the membrane *positive* with respect to the outside; it is sometimes called an **overshoot.** This action potential will propagate down the axon, as we'll discuss a little later.

What happens when we increase the level of depolarizing stimuli in successive pulses until they are well above threshold? This experiment displays another significant property of axonal membranes: With further increases in depolarizing stimulation, the amplitude of the nerve impulse does not change. The size of the nerve impulse is thus independent of stimulus magnitude. This characteristic is referred to as the **all-or-none property** of the nerve impulse. However, increases in stimulus strength are represented in the axon by changes in the *frequency* of nerve impulses rather than in the *amplitude.* That is, with stronger stimuli, more nerve impulses are produced but the size of each impulse remains the same.

A closer look at the form of the nerve impulse shows that the return to baseline is not simple. Rather, many axons show oscillations of potential following the nerve impulse. These changes are called **afterpotentials** or **undershoots,** and they are related to ion movements that we'll describe shortly.

Ionic Mechanisms Underlie the Action Potential

We just noted that when the membrane potential or voltage is changed by about 10 mV in a positive direction (depolarized), the membrane potential suddenly shifts in an explosive manner until the inside of the cell becomes transiently positive relative to the outside. The membrane potential then rapidly falls to somewhat less than the resting potential and then returns to the resting level. Why does this happen?

It used to be thought that the action potential resulted from a momentary increase in membrane permeability to all ions that caused the membrane potential to drop to zero. But Nobel Prize–winning research by English neurophysiologists Alan Hodgkin and Andrew Huxley revealed that an overshoot briefly makes the inside of the neuron positive with respect to the outside (see Figure 3.5c). Hodgkin and Huxley's experiments would have been hard to perform with just any axon. Most mammalian axons are less than 20 μm in diameter and quite difficult to pierce with an electrode. But nature provided Hodgkin and Huxley with an extraordinary solution to this problem: the giant axons of invertebrates, especially those of the squid.

Squid giant axons can attain a diameter of 1 mm, so thick and apparent to the unaided eye that observers originally thought these axons must be part of the circulatory or urinary system. Microelectrodes with tips about 0.2 μm in diameter can be inserted into a giant axon without altering its properties or activity. The membrane seems to seal around the inserted electrode tip. It is even possible to push the intracellular fluid out of the squid axon and replace it with other fluids to monitor the effect on the action potential.

The amplitude of the overshoot that occurs in response to changes in membrane potential is determined by the concentration of sodium ions (Na^+) (Hodgkin and Katz, 1949). At the peak of the nerve impulse, the potential across the membrane approaches that predicted by the Nernst equation with respect to the concentration of sodium ions: about +40 mV. This is the equilibrium potential for Na^+, the point at which the concentration gradient pushing Na^+ ions into the cell is exactly balanced by the positive charge pushing them out.

In its resting state the neural membrane can be thought of as a *potassium membrane* because it is permeable only to K^+ and the potential is about that of the potassium equilibrium potential. The active membrane, however, is a *sodium membrane,* permeable mainly to Na^+, so the membrane potential briefly tends toward the sodium equilibrium potential. Thus the action potential occurs during a sudden shift in membrane properties, which revert quickly to the resting state.

What causes the changes from K^+ permeability to Na^+ permeability and back again? A reduction in the resting potential of the membrane (depolarization) increases Na^+ permeability by opening "gates" in pores, or ion channels, that pass through the membrane (Figure 3.6).

A very special ion channel is responsible for the action potential. Like other ion channels, the **voltage-gated Na^+ channel** is a protein. But the voltage-gated Na^+ channel opens up in response to depolarization. So when we depolarize the axon to threshold, some of these Na^+ channels open (Figure 3.7). As some Na^+ ions enter the neuron, the resting potential is further reduced, causing still more Na^+ channels to open. Thus the process accelerates until all barriers to the entry of Na^+ are removed, and Na^+ ions rush in.

The voltage-gated Na^+ channels stay open for a little less than a millisecond; then they close again. By this time the membrane potential has reached the sodium equilibrium potential of about +40 mV. Now positive charges inside the nerve cell tend to push K^+ ions out, and the permeability to K^+ also increases, so the resting potential is soon restored.

If we continue the experiment on this axon by applying either very strong stimuli or stimulating pulses that are closely spaced in time, we observe another important property of axonal membranes. As we offer the beleaguered axon more and more stimuli, we note an upper limit to the frequency for nerve impulse activity, at about 1200 impulses per second. (Many neurons have even slower maximum rates

Alan Hodgkin

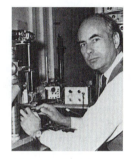

Andrew Huxley

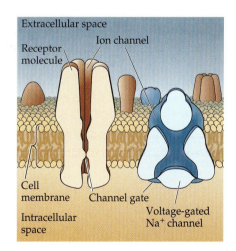

3.6 Ion Channels Neuronal membranes are studded with ion channels that consist of several large protein molecules linked together, floating in the fatty layers of the membrane. The voltage-gated Na^+ channel is essential to the action potential.

3.7 Mediation of the Action Potential by Voltage-Gated Sodium Channels

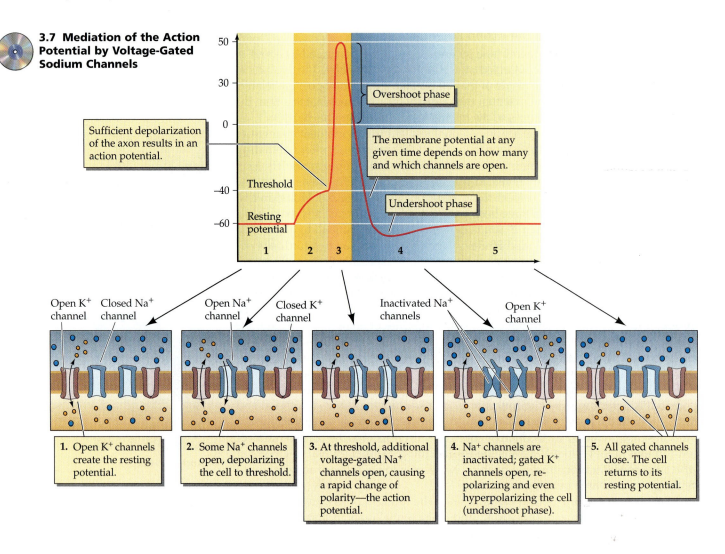

Sufficient depolarization of the axon results in an action potential.

Overshoot phase

The membrane potential at any given time depends on how many and which channels are open.

Threshold

Undershoot phase

Resting potential

Open K⁺ channel   Closed Na⁺ channel

Open Na⁺ channel   Closed K⁺ channel

Inactivated Na⁺ channels

Open K⁺ channel

1. Open K⁺ channels create the resting potential.

2. Some Na⁺ channels open, depolarizing the cell to threshold.

3. At threshold, additional voltage-gated Na⁺ channels open, causing a rapid change of polarity—the action potential.

4. Na⁺ channels are inactivated; gated K⁺ channels open, re-polarizing and even hyperpolarizing the cell (undershoot phase).

5. All gated channels close. The cell returns to its resting potential.

of response.) The same underlying property is shown when we compare the effects of varying the interval between two successive stimuli; that is, we space our stimuli closer and closer together until, at a particular brief interval, only the first pulse elicits a nerve impulse. In this case the axon membrane is said to be **refractory** (unresponsive) to the second stimulus. For a short while after the initiation of a nerve impulse, the membrane is totally insensitive to applied stimuli. This period is called the **absolute refractory phase** and is followed by a period of reduced sensitivity, the **relative refractory phase.**

The absolute and relative refractory phases can be related to changes in membrane permeability to Na⁺ as well. When the voltage-gated Na⁺ channels have opened completely during the rise of the nerve impulse, further stimulation does not affect the course of events. The Na⁺ channels, having opened during the action potential and then closed again, refuse to open again for a short time. Thus, during the rising and falling phases of an action potential, the neuron is *absolutely* refractory to elicitation of a second impulse. While K⁺ ions are flowing out and the resting potential is being restored, the neuron is *relatively* refractory, partly because some Na⁺ channels are still refractory, and partly because the cell is slightly hyperpolarized and therefore further from threshold, at the end of the action potential.

It's interesting to reflect that this protein molecule, the voltage-gated Na⁺ channel, is really a quite complicated machine. It monitors the axon's polarity, and at threshold the channel changes its shape to open the pore. But the channel also has a timing device that shuts the pore about a millisecond later. Finally, the channel somehow "remembers" that it was open lately and refuses to open again for a short time. These properties produce and enforce the properties of the action potential.

In general, cell bodies and most dendrites do not conduct action potentials, and this lack of conduction can be explained in terms of the kinds of membrane channels they contain. The cell body and dendrites have ion channels that are gated by certain chemicals, and they can therefore be stimulated chemically, as we'll discuss later in this chapter. But cell bodies and dendrites usually have few voltage-gated Na^+ channels (in an interesting exception to this rule, some dendrites actively propagate a potential to the cell body [Martina et al., 2000]). For this reason, a change in electrical potential cannot regenerate itself over the surface of the cell body by affecting voltage-gated channels in the adjacent stretch of cell membrane. The same is true for most dendrites. The voltage-gated ion channels of axons are what make them electrically excitable.

How Can We Study Ion Channels?

Let's look briefly at present concepts of the structure of ion channels and then consider how investigators have been able to determine these structures. The membrane is a double layer of lipids whose fatty nature tends to repel water. Because ions in water or body fluids are usually surrounded by clusters of water molecules, they cannot easily pass through neuronal membranes. Instead, they penetrate the cell through special channels, the inner surfaces of which do not repel water (see Figure 3.6).

The ion channels in neuronal membranes are too tiny to be seen in detail, even with the electron microscope. How, then, can investigators determine their structures and modes of operation? Three main techniques have been used, providing more complete knowledge about ion channels. Molecular genetic analysis of potassium and sodium channels in a variety of cells, including muscle cells and neurons, has yielded a detailed portrait of ion channel structure and function. Some of these studies have come from the scrutiny of abnormalities in sodium and potassium channel function that underlie particular human diseases. For example, some heritable muscle disorders characterized by loss of muscle tone or paralysis involve abnormalities in the sodium channels of muscle (S. C. Cannon, 1996). These studies reveal that multiple genes encode the structure and function of ion channel proteins. Other researchers use pharmacology or patch clamp techniques, which we describe next.

Pharmacological techniques. In pharmacological experiments, certain toxins of animal origin are used to block specific ion channels—some affecting the outer end of the channel, and others inhibiting the inner end of the channel. By specifically blocking only some channels, these toxins provide information about those channels, as well as about the remaining, unblocked channels.

Two animal toxins are known to block sodium channels when applied to the outer surface of the membrane; they do not affect other kinds of channels. These toxins are **tetrodotoxin** (**TTX**) and **saxitoxin** (**STX**). The size and structure of TTX and STX, together with those of other molecules that do or do not alter Na^+ permeability, indicate the dimensions of the sodium channel. Tetrodotoxin is found in the ovaries of the puffer fish, which is esteemed as a delicacy in Japan. If the ovaries of the puffer fish are not removed properly and if the fish is not cleaned with great care, people who eat it may be poisoned by TTX, which prevents their neurons from producing action potentials. Two kinds of scorpions have also evolved venoms that block the sodium channel.

Patch clamp recordings. In the **patch clamp** technique, a small patch of membrane is sealed by suction to the end of a micropipette, enabling investigators to record currents through single membrane channels (Figure 3.8). Erwin Neher and Bert Sakmann were awarded the 1991 Nobel Prize in physiology or medicine for devising this technique. Patch clamp recordings have been made not only in nerve cells but also in glial

Erwin Neher (left)
Bert Sakmann (right)

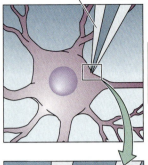

Patch-clamping pipette

A recording pipette filled with an electricity-conducting solution is placed in contact with a neuron's membrane.

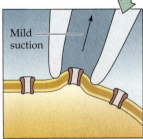

Mild suction

Slight suction clamps a patch of the membrane to the pipette tip.

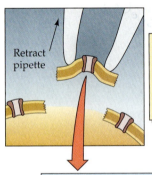

Retract pipette

Retracting the pipette removes the membrane patch, often with one or more ion channels in it; the opening and closing of ion channels can be recorded electrically through the pipette.

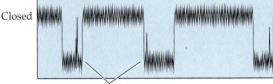

Closed

200 ms

Flow of electrical current as ion channel opens

3.8 Patch Clamp Recording from a Single Ion Channel

cells and muscle cells. The recordings show that the channels open abruptly and remain open only briefly (see Figure 3.8 *bottom*).

Opening of some channels is made more likely by changes in voltage; one example is the voltage-activated Na$^+$ channel that is responsible for the rising phase of the nerve impulse. This type of channel responds extremely rapidly. Channels of the other main family respond to chemical substances applied to the surface of the cell; their responses are slower than those of the voltage-gated channels. Examples of these chemically gated channels will be given a little later in this chapter when we discuss what happens at synapses.

Nerve Impulses Are Actively Propagated down the Axon

We have explored the characteristics of an action potential and the voltage-gated sodium channel that mediates it. Now we can ask how the action potential spreads down the length of the axon. To examine this process, we place recording electrodes at several points along the axon (Figure 3.9). The nerve impulse is initiated at one end of the axon, and recordings are made with electrodes placed along the length of the axon.

These recordings show that the nerve impulse appears with increasing delays at successive positions along the length of the axon. The nerve impulse initiated at one location on the axon spreads in a sort of chain reaction along the length, traveling at speeds that range from less than 1 meter per second (m/s) in some fibers to more than 100 m/s in others.

How does the nerve impulse travel? The nerve impulse is a change in membrane potential that is regenerated at successive axon locations. It spreads from one region to another because the flow of current associated with this small and rapid change in potential depolarizes and thus stimulates adjacent axon segments. That is (as noted earlier), the nerve impulse regenerates itself at successive points along the axon. An analogy is the spread of fire along a row of closely spaced match heads. When one match is lit, the heat associated with its flame can be hot enough to start fire in an adjacent match and so on along the row. Voltage-gated Na$^+$ channels open when the axon is depolarized to threshold. In turn, the influx of Na$^+$ ions—the movement into the cell of positive charges—depolarizes the adjacent segment of axon membrane and therefore opens new gates for the movement of Na$^+$ ions.

The axon normally conducts impulses in only one direction because the action potential starts at the **axon hillock,** the place where the axon emerges from the cell body (see Figure 2.4). Here voltage-gated Na$^+$ channels span the membrane. As the action potential progresses along the axon, it leaves in its wake a stretch of refractory membrane. Propagated activity does not spread from the hillock back over the cell body and dendrites because the membrane there does not possess voltage-gated Na$^+$ channels and so does not produce a regenerated impulse.

If we record the conduction speed of impulses in axons that differ in diameter, we see that the rate of conduction varies with the diameter of the axon. Larger axons allow the depolarization to spread faster through the interior. In mammals, relatively large, heavily myelinated fibers are found in sensory and motor nerves. In these neurons, conduction speed ranges from about 5 m/s in axons that are 2 μm in

[handwritten margin note:] Cell body & dendrites: no V-gated Na+ channels to propagate signal.

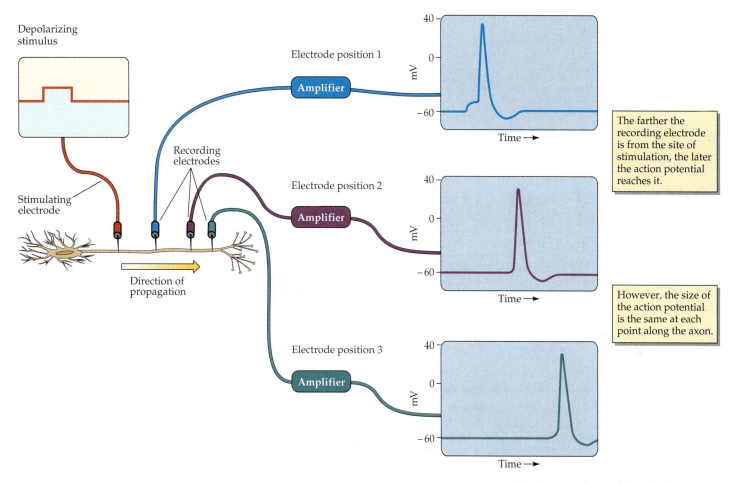

Depolarizing stimulus

Stimulating electrode

Recording electrodes

Direction of propagation

Electrode position 1

Amplifier

Electrode position 2

Amplifier

Electrode position 3

Amplifier

The farther the recording electrode is from the site of stimulation, the later the action potential reaches it.

However, the size of the action potential is the same at each point along the axon.

diameter to 120 m/s in axons that are 20 μm in diameter. Although once thought to be as great as the speed of light, the highest speed of neural conduction is "only" about one-third the speed of sound in air. This relatively high rate of conduction aids the speed of sensory and motor processes (Figure 3.10*a*).

The myelin sheathing on larger mammalian nerve fibers greatly speeds conduction. The myelin is interrupted by **nodes of Ranvier,** small gaps spaced about every millimeter along the axon (see Figure 2.6). Because the myelin insulation offers considerable resistance to the flow of ionic currents across the membrane, the impulse jumps from node to node. This process is called **saltatory conduction** (from the Latin *saltare,* "to leap or jump") (Figure 3.10*b*). The evolution of rapid saltatory conduction in vertebrates has given them a major behavioral advantage over invertebrates, in which axons are unmyelinated and mostly small in diameter, and thus slow in conduction.

One exception to this rule is that many invertebrates have a few giant axons, which mediate behaviorally significant motor responses, such as escape movements. In the invertebrate as in the vertebrate, the speed of conduction increases with axon diameter. The giant axon of the squid has an unusually high rate of conduction for an invertebrate, but the rate still is only about 20 m/s, about the rate of small myelinated axons only 5 μm in diameter. To conduct impulses as fast as a myelinated vertebrate axon does, an unmyelinated invertebrate axon would have to be 100 times larger in volume. It has been estimated that at least 10% of the volume of the human brain is occupied by myelinated axons. To maintain the conduction velocity of our cerebral neurons without the help of myelin, our brains would have to be ten times as large as they are.

The importance of myelin sheathing in promoting rapid conduction of neural impulses helps explain why myelination is an important index of maturation of the nervous system (see Chapter 7). It also helps explain the gravity of diseases that attack myelin, such as **multiple sclerosis.** In this disease the body mounts an immune

3.9 Propagation of the Action Potential

CLINICAL ISSUE

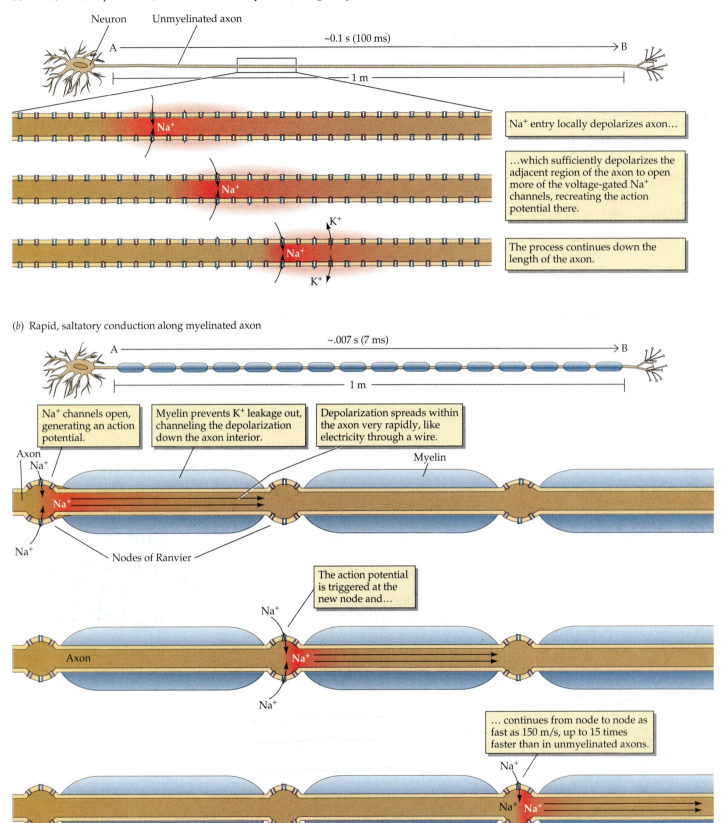

(a) Slow (10 meters per second) conduction of action potential along unmyelinated axon

Neuron   Unmyelinated axon

A ————————————— ~0.1 s (100 ms) ————————————→ B

|——————————————— 1 m ———————————————|

Na⁺ entry locally depolarizes axon…

…which sufficiently depolarizes the adjacent region of the axon to open more of the voltage-gated Na⁺ channels, recreating the action potential there.

The process continues down the length of the axon.

(b) Rapid, saltatory conduction along myelinated axon

A ———————————— ~.007 s (7 ms) ————————————→ B

|——————————————— 1 m ———————————————|

Na⁺ channels open, generating an action potential.

Myelin prevents K⁺ leakage out, channeling the depolarization down the axon interior.

Depolarization spreads within the axon very rapidly, like electricity through a wire.

Myelin

Axon
Na⁺
Na⁺
Na⁺
Nodes of Ranvier

The action potential is triggered at the new node and…

Na⁺
Axon
Na⁺
Na⁺

… continues from node to node as fast as 150 m/s, up to 15 times faster than in unmyelinated axons.

Na⁺
Na⁺   Na⁺

3.10 Conduction along Unmyelinated versus Myelinated Axons

response against its own myelin (Noseworthy, 1999), resulting in both motor and sensory impairments, including slowing of movements and loss of sensory abilities.

In Synaptic Transmission the Activity of Presynaptic Axon Terminals Elicits Postsynaptic Potentials

As we discussed in Chapter 2, neurons communicate with one another at tiny points of direct contact known as synapses. Until the early 1920s, vigorous dispute characterized discussions about the nature of communication across synapses in the nervous system. The big issue was whether synaptic communication was electrical or chemical: Either the electrical nerve impulse directly stimulates the adjacent cell, or the neuron secretes a substance that excites the adjacent cell.

Then one night in 1921, Otto Loewi awoke from a dream in which he had thought of an experiment that might answer the question. He excitedly scribbled some notes and returned to sleep. In the morning he was disappointed to find his notes indecipherable. When he had the dream again, Loewi got up and went straight to his lab to complete the relatively simple experiment.

He electrically stimulated the vagus nerve in a frog, which he knew would slow its heart rate. He then took the fluid bathing that heart and applied it to another, unstimulated heart. This second heart also slowed its beating, showing that stimulation of the first heart had released a chemical into the fluid. Loewi eventually proved that the chemical inhibiting the heart was acetylcholine—the first demonstrated **neurotransmitter** (or **transmitter**), a chemical released by a neuron to affect a postsynaptic cell. We will discuss transmitters later in this chapter and in Chapter 4. Although most synapses use a chemical signal such as acetylcholine, eventually it was found that the nervous system also employs electrical synapses (Box 3.1).

What all neurotransmitters have in common is that they briefly alter the resting potential of the postsynaptic cell. We call these brief changes **postsynaptic potentials.** A given neuron, receiving synapses from hundreds of other cells, is subject to hundreds of postsynaptic potentials. Taken together, these hundreds of potentials decide whether this neuron will reach threshold and therefore generate an action potential.

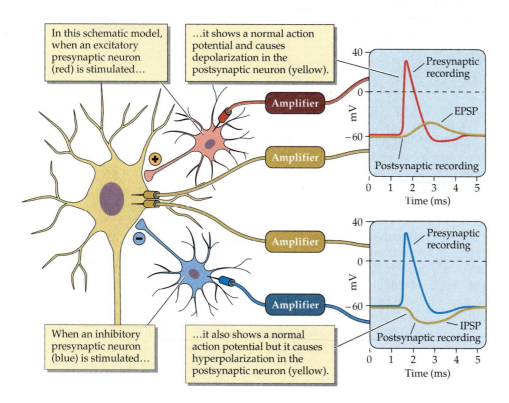

In this schematic model, when an excitatory presynaptic neuron (red) is stimulated…

…it shows a normal action potential and causes depolarization in the postsynaptic neuron (yellow).

Presynaptic recording

EPSP

Postsynaptic recording

When an inhibitory presynaptic neuron (blue) is stimulated…

…it also shows a normal action potential but it causes hyperpolarization in the postsynaptic neuron (yellow).

Presynaptic recording

IPSP
Postsynaptic recording

3.11 Recording Postsynaptic Potentials

BOX 3.1 *Electrical Synapses Work with No Time Delay*

Although most synapses require a chemical substance to mediate synaptic transmission, electrical synapses are also widespread in the brain (M. V. Bennett, 2000). At **electrical synapses** the presynaptic membrane comes even closer to the postsynaptic membrane than it does at chemical synapses; the cleft measures only 2 to 4 nm (see Figure A). In contrast, the gap is 20 to 40 nm at chemical synapses. At electrical synapses, the facing membranes of the two cells have relatively large channels that allow ions to flow from one neuron into the other (Figure B). As a consequence, the flow of electrical current that is associated with nerve impulses in the presynaptic axon terminal can travel across the presynaptic and the postsynaptic membranes.

Transmission at these synapses closely resembles conduction along the axon. Electrical synapses therefore work with practically no time delay, in contrast to chemical synapses, where the delay is on the order of a millisecond—slow in terms of neurons. Because of the speed of their transmission, electrical synapses are frequently found in neural circuits that mediate escape behaviors in invertebrates. They are also found where many fibers must be activated synchronously, as in the vertebrate oculomotor system, and they are found in mammalian neocortex (Gibson et al., 1999). (Figure A courtesy of Constantino Sotelo.)

(A) Electron micrograph of an electrical synapse

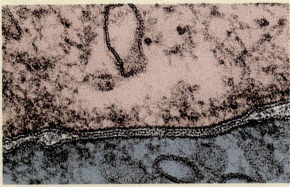

(B) Diagram of an electrical synapse

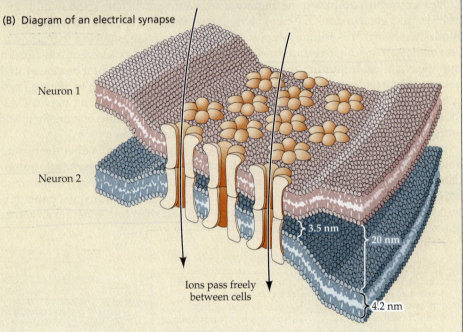

Neuron 1

Neuron 2

3.5 nm

20 nm

4.2 nm

Ions pass freely between cells

We can study postsynaptic potentials with a setup like that shown in Figure 3.11. By selecting the presynaptic (red) cell to stimulate, we can see how the postsynaptic (yellow) neuron responds to inputs from these varied connections. The responses of the presynaptic and postsynaptic cells are shown on the same graphs in Figure 3.11 for easy comparison of their time relations.

Stimulation of an excitatory presynaptic neuron leads to an all-or-none action potential in the presynaptic cell. In the postsynaptic cell, after a brief synaptic delay, a small local depolarization is seen. This postsynaptic membrane depolarization is known as an **excitatory postsynaptic potential** (**EPSP**) because it pushes the postsynaptic cell closer to the threshold for an action potential. Generally the combined effect of many excitatory synapses is required to elicit an action potential in a postsynaptic neuron. If EPSPs are elicited almost simultaneously by many neurons that converge on the motor cell, these potentials can summate and produce a depolarization that reaches the threshold and triggers an action potential. Note that there is a delay: In the fastest cases, the postsynaptic depolarization begins about half a millisecond after the presynaptic impulses. Most of this delay is due to the release and movement of neurotransmitter across the synapse, as we'll discuss later.

The action potential of an inhibitory presynaptic neuron looks exactly like that of the excitatory presynaptic fiber; neurons have only one kind of propagated signal. But the *postsynaptic* local potentials show opposite polarities. When the inhibitory neuron is stimulated, the postsynaptic signal is an *increase* of the resting potential. This hyperpolarization is inhibitory for the motoneuron—it decreases the probability that the neuron will fire an impulse—so it is called an **inhibitory postsynaptic potential (IPSP)**.

Usually IPSPs result from opening of channels that permit chloride (Cl^-) ions to enter the cell. Because Cl^- ions are much more concentrated outside the cell than inside (see Figure 3.4), they are driven inside the cell, making it even more negative. Although in this discussion we have been paying more attention to excitation, inhibition also plays a vital role in neural processing of information. Just as driving a car requires brakes as well as an accelerator, neural switches must be turned off as well as on. The nervous system treads a narrow path between overexcitation, leading to seizures (discussed later, in Box 3.2), and underexcitation, leading to coma and death.

What determines whether a synapse excites or inhibits the postsynaptic cell? One factor is the particular neurotransmitter released by the presynaptic cell. Some transmitters generate an EPSP in the postsynaptic cells; others generate an IPSP. Whether a neuron fires an action potential at any given moment is decided by the relation between the number of excitatory and the number of inhibitory signals it is receiving, and it receives many of both at all times. Some neurons and some synaptic transmitter chemicals are specialized to send inhibitory messages. In later chapters we will see specific neural circuits that involve inhibition—circuits for perception, motor control, and emotion.

Temporal Summation and Spatial Summation Integrate Synaptic Inputs

Synaptic transmission and impulse conduction not only communicate signals, but also integrate and transform messages in ways that make complex behavior possible. This means that the nerve cell, with its synaptic inputs, is able both to sum and to subtract input signals. These operations are possible because of the characteristics of synaptic inputs, the way in which the neuron integrates the postsynaptic potentials, and the trigger mechanism that determines whether a neuron will fire an impulse.

As we have seen, the postsynaptic potentials that are caused by the action of transmitter chemicals can be either depolarizing (excitatory) or hyperpolarizing (inhibitory). These EPSPs and IPSPs spread passively over the neuron from their points of origin on dendrites and on the cell body. The trigger mechanism for mammalian neurons is located at the initial segment of the axon, which in mammalian multipolar neurons is the axon hillock. Thus what determines whether the postsynaptic neuron will fire an action potential is whether depolarization reaches the critical threshold at the axon hillock.

The physical model in Figure 3.12 is analogous to information processing by the nerve cell. Here the cell body is represented by a metal ball. For simplicity, no dendrites are shown, and all input endings are on the cell body. The presynaptic terminals are represented by tubes through which blasts of hot or cold air can be delivered; hot air represents excitatory synaptic action, and cold air inhibitory synaptic action. The axon hillock contains a thermostat. If the temperature rises above a critical temperature (the threshold), the thermostat closes a circuit and triggers a propagated impulse.

Suppose impulses arrive at two excitatory endings, as shown in Figure 3.12*a*. The pulses of hot air are delivered, causing local heating of the cell body. This heat spreads out over the neuron (the ball in Figure 3.12), dissipating as it spreads so that only a small proportion of the heat reaches the axon hillock. Yet the two pulses together push the hillock region to threshold. Figure 3.12*b* shows what happens when blasts of cold air are also delivered. The resultant local cooling also spreads passively, so the change of temperature diminishes as it travels. Because some tubes

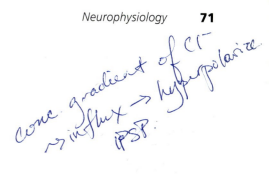

3.12 A Physical Model of Spatial Summation in a Postsynaptic Cell

(*a*) Excitatory inputs cause the cell to fire

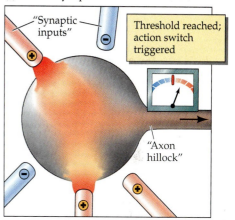

"Synaptic inputs"

Threshold reached; action switch triggered

"Axon hillock"

(*b*) Inhibition also plays a role

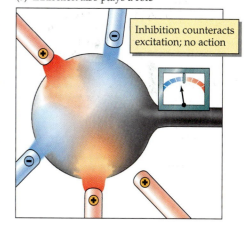

Inhibition counteracts excitation; no action

(*c*) The cell integrates excitation and inhibition

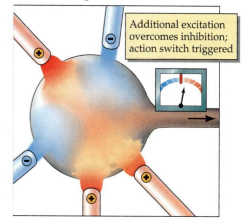

Additional excitation overcomes inhibition; action switch triggered cool and others warm the hillock, these effects partially cancel each other. Thus the net effect is the difference between the two: The neuron subtracts the IPSPs from the EPSPs.

If two excitatory terminals are activated simultaneously, their effects sum at the hillock: The neuron adds postsynaptic potentials that have the same sign. The summation of potentials across the cell body is called **spatial summation.** Only if the overall result of all the potentials is sufficient to raise the hillock temperature to the threshold level is an impulse triggered (Figure 3.12c). Usually the convergence of excitatory messages from many presynaptic fibers is required for a neuron to fire an action potential.

Postsynaptic effects that are not absolutely simultaneous can also be summed, because the effects last a few milliseconds. The closer they are in time, the greater is the overlap and the more complete is the summation, which in this case is called **temporal summation.** Temporal summation is easily understood if you imagine a neuron with only one input. If EPSPs arrive one right after the other, they sum and the postsynaptic cell eventually reaches threshold and produces an action potential. Thus although nerve impulses are all-or-none phenomena, the postsynaptic effect can be graded in size: A rapid barrage of impulses produces a larger postsynaptic potential than a single impulse does.

Dendrites have been omitted from Figure 3.12 for simplicity, but they add to the story. Dendrites augment the receptive surface of the neuron and increase the amount of input information the neuron can handle. All other things being equal, the farther out on a dendrite that a potential is produced, the less effect the potential will have on the trigger zone for action potentials—the axon hillock. (Interestingly, somehow distant synapses compensate for this by producing larger postsynaptic potentials than do synapses close to the hillock [Magee and Cook, 2000].) When the potential arises at a dendritic spine, its effect is further reduced because it has to spread down the shaft of the spine. Thus information arriving at various parts of the neuron is weighted in terms of the distance and path resistance to the axon hillock.

Finally, glial cells also play a role in synaptic transmission: They increase the strength of the postsynaptic potential (Pfrieger and Barres, 1997), perhaps by overlying the presynaptic terminal and thereby preventing neurotransmitter leakage out of the synaptic cleft.

Table 3.1 summarizes the many properties of action potentials and synaptic potentials, noting the principal similarities and differences among the three kinds of neural potentials.

TABLE 3.1 *Characteristics of Electrical Signals of Nerve Cells*

Type of signal	Signaling role	Typical duration (ms)	Amplitude	Character	Mode of propagation	Ion channel opening	Channel sensitive to:
Action potential (neural impulse)	Conduction along a neuron	1–2	Overshooting, 100 mV	All-or-nothing, digital	Actively propagated, regenerative	First Na⁺, then K⁺, in different channels	Voltage (depolarization)
Excitatory postsynaptic potential (EPSP)	Transmission between neurons	10–100	Depolarizing, from less than 1 to more than 20 mV	Graded, analog	Local, passive spread	Na⁺–K⁺	Chemical (neurotransmitter)
Inhibitory postsynaptic potential (IPSP)	Transmission between neurons	10–100	Hyperpolarizing, from less than 1 to about 15 mV	Graded, analog	Local, passive spread	K⁺–Cl⁻	Chemical (neurotransmitter)

The Sequence of Transmission Processes at Chemical Synapses

The sequence of events during chemical synaptic transmission, shown in Figure 3.13, includes the following main steps:

1. The nerve impulse is propagated into the presynaptic axon terminal.
2. A change in voltage-gated calcium channels in the axon terminal leads to the movement of calcium ions into the axon terminal.
3. Calcium causes synaptic vesicles, filled with neurotransmitter, to fuse with the presynaptic membrane, releasing the transmitter molecules into the synaptic cleft.
4. Some transmitter molecules bind onto special receptor molecules in the postsynaptic membrane, leading—directly or indirectly—to the opening of ion chan-

[handwritten notes: 1) action V to Axonterminal 2) Open Ca2+ channels 3) Ca2+ influx → NTs released → 4) NT bind receptor → open ion channels → response on postsynaptic neuron]

 3.13 Steps in Transmission at a Chemical Synapse

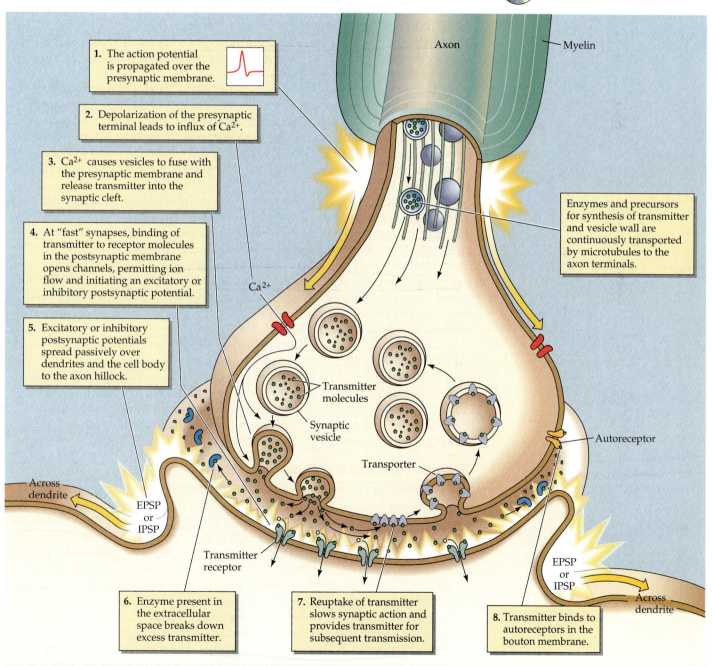

1. The action potential is propagated over the presynaptic membrane.

2. Depolarization of the presynaptic terminal leads to influx of Ca^{2+}.

3. Ca^{2+} causes vesicles to fuse with the presynaptic membrane and release transmitter into the synaptic cleft.

4. At "fast" synapses, binding of transmitter to receptor molecules in the postsynaptic membrane opens channels, permitting ion flow and initiating an excitatory or inhibitory postsynaptic potential.

5. Excitatory or inhibitory postsynaptic potentials spread passively over dendrites and the cell body to the axon hillock.

Enzymes and precursors for synthesis of transmitter and vesicle wall are continuously transported by microtubules to the axon terminals.

Axon

Myelin

Ca^{2+}

Transmitter molecules

Synaptic vesicle

Transporter

Autoreceptor

Across dendrite

EPSP or IPSP

Transmitter receptor

EPSP or IPSP

Across dendrite

6. Enzyme present in the extracellular space breaks down excess transmitter.

7. Reuptake of transmitter slows synaptic action and provides transmitter for subsequent transmission.

8. Transmitter binds to autoreceptors in the bouton membrane.

NT degraded by enzymes or recycled back into presynaptic neuron.

nels in the postsynaptic membrane. The resulting flow of ions alters the polarization of the postsynaptic neuron.

5. The IPSPs and EPSPs in the postsynaptic cell spread to the axon hillock. If the depolarization there is sufficient to reach threshold, the postsynaptic neuron will fire an action potential at its axon hillock.

6. Synaptic transmitter is inactivated (degraded) by enzymes, or

7. Synaptic transmitter is removed rapidly from the synaptic cleft by transporters, so the transmission is brief and accurately follows the presynaptic input signal.

The Nerve Impulse Causes the Release of Transmitter Molecules into the Synaptic Cleft

When a nerve impulse reaches a presynaptic terminal, how does it cause vesicles near the presynaptic membrane to discharge their contents into the synaptic cleft, where the transmitter molecules quickly diffuse to the receptor molecules on the other side (see Figure 3.13)? The arrival of the nerve impulse at the presynaptic terminal causes calcium ions (Ca^{2+}) to enter the terminal. The greater the influx of Ca^{2+}, the greater the number of vesicles released by the impulse. If the concentration of Ca^{2+} in the extracellular fluid is reduced, fewer Ca^{2+} ions enter the terminal and fewer vesicles are released.

Most synaptic delay is caused by the processes related to the entry of Ca^{2+} into the terminal. Small delays are also caused by diffusion of the transmitter across the cleft and reaction of the transmitter with the receptor. The structural components of the synaptic vesicle membrane are complex; one component is a protein called synaptotagmin that can bind calcium. Other vesicle components deal with the mechanism that places the vesicle in the right position for the release of its contents (Matthews, 1996).

All the vesicles for a given transmitter in a synapse appear to contain about the same number of molecules of transmitter chemical. The release of each vesicle causes the same change in potential in the postsynaptic membrane. Normally a nerve impulse causes release of the contents of several hundred vesicles at a time. But if the concentration of calcium is lowered at a synapse, only a few vesicles are released per impulse, and the size of unit depolarizations can then be measured. The number of molecules of transmitter per vesicle is probably in the tens of thousands. It has been difficult to determine whether this number is sufficient to occupy all of the postsynaptic receptors (Mainen et al., 1999).

The presynaptic terminal normally produces and stores enough transmitter to ensure that it is ready for activity. Intense stimulation of the neuron reduces the number of vesicles, but soon more vesicles are produced to replace those that were discharged. Neurons differ in their ability to keep pace with a rapid rate of incoming signals. The production of the transmitter chemical is governed by enzymes that are manufactured in the neuron cell body and transported actively down the axons to the terminals. If they were not, synaptic function could not continue.

Receptor Molecules Recognize Transmitters

The action of a key in a lock is a good analogy to the action of a transmitter on a receptor protein. Just as a particular key can open different doors, a particular chemical transmitter, called a *ligand* (see Chapter 4), can lead to the opening of different channels in the neural membrane. At excitatory synapses where it is the transmitter, **acetylcholine (ACh)** fits into recognition sites in **receptor molecules** located in the postsynaptic membrane (Figure 3.14).

This binding of ACh opens channels successively for Na^+ and K^+ ions, as Hodgkin and Huxley had shown for neural excitation. At inhibitory synapses, ACh opens a different door: It opens channels allowing chloride ions (Cl^-) to enter, thereby increasing the potential across the membrane (hyperpolarizing it). Thus, the receptor protein is different at different kinds of synapses, and a given transmitter may produce an EPSP or IPSP, depending on the receptor that receives it (see Chapter 4).

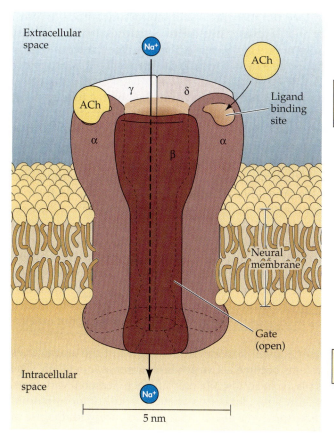

Extracellular space

Na+

ACh

γ

δ

ACh

α

β

α

Neural membrane

Ligand binding site

Gate (open)

Intracellular space

Na+

5 nm

When ACh molecules occupy both binding sites, the sodium channel opens…

…depolarizing the postsynaptic cell.

3.14 A Nicotinic Acetylcholine Receptor Each nicotinic ACh receptor consists of five subunits. Two of the subunits have ligand-binding sites that normally bind ACh molecules but also bind nicotine and other nicotinic drugs. The ACh molecule and Na+ ions are enlarged here for diagrammatic purposes.

The lock-and-key analogy is strengthened by the observation that various chemicals can fit onto receptor proteins and block the entrance of the key. Some of the preparations used in this research resemble the ingredients of a witch's brew. Two blocking agents for ACh are poisons: curare and bungarotoxin. Curare is the arrowhead poison used by native South Americans. Extracted from a plant, it greatly increases the efficiency of hunting: If the hunter hits any part of the prey, the arrow's poison soon paralyzes the animal. Bungarotoxin is a lethal poison produced by the bungarus snake of Taiwan. This toxin has proved very useful in studying acetylcholine receptors because a radioactive label can be attached to it without altering its action. With such labeling, it is possible to investigate the number and distribution of receptor molecules at synapses, as well as details of the binding of transmitter to receptor.

Another poison, muscarine, mimics the action of ACh at some synapses. This poison is extracted from the mushroom *Amanita muscaria*. Molecules such as muscarine and nicotine that act like a transmitter at a receptor are called **agonists** (from the Greek *agon*, "contest, struggle") of that transmitter. Conversely, molecules that interfere with or prevent the action of a transmitter, in such a manner as curare or bungarotoxin block the action of ACh, are called **antagonists.**

Just as there are master keys that fit many different locks, there are submaster keys that fit a certain group of locks, and keys that fit only a single lock. Similarly, each chemical transmitter binds to several different receptor molecules. ACh acts on at least four kinds of receptors. Nicotinic and muscarinic are the two main kinds of cholinergic receptors (all ACh receptors are referred to as **cholinergic**).

Nicotinic cholinergic receptors are found at synapses on skeletal muscles and in autonomic ganglia. Muscarinic cholinergic receptors are found on organs innervated by the parasympathetic division of the autonomic system (e.g., the heart muscle, the intestines, and the salivary gland). Most ACh receptors in the brain are muscarinic.

Most nicotinic sites are excitatory, but there are also inhibitory nicotinic synapses, and there are both excitatory and inhibitory muscarinic synapses, making at least four kinds of acetylcholine receptors. The existence of many types of receptors for each transmitter agent appears to be a device to produce specificity of action in the nervous system.

The nicotinic ACh receptor resembles a lopsided dumbbell with a tube running down its central axis (see Figure 3.14). The handle of the dumbbell spans the cell membrane (which is about 6 nm thick); the larger sphere extends about 5 nm above the surface of the membrane into the extracellular space, and the smaller sphere extends about 2 nm into the cell. The sides of the ion channel (the tube that runs through the handle) consist of five subunits arranged like staves in a barrel. Two units bind to ACh and are alike; the other three are all different. Both ACh-binding sites must be occupied for the channel to open. The genes for each of the four types of subunits have been isolated (Mishina et al., 1984), and neuroscientists have been able to assemble complete or incomplete receptors to study how they work.

After the structure of the nicotinic ACh receptor was determined, similar analyses were carried out for other receptors, including receptors for some of the synaptic transmitter molecules that we will be considering later, such as GABA (gamma-aminobutyric acid), glycine, and glutamate. Several of these receptors resemble each other, suggesting that they all belong to the same family and have a common evolutionary origin.

The number of receptors for a given transmitter in a region of the brain varies widely. Different receptor systems become active at different times in fetal life. The number of receptors remains plastic in adults: Not only are there seasonal variations, but many kinds of receptors show a regular daily variation of 50% or more in number. The numbers of some receptors have also been found to vary with the use of drugs (see Chapter 4). Chapter 18 describes how the number of some receptors increases with activity.

Transmitters Bind to Receptors, Gating Ion Channels

The recognition of transmitter molecules by receptor molecules leads to gating of ion channels in two different ways. **Ionotropic receptors** (Figure 3.15a) directly control an ion channel. When they bind to the released transmitter, the ion channel opens and ions flow across the membrane. (Ionotropic receptors are also known as chemically gated or **ligand-gated ion channels** because a chemical that binds a receptor is called a **ligand**.) **Metabotropic receptors** (Figure 3.15b) recognize the synaptic transmitter, but they do not directly control ion channels. Instead they activate molecules known as **G proteins.**

G protein is a convenient designation for proteins that bind the compounds guanosine diphosphate (GDP), guanosine triphosphate (GTP), and other guanine nucleotides. Sometimes the action of a G protein itself opens an ion channel, but in other cases the G protein activates another, internal chemical signal to affect ion channels. If we think of the transmitter-activated G protein as the first messenger inside the postsynaptic cell, then the next chemical activated within the cell is a **second messenger.** There are several different second messengers, such as cyclic AMP, diacylglycerol, or arachidonic acid, that amplify the effect of the first messenger and can initiate processes that lead to changes in electrical potential at the membrane. Second messengers can also lead to longer-lasting biochemical changes within the neuron.

Since about 80% of the known neurotransmitters and hormones activate cellular signal mechanisms through receptors coupled to G proteins, this coupling device is very important (Birnbaumer et al., 1990). The G protein is located on the inner side of the neural membrane. When a transmitter molecule binds to a receptor that is coupled to a G protein, parts of the G protein complex dissociate (i.e., separate from each other). One part, called the alpha subunit, migrates away within the cell and modulates the activity of its target molecules. Depending on the type of cell and re-

(*a*) Ligand-gated ion channel (fast, ionotropic)

(*b*) G protein–coupled receptor (slow, metabotropic)

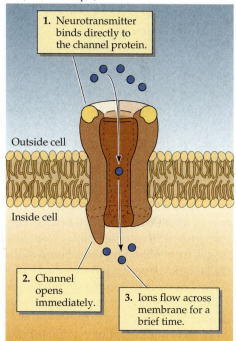

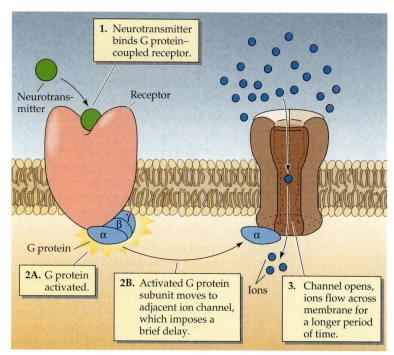

1. Neurotransmitter binds directly to the channel protein.

Outside cell

Inside cell

2. Channel opens immediately.

3. Ions flow across membrane for a brief time.

1. Neurotransmitter binds G protein–coupled receptor.

Neurotransmitter

Receptor

G protein

2A. G protein activated.

2B. Activated G protein subunit moves to adjacent ion channel, which imposes a brief delay.

Ions

3. Channel opens, ions flow across membrane for a longer period of time.

3.15 Two Types of Chemical Synapses

ceptor, the target may be a second-messenger system, an enzyme that works on an ion channel, or an ion pump. Many combinations of different receptors with different G proteins have already been identified, and more are being discovered at a rapid pace (Gudermann et al., 1997; Kobilka, 1992).

The Action of Synaptic Transmitters Is Stopped Rapidly

When a chemical transmitter such as ACh is released into the synaptic cleft, its postsynaptic action is not only prompt, but usually very brief as well. This brevity ensures that the message is repeated faithfully. Such accuracy of timing is necessary in many neural systems—for example, to ensure rapid changes of contraction and relaxation of muscles in coordinated behavior. The prompt cessation of transmitter effects is achieved in one of two ways (see Figure 3.13): (1) Some transmitters are rapidly broken down and thus inactivated by a special enzyme, a process known as **degradation.** (2) Other transmitters are rapidly cleared from the synaptic cleft by being taken up into the presynaptic terminal, a process known as **reuptake;** reuptake not only cuts off the synaptic activity promptly, but also allows the terminal to recycle transmitter molecules.

In an example of the first instance, the enzyme that inactivates ACh is acetylcholinesterase (AChE). Acetylcholinesterase hydrolyzes (breaks down) ACh very rapidly into choline and acetic acid, and these products are recycled (at least in part) to make more ACh in the end bouton. AChE is found especially at synapses, but also elsewhere in the nervous system. Thus, if any ACh escapes from a synapse where it is released, it is unlikely to survive and reach other synapses, where it could start false messages.

Norepinephrine, dopamine, and serotonin are examples of transmitters whose activity is terminated mainly by reuptake. In these cases, special receptors for the transmitter are located on the presynaptic axon terminal. These receptors, usually called **transporters,** take up the transmitter molecules and return them to the interior of the axon terminal, thus preventing them from making further contact with the postsynaptic receptors. Once taken up into the presynaptic terminal, some of the transmitter molecules are inserted into vesicles and can be released in response to further nerve impulses. Malfunction of reuptake mechanisms has been suspected to cause some kinds of mental illness, such as depression (see Chapter 16).

Sometimes neurons are influenced by hormones and neuromodulators, substances that by themselves do not produce significant neural effects but that bind to receptors to change the way they respond to a transmitter (see Chapter 4).

The Evolution of Ion Channels, Synapses, and Transmitters

Many investigators are interested in comparative aspects and the evolution of ion channels, synapses, and transmitters (Arbas et al., 1991; see also Hille, 2001). For example, certain voltage-gated ion channels for K^+ and Ca^{2+} are found in plants and in unicellular animals, as well as in multicellular animals, and thus must have evolved before the appearance of multicellular animals with nervous systems. Na^+ channels seem not to have evolved before the appearance of multicellular animals, and their structures suggest that they evolved from Ca^{2+} channels. The increased variety of ion channels may have been an important factor in promoting flexibility of neural circuits.

Electrical synapses are found in plants as well as animals and appear to be very ancient in an evolutionary sense. Chemical synapses add new flexibility: Transmission can be modulated by a variety of messages from adjoining cells. Some of the simpler compounds that function in multicellular animals as synaptic transmitters—such as ACh, GABA, glycine, and glutamate—are also present in plants and in unicellular animals, but it is doubtful that they act as transmitters there because plants and unicellular animals don't have nervous systems.

The transmitter functions these substances provide in multicellular animals probably evolved from and superseded their functions in plants and unicellular animals. The inhibitory ligand-gated receptors (for GABA and glycine) appear to have evolved from the excitatory nicotinic ACh receptor. The neuropeptide transmitters appear to have arisen first in multicellular animals. Thus, in communication of information in the body, as for other functions, evolution has proceeded by conserving and tinkering with the available raw material.

Neurons and Synapses Combine to Make Circuits

Now that we have discussed the basic properties of neurons and synapses, it is time for an initial look at how they can be connected into circuits to perform important functions. The use of the term *circuit* for an assemblage of neurons and their synaptic interconnections is an analogy to electrical or electronic circuits, in which an arrangement of components (such as resistors, capacitors, transistors, and their connecting wires) accomplishes a particular function, such as amplification, oscillation, or filtering.

Electrical or electronic circuits can represent signals in either analog or digital ways—that is, in terms of continuously varying values or in terms of integers. Neurons also have both analog signals (graded potentials) and digital signals (all-or-none action potentials). The nervous system comprises many different types of neural circuits that accomplish basic functions in cognition, emotion, and action—all the categories of behavior and experience. For now we will take up just three basic types of neural circuits: (1) the neural chain, (2) the feedback circuit, and (3) the oscillator circuit.

The Simplest Neural Circuit Is the Neural Chain

The first neural circuit that investigators proposed was the linking of neurons together in a chain. From the seventeenth century until well into the twentieth century, most attempts to understand behavior in neural terms were based on chains of neurons, which do account for some behaviors. For example, the basic circuit for the stretch reflex, such as the **knee jerk reflex,** consists of a sensory neuron, a motor neuron, and a single synapse where the sensory neuron joins the motor neuron. Hundreds or thousands of such circuits work in parallel to enable the stretch reflex.

Figure 3.16 shows the sequence and timing of events in the knee jerk reflex. Note that this reflex is extremely rapid: Only about 40 ms elapse between the stimulus

3.16 Events in the Knee Jerk Reflex

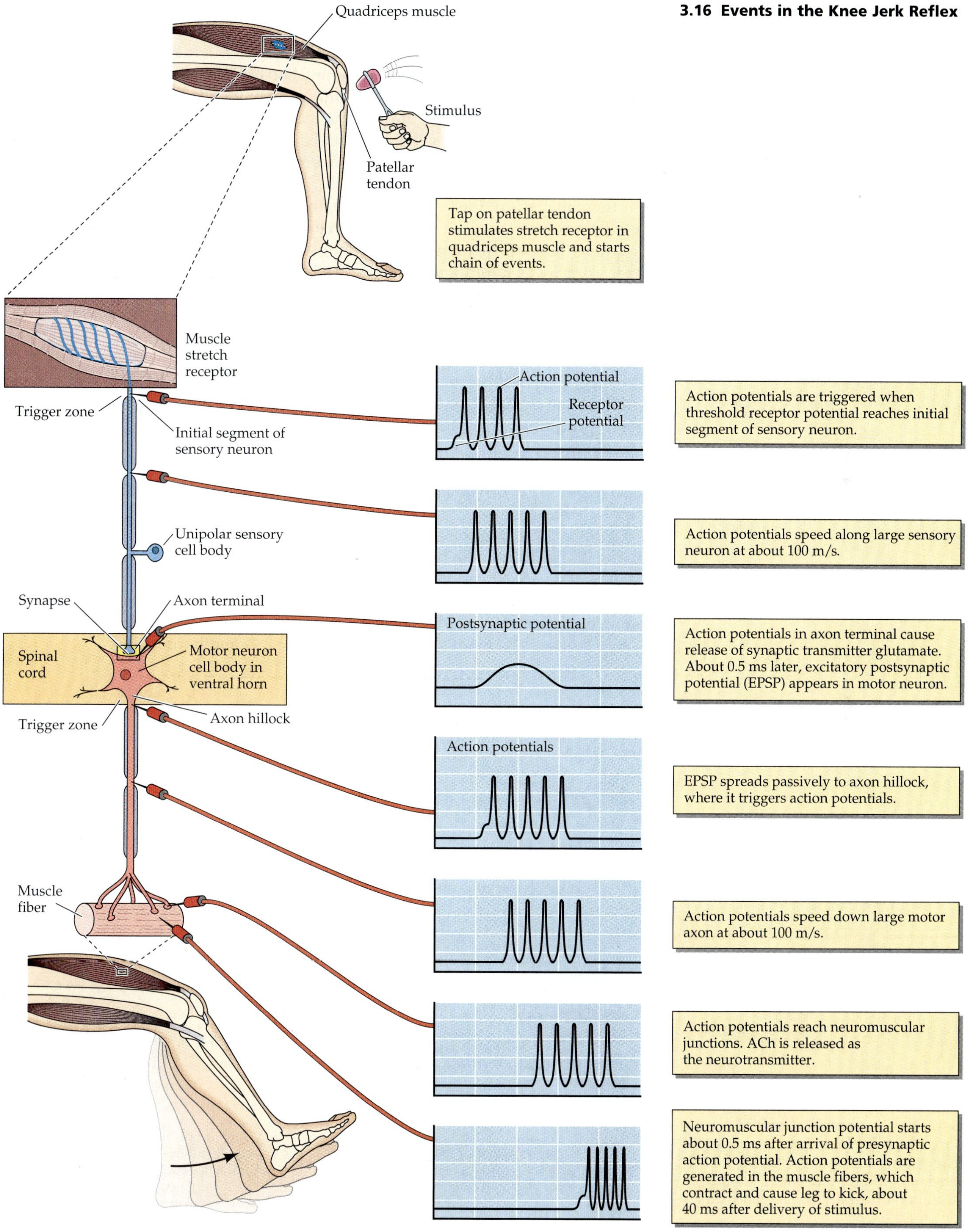

Quadriceps muscle
Stimulus
Patellar tendon
Tap on patellar tendon stimulates stretch receptor in quadriceps muscle and starts chain of events.
Muscle stretch receptor
Action potential
Receptor potential
Trigger zone
Initial segment of sensory neuron
Action potentials are triggered when threshold receptor potential reaches initial segment of sensory neuron.
Unipolar sensory cell body
Action potentials speed along large sensory neuron at about 100 m/s.
Synapse
Axon terminal
Spinal cord
Motor neuron cell body in ventral horn
Postsynaptic potential
Action potentials in axon terminal cause release of synaptic transmitter glutamate. About 0.5 ms later, excitatory postsynaptic potential (EPSP) appears in motor neuron.
Trigger zone
Axon hillock
Action potentials
EPSP spreads passively to axon hillock, where it triggers action potentials.
Muscle fiber
Action potentials speed down large motor axon at about 100 m/s.
Action potentials reach neuromuscular junctions. ACh is released as the neurotransmitter.
Neuromuscular junction potential starts about 0.5 ms after arrival of presynaptic action potential. Action potentials are generated in the muscle fibers, which contract and cause leg to kick, about 40 ms after delivery of stimulus.

and the initiation of the response. Several factors account for this rapidity: (1) Both the sensory and the motor axons involved are of large diameter and thus conduct rapidly, (2) the sensory cells synapse directly on the motor neurons, and (3) both the central synapse and the neuromuscular junction are fast synapses.

For some purposes, the afferent (input) parts of the visual system can be represented as a neural chain (Figure 3.17a; in reality, the retina contains many kinds of neural circuits, which we will discuss in Chapter 10). A more accurate schematic diagram of the visual system (Figure 3.17b) brings out two other features of many neural circuits: **convergence** and **divergence.**

In many parts of the nervous system, the axons from large numbers of neurons converge on certain cells. In the human eye, about 100 million receptor cells concentrate their information down on about 1 million ganglion cells; these ganglion cells convey the information from the eye to the brain. Higher in the visual system there is much divergence: The 1 million axons of the optic nerve communicate to billions of neurons in several different specialized regions of the cerebral cortex.

The Feedback Circuit Is a Regulator

In a feedback circuit, part of the output is *fed back* to the input. There are two types of feedback circuits: positive and negative. In **positive feedback circuits,** the effect of the output is to sustain or increase the activity of the initial input; in **negative feedback circuits,** the output inhibits the activity of the initial input. In some feedback circuits, a branch of the axon of a neuron loops back and contacts the same neuron (Figure 3.18a). In others, one or more intermediate neurons (interneurons) form the feedback loop.

Feedback circuits were first discovered in the nervous system in the 1940s, and psychologist Donald O. Hebb (1949) pointed out their relevance for psychological and neuroscience theory. For example, a positive feedback circuit can be used to sustain neural activity, which can contribute to maintaining a motivational state or to forming the cellular basis of memory. Negative feedback circuits help regulate many body functions by maintaining relatively constant conditions.

(a) The visual system represented as a neural chain

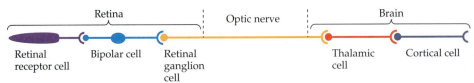

(b) A more realistic representation, showing convergence and divergence

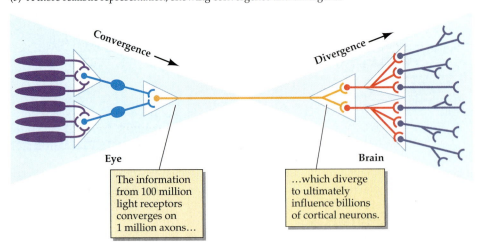

The information from 100 million light receptors converges on 1 million axons...

...which diverge to ultimately influence billions of cortical neurons.

3.17 Two Representations of Neural Circuitry (a) This simple representation shows the input part of the visual system. (b) This more complex representation illustrates convergence and divergence.

(a) Negative feedback loop within a single cell

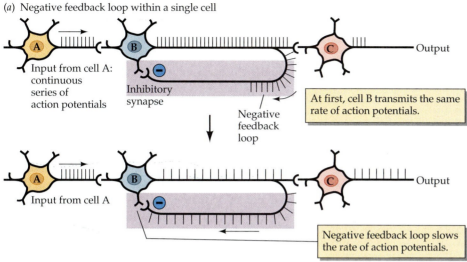

3.18 Negative Feedback Circuits
(*a*) A circuit within a single cell. (*b*) A simple oscillator circuit, in which a continuous series of action potentials from neuron A is modulated by inhibitory output from cell C to cell B, which ultimately causes rhythmic output from cells B and C.

Input from cell A: continuous series of action potentials

Inhibitory synapse

Negative feedback loop

At first, cell B transmits the same rate of action potentials.

Input from cell A

Negative feedback loop slows the rate of action potentials.

(b) A simple oscillator circuit

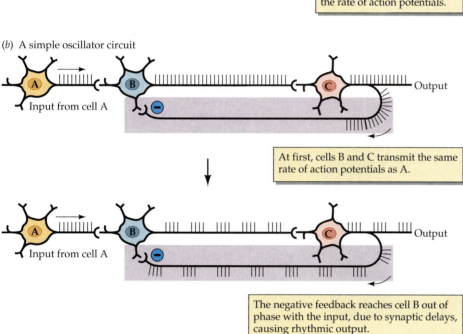

Input from cell A

At first, cells B and C transmit the same rate of action potentials as A.

Input from cell A

The negative feedback reaches cell B out of phase with the input, due to synaptic delays, causing rhythmic output.

A thermostat is an example of a negative feedback device; many neural circuits in the body function in the same basic manner. The stretch reflex (see Figure 3.16) serves as part of a negative feedback system in maintaining posture as you stand. Swaying a little to the front causes muscles in the back of the leg to stretch; the leg muscles respond by contracting, bringing the body again to the vertical. Similarly, swaying to the back stretches muscles in the front, and again the stretch reflex brings about the necessary compensation.

The Oscillator Circuit Controls Rhythmic Behavior

Many kinds of behavior—from beating of the heart, breathing, walking, sleeping, and waking, to annual migration—are rhythmic, and their cycles differ in duration from short to long. Some neurons, mostly in invertebrates, show inherent spontaneous rhythmicity of activity: The frequency of neural impulses of such *pacemaker* cells waxes and wanes in regular alternation. Rhythmic wing beating in some insects is controlled by such oscillation. In both invertebrates and vertebrates, however, oscillatory activity usually depends on circuits of neurons. Figure 3.18*b* shows a simple **oscillator circuit.**

3.19 Gross Potentials of the Human Nervous System

(a) *Top left:* Electrode array for EEG recording. *Bottom left:* Each electrode can be assigned a letter on a map of the scalp. *Right:* Typical EEG records showing potential measured between various points on the scalp.

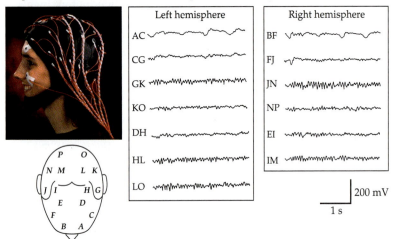

(b) BEAM images

Computer analysis of EEG signals can produce a color-coded map of brain activity.

These models combined with MRI yield 3-dimensional images.

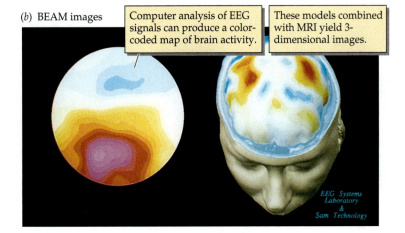

EEG Systems Laboratory & Sam Technology

(c) Event-related potentials (average of many stimulus presentations)

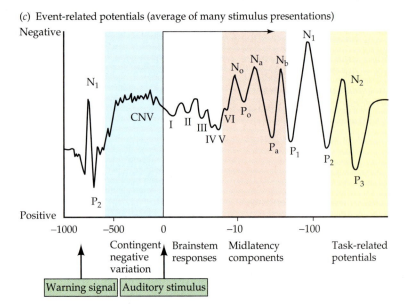

Gross Electrical Activity of the Human Brain

The brain is a large collection of separate elements, and the electrical activity of thousands of cells working together adds up to potentials that can be recorded even at the surface of the skull. Recordings of electrical activity in the brain that are made with large electrodes either on the scalp or within the brain can present useful glimpses of the simultaneous workings of populations of neurons. Investigators divide brain potentials into two principal classes: those that appear spontaneously without specific stimulation and those that are evoked by particular stimuli.

Electroencephalograms Measure Spontaneous Brain Potentials

A recording of spontaneous brain potentials is called an **electroencephalogram** (**EEG**), or more informally, *brain waves* (Figure 3.19a). As we will see in Chapter 14, EEG recordings of a sleeping person allow investigators to distinguish different kinds and stages of sleep. Brain potentials also provide significant diagnostic data—for example, in distinguishing forms of seizure disorders (Box 3.2). In addition, they provide prognostic data—for example, predictions of the functional effects of brain injury. In most states of the United States, EEGs are used to determine death according to the legal definition. One system for analyzing and displaying brain potentials is **brain electrical activity mapping** (**BEAM**) (Figure 3.19b) (F. H. Duffy et al., 1992).

Event-Related Potentials Measure Changes Resulting from Discrete Stimuli

Gross potential changes evoked by discrete stimuli—usually sensory stimuli, such as light flashes or clicks—are called **event-related potentials** (**ERPs**) (Figure 3.19c). In the usual experiment to study this phenomenon, many ERPs are averaged to obtain a reliable estimate of stimulus-elicited brain activity. Sensory-evoked potentials have distinctive characteristics of wave shape and latency that reflect the type of stimulus, the state of the subject, and the site of recording. Subtler psychological processes, such as expectancy, appear to influence some characteristics of evoked potentials.

Computer techniques enable researchers to record brain potentials at some distance from the sites at which they are generated. Such recording is akin to the ability of a sensitive heat detector to pick up minute sources of heat that are located at a distance. An example that has attracted considerable research and clinical attention is *auditory-evoked brainstem potentials* (see Figure 3.19c). The neural generators of these waves are located far from the site of recording—in the auditory nerve and successive levels of the auditory brainstem pathways. These responses

BOX 3.2 *Seizure Disorders*

Epilepsy (from the Greek *epilepsia*, a form of the verb meaning "to seize") has provoked wonder and worry since the dawn of civilization. Through the ages the seizures that accompany this disease have spawned much speculation about the cause—from demons to gods. Consequently, people afflicted with this disease have sometimes been shunned, sometimes exalted. Epidemiological studies indicate that 30 million people worldwide suffer from epilepsy. Because epilepsy affects so many people, the origin and possible cures of this disease are an important focus of research.

What causes seizures? The electrical character of nervous system signals offers the special biological advantages of rapid communication and the ability to generate, receive, and integrate a wide array of messages. However, this fundamental property also comes at a price. In addition to the high metabolic demands of nerve cells is the potential cost of seizures. Because of the extensive connections among its nerve cells, the brain can generate massive waves of intense nerve cell activity that seem to involve almost the entire brain. A **seizure** is the synchronized excitation of large groups of nerve cells. These unusual electrical events in the brain have a wide array of possible causes, including trauma or injury to the brain, as well as chemical changes derived from metabolic faults or exposure to toxins. Some heritable forms of epilepsy seem to be due to mutations in ion channels (McNamara, 1999).

Several types of seizure disorders can be distinguished both behaviorally and neurophysiologically. Generalized seizures are characterized by loss of consciousness and symmetrical involvement of body musculature. **Grand mal seizures** exhibit an EEG pattern that is evident at many places in the brain (Figure A). The behavior connected with this state is dramatic: The person loses consciousness, and the muscles of the entire body suddenly contract. This tonic phase of the seizure is followed 1 to 2 minutes later by a clonic phase consisting of sudden alternating jerks and relaxation of the body. Minutes or hours of confusion and sleep follow. When nonprofessionals refer to epilepsy, they generally mean grand mal seizures.

Petit mal seizures are a more subtle variant of generalized seizures. This condition is revealed by a distinctive electrical pattern in EEG recordings, called the spike-and-wave pattern, that lasts 5 to 15 seconds (Figure B). Periods of such unusual electrical activity can occur many times a day. During these periods the person is unaware of the environment and later cannot recall events that occurred during the petit mal episode. Behaviorally, the person does not show unusual muscle activity, except for a cessation of ongoing activity and sustained staring.

Complex partial seizures do not involve the entire brain; they produce a complex variety of symptoms. Often the person experiences an **aura,** some sensation that precedes the seizure. One woman felt an unusual sensation in the abdomen, a sense of foreboding, and tingling in both hands before the seizure spread. At the height of it, she was unresponsive, and rocked her body back and forth while speaking nonsensically, twisting her left arm, and looking toward the right. Figure C is a three-dimensional reconstruction showing where the seizures occurred in her brain.

Clinical neurologists have suggested a connection between complex partial seizures and certain personality attributes (Trimble, 1991). Some researchers argue that emotional changes observed in these disorders are a direct result of frequent activation by seizures of emotional circuits in the temporal lobe. Others believe that emotional changes arise as a result of psychological responses to the social trauma of having a life with unpredictable seizures. A few patients with complex partial seizures exhibit striking and varied aggressive behavior. Hindler (1989) described a person in whom strong aggression was elicited by the laughing of an infant, which appeared to trigger odd olfactory sensations and other features of temporal lobe seizure activity.

Seizures can occur in the brains of many nonhuman creatures. Spontaneous seizures characterize some animals—for example, some breeds of dog, especially beagles. One interesting model of seizure disorders uses repeated direct electrical stimulation of brain regions to provoke epileptic seizures. This process of establishing seizures is referred to as **kindling** (McNamara, 1984). To establish seizure activity in this model, an electrical stimulus that is too weak to cause a seizure on its own is delivered directly through implanted electrodes to a particular brain site in the animal. Over a period of days, this brief stimulus comes to produce both behavioral changes and signs of seizure activity in a progressive manner. Eventually seizures appear spontaneously. The phenomenon of kindling may be relevant to the finding that some human patients develop multiple foci for the initiation of seizures as a result of a history of seizure activity (Morrell, 1991). (Figure C courtesy of Hal Blumenfeld, Rik Stokking, Susan Spencer, and George Zubal, Yale School of Medicine.)

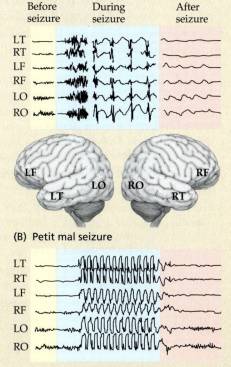

(A) Grand mal seizure

	Before seizure	During seizure	After seizure
LT			
RT			
LF			
RF			
LO			
RO			

LF　LO　LT　RO　RF　RT

(B) Petit mal seizure

LT			
RT			
LF			
RF			
LO			
RO			

(C) Complex partial seizure

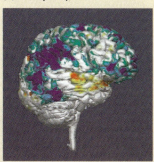

provide a way to assess the neural responsiveness of the brainstem and especially its auditory pathways. For example, decreases in the amplitude of certain waves or increases in their latency have been valuable in detecting hearing impairments in very young children and noncommunicative persons. Infants with impaired hearing produce reduced auditory ERPs or no ERP at all in response to sounds. Another use of ERPs is in the assessment of brainstem injury or damage, such as that produced by tumors or stroke.

Long-latency components of scalp-recorded ERPs tend to reflect the impact of information processing variables, such as attention, decision making, and other complex psychological dimensions. Another way of contrasting these events with short-latency events, such as the brainstem potentials, is to compare the sorts of factors that affect them. The later potentials are influenced more by endogenous factors, such as attention. In contrast, short-latency responses are determined more by exogenous factors. Because they are determined more by the stimulus, dimensions like stimulus intensity have a far more profound effect on early components of ERPs than on longer-latency components.

Although it is difficult to determine which brain region has produced a given component of the ERP, such changes are detected quickly, within a fraction of a second. In contrast, computer-coordinated imaging of brain activity, such as functional MRI (see Chapter 2), indicates clearly which brain region is active, but because such imaging techniques must average activity over seconds or minutes, they are much slower than ERPs. Perhaps the greatest promise for future research is a melding of the two techniques—using ERPs to detect changes in brain activity rapidly, and using fMRI or PET scans to indicate where those electrical changes originate within the brain (Abdullaev and Posner, 1998; A. Z. Snyder et al., 1995).

Summary

1. Nerve cells are specialized for receiving, processing, and transmitting signals.

2. Neural signals are changes in the resting potential, which is the normal small difference in voltage between the inside and outside of the cell membrane.

3. The different concentrations of ions inside and outside the neuron—especially potassium ions (K^+)—account for the resting potential. The inside of the neuron is about –60 to –70 mV compared to the outside. The resting membrane is mainly permeable to potassium ions and is thus a potassium membrane.

4. A propagated nerve impulse, also called an action potential, travels the length of the axon without diminishing in amplitude; the impulse is regenerated by successive segments of the axon.

5. Reduction of the resting potential (depolarization of the membrane) makes the axon membrane more permeable to sodium ions (Na^+); that is, voltage-gated channels open that admit mainly Na^+. If this depolarization reaches a threshold value, the membrane becomes briefly a sodium membrane, and the axon becomes briefly more positive inside than outside. Depolarization of a stretch of membrane stimulates the adjacent stretch of membrane to depolarize, so the action potential sweeps along the axon.

6. Postsynaptic (local) potentials spread very rapidly, but they are not propagated. Thus they diminish in amplitude as they spread passively along dendrites and the cell body.

7. Excitatory postsynaptic potentials (EPSPs) are depolarizing (they decrease the resting potential) and make it easier for the neuron to generate an action potential. Inhibitory postsynaptic potentials (IPSPs) are hyperpolarizing (they increase the resting potential) and make it harder for the neuron to fire.

8. Cell bodies process information by integrating (adding algebraically) postsynaptic potentials across their surfaces.

9. A propagated nerve impulse is initiated at the axon hillock when the excess of EPSPs over IPSPs reaches threshold.

Refer to the *Learning Biological Psychology* CD for the following study aids for this chapter:

10 Objectives

75 Study Questions

1 Activity

2 Animated Tutorials

10. During the action potential, the neuron cannot be excited by a second stimulus; it is absolutely refractory.

11. Some synapses use electrical transmission and do not require a chemical transmitter. At these electrical synapses, the cleft between presynaptic and postsynaptic cells is extremely narrow.

12. At most synapses, the transmission of information from one neuron to another requires a chemical transmitter that diffuses across the synaptic cleft and binds to receptor molecules in the postsynaptic membrane. Because the transmitter binds to the receptor, it is called a ligand.

13. At some synapses, the receptor molecule responds to recognition of a transmitter by opening an ion channel within its own structure. At other synapses, the binding of a transmitter molecule to a receptor molecule leads to opening of channels through the activity of G proteins and second messengers.

14. Evidence for the evolution of ion channels, synapses, and transmitters has been obtained from comparative studies. For example, certain ion channels and electrical synapses are found in plants as well as animals, but Na^+ channels and neuropeptide transmitters appear to have arisen first in multicellular animals.

15. Neurons and synapses can be assembled into circuits that process information. Three basic kinds of neural circuits are the neural chain, the feedback circuit, and the oscillator circuit.

16. The summation of electrical changes over millions of nerve cells can be detected by electrodes on the scalp. Electroencephalograms (EEGs) can reveal rapid changes in brain function, especially in response to a brief, controlled stimulus that evokes an event-related potential (ERP).

Recommended Reading

Hall, Z. W. (Ed.). (1992). *An introduction to molecular neurobiology.* Sunderland, MA: Sinauer.

Hille, B. (2001). *Ion channels of excitable membranes* (3rd ed.). Sunderland, MA: Sinauer.

Kandel, E. R., Schwartz, J. H., and Jessell, T. M. (2000). *Principles of neural science* (4th ed.). New York: McGraw-Hill.

Nicholls, J. G., Martin, A. R., Wallace, B. G., and Fuchs, P. A. (2000). *From neuron to brain* (4th ed.). Sunderland, MA: Sinauer.

Purves, D., Augustine, G. J., Fitzpatrick, D., Katz, L. C., et al. (2000). *Neuroscience* (2nd ed.). Sunderland, MA: Sinauer.

Shepherd, G. M. (Ed.). (1998). *The synaptic organization of the brain* (4th ed.). New York: Oxford University Press.

4

Psychopharmacology: Neurotransmitters, Drugs, and Behavior

Most drugs affect the brain and behavior by changing synaptic transmission. To begin our discussion about drugs and the nervous system, we review the varieties of transmitters, many of which we mentioned in Chapter 3. Then we consider examples of how drugs affect the nervous system and behavior. We also discuss drug dependency and the information that neuroscientists can offer to help deal with the personal and social problems associated with substance abuse.

As far back as we can trace human history, people have tasted, sipped, chewed, or swallowed all kinds of substances—animal, vegetable, and mineral. From these experiences, people have learned to consume some substances and shun others. Social customs and dietary codes evolved to protect people from consuming harmful substances. This long history of seeking, testing, and using different substances came not only from the need for nourishment but also from the desire to relieve pain, control anxiety, and pursue pleasure. Human consumption of drugs is so pervasive that one investigator characterizes human beings as "drug-taking animals" (B. E. Leonard, 1992). But we are not alone in this activity: "Almost every species of animal has engaged in the natural pursuit of intoxicants" (R. K. Siegel, 1989, p. viii).

Fred Tomaselli, *Brain with Flowers*, 1990–1997
Cannabis leaves, LSD, photos, acrylic, and resin on wood

The Search for Chemical Transmitters

We learned in Chapter 3 that neuronal axons release a chemical known as a **neurotransmitter** (or simply, **transmitter**) to communicate with target cells, usually other neurons. Identifying neurotransmitters and understanding how they act are continuing quests. Table 4.1 summarizes the various classes of currently known transmitters, some of which we mentioned in Chapter 3.

Amine transmitters—including acetylcholine, norepinephrine, and epinephrine (adrenaline)—were recognized in the 1940s. Beginning in the 1950s, investigators discovered that some amino acids, the building blocks of proteins, can also act as transmitters; these include glutamate, glycine, and GABA, among others. In the 1970s, investigators recognized that many peptides—short strings of amino acids—could be synaptic transmitters; some examples are the endogenous opioids, oxytocin, substance P, and vasopressin. As the search continued, the number of probable synaptic transmitters grew from a few to several dozen, and new discoveries continue to bring surprises.

What does it take for a substance to be considered a transmitter? The criteria come from the view of synaptic transmission that we discussed in Chapter 3. To prove that a particular substance is the chemical transmitter at a particular synapse, we must demonstrate that

- The chemical exists in the presynaptic terminals
- The enzymes for synthesizing the transmitter exist in the presynaptic terminals or, in the case of the peptides, in the cell body
- The transmitter is released when nerve impulses reach the terminals, and in sufficient quantities to produce normal changes in postsynaptic potentials
- Specific receptors for the released transmitter exist on the postsynaptic membrane
- Experimental application of appropriate amounts of the chemical at the synapse produces changes in postsynaptic potentials
- Blocking release of the substance prevents presynaptic nerve impulses from altering the activity of the postsynaptic cell

Substances that satisfy the criteria for transmitters include acetylcholine, norepinephrine, dopamine, serotonin, GABA, glutamate, and others (see Table 4.1). Even if a substance is known to be a transmitter in one location, it may be hard to prove that it acts as a transmitter at another location where it is found.

For example, acetylcholine was long accepted as a transmitter agent in the peripheral nervous system (its role at the vertebrate neuromuscular junction was well known; see Chapter 11), but it was harder to prove that it serves as a transmitter in the central nervous system as well. Now it is recognized that acetylcholine is widely distributed in the brain, and its possible relationship to the cognitive deficits seen in Alzheimer's disease is the subject of much current work. Considering the rate at which these substances are being discovered and characterized, it would not be surprising if there turned out to be several hundred different peptides conveying information at synapses in different subsets of neurons.

TABLE 4.1	Some Synaptic Transmitters and Families of Transmitters
Family and subfamily	**Transmitter(s)**
AMINES	
Quaternary amines	Acetylcholine (ACh)
Monoamines	*Catecholamines*
	Norepinephrine (NE)
	Epinephrine (adrenaline)
	Dopamine (DA)
	Indoleamines
	Serotonin (5-hydroxytryptamine; 5-HT)
	Melatonin
AMINO ACIDS	Gamma-aminobutyric acid (GABA)
	Glutamate
	Glycine
	Histamine
NEUROPEPTIDES	
Opioid peptides	*Enkephalins*
	Met-enkephalin
	Leu-enkephalin
	Endorphins
	β-endorphin
	Dynorphins
	Dynorphin A
Peptide hormones	Oxytocin
	Substance P
	Cholecystokinin (CCK)
	Vasopressin
	Neuropeptide Y (NPY)
	Hypothalamic releasing hormones

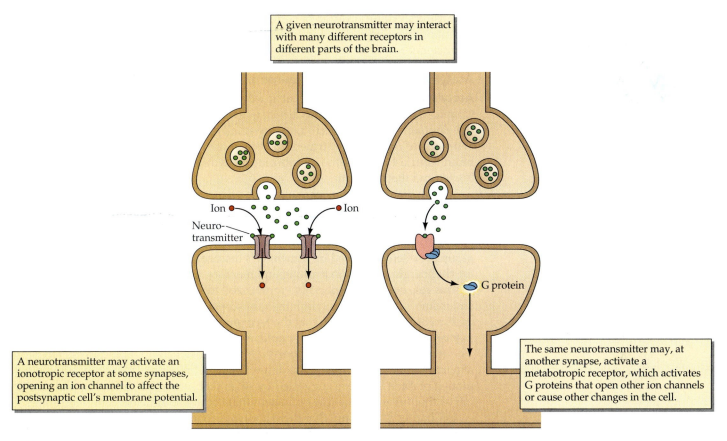

A given neurotransmitter may interact with many different receptors in different parts of the brain.

Ion

Neuro-transmitter

Ion

G protein

A neurotransmitter may activate an ionotropic receptor at some synapses, opening an ion channel to affect the postsynaptic cell's membrane potential.

The same neurotransmitter may, at another synapse, activate a metabotropic receptor, which activates G proteins that open other ion channels or cause other changes in the cell.

4.1 The Versatility of Neurotransmitters A single neurotransmitter may interact with many different receptors in different parts of the brain—binding to a fast, ionotropic receptor in some target cells, and a slow, metabotropic receptor in other cells. Either type of receptor may either excite or inhibit the target cell.

As we discussed in Chapter 3, neurotransmitters affect their targets by interacting with **receptors,** protein molecules embedded in the postsynaptic membrane that recognize the transmitter. The transmitter molecule binds to the receptor, changing its shape to open an ion channel (fast, **ionotropic receptors**), or altering chemical reactions within the target cell (slow, **metabotropic receptors**) (see Figure 3.15 and Table 3.2). Receptors add to the complexity of neural signaling because a single transmitter molecule may bind to hundreds of different types of receptor molecules, and these various receptors may trigger very different responses in the target cell (Figure 4.1). We'll begin this chapter by discussing various transmitters and their receptors, and this basic knowledge will help us understand how drugs affect the nervous system and behavior.

Neurotransmitter Systems Form a Complex Array in the Brain

The neurochemical complexity of the brain has become more evident as techniques such as immunocytochemistry (see Box 2.1) have provided a more complete appreciation of the location of these substances within the nervous system and the multiplicity of ways in which they interact. Although at one time in the recent past it was thought that each nerve cell contained only one transmitter, we now know that some nerve cells contain more than one transmitter—a phenomenon known as neu-

[handwritten margin note: transmitters w/in (neuron = colocalization)]

rotransmitter **co-localization** or co-release (Tsen et al., 2000). In this section we present maps showing where some neurotransmitters are found in the brain, and the character of receptors for these transmitters.

Acetylcholine Was the First Neurotransmitter to Be Identified

Acetylcholine (**ACh**), the chemical at work in Otto Loewi's classic experiment (see Chapter 3), was the first chemical substance to be known as a neurotransmitter. The development of techniques to measure small quantities of enzymes involved in the synthesis of ACh demonstrated the role of this compound as a transmitter in the brain. Figure 4.2 shows the distribution of ACh-containing (**cholinergic**) nerve cell bodies and their projections.

Several distinct clusters of cholinergic cells are apparent. The basal forebrain includes major groups of cholinergic cells in the medial septal nucleus, the nucleus of the diagonal band, and the nucleus basalis. These cholinergic cells project to the hippocampus and amygdala, as well as throughout the cerebral cortex. Cells in this group are often destroyed in Alzheimer's disease, which suggests an important role for cholinergic neurons in learning and memory, as will be discussed in Chapter 18.

This role of ACh is especially emphasized by the deleterious effects on learning and memory of the cholinergic antagonist scopolamine, a substance that blocks some ACh receptors. (Remember that the term **antagonist** refers to substances that bind to receptors but fail to initiate synaptic effects and therefore can block the action of a neurotransmitter; the term **agonist** refers to substances that bind to the receptors of a transmitter and initiate some of its effects.) A behavioral role of ACh in the regulation of sleep has been suggested by several observations, including the clustering of cholinergic cells in the brainstem that control some aspects of sleep states.

In Chapter 3 we noted that there are two broad classes of ACh receptors in the peripheral and central nervous systems: **nicotinic** and **muscarinic** receptors. Within each of these two groups are subgroups of receptor types. Most nicotinic receptors are ionotropic, responding rapidly and usually having an excitatory effect. These receptors can be blocked by the drug curare. Muscarinic receptors are G protein–coupled (metabotropic) receptors, so they have slower responses when activated,

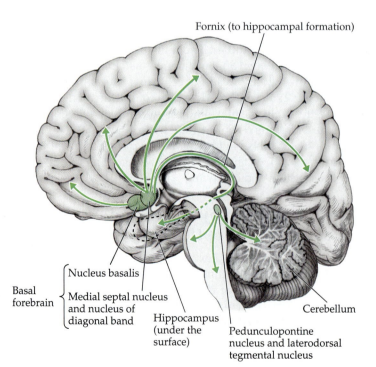

4.2 Cholinergic Pathways in the Brain
In this midsagittal view, the nuclei containing cell bodies of neurons that release ACh are shown in green; the projections of axons from these neurons are indicated by green arrows. Because they use ACh as a transmitter, these neurons are said to be cholinergic.

Fornix (to hippocampal formation)

Nucleus basalis

Basal forebrain

Medial septal nucleus and nucleus of diagonal band

Hippocampus (under the surface)

Pedunculopontine nucleus and laterodorsal tegmental nucleus

Cerebellum

BOX 4.1 *Pathways for Neurotransmitter Synthesis*

Many of the most-studied neurotransmitters, including the amine hormones, must be synthesized through the use of specialized enzymes. Therefore, we can gain some ideas about where these transmitters are produced by finding out where the associated enzymes occur. For example, the enzyme choline acetyltransferase (ChAT) causes a choline molecule to combine with an enzyme (acetyl coenzyme A, or acetyl CoA) to produce a molecule of ACh:

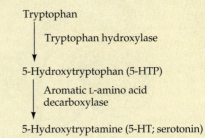

Acetyl CoA + choline

⬇ ChAT

ACh + coenzyme A

The enzyme **acetylcholinesterase** (**AChE**) breaks down the ACh, leaving choline and acetic acid:

ACh

⬇ AChE

Choline + acetic acid

By noting where ChAT and AChE are found, we can make inferences about where ACh might be made and released, respectively. As it turns out,

AChE is very widely distributed, but ChAT is found primarily in the nuclei shown in Figure 4.2.

All of the catecholamine transmitters (norepinephrine, epinephrine, and dopamine) are produced in successive steps in the same synthetic pathway, starting with the amino acid tyrosine and using several different enzymes:

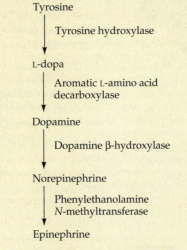

Tyrosine

⬇ Tyrosine hydroxylase

L-dopa

⬇ Aromatic L-amino acid decarboxylase

Dopamine

⬇ Dopamine β-hydroxylase

Norepinephrine

⬇ Phenylethanolamine *N*-methyltransferase

Epinephrine

Only neurons that possess the enzyme tyrosine hydroxylase have the capacity to produce these catecholamine transmitters. L-dopa is a precursor for all three.

The indoleamine serotonin is produced from the amino acid tryptophan in two chemical steps:

Tryptophan

⬇ Tryptophan hydroxylase

5-Hydroxytryptophan (5-HTP)

⬇ Aromatic L-amino acid decarboxylase

5-Hydroxytryptamine (5-HT; serotonin)

All of the monoamines (dopamine, norepinephrine, epinephrine, serotonin, and melatonin) are inactivated to a great extent by reuptake through the presynaptic transporters for each, but they are also enzymatically degraded. Most of the initial degradation of monoamines is carried out by a class of enzymes known as **monoamine oxidases** (**MAOs**).

Neuropeptides are synthesized like any other peptide or protein—through transcription of a gene and translation of messenger RNA (mRNA)—so we can find neurons making those transmitters by looking for the appropriate mRNA transcript—through the use of Northern blots or in situ hybridization (see the Appendix).

and they can be either excitatory or inhibitory (see Figure 3.15). They can be blocked by the drugs atropine or scopolamine.

Five Monoamines Act as Neurotransmitters

There are two principal classes of **monoamines**: catecholamines and indoleamines. The **catecholamine** neurotransmitters are dopamine, epinephrine, and norepinephrine. The **indoleamines** are melatonin and serotonin. Box 4.1 describes how neurons synthesize the monoamines and ACh. In the sections that follow we will take a closer look at three important monoamines: dopamine, norepinephrine, and serotonin.

Dopamine. Almost a million nerve cells in the human brain contain **dopamine** (**DA**). The locations of these cells and their projections in the brain are shown in Figure 4.3. Dopaminergic neurons are found in several main groups; Figure 4.3 focuses on two of these groups: the mesostriatal system and the mesolimbocortical system.

The **mesostriatal system,** as the name indicates, originates from the mesencephalon (midbrain)—specifically the **substantia nigra** and nearby areas—and ascends as part of the medial forebrain bundle to innervate the **striatum:** the caudate nucleus and putamen (see Figure 4.3). Although this group contains relatively few

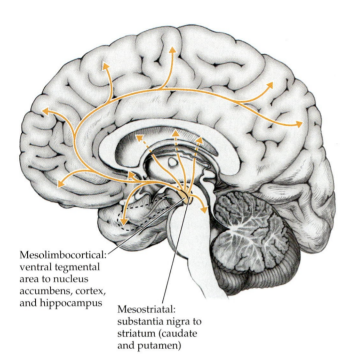

Mesolimbocortical:
ventral tegmental
area to nucleus
accumbens, cortex,
and hippocampus

Mesostriatal:
substantia nigra to
striatum (caudate
and putamen)

4.3 Dopaminergic Pathways in the Brain   The neurons
in the pathways represented in this midsagittal view release
dopamine and thus are called dopaminergic.

**CLINICAL
ISSUE**

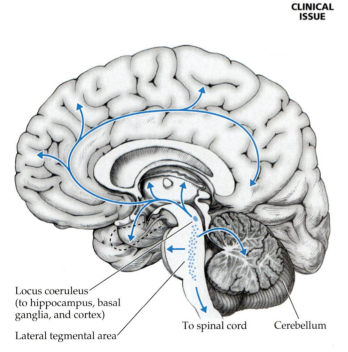

Locus coeruleus
(to hippocampus, basal
ganglia, and cortex)

Lateral tegmental area

To spinal cord   Cerebellum

4.4 Noradrenergic Pathways in the Brain   The neurons
shown in this midsagittal view release norepinephrine as a
transmitter.

nerve cells, a single axon can give rise to thousands of synapses. Degeneration of this system, through loss of neurons either with aging or illicit drug use, can result in the resting tremors or even complete paralysis of Parkinson's disease (see Chapter 11). In the early stages, loss of DA can be partially overcome by providing more L-dopa precursor molecules. Thus the mesostriatal DA system is thought normally to play a crucial role in motor control.

The **mesolimbocortical system** originates in a midbrain region designated the ventral tegmental area (see Figure 4.3), and projects to the limbic system (amygdala, nucleus accumbens, hippocampus) and the cortex. This pathway has been implicated in various theories that schizophrenia is mediated by overstimulation of DA pathways (see Chapter 16).

Several subtypes of DA receptors have been discovered and have been labeled D_1, D_2, D_3, D_4, and D_5, numbered in the order of their discovery. The D_1 and D_5 receptors are similar to each other but quite different from the D_2, D_3, and D_4 receptors, all three of which resemble each other. Drugs that are DA agonists or antagonists often act differently with respect to this array of receptor types. For example, haloperidol is a potent **antipsychotic** drug and is a DA receptor antagonist with a nearly 100-fold selectivity for D_2 over D_1 receptors. In fact, there is a strong correlation between the effectiveness of antipsychotics for relieving symptoms of schizophrenia and their tendency to bind D_2 receptors.

The antipsychotic drugs (also known as neuroleptics) revolutionized the treatment of schizophrenia because they greatly reduce many of the symptoms that prevent patients with this condition from living on their own. In addition, a rich research literature (e.g., Nader et al., 1997) connects DA, especially the D_2 receptor subtype, to reward and reinforcement, a topic we revisit at the end of this chapter. The 1990s saw the advent of so-called atypical or second-generation antipsychotics which, in addition to blocking D_2 receptors, also block a class of serotonin receptors. These newer drugs are just as effective antipsychotic agents, but they are less likely to cause unwanted side effects on motor function (see Chapter 16).

Norepinephrine.   Neurons that release **norepinephrine** (**NE**) are organized into three main clusters in the brainstem: the **locus coeruleus** complex in the pons, the lateral tegmental system of the midbrain, and the dorsal medullary group (Figure 4.4). Because norepinephrine is also known as noradrenaline, NE-producing cells are said to be **noradrenergic.**

The output of the noradrenergic locus coeruleus cells extends broadly throughout the cerebrum, including the cerebral cortex and thalamic nuclei. In addition, it projects prominently to the cerebellum and spinal cord. Because of this wide distribution of projection paths, noradrenergic cells of the locus coeruleus are believed to modulate many behavioral and physiologica processes.

Serotonin.   The second class of monoamines—the indoleamines—consists of melatonin and serotonin. Here we will discuss serotonin. **Serotonin** is abbreviated **5-HT** because its chemical name is 5-hydroxytryptamine. Large areas of the brain are

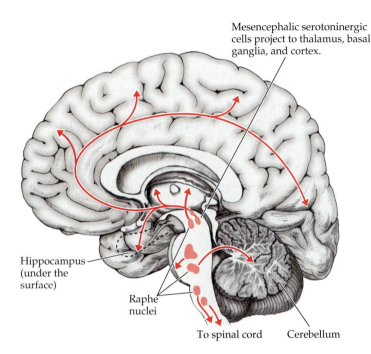

Mesencephalic serotoninergic cells project to thalamus, basal ganglia, and cortex.

Hippocampus (under the surface)

Raphe nuclei

To spinal cord

Cerebellum

4.5 Serotonergic Pathways in the Brain The neurons in the nuclei shown in this midsagittal view release serotonin (5-HT) and thus are said to be serotonergic.

innervated by **serotonergic** fibers, although 5-HT cell bodies are relatively few and are concentrated in the brainstem (most are found in the **raphe nuclei** near the midline). Figure 4.5 shows the distribution of cell bodies and fibers that release 5-HT in the brain. Humans have about 200,000 serotonergic cells, a minuscule number compared with the billions of nerve cells. However, tracts and fibers that release 5-HT extend throughout the brain. The most prominent serotonergic pathway emerges from the dorsal raphe (pronounced "ruh-FAY") nuclei in the brainstem.

Serotonin has been implicated in the control of sleep states (see Chapter 14). In addition, drugs that increase 5-HT activity are effective antidepressants; Prozac is an example (see Chapter 15). At least 15 types of 5-HT receptors ($5HT_1$, $5HT_2$, and so on) have been described.

CLINICAL ISSUE

Some Amino Acids Act as Neurotransmitters

The most common transmitters in the brain are members of a chemical class called amino acids. In this group are two prominent excitatory amino acids—**glutamate** and **aspartate**—and two prominent inhibitory amino acids—**gamma-aminobutyric acid (GABA)** and **glycine.** These transmitters are distributed throughout the central nervous system. Glutamate is the most common excitatory transmitter, and GABA is the major inhibitory transmitter in the brain.

Glutamate transmission employs a group of ionotropic receptors referred to as AMPA, kainate, and NMDA receptors (their names refer to drugs that act as selective agonists). Because NMDA-type glutamate receptors are active in a fascinating model of learning and memory (see Chapter 18), they have been studied very closely (Box 4.2). There are also several metabotropic glutamate receptors (which act more slowly because they work through second messengers).

Glutamate is associated with an interesting feature of synaptic transmission called **excitotoxicity,** a phenomenon in which prolonged depolarization produced by glutamate kills neurons. This condition can arise with neural injury and amplify the effects of injury or stroke. Another interesting feature of glutaminergic synapses is that nearby astrocytes seem to be responsible for taking up glutamate, clearing it from the cleft after synaptic transmission (Rothstein, 2000).

GABA receptors are divided into three large classes (designated GABA$_A$, GABA$_B$, and GABA$_C$), each exhibiting quite different properties. By mixing and matching various subunits, the brain may normally make hundreds of different GABA receptors. Receptors in the GABA$_A$ class contain a chloride channel and include several distinct binding sites, as we'll see later. GABA$_A$ receptors are ionotropic receptors (recall that ionotropic receptors react quickly because they contain an ion channel; see Figure 4.1), and therefore mediate fast inhibitory postsynaptic potentials. The drug sensitivities of GABA$_B$ receptors differ from those of GABA$_A$ recep-

BOX 4.2 *A Star among Receptor Molecules*

Because of its special role in many kinds of information processing, the NMDA receptor is getting star treatment; it is the subject of thousands of recent research articles, more than 100 review articles in the past few years (e.g., Daw et al., 1993), and a symposium volume (Watkins and Collingridge, 1994). The **NMDA receptor** is one of the two main kinds of receptors activated by glutamate, which is a major excitatory synaptic transmitter found in all parts of the nervous system. The name *NMDA receptor* reflects the fact that this receptor is especially sensitive to the glutamate agonist *N*-**m**ethyl-**D**-**a**spartate. The other main kind of glutamate receptor is called the **AMPA receptor** because it is particularly sensitive to α-*a*mino-3-hydroxy-5-*m*ethyl-4-isoxazole-*p*ropionic *a*cid.

The NMDA receptor acts differently from most receptor molecules because it is both ligand gated and voltage sensitive. When the NMDA receptor is activated, Ca^{2+} ions flow through its central channel into the neuron. But only very small amounts of Ca^{2+} flow

through the NMDA receptor at the resting potential of –75 mV or at any membrane potential between –75 and –35 mV. The reason for the low Ca^{2+} conductance at these membrane potentials is that magnesium ions (Mg^{2+}) block the NMDA channel, as the *left-hand panel* of the figure illustrates.

Sufficient activation of AMPA receptors or other excitatory receptors in the same neuronal membrane can partially depolarize the membrane to less than –35 mV. This depolarization removes the Mg^{2+} block (*middle panel* of the figure); the NMDA receptor now responds actively to glutamate and admits large amounts of Ca^{2+} through the channel. The Ca^{2+} starts a cascade of effects (described in more detail in Chapter 18) that results in more AMPA receptors (*right-hand panel*). Thus the NMDA receptor is fully active only when it is gated by a combination of voltage and its ligand. Patch clamp studies show that activation of NMDA receptors usually has a relatively slow onset and a prolonged effect (up to 500 ms), whereas non-NMDA receptors at

the same synapse act rapidly, and their channels remain open only a few milliseconds at a time.

We can study the contributions of NMDA receptors by observing which functions are impaired or abolished by an NMDA antagonist. One such agent is aminophosphonovalerate (APV), which antagonizes the binding of glutamate to the NMDA receptor. Experiments with APV demonstrate that NMDA receptors are not needed for the normal flow of synaptic messages. But when the activity of other receptors reaches a relatively high level and partially depolarizes the membrane, NMDA receptors amplify and prolong the synaptic activity.

Because of these special properties, NMDA receptors play a wide variety of important roles. In later chapters we will see examples of how the NMDA receptor is involved in visual, auditory, and pain perception; in regulating motor and circulatory functions; and in fostering memory formation. The drug PCP may act on the NMDA receptor (see Chapter 16).

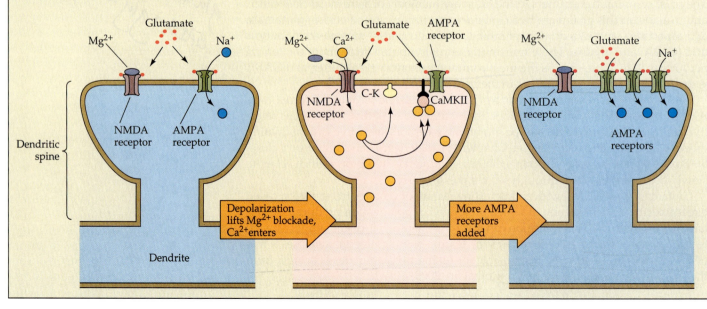

tors, and GABA$_B$ receptors are coupled to a G protein. In other words, GABA$_B$ receptors are metabotropic receptors, in contrast to the ionotropic GABA$_A$ receptors. GABA$_C$ receptors are ionotropic with a chloride channel, but they differ in subunit structure from other GABA receptors. Neural inhibition is the dominant story about GABA, and it is therefore not surprising that drugs that block the actions of GABA can provoke seizures.

Many Peptides Function as Neurotransmitters

Many different peptides are found in the brain; those that have a prominent role as neurotransmitters include (1) **opioid peptides** (peptides that can mimic opiate drugs such as morphine), including met-enkephalin, leu-enkephalin, β-endorphin, and dynorphin; (2) a group of peptides found in the gut and spinal cord or brain, including substance P, cholecystokinin (CCK), neurotensin, neuropeptide Y (NPY), and others; and (3) pituitary hormones such as oxytocin and vasopressin, among others. Many of these peptides act as neurotransmitters at certain synapses, but they also act as hormones (see Chapter 5).

Research on Drugs Ranges from Molecular Processes to Effects on Behavior

The subject of *neuropsychopharmacology*—how drugs affect the nervous system and behavior—is vast and changing at a rapid pace. The range and complexity of neuropsychopharmacology are suggested by the different meanings of the Greek word *pharmakon,* which is the root of the word *pharmacology. Pharmakon* has three principal meanings: (1) "a charm"—that is, an object thought to have a magical effect, (2) "a poison," and (3) "a remedy or medicine." Similarly, in English we use the term *drug* in different ways. One common meaning is "a medicine used in the treatment of a disease" (e.g., a *prescription drug* or an *over-the-counter drug*). Quite a different meaning of *drug,* but also a common one, is "a psychoactive agent," especially an addictive one—that is, a drug of abuse. The common element of these meanings is a substance that, taken in relatively small amounts, has clear effects on experience, mood, emotion, activity, and/or health.

Some drugs originally evolved in plants, probably to discourage animals from eating them. One example is the bitter-tasting morphine produced by the opium poppy (Figure 4.6). Almost all the drugs of interest to psychologists reliably alter behavior, and these drugs usually act on particular classes of neurotransmitter receptors, as we discuss in the next section.

To understand how drugs work, we must use many levels of analysis—from molecules to behavior and experience (see Figure 1.6). Because drugs exert their effects at the molecular level but have profound effects on behavior, we will encounter these different levels of analysis in this chapter.

4.6 The Source of Opium and Morphine The opium poppy has a distinctive flower and seedpod.

Drugs Fit like Keys into Molecular Locks

Some drugs are effective because they interact with lipid molecules that make up the membrane, but most drugs of interest to biological psychology react with specialized receptor molecules. Receptor molecules are proteins that may be situated either in the cell membrane (as are the receptor molecules in the postsynaptic membrane that we considered in Chapter 3) or inside the cell (as are the receptors for certain hormones that we will consider in Chapter 5).

Perhaps the most compelling single principle of neurotransmitters and their receptors is that a given neurotransmitter may normally act on several different receptors. We've seen that a single compound, GABA, may act on hundreds of different receptors. Apparently natural selection tinkers structurally with receptors more often than with transmitters. The resulting multiplicity of receptors offers an opportunity for pharmacological approaches because **synthetic** (human-made) compounds can be devised to affect some of the receptors that are normally activated by a neurotransmitter, but not others. Thus there is always a great deal of interest in which version of a receptor is the target of a given drug.

Drug molecules do not seek out particular receptor molecules; rather, drug molecules spread widely throughout the body, and when they contact receptor molecules with the specific shape that fits the drug molecule, the two molecules bind together briefly and begin a chain of events. The lock-and-key analogy is often used for this binding action, as we mentioned in Chapter 3. But now we have to think of keys (drug molecules) trying to insert themselves in all the locks (receptor molecules) in the neighborhood; each key unlocks only a particular set of doors.

Where a drug appears to bind to receptor molecules, investigators try to find the endogenous substance that is the natural **ligand** binding to that receptor. (the word **endogenous** means "occurring naturally within the body." Drugs are **exogenous** substances; that is, they are introduced from outside the body.) In some cases, such as the opioids, the key was identified before the structure of the lock was determined. In other cases, such as the receptor for the active ingredient of marijuana, the lock was identified before the endogenous key was found. Once the drug or transmitter (the key) binds to the receptor (the lock), it alters the shape of the receptor to set off a chain of events, often the flow of ions across the postsynaptic membrane. But the binding is usually temporary, and when the drug or transmitter breaks away from the receptor, the receptor resumes its unbound shape and ion flow stops.

Drug–Receptor Relations Vary in Specificity

The tuning of drug molecules to a receptor is not absolutely specific. That is, a particular drug molecule may bind strongly with one kind of receptor molecule, more weakly with some others, and not at all with many others. A drug molecule that has more than one kind of action in the body exhibits this flexibility because it affects more than one kind of receptor molecule. For example, some drugs combat anxiety at low doses without producing sedation (relaxation, drowsiness), but at higher doses they cause sedation, probably because at those doses they activate another type of receptor molecule.

Some drug molecules bind to the receptor for a long time; others bind for only a short time. All other things being equal, a drug that binds for a long time has a greater effect than one that binds for a short time because it activates the receptor longer. The compound that binds to the receptor longer is said to have a greater **binding affinity** (or, simply, **affinity**) for the receptor. To some extent you can compare the effectiveness of different drugs by comparing their affinity for the receptor of interest.

In principle, we would like to know how long a given drug molecule binds to a receptor molecule, but in practice it is easier to measure binding affinity in a different way. Continuous addition of molecules of the drug to a solution containing those receptors eventually produces a concentration of drug that binds half of the receptors present. At this point, for every drug molecule that is released by one receptor, another molecule will become bound to another receptor, and we say that the binding has reached equilibrium. If the drug has a very high affinity (and there-

IMPORTANT METHOD

fore binds to the receptor for a relatively long time), then a very low concentration of drug molecules will be sufficient to bind half the receptors (Figure 4.7). So pharmacologists tend to speak of a drug's affinity for the receptor in terms of the concentration of drug needed to bind half the receptors. The lower this concentration, the greater the drug's affinity.

Note that the binding of a ligand with a receptor molecule does not necessarily mean that the ligand *activates* the receptor. As we discussed in Chapter 3, there are some cases in which a drug merely occupies the receptor site and prevents the transmitter from activating the receptor; in such a scenario the drug is an *antagonist* of the transmitter. The drug competes with the transmitter for access to the receptor. If a drug binds the site and activates the same receptor as the transmitter does, then the drug is an *agonist* of the transmitter (Figure 4.8).

Sometimes a drug doesn't simply block the transmitter from occupying the binding site, as antagonists do. Sometimes the drug binds the site and causes the receptor to do the *opposite* of what the native neurotransmitter does (e.g., it may cause an inhibitory postsynaptic potential rather than an excitatory postsynaptic potential). We call such a drug, that makes a receptor do the opposite of an agonist, an **inverse agonist.**

To complicate things a bit further, some drugs bind to a part of the receptor that does not normally bind the transmitter (see Figure 4.8). That means that the drug does not compete with the transmitter for its binding site, and so we say that the drug is a **noncompetitive** ligand, binding to a **modulatory site** on the receptor. Noncompetitive ligands may either activate the receptor, thereby acting as noncompetitive agonists, or prevent the receptor from being activated by the transmitter, thus acting as noncompetitive antagonists. We'll discuss modulatory sites on the GABA receptor later in this chapter.

If a particular drug has a low affinity for a receptor, then it will quickly uncouple from the receptor. To bind half the receptors at any given time, a higher concentration of the drug is needed.

If a drug has a high affinity for a receptor, the two will stay together for a longer time, and a lower concentration of drug will be sufficient to bind half the receptors.

If equal concentrations of the two drugs are present, the high-affinity drug will be bound to more receptors at any given time. If the drugs activate the receptor equally, then the higher-affinity drug will have a more potent effect.

4.7 Using Binding Affinity to Compare Drug Effectiveness

 4.8 The Agonistic and Antagonistic Actions of Drugs

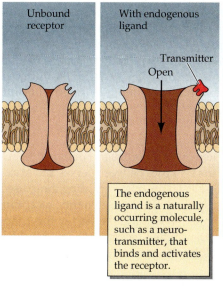 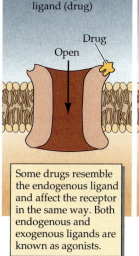 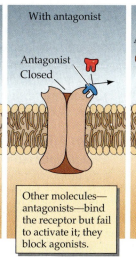 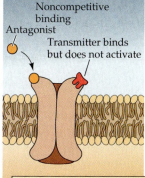

| Unbound receptor | With endogenous ligand | With exogenous ligand (drug) | With antagonist | Noncompetitive binding |

Transmitter
Open

Drug
Open

Antagonist
Closed

Antagonist
Transmitter binds but does not activate

The endogenous ligand is a naturally occurring molecule, such as a neurotransmitter, that binds and activates the receptor.

Some drugs resemble the endogenous ligand and affect the receptor in the same way. Both endogenous and exogenous ligands are known as agonists.

Other molecules—antagonists—bind the receptor but fail to activate it; they block agonists.

Some drugs bind to receptors at a site different from the site where that receptor's native ligand(s) bind. This binding may activate or block the activation of the receptor, without competing with the native transmitter for binding sites, so such drugs are known as noncompetitive agonists or antagonists.

Drugs Affect Each Stage of Neural Conduction and Synaptic Transmission

Almost all the behavioral effects that we discuss in this chapter are caused by the activities of drugs on synaptic events and processes and on neural conduction. Figure 4.9 explains how certain drugs affect the major steps in neural conduction and synaptic transmission (see Figure 3.13). In the discussion that follows we'll comment on some of these agents and their effects, as well as on related effects of other agents.

Drugs Affect Presynaptic Events

If axonal transport is inhibited by a drug (e.g., colchicine), enzymes that are manufactured in the cell body are not replaced in the presynaptic terminals. Because enzymes are needed to manufacture transmitter chemicals and vesicle walls, drugs that inhibit axonal transport prevent replenishment of the transmitter agent as it is used up and cause synaptic transmission to fail. The drug reserpine inhibits the storage of catecholamine transmitters (dopamine, epinephrine, and norepinephrine) in vesicles. Even if a presynaptic terminal has an adequate supply of transmitter stored in vesicles, various agents or conditions can prevent the release of transmitter when a nerve impulse reaches the terminal. A low concentration of calcium (Ca^{2+}) in the extracellular fluid is such a condition: Under these circumstances, transmitter is not released because too little Ca^{2+} enters.

Specific toxins prevent the release of specific kinds of transmitters (see Figure 4.9 for examples) (de Paiva et al., 1993). For instance, botulinum toxin, which is formed by bacteria that multiply in improperly canned food, poisons many people each year by blocking the release of ACh. The toxin binds to specialized receptors in nicotinic cholinergic neural membranes and is transported into the cell, where it blocks Ca^{2+}-dependent release of transmitter (McMahon et al., 1992). Tetanus (lockjaw) bacteria produce an often fatal toxin that blocks activity at inhibitory synapses and causes strong involuntary contractions of muscles.

**CLINICAL
ISSUE**

Other agents stimulate or facilitate the release of certain transmitters. **Neuromodulators** are compounds that are not transmitters themselves, but that modulate the effectiveness of synaptic transmission. The noncompetitive ligands discussed earlier (see Figure 4.8) are neuromodulators. In general, neuromodulators affect either the release of the transmitter or the receptor response to the transmitter. For example, black widow spider venom exaggerates the release of ACh.

The stimulant drug amphetamine facilitates the release of catecholamine transmitters, as well as inhibiting their reuptake, which further increases their synaptic action. Caffeine blocks the effect of an endogenous neuromodulator, adenosine. Because adenosine normally acts on presynaptic terminals to inhibit the release of catecholamine transmitters, caffeine increases catecholamine release, causing arousal.

Where does adenosine normally come from? It appears that at least some catecholaminergic synapses co-release adenosine along with the neurotransmitter. The adenosine binds to receptors on the same presynaptic terminal that released it, so we say that the adenosine acts on **autoreceptors**. It may seem odd that a neuron that is releasing transmitter would also release a neuromodulator to inhibit transmitter release, but this type of complicated modulation of transmitter release may be the rule, not the exception.

Drugs Affect Postsynaptic Events

Postsynaptic receptor molecules can be blocked by various drugs. For example, curare blocks nicotinic ACh receptors. Because the synapses between nerves and skeletal muscles are nicotinic, curare paralyzes all skeletal muscles, including those used in breathing. We discussed several other drugs that affect postsynaptic receptors when we described the different neurotransmitter systems at the start of this chapter. Behavior can be disrupted not only when transmitter–receptor action is blocked, but also when it is prolonged. Agents that inhibit the enzyme acetylcholinesterase

(*a*) Presynaptic mechanisms

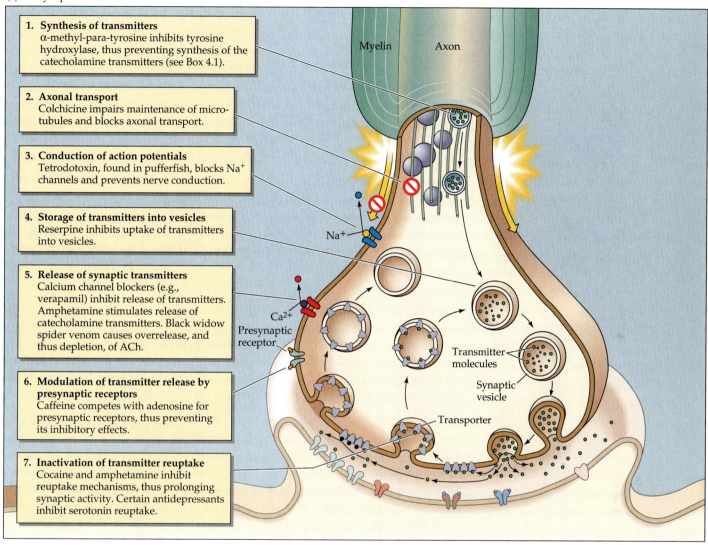

1. **Synthesis of transmitters**
   α-methyl-para-tyrosine inhibits tyrosine hydroxylase, thus preventing synthesis of the catecholamine transmitters (see Box 4.1).

2. **Axonal transport**
   Colchicine impairs maintenance of micro-tubules and blocks axonal transport.

3. **Conduction of action potentials**
   Tetrodotoxin, found in pufferfish, blocks Na^+ channels and prevents nerve conduction.

4. **Storage of transmitters into vesicles**
   Reserpine inhibits uptake of transmitters into vesicles.

5. **Release of synaptic transmitters**
   Calcium channel blockers (e.g., verapamil) inhibit release of transmitters. Amphetamine stimulates release of catecholamine transmitters. Black widow spider venom causes overrelease, and thus depletion, of ACh.

6. **Modulation of transmitter release by presynaptic receptors**
   Caffeine competes with adenosine for presynaptic receptors, thus preventing its inhibitory effects.

7. **Inactivation of transmitter reuptake**
   Cocaine and amphetamine inhibit reuptake mechanisms, thus prolonging synaptic activity. Certain antidepressants inhibit serotonin reuptake.

Myelin   Axon

Na^+

Ca^{2+}
Presynaptic receptor

Transmitter molecules

Synaptic vesicle

Transporter

(*b*) Postsynaptic mechanisms

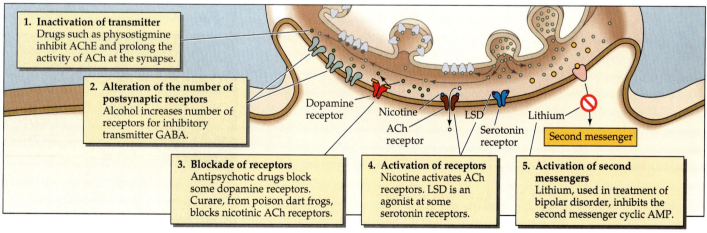

1. **Inactivation of transmitter**
   Drugs such as physostigmine inhibit AChE and prolong the activity of ACh at the synapse.

2. **Alteration of the number of postsynaptic receptors**
   Alcohol increases number of receptors for inhibitory transmitter GABA.

3. **Blockade of receptors**
   Antipsychotic drugs block some dopamine receptors. Curare, from poison dart frogs, blocks nicotinic ACh receptors.

4. **Activation of receptors**
   Nicotine activates ACh receptors. LSD is an agonist at some serotonin receptors.

5. **Activation of second messengers**
   Lithium, used in treatment of bipolar disorder, inhibits the second messenger cyclic AMP.

Dopamine receptor

Nicotine
ACh receptor

LSD
Serotonin receptor

Lithium

Second messenger

4.9 Steps in Synaptic Transmission That Are Affected by Drugs

(AChE) allow ACh to remain active at the synapse and alter the timing of synaptic transmission. Effects can range from mild to severe, depending on the anti-AChE agent and its dosage.

Drugs That Affect the Brain Can Be Divided into Functional Classes

Of the many drugs that affect the brain, several draw special attention because they contribute to social distress and personal disasters. These drugs are often classified on the basis of their effects on the brain. In the sections that follow, we will briefly review some of the major features of these substances.

Opiates Help Relieve Pain

Opium has a long history of human use, stretching back to the Stone Age. It is a mixture of many substances. Morphine, the major active substance in opium, was extracted from poppy flower seedpods (see Figure 4.6) in pure form starting at the beginning of the nineteenth century. Morphine continues to be used medically as a very effective **analgesic** (painkiller), but it also has a strong potential for addiction. Many people have become addicted to morphine and to an artificially modified form of morphine: **heroin** (diacetylmorphine).

In 1973, pharmacologists Candace Pert and Solomon Snyder found that opiate drugs such as morphine bind to receptor molecules that are concentrated in certain regions of the brain. Opiate receptors are found especially in the limbic and hypothalamic areas of the brain, and they are particularly rich in the locus coeruleus and in the gray matter that surrounds the aqueduct in the brainstem (known as the **periaqueductal gray**) (Figure 4.10). Injection of morphine directly into the periaqueductal gray causes analgesia, indicating that this is a region where morphine acts to reduce pain perception (see Chapter 8). After the discovery of opiate receptors, investigators began an intensive search for natural substances in the body that would normally bind to these receptors—in other words, the natural keys that fit the lock of the opiate receptors.

In 1975, pharmacologists John Hughes and Hans Kosterlitz isolated from pig brain two similar peptides that bind to the opiate receptor (Hughes et al., 1975). They called these substances **enkephalins** (from the Greek *en*, "in," and *kephale*, "head"). Research with animal subjects demonstrated that enkephalins relieve pain and are

Candace Pert

Solomon Snyder

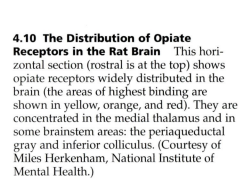

4.10 The Distribution of Opiate Receptors in the Rat Brain This horizontal section (rostral is at the top) shows opiate receptors widely distributed in the brain (the areas of highest binding are shown in yellow, orange, and red). They are concentrated in the medial thalamus and in some brainstem areas: the periaqueductal gray and inferior colliculus. (Courtesy of Miles Herkenham, National Institute of Mental Health.)

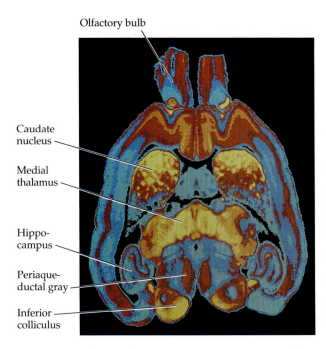

Olfactory bulb

Caudate nucleus

Medial thalamus

Hippocampus

Periaqueductal gray

Inferior colliculus

addictive. Only a small part of the enkephalin molecule is the same as the morphine molecule; this common part is what binds to the opioid receptor. Further research uncovered whole families of what are called **endogenous opioids**—that is, opioids that are found naturally in the brain. One of these families consists of compounds called **endorphins,** a contraction of *endogenous morphine*—literally, "the brain's own morphine."

Three main kinds of opioid receptors differ in terms of which drugs bind them most strongly: the δ, κ, and μ opioid receptors (Evans et al., 1992; J. B. Wang et al., 1993; Yasuda et al., 1993). All three are G protein–coupled receptors.

Marijuana Has a Wide Array of Effects

More people in the United States use **marijuana** than any other illegal drug. Marijuana is obtained from a plant, *Cannabis sativa* (Figure 4.11), which also furnishes other preparations, such as hashish. The main active ingredient in marijuana and hashish is the compound **tetrahydrocannabinol (THC)** (Gaoni and Mechoulam, 1964). THC, marijuana, hashish, and related preparations are called **cannabinoids.** Their effects on experience are highly variable among individuals, from stimulating and causing hallucinations to inducing relaxation, or sometimes initially causing almost no effect at all. Continued use of marijuana often causes addiction, although many people start using it without being aware of this potential. Smoking marijuana, like cigarettes, can also contribute to respiratory diseases.

In the case of marijuana, investigators deciphered the structure of the receptor molecules before they discovered the endogenous ligand—the body's own marijuana. For years investigators tried to locate THC receptors by placing THC tagged with a radioactive tracer onto slices of brain and observing where it accumulated. But THC turned out to be a "sticky" molecule that binds nonspecifically to surfaces all through the brain. This case is an example in which one molecule binds to another without activating it.

In subsequent experiments, scientists used a synthetic THC-like compound that has a more specific affinity for THC receptors. With this ligand they found that the receptor molecules for THC are concentrated in the substantia nigra, the hippocampus, the cerebellar cortex, and the cerebral cortex (Figure 4.12) (De-

4.11 Indoor Marijuana Farm
Although growing marijuana is illegal in the United States, this plant has been estimated to be the largest cash crop in several states. Growers have developed techniques for growing highly potent strains of cannabis indoors under "grow lights."

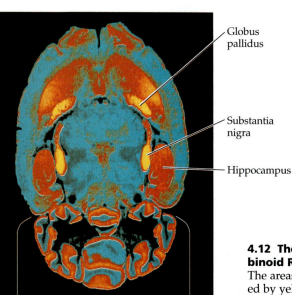

Globus pallidus

Substantia nigra

Hippocampus

Cerebellum

4.12 The Distribution of Cannabinoid Receptors in the Rat Brain
The areas of highest binding are indicated by yellow, orange, and red in this horizontal section. (Courtesy of Miles Herkenham, National Institute of Mental Health.)

vane et al., 1988); other regions, such as the brainstem, show few of these receptors. There are at least two cannabinoid receptors—CB_1 and CB_2 (Gerard et al., 1991; Pertwee, 1997)—both of which are G protein–coupled receptors. Genetic disruption of CB_1 is sufficient to make mice unresponsive to the rewarding properties of cannabinoid drugs (Ledent et al., 1999).

In 1992, investigators isolated an endogenous compound in brain tissue that binds to the THC receptor and that has at least some of the properties of THC (Devane et al., 1992). In the hope that they had found an endogenous equivalent to marijuana, the discoverers named this compound **anandamide** (from the Sanskrit *ananda*, "bliss"). Further research showed that anandamide and THC produce several of the same effects—reduced sensitivity to pain, hypothermia, hypomotility, and catalepsy—and these effects vary with dosage and route of administration (P. B. Smith et al., 1994).

COMPETING HYPOTHESES

Another endogenous ligand for the cannabinoid receptor was found to be 170 times more common than anandamide in the brain (Stella et al., 1997). If either substance really is an endogenous equivalent of THC, the discovery will allow researchers to identify the neurons that produce the substance and to study their functions in the nervous system; up to now, the mechanism(s) of the action of marijuana have not been clear. Identification of an endogenous ligand may also aid in the search for other drugs that have the clinical effects of marijuana (relieving pain, lowering blood pressure, combating nausea, and lowering eye pressure in glaucoma).

Alcohol Acts as a Depressant

Alcohol has traveled the full route of human history, no doubt because it is so easily produced by fermentation, which can readily occur when fruit or grains are left standing in a warm, damp place. Alcohol is the most commonly used psychoactive substance and frequently serves as the day's tension reducer. The action of alcohol on the nervous system is biphasic: An initial stimulant phase is followed by a more prolonged depressant phase.

Sustained use of alcohol can damage nerve cells. Cells of the superior frontal cortex, Purkinje cells of the cerebellum, and hippocampal pyramidal cells show particularly prominent pathological changes. These degenerative effects of chronic alcohol use may be due to a secondary consequence of alcoholism: poor diet. Chronic alcoholics suffer severe thiamine deficiency, which can lead to neural degeneration and Korsakoff's syndrome (see Chapter 17).

NEURAL PLASTICITY

Kril et al. (1997) reported that frontal lobes of alcoholics—especially superior frontal association cortex—are most affected by chronic alcohol use. However, some of the anatomical changes that are evident in the brains of chronic alcoholics may be reversible with abstinence. For example, chronic exposure to alcohol in experimental rats reduces the number of synapses on cerebellar neurons, but this number is restored to control levels after a period of recovery (Dlugos and Pentney, 1997). In human alcoholics, MRI studies of short-term effects of abstinence show an increase in the volume of cortical gray matter and a reduction in ventricular volume (Figure 4.13) (Pfefferbaum et al., 1995).

The nature of this reversibility remains a puzzle. It is clearly not due to rehydration, and it may well be a form of neural plasticity. PET scans also reveal a restorative effect in alcoholics who abstain from drinking (Johnson-Greene et al., 1997). The destructive effects of alcohol are mediated probably by the breakdown products of alcohol—aldehydes—rather than by the direct effects of alcohol on nerve cells (Seil et al., 1977). In Chapter 7 we will review the dramatic, permanent brain damage caused by prenatal exposure to alcohol (fetal alcohol syndrome).

Interactions between alcohol and GABA are a prominent basis of the effects of alcohol on the brain; alcohol activates the $GABA_A$ receptor–coupled chloride channel, which increases postsynaptic inhibition. Alcohol also affects other transmitters. For example, low doses of alcohol stimulate dopamine pathways, and the resulting increase in dopamine may be related to the euphoriant properties of alcohol. Opiate antagonists such as naloxone suppress alcohol consumption in rats (Froehlich et al., 1990), a result suggesting that opioid receptors mediate the effects of alcohol.

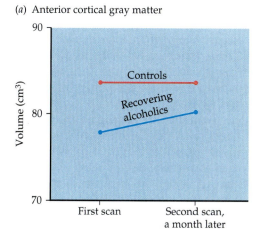

(a) Anterior cortical gray matter

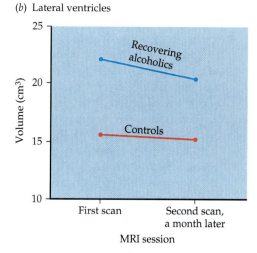

(b) Lateral ventricles

4.13 The Effects of Alcohol on the Brain MRI studies of alcoholics show that abstaining from alcohol for 30 days increases the volume of cortical gray matter (a) and decreases the volume of the lateral ventricles (b). (After Pfefferbaum et al., 1995.)

There is a strong hereditary component to alcoholism, as indicated by human studies and selective breeding experiments in rats. In humans, 20 to 50% of the sons of alcoholics and 3 to 8% of the daughters become alcoholics themselves. Rates of alcoholism in the first-degree relatives of alcoholics are several times higher than are rates for the general population (Schuckit and Smith, 1997). Some evidence suggests that a genetic vulnerability combined with a stressful environment can result in alcoholism (McGue, 1999).

GENES AND BEHAVIOR

Anxiolytics Combat Anxiety

Most of us occasionally suffer feelings of vague dissatisfaction or apprehension that we call anxiety, but here we will be concerned with the disabling emotional distress that resembles abject fear and terror. Severe anxiety that prevents people from carrying on normal daily activities is estimated to afflict about 8% of adult Americans. These clinical states of anxiety include phobias—such as the fear of taking an airplane or even of leaving the house—and frank attacks of panic (see Chapter 16).

Substances used to combat anxiety are called **anxiolytics** (from the word *anxiety* and the Greek *lytikos*, "able to loosen"). One substance that has long been used as an anxiolytic is alcohol. Alcohol decreases anxiety in some people, but it has some quite undesirable consequences, such as neuropsychological impairments with excessive use and a strong potential for addiction. Opiates and barbiturates have also been used to relieve anxiety, but they seem to sedate or, in higher doses, to produce stupor rather than being true anxiolytics.

In the early 1960s, an effective new family of anxiolytics was found: the **benzodiazepines.** Benzodiazepines are some of the most frequently prescribed drugs, especially diazepam (trade name Valium). Benzodiazepines bind to and enhance the activity of some GABA receptors (Walters et al., 2000). Because these GABA receptors are inhibitory, benzodiazepines produce larger inhibitory postsynaptic potentials than would be caused by GABA alone. In fact, there are several different binding sites on GABA receptors—some that facilitate and some that inhibit the effect of GABA (Figure 4.14). Note that benzodiazepines do not bind to the same site on the receptor as the transmitter GABA does; rather the drug binds to a modulatory site on the receptor.

Neuroscientists have been searching for a natural substance in the nervous system that binds to the so-called benzodiazepine receptor—an endogenous ligand for the receptor—but the quest continues. An endogenous factor binds to another site on the GABA receptor: the neurohormone **allopregnanolone,** a steroid derived from the hormone progesterone. This neurohormone is induced and released as a conse-

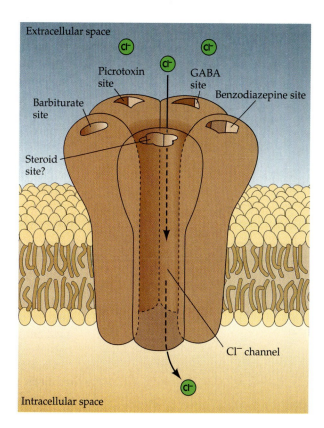

4.14 The GABA Receptor Has Many Different Binding Sites

quence of stress; it has a calming effect. Alcohol ingestion also increases brain concentrations of allopregnanolone (VanDoren et al., 2000), so this steroid may be responsible for some of alcohol's calming influence. Allopregnanolone binds to GABA receptors and increases the effectiveness of GABA. In turn, GABA inhibits the release of corticotropin-releasing hormone, which triggers stress responses. Thus allopregnanolone may be an endogenous anxiolytic substance whose actions can be mimicked by the benzodiazepine drugs.

Of course, some drugs have no endogenous counterpart. A drug molecule may happen to bind to a part of the receptor that does not normally interact with any endogenous compound. Natural selection may favor plants that produce new molecules affecting receptors in the nervous system as a way of discouraging predators. For example, chili peppers evolved a molecule, capsaicin, that activates heat receptors in humans, producing a burning sensation (see Chapter 8). This is the pepper's way of telling us to eat somebody else. We have no endogenous capsaicin; normally it is the increase in temperature that physically activates our heat receptors. By extension, there may be no endogenous benzodiazepine.

Stimulants Increase the Activity of the Nervous System

The degree of activity of the nervous system is determined by competing excitatory and inhibitory influences. Stimulants are drugs that tip the balance toward the excitatory side; they therefore have an alerting, activating effect. Many naturally occurring and artificial stimulants are widely used; examples include amphetamine, nicotine, caffeine, and cocaine. Some stimulants act directly by increasing excitatory synaptic potentials. Others act by blocking normal inhibitory processes; one example we've seen already is the blocking of adenosine by caffeine.

Nicotine. Tobacco is native to the Americas, where European explorers first encountered smoking. When smoking tobacco was introduced to England in the sixteenth century, King James banned it, but he was unable to prevent its growing use. However, tobacco was not used widely until about 1880, when a technological innovation in curing tobacco made it seem mild, so it could be readily inhaled in cigarettes (W. Bennett, 1983). Exposed to the large surface of the lungs, the **nicotine** from cigarettes enters the blood and brain much more rapidly than does nicotine from pipes, cigars, chewing tobacco, or snuff.

The stimulant nicotine activates one class of ACh receptors, which, as we learned earlier, are called *nicotinic receptors*. Most nicotinic receptors are found at neuromuscular junctions and in neurons of the autonomic ganglia, but many are also present in the central nervous system. When nicotine enters the bloodstream, it increases the heart rate—both directly, by stimulating sympathetic ganglia, and indirectly, by stimulating the adrenal gland to release the hormone epinephrine. Nicotine also increases blood pressure, secretion of hydrochloric acid in the stomach, and motor activity of the bowel. These neural effects, quite apart from the effects of tobacco tar on the lungs, contribute to the unhealthful consequences of heavy and prolonged use of tobacco products.

Cocaine. **Cocaine** is an alkaloid that comes from the leaves of the coca shrub, which is indigenous to Bolivia, Colombia, and Peru. Some people in these countries chew coca leaves or drink a tea brewed from the leaves to increase endurance, alleviate hunger, and promote a sense of well-being. This use of coca leaves does not seem to cause problems. However, the indigenous material has been purified by technological modifications into addictive forms such as cocaine powder and crack cocaine crystals.

Cocaine was isolated in 1859 and was soon added to beverages for its stimulant qualities. By the 1890s, cocaine was used as a local anesthetic and to relieve depression, until it was found to be addictive. It was widely used as a psychostimulant until 1932, when it gave way to amphetamine, which acts much like cocaine but was easier to obtain (amphetamine was sold in inhalers for nasal congestion, and some people cracked open inhalers to get the drug). When legal restrictions on amphetamine raised its price in the 1960s, cocaine use rose again. Many users inhale cocaine powder, which enters the bloodstream and takes effect rapidly by this route.

Crack is a smokable form of cocaine that appeared in the mid-1980s. Because cocaine in this form enters the blood and the brain even more rapidly, crack cocaine is even more addictive than cocaine powder. Cocaine seems to block monoamine transporters, especially those for norepinephrine (Figure 4.15), blocking reuptake of the transmitters and therefore boosting their effects. Cocaine can provoke an acute stroke in new or long-term users; it also causes long-term alterations in cerebral blood flow (Holman et al., 1993). Decreases in cerebral glucose metabolism are evident for several months after cocaine use is discontinued.

Some children are initially exposed to cocaine while in the womb, and there has been widespread fear that exposure during fetal life might produce irreversible harm to the development of brain and behavior (Vogel, 1997). Although the home environment of children who were exposed to cocaine prenatally has potent effects on intellectual development, fetal exposure to cocaine also impairs intellectual growth to some extent. One cocaine-related developmental effect on infants is decreased ability to focus attention, an effect seen in rats exposed to prenatal cocaine (Garavan et al., 2000). In rabbits exposed to cocaine, dendrites in the anterior cingulate area grow 30 to 50% longer and weave extensions through several planes (Levitt et al., 1997). These rabbits also show inefficient transmission involving some dopamine receptors.

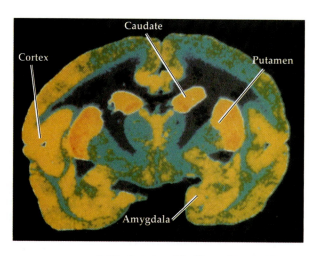

4.15 Cocaine-Binding Sites in the Monkey Brain This autoradiograph of a coronal section shows the distribution of cocaine-binding sites. The areas of the highest binding are shown by orange and yellow. (Courtesy of Bertha K. Madras.)

Amphetamine. A molecule of the artificial substance **amphetamine** resembles the structure of the catecholamine transmitters (norepinephrine, epinephrine, and dopamine). Amphetamine and the even more potent methamphetamine (*speed*) cause the release of these transmitters from the presynaptic terminals even when no nerve impulse arrives at the terminals, and potentiate the effects of nerve impulses in releasing them. After catecholamine transmitter molecules reach the synaptic cleft, amphetamine enhances their activity in two ways: (1) by blocking the reuptake of catecholamines into the presynaptic terminal, and (2) by competing with the catecholamines for the enzyme that inactivates them (monoamine oxidase).

These effects of amphetamine prolong the presence of the catecholamine transmitters in the synaptic cleft, thus increasing their effectiveness. The stimulant cocaine is similar to amphetamine in blocking the reuptake of catecholamines, but it does not have the other synaptic effects of amphetamine. Although first synthesized in 1887, amphetamine did not become widely abused until the 1930s.

Because amphetamine stimulates and enhances the activity of the catecholamine transmitters, it has a variety of behavioral effects. On a short-term basis, it produces heightened alertness and even euphoria, and it wards off boredom. Its short-term use can promote sustained effort without rest or sleep and with lowered fatigue. However, although a person may be able to accomplish more work and feel more confident by using amphetamine, most studies show that the quality of work is not improved by the drug; it appears to increase motivation but not cognitive ability. The activity of amphetamine at synapses of the autonomic nervous system may also produce high blood pressure, tremor, dizziness, sweating, rapid breathing, and nausea. Chronic speed abusers display symptoms of brain damage long after they quit using the drug (Ernst et al., 2000).

Cocaine and amphetamine treatments each induce the brain to produce a peptide called, naturally enough, **cocaine- and amphetamine-related peptide** (**CART**). Injections of CART in a particular brain region (the ventral tegmental area, which we discuss a little later in the chapter) is very rewarding for rats (Kimmel et al.,

2000), so the peptide may mediate some of the pleasurable effects of these drugs. CART injections to the brain also suppress appetite (Kristensen et al., 1998).

Prolonged use of amphetamine leads to an important pharmacological phenomenon: tolerance. **Tolerance** is the progressive loss of effectiveness of a drug that is administered repeatedly. Often tolerance develops because the number of receptors is reduced by repeated stimulation with the drug. Thus larger and larger doses of the drug are needed to achieve the same effect. Because of tolerance, amphetamine users take higher and higher doses, leading to sleeplessness, severe weight loss, and general deterioration of mental and physical condition. Prolonged use of amphetamine may lead to symptoms that closely resemble those of paranoid schizophrenia: compulsive, agitated behavior and irrational suspiciousness. In fact, some amphetamine users have been misdiagnosed as schizophrenic (see Chapter 16).

Interestingly, repeated use of some drugs, including cocaine and amphetamines, can lead to the opposite of tolerance: **sensitization.** In that case, the same dose of drug has a *greater* effect with repeated use. This heightened sensitivity may last for a prolonged period, and it seems to reflect long-term brain changes in response to drugs of abuse (Peris et al., 1990).

Hallucinogenic Drugs Alter Sensory Perception

Some drugs alter sensory perception, often in striking or dramatic ways, and produce peculiar experiences. These drugs are termed **hallucinogens**—agents that cause hallucinations. But some investigators feel that the term *hallucinogen* is not appropriate, because whereas a hallucination is a perception that takes place without sensory stimulation, hallucinogens such as LSD, mescaline, and psilocybin alter or distort perceptions. The effects of LSD and related substances are predominantly visual and can become frightening. Users often see fantastic pictures with intense colors, and they are often aware that these strangely altered perceptions are not real events.

Hallucinogenic agents are chemically diverse; several have been found to affect one or another of the amine synaptic transmitter systems. For example, mescaline, the drug extracted from the peyote plant, affects the norepinephrine system. LSD and psilocybin act on one kind of serotonin receptor. Other hallucinogens, such as muscarine, found in some mushrooms, affect the ACh system.

LSD (lysergic acid diethylamide) was synthesized in 1938 by Albert Hofmann, a Swiss pharmacologist who was looking for new therapeutic agents. Because tests with animals did not appear to show effects, he put the compound aside. Then one day in 1943, Dr. Hofmann experienced a peculiar dreamlike, almost drunken state. When he closed his eyes, fantastic pictures of intense color and extraordinary plasticity seemed to surge toward him. The state lasted about 2 hours. Correctly suspecting that he had accidentally ingested a small amount of LSD, Hofmann began to investigate the compound again. LSD proved to be amazingly potent: A fraction of a milligram is enough to induce hallucinations.

In the 1950s, many investigators worked on LSD, hoping it would provide a useful model of psychosis that would suggest clues about the biochemical processes in mental illnesses. The structure of LSD resembles that of serotonin, and LSD was soon found to act on serotonin receptors, but the mechanism by which LSD evokes hallucinations is still unknown. Many former users of LSD have reported flashbacks—that is, experiences as if they had taken a dose of drug, even though they are drug-free. These episodes can follow even brief use of LSD, but it is not yet clear whether they reflect permanent neural changes or a special form of memory.

Phencyclidine (commonly known as **PCP** or *angel dust*) was developed in 1956 as a potent analgesic and anesthetic agent. It was soon dropped from use as an anesthetic because patients reported effects such as agitation, excitement, delirium, hostility, and disorganization of perceptions. PCP is often sold illegally as a hallucinogen.

Toxic reactions to PCP include the *four Cs:* Low doses may produce (1) combativeness and (2) catatonia (a condition that may include stupor, stereotyped behavior, mania, and either rigidity or extreme flexibility of the limbs). Overdoses result in (3) convulsions or coma that may last for days and (4) confusion that may last for weeks. As with amphetamine, users sometimes develop a psychotic condition that resembles schizophrenia, so PCP may provide a useful chemical model of schizophrenia (see Chapter 16). PCP may also produce neurotoxic effects. Given over several days to animals, PCP produces extensive degeneration in the hippocampus and the cingulate gyrus.

PCP antagonizes the NMDA receptor (see Figure 16.8), perhaps at a special binding site, and it stimulates the release of the transmitter dopamine (Gorelick and Balster, 1995). Ketamine is a less potent NMDA antagonist that is used as an anesthetic agent with nonhumans. PET studies of the effects of ketamine on the brains of healthy volunteers showed focal increases of metabolic activity in the prefrontal cortex (Breier et al., 1997), so perhaps PCP acts there. Ketamine also produced transient psychotic symptoms in these volunteers.

Some "Recreational" Drugs May Have Long-Term Effects

The dangers of drug use widely heralded in public health campaigns usually focus on short-term changes. We all know about the heroin *rush*, the cocaine *high*, and the many other relatively short-term effects of recreational drugs described in newspapers, magazines, and textbooks. But do these drugs have enduring effects that persist well beyond a period of hours or days? Some ominous findings indicate that brain changes produced by recreational drugs may persist for months (McCann et al., 1997).

For example, *Ecstasy* is the street name for the hallucinogenic amphetamine derivative **MDMA** (3,4-methylenedioxymethamphetamine). In nonhumans, this drug produces persistent effects on serotonin-producing neurons: prolonged reduction in serotonin metabolites and the serotonin transporter. In addition, fine serotonin axons are damaged, but cell bodies in the brainstem are spared. Figure 4.16 shows a marked reduction in serotonin axons in the neocortex and hippocampus of a squirrel monkey treated with MDMA 18 months earlier (C. Fischer et al., 1995). Humans who take MDMA also display reduced serotonin binding in the cortex (Sem-

NEURAL PLASTICITY

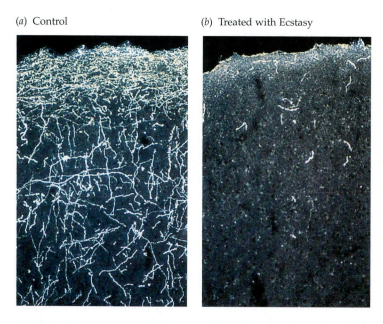

(*a*) Control   (*b*) Treated with Ecstasy

4.16 Long-Term Effects of a Single Dose of Ecstasy on the Monkey Brain
Serotonin axons in the dorsal neocortex of a control squirrel monkey (*a*) and a squirrel monkey treated with a single dose of MDMA (Ecstasy) 18 months earlier (*b*). (Courtesy of George Ricaurte.)

ple et al., 1989). These changes may be related to the persistent psychiatric and cognitive effects, including memory disturbances, seen after MDMA use (Wareing et al., 2000).

Drug Abuse Is Pervasive

Substance abuse and addiction have become a social problem that afflicts roughly 5 million Americans and disrupts the lives of their families, friends, and associates. The whole community is affected because (1) many people who use tobacco, alcohol, and other drugs run up medical expenses and die prematurely; (2) substance abusers commit crimes and cause traffic accidents, fires, and other social disorders; (3) the costs of helping addicts control their dependence and abuse, and of controlling drug trafficking are high; and (4) many babies whose mothers used psychoactive substances (including alcohol and nicotine) during pregnancy are born with brain impairments.

To gain some perspective on the relative importance of dependence on different substances as causes of death, consider these figures: Smoking is estimated to cause about 432,000 deaths annually in the United States—20% of all U.S. deaths—more than 100,000 of which are from lung cancer (Figure 4.17). Further evidence of the toxicity of smoking is that among people 55 years and older, it doubles the risk of dementia, especially of Alzheimer's disease (Ott et al., 1998). About 125,000 deaths annually in the United States are associated with the use of alcohol, many of them resulting from traffic accidents caused by drinking. Illegal drugs are estimated to cause about 20,000 deaths annually in the United States, and about 8000 more are attributed to drug-associated AIDS (Institute for Health Policy, Brandeis University, 1993, pp. 32–37; Mathias, 1994). Even if the number of deaths caused by illegal drugs has been underestimated, it is clear that the legal drugs—nicotine and alcohol—exact a far larger social cost than do illegal drugs.

In the discussion that follows, we will examine the mechanisms of drug abuse, the different approaches to understanding drug abuse, how individuals vary in their vulnerability to drug abuse, and how drug abuse can be prevented and treated.

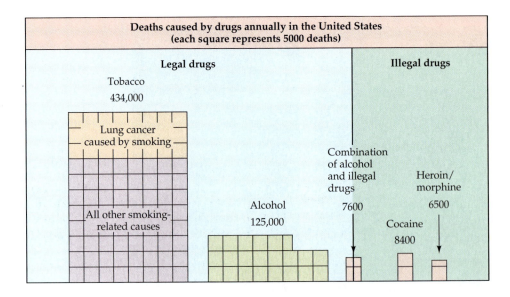

4.17 Deaths Caused by Drugs The number of deaths caused annually in the United States by the legal drugs tobacco and alcohol far exceeds the number caused by illegal drugs. (After Mathias, 1994.) On the other hand, illegal drugs tend to kill people at a younger age. Although more people use alcohol in a given month than smoke cigarettes, exposure to active smoking is a much greater risk factor than is drinking alcohol. (U.S. Department of Health and Human Services, 1991.)

The Mechanisms of Drug Abuse Have Been Studied Extensively

For more than a century, scientists have been investigating substance dependence. Physiological, behavioral, and environmental mechanisms for substance dependence have been proposed and investigated; some investigators put more emphasis on one or another of these types of mechanisms (M. Glantz and Pickens, 1992).

We will consider different kinds of mechanisms, taking examples mainly from dependence and abuse related to cocaine, the opiate drugs (such as morphine and heroin), nicotine, and alcohol, because these substances have been studied the most thoroughly. Scientists and clinicians engaged in this field have developed specific terminology that does not always coincide completely with the way the public uses terms related to substance dependence (addiction) and substance abuse. Box 4.3 clarifies some of this terminology.

Although we are concerned mainly with substance abuse by humans, many cases have been reported in which animals in the wild administer addictive substances to themselves and even become dependent on them (R. K. Siegel, 1989). For example, elephants have been observed becoming repeatedly intoxicated by eating fermented fruits. When confined to game preserves, elephants accept alcohol, and when their space is restricted—causing what is assumed to be a stressful condition for them—they increase their drinking. Baboons consume tobacco in the wild, and intoxicating mushrooms are eaten by cattle, reindeer, and rabbits. These observations suggest that the propensity for drug use, and possibly even addiction, is widespread among animals.

Because addictive substances are no exception to the general rule that drugs produce multiple effects, it is difficult to determine which mechanisms are most important in producing dependence. For example, cocaine has the following major characteristics: (1) It is a local anesthetic; (2) its administration promptly leads to

---

BOX 4.3 *The Terminology of Substance-Related Disorders*

For definitions of mental disorders, psychiatrists, psychologists, and neuroscientists rely on the *Diagnostic and Statistical Manual of Mental Disorders* (fourth edition), often called *DSM-IV* (American Psychiatric Association, 1994; all page numbers cited in this box refer to this manual). What the public usually calls *addiction*, the *DSM-IV* calls **substance-related disorders**. Within this category, **dependence** (commonly called addiction) is a more severe disorder than **abuse**.

The essential feature of dependence on psychoactive substances (e.g., alcohol, tobacco, cocaine, marijuana) is "a cluster of cognitive, behavioral, and physiological symptoms indicating that the individual continues use of the substance despite significant substance-related problems" (p. 176). To be diagnosed as dependent, a person must meet at least three of seven criteria, four of which are the following:

1. The substance is often taken in larger amounts or over a longer period than intended.

2. The persistent desire or efforts to cut down or control substance use are unsuccessful.

3. Much time is devoted to activities necessary to procure the substance (e.g., visiting multiple doctors or driving long distances), to use the substance (e.g., chain-smoking), or to recover from its effects.

4. Important social, occupational, or recreational activities are abandoned or reduced because of substance use.

We list these criteria only to give you an indication of the symptoms of substance-related dependence. Diagnosis should be left to qualified experts.

The severity of dependence varies from mild to moderate to severe, depending on how many of the seven criteria have been met. A person exhibiting mild dependence has few, if any, symptoms beyond the three required to make the diagnosis, and the symptoms result in only mild impairment in work or in usual social activities or relationships with others. Severe dependence is evidenced by many symptoms, which markedly interfere with work or with usual social activities or relationships.

When the criteria for dependence have not been met but there is evidence of maladaptive patterns of substance use that have persisted at least 1 month or have occurred repeatedly, the diagnosis is substance abuse. Some examples of situations in which a diagnosis of abuse is appropriate are as follows (p. 182):

1. A student has substance-related absences, suspensions, or expulsion from school.

2. A person is repeatedly intoxicated with alcohol in situations that are hazardous—for example, when driving a car, operating machinery, or engaging in risky recreations such as swimming or rock climbing.

3. A person has recurrent substance-related legal problems—for example, arrests for disorderly conduct, assault and battery, or driving under the influence.

pleasurable feelings, so it is a rewarding agent; and (3) it is a psychomotor stimulant, enhancing activity at synapses that use catecholamine transmitters, speeding the heart rate, and evoking other circulatory responses, which sometimes prove fatal.

Opiate drugs, such as morphine, also have a variety of effects, including but not limited to the following:

- They lead to predominance of parasympathetic activity and depression of the activity of the heart and respiratory system.
- They quickly have a pleasurable and rewarding effect.
- Their use leads to development of tolerance, so dosages must be increased to maintain effects.
- They lead to development of strong physical dependence; that is, after repeated use, abstinence from the drug causes a severe withdrawal syndrome, as we discuss a bit later.

An understanding of drug abuse must account for why drugs with such different effects can all lead to addiction.

Different Approaches Compete to Help Us Understand Drug Abuse

COMPETING HYPOTHESES

Attempts to explain drug abuse and addiction have changed widely during the last two centuries. The different explanations have different implications for our understanding of behavior and for treatment of addiction, and some explanations are better suited to one or another phase of drug abuse, as we'll see. Each explanation continues to be used by some people.

The moral model.   The earliest approach to explaining drug abuse was to blame the drug user for lack of moral character or lack of self-control. Explanations of this sort often have a religious character and hold that only divine help will free a person from addiction. Applications based on the moral model have been effective. For example, the temperance movement in the United States, beginning around the 1830s, is estimated to have cut per capita consumption of alcohol to about one-third its level in the period from 1800 to 1820 (Rorabaugh, 1976).

The disease model.   The disease model for addiction arose in the latter part of the nineteenth century, partly from concern about the abuse of drugs such as opium and morphine that were prescribed by physicians and included in many popular remedies. In this view, the person who abuses drugs requires medical treatment rather than moral exhortation or punishment. This view also justifies spending money on research on drug abuse in the same way that money is spent on other diseases. It is still not clear, however, what kind of a disease addiction is, or how a disease causes people to take psychoactive drugs.

Usually the term *disease* is reserved for a state in which we can identify an abnormal physical or biochemical condition; examples include the presence of an infectious agent such as the syphilis bacterium, damage to brain tissue such as that found in Parkinson's disease, or under- or overproduction of various hormones (see Chapter 5). Investigators have not been able to find such an abnormal physical or biochemical condition in the case of drug addiction (although mounting evidence suggests that some people are more susceptible to addiction than others, as we'll see later). Nevertheless, this approach continues to appeal to many. In 1995, the director of the U.S. National Institute on Alcohol Abuse and Alcoholism stated that ultimately scientific research will lead to "better treatment, better diagnosis, better prevention, and the putting to rest of the notion that alcoholism isn't a disease" (Azar, 1995).

The physical dependence model.   The physical dependence model is based on the unpleasant **withdrawal symptoms** that occur when a person stops taking a drug that he or she has used frequently. The specific withdrawal symptoms depend on the drug, but they are often the opposite of the effects produced by the drug itself. For example, the withdrawal symptoms of morphine include irritability, tremor, and elevated heart rate and blood pressure. Waves of goosebumps occur, and the skin resembles that of a plucked turkey, which is why abrupt withdrawal without any treatment is called *cold turkey*. Whereas most drugs of abuse produce pleasurable feelings, withdrawal usually induces the opposite: dysphoria.

Some of the user's physiological functions appear to have compensated for the actions of the drug, and withdrawing the drug appears to disturb these aspects of functioning. Withdrawal symptoms can be suppressed quickly (within 15 to 20 minutes in the case of morphine) by administration of the substance to which the person is addicted. This model provides one explanation of why addicts work compulsively to get drugs: to avoid or overcome withdrawal effects.

Withdrawal symptoms are so striking that some investigators have proposed that development of dependence is the basic characteristic of addiction. But it is clear that people can become dependent on drugs, like cocaine, that do not produce any dramatic withdrawal symptoms (R. A. Wise, 1996). Are these people *psychologically* addicted rather than *physically* addicted? So far such a distinction seems irrelevant because either form of addiction can have disastrous, even fatal, consequences. Indeed, the entire theme of this book is that *psychological* processes all have a physical basis in the brain, which is just as real as the muscular contractions that produce shivering or nausea. Clearly a better explanation is needed.

The positive reward model. The positive reward model of addictive behavior arose from animal research that was started in the 1950s (McKim, 1991), and it has been tested in humans. Before the 1950s, researchers believed that animals could not become addicted to drugs. Most of them did not know of observations that wild animals consume psychoactive substances in nature, and they thought (incorrectly) that animals were not capable of learning an association that spanned the 15 to 20 minutes between an injection and relief from withdrawal symptoms. Then a few simple technological and procedural breakthroughs made it possible for laboratory animals to perform tasks that led to self-administration of a drug through a fine flexible tube implanted into a vein (Figure 4.18).

The first investigators to use this technique believed that physical dependence was necessary if animals were to administer drugs to themselves. Therefore, they first made rats or monkeys dependent on morphine by giving them repeated injections over a period of days before giving them the opportunity to press a lever that caused delivery of morphine through the implanted tube. The animals quickly learned to respond, and it appeared that the drug infusion was acting as a typical experimental reward, such as food or water (T. Thompson and Schuster, 1964).

Subsequent experiments by psychopharmacologist Charles R. Schuster demonstrated that animals that had not been made dependent would self-administer doses of morphine so low that no physical dependence ever developed (Schuster, 1970). Animals would also press a lever to self-administer cocaine and other stimulants that do not produce marked withdrawal symptoms (Pickens and Thompson, 1968; Koob, 1995; Tanda et al., 2000).

These and other studies contradict the assumptions of both the disease model and the physical dependence model of drug addiction. Although physical dependence may be an important factor in the consumption of some drugs, it is not necessary for self-administration and cannot serve as the sole explanation for drug addiction. Furthermore, these studies indicate that the acquisition of drug self-administration can be interpreted according to principles that govern behavior controlled by positive rewards (operant conditioning theory; see Box 17.1), thus precluding the need to consider drug self-administration a disease.

A wide variety of addictive drugs cause the release of dopamine in the **nucleus accumbens,** just as do more traditional reinforcers, such as food for a hungry animal (Di Chiara et al., 1999). This dopamine appears to be released from axons that arise in a midbrain region known as the **ventral tegmental area** (Figure 4.19*a*),

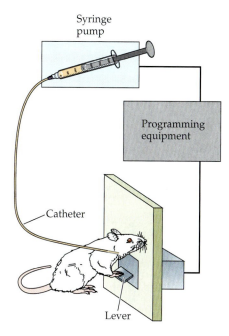

4.18 Experimental Setup for Self-Administration of a Drug by an Animal

Charles R. Schuster

IMPORTANT METHOD

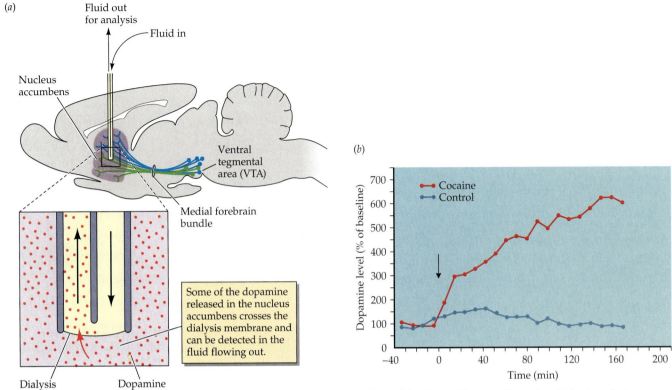

4.19 A Neural Pathway Implicated in Drug Abuse   The microdialysis technique makes use of a small, permanently implanted probe to monitor neurochemical changes in awake, behaving animals. (*a*) A microdialysis probe inserted into the nucleus accumbens can detect changes in dopamine levels in response to drug administration. (*b*) Dopamine levels in the nucleus accumbens rise sharply in rats during self-administration (begins at arrow) of cocaine. (Part *b* after Pettit and Justice, 1991.)

which is part of the ventral mesostriatal dopaminergic pathway seen in Figure 4.3.

Recall from our discussion of cocaine that injection of the peptide CART to the ventral tegmental area is rewarding for rats. If the dopaminergic pathway from the ventral tegmental area to the nucleus accumbens serves as a reward system for a wide variety of experiences, then the addictive power of drugs may come from their artificial stimulation of this pathway. Acting on this assumption, Pilla et al. (1999) found that a weak DA agonist reduced cocaine craving in rats; perhaps the mild DA stimulation produced by the agonist filled in for the DA that would have been released by cocaine.

People Differ in Their Vulnerability to Drug Abuse

The positive reward model of addiction does not try to account for the fact that most people who try addictive drugs do not become addicted. Under some circumstances, even prolonged use is not accompanied by addiction. For example, patients who have been given regular doses of opiates to relieve pain during hospital treatment show very low rates of use or abuse after release: fewer than one out of 2500 (Brownlee and Schrof, 1997). Of Vietnam veterans who had become addicted to heroin overseas, only 12% relapsed to dependence within 3 years after their return. Many investigators have tried to determine which factors in individuals and in their environments may account for vulnerability to the development of drug abuse (M. Glantz and Pickens, 1992).

The subject is complicated because different factors appear to operate for transitions between different conditions—from nonusers to moderate users to abusers to former abusers to relapse. In addition, factors appear to differ among different drugs of abuse. Some of the most revealing investigations of this subject are longitudinal studies, which follow individuals from infancy on, giving psychological tests and interviews at regular intervals. Some of these longitudinal studies have related personality variables and life experiences to drug use and abuse. Factors that have been demonstrated to be significant, at least for some drugs, fall into several categories:

- *Biological factors.* Sex is such a variable; males are more likely to abuse drugs than are females. There is also evidence for genetic predisposition. We mentioned earlier that having an alcoholic biological parent makes drug abuse more likely. This is true even in the case of children adopted away soon after birth (Cadoret et al., 1986).
- *Personal characteristics.* Characteristics related to drug abuse include aggressiveness and the tendency to act out emotional states. Characteristics that appear to discourage drug abuse include good school achievement, high educational goals, and religiousness. Age and maturity are important factors; youthful drug use often terminates in the midtwenties, when individuals assume adult roles of employment and marriage.
- *Family situation.* Factors related to drug abuse include divorce of parents and having an antisocial sibling. Strong ties to parents protect against drug abuse.
- *Social and community factors.* A high prevalence of drug use in the community, especially by the peer group, predisposes an individual toward drug abuse.

The greater the number of risk factors that apply, the more likely an individual will abuse alcohol or marijuana (Brook et al., 1992). Furthermore, these risk factors do not necessarily operate independently; in some cases they interact. For example, individuals who have high childhood ratings of aggression show a fairly strong tendency to move from moderate to heavy use of marijuana; the degree of social deviance of their peers has only a moderate effect, as the upper curve in Figure 4.20 shows. Individuals with low ratings of aggression, however, are much more likely to be influenced in marijuana abuse by the social deviance of their peers, as the lower curve in Figure 4.20 demonstrates. Although in this study only 2% of individuals with low aggression moved to heavy marijuana use if their peers were low in deviancy, those whose peers were high in deviancy had a 25% chance of becoming heavy users (Brook et al., 1992).

Drug Use, Abuse, and Dependence Can Be Prevented or Treated in Multiple Ways

Because drug use, abuse, and dependence cause many personal and social problems, health professionals and investigators have worked to develop a variety of ways to prevent or treat these conditions. Several of these methods are related to the various models used to explain drug use that we described earlier. For example, in keeping with the moral model, which employs exhortations such as "Just Say No," many people do abstain, and many others do not go beyond initial trials of cigarettes, alcohol, or illicit drugs. Even among those who become addicted, many overcome their problems without outside help (Peele and Brodsky, 1991): Investigators report that more than 90% of ex-smokers (S. Cohen et al., 1989) and about half of former problem drinkers (Institute of Medicine, 1990) appear to have quit on their own.

Several categories of medication may aid in the treatment of drug addiction (Nathan and Gorman, 1998), including the following:

- *Drugs for detoxification,* including those that are directed especially toward the control of withdrawal syndromes. Examples include benzodiazepines, methadone, and drugs that suppress central adrenergic activity (e.g., clonidine).

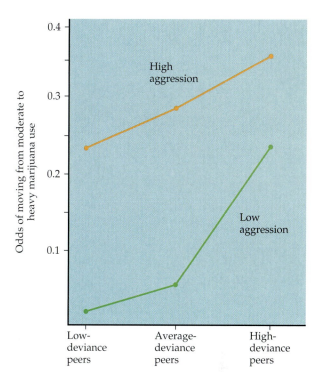

4.20 Social and Personality Factors in Marijuana Use Individuals who rate low in aggression are not likely to use marijuana if they do not associate with socially deviant peers, but they are much more likely to use marijuana if their peers are socially deviant. (After Brook et al., 1992.)

- *Agonists of drugs that produce common addiction states.* The prime example in this category is methadone, which is a μ opiate receptor agonist that constrains the craving for heroin. Unlike heroin, methadone does not affect cognition and alertness, and it may cause fewer withdrawal symptoms than heroin.
- *Antagonists to the addictive drug.* The administration of drugs that are specific antagonists for opiate receptors (e.g., naltrexone) can block the effects of opiate injections. Most addicts apparently prefer methadone to naltrexone because methadone produces a mild opioid effect.
- *Anticraving medications,* including several substances that especially affect the desire for alcohol. Examples include several antidepressants and several substances that are at the animal-testing stage of development.
- *Medication that blocks drug metabolism.* For alcohol abuse, some therapists prescribe the drug disulfiram (trade name Antabuse). This substance produces an accumulation of acetaldehyde, a toxic metabolite of alcohol that can be quite unpleasant. A person who takes this medication suffers unpleasant physiological reactions if he or she drinks alcohol; thus the effects of drinking are negative rather than rewarding.

The positive reward model attributes abuse and dependence to the extremely rewarding properties of drugs that many people experience, so some investigators have attempted either to reduce or abolish the reward provided by a drug or to disconnect the reward from some of the noxious side effects of the drug. Here are a few examples: Smokers who fear the withdrawal symptoms if they quit smoking "cold turkey" can use nicotine chewing gum or nicotine skin patches while they attempt to quit. The nicotine still has harmful effects on the body, but at least the lungs escape the effects of tobacco smoke. Moreover, nicotine delivered through gum or skin patches is less addictive than cigarette smoke is because these methods do not deliver pulses of nicotine as rapidly to the brain as smoking does (Figure 4.21). Antianxiety drugs can also be used to reduce withdrawal symptoms.

Could people be immunized against drug abuse? A monkey trained to self-administer low doses of heroin and cocaine on alternate sessions was then immunized by injection of a heroin-like compound (morphine) bound to a protein (Bonese et al., 1974). In later sessions, the monkey continued to self-administer cocaine, but it soon no longer took heroin. Apparently the antibodies produced in response to morphine immunization bound molecules of heroin, reducing its concentration to

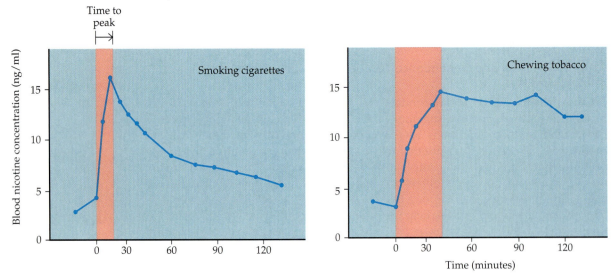

4.21 Variation in the Rise in Nicotine Concentrations with the Method of Use
These curves show concentrations during the first 2 hours after tobacco is ingested in various forms. Note how much more rapidly the concentration rises after a cigarette is smoked than after tobacco is chewed. (After W. Bennett, 1983.)

a level that was no longer addictive. The antibodies may slow drug entry to the brain sufficiently to blunt the pleasurable effects. Another promising prospect is the administration of antibodies to overdose victims to remove circulating drug molecules (Proksh et al., 2000).

Many of these types of treatment help at least some substance abusers, but no single approach appears to be uniformly effective (Institute of Medicine, 1990). Rates of relapse remain high, and a majority of clients in abstinence programs return to using the psychoactive substance within a year after completing a course of treatment. Research breakthroughs are therefore badly needed to overcome the painful and costly problems of drug abuse and dependence.

Summary

Refer to the ***Learning Biological Psychology*** CD for the following study aids for this chapter:

9 Objectives

72 Study Questions

1 Activity

1 Animated Tutorial

1. Because many drugs work by acting on receptor molecules, investigators search for the structure of the receptor molecules and for the endogenous substances that work on the receptors. A given neurotransmitter may normally bind several different receptors.

2. The tuning of receptor molecules is not absolutely specific. A particular drug molecule may act strongly with one kind of receptor molecule and more weakly with others.

3. Repeated use of some drugs produces tolerance, in which an increasingly large dose is needed to achieve a particular effect. Repeated use of other drugs produces sensitization, in which the effects increase wth use of the same dosage.

4. Some stimulants, such as nicotine, imitate an excitatory synaptic transmitter. Others, such as amphetamine, cause the release of excitatory synaptic transmitters and block the reuptake of transmitters. Still others, such as caffeine, block the activity of an inhibitory neuromodulator.

5. Substances that are used to combat anxiety, such as the benzodiazepines, are called anxiolytic drugs. The benzodiazepines synergize the activity of the inhibitory transmitter GABA at some of its receptors.

6. Some drugs are called hallucinogens because they alter sensory perception and produce peculiar experiences. Different hallucinogens act on different kinds of synaptic receptors, and it is not yet clear what causes the hallucinogenic effects.

7. Drug abuse and addiction are being studied intensively, and several models have been proposed: the moral model, the disease model, the physical dependence model, and the positive reward model.

8. People differ in their vulnerability to drug abuse according to several factors: genetic predisposition, personality characteristics, and family and social context.

9. The study of psychopharmacology using animal subjects is useful because many species of animals consume psychoactive substances in nature, and their responses to many substances are similar to those of humans.

Recommended Reading

Bloom, F. E., and Kupfer, D. (Eds.). (1995). *Psychopharmacology: The fourth generation of progress.* New York: Raven.

Cooper, J. R., Bloom, F. E., and Roth, R. H. (1996). *The biochemical basis of neuropharmacology* (7th ed.). New York: Oxford University Press.

Feldman, R. S., Meyer, J. S., and Quenzer, L. F. (1997). *Principles of neuropsychopharmacology.* Sunderland, MA: Sinauer.

Julien, R. J. (2000). *A primer of drug action* (9th ed.). New York: Freeman.

Stahl, S. M., and Munter, N. (2000). *Essential psychopharmacology: Neuroscientific basis and practical applications.* Cambridge, England: Cambridge University Press.

5

Hormones and the Brain

T he cells of the body communicate via chemicals, a major class of which is hormones. Without regular supplies of some hormones, our capacity to behave would be seriously impaired; without others, we would soon die. Deficiency or excess of some hormones can result in striking changes in our cognitive and emotional behavior. Tiny amounts of some hormones can markedly modify our moods and actions, our inclination to eat or drink, our aggressiveness or

Nachume Miller, *Untitled*, 1995, 10'6" × 18'2"

submissiveness, and our reproductive and parental behavior. Furthermore, hormones do more than influence adult behavior: Early in life and during adolescence they help determine the development of body form. Later in life the changing outputs of some endocrine glands and the body's changing sensitivity to some hormones are prominent aspects of aging.

In this chapter we will consider the mechanisms by which hormones accomplish their functions, the main endocrine glands and their hormones, and examples of hormonal influences on physiology and on behavior. After presenting a brief history of discoveries relevant to hormones and their actions, we will compare the ways in which the endocrine and nervous systems communicate and coordinate function. Effects on memory formation will be discussed briefly. Later chapters will include detailed discussion of the behavioral aspects of hormone activities.

Hormones Act in a Great Variety of Ways throughout the Body

Hormones (from the Greek *horman*, "to excite") are chemicals secreted into the bloodstream by one set of cells and carried to other parts of the body, where they act on specific target tissues to produce specific physiological effects. Specialists who study hormones are known as endocrinologists because many hormones are produced by **endocrine glands** (from the Greek *endon*, "within," and *krinein*, "to secrete"), so called because they release their hormones within the body. **Exocrine glands** (the Greek *exo* means "out"), such as the tear glands, the salivary glands, and the sweat glands, secrete their products through ducts to the outside of the body. Sometimes exocrine glands are called duct glands, in contrast to endocrine glands, which are ductless.

Endocrine glands come in a variety of sizes, shapes, and locations in the body (Figure 5.1). Although the endocrine glands and their hormones are important, today's definition of *hormone* is more inclusive, recognizing that other tissues, such as the heart and kidneys, secrete compounds known as hormones. Even plants, which have no endocrine glands, use chemical signals that are considered to be hormones.

In this chapter we introduce the basic mechanisms of action by which hormones affect target cells; then we review some of the many hormones that are known to influence behavior. In later chapters we will discuss specific examples of hormones influencing reproductive behavior (Chapter 12), eating and drinking (Chapter 13), biological rhythms (Chapter 14), and the stress response (Chapter 15).

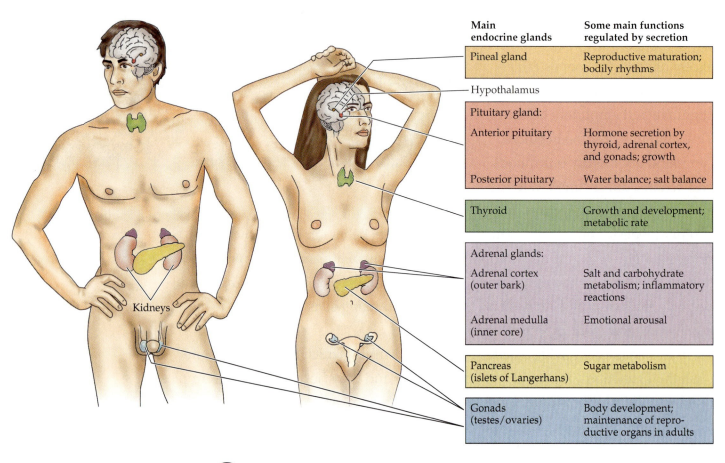

Main endocrine glands	Some main functions regulated by secretion
Pineal gland	Reproductive maturation; bodily rhythms
Hypothalamus	
Pituitary gland:	
Anterior pituitary	Hormone secretion by thyroid, adrenal cortex, and gonads; growth
Posterior pituitary	Water balance; salt balance
Thyroid	Growth and development; metabolic rate
Adrenal glands:	
Adrenal cortex (outer bark)	Salt and carbohydrate metabolism; inflammatory reactions
Adrenal medulla (inner core)	Emotional arousal
Pancreas (islets of Langerhans)	Sugar metabolism
Gonads (testes/ovaries)	Body development; maintenance of reproductive organs in adults

Kidneys

5.1 Major Endocrine Glands and Their Functions   Table 5.2 lists the hormones secreted by the glands shown here and the effects of those hormones in the body.

Our Current Understanding of Hormones Developed in Stages

Communication within the body and the integration of behavior were considered the exclusive province of the nervous system until the beginning of the twentieth century, when investigators became aware that the endocrine system is also important for these functions. However, the role of such body fluids was anticipated in several ancient civilizations in which endocrine glands were eaten to modify health or behavior. Ancient societies also noted some of the behavioral and physiological changes from obvious endocrine pathology, such as the disfiguring enlargement of the thyroid called goiter.

In the fourth century B.C.E., Aristotle accurately described the effects of **castration** (removal of the testes) in birds, and he compared the behavioral and bodily effects with those seen in eunuchs (castrated men). Although he did not know what mechanism was involved, clearly the testes were important for the reproductive capacity and sexual characteristics of the male. This observation was consistent with the ancient Greek emphasis on body humors, or fluids, as an explanation of temperament and emotions. It was believed that these fluids—phlegm, blood, yellow bile (also known as choler), and black bile—all interacted to produce health or disease (Figure 5.2). The notion of body fluids as the basis of human temperament lingered into the twentieth century with the continued use of terms such as *phlegmatic* ("sluggish"), *bilious* ("irritable"), and *choleric* ("hot-tempered") to describe personalities.

The first major endocrine experiment was carried out in 1849 by German physiologist Arnold Adolph Berthold. When Berthold castrated young roosters, they showed declines in both reproductive behavior and secondary sexual characteristics,

5.2 The Four Humors A medieval representation of the ancient view that excess amounts of any one of the four basic body fluids, or humors, resulted in particular temperaments. (*Clockwise from top left*) An excess of black bile was said to cause melancholia; phlegm was said to cause sluggishness; blood, a highly changeable temperament; choler or yellow bile, irascibility and anxiousness.

5.3 The First Experiment in Behavioral Endocrinology

Berthold's nineteenth-century experiment demonstrated the importance of hormones for behavior.

Group 1	Group 2	Group 3
Left undisturbed, young roosters grow up to have large red wattles and combs, to mount and mate with hens readily, and to fight one another and crow loudly.	Animals whose testes were removed during development displayed neither the appearance nor the behavior of normal roosters as adults.	However, if one of the testes was reimplanted into the abdominal cavity immediately after its removal, the rooster developed normal wattles and normal behavior.

	Group 1	Group 2	Group 3
Comb and wattles:	Large	Small	Large
Mount hens?	Yes	No	Yes
Aggressive?	Yes	No	Yes
Crowing?	Normal	Weak	Normal

Conclusion
Because the reimplanted testis in Group 3 was in an abnormal body site, disconnected from normal innervation, and yet still affected development, Berthold reasoned that the testes release a hormonal signal that has widespread effects.

such as the rooster's comb (Figure 5.3). Berthold observed that if he placed one testis into the body cavity of these castrates, sometimes it received a blood supply and restored both the normal behavior of these roosters and their combs. They began crowing and showed usual sexual behaviors. Because the nerve supply to the testis had not been reestablished, Berthold concluded that the testes release a chemical into the blood that affects both male behavior and male body structures. Today we know that the testes make and release the hormone testosterone, which exerts these effects.

The French physiologist Claude Bernard helped set the stage in the nineteenth century for the emergence of endocrinology as a science. Bernard stressed the importance of the internal environment ("internal milieu") in which cells exist and emphasized that this environment must be carefully regulated. He regarded a constant internal body environment as necessary for independent activity in the external environment.

This idea was later embedded in the concept of homeostasis, which was advanced by American physiologist Walter B. Cannon in the 1920s. **Homeostasis** is the maintenance of a relatively constant internal environment by an array of mechanisms in the body. Clinical and experimental observations starting in the late nineteenth century showed the importance of several glands—including the thyroid, the adrenal cortex, and the pituitary—for maintaining this constant environment inside our bodies.

Techniques that were developed in the twentieth century have enabled scientists to identify many different hormones. Several Nobel Prizes have been awarded for the determination of the structure of hormones. For example, Vincent du Vigneaud received the 1955 Nobel Prize in chemistry for synthesizing the hormones oxytocin and vasopressin. The discovery of a sensitive technique (called radioimmunoassay,

Vincent du Vigneaud

or RIA) for measuring small quantities of hormones (Box 5.1) earned Rosalyn Yalow the 1977 Nobel Prize in physiology or medicine. These techniques, together with earlier ones, give us a powerful set of tools to analyze the reciprocal relations between hormones and behavior.

Rosalyn Yalow

Organisms Use Several Types of Chemical Communication

The following are some categories of chemical signals in the body, classified according to the form of their communication or delivery:

- *Synaptic communication.* This form of communication was described in Chapters 3 and 4. In synaptic transmitter function (sometimes called **neurocrine** function), the released chemical signal diffuses across the synaptic cleft and causes a change in polarization of the postsynaptic membrane (Figure 5.4*a*). Typically, synaptic transmitter function is highly localized.
- *Autocrine communication.* In **autocrine** communication a released or secreted hormone acts on the releasing cell itself and thereby affects its own activity (Figure 5.4*b*). An example of autocrine function is seen in nerve cells that have autoreceptors that are affected by the released synaptic transmitter molecules and thus monitor their own activity. In this case, the signal molecule serves both an autocrine and a synaptic transmitter function.
- *Paracrine communication.* In **paracrine** regulation or communication, the released chemical signal diffuses to nearby target cells through the intermediate extracellular space (Figure 5.4*c*). The strongest impact is on the nearest cells.
- *Endocrine communication.* In **endocrine** regulation and communication, the chemical signal is a hormone released into the bloodstream and taken up selectively by target organs, which may be quite far away (Figure 5.4*d*). We will see later that some neurons release hormones into the bloodstream in this manner.
- *Pheromone communication.* Hormones can be used to communicate not only within an individual, but also between individuals. **Pheromones** (from the Greek *pherein*, "to carry") are hormones produced by one individual and then released outside the body to affect other individuals of the same species (Figure 5.4*e*). For example, many species of ants produce a variety of pheromones that are used to communicate the presence of intruders in the nest, or to mark the trail that leads to a rich food source. Dogs and wolves urinate on various landmarks to designate their territory; other members of the species smell the pheromones in the urine and either respect or challenge the ter-

(*a*) Neurocrine function (synaptic transmission)

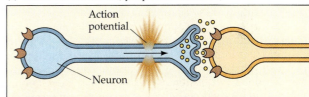

(*b*) Autocrine function

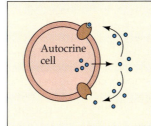

(*c*) Paracrine function

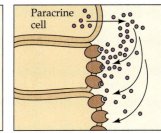

(*d*) Endocrine function

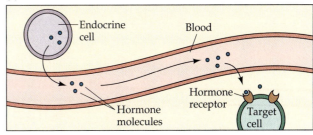

(*e*) Pheromone function

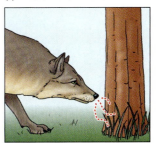

(*f*) Allomone function

5.4 Chemical Communication Systems (*a*) In synaptic transmitter (neurocrine) communication, a chemical signal is released from the presynaptic terminal of the neuron and binds to receptor molecules on a postsynaptic target cell. (*b*) Autocrine mechanisms are the feedback effects of a chemical signal on the very cell from which it was released. Some synaptic transmitters are also autocrine signals in that they affect receptors on the presynaptic terminal (autoreceptors). (*c*) In paracrine communication, chemical signals diffuse through extracellular space to nearby target cells. The strongest effects are produced in the nearest cells. (*d*) Endocrine glands produce chemical signals and release them into the bloodstream. Effects are produced in the body wherever receptors for the hormone are found. (*e*) Pheromones carry a message from one individual of the species to other individuals. Often pheromones indicate whether the individual emitting them is ready to mate. (*f*) Allomones are produced by individuals of one species to communicate with (and affect the behavior of) individuals of other species. Some plants even communicate with animals via allomones.

BOX 5.1 *Techniques of Modern Behavioral Endocrinology*

To establish that a particular hormone affects behavior, investigators usually begin with the type of experiment that Berthold performed in the nineteenth century: observing the behavior of the intact animal, then removing the endocrine gland and looking for a change in behavior (see Figure 5.3). Berthold was limited to this type of experiment, but modern scientists have many additional options available. Let's imagine we are investigating a particular effect of hormones on behavior to see how we might proceed.

Which Hormones Affect Which Behaviors?

First the investigator must carefully observe the behavior of several individuals, seeking ways to classify and quantify the different types of behavior and to place them in the context of the behavior of other individuals. For example, most adult male rats will try to mount and copulate with a female placed in their cage. Sometimes (about every fourth day) the female will respond to the male's advances by lifting her rump and pushing her tail to one side, allowing the male to mate with her. At such times the female is said to be receptive to the male.

If the testes are removed from the male rat, he will eventually stop copulating with females, even if they are receptive. We know that one of the hormones produced by the testes is testosterone. Is it the loss of testosterone that causes the loss of male copulatory be-

havior? To explore this question, we purchase some synthetic testosterone, inject it into castrated males, and observe whether the copulatory behavior returns. (It does.)

Next we might examine individual male rats and ask whether the ones that copulate a lot have more testosterone circulating in their blood than those who copulate only a little. To investigate this question we measure individual differences in the amount of copulatory behavior, take a sample of blood from each individual, and measure levels of testosterone. To take this measure we use **radioimmunoassay** (**RIA**), a technique that uses an antibody that binds to a particular hormone. By adding many such antibodies to each blood sample and measuring how many of the antibodies find a hormone molecule to bind, we can estimate the total number of molecules of the hormone per unit volume of blood. (We won't go into detail here about how we determine the number of antibodies that bind to hormone.)

It turns out that individual differences in the sexual behavior of normal male rats (and normal male humans) do *not* correlate with differences in testosterone levels in the blood. In both rats and humans, a drastic loss of testosterone, as after castration, results in a gradual decline in sexual behavior. All normal males, however, appear to make more than enough testosterone to maintain sexual behavior, so something else must modulate this behavior. In

other words, the hormone acts in a permissive manner: It permits the display of the behavior, but something else determines how much of the behavior each individual exhibits.

Where Are the Target Cells?

What does testosterone do to permit this behavior? One step toward answering this question is to ask another question: Which parts of the brain are normally affected by this hormone? We have two methods at our disposal for seeking the answer to this question.

First, we might inject a castrated animal with testosterone that has been radioactively labeled (one or more of the atoms in the molecule has been replaced with a radioactive atom). After waiting about an hour for the testosterone to accumulate in the brain regions that have receptors for the hormone, we would sacrifice the animal, remove the brain, freeze it, cut thin sections from it, and place the thin sections on photographic film. If the tissue were left in place for a few months, enough radioactive particles from the testosterone would hit the film to expose it. We would then develop the film to learn which brain regions had accumulated testosterone. This method is known as **autoradiography** because the tissue "takes its own picture" with radioactivity (see Box 2.1).

When the labeled hormone is a steroid like testosterone, the radioactivity accumulates in the nuclei of neurons and leaves small black specks on

ritory. In Chapter 12 we'll discuss evidence of pheromones that may synchronize menstrual cycles in women.

- *Allomone communication.* Some chemical signals are released by members of one species and affect the behavior of individuals of another species (W. L. Brown, 1968). These hormones are called **allomones** (from the Greek *allos,* "other"). Allomones can carry messages between animal species or from plants to animals (Figure 5.4*f*). Flowers exude scents to attract insects and birds in order to distribute pollen. Other plant agents inhibit insect growth hormones, thus interfering with the life cycle of potential predators. Skunks produce what may be the best-known allomone of all.

Hormone Actions Can Be Organized according to Ten General Principles

Although there are some exceptions, the following rules are general principles of hormone action:

1. Hormones frequently act in a gradual fashion, activating behavioral and physiological responses after weeks of treatment. Those responses may persist for several days after hormone treatment is stopped.

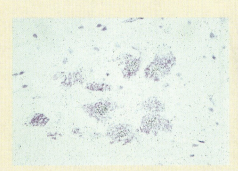

(A) An autoradiogram showing that spinal motoneurons accumulate testosterone

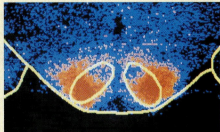

(B) An oxytocin autoradiogram showing the concentration of oxytocin receptors in the ventromedial hypothalamus (oval outlines)

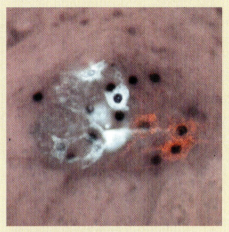

(C) Immunocytochemistry revealing testosterone receptors (dark circles over cell nuclei) in neurons labeled with fluorogold (white-filled somata) or fluororuby (red cells)

the film (Figure A). When the radiolabeled hormone is a protein hormone, the radioactivity accumulates in the membranes of cells and appears in particular layers of the brain. Computers can generate color maps that highlight regions with high densities of receptors (Figure B).

The second method for detecting hormone receptors is **immunocytochemistry.** In this method (which is described in more detail in Box 2.1) we use antibodies that recognize either the hormone or the hormone receptor (Figure C). This method allows us to map the distribution of hormone receptors in the brain. We put the antibodies on slices of brain tissue, wait for them to bind to the receptors, wash off the unbound antibodies, and use chemical methods to visualize the antibodies by creating a tiny dark spot at each one. When the antibodies recognize a steroid receptor, chemical reactions cause a dark coloration in the nuclei of target brain cells.

What Happens at the Target Cells?

Once we have used either autoradiography or immunocytochemistry (or, better yet, both) to identify brain regions that have receptors for the hormone, those regions become candidates for the places at which the hormone works to change behavior. Now we can take castrated males and implant tiny pellets of testosterone into one of those brain regions. We use RIA to ensure that the pellets are small enough that they have no effect on hormone levels in the blood. Then we ask whether the small implant in that brain region restores the behavior. If not, then in other animals we can implant pellets in a different region or try placing implants in a combination of brain sites.

It turns out that such implants can restore male sexual behavior in rats only if they are placed in the medial preoptic area (mPOA) of the hypothalamus. Thus we have found so far that testosterone does something to the mPOA to permit individual males to display sexual behavior. Now we can examine the mPOA in detail to learn what changes in the anatomy, physiology, or protein production of this region are caused by testosterone. We have more or less caught up to modern-day scientists who work on this very question. Some of the preliminary answers suggested by their research will be discussed in Chapter 12. (Figure B courtesy of Bruce McEwen; Figure C courtesy of Cynthia Jordan.)

2. When hormones alter behavior, they tend to act by changing the intensity or probability of evoked behaviors, rather than acting as a switch to turn behaviors on or off regardless of context (see Box 5.1).

3. Both the quantities and types of hormones released are influenced by environmental as well as endogenous factors. *The relationship between behavior and hormones is clearly reciprocal;* that is, hormones change behaviors and behaviors change hormone levels or responses. For example, high levels of testosterone are related to aggression, and in some species males who lose in aggressive encounters show a reduction in testosterone levels, while the winners in these bouts show little change in testosterone levels. This example shows the reciprocal relation between somatic and behavioral events that we discussed in Chapter 1 (see Figure 1.3).

4. Each hormone has multiple effects on different tissues, organs, and behaviors; conversely, a single type of behavior or physiological change can be affected by many different hormones (Figure 5.5).

5. Hormones are produced in small amounts and often are secreted in bursts. This *pulsatile* secretion pattern is sometimes crucial for the small amount of hormone to be effective.

5.5 The Multiplicity of Hormone Action A single hormone often has multiple effects (e.g., hormones A and C in this illustration) on several different groups of target cells. Similarly, a single process or body organ (yellow box) may be affected by several hormones.

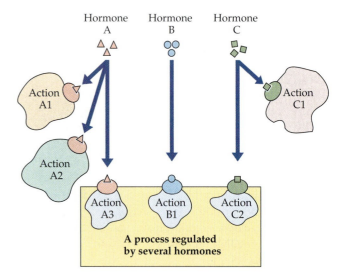

6. The levels of many hormones vary rhythmically throughout the day, and many hormonal systems are controlled by circadian "clocks" in the brain, as we'll see in Chapter 14.

7. Hormones affect metabolic processes in most cells, including the buildup and breakdown of carbohydrates, lipids, and proteins. In this sense, hormones induce long-term metabolic change.

8. Hormones interact; the effects of one hormone can be markedly changed by the actions of another hormone.

9. The chemical structure of a given hormone is similar in all vertebrates, but the functions served by that hormone can vary across species.

10. Hormones can affect only cells that possess a receptor protein that recognizes the hormone and alters cell function. Among different vertebrates, the same brain regions often possess the same hormone receptors.

Neural versus hormonal communication. There are four main differences between neural and hormonal communication:

1. *Neural communication* works somewhat like a telephone system: Messages travel over fixed channels to precise destinations. The anatomical connections between neurons determine the transmission of information from one cell to another. In contrast, *hormonal communication* works more like a TV broadcasting system: Many different endocrine messages spread throughout the body and can then be picked up by scattered cells that have receptors for them. Some hormones broadcast rather locally; for instance, the hypothalamus sends hormones only a few millimeters through the blood vessels to the anterior pituitary gland. Other hormones broadcast throughout the body, but because cells in only a particular organ have the proper receptors, these hormones influence only that organ.

2. Whereas neural messages are rapid and are measured in milliseconds, hormonal messages are slower and are measured in seconds and minutes.

3. Most neural messages are *digitized* (all-or-none) impulses. Hormonal messages are *analog*—that is, graded in strength.

4. Neural and hormonal communication also differ in terms of voluntary control. You cannot, at a command, increase or decrease the output of a hormone or a response mediated by the endocrine system, but you can voluntarily lift your arm, blink your eyelids, or perform many other acts under neuromuscular control. This distinction between neural and hormonal systems, however, is not absolute. Many muscular responses cannot be performed or changed at will, even though they are under neural control. An example is heart rate, which is regulated by the vagus nerve and can meet changing demands during exercise or stress, but which only very few people can alter promptly and directly on command. Later in this chapter we will note examples of conditioned responses that are controlled by hormones: the milk let-

down reflex mediated by oxytocin during breast-feeding, and the early release of insulin during eating.

Similarities in neural and hormonal communication.

In spite of the differences outlined in the previous section, the neural and hormonal systems show important similarities. The nervous system uses specialized biochemical substances (neurotransmitters) to communicate across synaptic junctions in much the same way that the endocrine system uses hormones (Figure 5.6). Of course, the distance traveled by the chemical messengers differs enormously in the two cases: The synaptic cleft is only about 30 nm (30×10^{-9} m) wide, but hormones may travel a meter or so from the site of secretion to the target organ. Nevertheless, the analogy between chemical transmission at synapses and hormonal communication holds up in several specific respects:

- The neuron produces particular transmitter chemicals and stores them for later release, just as an endocrine gland stores its hormones for secretion.
- Neurons are stimulated, usually by other neurons, to produce an action potential that causes the presynaptic terminal to release transmitter into the synaptic cleft. Similarly, endocrine glands are stimulated to secrete hormones into the bloodstream, some glands responding to neural messages and others to chemical messages.
- There are many different synaptic transmitter chemicals, and there are many different hormones. In fact, more and more chemicals are being found to serve as both. Norepinephrine and epinephrine, which act as transmitters at many brain synapses, are also secreted as hormones by the adrenal gland.
- The synaptic transmitter reacts with specific receptor molecules at the surface of the postsynaptic membrane. Similarly, hormones react with specific receptor molecules, either on the surface or in the interior of their target cells; most organs do not have receptors for a given hormone and therefore do not respond to it.
- Often when hormones act on receptor molecules on the cell surface, a second messenger is released within the target cells to bring about changes within the cell. This process has been studied extensively in the endocrine system. Some neural effects also involve the release of second messengers in the postsynaptic neuron. Moreover, the same chemicals act as second messengers in both the nervous and the endocrine systems.

A look at the neurons in the hypothalamus that synthesize hormones and release them into the bloodstream will highlight the similarities between neuronal and hormonal communication. These so-called **neurosecretory** (or **neuroendocrine**) **cells** make it hard to draw a firm line between neurons and endocrine cells (see Figure 5.6c). In fact, some investigators believe that the endocrine glands may have evolved from neurosecretory cells (Norman and Litwack, 1987).

Findings that certain chemicals in vertebrates—either hormonal peptides or **neuropeptides** (peptides used by neurons)—are also found in single-celled organisms suggest that both the nervous system and the endocrine system are derived from chemical communication systems in our remote single-celled ancestors (LeRoith et al., 1992). Much current research is devoted to determining the functions of peptide compounds in the brain (Björklund et al., 1992; Koob et al., 1990). Some peptides are used as neurotransmitters. On the other hand, because peptides typically have a slower onset of effect and a longer duration of action than do other

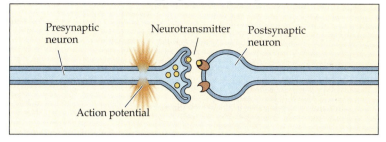

(*a*) Neurocrine communication (synaptic transmission)

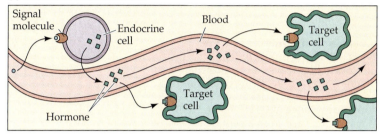

(*b*) Endocrine communication

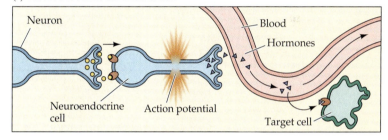

(*c*) Neuroendocrine communication

5.6 Neuroendocrine Cells Blend Neuronal and Endocrine Mechanisms

(*a*) Neurons communicate with other neurons or muscle cells or glands, and signal transmission is determined by the pattern of anatomical connections. (*b*) Endocrine signals are transmitted through the bloodstream and are recognized by appropriate receptors in specific locations in the body. (*c*) Neuroendocrine (neurosecretory) cells are the interface between neurons and endocrine glands. They receive neural signals from other neurons and secrete a hormone into the bloodstream. In this way electrical signals are converted into hormonal signals.

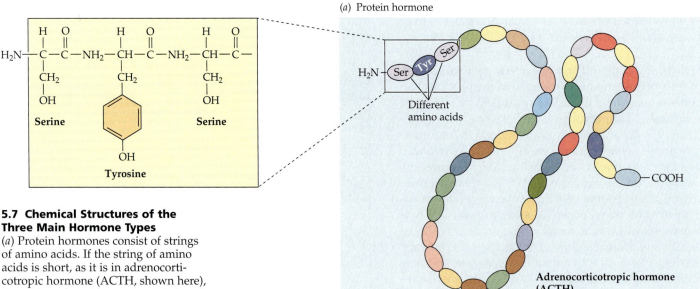

5.7 Chemical Structures of the Three Main Hormone Types
(*a*) Protein hormones consist of strings of amino acids. If the string of amino acids is short, as it is in adrenocorticotropic hormone (ACTH, shown here), it may be referred to as a peptide hormone. (*b*) Amine hormones, such as thyroxine (shown here), are modified single amino acids. (*c*) Steroid hormones, such as estradiol (shown here), are derived from cholesterol and consist of four interconnected rings of carbon atoms, to which are attached different numbers and types of atoms.

transmitters, it has been suggested that they often act as **neuromodulators** (see Chapter 4), substances that alter the reactivity of cells to specific transmitters.

Hormones Can Be Classified by Chemical Structure

Most hormones fall into one of three categories: protein hormones, amine hormones, or steroid hormones. Like all other proteins, **protein hormones** are composed of strings of amino acids (Figure 5.7*a*). (Recall that a peptide is simply a small protein—i.e., a short string of amino acids. In this chapter we will refer to both protein and peptide hormones as protein hormones.) Different protein hormones consist of different combinations of amino acids. **Amine hormones** have a simpler structure, each one consisting of a single amino acid (hence their alias, *monoamine* hormones) that has been modified into a related molecule (Figure 5.7*b*). **Steroid hormones** are composed not of amino acids, but of four interconnected rings of carbon atoms (Figure 5.7*c*). Different steroid hormones vary in the number and kinds of atoms attached to the rings. This structure allows steroids to dissolve readily in lipids, so they can cross cell membranes easily.

The distinction between protein or amine hormones and steroid hormones is important because these two hormone classes interact with different types of receptors and by different mechanisms. Table 5.1 gives examples of each class of hormones.

Hormones Act on a Wide Variety of Cellular Mechanisms

Later in the chapter we will be considering the effects of specific hormones on behavior. In preparation for that discussion, let's look briefly at three aspects of hormonal activity: the effects of hormones on cells, the mechanisms by which hormones exercise these effects, and the regulation of hormone secretion.

Hormones Affect Cells by Influencing Their Growth and Activity

By influencing cells in various tissues and organs, hormones affect many everyday behaviors in humans and other animals. Hormones exert these far-reaching effects by (1) promoting the proliferation, growth, and differentiation of cells, and (2) modulating cell activity. Early developmental processes are promoted by various hormones—for example, the thyroid hormones. Without these hormones, fewer cells are produced in the brain, and mental development is stunted. Although cells proliferate and differentiate mainly during early development in the brain, hormones cause cells in some organs to divide and grow at later stages of life, too. For example, male and female hormones cause secondary sex characteristics to appear during adolescence: breasts and broadening of the hips in women, and facial hair and enlargement of the Adam's apple in men.

In cells that are already differentiated, hormones can modulate the rate of function. For example, thyroid hormones and insulin promote the metabolic activity of most of the cells in the human body. Other hormones modulate activity in certain types of cells. For example, luteinizing hormone (a hormone from the anterior pituitary gland) promotes the secretion of sex hormones by the testes and ovaries.

Hormones Initiate Actions by Binding to Receptor Molecules

The three classes of hormones exert their influences on target organs in two different ways:

1. Protein hormones bind to specific receptors (proteins that recognize only one hormone or class of hormones). Such receptors are usually found *on the surface* of target cell membranes and, when stimulated by the appropriate hormone, cause the release of a second messenger in the cell. (As we saw in Chapter 3, the release of a second messenger can also be caused by some synaptic transmitters.) Protein hormones exert their effects by using this mechanism to alter proteins that already exist within the cell. Most amine hormones also act via surface receptors and second messengers, but as we'll see, the thyroid hormones are an exception.

2. Steroid hormones pass through the membrane and bind to specific receptor proteins *inside* the cell. The steroid–receptor complex then binds to DNA in the nucleus of the cell. This binding affects the transcription of specific genes, increasing the production of some proteins and decreasing the production of others. Hence these hormones act by affecting gene expression and thereby altering the production of proteins (see the Appendix).

Let's look at these two main modes of action in a little more detail and examine the ways in which hormones affect cellular function.

Protein and amine hormones act rapidly. What characteristic of a cell determines whether it responds to a particular protein hormone? Some proteins manufactured by a cell, such as the neurotransmitter receptors discussed in Chapters 3 and 4, become integrated into the membrane. Part of the receptor protein faces the outside of the cell to interact with extracellular chemical signals, while other parts of the protein remain inside the cell. Some of these proteins serve as receptors for protein hormones rather than for neurotransmitters. Thus only cells that produce the appropriate receptor proteins and insert them into the membrane respond to a specific hormone.

TABLE 5.1 *Major Classes of Hormones*	
Class	**Hormone**
PROTEIN HORMONES	Adrenocorticotropic hormone (ACTH)
	Follicle-stimulating hormone (FSH)
	Luteinizing hormone (LH)
	Thyroid-stimulating hormone (TSH)
	Growth hormone (GH)
	Prolactin
	Insulin
	Glucagon
	Oxytocin
	Vasopressin (arginine vasopressin, AVP; antidiuretic hormone, ADH)
	Releasing hormones, such as: Corticotropin-releasing hormone (CRH) Gonadotropin-releasing hormone (GnRH)
AMINE HORMONES	Epinephrine (adrenaline)
	Norepinephrine (NE)
	Thyroid hormones
	Melatonin
STEROID HORMONES	
Gonadal	Estrogens (e.g., estradiol)
	Progestins (e.g., progesterone)
	Androgens (e.g., testosterone, dihydrotestosterone)
Adrenal	Glucocorticoids (e.g., cortisol)
	Mineralocorticoids (e.g., aldosterone)

5.8 Two Main Mechanisms of Hormone Action   (*a*) Protein hormone receptors are found in the cell membrane. When the hormone binds to the receptor, a second-messenger system is activated, which affects different cellular processes. (*b*) Steroid hormones diffuse passively into cells. Inside the target cells are large receptor molecules that bind to the steroid hormone. The steroid–receptor complex then binds to DNA, causing an increase in the production of some gene products and a decrease in the production of others.

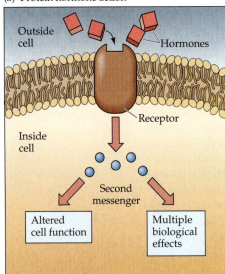

(*a*) Protein hormone action

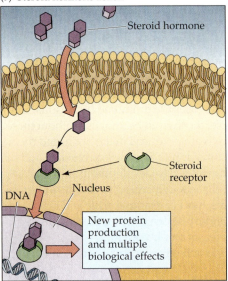

(*b*) Steroid hormone action

Hormone receptors can increase or decrease in number, and these changes are sometimes referred to as up-regulation and down-regulation, respectively. Sometimes continuous exposure to a specific hormone results in fewer receptors to bind the hormone to a cell; in other cases the reverse happens.

When a hormone binds to the extracellular portion of the receptor, the receptor molecule changes its overall shape. The alteration in the intracellular portion of the receptor then changes the internal chemistry of the cell, often by activating a second messenger (Figure 5.8*a*).

One second-messenger compound—cyclic adenosine monophosphate, commonly referred to as **cyclic AMP** or **cAMP**—transmits the messages of many of the peptide and amine hormones. It may seem surprising that the same second messenger can mediate the effects of many different hormones, but recall from Chapter 3 that the same kind of neural impulses can convey all sorts of neural messages. This situation is similar: A change in cAMP levels can cause very different outcomes, depending on which cells are affected, on which part of a cell is affected, and on the prior biochemical activity inside the cell. Other widespread second-messenger compounds include **cyclic guanosine monophosphate** (**cGMP**) and **phosphoinositides.**

The specificity of hormonal effects is determined in part by the selectivity of receptors; only a few cells produce the receptor that recognizes and reacts to the hormone, and only those cells respond. For example, adrenocorticotropic hormone (ACTH) interacts with receptors on the membranes of cells in the adrenal cortex, and in these cells an increase in cAMP leads to the synthesis and release of other hormones.

Protein hormones usually act relatively rapidly, within seconds to minutes. (Although rapid for a hormone, this action is much slower than neural activity.) There can also be prolonged effects. For example, ACTH promotes the proliferation and growth of adrenal cortical cells, thereby increasing the long-term capacity to sustain production of their hormones.

Steroid hormones act slowly.   Steroid hormones typically act more slowly than protein or amine hormones, requiring hours to take effect. The specificity of action of steroid hormones is determined by the receptors that reside inside target cells. A large "superfamily" of steroid receptor genes has been discovered (Ribeiro et al., 1995). Some of these receptors are orphans; that is, we don't yet know which steroid hormone binds them.

Steroid hormones pass in and out of many cells in which they have no effect. If there are appropriate receptor proteins inside, however, these receptors bind to the

(a) Autocrine feedback

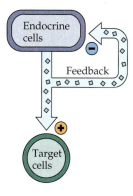

(b) Target cell feedback

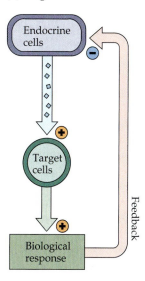

(c) Brain regulation

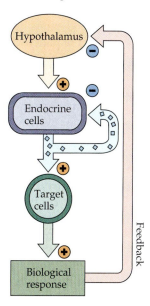

(d) Brain and pituitary regulation

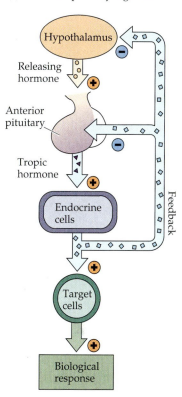

hormone, and the receptor–steroid complex then binds to DNA, so they become concentrated in the nuclei of target cells (Figure 5.8*b*). Thus, as Box 5.1 describes, one can study where a steroid hormone is active by observing where radioactively tagged molecules of the steroid are concentrated. For example, when tagged estradiol is administered into the circulatory system, it accumulates not only in the reproductive tract (as you might expect), but also in the nuclei of some neurons throughout the hypothalamus. By altering protein production, steroids have a slow but often long-lasting effect on the development or adult function of cells. We will discuss such effects of steroids further in Chapter 12.

When a cell possesses a steroid receptor, it *may* respond to the steroid hormone, but just having the steroid receptor is not enough to guarantee a response. Recently discovered **steroid receptor cofactors** are a variety of proteins that a cell may also make. Some cofactors appear to be needed, in addition to the steroid receptor, for a cell to respond. Two different cells, containing the same steroid receptors, may respond quite differently to the steroid hormone if they are producing different steroid receptor cofactors (Tetel, 2000). These cofactors seem to determine which genes will be regulated when the steroid hormone and its receptor reach the nucleus.

Steroids may be able to affect cells in other ways. For example, estradiol, in addition to its slow, long-lasting action on gene expression, can have a rapid, brief effect on some neurons. This nongenomic, rapid effect may involve a separate class of steroid receptors in the neuronal *membrane* (Wehling, 1997), modulating neural excitability. In Chapter 4 we discussed a related example in which the steroid allopregnanolone modulates activity of the GABA receptor.

Feedback Control Mechanisms Regulate the Secretion of Hormones

One of the major features of almost all hormonal systems is that they don't just manufacture a hormone; they also detect and evaluate the effects of the hormone. Thus secretion is usually monitored and regulated so that the rate is appropriate to ongoing activities and needs of the body. The basic control used is a negative feedback system: Output of the hormone *feeds back* to inhibit the drive for more hormone.

Figure 5.9*a* diagrams the simplest kind of system that regulates hormones: An endocrine cell releases a hormone that acts on target cells, but the same hormone also feeds back to inhibit the gland that released it. This is an autocrine response.

In other cases, the endocrine cell reacts not to its own hormone, but to the biological response the hormone elicits from the target cells (Figure 5.9*b*). This response is monitored by some cells in the circuit. If the initial effects are too small, addition-

5.9 Endocrine Feedback Loops
(*a*) In the simplest type of negative feedback control, an endocrine gland releases a hormone that not only acts on a target, but also feeds back in an autocrine fashion to inhibit further hormone secretion. (*b*) The hormone from the endocrine gland acts on target cells to produce a specific set of biological effects. The consequences of these effects may be detected by the endocrine gland, inhibiting further hormone release. (*c*) In many feedback systems the brain becomes involved. The hypothalamic region drives the endocrine gland via either neural or hormonal signals. The target organ signals the brain to inhibit this drive. (*d*) Highly complex feedback mechanisms involve the hypothalamus and the anterior pituitary, as well as the endocrine gland. Feedback regulation may involve a variety of routes and hormones.

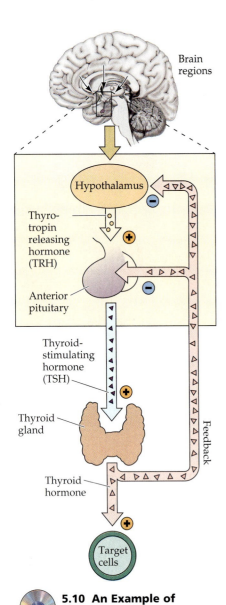

5.10 An Example of Complex Endocrine Regulation The brain funnels information to the hypothalamus, which then controls the anterior pituitary, which in turn stimulates the thyroid gland. Note that three hormones and at least four cell groups are interacting in this instance.

al hormone is released. For example, the hormone insulin helps control the level of glucose circulating in the blood in the following way: After a meal, glucose from the food enters the bloodstream and extracellular fluid, causing insulin to be released from the pancreas. The insulin causes extracellular glucose to enter muscle and fat cells and stimulates them to use the glucose. As the level of glucose in the blood falls, the pancreas secretes less insulin, so a balance tends to be maintained. Thus insulin is normally self-limiting: The more that is secreted, the more glucose is pulled out of circulation and the lower the call for insulin. This negative feedback action of a hormone system is like that of a thermostat, and just as the thermostat can be set to different temperatures at different times, the set points of a person's endocrine feedback systems can be changed to meet varying circumstances. We'll encounter negative feedback effects again in Chapter 13.

A more complex endocrine system includes the hypothalamus as part of the circuit that controls an endocrine gland (Figure 5.9c). This control may be exerted through a neural link, as in control of the adrenal medulla. The secretion of epinephrine by the adrenal medulla affects target cells, and the negative feedback goes directly to the hypothalamus, bypassing the endocrine gland (adrenal medulla) and reducing the demand for further hormone output.

An even greater degree of complexity is encountered when the anterior pituitary becomes involved (Figure 5.9d). As we'll see, several anterior pituitary hormones affect the secretion of other endocrine glands; all of these pituitary hormones are called **tropic hormones.** (*Tropic*, pronounced with a long *o* as in *toe*, means "directed toward.") The hypothalamus uses another set of hormones, called **releasing hormones,** to control the pituitary release of tropic hormones. Thus the brain's releasing hormones affect the pituitary's tropic hormones, which affect the release of hormone from another endocrine gland. Feedback in this case goes from the hormone of the endocrine gland to both the hypothalamus and the anterior pituitary (Figure 5.10).

Each Endocrine Gland Secretes Specific Hormones

We will restrict our account in this chapter to some of the main endocrine glands because a thorough treatment would fill an entire book (e.g., Hadley, 2000). Table 5.2 gives a fuller but far from complete listing of hormones and their functions. Keep in mind that most hormones have more functions than are mentioned here and that several hormones may act together to produce effects in the same target cells.

The Pituitary Gland Releases Many Important Hormones

Resting in a depression in the base of the skull is the **pituitary gland** (see Figure 5.1), about 1 cm³ in volume and weighing about 1 g. The hypothalamus sits just above it. The term *pituitary* comes from the Latin *pituita*, "mucus," reflecting the outmoded belief that waste products dripped down from the brain into the pituitary, which secreted them out through the nose. (The ancients may have thought you could literally sneeze your brains out.) The pituitary used to be referred to as the *master gland*, a reference to its regulatory role in regard to several other endocrine glands. But this gland is itself enslaved by the hypothalamus above it, as we'll see.

The pituitary gland consists of two main parts: the **anterior pituitary,** or adenohypophysis, and the **posterior pituitary,** or neurohypophysis. The term *hypophysis* comes from the Greek *hypophyein*, "to grow beneath," referring to the fact that the pituitary is situated under the brain. The adenohypophysis originates from glandular tissue (the Greek *aden* means "gland"). The neurohypophysis derives from neural tissue. The anterior and posterior pituitary are completely separate in function.

The pituitary is connected to the hypothalamus by a thin piece of tissue called the pituitary stalk (see Figure 5.11). The stalk contains many axons and is richly supplied with blood vessels. The axons extend only to the posterior pituitary, which we will consider next. The blood vessels, as we will see later, transmit information exclusively to the anterior pituitary.

TABLE 5.2   *Main Endocrine Glands, Their Hormone Products, and Principal Effects of Their Hormones*

Gland	Hormones	Principal effects
Posterior pituitary (storage organ for certain hormones produced by hypothalamus)	Oxytocin	Stimulates contraction of uterine muscles; stimulates release of milk by mammary glands
	Vasopressin (AVP; antidiuretic hormone, ADH)	Stimulates increased water reabsorption by kidneys; stimulates constriction of blood vessels
Anterior pituitary	Growth hormone (GH)	Stimulates growth
	Thyroid-stimulating hormone (TSH)	Stimulates the thyroid
	Adrenocorticotropic hormone (ACTH)	Stimulates the adrenal cortex
	Follicle-stimulating hormone (FSH)	Stimulates growth of ovarian follicles and of seminiferous tubules of the testes
	Luteinizing hormone (LH)	Stimulates conversion of follicles into corpora lutea; stimulates secretion of sex hormones by gonads
	Prolactin	Stimulates milk secretion by mammary glands
Hypothalamus	Releasing hormones	Regulate hormone secretion by anterior pituitary
	Oxytocin; vasopressin	*See under* Posterior pituitary
Pineal	Melatonin	Regulates seasonal changes; regulates puberty
Adrenal cortex	Glucocorticoids (corticosterone, cortisol, hydrocortisone, etc.)	Inhibit incorporation of amino acids into protein in muscle; stimulate formation and storage of glycogen; help maintain normal blood sugar level
	Mineralocorticoids (aldosterone, deoxycorticosterone, etc.)	Regulate metabolism of sodium and potassium
	Sex hormones (especially androstenedione)	Regulate facial and body hair
Gonads		
Testes	Androgens (testosterone, dihydrotestosterone, etc.)	Stimulate development and maintenance of male primary and secondary sexual characteristics and behavior
Ovaries	Estrogens (estradiol, estrone, etc.)	Stimulate development and maintenance of female secondary sexual characteristics and behavior
	Progestins (progesterone)	Stimulate female secondary sexual characteristics and behavior; maintain pregnancy
Thyroid	Thyroxine, triiodothyronine	Stimulate oxidative metabolism
	Calcitonin	Prevents excessive rise in blood calcium
Pancreas	Insulin	Stimulates glycogen formation and storage
	Glucagon	Stimulates conversion of glycogen into glucose
Stomach	Secretin	Stimulates secretion of pancreatic juice
	Cholecystokinin (CCK)	Stimulates release of bile by gallbladder
	Enterogastrone	Inhibits secretion of gastric juice
	Gastrin	Stimulates secretion of gastric juice
	Ghrelin	Stimulates the anterior pituitary to release growth hormone
Heart	Atrial natriuretic peptide	Promotes salt loss in urine

The posterior pituitary.   The posterior pituitary gland contains two principal hormones: **oxytocin** and **arginine vasopressin** (**AVP,** often called just **vasopressin**). Neurons in various hypothalamic nuclei, especially the supraoptic nucleus and the paraventricular nucleus, synthesize these two hormones and transport them along their axons to the axon terminals (Figure 5.11). Nerve impulses in these hypothalamic neurosecretory cells travel down the axons in the pituitary stalk and reach the axon terminals in the posterior pituitary, causing release of the hormone from the

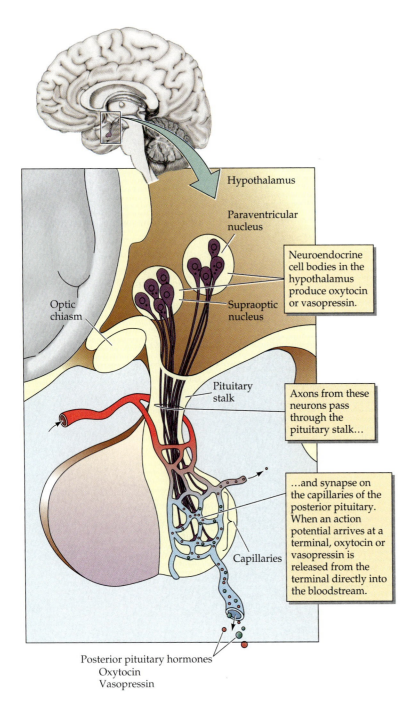

Neuroendocrine cell bodies in the hypothalamus produce oxytocin or vasopressin.

Axons from these neurons pass through the pituitary stalk...

...and synapse on the capillaries of the posterior pituitary. When an action potential arrives at a terminal, oxytocin or vasopressin is released from the terminal directly into the bloodstream.

Hypothalamus

Paraventricular nucleus

Optic chiasm

Supraoptic nucleus

Pituitary stalk

Capillaries

Posterior pituitary hormones
Oxytocin
Vasopressin

5.11 Hormone Production by the Posterior Pituitary

terminals into the rich vascular bed of the neurohypophysis. The axon terminals abut capillaries (small blood vessels), allowing the hormone to enter circulation immediately.

Some of the signals that activate the nerve cells of the supraoptic and paraventricular nuclei are related to thirst and water regulation, which we will discuss in Chapter 13. Secretion of AVP increases blood pressure by causing blood vessels to contract. AVP is also known as antidiuretic hormone (ADH) because it inhibits the formation of urine (which is the effect that defines an antidiuretic as such). This action of AVP helps conserve water. In fact, the major physiological role of AVP is its potent antidiuretic activity; it exerts this effect with less than one-thousandth of the dose needed to alter blood pressure. But because the name *vasopressin* was the first one applied to the hormone, that is the preferred name. AVP also acts as a neurotransmitter for some neurons that project within the brain.

Oxytocin is involved in many aspects of reproductive and parental behavior. One of its functions is to stimulate contractions of the uterine muscles and thus hasten birth (the word *oxytocin* is derived from the Greek *oxys,* "rapid," and *tokos,* "childbirth"). In fact, injections of oxytocin (or the synthetic version, Pitocin) are frequently used to accelerate delivery when prolonged labor threatens the health of the fetus.

Oxytocin also triggers the **milk letdown reflex,** the contraction of cells in the mammary glands. The mechanism that mediates this phenomenon is a good example of the interaction of behavior and hormone release. When an infant or young animal first begins to suckle, the arrival of milk at the nipple is delayed by 30 to 60 s. This delay is caused by the sequence of steps that precede letdown. Stimulation of the nipple activates receptors in the skin, which transmit this information through a chain of neurons and synapses to hypothalamic cells that contain oxytocin. Once these cells have been sufficiently stimulated, the hormone is released from the posterior pituitary and travels via the vascular system to the mammary glands, where it produces a contraction of the tissues storing milk, making it available at the nipple (Figure 5.12). For mothers this reflex response to suckling frequently becomes conditioned to baby cries, so milk appears promptly at the start of nursing.

Another perspective on this hormone is best summarized by the newspaper headline "A Potent Peptide Prompts an Urge to Cuddle" (Angier, 1992). Oxytocin is active in both sexes and appears to be part of the mechanism that mediates both sexual arousal and affectionate responses. Rodents given supplementary doses of oxytocin spend more time in physical contact with each other (Carter, 1992). Male mice with the oxytocin gene knocked out are unable to produce the hormone and display *social amnesia:* They seem unable to recognize the scent of female mice they've met before (Ferguson et al., 2000). Because a burst of oxytocin is released during orgasm in both men and women, oxytocin may contribute to the pleasurable feelings of sexual cli-

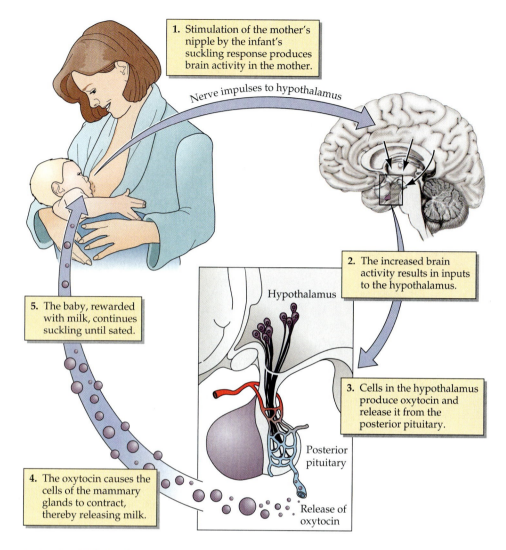

1. Stimulation of the mother's nipple by the infant's suckling response produces brain activity in the mother.

Nerve impulses to hypothalamus

2. The increased brain activity results in inputs to the hypothalamus.

Hypothalamus

3. Cells in the hypothalamus produce oxytocin and release it from the posterior pituitary.

5. The baby, rewarded with milk, continues suckling until sated.

Posterior pituitary

4. The oxytocin causes the cells of the mammary glands to contract, thereby releasing milk.

Release of oxytocin

5.12 The Milk Letdown Reflex

max. Oxytocin and vasopressin also serve as neurotransmitters from hypothalamic cells (Figure 5.13), projecting widely through the nervous system.

The anterior pituitary. Different cells of the anterior lobe of the pituitary synthesize and release different tropic hormones, which we'll discuss in the next section. Synthesis and release of the tropic hormones, however, are under the control of releasing hormones, as mentioned earlier. The releasing hormones are made by cells of the hypothalamus. We will briefly note some of the properties of these hypothalamic releasing hormones before further considering anterior pituitary actions.

Hypothalamic Releasing Hormones Govern the Anterior Pituitary

Neurons that synthesize different releasing hormones reside in different regions of the hypothalamus; like the neurons that produce oxytocin and vasopressin, these cells are considered neuroendocrine, or neurosecretory, cells. The axons of the neuroendocrine cells converge on the median eminence just above the pituitary stalk. This region contains an elaborate profusion of capillaries that form the **hypothalamic–pituitary portal system.**

Axons in this area contain large granules filled with hormones, which are released not into a synapse, but into the capillaries, where blood carries the releasing hormone

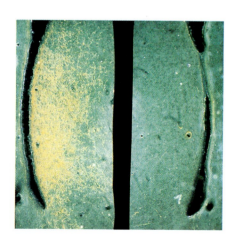

5.13 Vasopressin Can Serve as a Neurotransmitter Revealed here by immunocytochemistry are vasopressin fibers in the septum of intact (*left*) and castrated (*right*) male rats. (Courtesy of Geert DeVries.)

5.14 Hormone Production by the Anterior Pituitary

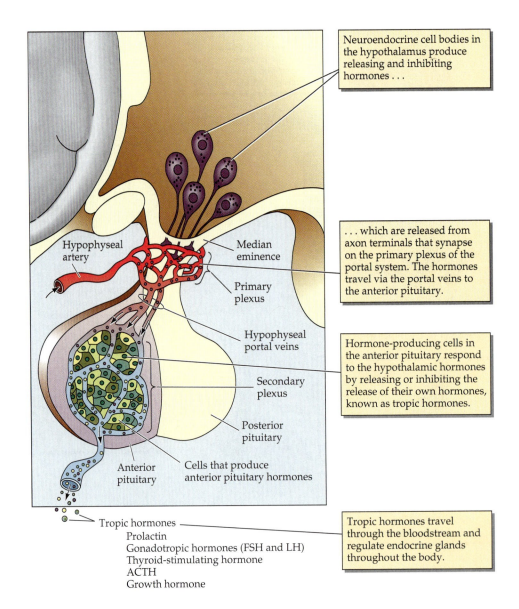

Neuroendocrine cell bodies in the hypothalamus produce releasing and inhibiting hormones . . .

. . . which are released from axon terminals that synapse on the primary plexus of the portal system. The hormones travel via the portal veins to the anterior pituitary.

Hormone-producing cells in the anterior pituitary respond to the hypothalamic hormones by releasing or inhibiting the release of their own hormones, known as tropic hormones.

Tropic hormones travel through the bloodstream and regulate endocrine glands throughout the body.

Hypophyseal artery

Median eminence

Primary plexus

Hypophyseal portal veins

Secondary plexus

Posterior pituitary

Anterior pituitary

Cells that produce anterior pituitary hormones

Tropic hormones
Prolactin
Gonadotropic hormones (FSH and LH)
Thyroid-stimulating hormone
ACTH
Growth hormone

a short distance into the anterior pituitary. The blood supply of the anterior pituitary thus contains many different releasing hormones that cause various anterior pituitary cells to change the rate at which they release their tropic hormone (Figure 5.14).

These types of controls apply to all the anterior pituitary hormones. Neuroendocrine cells in the hypothalamus make one releasing hormone or another, transport it down their axons to the median eminence, and when an action potential arrives at the terminals, dump the releasing hormone into the hypothalamic–pituitary portal system. When the releasing hormones reach the anterior pituitary, they cause the cells there to release more or less tropic hormone into the bloodstream. Thus the hypothalamic releasing hormones are an important control element in the regulation of secretions of endocrine organs throughout the body. Cutting the pituitary stalk interrupts the blood vessels and the flow of releasing hormones and leads to profound atrophy of the pituitary.

The neuroendocrine cells that synthesize the releasing hormones are themselves subject to two kinds of influences:

1. They receive *neural impulses* (either excitatory or inhibitory) from other brain regions via the synaptic contacts of these cells in the hypothalamus. In this manner a wide range of neural signals reflecting both internal and external events influence the endocrine system. Thus the outputs of endocrine glands can be regulated in accordance with ongoing events and can be conditioned by learning.

2. They are directly affected by *circulating messages,* such as other hormones (especially hormones that have themselves been secreted in response to tropic hormones), and by blood sugar and products of the immune system. In other words, these neuroendocrine cells are not shielded by a blood–brain barrier. (The blood–brain barrier was discussed in Chapter 2.)

Tropic hormones of the anterior pituitary. The anterior pituitary gland secretes six main tropic hormones (Figure 5.15; see also Table 5.2). The first two regulate the function of the adrenal cortex and thyroid gland:

1. Adrenocorticotropic hormone (**ACTH**) controls the production and release of hormones of the adrenal cortex. The adrenal cortex in turn releases steroid hormones. The levels of ACTH and adrenal steroids show a marked rhythm in the course of a day (see Chapter 14).

2. Thyroid-stimulating hormone (**TSH**) increases the release of thyroid hormones from the thyroid gland and markedly affects thyroid gland size.

Two other tropic hormones of the anterior pituitary influence the gonads:

1. Luteinizing hormone (**LH**) stimulates the release of eggs from the ovaries in females and prepares the uterine lining for the implantation of a fertilized egg. In males, LH stimulates interstitial cells of the testes to produce testosterone.

2. Follicle-stimulating hormone (**FSH**) stimulates the secretion of estrogens in females and of testosterone in males. It also influences both egg and sperm production.

The two remaining tropic hormones control milk production and body growth:

1. Prolactin is named after its role of promoting mammary development for lactation in female mammals. In other vertebrates prolactin plays other roles; for example, in ringdoves of both sexes it promotes the secretion of crop milk, which parents feed to their chicks.

5.15 Secretions of the Anterior Pituitary Hormones produced in the anterior pituitary include tropic hormones, which control endocrine glands and directly affect other body organs, such as bones.

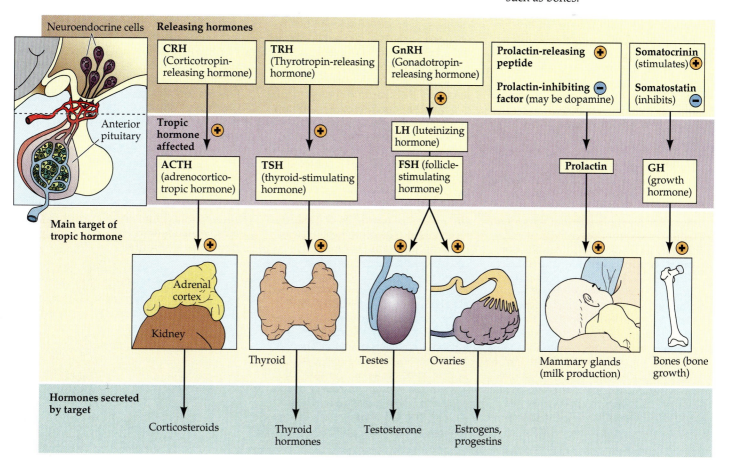

2. **Growth hormone** (**GH;** also known as somatotropin or somatotropic hormone) acts throughout the body to influence the growth of cells and tissues by affecting protein metabolism. The daily production and release of GH are especially prominent during the early stages of sleep. Several other factors influence the release of growth hormone, including a decrease in blood sugar, starvation, exercise, and stress (Box 5.2). In addition to hypothalamic factors that affect GH release, the stomach secretes a hormone, called ghrelin (from the proto-Indo-European root for "grow"), that evokes GH release from the anterior pituitary (Kojima et al., 1999).

Let's consider three of the target organs stimulated by tropic hormones of the anterior pituitary: the adrenal gland, the thyroid gland, and the gonads. Each of these glands secretes hormones of its own in response to the pituitary tropic hormones.

Two Divisions of the Adrenal Gland Produce Hormones

Resting on top of each kidney is an **adrenal gland,** which secretes a large variety of hormones (Figure 5.16). In mammals, the adrenal structure is divided into two major portions. In many nonmammalian vertebrates, these two portions are separate glands. In mammals, the outer bark of the gland, the **adrenal cortex,** is composed of distinct layers of cells, each producing different steroid hormones; this portion is about 80% of the gland. The core of this gland is the **adrenal medulla,** really a portion of the sympathetic nervous system because it is richly supplied with nerves from the autonomic ganglia.

BOX 5.2 *Stress and Growth: Psychosocial Dwarfism*

Genie had a horrifically deprived childhood. From the age of 20 months until the age of 13 years, she was isolated in a small, closed room, and much of the time she was tied to a chair. Her disturbed parents provided food, but nobody held Genie or spoke to her. When she was released from her confinement and observed by researchers at the age of 13 years 9 months, her size made her appear only 6 or 7 years old (Rymer, 1993).

Other less horrendous forms of family deprivation have also been shown to result in failure of growth. This syndrome is referred to as **psychosocial dwarfism** to emphasize that the growth failure arises from psychological and social factors mediated through the CNS and its control over endocrine functions (Green et al., 1984). When children suffering from psychosocial dwarfism are removed from stressful circumstances, many begin to grow rapidly. The growth rates of three such children, before and after periods of emotional deprivation, are shown in the figure (arrows indicate when each child was removed from the abusive situation). These children seem to have compensated for much of the growth deficit that occurred during prolonged stress periods.

How do stress and emotional deprivation impair growth? Growth impairments appear to be mediated by changed outputs of several hormones, including growth hormone (GH), cortisol, and other hormones, known as **somatomedins** (which are normally released by the liver in response to GH). GH and the somatomedins normally stimulate cell growth; high levels of cortisol inhibit growth.

Some children with psychosocial dwarfism show almost a complete lack of release of GH, which may be caused by an absence of the releasing hormone somatocrinin from the hypothalamus (Brasel and Blizzard, 1974). Disturbed sleep has also been suggested as a cause of this failure because GH is typically released during certain stages of sleep, as we will see in Chapter 14, and children under stress show disturbed sleep patterns (L. I. Gardner, 1972). Other children who exhibit psychosocial dwarfism show normal levels of GH but low levels of somatomedins, and these hormones, along with GH, appear to be necessary for normal growth. Still other children with this condition show elevated levels of steroids (probably as a result of stress) that inhibit growth. Some affected children show none of these hormonal disturbances. Thus there may be other routes through which emotional factors influence growth.

Growth is an example of a process that involves many factors—hormonal, metabolic, and dietary—and can therefore malfunction in a variety of ways. Cases of psychosocial dwarfism are more common than once was thought, and investigators who study this syndrome are calling for further awareness of and attention to it (Green et al., 1984). For Genie, relief came in time to restore much of her body growth, but her mental development remained severely limited; she never learned to say more than a few words, and she now lives in an institution.

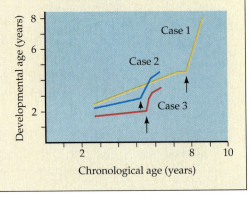

5.16 Regulation of Hormones Produced by the Adrenal Glands
Situated above the kidneys, each adrenal gland consists of an outer layer (the cortex) and an inner layer (the medulla). The main hormones of the cortical portion are corticosteroids, mineralocorticoids, and sex steroids (androgens and estrogens). The cells of the adrenal medulla release epinephrine and norepinephrine as a result of stimulation by the sympathetic nervous system. The level of circulating adrenal cortical hormones is regulated in several steps that involve both corticotropin-releasing hormone from the hypothalamus and adrenocorticotropic hormone (ACTH) secreted by the anterior pituitary.

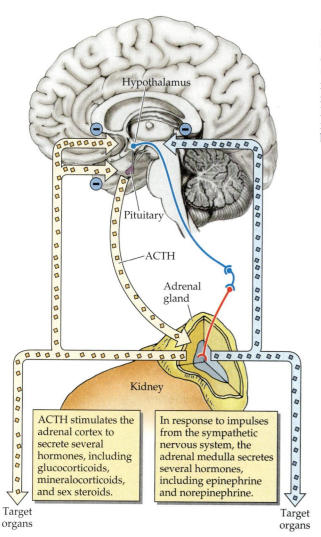

Hypothalamus

Pituitary

ACTH

Adrenal gland

Kidney

ACTH stimulates the adrenal cortex to secrete several hormones, including glucocorticoids, mineralocorticoids, and sex steroids.

In response to impulses from the sympathetic nervous system, the adrenal medulla secretes several hormones, including epinephrine and norepinephrine.

Target organs

Target organs

The adrenal medulla releases amine hormones—**epinephrine** (adrenaline) and **norepinephrine** (noradrenaline)—in response to nerve impulses of the sympathetic nervous system. In Chapter 4 we saw that epinephrine and norepinephrine are also synaptic transmitters at certain sites in the nervous system.

The adrenal cortex produces and secretes a variety of steroid hormones, collectively called the **adrenocorticoids** (or adrenal steroids). One subgroup is the **glucocorticoids,** so named because of their effects on the metabolism of carbohydrates, including glucose. Hormones of this type, such as **cortisol,** increase the level of blood glucose. They also accelerate the breakdown of proteins. In high concentrations, glucocorticoids have a marked anti-inflammatory effect; that is, they inhibit the swelling around injuries or infections. This action normally results in the temporary decrease of bodily responses to tissue injury. However, high levels of glucocorticoids can destroy nerve cells, as we'll see shortly and in Chapter 15. Glucocorticoids can also affect appetite and muscular activity.

A second subgroup of adrenal steroids is the **mineralocorticoids,** so named because of their effects on ion concentrations in some body tissues, especially the kidneys. The primary mineralocorticoid hormone is **aldosterone,** which acts on the kidneys to retain sodium and thus reduces the amount of urine produced, conserving water. This action helps maintain a homeostatic equilibrium of ions in blood and extracellular fluids.

The adrenal cortex also produces **sex steroids.** The molecular structure of these hormones is very similar to that of the other adrenal steroids. The chief sex hormone secreted by the human adrenal cortex is **androstenedione;** it contributes to the adult pattern of body hair in men and women. In some females the adrenal cortex produces more than the normal amounts of sex hormones, causing a more masculine appearance (see Chapter 12).

The level of circulating adrenal cortical hormones is regulated in several steps (see Figure 5.16). The pituitary hormone ACTH promotes steroid synthesis in the adrenal gland; cortisol is secreted by the adrenal cortex only when ACTH is present. Adrenal steroids in turn exert a negative feedback effect on ACTH release. As the level of adrenal cortical hormones increases, the secretion of ACTH is suppressed, so the output of hormones from the adrenal cortex diminishes. When the levels of adrenal steroids fall, the pituitary ACTH-secreting cells are released from suppression, and the concentration of ACTH in the blood rises, leading to increased output of adrenal cortical hormones.

A prominent influence on ACTH secretion is stress, both physiological and psychological. **Stress** is defined as any factor that throws us out of homeostatic balance. Such factors include unusual physiological states, such as exposure to extreme cold or heat, and an array of threatening psychological states. Stressors elicit a complex array of physiological changes; foremost among them is the activation of pathways from the brain to the hypothalamus, the outputs of which lead to activation of the pituitary. As we have noted, hormones released from the pituitary include ACTH, which triggers the release of glucocorticoids from the adrenal cortex. Robert Sapolsky (1992b) found that high levels of glucocorticoids released during stress can kill nerve cells in the hippocampus. (Stress and ACTH are discussed further in Chapter 15.)

Thyroid Hormones Regulate Growth and Metabolism

Situated just below the vocal apparatus in the throat is the **thyroid gland** (see Figure 5.1). This gland produces and secretes several hormones. Two of these—**thyroxine** and **triiodothyronine**—are usually referred to as thyroid hormones; a third—calcitonin—promotes calcium deposition in bones and will not be discussed further. Certain thyroid cells produce these hormones, and a saclike collection of cells called the thyroid colloid stores them.

The thyroid is unique among endocrine glands because it stores large amounts of hormone and releases it slowly; normally the thyroid has at least a 100 days' supply of hormones. Although thyroid hormones are amines—derived from amino acids—they behave like steroids. They bind to specialized receptors (part of the steroid receptor superfamily) found inside cells. The thyroid hormone–receptor complex then binds to DNA and regulates gene expression.

Figure 5.10 shows the control network for regulating thyroxine levels in blood. The major control is exerted by thyroid-stimulating hormone (TSH) from the anterior pituitary gland. The secretion of TSH by the pituitary is controlled by two factors. The dominant factor is the negative feedback from thyroid hormones circulating in the blood; they directly inhibit the pituitary, reducing TSH release. The second factor is the production (by the hypothalamus) of **thyrotropin-releasing hormone (TRH)**, which stimulates the release of TSH from the pituitary. When the level of circulating thyroid hormone falls, both TRH and TSH are secreted; when TSH reaches the thyroid gland, it stimulates the production and release of thyroid hormones.

CLINICAL ISSUE

Thyroid hormones are the only substances produced by the body that contain iodine, and their manufacture is critically dependent on the supply of iodine. In parts of the world where foods contain little iodine, many people suffer from hypothyroidism. In such cases the thyroid gland enlarges, driven by higher and higher TSH levels. In the attempt to produce more thyroid hormones, the gland swells, producing a **goiter.** The addition of a small amount of iodine to salt—producing *iodized salt*—is now a widespread practice designed to prevent this condition.

The major role of the thyroid is to regulate metabolic processes, especially carbohydrate use. The thyroid hormones also influence growth; this function is especially evident when thyroid deficiency starts early in life. Besides stunted body growth and characteristic facial malformation, thyroid deficiency produces a marked reduction in brain size and cellular structure (branching of axons and dendrites is reduced). This state, called **cretinism,** is accompanied by mental retardation.

The Gonads Produce Steroid Hormones, Regulating Reproduction

Almost all aspects of reproductive behavior, including mating and parental behavior, depend on hormones. Since Chapter 12 is devoted to reproductive behavior and physiology, at this point we will only briefly note relevant hormones and some pertinent aspects of anatomy and physiology. Female and male **gonads** (ovaries and testes, respectively; see Figure 5.1) consist of two different subcompartments—one to produce hormones (the sex steroids we mentioned earlier) and another to produce gametes (eggs or sperm). The gonadal hormones are critical for triggering both reproductive behavior controlled by the brain, and gamete production.

The testes. Within the **testes** are several cell types. Interspersed among the sperm-producing cells (the Sertoli cells) are the Leydig cells, which produce and secrete the sex steroid called **testosterone.** Testosterone and other male hormones are called **androgens** (from the Greek *andro-*, "man," and *gennan*, "to produce"). The production and release of testosterone are regulated by luteinizing hormone from the anterior pituitary. LH in turn is controlled by a hypothalamic releasing hormone, called **gonadotropin-releasing hormone (GnRH).**

Testosterone controls a wide range of body changes that become visible at puberty, including changes in voice, hair growth, and genital size. Levels of testosterone vary during the day in adult males, although the connection between these daily rhythms and behavior remains a mystery. In species that breed only in certain seasons of the year, testosterone has especially marked effects on appearance and behavior—for example, the antlers and fighting between males that are displayed by many species of deer (Figure 5.17). Figure 5.18*a* summarizes the regulation of testosterone secretion.

The ovaries. The paired female gonads, the **ovaries,** also produce both the mature gametes—called *ova* (singular *ovum*) or *eggs*—and sex steroid hormones. However, hormonal secretion by the ovaries is more complicated than by the testes. Ovarian hormones are produced in cycles, the duration of which varies with the species. Human ovarian cycles last about 4 weeks; rat cycles last only 4 days.

The ovary produces two major classes of steroid hormones: **progestins** (from the Latin *pro*, "favoring," and *gestare*, "to bear," because these hormones maintain pregnancy) and **estrogens** (from the Latin *oestrus*, "gadfly or frenzy," and the Greek *gennan*, "to produce"). If you suspect sexism in the naming of estrogens as though they induce frenzy, you're right. This term borrowed from the now discredited idea that women suffered hysteria because of secretions from their uterus. In fact, estrogens may improve cognitive functioning (Maki and Resnick, 2000). However misguided the origin of the term *estrogens* was, though, we're stuck with it now.

There are two different estrogen receptors, and both are expressed in the brain. The most important naturally occurring estrogen is **estradiol,** but many synthetic estrogens are tested in search of drugs that produce only the beneficial effects of the hormone (Christensen, 1999). The primary progestin is **progesterone.** Interestingly, estrogens make the brain sensitive to progesterone by promoting the production of progestin receptors there. Ovarian release of hormones is controlled by two tropic hormones of the anterior pituitary: FSH and LH. The release of these tropic hormones is controlled by GnRH from the hypothalamus (Figure 5.18*b*).

Relations among gonadal hormones. All three classes of sex hormones—androgens, estrogens, and progestins—have closely related chemical structures. They and the adrenal steroids are all derived from cholesterol, and all have the basic structure

5.17 The Influence of a Hormone
The antlers and combative behavior of male red deer, a subspecies of the North American Elk, are both seasonally affected by testosterone.

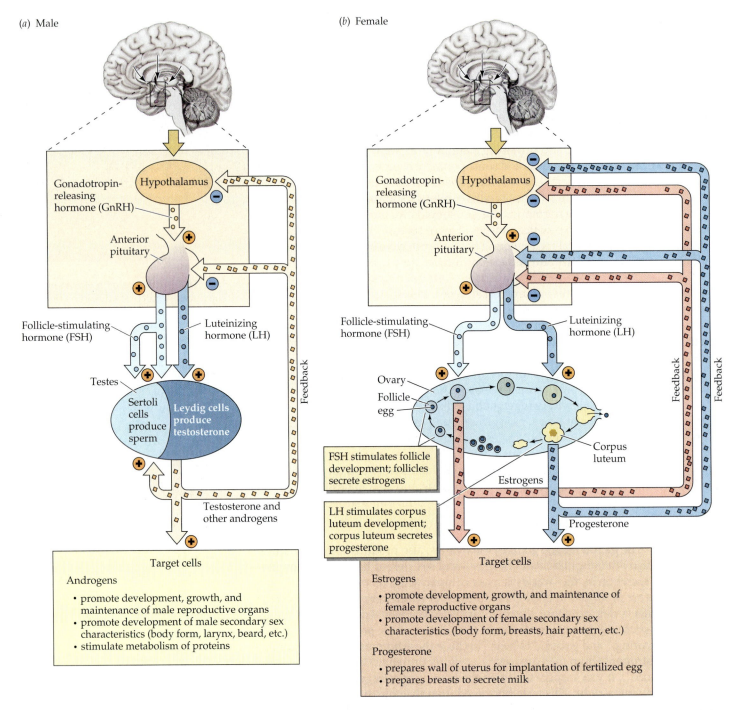

(a) Male

(b) Female

Gonadotropin-releasing hormone (GnRH)

Hypothalamus

Anterior pituitary

Follicle-stimulating hormone (FSH)

Luteinizing hormone (LH)

Feedback

Testes

Sertoli cells produce sperm

Leydig cells produce testosterone

Testosterone and other androgens

Target cells

Androgens

- promote development, growth, and maintenance of male reproductive organs
- promote development of male secondary sex characteristics (body form, larynx, beard, etc.)
- stimulate metabolism of proteins

Gonadotropin-releasing hormone (GnRH)

Hypothalamus

Anterior pituitary

Follicle-stimulating hormone (FSH)

Luteinizing hormone (LH)

Ovary

Follicle egg

Corpus luteum

FSH stimulates follicle development; follicles secrete estrogens

Estrogens

LH stimulates corpus luteum development; corpus luteum secretes progesterone

Progesterone

Feedback

Feedback

Target cells

Estrogens

- promote development, growth, and maintenance of female reproductive organs
- promote development of female secondary sex characteristics (body form, breasts, hair pattern, etc.)

Progesterone

- prepares wall of uterus for implantation of fertilized egg
- prepares breasts to secrete milk

5.18 Regulation of Gonadal Steroid Hormones   (a) In males the principal gonadal steroid secreted is testosterone. (b) The female gonads produce two classes of steroids: estrogens and progestins.

of four interconnected carbon rings (see Figure 5.7c). Furthermore, estrogens are synthesized from androgens, and androgens are synthesized from progestins.

Different organs differ in the relative amounts of these hormones they produce. For example, whereas the testis converts only a relatively small proportion of testosterone into estradiol, the ovary converts most of the testosterone it makes into estradiol. No steroid is found exclusively in either males or females; rather the two sexes differ in the proportion of these steroids. Some of the testosterone that enters brain cells is converted within those cells to estradiol, as we'll see in Chapter 12.

The Pineal Gland Secretes Melatonin

The **pineal gland** sits atop the brainstem and in mammals is overlaid by the cerebral hemispheres (Figure 5.19*a*). Whereas most other brain structures are paired (present on both left and right), the pineal gland is a single structure. This unusual aspect of the pineal may explain why the seventeenth-century philosopher René Descartes proposed that it could contain the soul.

Today we know that the pineal is innervated by the sympathetic nervous system, specifically by the superior cervical ganglion (see Figure 5.19*a*). In response to the activity of cells in this ganglion, the pineal releases an amine hormone called **melatonin.** The melatonin receptor is a G-coupled protein residing in cell membranes and is similar to receptors for peptide hormones. In many vertebrate species, the pineal secretion of melatonin controls whether animals are in breeding condition. Melatonin is released almost exclusively at night (Figure 5.19*b*).

In seasonally breeding mammals such as hamsters, the lengthening nights of autumn affect activity in the superior cervical ganglion, which in turn causes the pineal to prolong its nocturnal release of melatonin. The hypothalamus responds to the prolonged exposure to melatonin by becoming extremely sensitive to the negative feedback effects of gonadal steroids. Consequently, less and less GnRH is released, resulting in less gonadotropin release, as well as atrophy of the gonads. Lesion of the pineal prevents such regression, whereas prolonged treatment of normal animals with melatonin induces gonadal regression. In fact, one of the earliest hints of

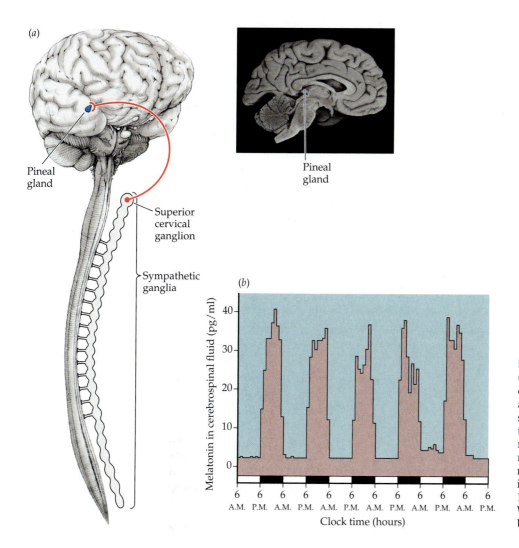

5.19 Regulation of the Pineal Gland (*a*) The pea-shaped pineal gland sits close to the floor of the third ventricle, atop the brainstem. Innervated by the sympathetic nervous system, specifically the superior cervical ganglion, the pineal releases melatonin. (*b*) Melatonin is released almost exclusively during the night in a wide variety of vertebrates, including humans. (After Reppert et al., 1979; photograph courtesy of S. Mark Williams and Dale Purves, Duke University Medical Center.)

pineal function was the report that a boy with a tumor that was destroying the pineal reached puberty early in life.

In birds, light from the environment penetrates the thin skull and reaches the pineal gland directly. Photosensitive cells in the bird pineal gland monitor daily light durations. In several reptile species the pineal is close to the skull and even has an extension of photoreceptors providing a "third eye" in the back of the head. (You may have noticed that the teacher who seemed to see everything that happened behind his back had a rather reptilian appearance.) The reptile pineal photoreceptors do not form images but act as simple photocells, monitoring day length to regulate seasonal functions. In seasonally breeding birds and mammals, the return of gonadal function is independent of melatonin secretion; after a fixed period of time, the hypothalamus becomes less sensitive to the negative feedback effects and the gonads grow and become functional again, no matter what the day length or amount of melatonin secretion. Specific brain regions ignore the melatonin signal and restore reproductive function (Larkin et al., 2001).

Humans are not, strictly speaking, seasonal breeders, but melatonin has been implicated in our daily cycles, such as sleep rhythms. Like other vertebrates, we release melatonin at night, and administering melatonin has been reported to induce sleep sooner at night. In fact, many recent studies indicate a role for melatonin in the timing of sleep. For example, melatonin has been used for treatment of jet lag (Lewy et al., 1992; Sack et al., 1992).

The Pancreas Secretes Two Main Hormones

Throughout the **pancreas** (which is located in the back of the abdominal cavity; see Figure 5.1) are clusters of cells called **islets of Langerhans,** which secrete hormones directly into the bloodstream. These endocrine cells are intermingled with other cells that perform an exocrine function, secreting digestive enzymes (such as bile) into ducts leading to the gastrointestinal tract. Hormones secreted by the islets of Langerhans include **insulin** and **glucagon,** both of which have potent and frequently reciprocal effects on glucose utilization. Insulin is produced in one type of cell within the islets (beta cells), and glucagon is secreted by another type (alpha cells).

Both nonneural and neural factors regulate the release of insulin. The level of glucose in the bloodstream, monitored by cells of the islets of Langerhans, is a critical determinant. As the level of blood sugar rises above a certain concentration, insulin is released. Among the effects of insulin are increased glucose uptake in some tissues, such as muscle, and reduced output of glucose from the liver. These effects lower blood glucose levels. As noted earlier, this reaction is a direct, negative feedback effect that does not involve a tropic hormone from the pituitary.

The effects of insulin directly antagonize those of glucagon, which increases blood glucose levels. Figure 5.20 summarizes the hormonal regulation of insulin and glucagon. In addition, there is paracrine action between adjacent alpha and beta cells of the islets of Langerhans; that is, glucagon and insulin can oppose each other locally within the pancreas, as well as by the endocrine route. The reciprocal action of insulin and glucagon helps keep blood glucose levels within the range necessary for proper functioning of the brain and other organs (see Chapter 13).

5.20 Regulation of Blood Glucose Levels Both glucagon (*a*) and insulin (*b*) are released by the pancreas, and each affects the availability of glucose in circulation. (*c*) Normally, both hormones are at work, in a reciprocal fashion.

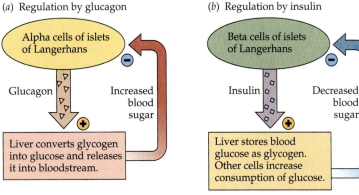

(*a*) Regulation by glucagon

Alpha cells of islets of Langerhans

Glucagon

Increased blood sugar

Liver converts glycogen into glucose and releases it into bloodstream.

(*b*) Regulation by insulin

Beta cells of islets of Langerhans

Insulin

Decreased blood sugar

Liver stores blood glucose as glycogen. Other cells increase consumption of glucose.

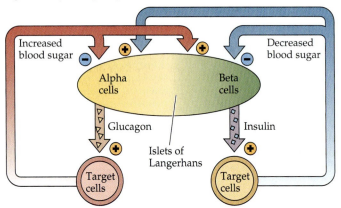

(*c*) Regulation by both glucagon and insulin

Increased blood sugar

Decreased blood sugar

Alpha cells

Beta cells

Glucagon

Insulin

Islets of Langerhans

Target cells

Target cells

The release of insulin is also controlled by neural impulses that arrive at the pancreas via the parasympathetic vagus nerve. When a person eats, insulin is released even before glucose reaches the bloodstream. This early release occurs in response to taste stimulation in the mouth. (Other stimuli that are normally associated with eating can also cause the release of insulin.) Cutting the vagus nerve in experimental animals prevents the early release of insulin in response to the taste of food, but it does not interfere with the later response to glucose in the bloodstream, showing that the conditioned response operates via the nervous system.

Hormones Affect Behavior in Many Different Ways

In later chapters we will discuss specific examples of the role of hormones in reproductive behavior (Chapter 12), eating and drinking (Chapter 13), biological rhythms (Chapter 14), and stress (Chapter 15). Hormonal effects on growth are considered in Box 5.2. For now, to get an idea of how hormones affect behavior, let's briefly consider the role of hormones in modulating memory formation, and the psychopathology that can result from too much or too little hormone.

Hormones Can Affect Learning and Memory

Hormones affect both the early development of capacities to learn and remember, and the efficient use of these capacities after they have formed. Thyroid hormones, as already indicated, are important in the early development of the nervous system. Insufficient thyroid secretion results in fewer synaptic connections than usual, leading to cretinism.

NEURAL PLASTICITY

Experimental studies have given us more information about this condition: If a drug that inhibits thyroid function is administered to infant rats, the result is a decrease in the formation of cortical synapses, as well as significantly impaired learning ability. Giving such experimental cretin rats enriched experience as they grow has been reported to diminish their behavioral deficiencies to a large extent (Davenport, 1976). (The effects of enriched experience on the brain will be discussed further in Chapter 18.)

The ability of animals to learn and remember can be affected by the hypothalamic hormones ACTH, AVP, and oxytocin, as well as by particular fractions or analogs of these hormones, and by the catecholaminergic hormones of the adrenal medulla: norepinephrine and epinephrine (McGaugh, 1992; Schulteis and Martinez, 1992). One hypothesis being tested is that the emotional aspects of a learning situation affect the release of hormones, and the hormones modulate the consolidation of memory after training. Perhaps the pleasure, pain, or stress involved in a learning episode will, through hormonal aftereffects, help determine how well the situation is remembered. Such hormonal effects may be important in reinforcing learning during crucial situations, as we will discuss in Chapter 18.

Endocrine Pathology Can Produce Extreme Effects on Human Behavior

Both deficient and excessive hormone secretion are associated with a variety of human physiological, anatomical, and behavioral disorders (Erhardt and Goldman, 1992). Some of these disorders have long been known, especially those that include either marked behavioral changes or anatomical abnormalities.

CLINICAL ISSUE

Many hormonal disorders resemble psychiatric disorders. For example, parathyroid deficiency results in calcium deposition in the basal ganglia and a symptom portrait that resembles a severe psychotic state, schizophrenia. Patients with excessive thyroid release frequently appear intensely anxious; those with decreased thyroid release may show cognitive impairments and depression. An inherited form of attention deficit disorder in children involves decreased sensitivity to thyroid hormone (Hauser et al., 1993).

Excessive release of glucocorticoids by the adrenal cortex, **Cushing's syndrome,** is accompanied by many bodily and psychological changes, including fatigue, de-

TABLE 5.3 *Hormonal Disorders and Associated Cognitive, Emotional, and Psychiatric Disorders*

Hormonal disorder	Impaired cognition	Anxiety	Depression	Psychosis and delirium
Hyperthyroidism	+	++	+	+
Hypothyroidism	+	+	++	++
Hypercortisolism	+	++	++	++
Hypocortisolism	—	+	++	++
Panhypopituitarism[a]	—	+	++	++
Hyperparathyroidism	+	+	++	++
Hypoparathyroidism	?	++	++	++
Hyperinsulinism	+	++	—	++
Hypoinsulinism	+	—	—	+

Note: +, sometimes; ++, often.
[a]Undersecretion of all or nearly all anterior pituitary hormones.

pression, unusual distribution of hair, and other autonomic changes. Several studies have indicated that affective changes, especially depression, frequently long precede other physiological effects of excessive cortisol secretion. In some people who take excessive amounts of glucocorticoids, such as athletes, psychiatric symptoms can emerge that include periods of intense psychotic behavior. Table 5.3 lists an array of hormonal disorders and their associated cognitive, emotional, and psychiatric changes.

Hormonal and Neural Systems Interact to Produce Integrated Responses

Although we have focused on the endocrine system in this chapter, the endocrine system participates in interactions with many other organs, including, of course, the brain. Figure 5.21 incorporates the endocrine system into a larger schema of reciprocal relations between body and behavior. Let's examine some of these relations.

Incoming sensory stimuli elicit nerve impulses that go to several brain regions, including the cerebral cortex, cerebellum, and hypothalamus. Behavioral responses bring further changes in stimulation. For example, a person may approach or go away from the original source of stimulation, and this action alters the size of a visual image, the loudness of a sound, and so forth. Meanwhile the endocrine system is altering the response characteristics of the person. If evaluation of the stimulus calls for action, energy is mobilized through hormonal routes. The state of some sensory receptor organs may also be altered, thus modifying further processing of stimuli.

Many behaviors require neural and hormonal coordination. For example, when a stressful situation is perceived through neural sensory channels, hormonal secretions prepare the individual to make energetic responses. The muscular movements for the fight-or-flight response (see Chapter 2) are controlled neurally, but the required energy is mobilized through hormonal routes. Another example of neural and hormonal coordination is the milk letdown reflex (see Figure 5.12).

Four kinds of signals from one cell to another are possible between nerve cells and endocrine cells: neural-to-neural, neural-to-endocrine, endocrine-to-endocrine, and endocrine-to-neural. All four kinds of signals can be found in the courtship behavior of the ringdove (M. B. Friedman, 1977). The visual stimulation and perception of a male dove that sees a female involve (1) neural-to-neural transmission. The particular visual stimulus activates (2) a neural-to-endocrine link, which causes some neurosecretory cells in the male's hypothalamus to secrete GnRH. (3) Endocrine-to-endocrine signals cause increased production and release of the hormone testosterone in response to GnRH. Testosterone, in turn, alters the excitability of some neurons through (4) an endocrine-to-neural link and thus causes the male to display courtship behavior. The female dove responds to this display, thus providing new visual stimulation to the male and further neural-to-neural signals within his brain.

Our circle schema in Figure 5.21 helps reveal how we discover relations between endocrine activity and behavior. The level of circulating hormones can be altered by experimental intervention, which can affect behavior. For example, removal of the adrenals, which deprives animals of aldosterone, causes excretion of salts, which greatly increases the animals' preference for salty water. But experience can also cause rapid changes in the output of endocrine glands.

For example, starting to exercise or stepping out in the cold increases the level of thyroxine in the circulation. Men rooting for a sports team have higher testosterone levels just after their team wins, and have lower levels if their team loses (Bernhardt et al., 1998). Conversely, physical stresses, pain, and unpleasant emotional situations decrease thyroid output and trigger the release of adrenal glucocorticoids (see Chapter 15). Any thorough understanding of the relationship of hormones to behavior must come to grips with these reciprocal interactions between the two.

Not only do the neural and endocrine systems interact, but both systems also interact with the immune system, as we will discuss in Chapter 15.

Summary

1. Hormones are chemical compounds that act as signals in the body. They are secreted by endocrine glands or specialized cells into the bloodstream and are taken up by receptor molecules in target cells.

2. Neural communication differs from hormonal communication in that neural signals travel rapidly over fixed pathways, whereas hormonal signals spread more slowly and throughout the body.

3. Neural and hormonal communication systems have several characteristics in common: Both utilize chemical messages; some substances act as a hormone in some locations and as a synaptic transmitter in others. Both systems manufacture, store, and release chemical messengers. Both use specific receptors and may employ second messengers.

4. Some hormones have receptors in a wide variety of cells and can therefore influence the activity of most cells in the body. Others have receptors in only certain special cells or organs.

5. Hormones act by promoting the proliferation and differentiation of cells and by modulating the activity of cells that have already differentiated.

6. Protein and amine hormones bind to specific receptor molecules at the surface of the target cell membrane and activate second-messenger molecules inside the cell. Steroid hormones pass through the membrane and bind to receptor molecules inside the cell.

7. A negative feedback system monitors and controls the rate of secretion of each hormone. In the simplest case the hormone acts on target cells, leading them to change the amount of a substance they release; this change in turn regulates the output of the endocrine gland.

8. Several hormones are controlled by a more complex feedback system: A releasing hormone from the hypothalamus regulates the release of an anterior pituitary tropic hormone, which in turn controls secretion by an endocrine gland. In this case, feedback of the endocrine hormone acts mainly at the hypothalamus and anterior pituitary.

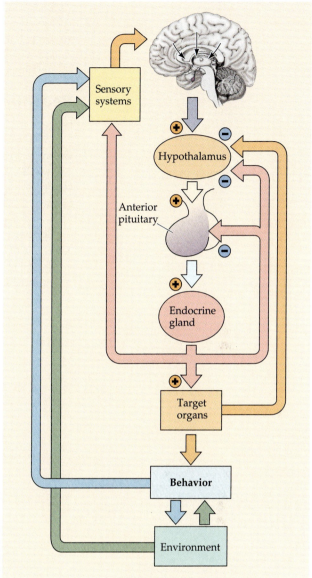

5.21 The Reciprocal Relations between Hormones and Behavior

Refer to the *Learning Biological Psychology* CD for the following study aids for this chapter:

7 Objectives

65 Study Questions

1 Activity

1 Animated Tutorial

9. Endocrine influences on structures and functions often involve more than one hormone, as in growth, homeostasis, metabolism, and learning and memory.

10. Many behaviors require the coordination of neural and hormonal components. Messages may be transmitted in the body via neural-to-neural, neural-to-endocrine, endocrine-to-endocrine, or endocrine-to-neural links.

Recommended Reading

Becker, J. B., Breedlove, S. M., Crews, D., and McCarthy, M. M. (Eds.). (in press). *Behavioral endocrinology* (2nd ed.). Cambridge, MA: MIT Press.

Greenspan, F. S., and Strewler, G. J. (1997). *Basic and clinical endocrinology* (5th ed.). Stamford, CT: Appleton & Lange.

Hadley, M. E. (2000). *Endocrinology* (5th ed.). Englewood Cliffs, NJ: Prentice Hall.

Litwack, G., and Norman, A. W. (1997). *Hormones* (2nd ed.). San Diego, CA: Academic Press.

Nelson, R. J. (2000). *An introduction to behavioral endocrinology* (2nd ed.). Sunderland, MA: Sinauer.

Norris, D. O. (1997). *Vertebrate endocrinology* (3rd ed.). San Diego, CA: Academic Press.

Wilson, J. D., and Foster, D. W. (1998). *Williams textbook of endocrinology* (9th ed.). Philadelphia: Saunders.

PART TWO

Evolution and Development of the Nervous System

Part 2 presents two viewpoints and two timescales for the development of brain and behavior. Chapter 6 considers the evolution of the brain and behavior over millions of years. Chapter 7 takes up the growth of the individual over the months and years of the life span. Both viewpoints contribute to our understanding of development, somewhat as an architect and a contractor make different but essential contributions to building a house.

The architect brings to the construction of houses the sort of perspective that evolution brings to the construction of animals. The information in the architect's plan is analogous to the information in the genome. In preparing plans, the architect calls on a long history of hard-won knowledge about structures that meet basic human needs. The contractor's perspective is more like that of the developing individual, using the plans to construct a particular house—translating the abstract information of the blueprints into a practical, working structure. The contractor's judgment and interpretation are necessary, so two houses built by different contractors from the same blueprint will not be identical, just as identical twins differ slightly.

The architect tries to foresee some of the problems of construction and to build safety factors into the plans, so that small deviations or errors will not seriously impair the safety or utility of the building. But the architect also relies on the contractor to fill in details and to improvise when external conditions require it. So, too, has evolutionary wisdom, distilled in the genome, come to rely on the environment and experience to guide the construction of the developing brain.

6

Evolution of Brain and Behavior

I n this chapter we consider the intriguing story of how brains and behavior have evolved. Research on this topic focuses on many species of animals, both extant and extinct. Since we share many biological and behavioral features with all other animals, it is not surprising that our search to understand ourselves leads us to study apes, monkeys, carnivores, rodents, birds, and amphibians. The brains of all these vertebrates reveal the same basic plan as ours, although in some ways theirs are simpler and in some ways theirs differ distinctively.

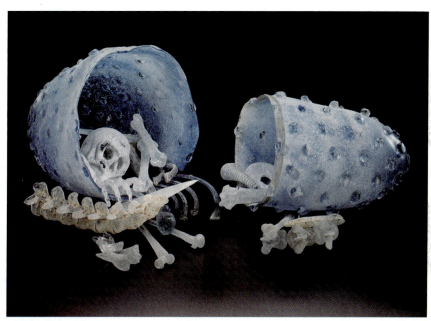

William Morris, *Artifact Series #9* (*Burial*), 1989

The quest to understand the nervous system has also led to the study of animals that are quite different from us: invertebrates and even single-celled animals. But describing, cataloging, and understanding the relationships between the nervous system and behavior in even a small fraction of Earth's inhabitants would be an awesome (and dull) task unless we had a rationale beyond mere completeness. As we'll see, studying and comparing well-chosen species throws much light on the principles of nervous system organization.

This chapter reflects two major traditions in biology. One is to discover the diversity of animal forms (including the structure of the nervous system) and to understand the relationships among species. The second major tradition is to study relationships between form and function, which we now understand in the context of adaptation and natural selection.

Why Should We Study Other Species?

One old-fashioned reason for comparing species was human centered, based on the question, Why does the human being end up on top of the animal order? This human-centered perspective was properly criticized because it implicitly pictured other animals as incomplete "little humans," a view that no modern scientists see as valid. It also embraced the old idea that animals vary along a single scale from simple to complex, whereas scientists now see a multibranching set of radiations. Today we see that comparisons of different species provide clues about our evolutionary history—the phylogeny of humans.

A **phylogeny** (from the Greek *phylon*, "tribe, kind," and *genes*, "born") is the evolutionary history of a particular group of organisms; it is often represented as a *family tree* that shows which species may have given rise to others. (Some scientists prefer to say *bush* rather than *tree* because the phylogeny branches so extensively.) Comparisons among extant animals, coupled with fragmentary but illuminating data from fossil remains, stimulate concepts about the history of the human body and brain, and the forces that shaped them.

Figure 6.1 shows a recent attempt to reconstruct the family tree of apes and humans. This diagram shows humans and chimpanzees as being more closely related to each other than either is to the gorilla. Not all investigators agree about the branching pattern, but all agree that these three species are closely related. We will say more about phylogenies a little later in the chapter.

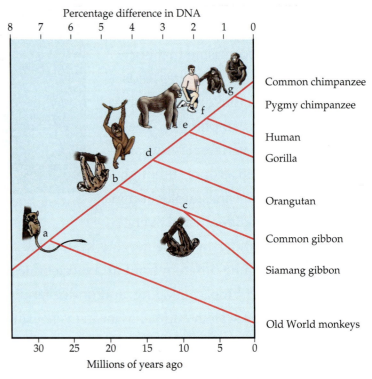

6.1 Family Tree of Apes and Humans   This tree was derived from measurements of differences between pairs of species in samples of their genetic material—molecules of deoxyribonucleic acid (DNA). To see how different two species are in their genetic endowments, trace the lines from the two members of a pair to the point that connects them, and match the point with the scale at the top. For example, the line from humans and the line from chimpanzees converge at point f, so the DNA of humans and of chimpanzees differs by only about 1.6%. The DNA of humans and of chimpanzees, in turn, differs from that of the gorilla (point e) by about 2.3%. The scale at the bottom gives the estimated number of millions of years since any pair of species shared a common ancestor. For example, humans and chimpanzees diverged from a common ancestor about 7 million years ago. (After M. Goodman et al., 1990; Horai et al., 1995; Sibley and Ahlquist, 1987; and Sibley et al., 1990.)

No animal is simply sitting around providing researchers with the details of human biological history; rather, each species is busily engaged in satisfying its needs for survival, which must include an active interchange with the environment. Species with varying biological histories show different solutions to the dilemmas of survival and reproduction. In many cases, adaptations to particular ecological niches can be related to differences in brain structure.

Understanding the neural structures and mechanisms that mediate specific behaviors in various other animals can provide a new perspective and intriguing clues about the neural bases of human behavior. For example, some relatively simple animals show changes in behavior that arise from experience. Understanding how the nervous systems of these simpler animals form and store memories provides insights into the workings of more complex animals, including human beings, as we will see in Chapter 18.

IMPORTANT METHOD

How Closely Related Are Two Species?

The attempt to construct the family trees of animals raises the question, How can we find out how closely related two species are? Some basic knowledge of this topic is important for the examples that we consider later in this chapter and in other chapters.

Early Views of Classification and Evolution

People have probably always classified the animals they saw around them and realized that some forms resemble each other more closely than others. The contact between Europe and the Americas beginning in 1492 prompted European scholars to question how best to classify the many newly discovered animals.

In the mid-eighteenth century the Swedish biologist Carolus Linnaeus (1707–1778) proposed the basic system we use today. In Linnaeus's system each species is assigned two names, the first name identifying the genus and the second name indicating the species. Both names are always italicized, and the genus name is capitalized. According to this system, the modern human species is *Homo sapiens*. Table 6.1 shows the classifications of some other species.

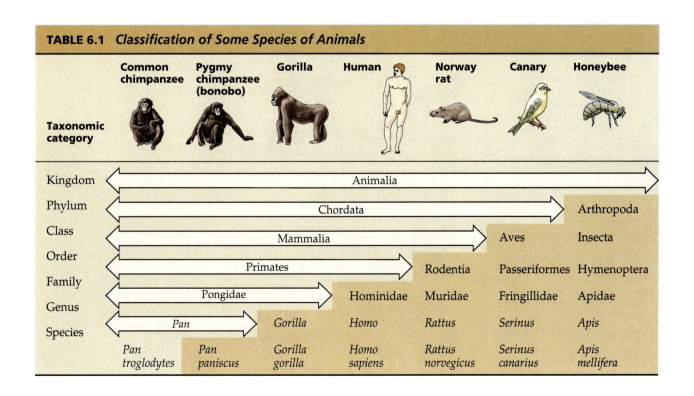

TABLE 6.1 *Classification of Some Species of Animals*

Taxonomic category	Common chimpanzee	Pygmy chimpanzee (bonobo)	Gorilla	Human	Norway rat	Canary	Honeybee
Kingdom	Animalia →						
Phylum	Chordata →						Arthropoda
Class	Mammalia →					Aves	Insecta
Order	Primates →				Rodentia	Passeriformes	Hymenoptera
Family	Pongidae →			Hominidae	Muridae	Fringillidae	Apidae
Genus	Pan →		Gorilla	Homo	Rattus	Serinus	Apis
Species	*Pan troglodytes*	*Pan paniscus*	*Gorilla gorilla*	*Homo sapiens*	*Rattus norvegicus*	*Serinus canarius*	*Apis mellifera*

The different levels of classification in Table 6.1 are illustrated and defined in Figure 6.2. Each successively broader category above the species level takes in more and more animals, so members of the higher categories show increasing variety. (Here's an aid to remembering the succession of classifications in Table 6.1: **K**indly **p**ut **c**lothes **o**n, **f**or **g**oodness **s**ake.) Linnaeus classified animals mainly on the basis of gross anatomical similarities and differences; the classification of animals was not at the start meant to imply anything about evolution or common ancestry.

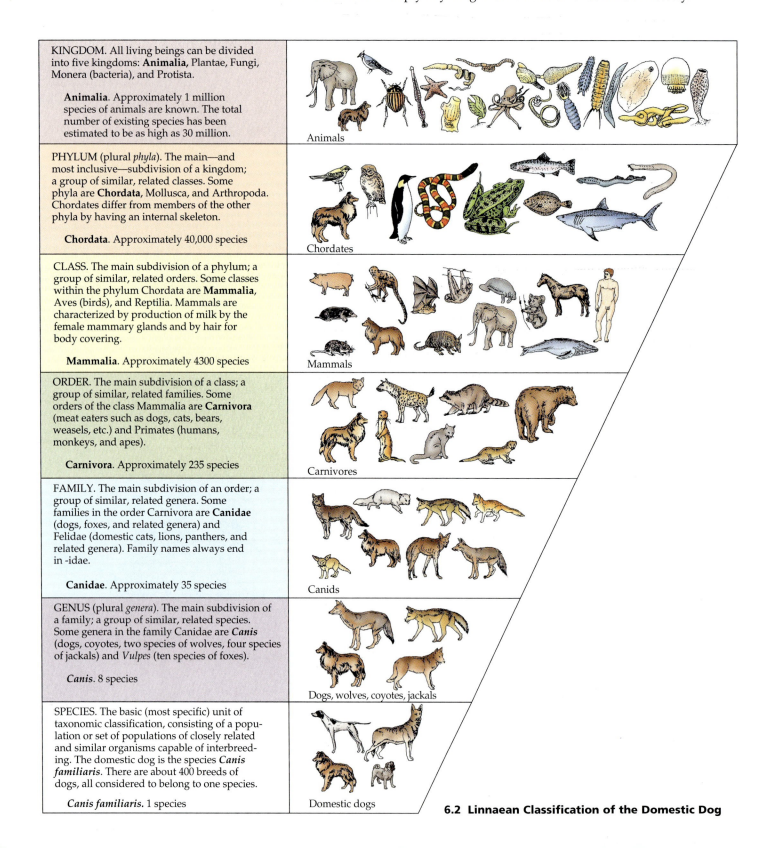

KINGDOM. All living beings can be divided into five kingdoms: **Animalia,** Plantae, Fungi, Monera (bacteria), and Protista.

Animalia. Approximately 1 million species of animals are known. The total number of existing species has been estimated to be as high as 30 million.

Animals

PHYLUM (plural *phyla*). The main—and most inclusive—subdivision of a kingdom; a group of similar, related classes. Some phyla are **Chordata**, Mollusca, and Arthropoda. Chordates differ from members of the other phyla by having an internal skeleton.

Chordata. Approximately 40,000 species

Chordates

CLASS. The main subdivision of a phylum; a group of similar, related orders. Some classes within the phylum Chordata are **Mammalia**, Aves (birds), and Reptilia. Mammals are characterized by production of milk by the female mammary glands and by hair for body covering.

Mammalia. Approximately 4300 species

Mammals

ORDER. The main subdivision of a class; a group of similar, related families. Some orders of the class Mammalia are **Carnivora** (meat eaters such as dogs, cats, bears, weasels, etc.) and Primates (humans, monkeys, and apes).

Carnivora. Approximately 235 species

Carnivores

FAMILY. The main subdivision of an order; a group of similar, related genera. Some families in the order Carnivora are **Canidae** (dogs, foxes, and related genera) and Felidae (domestic cats, lions, panthers, and related genera). Family names always end in -idae.

Canidae. Approximately 35 species

Canids

GENUS (plural *genera*). The main subdivision of a family; a group of similar, related species. Some genera in the family Canidae are *Canis* (dogs, coyotes, two species of wolves, four species of jackals) and *Vulpes* (ten species of foxes).

Canis. 8 species

Dogs, wolves, coyotes, jackals

SPECIES. The basic (most specific) unit of taxonomic classification, consisting of a population or set of populations of closely related and similar organisms capable of interbreeding. The domestic dog is the species *Canis familiaris*. There are about 400 breeds of dogs, all considered to belong to one species.

Canis familiaris. 1 species

Domestic dogs

6.2 Linnaean Classification of the Domestic Dog

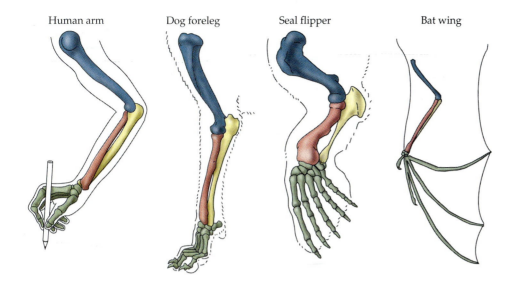

Human arm   Dog foreleg   Seal flipper   Bat wing

6.3 Homology of Forelimb Structures Bones of the same sort are shown here in the same color in all species. The sizes and shapes of the bones of the forelimb have evolved so that they are adapted to widely different functions: skilled manipulation in humans, locomotion in dogs, swimming in seals, flying in bats. The similarities among the sets of bones reflect descent from a common ancestor.

Until about 200 years ago, it was generally believed that each species had been created separately. Then, at about the time of Linnaeus, some naturalists—students of animal life and structure—began to have doubts. For example, some naturalists observed that the limb bones of all mammals, no matter what the animal's way of life, are remarkably similar in many details (Figure 6.3). If these species had been specifically created for different ways of locomotion, the naturalists reasoned, they should have been built on different plans rather than all being modifications of a single plan.

The idea of evolution slowly became more acceptable as naturalists adopted it and as nineteenth-century geologists showed that Earth had been changing for millions of years. The fossils discovered early in the nineteenth century and the inclusion of fossilized species in the Linnaean system provided additional evidence for evolution. But a plausible *mechanism* for evolution was lacking. Early in the nineteenth century the French naturalist Jean-Baptiste de Lamarck (1744–1829) promoted the idea of evolution and proposed that organisms evolve through the gradual accumulation of characteristics acquired by individuals throughout life as they exercise and stretch their bodies. But this idea proved to be incompatible with later discoveries about genetic inheritance.

Half a century after Lamarck, in 1858, Charles Darwin and Alfred Russel Wallace announced the hypothesis of **evolution by natural selection.** Darwin and Wallace each had hit upon the idea independently, and Darwin had been accumulating much evidence to support it ever since, as a young naturalist in the 1830s, he had voyaged on the HMS *Beagle* to South America and the Galapagos Islands. In 1859 Darwin published his revolutionary book *On the Origin of Species by Means of Natural Selection.* The hypothesis he stated was based on three main observations and one important inference. The facts were these: (1) Individuals of a given species are not identical, (2) some of this variation is heritable (i.e., can be inherited), and (3) not all offspring survive. The inference was that the variations among individuals affect the probabilities that they will survive, reproduce, and pass on their characteristics.

Darwin knew about variability from his studies of many species of plants and animals. As a naturalist and a pigeon fancier, he saw close parallels between artificial selection by breeders, which can produce differences in a few generations, and selection in nature, which may be less sharply defined but which can work over many generations.

The concept of evolution by natural selection has become one of the major organizing principles in all the life sciences, directing the study of behavior and its mechanisms, as well as the study of morphology (form and structure). Darwin (1859) wrote prophetically that because of his work, "Psychology will be based on a new foundation, that of the necessary acquirement of each mental power and capacity by gradation" (p. 113); that is, psychology will be based on evolution.

Charles Darwin
(1809–1892)

Alfred Russel Wallace
(1823–1913)

Darwin later added another evolutionary principle, that of **sexual selection** (1871). This principle holds that members of each sex exert selective pressures on the other in terms of both anatomical and behavioral features that favor reproductive success. Thus, for example, female choices have led to the ornamental but costly tails of peacocks. We will discuss this principle at greater length in Chapter 12 and will also call on it at the end of this chapter in relation to evolution of the human brain.

Modern Evolutionary Theory Combines Natural Selection and Genetics

A gap in Darwin's theory was that he could not specify the source of the variation upon which natural selection acts or the mechanism by which biological inheritance works. A major step to round out the theory of evolution was accomplished by the pioneering work of an Austrian monk and botanist named Gregor Johann Mendel (1822–1884). On the basis of his research with pea plants, Mendel published the laws of inheritance in an obscure journal in 1866 (Mendel, 1967). Only in 1900 were these laws brought into prominence and related to evolution when they were rediscovered independently by the Dutch biologist Hugo de Vries (1848–1935) and two other European biologists. Each of these investigators searched the scientific literature for any anticipation of his discovery and was surprised to find Mendel's papers. Each then heralded Mendel's discovery and reported his own work only as confirmation.

De Vries went beyond Mendel in an important respect: Working with primroses, he found that occasionally a new variety arose spontaneously and then perpetuated its characteristics in successive generations. In 1901 de Vries pointed out that in such cases evolution could occur by sudden jumps, or **mutations,** as he called these changes. (Nowadays, scientists deliberately induce mutations in plants and animals, as we will discuss in Box 7.3.) Thus de Vries discovered that evolution is not only the slow process that Darwin hypothesized; it can also occur rapidly.

Although **genetics,** the study of the mechanisms of inheritance, started with plants such as the pea and the primrose, investigators soon began to study organisms that reproduce more rapidly and that have other advantages for investigation. An example is the fruit fly *Drosophila,* whose generation time is 10 days and whose salivary glands produce giant chromosomes visible under a light microscope. (**Chromosomes** [from the Greek *chroma,* "color," and *soma,* "body"] are rod-shaped assemblies of DNA in the nucleus of each cell that bear genetic information. Since 1882 it had been known that chromosomes replicate themselves during cell division, but the significance of this phenomenon did not become apparent until Mendel's work was rediscovered.) Many of the findings about genetic mechanisms made with *Drosophila* and even with bacteria hold true for larger organisms, such as humans, that reproduce much more slowly.

By the 1940s, scientists realized that nucleic acids are the instruments of genetic inheritance. In 1953 Francis Crick and James D. Watson announced that the structure of the DNA molecule, which forms chromosomes, is a double helix. This discovery led in turn to the cracking of the genetic code, a topic taken up in the Appendix. Crick and Watson were awarded the Nobel Prize in physiology or medicine in 1962.

Both gradual evolutionary changes and larger evolutionary processes, such as the formation of new species, can now be understood in the light of modern evolutionary theory, which combines Darwin's hypothesis of natural selection with modern genetics and molecular biology. Further insights continue to be added by research in these and related fields, such as developmental biology, paleontology, and systematic biology.

Newer Methods Aid in Classifying Animals and Inferring Evolution

The field of **taxonomy** (from the Greek *taxis,* "arrangement," and *nomos,* "law"), or classification, of animals is an ongoing endeavor. Taxonomists continue to be challenged as previously unknown animals are discovered, as new techniques become available, and as new concepts arise. They disagree about how some species are classified and about the best overall methods of classification.

For example, some of the relationships among apes and humans are being debated. You may have noticed that Figure 6.1 and Table 6.1 differ in their placement of human beings. Figure 6.1, which is based on differences between samples of DNA, shows the chimpanzees closer to humans than to gorillas in their genetic endowment. Table 6.1, which is based on body measurements, puts both chimpanzees and gorillas in the family Pongidae (the great apes), whereas humans are traditionally placed in their own family, Hominidae. The difference between these two classifications of primates remains unresolved.

In addition to the patterns in gross anatomy that Linnaeus used, more recent developments help us classify animals and make inferences about their evolution. One such development is the recognition that fossils can be used to trace the families of many living species into the remote past and to clarify some classifications. The fossil record has been invaluable, but it is still very incomplete; important fossils are being discovered every year. The fossil record also reveals many extinct species. For example, it is estimated that since birds first evolved, about 150 million years ago, a total of about 150,000 species of birds have existed, but only about 9000 exist today (Sibley and Ahlquist, 1990).

A more recent aid to classification is the development of molecular techniques that allow us to study genetic material and to measure genetic variation with precision. Analysis of genetic material—fragments of DNA molecules—from many species has confirmed many classifications and improved others. Furthermore, quantification of the amount of difference between base pairs in DNA samples from two species allows investigators to estimate the genealogical distance between them. (The method used in this quantification—nucleic acid hybridization—is described briefly in the Appendix.) Thus DNA analyses and comparisons help in constructing phylogenetic trees such as the one in Figure 6.1.

**IMPORTANT
METHOD**

In addition, DNA appears to change at a relatively steady average rate in all lineages of a given order of animals (Hillis et al., 1996). Thus the proportion of differences between DNA samples from two species can be used as a "molecular clock" to estimate how long ago they diverged from a common ancestor. The absolute times on the horizontal axis in Figure 6.1 should be considered with caution, however, because scientists disagree about the calibration of the molecular clocks. This debate does not lessen the value of the relative time periods; that is, the overall picture appears to be accurate even if future research expands or contracts the timescale.

Recently, small fragments of DNA have been obtained from insects fossilized in amber as long as 40 million years ago, helping us to discriminate among possible lines of descent of some modern insects and to test further the "clock" of changes in DNA over time (Poinar, 1994). A fictionalized version of this technique helped make millions of dollars for the writers and producers of the *Jurassic Park* movies.

At present, investigators use both morphological and molecular analyses to determine the evolutionary relationships among animals. Instances in which responses to similar ecological features bring about similarities in behavior or structure among animals that are only distantly related (that differ in genetic heritage) are referred to as **convergent evolution.** For example, the body forms of a tuna and a dolphin resemble each other because they each evolved for efficient swimming, even though the tuna is a fish and the dolphin is a mammal descended from terrestrial ancestors. This is an example of **homoplasy,** features that look the same, often due to convergent evolution.

By contrast, a **homology** is a resemblance based on common ancestry, such as the similarities in forelimb structures of mammals that we described earlier (see Figure 6.3). **Analogy** refers to similar function, although the structures may look different (e.g., the hand of a human and the trunk of an elephant are analogous).

IMPORTANT METHOD

Comparative Methods Help Us Study the Biological Mechanisms of Behavior

Comparisons of behavior and of neural mechanisms across different kinds of animals and across different ecological niches are common in biological psychology and related disciplines. We use such comparisons in every chapter of this book. Although studying only one species may yield important information, comparing two or more carefully chosen species or a large representative sample of species leads to a much deeper understanding of the phenomena being observed because the evolutionary framework provides additional explanatory power. Let's look at a few examples.

Some Ways of Obtaining Food Require Bigger Brains Than Others

Most species of animals spend much of their time and energy in the pursuit of food, often using elaborate strategies. Researchers have found that the strategies that different species employ to obtain food are correlated to brain size and structure. For example, mammals that eat food distributed in clusters that are difficult to find (such as ripe fruit) tend to have brains larger than those of related species whose food is rather uniformly distributed and easy to find (such as grass or leaves). Within several families of mammals, species that eat leaves or grass have brains that are relatively smaller than those of species that feed on fruit or insects that are distributed less densely and less uniformly. This relationship has been found among families of rodents, insectivores (such as shrews and moles), lagomorphs (such as rabbits and pikas; Clutton-Brock and Harvey, 1980), and primates (Mace et al., 1981).

Finding novel ways of obtaining food is related to the size of the forebrain in different orders of birds (L. Lefebvre et al., 1997). Investigators collected accounts of novel behavior from several ornithological journals (e.g., magpies digging up potatoes, house sparrows searching car radiator grilles for insects, crows dropping palm nuts in the paths of cars that run over and open them). Separate data sets were prepared for North America and the British Isles, and the numbers of innovations differed among bird orders in a similar fashion in both geographic zones. In both areas, more innovative species have relatively larger forebrains. The results suggest a directional selection for increased size of the forebrain to cope with environmental challenges and opportunities in new, flexible ways.

Some behavioral adaptations have been related to differences in relative sizes of certain structures within the brain. For example, some species of bats find their way and locate prey by hearing; others rely almost entirely on vision. In the midbrain, the auditory center (the inferior colliculus) is much larger in bats that depend on hearing; bats that depend on sight have a larger visual center (the superior colliculus). Families of birds that store bits of food for later use (e.g., the acorn woodpecker, Clark's nutcracker, or the black-capped chickadee) have a larger hippocampus relative to the forebrain and to body weight than do families of birds that do not store food (Sherry, 1992). This difference has been found among both North American species (Figure 6.4) and European species.

We will see in Chapters 17 and 18 that the hippocampus is important for memory formation, and in some species especially for spatial memory, which is needed to recover stored food. The families of birds that store food are no more closely related to each other than they are to other, non-food-storing families and subfamilies of birds. Thus food storers are not all descendants of an ancestral species that stored food and that also happened to possess a large hippocampus. Rather the evidence suggests that a large hippocampus is necessary for successful storage and recovery of food, and that several families of birds show convergent evolution for these attributes (Sherry, 1992).

Investigators have pushed this analysis further by asking, Among closely related species of birds that all store food, but in which some species depend more on stored food than others, is

6.4 Food-Storing in Birds as Related to Hippocampal Size Food-storing species of birds have twice as large a hippocampus in relation to their forebrain (the telencephalon) as do species that do not store food. Note that both axes on this graph are logarithmic. (After Sherry et al., 1989.)

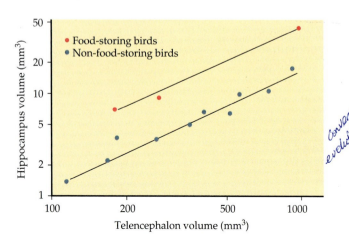

- Food-storing birds
- Non-food-storing birds

Hippocampus volume (mm³) vs. Telencephalon volume (mm³)

BOX 6.1 *To Each Its Own Sensory World*

Lifestyle differences among mammals are related to the organization of the cerebral cortex, as the examples here show. The rat (*Rattus norvegicus*) is nocturnal and uses its whiskers to find its way in the dark. About 28% of the representation of the rat's body surface in the cortex is devoted to the whiskers (vibrissae), whereas only about 9% of the body surface representation of the squirrel (*Sciurus carolinensis*) is devoted to the whiskers (see the figures; Huffman et al., 1999). In addition, the rat makes rather little use of vision, and its primary visual cortex (V1) is relatively small compared with that of the squirrel, which is diurnal.

The remarkable platypus (*Ornithorhynchus anatinus*) is an egg-laying mammal that lives in and around streams in eastern Australia and Tasmania. Because of its ducklike bill and webbed feet, some scientists thought it might be a hoax when the first skin preparations were brought to Europe at the beginning of the nineteenth century.

The platypus is largely nocturnal and dives into murky waters, closing its eyes, ears, and nostrils as it hunts for invertebrates, including insects, shrimp, and crayfish. How it senses its prey remained a mystery until the 1980s, when investigators found that

the main sensory organ of the platypus is its bill, which is about 7 cm long in a 160-cm-long adult. The bill has about 16 longitudinal stripes of receptors: stripes of touch receptors alternating with touch-electrical receptors (see the figure) (Manger et al., 1998). As the platypus moves its bill underwater, it can detect prey by both the mechanical ripples and the changes in electrical fields they cause. In keeping with the importance of the bill in locating prey, almost all of the somatosensory cortex (S1 and S2) of the platypus is devoted to the bill (see the figure), and the primary visual (V1) and auditory (A1) areas are small (Krubitzer et al., 1995).

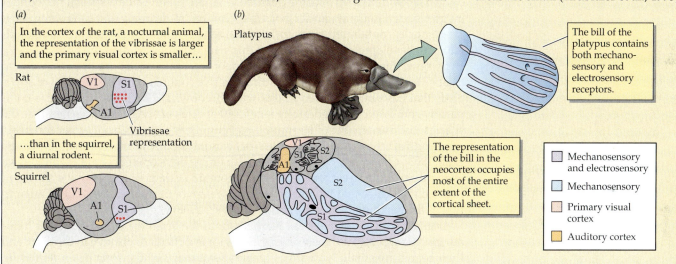

(a) In the cortex of the rat, a nocturnal animal, the representation of the vibrissae is larger and the primary visual cortex is smaller… …than in the squirrel, a diurnal rodent.

Rat — V1, S1, A1 — Vibrissae representation

Squirrel — V1, A1, S1

(b) Platypus

The bill of the platypus contains both mechanosensory and electrosensory receptors.

The representation of the bill in the neocortex occupies most of the entire extent of the cortical sheet.

V1, S1, S2, A1, S2, S1

☐ Mechanosensory and electrosensory
☐ Mechanosensory
☐ Primary visual cortex
☐ Auditory cortex

there a relationship between the amount of storing and the relative size of the hippocampus? The answer is yes for species of corvids (including jays and nutcrackers) (Basil et al., 996) and for species of parids (including chickadees and titmice) (Hampton et al., 1995). So even within closely related species, reliance on storing and recovering food appears to have been a selection pressure that has led to larger hippocampal size.

Box 6.1 provides other examples of solutions that different species employ to solve the dilemmas of adaptation. As a general rule, the relative size of a brain region is a good guide to the importance of the function of that region for the adaptations of the species. In this sense "more is better," but even small brain size is compatible with some complex behavior, as we will see in many instances in this book. Our understanding of how these differences in size and structure of the brain promote behavioral specializations should help us understand the neural basis of human behavior. For example, the size of some regions in the human temporal lobes seems to be related to language function (see Chapter 19).

EVOLUTION AT WORK

Birdsong Is Related to Brain Structure

In recent years songbirds that are able to learn their songs (rather than inheriting them) have become a model for studies of vocal learning. Of the 23 orders of birds, only three orders learn their songs: the perching birds (Passeriformes), such as canaries, mockingbirds, and crows; the hummingbirds (Trochiliformes); and the parrots (Psittaciformes). Vocal learning in these species is necessary for reproduction—for example, for attracting mates and defending territory. The other birds that sing develop their species-specific vocalizations even if they are raised in isolation and do not hear another bird. The three orders of birds that learn their songs include more species than all the 20 other orders together, suggesting that plasticity of brain and behavior permits extensive specialization for different ecological niches and consequently a greater variety of species.

A phylogenetic tree of the 9000 species of living birds, constructed on the basis of comparisons of DNA (Sibley and Ahlquist, 1990), shows that the three orders that exhibit vocal learning are not closely related and have not shared a common ancestor for tens of millions of years. In fact, each of the orders with vocal learning is more closely related to some orders that do not learn their song than to the other orders that do learn their songs. These relationships suggest that innate, unlearned development of vocalization is the primitive condition and that song learning is an example of convergent evolution in the three relevant orders—perching birds, hummingbirds, and parrots (Brenowitz, 1991).

In the 1970s, investigators began to study the brains of canaries to determine which structures govern their singing (Nottebohm et al., 1976). This and subsequent research (which we will take up in some detail in Chapter 19) revealed a special network of interconnected forebrain nuclei that are specialized for learning and controlling song. These nuclei contain receptors for gonadal sex hormones, and the hormones modulate the development and activity of this song control system in the brain.

By now, this hormone-sensitive system of forebrain nuclei has been found in at least 47 species of songbirds, including the five (out of six) main families of songbirds that have been studied in this way (Brenowitz, 1991). Furthermore, a comparative study of song repertoire size in 40 species of songbirds revealed that the species that are capable of learning larger numbers of songs have larger forebrain song control centers than do species that cannot acquire as many songs (DeVoogd et al., 1993). Only a few orders of birds with innate development of vocalization have been inspected for the presence of this forebrain system, and none have shown it. Research indicates that the forebrain song system of parrots is essentially similar to that of the perching birds (Durand et al., 1997, 1998).

Until recently, little had been learned about the brain regions involved in hummingbird songs because their singing behavior is difficult to observe in captivity and their brains are small. Now investigators have mapped the song brain regions in hummingbirds by monitoring messenger RNA (mRNA) synthesis for the transcriptional regulator *ZENK*, a gene that is expressed when neurons are activated (Jarvis et al., 2000). First the investigators used *ZENK* expression to map song regions in the brains of perching birds (Mello and Clayton, 1994) (Figure 6.5) and parrots (Jarvis and Mello, 2000). The results corresponded well with results of studies using electrophysiological mapping.

Hummingbirds were studied in a nature reserve in Brazil. Tree perches were located where individual birds sang frequently, and birds were trapped early in the morning in one of three conditions: silent controls (birds that were caught before the start of the dawn chorus), hearing-only (birds that were caught around the same time after hearing a half-hour recording of singing by an individual of the same species, but that did not sing in response), hearing and vocalizing (birds that were caught early in the morning after hearing song and singing one or more song bouts per minute during the half-hour period). The birds were sacrificed immediately upon capture, and their brains were processed for *ZENK* mRNA expression.

Compared to silent controls, hearing-only birds showed hearing-induced *ZENK* expression in seven brain areas. Compared to hearing-only birds, hearing and vocalizing birds showed vocalizing-induced *ZENK* expression in eight brain areas—seven in the telencephalon and one in the midbrain. *ZENK* expression in these eight structures was proportional to the number of song bouts produced in the half-hour song period.

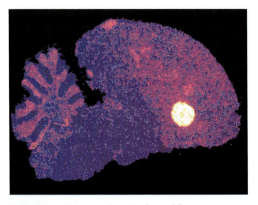

6.5 Gene Expression Induced by Singing In situ hybirdization of the brain of a zebra finch that had been singing shows high expression (white and yellow) of the *ZENK* gene in a song region known as area X (see Chapter 19). (Photograph courtesy of David Clayton.)

The seven telencephalic areas with vocalizing-induced *ZENK* expression in hummingbird brains correspond to the seven song regions found in parrots and perching birds. *ZENK* is an example of a class of genes called immediate early genes (IEGs)—that is, genes that show rapid but transient increases in response to extracellular signals such as neurotransmitters and growth factors, as we will discuss in Chapter 18.

To learn whether the pattern of activation of *ZENK* by song production is specific to *ZENK* or more general, the investigators studied the expression of both *ZENK* and another IEG, *c-jun*, in canaries. The regional patterns of vocalization-induced expression were similar for the two immediate early genes (Nastiuk et al., 1994). Mapping by gene expression was more rapid and economical than by other techniques. The power of the IEG expression technique is responsible for its increasing use to map functional circuits in the brain.

What are the evolutionary implications of the fact that the three song-learning orders of birds (out of 23 orders) have very similar brain song regions? Because the three song-learning orders are separated phylogenetically by nonlearners, it has been thought that the three avian learning groups evolved vocal learning independently. If so, the evolution of similar brain structures suggests strong constraints. Alternatively, vocal learning and the associated brain structures may have been present in a distant common ancestor and have been lost in most orders, possibly because of the expense of maintaining vocal learning and associated structures, with many orders evolving in adaptive zones that did not require complex learned vocalizations. Or, avian nonlearners may possess some rudimentary forebrain vocal areas that have not yet been identified.

Thus by investigating the brain structures of a relatively small number of species that have been carefully chosen for their phylogenetic relationships and their song ability, researchers are making important progress toward understanding the evolution of birdsong. If investigators had studied an equal number of species chosen at random among the 9000 current species of birds, the results would have been much less informative and less able to yield general conclusions.

Box 6.2 gives further answers to the question, Why should we study particular species?

Nervous Systems Differ Widely in Structure

Having compared aspects of the nervous systems of a few species, let's look more broadly at the variety of nervous systems of a few phyla of animals. Figure 6.6 shows the gross anatomy of the nervous system of some representative animals.

A leading researcher in comparative neurosciences, Theodore H. Bullock (1984), asserts, "We cannot expect truly to comprehend either ourselves or how the nervous system works until we gain insight into this range of nervous systems, from nerve nets and simple ganglia in sea anemones and flatworms to the optic lobes of dragon flies, octopuses, and lizards to the cerebral cortex in primates" (p. 473). Faced with the enormous complexity of the vertebrate brain, with its billions of nerve cells, researchers have turned instead to the nervous systems of some invertebrates that have only hundreds or thousands of neurons. An exhaustive description of the "wiring diagram" of the nervous system and how it relates to behavior may be possible with these invertebrates.

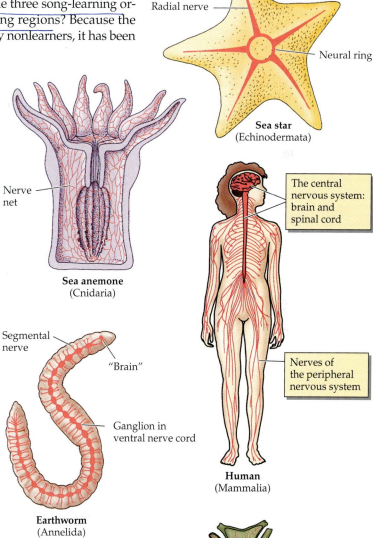

6.6 A Comparative View of Nervous Systems Gross anatomy of the nervous system in representative animals from five phyla shows some of the variety.

Radial nerve

Neural ring

Sea star
(Echinodermata)

The central nervous system: brain and spinal cord

Nerves of the peripheral nervous system

Human
(Mammalia)

Nerve net

Sea anemone
(Cnidaria)

Segmental nerve

"Brain"

Ganglion in ventral nerve cord

Earthworm
(Annelida)

Head ganglia

Abdominal ganglion

Aplysia
(Mollusca)

BOX 6.2 *Why Should We Study Particular Species?*

With all the species that are available, why should we choose certain ones for study? Investigators usually follow several criteria in selecting species for study. The following are several examples:

1. *Outstanding features.* Some species are champions at various behaviors and abilities, such as sensory discrimination (e.g., the acute auditory localization of the owl, or the extremely fine visual acuity of the eagle) or control of movement (e.g., the flight behavior of the housefly). These abilities are often linked to highly specialized neuronal structures. Such structures incorporate and optimize particular neuronal designs that may be less conspicuous in organisms that lack these superior capacities (Bullock, 1984, 1986). Study of such species may yield general principles that apply to other species. The female spotted hyena appears to have a penis and is dominant over the smaller male; this sex "reversal" is caused by unusual hormonal adaptations that help illuminate sexual development (see Chapter 12).

2. *Convenience.* Some species, such as the laboratory rat, are particularly convenient for study because they breed well in the laboratory, are relatively inexpensive to maintain, are not rare or endangered, have relatively short life spans, and have

been studied extensively already, so there is a good base of knowledge about them at the outset. In addition, they may serve as good models because their morphology and behavior show clear relationships to other species. Other species are convenient because they offer advantages for certain methods of study. For example, some mollusks have relatively simple nervous systems that aid in tracing neural circuits. The fruit fly *Drosophila* is excellent for genetic studies because it has a relatively simple genome and a short time period between generations; furthermore, investigators have been increasingly impressed by the large number of DNA sequences that *Drosophila* shares with mammals, including humans (R. Lewis, 1998).

3. *Comparison.* Close relationships between species that behave very differently enable the testing of hypotheses. For example, whereas in some closely related species of rodents the home ranges of males and females differ in size, in others they do not. Comparison of these species tests whether differences in maze-solving ability are associated with the size of the home range and with the size of the hippocampus (see Chapter 17).

4. *Preservation.* Studies of rare and/or endangered species can help pre-

serve these animals. Because of their predicament, these species are seldom studied in the laboratory, but they may be investigated in field studies or in zoos.

5. *Economic importance.* Species that are economically important include agricultural animals (e.g., sheep and cows), animals that furnish valuable products (e.g., fish), predators on agricultural animals (e.g., wolves), or destroyers of crops (e.g., elephants). Studying these animals can provide information that helps increase production and/or decrease losses.

6. *Treatment of disease.* Some species are subject to the same diseases as other species and therefore are valuable models for investigation (here we focus on diseases of the nervous system and endocrine [hormonal] system). Examples include certain kinds of mice, which provide a model for the behavior and anatomy of Down syndrome (see Chapter 7); baboons and certain breeds of dogs, which are prone to seizures (see Chapter 3); several breeds of dogs that are afflicted by narcolepsy (see Chapter 14); some strains of rodents that provide models for depression (see Chapter 16); and *Drosophila* and mice, which now provide models for investigations of Parkinson's disease (see Chapter 11).

Theodore H. Bullock

Complex aspects of behavior, such as memory and species-typical eating or aggressive behaviors, have been explored in an exciting manner in several invertebrates that have become laboratory favorites. First, however, let's start our comparison with brains closer to our own.

Mammals Share Main Brain Structures

A comparison of human and rat brains illustrates basic similarities and differences (Figure 6.7). Each of the main structures in the human brain has a counterpart in the rat brain. This comparison could be extended to much greater detail, down to nuclei, fiber tracts, and types of cells. Even small structures in the brains of one mammalian species are found to have exact correspondence in the brains of others. All mammals also have similar types of neurons and similar organization of the cerebellar cortex and the cerebral cortex.

The differences between the brains of humans and the brains of other mammals are mainly quantitative; that is, they concern both actual and relative sizes of the whole brain, brain regions, and brain cells. Whereas the brain of an adult human being weighs about 1400 g, that of an adult rat weighs a little less than 2 g. In each case,

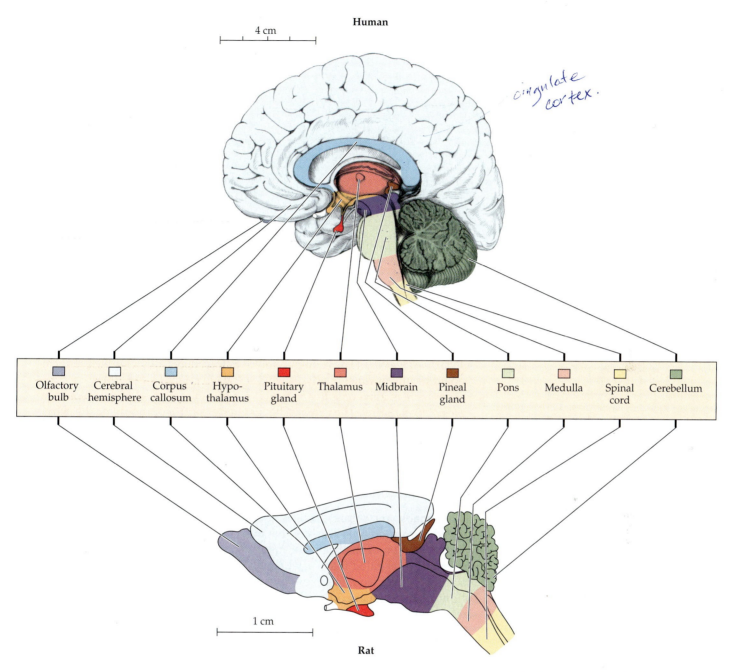

Human

4 cm

cingulate cortex.

| Olfactory bulb | Cerebral hemisphere | Corpus callosum | Hypo-thalamus | Pituitary gland | Thalamus | Midbrain | Pineal gland | Pons | Medulla | Spinal cord | Cerebellum |

1 cm

Rat

however, the brain represents about 2% of total body weight. The cerebral hemispheres occupy a much greater proportion of the brain in the human than in the rat, and the surface of the human brain shows prominent gyri and fissures, whereas the rat cerebral cortex is smooth and unfissured.

The rat has, relatively, much larger olfactory bulbs than the human. This difference is probably related to the rat's much greater use of the sense of smell. The size of neurons also differs significantly between human and rat; in general, human neurons are much larger than rat neurons. In addition, there are great differences in the extent of dendritic trees. Figure 6.7 gives some examples of size differences among neurons of different species.

All Vertebrate Nervous Systems Share Certain Main Features but Differ in Others

Now let's extend our view to the basic features of vertebrate nervous systems. The following are main features of the vertebrate nervous system, some of which are illustrated for humans in Figure 6.6:

6.7 Human and Rat Brains Compared   Midsagittal views of the right hemisphere of human and rat brains show that the main structures are the same in both, and they have the same topological relations to each other. Note, however, that the cerebral hemispheres are relatively much larger in the human brain, whereas the rat has a relatively larger midbrain and olfactory bulb. (The rat brain has been enlarged about six times in linear dimensions in relation to the human brain.)

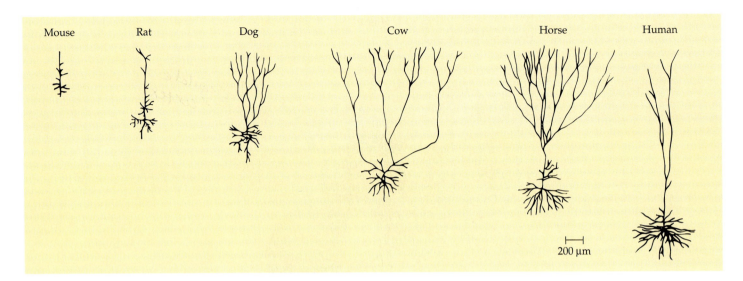

| Mouse | Rat | Dog | Cow | Horse | Human |

⊢——⊣
200 μm

6.8 The Same Kind of Neuron in Different Species   These pyramidal neurons from the motor cortices of different mammals are all drawn to the same scale. (After Barasa, 1960.)

EVOLUTION AT WORK

- *Development from a hollow dorsal neural tube* (see Chapters 2 and 7).
- *Bilateral symmetry.* (The human cerebral hemispheres are not quite identical anatomically or functionally, as we'll see in Chapters 18 and 19.)
- *Segmentation.* Pairs of spinal nerves extend from each level of the spinal cord.
- *Hierarchical control.* The cerebral hemispheres control or modulate the activity of the spinal cord.
- *Separate systems.* The central nervous system (brain and spinal cord) is clearly separate from the peripheral nervous system.
- *Localization of function.* Certain functions are controlled by certain locations in the central nervous system.

Presumably vertebrates have all of these features in common because they descended from a common ancestor that possessed the same neural features. Anatomical examination of the brains of many classes of the 10,000 to 20,000 vertebrate species have revealed that vertebrates with larger bodies tend to possess larger brains. No matter what the size, however, all vertebrate brains have the same major subdivisions. The main differences among vertebrates are the absolute and relative sizes of different regions.

Within the major subdivisions of the brain, there are also important differences in structure among the vertebrate classes. These differences are especially noticeable for the organization of the forebrain, which has led different investigators to give different answers to such questions as this: What part(s) of the telencephalon of birds correspond to the neocortex in mammals? In a recent review of this problem, Striedter (1997) proposes that it can be solved by the inclusion of embryological patterns of telencephalic organization in the comparative analysis. Because the early developmental stages of the vertebrate classes resemble each other more than the adults do, the embryological data reveal intermediate patterns of organization that provide support for a set of homologies of parts of the forebrain.

Invertebrates Show Enormous Diversity

Most of the animals on Earth are invertebrates, animals without backbones. (In fact, the order Coleoptera [the beetles] contains far more animal species than any other, so it's been said that, to a first approximation, every species is a beetle!) The invertebrates far exceed vertebrates in many ways, including number, diversity of appearance, and variety of habitat. Whereas invertebrates make up 17 phyla, the vertebrates are only a part of the phylum Chordata (the chordates). The abundance of invertebrates is clearly demonstrated by the following estimate: For each person on Earth, there are at least 1 billion insects, which are just one type of invertebrate.

Neuroscientists focus on certain invertebrates because of the relative simplicity of their nervous systems and the great varieties of behavioral adaptation they display. Simplicity of structure has not ruled out some forms of behavior, such as some types of learning and memory, that are also seen in more complex organisms. Furthermore, invertebrates possess elaborate sensory systems that permit detection of some stimuli with exquisite sensitivity. Every conceivable niche on land, sea, or air has been successfully exploited by one or more invertebrate species.

With all the diversity of invertebrate nervous systems, we cannot select a few as representative, but we will describe some features of the nervous systems of mollusks and insects in preparation for our treatment of research on these animals in later chapters.

The mollusk Aplysia. Slugs, snails, clams, and octopuses are a few of the almost 100,000 species of mollusks. These soft-bodied animals display an enormous range of complexity in both body and behavior. Some mollusks, such as the octopus, show excellent problem-solving capabilities; other mollusks exist in a near parasitic form. The head end of a mollusk usually consists of a mouth, tentacles, and eyes. The typical structure also includes a footlike appendage and a visceral section that is frequently covered by a protective envelope called the mantle. A simple marine mollusk, *Aplysia*, has gained considerable notoriety because it has been used extensively in cellular studies of learning and memory (see Chapter 18). Here we review briefly the principal structures of the nervous system of *Aplysia*.

The nervous system of *Aplysia* consists of four paired ganglia at the head end that form a ring around the esophagus (Figure 6.9a). Below these head ganglia is a fused abdominal ganglion. The ganglia are interconnected by tracts. One head ganglion innervates the eyes and the tentacles; a second head ganglion innervates the mouth muscles. The other two paired ganglia innervate the foot. The abdominal ganglion controls such major visceral functions as circulation, respiration, and reproduction.

Comprehensive research by Eric Kandel and his collaborators has led to detailed maps of **identifiable neurons** in these ganglia, especially the abdominal ganglion. (These cells are called identifiable because they are large and similar from one *Aplysia* to the next, so investigators can recognize them and give them code names.) Because the nervous system of *Aplysia* includes many identifiable cells (Figure 6.9b), it has become possible to trace the circuits that mediate various behaviors in this animal. Work with *Aplysia* has also provided much detailed understanding of the molecular basis of learning (Kandel et al., 1986; Krasne and Glanzman, 1995), supporting the view that simpler invertebrate nervous systems can provide useful models for examining complex features of the human brain.

Insect nervous systems. Insects, of which there are more than 1 million living species, are remarkable in the animal kingdom for color, form, and presence in a great variety of habitats. The life cycle of many insects includes striking morphological changes (e.g., from caterpillar to butterfly) that not only affect the external form of the animal but also involve a resculpturing of the nervous system.

The sensory organs of insects display great variety and sensitivity. Success in the battle for survival has affected this group of animals in many distinctive ways, and it is easy to appreciate why neuroscientists have focused much research on the neural mechanisms of the behavior of insects. In spite of the diversity of insect body form, the central nervous systems of insects are remarkably similar: They vary "astonishingly little from the most primitive to the most advanced" (Edwards and Palka, 1991, p. 391).

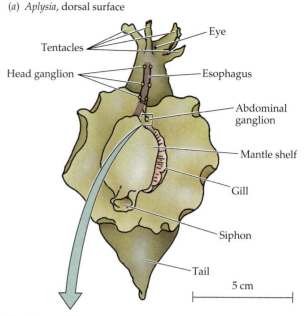

(a) Aplysia, dorsal surface

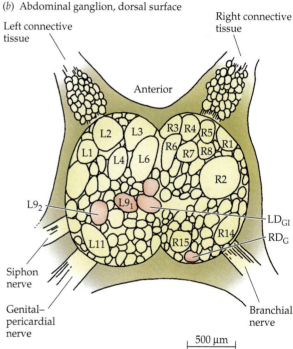

(b) Abdominal ganglion, dorsal surface

6.9 The Nervous System of *Aplysia*
The sea snail *Aplysia* has a relatively simple nervous system with large identifiable neurons, which has made it a popular species in research on the neural basis of learning and memory. (*a*) In this dorsal view of the entire organism, the neural ganglia are shown in yellow and connecting nerve cords in black. (*b*) In this dorsal view of an abdominal ganglion, several identified neurons are labeled. Neurons in the circuit that is involved in habituation, a learned decreased response to a repeated stimulus, are shown in pink. (Part *a* after Kandel, 1976; *b* from Frazier et al., 1967.)

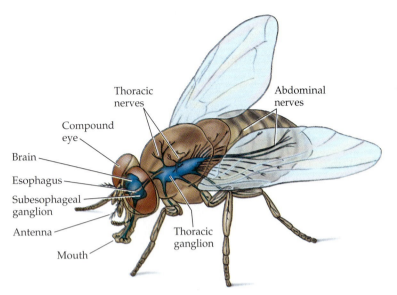

Thoracic nerves

Abdominal nerves

Compound eye

Brain

Esophagus

Subesophageal ganglion

Antenna

Mouth

Thoracic ganglion

6.10 The Nervous System of a Typical Insect, *Drosophila melanogaster* In insects, such as this fruit fly, the brain with its subdivisions is linked via bundles of axons (connectives) to groups of ganglia in the thorax and abdomen. The brain, connectives, and ganglia are shown here in blue.

The gross outline of the adult insect nervous system consists of a brain in the head end and ganglia in each body segment behind the head (Figure 6.10). Bundles of axons connect ganglia to the brain. The number of ganglia varies; in some insects all the ganglia of the chest and abdomen fuse into one major collection of cells. In other insects there are as many as eight ganglia in a chain. The brain itself contains three major compartments: protocerebrum, deutocerebrum, and tritocerebrum. The most complex part of the insect brain is the protocerebrum, which consists of a right and a left lobe, each continuous with a large optic lobe, an extension of the compound eye. Within the optic lobe are distinct masses of cells that receive input from the eye as well as from the brain. Electrical stimulation of sites within the protocerebrum of various insects elicits complex behaviors.

The relative sizes of different components of the protocerebrum differ among insects, and some of these variations may be particularly relevant to behavioral variations. For example, a portion of the protocerebrum called the corpus pedunculatum is especially well developed in social insects, and the behavior of these animals tends to be more elaborate than that displayed by solitary insects.

One prominent feature of the nerve cord of insects is **giant axons**—fibers much bigger in diameter than most. The properties of these giant fibers have been explored in some interesting studies, using many different orders of insects (Edwards and Palka, 1991). These insects have receptive organs (the cerci) in the tail that can be excited by movement of the air; these receptors connect to giant interneurons with very large axons that ascend the nerve cord to the head. Along the way, these axons excite some motor neurons.

This system originated to allow insects to escape from predation by retreating rapidly. In many insects (e.g., cockroaches) this system still functions as an escape system; in other insects the cerci and the connections of the giant interneurons have been modified so that they also play a role in reproductive behavior (in crickets) or help regulate flight maneuvers (in grasshoppers). Whatever its function in a particular species, the basic organization and cellular composition of this system appears to have remained the same for a very long time, perhaps as long as 400 million years (Edwards and Palka, 1991).

Vertebrate Nervous Systems Differ from Those of Invertebrates

To summarize some of the features of vertebrate and invertebrate nervous systems that we have described up to now, let's compare them:

- *Basic plan.* All vertebrates and most invertebrates have a basic plan that consists of a central nervous system and a peripheral nervous system.
- *Brain.* All vertebrates and many invertebrates, including mollusks and insects, have brains. The general evolutionary trend in both vertebrates and invertebrates is toward increasing brain control over ganglia at lower levels of the body.
- *Number of neurons.* Whereas vertebrate brains usually have many neurons devoted to information processing, invertebrate brains usually have fewer but larger and more complicated neurons that manage key integrative processes.
- *Identifiable neurons.* Some of the large invertebrate neurons are identifiable. In contrast, there are very few cases of identifiable neurons in vertebrates.
- *Ganglion structure.* Vertebrate ganglia have the cell bodies on the inside and the dendrites and axons on the outside. Ganglia in invertebrate nervous systems have a characteristic structure: an outer rind that consists of monopolar cell bodies and an inner core that consists of the extensions of the cell bodies forming a dense neuropil (a network of axons and dendrites).

- *Axons and neural conduction.* Many axons of mammalian neurons are surrounded by myelin, which helps them conduct impulses faster than the unmyelinated invertebrate axons (see Chapter 2). Invertebrates have no myelin to speed nerve conduction, but many have a few giant axons to convey messages rapidly in escape systems.
- *Structural changes.* The structure of the nervous system undergoes large-scale changes in some invertebrates during metamorphosis. Vertebrates show important changes in neural structure during development, but these changes are not as dramatic as the changes during invertebrate metamorphoses.
- *Location in the body.* In vertebrates the central nervous system is encased in the bony skull and spinal column. In many invertebrates the nervous system is built around the digestive tract.
- *Constancy.* The basic structure and connections of the insect nervous system have remained similar throughout hundreds of millions of years, even though body forms have varied greatly. The vertebrate nervous system has also maintained the same basic structure for hundreds of millions of years of evolution. Although differences in body form are less extreme among vertebrates than among insects, nevertheless many evolutionary changes have taken place in vertebrate brains.

The Evolution of Vertebrate Brains Can Be Related to Changes in Behavior

During the course of evolution the characteristics of the nervous system have changed progressively. One especially prominent change in the last 100 million years has been a general tendency for the brain size of vertebrates to increase, and the brains of our human ancestors showed a particularly striking increase in size during the last 2 million years. How, then, has the evolution of the brain been related to changes in behavioral capacity?

Present-Day Animals and Fossils Reveal Evolution of the Brain

We could learn more about the evolution of the brain by studying the brains of fossil animals. But brains themselves do not fossilize—at least, not literally. Two methods of analysis have proved helpful. One is to use the cranial cavity of a fossil skull to make a cast of the brain that once occupied that space. These casts (called **endo-casts;** the Greek *endon* means "within") give a reasonable indication of the size and shape of the brain.

The other method is to study present-day animals, choosing species that show various degrees of similarity to (or difference from) ancestral forms. Although no modern animal is an ancestor of any other living form, some present-day species resemble ancestral forms more closely than others do. For example, present-day salamanders are much more similar to vertebrates of 300 million years ago than are any mammals. Among the mammals, some species, such as the opossum, resemble fossil mammals of 50 million years ago more than do other species, such as the dog. Thus a species such as the opossum is said to retain primitive or ancestral states of particular anatomical features. Anatomists who study the brains of living species can obtain far more detailed information from such species than from endocasts because they can investigate the internal structure of the brain: its nuclei, fiber tracts, and the circuitry formed by connections of its neurons.

EVOLUTION AT WORK

We must be careful not to interpret the evolutionary record as if it were a linear sequence. The main classes of vertebrates in Figure 6.11, for example, represent different lines or radiations of evolution that have been proceeding separately for at least 200 million years. Thus a particular evolutionary development may not have been available to mammals even if it occurred before the first mammals appeared. For example, among the sharks, some complex forms long ago evolved much larger brains than primitive sharks had, but the evolution of large brains in sharks cannot account for the large brains of mammals. The line of descent that eventually led to mammals had separated from that of the sharks before the large-brained sharks evolved.

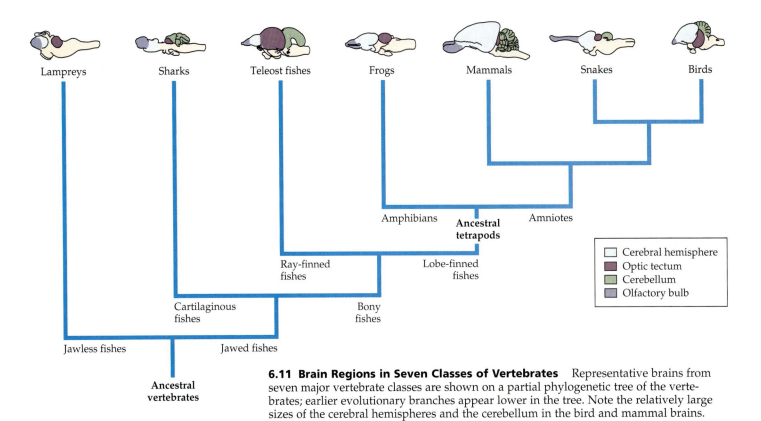

6.11 Brain Regions in Seven Classes of Vertebrates   Representative brains from seven major vertebrate classes are shown on a partial phylogenetic tree of the vertebrates; earlier evolutionary branches appear lower in the tree. Note the relatively large sizes of the cerebral hemispheres and the cerebellum in the bird and mammal brains. (Brains are not drawn to the same scale.)

Through Evolution, Vertebrate Brains Have Changed in Both Size and Organization

Let's consider some examples of changes in the size and organization of vertebrate brains. Even the living vertebrate that has the most primitive features—the lamprey (a jawless fish)—has a more complex brain than it used to be given credit for. The lamprey has not only the basic neural chassis of spinal cord, hindbrain, and midbrain, but also a diencephalon and a telencephalon. Its telencephalon has cerebral hemispheres and other subdivisions that are also found in the mammalian brain. So all vertebrate brains appear to have these regions.

One difference in basic brain structure between the lamprey and other vertebrates is that the cerebellum in the lamprey is very small and may consist of only some brainstem nuclei. The evolution of large cerebellar hemispheres in birds and mammals appears to be a case of parallel evolution from the small cerebellum in their common reptilian ancestor; the increased size of the cerebellum may be related to increased complexity of sensory processing and increased motor agility.

The differences among the brains of vertebrate species, then, lie not in the existence of basic subdivisions, but in their relative size and elaboration. At what stages of vertebrate evolution do various regions of the brain first become important? Large, paired optic lobes in its midbrain probably represent the lamprey's highest level of visual integration. In bony fishes, amphibians, and reptiles, the relatively large optic tectum in the midbrain is the main brain center for vision (see Figure 6.10). In birds and mammals, however, complex visual perception requires an enlarged telencephalon.

All mammals have a six-layered **neocortex** (from the Greek *neos*, "new," and the Latin *cortex*, "bark of a tree"). In more recent mammals the neocortex accounts for more than half the volume of the brain. In many larger mammals the neocortex is deeply fissured, so a large cortical surface covers the brain. In more recent mammals the cortex is the structure mainly responsible for many complex functions, such as the perception of objects. Regions of the brain that were responsible for perceptual functions in less encephalized animals—such as the midbrain optic lobes (in the lamprey) or the midbrain optic center (in the frog)—have in present-day mammals become visual reflex centers or way stations in the projection pathway to the cortex. (We will refer to the neocortex in almost every chapter, from Chapter 8 on, in connection with not only perception but also complex cognitive functions.)

Reptiles were the first vertebrates to exhibit relatively large cerebral hemispheres. Reptiles were also the first vertebrates to have a cerebral cortex, but their cortex has only three layers, unlike the six-layered neocortex of mammals. Part of the cortex in reptiles appears to be homologous to the three-layered hippocampus in mammals.

Brain Size Evolved Independently in Multiple Lineages

The brain is sometimes said to have increased in size with the appearance of each succeeding vertebrate class shown in Figure 6.11, but that statement is wrong in several respects. For one thing, there are exceptions among the present-day representatives of the various classes; for example, birds appeared later than mammals but do not have larger brains. For another, the generalization arose from the old way of viewing vertebrate evolution: as one linear series of increasing complexity rather than as a series of successive radiations.

If we compare animals of similar body size, there is considerable variation in brain size within each line of evolution. For example, within the ancient class of jawless fishes, the hagfishes, which are more recent members of that class, possess forebrains that are four times as large as those of lampreys of comparable body size. The increase of brain size in relation to behavioral capacity has been studied most thoroughly in the mammals.

EVOLUTION AT WORK

The encephalization factor.   The study of brain size is complicated by the wide range of body sizes. How are body size and brain size related? A general relationship was found first for present-day species and then applied successfully to fossil species. This function turns out to be useful in finding relationships between brain and behavior.

We humans long believed our own brains to be the largest, but this belief was upset in the seventeenth century when the elephant brain was found to weigh three times as much as our own. Later, whale brains were found to be even larger. These findings puzzled scholars, who took it for granted that human beings are the most intelligent of animals and therefore must have the largest brains.

To address this apparent discrepancy, they proposed that brain weight should be expressed as a fraction of body weight. On this basis humans outrank elephants, whales, and all other animals of large or moderate body size. But a mouse has about the same ratio of brain weight to body weight as a human, and the tiny shrew outranks a human on this measure. Without trying to prove that one species or another is "brainiest," we would like to know how much brain is needed to control and serve a body of a given size. From a comparative point of view, what is the general relation between brain size and body size?

When we plot brain weights and body weights for a large sample of mammals, we see some generalities (Figure 6.12a). All the plot points fall within a narrow polygon. Since both scales are logarithmic, the graph encompasses a great variety of animal sizes, and departures from the general rule tend to be minimized. The line drawn through the center of the polygon has a slope of about 0.69 (Harvey and Krebs, 1990). When the sample of mammals is divided into orders, each order shows a graph roughly like that of the mammalian class in Figure 6.12a, but the slopes vary. The overall slope of Figure 6.12a is largely determined by the differences among mammalian orders in brain weight–body weight relations (Harvey and Pagel, 1991).

COMPETING HYPOTHESES

Let's test the generality of this rule by examining the relation between brain weight and body weight for six vertebrate classes (Figure 6.12b). In each class except the mammals, the data yield a diagonal area with a slope of about three-fourths, so the relationship between brain weight and body weight is similar for all classes of vertebrates. But notice that the diagonal areas are displaced from each other vertically in Figure 6.12b: The mammals are highest, the bony fishes and reptiles clearly lower, and cyclostomes (e.g., the lamprey) the lowest. This configuration reflects the fact that

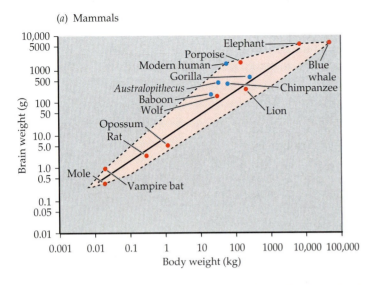

(a) Mammals

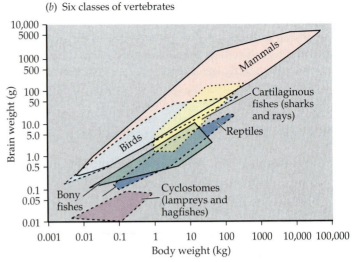

(b) Six classes of vertebrates

6.12 The Relation between Brain Weight and Body Weight (a) Brain weight is related here to body weight in several mammal species. Note that both axes are logarithmic, so the graph includes a wide range of brain weights and body weights. A polygon has been drawn to connect the extreme cases and include the whole sample. The diagonal line shows the basic relationship, with brain weight related to the 0.7 power of body weight. (b) Brain weight is plotted here against body weight for various species in six classes of vertebrates. Each class is represented by a polygon that includes a large sample of species in that class. The other classes of animals fall below the mammals, reflecting the fact that relative brain weight to body weight is smaller in those classes; they are less "brainy" than the mammals. (Part a after H. Stephan et al., 1981; b after Jerison, 1991.)

these classes have successively less brain weight for a body of the same size. Thus a mammal or a bird that weighs about 100 g (e.g., a rat or a blue jay) has a brain that weighs about 1 g, but a fish or a reptile of the same body weight has a brain that weighs only a little more than 0.1 g; a 100 g lamprey has a brain that weighs only about 0.03 g.

To take into account the variation both between classes and within classes, we need a measure of vertical distance above or below the diagonal line on the graph. This distance is usually called k and is different for each class and for each species. Because k indicates the relative amount of brain, it is called the **encephalization factor**. The greater the encephalization factor is for a species, the higher its value is above the diagonal line for its class. In Figure 6.12a the point for humans is farther above the diagonal line than the point for any other species. In terms of the encephalization factor, human beings rate higher than any other species. Figure 6.13 gives the values of the encephalization factor for several mammalian species.

Brain size has been studied in many species of mammals, both living and fossil. These studies have yielded clues about some selection pressures that have led to larger brains. For example, you may have heard the statement that dinosaurs became extinct because of the inadequacy of their small ("walnut-sized") brains (see Figure 6.14). Is this hypothesis correct?

COMPETING HYPOTHESES

Examination of endocasts of dinosaur brains and use of the equation that relates estimated brain weight to body weight show that dinosaur brain weights fit the relationship for reptiles shown in Figure 6.12b. For example, the brain of *Tyrannosaurus rex* probably weighed about 700 g—only half the size of the human brain, but much heavier than a walnut and appropriate for a reptile of its size—so it seems unlikely that dinosaurs perished because of a lack of brains (Jerison, 1991). A more likely cause of their demise is climate change, perhaps caused by collision of an asteroid with Earth.

Evolution of brain size. As the brain has evolved, it has shown adaptive size changes both in specific regions and overall; this adaptation illustrates both the

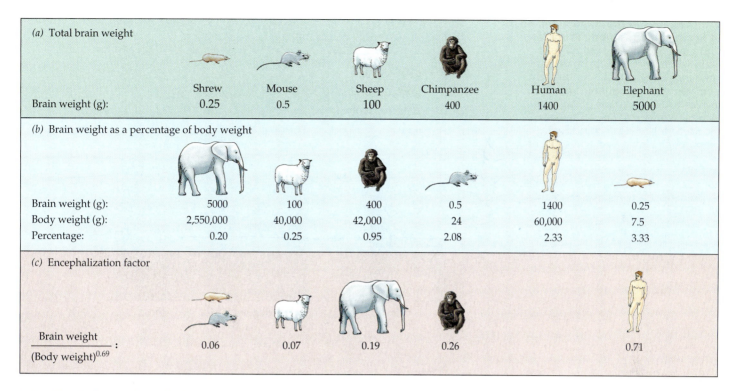

(a) Total brain weight						
	Shrew	Mouse	Sheep	Chimpanzee	Human	Elephant
Brain weight (g):	0.25	0.5	100	400	1400	5000

(b) Brain weight as a percentage of body weight						
Brain weight (g):	5000	100	400	0.5	1400	0.25
Body weight (g):	2,550,000	40,000	42,000	24	60,000	7.5
Percentage:	0.20	0.25	0.95	2.08	2.33	3.33

(c) Encephalization factor						
$\dfrac{\text{Brain weight}}{(\text{Body weight})^{0.69}}$:	0.06	0.07	0.19	0.26		0.71

6.13 Who Is the Brainiest? For this sample of small to large mammals, the answer depends on what measure is used: total brain weight (*a*), brain weight as a percentage of body weight (*b*), or the encephalization factor (*c*). For each measure, the animals are ranked here from lowest value to highest.

specificity and the continuity among species that we mentioned in Chapter 1. Certain capabilities, such as food foraging or birdsong, have been linked to sizes of particular brain regions, as we saw earlier in this chapter. In contrast, some other capabilities are related to overall neocortical volume rather than to the volume of any particular region of cortex; this relationship suggests that the amount of cortex devoted to some capabilities could increase only as the result of an increase in total cortical volume, although this seems like an inefficient and expensive way to increase the tissue related to a specific function.

The conclusion that changes occur in the overall size of the brain rather than in specific brain regions is consistent with the concept that overall developmental factors and programs (which we will consider in Chapter 7) severely constrain the magnitude of local adaptations. Supporting this conclusion is the finding that if the weight of the brain of any mammalian species is known, the weight of each of its parts can be predicted (Finlay and Darlington, 1995).

To study this relationship, investigators used data published by H. Stephan and coworkers (1981) on sizes of the main parts of the brain in 131 species of mammals—insectivores, bats, prosimians, and simians (including *Homo sapiens*). Their data set had the advantages, for comparative study, of including a large number of species, a wide range of ecological niches (including terrestrial, arboreal [tree-dwelling], burrowing, amphibious, and flying), and a wide range of body weights (2 to 105,000 g) and brain sizes (60 to 1,252,000 mm^3). Another advantage was the fact that the 11 brain divisions measured constitute the entire brain. Because of the wide range of sizes, the logarithms of the sizes were used in the analyses.

In logarithmic scales, the size of each brain structure, except for the olfactory bulb, showed a highly linear relation to brain weight. The size of each structure, except the olfactory bulb, correlated 0.96 or higher with to-

THE FAR SIDE By GARY LARSON

"The picture's pretty bleak gentlemen . . . The world's climates are changing, the mammals are taking over, and we all have a brain about the size of a walnut."

6.14 Was the Dinosaur Being Too Modest?

6.15 Changes in the Apportionment of Brain Regions among Primates

This graph shows the percentage of brain volume occupied by three different parts of the brain in four different primates. As the size of the brain increases, different parts of the brain increase at different rates. The size of the neocortex increases steadily as a proportion of brain size, while that of the cerebellum stays about the same, and the relative size of the medulla decreases. This generalization holds for all primates. (Data from H. Stephan et al., 1981.)

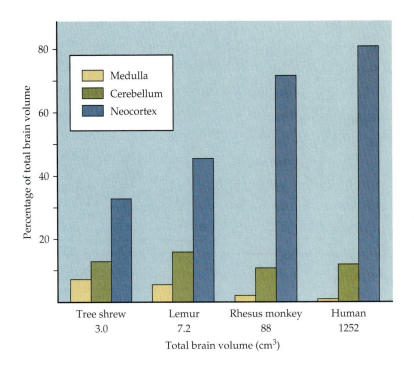

tal brain size; for the olfactory bulb the correlation was only 0.70. Thus for all parts of the brain except the olfactory bulb, a simple rule relates the size of the particular structure to total brain size.

Although the different parts of the brain increase regularly in size as total brain size increases, different parts increase at different rates. In a series of mammalian brains from small to large, the medulla becomes smaller relative to brain weight, the cerebellum keeps pace with brain weight, and the neocortex grows the most of all the parts; Figure 6.15 shows examples. Thus the proportion of brain devoted to each part differs in important ways from small to large brains.

The fact that the brain shows overall developmental constraints does not contradict the existence of some specific size adaptations of brain structures. For one thing, the logarithmic scales used by Finlay and Darlington tend to obscure subtle differences, so that even a threefold increase or decrease in size of a region is hardly noticed. For another thing, the brain divisions analyzed by Finlay and Darlington are relatively large, and most of them contain subdivisions that may vary in their development. For example, one of the brain divisions in their study is the mesencephalon, which includes both the inferior colliculus and the superior colliculus; as we have mentioned, the inferior colliculus is larger in animals that depend mainly on audition, whereas the superior colliculus is larger in animals that rely on vision. So although general constraints on development are strong, specific adaptations of brain regions do occur.

The rapid evolution of hominid brains.   Valuable information about evolutionary relationships between brain and behavior comes from the study of hominids—primates of the family Hominidae—of which we humans constitute the only living species. This approach is intriguing for the light it sheds on our distant ancestors, and it helps us understand how the body adapts to the environment through natural selection.

The structural and behavioral features that we consider characteristic of humans did not develop simultaneously (Falk, 1993). Our large brain is a relatively late development. According to one estimate, the trunk and arms of hominids reached their present form about 10 million years ago. (Note that the time span of human evolution and the dates of fossils have been altered by recent methods of dating. Not all authorities agree on these dates; they should be considered only approximate.)

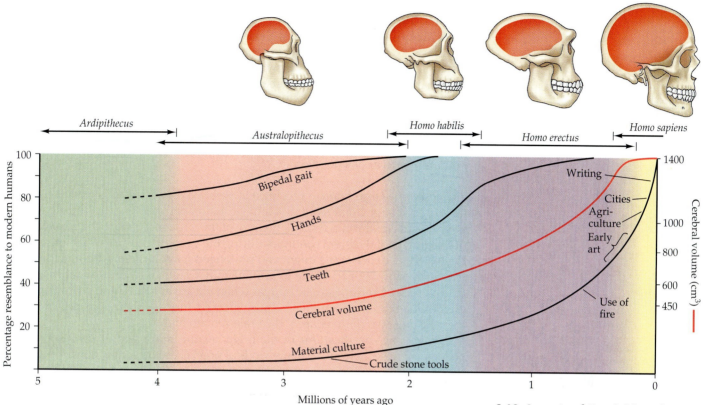

6.16 Aspects of Hominid Evolution
The bipedal (two-footed) gait was similar to that of modern humans even in *Australopithecus,* but cerebral volume reached its current size only in *Homo sapiens.* High culture (art, agriculture, cities, writing) emerged only relatively recently and was not associated with any further change in brain size. (After Tobias, 1980; updated with the assistance of Tim White.)

Hominids began walking on two feet more than 3.5 million years ago, and the oldest manufactured stone tools date back to about 2.6 million years ago (Figure 6.16).

The early toolmakers and users were bipedal hominids called australopithecines. Endocasts of their skulls show a brain volume of about 350 to 400 cm³ (see Figure 6.16), about the size of the modern chimpanzee brain. Chimpanzees do not make tools from stone, although some collect stones to use as tools, and a captive chimpanzee has been taught to make stone tools. But the australopithecines made and used crude stone tools in hunting and in breaking animal bones to eat. The ability to use tools reduced the selection pressure to maintain large jaws and teeth, and hominid jaws and teeth thus became steadily smaller than the ape's and more like those of modern human beings. Smaller teeth may also be related to increasing social tolerance, since canine teeth are often used in fighting among primate groups.

Even though the brain did not grow much among the australopithecines, never becoming larger than 600 cm³, they were successful animals, lasting—relatively unchanged—some 2 million years. Examination of ancient campsites suggests that these early hominids lived in nomadic groups of 20 to 50 individuals. They hunted and gathered plant foods—a new lifestyle that was continued by later hominids.

About 1.5 to 2 million years ago, when the australopithecines died out, *Homo erectus* appeared. This early representative of the genus *Homo* started with a cranial capacity of about 700 cm³ and a smaller face than *Australopithecus* had. As *Homo erectus* evolved, the brain became steadily larger, reaching the present-day volume of about 1400 cm³, and the face continued to become smaller. *Homo erectus* made elaborate stone tools, used fire, and killed large animals. Fossils and tools of *Homo erectus* are found throughout three continents, whereas those of the australopithecines are found only in Africa. *Homo erectus* may have represented a level of capacity and of cultural adaptation that allowed the hominids to expand into new environmental niches and to overcome barriers that kept earlier hominids in a narrower range.

Evolution of the brain and increased behavioral capacity advanced rapidly during the time of *Homo erectus* (see Figure 6.16). By the time *Homo sapiens* appeared, about 200,000 years ago, brain volume had reached the modern level. Thus after remaining little changed in size during about 2 million years of tool use by the australopithecines, the hominid brain almost tripled in volume during the next 1.5 million years.

The size of the human brain now appears to be at a plateau. The recent changes in human lifestyle shown in Figure 6.16—such as the appearance of language, the introduction of agriculture and animal husbandry (about 10,000 years ago), and urban living (the last few thousand years)—have all been accomplished and assimilated by a brain that does not seem to have altered in size since *Homo sapiens* appeared. The lack of further increase in brain size may be related to the costs of a large brain, a topic we consider next.

The costs of a large brain.   Having a large brain entails costs as well as benefits. Growth of a large brain requires a long gestation period, which is a burden on the mother, and childbirth is difficult because of the large size of the baby's head. Much of the growth of the brain continues during the years after birth, which means prolonged dependence of the infant and prolonged parental care. Although the brain makes up only about 2% of our total adult body weight, it requires about 15% of our cardiac output and metabolic budget when we are at rest. These percentages decrease when the body is active because muscles increase their demands, but even then the energy requirements of the brain remain high.

[handwritten margin note: uses 15% of all metabolized energy]

The genetic specifications of the brain require more than half of the human genome because there are so many kinds of brain cells and connections. These complex genetic messages are vulnerable to accidents; many of the known disorders of behavior are related to mutations of single genes. The evolution of large brains is especially remarkable when viewed in the context of these costs.

Selection pressures for increased brain size.   A change in any organ during evolution suggests that the change confers advantages with respect to survival. A rapid increase, as in the size of the hominid brain, implies strong advantages for survival. Can we then determine in what ways the evolution of the human brain accompanied and made possible certain changes in human behavior?

Unfortunately, we cannot directly examine the brains of australopithecines. All we have is the information about size and external shape that endocasts afford. Chimpanzees have brains of about the same size and shape as australopithecine brains, but chimpanzees in the wild have never been seen to fashion a stone tool, even crudely. They catch small game, but not in the frequent manner that is suggested by the collections of bones of prey found in association with australopithecine tools and fossils. Thus archaeological and behavioral evidence suggests that the australopithecine is our closer relative, further advanced toward human culture than is the chimpanzee.

Recent evidence, however, suggests that groups of chimpanzees at different sites in Africa do show cultural differences. Researchers from seven well-studied sites pooled their observations and found 39 different behaviors that are frequent at one or more but not at all seven locations (Whiten et al., 1999; see also de Waal, 1999, and Vogel, 1999). Most of these distinctive behaviors are related to obtaining food, including the use of stone and wooden tools, but others are social behaviors such as grooming or mating displays. Even monkey groups have been observed to develop and transmit cultural differences (Figure 6.17).

Keeping in mind that the brain organization, as well as the behavior, of the australopithecine probably differed somewhat from that of the chimpanzee, let's see how the modern human brain differs from the chimpanzee's brain to give us some clues about the evolution of the hominid brain. Prominent differences between the organization of the brain of *Homo sapiens* and that of the chimpanzee include the following:

- The human brain has larger motor and sensory cortical areas devoted to the hands.

6.17 Transmitting Culture
Culture has also been observed in non-human primates. For example, a population of Japanese macaques developed a set of behaviors that included washing food, playing in the water, and eating marine food items, and they transmitted this culture of water-related behaviors from generation to generation. (Courtesy of Frans B. M. de Waal.)

- In both the human brain and the chimpanzee brain, parts of the limbic system are involved in vocalization. However, the human brain shows, in addition, large neocortical regions devoted to the production and perception of speech. Nonhuman primates have relatively smaller neocortical regions controlling vocalization.
- For speech, manual dexterity, and other functions, the human brain shows striking hemispheric specialization of functions. In the chimpanzee the right and left hemispheres seem more equivalent in function.
- A controversial question is whether human prefrontal cortex (i.e., the cortex anterior to the motor cortex) is relatively larger in the human brain than would be predicted in an ape with a brain as large as a human's. Deacon (1997) estimates that it is about twice as large in the human brain, and he suggests that the development of the prefrontal cortex permitted more varied and more elaborate processing of information and may have underlain the emergence of symbolic thinking. On the other hand, Semendeferi and colleagues (Semendeferi et al., 1997; Semendeferi and Damasio, 2000) measured brains of humans and of apes by magnetic resonance scanning and found that neither the frontal cortex as a whole nor its main regions are relatively larger in the human brain than in the ape brain.

In trying to account for the evolution of the human brain and for the special capabilities of *Homo sapiens*, different theorists have emphasized different behavioral traits: "Dexterity and tool use, language, group hunting, various aspects of social structure, and the ability to plan for the future have all been proposed as primary in the cascade of changes leading to the constellation of traits we now possess" (Finlay and Darlington, 1995, p. 1583).

From their analysis of the evolution of the mammalian brain, Finlay and Darlington suggest that the multiple facets and rapid rate of human evolution may be explained by the fact that large primates are on the part of the curve relating neocortex weight to brain weight where small increases in brain weight are associated with large increases in neocortex weight. Selection for any single cognitive ability might therefore cause, in parallel, greater processing capacity for all the other abilities. They suggest that the neocortex, as a general-purpose processor, may allow "the organism to take advantage of the extra brain structure in ways not directly selected for during evolution." Charles Darwin (in F. Darwin, 1888) made almost the same point in the nineteenth century:

COMPETING HYPOTHESES

In many cases, the continued development of a part—for instance the beak of a bird or the teeth of a mammal—would not aid the species in gaining its food, or for any other object; but with man we can see no definite limit to the continual development of the brain and mental faculties, as far as advantage is concerned. (p. 169)

The survival advantage of larger brains does not hold only for human beings, or primates, or mammalian predators and prey. It would even be too limited to maintain, as Shaw's Don Juan does in the epigraph at the beginning of this book, that large brains are the specialty of the mammalian line. Within each line of vertebrate evolution relative brain size varies: The more recently arrived species usually has the larger encephalization factor. Furthermore, in each vertebrate line it is the dorsal part of the telencephalon that has expanded and differentiated in the species with more elaborated capabilities. As we find more such common responses to selection pressures, they may reveal the "rules" of how nervous systems adapt and evolve.

A different approach to the rapid expansion of the human brain over the last 1.5 million years is in terms of Darwin's second evolutionary principle, that of sexual selection. Geoffrey Miller (2000) suggests that natural selection to obtain food and shelter is not likely to account completely for the large brain and complex intelligence of *Homo sapiens*. In fact, he notes, brain size tripled in our ancestors between 2.5 million years ago and 200,000 years ago, yet during this period our ancestors continued to make the same kind of stone axes. Only after the human brain stopped expanding did technological progress develop, so brain growth did not correlate well with the supposed survival benefit of enlarged brains.

Rather, Miller proposes an additional factor to account for large human brains: In humans much creativity, and related brain growth, is due to sexual selection for abilities to attract attention, stimulate, and surprise a potential mate. This hypothesis, Miller claims, has the further value of presenting an evolutionary theory for such characteristic human traits as humor, art, music, language, and creativity.

The hypothesis that sexual selection for artistry and creativity may lead to increased brain size is supported by recent findings from the family of bowerbirds (Paradisaeidae). In order to attract and impress females, male bowerbirds construct elaborate structures of twigs, decorated with colorful objects such as shiny beetles, shells, and petals (Figure 6.18). Zoologist Joah Madden found that bowerbirds have large brains, compared with other birds (Madden, 2001). Even within the bowerbirds, species that build more elaborate bowers have larger brains.

Sexual selection stimulates more culture & creativity?

6.18 Bowerbird Nests
In order to attract mates, male bowerbirds build elaborate bowers of twigs, such as this structure, and decorate them with colorful objects. The architectural complexity and ornate decoration of the bowers may be the reason for the relatively large brains of bowerbirds. (Courtesy of Will Betz and Adrian Forsyth.)

Summary

1. Studies of the classification of animals help determine how close the relationships between different species are. Knowing this relationship, in turn, helps us interpret similarities and differences in the behavior and structure of different species.

2. Comparative studies of the nervous system help us understand the evolution of the nervous system, including the human brain. They also provide a perspective for understanding species-typical behavioral adaptations.

3. The nervous systems of invertebrate animals range in complexity from a simple nerve net to the complex structures of the octopus. The nervous systems of certain invertebrates may provide a simplified model for understanding some aspects of vertebrate nervous systems.

4. Some of the distinctive features of invertebrate nervous systems include large, identifiable neurons and large axons that are frequently components of circuits mediating rapid escape behaviors.

5. The main divisions of the brain are the same in all vertebrates. Differences among these animals are largely quantitative, as reflected in differences in the relative sizes of nerve cells and brain regions.

6. Size differences in brain regions among various mammals are frequently related to distinctive forms of behavioral adaptation.

7. Evolutionary changes in brain size are apparent in comparisons of fossils and contemporary animals.

8. The brain size of a species must be interpreted in terms of body size. The overall rule for vertebrates is that brain weight is proportional to the 0.7 power of body weight.

9. Some animals have larger brains and some have smaller brains than is predicted by the general relation between brain and body weights; that is, they differ in encephalization factor. Humans, in particular, have larger brains than would be predicted from their body size.

10. Within each of the lines of vertebrate evolution, relative brain size varies, and the more recently evolved species usually have the larger encephalization factors.

11. The human brain, compared to brains of nonhuman primates, has larger motor and sensory cortical areas devoted to the hands, larger cortical regions devoted to the production and perception of speech, a larger proportion of the brain devoted to varied and elaborate processing of information, and striking hemispheric specializations of function.

12. Not only natural selection but also sexual selection has been proposed to account for the large size of the human brain.

Refer to the *Learning Biological Psychology* CD for the following study aids for this chapter:

6 Objectives

45 Study Questions

Recommended Reading

Alcock, J. A. (2001). *Animal behavior: An evolutionary approach* (7th ed.). Sunderland, MA: Sinauer.

Butler, A. B., and Hodos, W. (1996). *Comparative vertebrate anatomy: Evolution and adaptation.* New York: Wiley-Liss.

de Waal, F. (2001). *The ape and the sushi master.* New York: Basic Books.

Futuyma, D. J. (1998). *Evolutionary biology* (3rd ed.). Sunderland, MA: Sinauer.

Krebs, J. R., and Davies, N. B. (Eds.). (1997). *Behavioral ecology: An evolutionary approach.* Cambridge, MA: Blackwell Science.

Li, W., and Graur, D. (1991). *Fundamentals of molecular evolution.* Sunderland, MA: Sinauer.

Mayr, E., and Ashlock, P. D. (1991). *Principles of systematic zoology* (2nd ed.). New York: McGraw-Hill.

Miller, G. F. (2000). *The mating mind: How sexual choice shaped the evolution of human nature.* New York: Doubleday.

Shettleworth, S. A. (1998). *Cognition, evolution, and behavior.* New York: Oxford University Press.

7

Life-Span Development of the Brain and Behavior

Age puts its stamp on the behavior of all animals. Although the pace, progression, and orderliness of changes are especially prominent early in life, change is a feature of the entire span of life. Shakespeare put it well in his play *As You Like It* when he said

> . . . from hour to hour, we ripe and ripe,
> And then, from hour to hour, we rot and rot . . .

In this chapter we will describe the features of adult brains that we introduced in Chapters 2 and 3 in terms of their progress through life from the womb to the tomb. The fertilization of an egg leads to a body with a brain that contains billions of neurons with an incredible number of connections. The pace of this process is extraordinary: During the height of prenatal growth of the human brain, more than 250,000 neurons are added per minute! Our discussion of this developmental process will range widely: We will describe the emergence of nerve cells, the formation of their connections, and the role of genes in shaping the nervous system. But we'll see that experience, gained through behavioral interactions with the environment, also sculpts the developing brain.

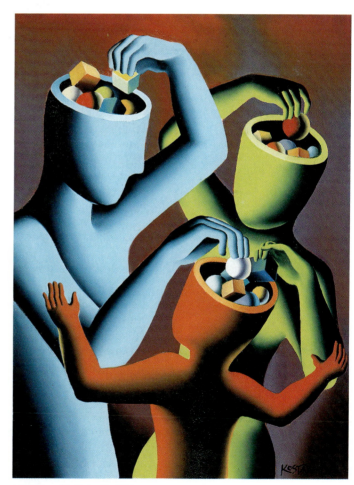

Mark Kostabi, *Bit by Bit*, 1992

7.1 Human Brain Weight as a Function of Age
Note that the age scale on this graph has been expanded for the first 5 years to show data more clearly during this period of rapid growth. (After Dekaban and Sadowsky, 1978.)

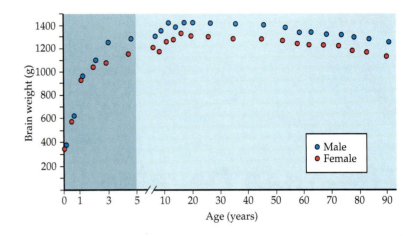

Growth and Development of the Brain Are Orderly Processes

Picture, if you can, the number of neurons in the mature human brain—about 100 billion, and at least as many glial cells. There are many types of neurons, each forming a vast array of hundreds or thousands of connections. The overall number of connections in the brain is about 100 trillion. Yet each of us began as a single microscopic cell—the fertilized egg. How can one cell divide and grow to form the most complicated machines on Earth, perhaps in the universe? Of course, some vital information was packed in the genes of that single cell, but we'll see that the developing nervous system also relies on its environment to guide the construction of this fabulous gadget between our ears.

One measure of brain development is weight, a summary of many developmental processes. Dekaban and Sadowsky (1978) give a definitive portrait of the weight of the human brain over the life span. Figure 7.1 shows the changes with age in the weight of the brain in males and females. Note the rapid increase during the first 5 years. Let's explore at the cellular level what happens in the developing brain.

The Brain Emerges from the Neural Tube

A new human being begins when a sperm about 60 µm long penetrates the wall of an egg cell 100 to 150 µm in diameter. The fertilized egg, or **zygote,** has 46 chromosomes, which contain genetic recipes for the development of a new individual. (A summary of the life cycle of cells, including a discussion of the basic genetic materials and how they direct cell activities, is provided in the Appendix.) Rapid cell division begins the developmental program. Within 12 hours after conception the single cell has divided into two cells, and after 3 days these two cells have become a small mass of homogeneous cells, like a cluster of grapes, about 200 µm in diameter.

Within a week the emerging human embryo shows three distinct cell layers (Figure 7.2a). These layers are the beginnings of all the tissues of the embryo. The nervous system develops from the outer layer, called the **ectoderm** (from the Greek *ektos,* "out," and *derma,* "skin"). As the cell layers thicken, they grow into a flat oval plate. Uneven rates of cell division form a groove—the primitive streak—which will form the midline. At the head end of the groove, a thickened collection of cells forms 2 weeks after fertilization. Ridges of ectoderm continue to bulge on both sides of the middle position. The groove between them is called the **neural groove** (Figure 7.2b).

The pace of events now increases. The neural ridges come together to form the **neural tube** (Figure 7.2c). At the anterior part of the neural tube, three subdivisions become apparent. These subdivisions correspond to the future **forebrain** (prosencephalon, consisting of the telencephalon and the diencephalon), **midbrain** (mesen-

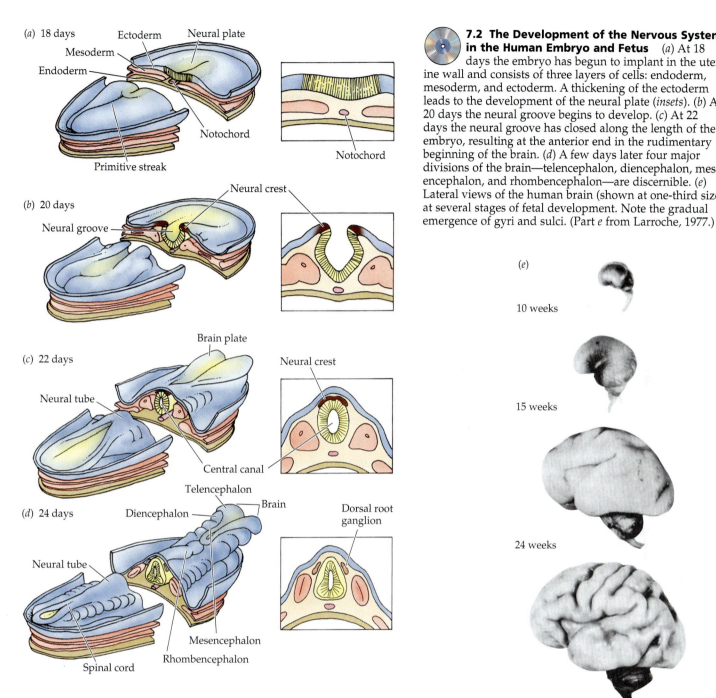

(a) 18 days

Ectoderm
Mesoderm
Endoderm
Neural plate
Notochord
Primitive streak

Notochord

(b) 20 days

Neural crest
Neural groove

(c) 22 days

Brain plate
Neural crest
Neural tube
Central canal

(d) 24 days

Telencephalon
Diencephalon
Brain
Neural tube
Mesencephalon
Rhombencephalon
Spinal cord
Dorsal root ganglion

7.2 The Development of the Nervous System in the Human Embryo and Fetus (a) At 18 days the embryo has begun to implant in the uterine wall and consists of three layers of cells: endoderm, mesoderm, and ectoderm. A thickening of the ectoderm leads to the development of the neural plate (*insets*). (b) At 20 days the neural groove begins to develop. (c) At 22 days the neural groove has closed along the length of the embryo, resulting at the anterior end in the rudimentary beginning of the brain. (d) A few days later four major divisions of the brain—telencephalon, diencephalon, mesencephalon, and rhombencephalon—are discernible. (e) Lateral views of the human brain (shown at one-third size) at several stages of fetal development. Note the gradual emergence of gyri and sulci. (Part *e* from Larroche, 1977.)

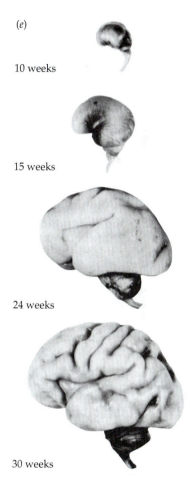

(e)

10 weeks

15 weeks

24 weeks

30 weeks

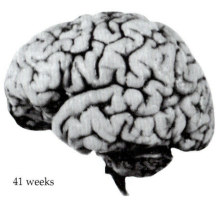

41 weeks

cephalon), and **hindbrain** (rhombencephalon, consisting of the metencephalon and the myelencephalon), which were discussed in Chapter 2 (Figure 7.2*d*). The interior of the neural tube becomes the cerebral ventricles of the brain, the central canal of the spinal cord, and the passages that connect them.

By the end of the eighth week, the human embryo shows the rudimentary beginnings of most body organs. The rapid development of the brain is reflected in the fact that by this time the head is one-half the total size of the embryo. (Note that the developing human is called an **embryo** during the first 10 weeks after fertilization; thereafter it is called a **fetus**.) Figure 7.2*e* shows the prenatal development of the human brain from weeks 10 through 41. Even after this period, there are dramatic local changes as some brain regions grow more than others, well into the teenage years (P. M. Thompson et al., 2000).

Development of the Nervous System Can Be Divided into Six Distinct Stages

From a cellular viewpoint it is useful to consider brain development as a sequence of distinct stages, most of which occur during prenatal life:

1. *Neurogenesis,* the mitotic division of nonneuronal cells to produce neurons.
2. *Cell migration,* the massive movements of nerve cells or their precursors to establish distinctive nerve cell populations (nuclei in the CNS, layers of the cerebral cortex, etc.).
3. *Differentiation* of cells into distinctive types of neurons.
4. *Synaptogenesis,* the establishment of synaptic connections as axons and dendrites grow.
5. *Neuronal cell death,* the selective death of many nerve cells.
6. *Synapse rearrangement,* the loss of some synapses and development of others, to refine synaptic connections.

This sequence is portrayed in Figure 7.3. The six stages proceed at different rates and times in different parts of the nervous system. Some of the stages may overlap even within a region. In the discussion that follows we will take up each stage in succession.

7.3 The Six Stages of Neural Development

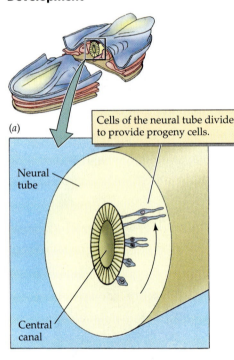

(a) Cells of the neural tube divide to provide progeny cells.

Neural tube

Central canal

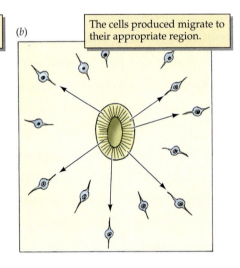

(b) The cells produced migrate to their appropriate region.

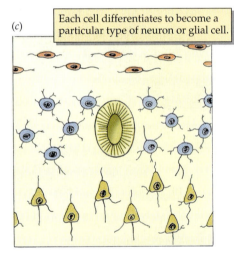

(c) Each cell differentiates to become a particular type of neuron or glial cell.

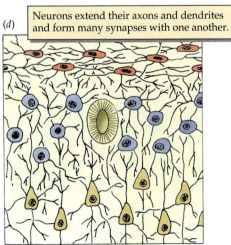

(d) Neurons extend their axons and dendrites and form many synapses with one another.

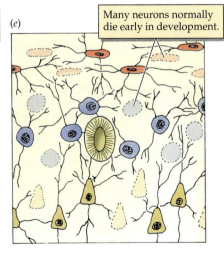

(e) Many neurons normally die early in development.

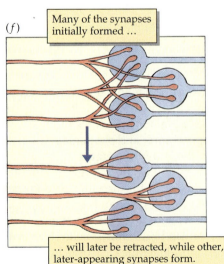

(f) Many of the synapses initially formed …

… will later be retracted, while other, later-appearing synapses form.

Cell Proliferation Produces Cells That Become Neurons or Glial Cells

The production of nerve cells is called **neurogenesis.** Nerve cells themselves do not divide, but the cells that will give rise to neurons begin as a single layer of cells along the inner surface of the neural tube. These cells divide (in a process called **mitosis**) and gradually form a closely packed layer of cells, the **ventricular zone** (Figure 7.4). These cells continue to divide, giving rise to *daughter cells,* which also divide. All neurons and glial cells are derived from cells that originate from such ventricular mitosis. Eventually some daughter cells leave the ventricular zone and begin expressing genes that transform the cell into either a neuron or a glial cell. These two types of cells separate early in the ventricular zone. In most mammals neural cells in the ventricular layer continue to form until birth; relatively few are added after birth.

Each part of an animal's brain has a species-characteristic "birth date." That is, there is an orderly chronological program for brain development, and it is possible to state the approximate days during development on which particular cell groups stop dividing. Of course, given the complexity of vertebrate brains, it is difficult to trace individual cell development from the initial small population of ventricular cells. Descendants disappear in the crowd. However, in some simpler invertebrate nervous systems that have very few neurons, mitotic lineages can be traced more easily and completely.

A favorite animal of researchers who study the lineage of nerve cells is the nematode *Caenorhabditis elegans,* a tiny worm with fewer than a thousand cells, 302 of which are nerve cells. Because the body of *C. elegans* is almost transparent (Figure 7.5*a*), researchers have been able to map the origins of each nerve cell, and they have identified several of the genes that control the paths of this worm's neural development (Wolinsky and Way, 1990). By observing the successive cell divisions of a *C. elegans* zygote, investigators can predict exactly the fate of each cell in the adult—whether it will be a sensory neuron, muscle cell, skin cell, and so on—on the basis of its mitotic "ancestors."

Whereas cell fate in *C. elegans* is a highly determined and stereotypical result of mitotic lineage (Figure 7.5*b*), in vertebrates the paths that cells take to form the com-

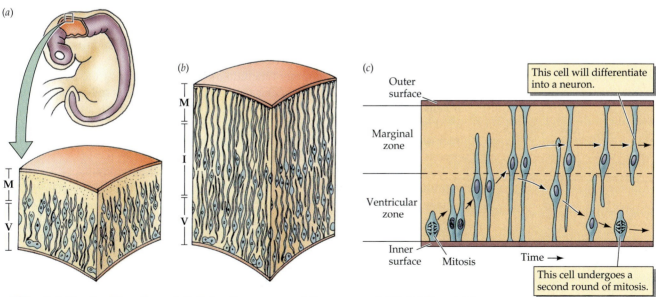

7.4 The Proliferation of Cellular Precursors of Neurons and Glial Cells (*a*) In this small section of the wall of the neural tube at an early stage of embryonic development, only ventricular (V) and marginal (M) layers are visible. (*b*) Later an intermediate (I) layer develops as the wall thickens. (*c*) Nuclei (within their cells) migrate from the ventricular layer to the outer layers. Some cells, however, return to the ventricular zone and divide, and the resulting daughter cells migrate to the outer layers, repeating the cycle.

(a)

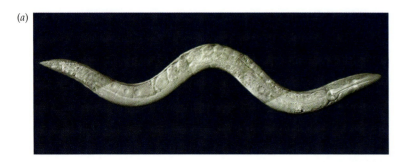

7.5 Cell Fate in a Simple Organism (a) This montage of photomicrographs shows the transparent body of *C. elegans*. (b) In this mitotic lineage of cells that give rise to the body of the adult *C. elegans*, nervous system cells are highlighted in blue. The structure and function of every cell can be predicted from its mitotic lineage. Such mitotic determination of cell differentiation does not seem important to the development of vertebrates. (Part *a* courtesy of Paola Dal Santo and Erik M. Jorgensen, University of Utah; *b* after Pines, 1992.)

(b)

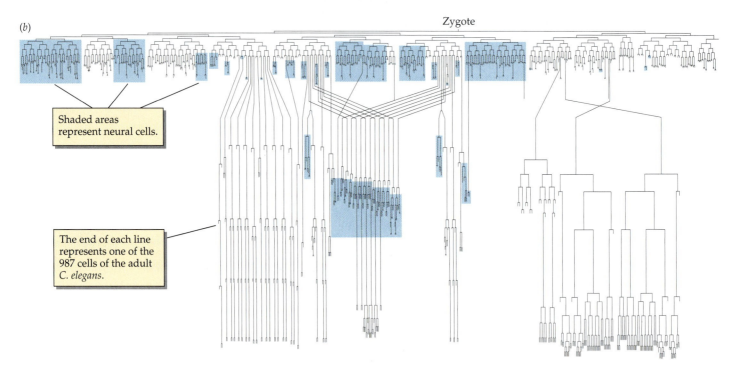

Zygote

Shaded areas represent neural cells.

The end of each line represents one of the 987 cells of the adult *C. elegans*.

pleted nervous system are more complex. Various techniques, such as the injection of substances that act as markers or the use of induced mutations, show that in vertebrates the paths of development include more local regulatory mechanisms. The hallmark of vertebrate development is that cell fate is affected by **cell–cell interactions** as cells sort themselves out and take on fates that are appropriate in the context of what neighboring cells are doing. Thus vertebrate development is less determined intrinsically; that is, it is more subject to environmental signals and, as we'll see, experience.

Traditionally, investigators of nervous system development believed that most mammals had at birth all the nerve cells they would ever have. Researchers have usually attributed the postnatal growth of human brain weight to growth in the size of neurons, branching of dendrites, elaboration of synapses, increase in myelin, and addition of nonneuronal (glial) cells. But early reports that new neurons are added just after birth in some brain regions (Altman, 1969) have been supplemented with recent findings that new neurons are added even in adulthood in humans (Eriksson et al., 1998) and other animals (E. Gould, Beylin, et al., 1999; E. Gould, Reeves, et al., 1999; Magavi et al., 2000).

Likewise, nerve cells of the olfactory organ (which we use to detect odors) are normally replaced throughout life (Jacobson, 1991). Furthermore, neurons are added to the adult nervous system in songbirds (discussed in Chapters 12 and 19). In canaries, one part of the brain circuit for birdsong is large in spring and shrinks to half that size in the fall (Nottebohm, 1991). Most of this seasonal variation in the size of brain regions is caused by variations in dendritic length and branching, but the production of new neurons also contributes to these changes.

New Nerve Cells Migrate

Neurons of the developing nervous system are always on the move. At some stage the cells that form in the ventricular layer through mitotic division move away, in a process known as **cell migration.** The cells acquire short extensions at the "head" and "tail" ends. Some descriptions of migrating cells compare them to a trail of active ants. In primates, by the time of birth almost all presumptive nerve cells have completed their migration, but in rats, cells that will become neurons continue to migrate in some regions for several weeks following birth.

Cells do not move in an aimless, haphazard manner. Many elegant studies (reviewed in Rakic, 1985) show that some cells in the developing brain move along the surface of a particular type of glial cell that appears early. Like spokes (radii) of a wheel, these **radial glial cells** extend from the inner to the outer surfaces of the emerging nervous system (Figure 7.6). The radial glial cells act as a series of guide wires, and the newly formed cells creep along them, as if they were "riding the glial monorail" (Hatten, 1990) when observed **in vitro** (in a laboratory dish; Figure 7.6c). Some migrating cells move in a direction perpendicular to the radial glial cells (S. A. Anderson et al., 1997) like Tarzan swinging from vine to vine; others move in a rostral stream to produce the olfactory bulbs (C. M. Smith and Luskin, 1998).

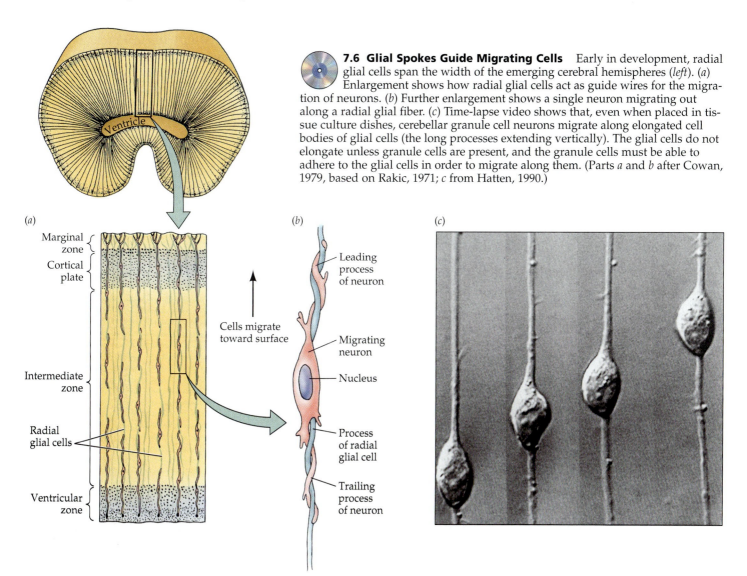

7.6 Glial Spokes Guide Migrating Cells   Early in development, radial glial cells span the width of the emerging cerebral hemispheres (*left*). (*a*) Enlargement shows how radial glial cells act as guide wires for the migration of neurons. (*b*) Further enlargement shows a single neuron migrating out along a radial glial fiber. (*c*) Time-lapse video shows that, even when placed in tissue culture dishes, cerebellar granule cell neurons migrate along elongated cell bodies of glial cells (the long processes extending vertically). The glial cells do not elongate unless granule cells are present, and the granule cells must be able to adhere to the glial cells in order to migrate along them. (Parts *a* and *b* after Cowan, 1979, based on Rakic, 1971; *c* from Hatten, 1990.)

Ventricle

(*a*)

Marginal zone
Cortical plate

Cells migrate toward surface

(*b*)

Leading process of neuron

Migrating neuron

Nucleus

Intermediate zone

Radial glial cells

Process of radial glial cell

Ventricular zone

Trailing process of neuron

(*c*)

Failures in the mechanism of cell migration result in either a vastly reduced population of neurons or a disorderly arrangement and, not surprisingly, behavioral disorders. The migration of cells and the outgrowth of nerve cell extensions (dendrites and axons) involve various chemicals. Molecules that promote the adhesion of developing elements of the nervous system, and thereby guide migrating cells and growing axons, are called **cell adhesion molecules** (**CAMs**). Knowledge about CAMs and other components of the extracellular matrix surrounding developing cells is important for understanding the major steps in neural development (Reichardt and Tomaselli, 1991). CAMs may also guide axons to regenerate when they are cut in adulthood (Box 7.1).

The single-file appearance of nerve cell precursors during cell migration (see Figure 7.6a) is followed by the aggregation, or grouping, of cells in a manner that foreshadows the nuclei of the adult brain that we discussed in Chapter 2. For example, cells of the cerebral cortex arrive in waves during fetal development, each successive wave forming a new outer layer, until the six layers of the adult cortex are formed, with the latest arrivals on the outside.

Once the cells are in place, an intense phase of dendritic growth and synapse formation in the cerebral cortex occurs after birth, as Figure 7.7 illustrates. In the next section we will discuss how the young, relatively simple cells in Figure 7.7a become the more complex neurons of Figure 7.7c.

Cells in Newly Formed Brain Regions Differentiate into Neurons

Newly arrived cells in the brain bear no more resemblance to mature nerve cells than they do to the cells of other organs. Once they reach their destinations, however, the cells begin to use (*express*) particular genes to make the particular proteins a neuron needs. This process of **differentiation** allows the cell to acquire the distinctive appearance of neurons to characteristic of the particular region. Figure 7.8 shows the progressive unfolding of Purkinje cells of the cerebellar cortex. Outgrowths of the dendrites of these cells appear soon after the cells have aligned into a single row. Slowly more and more branches form, progressively expanding the receptive surface of the Purkinje cell.

What controls differentiation is not completely understood, but two classes of influence are known. First, intrinsic self-organization is an important factor; both granule cells and Purkinje cells in tissue culture grow in a typical manner, although they are deprived of some normal connections (Seil et al., 1974). When a cell shows

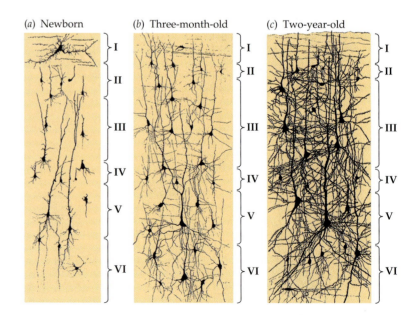

(a) Newborn   (b) Three-month-old   (c) Two-year-old

7.7 Cerebral Cortex Tissue in the Early Development of Humans These representations of cerebral cortex show the extent of neural connections at birth (a), at 3 months of age (b), and at 2 years of age (c). Numerals refer to the six cortical layers. (From Conel, 1939, 1947, 1959.)

BOX 7.1 *Degeneration and Regeneration of Nervous Tissue*

When a mature nerve cell is injured, it can regrow in several ways. Complete replacement of injured nerve cells is rare in mammals, but Figures A and B illustrate two characteristic forms of degeneration and regeneration in the mammalian peripheral and central nervous systems. Injury close to the cell body of a neuron produces a series of changes that results in the eventual destruction of the cell. This process is called **retrograde degeneration** (Figure A, 2 and 3). If the injured neuron dies, the target cells formerly innervated by that neuron may show signs of **transneuronal degeneration** (Figure A, 4).

Cutting through the axon also produces loss of the *distal* part of the axon (the part that is separated from the cell body). This process is called wallerian, or **anterograde, degeneration** (Figure B, 2 and 3). The part of the axon that remains connected to the cell body may regrow. Severed axons in the peripheral nervous system regrow readily. Sprouts emerge from the part of the axon that is still connected to the nerve cell body and advance slowly toward the periphery (Figure B, 4). Cell adhesion molecules (CAMs) help guide the regenerating axons. Some fish and amphibians have an enviable advantage over humans: After an

injury to the brain they can regenerate many of the lost connections. In these cases, CAMs appear to guide this regeneration (as we'll see in Box 7.2).

One interesting thing about regeneration of the nervous system is that it involves processes that seem similar to those that take place during an organism's original development. Studying regeneration, then, may increase our understanding of the original processes of growth of the nervous system, and vice versa. From a therapeutic viewpoint, these studies may help scientists learn how to induce repair and regrowth of damaged neural tissue in humans.

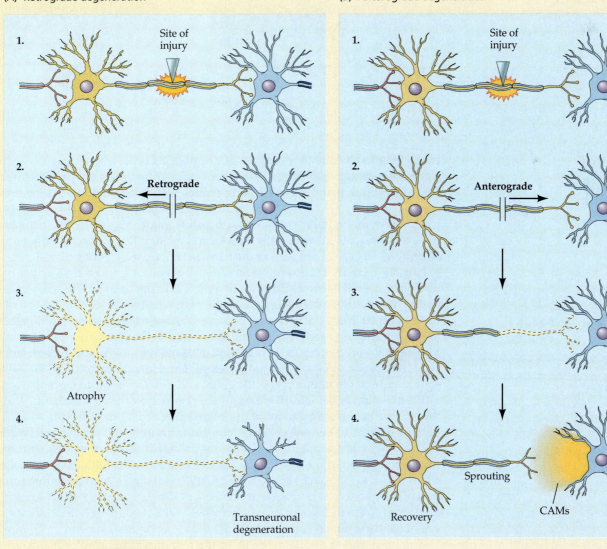

(A) Retrograde degeneration

(B) Anterograde degeneration

7.8 The Development of Purkinje Cells in the Human Cerebellum   (After Zecevic and Rakic, 1976.)

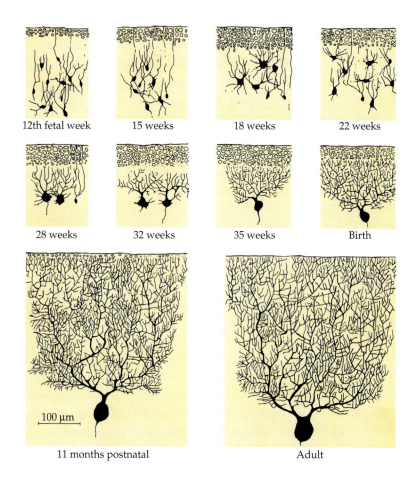

12th fetal week   15 weeks   18 weeks   22 weeks

28 weeks   32 weeks   35 weeks   Birth

100 μm

11 months postnatal   Adult

characteristics that are independent of neighboring cells, we say that it is acting in a **cell-autonomous** manner. In cell-autonomous differentiation, presumably only the genes within that cell are directing events. Some examples exist in the nervous system.

However, the neural environment also greatly influences nerve cell differentiation. In other words, neighboring cells are a second major influence on the differentiation of neurons. In vertebrates (unlike the nematode *C. elegans*), young neural cells seem to have the capacity to become many varieties of neurons, and the particular type of neuron that a cell becomes depends on where it happens to be and what its neighboring cells are. For example, consider spinal motoneurons—cells in the spinal cord that send their axons out to control muscles. Motoneurons are large, multipolar cells found in the left and right sides of the spinal cord in the ventral horn of gray matter. Motoneurons are among the first recognizable neurons in the spinal cord, and they send their axons out early in fetal development. How do these cells "know" they should express motoneuron-specific genes and differentiate into motoneurons?

Examination of the late divisions giving rise to motoneurons makes it clear that the cells are not attending to mitotic lineage (Leber et al., 1990). Instead, some spinal cells are directed to become motoneurons under the influence of other cells lying just ventral to the developing spinal cord—in the **notochord,** a rodlike structure that forms along the midline (see Figure 7.2*a*). If we insert an additional length of notochord dorsal to the spinal cord, cells begin differentiating into motoneurons on each side of the spinal cord near the extra notochord (Roelink et al., 1994). The notochord releases a protein messenger (playfully named "Sonic hedgehog") that diffuses to the spinal cord and directs some (but not all) cells to become motoneurons (Figure 7.9).

The influence of one set of cells on the fate of neighboring cells is known as **induction;** the notochord induces some spinal cord cells to differentiate into motoneurons. Induction of this sort has been demonstrated many times in the developing vertebrate body and brain. Another way to describe the situation is that there is extensive cell–cell interaction, each cell taking cues from its neighbors. Because each cell influences the differentiation of others, neural development is very complex, but also very flexible.

For example, cells differentiate into the type of neuron that is appropriate for wherever they happen to be in the brain; thus cell–cell interaction coordinates development—directing differentiation to provide the right type of neuron for each part of the brain. Another consequence of the reliance of development on cell–cell interactions such as induction is that if a few cells are injured or lost, other cells will "answer the call" of inducing factors and fill in for the missing cells.

This phenomenon can be observed in any vertebrate and in many invertebrate embryos from which some cells have been removed. For example, if cells are removed early enough from a developing limb bud in a chick embryo, other cells pitch in, and by the time the chick hatches, the limb looks normal—with no parts missing. Embryologists refer to such adaptive responses to early injury as **regulation:** The developing animal compensates for missing or injured cells. Because cell fate is so tightly coupled with mitotic lineage in *C. elegans,* this organism shows little or no regulation. If a cell in *C. elegans* is killed (with a laser through the microscope), no other cells take its place; the worm must do without that cell.

There is another consequence of this system of cells taking cues from their neighbors as to what genes they should express and what function they should fulfill: If you can obtain cells that have not yet differentiated extensively, and place them into a particular brain region, they will differentiate in an appropriate way and become properly integrated. Such undifferentiated cells, called **stem cells,** are present throughout embryonic tissues and so can be gathered from umbilical cord blood or miscarried embryos.

It may be possible to take cells from adult tissue and, by treating them with various factors in a dish, transform them into "adult" stem cells. Research is being done to determine whether placing stem cells in areas of brain degeneration, such as loss of myelination in multiple sclerosis, or of dopaminergic neurons in Parkinson's disease, might reverse such degeneration as the implanted cells differentiate to fill in for the missing components (S. Liu et al., 2000).

The Axons and Dendrites of Young Neurons Grow Extensively and Form Synapses

The biggest changes in brain cells early in life take place in axons, dendrites, and synapses. There are huge increases in the length of dendrites, which seem to involve processes akin to those involved in the growth of axons. Collectively these processes are known as **synaptogenesis.** At the tips of both axons and dendrites are **growth cones,** swollen ends from which extensions emerge (Figure 7.10*a*). The very fine outgrowths, called **filopodia** (singular *filopodium,* from the Latin *filum,* "thread," and the Greek *pous,* "foot"), are spikelike; the sheetlike extensions are called **lamellipodia** (singular *lamellipodium,* from a form of the Latin *lamina,* "thin plate"). Both the filopodia and lamellipodia seem to adhere to the extracellular environment, and then they contract to pull the growth cone in a particular direction (the growing axon or dendrite follows behind it). Dendrite growth cones in adults attest to the continued elongation and change in dendrites throughout life in response to functional demands.

What guides axons along the paths they take? Axons are guided by chemicals released by the target nerve cells or other tissues, such as muscles (C. S. Goodman, 1996; Tessier-Lavigne and Placzek, 1991). The axon growth cone responds to the concentration gradients of these chemicals that provide directional guidance, as in Figure 7.10*b* and *c*. Chemical signals that attract certain growth cones are called **chemoattractants** (Hiramoto, et al., 2000); chemicals that repel growth cones are **chemorepellents** (Chen et al., 2000; Keynes and Cook, 1992). For example, because it is important for some axons to remain on one side of the body and for others to cross over, a protein called Slit repels some axons to prevent them from crossing the midline (Figure 7.10*d*) (Brose et al., 1999). Some secreted proteins, such as the sem-

7.9 The Induction of Spinal Motoneurons Spinal motoneurons normally cluster in the ventral region on either side of the spinal cord. In this section of labeled cells from the chick embryo, the notochord (green circle at bottom) lies just beneath the spinal cord and secretes a protein called Sonic hedgehog. The concentration of this protein in the ventral spinal cord induces the cells there to develop as motoneurons (gold). Another protein (blue) is expressed only in the dorsal spinal cord. (Courtesy of Thomas Jessell.)

(a)

(b)

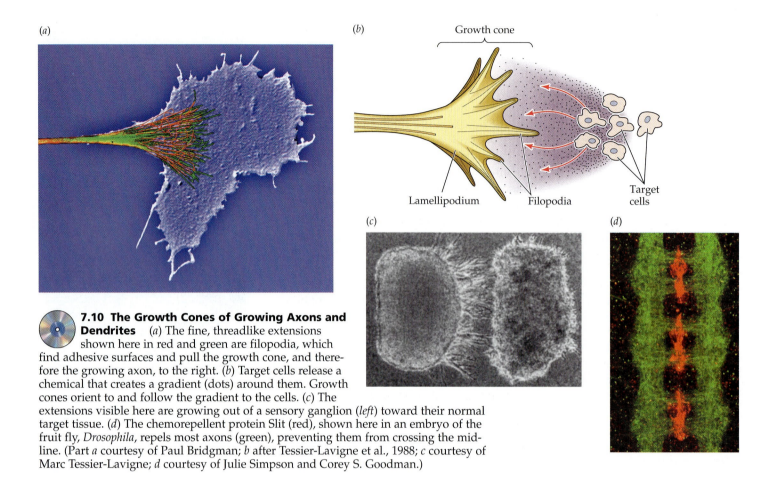

7.10 The Growth Cones of Growing Axons and Dendrites (*a*) The fine, threadlike extensions shown here in red and green are filopodia, which find adhesive surfaces and pull the growth cone, and therefore the growing axon, to the right. (*b*) Target cells release a chemical that creates a gradient (dots) around them. Growth cones orient to and follow the gradient to the cells. (*c*) The extensions visible here are growing out of a sensory ganglion (*left*) toward their normal target tissue. (*d*) The chemorepellent protein Slit (red), shown here in an embryo of the fruit fly, *Drosophila*, repels most axons (green), preventing them from crossing the midline. (Part *a* courtesy of Paul Bridgman; *b* after Tessier-Lavigne et al., 1988; *c* courtesy of Marc Tessier-Lavigne; *d* courtesy of Julie Simpson and Corey S. Goodman.)

7.11 The Postnatal Development of Synapses The rate of synapse development in the visual cortex of rats (*a*) and humans (*b*). In humans, note the decline in the density of synapses after the first year of life. (Part *a* after Blue and Parnavelas, 1983; *b* from Huttenlocher et al., 1982.)

aphorins, act as chemoattractants to some growth cones and chemorepellents to others (Polleux et al., 2000). Dendritic growth is also affected by both intrinsic factors and cell–cell interactions, especially the approach of axons from other cells (T. H. Brown et al., 1992).

Synapses can form rapidly on dendrites and dendritic spines (Figure 7.11). The spines themselves proliferate rapidly after birth. These connections can be affected by postnatal experience, as we will see in Chapter 18. To support the metabolic needs of the expanded dendritic tree, the nerve cell body greatly increases in volume.

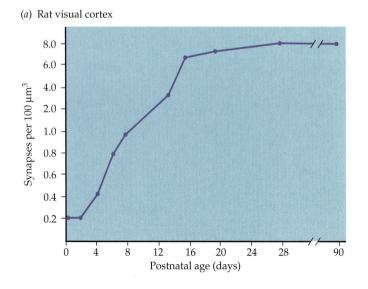

(a) Rat visual cortex

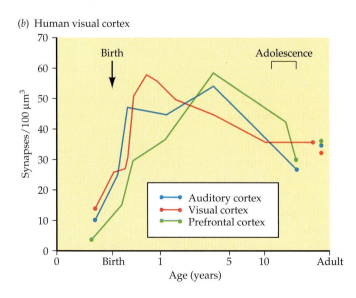

(b) Human visual cortex

Why is a synapse created at any single site on a neuron or other targets, such as muscle? Undoubtedly some type of chemical recognition bonds a presynaptic ending to a particular postsynaptic site; the molecular features of this recognition mechanism are slowly unfolding.

The Death of Many Neurons Is a Normal Part of Development

As strange as it may seem, **neuronal cell death** is a crucial phase of brain development, especially during embryonic stages. This developmental stage is not unique to the nervous system. Naturally occurring cell death, also called **apoptosis** (from the Greek *apo,* "away from," and *ptosis,* "act of falling"), is evident as a kind of sculpting process in the emergence of other tissues in both animals and plants (Oppenheim, 1991).

In the nervous system, however, the number of cells that die during early development is quite large. In some regions of the brain and spinal cord, most of the nerve cells die during prenatal development. Figure 7.12 illustrates the magnitude of this developmental phenomenon. The proportion of nerve cells that die varies from region to region and ranges from 20 to 80% of the cells. Naturally occurring neuronal cell death was first described by Viktor Hamburger (1958) in chicks, in which about half the originally produced spinal motoneurons die before hatching.

Several factors influence this massive cell death in the nervous system. The extent of cell death is regulated in part by factors associated with the synaptic targets of cells. Reduction of the size of the synaptic target invariably reduces the number of surviving nerve cells. For example, if the leg of a tadpole is removed early in development, many more developing spinal motoneurons die than if the leg had remained in position. Conversely, grafting on an extra leg—a technique that is possible with chicken embryos and tadpoles—appreciably reduces the usual loss of cells; in such cases the mature spinal cord has more than the usual number of neurons.

These observations suggest that the target of a developing population of nerve cells influences the survival of these neurons and that the neurons are competing for something in order to survive. These results also suggest that some of the cells that would have died in the absence of the extra leg are perfectly capable of performing the job of motoneurons, so we can conclude that these cells are not dying because of a defect. Rather, it appears that these cells have "decided" to die and are actively committing suicide.

For example, all cells carry **death genes**—genes that are expressed only when a cell undergoes apoptosis (Peter et al., 1997). Apoptosis appears to begin with the sudden influx and release of Ca^{2+} ions that cause the mitochondria inside the cell to release a protein called, devilishly enough, **Diablo** (Verhagen et al., 2000). Diablo binds to a family of proteins, the well-named **inhibitors of apoptosis proteins (IAPs)** (Earnshaw et al., 1999). The IAPs, in turn, have been inhibiting a family of proteins, the **caspases,** which are proteases (protein-dissolving enzymes) that cut up proteins

Viktor Hamburger
(1900–2001)

7.12 Many Neurons Die during Normal Early Development   The pattern of neuronal cell death in spinal motoneurons of chicks (*a*) and humans (*b*). Many neuronal populations show a similar pattern of apoptosis. (Part *a* from Hamburger, 1975; *b* from Forger and Breedlove, 1987.)

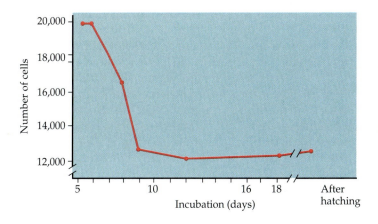

(*a*) Chick spinal motoneurons

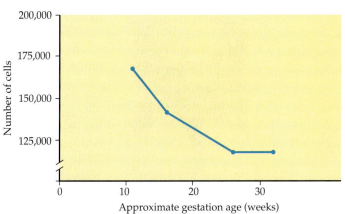

(*b*) Human spinal motoneurons

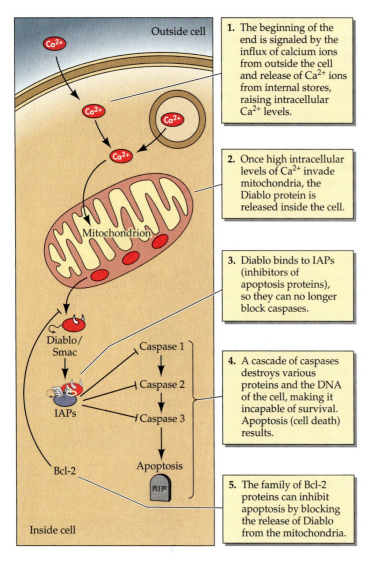

1. The beginning of the end is signaled by the influx of calcium ions from outside the cell and release of Ca^{2+} ions from internal stores, raising intracellular Ca^{2+} levels.

2. Once high intracellular levels of Ca^{2+} invade mitochondria, the Diablo protein is released inside the cell.

3. Diablo binds to IAPs (inhibitors of apoptosis proteins), so they can no longer block caspases.

4. A cascade of caspases destroys various proteins and the DNA of the cell, making it incapable of survival. Apoptosis (cell death) results.

5. The family of Bcl-2 proteins can inhibit apoptosis by blocking the release of Diablo from the mitochondria.

7.13 Death Genes Regulate Apoptosis

and nuclear DNA. So when Diablo binds the IAPs, the caspases are free to dismantle the cell. **Bcl-2** proteins (another family) block apoptosis by preventing Diablo release from the mitochondria. This intricate system of checks and balances, which determines whether a cell gives up the ghost (Figure 7.13), must have been established long ago in evolution, since homologs of the genes that produce these proteins function similarly in *C. elegans*.

Afferents (axons that provide synaptic input to a neuron) exert some influence on neuronal death during development. Reducing afferent input significantly increases neuronal death in various nervous system regions (Oppenheim, 1991). Sometimes hormones in general circulation affect cell death. Nerve cell death in moth nervous systems, for example, is triggered by the same hormones that produce the transformation from caterpillar to moth (Truman, 1983; Weeks and Levine, 1990). And the Mauthner cell (a specialized cell in the medulla) of some amphibians changes as a result of the secretion of thyroid hormones; the cell degenerates as the animal's lifestyle changes from aquatic to terrestrial. In Chapter 12 we will note the importance of certain sex hormones in controlling cell death in the spinal cord of mammals. But the most important factor regulating neuronal cell death seems to be competition among neurons.

According to one view, neurons compete for connections to target structures (other nerve cells or end organs, such as muscle). Cells that make adequate synapses remain; those without a place to form synaptic connections die. Another view is that the cells compete not just for synaptic sites, but for a chemical that the target structure makes and releases. Neurons that receive enough of the chemical survive; those that do not, die.

Such target-derived chemicals are called **neurotrophic factors** (or simply *trophic factors*) because they act as if they "feed" the neurons to help them survive (in Greek, *trophe* means "nourishment"). The neurotrophic factor that was the first to be identified keeps developing sympathetic neurons alive, as we'll discuss next. It is widely assumed that there are many neurotrophic factors, each specifically maintaining a particular population of neurons during a period of neuronal cell death.

Neurotrophic Factors Allow Neurons to Survive and Grow

More than 30 years ago, investigators discovered a substance—called **nerve growth factor (NGF)**—that markedly affects the growth of neurons in spinal ganglia and in the ganglia of the sympathetic nervous system (Bothwell, 1995; Levi-Montalcini, 1982). Administered to a chick embryo, NGF caused the formation of sympathetic ganglia with many more cells than usual. These cells were also larger and had many extensive processes (Figure 7.14).

The discovery of NGF earned Rita Levi-Montalcini and Stanley Cohen the 1986 Nobel Prize in physiology or medicine. Originally, NGF was found in a variety of unusual places, including the salivary glands of mice, certain skin tumors, and the venom of a snake. Later, precise biochemical techniques revealed that various target organs normally produce NGF during development. NGF is taken up by the axons of sympathetic neurons innervating the organs and transported back to the cell body, and it prevents some of the sympathetic neurons from dying. The amount of NGF produced by targets during development is roughly correlated with the amount of sympathetic innervation the targets receive in adulthood. This relation-

Rita Levi-Montalcini

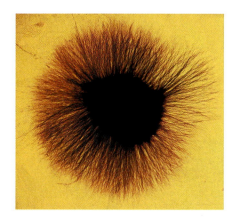

7.14 The Effects of Nerve Growth Factor
If NGF is added to the solution bathing a spinal ganglion grown in a glass dish outside the body (in vitro), neuronal processes grow outward in an exuberant, radiating fashion. (From Levi-Montalcini, 1963.)

ship suggests that differing extents of cell death, controlled by access to NGF, match the sympathetic innervation to each target.

Part of the interest in NGF arose from the possibility that there were more neurotrophic factors, each one affecting the survival of a particular cell type during a specific developmental period. After the discovery of NGF, investigators began searching for other neurotrophic factors. One such factor, purified from the brains of many animals, was named **brain-derived neurotrophic factor** (**BDNF**). The gene for BDNF turned out to be very similar to the gene for NGF. Investigators used molecular techniques to search for other NGF-related molecules and found several more.

The family of NGF-like molecules was named the neurotrophin family, and its members are numbered: neurotrophin-1 (NGF), -2 (BDNF), -3, and -4/5 (it turned out that the fifth neurotrophin discovered was identical with the fourth). Neurotrophic factors that are unrelated to NGF also have been found, including ciliary neurotrophic factor (named after its ability to keep neurons from ciliary ganglia alive in vitro).

The exact role of these various factors (and other neurotrophic factors yet to be discovered) is under intense scientific scrutiny (Lewin and Barde, 1996; Kafitz et al., 1999). Figure 7.15 depicts our current model of how neurotrophic factors influence the survival of neurons and/or their connections. The decline in production of neurotrophins has been related to the decline of memory formation. We'll see in Chapter 18 that treatments that restore neurotrophin production have restored memory formation in aged animals.

7.15 A Model for the Action of Neurotrophic Factors

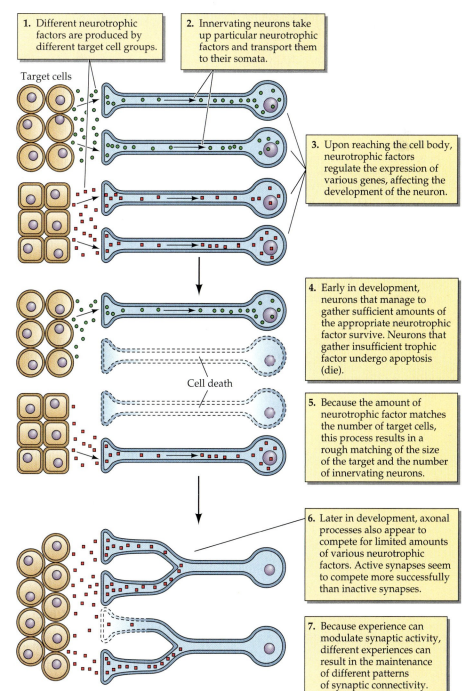

1. Different neurotrophic factors are produced by different target cell groups.

2. Innervating neurons take up particular neurotrophic factors and transport them to their somata.

Target cells

3. Upon reaching the cell body, neurotrophic factors regulate the expression of various genes, affecting the development of the neuron.

4. Early in development, neurons that manage to gather sufficient amounts of the appropriate neurotrophic factor survive. Neurons that gather insufficient trophic factor undergo apoptosis (die).

Cell death

5. Because the amount of neurotrophic factor matches the number of target cells, this process results in a rough matching of the size of the target and the number of innervating neurons.

6. Later in development, axonal processes also appear to compete for limited amounts of various neurotrophic factors. Active synapses seem to compete more successfully than inactive synapses.

7. Because experience can modulate synaptic activity, different experiences can result in the maintenance of different patterns of synaptic connectivity.

BOX 7.2 *The Frog Retinotectal System Demonstrates Intrinsic and Extrinsic Factors in Neural Development*

In the 1940s Roger Sperry began a series of experiments that seemed to emphasize the importance of intrinsic factors, such as genes, for determining the pattern of connections in the brain. If the optic nerve that connects an eye to the brain is cut in an adult mammal, the animal is blinded in that eye and never recovers. In fish and amphibians such as frogs, however, the animal is only temporarily blinded; in a few months the axons from the eye (specifically, from the ganglion cells of the retina) reinnervate the brain (specifically the dorsal portion of the midbrain, called the *tectum*) and the animal recovers its eyesight. When food is presented on the left or right, above or below, the animal flicks its tongue accurately to retrieve it. Thus either (1) the retina reestablishes the same pattern of connections to the tectum that was there before surgery and the brain interprets visual information as before, or (2) the retina reinnervates the tectum at random but the rest of the brain learns to interpret the information presented in this new pattern.

Several lines of evidence established that the first hypothesis is correct. One such piece of evidence is that the first-arriving retinal axons sometimes pass over uninnervated tectum to reach their original position. In the classic case illustrating this phenomenon, the optic nerve was cut and the eye was ro-

(A) Two possible mechanisms of chemoaffinity

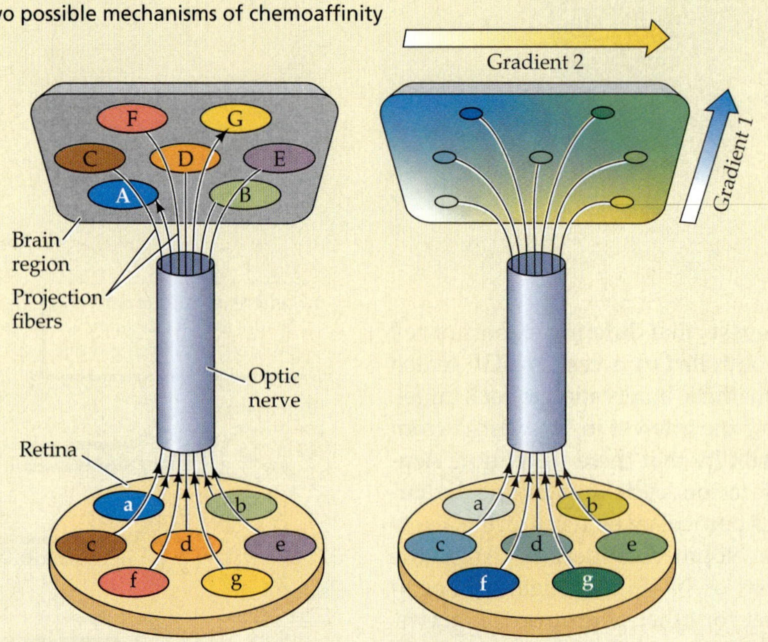

tated 180°; when the animal recovered eyesight, it behaved as if the visual image had been rotated 180°: It moved to the left when trying to get food presented on the right, and it flicked its tongue up when food was presented below. The only explanation for this behavior is that the retinal axons had grown back to their original positions on the tectum, ignoring the rotation of

the eye. Furthermore, once the original connections had been reestablished, the brain interpreted the information as if the eye were in its original position. Even years later, animals that underwent this treatment had not learned to make sense of information from the rotated eye.

Sperry proposed the **chemoaffinity hypothesis** to explain how retinal ax-

Synaptic Connections Are Refined by Synapse Rearrangement

Just as not all the neurons produced by a developing individual are kept into adulthood, some of the synapses formed early in development are later retracted. Originally this process was described as synapse elimination, but later studies found that although some original synapses are lost, new synapses are also formed. Thus a more accurate term is **synapse rearrangement,** or *synaptic remodeling.* In most cases synapse rearrangement takes place after the period of cell death.

For example, as we learned already, about half of the spinal motoneurons that form die later (see Figure 7.12). By the end of the cell death period, each surviving motoneuron innervates many muscle fibers, and every muscle fiber is innervated by several motoneurons. But later the surviving motoneurons retract many of their axon collaterals, until each muscle fiber comes to be innervated by only one motoneuron. Then each motoneuron enlarges the remaining synapse.

Similar events have been documented in several neural regions, including the cerebellum (Mariani and Changeaux, 1981), the brainstem (Jackson and Parks, 1982),

ons know which part of the tectum to innervate. Suppose each retinal cell and each tectal cell had a specific chemical identity—an address of sorts. Then each retinal cell would need only to seek out the proper address in the tectum and the entire pattern would be reestablished; many chemical cues (represented by many colors in Figure A *left*) or only a few (two colors in Figure A *right*) may be involved.

Several preparations indicated that there are limits to how accurately retinal cells can find their original target, but there is one dramatic demonstration: When retinal cells are placed in culture dishes, their axons grow and show preferences. The axons of ganglion cells from lateral retina prefer to grow over cell membranes from rostral tectum (their normal target) rather than over cell membranes from caudal tectum (F. Bonhoeffer and Huf, 1985). Axons from medial retina, however, show no preference. Thus apparently cell adhesion molecules in tectal membranes direct the retinal axons to the roughly appropriate region of tectum.

Having arrived at the roughly appropriate region of tectum, retinal connections are fine-tuned by extrinsic factors, specifically by *experience.* Normally each retina innervates only the tectum on the opposite side. When implantation of a third eye forces two retinas to innervate a single tectum (Figure B *left*), they each do so in the same rough pattern, but they segregate; axons from one retina predominate in one area, and axons from the other retina predominate in neighboring tectum, so there are alternating stripes of innervation from the two eyes (Figure B *right*).

This segregation depends on activity (Constantine-Paton et al., 1990). If neural activity in one eye is silenced (by injection of drugs), the eye loses its connections to the tectum and the other eye takes over, innervating the entire tectum. If both eyes are silenced (by the animal's being kept in the dark), neither eye predominates, their axons fail to segregate in the tectum, and the detailed pattern of innervation fails to appear. Presumably the two eyes are competing for limited supplies of a neurotrophic factor from the tectum, and active synapses take up more of the factor(s).

Thus, the retinotectal system appears to reestablish the original pattern of innervation in two steps: (1) Chemical cues bring retinal axons to the *approximately* correct region of tectum. (2) The neural activity of the retinal cells, normally driven by patterned visual stimulation, directs these axons to innervate or maintain innervation of the *precise* tectal region. (Figure B courtesy of Martha Constantine-Paton.)

(B) A three-eyed frog has two eyes innervating the left tectum.

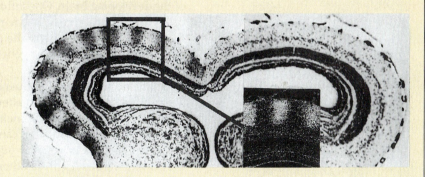

the visual cortex (Hubel et al., 1977), and several autonomic ganglia (Lichtman and Purves, 1980). In human cerebral cortex there seems to be a net loss of synapses from late childhood until midadolescence (see Figure 7.11*b*). What determines which synapses are kept and which are lost? Although we don't know all the factors, one important influence is neural activity (Box 7.2 shows an example). One theory is that active synapses take up some neurotrophic factor that maintains the synapse, while inactive synapses get too little trophic factor to remain stable.

Later in this chapter we'll see specific examples in which active synapses are maintained and inactive synapses are retracted in the mammalian visual system. In Chapter 8 we'll review evidence that synapse rearrangement in the cerebral cortex can continue throughout life.

Glial Cells Provide Myelin, Which Is Vital for Brain Function

As already noted, glial cells develop from the same populations of immature cells as neurons. The factors that determine whether a cell differentiates into a neuron or

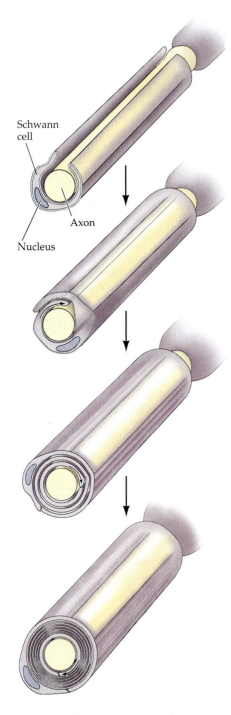

Schwann cell

Axon

Nucleus

7.16 Myelin Formation The repeated wrapping of a Schwann cell cytoplasm around an axon results in a many-layered sheath that insulates the axon electrically, speeding the conduction of electrical signals along its length.

a glial cell remain unknown. Glial cells continue to be added to the nervous system throughout life. (Sometimes the process becomes aberrant, resulting in glial tumors, or gliomas, of the brain.) In fact, the most intense phase of glial cell proliferation in many animals occurs after birth, when glial cells are added from immature cells located in the ventricular zone.

The development of sheaths around axons—the process of myelination (Figure 7.16)—greatly changes the rate at which axons conduct messages (see Figure 3.10). Myelination has a strong impact on behavior because it profoundly affects the velocity of the nerve impulse and thereby affects the temporal order of events in the nervous system. **Multiple sclerosis** is a disorder in which myelin is destroyed, probably by the patient's own immune system (Manova and Kostadinova, 2000), with devastating disruptions of sensory and motor function.

In humans, the earliest myelination in the peripheral nervous system is evident in cranial and spinal nerves about 24 weeks after conception. But the most intense phase of myelination occurs shortly after birth. Furthermore, some investigators believe that myelin can be added to axons throughout life. The first nerve tracts in the human nervous system to become myelinated are in the spinal cord. Myelination then spreads successively into the hindbrain, midbrain, and forebrain. Within the cerebral cortex, sensory zones are myelinated before motor zones; correspondingly, sensory functions mature before motor functions.

Growth and Development of the Brain Reflect the Interaction of Intrinsic and Extrinsic Factors

Many factors influence the emergence of the form, arrangements, and connections of the developing brain. One influence is genes, which direct the production of every protein the cell can make. In the nematode *C. elegans*, genes are almost the only factors affecting development; the cells somehow keep track of their mitotic lineage and then simply express the genes that are appropriate for the cell fate that their lineage directs.

Genes are also a major influence on the development of the vertebrate brain. An animal that has inherited an altered gene will make an altered protein, which will affect any cell structure that includes that protein. Thus every neuronal structure, and therefore every behavior, can be altered by changes in the appropriate gene(s). It is useful to think of genes as *intrinsic* factors—that is, factors that originate within the developing cell itself. All other influences we can consider *extrinsic*—that is, originating outside of the developing cell.

What are the extrinsic factors? For mammals, which depend on nutrients supplied from the mother during development, an important extrinsic factor is whether the fetus is provided with the nutrients needed to carry out the genetic instructions. As we'll see, the lack of nutrients or the presence of chemicals that interfere with the delivery of nutrients can have a profound effect on brain development.

Another important class of extrinsic factors for all vertebrates is cell–cell interactions: Whether a cell expresses a particular gene, takes a particular shape, or performs a particular task may depend on whether neighboring cells exert an inductive influence. The recognition that cell–cell interactions are very important for brain development led to the discovery of another extrinsic factor—neural activity.

As we'll see, sometimes the electrical activity of a neuron can affect the fate of other cells (whether they live or die) and can determine whether or not synapses are maintained. Finally, the ability of neural activity to direct brain development identifies another influence: experience.

First, the developing organism's own behavior generates sensory experience. Furthermore, events in the environment (sounds, lights, odors, and so on) also affect the activity of sensory neurons; in several cases the activity of the sensory neurons determines which synapses are maintained and which are lost. In this way experience can alter the connections of the developing brain, thereby affecting an

TABLE 7.1 *Intrinsic and Extrinsic Factors That Affect Neural Development*

Factors	Examples of effects
INTRINSIC FACTORS (GENES)	
Chromosomal aberrations	Down syndrome, fragile X syndrome
Single-gene effects	Phenylketonuria, various *Drosophila* mutants, Tay-Sachs disease
EXTRINSIC FACTORS	
Nutrients	Malnutrition
Drugs, toxins	Fetal alcohol syndrome
Cell–cell interactions	
Induction directs differentiation	Motoneuron differentiation induced by notochord
Trophic factors direct cell death or synapse loss	Developing sympathetic neurons spared by NGF from death
Neural activity affects synapse maintenance and loss	
Non-sensory-driven	Eye segregation in layer IV cortex before birth
Sensory-driven (experience)	Ocular dominance outside layer IV after birth
	Increased IQ resulting from childhood enrichment
Birth process in mammals	Hypoxia-induced mental retardation

individual's behavior in adulthood. Table 7.1 lists these intrinsic and extrinsic factors and some of the examples we'll use to illustrate each.

Genes Are the Intrinsic Factors That Influence Brain Development

Psychologists have shown the importance of genetic factors in a variety of behaviors in many species, including humans (Rende and Plomin, 1995). Of course, genes do not work in isolation. Development should be viewed as the interaction of genetic instructions with the other, extrinsic influences, such as those listed in Table 7.1.

The sum of all the intrinsic, genetic information an individual has is its **genotype,** or **genome.** The sum of all the physical characteristics that make up an individual is its **phenotype.** Your genotype was determined at the moment of fertilization and remains the same throughout your life. But your phenotype changes constantly, as you grow up and grow old and even, in a tiny way, as you take each breath.

Phenotype is determined by the interaction of genotype and extrinsic factors, including experience. Thus we'll see that twins who have identical genotypes do not have identical phenotypes, because they have not received identical extrinsic influences. Because their nervous system phenotypes are somewhat different, twins do not behave exactly the same. A related term, **congenital,** is often misunderstood to mean "inherited," but really it refers to a character that is "present at birth," whether inherited or not.

Identical genes, different nervous systems. One breeding technique produces genetically identical animals, called **clones,** which used to be known mainly in science fiction and horror films. But life imitates fiction. Although the sheep Dolly was the first successfully cloned mammal, she was not the first animal to be cloned. Using grasshopper clones, Corey Goodman (1979) compared the uniformity and variability in the growth and development of different neurons. Although the basic shape of larger cells showed considerable uniformity, many neurons of cloned grasshoppers showed differences in neural connections among these genetically identical individuals.

GENES AND BEHAVIOR

Similar results were derived from a tiny crustacean, the daphnia, well known to aquarium owners (Macagno et al., 1973). Female daphnias can reproduce without fertilization by males, and lines of genetically identical female offspring are the result. The daphnia eye contains exactly 176 sensory neurons, which make synaptic contacts with exactly 110 neurons of the optic ganglion. But the exact number of synapses established between a particular sensory neuron and a specific neuron in the ganglion can vary by more than threefold between individual daphnia clones. Presumably, the variations are due to variation in extrinsic factors.

Among vertebrates, identical neurons for comparing synaptic connections among twins are harder to find. But some fish have identifiable neurons—Mauthner cells—and some of these fish reproduce as daphnias do; that is, females produce daughters that are genetically identical to each other and to their mother. Each fish has a single giant Mauthner cell on each side of the brain. Although the pattern of dendritic branching of the Mauthner cells is similar from individual to individual among clones, there are individual differences in the detail of branching and of synapses (Levinthal et al., 1976).

Genetically identical mice raised in different laboratories behave in markedly different fashions on a variety of tests (Crabbe et al., 1999; Finch and Kirkwood, 2000). For human identical twins, the branching pattern of nerve endings in the skin must differ, since even identical twins show some differences in their fingerprints (although their prints are more similar than are those of fraternal twins).

Further differences between the nervous systems of identical twins may be caused by responses to differential experiences, as we will see in Chapters 17 and 18 when we consider the effects of experience and learning on the anatomy of the nervous system. Indeed, in several places in this book we'll find that human identical twins do not always share such traits as schizophrenia (see Figure 1.9), sexual orientation, or depression, and these differences between twins cannot be attributed to the genome.

Effects of mutations.   In rare instances an animal inherits a sudden change in genetic structure, a **mutation,** that is related to marked anatomical or physiological change. Researchers can increase the frequency of mutations by exposing animals to chemicals or radiation that produce changes in genes.

Mutants—animals that display these altered genes—are interesting to study because their changed genetic characteristics may be quite specific and striking. For example, Greenspan et al. (1980) described mutants of the fruit fly *Drosophila* that seemed normal in every way except that they had memory problems. These mutants—affectionately labeled *dunce, amnesiac,* and *turnip*—either failed to learn or could learn but forgot rapidly. Biochemical deficits in these mutants (due to mutations that render specific genes and therefore specific proteins ineffective) cause the failures of memory (Dudai, 1988). The strength of research on *Drosophila* mutants derives from the wealth of specific mutations, each one involving a distinct defect in part of the fly's nervous system (J. C. Hall and Greenspan, 1979). For example, a lethal *Drosophila* mutant, *Notch,* has an enlarged nervous system because too many precursor cells are produced.

Many mutations in mice affect the nervous system. Some mutant mice fail to produce particular brain regions. Others show specific anatomical derangements, such as a failure to myelinate or to arrange cells in their characteristic alignments. Mutants of one group that is especially intriguing to researchers all have single-gene mutations that affect postnatal development of the cerebellum. The names of these mutant animals—*reeler, staggerer,* and *weaver*—reflect the locomotor impairment that characterizes them. Figure 7.17 illustrates the impact of these mutations on the size and arrangement of the cerebellum.

The cerebellum of *reeler* (Figure 7.17c) shows an abnormal positioning of cells. There are no characteristic layers in the cerebellum, hippocampus, or cerebral cortex (Caviness, 1980). The cerebellum of *weaver* (Figure 7.17b) has far fewer granule cells than a normal cerebellum (Figure 7.17a), which arises from a failure of granule cells to mi-

(a) Normal   (b) *weaver*   (c) *reeler*

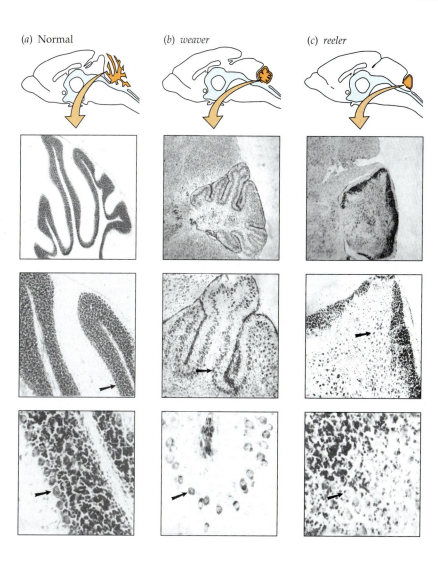

7.17 Cerebellar Mutants among Mice (a) The cerebellum in a normal mouse at three levels of magnification (×25, ×66, and ×250, from top to bottom). (b) Comparable views in the mutant *weaver*. Note the almost complete absence of granule cells, while the alignment of Purkinje cells (arrows) is normal. (c) Sections from the mutant *reeler*. Marked derangement of the customary layering of cells is evident. Both mutants show overall shrinkage of the cerebellum. (From A. L. Leiman, unpublished observations.)

grate properly. The granule cells from *weaver* mice fail to make the CAM that would allow them to attach to and migrate along glial cells; therefore they fail to reach their appropriate levels, and the cerebellum fails to develop the normal laminar (layered) organization. Today scientists sometimes deliberately delete or introduce a particular gene in mice in order to study the effect of that gene on the nervous system (Box 7.3).

Despite the importance of genes for nervous system development, understanding the genome alone could never enable an understanding of the developing brain because, as we'll see next, experience also directs developing neurons.

Experience Is an Important Influence on Brain Development

The young of many species are born in a highly immature state, both anatomically and behaviorally. For example, in humans the weight of the brain at birth is only one-fourth of its adult weight. Infants of such species are totally dependent on their parents. In these species developments in brain and in behavior seem to vary together. The successes and failures of early experience can affect the growth and development of brain circuits.

Varying an individual's experience during early development has been found to alter many aspects of behavior, brain anatomy, and brain chemistry in animal models (E. L. Bennett, et al., 1964; Gottlieb, 1976; Rosenzweig and Bennett, 1977, 1978). Presumably, similar neural processes are affected by the early childhood enrichment programs that produce a long-lasting increase in IQ in humans, especially those from deprived backgrounds (Ramey et al., 2000).

NEURAL PLASTICITY

BOX 7.3 *Transgenic and Knockout Mice*

In the text we have discussed several instances in which animals with mutations in specific genes can offer clues about the role of genes in development and brain function. Until recently the only types of mutants one could study were the very rare cases of spontaneous mutations or mutations caused by animals being treated with radiation or chemicals to increase the rate of mutation. Unless very small, short-lived animals like *Drosophila* were the subject of the research, this process was tedious because very few of the induced mutations were in the gene of interest.

Among the many new tools brought to us by the revolution in molecular biology is *site-directed mutagenesis*, the ability to cause a mutation in a particular gene. Researchers using this technique must know the sequence of nucleotides in the gene of interest. Then they can use the tendency of complementary nucleotides to hybridize with that part of the gene to induce changes (see the Appendix for a refresher on hybridization). The easiest change to make is total disruption of the gene, making it nonfunctional. If this is done in special embryonic mouse cells, there are ways to introduce the manipulated gene into the testes or ovaries of a developing mouse. That mouse can then produce offspring that are missing one copy of the gene and, through inbreeding, grandchildren missing both copies

of the gene. We call the resulting animal a **knockout mouse** because the gene of interest has been *knocked out.*

By following the development of knockout mice, we can obtain clues about the role of particular genes in normal animals. For example, the motoneurons of brain-derived neurotrophic factor (BDNF) knockout mice survive despite the absence of BDNF (Sendtner et al., 1996), so we know that trophic factor is not crucial for motoneuron survival. On the other hand, some parasympathetic ganglia fail to form in BDNF knockout mice (J. T. Erickson et al., 1996), suggesting that these neurons depend on BDNF for survival. As we'll see in Chapter 18, several genes suspected of playing a role in learning have been knocked out in mice, and the resulting animals indeed show deficits in learning.

There are some problems in interpreting such results because the missing gene may have contributed only very indirectly to the learning process, or the animal's poor performance may have been due to a distraction caused by the knockout. For that matter, even normal behavior by animals missing the gene does not prove that the gene is unimportant for behavior. Perhaps the developing animal, in the absence of that gene, somehow has compensated for the loss and found a new way to solve the problem. This would be an-

other example of the embryonic regulation that is so common in vertebrate development.

In other cases, a functional, manipulated copy of a gene can be introduced into the mouse. Such an animal is called **transgenic** because a gene has been transferred into its genome. This approach is often used as a method for improving our understanding of genetic disorders. For example, in Chapter 11 we'll learn that when a human gene that causes severe motor impairments is transferred into mice, the mice develop very similar symptoms to those that appear in humans. It may be possible to study the disease more closely in these mice and test possible therapies.

So far, knockout and transgenic animals have one limitation: They possess the genetic manipulation from the moment of conception and in every cell in the body. More recently, molecular neurobiologists have begun knocking out or replacing a gene in an animal after it has reached adulthood (by injecting the animal with a triggering substance such as tetracycline), or replacing or knocking out a gene in only one region of the brain. These manipulations allow the animals to develop with a normal genotype, thereby making it easier to interpret the result of the gene manipulation in adulthood. It may even be possible to knock out and then restore a gene.

Visual Deprivation Can Lead to Blindness

The role of experience in guiding neural development is best understood in the visual system. Some people do not see forms clearly with one of their eyes, even though the eye is intact and a sharp image is focused on the retina. Such impairments of vision are known as **amblyopia** (from the Greek *amblys,* "dull, blunt," and *ops,* "eye"). Some people with this disorder have a *lazy eye,* one that is turned inward (cross-eyed) or outward. Children born with such a misalignment see a double image rather than a single fused image. If the deviated eye is not surgically realigned early in childhood, vision becomes impaired. By the time an untreated person reaches the age of 7 or 8, pattern vision in the deviated eye is almost completely suppressed. Realignment of the eyes in adulthood does not restore acute vision to the turned eye.

CLINICAL ISSUE

The inability in these cases to correct the problem in adulthood is quite striking, since throughout the person's development light enters this eye in a normal manner and the nerve cells of the eye continue to be excited. Similar misalignment of the eyes, when it appears for the first time in adulthood, produces double vision, a condition that shows no change with further aging. These clinical observations of humans suggest that unusual positioning of the eyes during early development changes

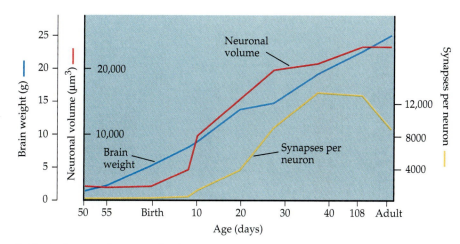

7.18 Brain Development in the Visual Cortex of Cats   Synaptic development in cats is most intense from 8 to 37 days after birth, a period during which visual experience can have profound influence. Note that brain weight and cell volume rise in a parallel fashion and precede synaptic development. Note also the decline in synapse numbers after 108 days of age—evidence of synapse rearrangement. (After Cragg, 1975.)

neural connections in the brain. (However, the connections may change further, even in adults, if the weak eye is exercised sufficiently [Romero-Apis et al., 1982]. We'll discuss amblyopia in more detail in Chapter 10.)

Understanding the cause of amblyopia in people has been greatly advanced by visual-deprivation experiments with animals. These experiments revealed startling changes related to disuse of the visual system during early critical periods. Depriving animals of light to both eyes (**binocular deprivation**) produces structural changes in visual cortical neurons: a loss of dendritic spines and a reduction in synaptic density.

If such deprivation is maintained for several weeks during development, when the animal's eyes are opened, it will be blind. Although light enters its eyes and the cells of the eyes send messages to the brain, the brain seems to ignore the messages, and the animal is unable to detect visual stimuli. If the deprivation lasts long enough, the animal is never able to recover eyesight. Thus early visual experience is crucial for the proper development of vision. There appears to be a **sensitive period** during which these manipulations of experience can exert long-lasting effects on the system. These effects are most extensive during the early period of synaptic development in the visual cortex (Figure 7.18). After the sensitive period, the manipulations have little or no effect. The exact timing of the sensitive period depends on the manipulation exerted and the species examined.

Even subtle manipulations of visual experience have profound effects on the developing visual system. Pioneering work by David Hubel and Torsten Wiesel, who shared the 1981 Nobel Prize in physiology or medicine, showed that depriving only one eye of light (**monocular deprivation**) produces profound structural and functional changes in the thalamus and visual cortex. Monocular deprivation in an infant cat or monkey causes the deprived eye not to respond when the animal reaches adulthood.

The effect of visual deprivation can be illustrated graphically by an **ocular dominance histogram,** which portrays the strength of response of a brain neuron to stimuli presented to either the left or the right eye. Normally, most cortical neurons (except those in layer IV) are excited equally by light presented to either eye (Figure 7.19*a*).

Few neurons are activated solely by inputs to one eye. Monocular deprivation early in development, by keeping one eye closed or covered, results in a striking shift in this graph; most cortical neurons respond only to input from the nondeprived eye (Figure 7.19*b*). In cats the susceptible period for this effect is the first 4 months of life. In rhesus monkeys the sensitive period extends to age 6 months. After these ages visual deprivation has little effect.

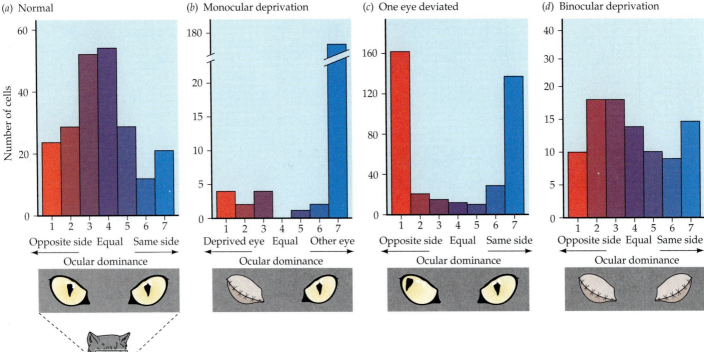

(a) Normal

Number of cells

1 2 3 4 5 6 7
Opposite side   Equal   Same side
Ocular dominance

(b) Monocular deprivation

1 2 3 4 5 6 7
Deprived eye   Equal   Other eye
Ocular dominance

(c) One eye deviated

1 2 3 4 5 6 7
Opposite side   Equal   Same side
Ocular dominance

(d) Binocular deprivation

1 2 3 4 5 6 7
Opposite side   Equal   Same side
Ocular dominance

7.19 Ocular Dominance Histograms
These histograms show responses of cells in the visual cortex of cats in normal adults (*a*), after monocular deprivation through the early critical period (*b*), after early deviation of one eye—that is, squint (*c*), and after binocular deprivation (*d*). The numbers along the *x*-axis represent a gradation in response: Cells that respond *only* to stimulation of the opposite eye are class 1 cells. Cells that respond *mainly* to stimulation of the opposite eye are class 2. Cells that respond equally to either eye are class 4. Cells that respond only to stimulation of the eye on the same side are class 7, and so on. (After Hubel and Wiesel, 1965; Wiesel and Hubel, 1965.)

NEURAL PLASTICITY

The mechanisms proposed for this phenomenon bring us to a possible understanding of the forms of amblyopia we have described. During early development, synapses are rearranged in the visual cortex, and axons representing input from each eye "compete" for synaptic places. Active, effective synapses predominate over inactive synapses. Thus if one eye is "silenced," synapses carrying information from that eye are retracted while synapses derived from the other eye are maintained. D. O. Hebb (1949) proposed that effective synapses (those that successfully drive the postsynaptic cell) might grow stronger at the expense of ineffective synapses. Thus synapses that grow stronger or weaker depending on their effectiveness in driving their target cell are known as **Hebbian synapses** (Figure 7.20). In Chapter 18 we will see that the maintenance of active synapses and retraction of inactive synapses may also play a role in learning and memory.

Researchers offer a similar explanation for amblyopia produced by misalignment of the eyes. Hubel and Wiesel (1965) produced an animal replica of this human condition by cutting muscles on one side of the eye in young cats, causing the eyes to diverge. The ocular dominance histogram of these animals reveals that the normal binocular sensitivity of visual cortical cells is greatly reduced (see Figure 7.19c). A much larger proportion of visual cortical cells are excited by stimulation of either the right or the left eye than in control animals. This effect occurs because after surgery, visual stimuli falling on the misaligned eyes no longer provide simultaneous, convergent input to the cells of the visual cortex.

The competitive interaction between the eyes results in a paradox: Brief deprivation of *both* eyes can have less of an effect on neuronal connections than an equal period of deprivation to only one eye (compare panels *a, b,* and *d* in Figure 7.19). Presumably the binocular deprivation keeps both eyes on an equal footing for stimulating cells in the visual cortex, so the predominantly binocular input to the cortical cells is retained.

One popular notion is that neurotrophic factors may be playing a role in experience-driven synapse rearrangement. For example, if the postsynaptic cells are making a limited supply of a neurotrophic factor, and if active synapses take up more of the factor than inactive synapses do, then perhaps the inactive axons retract for lack of neurotrophic factor. If this were the case, then providing all the presynaptic axon terminals with excess neurotrophic factor might delay synapse rearrangement in response to manipulations of visual experience.

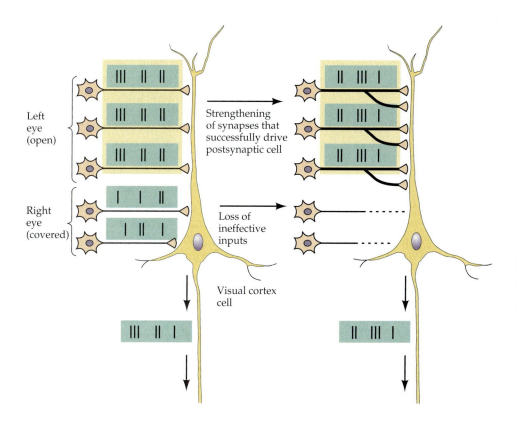

7.20 Hebbian Synapses Can Account for Changes After Monocular Deprivation (*Left*) If only one eye is open, clusters of neurons in that eye will sometimes fire at the same time because they have been stimulated by some image falling on the retina. Since neighboring cells on the retina tend to send their information to the same region of visual cortex, these simultaneously firing retinal cells will excite a single cortical cell all at once, causing the cortical cell to fire. (*Right*) Under the rules of a Hebbian synapse, these synapses that successfully drive the cortical cell will be strengthened. Meanwhile, the competing neurons from the other eye never fire together (because the eye is closed and no form vision reaches the retina), never successfully drive the cortical cell, and therefore those synapses are weakened or lost.

Indeed, Cabelli et al. (1995) found that infusions of BDNF (neurotrophin-2) or neurotrophin-4 into the visual cortex of kittens inhibited the formation of ocular dominance columns. Neither NGF (neurotrophin-1) nor neurotrophin-3 had this effect. Conversely, interfering with the action of BDNF causes the dendrites of neurons in visual cortex to shrink (McAllister et al., 1997), suggesting that this neurotrophic factor normally favors the retention of synapses. So perhaps presynaptic uptake of neurotrophic factors depends on synaptic activity, such that ineffective synapses wither for lack of neurotrophic factor.

Early Exposure to Visual Patterns Helps Fine-Tune Connections in the Visual System

At birth the visual cortex is quite immature, and most synapses have yet to form. Evidence cited in the previous sections shows that profound disuse results in changes in both structure and response of visual pathways. The modifiability of the developing brain is also evidenced when animals are exposed to certain visual patterns during early development.

Experiments in which visual patterns are manipulated early in an animal's life have used patterns such as horizontal or vertical lines (Blakemore, 1976), a field of such stripes seen through goggles (H. V. B. Hirsch and Spinelli, 1971), or small spots of light (Pettigrew and Freeman, 1973). In each case, experimenters try to ensure that the animals are exposed to visual stimuli of only one particular type. Then the animals' behavioral responses and/or their brain responses to the visual stimuli are recorded. The question is whether the animals can see stimuli to which they were exposed during a sensitive developmental period better than they see novel stimuli.

Although controversial (Movshon and van Sluyters, 1981), the results of such experiments suggest that visual experiences during the critical early periods of life can modify the responses of nerve cells in the visual cortex. The effects are subtler than those seen with complete deprivation, but the ability of animals to detect visual stimuli of a particular, general pattern (e.g., horizontal lines versus vertical lines) depends on their exposure to such visual patterns during development. These expe-

NEURAL PLASTICITY

Colin Blakemore

rience-dependent effects are probably mediated by synapse rearrangement within the visual cortex (Katz and Shatz, 1996).

Perhaps the most dramatic demonstration that sensory input organizes brain circuits comes from experiments that redirect visual information, which normally goes to visual cortex, into the auditory cortex in developing ferrets (Sharma et al., 2000). In such cases the auditory cortical cells are organized by the visual inputs into a pattern almost identical with normal visual cortex. This is also another demonstration of how cell–cell interactions guide the developing brain: The cortex seems ready to organize itself into whatever pattern is appropriate for the inputs it receives.

Experiences in Other Senses Also Affect Neural Development

Development of the brain also can be affected by early manipulation of nonvisual sensory inputs—a mouse's whiskers, for example. Thomas Woolsey and collaborators (T. A. Woolsey and Wann, 1976; T. A. Woolsey et al., 1981) found a unique clustering of nerve cells in a region of the cerebral cortex of the mouse that receives input from the whiskers.

The arrangement of whiskers on the skin is distinctive, and whiskers are arrayed similarly in all animals of the same species. The region of the cortex in which the whiskers are represented contains clusters of cells, called **whisker barrels** because their arrangement makes them look like barrels squeezed together in the cortex. The layout of these cortical barrels corresponds to the map of the whiskers (Figure 7.21). If a whisker is cut a few days after birth, sensory information from that whisker is silenced (because the shortened whisker doesn't brush against anything), and its cortical barrel does not develop. Furthermore, the whisker barrels that represent adjacent, intact whiskers tend to be enlarged, as neurons carrying information from intact whiskers expand cortical synapses at the expense of the missing whiskers (see Figure 7.21c and d; Lendvai et al., 2000). This activity-driven plasticity in cortex may be mediated by glutaminergic afferents because mice with defective NMDA-type glutamate receptors (see Box 4.2) do not form whisker barrels (Iwasato et al., 2000).

There are many other examples of early experience altering brain sensory systems. For instance, restricting salt intake in developing rats alters their later sensitivity to salty fluids (Thaw et al., 2000). And closing one nostril in newborn rats prevents the developing olfactory receptors on that side from being stimulated by odors, causing the olfactory bulb on that side of the brain to be reduced by about 25% (Brunjes, 1994).

Thomas Woolsey

NEURAL PLASTICITY

Maldevelopment of the Human Brain Impairs Behavior

Because the processes that guide development of the human brain are so various and complex, there are many ways in which they can go wrong. For example, children who experience complicated delivery at birth, when a transient lack of oxygen (**hypoxia**) may affect the brain, are at greater risk for mental retardation than are children who have a problem-free birth. The many factors that control brain development—those that govern cell proliferation, migration, and differentiation, as well as the formation of synapses—are subject to failures that can have catastrophic consequences for adaptive behavior.

The magnitude of this problem is reflected in the incidence of disorders that produce marked cognitive impairment. In the United States approximately 3.6 children per 1000 between the ages of 5 and 17 have IQ levels below 50. In this section we discuss some examples of behavioral impairment related to genetically controlled states and prenatal maternal conditions.

Some Genetic Disorders Have Widespread Effects on the Nervous System

Many genetic disorders affect metabolism and profoundly affect the developing brain. In this category are 100 to 200 different disorders involving disturbances in the metabolism of proteins, carbohydrates, or lipids. Characteristically, the genetic

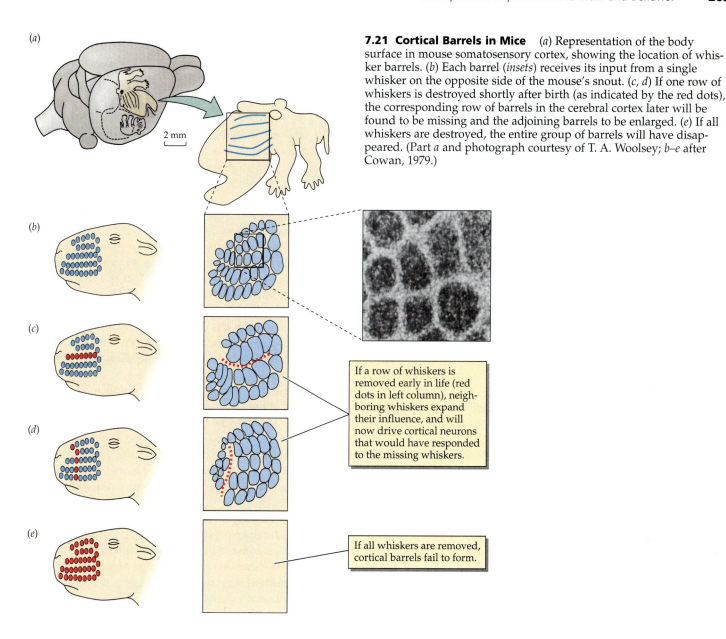

(a)

2 mm

7.21 Cortical Barrels in Mice (*a*) Representation of the body surface in mouse somatosensory cortex, showing the location of whisker barrels. (*b*) Each barrel (*insets*) receives its input from a single whisker on the opposite side of the mouse's snout. (*c, d*) If one row of whiskers is destroyed shortly after birth (as indicated by the red dots), the corresponding row of barrels in the cerebral cortex later will be found to be missing and the adjoining barrels to be enlarged. (*e*) If all whiskers are destroyed, the entire group of barrels will have disappeared. (Part *a* and photograph courtesy of T. A. Woolsey; *b–e* after Cowan, 1979.)

(b)

(c)

If a row of whiskers is removed early in life (red dots in left column), neighboring whiskers expand their influence, and will now drive cortical neurons that would have responded to the missing whiskers.

(d)

(e)

If all whiskers are removed, cortical barrels fail to form.

defect is the absence of a particular enzyme that controls a critical biochemical step in the synthesis or breakdown of a vital body product. Enzymatic deficits can affect the brain in two ways: Either (1) certain compounds build up to toxic levels, or (2) compounds needed for function or structure fail to be synthesized.

An example of the first type of deficit is **phenylketonuria** (**PKU**), a recessive hereditary disorder of protein metabolism that at one time resulted in many people with mental retardation. One out of 50 persons is a carrier; one in 10,000 births produces an affected victim. The basic defect is the absence of an enzyme necessary to metabolize phenylalanine, an amino acid that is present in many foods. The brain damage caused by phenylketonuria is probably due to an enormous buildup of phenylalanine.

The discovery of PKU marked the first time that an inborn error of metabolism was associated with mental retardation. Nowadays screening methods, required by law throughout the United States, assess the level of phenylalanine in children a few days after birth. Early detection is important because brain impairment can be prevented by a diet low in phenylalanine. Such dietary control of phenylketonuria is critical during early years, especially before age 2; after that, diet can be relaxed somewhat.

GENES AND BEHAVIOR

**CLINICAL
ISSUE**

New syndromes that probably involve inherited metabolic disorders are constantly being discovered. Researchers have become interested in a disorder called **Williams syndrome** (see Figure 19.13). Patients with this disorder have largely intact linguistic functioning, a large vocabulary, and very fluent speech. Yet they also show clear mental retardation on standard IQ tests: They have great difficulty in copying a pattern of blocks or assembling a picture from its parts (Lenhoff et al., 1997). MRI studies reveal a selective effect on brain development. Patients who suffer from Williams syndrome show reduced cerebral size, but normal cerebellar and subcortical structure (Jernigan et al., 1993). An autopsy of one such patient revealed increased cell packing and abnormally clustered and oriented neurons throughout the brain (Galaburda et al., 1994).

A more common form of cognitive disorder, resulting from a chromosomal abnormality, is **Down syndrome.** The disorder associated with 95% of these cases is an extra chromosome 21 (for a total of three). This disorder is strikingly related to the age of the mother at the time of conception: For women over 45 years of age, the chance of having a baby with Down syndrome is nearly 1 in 40 (Karp, 1976). The behavioral dysfunctions are quite varied. Most individuals who have Down syndrome have a very low IQ, but some rare individuals attain an IQ of 80. Brain abnormalities in Down syndrome also vary. Biopsies of the cerebral cortex of patients with Down syndrome show abnormal formation of dendritic spines. A mouse model that involves an extra chromosome results in structural and behavioral changes that are analogous to Down syndrome in humans (C. J. Epstein, 1986; Siarey et al., 1997).

Very likely, the most frequent cause of inherited mental retardation is the condition **fragile X syndrome.** At the end of the long arm of the X chromosome is a site that seems fragile—prone to breaking because the DNA there is unstable (Yu et al., 1991). Persons with this abnormality have a modified facial appearance, including elongation of the face, large prominent ears, and a prominent chin. A wide range of cognitive impairments—from mild to severe retardation—are associated with this syndrome (Baumgardner et al., 1994). The disorder is more common in males than in females.

**GENES AND
BEHAVIOR**

The molecular basis of fragile X syndrome provided a surprise for geneticists because it demonstrated that we don't always pass on a faithful copy of our DNA to our offspring. The fragile site in the DNA consists of three nucleotides (CGG; see the Appendix for a review of nucleotides) repeated over and over. Most people have only 6 to 50 of these **trinucleotide repeats** at this site (Laxova, 1994). But during the production of sperm or eggs, the number of repeats sometimes changes, so a father who has only 50 trinucleotide repeats may provide 100 repeats to his daughter.

People who have between 51 and 200 of the CGG repeats are themselves unaffected, but any of their children who receive more than 200 repeats will display fragile X syndrome. No one knows why the number of repeats changes from one generation to the next or what determines whether more or fewer repeats will appear (Paulson and Fischbeck, 1996). Trinucleotide repeats of another gene are also at the heart of another behavioral disorder: Huntington's disease (see Chapter 11).

Exposure to Drugs during Pregnancy Can Impair Neural Development

Even in the protected environment of the womb, the embryo and fetus are not immune to outside influence; what is taking place in the mother's body directly affects them. Maternal conditions such as viral infection, exposure to drugs, and malnutrition are especially likely to result in developmental disorders in the unborn child. Concern with the maternal environment as a determinant of brain development spawned the field of **behavioral teratology** (*teratology*—from the Greek *teras*, "monster"—is the study of malformations). Investigators in this field are especially concerned with the pathological effects of drugs ingested during pregnancy.

There is a long history of concern about alcohol and pregnancy, dating back to classical times. Aristotle warned that "foolish, drunken . . . women . . . bring forth children like unto themselves, morose and languid" (cited in Abel, 1982). By now, the wisdom of this observation (if not the misogyny) is well supported by abundant

(a) Normal infant　　　Corpus callosum　　　(b) Infant with FAS

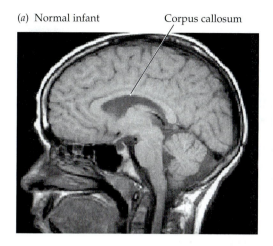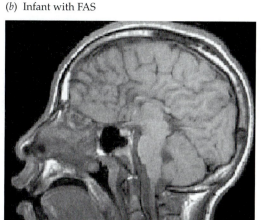

7.22 Abnormal Brain Development Associated with Fetal Alcohol Syndrome A brain from a normal infant (a) compared to a brain from an infant with FAS of the same age (b). The FAS brain shows microcephaly (abnormal smallness), fewer cerebral cortical gyri, and the absence of a corpus callosum connecting the two hemispheres. (Courtesy of E. Riley.)

research. About 40% of children born to alcoholic mothers show a distinctive profile of anatomical, physiological, and behavioral impairments known as **fetal alcohol syndrome (FAS)** (Abel, 1984; Colangelo and Jones, 1982).

Prominent anatomical effects of fetal exposure to alcohol include distinctive changes in facial features (e.g., a sunken nasal bridge and altered shape of the nose and eyelids) and stunted growth. Few of these children catch up in the years following birth. The most common problem associated with FAS is mental retardation, which varies in severity. No alcohol threshold has yet been established for this syndrome, but it can occur with relatively moderate intake during pregnancy.

In addition to mental retardation, children with fetal alcohol syndrome show other neurological abnormalities, such as hyperactivity, irritability, tremulousness, and other signs of motor instability. In some cases, they lack a corpus callosum (Figure 7.22). Even children of alcoholic mothers who do not show physical symptoms and are therefore not diagnosed as having FAS often have neurophysiological impairments (Mattson et al., 1998). This syndrome may not be restricted to alcohol; heavy use of marijuana seems to exert a similar effect on fetal growth and development (Hingson et al., 1982).

CLINICAL ISSUE

The Brain Continues to Change As We Grow Older

The passage of time brings us an accumulation of joys and sorrows—perhaps riches and fame—and a progressive decline in many of our abilities. Although slower responses seem inevitable with aging, many of our cognitive abilities show little change during the adult years, until we reach an advanced age. What happens to brain structure from adolescence to the day when we all become a little forgetful and walk more hesitantly? Does the structure of the brain change continuously throughout the life span?

Changes in the structure of the brain with aging can be viewed at different levels, from subcellular structures to overall brain morphology. Brain weight declines with age, but some people have questioned the relevance of aging to these weight changes because it is hard to distinguish changes due to aging from changes that arise from disease states shortly before death. An excellent study that eliminated such confounding factors showed that changes are very small up to the age of 45, after which time the weight of the brain begins to decline significantly (see Figure 7.1). The course of these changes is the same for men and women, even though women generally live 7 to 10 years longer than men. Data also emphasize that aging is a variable state. Declines are evident in many people, and exaggerated in some. This variability highlights the genetic contribution to aging and reinforces the idea that if you want to live long, choose parents and grandparents who have lived long.

Another measure used in studies of brain aging is the number of neural and glial cells in particular volumes of tissue. Investigators map specific regions and count the number of cells in various areas, using tissue taken from people who have died at different ages. These studies suggest that cell changes begin as early as the third decade of life and are specific to particular regions. Even more noticeable than the decrease in the number of cells is the loss of synaptic connections, which is especially prominent in the frontal cortical regions. However, growth cones can be found in the dendritic terminals of cortical cells of old people, suggesting that some forms of synaptic plasticity continue throughout life.

Memory Impairment Correlates with Hippocampal Shrinkage during Aging

In a recent study of healthy and cognitively normal people, aged 55 to 87, investigators asked whether mild impairment in memory is specifically related to reduction in size of the hippocampal formation (HF) or is better explained by generalized shrinkage of brain tissue (Golomb et al., 1994). (In Chapter 18 we'll see that the HF is implicated in memory.) Loss of HF tissue has been reported in cases of mild Alzheimer's disease and in elderly individuals who show cognitive impairment (Convit et al., 1993; de Leon et al., 1993; Killiany et al., 1993), but it is unclear to what extent atrophy of the HF can account for milder declines in memory that many neurologically healthy older people experience.

In one study, volunteers took a series of memory tests and were scored for both immediate recall and delayed recall. A series of ten coronal MRI images for each subject was measured for three variables (Figure 7.23): (1) volume of the HF; (2) volume of the supratemporal gyrus, a region that is close to the HF and is known to shrink with age but has not been implicated in memory; and (3) volume of the subarachnoid cerebrospinal fluid (that is, the fluid-filled space between the interior of the skull and the surface of the brain), which yields a measure of overall shrinkage of the brain. Immediate memory showed very little decline with age, but delayed memory did decline. When effects of sex, age, IQ, and overall brain atrophy were eliminated statistically, HF volume was the only brain measure that correlated significantly with the delayed memory score.

Of course, brain regions not included in this study also may correlate with memory, so other areas of the brain should be included in future measurements. In addition, the techniques of this experiment did not allow the researchers to measure small regions, such as the entorhinal cortex, that animal experiments show are also important for memory.

Two regions of the motor system show how different the effects of aging can be. In the motor cortex a type of large neuron—the Betz cell—starts to decline in number by about age 50, and by the time a person reaches age 80, many of these cells have shriveled away (M. E. Scheibel et al., 1977). In contrast, other cells involved in motor circuitry—for example, those in an area of the brainstem called the inferior olive—remain about the same in number through at least eight decades of life.

7.23 Hippocampal Shrinkage Correlates with Memory Decline in Aging (*Left*) MRI images that illustrate the variables tested for correlation with memory decline in normal aged people, such as the one on the right, are taken from the plane of section shown here. (*Right*) The hippocampal formation is shaded red, the supratemporal gyrus orange, and the space between brain and skull yellow-green. Only shrinkage of the hippocampal formation correlated with memory decline. (From Golomb et al., 1994; MRI courtesy of James Golomb.)

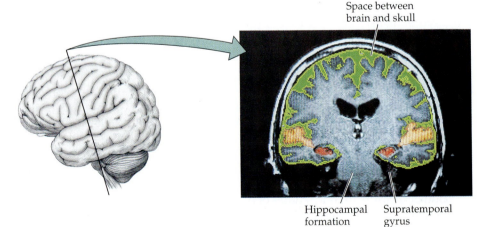

Space between brain and skull

Hippocampal formation   Supratemporal gyrus

PET scans of elderly people add a new perspective to aging-related changes. Studies of normal cases reveal that cerebral metabolism remains almost constant. This stability is in marked contrast to the decline of cerebral metabolism in Alzheimer's disease, which we will consider next.

Alzheimer's Disease Is Associated with a Decline in Cerebral Metabolism

Since 1900, the population of people over the age of 65 in the United States has increased dramatically. Most people reaching this age lead happy, productive lives, although at a slower pace than they did in earlier years. In a growing number of elderly people, however, age has brought a particular agony—the disorder called **Alzheimer's disease,** named after the neurologist who first described a type of **dementia** (drastic failure of cognitive ability, including memory failure and loss of orientation) appearing before the age of 65. Alzheimer's disease is sometimes called *senile dementia.*

Over 4 million Americans suffer from Alzheimer's disease, and the progressive aging of our population means that these ranks will continue to swell. This disorder is found worldwide with almost no geographic differences. The frequency of Alzheimer's increases with aging up to age 85 to 90 (Rocca et al., 1991), but people who reach that age without symptoms become increasingly less likely ever to develop them (Breitner et al., 1999). This last finding indicates that Alzheimer's is in fact a disease, and not simply the result of wear and tear in the brain.

Alzheimer's disease is characterized by a progressive decline in intellectual functioning. It begins as a loss of memory of recent events. Eventually this memory impairment becomes all-encompassing, so extensive that Alzheimer's patients cannot maintain any form of conversation because both the context and prior information are rapidly lost. They cannot answer simple questions such as, What year is it? Who is the president of the United States? or Where are you now? Cognitive decline is progressive and relentless. In time, patients become disoriented and easily lose themselves in familiar surroundings. Very commonly, this drastic loss of cognitive functioning is unaccompanied by any other readily apparent mark of debility, such as loss of motor coordination.

Observations of the whole brain of Alzheimer's patients reveal striking cortical atrophy, especially in frontal, temporal, and parietal areas. PET scans following the administration of a radioactive form of glucose show marked reduction of metabolism in posterior parietal cortex and some portions of the temporal lobe (Figure 7.24; Foster et al., 1984). Functional MRI reveals a disruption of the normal columnar organization of the cortex (Buldyrev et al., 2000), which we described in Chapter 2.

The brains of Alzheimer's patients reveal three characteristic cellular changes:

1. Strange patches of degenerating axon terminals and dendrites, termed **senile plaques** (Figure 7.25*a*), appear in frontal and temporoparietal cortex, the hippocampus, and associated limbic system sites. The plaques are formed by the buildup of a substance called β-**amyloid** (Selkoe, 1991), so they are sometimes called amyloid plaques.
2. Some cells show abnormalities called **neurofibrillary tangles,** which are abnormal whorls of neurofilaments, including a protein called **tau,** that form a tangled array in the cell. The number of senile plaques is directly related to the magnitude of cognitive impairment. Because neurofibrillary tangles appear in other brain disorders, in Alzheimer's they are probably a secondary response to amyloid plaques.
3. These degenerative events cause the basal forebrain nuclei to disappear in Alzheimer's patients (Figure 7.25*b*), either because the cells die or because they stop producing their transmitter, acetylcholine. The latter possibility is more likely, because providing these neurons with NGF restores their cholinergic characteristics in aged monkeys (D. E. Smith et al., 1999).

CLINICAL ISSUE

Alois Alzheimer (1864–1915)

7.24 Patients with Alzheimer's Show Reduced Activity in the Brain When compared with normal elderly subjects (*a*), patients with Alzheimer's disease (*b*) show less widespread brain activation in PET scans. The dots in right column highlight regions where this difference is particularly apparent. (Courtesy of John Mazziotta.)

(*a*) Normal (*b*) Person with Alzheimer's

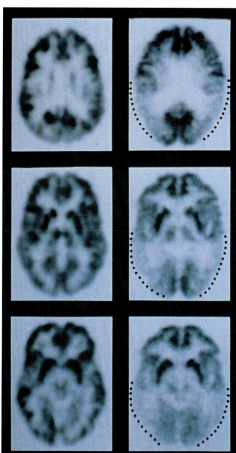

7.25 Patients with Alzheimer's Show Structural Changes in the Brain (*a*) Neurofibrillary tangles (the flame-shaped objects) and senile plaques (the darkly stained clusters) are visible in this micrograph of the cerebral cortex of an aged patient with Alzheimer's. (*b*) This representation of the brain shows the location of the basal forebrain nuclei and the distribution of their axons, which use acetylcholine as a neurotransmitter. These cells seem to disappear in Alzheimer's patients. (From Roses, 1995; micrograph courtesy of Gary W. Van Hoesen.)

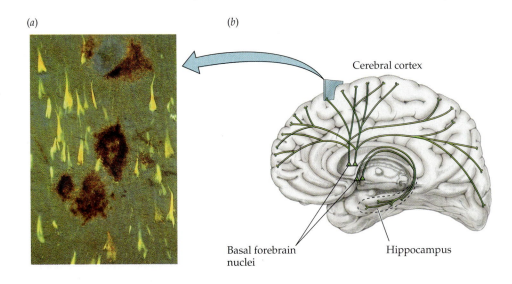

(*a*)

(*b*)

Cerebral cortex

Basal forebrain nuclei

Hippocampus

If amyloid plaques are the primary cause of Alzheimer's, what causes the buildup of β-amyloid? **Amyloid precursor protein** (**APP**) is cleaved by two enzymes—**β-secretase** and **presenilin**—to form extracellular β-amyloid that builds up. Mutations in each of the genes that produce these proteins have been associated with Alzheimer's disease, with presenilin mutations by far the most common cause (Selkoe, 1999). This scenario, depicted in Figure 7.26, suggests several treatment strategies, such as injection of antibodies that will bind β-amyloid and slow the formation of plaques (Bard et al., 2000).

A gene called *ApoE* (for *apolipoprotein E*) has been associated with Alzheimer's disease (Raber et al., 2000; Strittmatter and Roses, 1996). The most common forms of the gene are *ApoE2, ApoE3,* and *ApoE4.* Everyone has two copies of the gene, but people who have one or two copies of the *ApoE4* version are at much higher risk for Alzheimer's. One theory is that the *ApoE* proteins normally break down β-amyloid, but the *E4* version is less effective.

Two Timescales Are Needed to Describe Brain Development

In the introduction to this part of the book, we warned that Chapters 6 and 7 would present two very different timescales for the development of brain and behavior—the eons of evolution versus the days and years of ontogeny. These different timescales are analogous to the different but equally essential contributions of an architect and a contractor, respectively, in building a house.

In preparing his plans, the architect calls on a long history of human knowledge about structures that meet basic human needs. These plans incorporate hard-won information gathered over the centuries. Similarly, our genes carry a basic plan that has worked for millions of generations (absolutely every one of your millions of ancestors managed to reproduce!).

The contractor's perspective is more like that of a developing individual. He must use the general plans of the architect to construct a particular house here and now. As he builds, the contractor's judgment and interpretation are necessary, so two houses built from the same blueprints will not be identical, just as two monozygotic twins will show differences. In fact, even the best architects rely on contractors to adjust and improvise to make their plans work. Similarly, the information in our genome relies on extrinsic factors such as experience to determine the fine wiring of the nervous system.

Long ago, well before the common ancestor of all the vertebrates emerged, developing animals began relying on cell–cell interactions to adjust the fate of indi-

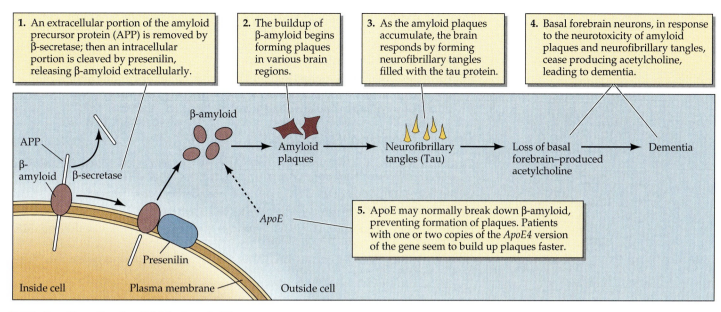

1. An extracellular portion of the amyloid precursor protein (APP) is removed by β-secretase; then an intracellular portion is cleaved by presenilin, releasing β-amyloid extracellularly.

2. The buildup of β-amyloid begins forming plaques in various brain regions.

3. As the amyloid plaques accumulate, the brain responds by forming neurofibrillary tangles filled with the tau protein.

4. Basal forebrain neurons, in response to the neurotoxicity of amyloid plaques and neurofibrillary tangles, cease producing acetylcholine, leading to dementia.

5. ApoE may normally break down β-amyloid, preventing formation of plaques. Patients with one or two copies of the *ApoE4* version of the gene seem to build up plaques faster.

7.26 One Hypothesis of Alzheimer's Disease

vidual cells on the basis of their position in the organism as a whole. Once this strategy was adopted, it was only a matter of time before the fate of some neurons would be affected by neural activity. So neural activity began determining which synapses and neurons would be retained and which would be eliminated. Eventually, it would be the neural activity derived from sensory neurons—experience itself—that would affect these decisions. That is how we humans came to have a nervous system so malleable, so plastic, that we can write, read, and think about our own origins.

Summary

1. Early embryological events in the formation of the nervous system include a sequence of six cellular processes: (1) the production of nerve cells (neurogenesis); (2) the movement of cells away from regions of mitotic division (cell migration); (3) the acquisition, by these cells, of distinctive neuronal forms (cell differentiation); (4) the establishment of synaptic connections (synaptogenesis); (5) the selective loss of some cells (neuronal cell death); and (6) the selective rearrangement of previously formed synapses.

2. Fetal and postnatal changes in the brain include the myelination of axons by glial cells and the development of dendrites and synapses by neurons. Although in humans most neurons are present at birth, most synapses develop after birth and continue developing into adulthood.

3. In simple animals such as the nematode *Caenorhabditis elegans*, neural pathways and synapses form according to an innate, genetic plan that specifies the precise relations between growing axons and particular target cells. In more complicated animals, however, including all vertebrates, genes do not exert such rigid control on specific neural connections.

4. Among the many determinants of brain development are (1) genetic information and (2) a multitude of extrinsic factors, such as neurotrophic factors, nutrition, and experience.

5. Experience affects the growth and development of the nervous system. Experience can induce and modulate the formation of synapses, maintain synapses that are already formed, or determine which neurons and synapses will survive and which will be eliminated.

6. Maldevelopment of the brain can occur as a result of genetically controlled disorders. Some are metabolic disorders, such as phenylketonuria; others, such as Down syndrome, are related to disorders of chromosomes.

7. Impairments of fetal development that lead to mental retardation can be caused by the use of drugs such as alcohol or marijuana during pregnancy.

Refer to the *Learning Biological Psychology* CD for the following study aids for this chapter:

6 Objectives

74 Study Questions

1 Activity

6 Videos

8. The brain continues to change throughout life. Old age is accompanied by the loss of neurons and synaptic connections in some regions of the brain. In some people the changes are more severe than in others; pathological changes characterize the condition known as Alzheimer's disease.

9. Alzheimer's seems to be caused by a buildup of β-amyloid, causing degenerative plaques and tangles through much of the cortex. Several genes, such as *ApoE*, influence the rate of amyloid accumulation and therefore the risk of Alzheimer's.

Recommended Reading

Cowan, W. M., Jessell, T. M., and Zipursky, S. L. (1997). *Molecular and cellular approaches to neural development*. New York: Oxford University Press.

Gilbert, S. F. (2000). *Developmental biology* (6th ed.). Sunderland, MA: Sinauer.

Jacobson, M. (1991). *Developmental neurobiology*. New York: Plenum.

Purves, D., and Lichtman, J. W. (1985). *Principles of neural development*. Sunderland, MA: Sinauer.

Sanes, D. H., Reh, T.A., and Harris, W.A. (2000). *Development of the nervous system*. San Diego, CA: Academic Press.

PART THREE

Perception and Action

L ight from the sun warms our skin and stimulates our eyes. A chorus of sounds, ranging from the songs of insects to the hearty performances of opera singers stimulates our ears. Winds bend the hairs on our skin and carry pleasant or unpleasant odors. The food we eat affects receptors in the mouth, the stomach, and the brain. All about us a wide range of energies and substances excites our senses and supplies our brains with a vast array of information about external and internal happenings.

The success of any animal—including humans—in dealing with the tasks of survival depends on its ability to construct reliable representations of some of the physical characteristics of its environment. In most cases, however, sensory systems are not slavish, passive copiers and reflectors of impinging stimuli—quite the contrary. Evolutionary success calls for far more selective action. For any species, sensory systems construct only partial and selective portraits of the world.

Sensory inputs to the brain do not merely provide "pictures in the head"; they often incite the individual to act. Consider the simple case of a sound that occurs suddenly: Our eyes almost automatically turn toward the source of the sound. Some movements are not directly driven or triggered by sensory events but reflect intrinsic programs of action, which may involve sensory inputs only as modulators. How information is processed in perceptual systems (the topic addressed in Chapters 8 through 10) and then used to choose particular motor responses (Chapter 11) is our theme in Part 3.

8

General Principles of Sensory Processing, Touch, and Pain

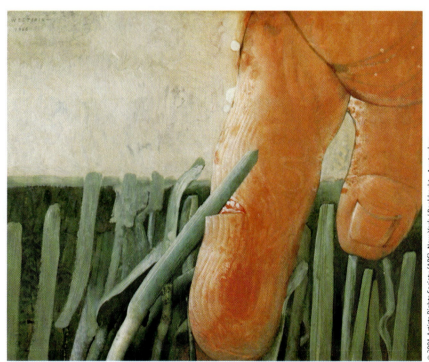

Co Westerik, *Cut by Grass* (1), 1966, oil and tempera on panel, 60 × 75 cm

*A*ll around us are many different types of energy that affect us in various ways. Some molecules traveling through the air cause us to note particular odors. We detect waves of compression and expansion of air as sounds. Our abilities to detect, recognize, and appreciate these varied energies depend on the characteristics of sensory systems. These systems include receptors specialized to detect specific energies and the neural pathways of the spinal cord and the brain that receive input from these receptors.

For each species, however, certain features of surrounding energies have become especially significant for adaptive success. For example, the bat darting through the evening sky is specially equipped to detect ultrasonic cries. Most humans, on the other hand, are hardly able to detect such sounds. Some snakes, such as boa constrictors, have infrared-sensing organs that enable them to generate an image of heat sources in their surroundings, thus enabling them to locate warm-blooded prey.

Sensory Processing

Each species has distinctive windows on the world based on the energy sensitivities of its receptors and on how its nervous system processes information from the receptors. In the first portion of this chapter we will consider some of the basic principles of sensory processing. In the second half we'll see how those principles apply to touch and pain sensation.

All Sensory Systems Follow the Same Basic Plan

All animals have specialized body parts that are particularly sensitive to some forms of energy. These **sensory receptor organs** act as filters of the environment: They detect and respond to some stimuli but not others. Furthermore, receptors convert energy into the language of the nervous system: electrical signals. Eventually information from sensory receptor organs enters the brain as a series of action potentials traveling along millions of axons, and our brains must make sense of it all.

Across the animal kingdom, receptor organs offer enormous diversity. A wide array of sizes, shapes, and forms reflects the varying survival needs of different animals (Figure 8.1). For some snakes, detectors of infrared radiation are essential, and several species of fish depend on receptors of electrical energy. Several migratory animals detect Earth's magnetic field (Deutschlander et al., 1999; Diebel et al., 2000). These specialized sensors have evolved to detect signals that are crucial for partic-

(a)

(b)

(c)

(d)

8.1 The Variety of Eyes (*a*) The compound eyes of a tabanid fly are specially adapted for detecting motion. (*b*) The panther chameleon can move its eyes independently. (*c*) The eyes of the Philippine tarsier are specialized for nocturnal foraging. (*d*) The eyes of the American bald eagle demonstrate high acuity.

ular environmental niches. Thus receptor organs reflect strategies for success in particular worlds.

We will begin by considering some ideal properties of sensory systems from both biological and engineering perspectives. These perspectives help us understand the characteristics of sensory systems, the evolutionary forces that have generated them, and the costs and benefits of various sensory mechanisms.

**EVOLUTION
AT WORK**

A Sensory System Requires Different Receptors to Discriminate among Forms of Energy

The types of energies and the range of substances in the world are quite broad. Different kinds of energy, such as light and sound, need different receptors to convert them into neural activity, just as taking a photograph requires a camera, not an audiotape recorder. We gain information by distinguishing among types of stimulus energy. We may appreciate the poet who writes, "The dawn came up like thunder," but most of the time we want to know whether a sudden dramatic sensory event was auditory or visual, a touch or a smell. Furthermore, different senses furnish us with quite different information: We may see a car hurtling toward us, hear the whine of a mosquito circling us, or smell gas escaping, but we might not hear the car until it is too late, and we would not smell the mosquito or see the gas. Thus our model sensory system should provide us with the means of detecting and distinguishing among different forms of energy.

The pioneer physiologist Johannes Müller explored this requirement of sensory systems early in the nineteenth century. He proposed the doctrine of **specific nerve energies,** which states that the receptors and neural channels for the different senses are independent and operate in their own special ways. For example, no matter how the eye is stimulated—by light or mechanical pressure or by electrical shock—the resulting sensation is always visual. Müller formulated his hypothesis before the nature of nervous transmission was known. Today, we know that the messages for the different senses—such as seeing, hearing, touching, sensing pain, and sensing temperature—are kept separate and distinct not by the use of different "nerve energies," but by the use of separate nerve tracts.

A Sensory System Should Discriminate among Different Intensities of Stimulation

Many forms of energy have a broad range of intensities. For example, a sonic boom brings to the ear millions of times more energy than the tick of a watch, and sunlight at noon has 10 million times more energy than the wan light of the first quarter moon. The optimal visual sensory system would be able to represent stimulus values over these broad ranges so that the viewer could always discriminate accurately, neither groping in the dark nor being blinded by the glare of intense light. However, because sensitivity to very feeble stimuli may require highly specialized, and therefore costly, sensory detectors, we must settle for a realistic lower limit.

If the system is to respond to a wide range of intensities, it should be sensitive to differences in intensity; that is, it should be able to provide large responses for small changes in the strength of a stimulus. The absolute value of a stimulus is seldom of major adaptive significance. In most instances the important signal for survival is a *change* in the stimulus. We respond mainly to changes—whether they are changes in intensity, quality, or location of the stimulus.

A Sensory System Should Respond Reliably

In a reliable sensory system, the relation between any signal in the external or internal environment and the response of the sensory system to that signal is consistent. Imagine your confusion if a cold stimulus randomly elicited the responses cold, warm, painful, and slippery. To establish useful representations of the world, our sensory system must produce the same sensations for the same stimuli.

A customary way to improve the reliability of a system is to increase the number of its components. Using several different circuits to process the same stimulus (parallel processing) is a conventional way to ensure reliability. However, increasing the number of components in biological systems comes at greater metabolic expense and may compromise speed.

A Sensory System Should Respond Rapidly

Optimal adjustment to the world requires that sensory information be processed rapidly. As a driver, you have to perceive the motion of other cars swiftly and correctly to avoid collisions. Similarly, it does not do a predator much good to recognize prey unless it can do so both rapidly and accurately. Thus we have come up against a conflict between optimal properties: They must be able to respond both reliably and rapidly.

A Sensory System Should Suppress Extraneous Information

Have you ever tried to hold a conversation on a dance floor? Could you hear anything besides the overwhelming input of the music? This example illustrates a paradox. In describing the optimal sensory system, we have emphasized the need for exquisite sensitivity and reliability, but now we argue that this extraordinary system should also be able to ignore some of the world. From moment to moment, particular stimuli may be especially important, while other stimuli fade into insignificance. The fragrance of perfume may be quite compelling in an intimate situation, but it may go undetected when we are frantically reading a road map. As we will see, different sensory devices suppress stimuli in different ways.

How are the optimal properties that we have just discussed realized in the sensory systems of human beings and other species? What compromises has natural selection settled upon? Let's examine some basic features of all actual sensory systems.

Different Species Detect Different Aspects of the World with Similar Sensory Systems

From the physicist's point of view, the stimuli that animals detect are forms of physical energy or chemical substances that can be defined and described by measures of physics and chemistry. For example, a sound meter can measure the intensity of an acoustic stimulus, and a light meter can measure visual stimuli. Likewise, different sensory receptors respond to different types of stimuli.

Table 8.1 classifies sensory systems, identifying the kinds of stimuli related to each system. An **adequate stimulus** is the type of stimulus for which a given sensory organ is particularly adapted. The adequate stimulus for the eye is photic (light) energy; although mechanical pressure on the eye or an electrical shock can stimulate the retina and produce sensations of light, these are not adequate stimuli for the eye.

Sensory Systems of Particular Animals Have a Restricted Range of Responsiveness

For any single form of physical energy, the sensory systems of a particular animal are quite selective. For example, humans do not hear sounds in the frequency range above 20,000 cycles per second (hertz [Hz]), a range we call ultrasonic. To a bat, however, air vibrations of 50,000 Hz would be sound waves, just as vibrations of 10,000 Hz would. The range of hearing for larger mammals is even lower than that of humans. Figure 8.2 compares the auditory ranges of some animals. In the visual realm, too, some animals can detect stimuli that humans cannot. For example, birds and bees see in the ultraviolet range of light.

Sensory Processing Begins in Receptor Cells

Detection of energy starts with the properties of **receptor cells.** A given receptor cell is specialized to detect particular energies or chemicals. Upon exposure to a stim-

TABLE 8.1   *Classification of Sensory Systems*

Type of sensory system	Modality	Adequate stimuli
Mechanical	Touch	Contact with or deformation of body surface
	Hearing	Sound vibrations in air or water
	Vestibular	Head movement and orientation
	Joint	Position and movement
	Muscle	Tension
Photic	Seeing	Visible radiant energy
Thermal	Cold	Decrement of skin temperature
	Warmth	Increment of skin temperature
Chemical	Smell	Odorous substances dissolved in air or water in the nasal cavity
	Taste	Substances in contact with the tongue or other taste receptor; in mammals the categories of taste experience are sweet, sour, salty, bitter (and possibly umami)
	Common chemical	Changes in CO_2, pH, osmotic pressure
	Vomeronasal	Pheromones in air or water (see Chapters 5 and 9)
Electrical	Electroreception	Differences in density of electrical currents

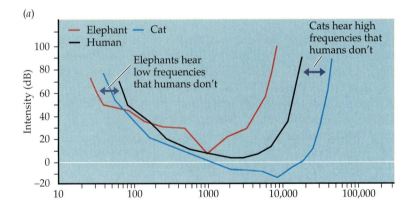

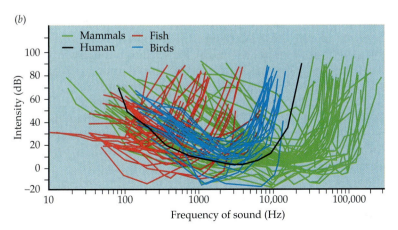

8.2 Do You Hear What I Hear?   For comparison, the auditory sensitivity ranges of three mammals (*a*) and of many species of fish, birds, and mammals (*b*) are plotted here together. Note that the species within a class detect a similar range of frequencies. For a discussion of the measurement of sound, see Box 9.1.

8.3 Receptors in Skin
The different functions of several of these receptors are compared in Figure 8.14.

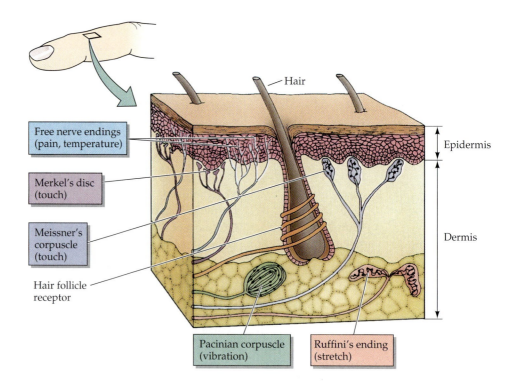

Free nerve endings (pain, temperature)

Merkel's disc (touch)

Meissner's corpuscle (touch)

Hair follicle receptor

Hair

Epidermis

Dermis

Pacinian corpuscle (vibration)

Ruffini's ending (stretch)

ulus, a receptor cell converts the energy into a change in the electrical potential across its membrane. Changing the signal in this way is called **sensory transduction** (devices that convert energy from one form to another are known as *transducers,* and the process is called *transduction*). Receptors are transducers that are the starting points for the neural activity that leads to sensory perception. Figure 8.3 shows some different receptor cells in skin. We will look at these types in more detail later in the chapter.

Some receptor cells have axons to transmit information. Other receptor cells have no axon of their own, but stimulate an associated nerve ending, either mechanically or chemically. For example, various kinds of corpuscles are associated with nerve endings in the skin. The eye has specialized receptor cells that convert photic energy into electrical changes that cause neurotransmitter to be released upon nearby neurons. The inner ear has specialized hair cells that transduce mechanical energy into electrical signals that stimulate the fibers of the auditory nerve.

The Initial Stage of Sensory Processing Is a Change in Electrical Potential in Receptor Cells

The structure of a receptor determines the forms of energy to which it will respond. In all cases the steps between the impact of energy at a receptor cell and the initiation of nerve impulses in a nerve fiber leading away from the receptor involve local changes of membrane potential; these are referred to as **generator potentials.** (In most instances, the generator potential resembles the excitatory postsynaptic potentials discussed in Chapter 3.) These electrical changes are the necessary and sufficient conditions for generating nerve impulses (action potentials).

One example of the generator potential can be studied in a receptor called the **pacinian corpuscle** (Loewenstein, 1971). This receptor is found throughout the body in skin and muscle, but it is especially prominent in tissue overlying the abdominal cavity. It is made of a neural fiber that enters a structure that resembles a tiny onion consisting of concentric layers of tissue separated by fluid (Figure 8.4*a*).

Mechanical stimuli (in this case vibration) delivered to the corpuscle produce a graded electrical potential with an amplitude that is directly proportional to the strength of the stimulus. When this electrical event reaches sufficient amplitude, the

(a) Innervation of a pacinian corpuscle

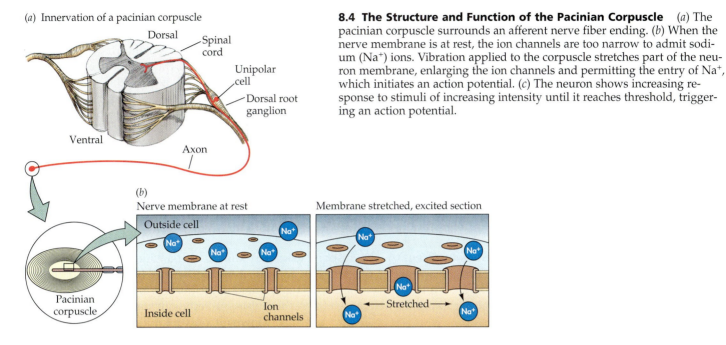

8.4 The Structure and Function of the Pacinian Corpuscle (a) The pacinian corpuscle surrounds an afferent nerve fiber ending. (b) When the nerve membrane is at rest, the ion channels are too narrow to admit sodium (Na^+) ions. Vibration applied to the corpuscle stretches part of the neuron membrane, enlarging the ion channels and permitting the entry of Na^+, which initiates an action potential. (c) The neuron shows increasing response to stimuli of increasing intensity until it reaches threshold, triggering an action potential.

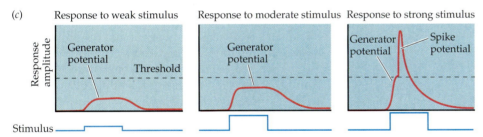

nerve impulse is generated. Careful dissection of the corpuscle, leaving the bared axon terminal intact, shows that this graded potential—the generator potential—is initiated in the nerve terminal. Pressing the corpuscle bends this terminal, which leads to the generator event. The sequence of excitatory events is as follows:

1. Mechanical stimulation deforms the corpuscle.
2. This deformation leads to mechanical stretch of the tip of the axon.
3. Stretching the axon enlarges pores in the membrane, allowing sodium ions to enter (Figure 8.4b).
4. When the generator potential reaches **threshold** amplitude, the axon produces one or more nerve impulses (Figure 8.4c).

Sensory Information Processing Is Selective and Analytical

Thinkers in ancient Greece believed that the nerves were tubes through which tiny bits of stimulus objects traveled to the brain, to be analyzed and recognized there. Even after gaining accurate knowledge of neural conduction in the twentieth century, many investigators thought that the sensory nerves simply transmitted accurate information about stimulation to the brain centers. Now, however, it is clear that the sensory organs and peripheral sensory pathways convey only limited—even distorted—information to the centers. A good deal of selection and analysis takes place in the peripheral sensory pathways. In the discussion that follows we will examine some basic aspects of this processing: coding, sensory adaptation, suppression, receptive fields, and attention.

Sensory Events Are Represented by Neural Codes

Information about the world is represented in the circuits of the nervous system by electrical potentials in cells. We have already considered the first step in this process—the transformation of energy at receptors (i.e., transduction) and the generator potential. But once action potentials are produced, how do they represent the stimulus? In some manner electrical events in nerve cells "stand for" (represent) stimuli impinging on an organism. This system of representation is often referred to as **coding.** (A *code* is a set of rules for translating information from one form to another. For example, we can code a message in English for telegraphic transmission by using the set of rules that make up the dot–dash Morse code.)

Sensory information can be encoded into all-or-none action potentials according to several criteria: the frequency of the impulses, the rhythm in which clusters of impulses occur, and so forth. Here we will examine possible neural representations of the intensity, quality (type), position (location), and pattern (identity) of stimuli.

Stimulus intensity. We respond to sensory stimuli over a wide range of intensities. Furthermore, within this range we can detect small differences of intensity. How are different intensities of a stimulus represented in the nervous system? Within a single nerve cell the frequency of nerve impulses can represent stimulus intensity (Figure 8.5*a*). However, only a limited range of different sensory intensities can be represented in this manner.

As we noted in Chapter 3, the maximal rate of firing for a single nerve cell is about 1200 impulses per second, and most sensory fibers do not fire more than a few hundred impulses per second. But the number of differences in intensity that can be detected in vision and hearing is much greater than this code can offer. For example, we can see both in very, very dim light and when the light is 10 billion–fold brighter. A single receptor that could change activity only a few hundred–fold could never represent that entire range. Therefore, variations in the firing rate of a *single* cell simply cannot account for the full range of intensity perception.

Multiple nerve cells acting in a parallel manner provide a broader range for coding the intensity of a stimulus. As the strength of a stimulus increases, new nerve cells are "recruited"; thus intensity can be represented by the number of active cells. A variant of this idea is the principle of intensity coding called **range fractionation** (Figure 8.5*b*). According to this hypothesis, a wide range of intensity values can be accurately noted in the nervous system by cells that are "specialists" in particular segments or fractions of an intensity scale. This mode of stimulus coding requires an array of receptors and nerve cells with a wide distribution of thresholds, some with very high sensitivity (lower thresholds) and others with much lower sensitivity (higher thresholds).

Stimulus type. Within any sensory modality, we can readily discriminate the many qualitative differences among stimuli. For example, we can discriminate among wavelengths of light, frequencies of sound, and a variety of skin sensations, such as touch, warmth, cold, and pain. What kind of coding underlies these

8.5 Intensity Coding (*a*) Each of the three nerve cells represented here has a different threshold—low, medium, or high—and thus a different rate of firing. Each cell varies its response over a fraction of the total range of stimulus intensities. (*b*) Although none of these nerve cells can respond faster than 150 times per second, the sum of all three can vary in response rate from 0 to 450 impulses per second, accurately indicating the intensity of the stimulus.

(*a*) Response rate versus stimulus intensity for three neurons with different thresholds

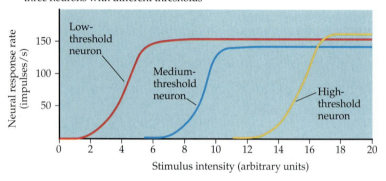

(*b*) Simulation of responses for the three neurons

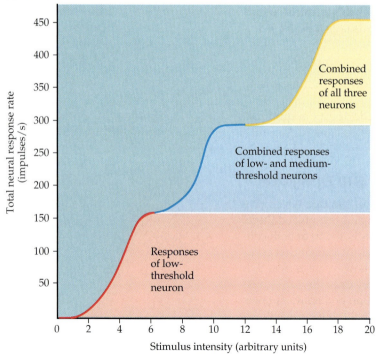

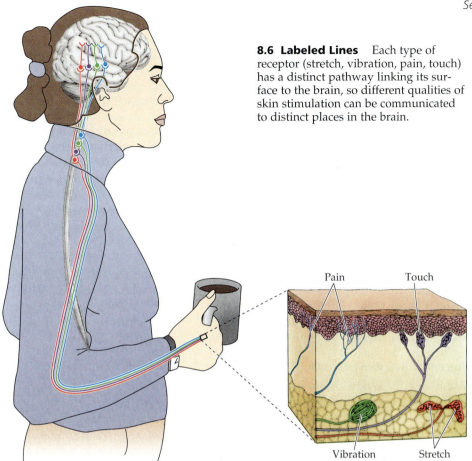

8.6 Labeled Lines   Each type of receptor (stretch, vibration, pain, touch) has a distinct pathway linking its surface to the brain, so different qualities of skin stimulation can be communicated to distinct places in the brain.

qualitative differences? An important part of the answer is the concept of **labeled lines.** This view states that particular nerve cells are, at the outset, labeled for distinctive sensory experiences (Figure 8.6). Neural activity in this *line* provides the basis for our detection of the experience.

Major separation of sensory experiences into modalities clearly involves labeled lines; stimulation of the optic nerve, for instance, always yields vision and never gives us sounds or touch sensations. These labeled lines do not use different "nerve energies" as Müller thought. They each use action potentials, but we interpret action potentials differently depending on the line along which they travel.

Stimulus location.   The position of an object or event, either outside or inside the body, is an important feature of the information that a person or animal gains by sensory analysis. Some sensory systems reveal this information by the position of excited receptors on the sensory surface. This feature is most evident in the **somatosensory** ("body sensation") system.

You know an object is on your back if a receptor in the skin there is stimulated. If a receptor on your palm is stimulated, then the object must be there. Each receptor activates pathways that convey unique positional information. The spatial properties of a stimulus are represented by labeled lines that uniquely convey spatial information. Similarly, in the visual system an object's spatial location determines which receptors in the eye are stimulated.

In both the visual and the tactile system, cells at all levels of the nervous system—from the surface sheet of receptors to the cerebral cortex—are arranged in an orderly, maplike manner. The map at each level is not exact but reflects both position and receptor density. Thus more cells are allocated to the spatial representation of sensitive, densely innervated sites like the skin of the lips or the center of the eye, than to sites that are less sensitive, such as the skin of the back or the periphery of the eye.

Information about location is not restricted to sensory systems that are laid out like a map. We all know that we can detect quite accurately the source of a sound or an odor. For one thing, we might move our head about to detect variation in stimulus strength. But for both odor and sound localization, we rely heavily on bilateral receptors: two ears or two nostrils.

With bilateral receptor systems—the two ears or the two nostrils—the relative time of arrival of the stimulus at the two receptors, or the relative intensity, is directly related to the location of the stimulus. For example, the only time when both ears are excited identically is when the sound source is equidistant from the ears, in the median plane of the head. As the stimulus moves to the left or right, receptors of the left and right sides are excited asymmetrically. Specialized nerve cells that receive inputs from both left and right ears, and measure stimulus disparities between the two sides, are discussed in Chapter 9.

Stimulus identity. Being able to recognize stimuli requires the ability both to perceive patterns of stimulation and to recall patterns that have been learned previously. Usually these abilities go together, but in some cases of brain damage, they become divorced. In Chapter 19, for example, we will consider some rare cases of people who can see and describe faces but can no longer recognize familiar faces.

Receptor Response Can Decline with Maintained Stimuli

Many receptors show progressive loss of response when stimulation is maintained. This process is called **adaptation.** We can demonstrate adaptation by recording nerve impulses in a fiber leading from a receptor. Observations of the time course of nerve impulses show a progressive decline in the rate of discharges as the stimulus is continued (Figure 8.7). In terms of adaptation, there are two kinds of receptors: **Tonic receptors** show a slow or nonexistent decline in the frequency of nerve impulses as stimulation is maintained. In other words, these receptors show relatively little adaptation. **Phasic receptors** show a rapid decrease in the frequency of nerve impulses.

Adaptation means that there is a progressive shift in neural activity *away from accurate portrayal* of maintained physical events. Thus the nervous system may fail to register neural activity even though the stimulus continues. Such a striking discrepancy is no accident; sensory systems emphasize *change* in stimuli because changes are more likely to be significant for survival. Sensory adaptation is a form of information suppression that prevents the nervous system from becoming overwhelmed by stimuli that offer very little "news" about the world. For example, the pressing of a hair on the leg by pants may be continuous, but we are saved from a

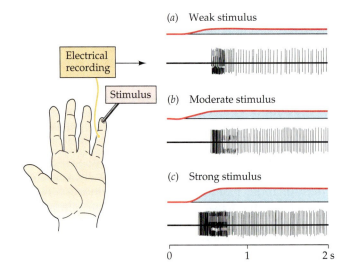

8.7 Sensory Adaptation The rate of firing of the neuron represented here, the receptive field for which is located on the fifth finger, is rapid when the stimulus—whether weak (*a*), moderate (*b*), or strong (*c*)—is first applied, but then it adapts, slowing to a steady rate. (After Knibestol and Valbo, 1970.)

(*a*) Weak stimulus

Electrical recording

Stimulus

(*b*) Moderate stimulus

(*c*) Strong stimulus

0   1   2 s

constant neural barrage from this stimulus by several suppression mechanisms, including adaptation.

The bases of adaptation include both neural and nonneural events. For example, in some mechanical receptors, adaptation develops from the elasticity of the receptor cell itself. This situation is especially evident in the pacinian corpuscle, which detects vibration. Maintained vibration on the receptor results in an initial burst of neural activity and a rapid decrease to almost nothing. But when the corpuscle (which is a separate, accessory cell) is removed, the same constant stimulus applied to the uncovered sensory nerve fiber produces a continuing discharge of nerve impulses. So for this receptor, adaptation is a mechanical property of the nonneural component, the corpuscle.

In some receptors, adaptation reflects a change in the generator potential of the cell. Changes in this electrical property of a receptor may be produced by ionic changes that result in hyperpolarization.

Sensory Inputs Can Be Suppressed

We have noted that successful survival does not depend on exact copying of external and internal stimuli. Rather, our success as a species demands that our sensory systems accentuate, from among the many things happening about us, the important *changes* of stimuli. Without selectivity we would suffer from an overload of information and would end up with a confusing picture of the world.

Information in sensory systems is constrained or suppressed in at least two ways. In many sensory systems, accessory structures can reduce the level of input in the sensory pathway. For example, closure of the eyelid reduces the level of illumination that reaches the retina. In the auditory system, contraction of the middle-ear muscles reduces the intensity of sounds that reach the inner ear. In this form of sensory control, the relevant mechanisms change the intensity of the stimulus before it reaches the receptors.

A second form of information control involves neural connections that descend from the brain to lower levels in the sensory pathway, in some cases as far as the receptor surface. For example, higher centers in the pain system (discussed later in this chapter) send axons down the spinal cord, where they can inhibit incoming pain signals. Such central modulation of sensory input is also evident in the auditory system, where a small group of cells in the brainstem send axons along the auditory nerve to connect with the base of the receptor cells. Stimulation of this pathway can dampen sounds in a selective manner.

Successive Levels of the CNS Process Sensory Information

Sensory stimulation leads to responses and perceptions. How? In brief, different levels and regions of the brain process information from receptor surfaces in different ways. These sites of information processing are located along pathways that lead from the sensory surface to the highest levels of the brain, and each sensory system has its own distinctive pathways. Specifically, pathways from receptors lead into the spinal cord or brainstem, where they connect to distinct clusters of nerve cells. These cells, in turn, have axons that connect to other nerve cell groups. Eventually the pathway terminates in sets of neurons in regions of the cerebral cortex. Each sensory modality—such as touch, vision, or hearing—has a distinct collection of tracts and stations in the brain that are collectively known as the **sensory pathway** for that modality.

Each station in any pathway is thought to accomplish a basic aspect of information processing. For example, painful stimulation of the finger leads to reflex withdrawal of the hand, which is mediated by spinal circuits. At the brainstem level, other circuits can turn the head toward the source of pain. The most complex aspects of sensory representations are at the level of the cerebral cortex. For most senses, information reaches the thalamus before being relayed to the cortex; the somatosensory pathway is one example (Figure 8.8).

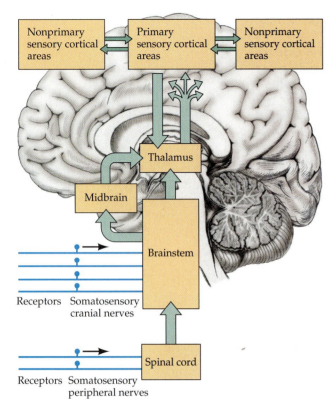

8.8 Levels of Somatosensory Processing
Sensory information enters the CNS through the brainstem or spinal cord, then reaches the thalamus. The thalamus shares the information with the cerebral cortex; the cortex directs the thalamus to supress some sensations.

As sensory information enters the nervous system, it travels in divergent pathways, so there is more than one representation of that modality at each level of the nervous system. Figure 8.9 shows six different somatosensory regions in the monkey cortex. Each of them is a full, orderly representation of either the body surface or deep body tissues.

Neurophysiologist Clinton Woolsey was a pioneer in mapping these multiple somatosensory regions. Similar collections of maps are found at different levels of the auditory and visual pathways. One way of studying these brain maps is to record the electrical activity of the neurons that constitute them. Let's take a closer look at the different levels of sensory representation in the central nervous system.

Receptive fields of sensory neurons. The **receptive field** of a sensory neuron consists of the stimulus region and the features that cause that cell to alter its firing rate. To determine the receptive field of a neuron, investigators record its electrical responses to a variety of stimuli to learn what makes the activity of the cell change from its resting rate (Figure 8.10). Such experiments show that somatosensory receptive fields have either an excitatory center and an inhibitory surround, or an inhibitory center and an excitatory surround. These receptive fields make it easier to detect edges and discontinuities on the objects we feel.

Receptive fields differ also in size and shape, and in the quality of stimulation that activates them. For example, some cells respond preferentially to light touch, while other cells fire most rapidly in response to painful stimuli. Receptive fields have been studied for cells at all levels, and we will see examples in other brain regions later in this chapter and in the next two chapters.

Regions of the cerebral cortex. For a given sensory modality we can find several different regions of cortex that receive information about that sense. Each of these cortical regions has a separate map of the same receptive surface, but the different cortical regions process the information differently and make different contributions to perceptual experiences (Miyashita, 1993; Zeki, 1993). For example, these areas receive fibers from different divisions of the thalamus (see Figure 8.9). and the maps, although orderly, differ in internal arrangement.

By convention, one of the cortical maps is designated as **primary sensory cortex** for that particular modality. Thus there is primary somatosensory cortex, primary auditory cortex, and so on. The other cortical maps for a given modality are said to be **secondary sensory cortex** or **nonprimary sensory cortex** (see Figure 8.8). The primary cortical area is the main source of input to the other fields for the same modality, even though these other fields also have direct thalamic inputs.

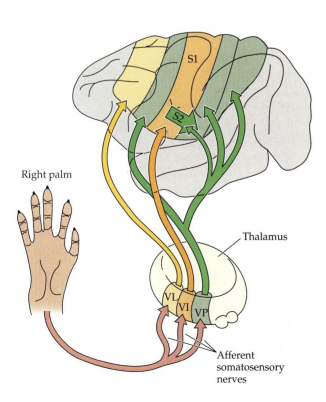

8.9 Thalamic Relays Some of the connections between thalamus and cortex in the somatosensory system of monkeys. (The thalamus is shown here removed from the brain for clarity.) Different divisions of the thalamus—ventrolateral (VL), ventralis intermedius (VI), and ventroposterior (VP)—send axons to different somatosensory regions of the cerebral cortex. S1, primary somatosensory cortex; S2, secondary somatosensory cortex. (After Merzenich and Kaas, 1980.)

(*a*) Experimental setup

(*b*) Cortical cell with receptive field on forelimb

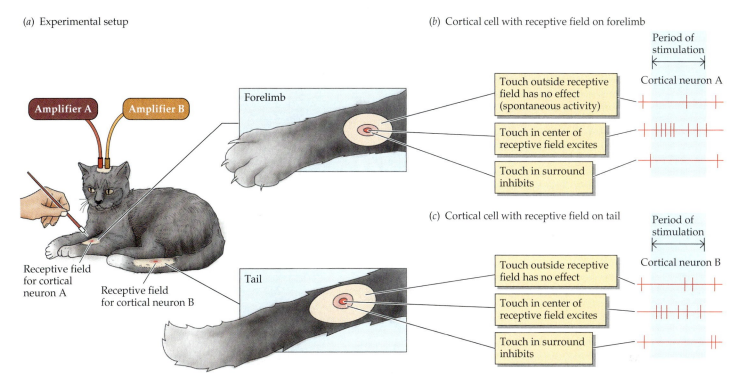

8.10 Identifying Somatosensory Receptive Fields The procedures illustrated here are used to record from somatosensory neurons of the cerebral cortex. Changes in the position of the stimulus affect the rate of neural impulses. Neuron A responds to touch on a region of the forepaw; neuron B, only a few centimeters away in the somatosensory cortex, responds to stimulation of the tail. The receptive fields of these neurons include an excitatory center and an inhibitory surround, but other neurons have receptive fields with the reverse organization: inhibitory centers and excitatory surrounds.

Primary somatosensory cortex, known as **somatosensory 1,** or **S1** (see Figure 8.9), maps the opposite side of the body. Secondary somatosensory cortex (S2) maps both sides of the body in registered overlay; that is, the left-arm and right-arm representations occupy the same part of the map, and so forth. Different cortical regions simultaneously process different aspects of perceptual experience, but the cortical and thalamic regions exchange information back and forth. Information is also exchanged between the primary and nonprimary sensory cortex through subcortical loops.

Plasticity in cortical maps. At one time most researchers thought that cortical maps were fixed and invariant among all members of the same species. But contemporary research shows that cortical maps can change with experience. At least some of these changes in cortical maps are due to new synapses between cortical neurons (Florence et al., 1998). Three experiments with monkeys illustrate the plasticity of sensory representation (Merzenich and Jenkins, 1993).

In the first, the receptive field of a monkey's hand was mapped in detail in the somatosensory cortex (Figure 8.11*a*). Then the nerve to the thumb and index finger was severed. After a few weeks, remapping the same somatosensory cortex revealed that the area representing those fingers had shrunk, and stimulating the back of the hand activated the territory formerly held by the denervated fingers (Figure 8.11*b*).

In the second experiment, the middle finger was surgically removed. This treatment expanded the cortical representation of each adjacent finger (Figure 8.11*c*).

In a third experiment, the monkey was trained to maintain contact with a rotating disc with one or two fingers in order to obtain food rewards. After several weeks

Clinton Woolsey
(1904–1993)

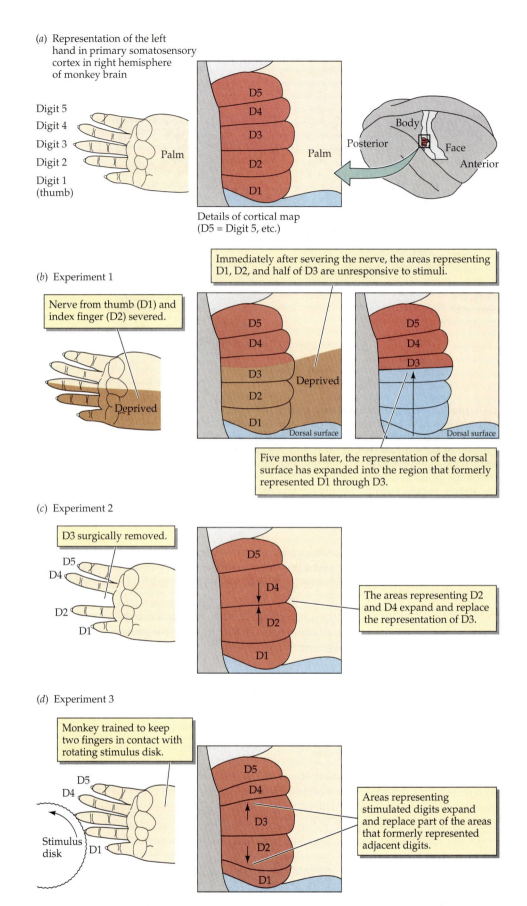

(a) Representation of the left hand in primary somatosensory cortex in right hemisphere of monkey brain

Digit 5
Digit 4
Digit 3
Digit 2
Digit 1 (thumb)

Palm

D5
D4
D3
D2
D1

Palm

Body
Posterior
Face
Anterior

Details of cortical map (D5 = Digit 5, etc.)

(b) Experiment 1

Nerve from thumb (D1) and index finger (D2) severed.

Deprived

Immediately after severing the nerve, the areas representing D1, D2, and half of D3 are unresponsive to stimuli.

D5
D4
D3
D2
D1

Deprived

Dorsal surface

D5
D4
D3

Dorsal surface

Five months later, the representation of the dorsal surface has expanded into the region that formerly represented D1 through D3.

(c) Experiment 2

D3 surgically removed.

D5
D4
D2
D1

D5
D4
D2
D1

The areas representing D2 and D4 expand and replace the representation of D3.

(d) Experiment 3

Monkey trained to keep two fingers in contact with rotating stimulus disk.

D5
D4
Stimulus disk
D1

D5
D4
D3
D2
D1

Areas representing stimulated digits expand and replace part of the areas that formerly represented adjacent digits.

8.11 The Plasticity of Somatosensory Representations These experiments demonstrate that the adult brain can be altered by experience. (After Merzenich and Jenkins, 1993.)

of training, the hand area was mapped again, and the trained fingers were found to have considerably enlarged representations over their previous areas (Figure 8.11*d*).

Similar findings were noted in rats exposed to differential tactile experience (Xerri et al., 1996). Professional musicians who play stringed instruments have expanded cortical representations of their left fingers, presumably because they have been using these fingers to depress the strings for precisely the right note (Elbert et al., 1995). Brain imaging also reveals cortical reorganization in people who lose a hand in adulthood (Figure 8.12).

Some changes in cortical maps occur after weeks or months of use or disuse; they may arise from the production of new synapses (sprouting) or the loss of others. On the other hand, some changes are so rapid, occurring within hours, that they probably arise from changes in the strength of existing synapses. Rapid changes in cortical maps may also result from a loss of sustained inhibition of some synapses; these changes could be thought of as the unmasking of "hidden synapses."

In a review of the topic of plasticity of sensory representation, Kaas (2000) concluded the following:

NEURAL PLASTICITY

- The detailed cortical sensory maps are dynamically maintained, capable of both rapid and gradual change with experience and use.
- Prolonged sensory manipulations can lead to activity-induced modifications in neurotransmitter expression, the growth of axons and dendrites, and synaptic strength.
- Reorganizations occur in all major sensory (and motor) systems at subcortical and cortical levels.
- Even rather limited reorganization in subcortical regions can result in impressively large reorganization of cortical maps.
- Some types of reorganization, such as after major sensory nerve loss, may take months to emerge, and they appear to depend on extensive sprouting and growth of axons to form new connections.

Sensory Systems Influence One Another

Many research observations and individual experiences show that the use of one sensory system influences perception derived from another sensory system. For example, cats often do not respond to birds unless they can both see and hear them; neither sense alone is sufficient to elicit a response (B. Stein and Meredith, 1993).

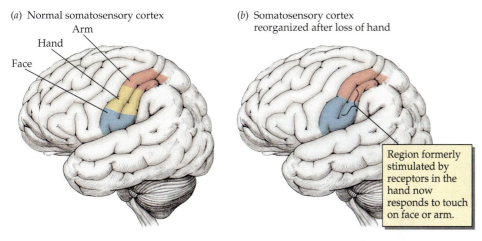

(*a*) Normal somatosensory cortex
Arm
Hand
Face

(*b*) Somatosensory cortex reorganized after loss of hand

Region formerly stimulated by receptors in the hand now responds to touch on face or arm.

8.12 Cortical Reorganization after Amputation of a Hand   Normally the cortical region receiving information from the hand is interposed between the regions representing the upper arm and the face. But in a person who, as an adult, lost one hand, the cortical regions representing the upper arm and face expand, taking over the cortical region previously representing the missing hand. Presumably the loss of sensory input from the lost hand allows those cortical neurons to become innervated by neighboring cortical neurons. (After Yang et al., 1994.)

Similarly, humans detect a visual signal more accurately if it is accompanied by a sound from the same part of space (J. J. McDonald et al., 2000).

Many sensory areas in the brain, so-called association areas, do not represent exclusively a single modality but show a mixture of inputs from different modalities. Some "visual" cells, for instance, also respond to auditory or tactile stimuli. Perhaps loss of input from one modality allows these cells to better analyze input from remaining senses as, for example, in cases of people who become blind early in life and are better than sighted people at localizing auditory stimuli (Lessard et al., 1998). The normal stimulus convergence on such polymodal cells provides a mechanism for intersensory interactions (Fuster et al., 2000).

Attention. In 1890 William James wrote, "Everyone knows what attention is. It is the taking possession by the mind in clear and vivid form one out of what seem several simultaneous objects or trains of thought." In fact, however, not everyone agrees about the definition of **attention.** This important aspect of sensory processing has a multiplicity of meanings.

One view emphasizes the state of alertness or vigilance that enables animals to detect signals. In this view, attention is a generalized activation that attunes us to inputs. According to another view, attention is the process that allows the selection of some sensory inputs from among many competing ones. Some investigators view attention in a more introspective manner, arguing that it is a state of mental concentration or effort that makes it possible to focus on a particular task. As you can see, a notion that may seem self-evident to some has considerable complexity.

Certain regions of the cerebral cortex have been particularly implicated in attention, as evidenced by the impairment of attention in people and animals with localized cortical damage and by recordings of electrical activity of cells in different cortical regions while animals attend to stimuli or await stimuli in order to obtain rewards.

One cortical region that appears to play a special role in attention is a part of the posterior parietal lobe. Many cells here are polymodal. Some of them are especially responsive when a trained monkey is expecting the appearance of a stimulus (Mountcastle, Andersen, and Motter, 1981). Lesions of this area in monkeys result in inattention or neglect of stimuli on the opposite side. (In Chapter 19 we will see that this symptom is especially severe in people with lesions of the right parietal lobe.) The frontal eye fields seem to be involved in attentive visual exploration of space. The posterior part of the cingulate cortex (around the posterior part of the corpus callosum) has been implicated in motivational aspects of attention. These three cortical areas have especially prominent anatomical connections with each other, and each receives strong input from sensory fibers (Mesulam, 1989).

Figure 8.13 shows activation in the anterior cingulate cortex (especially on the right side) during a task involving a shift in spatial orientation (Gitelman et al., 1996; Nobre et al., 1997). This region has been hypothesized to play a significant role in an "executive" attention system (Posner and Raichle, 1994).

8.13 Brain Regions Activated When We Are Attending Functional-MRI images of a subject cued to expect a stimulus in a particular portion of the visual field show right-hemisphere activation in the cingulate cortex in midsagittal (*left*) and frontal (*right*) views. Areas of highest activation are shown in yellow. CG, cingulate gyrus; CS, cingulate sulcus. (Courtesy of Darren Gitelman.)

Touch and Pain

Skin envelops our bodies and provides a boundary with our surroundings. This delicate boundary harbors an array of receptors that enable us to detect and discriminate among many types of impinging stimuli. Among primates, an important aspect of skin sensations is the active manipulation of objects by the hands, which enables identification and use of

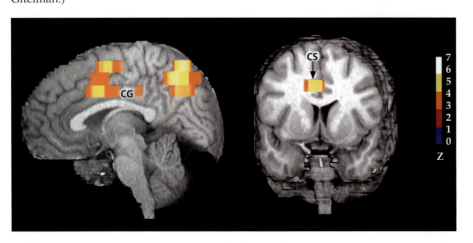

various shapes. More complex aspects of skin sensations are evident in the worlds of pain with which we are all too familiar. After examining how skin senses work—looking specifically at sensory receptors in the skin, at how sensory information from the skin is transmitted to the brain, and at how that information is processed in the brain—we will discuss pain.

Touch Includes a Variety of Sensations

Touch is not just touch. Careful studies of skin sensations reveal qualitatively different sensory experiences: pressure, vibration, tickle, "pins and needles," and more complex dimensions, such as smoothness or wetness. All forms of touch are recorded by receptors in the skin.

Skin Is a Complex Organ That Contains a Variety of Sensory Receptors

Because the average person has about 1 to 2 m^2 (10 to 20 square feet) of skin, it is sometimes considered the largest human organ. Skin is made up of three separate layers; the relative thickness of each varies over the body surface. The outermost layer—the **epidermis**—is the thinnest and varies most widely, ranging from a very flexible, relatively thick layer on the surface of the hands and feet to the delicate outer layer of the eyelid. Each day millions of new cells are added to the outermost layer. The middle layer—the **dermis**—contains a rich network of nerve fibers and blood vessels, in addition to a network of connective tissue that is rich in the protein collagen, which gives skin its strength. The character of skin is further complicated by other specialized outgrowths, such as hair or feathers, claws, hooves, and horns. The innermost layer—**subcutaneous tissue**—contains fat cells, which act as thermal insulators and cushion internal organs from mechanical shock.

Detection of pain, heat, and cold at the skin has been associated with the activation of free **nerve endings** (see Figure 8.3). Later in this chapter we'll discuss the details of pain signals and their use of both fast and slow axons (see Table 8.2).

Within the skin are four highly sensitive touch receptors (Figure 8.14). The pacinian corpuscles are found deep within the dermis. The onionlike outer portion of the

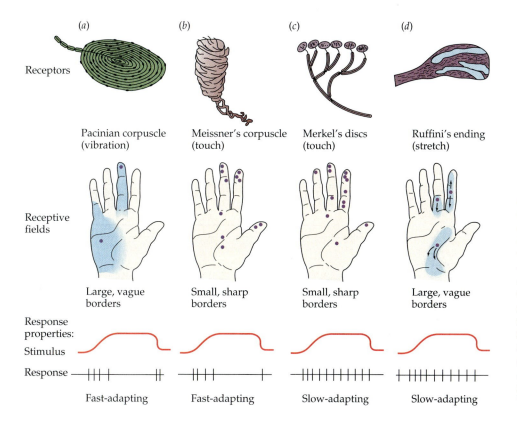

Receptors

(a) Pacinian corpuscle (vibration)
(b) Meissner's corpuscle (touch)
(c) Merkel's discs (touch)
(d) Ruffini's ending (stretch)

Receptive fields

Large, vague borders — Small, sharp borders — Small, sharp borders — Large, vague borders

Response properties:
Stimulus

Response

Fast-adapting — Fast-adapting — Slow-adapting — Slow-adapting

8.14 Properties of Skin Receptors Related to Touch Shown here for each skin receptor is the type of receptor (*top*), the size and type of the receptive field (*middle*), and the electrophysiological response (*bottom*). (*a*) Pacinian corpuscles activate fast-adapting fibers with large receptive fields. (*b*) Meissner's corpuscles are fast-adapting mechanoreceptors with small receptive fields. (*c*) Merkel's discs are slow-adapting receptors with small receptive fields. (*d*) Ruffini's endings are slow-adapting receptors with large receptive fields. (After Valbo and Johansson, 1984.)

corpuscle acts as a filter, shielding the underlying nerve fiber from most stimulation. Only vibrating stimuli of more than 200 Hz will pass through the corpuscle and stretch the nerve fiber to reach threshold. Normally the skin receives such rapid vibration when it is moving across the textured surface of an object. Pacinian corpuscles are fast-responding and fast-adapting receptors (see Figure 8.14*a*).

The touch receptors that mediate most of our ability to perceive form are the fast-adapting **Meissner's corpuscles** (see Figure 8.14*b*) and the slow-adapting, oval **Merkel's discs** (see Figure 8.14*c*). These receptors are especially densely distributed in skin regions where sensitive spatial discrimination is possible (fingertips, tongue, and lips).

The receptive fields of Merkel's discs usually have an inhibitory surround (an example of lateral inhibition), which increases their spatial resolution. This field also makes them especially responsive to edges and to isolated points on a surface (such as the dots for Braille characters).

Meissner's corpuscles are more numerous than Merkel's discs but offer less spatial resolution. Meissner's corpuscles seem specialized to respond to *change* in stimuli (as you'd expect from rapidly adapting receptors) to detect localized movement between the skin and a surface. This provides detailed information about texture (Johnson and Hsiao, 1992). The low-threshold, rapidly adapting characteristics of Meissner's corpuscles may be due to a specialized Na$^+$ channel (M. P. Price et al., 2000).

The final touch receptors are the slow-adapting **Ruffini's endings,** which detect stretching of the skin when we move fingers or limbs (see Figure 8.14*d*). Figure 8.15 compares how each of these four touch receptors respond when a finger is moved across the raised dots of Braille. All four of these touch receptors utilize moderately large (so called Aβ), myelinated fibers, so they deliver information to the CNS rapidly (see Table 8.2).

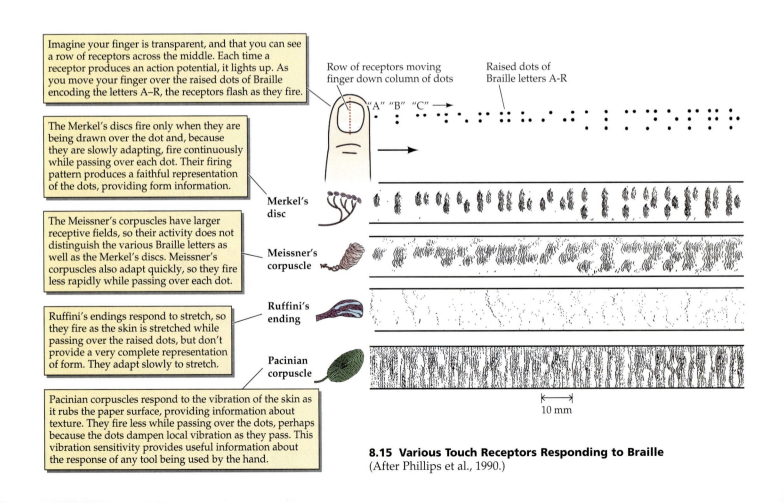

Imagine your finger is transparent, and that you can see a row of receptors across the middle. Each time a receptor produces an action potential, it lights up. As you move your finger over the raised dots of Braille encoding the letters A–R, the receptors flash as they fire.

The Merkel's discs fire only when they are being drawn over the dot and, because they are slowly adapting, fire continuously while passing over each dot. Their firing pattern produces a faithful representation of the dots, providing form information.

The Meissner's corpuscles have larger receptive fields, so their activity does not distinguish the various Braille letters as well as the Merkel's discs. Meissner's corpuscles also adapt quickly, so they fire less rapidly while passing over each dot.

Ruffini's endings respond to stretch, so they fire as the skin is stretched while passing over the raised dots, but don't provide a very complete representation of form. They adapt slowly to stretch.

Pacinian corpuscles respond to the vibration of the skin as it rubs the paper surface, providing information about texture. They fire less while passing over the dots, perhaps because the dots dampen local vibration as they pass. This vibration sensitivity provides useful information about the response of any tool being used by the hand.

Row of receptors moving finger down column of dots

Raised dots of Braille letters A-R

"A" "B" "C"

Merkel's disc

Meissner's corpuscle

Ruffini's ending

Pacinian corpuscle

10 mm

8.15 Various Touch Receptors Responding to Braille (After Phillips et al., 1990.)

Two Pathways Carry Sensory Information from the Skin to the Brain

Nerve fibers from the skin surface run to the spinal cord. Within the cord, somatosensory fibers ascend to the brain in at least two major pathways: (1) the dorsal column system and (2) the anterolateral (spinothalamic) system (Figure 8.16). Inputs to the **dorsal column system** enter the spinal cord and ascend to the medulla, where they synapse. The axons of postsynaptic cells form a fiber bundle that crosses in the brainstem to the opposite side and ascends to a group of nuclei of the thalamus. Outputs of the thalamus are directed to postcentral cortical regions referred to as the somatosensory cortex.

The **anterolateral,** or **spinothalamic, system** has a different arrangement. Inputs from the skin to this system synapse on cells in the spinal cord, whose axons cross to the opposite side and ascend in the anterolateral columns of the spinal cord. At least some of the input to this system mediates pain and temperature sensations (see Figure 8.23).

The skin surface can be divided into bands called *dermatomes* according to which spinal nerve carries the most axons from each region (Figure 8.17a). A **dermatome** (from the Greek *derma,* "skin," and *tome,* "part, segment") is a strip of skin innervated by a particular spinal root. The pattern of dermatomes is hard to understand in an upright human, but we must remember that erect posture is a recent evolutionary development in mammals. The mammalian dermatomal pattern evolved

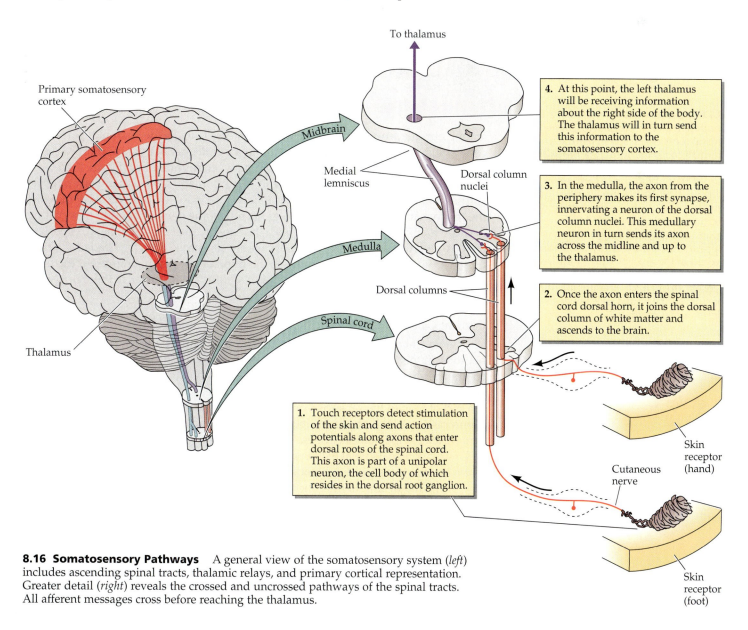

8.16 Somatosensory Pathways   A general view of the somatosensory system (*left*) includes ascending spinal tracts, thalamic relays, and primary cortical representation. Greater detail (*right*) reveals the crossed and uncrossed pathways of the spinal tracts. All afferent messages cross before reaching the thalamus.

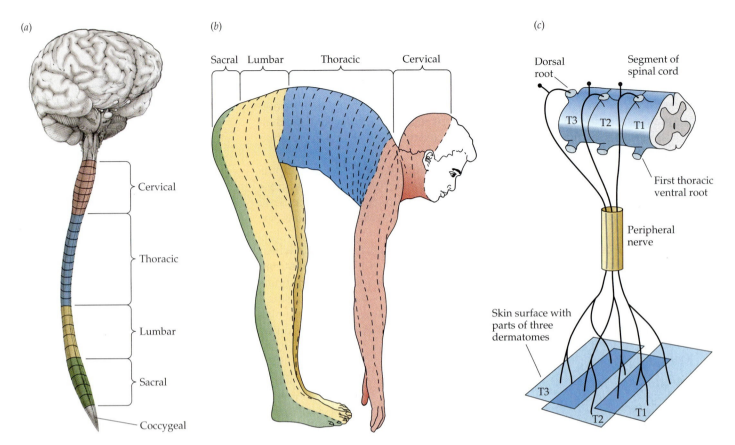

(a)

Cervical

Thoracic

Lumbar

Sacral

Coccygeal

(b) Sacral Lumbar Thoracic Cervical

(c) Dorsal root Segment of spinal cord

T3 T2 T1

First thoracic ventral root

Peripheral nerve

Skin surface with parts of three dermatomes

T3 T2 T1

8.17 Dermatomes (*a*) Bands of skin send their sensory inputs to different dorsal roots of the spinal cord. Each dermatome is the section of the skin that is innervated primarily by a given dorsal root of the spinal cord. (*b*) In this side view of the human body in quadrupedal position, the pattern of dermatomes is color-coded to correspond to the spinal regions in *a,* and it appears more straightforward than it would in the erect posture. (*c*) Adjacent dorsal roots of the spinal cord collect sensory fibers from overlapping strips of skin, so the boundaries between the dermatomes overlap.

among our quadrupedal (four-legged) ancestors. Thus the dermatomal pattern becomes clear when depicted on a person in a quadrupedal posture (Figure 8.17*b*). There is also a modest amount of overlap between dermatomes (Figure 8.17*c*).

The cells in all brain regions concerned with somatic sensation are arranged according to the plan of the body surface. Each region is a map of the body in which the relative areas devoted to body regions reflect the density of body innervation. Because many fibers are involved with the sensory surface of the head, especially the lips, a particularly large number of cells are concerned with the head; in contrast, far fewer fibers innervate the trunk, so the number of cells that represent the trunk is much lower (Figure 8.18). This map is a simplification because there is overlap among representations of different body areas.

Cortical Columns Show Specificity for Modality and Location

We saw in Chapter 2 that the cerebral cortex is organized into vertical columns of neurons; in this section we will examine the functional significance of these cortical columns. It had long been known that the cortex contains large functional regions, such as the somatosensory areas and the visual areas, and that each of these regions is a sort of map of the sensory world. Then, in pioneering work begun in the 1950s, Mountcastle (1984) mapped the receptive fields of individual neurons in somatosensory cortex using microelectrodes.

This work revealed that each cortical cell not only has a precise receptive field, but also responds to only one submodality. For example, a particular cell responds only to a given kind of stimulation, such as light touch, and another cell responds only to deep pressure. Furthermore, within a given column of neurons all the cells respond to the same location and quality of stimulation. All the columns in a band of adjacent columns respond to the same quality of stimulation, and another band of columns is devoted to another kind of stimulation (Figure 8.19).

Each column extends from the surface of the cortex (layer I in Figure 8.19) down to the base of the cortex (layer VI). Area 3b of the cortex receives input from both

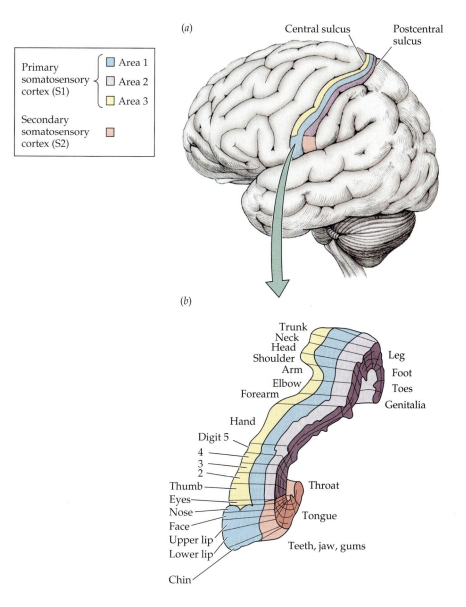

(a)

Central sulcus

Postcentral sulcus

Primary somatosensory cortex (S1)
- Area 1
- Area 2
- Area 3

Secondary somatosensory cortex (S2)

(b)

Trunk
Neck
Head
Shoulder
Arm
Elbow
Forearm
Hand
Digit 5
4
3
2
Thumb
Eyes
Nose
Face
Upper lip
Lower lip
Chin

Leg
Foot
Toes
Genitalia

Throat

Tongue

Teeth, jaw, gums

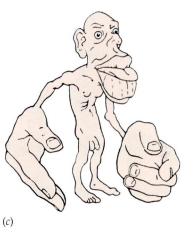

(c)

8.18 Representation of the Body Surface in Somatosensory Cortex (*a*) The location of primary (S1) and secondary (S2) somatosensory cortical areas on the lateral surface of the human brain. (*b*) The order and size of cortical representations of different regions of skin. (*c*) The homunculus (literally, "little man") depicts the body surface with each area drawn in proportion to the size of its representation in the primary somatosensory cortex.

8.19 The Columnar Organization of the Somatosensory Cortex This part of the somatosensory cortex represents some of the fingers of the right hand. The different regions of somatosensory cortex—Brodmann's areas 3a, 3b, 1, and 2—receive their main inputs from different kinds of receptors. Area 3b receives most of its projections from the superficial skin, including both fast-adapting and slow-adapting receptors; these projections are represented in separate cortical columns or slabs. Area 3a receives input from receptors in the muscle spindles. The cortex is organized vertically in columns and horizontally in layers. Input from the thalamus arrives at layer IV, where neurons distribute information up and down layers. (After Kaas et al., 1979.)

fast-adapting and slow-adapting receptors near the surface of the skin. Each type of receptor feeds information to a different cortical column. Moving the stimulation to a slightly different region on the skin shifts the excitation to a different cortical column. Area 3a of the cortex contains cells that respond to stimulation of the stretch receptors in the muscles, and within area 3a each change in location means stimulation of a different column. Thus the columns code for both location and quality of stimulation.

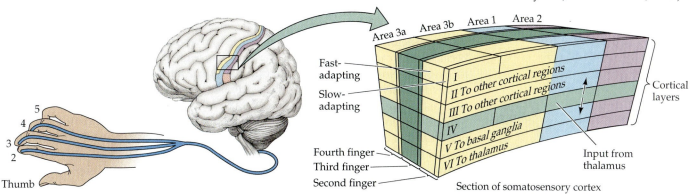

5
4
3
2
Thumb

Area 3a
Area 3b
Area 1
Area 2

Fast-adapting
Slow-adapting

I
II To other cortical regions
III To other cortical regions
IV
V To basal ganglia
VI To thalamus

Cortical layers

Input from thalamus

Fourth finger
Third finger
Second finger

Section of somatosensory cortex

In Chapters 9 and 10 we will see that the auditory and visual areas of the cerebral cortex have a similar kind of columnar organization. Interestingly, the cells in more caudal somatosensory cortex often respond to more than one modality, as though integrating information as the information is processed beyond primary cortex.

Somatosensory Perception of Objects Requires Active Manipulation

The functions of the somatosensory cortex in discriminating forms have been studied in monkeys in two ways: (1) The effects of lesions in this region have been observed. (2) Responses of individual neurons have been recorded while the monkeys' hands were stimulated. Lesions impaired the ability of the animal to discriminate the form, size, and roughness of tactile objects (Norsell, 1980). Each of these impairments could be localized to a subregion of somatosensory cortex: Lesions in one area affected mainly the discrimination of texture, lesions in a second area impaired mainly the discrimination of angles, and lesions in a third area affected all forms of tactile discrimination (Randolf and Semmes, 1974).

Temporal and spatial aspects of touch have been studied through the use of complex stimuli (Darian-Smith et al., 1980). In this research, metal strips of varied widths and spacing were moved at different rates of speed under the fingertips of monkeys while recordings were made from sensory nerves. No single fiber could give an accurate record of each ridge and depression in the stimulus, but the ensemble of fibers provided an accurate representation.

Some somatosensory cortical cells could not be activated when the experimenter stimulated either skin or joints but responded strongly when the animal grasped an object and manipulated it. Some of these "active touch" cells had highly specific response characteristics (Iwamura and Tanaka, 1978). For example, one unit responded actively when the monkey felt a straight-edged ruler or a small rectangular block but did not respond when the monkey grasped a ball or bottle. The presence of two parallel edges appeared to be crucial for effective activation of this cell. The same electrode penetration identified another cell that responded best when the monkey grasped a ball and responded well to a bottle, but did not respond at all when the monkey manipulated a rectangular block.

PET studies have shown that in humans the posterior part of the parietal cortex is activated during exploration of objects by touch (Roland and Larson, 1976). This result was obtained by the recording of blood flow in the cortex under three conditions:

1. The experimenter moved the passive hand of the subject over the stimulus object.
2. The subject moved his or her hand energetically but did not touch an object.
3. The subject explored an object by touch.

Only in the last of these conditions was there specific activation of the posterior parietal cortex, suggesting that this region is particularly involved in active touch.

Pain Is an Unpleasant but Adaptive Experience

Pain has been defined as "an unpleasant sensory and emotional experience associated with actual or potential tissue damage, or described in terms of such damage." Because of its capacity to be unpleasant and cause great suffering, it may be difficult to imagine a biological role for pain. But clues to the adaptive significance of pain can be gleaned from the study of rare individuals who never experience pain. The **congenital insensitivity to pain** that such people exhibit is probably inherited, since the pain insensitivity syndrome is sometimes seen in siblings (E. Hirsch et al., 1995), and one version of insensitivity has been traced to a defect in a gene for a receptor to nerve growth factor (Indo et al., 1996), suggesting that pain fibers in these individuals fail to grow out for lack of response to a neurotrophic signal.

**CLINICAL
ISSUE**

Some people who display this insensitivity can discriminate between the touch of the point or head of a pin but experience no pain when pricked with the point. Case descriptions note that the bodies of such people show extensive scarring from injuries to fingers, hands, and legs (Manfredi et al., 1981). One little girl had deliberately pulled out most of her teeth by 8 years of age and had to be instructed to leave her teeth alone (Rasmussen, 1996). The first clinically reported person with congenital insensitivity to pain worked on the stage as a "human pincushion" (Figure 8.20) (Dearborn, 1932).

Many people with congenital insensitivity to pain die young, frequently from extreme trauma to the body. These cases suggest that pain guides adaptive behavior by indicating potential harm. Pain is so commonplace for most of us that we easily forget its guiding role: The experience of pain leads to behavior that removes the body from a source of injury.

Dennis and Melzack (1983) argue that pain serves three purposes:

1. Short-lasting pain causes us to withdraw from the source, often reflexively, thus preventing further damage.
2. Long-lasting pain promotes behaviors such as sleep, inactivity, grooming, feeding, and drinking that promote recuperation.
3. The expression of pain may serve as a social signal to other animals. For example, screeching after a painful stimulus may have significant adaptive value by signaling the potential of harm to genetically related members of the same species or eliciting certain caregiving behavior from others—such as grooming, defending, and feeding—that could mean the survival of the victim.

Human Pain Can Be Measured

In some parts of the world people endure, with stoic indifference, rituals (including body mutilation) that would cause most other humans to cry out in pain. Incisions of the face, hands, arms, legs, or chest; walking on hot coals; and other treatments clearly harmful to the body can be part of the ritual. Comparable experiences are also seen in more ordinary circumstances, such as the occasions when a highly excited athlete continues to play a game with a broken arm or leg. Learning, experience, emotion, and culture all seem to affect pain in striking ways.

Detailed psychological studies of the experience of pain further emphasize its complexity. The mere terms *mild* and *intense* are inadequate to describe the sensation that is distinctive to a particular disease or injury. Furthermore, assessment of the need for pain relief intervention requires some kind of quantitative measurement (Chapman et al., 1985). For example, Melzack (1984) has provided a detailed quantitative rating scale that examines the language of pain.

This rating scale—called the McGill Pain Questionnaire—consists of a list of words arranged into classes that describe three different aspects of the pain experience: (1) the sensory–discriminative quality, (2) the motivational–affective (emotional) quality, and (3) an overall cognitive evaluative quality (Figure 8.21). Patients are asked to select the set of words that best describes their pain, and within the selected sets, to identify the word that is relevant to their condition. Quantitative treatment of this scale includes adding up the number of selected words and the rank value.

One of the interesting aspects of the McGill scale is that it can distinguish among pain syndromes, meaning that patients use a distinctive constellation of words to describe a particular pain experience. For example, data obtained from different groups of patients show that the pain of toothache is described differently from the

THE HUMAN PINCUSHION WHO INCURS CONSTANT RISKS OF BLOOD POISONING.

8.20 Doesn't That Hurt? The earliest scientific report of a person with congenital insensitivity to pain was of a man working in the theater, like the man shown here, as a "human pincushion." (Photo by Culver Pictures, Inc.)

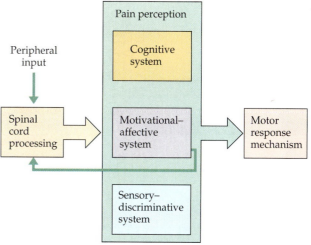

8.21 The Multifaceted Character of Pain

pain of arthritis, which in turn is described differently from menstrual pain. The simple query by a physician "Is the pain still there?" has been replaced by a more detailed analysis that provides better clues about the effectiveness of pain control.

Pain Information Is Transmitted through Special Neural Systems

Contemporary studies of pain mechanisms have described the characteristics of receptors in the skin that transmit pain information and the relevant pathways of the central nervous system. Many unknowns remain in our understanding of pain pathways, and research continues to elaborate on the complexity of the distribution of neural activity initiated by pain stimuli. In this section we will discuss some features of peripheral and central nervous system pathways that mediate pain.

Peripheral origins of pain information.   In most cases the initial stimulus for pain is the partial destruction of or injury to tissue adjacent to certain nerve fibers. This tissue change results in the release of chemical substances that activate pain fibers in the skin. Various substances have been suggested as the chemical mediators of pain, including neuropeptides, serotonin, histamine, various proteolytic (protein-metabolizing) enzymes, and prostaglandins (a group of widespread hormones) (Figure 8.22). This area of research is very important because it may lead to the development of new pain relief drugs that act at the periphery.

Are some peripheral receptors and nerve fibers specialized for the signaling of noxious stimulation? Over the years this question has generated considerable controversy. Some researchers have argued that there are no **nociceptors,** specialized receptors or fibers that respond to noxious stimulation; they suggest instead that pain is initiated by a *pattern* of stimulation of a broad class of peripheral afferent fibers. Perl (1980) clarified this issue by showing that two classes of peripheral afferent fibers respond to noxious stimulation.

One class (type **Aδ fibers**) includes large-diameter, myelinated, high-threshold receptors. Because of the relatively large axon diameter and myelination, these fibers report very quickly. When you stub your toe, the first, sharp pain you feel is conducted by these fibers. A second class of pain receptors of the skin consists of thin, unmyelinated fibers (called **C fibers**). These fibers conduct slowly and adapt slowly, providing us with the second wave of pain—the dull, lasting ache in that darned toe. Table 8.2 compares these different fibers.

8.22 Peripheral Mediation of Pain
When the skin is injured, activity of the peripheral nervous system causes the local release of various substances.

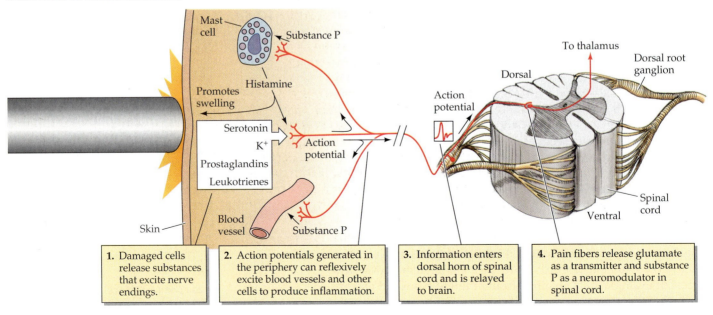

1. Damaged cells release substances that excite nerve endings.

2. Action potentials generated in the periphery can reflexively excite blood vessels and other cells to produce inflammation.

3. Information enters dorsal horn of spinal cord and is relayed to brain.

4. Pain fibers release glutamate as a transmitter and substance P as a neuromodulator in spinal cord.

TABLE 8.2 *Fibers That Link Receptors to the CNS*

Receptor type	Axon type	Diameter (μm)	Conduction speed (m/s)
Proprioceptors of skeletal muscles	Aα	13–20	80–120
Mechanoreceptors of skin	Aβ	6–12	35–75
Pain, temperature	Aδ	1–5	5–30
Temperature, pain, itch	C	0.02–1.5	0.5–2

Another indication that there are specialized pain fibers in the periphery comes from studies of **capsaicin,** the ingredient that makes chili peppers spicy. When investigators isolated the receptor that is bound by capsaicin, they found that the receptor also responds to sudden increases in temperature (Caterina et al., 1997). The receptor was cloned and named the **vanilloid receptor 1** (**VR1**) because the crucial component of the capsaicin molecule is a chemical known as vanilloid. Mice lacking the gene for this receptor still responded to mechanosensory pain, but not to heat or capsaicin (Caterina et al., 2000). So the reason that chili peppers taste "hot" is that the capsaicin in the peppers activates VR1 receptors in the body that normally detect noxious heat. Paradoxically, rubbing capsaicin into the skin overlying arthritic joints brings some pain relief, perhaps because overactivated pain fibers temporarily run out of transmitter.

Thus contemporary research has clearly established that there are specific groups of nociceptors—receptor cells that respond selectively to noxious stimulation. Information about pain is then transmitted along specialized pain fibers.

Special CNS pathways mediate pain.   In the central nervous system, special pathways mediate pain. Afferent fibers from the periphery that carry nociceptive information probably use **glutamate** as a neurotransmitter to excite cells (S. Li and Tator, 2000), but they also release the neuromodulator **substance P** in the superficial layers of the dorsal horn of the spinal cord. Substance P is a neuropeptide (the *P* originally stood for *peptide*). Injection of capsaicin into the skin provides a specific painful stimulus that leads to the release of substance P in the dorsal horn. There the postsynaptic neurons take up the substance P and begin remodeling their dendrites; investigators have speculated that this neural plasticity later affects pain perception, as we'll see shortly (Mantyh et al., 1997).

Further evidence that substance P plays a role in pain comes from experiments with knockout mice that lack either the gene for the precursor to substance P (Cao et al., 1998) or a gene for the substance P receptor (De Felipe et al., 1998). (See Box 7.3 to review experimental techniques using knockout mice.) These mice are unresponsive to certain kinds of intense pain. Interestingly, they still responded to mildly painful stimuli, suggesting that other signals, perhaps the glutamate neurotransmitter, can carry that information. The dorsal horn neurons that receive this information, part of the spinothalamic system we mentioned earlier, send their axons across the midline and up the spinal cord to terminate in several nuclei of the thalamus (Figure 8.23).

GENES AND BEHAVIOR

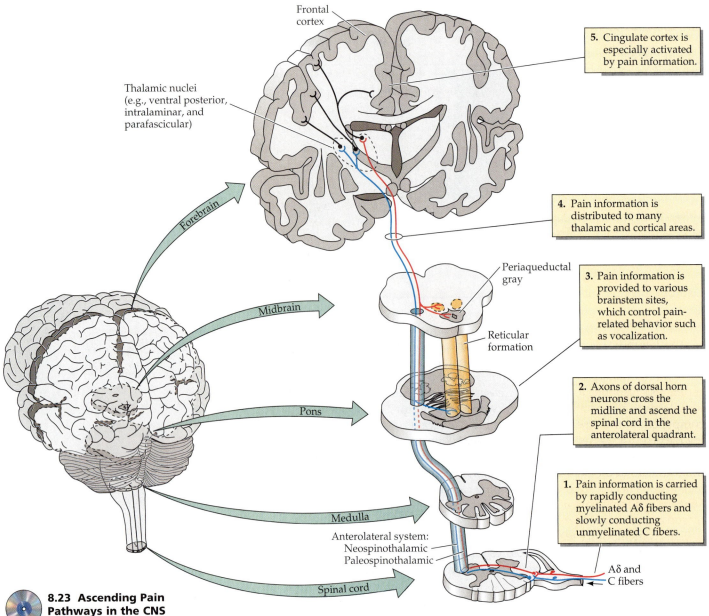

Frontal cortex

5. Cingulate cortex is especially activated by pain information.

Thalamic nuclei (e.g., ventral posterior, intralaminar, and parafascicular)

4. Pain information is distributed to many thalamic and cortical areas.

Periaqueductal gray

3. Pain information is provided to various brainstem sites, which control pain-related behavior such as vocalization.

Reticular formation

2. Axons of dorsal horn neurons cross the midline and ascend the spinal cord in the anterolateral quadrant.

Forebrain

Midbrain

Pons

1. Pain information is carried by rapidly conducting myelinated Aδ fibers and slowly conducting unmyelinated C fibers.

Medulla

Anterolateral system:
Neospinothalamic
Paleospinothalamic

Aδ and C fibers

Spinal cord

8.23 Ascending Pain Pathways in the CNS Pain sensation travels from its origin to the brain via the spinothalamic system.

CLINICAL ISSUE

Sometimes pain persists long after the injury that gave rise to it has healed. The most dramatic example is a person's continued perception of chronic pain coming from a missing limb after loss of an arm or leg. Called *phantom limb pain*, it is an example of **neuropathic pain,** so called because the pain seems to be due to inappropriate signaling of pain by neurons (rather than to tissue damage). Such cases can be seen as a disagreeable manifestation of neural plasticity because the nervous system seems to have amplified its response to the pain signal. In some cases, the plasticity seems to reflect long-lasting changes in the expression of transmitters and/or receptors (Woolf and Salter, 2000).

These cases are notoriously difficult to treat. In one type of phantom limb pain, the patient perceives that his missing limb is twisted and therefore hurts. A controversial treatment for this condition is to have the patient look at himself in a mirror, so that the reflection of the intact limb seems to have filled in for the missing limb. The patient then repeatedly moves "both limbs" (by moving the remaining one), watching closely the whole while, and sometimes reports that the phantom limb feels as though it has straightened out and no longer hurts (Ramachandran and Rogers-Ramachandran, 2000). This result also suggests that neuropathic pain is due to neural plasticity. The brain interpreted the signals coming from the limb stump as painful, but visual stimuli may lead to a reinterpretation.

The pain information is eventually integrated in the **cingulate cortex.** Recall from Chapter 1 that the cingulate cortex is much more likely to be activated by a stimulus if people are led to believe that the stimulus will be painful (see Figure 1.5) (Rainville et al., 1997). A sensory illusion further confirms the role of the cingulate cortex in pain perception: Placing your hand over alternating pipes of cool and warm (not hot) water produces the sensation of pain, as though the pipes were hot. This is a wonderful illustration that "pain is in the brain" because no tissue is actually being damaged. The cingulate cortex is also activated in people experiencing this illusory pain (Craig et al., 1996).

Pain Can Be Controlled by a Variety of Mechanisms and Pathways

Relief from the suffering of pain has long been a dominant concern of humans. Throughout history different remedies have been offered. One interesting, puzzling aspect of pain pathways is that their interruption reduces pain perception only temporarily. After a pathway in the spinal cord is cut, pain is diminished, but it returns after an interval of weeks or months.

The usual way of interpreting these data is that nociceptive input from the remaining intact pathways becomes abnormally effective. Pain relief received renewed attention after the publication of an insightful paper by Melzack and Wall (1965). They suggested that pain is subject to many modulating influences, including some that can close spinal "gates" controlling the flow of pain information from the spinal cord to the brain.

Additional control is exerted by higher centers in the pain system, which send axons down the spinal cord, where they terminate on the first synapses of the pain system in the superficial layers of the dorsal horn. The modulatory signals above the spinal cord can inhibit the transmission of incoming pain impulses. The discovery of the brain's power to control the flow of pain signals has inspired many new approaches for the alleviation of pain. In the sections that follow, we will discuss some of these strategies, which are examples of the interaction between basic research and application.

Ronald Melzack

P. D. Wall
(1925–2001)

Opiate drugs.   Over the centuries opium has been exploited for its pain-relieving effects. For years researchers attempted to determine how opiate drugs (drugs such as morphine, derived from or related to opium) control pain; finally they successfully showed that the brain contains natural opiate-like substances, or opioids. This finding suggested that the brain has built-in mechanisms to control the transmission of pain information. In effect, the brain might modulate pain in a manner akin to how exogenous opiates such as morphine do. Several classes of **endogenous opioids,** such as **endorphin** and the **enkephalins,** have now been discovered (see Chapter 4), and several classes of **opiate receptors** have been identified and designated by Greek letters. For example, the μ opiate receptor seems to be most affected by morphine.

Early observations showed that electrical stimulation of the **periaqueductal gray** area (see Figure 8.23) of the brainstem in rats produces potent **analgesia** (loss of pain sensation; from the Greek *an-*, "not," and *algesis*, "feeling of pain"). Injection of opiates into this area also relieves pain, suggesting that the region contains synaptic receptors for opiate-like substances. Neural inputs to the periaqueductal gray area are diverse, including axons that arise from some cerebral cortical sites, the amygdala, and the hypothalamus. Most important is a strong input from the spinal cord, which presumably delivers nociceptive information.

According to one model of the control of pain transmission in the spinal cord by the brainstem (Basbaum and Fields, 1978, 1984), excitation of periaqueductal gray neurons leads via endorphin-containing axons to the stimulation of neurons in the medulla. These medullary neurons have serotonin-containing axons that innervate the spinal cord and inhibit neurons that transmit information from the periphery. In this way, pain information is blocked by a direct gating action in the spinal cord.

Electrical stimulation of the descending tract elicits inhibition of the response of spinal cord sensory relay cells to noxious stimulation of the skin. Figure 8.24 shows both the ascending pain communication system and the descending pain control system.

In addition to their beneficial pain-relieving effects, opiates and other analgesics (painkillers) often produce side effects such as confusion, drowsiness, vomiting, constipation, and depression of the respiratory system. Now that we know the circuitry of the pain relief system, why give large doses of the drug systemically (i.e., throughout the body)? Instead, physicians can now administer very small doses of opiates directly to the spinal cord to relieve pain, thus avoiding many of the side effects. The drugs can be administered epidurally (just outside the spinal cord's dura mater) or intrathecally (between the dura mater and the spinal cord). Both routes are somewhat invasive and therefore are restricted to surgical anesthesia, childbirth, or the management of severe chronic pain (Landau and Levy, 1993).

8.24 Ascending and Descending Pain Pathways Pain sensation is projected up to the brain (*a*), but the brain can inhibit these signals to control pain (*b*). (After Basbaum and Fields, 1984.)

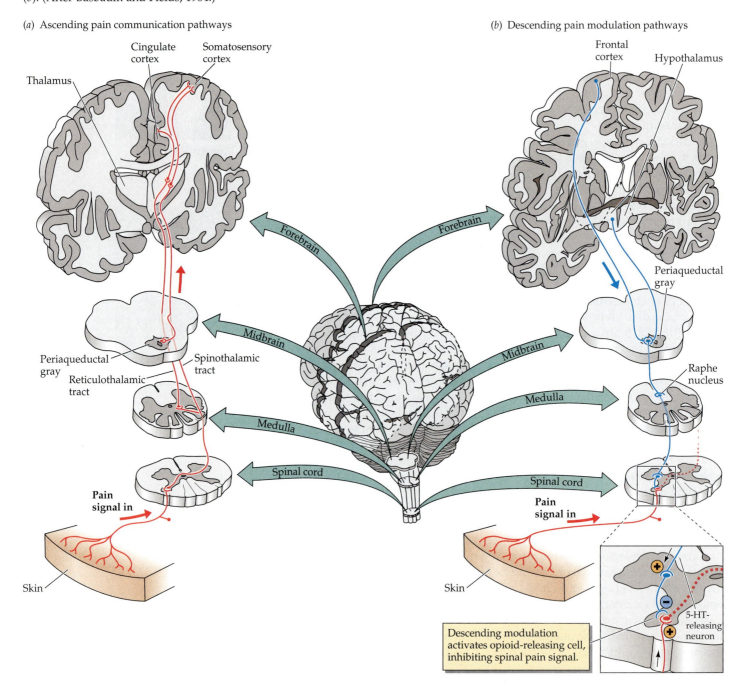

(*a*) Ascending pain communication pathways

(*b*) Descending pain modulation pathways

Descending modulation activates opioid-releasing cell, inhibiting spinal pain signal.

In the clinical context there have been long-standing concerns about the use of morphine and other opiates for the relief of pain because of their addictive potential. Low doses and infrequent use have been the common standard. However, a report of the Agency for Health Care Policy and Research urges swift and aggressive use of painkillers after surgery to relieve pain and speed recovery. Several studies show that the danger of addiction from the use of morphine to relieve surgical pain had been vastly overexaggerated (Melzack, 1990); it is now estimated to be no more than 0.04% (Brownlee and Schrof, 1997). Moreover, once chronic pain develops, it is extremely difficult to overcome, so the best approach is to prevent the onset of chronic pain by early, aggressive treatment.

CLINICAL ISSUE

There is some evidence that the rewarding effects of opiates are mediated by the substance P receptor (Murtra et al., 2000), so future drugs may be able to block this side effect of opiate drugs. Other, nonopioid analgesics may be available soon. For example, a drug called epibatidine that is isolated from frog skin is a very potent analgesic that seems to act on nicotinic cholinergic receptors in the dorsal horn of the spinal cord (Bannon et al., 1998).

Stimulation of the skin. Human history is filled with examples of the use of strange techniques to achieve relief from pain. One of the more unusual procedures is the administration of electrical currents to the body. Centuries ago this technique included the application of electric fish or eels to sites of pain. More recently, a procedure called **transcutaneous electrical nerve stimulation (TENS)** has gained prominence as a way to suppress certain types of pain that have proven difficult to control.

In TENS treatment, electrical pulses are delivered through electrodes attached to the skin, which excite nerves that supply the region that hurts. The stimulation itself produces a sense of tingling rather than pain. In some cases dramatic relief of pain can outlast the duration of stimulation by a factor of hours. The best pain relief is produced when the electrical stimulation is delivered close to the source of pain.

TENS has been especially successful in the treatment of patients whose pain is derived from peripheral nerve injuries. The analgesic action of this technique is at least partially mediated by endogenous opioids, since administration of **naloxone,** an opioid antagonist, partially blocks this analgesic action. Recall, for example, the last time you stubbed your toe. In addition to a string of expletives, a frequent result of such incidents is the self-administration of skin stimulation; that is, you react by vigorously rubbing the injured area, which brings a little relief.

Placebos. The search for relief from pain has led people to consume many unusual substances; even chemically inert pills have been reported to alleviate pain in many patients. The term **placebo** (Latin for "I shall please") has been applied to such inert substances or other treatments that have no obvious direct physiological effect. Because placebo effects are strong in many circumstances, many investigators have studied them (W. A. Brown, 1998). Whenever a placebo appears to alleviate pain, investigators try to determine the indirect effects of the placebo treatment or of the circumstances in which it was administered.

Research has yielded striking observations providing clues about why placebos relieve pain in some patients. Volunteer subjects who had just had their wisdom teeth extracted were told that they were being given an analgesic but were not told what kind (J. D. Levine et al., 1978). Some of these patients received morphine-based drugs, and some were given saline solutions—the placebo. One out of three patients given the placebo experienced pain relief. (Morphine produced relief in most of the patients but, as has been shown before, not in all patients.)

To explore the mechanisms of the placebo effect, the researchers gave naloxone to other patients who were also administered the placebo. Recall that naloxone blocks the effects of both exogenous opiates and endogenous opioids, or opiate-like substances. Patients given the placebo and naloxone did not experience pain relief; this result implies that placebo relief of pain is mediated by an endogenous opioid system. But Grevert et al. (1983) showed that naloxone did not completely prevent placebo-induced analgesia but rather reduced the effectiveness of a placebo. The results suggest that both opioid and nonopioid mechanisms contribute to placebo analgesia; the same conclusion comes from studies of stress-induced analgesia that we will discuss shortly.

Acupuncture.   The earliest description of pain relief from **acupuncture** is at least 3000 years old. In some acupuncture procedures the needles are manipulated once they are in position; in other instances electrical or heat stimulation is delivered through the inserted needles. The points at which needles are inserted are related to the locus of pain and to some of the characteristics of the pain condition.

Acupuncture has gained popularity, but detailed clinical assessments indicate that only some people achieve continued relief from chronic pain. At least part of the pain-blocking character of acupuncture appears to be mediated by the release of endorphins (N. M. Tang et al., 1997). Administering opioid antagonists such as naloxone prior to acupuncture blocks or reduces its pain control effects. More research is needed in clinical settings to identify the limits of this type of pain control. Animal models of the procedures used with human patients are also promoting an understanding of this ancient but enduring remedy.

Stress.   A deer fleeing from an encounter with a mountain lion would do well to ignore any pain from injuries for the moment. Sometimes people badly hurt in traumatic circumstances report little or no immediate pain, suggesting that the injured deer indeed feels no pain. Inhibition of pain has been shown in many laboratory situations that involve unusual treatments, such as electrical stimulation of the brain. Such studies demonstrate the existence of pain control circuitry, but they do not provide information about the customary ways in which inhibitory systems are activated.

What conditions normally activate endorphin-mediated pain control? To answer this question, researchers have examined pain inhibition that might arise in stressful circumstances. Some researchers have suggested that stress induces activation of the brain systems that produce analgesia when pain threatens to overwhelm effective coping strategies. Studies concerned with how pain might control pain itself have revealed some new perspectives on mechanisms that mediate these effects.

Researchers found that exposure of rats to mild foot shock produced analgesia. Many other forms of stress, such as swimming in cold water, also inhibited pain responses. Other observations suggested that such stress-induced analgesia is mediated by endogenous opioids in the brain. In fact, the analgesia produced by stress was similar in several respects to that produced by opiates (Bodnar et al., 1980).

Like opiates, repeated exposure to stress resulted in declining analgesic effectiveness. In addition, cross-tolerance is observed between opiates and stressors; that is, diminished analgesia to repeated stress is accompanied by reduced pain inhibition by opiate drugs. However, antagonists to opiates, such as naloxone, have had variable effects on stress-induced analgesia, suggesting that some part of stress-induced analgesia is not mediated by endogenous opioids. More recent research has explored this theme more completely.

John Liebeskind—who was for many years a leading researcher in the area of pain—and his colleagues studied rats in stress situations that consisted of inescapable foot shock (Terman et al., 1984). Different groups of rats were exposed to different regimens of foot shock, and changes in pain threshold were assessed by a technique called the tail-flick test. This assessment is a measure of the level of radiant heat that produces a quick flick of a rat's tail away from the heat. In these studies the role of endogenous opioids was assessed by the administration of an opiate antagonist—naltrexone.

In this experimental situation the stress of inescapable shock produces an increase in tail-flick latency, which shows that the shock stress produces an analgesic effect. However, administration of naltrexone produces a curious complication: When analgesia is produced by short periods of foot shock, naltrexone reverses the analgesic response, a result demonstrating that the source of analgesia is an opioid system in the brain.

John Liebeskind
(1935–1997)

However, antagonists to opiates have little effect on stress-induced analgesia if the duration or intensity of foot shock is altered. This finding demonstrates that stress activates both an opioid-sensitive analgesic system and a pain control system that does not involve opioids. Relatively precise parameters of the stress-inducing stimuli seem to determine which system is activated.

Similar elements are probably involved in both of these pain control circuits because spinal lesions disrupt both forms of stress-induced analgesia. But the pathways must be separated to some extent, for some brainstem lesions can affect the opiate-mediated analgesia without affecting the nonopiate-mediated analgesia. These findings are very important in suggesting clinical strategies for pain relief intervention in humans. Further research should clarify whether additional forms of pain relief are controlled by other circuits.

Table 8.3 summarizes the many types of pain relief strategies and interventions, including surgical and pharmacological strategies, psychological brain and spinal cord stimulation, and sensory stimulation. The elusive nature of pain is evident in this range of potential interventions, some of which reflect desperation in the face of great anguish. Of course, the persistence of pain often leads to the testing of new tools, some of which are readily denounced as quackery. However, some techniques that elicit initial skepticism may later be supported with better evidence.

TABLE 8.3 *Types of Pain Relief Intervention*

Measure	Mechanism	Limitations/comments
PSYCHOGENIC		
Placebo	May activate endorphin-mediated pain control system	Sometimes inhibited by opiate antagonists
Hypnosis	Alters brain's perception of pain	Control unaffected by opiate antagonists
Stress	Both opioid and nonopioid mechanisms	Clinically impractical and inappropriate
Cognitive (learning, coping strategies)	May activate endorphin-mediated pain control system	Limited usefulness in severe pain
PHARMACOLOGICAL		
Opiates	Bind to opioid receptors in periaqueductal gray and spinal cord	Severe side effects due to binding in other brain regions
Spinal block	Drugs block pain signals in spinal cord	Avoids side effects of systemic administration
Anti-inflammatory drugs	Block prostaglandin and leukotriene synthesis at site of injury	Major side effects
Aspirin	Blocks prostaglandin (see Figure 8.22) synthesis at site of injury	Does not block leukotriene synthesis
STIMULATION		
TENS/mechanical	Tactile or electrical stimulation of large fibers blocks or alters pain signal to brain	Segmental control; must be applied at site of pain
Acupuncture	Seems similar to TENS	Sometimes affected by opiate antagonists
Central gray	Electrical stimulation activates endorphin-mediated pain control systems, blocking pain signal in spinal cord	Control inhibited by opiate antagonists
SURGICAL		
Cut peripheral nerve cord Rhizotomy (cutting dorsal root) Cord hemisection Frontal lobotomy	Create physical break in pain pathway	Considerable risk of failure or return of pain

For example, researchers examined the potential pain relief provided by magnets (Vallbona et al., 1997). Small magnets slightly stronger than the ones on your refrigerator door were strapped to sensitive pain-generating areas of the body. In the control condition, inactive magnets were strapped over painful areas in other patients. A marked reduction in scores on a pain questionnaire were evident in the group that was exposed to the active as opposed to inactive magnets. No ready explanation of this effect was provided by these researchers, but other researchers have shown that somatosensory-evoked potentials elicited by pain-related stimuli are reduced when subjects are exposed to oscillating magnetic fields (Sartucci et al., 1997).

Summary

Sensory Processing

Refer to the *Learning Biological Psychology* CD for the following study aids for this chapter:

7 Objectives

73 Study Questions

2 Activities

1. A sensory system furnishes selected information to the brain about internal and external events and conditions. It captures and processes only information that is significant for the particular organism.

2. Ideal sensory systems discriminate among some of the available forms of energy, respond over a wide range of intensities, are highly sensitive to a change of stimuli, respond reliably and rapidly, and suppress unwanted information.

3. Stimuli that some species detect readily have no effect on other species that lack the necessary receptors.

4. Some receptors are simple free nerve endings, but most include cells that are specialized to transduce particular kinds of energy.

5. Energy is transduced at sensory receptors by the production of a generator potential that stimulates the sensory neurons.

6. Coding translates receptor information into patterns of neural activity.

7. In adaptation, the rate of impulses progressively decreases as the same stimulation is maintained. This decline is slow in the case of tonic receptors but rapid for phasic receptors. Adaptation protects the nervous system from redundant stimulation.

8. Mechanisms of information suppression include accessory structures, descending pathways from neural centers to the receptor, and central circuits.

9. The receptive field of a cell is the stimulus region that changes the response of the cell.

10. The succession of levels in a sensory pathway is thought to allow for different and perhaps successively more elaborate kinds of processing.

11. Attention is the temporary enhancement of certain sensory messages during particular states of the individual.

Touch and Pain

1. The skin contains several distinct types of receptors that have specific sensitivities. Inputs from the skin course through distinct spinal pathways, including the dorsal column system and the anterolateral (spinothalamic) system.

2. The surface of the body is represented at each level of the somatosensory system, and at the level of the cerebral cortex are multiple maps of the body surface.

3. Pain guides adaptive behavior by providing indications of harmful stimuli. Pain is a complex state that is strongly influenced by cultural factors and many aspects of individual experience.

4. Pain sensation is subject to many controlling or modulating conditions, including circuitry within the brain and spinal cord that employs opioid synapses. One component in the modulation of pain is made up of the descending pathways arising in the brain that inhibit incoming neural activity at synapses within the spinal cord.

5. Pain control has been achieved by the administration of drugs (including placebos), electrical and mechanical stimulation of the skin, acupuncture, and surgery, among other methods.

Recommended Reading

Aronoff, G. M. (Ed.). (1999). *Evaluation and treatment of chronic pain* (3rd ed.). Baltimore: Williams & Wilkins.

Carli, G., and Zimmerman, M. (Eds.). (1996). *Towards the neurobiology of chronic pain*. Amsterdam: Elsevier.

Fishman, S., and Berger, L. (2000). *The war on pain: How breakthroughs in the new field of pain medicine are turning the tide against suffering.* New York: HarperCollins.

Goldstein, E. B. (1999). *Sensation and perception* (5th ed.). Pacific Grove, CA: Brooks/Cole.

Johnson, K. O., Hsiao, S. S., and Twombly, I. A. (1995). Neural mechanisms of tactile form recognition. In M. S. Gazzaniga (Ed.), *The cognitive neurosciences* (pp. 253–269). Cambridge, MA: MIT Press.

Mogil, J. S., Yu, L., and Basbaum, A. I. (2000). Pain genes?: Natural variation and transgenic mutants. *Annual Review of Neuroscience, 23,* 777–811.

Vertosick, F. T. (2000). *Why we hurt: The natural history of pain.* New York: Harcourt.

Wall, P. D. (1999). *Pain: The science of suffering.* London: Weidenfeld & Nicolson.

Wall, P. D., and Melzack, R. (Eds.). (1999). *Textbook of pain* (4th ed.). Edinburgh, Scotland: Churchill Livingstone.

9

Hearing, Vestibular Perception, Taste, and Smell

Y ou exist only because your ancestors had keen senses that allowed them to find food and to avoid predators and other dangers. In this chapter we will continue our consideration of sensory worlds by discussing the perception of signals from distant sources, including hearing (audition) and smell (olfaction). We will also explore two related sensory systems: (1) the vestibular system, which detects orientation and movement of the body, and which is related to the auditory system; and (2) the sense of taste, which, like smell, is a chemical sense.

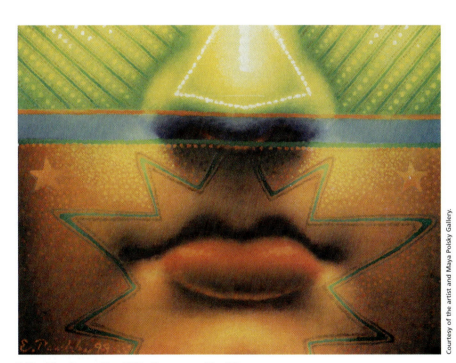

Ed Paschke, *Orange Star*, 1999, oil on canvas, 9″ × 12″

Recent discoveries have greatly expanded our understanding of both receptor mechanisms and central processing, especially in audition and olfaction. Both of these senses are extremely acute, and we will explore some of the special mechanisms that make them so sensitive. We begin with hearing because audition evolved from special mechanical receptors related to the somatosensory elements discussed in Chapter 8.

Hearing

Hearing is an important part of the adaptive behavior of many animals. For humans, the sounds of speech form the basic elements of languages and therefore of social relations. Helen Keller, who was both blind and deaf, said, "Blindness deprives you of contact with things; deafness deprives you of contact with people."

The sounds of any single language are only a small subset of the enormous possibilities of sounds that can be produced by human vocal cavities. The sounds produced by animals—from insects to whales—also have a wide range of complexity. The adaptive successes of many animals are linked to their ability to make and perceive these sounds, with which they probe the environment.

For example, the melodic songs of male birds and the chirps of male crickets attract females of their species. The grunts, screeches, and burbly sounds of primates signal danger or the need for comfort or satisfaction. Owls and bats exploit the directional property of sound to locate prey and avoid obstacles in the dark. Elephants can recognize individuals by their calls (McComb et al., 2000). Whales communicate with sounds that can travel hundreds of miles in the ocean. Unlike sights, sounds

---

BOX 9.1 *The Basics of Sound*

Sound is a repetitive change in the pressure of a particular medium, commonly air or water. In air the change arises because air particles are moved by a vibrating mechanical system, such as the glottis of the larynx in speech, the cone of a loudspeaker, or a tuning fork. In the last case, as the tuning fork moves away from a resting position it compresses air particles, causing the air pressure to rise above atmospheric pressure. As the tuning fork swings to the other side of its resting position, air particle density is briefly reduced with respect to atmospheric pressure. A single alternation of compression and expansion of air is called one *cycle.*

Figure A illustrates the changes in the spacing of air particles produced by a vibrating tuning fork. Because the sound produced by a tuning fork has only one frequency of vibration, it is called a *pure tone* and can be represented by a sine wave. A pure tone is described physically in terms of two measures:

1. **Frequency,** or the number of cycles per second, measured in hertz (Hz). For example, middle A on a piano has a frequency of 440 Hz.

2. **Amplitude,** or intensity—the distance of particle movement in a defined period of time, usually measured as pressure, or force per unit area, in dynes per square centimeter (dyn/cm^2).

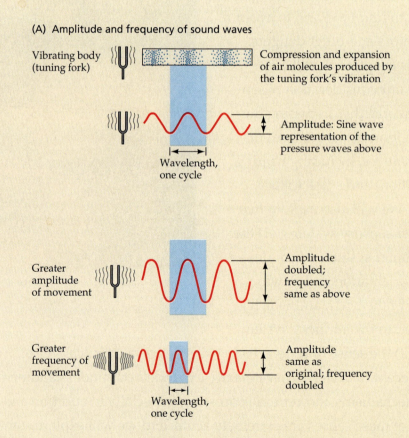

(A) Amplitude and frequency of sound waves

Vibrating body (tuning fork)

Compression and expansion of air molecules produced by the tuning fork's vibration

Amplitude: Sine wave representation of the pressure waves above

Wavelength, one cycle

Greater amplitude of movement

Amplitude doubled; frequency same as above

Greater frequency of movement

Amplitude same as original; frequency doubled

Wavelength, one cycle

Most sounds are more complicated than a pure tone. For example, a sound made by a musical instrument contains a fundamental frequency and harmonics. The **fundamental** is the basic frequency, and the **harmonics** are multiples of the fundamental. Thus if the fundamental is 440 Hz, the harmonics are 880, 1320, 1760, and so on. When different instruments play the same note, the notes differ in the relative intensities of the various harmonics; this difference is what gives each instrument its characteristic sound quality, or **timbre.**

can turn corners and go around obstacles, and they work as well in the dark as in the light.

Your auditory system can detect rapid changes of sound intensity (measured in **decibels, dB**) and frequency (measured in **hertz, Hz**). In fact, the speed of auditory information processing is so good that the analysis of frequency by the human ear rivals that of modern electronic gadgets. Your ear is also as sensitive as possible to weak sounds at frequencies in the range from 1000 to 2000 Hz. If it were any more sensitive, you would be distracted by the noise of air molecules bouncing against each other in your ear canal. Box 9.1 describes the basic principles of sound.

Each Part of the Ear Performs a Specific Function in Hearing

How do the small vibrations of air particles become the speech, music, and other sounds we hear? By shaping the mechanical forces that act on auditory end organs, the peripheral components of the auditory system determine the beginnings of auditory perception. In this section we discuss these initial stages of auditory processing.

Any complex pattern can be analyzed into a sum of sine waves, a process called **Fourier analysis.** (We will see in Chapter 10 that Fourier analysis can also be applied to visual patterns.) Figure B shows how a complex, square wave (**2**) can be analyzed into component sine waves of different frequencies. Using only the fundamental (**3**) and two harmonic frequencies (**4** and **5**) we can come close to restructuring the square wave (**6**). By using additional frequencies, we could eventually duplicate the square wave perfectly.

Because the ear is sensitive to a huge range of sound pressures, sound intensity (a measure of the difference between two pressures) is usually expressed in decibels (dB), a logarithmic scale. The definition of a decibel is as follows:

$$N = 20 \log P_1/P_2$$

where N is the number of decibels and P_1 and P_2 are the two pressures to be compared. The common reference level, or threshold, in hearing studies (P_2 in the notation above) is 0.0002 dyn/cm²; this is the least amount of pressure necessary for an average human to hear a 1000 Hz tone. A whisper is about ten times as intense and a jet airliner 500 feet overhead about a million times as intense. The whisper is about 20 dB above threshold, and the jetliner is about 120 dB above threshold. Normal conversation is about 60 dB above the reference level.

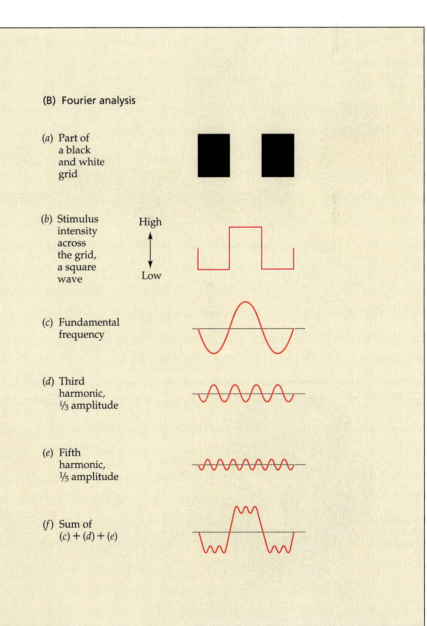

(B) Fourier analysis

(a) Part of a black and white grid

(b) Stimulus intensity across the grid, a square wave — High / Low

(c) Fundamental frequency

(d) Third harmonic, ⅓ amplitude

(e) Fifth harmonic, ⅕ amplitude

(f) Sum of (c) + (d) + (e)

The External Ear Captures, Focuses, and Filters Sound

Sound waves are collected by the external ear, which consists of the part we readily see, called the **pinna** (plural *pinnae;* Latin for "wing"), and a canal that leads to the eardrum (Figure 9.1*a* and *b*). The external ear is a distinctly mammalian characteristic, and mammals show a wide array of ear shapes and sizes. The acoustic properties of the external ear are important because its shape physically transforms sound energies.

The "hills and valleys" of the pinna modify the character of sound that reaches the middle and inner ear. Some frequencies of sound are enhanced; others are dimmed. For example, the shape of the human ear especially increases the efficiency of sounds in the frequency range of 2000 to 5000 Hz, a range that is important for speech perception. The shape of the external ear is also important in sound localization—that is, identifying the direction and distance of the source of a sound (discussed later in this chapter).

Few humans can move their ears, but many other mammals have an elaborate set of muscles associated with the external ear, enabling them to change the shape of the pinna and to point it toward the source of sound. Animals with acute auditory localization abilities, such as bats, have especially mobile ears. Of course, animals with mobile ears have to take into account the position of the pinna when interpreting sounds around them. Information about the position of the external ear in such animals is conveyed to the au-

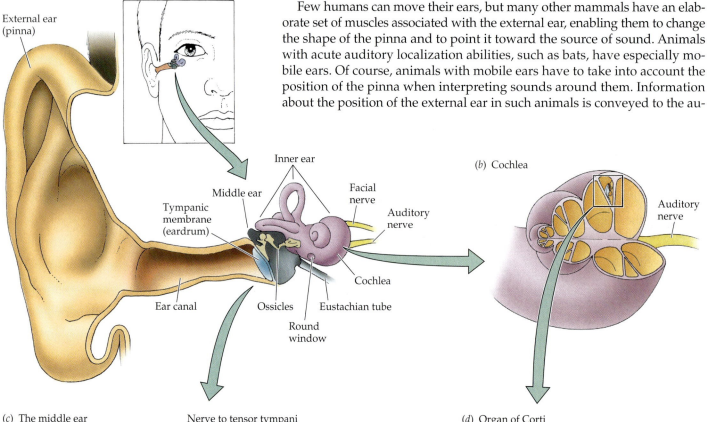

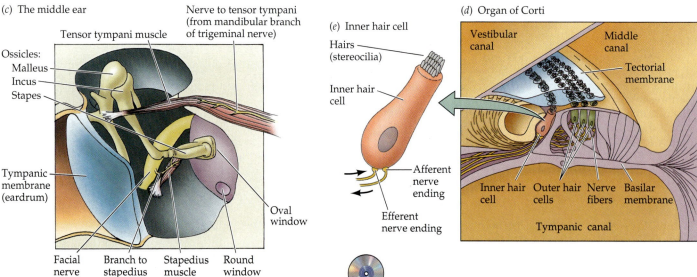

9.1 External and Internal Structures of the Human Ear

ditory pathways in several forms, including feedback information from receptors in the muscles around the pinna.

The Middle Ear Concentrates Sound Energies

Between the external ear and the receptor cells of the inner ear is a group of structures, including bones and muscles, that constitute the **middle ear** (see Figure 9.1*c*). A chain of three tiny bones, or **ossicles,** connects the eardrum (**tympanic membrane**) at the end of the ear canal to an opening of the inner ear called the **oval window.** These ossicles, the smallest bones in the body, are called the **malleus** (hammer), the **incus** (anvil), and the **stapes** (stirrup).

Small displacements of the tympanic membrane move the chain of ossicles. These bones help the minute mechanical forces of air particles perform the difficult task of perturbing the fluid in the inner ear by focusing the pressures from the relatively large tympanic membrane onto the small oval window. This arrangement vastly amplifies sound pressure so that it is capable of stimulating the fluid-filled inner ear.

The mechanical linkage of the ossicles is not fixed; it is modulated by two muscles in ways that improve auditory perception and protect the delicate inner ear from loud, potentially damaging sounds. One of these muscles, the **tensor tympani** (see Figure 9.1*c*), is attached to the malleus, which is connected to the tympanic membrane. The other muscle of the middle ear is attached to the stapes and thus is called the **stapedius.** When activated, these muscles stiffen the linkages of the middle-ear bones, thus limiting the effectiveness of sounds. The muscles of the middle ear are activated by sounds that are 80 to 90 dB above a person's hearing threshold—about as loud as a noisy street. When a loud sound occurs, the stapedius muscle starts to contract about 200 ms later.

The muscles of the middle ear also become active during body movement, swallowing, and vocalization; they are the reason we hear few of the sounds produced by the workings of our own bodies. In some animals, activation of these muscles prevents damage to receptors from very loud, self-produced vocalizations (Avan et al., 1992). For example, some birds and bats (and some babies) produce vocalizations at intense levels of sound pressure; activation of the stapedius muscle dramatically reduces the effect of the vocalization on the individual's own auditory receptors. In the case of sounds produced by our own bodies, the stapedius muscle contracts automatically just before the sound-producing movement. People whose middle-ear muscles have been damaged by disease complain about the annoying loudness of sounds they formerly ignored.

The Inner Ear Transduces Mechanical Energy into Neural Activity

The complex structures of the **inner ear** (Figure 9.1*b*) convert sound into neural activity. To understand how the inner ear accomplishes this transduction, let's look at the details of the inner ear. In mammals the auditory portion of the inner ear is a coiled structure called the **cochlea** (from the Greek *kochlos,* "snail") (see Figure 9.1*b* and *d*). The human cochlea is embedded in the temporal bone of the skull and is a marvel of miniaturization. In an adult, the cochlea measures only about 4 mm in diameter—about the size of a pea. Unrolled, the cochlea would measure about 35 to 40 mm in length.

The region nearest the oval-window membrane is the base of the spiral; the other end, or top, is referred to as the apex. Along the length of the cochlea are three parallel canals: (1) the **tympanic canal,** (2) the **vestibular canal,** and (3) the **middle canal** (see Figure 9.1*d*). Because the entire structure is filled with noncompressible fluid, movement within the cochlea in response to a push on the oval window requires the presence of a movable outlet membrane. This membrane is the **round window,** which separates the tympanic canal from the middle ear (see Figure 9.1*c*).

The principal elements for converting sounds into neural activity are found on the **basilar membrane,** a flexible structure that separates the tympanic canal from the middle canal (see Figure 9.1*d*). This membrane vibrates in response to sound. It is about five times wider at the apex of the cochlea than at the base, even though the cochlea itself narrows toward its apex. Within the middle canal and atop the basilar membrane is the **organ of Corti**—the collective term for all the elements involved in the transduction of sounds. The organ of Corti includes three main structures: (1) the sensory cells (hair cells), (2) an elaborate framework of supporting cells, and (3) the terminations of the auditory nerve fibers (see Figure 9.1d).

Each ear contains two sets of sensory cells: a single row of about 3500 **inner hair cells** (**IHCs;** called *inner* because they are closer to the central axis of the cochlea) and about 12,000 **outer hair cells** (**OHCs**) in three rows (see Figure 9.1d). The IHCs are flask shaped, and the OHCs are cylindrical, with a diameter of approximately 5 μm and a length of 20 to 70 μm. From the upper end of each hair cell protrude tiny hairs whose length ranges from 2 to 6 μm (see Figure 9.1e). Each hair cell has 50 to 200 of these relatively stiff hairs, called **stereocilia** (singular *stereocilium;* from the Greek *stereos,* "solid," and the Latin *cilium,* "eyelid") or simply *cilia.* The heights of the stereocilia increase progressively across the hair cell, so the tops approximate an inclined plane. Atop the organ of Corti is the **tectorial membrane** (see Figure 9.1d). The stereocilia of the OHCs extend into indentations in the bottom of the tectorial membrane.

Auditory nerve fibers contact the base of the hair cells (see Figure 9.1e). Each IHC is associated with 16 to 20 auditory nerve fibers; relatively few nerve fibers contact the many OHCs. In fact, the nerve fibers running from the IHCs account for 90 to 95% of the afferent auditory fibers. These auditory afferents from the cochlea synapse upon neurons in the cochlear nuclei of the pons.

The OHCs have a different function: modulating acoustic stimulation. They send messages out the auditory nerve to the CNS, but they are also contacted by efferent nerve fibers from the CNS. When these efferent nerve fibers are excited, the OHCs change their length (Zheng et al., 2000), thereby influencing the mechanics of the cochlea. Changes in length of the OHCs during the basic responses to sound sharpen the tuning to different frequencies, as we will see later in this chapter (Ashmore, 1994). The IHCs also receive efferent messages, perhaps to inhibit some of the input from loud sounds. Further evidence of the different roles of the inner and outer hair cells comes from studies of a mutant strain of mice that lack IHCs but have normal OHCs; these mice appear to be deaf (Deol and Gluecksohn-Waelsch, 1979).

Synapses in the Organ of Corti Convey Messages to and from the Brain

The organ of Corti has four kinds of synapses and nerve fibers. Two of these (1 and 3 in Figure 9.2a) are afferents that convey messages from the hair cells to the brain;

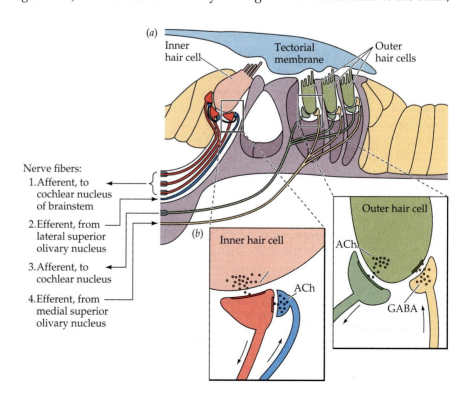

9.2 Auditory Nerve Fibers and Synapses in the Organ of Corti (*a*) The inner and outer hair cells form synaptic connections to and from the brain. (*b*) Different synaptic transmitters are hypothesized to be active at the synapses of inner and outer hair cells in the organ of Corti.

Nerve fibers:
1. Afferent, to cochlear nucleus of brainstem
2. Efferent, from lateral superior olivary nucleus
3. Afferent, to cochlear nucleus
4. Efferent, from medial superior olivary nucleus

the other two (2 and 4 in Figure 9.2*a*) are efferents that convey messages from the brain to the hair cells. Different synaptic transmitters are active at each type of synapse (Figure 9.2*b*) (Eybalin, 1993).

Sounds Produce Waves of Fluid in the Cochlea

When the stapes moves in and out as a result of acoustic vibrations, it exerts varying pressure on the fluid of the vestibular canal, which in turn causes oscillating movements of the basilar membrane. Late in the nineteenth century, it was suggested that the cochlea might be "tuned"; that is, different parts of the basilar membrane might be affected by different frequencies of auditory stimulation.

In the 1930s and 1940s the Hungarian scientist Georg von Békésy tested this hypothesis, using ingenious physical techniques to make direct observations on cochleas that had been surgically removed from cadavers or dead animals. Békésy, who ultimately won a Nobel Prize for his work, found that sounds initiate traveling waves that sweep along the basilar membrane, and the site of the largest amplitude of displacement of the basilar membrane depends on the frequency of the stimulus (Figure 9.3). For high frequencies the displacement of the basilar membrane peaks in the region where the basilar membrane is narrow—the base of the cochlea. For low-frequency stimuli the amplitudes of membrane displacement peak at the widest portion of the basilar membrane—the apex (Ashmore, 1994).

The Hair Cells Transduce Auditory Vibrations into Electrical Signals

Modern techniques reveal intimate details of the principal elements of transduction—the hair cells (Hudspeth, 1989, 1992). The movements of fluid in the cochlea, excited by sounds, produce vibrations of the basilar membrane. These vibrations bend the hair cell cilia that are inserted into the tectorial membrane (see Figure 9.1*d*). Recordings from isolated individual hair cells have shown that very small displacements of hair bundles cause rapid changes in ionic channels of the stereocilia. These changes initiate excitation of the hair cells and then of the afferent axons.

The ion channels in the stereocilia are believed to be gated by mechanical energy, as are those in touch receptors (see Chapter 8), but the gates in the channels for hearing are also specialized for rapid response: They can open and close thousands of times per second. This rapidity rules out the use of second messengers, which are found in receptors for smell, taste, and sight (as we'll see later in this chapter and in Chapter 10).

The number of channels per hair cell has been estimated by measurements of the variability of response in relation to the size of response. These measures suggest that there are only about 100 ion channels per hair cell,

Georg von Békésy
(1890–1972)

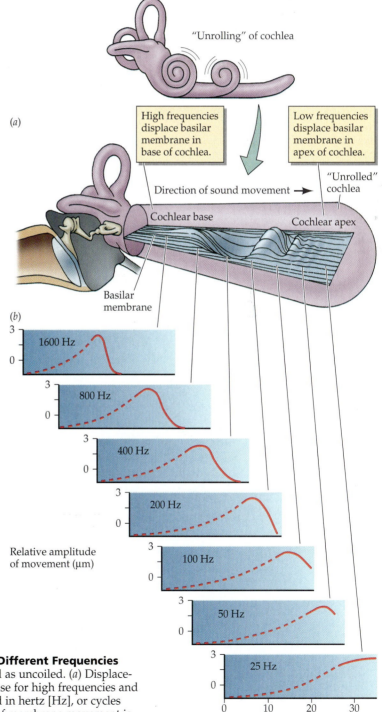

"Unrolling" of cochlea

High frequencies displace basilar membrane in base of cochlea.

Low frequencies displace basilar membrane in apex of cochlea.

Direction of sound movement →

"Unrolled" cochlea

(*a*)

Cochlear base

Cochlear apex

Basilar membrane

(*b*)

1600 Hz

800 Hz

400 Hz

200 Hz

100 Hz

Relative amplitude of movement (µm)

50 Hz

25 Hz

Distance from stapes (mm)

9.3 Basilar Membrane Movement for Sounds of Different Frequencies
In this illustration the basilar membrane is represented as uncoiled. (*a*) Displacement of the basilar membrane peaks at the cochlear base for high frequencies and at the apex for low frequencies. (*b*) As the frequency (measured in hertz [Hz], or cycles per second) of stimulation decreases, the position of the peak of membrane movement is displaced progressively toward the apex of the cochlea.

(a)

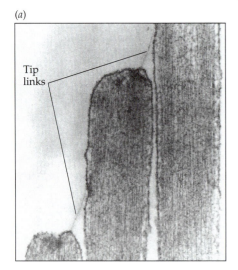

Tip links

(b)

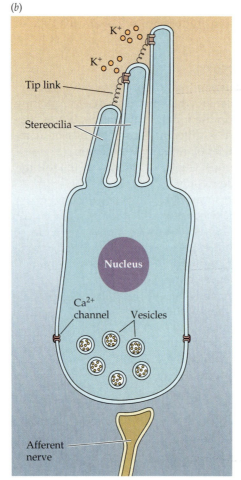

K+
K+
Tip link
Stereocilia
Nucleus
Ca²⁺ channel
Vesicles
Afferent nerve

(c)

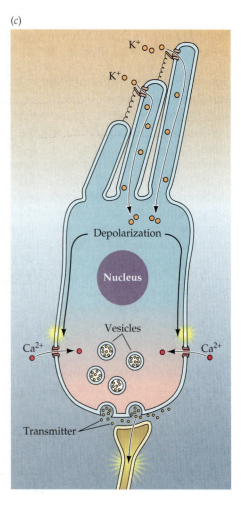

K+
K+
Depolarization
Nucleus
Vesicles
Ca²⁺
Ca²⁺
Transmitter

9.4 How Auditory Stimulation Affects the Stereocilia on Cochlear Hair Cells (a) This micrograph of stereocilia shows the tip links as thread-like structures. (b) Hudspeth (1992) proposed the model of hair cell stimulation illustrated here. (c) Displacement of the stereocilia opens K⁺ channels. This depolarization opens Ca²⁺ channels in the cell's base, which causes neurotransmitter release to excite afferent axons. (Micrograph courtesy of A. J. Hudspeth.)

[Handwritten margin notes:] mechanical gates. Open → K⁺ rush in. depolarize → V-gated Ca channels open @ base. → then NB transmitters out to stimulate the neuron.

or about one or two per stereocilium. Comparing the recordings from different parts of the cell indicates that some ion channels are near the tops of the cilia. Fine, thread-like fibers called **tip links** run along the tips of the stereocilia (Figure 9.4a).

According to one model (Hudspeth, 1997), a sound that makes the hair cells sway only slightly will increase the tension on the elastic tip links and pull open a "trap-door," opening the ion channel, which closes again in a fraction of a millisecond as the hair cell sways back (Figure 9.4b). Opening of the channels allows an inrush of potassium (K⁺) ions and a rapid depolarization of the entire hair cell. This initial depolarization leads to a rapid influx of calcium ions (Ca²⁺) at the *base* of the hair cell, which causes synaptic vesicles there to fuse with the presynaptic membrane and release their chemical contents—probably the synaptic transmitter glutamate—from the base of the hair cell, and stimulate the afferent nerve fiber (Figure 9.4c).

The ion pores in the cilia are large and do not discriminate among kinds of ions. They let even small organic molecules pass through, which is why some drugs, such as aspirin and antibiotics, can impair hair cells by attacking their mitochondria. Susceptibility to this kind of damage of the receptor is inherited maternally, as are the mitochondria.

Active Electromechanical Processes in the Cochlea Enhance Frequency Discrimination

As Georg von Békésy realized, the broad peaks of tuning for different frequencies that he observed along the basilar membrane (see Figure 9.3) are not sharp enough to account for our ability to discriminate frequencies only 2 Hz apart. Békésy and others suggested that the broad patterns of excitation along the basilar membrane are "sharpened" somehow.

Even in the 1940s, recordings from auditory nerve fibers showed much more precise tuning than Békésy had found in his measurements of the basilar membrane. The **tuning curves** (or receptive fields) of single auditory nerve fibers were studied through recordings of their responses to sounds that varied in frequency and intensity (Figure 9.5). The fact that auditory nerve fibers are tuned much more precisely than the basilar membrane suggests that the cochlea itself has a way of enhancing the tuning.

We mentioned earlier that OHCs show the surprising property of changing length when they are stimulated electrically—an electromechanical response (Brownell et al., 1985). Hyperpolarization causes the OHCs to lengthen, while depolarization causes them to shorten. These changes, which amount to as much as 4% of the length of the cell, occur almost instantaneously. Investigators hypothesize that these mechanical responses of the OHCs serve as a **cochlear amplifier**, amplifying the movements of the basilar membrane in some regions and dampening basilar membrane movements in other regions. This selective regulation of the basilar membrane sharpens the tuning of the cochlea (Ashmore, 1994; Hubbard, 1993). Other evidence of the active nature of the cochlea is that the ear can emit sounds (see the next section).

But whereas each neuron responds to a very precise frequency at its threshold, as more intense stimuli are used the neuron responds to a broader range of frequencies. For example, the fiber whose responses are shown in red in Figure 9.5 has its *best frequency* at 1200 Hz; that is, it responds to a very weak tone at 1200 Hz. When sounds are 20 dB stronger, however, the fiber responds to any frequency from 500 to 1800 Hz. Thus an auditory nerve fiber is not a labeled line of the sort we discussed in Chapter 8; that is, it does not respond to just one frequency of stimulation. If the brain received a signal from only one such fiber, it would not be able to tell whether the stimulus was a weak tone of 1200 Hz or a stronger tone of 500 or 1800 Hz or any frequency in between.

The ability to discriminate frequencies is even sharper at higher stations of the auditory nervous system, as Békésy hypothesized. At the medial geniculate nucleus and the auditory cortex, neurons are excited by certain frequencies and inhibited by neighboring frequencies. This interplay of excitation and inhibition further sharpens the frequency responses, allowing us to discriminate very small frequency differences.

The Ears Emit Sounds as Part of the Hearing Process

The cochlea is not only the first stage in the analysis of sounds; in most people it also *produces* sounds. If you make a brief sound—a click or a short burst of tone—in the external ear canal, a few milliseconds later a similar sound comes back from the inner ear. This is not just an echo from the eardrum or middle ear, although such echoes exist. The cochlea produces this sound. The sounds that the cochlea produces in response to acoustic stimulation are called **evoked otoacoustic emissions** (**EOAEs**). They occur in all people who have normal hearing and are thought to reflect the action of the cochlear amplifier discussed earlier, selectively boosting response to particular frequencies.

In addition to evoked otoacoustic emissions, the ears of many people also produce continuous low-level sounds at one or more frequencies; these sounds are called **spontaneous otoacoustic emissions** (**SOAEs**) (D. T. Kemp, 1979; Zurek, 1981). These spontaneous emissions are usually less than 20 dB above threshold; they can be detected by sensitive microphones in quiet environments, but the people who produce these sounds do not perceive them.

About two-thirds of women and half of men under 60 produce SOAEs (McFadden, 1993a). Because they are observed in infants as well as in adults, SOAEs don't seem to require prior auditory experience. Usually people who have SOAEs have more sensitive hearing than persons without them, which is consistent with the idea that these emissions are part of the cochlear amplifier (McFadden, 1993b).

9.5 Examples of Tuning Curves of Auditory Nerve Cells These curves are obtained by measurement of neural responses to sounds of different intensities and frequencies. They represent threshold measurements. Illustrated here are responses of six neural units recorded from the auditory nerve of the cat. (After Kiang, 1965.)

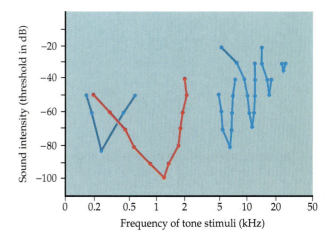

McFadden (1993b) reported a startling finding: Women who have a twin brother show significantly fewer SOAEs, and weaker EOAEs, than singleton females or females who have a female twin. McFadden suggested that the reason for the lower incidence of SOAEs in females with male twins is that in the womb, the female is exposed to androgens secreted by the male—a prenatal masculinizing effect (see Chapter 12). Lesbians, on average, have weaker EOAEs than heterosexual women (McFadden and Pasanen, 1998), suggesting that prenatal androgens may increase the probability of homosexuality in females.

Evoked otoacoustic emissions may aid the screening of young children, especially newborns, for hearing impairments. Several studies have shown that EOAEs can be observed in human infants and that observation of EOAEs is as useful as a commonly used electrophysiological technique for detecting hearing impairments (Doyle et al., 1997; Nozza, et al., 1997). The electrophysiological technique employed to compare with otoacoustic emissions is known as **auditory-evoked potentials,** like those mentioned in Chapter 3. These electrical responses are obtained from an electrode on the scalp and include a series of waveforms generated at successive places in the auditory pathway that extends from cochlea to cortex, which we discuss next.

Auditory System Pathways Run from the Brainstem to the Cortex

On each side of your head, about 30,000 to 50,000 auditory fibers from the cochlea make up the auditory part of the eighth (vestibulocochlear) cranial nerve. Recall that most of these afferent fibers are carrying messages from the IHCs, each of which stimulates several nerve fibers. Input from the auditory nerve is distributed in a complex manner to both sides of the brain (Figure 9.6). Each auditory nerve fiber divides into two main branches as it enters the brainstem. Each branch then goes to separate groups of cells in the dorsal and ventral **cochlear nuclei.**

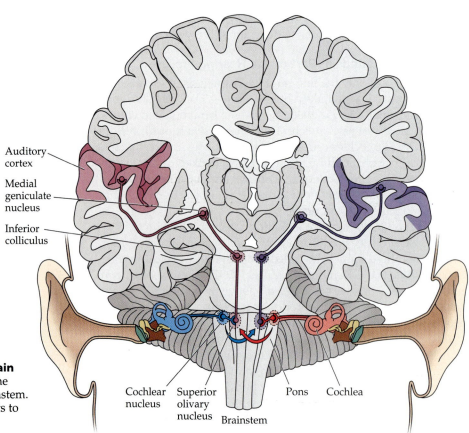

9.6 Auditory Pathways of the Human Brain
This view from the front of the head shows the first binaural afferent interactions in the brainstem. Most of the information from each ear projects to the cortex on the opposite side of the brain.

Auditory cortex

Medial geniculate nucleus

Inferior colliculus

Cochlear nucleus Superior olivary nucleus Pons Cochlea Brainstem

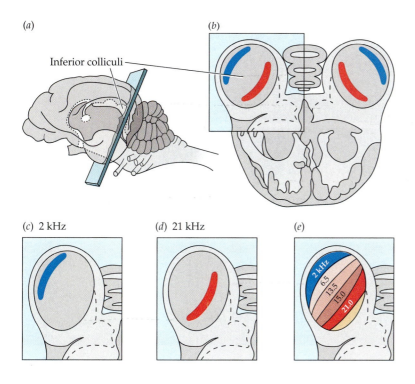

(a)

Inferior colliculi

(b)

(c) 2 kHz

(d) 21 kHz

(e)

2 kHz
6.5
13.5
15.0
21.0

9.7 Mapping Auditory Frequencies in the Cat Inferior Colliculus (*a*) This lateral view of the cat brain shows the plane of the transverse section in part *b* through the inferior colliculi. (*c, d*) Locations of the cells labeled with 2-DG via 2000 Hz stimulation (*c*) and 21,000 Hz stimulation (*d*) are indicated here by blue and red, respectively. (*e*) Complete tonotopic mapping shows the range of frequencies that can stimulate the cat's auditory system. (After Serviere et al., 1984.)

The output of the cochlear nuclei also travels via multiple paths. One path goes to the **superior olivary nuclei,** which receive inputs from both right and left cochlear nuclei. The bilateral input to this set of cells is the first level for **binaural** (two-ear) **interaction** of afferents in the auditory system and is therefore of primary importance for mechanisms of auditory localization, which we'll discuss shortly. Several other parallel paths converge on the **inferior colliculus,** which is the auditory center of the midbrain. Outputs of the inferior colliculus go to the **medial geniculate nucleus** of the thalamus. At least two different pathways from the medial geniculate extend to several auditory cortical areas.

At each level of the auditory system, from cochlea to auditory cortex, a major feature is that the neurons are arranged in an orderly map that reflects the frequencies of stimuli; cells responsive to high frequency sound are located at a distance from those responsive to low frequencies. This mapping of neural regions of the auditory system according to stimulus frequency is called **tonotopic organization.**

Tonotopic organization is obvious in mapping of the tuning curves of neurons as the auditory brain centers are traversed. We can also demonstrate tonotopic organization anatomically by injecting an animal with 2-deoxyglucose (2-DG) and exposing it to a tone of a particular frequency. 2-DG is taken up by cells as though it were glucose, but 2-DG is not metabolized, so it remains in the cells. The neurons that are most active at the time 2-DG is injected take up more 2-DG than other cells, so postmortem processing reveals the regions of greatest activity in response to that frequency (Figure 9.7).

Most animals have several auditory cortical fields. Different fields of the auditory cortex may be specialized for location of sounds in space, movement of sound sources, perception of species-specific sounds, and so on (Figure 9.8). PET and fMRI studies show that stimulation with pure tones or noise activates chiefly the primary auditory cortex on the

9.8 Tonotopic Organization of Auditory Cortical Regions in Three Species of Mammals The arrows show the direction of tonotopic representation, from low to high frequencies. (After Merzenich et al., 1993.)

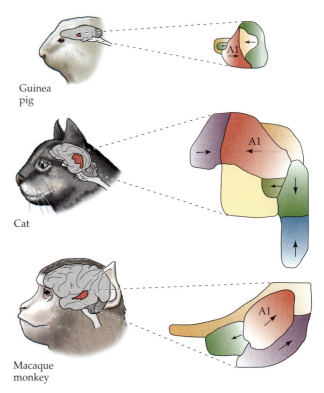

Guinea pig

A1

Cat

A1

Macaque monkey

A1

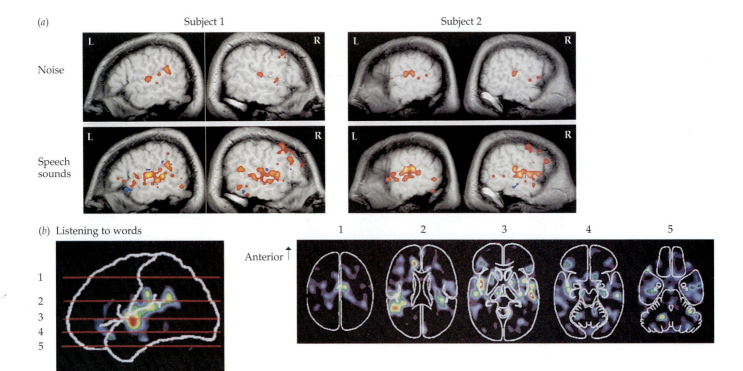

(a)

Subject 1   Subject 2

Noise

Speech sounds

(b) Listening to words

1
2
3
4
5

Anterior ↑   1   2   3   4   5

9.9 Responses of the Human Auditory Cortex to Random Sounds versus Speech

(a) Functional-MRI scans of the cerebral hemispheres show that pure tones or noise (*top*) activate chiefly the primary auditory area on the superior aspect of the temporal lobe, while listening to speech sounds (*bottom*) activates other auditory cortical regions as well as the primary auditory area. (b) Lateral (*left*) and horizontal (*right*) PET scans show that listening to words activates not only several regions of the cerebral cortex but also regions of the thalamus and the cerebellum. The numbered horizontal lines in the left panel correspond to the levels of the horizontal sections in the right panel. (Part *a* from Binder et al., 1994, courtesy of Jeffrey Binder; *b* from Posner and Raichle, 1994, courtesy of Marcus Raichle.)

superior temporal lobe (Figure 9.9*a*). Speech activates this and other auditory areas (Figure 9.9*a* and *b*). Interestingly, the same regions are activated when normal subjects try to lip-read—that is, to understand someone by watching their lips without auditory cues (Calvert et al., 1997)—a result that suggests that the auditory cortex integrates other, nonauditory, information with sounds. We'll discuss the auditory cortex in more detail shortly.

Two Main Theories Describe How We Discriminate Pitch

Most of us can discriminate very small differences in frequency of sound over the entire audible range—from 20 Hz to 15,000 or even 20,000 Hz. The ability to detect a change in frequency is usually measured as the **minimal discriminable frequency difference** between two tones. The detectable difference is about 2 Hz for sounds up to 2000 Hz; above these frequencies it grows larger.

Note that *frequency* and *pitch* are not synonymous terms. **Frequency** describes a physical property of sounds (see Box 9.1); **pitch** relates solely to sensory experience—that is, the responses of subjects to sounds. There are important reasons to emphasize this distinction, including the fact that frequency is not the sole determinant of pitch experience (at some frequencies, sounds seem to increase in pitch as they become more intense), and changes in pitch do not precisely parallel changes in frequency.

How do we account for the ability to discriminate pitches? Two main theories have been offered. One, described as **place theory**, argues that our perception of pitch depends on where the sound causes maximal displacement of the basilar membrane. Recall that high frequencies displace the basilar membrane at the base of the cochlea, and low frequencies displace the basilar membrane in the apex of the cochlea. But place theory also identifies the neurons that are stimulated in the central auditory pathways; that is, particular nerve cells receive excitation from a particular part of the basilar membrane and therefore respond to particular stimulus frequencies.

The alternative idea, **volley theory,** emphasizes the relations between the frequency of auditory stimuli and the pattern or timing of neural discharges. According to this perspective, the firing pattern of a single nerve cell reveals the frequency of the stimulus because each time the stimulus changes frequency, the pattern of neuronal discharge is altered. The crudest representation of this idea suggests a one-to-one relationship; that is, a 500 Hz tone is represented by 500 nerve impulses per second, and a 1000 Hz tone stimulating the same neuron is represented by a frequency of 1000 nerve impulses per second. In both cases the firing of the nerve impulse is *phase-locked* to the stimulus; that is, it occurs at a particular portion of the cycle. Such a phase-locked representation can be accomplished more accurately by several fibers than by a single fiber—hence the term *volley,* as in a volley of nerve impulses.

Are these views—place and volley theories—necessarily antagonistic? No. In fact, the contemporary view of pitch perception incorporates *both* perspectives.

As place theory predicts, the region of maximal vibration along the basilar membrane indeed varies with the frequency of the stimulus: A change in frequency is accompanied by a change in the region of maximal disturbance (see Figure 9.3; Rhode, 1984). For complex sounds with several frequency components, the cochlea accomplishes a sort of Fourier analysis (see Box 9.1), with the different frequencies represented by peaks of vibration at different places along the basilar membrane. The accuracy of such place representation of auditory frequency has improved over the course of evolution as the basilar membrane has lengthened and the number of hair cells and auditory nerve fibers has increased.

And as volley theory predicts, neurophysiological data suggest that pitch sensation also involves temporal patterns of nerve discharge. In these experiments the measurement of temporal pattern is usually the distribution of the intervals between the nerve impulses elicited by a sound. A neuron can be said to code the frequency of a sound if this distribution is either the same as the interval between successive cycles of the sound or an integral multiple of it. This kind of coding is quite prominent at frequencies below about 1500 Hz, although it has also been noted for sounds with frequencies up to 4000 Hz.

So the frequency properties of a sound are coded in two ways: (1) according to the distribution of excitation among cells—that is, place coding or tonotopic representation—and (2) according to the temporal pattern (volley) of discharge in cells extending from the auditory nerve to the auditory cortex.

One Ear Can Localize Sounds, but Two Ears Can Do It Better

Normally, we can locate the position of a sound source with great accuracy (within about 1°) by using both ears. This **binaural detection** relies on differences between the stimuli that reach the two ears. We call stimuli that differ at the two ears **dichotic stimuli.** People who were born blind can localize sound sources even better than sighted people, apparently because they utilize more of the brain to process sound (Röder et al., 1999).

What features of the stimulus are important for binaural localization? Two main binaural cues for auditory localization are (1) **intensity differences,** the difference in sound intensity at the two ears, and (2) **latency differences,** the difference in the time of arrival of a sound at the two ears. Early in the twentieth century, some investigators stressed the importance of intensity differences in dichotic stimuli, while others emphasized time differences. As often happens, both were correct. The idea that we use both intensity differences and arrival distances to localize sound is known as the **duplex theory.**

Some sounds show intensity differences at the two ears because the head casts a sound shadow (Figure 9.10). The sound frequencies that are blocked depend on the size of the head because low-frequency sounds have long waves that go around the head. At low frequencies, no matter where sounds are presented in the horizontal plane, there are virtually no intensity differences between the ears. For these frequencies, differences in times of arrival are the principal cues for sound position. At higher frequencies, the sound shadow cast by the head produces significant binaural intensity

9.10 Cues for Binaural Hearing
The two ears receive somewhat different information from sound sources located to one side or the other of the observer's midline. The head blocks frequencies greater than 1000 Hz, producing binaural differences in sound intensity. Sounds also take longer to reach the more distant ear, resulting in binaural differences in time of arrival.

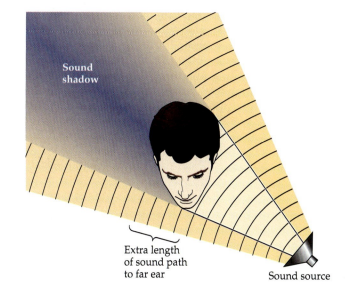

Sound shadow

Extra length of sound path to far ear

Sound source

differences. We cannot tell by monitoring our own performance that we are using one cue to localize high-frequency sounds and another cue to localize low-frequency sounds. In general we are aware of the results of neural processing but not the processing itself.

How are the binaural features of an acoustic environment analyzed by the nervous system? There are many opportunities for binaural interaction at various levels of the brainstem—regions where single nerve cells receive inputs derived from both ears, including the superior olivary complex and the inferior colliculus. Bipolar neurons in these regions can detect small differences in arrival time of low-frequency stimuli to the two ears, apparently by comparing input to their two dendrites (Agmon-Snir et al., 1998).

Tests for spatial sensitivity in neurons use a setup like that shown in Figure 9.11. Some auditory neurons respond to a sound that originates almost anywhere in the opposite hemifield. Other, location-sensitive neurons have relatively small receptive fields that respond only to sounds at a particular location. Models suggest that if you mapped the receptive fields of only 128 such cortical neurons, you could use that information to predict the source of a sound as well as the cat does (Furukawa et al., 2000). In mammals, there does not seem to be a systematic map of auditory space in any brain centers, but later we'll discuss such maps in the brains of owls.

If you know someone who is deaf in one ear, you may have noticed that deaf people, too, can localize sounds to some extent. Such **monaural** (one-ear) **detection** relies on a very different cue. Most natural sounds consist of a mix of many different frequencies. But as we mentioned at the start of this chapter, the hills and valleys of your outer ear (and your head) will dampen some frequencies more than others before the sound enters the ear canal. The frequencies that will be modulated depend on where the sound is coming from (Kulkarni and Colburn, 1998).

As the head and ears grow, we learn how this *spectral filtering* varies with the location of sound sources and use this as another cue. Researchers can place a speaker directly in the ear canal and, by varying the spectral filtering of natural sounds, fool a person or animal into believing it came from a particular point in space (Xu et al., 1999). In fact, for sounds from the midline (directly above, below, in front of, or behind us), we rely heavily on such cues because there are no dif-

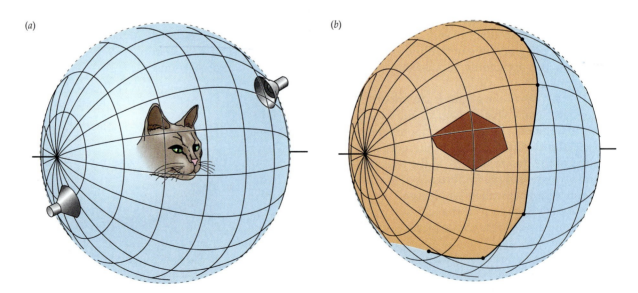

(a)   (b)

9.11 Spatial Sensitivity of the Auditory Neurons in Cat Cortex   (a) A loudspeaker emitting sound was moved along the surface of an imaginary sphere with a radius of 1 m while the responses of individual neurons were recorded. (b) About half the neurons showed some spatial sensitivity. Of these neurons, half responded to sounds that originated anywhere in the opposite hemifield (tan), and the other half showed relatively small receptive fields, responding only to sounds at a particular location on the side of the opposite ear (brown). (After Middlebrooks and Pettigrew, 1981.)

ferences in the intensity or latency of sound stimuli to the two ears. This is one reason why we are not as good at detecting the sources of sounds from the midline as elsewhere.

Orchestra conductors are especially good at localizing the sources of sounds (Münte et al., 2001), presumably because of extensive practice ("Mr. Breedlove, could you please play in tune?").

The Auditory Cortex Performs Complex Tasks in the Perception of Sound

Most investigators of hearing, from the late nineteenth century until recently, believed that auditory sensation and discrimination depend on the auditory cortex. The noncortical auditory nuclei were considered to be mere relay stations or stepping-stones in a pathway to the cortex (Masterton, 1993). But behavioral testing after surgical removal of auditory cortex showed that cats do not *need* auditory cortex to discriminate intensity (Raab and Ades, 1946; Rosenzweig, 1946), frequency (Butler et al., 1957), or duration of tones (for a review, see Neff and Casseday, 1977). If the auditory cortex is not involved in these basic kinds of auditory discrimination, then what *does* it do?

For one thing, the early studies relied on simple, but unnatural, pure tones (Masterton, 1993, 1997). But most of the sounds in nature contain many frequencies and change rapidly—such as vocalizations of animals, footsteps, snaps, crackles, and pops—and the auditory nervous system likely evolved to deal with such sounds. Indeed, most central auditory neurons habituate rapidly to continuous sound, ceasing to respond after only a few milliseconds, but brief sounds or abrupt onsets of sound usually evoke responses from many neurons, from the cochlear nuclei to the auditory cortex. Ablation of the auditory cortex in cats does impair discrimination of temporal *patterns* of sound (Neff and Casseday, 1977). Similarly, in monkeys, bilateral ablation of the auditory cortex impairs the ability to discriminate species-specific vocalizations (Heffner and Heffner, 1989). So auditory cortex is required to analyze complex sounds encountered in everyday life.

There seem to be two main streams of auditory processing in cortex (Kaas and Hackett, 1999). A dorsal stream, involving the parietal lobe, may be concerned with spatial location of sounds, while a ventral stream through the temporal lobe may analyze the various components of sounds (Romanski et al., 1999). The two streams project to different regions of prefrontal cortex. This division of cortical processing into *where* sound arises and *what* produced the sound echoes hypotheses about the analysis of visual stimuli that will be discussed in Chapter 10.

Experience Affects Auditory Perception and the Auditory Pathways

Aspects of auditory discrimination and the neural circuits involved in hearing change as we grow. At birth the human infant has diverse hearing abilities. Postnatal developments involve elaborate structural changes throughout auditory pathways. Accompanying these changes are progressive improvements in the perception of complex sounds, such as speech. Because the world after birth is filled with a complex array of sounds, it is reasonable to ask whether experience shapes or modulates the forming of connections in the auditory system.

One demonstration of the role of early auditory experience comes from studies of musicians (Pantev et al., 1998). In these studies the evoked brain activity from musicians and nonmusicians was identical in response to pure tones. But if, instead of pure tones, the more complex and musically relevant sounds from a piano were used, musicians displayed a greater brain response than did nonmusicians. Now maybe these people became musicians because their brains were more responsive to complex tones to begin with. However, there was a significant correlation between the magnitude of brain response to piano tones and the age at which the musicians began studying music. The earlier the musician had begun her studies, the greater the brain response to piano tones, suggesting that exposure to musical training affects brain auditory responsiveness.

NEURAL PLASTICITY

The role of auditory experience in the development of sound localization is implied by observations in bilaterally deaf children who were fitted with different types of hearing aids (Beggs and Foreman, 1980). The children in one group were given a hearing aid that delivered the very same sounds to both ears. In a second group children were fitted with a separate hearing aid for each ear so that they experienced dichotic stimuli. When examined years later, the children who had been fitted with dichotic hearing aids were able to localize sounds with significantly greater accuracy than that shown by the children who had experienced comparable overall levels of sounds but were deprived of dichotic stimuli.

Knudsen and colleagues (1984) performed some elegant studies using an especially acute binaural perceiver—the owl. When hunting, owls use both arrival differences and intensity differences to accurately localize sounds at night (Pena and Konishi, 2001). In the avian equivalent to the inferior colliculus (the dorsal "roof" of the midbrain called the *tectum*), some cells are arranged in a roughly spherical representation of space. In other words, each space-specific cell has a receptive field that includes sounds coming from a small cone of space centering on the owl's head. Neighboring cells in the tectum respond to neighboring regions of auditory space (Knudsen, 1984b; Knudsen and Konishi, 1978).

In the owl tectum, both auditory and visual space are represented, and the maps for the two senses correspond closely (Knudsen, 1982). Most cells in this region respond to both auditory and visual stimuli. In most cases the visual receptive field of a cell is enclosed within the auditory receptive field of the same cell. This close alignment of auditory and visual maps of space may help guide motor responses to the position of the stimulus.

To assess the impact of early experience on the development of these maps, investigators placed a plug in one ear of the owl, which reduced sound intensity in that ear by 20 to 40 dB. This treatment was applied to owls of various ages. When the plug was first placed in the ear, the animal made large localization errors to the side of the open ear. For example, if a sound was made directly in front of the owl, the owl responded as if the sound had come from the side of the open ear—presumably because the sound was more intense in that ear, which would normally mean that it came from that side.

Adult animals never seemed to adjust to the ear plug, but owls younger than 8 weeks at the time of plugging slowly began to compensate for the distortion produced by the blockage of one ear. Then when the ear plugs were removed, these animals made large localization errors to the opposite side. Knudsen and Knudsen (1985) showed the critical role of vision in this process of adjustment of auditory localization. Barn owls with one ear plugged did not correct their auditory localization errors if deprived of vision. Furthermore, if owls were fitted with prisms that deviated vision by 10° (Figure 9.12), the adjustment of auditory localization was matched to this visual error.

Eric Knudsen

NEURAL PLASTICITY

9.12 The Role of Vision in Auditory Localization This young owl has had prisms fitted over its eyes to deviate vision by about 10° to the side. At first, it makes mistakes when reaching for a visual target, but eventually it learns to adapt to the prisms. The neurons in its tectum also adapt, so now neurons excited by a sound from a particular location in space are also excited by visual stimuli presented 10° to the left of that location. (Courtesy of Eric Knudsen.)

Neurophysiological studies of these owls reveal some features of the underlying mechanisms (Knudsen, 1985). As mentioned earlier, within the tectum of barn owls are nerve cells that are bimodal; that is, they respond to both visual and auditory stimuli, and the auditory and visual spatial sensitivities are aligned; that is, they correspond to approximately the same positions in space. So either a sound or a visual cue in one location will activate neurons in a particular region of the tectum.

When the correspondence between auditory localization cues and visual position was changed by the use of an ear plug in young owls, an interesting finding was noted. Even though correspondence was altered by the ear plug, when tested months later, the auditory receptive fields aligned well with the visual receptive fields. But removal of the ear plug caused the cells' most sensitive auditory receptive areas to shift away from the alignment with the visual fields of a nerve cell. These changes in auditory spatial tuning did not occur in an adult animal that had been similarly treated, which suggests that this experience-dependent process involves a critical period during early development. These changes might arise either from structural modifications of growing neural circuits or from modulations of synaptic effectiveness (Knudsen, 1998).

Maps of mammalian auditory areas also show plasticity. For example, monkeys were trained by means of a food reward to perform a difficult auditory frequency discrimination task. After several months of training, the cortical surface area representing the frequency band in which they had learned to discriminate had increased. Other subjects that heard the same tones but were not required to engage in the discrimination task did not develop an enlarged representation for these frequencies (Recanzone et al., 1993). Conditioning a guinea pig to tones of a particular frequency can cause cortical neurons to shift their response to favor that frequency (Figure 9.13) (N. M. Weinberger, 1998). Thus the auditory cortical map remains plastic even in adult mammals.

Deafness Is a Major Disorder of the Nervous System

There are about 18 million cases of deafness or hearing impairment in the United States (Travis, 1992). These disabilities range in severity from occasional difficulties in speech perception (a drop in sensitivity of 41 to 55 dB between 500 and 2000 Hz) to the inability to hear anything (a 90 dB drop between 500 and 2000 Hz). In this sec-

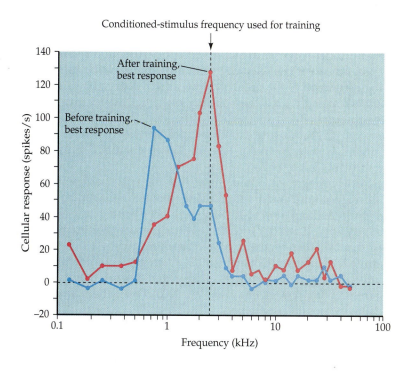

9.13 Long-Term Retention of a Trained Shift in Tuning of an Auditory Receptive Field Before training, the best frequency of this auditory cortex cell of an adult guinea pig was about 0.7 kHz. After training with a 1.1 kHz tone, the best frequency shifted to 1.1 kHz. After 2 and 4 weeks, the shift had remained stable. (From N. M. Weinberger, 1998.)

tion, after looking at the different kinds of deafness, we will discuss a promising treatment for this disability.

There Are Three Main Causes of Deafness

Many severe hearing impairments arise early in life and impair language acquisition. There are three general categories of deafness:

1. **Conduction deafness** arises when disorders of the outer or middle ear prevent vibrations produced by auditory stimuli from reaching the cochlea.
2. **Sensorineural deafness** results from disorders of the cochlea or the eighth-nerve fibers that conduct information from the cochlea to the brain.
3. **Central deafness** is due to disorders in brain auditory regions.

In the subsections that follow, we'll look at the latter two forms of deafness in more detail.

Sensorineural deafness.   This type of deafness starts at 10 years of age and results in total bilateral deafness by the age of 30. The conditions that cause sensorineural deafness are quite varied and include hundreds of hereditary disorders (Pennisi, 1997), metabolic dysfunctions, exposure to toxic substances, trauma, and loud sounds. The end result is the same: Auditory nerve fibers are unable to become excited in a normal manner. E. D. Lynch et al. (1997) isolated a gene responsible for sensorineural deafness in a large family in Costa Rica. The defective gene normally encodes one of the structural proteins that stiffen the hair cells. Other genetic forms of deafness involve other genes that control hair cell structure (Littlewood et al., 2000).

Drug-induced deafness results from the toxic properties of a group of antibiotics that includes streptomycin and gentamicin. The **ototoxic** (ear-damaging) properties of streptomycin were discovered because this antibiotic is remarkably effective in the treatment of tuberculosis, but there was a tremendous price to pay for the cure: Many patients showed severe cochlear and/or vestibular damage. In some patients, streptomycin produced total, irreversible loss of hearing caused by the almost complete destruction of hair cells in the cochlea.

Noise-induced hearing impairments also involve primarily inner-ear mechanisms. Noise pollution and the advent of recreational sounds—such as those from intense music, motorcycles and other loud engines, and especially the firing of guns—have made hearing loss a prominent problem and have given **audiologists** (hearing therapists) and **otologists** (ear doctors) a lot of business (Clark, 1991).

The cochlea can be damaged by exposure to intense sudden sounds or to chronic sounds of high intensity. The initial histological changes in the inner ear involve primarily hair cells, and the outer hair cells are more susceptible to sound trauma than the inner cells. The progression of changes with continued sound exposure leads in some individuals to destruction of the organ of Corti and the nerve fibers that innervate it. Loud sounds coupled with the use of some over-the-counter drugs, such as aspirin, can have profound effects on hearing (McFadden and Champlin, 1990). The hearing loss caused by chronic use of aspirin can be impressive—a reduction of up to 40 dB for high tones, coupled with the development of **tinnitus,** a sensation of noises or ringing in the ears (Brien, 1993).

Can damaged hair cells be regrown in mammals? Although fish and amphibians produce hair cells throughout life and are thus able to replace damaged hair cells, mammals traditionally were thought to be incapable of regenerating hair cells. But more recent findings have called this traditional idea into question. For example, researchers discovered that birds can regenerate hair cells damaged by acoustic overstimulation or by ototoxic chemicals (Cotanche, 1987). And gene manipulation induced the regeneration of hair cells in cultures of the organ of Corti that had been surgically removed from young rats (Zheng and Gao, 2000), so regeneration of hair cells in deaf people may be possible someday.

Central deafness.   Central deafness (hearing loss caused by brain lesions or impairments) is seldom a simple loss of sensitivity. An example of the complexity of changes in auditory perception following cerebral cortical damage is **word deafness,** a disorder in which people show normal speech and hearing for simple sounds but cannot recognize spoken words. Some researchers have suggested that the basis of word deafness is an abnormally slow analysis of auditory inputs. Another example of central deafness is **cortical deafness,** in which patients have difficulty recognizing both verbal and nonverbal auditory stimuli. Cortical deafness is a rare syndrome that arises from a bilateral destruction of inputs to the auditory cortex.

Strokes that interrupt all of the projection fibers (white matter) from the medial geniculate nucleus to the various auditory cortical regions cause deafness (Y. Tanaka et al., 1991). Patients who have experienced such strokes still show various acoustic reflexes mediated by the brainstem—such as bodily responses to environmental sounds—although they deny hearing the sounds to which they are reacting. In contrast, patients with bilateral destruction of only the *primary* auditory cortex often have less severe hearing loss, presumably because other auditory cortical regions contribute to hearing, as discussed earlier.

Electrical Stimulation of the Auditory Nerve Can Alleviate Deafness

Researchers have tried to restore hearing in profoundly deaf individuals by directly stimulating the auditory nerve with electrical currents (Loeb, 1990; J. M. Miller and Spelman, 1990). Progress in the development of **cochlear implants** that deliver such electrical stimulation has been rapid (Figure 9.14).

Who gains by the use of such devices? In several types of sensorineural hearing loss, including those caused by ototoxic drugs and childhood meningitis, the damage that produces deafness involves the hair cells. Although the hair cells may be completely destroyed, the electrical excitability of the auditory nerve often remains unchanged. Some of the most enthusiastic recipients of this clinical aid are patients who became deaf before acquiring language (Loeb, 1990). However, some deaf people and advocates of the deaf oppose the use of such prostheses (Crouch, 1997). They believe that deaf people should accept their disability and use sign language to communicate, rather than become imperfect hearers. Nevertheless, analytical studies reveal an increase in speech perception with continued use of cochlear prostheses (Skinner et al., 1997).

What kinds of sensory responses does electrical stimulation of the auditory nerve provoke? The usual technique employed in these studies is to insert a small group of wires through the cochlea to the endings of the auditory nerve. In these patients electrical stimulation produces pitch sensations that are partially related to the tonotopic organization of the cochlea. Unfortunately, the effective number of channels is limited by technical factors, so the range of frequencies that can be excited is also limited. With successive technical ad-

9.14 Cochlear Implants Provide Hearing in Some Deaf People
A microphone detects sound and directs the cochlear implant circuitry to stimulate the auditory nerve. Although this provides only a crude simulation of ordinary auditory nerve activity, the brain can learn to use the information to decipher speech.

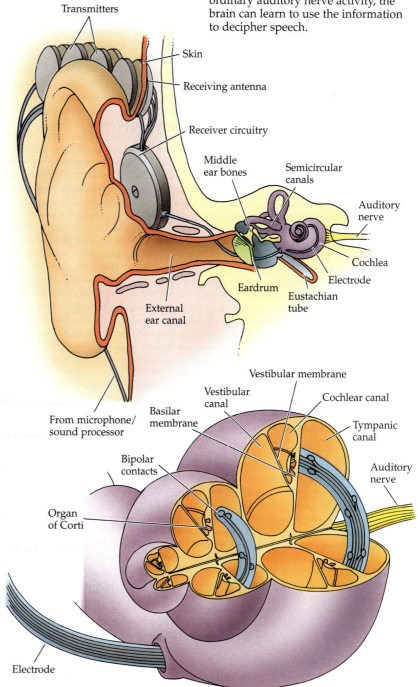

vances, the number has increased from 6 different frequencies to 32, but this range is still very limited compared with normal hearing. Dynamic range is also limited because intensities of electrical stimulation barely above the thresholds for sound produce discomfort.

Nevertheless, the pattern of electrical stimulation of the auditory nerve provided by cochlear implants can greatly facilitate acoustically mediated behaviors. For example, this treatment makes it possible to distinguish voiced and unvoiced speech sounds (e.g., "v" and "f"), which cannot be distinguished in lip-reading. In addition, thanks to cochlear implants, some formerly deaf people can converse over the telephone with absolutely no visual aids.

When the cochlear implants are turned on, auditory cortex is activated (J. Ito et al., 1993; Klinke et al., 1999), indicating that this region is processing the information. Cochlear implants also demonstrate the plasticity of the auditory cortex because patients must learn to interpret the signals provided by the implants. Furthermore, the earlier the implants are provided, the better the eventual performance (Rauschecker, 1999). The success of these implants is due mainly to the cleverness of the brain, not the implant. Because the prosthesis stimulates the auditory nerve directly, investigators have used the implants to study how loudness, pitch, and temporal discrimination of sounds are encoded in cochlear activity (Zeng and Shannon, 1999).

Vestibular Perception

The vestibular system provides information about the force of gravity on the body and the acceleration of the head. When you go up in an elevator, you feel the acceleration clearly. When you turn your head or ride in a car going around a tight curve, you feel the change of direction. If you are not used to these kinds of stimulation, sensitivity to motion can make you "seasick." The receptors of the vestibular system inform the brain about mechanical forces, such as gravity and acceleration, that act on the body.

The Receptor Mechanisms for the Vestibular System Are in the Inner Ear

The receptors of the vestibular system lie within the inner ear next to the cochlea. (The term *vestibular* comes from the Latin *vestibulum*, "entrance hall," and reflects the fact that the system lies in hollow spaces in the temporal bone.) In mammals, one portion of the vestibular system consists of three **semicircular canals,** fluid-filled tubes that are each oriented in a different plane (Figure 9.15*a* and *b*). The three canals are connected at their ends to a saclike structure called the **utricle** (literally, "little uterus"). Lying below the utricle is another small fluid-filled sac, the **saccule** ("little sac").

Receptors in these structures, like those of the auditory system, are groups of hair cells whose bending leads to the excitation of nerve fibers. In each semicircular canal, the hair cells are in an enlarged region, the **ampulla** (plural *ampullae*), that lies at the junction between each canal and the utricle (Figure 9.15*b* and *e*). Here the cilia of the hair cells are embedded in a gelatinous mass. The orientation of the hairs is quite precise and determines the kind of mechanical force to which they are especially sensitive.

The three semicircular canals are at right angles to each other; thus, one or another detects angular acceleration in any direction. The receptors in the saccule and utricle respond to static positions of the head. Small bony crystals on the gelatinous membrane, called **otoliths** (from the Greek *ot-*, "ear," and *lithos*, "stone"), increase the sensitivity of these receptors to movement (Figure 9.15*c* and *d*). At the base of the hair cells in these receptors are nerve fibers connected much like those that connect auditory hair cells (Figure 9.15*f*).

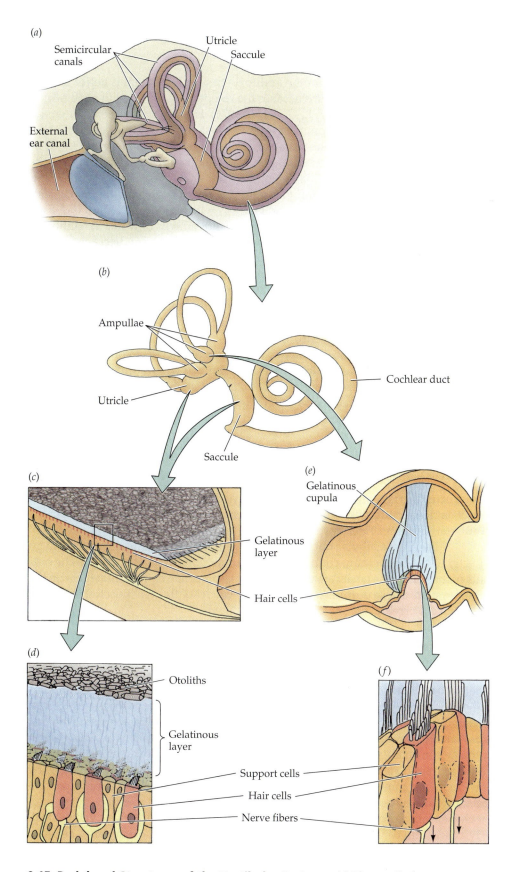

(a)

Semicircular canals

Utricle

Saccule

External ear canal

(b)

Ampullae

Cochlear duct

Utricle

Saccule

(c)

Gelatinous layer

Hair cells

(e)

Gelatinous cupula

Hair cells

(d)

Otoliths

Gelatinous layer

Support cells

Hair cells

Nerve fibers

(f)

9.15 Peripheral Structures of the Vestibular System (*a*) The vestibular apparatus is located in the temporal bone. (*b*) The semicircular canals are connected through ampullae to the utricle, which connects to the saccule. (*c–f*) Embedded in a gelatinous layer, hair cells in the ampullae, utricle, and saccule are the receptors of the vestibular system. Otoliths increase the sensitivity of these hair cells to movement.

**EVOLUTION
AT WORK**

Evolution Has Shaped the Auditory and Vestibular End Organs

The long evolutionary history of the auditory–vestibular system is better known than that of other sensory systems because the receptors are encased in bone, which can fossilize (van Bergeijk, 1967; E. G. Wever, 1974). It is generally accepted that the auditory end organ evolved from the vestibular system. In turn, the vestibular system evolved from the **lateral-line system,** a sensory system found in many kinds of fish and some amphibians. The lateral-line system consists of an array of receptors along the side of the body; tiny hairs emerge from sensory cells in the skin. These hairs are embedded in small gelatinous columns called **cupulae** (singular *cupula*), like those in mammals (Figure 9.15*e* and *f*).

In aquatic animals with lateral-line systems, movements of water in relation to the body surface stimulate these receptors so that the animal can detect currents of water and movements of other animals, prey, or predators. Information from the lateral line helps schools of fish stay in formation; each fish feels the currents made by the others. A specialized form of lateral-line organ is the lateral-line canal, a groove that partially encloses the cupulae. It is speculated that the first semicircular canals developed from a stretch of lateral-line canal that migrated into the body. This development gave the animal a sensor for turns to the right or left, and this receptor, being away from the surface of the body, was free of effects of stimulation of the skin. Sensitivity to change of direction was optimized when the canal developed into a roughly circular form. From the vestibular system that arose out of the lateral-line system evolved the auditory system (Figure 9.16). Note that in birds the auditory receptor organ (the lagena) never coiled into a snail shape.

Nerve Fibers from the Vestibular Portion of the Vestibulocochlear Nerve Synapse in the Brainstem

The structural arrangements of brain pathways dealing with the vestibular system reflect its close connection to muscle adjustments in the body. Nerve fibers from the vestibular receptors enter lower levels of the brainstem and synapse in a group of nuclei, called the **vestibular nuclei.** Some of the fibers bypass this structure and go directly to the cerebellum, contributing to its functions in motor control. The outputs of the vestibular nuclei are complex, as is appropriate to their influences on the motor system. These outputs go to the motor nuclei of the eye muscles, the thalamus, and the cerebral cortex, among others.

Some Forms of Vestibular Excitation Produce Motion Sickness

There is one aspect of vestibular activation that many of us would gladly lose. Certain types of body acceleration—such as those we experience as a passenger in an oceangoing boat, an airplane, a car, or an amusement park ride—can produce distress known as **motion sickness.** Caloric stimulation—the pouring of warm water into one ear canal—produces the same effect by initiating movements of inner ear fluids that simulate mechanical stimulation. Motion sickness is caused especially by low-frequency movements that an individual cannot control. For example, passengers in a car may suffer from motion sickness, but the driver does not.

One major theory of motion sickness—**sensory conflict theory**—says that the malady arises from contradictory sensory messages, especially a discrepancy between vestibular and visual information. For instance, as an airplane suddenly moves up, the vestibular system is excited, but the eyes see the constancy of the plane's interior; the resulting disorientation is distressing (Benson, 1990).

Why do we experience motion sickness? Michel Treisman (1977) hypothesized that the sensory conflict of some conditions of motion sets off responses that evolved to rid the body of swallowed poison. According to this hypothesis, discrepancies in

(*a*) Fish

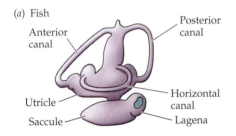

Anterior canal
Posterior canal
Horizontal canal
Utricle
Saccule
Lagena

(*b*) Reptile

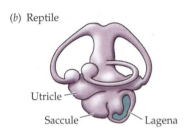

Utricle
Saccule
Lagena

(*c*) Bird

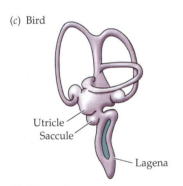

Utricle
Saccule
Lagena

(*d*) Mammal

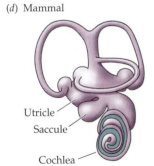

Utricle
Saccule
Cochlea

Auditory receptor cells

9.16 Evolution of the Vestibular and Auditory End Organs

sensory information normally signal danger and cause dizziness and vomiting to eliminate potentially toxic food. Such a response has obvious significance for preservation of life, although it is not helpful as a response to movements of vehicles.

The Chemical Senses: Taste and Smell

Sensitivity to chemical stimuli in the environment is vital for the survival of organisms throughout the animal kingdom. The sense of taste provides an assessment of foods (Lindemann, 1995): Sweet indicates high-calorie foods; salty and sour relate to important aspects of homeostasis; bitter warns of toxic constituents. Many animals also use chemical sensitivity to detect the odor trails of other animals, thus informing themselves about prey, predators, and locations of mates. This section will explore the many roles of the chemical senses—taste and smell—in guiding behavior.

Smell is the more complicated and puzzling chemical sense, but recent discoveries described later in the chapter have increased our understanding of olfaction.

Chemicals in Tastants Elicit Taste Sensations

We start our review of the chemical senses with taste, which is somewhat simpler and in some ways has been more thoroughly investigated than smell.

Humans Detect Four (or Five?) Basic Tastes

Because we recognize many substances by their distinct flavor, we tend to think that we can discriminate many tastes. But traditionally humans have been said to detect only four basic tastes: salty, sour, sweet, and bitter. We can qualify that limitation a bit because, as we will see, there is probably more than one sweet taste, and there is evidence for a fifth taste, but in any case, there are only a few tastes.

The sensations aroused by an apple, a steak, or an olive are *flavors* rather than simple tastes; they involve smell as well as taste. Block your nose, and a potato tastes the same as an apple. Our ability to respond to many odors—it is estimated that humans can detect more than 10,000 different odors and can discriminate as many as 5000 (Ressler et al., 1994)—is what produces the complex array of flavors that we normally think of as tastes. Ordinarily, smell and taste work together, such that detecting certain tastes makes it easier to detect certain odors (Dalton et al., 2000). Most mammals seem to have the four basic tastes, but members of the cat family have only three: Cats are not sensitive to sweet.

The ability to taste many substances is already well developed at birth. Even premature infants show characteristic responses to different tastes, sucking in response to a sweet substance but trying to spit out a bitter substance. Newborns seem to be relatively insensitive to salty tastes, but a preference for mildly salty substances develops in the first few months. This preference does not seem to be related to experience with salty tastes; rather it probably indicates maturation of the mechanisms of salt perception (Beauchamp et al., 1994).

Tastes Excite Specialized Receptor Cells on the Tongue

In mammals, most taste receptor cells are located on small projections from the surface of the tongue; these little bumps are called **papillae** (singular *papilla*; Latin for "nipples"). Each papilla holds one or more clusters of 50 to 150 cells, which are the **taste buds** (Figure 9.17a). At the surface end of the taste bud is an opening, the taste pore. The taste cells extend fine cilia into the taste pore, which come into contact with **tastants** (substances that can be tasted).

Not all the sensory cells in taste buds signal taste sensations; some are pain receptors, responding to stimuli such as "hot" red pepper, and others are touch receptors. With a life span of only 10 to 14 days, taste cells are constantly being replaced. A single taste bud has receptor cells that are at many different stages of development (Figure 9.17b).

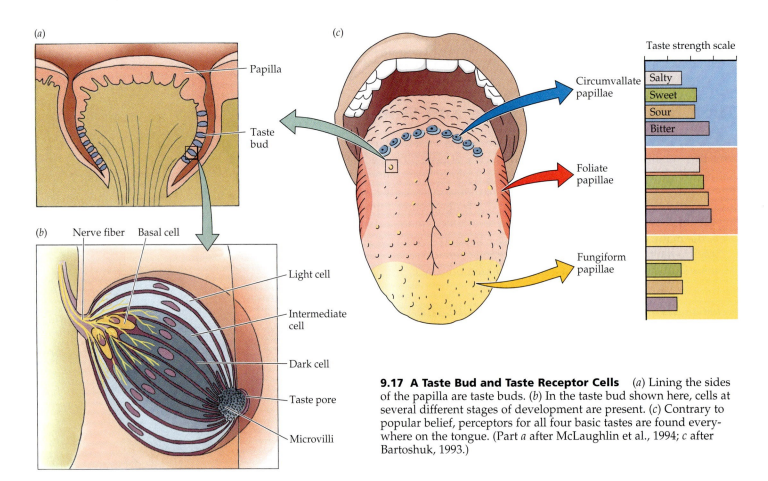

9.17 A Taste Bud and Taste Receptor Cells   (*a*) Lining the sides of the papilla are taste buds. (*b*) In the taste bud shown here, cells at several different stages of development are present. (*c*) Contrary to popular belief, perceptors for all four basic tastes are found everywhere on the tongue. (Part *a* after McLaughlin et al., 1994; *c* after Bartoshuk, 1993.)

There are three kinds of taste papillae; Figure 9.17*c* shows their distribution on the tongue. The most numerous are **fungiform papillae,** which resemble button mushrooms in shape (*fungus* is Latin for "mushroom"). There are hundreds of fungiform papillae on the tongue, but the numbers vary greatly among individuals. A fungiform papilla usually contains only a single taste bud. Each of the few **circumvallate papillae** and **foliate papillae** contains several taste buds.

Many books show a map of the tongue indicating that each taste is perceived mainly in one region (sweet at the tip of the tongue, bitter at the back, and so on), but Linda Bartoshuk (1993), a specialist in taste psychophysics, states that this map is erroneous: "The [usual] tongue map has become an enduring scientific myth" (p. 253). Work of Collings (1974) and Yanagisawa et al. (1992) shows that all four basic tastes can be perceived anywhere on the tongue where there are taste receptors. The areas do not differ greatly in the strength of taste sensations they mediate (see Figure 9.17*c*).

Different Cellular Processes Transduce the Basic Tastes

The tastes salty and sour are evoked when taste cells are stimulated by simple ions acting on ion channels in the membranes of the taste cells. Sweet and bitter tastes are perceived by specialized receptor molecules and communicated by second messengers. In the subsections that follow we will examine the mechanisms of each taste, proceeding from simple to complex.

Salty.   Sodium ions (Na^+) are transported across the membranes of taste cells by sodium ion channels. Blocking these channels with a drug prevents the salty taste of sodium chloride in both humans and rats; facilitating the passage of Na^+ across the membrane with another drug intensifies salty tastes (Schiffman et al., 1986). The entry of sodium ions partially depolarizes the taste cells and causes them to release neurotransmitters that stimulate the afferent neurons that relay the information to the brain.

Sour. An acid tastes sour, whether it is a simple inorganic compound, such as hydrogen chloride, or a more complex organic compound, such as lactic acid. The property that all acids share is that each releases a hydrogen ion (H^+). The hydrogen ions block potassium channels in cell membranes, preventing the release of potassium ions (K^+) from taste cells. The buildup of K^+ in the cell leads to depolarization and to neurotransmitter release. The afferent fibers stimulated by these taste cells report the acidic stimulation to the brain.

Sweet. The molecular mechanisms in the transduction of sweet and bitter tastes are more complex than those responsible for salty and sour tastes. There are good reasons to believe that sweet and bitter tastants stimulate specialized receptor molecules on membranes of the taste cells, causing a cascade of internal cellular events involving G proteins and second messengers.

These receptors are probably like the slow, metabotropic synaptic receptors we considered in Chapter 3. A novel G protein α subunit has been isolated in taste cells (McLaughlin et al., 1994). Investigators have not yet identified the receptor molecules for sweet or bitter tastes. A variety of molecules taste sweet, and psychophysiological experiments show that there is probably more than one kind of sweet taste.

Bitter. Bitter sensations are evoked by even more different tastants than are sweet sensations. The bitter taste of many toxic substances—such as nicotine, caffeine, strychnine, and morphine—provided strong evolutionary pressure to develop a high sensitivity to bitterness. Different bitter substances can be discriminated from each other—in psychophysical work with human tasters (McBurney et al., 1972) and with animal subjects (Lush, 1989)—suggesting that there is more than one receptor for bitterness.

Further evidence of the existence of multiple receptors for bitterness is the specific inability of some individuals to taste certain bitter substances. For example, about 25% of people in the United States cannot taste the chemical phenylthiocarbamide (PTC) and the related compound 6-*n*-propylthiouracil (PROP), even though they can taste other bitter substances. Family genetic studies have suggested that the ability to taste PTC and PROP requires a gene that can take two forms (which are referred to as *alleles*): *T* and *t*. Individuals with the *T* allele can taste these substances. Individuals with two *t* alleles (*tt*) are nontasters. Those carrying one of each allele (*Tt*) are tasters, which is why the *T* gene is called dominant. But people with two *T* alleles (*TT*) are supertasters, who perceive stronger taste intensities from some (but not all) bitter compounds and from some sweet compounds (Bartoshuk and Beauchamp, 1994).

Counts of the number of taste buds in people with varying sensitivity to PROP show that nontasters have the fewest taste buds (averaging 96 per square centimeter) on the tongue tip, medium tasters have an intermediate number (184), and supertasters have the most (425; Reedy et al., 1993). A recently discovered bitter receptor expressed in some taste buds (Matsunami et al., 2000) may be the *T* gene, and it is one of a family of at least a dozen receptors expressed in taste buds. Interestingly, a given taste bud may express more than one of these receptors (Firestein, 2000), so the brain may have to gauge responses from an array of taste buds to actively discriminate tastes.

Umami? There is mounting evidence of a fifth taste, called *umami* (Japanese for "good taste"), which has been described as a meaty, savory flavor. For most of the twentieth century, researchers argued about whether such a distinct umami taste existed, but the discovery of a gene that produces a variant of the metabotropic glutamate receptor and is expressed in taste buds (Chaudhari et al., 2000) strongly supports the idea.

Probably the normal stimulus for activating taste buds that express the gene for this receptor is the amino acid glutamate. Foods rich in protein will of course also be rich in such amino acids, and this seems like useful information for the organism. Monosodium glutamate (MSG), which is used widely in cooking, undoubtedly stimulates this taste receptor.

Neural Coding for Tastes Is Complex

Because different taste cells appear to be responsible for each of the four main tastes, it might seem obvious that each afferent axon from the taste buds carries information about only one taste. This idea is known as the labeled-line hypothesis, or **specific-pathway hypothesis.** (Recall our discussion of labeled lines for the skin senses in Chapter 8.) According to another hypothesis, **pattern coding,** each axon responds to some extent to more than one taste, and taste discrimination requires central processing based on relative activity coming from different afferent axons.

Recording from individual taste axons shows that each axon responds to a low concentration of one taste stimulus but also responds to higher concentrations of other tastes (Pfaffmann et al., 1979). For example, one axon responds most readily to sweet stimuli but also responds to a concentrated salty or bitter solution. Thus the fact that this cell is active does not indicate whether it is responding to a dilute sugar solution or a strong salt solution. Only central analysis of the pattern of responses across several neurons reveals the identity of the stimulus. This situation is similar to what we saw in audition: The response of a single axon can be evoked by a weak stimulus at its best frequency or by stronger stimuli anywhere in a broad range.

Taste Information Is Transmitted to Several Parts of the Brain

The **gustatory system** (from the Latin *gustare*, "to taste") extends from the taste receptor cells through brainstem nuclei and the thalamus to the cerebral cortex (Figure 9.18). Each taste cell transmits information to several afferent fibers, and each afferent fiber receives information from several taste cells. The afferent fibers run along three different cranial nerves—the facial (VII), glossopharyngeal (IX), and vagus (X) nerves (see Figure 2.8). The gustatory fibers in each of these nerves run to the brainstem. Here they synapse with second-order gustatory fibers that run to the ventral posterior medial nucleus of the thalamus. After another synapse, third-order gustatory fibers run to the cortical taste areas in the somatosensory cortex.

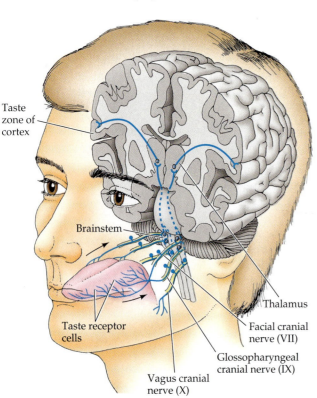

9.18 Anatomy and Main Pathways of the Human Gustatory System

Taste zone of cortex

Brainstem

Taste receptor cells

Thalamus

Facial cranial nerve (VII)

Glossopharyngeal cranial nerve (IX)

Vagus cranial nerve (X)

Chemicals in the Air Elicit Odor Sensations

We have already noted that many aspects of an animal's world are determined by chemicals carried in the air. A survey sponsored by *National Geographic* magazine elicited responses from more than 1.5 million individuals who smelled scents released when the surface of a piece of paper containing six different odors was scratched (Gilbert and Wyslocki, 1987). Half of the respondents were able to detect all six odors presented, and only about 1% were unable to smell three or more samples. But there was widespread partial **anosmia** (odor blindness): A third of the respondents could not detect androsterone (sweat), and 29% could not detect galaxolide (musk). Women were slightly better than men in both detecting and identifying odors. The ability to detect odors declined somewhat with age. Smokers showed a dulled sense of smell; they found pleasant odors to be less pleasant and unpleasant odors less unpleasant than nonsmokers did.

The Sense of Smell Starts with Receptor Neurons in the Nose

In humans, a sheet of cells called the **olfactory epithelium** (Figure 9.19) lines the dorsal portion of the nasal cavities and adjacent regions, including the septum that separates the left and right nasal cavities. Within the olfactory epithelium of the nasal cavity are three types of cells: receptor neurons, supporting cells, and basal cells. At least 6 million olfactory receptor neurons are found in the 2 cm² area of human olfactory epithelium; in many other mammals this number is an order of magnitude greater; for example, rabbits have about 40 million receptor neurons in the olfactory epithelium.

Each receptor cell has a long slender apical dendrite that extends to the outermost layer of the epithelium, the mucosal surface. There, numerous **cilia** emerge from the **dendritic knob** and extend along the mucosal surface. At the opposite end of each bipolar olfactory receptor cell, a fine, unmyelinated axon, which is among the smallest-diameter axons in the nervous system, runs to the olfactory bulb (which we will discuss shortly).

In contrast with many other receptor neurons in the body, olfactory receptor neurons can be replaced in adulthood (Costanzo, 1991). One theory is that these receptor neurons normally degenerate after a few weeks because they are in direct contact with external irritants, such as chemicals and viruses, and so must constantly be replaced. It's clear that, if destroyed, an olfactory receptor cell will be replaced as an adjacent basal cell differentiates into a neuron and extends dendrites to the mucosal surface and an axon into the brain. What's not clear is whether receptor cells are *normally* "disposable," subject to constant turnover even in the absence of a particular trauma.

If the olfactory epithelium is damaged, it can be regenerated and will properly reconnect to the olfactory bulb. The functional capability of these new connections has

9.19 Anatomy and Main Pathways of the Human Olfactory System
The schematic diagram at lower right indicates the main olfactory pathways in the brain.

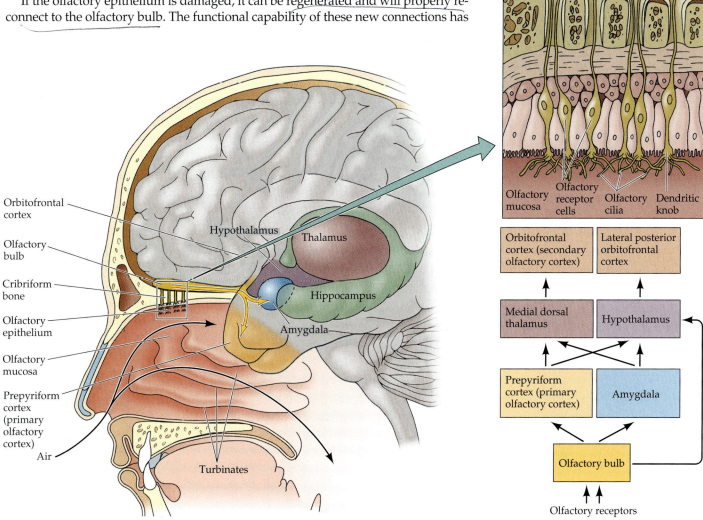

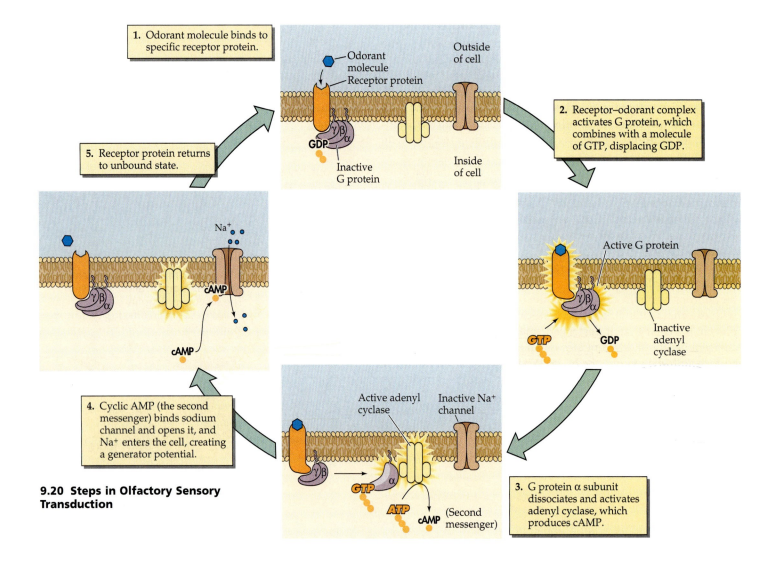

1. Odorant molecule binds to specific receptor protein.

5. Receptor protein returns to unbound state.

2. Receptor–odorant complex activates G protein, which combines with a molecule of GTP, displacing GDP.

3. G protein α subunit dissociates and activates adenyl cyclase, which produces cAMP.

4. Cyclic AMP (the second messenger) binds sodium channel and opens it, and Na⁺ enters the cell, creating a generator potential.

9.20 Steps in Olfactory Sensory Transduction

been clearly demonstrated in both behavioral and electrophysiological studies of animals with completely regenerated olfactory epithelium. Investigators are trying to determine how these neurons can regenerate while those in most other parts of the nervous system cannot.

Odorants Excite Specialized Receptor Molecules on Olfactory Receptor Cells

Odorants enter the nasal cavity during inhalation and especially during periods of sniffing; they also rise to the nasal cavity from the mouth when we chew food. The direction of airflow in the nose is determined by complex curved surfaces called **turbinates** that form the nasal cavity (see Figure 9.19). Airborne molecules initially encounter the fluids of the mucosal layer, which contain binding proteins that transport odorants to receptor surfaces (Farbman, 1994). The viscosity (stickiness) of the mucous layer determines how rapidly odorants reach the cilia of olfactory receptor cells (Kinnamon and Cummings, 1992).

The odorant stimulus then interacts with receptor proteins located on the surface of the olfactory cilia and the dendritic knob of the receptor cells. These receptor proteins are members of a superfamily of G protein–linked receptors. Interactions of odorants with the receptor trigger the synthesis of second messengers, including cyclic AMP (cAMP) and inositol trisphosphate (IP$_3$). Cyclic AMP opens a cation channel (Brunet et al., 1996) to elicit the generator current that depolarizes the olfactory receptor cell, and the depolarization in turn leads to action potentials.

This sensory transduction process, portrayed in Figure 9.20, is similar to the activation of other sensory systems, such as those for sweet and bitter tastes, and those in the eye (see Chapter 10). A specific G protein must be used by all the olfactory receptors because mice in which the gene for this particular G protein is knocked out are generally anosmic (Belluscio et al., 1998).

The members of the olfactory receptor protein family are diverse, although they have certain regions in common (Buck, 1996; Mombaerts, 1999). Zhao et al. (1998) proved that these proteins are indeed odor receptors by transfecting rat olfactory epithelial cells with a gene to produce more copies of one of the proteins; as a result the animals were more sensitive to a particular set of odorants.

In mice there are about 2 million receptor cells, and each of them expresses only one of about 1000 different receptor proteins. These receptor proteins can be divided into four different subfamilies of about 250 proteins each (K. Mori et al., 1999). Within each subfamily, members have a very similar structure and presumably recognize similar odorants. Each subfamily of receptors is synthesized in a separate band of the epithelium (Figure 9.21) (Vassar et al., 1993).

The human genome is estimated to contain about 500 to 1000 different odorant receptor genes (Ressler et al., 1994). Comparisons of the estimated 5000 odors that humans can discriminate suggest that each odorant receptor interacts with a small number of different odorants. Although some odorants may be "recognized" by a single kind of receptor molecule, most odorants probably are recognized by a combination of a few different kinds of receptor molecules. In other words, most odorants activate a particular array of receptor cells (Duchamp-Viret et al., 1999).

Olfactory Axons Connect with the Olfactory Bulb, Which Sends Its Output to Several Brain Regions

The numerous axons of the olfactory nerve terminate in a complex structure at the anterior end of the brain called the **olfactory bulb** (see Figures 9.19 and 9.21). The olfactory bulb is organized into many roughly spherically shaped neural circuits called **glomeruli** (singular *glomerulus*; from the Latin *glomus*, "ball"). The intrinsic circuitry within these glomeruli contributes to an elaborate feedback control and modulation of olfactory bulb activity. Mice have about 1800 glomeruli, and each one receives input from receptor cells expressing only one of the four receptor protein families described in the previous section (K. Mori et al., 1999). So there appears to be a topographic distribution of smells in the bulb, but so far we don't understand the relationship between neighboring glomeruli.

Experiments with knockout mice (see Box 7.3) suggest that the olfactory receptor proteins help guide the innervating axons to the proper target when new olfactory receptors are generated. Disruptions of the receptor protein prevent newly generated olfactory receptor axons from reaching their normal glomerulus (F. Wang et al., 1998). The olfactory bulb, in relation to the rest of the brain, is much smaller in humans than in animals such as rats that depend extensively on olfaction (compare Figures 9.19 and 9.21).

Outputs from the olfactory bulb extend to prepyriform cortex (note that smell is the only sensory modality that can synapse directly in the cortex rather than in the thalamus), the amygdala, and the hypothalamus, among other brain regions.

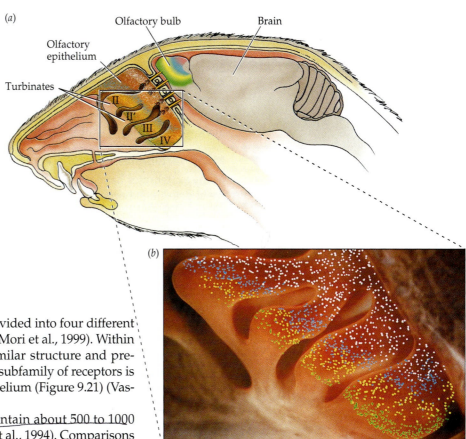

(a)

Olfactory bulb Brain

Olfactory epithelium

Turbinates

II
II'
III
IV

(b)

9.21 Different Kinds of Olfactory Receptor Molecules on the Olfactory Epithelium (*a*) In this diagram showing the anatomy of the rat olfactory organ, the Roman numerals designate different turbinates. (*b*) The different colors in this photograph of rat olfactory epithelium show receptor locations for four receptor subfamilies (and also correspond to those on the olfactory bulb, which illustrate the probable topographic innervation of that structure). The different receptor types have distinct but overlapping spatial distributions. (After Vassar et al., 1993; *b* courtesy of Robert Vassar.)

Functional-MRI studies suggest that the human prepyriform cortex is activated during sniffing, whether or not an odor is present (Sobel et al., 1998), because the airflow induced by sniffing provides somatosensory stimulation. When an odor is present, primary olfactory cortex (prepyriform cortex) and secondary olfactory cortex (orbitofrontal cortex) are both activated during a sniff (Sobel et al., 2000). Furthermore, the same chemical mix may produce a different odor perception, depending on how fast the air enters during a sniff (Sobel et al., 1999). So the brain gauges the airflow rate during a sniff in order to properly interpret olfactory information.

Many Vertebrates Possess a Vomeronasal System

Many vertebrates have a second chemical detection system that appears to specialize in detecting **pheromones,** the odor signals or trails that many animals secrete (see Chapter 5). This **vomeronasal system** (Figure 9.22), as it is called, is present in most terrestrial mammals, amphibians, and reptiles (Box 9.2). The receptors for the system are found in a **vomeronasal organ** (**VNO**) of epithelial cells near the olfactory epithelium.

Rodents have a family of receptor proteins that are similar to, but distinct from, the receptor proteins in the olfactory epithelium that we discussed earlier (Keverne, 1999). VNO receptors are remarkably sensitive, detecting even a few pheromone molecules (Leinders-Zufall et al., 2000). The receptors send their information to the accessory olfactory bulb (adjacent to the main olfactory bulb), which projects to the medial amygdala, which in turn projects to the hypothalamus. Hamsters (Mateo and Johnston, 2000) and mice (Isles et al., 2001) can distinguish relatives from nonrelatives just by smell, even if they were raised by foster parents. Presumably they compare whether other animals smell like themselves, perhaps to avoid mating with kin. Whether the main olfactory bulb or the VNO mediates this ability is unknown.

The VNO is usually said to be absent or vestigial in fishes, birds, and higher primates, including humans (M. Halpern, 1987). However, there is anatomical (D. T. Moran et al., 1991) and electrophysiological (Monti-Bloch et al., 1994) evidence of a vomeronasal system in adult humans. The report that extracts of human sweat, when applied to the upper lip of women, can adjust their menstrual cycle by 1 to

Vomeronasal & Pheromone detection

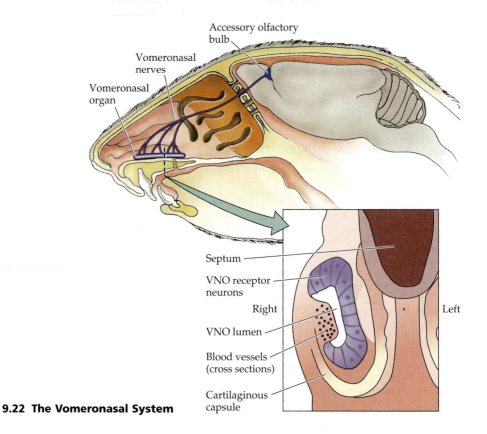

9.22 The Vomeronasal System

BOX 9.2 *Why Do Snakes Have Forked Tongues?*

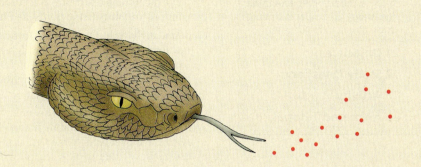

The forked tongue of snakes (see figure) has intrigued people for millennia, inspiring many hypotheses about its function (Schwenk, 1994). In many cultures and religions the forked tongue symbolizes malevolence and deceit. The first person known to inquire about the functional significance of the forked tongue was Aristotle; he suggested that this feature would double the pleasure of gustatory sensations. By the beginning of the twentieth century, the consensus was that the snake's tongue is a tactile organ; that is, the snake uses it to tap the ground much as a blind person uses a cane.

In 1920, L. G. Browman suggested what seemed to be a winning hypothesis: When the snake retracts its tongue, the tips (or tines) of the forked tongue are inserted into openings on both sides of the roof of the mouth; through these openings chemical stimuli reach special olfactory organs—the vomeronasal organs (VNOs). These organs are highly developed in snakes, lizards, and many mammals. They are a second olfactory system that appears to have evolved specifically to detect pheromones, the chemical signals that animals secrete as messages to other animals of their species. (We will refer to VNOs and pheromones again when we discuss sex in Chapter 12.) Browman suggested that the forked tongue flicks out, picking up chemical signals, and then delivers these signals to the VNOs. Later demonstrations that cutting the vomeronasal nerve reduces the frequency of tongue flicks (M. Halpern et al., 1997) fit this hypothesis.

But X-ray movie studies of tongue flicks in snakes and lizards with forked tongues disproved the hypothesis; they showed that when the tongue is withdrawn into the mouth, it enters a sheath and the tips do not go into the openings to the VNOs (Gillingham and Clark, 1981). Instead, the chemical molecules are deposited on pads at the bottom of the mouth, and closing the mouth presses the pads and molecules against the VNO openings.

If the tongue is not forked to fit into the VNOs, then what function could the forked shape serve? Schwenk (1994) proposed a solution that encompasses observations from several fields—animal behavior, ecology, sensory physiology, and neuroanatomy. He hypothesized that the forked tongue allows the snake to sense chemical stimuli at two points simultaneously, thereby giving it the ability to detect gradients in an odor trail. Obtaining two simultaneous readings enhances the ability of the snake to follow pheromone trails accurately, as depicted in the figure. This ability is important in seeking both prey and mates. (The split allows the right and left sides of the tongue to be farther apart.)

This accurate spatial chemical perception is like other systems for spatial perception that are based on simultaneous stimulation of two separated sense organs—for example, auditory localization, which depends on differential stimulation at the two ears, as discussed earlier in this chapter, or stereovision, which is made possible by the use of two eyes (see Chapter 10).

Species in other orders have also evolved paired chemical receptors to guide individuals to mates or prey. For example, male gypsy moths have large, elaborate, odor-detecting antennae with which they track potential mates over large distances. And the ant nest beetle has spoon-shaped antennae extending from each side of the head with which it detects and follows the pheromones of the ants that are its food.

---

2 days (K. Stern and McClintock, 1998) suggests that humans detect pheromones. In this study the donor sweat was gathered from other women, and depending on where the donors were in their menstrual cycles, the recipients' cycles were either accelerated or retarded in response. Sex pheromones enable males of many species to discriminate ovulating from nonovulating females, and mothers and their offspring recognize each other through airborne cues. Many of the cues are emitted in urine and distinctive body glands.

The role of olfaction in human social behavior is less obvious. Humans have distinctive odors, as shown by the ability of police dogs to readily distinguish one person from another, but do people respond to human odors? Human infants recognize their mothers by odors of the breast, and human mothers can distinguish the odors of their babies from others. In contrast to other animals, humans show no clear role for pheromones in their copulatory behavior, but the allure of perfumes (in fact, *Pheromone* is the name of a perfume) and colognes suggests that in this respect humans might not be all that different from other animals (Takagi, 1989).

Refer to the *Learning Biological Psychology* CD for the following study aids for this chapter:

21 Objectives

72 Study Questions

1 Activity

1 Animated Tutorial

Summary

Hearing

1. The external ear captures, focuses, and filters sound. The sound arriving at the tympanic membrane (eardrum) is focused by the ossicles of the middle ear onto the oval window to stimulate the fluid-filled inner ear (cochlea).

2. Sound arriving at the oval window causes traveling waves to sweep along the basilar membrane of the inner ear. For high-frequency sounds, the largest displacement of the basilar membrane is at the base of the cochlea, near the oval window; for low-frequency sounds, the largest amplitude is near the apex of the cochlea.

3. The organ of Corti has both inner hair cells (about 3500 in humans) and outer hair cells (about 12,000 in humans). The inner hair cells convey most of the information about sounds; each is associated with about 20 nerve fibers. The outer hair cells move, amplifying the movements of the basilar membrane in response to sound, thus sharpening the frequency tuning of the cochlea.

4. Vibration of the hair cells causes the opening and closing of ion channels, thereby transducing mechanical movement into changes in electrical potential. These changes in potential stimulate the nerve cell endings that contact the hair cells.

5. At each level of the auditory system, sound frequencies are mapped in an orderly succession; this is called tonotopic mapping.

6. Two theories explain the discrimination of auditory frequency. According to place theory, our perception of pitch depends on where the sound causes maximal displacement of the basilar membrane. Volley theory argues that the relations between the frequencies of auditory stimuli and the pattern or timing of neural discharges are the important criteria for pitch discrimination.

7. Auditory localization depends on differences in the sounds arriving at the two ears. For low-frequency sounds, differences in time of arrival at the two ears are especially important. For high-frequency sounds, differences in intensity are especially important.

8. Sound experiences early in life can influence later auditory localization and the responses of neurons in auditory pathways. Experiences later in life can also lead to changes in responses of auditory neurons.

9. Deafness can be caused by pathological changes at any level of the auditory system. Conduction deafness consists of impairments in the transmission of sound to the cochlea that are produced by changes in the external or middle ear. Sensorineural deafness arises in the cochlea or auditory nerve. Central deafness arises in the brain.

10. Some forms of deafness can now be alleviated by direct electrical stimulation of the auditory nerve by an implanted prosthesis (a cochlear implant) that records and transforms acoustic stimuli.

Vestibular Perception

1. The receptors of the vestibular system lie within the inner ear next to the cochlea. In mammals the vestibular system consists of three semicircular canals, the utricle, and the saccule.

2. Within each of these structures, the receptors, like those of the auditory system, are groups of hair cells whose bending leads to the excitation of nerve fibers.

3. The vestibular system appears to have evolved from the lateral-line system, found in many kinds of fish and some amphibians. It is generally accepted that the auditory end organ evolved from the vestibular system.

The Chemical Senses: Taste and Smell

1. Humans detect only four or five main tastes: salty, sour, sweet, bitter, and perhaps umami.

2. In mammals, most taste receptor cells are located in clusters of cells called taste buds. Taste cells extend fine cilia into the taste pore of the bud, where tastants come into contact with them. The taste buds are situated on small projections from the surface of the tongue called papillae.

3. The tastes of salty and sour are evoked by simple ions acting on ion channels in the membranes of taste cells. Sweet and bitter tastes are perceived by specialized receptor molecules and communicated by second messengers. Taste buds detecting umami respond to glutamate.

4. Each taste axon responds most strongly to one taste but also to other tastes. Taste discrimination requires central processing based on relative activity coming from different afferent axons.

5. Each taste cell transmits information to several afferent fibers, and each afferent fiber receives information from several taste cells. The afferent fibers run along cranial nerves to brainstem nuclei. The gustatory system extends from the taste receptor cells through brainstem nuclei to the thalamus and then to the cerebral cortex.

6. In contrast to the ability to detect only a few tastes, humans can detect thousands of different odors. Many species depend more on smell than humans do; such species have more olfactory receptor cells, larger olfactory bulbs, and lower thresholds for odorants.

7. Each olfactory receptor cell is a small bipolar cell whose dendrites extend to the olfactory epithelium in the nose. The fine, unmyelinated axon runs to the olfactory bulb. If an olfactory receptor cell dies, an adjacent cell will replace it.

8. There is a large family of odor receptor molecules. Each of these receptor molecules utilizes G proteins and second messengers.

9. Neurons that express the same receptor gene are not closely clustered in the olfactory epithelium, but they are limited to distinct regions of the epithelium. Each subfamily of receptors is synthesized in a different band of the epithelium.

10. The axons of the olfactory nerve terminate in the olfactory bulb. The projection from the epithelium to the bulb maintains a zonal distribution for different kinds of receptor molecules.

11. Outputs from the olfactory bulb extend to prepyriform cortex, the amygdala, and the hypothalamus, among other brain regions.

12. The vomeronasal organ contains receptors to detect pheromones released from other individuals of the species. These receptors transmit signals to the accessory olfactory bulb, which in turn communicates with the amygdala.

Recommended Reading

Bartoshuk, L. M., and Beauchamp, G. K. (1994). Chemical senses. *Annual Review of Psychology, 45,* 419–449.

Buck, L. B. (1996). Information coding in the vertebrate olfactory system. *Annual Review of Neuroscience, 19,* 517–545.

Doty, R. L. (In press). *Handbook of gustation and olfaction.* New York: Dekker.

Farbman, A. I. (1992). *Cell biology of olfaction.* Cambridge, England: Cambridge University Press.

Hildebrand, J. G., and Shepherd, G. M. (1997). Mechanisms of olfactory discrimination: Converging evidence for common principles across phyla. *Annual Review of Neuroscience, 20,* 595–631.

Masterton, R. B. (1993). Neurobehavioral studies of the central auditory system. *Annals of Otology, Rhinology, and Laryngology, Supplement, 168,* 31–34.

Murphy, C. (Ed.). (1998) *Olfaction and taste XII: An international symposium.* New York: New York Academy of Sciences.

Yost, W. A. (2000). *Fundamentals of hearing* (4th ed.). San Diego, CA: Academic Press.

10

Vision: From Eye to Brain

Seeing the world around you has been compared to drinking from a waterfall. How does the visual system avoid being overwhelmed by the flood of information that enters the eyes? The answer seems to be that the visual perceptions of each species depend on how their eyes and brains evolved to process information about the spatial distribution of various wavelengths of light, and to attend to the aspects likely to be important for survival.

Different kinds of processing allow us to see the form, color, position, and distance of objects in the visual field and to recognize objects. Research on visual-information processing is one of the most active fields of biological psychology and neuroscience, as it should be, since about one-fourth of the human cerebral cortex is devoted to visual analysis and perception. Our aim in this chapter is to convey some of the major challenges, accomplishments, and excitement of this field.

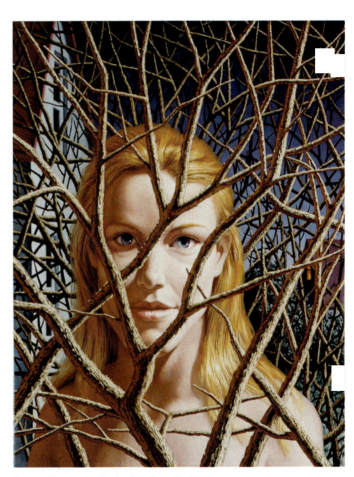

Leonard Koscianski, *Carrie of Cockeysville*, 1998

After introducing some of the main phenomena of visual perception, we will examine the bases of vision—structures and functions of the visual system, from the eye to the cerebral cortex. Different parts of the brain process different aspects of visual perception, as we will see from experiments using brain imaging during perception and from evidence connecting specific impairments of vision with brain lesions or with congenital absence of cone receptors in the retina.

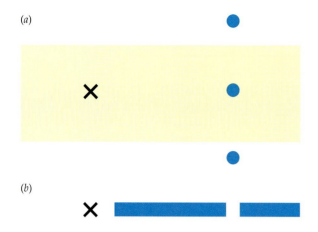

(a)

(b)

10.1 The Blind Spot   To locate your blind spot, hold the page about 10 to 12 cm (4 to 5 inches) away. Close your left eye and focus your right eye on the X. In part *a,* the middle dot on the right should disappear. In part *b,* when you place the gap at your blind spot, you will see a solid line rather than a broken line. (You may need to adjust the page closer or farther away to locate your blind spot.)

Vision Provides Information about the Form, Color, Location, Movement, and Identity of Objects

Although we're familiar with vision because we use it every day, some features of visual perception are not immediately apparent. A good grasp of the visual system will help us understand many of these surprising phenomena.

Perception of Form and Identification of Objects Are Complex Accomplishments

The whole area that you can see without moving your head or eyes is called your **visual field.** In a single glance, you can perceive the details of objects accurately only in the center of your visual field. We are usually not aware of this phenomenon because we move the direction of our gaze rapidly as we scan a scene or read a line of print. Thus we build up a sort of collage of detailed views.

But try keeping your eyes fixed on a letter in the center of a line and then attempt to read a word on the opposite page. You'll find it difficult because **visual acuity** (the sharpness of vision) falls off rapidly from the center of the visual field toward the periphery. This difference in acuity across the visual field is the reason your gaze has to jump from place to place in a line as you read.

If a stimulus suddenly appears away from the center of the visual field, we shift our direction of view, placing the new stimulus in the center of the visual field, where we can see it clearly. When we examine the circuitry of the retina and of higher stations of the visual system a little later, we will learn why vision is so much more acute in the center of the visual field.

If we examine the visual field of each eye separately, we find a **blind spot** about 16° to the temporal (lateral) side of the fixation point. This blind spot is relatively large, about 5° in diameter, ten times the diameter of the image cast on the retina by the full moon. (Because the eye is roughly spherical, it's conventional to refer to locations within it by using degrees.) Use Figure 10.1 to find the blind spot in the visual field of your right eye. The retina, a sheet of tissue covering the inside of the eye, contains millions of light-sensitive receptors, and the reason for the blind spot is that there are no receptors in a region called the **optic disc** (Figure 10.2). The optic disc, located about 16° to the nasal (nose) side of the retinal center, is where the fibers of the optic nerve exit the eye. Because there are no receptors in this region, nothing can be seen in the corresponding temporal part of the visual field. The optic disc on the nasal side of the retina causes the blind spot in the temporal side of the visual field because the pupil and the lens reverse the retinal image, left to right, as Figure 10.2 shows; the retinal image is also inverted top to bottom.

10.2 Structures of the Human Eye   Here the right eye is viewed in cross section from above. The visual image focused on the retina is inverted top to bottom and reversed right to left. The gap in the retina where the optic nerve leaves the eyeball is the optic disc.

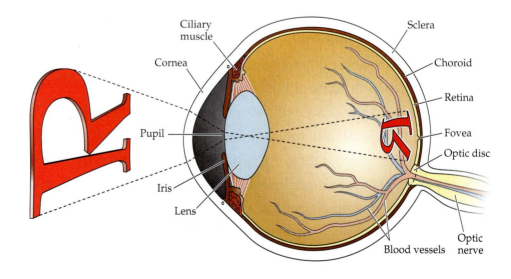

The blind spot does not appear as a dark spot; it is simply a region from which we cannot obtain visual information. Find your blind spot again using Figure 10.1*a* and place a pencil so that its center runs vertically through the blind spot. Do you see a gap in the pencil where it intersects the blind spot? No. You receive no information from the blind spot, yet you *perceive* a complete pencil; your perceptual system fills in from the surrounding area. If you place the gap in the line in Figure 10.1*b* in your blind spot, you will see the line as complete because the gap is invisible. Similarly, if you keep your left eye closed and look at a uniform area or most patterns with your right eye, you will not be aware of any gap in your visual field. An isolated stimulus, however (such as the dot in Figure 10.1*a*), may disappear in the blind spot. King Charles I of England is said to have amused himself by "beheading" some courtiers in this way, before he was literally beheaded himself.

We perceive a simple form like a triangle or recognize the face of a friend so rapidly and easily that we do not appreciate that these are exceedingly complex events that require processing in several parts of the brain. Most of the forms we see are embedded in complicated fields of objects; separating out a particular form for attention and identification requires practice and skill. It has been very difficult to achieve even primitive object recognition with artificial systems such as computers. Furthermore, recognition requires more than the accurate perception of objects. For example, as we will see in Chapter 19, some people with brain damage lose their ability to recognize familiar faces, even though they can still describe them accurately.

Consider the complexity of visual perception at the level of the nervous system. Each receptor in the retina is in a particular state of excitation at each instant. In effect, each receptor is signaling a quantitative index of excitation that can be represented by a number. About three times per second, the nervous system takes in a number from each of the approximately 100 million photoreceptors, and it faces the stupendous task of trying to figure out what in the outside world could have produced that particular array of values.

Figure 10.3 illustrates a simple example of such a task. The numbers in this array represent shades of gray from darkest (2) to lightest (9). As you inspect this grid, you may notice that the numbers representing lighter shades appear mainly in the upper half of the array, but you don't perceive a form. Now look at Figure 10.4, which shows the shades of gray that correspond to the numbers in the array in Figure 10.3; the form and identity leap out. Your nervous system processes data such as those in Figure 10.3 to achieve the perception of the form in Figure 10.4 in an instant. How the nervous system processes so much data so quickly is the staggering problem that confronts anyone who tries to understand vision.

Color Is Created by the Visual System

For most of us, the visible world has several distinguishable hues: blue, green, yellow, red, and their intermediates. These hues appear different because the reflected light that reaches our eyes can vary in wavelength (Box 10.1), and we can detect some of these differences. For about 8% of human males and about 0.5% of females, however, some of these color distinctions are either absent or at least less striking.

Although the term *color blindness* is commonly used to describe impairments in color perception, most people with impaired color vision distinguish some hues. Complete color blindness in humans is extremely rare, although it can be caused by brain lesions or by congenital absence of specialized receptors. Animals exhibit different degrees of color vision. Many species of birds, fish, and insects have excellent color vision. Humans and Old World monkeys also have an excellent ability to discriminate wavelengths, but many other mammals (e.g., cats) cannot discriminate wavelengths very well. We'll see more about the distribution of color vision among mammals later in this chapter.

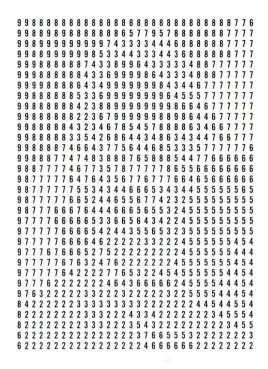

10.3 Can You Identify the Subject? This array of numbers represents the point-to-point illumination of a picture, from darkest (2) to lightest (9).

10.4 The Subject of Figure 10.3

BOX 10.1 *The Basics of Light*

The physical energy to which our visual system responds is a band of electromagnetic radiation. This radiation comes in very small packets of energy called **quanta** (singular *quantum*). Each quantum can be described by a single number, its **wavelength** (the distance between two adjacent crests of vibratory activity). The human visual system responds only to quanta whose wavelengths lie within a very narrow section of the total electromagnetic range, from about 400 to 700 nm, as the figure shows. Such quanta of light energy are called **photons** (from the Greek *phos*, "light"). The band of radiant energy visible to animals may be narrow, but it must provide for accurate reflection from the surface of objects in the size range that matters for survival. Radio waves are good for imaging objects of astronomical size; X-rays penetrate below the surface of objects.

Each photon is a very small amount of energy; the exact amount depends on the wavelength. A single photon of

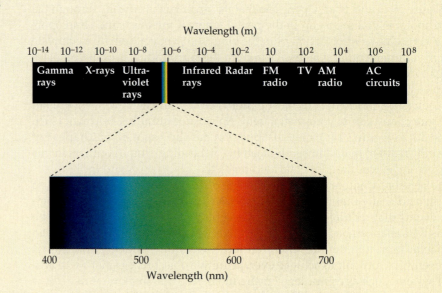

wavelength 560 nm contains only a tiny amount of energy. A 100-watt (W) light bulb gives off only about 3 W of visible light; the rest is heat. But even the 3 W of light amounts to 8 quintillion (8×10^{18}) photons per second. When quanta within the visible spectrum enter the eye, they can evoke visual sensations. The exact nature of such sensations depends both on the wavelengths of the quanta and on the number of quanta per second.

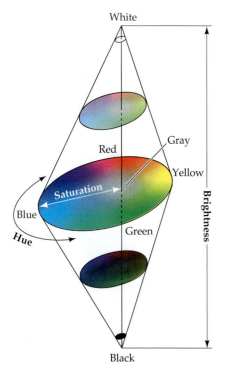

10.5 The Color Solid The three basic dimensions of the perception of light are brightness, hue, and saturation.

A patch of light has other aspects besides hue. The color solid shown in Figure 10.5 illustrates the basic dimensions of our perception of light when the visual system is adapted to daylight illumination; the figure is deliberately asymmetrical, for reasons we will mention. The three dimensions of color are as follows:

1. **Brightness**, which varies from dark to light; it is the vertical dimension in Figure 10.5. The middle plane of the figure is tipped up for yellow and down for blue because yellow in the spectrum is perceived as lighter and blue as darker than the other hues.
2. **Hue**, which varies continuously around the color circle through blue, green, yellow, orange, and red. (Hue is what most people mean when they use the term *color*.)
3. **Saturation**, which varies from rich full colors at the periphery of the color solid to gray at the center. For example, starting with red at the periphery, the colors become paler toward the center, going through pink to gray. Yellow is shown closer to the central axis than the other saturated hues because yellow is perceived as less saturated than the other spectral hues.

It is important not to equate perception of a particular hue with a particular stimulus—a wavelength of light—because, depending on the intensity of illumination and on the surrounding field, and on prior exposure to a different stimulus, a patch illuminated by a particular wavelength is seen as various different hues. As illumination fades, the blues in a painting or a rug appear more prominent and the reds appear duller, even though the wavelength distribution in the light has not changed. In addition, the hue perceived at a particular point is strongly affected by the pattern of wavelengths and intensities in other parts of the visual field.

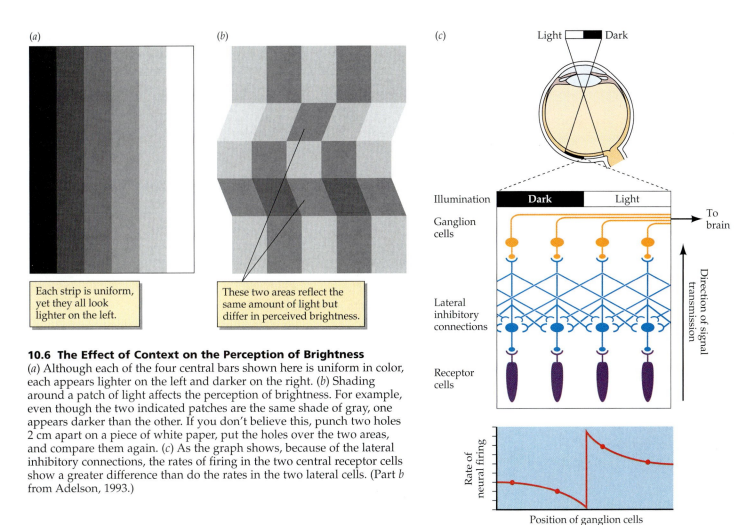

(a)

(b)

Each strip is uniform, yet they all look lighter on the left.

These two areas reflect the same amount of light but differ in perceived brightness.

(c)

Light ☐ ■ Dark

Illumination | Dark | Light

Ganglion cells

To brain

Lateral inhibitory connections

Direction of signal transmission

Receptor cells

Rate of neural firing

Position of ganglion cells

10.6 The Effect of Context on the Perception of Brightness
(*a*) Although each of the four central bars shown here is uniform in color, each appears lighter on the left and darker on the right. (*b*) Shading around a patch of light affects the perception of brightness. For example, even though the two indicated patches are the same shade of gray, one appears darker than the other. If you don't believe this, punch two holes 2 cm apart on a piece of white paper, put the holes over the two areas, and compare them again. (*c*) As the graph shows, because of the lateral inhibitory connections, the rates of firing in the two central receptor cells show a greater difference than do the rates in the two lateral cells. (Part *b* from Adelson, 1993.)

Brightness Is Created by the Visual System

The brightness dimension of visual perception is also created by the visual system rather than being determined simply by the amount of illumination reflected. Figure 10.6 presents two examples as illustration. The enhancement of the boundaries of the bars in Figure 10.6*a*, each of which is uniformly gray but looks as though the color varies in brightness, is based on a neural process called **lateral inhibition.**

Lateral inhibition occurs where the neurons in a region—in this case, retinal cells—are interconnected, either through their own axons or by means of intermediary neurons (interneurons), and each neuron tends to inhibit its neighbors (Figure 10.6*c*). Lateral inhibition occurs in the skin senses, too; if you press the end of a ruler against the skin of your forearm, for example, you will probably feel the pressure at the corners of the ruler more strongly than you feel the pressure along the line of contact.

In Figure 10.6*b*, two patches that clearly differ in brightness *reflect the same amount of light*. If you use your hands to cover the surrounding pattern to the left and right of the two patches, they appear the same. How are such puzzling effects produced? Although the contrast effect in Figure 10.6*a* is determined, at least in part, by interactions among adjacent retinal cells, the two areas indicated in Figure 10.6*b* are not adjacent, so the effect must be produced higher in the visual system (Adelson, 1993).

Motion Can Enhance the Perception of Objects

Movement enhances the visibility of objects, which is an important adaptation in the visual system because predators and prey both must be sensitive to moving objects in order to survive. In the periphery of our visual field, we may not be able to see stationary objects, but we can detect motion. We detect motion only within a range of speed that is appropriate to the locomotion of animals. Anything that moves faster is a blur or may be invisible, as is a bullet speeding by. Anything that moves too slowly—such as the hands of a clock—is not seen as moving, although we can note from time to time that it has changed position. A succession of still pictures, presented at the proper rate, can cause apparent motion, as in motion pictures. The investigation of apparent visual motion by psychologist Max Wertheimer in the 1920s led to the Gestalt movement in psychology. Perception of motion is analyzed by special areas of the brain, as we will see later in this chapter.

The Eye Is Both an Optical Device and a Neural Organ

The eye is an elaborate structure with optical functions (capturing light and forming detailed spatial images) and neural functions (transducing light into neural signals and beginning the processing that enables us to perceive objects and scenes). Our examination of the eye will lead us to a discussion about how this elaborate organ evolved.

The Vertebrate Eye Acts in Some Ways like a Camera

Our ability to see depends on numerous structures and processes. First among these are the structures and processes that enable the eye to form relatively accurate optical images on the light-sensitive cells of the retina. Accurate optical images are necessary for us to be able to see the shapes of objects; that is, light from a point on a target object must end up as a point—rather than a blur—in the retinal image. Without optical images, light-sensitive cells would be able to detect only the presence or absence of light and would not be able to see forms, just as exposing photographic film to light outside a camera does not produce an image of the surroundings.

To produce optical images, the eye has many of the features of a camera, starting with a **lens** to focus light (see Figure 10.2). Light travels in a straight line until it encounters a change in the density of the medium, which causes light rays to bend. This bending of light rays, called **refraction,** is the basis of such instruments as eyeglasses, telescopes, and microscopes. The **cornea** of the eye, the curvature of which is fixed, bends light rays, and is primarily responsible for forming the image on the retina. The lens, the shape of which is controlled by the **ciliary muscles** inside the eye, adjusts that focus. As the degree of contraction of the ciliary muscles varies, the lens focuses images of nearer or farther objects so that they form sharp images on the retina; this process of focusing is called **accommodation.**

The cornea in aquatic animals has little or no refractive power because the indices of refraction of water and the cornea are very similar. For the same reason, human vision is fuzzy underwater, although acuity can be restored with goggles that recreate the air–cornea interface. In aquatic animals, the lens is responsible for almost all the refractive power of the eye, so the lens in a fish eye is nearly spherical.

In many people the eyeball is either too long or too short to allow the lens to bring images into sharp focus on the retina. Eyeglasses or contact lenses can correct such conditions. Near the end of this chapter we'll see that preventive steps can be taken during childhood to avoid overlengthening of the eyeball. As mammals age, their lenses become less elastic and therefore less able to change curvature to bring nearby objects into focus. Humans correct this problem by wearing bifocal, trifocal, or continuously variable eyeglasses, in which segments of the lens refract differently, permitting accurate viewing at various distances.

The amount of light that enters the eye is controlled by the size of the **pupil,** just as the aperture controls the light that enters a camera. The pupil is an opening in the structure called the **iris** (see Figure 10.2). In Chapter 2 we mentioned that dilation of the pupils is controlled by the sympathetic division of the autonomic system, and constriction by the parasympathetic division. Because both divisions usually are active, pupil size reflects a balance of influences.

During an eye examination, the doctor may use a drug to block acetylcholine transmission in the parasympathetic synapses of your iris; this drug relaxes the

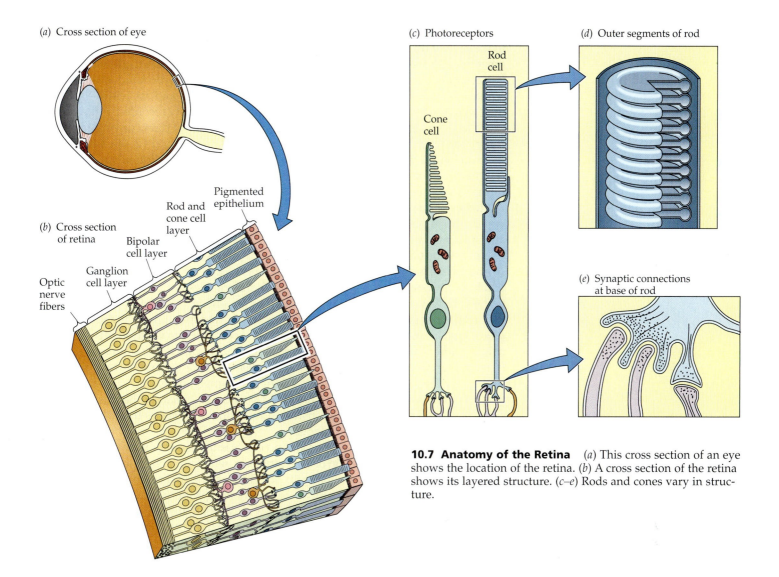

(a) Cross section of eye

(b) Cross section of retina

Optic nerve fibers

Ganglion cell layer

Bipolar cell layer

Rod and cone cell layer

Pigmented epithelium

(c) Photoreceptors

Rod cell

Cone cell

(d) Outer segments of rod

(e) Synaptic connections at base of rod

10.7 Anatomy of the Retina   (a) This cross section of an eye shows the location of the retina. (b) A cross section of the retina shows its layered structure. (c–e) Rods and cones vary in structure.

sphincter muscle fibers and permits the pupil to open widely. One drug that has this effect, belladonna (which is Italian for "beautiful lady"), got its name because it was thought to make a woman more beautiful by giving her the wide-open pupils of an attentive person. Other drugs, such as morphine, constrict the pupils.

The movement of the eyes is controlled by the **extraocular muscles,** three pairs of muscles that extend from the outside of the eyeball to the bony socket of the eye. Fixating (focusing on) still or moving targets requires delicate control of these muscles.

Visual Processing Begins in the Retina

The first stages of the processing of visual information occur in the **retina,** the receptive surface inside the back of the eye (Figure 10.7a). The retina is only 200 to 300 μm thick—not much thicker than the edge of a razor blade—but it contains several types of cells in distinct layers (Figure 10.7b). The receptive cells are modified neurons; some are called **rods** because of their relatively long, narrow form, others are called **cones** (Figure 10.7c). The rods and cones release neurotransmitter molecules that modulate the activity of the **bipolar cells** that synapse with them (Figure 10.7b). The bipolar cells in turn connect with **ganglion cells.** The axons of the ganglion cells form the **optic nerve,** which carries information to the brain.

Horizontal cells and **amacrine cells** are especially significant in interactions within the retina. The horizontal cells make contacts among the receptor cells; the amacrine cells contact both the bipolar and the ganglion cells. An example of interaction in the retina is lateral inhibition (see Figure 10.6c).

The rods, cones, bipolar cells, and horizontal cells generate only graded local potentials; they do not generate or conduct action potentials. These cells affect each other through the graded release of neurotransmitters in response to graded changes in electrical potentials. The ganglion cells, on the other hand, do conduct action potentials. Because the ganglion cells have action potentials and are relatively large, they were the first retinal cells to have their electrical activity recorded. From the receptive cells to the ganglion cells an enormous number of data converge and are compressed; the human eye contains about 100 million rods and 4 million cones, but there are only 1 million ganglion cells to transmit that information to the brain. The multitude of retinal cells and the connections among them permit a great deal of information processing in the eye.

Studies of human sensitivity to light reveal the existence of two different functional systems corresponding to the two different populations of receptors (rods and cones) and associated neural elements in the retina. One system works in dim light and involves the rods and highly convergent neural processing; this system is called the **scotopic system** (from the Greek *skotos,* "darkness," and *ops,* "eye"). The scotopic system has only one receptor type (rods) and therefore does not respond differentially to different wavelengths, which is the basis for the saying "at night, all cats are gray."

The other system requires more light and involves much more detailed neural processing; in some species, it shows differential sensitivity to wavelengths, enabling color vision. This system involves the cones and is called the **photopic system** (which, like *photon,* comes from the Greek *phos,* "light"). At moderate levels of illumination, both rods and cones function, and some ganglion cells receive input from both types of receptors. Having these two systems is part of the reason we can see over a wide range of light intensities. Table 10.1 summarizes the characteristics of the photopic and scotopic systems.

The extraordinary sensitivity of rods and cones is the result of their unusual structure and biochemistry. A portion of their structure, when magnified, looks like a large stack of pancakes or discs (see Figure 10.7d). The stacking of discs increases the probability of capturing quanta of light, an especially important function because light is reflected in many directions by the surface of the eyeball, the lens, and the fluid media inside the eye. The reflection and absorption of light at all these surfaces mean that only a fraction of the light that strikes the cornea actually reaches the retina.

TABLE 10.1 *Properties of the Human Photopic and Scotopic Visual Systems*

Property	Photopic system	Scotopic system
Receptors[a]	Cones	Rods
Approximate number of receptors per eye	4 million	100 million
Photopigments[b]	Three classes of cone opsins; the basis of color vision	Rhodopsin
Sensitivity	Low; needs relatively strong stimulation; used for day vision	High; can be stimulated by weak light intensity; used for night vision
Location in retina[c]	Concentrated in and near fovea; present less densely throughout retina	Outside fovea
Receptive field size and visual acuity	Small in fovea, so acuity is high; larger outside fovea	Larger, so acuity is lower
Temporal responses	Relatively rapid	Slow; long latency

[a]Cones and rods are illustrated in Figure 10.7c.
[b]Figure 10.23 shows the spectral sensitivities of the photopigments.
[c]See Figure 10.11.

The quanta of light that strike the discs are captured by special photopigment receptor molecules. In the rods this photopigment is **rhodopsin** (from the Greek *rhodon,* "rose," and *opsis,* "vision"). Cones use similar photopigments, as we will see later. All the photopigments in the eye consist of two parts: **retinal** (an abbreviated form of *retinaldehyde,* which is vitamin A aldehyde) and **opsin.** (From this point forward the noun *retinal,* standing for the molecule, will be printed in small capital letters—RETINAL—to distinguish it from the adjective *retinal,* meaning "pertaining to the retina.") The pioneering studies of George Wald (1964) established the chemical structure of rhodopsin and the related visual pigments of the cone receptors, earning him the 1967 Nobel Prize in physiology or medicine. The visual receptor molecules span the membranes of receptor discs and have structures that are similar to those of the G protein–coupled neurotransmitter receptors that we discussed in Chapter 3.

When light activates a rhodopsin molecule, the RETINAL dissociates rapidly from the opsin, revealing an enzymatic site on the opsin molecule. The activated opsin combines rapidly with many molecules of the G protein transducin (Figure 10.8). Transducin in turn acts through an enzyme, phosphodiesterase (PDE), to transform cyclic GMP (cyclic guanosine monophosphate) to 5'-GMP. Cyclic GMP holds channels for sodium ions (Na^+) open; light stimulation initiates a cascade of events that closes these channels. Capture of a single quantum of light can lead to the closing of hundreds of sodium channels in the photoreceptor membrane and block the entry of more than 1 million Na^+ ions (Schnapf and Baylor, 1987). Closing the Na^+ channels creates a hyperpolarizing generator potential (Figure 10.8*b*).

This change of potential represents the initial electrical signal of activation of the visual pathway. Light stimulation of rhodopsin hyperpolarizes the rods, just as light stimulation of the cone pigments hyperpolarizes the cones. And for rods and cones, the size of the hyperpolarizing photoreceptor potential determines the magnitude of the reduction in the rate of release of synaptic transmitter.

It may seem puzzling at first that light stimulation hyperpolarizes vertebrate retinal photoreceptors, since sensory stimulation depolarizes most other receptor cells. But remember that the visual system responds to *changes* in light. Either an increase or a decrease in light intensity can stimulate the visual system, and hyperpolarization is just as much a neural signal as depolarization is.

The cascade of processes required to stimulate the visual receptors helps account for three major characteristics of the visual system:

1. Its *sensitivity,* because weak stimuli are amplified to produce physiological effects
2. The *integration* of the stimulus over time, which makes vision relatively slow (compared, for example, to audition) but increases its sensitivity
3. The *adaptation* of the visual system to a wide range of light intensities, as we will discuss a little later

Photoreceptors Excite Some Retinal Cells and Inhibit Others

At their resting potentials, both rod and cone photoreceptors steadily release the synaptic neurotransmitter glutamate. Glutamate depolarizes one group of bipolar cells but hyperpolarizes another group. (We saw in Chapter 3 that the same neurotransmitter can have opposite effects when it acts at different chemical receptors in the neural membrane; the retinal bipolar cells offer an example.)

The first group are called **off-center bipolar cells:** Turning off light in the center of their receptive fields depolarizes the photoreceptor cells, causing them to release more glutamate, which depolarizes the off-center bipolar cells. The second group are called **on-center bipolar cells:** Turning on a light in the center of the receptive fields of their photoreceptor cells hyperpolarizes the photoreceptor cells, which release less glutamate, which depolarizes the on-center bipolar cells.

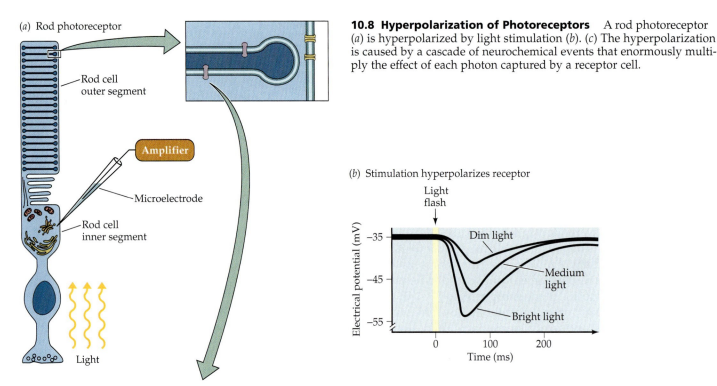

(a) Rod photoreceptor

Rod cell outer segment

Amplifier

Microelectrode

Rod cell inner segment

Light

10.8 Hyperpolarization of Photoreceptors A rod photoreceptor (a) is hyperpolarized by light stimulation (b). (c) The hyperpolarization is caused by a cascade of neurochemical events that enormously multiply the effect of each photon captured by a receptor cell.

(b) Stimulation hyperpolarizes receptor

Light flash

Dim light

Medium light

Bright light

Electrical potential (mV)

Time (ms)

(c) Photochemical amplification of stimulus

1. Light stimulation of a molecule of rhodopsin activates about 500 molecules of the G protein transducin. This activation causes a GTP molecule to replace the GDP molecule that binds to a subunit of transducin.

2. The activated G protein activates a phosphodiesterase (PDE).

3. Each PDE molecule hydrolyzes more than 2000 molecules of cGMP, reducing its concentration.

Outer-segment membrane

5′-**GMP**

cGMP

Na⁺

Na⁺

Open Na⁺ channel

Closed Na⁺ channel

Light

Rhodopsin

Disc membrane

Transducin

GTP   **GDP**

GTP

PDE

Disc

4. The reduction in cGMP leads to closure of Na⁺ channels and hyperpolarization of the receptor. One photon of light can block the entry of more than 1 million Na⁺ molecules.

Inside rod cell   Outside cell

Each cone in the central retina connects to four types of bipolar cells (Figure 10.9): one on-center **midget bipolar cell,** one off-center midget bipolar cell, and several on-center and off-center **diffuse bipolar cells.** Each midget bipolar cell in the central retina connects to just one cone, whereas each diffuse bipolar cell collects signals from many cones.

Bipolar cells also release glutamate, but glutamate always depolarizes the ganglion cells. Therefore, when light is turned on, on-center bipolar cells depolarize (excite) **on-center ganglion cells;** when light is turned off, off-center bipolar cells de-

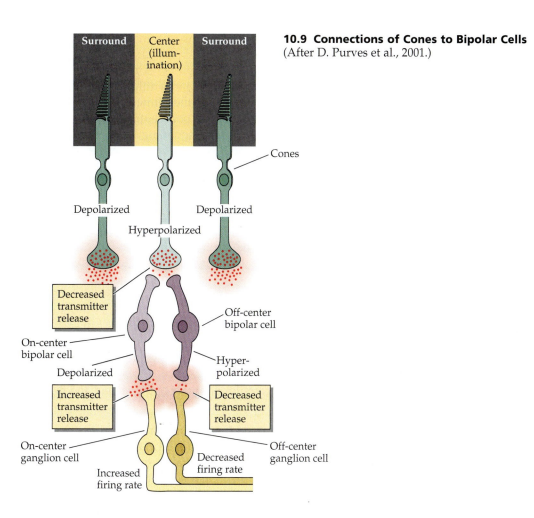

10.9 Connections of Cones to Bipolar Cells
(After D. Purves et al., 2001.)

polarize (excite) **off-center ganglion cells.** The stimulated on-center and off-center ganglion cells then fire nerve impulses and report "light" or "dark" to higher visual centers. Just as there are different types of bipolar cells—midget and diffuse—there are different types of ganglion cells, which we will describe shortly.

A small stimulus in a particular part of the visual field affects only those visual cells whose receptive fields are in the corresponding part of the retina. A mosaic of receptive fields covers the whole retina (except for the blind spot). This situation is similar to what occurs in the somatosensory system, where cells with different somatosensory receptive fields serve different parts of the body surface (see Figure 8.10), and the ensemble covers the whole body.

Different Mechanisms Enable the Eyes to Work over a Wide Range of Light Intensities

Many sensory systems have to work over wide ranges of stimulus intensity, as we learned in Chapter 8. This is certainly true of the visual system: A very bright light is about 10 billion times as intense as the weakest lights we can see (Figure 10.10). At any given time, however, we can discriminate over only a small fraction of this range of light intensity. Let's discuss the mechanisms by which the eye adapts to the prevailing level of illumination.

One way the visual system deals with a large range of intensities is by adjusting the size of the pupil. In bright light the pupil contracts quickly to admit only about one-sixteenth as much light as when il-

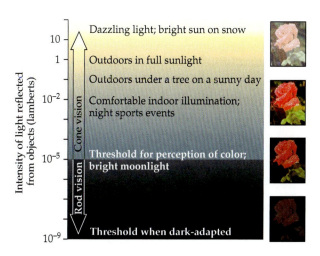

10.10 The Wide Range of Sensitivity to Light Intensity

lumination is dim. Although rapid, this pupil response cannot account for the billionfold range of visual sensitivity. Another mechanism for handling different light intensities is *range fractionation;* that is, different receptors—some with low thresholds (rods) and others with high thresholds (cones) handle different intensities (see Table 10.1). Figure 8.5 illustrated this mechanism for the somatosensory system.

But additional range fractionation would carry an unacceptable cost: If, at a particular light level, several sets of receptors were not responding, acuity would be impaired. If only a fraction of the receptors responded to the small changes in light intensity around a given level, the active receptors would be spaced apart from each other in the retina, and the "grain" of the retina would be coarse. The eye solves this problem by having receptors adapt to the prevailing level of illumination; that is, each receptor adjusts its sensitivity to match the average level of ambient illumination. Thus the visual system is concerned with differences, or changes, in brightness—not with the absolute level of illumination.

At any given time a photoreceptor operates over a range of intensities of about a hundredfold; that is, it is completely depolarized by a stimulus about one-tenth the ambient level of illumination, and a light ten times more intense than the ambient level will completely hyperpolarize it. The fact that the sensitivity of the visual receptors adapts to the level of illumination means that the receptors can shift their whole range of response to work around the prevailing level of illumination. Further adaptation occurs in the ganglion cells and the lateral geniculate nucleus, and probably at higher levels too.

Three main factors help account for receptor adaptation; the second and third of these mechanisms are specific to the visual system:

1. *The role of calcium.* Probably the most important factor is one shared by other sensory modalities: the role(s) of calcium (Ca^{2+}) ions (E. N. Pugh and Lamb, 1990). When intracellular Ca^{2+} ions are bound experimentally and thus made unavailable for reactions, the visual system can no longer adapt to higher levels of illumination.
2. *The balance between* RETINAL *and opsin.* When the photoreceptor pigment is split apart by light, its two components—RETINAL and opsin—slowly recombine, so the balance between the rate of breakdown of the pigment and its rate of recombination determines how much photopigment is available at any given time to respond to stimulation by light. If you go from bright daylight into a dark theater, it takes several minutes until enough rhodopsin becomes available to restore your dark vision.
3. *The availability of retinal chemicals for transduction.* Several retinal chemicals are required for transduction. They tend to be abundant at low levels of illumination but increasingly rare at higher levels of illumination, so increasing numbers of photons are required to activate them and hyperpolarize the receptors (E. N. Pugh and Lamb, 1993).

Acuity Is Best in Foveal Vision Because of the Dense Array of Cones and Ganglion Cells in the Fovea

We noted early in this chapter that acuity is especially fine in the center of the visual field and falls off rapidly toward the periphery. Reasons for this difference have been found in the retina and successive levels of the visual system, each of which is a detailed map of the visible world. Although the neural maps preserve the order of the visual field, each map emphasizes some regions at the expense of others; that is, each map is *topographic.*

One reason that the maps are topographic is that the concentration of cone receptors is greater in the center of the retinal surface than on the periphery (Figure 10.11*a*). The central region, called the **fovea** (Latin for "pit"), has a dense concentration of cones, and in this region light reaches the cone without having to pass through other layers of cells (Figure 10.11*c*) and the blood vessels that supply them.

Furthermore, each central cone has its own two ganglion cells. These structural arrangements provide for maximal acuity in the fovea.

The data on cone concentration in Figure 10.11*a* come from a classic study of only one retina by Østerberg (1935). More recently, Curcio et al. (1987) measured four other retinas. Østerberg's data fall in the same range, but the four retinas in Curcio's study differed by as much as three to one in the number of cones per square millimeter in the fovea. This variation may be related to individual differences in visual acuity. Species differences in visual acuity are known to reflect the density of cones in the fovea. For example, hawks, whose acuity is much greater than that of humans, have much narrower and more densely packed cones in the fovea than humans do. In the human retina, both cones and rods increase their diameter toward the periphery.

(*a*) Distributions of rods and cones across the retina

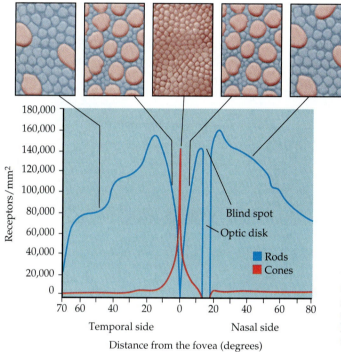

(*b*) Variation of visual acuity across the retina

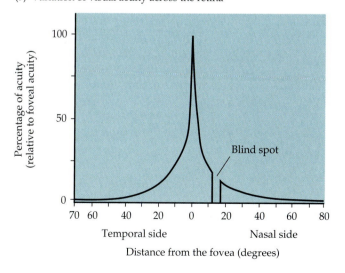

(*c*) Cross section of the central retina

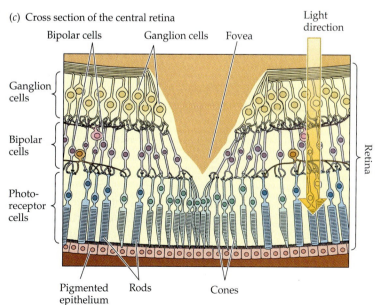

10.11 Frequencies of Retinal Receptors and Visual Acuity
(*a*) Rods and cones show variation in size and distribution across the retina. (*b*) The variation of visual acuity across the retina reflects the distribution of cones. (*c*) In the fovea, light reaches the cones without having to pass through other layers of cells. (Photographs in *a* courtesy of Christine Curcio.)

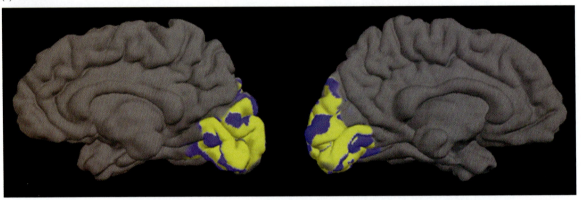

The small central region of the visual field projects to a large part of primary visual cortex.

(*a*) Macaque

1 cm

(*b*) Human

10.12 Location of the Primary Visual Cortex   (*a*) A pattern of flickering lights (*left*) was shown in a macaque's visual field, and a map of the visual field was revealed by autoradiography in a flattened section of the primary visual cortex (*right*). (*b*) Maps of human visual cortex derived from functional-MRI measurements show primary visual cortex as the innermost yellow band on each medial view. (Part *a* from Tootell et al., 1988; *b* from Tootell et al., 1998; both courtesy of Roger Tootell.)

The rods show a different distribution from the cones: They are absent in the fovea but more numerous than cones in the periphery of the retina. They are the most concentrated in a ring about 20° away from the center of the retina. That is why, if you want to see a dim star, you do best to search for it a little off to the side of your center of gaze. Not only are the rods more sensitive to dim light than the cones, but input from more rods converges on ganglion cells in the scotopic system, further increasing its sensitivity to weak stimuli. As mentioned earlier, there are no rods or cones in the optic disc (the *blind spot*), where the axons of the ganglion cells leave the retina and where blood vessels enter the retina.

A major part of the projection of visual space onto topographic brain maps is devoted to the foveal region (Figure 10.12*a*) (Tootell et al., 1982). Although the **primary visual cortex** (abbreviated **V1**) of the macaque is located on the lateral surface of the occipital area, human V1 is located mainly on the medial surface of the cortex (Figure 10.12*b*; see also Figure 10.18*d*). The fact that, as in the monkey, about half the human V1 is devoted to the fovea and the retinal region just around the fovea does not mean that our spatial perception is distorted. Rather, this representation makes possible the great acuity of spatial discrimination in the central part of the visual field.

Our acuity falls off about as rapidly in the horizontal direction as in the vertical direction, but species that live in open, flat environments (such as the cheetah and the rabbit) have fields of acute vision that extend farther horizontally than vertically.

Studying the regions of blindness caused by brain injuries reveals the extreme orderliness of the mapping of the visual field. If we know the site of injury in the visual pathway, we can predict the location of such a perceptual gap, or **scotoma** (plural *scotomata*), in the visual field. Although the word *scotoma* comes from the Greek *skotos*, meaning "darkness," a scotoma is not perceived as a dark patch in the visual field; rather it is a spot where nothing can be perceived, and usually rigorous testing is required to demonstrate its existence.

Within a scotoma, a person cannot perceive visual cues, but some visual discrimination in this region may still be possible; this paradoxical phenomenon has been called *blindsight*. In other cases, stimuli that cannot be seen within a scotoma affect judgments of stimuli outside it (Stoerig and Cowey, 1997). Blindsight may also be related to the phenomenon of *hemispatial neglect*—neglect of the side opposite to an injured cerebral hemisphere—which we will discuss in Chapter 19.

When we look at a complex organ like the eye of a mammal, an octopus, or a fly, it is hard at first to understand how it could have evolved. But inspection of different living species reveals a gradation from very simple light-sensitive cells to increasingly complex organs with focusing devices (Box 10.2).

**EVOLUTION
AT WORK**

Neural Signals Travel from the Retina to Several Brain Regions

The signals that result from visual processing in the retina converge on the ganglion cells, from which they then diverge to several brain structures (see Figure 3.17*b*). The optic nerves, which are made up of the axons of the ganglion cells in each eye, convey visual information to the brain (Figure 10.13). In all vertebrates, some or all of the axons of each optic nerve cross to the opposite cerebral hemisphere.

The optic nerves cross at the **optic chiasm** (named for the Greek letter X [*chi*] because of its crossover shape), which is located just anterior to the stalk of the pituitary gland. In humans, axons from the half of the retina toward the nose (the nasal retina) cross over to the opposite side of the brain. The half of the retina toward the side of the head (the temporal retina) projects its axons to its own side of the head. Proportionally more axons cross over in animals, such as rodents, that have laterally placed eyes with little binocular overlap in their fields of vision. After they pass the optic chiasm, the axons of the retinal ganglion cells are known collectively as the **optic tract.**

Most axons of the optic tract terminate on cells in the **lateral geniculate nucleus (LGN)**, which is the visual part of the thalamus. Most of the axons of postsynaptic cells in the LGN form the **optic radiations,** which terminate in the visual areas, mainly or exclusively in primary visual cortex, in the **occipital cortex** at the back of the brain. The primary visual cortex is often called the **striate cortex** because a broad stripe, or striation, is visible in anatomical sections through this region; the stripe represents layer IV of the cortex where the optic radiation fibers arrive. Inputs from the two eyes converge on cells beyond layer IV of the primary visual cortex, making binocular and stereo vision possible.

In addition to the primary visual cortex (V1) shown in Figures 10.12 and 10.13, numerous surrounding regions of the cortex are also largely visual in function (see Figure 10.18*c*). Visual cortical areas outside the striate cortex are sometimes called **extrastriate cortex.** As Figure 10.13 shows, the visual cortex in the right cerebral hemisphere receives its input from the left half of the visual field, and the visual cortex in the left hemisphere receives its input from the right half of the visual field. Because of the orderly mapping of the visual field (known as *retinotopic mapping*) at the various levels of the visual system, damage to parts of the visual system can be diagnosed from defects in perception of the visual field.

BOX 10.2 *Eyes with Lenses Have Evolved in Several Phyla*

Phylogenetic studies indicate that some of the steps in the evolution of eyes with lenses, like those of a mammal or an octopus, were the following (Fernald, 2000; Oyster, 1999):

1. Concentrating light-sensitive cells into *localized groups* that serve as photoreceptor organs (Figure A). Animals with such photoreceptor organs have better chances of surviving and reproducing than do similar animals with scattered receptor cells because photoreceptor organs facilitate responding differently to stimuli that strike different parts of the body surface.

2. Clustering light receptors at the bottom of pitlike or cuplike depressions in the skin (Figure B). Animals with this adaptation can discriminate better among stimuli that come from different directions. They also perceive increased contrast of stimuli against a background of ambient light.

3. Narrowing the top of the cup into a *small aperture* so that, like a pinhole camera, the eye can focus well (Figure C).

4. Closing the opening with *transparent skin* or filling the cup with a transparent substance (Figure D). This covering protects the eye against the entry of foreign substances that might injure the receptor cells or block vision.

5. Forming a *lens* either by thickening the transparent skin or by modifying other tissue in the eye (Figure E). This adaptation improves the focusing of the eye while allowing the aperture to be relatively large to let in more light; thus vision can be acute even when light is not intense.

The only requirement for the evolution of eyes to begin appears to be the existence of light-sensitive cells. Natural selection then favors the development of auxiliary mechanisms needed to improve vision. Many kinds of cells show some light sensitivity, and different phyla have modified different types of cells for specialized photoreceptors.

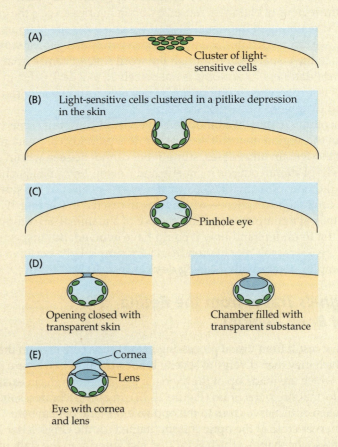

(A) Cluster of light-sensitive cells

(B) Light-sensitive cells clustered in a pitlike depression in the skin

(C) Pinhole eye

(D) Opening closed with transparent skin

Chamber filled with transparent substance

(E) Cornea — Lens

Eye with cornea and lens

The most common starting point has been cells of epidermal (skin) origin, but some lines (including that of our chordate vertebrate ancestors) derived their visual receptors from cells of neural origin. All known visual systems use a light-receptor molecule similar to rhodopsin, indicating a basic similarity among them.

Phylogenetic studies of the structure and development of eyes led investigators to conclude that eyes evolved independently in many different phyla (Salvini-Plawen and Mayr, 1977). A competent optical system with a lens, however, has evolved in only 6 of the 33 phyla of multicellular animals. These few phyla have been very successful; they account for about 96% of known species of multicellular animals. An effective optical system may have contributed to this success (Land and Fernald, 1992).

The fact that the cephalopods (such as squid and octopuses) evolved a visual system that in many ways resembles that of vertebrates (from fish to humans) suggests that there are major constraints on the development of a visual system for a large, rapidly moving animal. Let's look at some of the major similarities and differences between the eyes of cephalopods and those of vertebrates. In both, the eyes are relatively large, allowing for many receptors and the ability to gather large amounts of light. The incoming light is regulated by a pupil and focused by a lens. In both cephalopods and vertebrates, three sets of extraocular muscles move the eyeballs.

An important difference in eye structure between cephalopods and vertebrates is the organization of the retina. In the vertebrate eye, light must travel through neurons and blood ves-

BOX 10.2 (continued)

sels to reach the receptors, and the area where the neural axons and blood vessels enter and leave the retina forms the blind spot. In cephalopods the organization is more efficient in some respects: Light reaches the receptors directly, and the neurons and blood vessels lie behind the receptors; thus there is no blind spot. The detailed structure of the receptor cells is quite different in cephalopods and vertebrates. In addition, the visual stimulus causes depolarization of cephalopod

(and most invertebrate) retinal receptor cells, but it causes hyperpolarization of fish and mammalian retinal receptors.

It is still uncertain whether eyes of all species evolved from a single progenitor or have arisen more than once during evolution (Fernald, 2000). The major similarities between cephalopod and vertebrate eyes have often been cited as examples of convergent evolution, showing ways in which similar functions can be achieved with different structures and processes, starting

from different origins. Recent research suggests, however, that the eyes of all seeing animals share at least two important genetic features: First, they all use opsin pigments. Second, the compound eye of the fruit fly *Drosophila*, the vertebrate eye, and the cephalopod eye all develop through genes of the *Pax* family. The finding that highly homologous molecules are key regulators of eye development in different phyla argues that eyes in all phyla share a common origin.

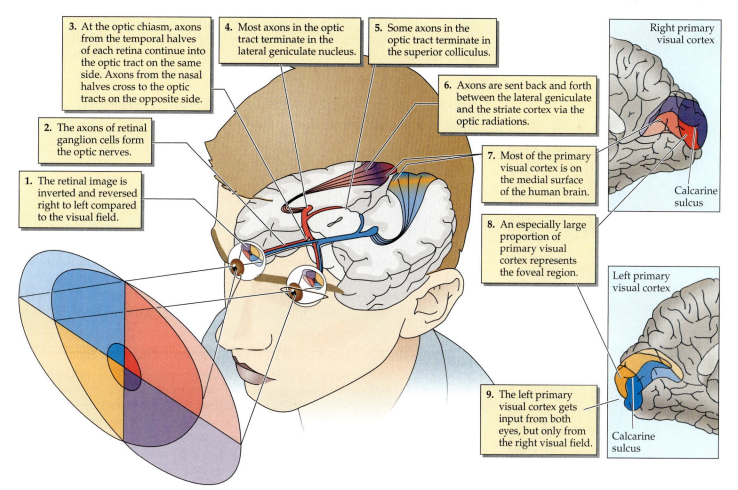

3. At the optic chiasm, axons from the temporal halves of each retina continue into the optic tract on the same side. Axons from the nasal halves cross to the optic tracts on the opposite side.

4. Most axons in the optic tract terminate in the lateral geniculate nucleus.

5. Some axons in the optic tract terminate in the superior colliculus.

2. The axons of retinal ganglion cells form the optic nerves.

6. Axons are sent back and forth between the lateral geniculate and the striate cortex via the optic radiations.

1. The retinal image is inverted and reversed right to left compared to the visual field.

7. Most of the primary visual cortex is on the medial surface of the human brain.

8. An especially large proportion of primary visual cortex represents the foveal region.

9. The left primary visual cortex gets input from both eyes, but only from the right visual field.

Right primary visual cortex

Calcarine sulcus

Left primary visual cortex

Calcarine sulcus

10.13 Visual Pathways in the Human Brain   Visual fields are represented on the retinas and project to the cerebral hemispheres. The right visual field projects to the left cerebral hemisphere, the left visual field to the right cerebral hemisphere.

Figure 10.13 shows that some retinal ganglion cells send their optic-tract axons to the superior colliculus in the midbrain. In Chapter 8 we saw that cells in the deeper layers of the superior colliculus form maps of visual, somatosensory, and auditory space, as well as of the motor system—and that all these maps are aligned with each other. The superior colliculus helps coordinate rapid movements of the eyes toward a target.

A minority of ganglion cells send their axons to nuclei in the hypothalamus that are involved in the control of daily cycles of behavior, called *circadian rhythms,* which we will discuss in Chapter 14. Optic-tract axons from still other ganglion cells go to the midbrain nuclei that regulate the size of the pupil and help coordinate the movements of the eyes. Some of the midbrain visual nuclei also project axons to the cerebellum, where the activity maps visual space.

Investigators have found several cortical areas for each sensory modality, and most of these areas are laid out in an orderly topographic map of the receptor surface (C. N. Woolsey, 1981a, 1981b, 1981c). Examination of the cortex of the macaque (an Old World monkey) reveals more than 30 visual areas, many of which contain a topographic representation of the retina (see Figure 10.18*c*). The different cortical regions work in parallel to process different aspects of visual perception, such as form, color, location, and movement, as we will take up later in this chapter.

Investigators use a variety of techniques to map the visual system: anatomical tracing of fibers, electrophysiological recording of activity evoked by specific kinds of visual stimulation, PET (positron emission tomography) and other noninvasive measures of regional activity in the brain, and experimental and clinical lesions of the visual system. Integrating the findings from these techniques provides us with our current understanding of the structure and functions of the visual system.

Neurons at Different Levels of the Visual System Have Very Different Receptive Fields

In the visual system, a neuron's **receptive field** consists of the stimuli in visual space that increase or decrease that neuron's firing. A small stimulus in a particular part of the visual field affects only those visual cells whose receptive fields are in the corresponding part of the retina. A mosaic of receptive fields covers the whole retina, except for the blind spot. Spots of light that are lighter or darker than surrounding areas are sufficient to activate cells in the retina or LGN, but many cells in the visual cortex are more demanding and respond only to more complicated stimuli.

The nature of the receptive field of a cell gives us good clues about its function(s) in perception. In the next sections we will see some cases in which neurons at lower levels in the visual system seem to account for particular perceptual phenomena and other cases in which solutions need to be sought at higher levels in the visual system.

Stephen Kuffler
(1913–1980)

Neurons in the Retina and the LGN Have Concentric Receptive Fields

Two scientists discovered the main features of the receptive fields of vertebrate retinal ganglion cells independently within a few months of each other: Stephen Kuffler (1953), studying the cat, and Horace Barlow (1953), studying the frog. They recorded from single ganglion cells while they moved a small spot of light across the visual field, keeping the animal's eye still. Results showed that the receptive fields of retinal ganglion cells are concentric, consisting of a roughly circular central area and a ring around it. Similar receptive fields were later obtained for retinal bipolar cells, but whereas the responses of the ganglion cells are nerve impulses, the responses of the bipolar cells are depolarization and hyperpolarization.

Horace Barlow

Both bipolar cells and ganglion cells have two basic types of retinal receptive fields: **on-center/off-surround** (Figure 10.14*a*) and **off-center/on-surround** (Figure 10.14*b*). The center and its surround are always antagonistic. These antagonistic effects explain why uniform illumination of the visual field is less effective in acti-

(a) An on-center/off-surround cell

(b) An off-center/on-surround cell

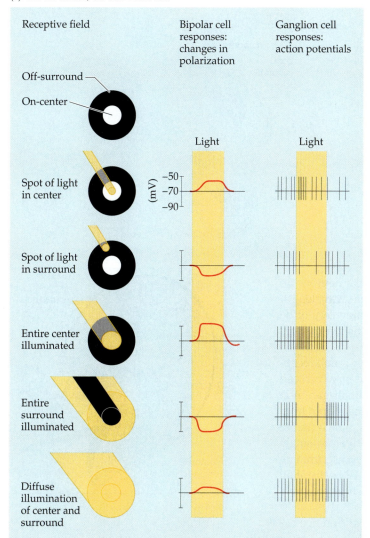

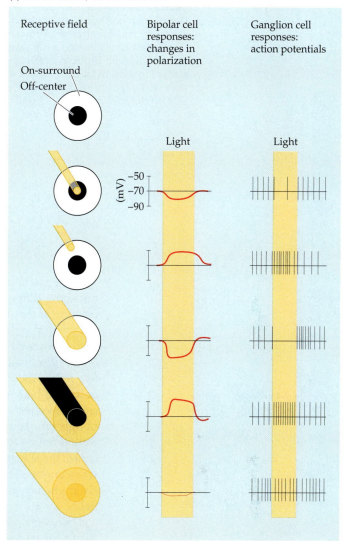

10.14 Receptive Fields of Retinal Cells   In primates, each retinal bipolar cell and each retinal ganglion cell has a concentric receptive field, with antagonistic center and surround. Here cells are shown responding to narrow or broad beams of light. Bipolar cells respond by changes in local membrane potentials; ganglion cells respond with action potentials. (a) An on-center/off-surround cell is excited by an increase of illumination in the center of its receptive field and inhibited by an increase of illumination in the surround. (b) Changes in illumination have the opposite effects on an off-center/on-surround cell.

vating a ganglion cell than is a well-placed small spot or a line or edge passing through the center of the cell's receptive field.

Investigators who study primate visual systems take the organization of the LGN as their key. The primate LGN has six layers (Figure 10.15). The structure is called *geniculate* because the layers are bent like a knee, for which the Latin word is *genu*.

The four dorsal, or outer, layers of the primate LGN are called **parvocellular** (from the Latin *parvus*, "small") because their cells are relatively small. The two ventral, or inner, layers are called **magnocellular** (from the Latin *magnus*, "large") because their cells are large. Most of the neurons in the magnocellular layers have relatively large receptive fields, the input of which can be traced back to large ganglion cells, which receive their input from diffuse retinal bipolar cells that contact many neighboring receptor cells.

10.15 Cross Section of the Monkey Lateral Geniculate Nucleus   In the four dorsal (parvocellular) layers, the cells are relatively small; in the two ventral (magnocellular) layers, the cells are relatively large. Cells with input from the opposite eye are located in layers 1, 4, and 6 (pink); cells with input from the eye on the same side are located in layers 2, 3, and 5 (blue).

Most magnocellular neurons do not show differential wavelength responses; that is, they cannot be involved in color discrimination. The neurons of the parvocellular layers have relatively small receptive fields, the input of which can be traced back to small ganglion cells, which receive their input from midget bipolar cells, which (in the central retina) are driven by single cones; these neurons discriminate wavelengths. The LGN cells of all six layers have concentric receptive fields.

Discovery of the difference between the parvocellular and magnocellular neurons of the primate LGN led investigators to take a fresh look at primate ganglion cells; they found two main types (Leventhal, 1979; Perry et al., 1984). The two types are sometimes called M and P ganglion cells because they project their axons, respectively, to the magnocellular or parvocellular layers of the LGN. As noted already, M ganglion cells are relatively large cells with large dendritic fields and thus large receptive fields. M ganglion cells can detect stimuli with low contrast and are sensitive to rapid temporal change; they respond transiently, and they have large-diameter axons that conduct very rapidly. M ganglion cells make up about 10% of primate retinal ganglion cells.

About 80% of primate retinal ganglion cells send their axons to the P layers of the LGN. These P ganglion cells are relatively small and have small dendritic and receptive fields. Several properties of the P ganglion cells distinguish them from the M ganglion cells:

- P cells require high contrast to be stimulated, but M cells respond to low contrast.
- P cells are relatively insensitive to rapid temporal change (flicker), but M cells respond at high flicker frequencies and to movement.
- Most P ganglion cells show differential responses to different wavelengths, so they provide a basis for color vision, but most M cells are achromatic.
- P cells have sustained, or tonic, responses, whereas M cells have transient responses.
- P cells have high acuity, but M cells respond best to coarse features (or low spatial frequencies).

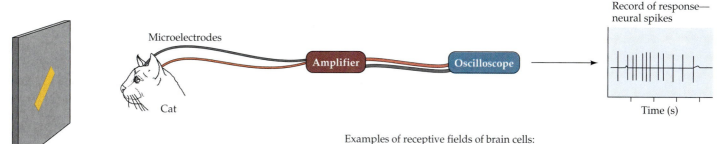

Record of response—
neural spikes

Time (s)

Microelectrodes

Amplifier

Oscilloscope

Cat

Stimulus projected
on screen

10.16 Receptive Fields of Cells at Various Levels in the Cat Visual System Microelectrode recordings reveal that cells differ greatly in their receptive fields. (*a*) Visual cells in the thalamus (LGN) have concentric receptive fields. (*b*, *c*) Visual cells in the cerebral cortex may show orientation specificity (*b*) or respond only to motion, or they may respond only to motion in a particular direction (*c*).

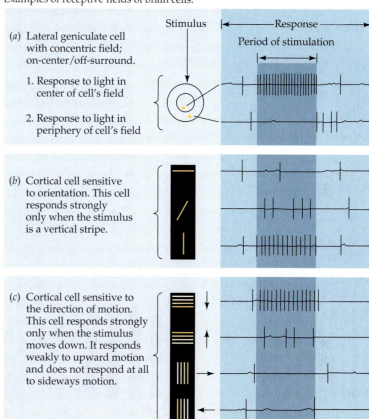

Examples of receptive fields of brain cells:

Stimulus　Response
Period of stimulation

(*a*) Lateral geniculate cell with concentric field; on-center/off-surround.

1. Response to light in center of cell's field

2. Response to light in periphery of cell's field

(*b*) Cortical cell sensitive to orientation. This cell responds strongly only when the stimulus is a vertical stripe.

(*c*) Cortical cell sensitive to the direction of motion. This cell responds strongly only when the stimulus moves down. It responds weakly to upward motion and does not respond at all to sideways motion.

The remaining 10% of the primate ganglion cells, which are neither M nor P type, will not concern us here.

Neurons in the Visual Cortex Have Varied and Complicated Receptive Fields

The next level of the visual system, the primary visual cortex, provided a puzzle. Neurons from the LGN send their axons to cells in the primary visual cortex (V1), but the spots of light that are effective stimuli for LGN cells are not very effective at the cortical level. After much unfruitful work, success in stimulating cortical visual cells was finally announced in 1959: David Hubel and Torsten Wiesel reported that visual cortical cells require more specific, elongated stimuli than those that activate LGN cells. Most cells in area V1 respond best to lines or bars in a particular position and at a particular orientation in the visual field (Figure 10.16*b*). Some cortical cells also require movement of the stimulus to make them respond actively. For some of these cells, any movement in their field is sufficient; others are even more demanding, requiring motion in a specific direction (Figure 10.16*c*).

For this and related research, Hubel and Wiesel were awarded the Nobel Prize in physiology or medicine in 1981. The success of this research also led many researchers to accept the theoretical model proposed by Hubel and Wiesel, but challenges have emerged. Let's examine a few more of Hubel and Wiesel's findings and look at their theoretical model.

Hubel and Wiesel categorized cortical cells into classes according to the types of stimuli required to produce maximum responses. So-called **simple cortical cells** responded best to an edge or a bar of a particular width and with a particular orientation and location in the visual field. These cells were therefore sometimes called bar detectors or edge detectors. Like the simple cells, **complex cortical cells** had elongated receptive fields, but they also showed some latitude for location; that is, they responded to a bar of a particular size and orientation anywhere within a particular area of the visual field.

Hubel and Wiesel's theoretical model can be described as hierarchical; that is, more complex events are built up from inputs of simpler ones. For example, a simple cortical cell can be thought of as receiving input from a row of LGN cells, and a

David Hubel

Torsten Wiesel

complex cortical cell can be thought of as receiving its input from a row of simple cortical cells. Other theorists extrapolated from this model, suggesting higher-order circuits of cells to detect any possible form. Thus it was suggested that by integration of enough successive levels of analysis, a unit could be constructed that would enable a person to recognize his or her grandmother, and such hypothetical "grandmother cells" were frequently mentioned in the literature. According to this view, any time such a cell was excited, up would pop a picture of one's grandmother. This hypothesis was given as a possible explanation for facial recognition.

Critics soon pointed out both theoretical and empirical problems with the hierarchical model. For one thing, a "grandmother-recognizing" circuit would require vast numbers of cells, perhaps even more than the number available in the cerebral cortex. At the same time that difficulties with this model were being shown, an alternative model was emerging, which we will describe next.

**COMPETING
HYPOTHESES**

Most Cells in the Primary Visual Cortex Are Tuned to Particular Spatial Frequencies

Concepts of pattern analysis in terms of lines and edges at various orientations have largely given way to what is known as the **spatial-frequency filter model.** To discuss this model, we must become familiar with a way of regarding spatial vision that is quite different from our intuitive thinking (F. W. Campbell and Robson, 1968; R. L. De Valois and De Valois, 1988). By *spatial frequency of a visual stimulus,* we mean the number of light–dark (or color) cycles the stimulus shows per degree of visual space.

For example, Figure 10.17*a* and *b* differ in the spacing of the bars; Figure 10.17*a* has twice as many bars in the same horizontal space and is therefore said to have

10.17 Spatial Frequencies
(*a, b*) The spacing between dark and light stripes shows that part *a* has double the spatial frequency of part *b*. (*c, d*) These visual grids show sinusoidal modulation of intensity: (*c*) high contrast; (*d*) low contrast. (*e–g*) A photograph of Groucho Marx subjected to spatial filtering: (*e*) normal photograph; (*f*) high spatial frequencies filtered out; (*g*) low spatial frequencies filtered out. (Parts *e–g* courtesy of John Frisby.)

(*a*) High-frequency square wave

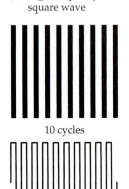

10 cycles

(*b*) Low-frequency square wave

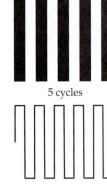

5 cycles

(*c*) High-contrast sinusoidal spatial grid

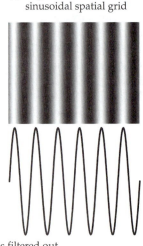

(*d*) Low-contrast sinusoidal spatial grid

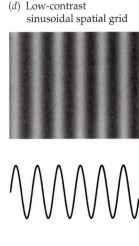

(*e*) Normal

(*f*) High frequencies filtered out

(*g*) Low frequencies filtered out

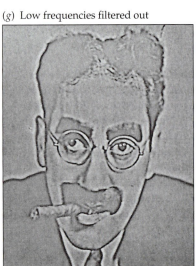

double the spatial frequency of Figure 10.17*b*. The spatial-frequency technique applies Fourier analysis (see Box 9.1) or linear systems theory rather than analyzing visual patterns into bars and angles.

In Box 9.1 we saw that we can produce any complex, repeating auditory stimulus by adding together simple sine waves. Conversely, using Fourier analysis, we can determine which sine waves would be needed to make any particular complex waveform. The same principle of Fourier analysis can be applied to visual patterns. If the dimension from dark to light is made to vary according to a sine wave function, the result is visual patterns like the ones in Figure 10.17*c* and *d*. A series of dark and light stripes, like those in Figure 10.17*a* and *b*, can be analyzed into the sum of a visual sine wave and its odd harmonics—that is, multiples of the basic frequency.

A complex visual pattern or scene can also be analyzed by the Fourier technique; in this case frequency components at different angles of orientation are also used. A given spatial frequency can exist at any level of contrast; Figure 10.17*c* and *d* show examples of high and low contrast, respectively.

To reproduce or perceive the complex pattern or scene accurately, the system has to handle all the spatial frequencies that are present in it. If the high frequencies are filtered out, the small details and sharp contrasts are lost; if the low frequencies are filtered out, the large uniform areas and gradual transitions are lost. Figure 10.17*e–g* show how the filtering of spatial frequencies affects a photograph. The photograph is still recognizable after the high visual frequencies are filtered out (Figure 10.17*f*) or when the low frequencies are filtered out (Figure 10.17*g*). (Similarly, speech is still recognizable, although it sounds distorted, after either the high audio frequencies or the low frequencies are filtered out.)

F. W. Campbell and Robson (1968) suggested that the visual system includes many channels that are tuned to different spatial frequencies, just as the auditory system has channels for different acoustic frequencies. The term *channel* is used here to mean a mechanism that accepts or deals with only a particular band or class of information. This concept is analogous to the transmission of information by a particular radio or television station, which occurs through an assigned channel or band of wavelengths; to receive this information, you must tune your receiving device to the particular channel.

The suggestion that the nervous system has different spatial-frequency channels was soon supported by results of experiments on selective adaptation to spatial patterns (Blakemore and Campbell, 1969; Pantle and Sekuler, 1968). In these experiments a person spent a minute or more inspecting a visual grating with a given spacing (or spatial frequency), such as those in Figure 10.17*a* and *b*. Looking at the grating made the cells that are tuned to that frequency adapt (become less sensitive). Then the person's sensitivity to gratings of different spacings was determined.

The results showed that sensitivity to the subsequent gratings was depressed briefly at the particular frequency to which the person had adapted. According to Russell De Valois and Karen De Valois (1980), the suggestion of multiple spatial-frequency channels

> had revolutionary impact because it led to entirely different conceptions of the way in which the visual system might function in dealing with spatial stimuli. It suggests that rather than specifically detecting such seminaturalistic features as bars and edges, the system is breaking down complex stimuli into their individual spatial frequency components in a kind of crude Fourier analysis. (p. 320)

The responses of cortical cells to spatial-frequency stimuli were found to be tuned more accurately to the dimensions of spatial-frequency grids than to the widths of bars (R. L. De Valois et al., 1977; Hochstein and Shapley, 1976; Maffei and Fiorentini, 1973). The receptive field of a cortical cell typically shows an excitatory axis and bands of inhibition on each side; the spacing of these components shows the frequency tuning. The spatial-frequency approach has proved useful in the analysis of many aspects of human pattern vision (K. K. De Valois et al., 1979) and provides the basis of high-definition TV.

Neurons of V1 may be involved not only in perceiving objects and events, but also in forming mental images (Box 10.3).

Neurons in the Visual Cortex beyond Area V1 Have Complex Receptive Fields and Contribute to the Identification of Forms

Area V1 is only a small part of the portion of cortex that is devoted to vision. Area V1 sends axons to other visual cortical areas, including areas that appear to be involved in the perception of form: area V2, area V4, and the inferior temporal area (see Figure 10.18c). Some of these extrastriate areas also receive direct input from the LGN. The receptive fields of the cells in many of these extrastriate visual areas are even more complex than those in cells of area V1. As Figure 10.18a–c reflect, on the basis of anatomical, physiological, and behavioral investigations with macaque mon-

---

BOX 10.3 *Does Forming a Mental Image Require Activation of Primary Visual Cortex?*

When you form a mental image of a visual object or scene, does the primary visual cortex (V1) have to be activated? A variety of previous observations have implicated V1 in mental imagery, but perhaps activation of this area is simply a by-product of activation of other brain regions and is not *required* for imagery to occur. Psychologist Stephen Kosslyn (1994) reviewed a variety of studies and concluded that perceiving a visual object and forming a visual image involve essentially the same cortical regions and processes. For example, imagined objects activate regions that corresponded to the retinotopic mapping of V1; when people imagined small letters (in order to be able to answer questions about them), PET recording showed activation of the foveal representation; when they imagined large letters, the parafoveal representation was activated (Kosslyn et al., 1993). Activation is also frequently seen in other visual areas beyond V1.

To obtain convergent evidence about the role of V1 in forming mental images, Kosslyn et al. (1999) used PET and also studied how impairing the function of V1 affected mental images. To impair function, they gave subjects repetitive **transcranial magnetic stimulation** (rTMS) directed to V1. Before each set of trials in which subjects formed and inspected mental images, the rTMS was administered at 1 Hz for 10 minutes; the effects were presumed to last for about 10 minutes after the conclusion of rTMS. A block of trials lasted about 85 seconds.

Before performing the imagery condition, subjects were exposed to and asked to remember a visual display that consisted of four quadrants, each quadrant containing a set of two to five parallel stripes that differed among quadrants in number, length, width, spacing, and orientation (see the figure). On each trial, the subject was asked to form a mental image of the display, and then was asked to respond as rapidly as possible to a question of this sort: Are the stripes in quadrant 1 longer than those in quadrant 4? Shortly before half of the imagery trials, the subject received rTMS that targeted V1; on the other trials, rTMS was directed to the skull and did not enter the brain. Similar trials were conducted in which the subjects actually saw the display rather than imagining it. In another set of trials, PET recordings were made while subjects imagined the display; the PET recordings showed activation of V1, V2, and other brain regions.

In all five subjects, rTMS impaired the reaction time by a small but significant amount, about 10 to 20%. Nevertheless, the responses were correct most of the time, whether or not rTMS was delivered preceding that trial. The weak TMS that was employed did not dim vision or cause any effect noticeable to the subjects during the imagery or perceptual trials. It was estimated to affect about 1 cm³ of cortex and did not impinge on V2.

The authors of this study concluded that the activation of V1 when subjects visualized and compared sets of stripes

is indeed causally linked to performance of the task. This study may foreshadow a time when TMS will be a familiar tool for cognitive neuroscientists (Barinaga, 1999); Pascual-Leone et al. (1999) have reviewed other work studying brain–behavior relationships by using TMS to induce "virtual lesions."

The fact that visual perception and visual imagery involve V1 in similar ways should not lead us to conclude that perceiving and imagining are identical or that their brain mechanisms are identical. Perceptual illusions provide an example of possible differences between the two. Although some earlier studies indicated that visual illusions occur in imagery, a recent study reports that this is not the case. The authors conclude that visual illusions are mediated by early, precortical mechanisms of information processing, whereas generation of a mental image involves only later, cortical mechanisms (Giusberti et al., 1998).

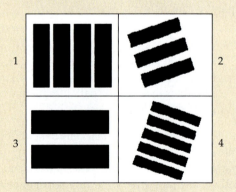

(From Kosslyn et al., 1999.)

(a) Macaque brain, lateral view

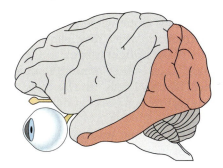

(b) Macaque brain, medial view

(c) Visual areas in the macaque cortex, unfolded view

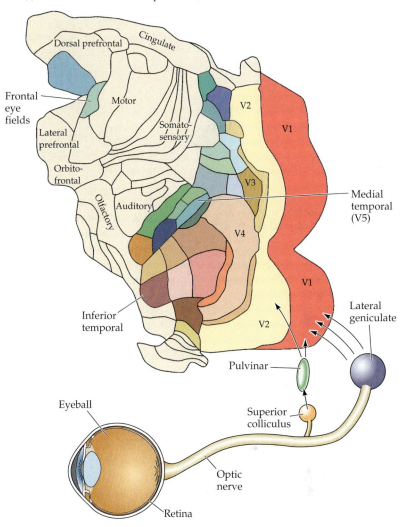

(d) Visual areas in the human occipital cortex, "flattened" by computational techniques

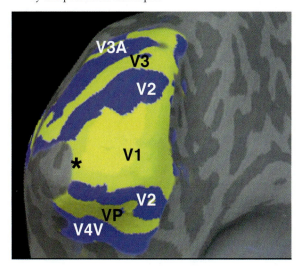

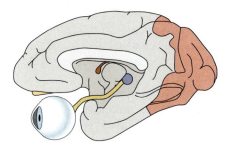

10.18 Main Visual Areas in Monkey and Human Brains (a, b) Macaque visual areas in occipital and temporal cortex are shown in pink. Part c shows all the known visual areas of the macaque on a flattened cortex in color. (d) Through computational techniques, the occipital regions of human brain shown in Figure 10.12b were "inflated," flattening the brain and bringing sulci in the cortex to the surface, which reveals the relative size and extent of various cortical visual areas. The asterisk identifies the representation of the center of the fovea. (Parts *a–c* after Van Essen and Drury, 1997; *d* from Tootell et al., 1998; courtesy of Roger Tootell.)

keys we know that at least 32 distinct cortical areas are directly involved in visual function (Van Essen and Drury, 1997).

The visual areas of the human brain have been less thoroughly mapped than those of the monkey brain, and mainly by neuroimaging, which does not have as fine spatial resolution as the electrophysiological recording used in the monkey brain, but the general layout appears to be similar in the two species (Figure 10.18d). However, there are important differences in proportions of cortical areas between the two species. In macaque monkeys, the occipital lobe occupies 32% of the neo-cortex and the frontal lobe 26%; in humans, the occipital lobe occupies 19% and the frontal lobe 36%. Whereas the 32 areas that are largely or entirely visual in function occupy 54% of the surface of the macaque neocortex, the visual areas account for

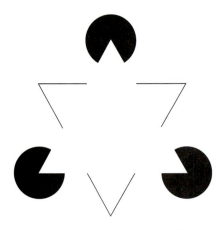

10.19 A Geometric Figure with "Illusory" or "Subjective" Contours Cells have been found in visual cortical areas that respond to illusory contours such as those of the upright triangle shown here. These contours thus have neurophysiological meaning.

10.20 Complex Stimuli Evoke Strong Responses in Visual Cortex (*a*) These concentric and radial stimuli evoke maximal responses from some cells in visual cortical area V4. The stimuli that evoked the highest response rates (see scale bar) are shown in red and orange. (*b*) These 12 examples illustrate the critical features of stimuli that evoke maximal responses from cells in the anterior inferior temporal area. (Part *a* from Gallant et al., 1993, courtesy of Jack Gallant; *b* from K. Tanaka, 1993, courtesy of Keiji Tanaka.)

only about 23% of human neocortex. We will discuss only a few of the main visual cortical areas and their functions.

Area V2 is adjacent to V1, and many of its cells show properties similar to those of V1 cells. Many V2 cells can respond to illusory contours, which may help explain how we perceive contours such as the boundaries of the upright triangle in Figure 10.19 (Peterhans and von der Heydt, 1989). Clearly such cells respond to complex relations among the parts of their receptive fields. Some V1 cells can also respond to illusory contours (Grosof et al., 1993), but this feature is more common in area V2.

Area V4 receives axons from V2 and has cells that give their strongest responses to the sinusoidal frequency gratings that we discussed in the previous section. Many V4 cells respond even better, however, to concentric and radial stimuli, such as those in Figure 10.20*a* (Gallant et al., 1993). Investigators have suggested that these V4 cells show an intermediate stage between the spatial-frequency processing in V1 and V2 cells and the recognition of pattern and form in cells of the inferior temporal area. Area V4 also has many cells that respond preferentially (most strongly) to wavelength differences, as we will see later when we discuss color vision. Area V5, also called the medial temporal (MT) area, appears to be specialized for the perception of motion, as we will also discuss later in this chapter.

The inferior temporal (IT) visual cortex has many cells that respond best to particular complex forms, including forms that the subject has learned to recognize. Because many cells in IT cortex have highly specific receptive fields, it is hard to find the exact stimuli that can activate a particular cell. Experimenters start by presenting many three-dimensional animal and plant objects (Desimone et al., 1984; K. Tanaka, 1993). When a stimulus elicits a strong response, the experimenters then simplify the image by sequentially removing parts of the features to determine the necessary and sufficient features for maximal activation of the cell.

Most cells in IT cortex do not require a natural object such as a face to activate them; instead they require moderately complex shapes, sometimes combined with color or texture, such as those in Figure 10.20*b*. K. Tanaka (1993) reports that IT cortex has a columnar organization like that of V1 (as we will see shortly), with adjacent cells often having similar receptive fields. He proposes that simultaneous activation of tens of such cells may be sufficient to specify a natural object. The complex

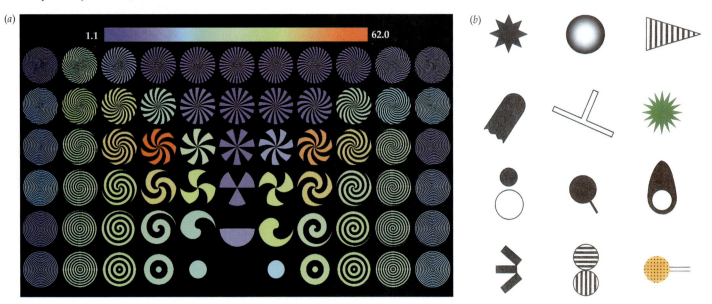

receptive fields in IT cortex probably develop through experience and learning. When a monkey was trained for a year to discriminate a set of 28 moderately complex shapes, 39% of the cells in the anterior IT cortex responded significantly to some of these shapes, whereas in control monkeys only 9% of the cells responded strongly to these forms (Kobatake and Tanaka, 1994).

The prefrontal cortex also contains a restricted region of neurons that are activated by faces but not by other visual stimuli, as found both by noninvasive recording of human subjects (Ungerleider et al., 1998) and by electrical recording of neurons in the monkey brain (Scalaidhe et al., 1997). These neurons receive connections from the superior temporal sulcus and adjacent cortex on the inferior temporal gyrus. These findings indicate that the ventral visual pathway that processes stimulus identification extends from the primary visual cortex through temporal cortical regions to the prefrontal cortex.

NEURAL PLASTICITY

Area V1 Is Organized in Columns and Slabs

Area V1 is organized with a richness of representation unimagined only a few years ago. The primary visual cortex has separate representations for at least four dimensions of the visual stimulus: (1) location in the visual field, with larger, finer mapping of the central region of the visual field than of the periphery; (2) orientation; (3) color; and (4) ocular dominance.

Ocular dominance columns were first discovered by electrophysiological recording. Although the receptive field of an individual neuron is the same for vision through either eye, some cells are equally activated by the two eyes but other cells respond preferentially (i.e., more strongly) to stimulation of one eye. However, all the cells in a vertical column of cells have the same ocular dominance. The vertical columns are arranged into **ocular dominance slabs** about 0.5 mm wide, all cells of which respond preferentially to stimulation of one eye. A given point in the visual field elicits responses in cells in adjacent left-eye-preferring and right-eye-preferring ocular dominance slabs.

The ocular dominance is especially clear in the broad layer IV of area V1, where each cell is monocular, responding to only one eye. Above and below the (monocular) ocular dominance stripes in layer IV, most of the cells respond to stimulation of both eyes. However, even though ocular dominance is expressed less strongly above and below layer IV, the cells in that slab still prefer the one eye over the other.

Anatomical tracing techniques in the 1970s furnished additional information about the ocular dominance organization. For example, when a small dose of radioactive amino acid is injected into one eye, some of it is transported along neurons, crossing synapses and reaching layer IV of primary visual cortex. Autoradiographic examination of the cortex then reveals parallel bands of radioactivity in layer IV that correspond to the ocular dominance stripes driven by the injected eye.

IMPORTANT METHOD

In another experiment, a monkey had one eye covered and the other eye open while radioactive 2-deoxyglucose (2-DG) was administered. Subsequent autoradiography of the cortical tissue showed not only stripes about 350 μm wide in layer IV, but also dots of radioactivity about 150 μm wide in the other layers, indicating responses to stimulation of the one eye. These dots ran along the centers of the ocular dominance slabs. The presence of these dots shows that some of the neurons in other layers of the columns are also mainly monocular.

Techniques of optical imaging of cortical activity (T. Bonhoeffer and Grinvald, 1991; Ts'o et al., 1990) allow us to see the ocular dominance stripes in the primary visual cortex of an awake monkey when visual patterns are presented to one eye (Figure 10.21a and b). The imaging is based on small changes in the light reflected from the cortex during activity. These changes are of two types: (1) changes in blood volume, probably in the capillaries of the activated area; and (2) changes in cortical tissue, such as the movement of ions and water or the expansion and contraction of

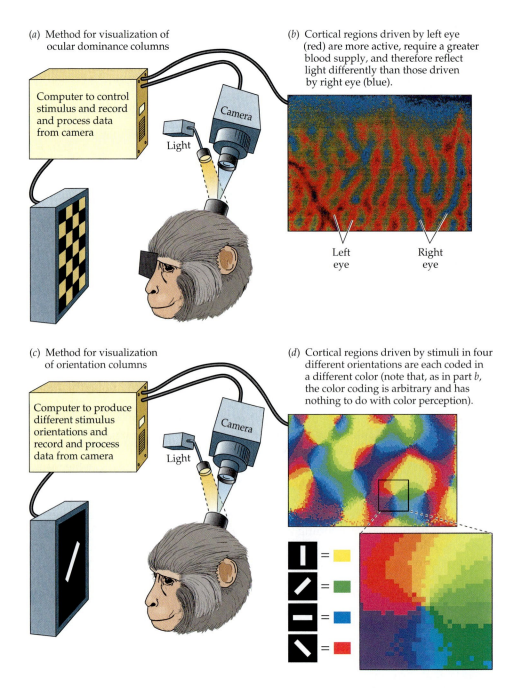

(a) Method for visualization of ocular dominance columns

(b) Cortical regions driven by left eye (red) are more active, require a greater blood supply, and therefore reflect light differently than those driven by right eye (blue).

Computer to control stimulus and record and process data from camera

Camera

Light

Left eye

Right eye

(c) Method for visualization of orientation columns

(d) Cortical regions driven by stimuli in four different orientations are each coded in a different color (note that, as in part b, the color coding is arbitrary and has nothing to do with color perception).

Computer to produce different stimulus orientations and record and process data from camera

Camera

Light

10.21 Visualization of Ocular Dominance Columns and Orientation Columns by Optical Imaging (a) In this method for visualization of ocular dominance, a camera records changes in light reflected from the cortex when the monkey views a twinkling checkerboard with one eye. Small differences in reflected light are amplified, and intensity is coded by color (red for strong intensity, blue for weak). (b) After the recording is processed, regions activated by the active eye are seen as red stripes. (c) In this method for visualization of orientation preference, stimuli at different orientations (vertical, horizontal, diagonal) are presented to reveal groups of neurons that respond most strongly to a particular orientation. The stimuli are usually black or white, but here they are color-coded to correspond to color-coded responses to four different orientations combined into a single pattern (d). Although the pattern at first seems disorderly, closer inspection reveals several regions at which all four orientations converge in a pinwheel pattern (inset). Note that the foci of pinwheels occur at regular intervals, that each orientation is represented only once within a pinwheel, and that the sequence of orientations is consistent across pinwheels. (After T. Bonhoeffer and Grinvald, 1991; b and d courtesy of A. Grinvald.)

extracellular spaces. Experimenters can combine optical imaging with electrophysiological recording to obtain visual guidance for placing microelectrodes in particular parts of ocular dominance slabs. Figure 10.21*b* shows the ocular dominance slabs that were activated when one eye was stimulated. This recording technique may prove useful as a mapping tool in human neurosurgery.

Ocular dominance slabs develop during the first 4 months in the cat and during the first 6 months in the macaque monkey. As we saw in Chapter 7, both eyes must be exposed to the visual environment if each eye is to obtain its own cortical representation (see Figure 7.20). Up to the age of 3 or 4 months, human infants are unimpressed by stereograms (pairs of pictures showing somewhat different left-eye and right-eye views that most adult observers perceive as a three-dimensional view). Beginning at the age of 3 or 4 months, however, most infants are captivated by stereograms (Held, 1993). Presumably, before that age the cortex is unable to separate the information from the two eyes because the information reaches the same cortical neurons.

Primary visual cortex also has a columnar organization for stimulus orientation: A microelectrode that follows a path perpendicular to the surface records cells that all prefer the same stimulus orientation within the visual field (Figure 10.21*c* and *d*). As the recording electrode is moved from one **orientation column** to the next, the preferred axis of orientation shifts by a few degrees. That is, in one column all the cells may be "tuned" to upright stimuli (at an orientation of 0°); in an adjacent column, all cells respond best to another orientation, perhaps at 10° from the vertical; in the next column, perhaps at 25°; and so forth.

In Figure 10.21*d* we see how these columns are organized parallel to the surface of the cortex. In this figure, optical recordings show the regions of primary visual cortex that respond best to stimuli of four different orientations. Inspection reveals that the columns are organized into slabs that run perpendicular to the borders of ocular dominance slabs. These slabs, however, stretch only from the center of one ocular stripe to the center of the adjacent one. Along the center of the ocular dominance stripes, preferred orientation shifts by 90°, creating regularly spaced "pinwheels" in which responses to the different stimulus orientations pivot around a center. A striking recent technical advance in the functional-MRI technique has made it possible to visualize individual orientation columns in the visual cortex of cats (D.-S. Kim et al., 2000). Mapping the distribution of columns in this way showed excellent agreement with data from electrical recording and optical imaging studies.

Also within the ocular dominance slabs of primate visual areas are vertical *blobs* (sometimes called *pegs*) that can be seen when the tissue is stained to reveal the enzyme cytochrome oxidase. Early experiments suggested that the blobs were related to color vision (Hendrickson, 1985; Livingstone and Hubel, 1984), but later work has cast doubt on this hypothesis. Quantitative studies show that neurons in the blobs cannot be readily distinguished from neurons outside the blobs on the basis of either chromatic tuning (Lennie et al., 1990) or orientation tuning (A. G. Leventhal et al., 1995). In addition, even nocturnal primates, whose retinas are poor in cones, and cats, which have little or no color vision, have blobs; and cone-rich rodents, such as ground squirrels, do not have blobs.

Blobs extend above and below layer IV but are not seen in layer IV itself. Figure 10.22 diagrams the organization of the primate visual cortex, including the large ocular dominance slabs, the orientation slabs, and the blobs. (Compare these diagrams with Figure 8.19, which shows the similar columnar organization of the somatosensory cortex.) Along the centers of the ocular dominance slabs, the orientation slabs are arranged radially, like the "pinwheels" in Figure 10.21*d,* with blobs at the centers of the pinwheels, but elsewhere the orientation slabs are laid out in a rectangular arrangement, like city blocks that cross the borders of the ocular dominance slabs.

10.22 Organization of the Primate Primary Visual Cortex These two partial ocular dominance slabs represent the left and right eyes, respectively. Blobs extend vertically through layers I through III and V through VI, located in the centers of ocular dominance slabs. Small columns represent the preferred orientations of groups of cells; these orientation columns radiate out from the centers of the blobs. The orientation is color-coded here as in Figure 10.21*d*. For simplification, this diagram does not represent spatial frequency (higher spatial frequencies are represented at the edges of the blocks and lower frequencies in the centers), nor does it represent the spectrally opponent cells (which we'll discuss shortly) that occur irregularly in the columns.

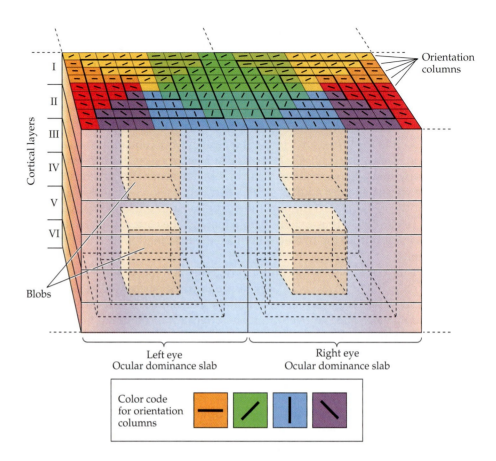

Color Vision Depends on Special Channels from the Retinal Cones through Cortical Area V4

For most people, different hues are a striking aspect of vision. The system for color perception appears to have at least four stages. In the first stage the cones, the retinal receptor cells that are specialized to respond to certain wavelengths of light, receive visual information. In the second stage this information is processed by neurons in the local circuits of the retina, leading to retinal ganglion cells that are excited by light of some wavelengths and inhibited by light of other wavelengths. The ganglion cells send the wavelength information via their axons to the LGN, mainly in the parvocellular layers. From there this information goes to area V1, from which it is relayed to other visual cortical areas, where the third and fourth stages of color perception take place.

Color Perception Requires Receptor Cells That Differ in Their Sensitivities to Different Wavelengths

Artists have long known that all the hues can be obtained from a small number of primary colors. On the basis of observations of mixing pigments and lights, scientists at the start of the nineteenth century hypothesized that three separate kinds of receptors in the retina provide the basis for color vision. This **trichromatic hypothesis** (from the Greek *tri-*, "three," and *chroma*, "color") was endorsed in 1852 by the great physiologist-physicist-psychologist Hermann von Helmholtz and became the dominant position.

Helmholtz predicted that blue-sensitive, green-sensitive, and red-sensitive cones would be found, that each would be sharply tuned to its part of the spectrum, and that each type would have a separate path to the brain. The color of an object would be recognized, then, on the basis of which color receptor was activated. This system would be like the mechanisms for discriminating touch and temperature on the basis of which skin receptors and labeled neural lines are activated (see Chapter 8).

Later in the nineteenth century, physiologist Ewald Hering proposed a different explanation. He argued, on the basis of visual experience, that there are four unique hues and three opposed pairs of colors—blue and yellow, green and red, and black and white—and that three physiological processes with opposed positive and negative values must therefore be the basis of color vision. As we will see, both this **opponent-process hypothesis** and the trichromatic hypothesis are encompassed in current color vision theory, but neither of the old hypotheses is sufficient by itself.

**COMPETING
HYPOTHESES**

Measurements of photopigments in cones have borne out the trichromatic hypothesis in part. Each cone of the human retina has one of three classes of pigments. These pigments do not, however, have the narrow spectral distributions that Helmholtz predicted. The color system that Helmholtz postulated would have given rather poor color vision and poor visual acuity. Color vision would be poor because only a few different hues could be discriminated; within the long-wavelength region of the spectrum there would be only red, and not all the range of hues that we see. Acuity would be poor because the grain of the retinal mosaic would be coarse; a red stimulus could affect only one-third of the receptors. (Actually, acuity is as good in red light as it is in white light.)

The human visual system does not have receptors that are sensitive to only a narrow part of the visible spectrum. Two of the three retinal cone pigments give some response to light of almost *any* wavelength. The pigments have different *peaks* of sensitivity, but the peaks are not as far apart as Helmholtz predicted. As Figure 10.23 shows, the peaks occur at about 420 nm (in the part of the spectrum where we usually see violet under photopic conditions), about 530 nm (where most of us see green), and about 560 nm (where most of us see yellow-green). Despite Helmholtz's prediction, none of the curves peak in the long-wavelength part of the spectrum, where most of us see red (around 630 nm).

Under ordinary conditions almost any visual object stimulates at least two kinds of cones, thus ensuring high visual acuity and good perception of form. The spectral sensitivities of the three cone types differ from each other, and the nervous system detects and processes these differences to extract the color information. Thus, certain ganglion cells and certain cells at higher stations in the visual system are color specific, even though the receptor cells are not. Similarly, visual receptors are not form specific, but form is detected later in the visual centers by comparison of the outputs of different receptors.

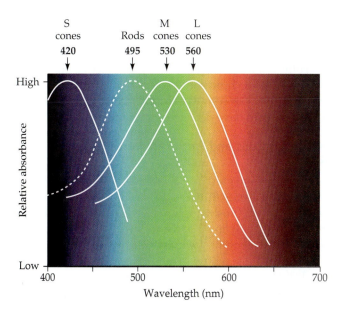

10.23 Spectral Sensitivities of Human Photopigments Each pigment has a peak sensitivity but responds to a wide range of wavelengths. S, short-wavelength; M, medium-wavelength; L, long-wavelength.

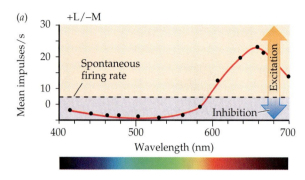

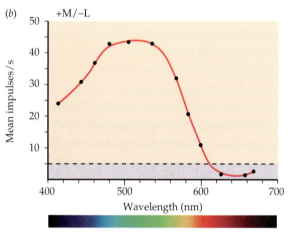

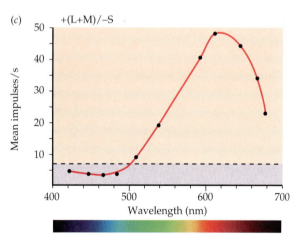

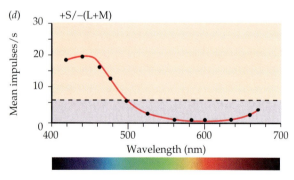

10.24 Responses of the Four Main Types of Spectrally Opponent Cells in Monkey LGN Each type is excited by one band of wavelengths and inhibited by another.

Because the cones are not color detectors, the most appropriate brief names for them can be taken from their peak areas of wavelength sensitivity: *short* (S) for the receptor with peak sensitivity at about 420 nm, *medium* (M) at 530 nm, and *long* (L) at 560 nm (see Figure 10.23). There are typically twice as many L as M receptors, but far fewer S receptors (Brainard et al., 2000; Carroll et al., 2000; Hagstrom et al., 1998); this difference explains why acuity is much lower with short-wavelength illumination than in the other parts of the visible spectrum.

The genes for wavelength-sensitive pigments in the retina have been analyzed, and the similarities in structure of the three genes suggest that they are all derived from a common ancestral gene (Nathans, 1987). In addition, the genes for the medium- and long-wavelength pigments occupy adjacent positions on the X chromosome and are much more similar to each other than either is to the gene for the short-wavelength pigment on chromosome 6.

The fact that humans and Old World monkeys have both M and L pigments, whereas most New World monkeys have only a single longer-wavelength pigment, suggests that the M and L pigments differentiated recently in evolutionary terms. Furthermore, the genes for the M and L pigments are variable among individuals, and particular variants in these pigment genes correspond to variants in color vision: so-called color blindness.

Thus, detailed examination of a person's photopigment genes can now show whether that person has normal color vision or has one of the recognized congenital deficiencies of color discrimination. In animal experiments, a fluorescently colored antibody has been developed for the S cone pigment, making it relatively easy to locate this kind of cone and to study its distribution over the retina (Wikler and Rakic, 1990).

The L and M cones are too similar to be distinguished from each other by antibodies, but a combination of differentially bleaching the retina with strong blue or red light and a highly precise optical system has allowed investigators to map the arrangement of S, M, and L cones in the eyes of two human subjects (Roorda and Williams, 1999). Both subjects had normal color vision, but in one the proportion of L to M cones was nearly 4:1, whereas in the other it was close to 1:1, so further sampling is in order. At a first approximation, the spatial distribution of the L and M cones seems random, but the S cones are regularly spaced.

The fact that the genes for the M and L pigments are on the X chromosome explains why defects of red/green color vision are much more frequent in human males than in human females. Because males have only one X chromosome, a mutation in the genes for the M or L pigments can impair color vision. But if a female has a defective photopigment gene in one of her two X chromosomes, a normal copy of the gene on the other X chromosome can compensate. Only very rarely do both of a female's X chromosomes have defective genes for color receptors.

Some Retinal Ganglion Cells and Parvocellular LGN Cells Show Spectral Opponency

Recordings made from retinal ganglion cells in Old World monkeys, which can discriminate colors as humans do, reveal the second stage of processing of color vision. Most ganglion cells and cells in the parvocellular layers of the LGN fire in response to some wavelengths and are inhibited by other wavelengths. Leading this research are Russell De Valois and Karen De Valois, whose results provide much of the information in this discussion.

Figure 10.24a shows the response of a parvocellular LGN cell as a large spot of light centered on the receptive field of the cell is changed from one wavelength to another. Firing is stimulated by wavelengths above 600 nm, where the L cones are most sensitive, then inhibited below 600 nm, where the M cones are most sensitive. A cell exhibiting this response pattern is therefore called a plus L/minus M cell (+L/–M). This is an example of a **spectrally opponent cell** because two regions of the spectrum have opposite effects on the cell's rate of firing. Figure 10.24 shows examples of responses of the four main kinds of spectrally opponent cells.

Each spectrally opponent ganglion cell presumably receives input from two or three different kinds of cones through bipolar cells. The connections from at least one type of cone are excitatory, and those from at least one other type are inhibitory (Figure 10.25). The spectrally opponent ganglion cells thus record the difference in stimulation of different populations of cones. For example, a +M/–L cell responds to the difference in the excitation of M and L cones. (Recall from Chapter 3 that a neuron can process information by subtracting one input from another; spectral opponency is an example of such information processing.)

Although the peaks of the sensitivity curves of the M and L cones are not very different (see Figure 10.23), the M-minus-L *difference* curve (see Figure 10.24*b*) shows a clear peak around 500 nm (in the green part of the spectrum), while the L-minus-M difference function (see Figure 10.24*a*) shows a peak around 650 nm (in the red part of the spectrum). Thus +M/–L and +L/–M cells yield distinctly different neural response curves.

Spectrally opponent neurons are the second stage in the system for color perception, but they still cannot be called color cells, for the following reasons: (1) They send their outputs into many higher circuits—for detection of form, depth, and movement, as well as hue; and (2) their peak wavelength sensitivities do not correspond precisely to the wavelengths that we see as the principal hues.

Russell De Valois

Karen De Valois

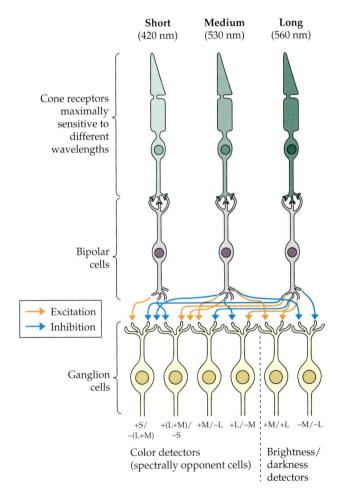

10.25 A Model of the Connections of the Wavelength Discrimination Systems in the Primate Retina The connections from the cones yield four kinds of spectrally opponent ganglion cells, as well as ganglion cells that detect brightness or darkness. (After R. L. De Valois and K. De Valois, 1980.)

In addition to the four kinds of spectrally opponent ganglion cells, Figure 10.25 diagrams the presumed inputs of ganglion cells that detect brightness and darkness. The brightness detectors receive stimulation from both M and L cones (+M/+L); the darkness detectors are inhibited by both M and L cones (–M/–L).

In the monkey LGN, 70 to 80% of the cells are spectrally opponent; in the cat, very few spectrally opponent cells are found—only about 1%. This difference explains the ease with which monkeys discriminate wavelengths and the difficulty in training cats to discriminate even large differences in wavelength.

Some Visual Cortical Cells and Regions Appear to Be Specialized for Color Perception

In the cortex, spectral information appears to be used for various kinds of information processing. Forms are segregated from their background by differences in color or intensity (or both). The most important role that color plays in our perception is to denote which parts of a complex image belong to one object and which belong to another. Some animals use displays of brightly colored body parts to call attention to themselves, but color can also be used as camouflage.

Some spectrally opponent cortical cells contribute to the perception of color, providing the third stage of the color vision system. R. L. De Valois and K. De Valois (1993) have suggested ways in which adding and subtracting the outputs of spectrally opponent ganglion cells could yield cortical cells that are perceptually opponent: red versus green, blue versus yellow, and black versus white. The spectral responses of these cells correspond to the wavelengths of the principal hues specified by human observers, and their characteristics also help explain other color phenomena.

Visual cortical region V4 is particularly rich in color-sensitive cells. Electrophysiological recording in monkeys shows that only some V4 cells (probably a minority) are selective for color (Schein et al., 1982). Evidence that this area is normally involved in the perception of color comes from electrophysiological studies showing that some V4 cells respond best if the color outside the receptive field is different from the color preferred in the receptive field (Schein and Desimone, 1990). These cells provide a fourth stage of color perception that may be important for color constancy and for figure/ground discrimination. Additional evidence of the role of V4 in color vision comes from PET studies in humans. Area V4 is activated when subjects view colored stimuli but not when they view black-and-white stimuli (Zeki et al., 1991).

It would probably be wrong to think of V4 as devoted exclusively to color perception. Cells in V4 are also tuned in the spatial domain, for orientation and for spatial frequency (Desimone and Schein, 1987). Schiller (1993) lesioned V4 in monkeys and found color vision relatively unaffected. V4 is the main pathway between the secondary visual area (V2) and the inferior temporal visual region, and it probably serves several aspects of visual perception.

Most Mammalian Species Have Some Color Vision

In 1942, Gordon Walls concluded from a survey that among mammals, color vision is by no means widespread, and this conclusion has been repeated in many books and articles. A much more extensive survey by Gerald Jacobs (1993), however, indicates that almost all mammals probably have at least some degree of color vision, which he defines as the ability to discriminate among stimuli that differ in wavelength distributions of spectral energy. Among mammals, only certain primates have good trichromatic color vision (i.e., based on three classes of cone photopigments), but many species have dichromatic color vision (based on two classes of cone pigments). Many so-called color-blind humans (actually color-*deficient* humans) have dichromatic vision and can distinguish short-wavelength stimuli (blue) from long-wavelength stimuli (not blue).

The ability of animals to discriminate visual cues on the basis of wavelength can be measured by behavioral tests (Neitz et al., 1989). Indirect approaches include

**COMPETING
HYPOTHESES**

measuring the electrical responses of the eye to flashes of different stimuli (Goldsmith, 1986; Neitz and Jacobs, 1984) or measuring the pigment in individual photoreceptors (Bowmaker, 1984; J. S. Levine and MacNichol, 1982). No species that possesses multiple cone pigments has been found to lack the central neural mechanisms for using them in color vision. In a few species, all three of the methods mentioned here have been used to study color vision, and because in these test cases the results of the three methods agreed, clear evidence from any one of these methods is accepted as proof of color vision.

**IMPORTANT
METHOD**

On the basis of his survey, G. H. Jacobs (1993) suggested that it is better to think of a continuum of color capabilities than to use an all-or-none criterion, and he proposed that four categories cover all mammalian species:

1. *Excellent trichromatic color vision* is found in diurnal primates such as humans and the rhesus monkey (*Macaca mulatta*).
2. *Robust dichromatic color vision* is found in species that have two kinds of cone photopigments and a reasonably large population of cones. Examples of such species are the dog, the pig, and many male New World monkeys, such as the squirrel monkey (*Saimiri sciureus*) and the marmoset monkey (*Callithrix jaccus*). (The females may be trichromatic as a result of having genes encoding for differing long-wavelength cones on their two X chromosomes.)
3. *Feeble dichromatic color vision* occurs in species that have two kinds of cone pigments but have very few cones. Examples are the domestic cat and the coati (*Nasua nasua*).
4. *Minimal color vision* is possessed by species that have only a single kind of cone pigment and that must rely on interactions between rods and cones to discriminate wavelength. Examples are the owl monkey (*Aotes trivirgatus*) and the raccoon (*Procyon lotor*).

When both diurnal and nocturnal species of a given taxonomic family have been tested for color vision (e.g., the coati and the raccoon), the diurnal species (in this case the coati) usually has had the better color vision.

Perception of Visual Motion Is Analyzed by a Special System That Includes Cortical Area V5

Some retinal ganglion cells respond preferentially to a certain direction of motion of objects; for example, certain ganglion cells respond to stimuli that move to the left but not to stimuli that move to the right (Barlow and Levick, 1965). Investigators have hypothesized that the direction-selective responses require retinal circuits involving both excitation and inhibition: Whereas movement in the preferred direction stimulates excitatory units before inhibitory units, movement in the nonpreferred direction reaches inhibitory units first.

Motion is analyzed by the cortex, partly in regions close to those that control eye movements. All the neurons in area V5 (also called the medial temporal [MT] area; see Figure 10.18c) in the monkey respond to moving visual stimuli, but they do not respond differentially to the wavelength of stimulation. A variety of studies provide converging evidence that area V5 is specialized for the perception of motion and direction of motion. As mentioned previously, PET studies of human subjects show that moving stimuli, rather than colored stimuli, evoke responses in area V5.

When monkeys are trained to report the direction of perceived motion, experimental lesions of area V5 impair their performance, at least temporarily (Newsome et al., 1985). Electrical stimulation of clusters of V5 neurons with similar preferred directions of motion can affect the monkeys' judgments of direction of motion: Weak stimulation biases the judgments toward the preferred direction of the neurons (Salzman et al., 1992); stronger stimulation impairs performance, presumably because its effects spread to neurons representing all directions of motion (Murasugi et al., 1993). Recent research has focused on Meynert cells, special cortical pyramidal cells whose dendrites extend much farther in one direction than in other directions; these cells might provide the basis for preferential responses to a given direction of motion (Ferster, 1998; Livingstone, 1998).

One striking report described a woman who had lost the ability to perceive motion after a stroke that had damaged area V5 (Zihl et al., 1983). The woman was unable to perceive continuous motion and saw only separate, successive positions. This impairment led to many problems in her daily life. She had difficulty crossing streets because she could not follow the positions of automobiles in motion: "When I'm looking at the car first, it seems far away. But then, when I want to cross the road, suddenly the car is very near." She complained of difficulties in following conversations because she could not see the movements of speakers' lips. Except for her inability to perceive motion, this woman's visual perception appeared normal.

Visual Attention Involves Both Striate and Extrastriate Cortex

In most visual scenes, many objects compete for attention. Studies using several complementary techniques are revealing the importance of extrastriate as well as striate cortical areas in visual attention. The techniques include brain imaging, experimental brain lesions, and event-related potentials (ERP).

In a study using functional MRI (Kastner et al., 1998), human observers looked at a fixation point while stimuli appeared either simultaneously or sequentially 6 to 8° from the fixation point. The strength of fMRI responses was measured in striate cortical areas V1 and V2 and in extrastriate areas V4 and posterior inferior temporal cortex. (For locations of these areas, see Figure 10.18c.) The observers concentrated on discriminating a rapid succession of the letters *T* or *L* appearing at the fixation point—a demanding task.

The fMRI responses were significantly stronger for sequential than for simultaneous presentation, suggesting that the cortical representation of each stimulus tends to suppress the representation of the other stimuli. The suppression effect was stronger in the extrastriate areas than in the striate areas. When the observers were instructed to attend to the stimulus closest to the fixation point, while continuing to count *T*s and *L*s, the suppression effect was reduced, especially in areas V4 and posterior inferior temporal cortex.

The investigators then conducted a related study in which monkeys were trained to look at a fixation point and judge whether a target that was projected to one of the four quadrants deviated from the vertical. Lesions were made in the representation of one quadrant in area V4, in that of another quadrant in inferior posterior temporal cortex, and of a third quadrant in both V4 and inferior posterior temporal cortex; the cortical representation of the fourth quadrant was left intact. The lesions caused deficits in discrimination of target orientation, but the presence of additional distracting stimuli increased the errors significantly in the lesion-affected quadrants. It appeared that in the absence of V4 and inferior posterior temporal cortex, selective attention was impaired and attention was captured by strong stimuli, regardless of their behavioral relevance (De Weerd et al., 1999).

IMPORTANT METHOD

The poor temporal resolution of fMRI doesn't reveal the functional neuroanatomy of visual attention, so A. Martinez et al. (1999) supplemented fMRI with ERP. Observers tried to detect changes in a stimulus presented away from the fixation point while their attention was directed to one or another part of the visual field. When the stimulus occurred in an attended location, fMRI responses were enhanced in both striate and extrastriate cortical areas. The ERP recordings provided critical temporal information. They showed that the initial responses, occurring in the striate cortex 50 to 55 ms after the stimulus, were not modulated by attention. The earliest facilitation of attended signals was observed in extrastriate areas at 70 to 75 ms. The investigators suggest that the later modulation observed with fMRI at striate cortex represents feedback from extrastriate areas.

Are the Many Cortical Visual Areas Organized into Two Major Systems?

Many investigators have wondered why primate visual systems contain so many distinct regions. The research just discussed indicates that certain regions specialize in processing different attributes or dimensions of visual experience (such as shape, location, color, motion, and orientation). But the number of visual fields—over 30—is larger than the number of basic attributes. Perhaps the reason that so many separate visual regions have been found is simply that investigators, being visually oriented primates themselves, have lavished special attention on the visual system.

Some investigators (e.g., Schiller, 1996), however, have claimed that many of the visual regions overlap in function and that neurons in many regions perform several different tasks rather than analyzing a single attribute. Others (e.g., Orban et al., 1996) have suggested that a particular attribute is processed in different areas along with other attributes (e.g., motion and color in one area, motion and form in another, and so on). Such multiple representation of different attributes within an area might help account for the large number of visual areas, as well as for the multifunctional properties of neurons.

Other workers have suggested that the many cortical visual areas can be grouped into two major systems. Earlier work with hamsters led to the hypothesis that there are two visual systems: One, for *identification* of objects, involves especially the visual cortex; the other, for *location* of objects, involves especially the superior colliculus (G. E. Schneider, 1969).

This hypothesis was later extended to primates, drawing on research on localized brain lesions in monkeys. Mishkin and Ungerleider (1982) proposed that primates have two main cortical processing streams, both originating in primary visual cortex: a ventral processing stream responsible for visual identification of objects, and a dorsal stream responsible for appreciating the spatial location of objects and visual guidance of movement toward objects. These processing streams were called, respectively, the *what* and the *where* streams.

PET studies, as well as brain lesions in patients, indicate that the human brain also possesses *what* and *where* visual processing streams similar to those found in monkeys (Figure 10.26*a*) (Ungerleider et al., 1998). In the ventral stream, including regions of the occipitotemporal, inferior temporal, and inferior frontal areas, information about faces becomes more specific as one proceeds farther forward. PET studies show that whereas general information about facial features and gender are extracted more posteriorly, the more anterior parts of the stream provide representations of individual faces (Courtney et al., 1996).

Later came the suggestion that the ventral processing stream, which is mainly responsible for analysis of form and color and for recognition of objects, is an extension of the parvocellular (P) pathway, whereas the dorsal processing stream, which is mainly responsible for perception of location, depth, and movement, is an extension of the magnocellular (M) system (Livingstone and Hubel, 1988). From the LGN, the P and M divisions were thought to project to different layers and areas of the cerebral cortex (Figure 10.26*b*). In area V1, the P and M projections are segregated but intertwined with each pathway leading to a different region of layer IV in area V1. In area V2 as well, the M and P systems occupy separate but intermixed small regions. It was proposed that beyond area V2 the two systems segregate completely—the P pathway going to inferior temporal regions of the cortex, the M pathway to parietal regions.

In a review of this topic, Merigan and Maunsell (1993) stated, "The notion of parallel visual subsystems has been broadly disseminated and popularized . . . and has quickly become widely accepted, owing in part to its great explanatory power and its appealing simplicity"(p. 370). But these reviewers point out that increasing evidence—anatomical, neurophysiological, and behavioral—suggests that the two systems overlap and intermingle considerably, beginning in layer IVb of V1, and the

Mortimer Mishkin

Leslie Ungerleider

COMPETING HYPOTHESES

(a) Broad locations of the ventral and dorsal pathways in the human brain

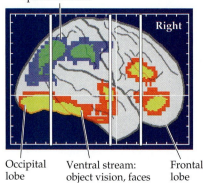

Dorsal stream: spatial location

Right

Occipital lobe

Ventral stream: object vision, faces

Frontal lobe

10.26 Parallel Processing Pathways in the Visual System (a) The ventral (*what*) pathway shown in yellow and red and the dorsal (*where*) pathway shown in green and blue serve different functions. (b) The magnocellular (dorsal) and parvocellular (ventral) pathways from the retina to the higher levels of the visual cerebral cortex are separate at the lower levels of the visual system, but they show increasing overlap at the higher levels. (Part *a* courtesy of Leslie Ungerleider.)

(b) The magnocellular and parvocellular pathways, from the retina to the higher levels of the visual cerebral cortex

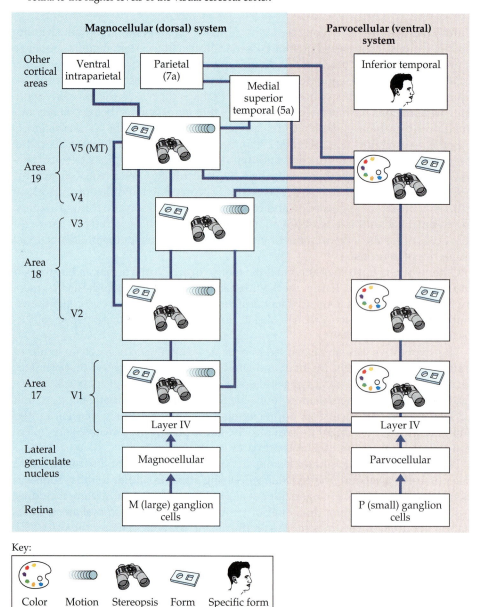

systems become increasingly merged at higher levels, so the cortical M and P pathways are only partially separate.

Visual Neuroscience Can Be Applied to Alleviate Some Visual Deficiencies

Vision is so important that many investigators have sought ways to prevent impairment, to improve inadequate vision, and to restore sight to the blind. In the United States, half a million people are blind. Recent medical advances have reduced some causes of blindness but have increased blindness from other causes. For example, improved treatment resulting in the increased survival of diabetics does not overcome all effects of this disease, one of which in many cases is blindness, and diabetes causes half the cases of blindness in the United States. In the discussion that follows we will first consider ways of avoiding impairment of vision. Then we will take up ways of exercising and training that are designed to improve an impaired visual system.

Impairment of Vision Often Can Be Prevented or Reduced

Studies of the development of vision in children and other animals show that the incidence of **myopia** ("nearsightedness") can be reduced. Myopia develops if the eyeball is too long, forcing the eye to focus objects in front of the retina rather than on the retina. As a result, distant objects appear blurred. Considerable evidence suggests that myopia develops when children spend much time looking at targets close up rather than at objects far away (Marzani and Wallman, 1997).

CLINICAL ISSUE

Before civilization, most people spent most of their time looking at objects far away, such as predators, prey, sources of water, and so on. Thus they kept the eye relaxed most of the time. Now, however, people spend long periods of time gazing at objects close at hand, such as books and computer screens. This constant close focusing requires that the lens be kept thick (unrelaxed). The developing eyeball compensates by elongating to make focusing easier, thus causing progressive myopia. Preventive steps can be taken, especially during childhood and adolescence:

- Read only in adequate light—enough that you can hold the book as far away as possible and still discern the words.
- Avoid small type.
- If you already have a prescription for myopia but you can read without using glasses, do so, because the glasses force you to thicken your lens more, thus accelerating the problem.

Increased Exercise Can Restore Function to a Previously Deprived or Neglected Eye

In Chapter 7 we considered the misalignment of the two eyes (*lazy eye*), which can lead to the condition called **amblyopia**, in which acuity is poor in one eye even though the eye and retina are normal. If the two eyes are not aligned properly during the first few years of life, the primary visual cortex of the child tends to suppress the information that arrives from one eye to the cortex, and that eye becomes functionally blind. Studies of the development of vision in children and other animals also show that most cases of amblyopia are avoidable.

The balance of the eye muscles can be surgically adjusted to bring the two eyes into better alignment. Alternatively, if the weak eye is given regular practice, with the good eye covered, then vision can be preserved in both eyes. Attempts to alleviate amblyopia by training, however, have produced mixed results and a great deal of controversy. The treatment recommended most often is, beginning at as early an age as possible, giving the weak eye extensive training and experience while obstructing the good eye (American Academy of Ophthalmology, 1994). (Although we follow the usual practice in referring to the "good eye" and the "weak eye," the difference lies not in the eyes but in the higher visual centers to which they send their neural messages. Even in an eye deprived of experience of visual patterns, the retinal cells often have normal receptive fields.) Children with amblyopia often wear a patch or opaque contact lens over the good eye to force use of the weak eye.

Some investigators (e.g., Epelbaum et al., 1993) have concluded that only treatment during the first few years of life can be effective. Others report considerable improvement, even with adults, if they exercise the weak eye sufficiently and if the amblyopia is not too severe. One study reported considerable recovery from long-standing amblyopia when the good eye was lost or severely damaged (Romero-Apis et al., 1982). In all eight patients in this study, aged 16 to 69 at the time they lost the good eye, the vision in the amblyopic eye improved markedly, thus revealing plasticity of the adult brain.

A remarkable study by Chow and Stewart (1972) encouraged much subsequent work on rehabilitation, even in adult animals and people. Chow and Stewart studied kittens, depriving one or both eyes of pattern vision for about the first 20 months after birth—longer than the critical period for development of visual function (from about 3 to 12 weeks of age). When a unilaterally deprived kitten was then tested for pattern perception with the previously deprived eye, it showed almost no discrimination on formal tests and it was not able to guide its locomotion visually, although it performed well using its other eye.

NEURAL PLASTICITY

The investigators then undertook an intensive program of rehabilitation with some of the kittens. They "gentled" and petted these animals frequently to keep them working on the demanding program. Over time the kittens developed some pattern discrimination with the previously deprived eye, and they could use it to guide their locomotion.

Furthermore, recovery of vision was accompanied by morphological changes in the LGN. After monocular deprivation, the LGN cells that had received input from the deprived eye were about one-third smaller than those that had been stimulated by pattern vision. When the previously deprived eye was retrained, the difference in size of LGN cells disappeared. Electrical recording showed that retraining also increased the number of binocular cells (those that respond to stimulation of either eye) in the visual cortex, in comparison with kittens that were not retrained. Such animal research, as well as research with human patients, provides encouraging examples for programs of rehabilitation (Bach-y-Rita, 1992).

Most of us can expect our visual acuity to decline steadily, although not severely, after age 40. Recent research suggests that much of this decline is caused by changes in cortical visual pathways (Schmolesky et al., 2000). The investigators measured electrical responses of single neurons in primary visual cortex of young adult or old macaque monkeys. The neurons of the old monkeys showed increased spontaneous activity and decreased selectivity for orientation of stimuli, both of which may be caused by age-related degeneration of intracortical inhibition. Might visual exercise counteract these changes?

The evidence for continuing plasticity in the visual system is consistent with similar evidence from the somatosensory system, presented in Chapter 8, and from the auditory system, presented in Chapter 9. Evidence of plasticity in other parts of the adult nervous system will be presented in Chapter 18.

Summary

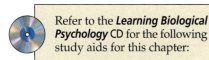

Refer to the *Learning Biological Psychology* CD for the following study aids for this chapter:

7	**Objectives**
68	**Study Questions**
1	**Activity**
3	**Animated Tutorials**

1. The perception of forms and the recognition of objects are complex accomplishments that require processing in many parts of the visual system.

2. The vertebrate eye is an elaborate structure that forms detailed and accurate optical images on the receptive cells of the retina.

3. Many different phyla have independently evolved photoreceptor organs; several have evolved eyes with lenses to focus light.

4. Visual-information processing begins in the retina, where cells that contain photopigments capture light and initiate neural activity. Two kinds of retinal receptor cells—rods and cones—represent the initial stages of two systems: the scotopic (dim light) and photopic (bright light) systems, respectively.

5. Each receptor reports only how strongly it has been excited, so at any given instant the visual nervous system receives an enormous array of quantitative information and has to determine what patterns in the outside world could have produced a particular set of "numbers." About one-fourth of the human neocortex is devoted to this computation.

6. Brain pathways of the visual system include the lateral geniculate nucleus in the thalamus, the primary visual cortex (striate cortex, or V1), and other cortical regions. Some axons of retinal ganglion cells extend to the superior colliculus in the midbrain.

7. Recordings from cells at successively higher levels in the visual system reveal that the receptive fields change in two main ways: (1) They become larger (occupy larger parts of the visual field), and (2) they require increasingly specific stimuli to evoke responses.

8. The cortex contains several visual areas, each presenting a topographic map of the visual field, but each somewhat specialized for processing one or more different aspects of visual information, such as form, color, or movement.

9. For the perception of visual patterns and forms, the stimulus pattern is analyzed at the primary visual cortex according to the orientation and spatial frequency of stimuli.

10. Like the somatosensory and auditory cortices, the primary visual cortex is organized in columns perpendicular to the surface. Columns, groups of columns, and slabs provide separate representations of the angular orientation of stimuli, of position in the visual field, of color, and of the two eyes.

11. In both cats and primates, parallel magnocellular and parvocellular projective systems from the retina to the brain mediate different aspects of visual projection, but these systems show increasing overlap in the cortical visual areas.

12. The ability to locate visual stimuli in space is aided by detailed spatial maps in some regions of the visual system.

13. The discrimination of hue in Old World primates and in humans depends on the existence of three different cone photopigments and on the fact that retinal connections yield four different kinds of spectrally opponent retinal ganglion cells.

14. Clinical evidence supports the concept of parallel processing because genetic anomalies or injury to the brain may impair some aspects of visual perception while leaving others intact. An example is the impaired ability to detect direction of motion after injury to area V5.

15. Selective attention involves extrastriate as well as striate visual areas.

16. The main pathways of the visual system appear to be determined genetically, but many aspects of the visual system develop in interaction with the environment and visual experience.

17. Attempts to treat amblyopia work best when retraining starts early in life, but success with some older patients demonstrates that the visual nervous system remains plastic even in adults.

Recommended Reading

Atkinson, J. (2000). *The developing visual brain.* Oxford, England: Oxford University Press.

De Valois, R. L., and De Valois, K. K. (1988). *Spatial vision.* New York: Oxford University Press.

Kaiser, P. K., and Boynton, R. M. (1996). *Human color vision.* Washington, DC: Optical Society of America.

Oyster, C. W. (1999). *The human eye: Structure and function.* Sunderland, MA: Sinauer.

Palmer, S. E. (1999). *Vision science: Photons to phenomenology.* Cambridge, MA: MIT Press.

Rodieck, R. W. (1998). *The first steps in seeing.* Sunderland, MA: Sinauer.

Wandell, B. A. (1995). *Foundations of vision.* Sunderland, MA: Sinauer

11

Motor Control and Plasticity

O ur emphasis shifts in this chapter to the motor system, allowing us to complete the circuit from sensory input to behavior. It is important to consider sensory and motor functions together. Just as we saw in Chapters 8 through 10 that motor activities are important for sensory and perceptual functions—movements of the fingers in active touch perception, sniffing in smell, and movements of the eyes and head in vision—so we will see in this chapter that sensory and perceptual processes set targets and goals for motor activities and help guide and correct our actions.

And just as our apparently effortless perception turns out to depend on intricate sensory mechanisms and perceptual processes, so too our apparently effortless adult motor abilities—such as reaching out and picking up an object, walking across the room, or even talking—require the development of complex muscular systems and their control and coordination by several parts and levels of the nervous system. Think, for example, of all the muscles involved when you say a single word. The tongue, larynx, throat, lips, chest, and diaphragm must work in a highly coordinated manner to produce even the simplest speech sound. And there is little room for error if you are to be understood.

Francesco Clemente, *Twins*, 1978, gouache, ink, and colored pencil on four sheets of paper, mounted on linen, 93" × 59" (236.2 × 149.9 cm)

What enables us to perform the movements and acts that make up our behavior? Any coordinated movement implies that there are underlying neural mechanisms for choosing the appropriate muscles and how they should act. These mechanisms require motoneurons to be activated in the proper order. Voluntary behavior adds another level of complexity: how the initial idea for a movement or act is translated into the selection of muscles. This process must involve at some places in the nervous system a plan for action—a motor plan. Furthermore, the motor system is plastic, changing some of its properties to meet new demands.

We begin our discussion by looking at movements and their coordination from different points of view—the behavioral view, the control systems view, and especially the neurobiological view.

The Behavioral View

Walking, crawling, swimming, and flying are some of the many ways to move from one place to another. Detailed analysis of different animals suggests some ideas about the underlying mechanisms of these behaviors. For example, the vigorous, regular beating of insect or bird wings suggests that the nervous system contains a rhythm generator, an oscillator. The varied gaits of four-legged animals suggest that different oscillators are coupled in precise but flexible ways to produce coordinated movement. The great versatility of learned movements in humans shows the range of complex adjustments made possible by the motor system.

Movements and Acts Can Be Classified into Categories

Sir Charles Sherrington
(1857–1957)

By the early nineteenth century, scientists knew that the dorsal roots of the spinal cord serve sensory functions and that the ventral roots contain motor fibers; connections between the two seemed to provide the basis for simple movements. In the late nineteenth and early twentieth centuries, British physiologist Charles Sherrington conducted extensive studies of spinal animals (animals in which the spinal cord has been disconnected from the brain). He showed that skin stimulation, such as pinching, provokes simple acts such as limb withdrawal. Many such observations led him to argue that the basic units of movement are **reflexes,** which he defined as simple, highly stereotyped, and unlearned responses to external stimuli.

Sherrington showed that the magnitude of a reflex is directly related to the intensity of the stimulus. His work ushered in an era of intensive attempts to identify the different reflexes and to chart their pathways in the nervous system, particularly in the spinal cord. Some reflexes involve only short pathways in the spinal cord linking dorsal and ventral roots; others involve longer loops connecting spinal cord segments to each other, or to brain regions.

Are reflexes the basic units of more complex movements and acts? Can every act be broken down into reflexes? The reflex perspective evoked criticism when it tried in a rather simple fashion to explain complex behaviors. For instance, Sherrington thought that complex acts were simply combinations of simpler reflexes strung out in a particular temporal order. The limitations of this perspective are apparent in attempts to analyze complex sequences of behavior, such as speech, in reflex terms. For example, explanations of speech in terms of reflexes hold that the movements and sounds associated with each element of speech provide the stimuli for the next element. If this were true, speech would be a series of stimulus–response units chained together, each response triggering the next.

On the contrary, it appears that the speaker has a plan in which several units (speech sounds and words) are placed in a larger pattern. Sometimes the units are misplaced, although the pattern is preserved: "Our queer old dean," said English clergyman William Spooner, when he meant, "Our dear old queen." Or "You hissed all my mystery lectures." (Spooner was so prone to mixing up the order of sounds in his sentences that this type of error is called a *spoonerism.*) Such mistakes reveal a plan: The speaker is anticipating a later sound and executing it too soon. A chain of reflexes would not be subject to such an error.

TABLE 11.1 *A Classification of Motor Behaviors*	
Category	**Examples**
MOVEMENTS	
Simple reflex pupillary contraction	Stretch, knee jerk, sneezing, startle, eye blink,
Posture and postural changes	Standing, rearing, lying, balancing, sitting, urination posture
Sensory orientation ear movement, tasting	Head turning, touching, eye fixation, sniffing,
ACTS	
Locomotion stalking, flying, hopping	Walking, creeping, running, crawling, swimming,
Species-typical action patterns	
Ingestion	Tasting, chewing, biting, sipping, drinking
Courtship display	Sniffing, chasing, retreating
Escape and defense	Hissing, spitting, submission posture, cowering
Grooming	Washing, preening, licking
Gestures	Grimacing, tail erection, squinting, tooth baring, smiling
Acquired skills	Speech, tool use, dressing, painting, sculpting, driving a car, skiing, dancing

The concept of a **motor plan,** or *motor program,* holds that complex movements and acts are controlled and produced by a set of commands to muscles that is completely established *before* an act occurs. Feedback from movements may inform the motor program about how the execution is unfolding. Examples of behaviors that exhibit this kind of internal plan for action range from skilled acts, such as piano playing, to a wide repertoire of simple escape behaviors of animals such as crayfish.

Table 11.1 gives a scheme for classifying movements and acts that focuses on their functional properties rather than on their exact muscle relations. We can use this table to distinguish between movements and acts. Simple reflexes include brief, unitary activities of muscle that we commonly call **movements.** These events are discrete, in many cases limited to a single part of the body, such as a limb. Listed in the bottom half of the table are complex, sequential behaviors, frequently oriented toward a goal. Different movements of several body parts might be included in such behaviors. These more complex events we distinguish as **acts,** or *action patterns.* Later in this chapter we will see that the regions of the nervous system that control movements are more restricted than those that control acts.

Movements and Acts Can Be Analyzed and Measured in a Variety of Ways

Movements and acts are readily visible in motion pictures, and high-speed photography provides an intimate portrait of even the most rapid events. To deal with the large amounts of data furnished by high-speed photography, methods of simplification or numerical analysis have been devised. Photographic techniques such as multiple exposures offer simple portraits of human movement. Computer graphic simulation techniques also provide striking examples of the representation of movements.

For example, sports trainers use detailed analyses of athletic acts based on time-lapse photographs or information derived from sensors attached at joints. Computer programs process digital photos to help quantify the performance, thereby enabling detailed measurement of the positions of different body parts in successive instants. Other devices record the direction, strength, and speed of motions. Figure 11.1 illustrates the paths of normal and impaired reaching movements, a kind of movment considered at several points in this chapter.

(a) Visually guided reaching task

These lights are not yet visible

To start a trial, subject places cursor (a glowing light) on center point.

Center point

← 10 cm →

Cursor

When a target light goes on (yellow), subject moves cursor rapidly to reach it. Cameras monitor and record movements of the glowing cursor.

(b) Examples of arm movements after 200 practice trials...

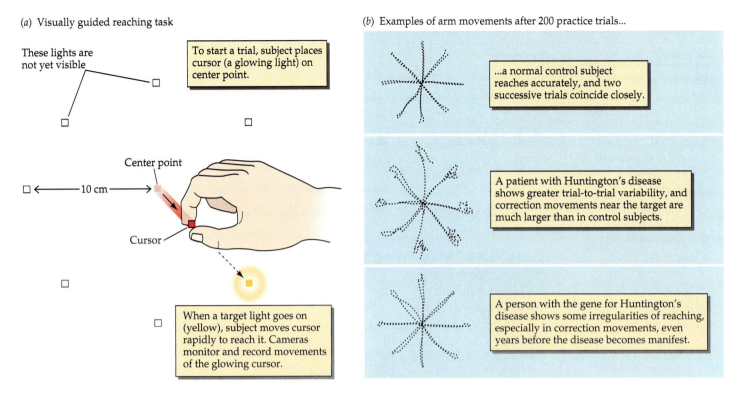

...a normal control subject reaches accurately, and two successive trials coincide closely.

A patient with Huntington's disease shows greater trial-to-trial variability, and correction movements near the target are much larger than in control subjects.

A person with the gene for Huntington's disease shows some irregularities of reaching, especially in correction movements, even years before the disease becomes manifest.

11.1 Measurement of Reaching Movements (a) An experimental setup to study reaching movements. (b) Recorded movement trajectories of normal subject (*top*), patient with Huntington's disease (*middle*), and a carrier of the gene for Huntington's disease (bottom). (Part *b* courtesy of Maurice R. Smith.)

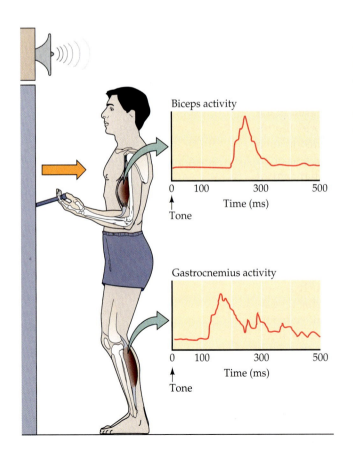

Biceps activity

0   100   300   500
          Time (ms)
↑
Tone

Gastrocnemius activity

0   100   300   500
          Time (ms)
↑
Tone

Another approach to the fine-grain analysis of movements is to record the electrical activity of muscles, a procedure called **electromyography** (**EMG**). Because the contraction of muscles involves electrical potentials generated by the muscle fibers, fine needle electrodes placed in a muscle, or electrodes placed on the skin over a muscle, provide electrical indications of muscle activity (Figure 11.2). If electrodes are placed over several different muscles, we get a record of the contraction of the muscles involved in an act, including the progressive buildup and decay of their activity. This technique is useful in diagnosing neuromuscular disorders. In Figure 11.2 the EMGs show that a postural response precedes the voluntary movement of the arm.

The Control Systems View

Engineering descriptions of the regulation and control of machines provide a useful way of looking at the mechanisms that regulate and control our movements. In designing machines, engineers commonly encounter two problems: (1) accuracy—how to prevent or minimize error; and (2) speed—how to accomplish a task quickly and efficiently. Two forms of control mechanisms—closed-loop and open-loop—are commonly employed to optimize performance according to these criteria.

11.2 Electromyography For these recordings made from biceps and gastrocnemius (calf) muscles, the subject was instructed to pull the handle as soon as a tone sounded. (After D. Purves et al., 2001.)

(a) Feedback control during driving

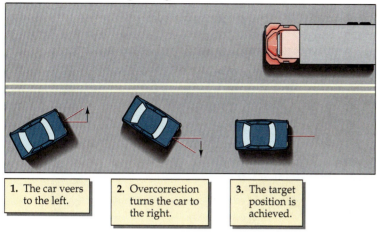

| **1.** The car veers to the left. | **2.** Overcorrection turns the car to the right. | **3.** The target position is achieved. |

(b) Schematic of closed-loop system

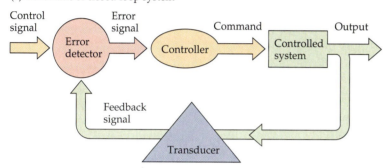

11.3 A Closed-Loop System (a) Auto driving provides an example of feedback control. (b) In the example in part a, the controlled system is the automobile. The input to the controlled system is the position of the steering wheel; the output is the position on the road. In any closed-loop system, the transducer is an element that measures output, and the error detector measures differences between actual output and desired output (control signal). In this example the transducer (the visual system), the error detector (the perceptual system), and the controller (the muscles) are all properties of the person driving the car. The driver compares the actual position of the car with its desired position on the road and makes corrections to minimize the discrepancy. Closed-loop systems emphasize accuracy and flexibility at the expense of speed.

In **closed-loop control mechanisms,** information flows from whatever is being controlled back to the device that controls it. The control of endocrine secretion, which we discussed in Chapter 5, is a closed-loop mechanism (see Figures 5.9 and 5.10). Driving a car provides a more complex example of a closed-loop system. In this case the variable being controlled is the position of an automobile on the road (Figure 11.3). Continuous information is provided by the driver's visual system, which guides corrections. Slow, sustained movements, sometimes called **ramp movements** (or *smooth movements*) are usually closed-loop in character, continuously guided by feedback.

The only way the car could stay on the road without feedback control (e.g., if you were driving with your eyes closed) would be with the aid of accurate memory of all the turns and bends in the road. But the car would not be able to deal with anything new, such as other moving cars. Such a memory system could be considered a form of open-loop control.

In **open-loop control mechanisms** there are no external forms of feedback; output is measured by a sensor, but the activity is preprogrammed. Open-loop controls are needed in systems that must respond so rapidly that no time is available for the delay of a feedback pathway. For example, once a baseball pitcher begins throwing a fastball, the pitch is completed no matter what sensory feedback is received. Such

BOX 11.1 *Movements and Acts Are Shaped and Modified by Learning*

We don't have to learn how to withdraw a hand from a hot stove, or how to breathe or swallow. These and many other acts are highly stereotyped, *involuntary* reflexes; no aspect of a person's attention changes their essential character. In contrast, we need explicit training to play tennis, use a keyboard, and perform many other acts. The characteristics of these acts are highly variable and frequently idiosyncratic, and they show considerable variability among individuals. These acts are commonly referred to as *voluntary* motor skills. How are such skills acquired? A comprehensive review of motor learning by Ivry (1993) notes that many variables affect skill acquisition or motor learning. This variability may account for why there are so many theoretical views in this field.

A simple example, in which a subject uses a joystick to move a cursor on a screen to follow a moving spot of light, helps focus on issues in motor learning. Large errors are evident in the initial trials; the subject is slow to change course and overshoots the path of the spot. On successive trials, the subject tracks the spot faster and with very few errors. What has happened during the acquisition of this motor skill? According to Paul Fitts (Fitts and Posner, 1967), a pioneer in the modern study of motor learning, there are three stages in skill acquisition:

1. *The cognitive stage.* Thoughts are developed about different features of the task and the effects of actions.

2. *The associative stage.* Trial-and-error solutions are attempted and successful strategies are defined.

3. *The automatic stage.* Acts are performed with little conscious recognition, and variability in performance is reduced. In this stage, behavior relies less on continuous feedback, and it has become more open-loop in character.

Another view is that skill acquisition involves the development of a **schema** for action—the formation of a

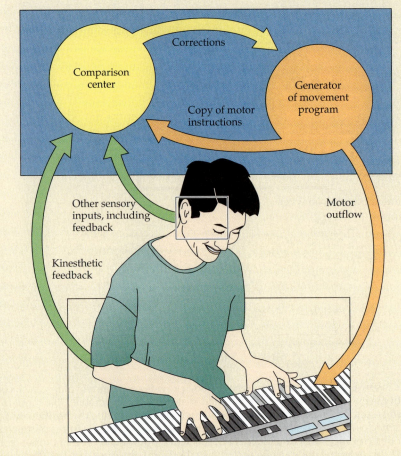

higher-level program. The performance of any skilled movement shows that several types of information are essential to the acquisition of a motor skill. One model of skill learning (Keele and Summers, 1976) posits that input to muscles is provided by a hypothetical movement program in the brain that directs the timing and force of neural outputs to muscles (the motor outflow). Feedback from receptors in joints, along with other modes of information about movements—visual or auditory—are matched to a model of skilled performance, as the figure shows.

Feedback information thus provides input about errors, which are gradually reduced. In some cases the need for monitoring the movement is eliminat-

ed; that is, Fitts's third stage is reached. At this stage in the learning of a skilled movement, the subject becomes unaware of the act; execution is automatic. Faster performance becomes possible because feedback control loops have less impact.

The brain may also be changed by such training. For example, investigators used MRI to measure the width of the precentral sulcus (the site of the primary motor area) in piano players and a control group. The sulcus was significantly wider in the musicians, especially in the hand representation, which was larger in the musicians who had started musical training at an early age; the younger the musician was at the start of musical training, the larger the sulcus was (Amunts et al., 1997).

open-loop movements are called **ballistic movements**. Because there is no feedback, open-loop systems need other ways to reduce error and variability. They must anticipate potential error. In living systems, prior learning may be the basis for accurate anticipation (Box 11.1).

The Neurobiological View

Neuroscientists have distinguished several different levels of hierarchically organized motor control systems:

- The *skeletal system* and the muscles attached to it determine which movements are possible.
- The *spinal cord* controls skeletal muscles in response to sensory information. In the simplest case, the response may be a reflex. The spinal cord also implements motor commands from the brain.
- The *brainstem* integrates motor commands from higher levels of the brain and transmits them to the spinal cord. It also relays sensory information about the body from the spinal cord to the forebrain.
- Some of the main commands for action are initiated in the *primary motor cortex*.
- The areas adjacent to primary motor cortex, *nonprimary motor cortex*, initiate another level of cortical processing.
- Other brain regions—the *cerebellum* and *basal ganglia*—modulate the activities of these hierarchically organized control systems.

We will examine each of these levels of control in more detail. This organizational scheme, outlined in Figure 11.4, will guide the discussion.

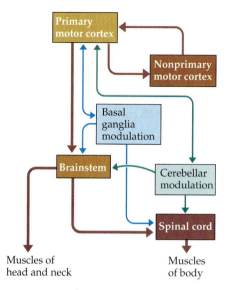

11.4 The Hierarchy of Movement Control   The primary motor cortex receives information from other cortical areas and sends commands to the brainstem, which passes commands to the spinal cord. Both the cerebellum and the basal ganglia adjust these commands.

The Skeletal System Enables Particular Movements and Precludes Others

Some properties of behavior arise from characteristics of the skeleton and muscles themselves. For example, the length, form, and weight of the limbs shape an animal's stride. The primary sites for bending are the joints, where bones meet. Figure 11.5 illustrates the human skeleton and shows examples of some joints and their

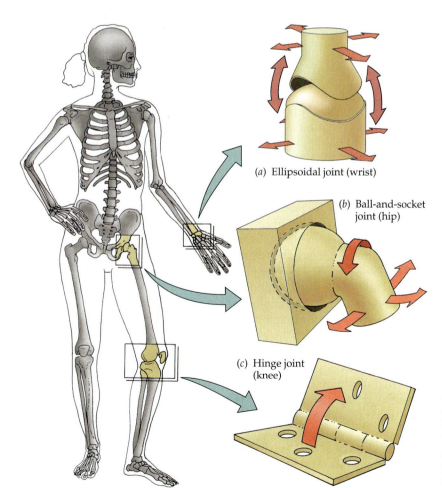

(*a*) Ellipsoidal joint (wrist)

(*b*) Ball-and-socket joint (hip)

(*c*) Hinge joint (knee)

11.5 Joints and Movements   Shown next to each joint is an enlarged mechanical model that indicates the kinds of movements the joint can perform. (*a*) The wrist joint moves in two principal planes: lateral and vertical. (*b*) The hip joint is a "universal" joint, moving in all three planes. (*c*) The knee joint has a single plane of motion.

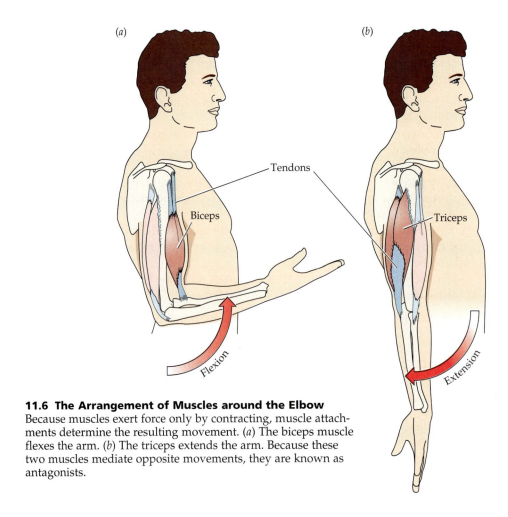

11.6 The Arrangement of Muscles around the Elbow
Because muscles exert force only by contracting, muscle attachments determine the resulting movement. (*a*) The biceps muscle flexes the arm. (*b*) The triceps extends the arm. Because these two muscles mediate opposite movements, they are known as antagonists.

possible movements. Some joints, such as the hip, are almost "universal" joints, permitting movement in many planes. Others, like the elbow or knee, are more limited and tolerate little deviation from the principal axis of rotation.

Muscles Control the Actions of the Skeletal System

Our bare skeleton must now be clothed with muscles. How a muscle attaches to bones is a direct indication of the movement it mediates. Muscles generate force only by contracting. Some muscles produce forces that maintain body posture; others produce movement around a joint. In contrast, some muscles do not act on the skeleton at all; examples include the muscles that move the eyes, lips, and tongue and those that contract the abdomen. Muscles have springlike properties that influence the timing of behavior and the forces that can be generated; the rate and force of muscular contractions limit some responses.

Muscles are connected to bone by **tendons.** Around a joint, different muscles are arranged in a reciprocal fashion: When one muscle group contracts (shortens), the other is extended; that is, the muscles are **antagonists** (Figure 11.6). Muscles that act together are said to be **synergists.** For example, four synergistic muscles act together to extend the leg at the knee. Three other antagonistic muscles flex the leg at the knee. Coordinated action around a joint may require one set of motoneurons to be excited while the antagonistic set of motoneurons is inhibited. The limb can be locked in position by co-contraction of the opposed muscles.

The molecular machinery of muscles. A muscle is composed of thousands of individual muscle fibers. Each muscle fiber is made up of many filaments of two kinds arranged in a regular manner (Figure 11.7). Bands of relatively thick filaments alternate with bands of thinner filaments, giving the fibers a striped appearance. The thick

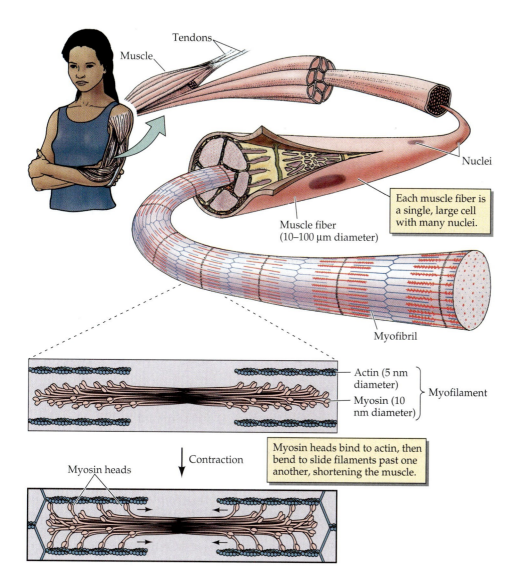

11.7 The Composition of Muscles and the Mechanism of Muscle Contraction Muscle fibers are shown here at progressively greater magnifications, from life size to 2 million times life size. The actions of myosin and actin cause muscle contraction.

Tendons

Muscle

Nuclei

Each muscle fiber is a single, large cell with many nuclei.

Muscle fiber (10–100 µm diameter)

Myofibril

Actin (5 nm diameter)

Myosin (10 nm diameter)

Myofilament

Myosin heads

Contraction

Myosin heads bind to actin, then bend to slide filaments past one another, shortening the muscle.

and thin filaments (made up of the complex proteins **myosin** and **actin,** respectively) always overlap. Contraction of the muscle increases the overlap: The filaments slide past each other, shortening the overall length of the muscle fiber (Figure 11.7).

Muscle types. Many of the muscles in your body, such as those in your stomach, are not under your direct control. Because of their appearance, these muscles are called **smooth muscle,** and because their contractions are regulated by the autonomic nervous system, we will not discuss them further. Rather, we will concern ourselves with a second class of muscle, called **striated muscles** (because they have a striped appearance), which are under voluntary control.

Because of the varying tasks they perform, different muscles require different speeds, precision, strength, and endurance. Matched to these requirements are at least two main types of striated muscle fibers: *fast* and *slow.* Eye movements, for example, must be quick and accurate so that we can follow moving objects and shift our gaze from one target to another. But fibers in the extraocular muscles do not have to maintain tension for long periods of time because some fibers relax while others contract. The extraocular muscles are therefore made up of **fast muscle fibers.** In leg muscles, fast fibers react promptly and strongly but fatigue rapidly; they are used mainly for activities in which muscle tension changes frequently, as in walking or running. Mixed in with the fast muscle fibers are **slow muscle fibers,** which are not as fast but have greater resistance to fatigue; they are used chiefly to maintain posture.

Neural Messages Reach Muscle Fibers at the Neuromuscular Junction

Once a motoneuron has integrated all the information bombarding it through hundreds or thousands of synapses (Figure 11.8*a*), it may produce an action potential. As the axon splits into many branches near the target muscle (Figure 11.8*b*), each branch carries an action potential to its terminal, which then (in vertebrates) releases the neurotransmitter **acetylcholine (ACh)**. Then all the muscle fibers innervated by that motoneuron respond to the ACh by producing action potentials of their own. The action potentials travel along each muscle fiber, permitting sodium (Na^+) and calcium (Ca^{2+}) ions to enter and then trigger the molecular changes that produce contraction.

The region where the motoneuron terminal and the adjoining muscle fiber meet—and produce distinctive structures for communication—is called the **neuromuscular junction (NMJ)** (Figure 11.8*c* and *d*). The NMJ is large and very effective: Almost every action potential that reaches an axon terminal releases enough ACh to cause a depolarization in the innervated muscle fiber that is large enough to produce another action potential. Thus every action potential in the motoneuron normally elicits a contraction in the postsynaptic fiber. In vertebrates, muscles can only be excited (by ACh), so the only way to prevent a muscle from contracting is to inhibit its motoneuron and prevent it from sending an action potential to the NMJ. Because it is large and accessible, the NMJ is a very well studied synapse, and much of what we know about synapses and synaptic plasticity was first established at the NMJ.

Even though the NMJ is a large and reliable synapse, its properties can change with use. All of us are familiar with muscle fatigue from extended use; some of the reduced responsiveness of the fatigued muscle is due to diminished effectiveness of neuromuscular junctions. Another well-known example of neural plasticity is **posttetanic potentiation.** When a rapid series of action potentials (a *tetanus*) is induced in a motor nerve, the NMJs are altered for a period so that subsequent single action potentials cause a stronger end-plate potential in the muscle. This potentiation is caused by a buildup of Ca^{2+} ions in the presynaptic terminal and therefore the release of more ACh. The study of several types of NMJ plasticity led to other studies of synaptic plasticity that may underlie learning, as will be discussed in Chapter 18.

Early in embryogenesis, young muscle fibers have ACh receptors along their entire length, so application of ACh anywhere along the fiber causes a response. But as the growing axon tip (the growth cone; see Figure 7.10) from a motoneuron contacts the fiber, ACh receptors migrate from other parts of the muscle fiber to cluster opposite the axon tip. (Remember that receptors and ion channels "float" in the fatty membrane of cells.) From this point on, the muscle fiber preferentially inserts additional ACh receptors beneath the motoneuron terminal at the newly formed NMJ. In adults, ACh receptors are densely packed, and so are molecules of AChE (acetylcholinesterase), so that muscle fibers can be activated repeatedly (J. R. Sanes and Lichtman, 1999).

Another interesting aspect of the development of the NMJ is that early in life, every muscle fiber is contacted by several motoneurons. During a postnatal period of **neuromuscular synapse elimination,** however, all motoneurons withdraw some of their terminal branches until every muscle fiber is innervated by only a single motoneuron. Researchers are studying how the motoneurons and muscle fibers eliminate just the right number of synapses to accomplish this task (C. L. Jordan et al., 1988; D. Purves, 1988). The net result is that each motoneuron has exclusive control of a pool of muscle fibers, enabling finely graded contractions of muscles.

The ratio of motor axons to muscle groups affects the precision of the control of movements. Fine neural control results when each axon connects to only a few muscle fibers. The **motor unit** consists of a single motor axon and all the muscle fibers it innervates (see Figure 11.8*b*). The **innervation ratio** is the ratio of motor axons to muscle fibers. High innervation ratios characterize muscles involved in fine movements, like those of the eye—one motoneuron for every three fibers (a 1:3 ratio).

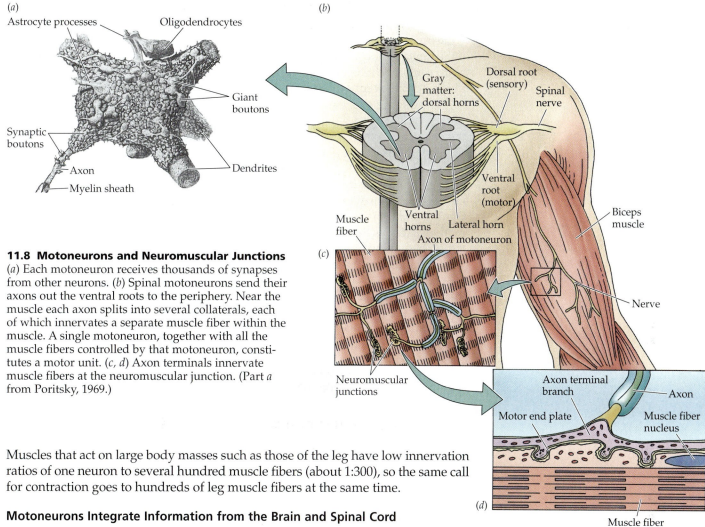

(a)
Astrocyte processes   Oligodendrocytes
Giant boutons
Synaptic boutons
Axon
Myelin sheath
Dendrites

(b)
Gray matter: dorsal horns   Dorsal root (sensory)   Spinal nerve
Muscle fiber   Ventral horns   Lateral horn   Axon of motoneuron   Ventral root (motor)   Biceps muscle

(c)
Nerve
Neuromuscular junctions

(d)
Axon terminal branch   Axon
Motor end plate   Muscle fiber nucleus
Muscle fiber

11.8 Motoneurons and Neuromuscular Junctions
(*a*) Each motoneuron receives thousands of synapses from other neurons. (*b*) Spinal motoneurons send their axons out the ventral roots to the periphery. Near the muscle each axon splits into several collaterals, each of which innervates a separate muscle fiber within the muscle. A single motoneuron, together with all the muscle fibers controlled by that motoneuron, constitutes a motor unit. (*c, d*) Axon terminals innervate muscle fibers at the neuromuscular junction. (Part *a* from Poritsky, 1969.)

Muscles that act on large body masses such as those of the leg have low innervation ratios of one neuron to several hundred muscle fibers (about 1:300), so the same call for contraction goes to hundreds of leg muscle fibers at the same time.

Motoneurons Integrate Information from the Brain and Spinal Cord

Muscles contract because motoneurons of the spinal cord and cranial nerve nuclei send action potentials along motor axons to muscles. These motoneurons are the **final common pathway** that links the activity of the rest of the spinal cord and brain to our many muscles. Because they respond to inputs from so many sources (see Figure 11.8*a*), motoneurons often have very widespread dendritic fields, and they are the largest cells in the spinal cord. Furthermore, motoneurons must respond to a tremendous variety of synaptic transmitters, both excitatory and inhibitory.

Motor cells of the spinal cord are not uniform in size or electrophysiological properties. Large motoneurons have axons of wide diameter and therefore conduct impulses faster. In general, small motoneurons innervate slow muscles and are more easily excited by synaptic currents; therefore they are activated before large motoneurons (Jones et al., 1994). Large motoneurons innervate fast muscles and tend to respond after small cells because, being large, they are less readily excited by synaptic currents. Their discharge characteristics are more phasic or abrupt.

In the 1960s Elwood Henneman (1991) found that muscle tension is increased by recruitment of increasing numbers of motor units in fixed order according to their size. Weak stimulation activates only small, low-threshold neurons for the slow muscle fibers defined earlier. Stronger stimulation excites larger, higher-threshold neurons that control fast muscle fibers. Evidence for the orderly recruitment of motor units has been found in a variety of voluntary and reflexive movements, and this systematic relationship is known as the **size principle.** It is similar to the principle of range fractionation for coding of sensory intensity that we discussed in Chapter 8 (see Figure 8.5).

Sensory Feedback from Muscles, Tendons, and Joints Monitors Movements

To produce rapid coordinated movements of the body, the integrative mechanisms of the brain and spinal cord must continuously gather information about the state of the muscles, the positions of the limbs, and the instructions being issued by the motor centers. This collecting of information about body movements and positions is called **proprioception** (from the Latin *proprius,* "own," and *recipere,* "to receive").

The sequence and intensity of muscle activation are monitored by sensory receptors, which report the state of muscles and joints to circuits that initiate and guide movements. Two major kinds of receptors are **muscle spindles,** which lie in parallel with the muscle fibers (Figure 11.9a and c), and **Golgi tendon organs,** which lie in series with muscles—one end attached to tendon, the other to muscle (Figure 11.9a and b). The mechanical sensitivities of the spindles and tendon organs differ. The stretching of a muscle, which occurs in most movements, activates especially the spindles and transiently the tendon organs. The shortening of a muscle during contraction activates the tendon organs because they lie in series with the muscle. Together these two kinds of receptors transmit to the central nervous system a range of information about muscle activities.

The muscle spindle. The **muscle spindle** of vertebrates is a complicated structure consisting of both afferent and efferent elements (see Figure 11.9c). The spindle gets its name from its shape: a sort of cylinder that is thicker in the middle and tapers at its two ends. The Latin for "spindle," *fusus,* is used to form adjectives referring to the muscle spindle; thus the small muscle fibers *within* each spindle are called **intrafusal fibers,** and the ordinary muscle fibers that lie *outside* the spindles are called **extrafusal fibers.**

The muscle spindle contains two kinds of receptor endings: **primary sensory endings** (also called *annulospiral endings*) and **secondary sensory endings** (also called *flower spray endings*). These endings are related to different parts of the spindle (see Figure 11.9c). The primary ending wraps in a spiral fashion around a region called the *nuclear bag* (the central region of the intrafusal fiber). The secondary endings terminate toward the thin ends of the spindle.

How do these elements become excited? Suppose a muscle is stretched, as when a load is placed on it. For example, if you were trying to hold your arm straight out in front of you, palm up, and someone put a book in your hand, that would put an additional load on your biceps. Your arm would move down transiently, stretching the biceps muscle. The muscle spindle would also stretch, and the resulting deformation of the endings on the spindle would trigger nerve impulses in the afferent fibers. These afferents would inform the spinal cord, and the spinal cord would then inform the brain about the muscle stretch and therefore about the load imposed (see Figure 11.9d).

Two important factors affect the stretch of the muscle. One is the *rate of change* of muscle length. In our example the rate of change is jointly a function of the weight of the load and the rate at which the load is applied. The second factor is the *force* you must continually exert with the muscle to prevent dropping the load. In our example this force is a function only of the weight of the book.

The different receptor elements of the muscle spindle are differentially sensitive to these two features of muscle length changes. The primary (central) endings show a maximum discharge early in stretch and then adapt to a lower discharge rate. In contrast, the secondary (distal) endings are maximally sensitive to maintained length and are slow to change their rate during the early phase of stretch. Because of this differential sensitivity, the primary endings are called *dynamic* and the secondary endings are called *static* indicators of muscle length. This distinction arises from the difference in how these receptors are embedded in the spindle rather than from a difference in the nerve fibers themselves.

Regulation of muscle spindle sensitivity. Muscle spindles not only help maintain posture; they also coordinate movement. Spindles are informed of planned and ongoing actions through innervation by special motoneurons that alter the tension

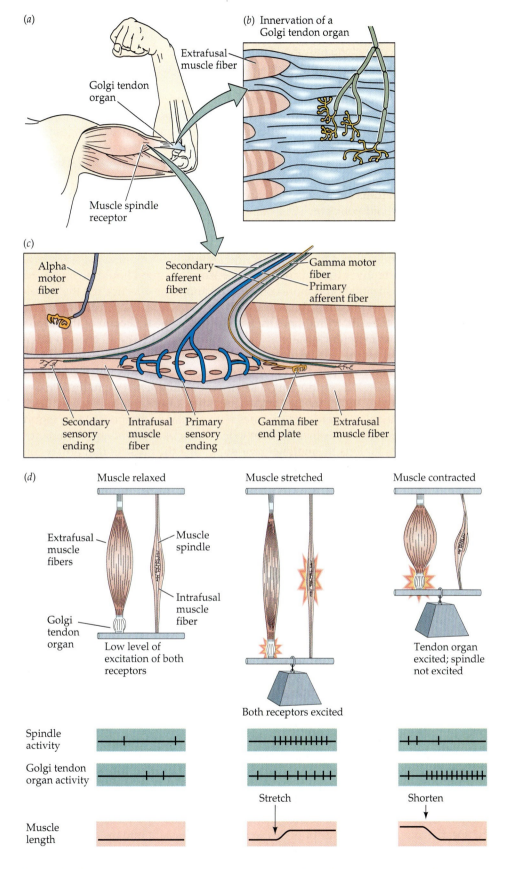

(a)

(b) Innervation of a Golgi tendon organ

Extrafusal muscle fiber

Golgi tendon organ

Muscle spindle receptor

(c)

Alpha motor fiber

Secondary afferent fiber

Gamma motor fiber

Primary afferent fiber

Secondary sensory ending

Intrafusal muscle fiber

Primary sensory ending

Gamma fiber end plate

Extrafusal muscle fiber

(d) Muscle relaxed — Muscle stretched — Muscle contracted

Extrafusal muscle fibers

Muscle spindle

Intrafusal muscle fiber

Golgi tendon organ

Low level of excitation of both receptors

Both receptors excited

Tendon organ excited; spindle not excited

Spindle activity

Golgi tendon organ activity

Stretch

Shorten

Muscle length

11.9 Muscle Receptors (*a*) The receptors in the body of the muscle are muscle spindles; those in the tendons are Golgi tendon organs. (*b*) This sensory ending is typical of a Golgi tendon organ. (*c*) A typical muscle spindle has two types of receptor endings: primary and secondary. Gamma motor fibers control a contractile portion of the spindle. (*d*) When a load is imposed on the muscle, muscle receptors are excited as shown here.

within the spindle and thus control the sensitivity of its receptors. These motoneurons are called **gamma efferents,** or *gamma motoneurons,* to distinguish them from the faster-conducting **alpha motoneurons,** which go to extrafusal muscle fibers (see Figure 11.9c). The cell bodies of gamma efferents are found in the ventral horns of the spinal cord.

The gamma efferent axon fibers connect to a contractile region of the spindle (called the *myotube region*). The activity in the gamma fibers causes a change in the length and tension of the spindle, which modifies its sensitivity to changes in the length of adjacent extrafusal muscle fibers. Hence the number of impulses elicited in the spindle afferents is a function of two factors: (1) muscle stretch and (2) the resting tension in the muscle spindle.

How do the gamma efferents help coordinate movements? Suppose that instead of continuing to hold your arm out straight ahead, you move your forearm up and down. If the muscle spindle had only one fixed degree of internal tension, it would not be able to help monitor and coordinate this movement. As the forearm moves up, both the extrafusal and the intrafusal fibers shorten. Shortening the spindle, as we have noted, removes the tension, so the sensory endings should no longer respond. But the real situation is more complicated and more effective. As the muscle shortens, the gamma efferents must correspondingly increase the tension on the intrafusal fibers if they are to maintain their sensitivity. One reflection of the importance of the gamma efferent system is the fact that about 30% of all efferent fibers are gamma efferents (the rest are alpha motoneurons).

The muscle spindles respond primarily to *stretch;* the other receptors that respond to muscle tension—Golgi tendon organs—are especially sensitive to muscle *contraction,* or shortening. **Golgi tendon organs** are rather insensitive to passive muscle stretch because they are connected in series with an elastic component (see Figure 11.9d). They detect overloads that threaten to tear muscles and tendons. Stimulation of these receptors inhibits the motoneurons supplying the muscles that pull on the tendon and thus, by relaxing the tension, prevents mechanical damage.

Classic studies in physiology emphasized the importance of these receptors for movement. Mott (1895) and Sherrington (1898) showed that after they cut the afferent fibers from muscles, monkeys failed to use the deafferented limb, even if the efferent connections from motoneurons to muscles were preserved. The deafferented limb is not paralyzed, since it can be activated (the motoneurons still innervate the muscles), but lack of information from the muscle leads to relative disuse. Monkeys can learn to flex a deafferented limb in response to a visual signal to avoid a shock to the body, even though during free behavior the arm looks paralyzed.

Although deafferenting one forearm leads to apparent paralysis of that limb, the result is quite different if both forearms are deafferented. In the latter case the monkey recovers coordinated use of its forearms over a few months (Taub, 1976). When one limb is deafferented, the monkey makes do with the other, but when *both* are deafferented, the monkey has to learn to use them and is able to do so. Even if only one arm is deafferented, forced use of it can lead to the return of coordinated use of the two arms.

This effect was shown in experiments in which the hand of the intact limb was placed inside a ball, which prevented the monkey from grasping objects with the hand but allowed finger movements and thus prevented atrophy. Slowly the deafferented limb gained dexterity, and over several weeks fine movements returned. After several months the ball on the intact hand was removed, and the monkey made coordinated movements of both limbs. However, if the forced usage lasted less than 4 months, movements of the deafferented limb subsequently regressed rapidly.

Deafferentation in humans provides some striking insight into the significance of sensory feedback. One patient suffered loss of sensory input from muscles, joints, and skin, but his motor functions were spared (Marsden et al., 1984). He engaged in a wide range of manual activities, including repetitive alternating hand movements and some grasping movements. A striking example of preserved motor skills was his ability to drive his manual-transmission car. In contrast, fine movements of the fingers, such as writing or fastening buttons, were drastically impaired. In addition,

**CLINICAL
ISSUE**

acquiring new movements of the hand was quite difficult. For example, after buying a new car, the patient found he was unable to acquire the arm movements necessary to drive it and had to revert to his old car. Thus sensory feedback is an important ingredient in skilled performance and in motor learning.

People who lose their proprioceptive sense can sometimes compensate by using other sensory modalities for feedback. For example, two deafferented patients were found to rely heavily on visual feedback for walking and picking up objects (Nougier et al., 1996). In fact, there may be channels of visual information to the motor system of which we are unaware. One patient with damage to the visual cortex could not report whether a slot was vertical or horizontal, yet when she was asked to insert a card in the slot, she consistently rotated her hand to put the card in smoothly. Similar experiments suggest that even neurologically intact people sometimes use visual cues of which they are unaware to guide their movements (Goodale and Haffenden, 1998).

Movements Are Controlled at Several Nervous System Levels

The nerve cells directly responsible for excitation of muscle are the motoneurons in the ventral region of the spinal cord and in the brainstem nuclei of several cranial nerves. (See Figures 2.8 and 2.9 for the anatomy of the cranial nerves and spinal cord.) Firing patterns of these cells determine the onset, coordination, and termination of muscle activity. To understand the physiology of movement, we need to know the source of the inputs to motoneurons. A variety of influences converge on the motoneurons. Some arise solely at the spinal level from muscle afferents and the intrinsic circuitry of the spinal cord. Other influences are directed to motor cells from several brain pathways. This is another reason that spinal and cranial motoneurons are called the *final common pathway*.

Spinal Reflexes Mediate "Automatic" Responses

One way to study spinal mechanisms is to sever the connections between the brain and the spinal cord (producing a spinal animal) and then observe the forms of behavior that can be elicited below the level of the cut. (All voluntary movements that depend on brain mechanisms are lost, of course, as is sensation from the regions below the cut.) Immediately after the cord is severed, there is an interval of decreased synaptic excitability in spinal cord neurons because they are isolated from brain communication. This condition is known as **spinal shock.** The period may last for months in humans, although for cats and dogs it may last only a few hours. During this period no reflexes mediated by the spinal cord can be elicited by either skin stimulation or excitation of muscle afferents.

As spinal shock fades, various kinds of reflexes can be elicited; their properties help us understand the basic functional organization of the spinal cord. The spinal animal can show various stretch reflexes that may function well enough to support its weight standing for brief periods. Stimulation of the skin of a spinal animal can also elicit reflex effects, which can be readily demonstrated in a spinal cat or dog by intense stimulation of the toe pad. This stimulation results in abrupt withdrawal of the stimulated limb, a response called the **flexion reflex** that is controlled by a multisynaptic pathway within the spinal cord. Other reflexive behaviors evident in the spinal animal include bladder emptying and penile erection. Thus some very basic properties of movement are "wired in" to the organization of the spinal cord itself and do not require the brain.

The behavior of the spinal animal also reveals the presence of pattern generator circuits in the spinal cord, which we'll describe later in this chapter. For example, mechanical stimulation of the feet or electrical stimulation of the spinal cord can elicit rhythmic movements of the legs. If the cut is high on the spinal cord, the alternating movements of the limbs are coordinated as in walking; this coordination indicates that the pattern generators for the different limbs are linked within the spinal cord (P. Grillner et al., 1991).

The stretch reflex. A good example of automatic control at the spinal level is the **stretch reflex**—the contraction that results when a muscle stretches. The physiological condition for muscle stretch can be readily understood under conditions of an imposed weight or load. For example, in Figure 11.10 a weight added to the hand imposes sudden stretch on muscle 1 (M_1). The circuit that keeps us from dropping the load is one that links muscle spindles and the relevant muscles. The simplest depiction of the events portrayed in Figure 11.10 is the following (steps 1 to 3 we saw already in Figure 11.9*d*, which described the activity of the muscle spindle):

1. A disturbance is imposed.
2. The muscle is stretched.
3. Afferent elements of the muscle spindle are excited.
4. The spindle afferents connect directly—that is, monosynaptically—to the motoneurons that control the stretched muscle, exciting them.
5. The motoneurons stimulate the muscle to oppose muscle stretch.

This sequence describes a simple negative feedback system that tends to restore the limb to its "desired" position. Activation of the muscle spindle also inhibits the motoneurons that supply the antagonistic muscle (M_2). Two synapses are required to inhibit the antagonistic motoneuron. Thus in the situation illustrated in Figure 11.10, spindle information terminates on the interneuron, which inhibits the motoneuron that supplies M_2. During this action the spindle excites the stretched muscle (and its synergists) and inhibits the antagonistic muscles. The relaxation of antagonistic muscles ensures that they are not injured by the sudden movement. A familiar example of the stretch reflex is the knee jerk used in medical examinations to test the integrity of the neural circuit just described (see Figure 3.16).

Spinal reflexes do not usually function in isolation. They are integrated and modulated by the activity of brain circuits. Control of movements involves **selective potentiation** of spinal neural circuits; that is, the activity of certain spinal circuits is enhanced by the brain, while the activity of other spinal circuits is inhibited.

Pathways from the Brain Control Different Aspects of Movements

There are many pathways from the brain to cranial and spinal motoneurons (Figure 11.11). Some pathways deliver discrete information; for example, the vestibulospinal

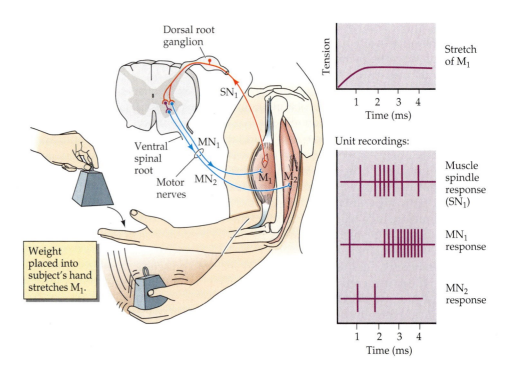

11.10 The Stretch Reflex Circuit
MN_1 is the motor nerve to muscle 1 (M_1); MN_2 is the motor nerve to muscle 2 (M_2), an antagonist to muscle 1. SN_1 is the sensory nerve from the muscle spindle of M_1. Characteristic responses at different stages in the circuit are shown at right.

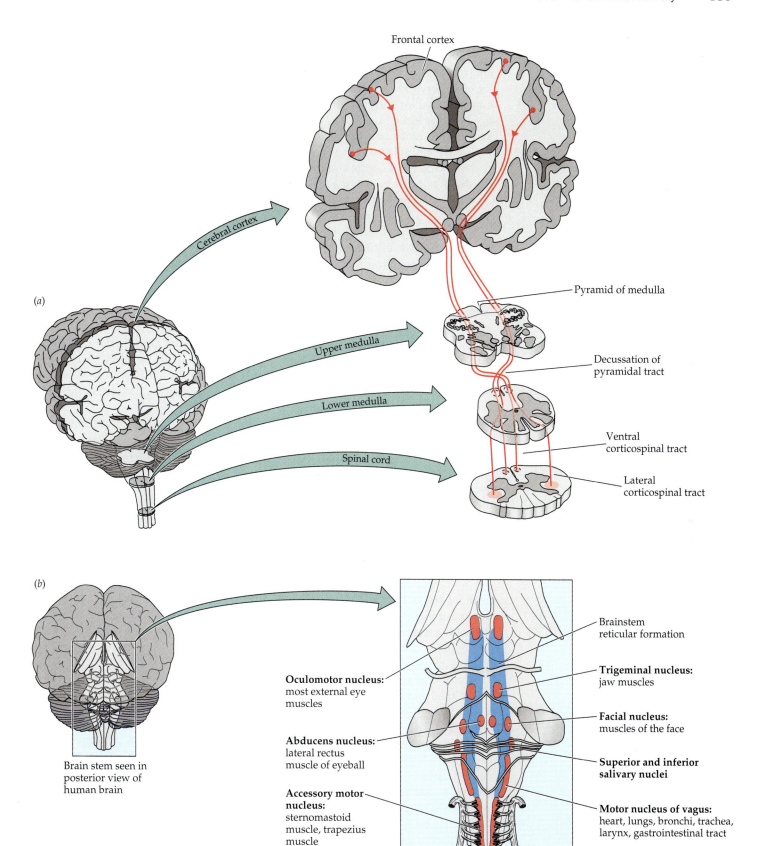

Frontal cortex

Cerebral cortex

Upper medulla

Lower medulla

Spinal cord

Pyramid of medulla

Decussation of pyramidal tract

Ventral corticospinal tract

Lateral corticospinal tract

(a)

(b)

Brain stem seen in posterior view of human brain

Oculomotor nucleus: most external eye muscles

Abducens nucleus: lateral rectus muscle of eyeball

Accessory motor nucleus: sternomastoid muscle, trapezius muscle

Brainstem reticular formation

Trigeminal nucleus: jaw muscles

Facial nucleus: muscles of the face

Superior and inferior salivary nuclei

Motor nucleus of vagus: heart, lungs, bronchi, trachea, larynx, gastrointestinal tract

11.11 The Pyramidal System (*a*) In the pyramidal (or corticospinal) motor system, most of the fibers cross to the opposite side in the medulla (at the decussation of the pyramidal tract) and descend the spinal cord in the lateral corticospinal tract. (*b*) The pyramidal system passes through some motor nuclei in the brainstem, shown here from the rear along with the reticular formation. The cranial nerves corresponding to these muscles are shown in Figure 2.8.

tract (see Figure 11.12) provides important information about head position, and this information influences postural muscles to adjust the body. Ideas about the different roles of each pathway in integrating and controlling movement have relied heavily on observations of changes in posture and locomotion produced by natural or experimental interferences in the brain. Clinical data from people with brain damage have generated useful anatomical and functional distinctions between two major divisions of the motor system: the pyramidal and extrapyramidal motor systems.

The **pyramidal system** (or **corticospinal system**) consists of neuron cell bodies within the cerebral cortex and their axons, which pass through the brainstem, forming the pyramidal tract to the spinal cord (see Figure 11.11*a*). Many of these cell bodies are located in the **primary motor cortex** (**M1**), the cortical region just anterior to the central sulcus (see Figure 11.13*a*). M1 can be distinguished from the adjacent *premotor* areas both cytoarchitectonically and by the lower intensity of electrical stimulation needed to elicit movements. Many of the axons of the pyramidal tract originate from large pyramidal neurons (called Betz cells) in layer V of M1.

The pyramidal tract is most clearly seen where it passes through the anterior aspect of the medulla. In a cross section of the medulla, the tract is a wedge-shaped anterior protuberance (pyramid) on each side of the midline. In the medulla the pyramidal tract from the right hemisphere crosses the midline to innervate the left spinal cord. The pyramidal tract consists of large-diameter (and therefore fast-conducting) axons and is a relatively recent development in evolution. It has been likened to a superhighway pushed through after the network of local routes has been established. Lesions of the pyramidal system deprive the patient of the ability to move individual joints and limbs.

In addition to the corticospinal outflow through the pyramidal tract, many other motor tracts run from the forebrain to the brainstem and spinal cord. Because these tracts are outside of the pyramids of the medulla, they and their connections are called the **extrapyramidal system** (Figure 11.12). In general, lesions of the extrapyramidal system do not prevent movement of individual joints and limbs, but they do interfere with spinal reflexes, usually exaggerating them.

Information flows from the extrapyramidal system to the spinal cord through two principal pathways: the reticulospinal and rubrospinal tracts. The extensive pool of interconnected neurons called the **reticular formation** modulates various aspects of movements. Some zones of the reticular formation facilitate movements; other zones are inhibitory. These effects are transmitted in descending tracts known as **reticulospinal tracts** that arise from the reticular formation and connect to spinal interneurons, where they influence the excitability of spinal motor circuitry. Some neurons of the reticular formation also help regulate the activation of muscles responsible for breathing. The second extrapyramidal outflow originates from the midbrain's **red nucleus** and so is called the **rubrospinal tract** (the Latin *ruber* means "red").

Also found in the brainstem are cranial motor nuclei whose axons innervate muscles of the head and neck (see Figures 11.11*b* and 2.9).

Primary Motor Cortex Is an Executive Motor Control Mechanism—and More

Initial information about sites of motor control came from the study of brain injuries. In humans, brain injuries involving the primary motor cortex (M1) produce partial paralysis on the side of the body opposite the brain lesion. This disturbance is greatest in distal muscles, such as those of the hand. Humans with these lesions are generally disinclined to use the affected limb.

Because human lesions arise from accidental injury or disease, they are usually not limited to a single neural system. The symptoms of corticospinal injury and the complexity of the observed changes may arise in part from loss of adjacent motor control systems. In other primates, experimental lesions restricted to the pyramidal tracts produce changes similar to those seen in humans, although the overall picture is less severe. Six weeks after bilateral interruption of the pyramidal tracts, monkeys can run, climb, and reach accurately for food. The persistent deficits they display are a limited ability to move individual fingers and an overall tendency for slower-than-

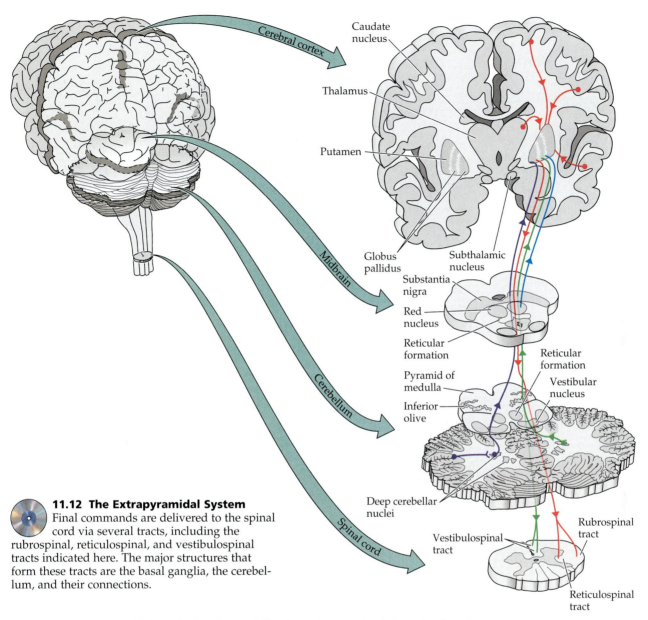

11.12 The Extrapyramidal System
Final commands are delivered to the spinal cord via several tracts, including the rubrospinal, reticulospinal, and vestibulospinal tracts indicated here. The major structures that form these tracts are the basal ganglia, the cerebellum, and their connections.

normal movements. Although they have difficulty releasing food from the hand, they can readily release their grip while climbing. In mammals other than primates, the impairments following pyramidal lesions are even less severe.

In the late nineteenth century, several experimenters showed that electrical stimulation of some regions of the cerebral cortex could elicit body movements, particularly flexion of the limbs. These and later findings helped scientists develop maps of movements elicited by cortical stimulation. Figure 11.13*b* shows a map of human primary motor cortex. The largest motor regions in these maps are devoted to the body parts involved in the most elaborate and complex movements in any species. For example, humans and other primates have extremely large cortical fields concerned with hand movements. "Colonies" of cells are related to particular muscle groups, and they form vertical columns in the cortex (Ghez et al., 1991)—an organizational principle similar to that of cortical sensory systems (see Chapter 10).

Maps like the one in Figure 11.13*b* gave rise to the idea that the primary motor cortex is like a piano keyboard, with each strip of neurons representing a particular muscle. Further research showed that this idea is wrong in two respects: (1) Although the centers of representation of body parts are separated in orderly fashion, the detailed sites that activate each body part are widely distributed, multiple, and overlapping. That is, the subregional organization of M1 is distributed, and each M1

COMPETING HYPOTHESES

(a) Lateral view of brain showing location of primary motor cortex

(b) Representation of the body in primary motor cortex

(c) Motor homunculus

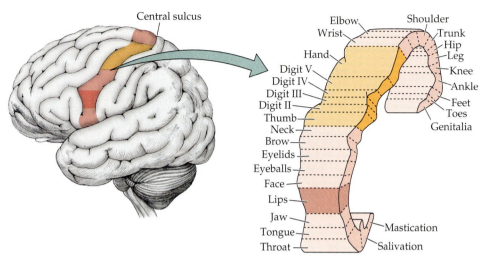

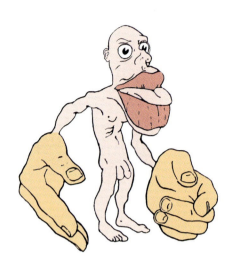

11.13 Human Primary Motor Cortex (a) This lateral view of the human brain shows the location of primary motor cortex (M1). (b) Regions controlling motor responses of different parts of the body are shown here in relative sequence and size. (c) The proportions of this homunculus show the relative sizes of motor representations of parts of the body.

neuron influences many muscles. (2) The strengths of connections between M1 neurons and muscles can change, as we will see a little later in this chapter.

Single muscles are actually represented multiple times over a wide region of the motor cortex (about 2–3 mm in primates) in a complex, mosaic fashion. Horizontal connections within the motor cortex create ensembles of neurons that coordinate the activity of muscles that generate movements. About one-third of human pyramidal tract fibers originate in the so-called motor area of the cortex. Another one-fifth come from the postcentral gyrus (somatosensory cortex). The remaining pyramidal fibers arise from many other cortical regions. Thus control of motor function is dispersed among cortical areas, leading to controversies about the boundaries of the primary motor cortex (Rothwell, 1994).

The motor cortex–pyramidal tract system may be the executive mechanism for voluntary movements. According to this view, the motor cortex represents particular kinds of movement, especially fine movements of the limbs, and the activation of these cells commands the excitation of relevant spinal and cranial motoneurons. In primates the pyramidal tract has some monosynaptic connections with spinal motoneurons, but most pyramidal tract neurons influence spinal motoneurons through polysynaptic routes and share control of these motor cells with other descending influences.

Apostolos Georgopoulos has focused on the properties of populations of motor cortex neurons (Georgopoulos et al., 1993). He recorded from M1 neurons of monkeys that were trained to make free arm movements in eight possible target directions (Figure 11.14a). Many cells changed their firing rates according to the direction of the movement, and for any one cell, discharge rates were highest in one particular direction (Figure 11.14b). Although different cells prefer different directions, each cell carries only partial information about the direction of reaching. When the activity of several hundred neurons is combined, the overall vector shows a good relation to the actual direction of the reaching arm. Given the millions of neurons in this region, a larger sampling would presumably provide an even more accurate prediction (Georgopoulos et al., 1993).

A long-standing controversy has raged over whether muscles or movements are represented in M1. That is, does activity of a cortical motor neuron encode a rela-

Apostolos Georgopoulos

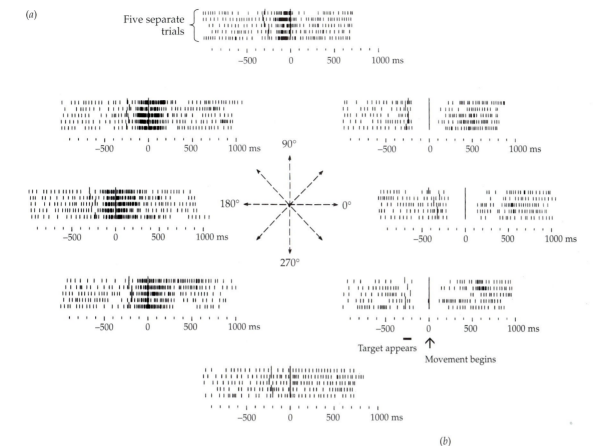

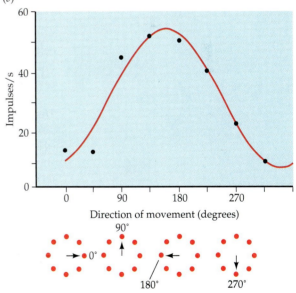

11.14 Directional Tuning of Motor Cortex Cells (*a*) Shown here is the activity of a single neuron during arm movement toward a target in eight different directions. Each horizontal record in the eight blocks of data represents one of five trials. Note that this cell consistently fires before the arm moves in the direction from 90° to 180° to 270°, and it is silent before movements in the other directions. (*b*) The average frequency of discharge during the interval before movement in the various directions. (From Georgopoulos et al., 1982.)

tively simple parameter such as force of contraction of a muscle or a more abstract parameter such as the path of the hand through space? To address this controversy, experimenters trained a monkey to perform rapid tracking movements of the wrist to obtain liquid rewards (Kakei et al., 1999). As shown in Figure 11.15, the animal grasped a handle that could be rotated along the two axes of wrist motion: flexion–extension and radial–ulnar deviation. Movement of the handle controlled the position of a cursor on a computer screen.

At the start of a trial, the forearm and hand were placed in one of three positions: pronated (palm down), supinated (palm up), or midway between these two positions. The monkey moved the cursor to a target in the center of the circle; then after 0.75 to 1.5 s, a second target appeared on the periphery of the circle. As soon as the central target disappeared, the monkey had to move the cursor rapidly to the new target. After much training over 8 years, the monkey performed well.

The experimenters then recorded activity of single cells in M1 as the monkey performed from different starting positions. A substantial group of M1 neurons (28 of 88, or 32%) displayed changes in activity that corresponded to muscle movements, but an even larger group of neurons (44 of 88, 50%) showed activity that corresponded to movement in space, regardless of hand posture. In other words, these

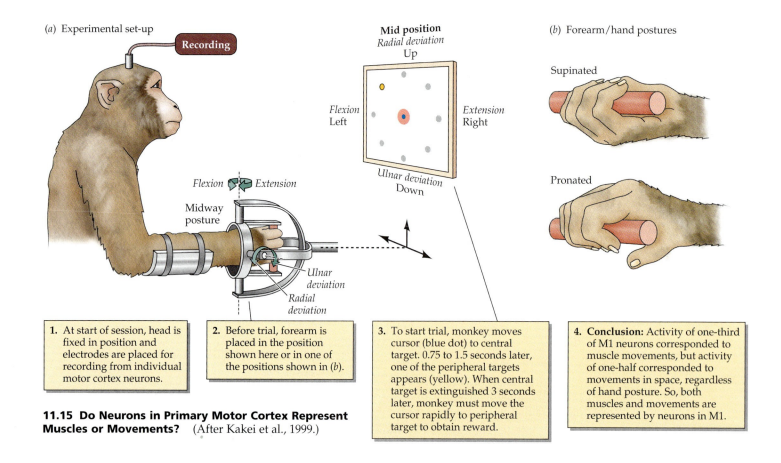

(*a*) Experimental set-up

Recording

Flexion ⟷ *Extension*

Midway posture

Ulnar deviation
Radial deviation

Mid position
Radial deviation
Up

Flexion
Left

Extension
Right

Ulnar deviation
Down

(*b*) Forearm/hand postures

Supinated

Pronated

1. At start of session, head is fixed in position and electrodes are placed for recording from individual motor cortex neurons.

2. Before trial, forearm is placed in the position shown here or in one of the positions shown in (*b*).

3. To start trial, monkey moves cursor (blue dot) to central target. 0.75 to 1.5 seconds later, one of the peripheral targets appears (yellow). When central target is extinguished 3 seconds later, monkey must move the cursor rapidly to peripheral target to obtain reward.

4. **Conclusion:** Activity of one-third of M1 neurons corresponded to muscle movements, but activity of one-half corresponded to movements in space, regardless of hand posture. So, both muscles and movements are represented by neurons in M1.

11.15 Do Neurons in Primary Motor Cortex Represent Muscles or Movements?   (After Kakei et al., 1999.)

cells were active whenever the monkey moved its hand in a particular *direction*, no matter which muscles it needed to use to accomplish that movement. Thus both muscles and movements appear to be strongly represented in M1.

The role of primary motor cortex in learning.   Several recent studies with both experimental animals and humans have demonstrated that motor representations in M1 change as a result of training. Maps prepared from electrical stimulation in M1 show changes in relation to acquisition of new skills—a visually guided tracking movement with the arm (J. N. Sanes and Donoghue, 2000) or a precision grasping task (Nudo et al., 1996) in monkeys, or a skilled reaching movement in rats (Kleim et al., 1998).

Focal **transcranial magnetic stimulation** (**TMS**) uses coils of wire placed near the head to induce a brief magnetic field that can stimulate neurons in the brain, beneath the skin and skull. TMS was used in human volunteers to evoke isolated thumb movements in a particular direction. Then the subjects practiced moving the thumb in a different direction for 15 to 30 minutes. The same TMS was then found to evoke thumb movement in the *new* direction for several minutes before the response reverted to the original direction (Classen et al., 1998). (This rapid change seems similar to the retuning of auditory cortical receptors during stimulation at another frequency, as noted in Chapter 9.)

NEURAL PLASTICITY

The role of primary motor cortex in encoding serial order.   Many kinds of behavior must be done in the correct temporal sequence to be effective; examples include dressing, eating, reading, and social interactions. How and where serial order is encoded in the nervous system has been a mystery. Now it appears that neurons in M1 can recognize the sequence of events in time, at least as a prelude to movement (Carpenter et al., 1999).

Monkeys were trained to hold a cursor on a central target and watch while three to five yellow spots appeared successively, 0.4 s apart, in any of eight positions around a peripheral circle. Then one of the spots, but not the last, would turn blue, and the monkey had to move the cursor to the spot that had appeared right after the blue spot. Not surprisingly, the activity of many M1 cells was related to the direction of the motor response, but some M1 cells also responded in terms of the serial position or location of the stimuli. And some cells showed a serial position effect in the absence of a motor directional effect. The influence of serial order on activity of M1 cells was at least as strong as the influence of direction of motor movement, challenging the view that M1 cortex is simply motor in function.

Nonprimary Motor Cortex Aids Motor Sequencing

Recordings of single nonprimary motor cortex neurons in awake monkeys have shown that many nerve cells in nonprimary motor cortex change their discharge rate just before the onset of conditioned movements, such as pressing a key in response to a sensory stimulus. Some nerve cells in these regions also respond to a sensory stimulus without evidence of elicited movement (S. P. Wise and Strick, 1984). Such data suggest that these regions are involved in the sensory guidance of movements, or that they represent higher-level intentions for movement. Favoring the latter hypothesis is the fact that nonprimary motor cortical areas are especially active during the preparation of skilled movements, typically sequences of movements.

Nonprimary motor cortex consists of two main regions: the **supplementary motor area (SMA)**, which lies mainly on the medial aspect of the hemisphere, and the **premotor cortex,** which is anterior to the primary motor cortex (Figure 11.16). Patients with unilateral lesions of premotor cortex retain fine motor control of the fingers but are impaired in the stability of stance and gait and in the coordination of the two hands. Patients with bilateral damage to the SMA are unable to move voluntarily, although some automatic and reflex movements remain. These long-lasting effects suggest that this region is involved in the conception and initiation of movement and movement sequences (Freund, 1984).

Studies of localized cerebral blood flow and metabolism reveal that in simple tasks, such as keeping a spring compressed between two fingers of one hand, blood flow increases markedly in the hand area of the opposite M1 (Roland, 1980, 1984). Increasing the complexity of motor tasks to a sequence of behaviors extends the area of blood flow increase to SMA. Finally, when subjects mentally *rehearse* the complex movement sequence, the enhanced blood flow is restricted to the SMA.

Whereas the SMA is especially activated during *internally* generated finger sequences, the premotor cortex is activated when motor sequences are guided *exter-*

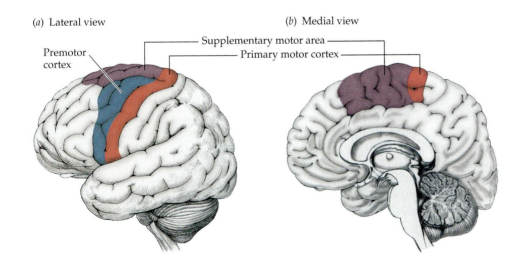

(*a*) Lateral view   (*b*) Medial view

Premotor cortex — Supplementary motor area — Primary motor cortex —

11.16 Human Motor Cortical Areas
(*a*) The primary motor cortex lies just anterior to the central sulcus. Anterior to the primary motor cortex are the premotor cortex and the supplementary motor area (SMA), which together make up the nonprimary motor cortex. The SMA lies mainly on the medial surface of the cerebral hemispheres (*b*).

nally by stimuli (Larsson et al., 1996)—a distinction that is also revealed by recordings of neuronal activity in behaving monkeys (Halsband et al., 1994).

A related distinction between SMA and premotor cortex is suggested by a study in which people learned the same sequence of finger movements under two conditions. In one condition the subjects soon became aware of the repeating sequence and began anticipating the next finger movement. In the other condition, subjects were distracted by another task and therefore never became aware of the repeating sequence, but nevertheless they learned it (as evidenced by their improved performance). Thus both groups learned to perform the same sequence of finger movements, but different brain regions were activated in these two conditions. The undistracted subjects, explicitly aware of the sequence they were learning, showed activation of the premotor cortex, but the distracted subjects, unaware that they were (implicitly) learning the sequence, showed activation of the SMA (Hazeltine et al., 1997). Perhaps, then, the premotor cortex participates in *explicit* motor learning, while the SMA mediates *implicit* motor learning.

Charles Gross

A subset of premotor neurons is also activated when objects are brought close to monkey's face or hand. If the lights are then turned out, some of these neurons continue to fire even if the object is silently moved, suggesting to Charles Gross and colleagues (Graziano et al., 1997) that the cells are coding for where the monkey *thinks* the object is. When the lights are turned back on and the monkey sees that the object is gone, the neurons cease firing. Such neurons may help us reach out for objects that are no longer visible.

Distributed activity in motor areas.   Motor areas of the cerebral cortex overlap in the control of muscular activity. Box 11.2 gives an example of this distributed control. Control of movements is not encoded in the successive or coordinated activation of individual neurons in M1; rather it emerges from the collective activation of a large distributed population of neurons—not only in M1 but also in the SMA and premotor cortex, and in the basal ganglia and cerebellum, to which we turn next.

The Basal Ganglia Modulate Movements

The **basal ganglia** include a group of interconnected forebrain nuclei: the caudate nucleus, putamen, and globus pallidus. Closely associated with these structures are two nuclei in the midbrain: the substantia nigra and subthalamic nucleus. Figure 11.12 shows the locations of these structures. The caudate nucleus and putamen together are referred to as the **striatum.**

Each of these structures receives input from wide areas of the cerebral cortex and sends much of its output back to the cerebral cortex via the thalamus in what can be described as a cortex–basal ganglia–thalamus–cortex loop. Lesions of these regions in humans produce movement impairments that seem quite different from those that follow interruption of the pyramidal system. Two disorders that we will discuss later in the chapter—Parkinson's disease and Huntington's disease—are caused by basal ganglia degeneration.

Inputs to the basal ganglia come from an extensive region of the cerebral cortex, as well as from thalamic nuclei and the substantia nigra. The sources of inputs suggest a subdivision of the basal ganglia into two major systems. One includes the caudate nucleus, the inputs of which are derived especially from frontal association cortex. The other system includes the putamen; inputs to this system come from sensorimotor cortical zones. Lesions within these subdivisions have different effects: Lesions of the caudate impair relatively complex behavior; lesions of the putamen cause more exclusively motor impairments, affecting the strength and rate of response rather than the direction of response (DeLong et al., 1984).

Animal studies of the basal ganglia use both lesions and recordings of single neurons during motor responses (DeLong et al., 1984). Each structure of the basal ganglia contains a topographic representation of body musculature. Studies suggest that the basal ganglia play a role in determining the amplitude and direction of movement rather than affecting the initiation of actions. The basal ganglia networks thus seem to modulate the patterns of activity initiated in other brain circuits that con-

BOX 11.2 *Cortical Neurons Control Movements of a Robotic Arm*

Signals from rat motor cortex can be used to control one-dimensional movements of a robotic arm, paralleling the movement of the rat's own arm (Chapin et al., 1999). If the rats receive visual feedback and are rewarded for successful movements of the robotic arm, they progressively cease to produce overt arm movements and let the robotic arm accomplish the task. This result suggests that paralyzed patients might learn to operate a robotic arm by cortical activity even though they can no longer move their own limbs.

Investigators have also used microwires implanted in two or more regions of the cortex of two owl monkeys to control a robotic arm in three dimensions, reproducing movements to reach for pieces of food placed in different positions, pick them up, carry them to the mouth, and return to the start position (Wessberg et al., 2000). In the first monkey, 16 microwires were implanted in each of the following areas: left dorsal premotor cortex (PMd), which is believed to plan the general temporal and spatial features of movements; left primary motor cortex (M1), which presides over the generation of movement commands for the right arm; left poste-

rior parietal cortex (PP), which is thought to integrate visual, somatosensory, and motor information to determine the location of a movement target and how to reach it; and right PMd, M1, and PP. In the other monkey, 16 microwires were implanted in each of two areas: left PMd and M1.

Training and recording were continued for 12 months in the first monkey

Owl monkey perched atop a robotic arm. (Courtesy of Miguel Nicolelis.)

and for 24 months in the second. Algorithms were developed to predict the hand motions from the cortical signals, as well as to predict hand trajectories to other directions—for example, to the left instead of to the right. The algorithms were used to control movements of robotic arms in real time both locally and, over the Internet, at a distance.

Analysis of the effects of excluding particular neurons from the calculations showed, somewhat unexpectedly, that PMd neurons contributed the most to the predictions and, as expected, ipsilateral M1 neurons contributed the least. Each area could be used for accurate predictions, provided enough neurons in that area were sampled.

The investigators suggest that this research could lead to voluntary control of prosthetic limbs in paralyzed patients. They note that implanted microwires yielded reliable recordings for at least 24 months. This result suggests that microwire arrays with implantable integrated circuits, designed to handle the signal processing and mathematical analysis, could form the basis of a brain–machine interface to control prosthetic devices (Mussa-Ivaldi, 2000; Nicolelis, 2001).

---

trol movements, such as motor and premotor cortical systems (see Figure 11.4). The basal ganglia are especially important in the generation of movements influenced by memories, in contrast to those guided by sensory control (Evarts et al., 1984). This point is also emphasized by Graybiel et al. (1994), who indicate that the multiple loops that connect the basal ganglia and neocortex are important in sensorimotor learning.

The Cerebellum Affects Programs, Timing, and Coordination of Acts

The cerebellum is a brain structure found in almost all vertebrates. In some vertebrate groups its size varies according to the range and complexity of movements. For example, the cerebellum is much larger in fish with extensive locomotor behavior than it is in less active fish; it is also larger in flying birds than in bird species that do not fly.

Recall from Chapter 2 that the outer layers of the cerebellum are called the cerebellar cortex and are dominated by a sheet of large multipolar cells called Purkinje cells (see Figure 2.16). All output of the cerebellar cortex travels via the axons of Purkinje cells, all of which synapse with the deep cerebellar nuclei. At these synapses, Purkinje cells produce only inhibitory postsynaptic potentials. Hence all the circuitry of the extensive cortical portion of the cerebellum, which also includes 10 billion to 20 billion granule cells in humans, guides movement by inhibiting neurons.

Inputs to the cerebellar cortex are derived both from sensory sources and from other brain motor systems. Sensory inputs include the muscle and joint receptors, and the vestibular, somatosensory, visual, and auditory systems. Both pyramidal and nonpyramidal pathways contribute inputs to the cerebellum and in turn receive

Masao Ito

outputs from the deep nuclei of the cerebellum. Thus the cerebellum receives elaborate information both from systems that monitor movements and from systems that execute movements. For this reason the cerebellum has long been believed to play a role in the feedback control of movements. It has also been suggested that the cerebellum elaborates neural "programs" for the control of skilled movements, particularly rapid, repeated movements that become automatic. This role of the cerebellum in the acquisition and retention of learned motor responses will be discussed in Chapter 18.

Various theories and experiments have suggested that cerebellar circuitry includes memory-like devices that might be important for motor learning. Masao Ito (1987) described a long-term depression of Purkinje cell activity that occurs when two different kinds of inputs to these cells are stimulated together. The depression of firing can last as long as 1 hour. This kind of memory change in the cerebellar cortex might be important for adaptive changes that involve interactions between the vestibular and visual systems, such as those that accompany the changing orientation of the head.

The Cerebellum and the Basal Ganglia Contribute Differently to Modulation of Motor Functions

The foregoing discussion and Figure 11.4 indicate that the cerebellum and the basal ganglia occupy rather similar positions in modulating motor functions. However, Y. Liu et al. (1999) found differences in the activity of these brain regions when they examined functional-MRI responses of subjects performing a tactile discrimination task. The subjects were given two similarly shaped objects—one in each hand—and they had to decide by active touching whether the objects were the same or different. Sustained activity was observed in the dorsolateral prefrontal cortex during this task. Changing patterns of activity were found in M1, the SMA, the cerebellum, and the basal ganglia. Cerebellar activity correlated significantly with activity of the SMA but not M1, whereas basal ganglia activity correlated more strongly with activity of M1 than of the SMA. Thus although the task appears to require activity of five brain regions (Figure 11.17), the cerebellum and basal ganglia show temporally and anatomically differentiated contributions.

The cerebellum and basal ganglia also contribute differently to the task of reaching. As we saw in Figure 11.1*b*, patients with Huntington's disease, who suffer from damage to the basal ganglia, show impairment especially toward the end of a reach, when corrections are made. In contrast, patients with cerebellar damage show errors especially in the initial direction of reach (M. A. Smith et al., 2000).

Endogenous Oscillators Drive Many Repetitive Movements

However it is accomplished, most locomotion is rhythmic. For all animals, moving about consists of repetitive cycles of the same act, be it the beating of wings or the repetitive swinging of legs. In Chapter 3 we presented an example of a basic neural circuit that could act as an **endogenous oscillator** (see Figure 3.18*c*), generating regularly repeating sequences of behavior. Do such endogenous oscillators provide the basic locomotor programs that motoneurons obligingly obey?

Early theories did not favor endogenous oscillators, emphasizing instead the role of sensory feedback and a reflex chain. According to this view, each act provides the sensory feedback from muscles that stimulates the next component. As with Sherrington's attempt to reduce complex behavior to a series of reflexes (discussed earlier in this chapter), this explanation is inadequate. Later experiments showed that eliminating the sensory feedback in locomotor acts such as walking or flying did not affect the basic rhythmic aspect of the act.

We now know that rhythmic movements are generated by mechanisms within the spinal cord. These endogenous rhythms are normally modulated by feedback, but they can function independently of brain influences or afferents. The term **central pattern generator** is used to refer to the neural circuitry responsible for generating rhythmic patterns of behavior as seen in walking. Typically neurons in a cen-

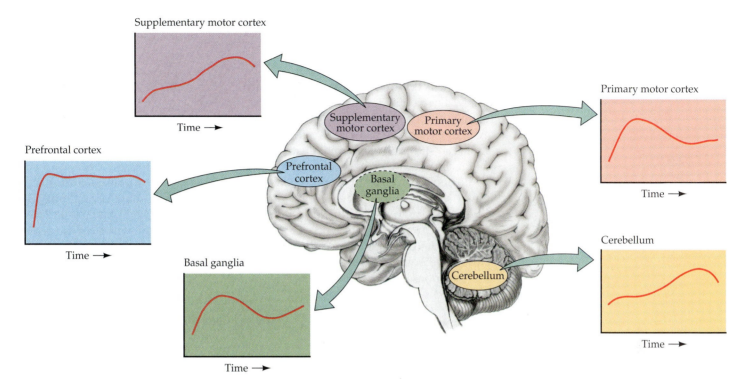

11.17 Contributions of the Cerebellum and Basal Ganglia to the Modulation of Movements Cerebellar activity correlates with that of the supplementary motor area, whereas basal ganglia activity correlates with that of primary motor cortex. (From Y. Liu.)

tral pattern generator circuit display reciprocal inhibitory innervation. Electromyographic records of hindlimb muscles of cats with spinal cord section and dorsal root cuts reveal a "walking" pattern that lasts for seconds when a single dorsal root is briefly stimulated electrically (P. Grillner et al., 1991; S. Grillner, 1985).

Outputs from spinal motoneurons also show different types of coordination with different locomotor patterns, like galloping. Three intact adjacent spinal segments provide the minimal amount of spinal processing necessary for generation of part of the locomotor rhythm. Thus the brain does not generate the essential rhythm in the spinal cord, but it may control the onset of the rhythm and provide corrections arising from other influences registered by the brain.

Disorders of Muscle, Spinal Cord, or Brain Can Disrupt Movement

CLINICAL ISSUE

Disorders at any level in the motor system—muscles, neuromuscular junctions, spinal cord, or brain regions—can impair movement. In the discussion that follows we will consider examples at each of these levels.

In Muscular Dystrophy, Biochemical Abnormalities Cause Muscles to Waste Away

Several muscle diseases involve biochemical abnormalities that lead to structural changes in muscle; these disorders are referred to as **muscular dystrophy.** As the name implies, a symptom that the various muscular dystrophies share is the wasting away of muscles.

Duchenne's muscular dystrophy strikes almost exclusively boys, beginning at the age of about 4 to 6 years and leading to death within a decade. Pedigrees suggest that the disorder is a simple Mendelian trait—caused by a single gene, in this case carried on the X chromosome. When researchers examined the X chromosomes in members of families afflicted with the disorder, they found that a single gene was

GENES AND BEHAVIOR

indeed abnormal in all the boys carrying the disorder and on one of the two X chromosomes carried by their mothers, but the same gene was normal in the fathers and in all unafflicted brothers.

The gene and its normal protein product were named **dystrophin.** In some ways the name is unfortunate because this protein, when normal, does *not* lead to dystrophy. Dystrophin is normally produced in muscle cells and may play a role in regulating internal calcium (Ca^{2+}) stores. Because females have two X chromosomes, even if one carries the defective copy of the dystrophin gene, the other X chromosome can still produce normal dystrophin. But about half the sons of such females will receive the defective gene and will be afflicted with the disease.

No one knows why the defective dystrophin protein shows no effects during the first few years of life. Mice with a mutation in this gene also show normal muscle function early in life and dystrophy in adulthood, but unlike humans with Duchenne's, the mice recover without intervention. Results from studies of the gene that encodes dystrophin have suggested that administering dystrophin protein to afflicted boys might enable their muscles to function properly. To date, however, immune responses to dystrophin in patients and in animal models have prevented use of this technique (Ferrer et al., 2000).

The Immune System May Impair Motor Function by Attacking Neuromuscular Junctions

Movement disorders involving the neuromuscular junction include a variety of reversible poison states. For example, snake bites can cause neuromuscular blocks because the venom of some highly poisonous snakes contains substances (such as bungarotoxin) that block postsynaptic acetylcholine receptors.

Studies of bungarotoxin have led to an understanding of one of the more debilitating neuromuscular disorders, **myasthenia gravis** (from the Greek *mys,* "muscle," and *asthenes,* "weak"; and the Latin *gravis,* "grave" or "serious"). This disorder is characterized by a profound weakness of skeletal muscles. The disease often first affects the muscles of the head, producing symptoms such as drooping of the eyelids, double vision, and slowing of speech. In later stages, paralysis of the muscles that control swallowing and respiration can become life-threatening. Antibodies directed against acetylcholine receptors cause these changes. Apparently myasthenic patients spontaneously develop these antibodies, which attack their own postsynaptic membranes (A. G. Engel, 1984).

Motoneuron Pathology Causes Some Motor Impairments

In the late 1930s the sad end of the brilliant baseball career of New York Yankees star Lou Gehrig brought public awareness to an unusual degenerative disorder in which the motoneurons of the brainstem and spinal cord are destroyed and their target muscles waste away. This syndrome is formally known as **amyotrophic lateral sclerosis (ALS),** although journalists more commonly refer to it as Lou Gehrig's disease.

The plight of U.S. Senator Jacob Javits (1904–1986) also drew attention to the personal struggles that accompany this disease, which progressively paralyzes a person while leaving intellectual abilities intact. The origins of the disease remain a mystery, but a wide range of causal factors are under investigation, including premature aging, toxic minerals, viruses, immune responses, and endocrine dysfunction.

About 10% of ALS cases are hereditary; that is, there is a clear family history of the disease, indicating that gene defects are involved. The pedigrees of several afflicted families indicate a single-gene disorder. The particular gene has been isolated (Andersen et al., 1995) and found to encode an enzyme—copper/zinc superoxide dismutase—that can convert highly reactive compounds (carrying what chemists call a *free radical*) into more ordinary compounds that can react in only a few ways. Some investigators speculate that this enzyme protects the muscles and/or motoneurons from the cellular damage that free radicals might cause. Thus the nonhereditary cases of ALS might stem from the buildup of similar damage from other sources, and this damage may accumulate despite the efforts of such enzymes.

GENES AND BEHAVIOR

When scientists produced transgenic mice that, in addition to their own normal copies of the enzyme, carried a copy of the defective human gene, these animals displayed an ALS-like syndrome (Gurney et al., 1994). Their muscles wasted away and their motoneurons died, leading to an early death. These results suggest that the abnormal gene actively damages part of the neuromuscular system. These molecular genetic changes may also lead to high levels of the transmitter glutamate. In high concentrations this excitatory amino acid can cause neurons to die.

Spinal Cord Pathology Causes Some Motor Impairments

Pathological changes in motoneurons also produce movement paralysis or weakness. Virus-induced destruction of motoneurons—for example, by the disease polio—was once a frightening prospect in the United States and western Europe. Polioviruses destroy motoneurons of the spinal cord and, in more severe types of the disease, cranial motoneurons of the brainstem. Because the muscles can no longer be called on to contract, they atrophy.

Vehicular accidents, violence, falls, and sports injuries cause many human spinal injuries that result in motor impairment. Injuries to the human spinal cord commonly develop from forces to the neck or back that break bone and compress the spinal cord. If the spinal cord is severed completely, immediate paralysis results, and reflexes below the level of injury are lost—a condition known as **flaccid paralysis.** Flaccid paralysis generally results only when a considerable stretch of the spinal cord has been destroyed. When the injury severs the spinal cord without causing widespread destruction of tissue, reflexes below the level of injury frequently become excessive because the intact tissue lacks the dampening influence of brain inhibitory pathways.

An estimated 250,000 to 400,000 individuals in the United States have spinal cord injuries. Probably the best known of these is the actor Christopher Reeve, star in the *Superman* movies of the 1970s and 1980s. Injured in 1995 in an equestrian accident, Reeve established a foundation to promote research on spinal cord injuries and to provide grants to improve the quality of life for people with disabilities (Figure 11.18).

The hope of reconnecting the injured spinal cord no longer seems as far-fetched as it once did. Months after the spinal cord is severed in lampreys, the animals can swim again without any therapeutic intervention (A. H. Cohen et al., 1989), but they seem unique among vertebrates in this regard. In rats, implants of peripheral nerve or fetal nervous tissue may provide a "bridge" across the injury to allow reconnection of the spinal cord (Bernstein-Goral and Bregman, 1993).

Recall from Chapter 9 that olfactory receptor neurons can be continuously produced throughout life and send out new axons. When Y. Li et al. (1997) took glial cells (called *ensheathing cells*) from the olfactory bulb and used them as a bridge across spinal cord cuts in rats, the corticospinal axons regenerated across the injury and the animals eventually regained use of their forepaws. Providing neurotrophic factors such as neurotrophin-3 to severed spinal cord axons also seems to promote regeneration (H. Cheng et al., 1996; Grill et al., 1997). These observations buoy the hope that regeneration in the injured spinal cord of humans will become possible.

Cerebral Cortex Pathology Causes Some Motor Impairments

The most common motor impairments that follow strokes or injury to the human cerebral cortex are paralysis or partial paralysis (**paresis**) of voluntary movements on one side of the body. Usually the paralysis appears on the side of the body opposite the injured hemisphere. In addition, affected patients show some **spasticity,** especially increased rigidity in response to forced movement of the limbs.

The spasticity reflects the exaggeration of stretch reflexes. Abnormal reflexes occur, such as the flaring and extension of the toes elicited by stroking the sole of the foot (the Babinski reflex). In the months following cerebral cortical injury, the clinical picture changes. The initial paralysis slowly diminishes, and some voluntary movements of the proximal portion of limbs return, although fine motor control of fingers is seldom regained. As noted earlier, in humans the symptoms are more severe than in many other mammals.

11.18 Leaders in the Campaign to Aid Victims of Spinal Paralysis Actor Christopher Reeve and his wife Dana were guests of honor at a meeting held in 1999 by the Society for Neuroscience to mark the achievements of the Decade of the Brain. Reeve received the Special Achievement Award for his efforts to raise public awareness of spinal cord injury and for promoting research funding. (Courtesy of the Society for Neuroscience.)

Damage to nonmotor zones of the cerebral cortex, such as some regions of parietal or frontal association cortex, produces more complicated changes in motor control. One such condition is **apraxia** (from the Greek *a-,* "not," and *praxis,* "action"), the inability to carry out certain acts even though paralysis or weakness is not evident and comprehension and motivation are intact. Apraxia is illustrated in the following example: When asked to smile, a patient is unable to do so, although he certainly attempts to. If asked to use a comb placed in front of him, he seems unable to figure out what to do. But things aren't as simple as they might appear. At one point in the discussion the patient spontaneously smiles, and at another point he retrieves a comb from his pocket and combs his hair with ease and accuracy.

Apraxia was first described by the nineteenth-century neurologist John Hughlings Jackson, who noted that some patients could not protrude their tongue on command even though they could use it in a variety of spontaneous acts, such as speech, licking their lips, and eating. Apraxia is a symptom of a variety of disorders, including stroke, Alzheimer's disease, and developmental disorders of children.

Neurologists studying patients who have suffered strokes have discovered several different types of apraxia. **Ideomotor apraxia** is characterized by the inability to carry out a *simple* motor activity in response to a verbal command (e.g., "smile," or "use this comb"), even though this same activity is readily performed spontaneously. Some researchers emphasize that this type of apraxia is characterized by the inability to select responses, arrange them in an appropriate order, and orient them properly; these processes are crucial in gestures. Other researchers emphasize the connection between this disorder and aphasia (disturbances of language that follow injury or diseases of the cerebral hemispheres).

Ideational apraxia is an impairment in the carrying out of a *sequence* of actions that are components of a behavioral script, although each element or step can be performed correctly. For example, one patient was asked to go through the sequence of acts involved in lighting a candle with a match. Although she was unable to comply with this request, when the lights went out during a storm she found a candle and lit it (Kosslyn et al., 1992). Such patients have difficulty carrying out instructions for a sequence of acts—"Push the button, then pull the handle, then depress the switch"—but they can do each of these tasks in isolation.

Parkinson's Disease Results from Lack of Stimulation of the Basal Ganglia

Diseases of the basal ganglia can produce a variety of effects, some almost opposite to others. Some disorders reflect release from the constraints that the basal ganglia usually impose on motor control. In the absence of these constraints, the activity initiated by other brain regions appears unchecked and yields dramatic, persistent excesses of movement. Other basal ganglia disorders produce slowness of movement and marked changes in muscle tone.

About 200 years ago, physician James Parkinson noted people in London who moved quite slowly, showed regular tremors of the hands and face while at rest, and walked with a rigid bearing. Another feature of what is now known as **Parkinson's disease** is a loss of facial muscle tone, which gives the face a masklike appearance. Patients who suffer from Parkinson's also show few spontaneous actions and have great difficulty in all motor efforts, no matter how routine. The hands may display tremors while at rest but move smoothly while performing a task. Parkinson's disease afflicts almost 1% of the U.S. population aged 65 and older, so there is active research on its causes and possible ways to prevent or alleviate it.

Patients with Parkinson's show progressive degeneration of dopamine-containing cells in the **substantia nigra** that project to the striatum. The loss of cells in this area is continuous, but symptoms appear only after a major loss. The discovery of a form of the disorder induced by illicit drugs (described in Box 11.3) has suggested that exposures to toxins over a prolonged period underlie the development of the disorder.

Most cases of Parkinson's disease are probably not inherited, but in one large Italian family Parkinson's disease develops in members who inherit a defective copy of the gene that encodes α-synuclein (Polymeropoulos et al., 1997), a protein normally expressed in the basal ganglia. Researchers hope that determining how this defective protein causes Parkinson's in this family will suggest clues to the onset of nonhereditary Parkinson's.

For years, there was no treatment for Parkinson's disease, but a pharmacological therapy emerged from the discovery in the late 1960s that patients suffering from Parkinson's show a loss of dopamine levels in the substantia nigra. This treatment was the administration of a precursor to dopamine to enhance the dopamine levels of surviving cells. The substance, called **L-dopa,** markedly reduces symptoms in patients with Parkinson's, including a decrease in tremor and an increase in the speed of movements.

Although L-dopa can reverse some symptoms of Parkinson's disease, nerve cell degeneration in the substantia nigra is relentless. Because the cell bodies in the brainstem degenerate, dopamine-containing terminals in the caudate nucleus and putamen also disappear. Eventually, too few dopamine-containing neurons remain in the substantia nigra to be influenced by the intake of L-dopa.

BOX 11.3 *The Frozen Addicts*

Parkinson's disease has been difficult to study because until recently it was not possible to find or produce a similar disorder in laboratory animals. Sloppy synthesis of illegal drugs led to the first valuable model of Parkinson's disease. This saga began when several drug addicts were admitted to a hospital in California with an unusual array of symptoms. Especially puzzling was the fact that although they were in their twenties, they presented an unmistakable portrait of Parkinson's disease, which is usually restricted to people 50 or older. The movements of these young patients were slow, they had tremors of the hands, and their faces were frozen without expression. In addition, the diagnosis of Parkinson's disease in these cases was confirmed by the therapeutic response to the drug L-dopa.

All of these drug addicts had recently used a "home-brewed" synthetic form of heroin. That fact, coupled with the recollection of a report of an unusual disorder that had arisen from a laboratory accident several years earlier, led to the conclusion that the synthetic heroin contained a neurotoxin that produced brain damage typical of Parkinson's disease (Kopin and Markey, 1988; Langston, 1985).

Moving step-by-step in a trail that resembles a detective story, researchers pieced together what had happened. Chemical studies led to the identification of a contaminant in the synthetic heroin, now known as MPTP (an abbreviation of a much longer chemical name). Many addicts have been exposed to this substance, but relatively few exhibit this parkinsonian disorder. Patients with symptoms show a decline in dopamine concentrations in the brain, as revealed by PET scans (W. R. Martin and Hayden, 1987).

The injection of MPTP into various research animals yielded a startling result: Although rats and rabbits showed only minimal and transient motor impairments, monkeys were as sensitive to the toxin as humans are, developing a permanent set of motor changes identical to those of humans with Parkinson's disease. Furthermore, the sites of damage in the brain were identical to those in the frozen addicts and in patients suffering from Parkinson's.

MPTP accumulates in the substantia nigra and caudate nucleus because it binds selectively to a form of the enzyme monoamine oxidase (MAO), which is plentiful in these regions. MPTP interacts with this enzyme to form a highly toxic metabolite: MPP^+. Researchers have suggested that the natural pigment neuromelanin, found in the substantia nigra, accounts for the selectivity of damage produced by MPTP (S. H. Snyder and D'Amato, 1985). They have shown that MPP^+ binds with special affinity to this pigment. Thus cells with neuromelanin accumulate MPP^+ to toxic levels, and because cells of the substantia nigra contain large amounts of the pigment, they are particularly vulnerable to the destructive impact of MPP^+.

In other parts of the brain, MPP^+ levels decline following exposure; in contrast, MPP^+ levels in substantia nigra cells may continue to increase for some time following exposure. In view of this binding mechanism, differences among species become more comprehensible. Nigral cells of monkeys and humans have pigment, while those of rodents are unpigmented.

Monkeys can be protected against the toxic effects of MPP^+ by oxidase inhibitors and certain other drugs (D'Amato et al., 1987). This drug model has already resulted in new drug treatments that hold considerable promise for human sufferers of Parkinson's disease. For example, the MAO inhibitor deprenyl slows the progression of Parkinson's. Discovering a primate model of this disease opened an exciting set of research opportunities that is removing the shroud of mystery around Parkinson's disease. Experiments with primates have also provided an opportunity to test other therapies, such as neural transplants. This research has led to successful transplants in human patients (see Figure 11.18), including some of the original frozen addicts.

Some researchers have speculated that Parkinson's disease in humans arises from exposure to an unknown toxin or toxins. In two cases involving laboratory workers, MPTP-induced disease arose from either inhalation of or skin contact with MPTP, suggesting that brief and almost trivial contact with MPTP is sufficient to begin the disease. Recent animal experiments indicate that some environmental toxins, such as certain herbicides (Betarbet et al., 2000) or combinations of herbicides (Thiruchelvam et al., 2000), may cause Parkinson's disease. Announcement of a *Drosophila* model of Parkinson's disease may speed research toward prevention or alleviation of this disorder (Feany and Bender, 2000; Haass and Kahle, 2000).

11.19 Brain Implants to Treat Parkinson's Disease The injection of human fetal cells into patients with Parkinson's disease led to increased dopamine receptors (coded in yellow and red) in the striatum 1 and 3 years later, as these PET scans reveal. (From Lindvall et al., 1994.)

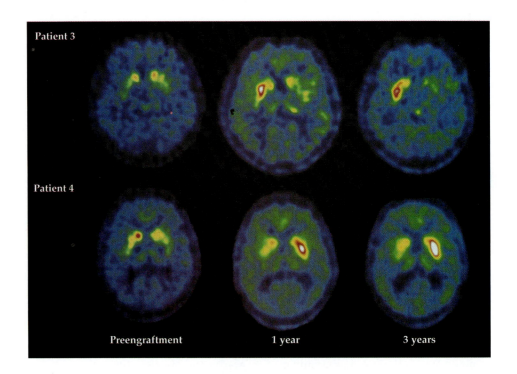

Patient 3

Patient 4

Preengraftment   1 year   3 years

Until recently, no surgical treatments to address this terminal condition were available. By the 1980s, however, researchers had begun to use transplants of dopamine-containing cells as a form of treatment in humans. The refinement of techniques led to the transplantation of human fetal cells derived from the brainstem. Direct injection of these cells into the corpus striatum (Figure 11.19) (Peschanski et al., 1994) has been reported to produce remarkable symptom relief in some patients with Parkinson's Animal research on such grafts indicates that these fetal brainstem cells become integrated into the circuitry of the corpus striatum; thus transplants result in a rewiring of the damaged brains in addition to the effects they produce by the release of synaptic transmitter.

Such transplants appear to have helped patients who suffer from drug-induced Parkinson's disease (see Box 11.3). In the first double-blind placebo-controlled clinical study of this procedure, the fetal cells produced dopamine in the brains of patients and improved the condition of some patients, but some patients with grafts became afflicted with severe involuntary movements, so this implant procedure is now under question (Freed et al., 2001).

An aspect of Parkinson's disease that may be independent of the degree of motor impairment is the appearance of cognitive and emotional changes. Some patients show marked cognitive decline during the course of their illness (Cummings, 1995). Depression in patients with Parkinson's is also common; some researchers have attributed such depression to the consequences of diminished movement capabilities and the general stress of such incapacity. Other researchers have attributed it to a diminished responsiveness of the serotonergic system (Sano et al., 1991).

Huntington's Disease Is Characterized by Excessive Movement Caused by Deterioration of the Basal Ganglia

Whereas damage to the basal ganglia in Parkinson's disease slows movement, other kinds of basal ganglia disorders cause excessive movement. An example of the latter type was reported by George Huntington, a physician whose only publication (1872) described a strange motor affliction. He correctly noticed that this disorder was inherited, passed from generation to generation. We now know that **Huntington's disease** is transmitted by a single dominant gene, so each child of a victim has a 50% chance of developing the disease.

The first symptoms of this disease are subtle behavioral changes: clumsiness, twitches in fingers and the face. Subtlety is rapidly lost as the illness progresses; a continuing stream of involuntary jerks engulfs the entire body. Aimless movements of the eyes, jerky leg movements, and writhing of the body turn the routine activities of the day into insurmountable obstacles. Worse yet, as the disease progresses, marked behavioral changes include intellectual deterioration, depression, and in a minority of patients, a psychotic state that resembles schizophrenia. In some patients, cognitive and emotional changes may appear many years before obvious motor impairments do (N. S. Wexler et al., 1991). Huntington's disease usually develops over a period of 15 to 20 years.

The neuroanatomical basis of this disorder is the profound, progressive destruction of the basal ganglia, especially the caudate nucleus and the putamen (Figure 11.20), as well as impairment of the cerebral cortex. Several types of cells are particularly vulnerable, including neurons that contain the transmitter GABA. Acetylcholine-containing neurons are relatively spared.

Because the symptoms of Huntington's disease usually first appear between the ages of 30 and 45 years, many victims have children before knowing whether they will ultimately contract the disease. Until quite recently this meant continuing generations of ravaged individuals. After losing her mother to this disease, psychologist Nancy Wexler organized a team of investigators that prepared a pedigree map of more than 10,000 individuals, including more than 300 Huntington's patients, from a community in Venezuela where Huntington's disease is relatively common. After years of work, she and her collaborators (including David Housman, James Gusella, and Venezuelan physician Ernesto Bonilla) were able to pinpoint the gene, on chromosome 4, that is responsible for the disorder (Gusella and MacDonald, 1993).

The function of the protein is still unknown, but the nature of the mutation in this gene (called *HD* for Huntington's disease) provides unexpected insight into the inheritance of the disorder. In afflicted individuals the *HD* gene is interrupted by a series of three nucleotides—CAG—repeated over and over (see the Appendix). This **trinucleotide repeat** can vary in length; if there are fewer than 30 repeats, no symptoms appear, but if there are 38 or more trinucleotide repeats in the *HD* gene, the person will develop Huntington's disease (A. B. Young, 1993).

The longer the string of trinucleotide repeats, the earlier in life Huntington's disease symptoms commence. When the repeats are carried by the mother, the gene with its repeats is copied faithfully in eggs and transmitted to the offspring, but in the production of sperm, a father may transmit more or fewer repeats than he himself carries. Unfortunately, it is more common for the father to transmit more repeats than fewer repeats. Thus in some cases an asymptomatic father may transmit Huntington's disease to his offspring.

Nancy Wexler

GENES AND BEHAVIOR

(*a*) Control
   Caudate nucleus   Putamen

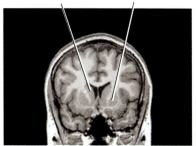

(*b*) Patient with Huntington's disease
   Lateral ventricles

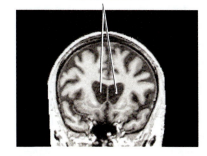

11.20 Neuropathology in Huntington's Disease Compared with the control (*a*), coronal MRI section through the brain of a patient suffering from Huntington's disease (*b*) shows marked enlargement of the lateral ventricles, caused by atrophy of the neighboring caudate nucleus and putamen. Note also the shrunken cortical gyri and enlarged sulci of the patient compared with those of the brain of a healthy person. (MRI images courtesy of Terry L. Jernigan and C. Fennema Notestine.)

How does carrying a copy of *HD* with extended repeats cause degeneration of the striatum and the symptoms of Huntington's disease? One hypothesis was that only striatal cells normally make the protein encoded by *HD* (which has been named **huntingtin**), so only these cells die when it is defective. But huntingtin, whether normal or defective, is produced not just in the striatum, but throughout the brain, by both neurons and glial cells. Huntingtin is also made in the muscles, liver, pancreas, and testes (A. B. Young, 1993). Thus the reason that the defective *HD* gene affects only striatal cells remains a mystery. Transgenic mice expressing the human *HD* gene develop a progressive syndrome with many of the characteristics of Huntington's disease (Mangiarini et al., 1996), and research with this mouse model is beginning to show ways of slowing progression of the disease (e.g., Ona et al., 1999).

The example of Huntington's disease, with its increased movements, demonstrates the major role that inhibition plays in normal motor control. Without adequate inhibition, a person is compelled to perform a variety of unwanted movements. We saw in Figure 11.1*b* that patients with Huntington's disease are less accurate in reaching for a target. People whose genetic tests reveal that they will develop Huntington's disease show some impairment in accuracy of reaching several years before predicted onset of the disease (M. A. Smith et al., 2000).

Cerebellar Damage Leads to Many Motor Impairments

Because the cerebellum modulates many aspects of motor performance, it is not surprising that its impairment leads to many abnormalities of behavior. These symptoms permit an examiner to identify with considerable accuracy the part of the cerebellum that is involved (Dichgans, 1984).

A relatively common lesion of the cerebellum results from a tumor that usually occurs in childhood. The tumor damages a part of the cerebellum—the vermis—that has close connections to the vestibular system and therefore causes disturbances of balance. The patient walks as if drunk and has difficulty even standing erect. Often patients afflicted in this way place their feet widely apart in an attempt to maintain balance. The abnormalities usually involve the legs and trunk but not the arms.

Normally the world seems to hold still as we walk because movements of our eyes compensate for movements of the head. Some patients with lesions of the cerebellum, however, see the world around them move whenever they move their heads. If normal subjects wear prismatic lenses, they learn to compensate for the new relationship between movement of the eyes and perceived change of direction. Patients with lesions of the vestibular part of the cerebellum cannot make this adjustment, suggesting that this part of the cerebellum is important for such learning.

Some alcoholic patients show degeneration of the cortex of the anterior lobe of the cerebellum. When this region is damaged, abnormalities of gait and posture are common. The legs show **ataxia** (loss of coordination), but the arms do not. Loss of coordination and swaying indicate that the patient is not compensating normally for the usual deviations of position and posture.

Several investigators have proposed that the cerebellum works like a comparator in a negative feedback circuit, comparing ongoing movements with target levels and sending corrective instructions to overcome any departures from planned values. (Such a feedback system is diagrammed in Figure 11.3*b*.) The cerebellar cortex has motor and sensory maps of the body that are in register (i.e., that are perfectly superimposed), which may allow the comparison of ongoing acts with planned positions and motions of body parts.

Difficulties of motor coordination are common after damage to the lateral aspects of the cerebellum. One such problem is called **decomposition of movement** because gestures are broken up into individual segments instead of being executed smoothly. A patient who had this problem after damage to his right cerebellar hemisphere described his condition in this way: "The movements of my left hand are done subconsciously, but I have to think out each movement of my right arm.

I come to a dead stop in turning and have to think it out before I start again." Thus the cerebellum is needed not to initiate acts or to plan the sequence of movements, but to facilitate activation and to "package" movements economically (V. B. Brooks, 1984).

Sensory and Motor Representations Overlap in Some Places

We started this chapter by noting reciprocal interactions between sensory and motor systems, and we conclude by describing some cases in which sensory and motor representation overlap or are even shared. One case is the superior colliculus, which we discussed in Chapter 10 as a midbrain station in the visual system. Actually, although the superficial layer of the superior colliculus receives visual input and forms a map of the visual field, the deeper layer is motor in function. Excitation of cells in the deeper layer causes saccadic movements of the eyes.

Moreover, the map of the motor layer is in register with the overlying sensory map, so stimulation at a point in visual space tends to evoke rapid eye movement toward that stimulus. There are direct connections between the visual and motor cells in the colliculus (P. H. Lee et al., 1997). Other visual and nonvisual inputs also reach these motor cells, helping to explain why saccadic eye movements do not occur in response to all visual stimuli.

More surprising is the discovery of cells in dorsal premotor cortex of monkeys that are both motor and sensory in function. The same cells respond when the monkey performs a particular action or when it sees another monkey performing a similar action, so they have been called *mirror cells* (Rizzolatti et al., 1996, 1999). Evidence for similar activation has been obtained in human subjects, and the investigators suggest that such findings may help us understand how the "motor" cortex participates when we recognize and understand the actions of others (Hari et al., 1998). The mirror system in humans includes Broca's area. The presence of a function such as this that matches observation with execution in a brain area critical for language invites speculation on its role in the evolution of the human communication system (Rizzolatti and Arbib, 1998).

The fact that some cells respond both to the observer's own behavior and to similar behavior in others does not mean that these two circumstances evoke similar action throughout the brain. PET imaging revealed different patterns of activity when subjects imagined themselves acting or another person acting in the same way (Ruby and Decety, 2001). Both patterns involved the secondary motor area, but imagining the subject's own activity also increased cerebral blood flow in the inferior parietal lobe, whereas imagining similar behavior of another person also increased blood flow in cingulate cortex.

We Can Trace a Choice Response from Input to Output

Now that we have reviewed the sensory and motor systems, it will be helpful to consider an example that includes sensory input, central processing, and a choice response. In Chapter 3 we considered the sequence and timing of events in a simple response, the knee jerk reflex (see Figure 3.16). Now let's consider the sequence and timing of events in a more complicated situation, in which a person is presented with two visual stimuli and has to signal, by pressing one of two buttons, whether the stimuli belonged to the same category.

Reaction times in such an experiment averaged about 310 ms. A review of research on this topic suggests the sequence and timing of events at several stations in the nervous system for this task (Figure 11.21) (Thorpe and Fabre-Thorpe, 2001). The time shown at each station in Figure 11.21 is a typical average latency. Activity proceeds from the primary visual cortex through the ventral *what* pathway to prefrontal cortex, then through premotor and primary motor cortex, down to the spinal motoneurons, and out to the finger muscles.

11.21 Input to Output The sequence and timing of brain events, from presentation of visual stimuli to a discrimination response. LGN, lateral geniculate nucleus; V1, primary visual cortex; V2 and V4, extrastriate visual areas.

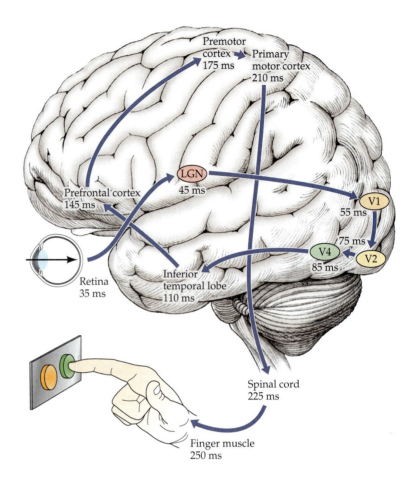

Summary

1. Two broad categories of motor activity—movements and acts—are divided into subcategories. Reflexes are movements; more complex motor behaviors are acts. Complex acts suggest the existence of a motor plan.

2. Reflexes are patterns of relatively simple and stereotyped movements that are elicited by stimulation of sensory receptors; their amplitude is proportional to the intensity of the stimulation.

3. Many reflexes are controlled by closed-loop, negative feedback circuits. Some behaviors are so rapid, however, that they are controlled by open-loop systems; that is, the pattern is preset and does not respond to feedback.

4. Motor control systems are organized into a hierarchy that consists of the skeletal system and associated muscles, the spinal cord, the brainstem, and various parts of the brain, including the primary and nonprimary motor cortices, the cerebellum, and the basal ganglia.

5. Muscles around a joint work in pairs. Antagonists work in opposite ways; synergists work together.

6. Smooth muscles, such as the stomach, are under involuntary control; striated muscles are under voluntary control.

7. Action potentials travel over motor nerve fibers (axons from motoneurons) and reach muscle fibers at the neuromuscular junction, releasing acetylcholine to trigger muscle contraction.

8. The final common pathway for impulses to skeletal muscles consists of motoneurons whose cell bodies in vertebrates are located in the ventral horn of the spinal cord and within the brainstem. The motoneurons receive impulses from a variety of sources, including sensory input from the dorsal spinal roots, other spinal cord neurons, and descending fibers from the brain.

9. Muscle spindles and Golgi tendon organs—sensory receptors in the muscles and tendons, respectively—transmit a wide range of information about muscle activities to the central nervous system. The sensitivity of the muscle spindle can be adjusted by efferent impulses that control the length of the muscle spindle. This adjustment allows flexible control of posture and movement.

10. Circuits within the spinal cord underlie the spinal reflexes, which can occur even when connections to the brain are severed.

11. When a muscle is stretched, a reflex circuit often causes contraction, which works to restore the muscle to its original length; this response is called the stretch reflex. The stretch of the muscle is detected by muscle spindles.

12. The corticospinal tract is especially well developed in primates and is mainly involved in controlling fine movements of the extremities. Its fibers originate mainly in the primary motor cortex (M1) and adjacent regions, and they run directly to spinal motoneurons or to interneurons in the spinal cord. Nonprimary motor cortex helps control the sequence of movements.

13. Although the centers of representation of body parts are separated in orderly fashion in M1, the subregional organization is broadly distributed, and each M1 neuron influences many muscles.

14. Primary motor cortex is involved in learning motor responses and in cognitive processes such as encoding serial order.

15. Control of movements involves the collective activation of a large distributed population of neurons in the different cortical motor areas.

16. Brain regions that modulate movement include the basal ganglia (caudate nucleus, putamen, and globus pallidus), some major brainstem nuclei (substantia nigra, thalamic nuclei, and red nucleus), and the cerebellum.

17. Central pattern generators, such as endogenous oscillators, are responsible for generating rhythmic patterns of behavior in locomotion.

18. Movement disorders can result from impairment at any of several levels of the motor system: muscles, neuromuscular junctions, motoneurons, spinal cord, brainstem, cerebral cortex, basal ganglia, or cerebellum. The characteristics of these disorders depend on and permit diagnosis of the locus of impairment.

19. Not only do sensory and motor systems interact reciprocally, but in some parts of the brain, such as the superior colliculus and the premotor cortex, sensory and motor representations overlap.

Recommended Reading

Georgopoulos, A. P. (1997). Voluntary movement: Computational principles and neural mechanisms. In M. D. Rugg (Ed.), *Cognitive neuroscience* (pp. 131–168). Cambridge, MA: MIT Press.

Purves, D., Augustine, G. J., Fitzpatrick, D., Katz, L., et al. (Eds.). (2001). *Neuroscience* (2nd ed.). Sunderland, MA: Sinauer. (See Unit III. "Movement and Its Central Control," Chapters 16–21.)

Rothwell, J. (1994). *Control of human voluntary movement* (2nd ed.). London: Chapman and Hall.

Sanes, J. N., and Donoghue, J. P. (2000). Plasticity and primary motor cortex. *Annual Review of Neuroscience, 23,* 393–415.

Stein, P. S. G., Grillner, S., and Selverston, A. I. (1998). *Neurons, networks, and motor behavior.* Cambridge, MA: MIT Press.

PART FOUR

Regulation and Behavior

S o far, we have reviewed the basic structure and function of the nervous system, the specialized organs that gather information about the environment, and the specialized motor systems that allow us to respond to that information. Now we come to a problem—given the information we have, which response should we make? The number of possible responses is infinite. But natural selection favors some responses in some situations, and other responses in others. A food-deprived animal should eat, an animal that has lost water should drink, an animal that is not adapted to function in darkness should sleep at night, and so on. When an animal consistently displays the same response, even in slightly inappropriate circumstances, we can infer that the animal is motivated to make that response.

The brain plays a pivotal role in the decision about which response to make. To some extent we can identify the different brain regions that are involved in deciding whether to reproduce (Chapter 12); eat, drink, seek shelter (Chapter 13); sleep (Chapter 14); be afraid, panic, or fight (Chapter 15). In each of these cases, we catalog the situations that usually elicit a particular response from members of a particular species, and we ask which brain regions are required for the response to be elicited, which brain regions are activated by the situation, and how various responses are integrated. As we'll see, many brain regions are involved in each of these responses. The involvement of multiple brain regions is a recurring theme in this book.

12

Sex: Evolutionary, Hormonal, and Neural Bases

Sexuality is such an important part of our lives that we take for granted some of its most basic properties—for example, the facts that two and only two sexes are required for reproduction, that in most species males are somewhat larger and more aggressive than females, and that most adult humans are, in some core sense, either a man or a woman. We will learn, however, that there are exceptions to each of these rules.

This chapter is divided into three main sections:

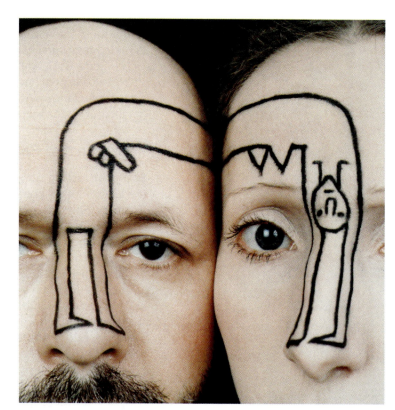

Rimma Gerlovina and Valeriy Gerlovin, *Romulus and Remus*, 1989, color photograph © by the artists

1. First we'll review sexual behaviors, which includes the sex act itself, copulation.

2. Next, the bewildering variety of sexual behaviors across species (and within our own species) will lead us to consider why such a messy and confusing process as sexual reproduction evolved. We'll find that sexual reproduction eventually gave rise to two sexes, which can sometimes be remarkably divergent in structure and behavior.

3. The evolution of two different sexes will lead us to the final topic: sexual differentiation, the process by which an individual's body and brain develop in a male or female fashion.

12.1 Sex According to Thurber and White In *Is Sex Necessary?* (1929), James Thurber and E. B. White explain, "It is customary to illustrate sexology chapters with a cross section of the human body. The authors have chosen to substitute in its place a chart of the North Atlantic, showing airplane routes. The authors realize that this will be of no help to the sex novice, but neither is a cross section of the human body." (If you insist on a cross section, see Figure 12.7.)

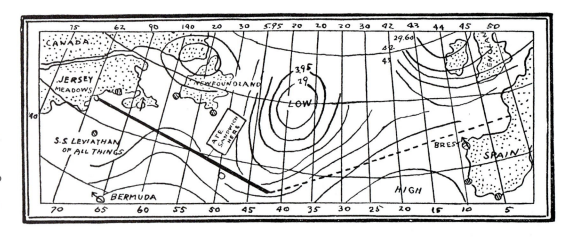

Sexual Behavior

We wish we could explain exactly why and how humans and other animals engage in the three Cs—courting, copulating, and cohabiting—but very little practical knowledge of such matters exists, as James Thurber and E. B. White lamented in 1929 (Figure 12.1). You may feel that there has been little improvement in the years since. Two barriers have blocked our understanding of sexual behavior: (1) a deep-seated reluctance within our culture to disseminate knowledge about sexual behavior and (2) the remarkable variety of sexual behaviors in existence.

Reproductive Behavior Can Be Divided into Four Stages

Sexual attraction is the first stage in bringing the male and female together (Figure 12.2). In many species an individual is attractive to others, and is itself attracted to others, only when its body is ready to reproduce. We can gauge how attractive a female is by observing how males respond to her—how rapidly they approach, how hard they work to gain access to her, and so on. The same measures show how attractive a male is to females. By manipulating the appearance of females, we can deduce which features males find attractive.

Such methods have demonstrated that in many species of apes and monkeys the male is attracted by the sight of the female's "sex skin," which swells under the influence of steroid hormones—estrogens. Most male mammals are also attracted by particular odors emitted by females of their species; many such odors are also the result of the action of estrogens. Thus estrogens simultaneously instigate the release of eggs (ovulation) and attract males to fertilize them. Of course, the female may find some of the males that approach her unattractive and refuse to mate with them. Despite a few descriptions of what may or may not be rape in nonhuman animals, for most species copulation is not possible without the female's active cooperation.

If the animals are mutually attracted, they may progress to the second stage of reproductive behavior: **appetitive behaviors** (behaviors that establish, maintain, or promote sexual interaction). A female mammal that engages in such behaviors is said to be **proceptive:** She may approach males, remain close to them, or show alternating approach and retreat behavior. In rats, the female may run away from the male with a distinctive hopping and darting gait, to which the male often responds by mounting the female. Male appetitive behaviors usually consist of staying near the female. In many mammals the male may sniff around the female's face and vagina. Male birds may engage in elaborate songs or nest-building behaviors.

If both animals display appetitive behaviors, they may progress to the third stage of reproduction: **copulation,** also known as *coitus.* In many vertebrates, including all mammals, copulation begins when the male puts his penis inside the female's vagina—a behavior referred to as **intromission.** Then the male ejaculates, rhythmically squirting a fluid mixture called **semen** inside the female. The semen contains sperm cells for reproduction.

After one bout of copulation the animals will not mate again for a period of time, which is called the **refractory phase.** The refractory phase varies from minutes to months, depending on the species and circumstances. Many animals show a shorter refractory phase if they are provided with a new partner—a phenomenon that is known as the **Coolidge effect.**

The female often appears to be the one to choose whether or not copulation will take place; when she is willing to copulate she is said to be **sexually receptive,** in heat, or in estrus. In some species, the female may show proceptive behaviors days before she will participate in copulation itself. In that case she is said to be proceptive but not (yet) receptive (see Figure 12.2). Usually females are receptive only during periods when mating is likely to result in reproduction. Because most animals are seasonal breeders (see Chapter 14), females are usually receptive only during the breeding season, which varies considerably from species to species. Many species, such as salmon, octopuses, and cicadas, reproduce only once, during a single season at the end of life.

Finally, the fourth stage of reproductive behavior consists of **postcopulatory behaviors.** These behaviors are especially varied across species. In some mammals—dogs and southern grasshopper mice, for example—the male's penis swells so much after ejaculation that he can't remove it from the female for a while (10 to 15 minutes in dogs), and the animals are said to be in a **copulatory lock** (Dewsbury, 1972). (Despite wild stories you may have heard or read, humans never experience copulatory lock, not even with Viagra.) Postcopulatory behaviors also include parental behaviors in many vertebrate species.

Copulation Brings Gametes Together for Reproduction

Sexually mature females are animals that can produce **gametes** (sex cells) called *eggs,* or **ova** (singular *ovum*); sexually mature males produce gametes called **sperm.** Successful reproduction requires that a sperm cell contact and fuse with an egg cell—a process known as **fertilization.** The resulting single cell is called a fertilized egg, or **zygote,** which may eventually divide and grow to make a new individual.

For many vertebrates, fertilization takes place outside the female's body—a process known as **external fertilization.** In most fishes and frogs, for example, males and females release their gametes in water, where fertilization takes place. In some fishes, such as guppies and swordtails, the male uses a modified fin to direct his sperm to swim into the female's body, where the sperm fertilize the female's eggs. Such **internal fertilization,** a feature of all mammals, birds, and reptiles, allows the zygotes to remain moist even in a desert, and the resulting offspring may gain nutrients from the mother.

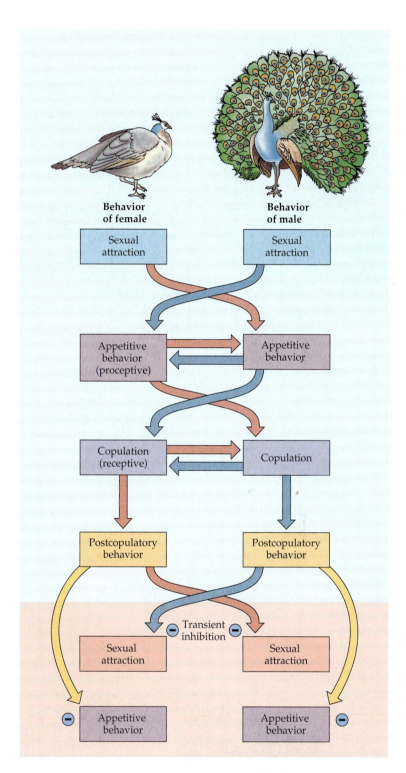

12.2 Stages of Reproductive Behavior Interaction between male and female partners in sexual reproduction is extensive, progressing in four stages: sexual attraction, appetitive behavior, copulation, and postcopulatory behavior. The postcopulatory phase (pink background) includes a temporary decrease in the sexual attractiveness of the partner and inhibition of appetitive behavior. (After Beach, 1977.)

TABLE 12.1 *Types of Sexual Reproduction in Animals*	
Type	**Examples of animals that follow this pattern**
EXTERNAL FERTILIZATION (requires aquatic environment)	Many invertebrates, fishes, amphibians
INTERNAL FERTILIZATION	
Oviparity	Insects, birds, many reptiles, monotremes
Viviparity	Some fishes, reptiles, all mammals except monotremes

Birds use internal fertilization even though most male birds do not have a penis. Semen is discharged and eggs are laid through the **cloaca** (plural *cloacae*), the same passage through which birds eliminate wastes. The female squats low; the male mounts her back, pushes his cloaca against hers, and squirts in the semen. After the sperm swim up the reproductive tract and fertilize an ovum, the female bird assembles rich nutrients and a tough shell around the zygote, which she later extrudes as an egg. This process is known as **oviparity** (from the Latin *ovum*, "egg," and *parere*, "to bring forth"). In live birth, or **viviparity** (the Latin *vivus* means "alive"), the zygote develops extensively within the female until a well-formed individual emerges.

All mammals use internal fertilization, and all but a few species (the monotremes—that is, the echidnas and the platypus of Australia—which are oviparous) give birth to live young. Table 12.1 summarizes the different types of sexual reproduction.

Copulation in Rats Is but a Brief Interlude

Like most other rodents, rats do not engage in lengthy courtship, nor do the partners tend to remain together after copulation. Rats are attracted to each other largely through odors. Females are spontaneous ovulators; that is, even when left alone they ovulate every 4 to 5 days. For a few hours during each cycle, the female seeks out a male and displays proceptive behaviors: hopping and darting, which we mentioned earlier, and ear wiggling. Both animals produce vocalizations at frequencies too high for humans to detect but audible to each other.

These behaviors prompt the male to mount the female from the rear, grasp her hind flanks with his forelegs, and rhythmically thrust his hips. If the female is receptive, she stands still and assumes a posture that allows intromission: She lifts her head and rump and moves her tail to one side. This posture is called **lordosis** (Figure 12.3). Once intromission has been achieved, the male rat makes a single thrust, lasting half a second or so, and then springs back off the female. During the next 6 to 7 minutes the male and female orchestrate seven to nine such intromissions; then, instead of springing away, the male raises the front half of his body up for a second or two while he ejaculates. Finally, he falls backward off the female.

After copulation the male almost immediately begins grooming his penis with his tongue and forepaws, while the female typically remains still for a few minutes before grooming her vagina. The male pays little attention to the female for the next 5 minutes or so, until, often in response to the female's proceptive behaviors, he mounts for another round of multiple intromissions and another ejaculation. The multiple intromissions before an ejaculation are not mere idle dawdling on the part of the male. If a male rat ejaculates the first time he enters the female (say, because he engaged in several intromissions with another female first), the female that receives his sperm will not become pregnant. Only if the female receives enough vaginal stimulation from multiple intromissions will her brain later cause the release of hormones to support pregnancy. In this instance, then, the behavior of one rat (the male) affects the hormonal secretions of its mate.

In other rodent species, intromission may be accompanied by more prolonged thrusting, or the penis may swell to form a copulatory lock. The northern pygmy mouse has only a single ejaculation during a mating session (talk about pressure!). In some rodent species a male and a female live together before and long after copulation; such animals are said to form **pair bonds.**

12.3 Copulation in Rats The raised rump and deflected tail of the female (the lordosis posture) make intromission possible. (After Barnett, 1975.)

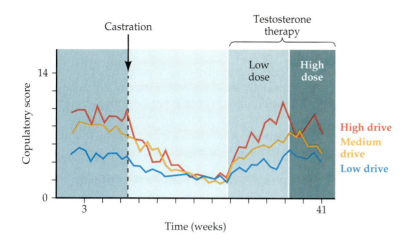

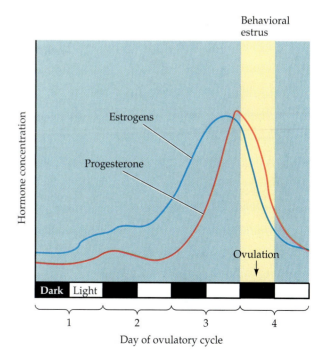

12.4 Androgens Permit Male Copulatory Behavior Although androgens have an effect, hormone level does not completely determine the amount of male sexual behavior, even in rodents. In the experiment whose results are shown here, after castration caused the sex activity of male guinea pigs to decrease, the same amount of testosterone was given to each animal, beginning at week 26. Each group returned to the level of sexual activity it had exhibited before castration. Doubling the amount of hormone at week 36 did not increase the mating activity of any group. (After Grunt and Young, 1953.)

Hormones play an important role in rat mating behaviors. Testosterone increases the male's interest in females, causes him to mount females more rapidly and more often, and allows him to achieve ejaculation. If an adult male rat is **castrated** (has his testes removed), he will stop ejaculating within a few weeks and will eventually stop mounting receptive females. Although testosterone disappears from the bloodstream within a few hours after castration, whatever effects the hormone had on the nervous system take several days to dissipate. Treating a castrated male with testosterone eventually restores mating behavior; if the administration of testosterone is then stopped, the mating behavior fades again. This is an example of a hormone exerting an **activational effect:** the hormone transiently influences behavior. In normal development, the rise of androgen secretion at puberty activates masculine behavior in male rats.

Interestingly, although individual male rats differ considerably in the vigor with which they mate with a receptive female, blood levels of testosterone clearly are *not* responsible for these differences. Evidence of this effect comes from experiments in which many male rats are classified on the basis of how often they mount females. Among scientists, such males (rats, we mean) are referred to as either *studs* or *duds.* These groups show no significant differences in blood testosterone levels. Furthermore, when castrated male rats or guinea pigs are given identical amounts of testosterone, the former studs remain studs and the duds are still duds (Figure 12.4). In fact, a very small amount of testosterone—one-tenth the amount normally produced by the animals—is enough to maintain the mating behavior of stud rats. Thus since all rats make more testosterone than is required to maintain their copulatory behavior, something else appears to be responsible for individual differences in mating activity.

Adult female rats release eggs (**ovulate**) every 4 or 5 days. Estrogens secreted at the beginning of this **ovulatory cycle** facilitate the proceptive behavior of the female rat, and the subsequent production of progesterone increases proceptive behavior and activates receptivity (Figure 12.5). An adult female whose ovaries have been removed will show neither proceptive nor receptive behaviors, and neither estrogen nor progesterone treatment alone will restore them. However, 2 days of estrogen treatment followed by a single injection of progesterone will, about 6 hours later, make the female rat proceptive and receptive for a few hours. Only the combination of estrogens followed by progesterone will activate copulatory behaviors in female rats. So we've now seen two examples of activational effects of hormone: Androgens activate masculine behavior in male rats, and the sequence of estrogens followed by progesterone activates feminine behavior in female rats.

12.5 The Ovulatory Cycle of Rats Changes in hormone levels indicate when the female rat will display lordosis. This behavioral receptivity, or estrus, occurs after the animal has been exposed first to estrogens, then to progesterone. In spontaneous ovulators such as rats, the cycle of hormone secretion repeats unless eggs are fertilized. In that case, the embryos secrete hormones to interrupt the cycle and maintain pregnancy.

Donald Pfaff

The Neural Circuitry of the Brain Regulates Reproductive Behavior

Most of what we know about the neural circuitry underlying reproductive behaviors comes from animal models, especially rats. In a wide range of vertebrate species, steroid receptors are consistently found in many brain regions, including the hypothalamus, medial amygdala, and hippocampus, among many others. As we'll see, steroid effects in the hypothalamus play a central role in regulating copulatory behavior, and there's reason to believe that this is true of humans as well.

Steroids Act on the Hypothalamus to Promote Female Receptivity

Recall that we can induce sexual receptivity in female rats by injecting them with an estrogen, such as estradiol, for a few days, then injecting them with progesterone. Donald Pfaff (1997) and colleagues have exploited this steroid sensitivity of the lordosis response to map out the neural centers that mediate this behavior (see Figure 12.6b).

Steroid autoradiography indicated that the hypothalamus contains a center for estrogen- and progesterone-sensitive neurons, and specifically the **ventromedial hypothalamus** (**VMH**) was found to be crucial for lordosis because lesions there abolish the response. Furthermore, tiny implants of estradiol in the brain can induce receptivity, but only if they are placed in the VMH region (Lisk, 1962; Pleim and Barfield, 1988). One of the actions of estrogen treatment is to increase the size of the dendritic trees of VMH neurons (Meisel and Luttrell, 1990). Another important function of estrogen treatment is to induce the production of progesterone receptors so that the animal will respond to that hormone. Activated progesterone receptors in turn increase the production of proteins that must be present for lordosis to result (Mani et al., 2000).

The VMH sends axons to the **periaqueductal gray** region of the midbrain, where again lesions greatly diminish lordosis. The periaqueductal gray neurons project to the **medullary reticular formation,** which in turn projects to the spinal cord via the reticulospinal tract. In the spinal cord the sensory information provided by the mounting male will now evoke the motor response of lordosis. Thus the role of the VMH is to monitor steroid hormone concentrations and, at the right time in the ovulatory cycle, activate a multisynaptic pathway that induces the spinal cord to contract back muscles, producing a lordosis response that is otherwise absent (Pfaff 1997). Figure 12.6b, which is based on many studies, schematically represents this neural pathway and the steroid-responsive components.

Androgens Activate a Neural System for Male Reproductive Behavior

Steroid hormones also activate male copulatory behavior in rodents, and again the sites of steroid action provided important clues revealing the neural circuitry involved. The hypothalamic **medial preoptic area** (**mPOA**) is chock-full of steroid-sensitive neurons, and lesions of the mPOA abolish male copulatory behavior in a wide variety of vertebrate species (Meisel and Sachs, 1994). Furthermore, mating can be reinstated in castrated males by small implants of androgens in the mPOA but not in other brain regions.

Neurons in the mPOA send their axons to the ventral midbrain via the medial forebrain bundle. From the ventral midbrain, information goes to the basal ganglia (presumably to coordinate mounting behaviors) and, through a diffuse multisynaptic pathway, to the spinal cord. The spinal cord, in turn, mediates the various reflexes of intromission and ejaculation.

Surprisingly, when testosterone activates the mPOA in an adult male rat, it does so after being converted to an estrogen, which then acts on estrogen receptors. On the other hand, the activation of androgen receptors in the periphery and spinal cord is what induces the intromission and ejaculation reflexes.

We can gather information about male copulatory neural systems also by investigating a sensory system that activates male arousal in rodents—the vomeronasal

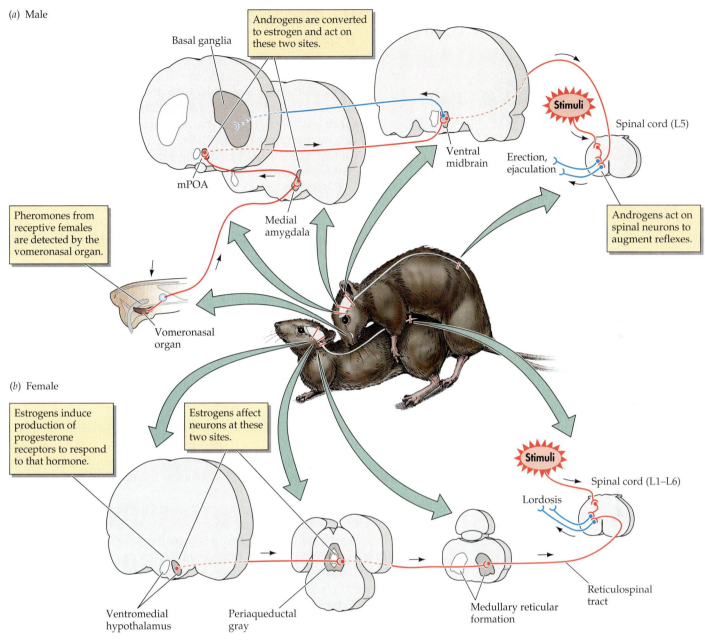

(a) Male

Basal ganglia

Androgens are converted to estrogen and act on these two sites.

Stimuli

Spinal cord (L5)

mPOA

Ventral midbrain

Erection, ejaculation

Androgens act on spinal neurons to augment reflexes.

Medial amygdala

Pheromones from receptive females are detected by the vomeronasal organ.

Vomeronasal organ

(b) Female

Estrogens induce production of progesterone receptors to respond to that hormone.

Estrogens affect neurons at these two sites.

Stimuli

Spinal cord (L1–L6)

Lordosis

Reticulospinal tract

Ventromedial hypothalamus

Periaqueductal gray

Medullary reticular formation

12.6 Neural Circuits for Reproduction in Rodents (Part *b* after Pfaff, 1980.)

system. The **vomeronasal organ** (see Chapter 9) consists of specialized receptor cells near but separate from the olfactory epithelium. These sensory cells detect chemicals called **pheromones** (see Chapters 5 and 9), which are released from one individual and detected by another. Vomeronasal receptor cells send electrical signals to the accessory olfactory bulb in the brain.

Receptive female rats release pheromones that can be detected by the male rat's vomeronasal organ and arouse the male, as evidenced by penile erections. The vomeronasal information from the accessory olfactory bulb projects to the **medial amygdala,** where lesions will abolish penile erections in response to receptive females (Kondo et al., 1997). The medial amygdala in turn sends axons to the mPOA. So the mPOA appears to integrate hormonal and sensory information such as pheromones, and to coordinate the motor patterns of copulation. Figure 12.6*a* summarizes the neural circuitry for male rat copulatory behavior.

We will see later that androgens, acting perhaps on the hypothalamus and/or the medial amygdala, activate sexual arousal in humans as well.

(a) Female

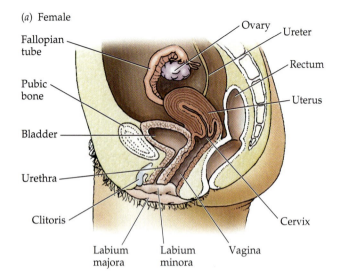

Fallopian tube
Pubic bone
Bladder
Urethra
Clitoris
Labium majora
Labium minora
Ovary
Ureter
Rectum
Uterus
Cervix
Vagina

(b) Male

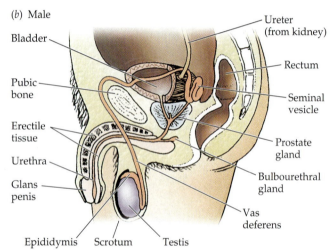

Bladder
Pubic bone
Erectile tissue
Urethra
Glans penis
Epididymis
Scrotum
Testis
Ureter (from kidney)
Rectum
Seminal vesicle
Prostate gland
Bulbourethral gland
Vas deferens

12.7 Adult Human Reproductive Anatomy (For an interesting chart of the North Atlantic, see Figure 12.1.)

Alfred Kinsey (1894–1956)

Human Reproduction Brings Gametes Together

In women, the **ovaries** release an egg every 28 days or so. The released egg enters the adjacent **fallopian tube** (named after the sixteenth-century anatomist who discovered its function; it is also called the *uterine tube*). The walls of the fallopian tube have specialized hairs, or cilia, that wave back and forth, moving the egg into the **uterus** (Figure 12.7a). The walls of the uterus are specialized to allow implantation of a developing embryo and support the **placenta,** which will nourish the embryo and fetus.

For a baby to result, copulation must take place around the time of ovulation, so that fertilization takes place in the fallopian tubes. Otherwise the zygote will not have enough time to divide to form an embryo that is sufficiently developed to implant into the walls of the uterus. If not implanted, the embryo will drift into the connecting vagina and outside the body.

Surrounding the opening of the human vagina are folds of skin known as **labia** (singular *labium*), and rostral to the vaginal opening is a mound of tissue called the **clitoris** (plural *clitorides,* honestly). This region surrounding the vaginal opening is sometimes called the **vulva.** In all mammals the walls of the uterus thicken before ovulation to allow implantation of a newly formed embryo. In some mammals, including humans and dogs, so many cells lining the walls of the uterus are shed between ovulations that a visible flow of cells and blood exits through the vagina—a process known as **menstruation.** In most mammals, however, many fewer cells are shed and there is no visible flow. Thus although all vertebrate species have ovulatory cycles (the periodic release of eggs), only a few mammalian species display menstrual cycles.

In males, the sperm are produced in the **testis** (plural *testes*) and mature in the adjacent, crescent-shaped **epididymis** (Figure 12.7b). Attached to the epididymis is a small tube called the **vas deferens** (plural *vasa deferentia*) or *ductus deferens.* Muscles lining the vas deferens contract to propel sperm to the **urethra,** a tube that travels through the penis to reach the outside. (The urethra also connects to the bladder and conducts urine outside the body.)

At the point at which the vas deferentia from the left and right testes join with the urethra, several glands are attached: The **seminal vesicles** produce and store a cloudy, viscous fluid; the **prostate,** which encircles the urethra at this point, produces a clear, astringent fluid; and other glands contribute other fluids. During copulation, sperm are expelled from the epididymis via the vas deferens and mixed with these various fluids in the urethra; the mixture (semen) is expelled from the penis during ejaculation.

The Hallmark of Human Sexual Behavior Is Diversity

For as long as humans have written, they have written about sex. But little scientific information was available about human sexual behavior until the 1940s, when biology professor Alfred Kinsey began to ask friends and colleagues about their sexual histories. Kinsey constructed a standardized set of questions and procedures to obtain information for representative samples of the U.S. population categorized by sex, age, religion, and education. Eventually he and his collaborators were able to publish extensive surveys (based on tens of thousands of respondents) of the sexual behavior of American males (Kinsey et al., 1948) and females (Kinsey et al., 1953).

Controversial in their time, these surveys indicated that nearly all men masturbated, that college-educated people were more likely to engage in oral sex than were non-college-educated people, that many people had at one time or other engaged in homosexual behaviors, and that as much as 10% of the population preferred homosexual sex. Although recently it has been suggested that the last figure is an overestimate, these surveys revealed much about human sexual behavior.

A further step is to make behavioral and physiological observations of people engaged in sexual intercourse or masturbation, but such studies are perilous for a scientist: John B. Watson, the founder of behaviorism, attempted such studies in the early 1920s, and the ensuing scandal cost him his professorship. After Kinsey's surveys were published, however, physician William Masters and psychologist Virginia Johnson began a large, well-known project of this kind (1966, 1970; Masters et al., 1994) that greatly increased our knowledge about the physiological responses in various parts of the body during intercourse, their time courses, and their relations to what is experienced.

Among most mammalian species, including nonhuman primates, the male mounts the female from the rear, but among humans, face-to-face postures are most common. A great variety of coital postures have been described, and many couples vary their postures from session to session or even within a session. This variety of reproductive behaviors, both within and between individuals, is a characteristic that differentiates humans from all other species.

Masters and Johnson (1966) summarized the typical response patterns of men and women as consisting of four phases: increasing excitement, plateau, **orgasm** (the brief, extremely pleasurable sensations experienced by most men during ejaculation and by most women during copulation), and resolution (Figure 12.8). During the excitement phase, the **phallus** (the penis in men, the clitoris in women) becomes engorged with blood, making it erect.

We now know some details about phallic erection. The **paragigantocellular nucleus (PGN)** in the pons sends serotonergic fibers down the spinal cord that inhibit erection (McKenna, 1999), and the sexually aroused forebrain inhibits the PGN, permitting erection. Antidepressant drugs that enhance the activity of brain serotonin receptors (see Chapter 16) can have side effects of difficulty achieving erection, ejaculation, and/or orgasm. These side effects may be due to enhancement of the effectiveness of PGN-released serotonin in spinal cord centers. (If you're wondering, the famous drug sildenafil [Viagra] acts directly on tissue in the penis to promote erection by inhibiting a second-messenger enzyme, phosphodiesterase-5 [Boolell et al., 1996].)

In women, the excitement phase also causes the vagina to secrete lubricating fluids, which facilitates intromission. Stimulation of the penis and clitoris during rhythmic thrusting accompanying intromission may lead to orgasm. In both men and women, orgasm is accompanied by rhythmic contractions of genital muscles (mediating ejaculation in men and contracting the opening of the vagina in women). In spite of the basic similarity, there are some typical differences between male and female sexual responses.

One important difference is the greater variety of commonly observed sequences in women. Whereas men have only one basic pattern, women have three typical patterns (see Figure 12.8b). The second main difference between the

William Masters

Virginia Johnson

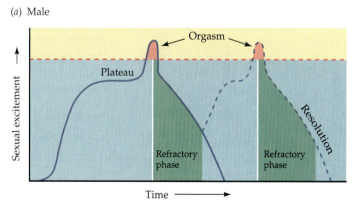

(a) Male

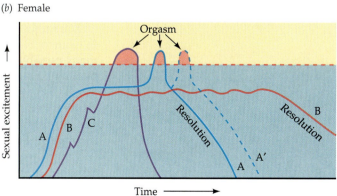

(b) Female

12.8 Human Sexual Response Cycles   (a) The typical male pattern includes an absolute refractory phase after orgasm. (b) These three patterns are often observed in women. These diagrams are schematic and do not represent a particular physiological measure, although heart rate varies in roughly this manner. The patterns vary considerably from one individual to another. (After Masters and Johnson, 1966.)

sexes is that most men, but not most women, have an absolute refractory phase following orgasm (see Figure 12.8a). That is, most men cannot achieve full erection and another orgasm until some time has elapsed, the length of time varying from minutes to hours, depending on individual differences and other factors. Many women, on the other hand, can have multiple orgasms in rapid succession.

The similarities and differences in sexual responses exemplify the generalization of Chapter 1 that in some ways each person is like all other people, in some ways like some other people, and in some ways like no other person. Some behavioral differences are related to differences in genetic makeup; some may be related to differences in hormone levels. But some are certainly due to differences in experience and learning; sexual therapy, for example, usually consists of helping the person relax, recognize the sensations associated with coitus, and learn the behaviors that produce the desired effects in both partners. Masturbation during adolescence, rather than being harmful as suggested in previous times, may help avoid sexual problems in adulthood. As in other behaviors, practice, practice, practice helps. Sexual behavior may also aid overall health; epidemiological studies indicate that men who have frequent sex tend to live longer than men who do not (Davey-Smith et al., 1997).

Some Diseases Can Be Transmitted through Sexual Behavior

Many serious diseases, including syphilis and gonorrhea, can be communicated through sexual intercourse. The **human immunodeficiency virus (HIV)** can be passed through genital, anal, or oral sex and causes **acquired immune deficiency syndrome (AIDS)**, an insidious, fatal disease. Proper use of **condoms** (rubber sheaths fitted over the penis to trap semen) during sexual intercourse can prevent the transmission of HIV and other sexually transmitted diseases. Condoms can also be effective birth control devices, preventing unwanted pregnancies that lead to serious social and moral problems.

Hormones Play Only a Permissive Role in Human Sexual Behavior

In male rodents a little bit of testosterone must be in circulation to activate male-typical mating behavior. The same relation seems to hold for human males. For example, boys who fail to produce testosterone at puberty show little interest in sex unless they are treated with synthetic androgens. These males, as well as men who have lost their testes as a result of cancer or accident, have made possible double-blind tests of whether androgens affect human copulatory behavior. (In *double-blind tests*, neither the subjects nor the investigator knows which subjects are receiving the drug and which are receiving a placebo until after the treatment is over.) Julian Davidson and colleagues (1979) demonstrated that androgens indeed stimulate sexual activity in men.

Julian Davidson

Recall that in rats, additional testosterone has no effect on the vigor of mating. Consequently, there is no correlation between the amount of androgens produced by an individual male rat and his tendency to copulate. In humans, too, testosterone levels below normal are sufficient to restore behavior, and there is no correlation between systemic androgen levels and sexual activity among men who have *some* androgen. In men over 60 years old, testosterone levels gradually decline as gonadotropin levels rise, indicating that the decline is in gonadal response to pituitary hormones.

You might be surprised to learn that androgens may also activate sexual interest in women. Some women report reduced interest in sex after menopause. There are many possible reasons for such a change, including several hormonal changes. As mentioned earlier, estrogens increase a woman's ability to produce lubricants, and indeed estrogen treatment of menopausal women aids lubrication, but it does not change their interest in sex. On the other hand, double-blind studies show that a very low regimen of androgens can revive sexual interest in postmenopausal women (Sherwin, 1998).

There have been several attempts to determine whether women's interest or participation in sexual behavior varies with the menstrual cycle. Some researchers have found a slight increase in sexual behavior around the time of ovulation, but the effect is small, and several studies have failed to see any significant change in interest in sex across the menstrual cycle.

Pheromones Both Prime and Activate Reproductive Behaviors

When steroid hormones from the gonads affect the brain to activate mating behavior, the activation is not absolute; individuals are simply more likely to engage in mating behaviors when gonadal steroid levels are adequate. This activation can be thought of as communication between the gonads and the brain: By producing steroids to make gametes, the gonads also inform the brain that the body is ready to mate. This signaling takes place inside the individual, but hormones can also provide information *between* animals.

For example, during ovulation, female goldfish produce a hormone called F prostaglandin. Some F prostaglandin escapes the female's body and passes through the water to a male. The F prostaglandin is detected by the male and stimulates his mating behavior (Sorensen and Goetz, 1993). The most likely scenario for the evolution of this relationship is that long ago females released F prostaglandin only as a by-product of ovulation, but because the presence of the hormone conveyed important information about the female's condition, natural selection favored males who detected the hormone and began courting in response to the signal. Even very simple unicellular organisms, such as yeasts, prepare each other for mating by releasing and detecting chemicals (Fields, 1990).

EVOLUTION AT WORK

In the case of the goldfish, a single chemical acts both as a hormone (in the female), and as a pheromone communicating to males. This pheromone **activates** another individual's behavior in a rapid and brief manner. But other pheromones act more gradually and have a longer-lasting effect. In these slower cases the pheromone **primes** potential mates, readying them for copulation and reproduction.

Two well-characterized pheromone systems in mammals are the activation of aggression in mice and the blocking of pregnancy in several rodent species. Male mice placed in a cage together will often fight; pheromones in the urine of one mouse determine whether the other mouse will attack. If one of the mice is a female or a male that has been castrated, the normal male mouse will not attack. If the castrated male is smeared with urine from an intact male (or from a female who has been injected with androgens), however, other males will attack him. Thus, circulating androgens appear to cause chemical(s) to be released in the urine (Novikov, 1993), and other male mice can detect this signal. Male mice attack only mice that produce these pheromones because only these mice are rivals for mating with females.

Pheromones in the urine of male mice can also accelerate puberty in young females (Drickamer, 1992; M. A. Price and Vandenbergh, 1992) and can halt pregnancy in mature females (Brennan et al., 1990). Female mice can even identify an individual male by the particular mix of pheromones in his urine. When prairie voles mate, the female is exposed to pheromones from her mate's mouth and urine. If she is then isolated and has urine from that male or any other male applied to her snout, pregnancy will be blocked; the fetuses are resorbed by the female, and she is soon ready to mate again.

Yet if the female remains with the original male from copulation on, pregnancy continues, apparently because the female is careful not to apply her mate's urine to her vomeronasal organ (Smale et al., 1990). The female not only distinguishes males by their pheromones, but remembers which male mated with her and avoids using his urine to interrupt pregnancy. Resorption of the young in the presence of a new male may be an attempt to make the best of a bad situation: If her original mate is gone, she may be better off beginning a new litter with a different male.

Do Pheromones Synchronize Menstrual Cycles in Women?

Martha McClintock (1971) reported that women residing together in a college dormitory were more likely to have their menstrual cycles in synchrony than would be expected by chance; that is, women who spend more time with each other are more likely to menstruate at the same time. McClintock hypothesized that pheromones passing between the women serve as a signal of the ovulatory cycle, enabling synchronization.

It has been difficult to prove that women show menstrual synchrony, but most studies confirm this idea (Weller and Weller, 1993). Whether the synchronization relies on social signals or pheromone signals between the women has been even more difficult to determine. However, women who have extracts of sweat from other women applied to their upper lip do display an acceleration or delay of their menstrual cycles, depending on where the donors were in their cycle (K. Stern and McClintock, 1998).

Why Are There Two Sexes?

Having talked about sex and some of its many complications, we may wonder how such an outlandish system ever got started, yet many animals come in two sexes. Author William Tenn (1968) imagined an exotic animal species that had seven different sexes. The sexes had wildly divergent bodies and behavior, allowing each to occupy a particular ecological niche, including both predator and prey. One problem with such an arrangement is reproduction: How do members of each of the seven sexes get together for mating when some are predators, some prey? In Tenn's scenario, one of the seven sexes was highly adapted for the tricky diplomacy of arranging suitable orgies.

In real life no creatures have more than two sexes, so perhaps even natural selection cannot solve diplomatic problems involving more than two parties. As we'll see next, however, species with only one sex reproduce perfectly well. Why should any species bother with two?

Sexual Reproduction Helps Combine Beneficial Mutations

If in a given population of animals one individual has a very rare, *beneficial* mutation, the mutation can be spread to other individuals in only two ways. One way is for that individual to make clones of itself, to give birth to individuals that have only its genes, including the mutated one. In unicellular organisms this process is known as **fission,** the simple splitting of one individual cell into two. In multicellular animals this process is known as **parthenogenesis** (from the Greek *parthenos*, "virgin," and *genesis*, "production"; the Parthenon was a Greek temple to the virgin goddess Athena). If the mutation is especially useful, future generations will consist mostly of this individual's progeny. Eventually other beneficial mutations may arise. Thus it is possible for a species to evolve without sexual reproduction.

**EVOLUTION
AT WORK**

But consider the other method of spreading the new gene: sexual reproduction. In this process the original holder of a helpful new gene produces offspring that have both the new gene and genes from other individuals. Some of these other genes may also be beneficial. The *function of sexual reproduction* is to bring together, in a single individual, many beneficial mutations, each of which arose in different individuals. This mixing of beneficial genes certainly generates biological diversity. But evolutionary theorists still debate why any particular individual, if capable of either parthenogenesis or sexual reproduction, would benefit by producing offspring that carry only half of its genes (Peck and Waxman, 2000).

Some animals can reproduce by either method. Aphids, the small green insects that probably infest your garden every year, reproduce by parthenogenesis when the food supply is ample and the conditions are favorable for growth and unchecked reproduction. When conditions worsen, though, the aphids begin sexually reproducing, effectively swapping genes to produce offspring that begin migrating away, looking for a more hospitable environment. Perhaps the advantage of reproducing

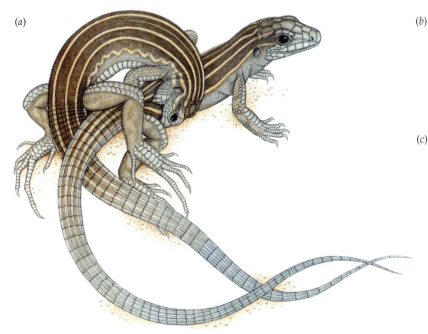

12.9 Are Males Necessary? Whiptail lizards (*a*) and Amazon mollies (*b*) are two of the rare vertebrate species that reproduce by parthenogenesis. All individuals are females that produce daughters with only the mother's genes. Nevertheless, these animals exhibit mock mating behaviors (such as those displayed by the lizards shown here) that greatly resemble the mating behaviors of related species that reproduce sexually. (*c*) Black molly females can, in the absence of a male, transform into fertile males. (Part *a* by Patricia J. Wynne; *b* courtesy of Michael Ryan.)

sexually is that, despite cutting in half your gene contribution to the next generation, by producing new combinations of genes that might better survive the new conditions you enhance the chance that at least some offspring will survive.

Nevertheless, parthenogenesis has been documented to occur on rare occasions in some vertebrate species, such as chickens and turkeys, and there are several species of whiptail lizards in the southwestern United States in which all individuals are females that reproduce exclusively via parthenogenesis (Figure 12.9*a*) (Crews, 1994). Aquarium fanciers know a species of tropical fish, the Amazon molly (Figure 12.9*b*), that consists solely of females reproducing by parthenogenesis. Apparently, then, nothing inherent in the vertebrate body requires sexual reproduction, but this method of reproduction among vertebrates is so pervasive that it must convey some advantage.

Even sexual reproduction does not require that animals come in two different sexes. In many sexually reproducing species, each individual produces both sperm and eggs, and sex consists of donating sperm to a partner while accepting sperm in return. Individuals that can reproduce as either males or females are known as **hermaphrodites** (a term derived from the Greek *Hermaphrodites*—the son of the god Hermes and goddess Aphrodite—who, while bathing, became joined in one body with a nymph). Although hermaphrodites, such as the sea slug *Aplysia,* are common among invertebrates, very few vertebrates (and all of them are fishes) are true hermaphrodites. Early in the evolution of our prevertebrate ancestors, the male and female roles became so divergent that the sexes eventually split—some individuals reproducing exclusively via sperm, while others produced only eggs.

In many species of fish, individuals may spend some parts of their life behaving and reproducing as females and other parts of their life reproducing in a male fashion. Although these individuals never produce both sperm and eggs *at the same time,* they may be regarded as *serial* hermaphrodites. In some cases the switch in sex has obvious reproductive advantages: Most such fish reproduce as females when young and switch to the more aggressive, territorial behavior needed to reproduce as males only after they grow large enough to compete with others (Francis, 1992). In other fishes, social stimuli may drive the sexual switch. For example, if you remove all the males from a tank of black molly fish (related to but different from Amazon mollies), one of the females, usually the largest, will transform into a male and successfully reproduce as that sex (Figure 12.9c).

Males and Females Often Adopt Different Reproductive Strategies

When our ancestors began reproducing through separate male and female individuals, the two sexes came to diverge in form and behavior (Figure 12.10). Today many species are **sexually dimorphic,** the term Darwin used to describe species in which males and females have very different bodies. Species in which the sexes look very similar are referred to as sexually monomorphic, even though they are different internally—for example, in the production of eggs or sperm. Table 12.2 reviews the various reproductive strategies.

12.10 Males Are Not Always the Larger Sex In mandrill baboons (*a*) and peafowl (*b*), the male is larger and more brightly colored than the female. In ringdoves (*c*), males and females appear identical but behave differently. Among praying mantises (*d*) and jacanas (*e*), females are larger than males.

(a) Mandrill baboons

(b) Peafowl

(c) Ringdoves

(d) Praying mantises

(e) Jacanas

TABLE 12.2 *Reproductive Strategies of Animals*

Type of reproduction	Strategy	Examples of animals that use the strategy
Asexual	Fission	Unicellular animals
	Parthenogenesis (virgin birth)	
	Obligatory	Amazon mollies, some whiptail lizards
	Occasional	Aphids
Sexual	Hermaphroditism (each individual produces both sperm and eggs)	
	Simultaneous	Many invertebrates (e.g., *Aplysia*)
	Serial	Some fishes
	Separate sexes (each individual produces either sperm or eggs)	
	Sexually monomorphic	Many birds (e.g., seagulls, ringdoves)
	Sexually dimorphic	Most mammals

The most obvious sexual dimorphism is the larger body size of males in many vertebrate species (see Figure 12.10*a* and *b*). Later in this chapter we will learn that the nervous systems of rats, humans, and other vertebrates also display sexual dimorphism. One example of sexual dimorphism that appears to have had profound effects on vertebrate evolution is the difference in the size of male gametes (sperm) and female gametes (ova): Male gametes are small and cheap; female gametes are large and expensive.

Figure 12.11 demonstrates the difference in size between male and female vertebrate gametes—a well-known fact—but the difference in cost is less familiar. Every animal must gain scarce resources to live, including nutrients to support growth. Unless individuals budget their use of nutrients and energy wisely, they cannot succeed at reproduction. An individual specialized for producing sperm can produce many millions of gametes for the same cost, in terms of nutrients and energy, as that of a single egg.

Because of the low cost of producing sperm, a single male individual can gather enough energy and nutrients to produce sufficient sperm to inseminate millions of females, potentially providing the entire next generation. Females, on the other hand, must be more selective in order to reproduce successfully. Females that carefully nurture their costly eggs (in whatever manner is appropriate for that species) reproduce more often than less cautious females and come to predominate in future generations. One of the most important ways that females of any species can nurture their egg investments is to choose a mate carefully. Males that carry many beneficial genes are more likely to provide the female's offspring with favorable genes. Therefore, females that discover and mate with such males should come to predominate in future generations, while females that mate indiscriminately will have fewer descendants.

The difficulty for a female, of course, is how to determine whether a potential mate has beneficial genes. (Until recently, she could not count on training in molecular biology.)

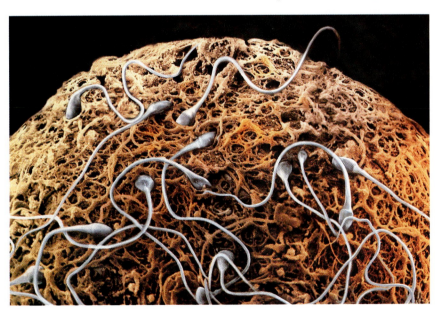

12.11 Male Gametes Are Small and Cheap, Female Gametes Large and Expensive   Sperm cluster around a human ovum, magnified about 1900 times. Because they are so much smaller than ova, sperm are easier to produce.

The female must closely observe the appearance and behavior of the male. A vigorous, healthy male must be doing something right, and in general, an unhealthy looking male is more likely (although by no means certain) to carry harmful genes. On the other hand, inseminating a female is rarely dangerous to a male. Even if the offspring do not survive, ample sperm will be left for the next female. The only real dangers for males come with mating in species such as black widow spiders and praying mantises, in which the female kills the male afterward, and with contracting sexually transmitted diseases.

From this perspective, **courtship** is a period during which the female indirectly assesses the genetic makeup of a male to judge his suitability as a mate. For mammalian females, which carry their young in utero for a prolonged period and then provide milk for an additional time, the investment in each fertilized egg is tremendous, and therefore the pressure to select a good mate is intense. In most vertebrates, nearly all the females who reach reproductive age manage to mate, but only a minority of mature males ever persuade anyone to mate with them. Some interesting exceptions to this pattern are described in the next section.

Mating Systems Can Be Classified into Four Basic Types

The mating strategies of males and females across species can be classified into four different mating systems: promiscuity, polygyny, polyandry, and monogamy. These different systems seem to be related to species differences in the investment of males and females in their offspring.

**EVOLUTION
AT WORK**

1. **Promiscuity**. Recall that among mammals, most females are very selective in mating and most males never mate. Thus a few males are doing most of the mating, and because the number of males and females is roughly equal, these males must be mating with more than one female. But most female mammals also mate with more than one male. Such a mating system, in which animals mate with several partners and do not establish long-lasting associations, is called promiscuity.
2. **Polygyny** (from the Greek *polys*, "many," and *gyne*, "woman"). With some animals, such as elephant seals and gorillas, a long-lasting association between mates develops—one male mating with a group of females (a harem). Each female mates with only one male, but that male mates with several females.
3. **Polyandry** (the Greek *aner* means "man"). In this system, which is much rarer than polygyny, each female of the species mates with several males, but each male mates with only one female. The jacana (see Figure 12.10*e*) is an example of a polyandrous species; in this species the females compete for mates. The females are larger and more colorful than the males, and they defend the nest site from other females. Once the female jacana lays the eggs, she departs, leaving the male to incubate the eggs and raise the young. The term *polygamy* (literally "many spouses"; the Greek *gamos* means "marriage") is sometimes used to refer to polygyny and polyandry collectively. (*Bigamy* means "having two spouses.")
4. **Monogamy** (literally "one spouse"). This mating system is characterized by one male and one female forming a breeding pair and mating exclusively (or almost exclusively) with one another. Monogamy is far more common among birds than among mammals (Figure 12.12*a*). It has been suggested that because birds have a high metabolic rate and their young tend to be very immature at hatching, a single parent could not provide enough food for the chicks to survive (see Figure 12.12*b*). In that case, males that did not care for eggs and chicks would make little or no contribution to the next generation; thus, the development of monogamy would be expected. Yet there seems to be a distinction between social monogamy and sexual monogamy because even among birds thought to be monogamous, the chicks are not always genetically related to the male that is caring for them (Johnsen et al., 2000). So the adults sometimes copulate outside the pair.

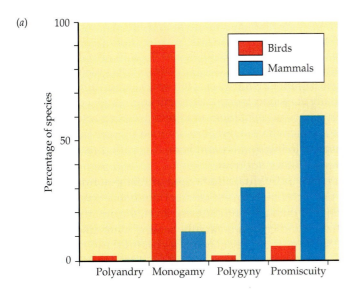

(a)

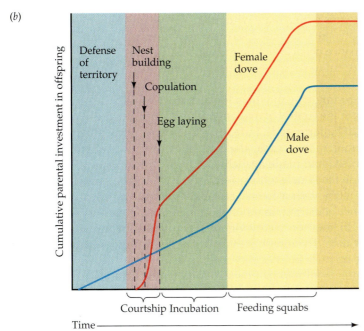

(b)

12.12 Mating Systems and Parental Investment in Offspring
(*a*) These estimates of mating-system types show that birds are far more likely than mammals to be monogamous. (*b*) Hypothetical curves of the cumulative investment of a female and a male ring-dove in their offspring throughout the reproductive cycle. Both parents incubate eggs and feed hatchlings (squabs). (Part *a* estimates for birds are based on data from Lack, 1968; estimates for mammals from Daly and Wilson, 1978. Both should be regarded as only rough estimates. Part *b* adapted from C. J. Erickson, 1978, and Trivers, 1985.)

Sexual Selection Accentuates Differences between the Sexes

As we learned in Chapter 6, Charles Darwin was the first to recognize that competition between males and the tendency of females to be very selective in mating affect the course of natural selection. He coined the term **sexual selection** to refer to the selective pressures that each sex exerts on the other. Darwin regarded sexual selection as a special type of natural selection and used the concept to explain certain features that were not easy to explain on the basis of natural selection alone. For example, why do male lions have manes, male birds of paradise display elaborate tail feathers, and male moose sport enormous antlers? These features do not seem to help the animal gather food, elude predators, or find shelter. Indeed, in many cases such features seem to hinder those functions.

The only advantage Darwin could imagine that these features might confer on animals was in procuring mates. Why? Because members of the other sex display a

EVOLUTION AT WORK

12.13 The Results of Sexual Selection
The male Wilson's bird of paradise puts
on a colorful tail display. Although such
bright colors and elaborate feathers may
interfere with the bird's ability to avoid
predators, they definitely attract female
birds of paradise.

preference for mates with those features. Darwin also realized that sexual selection, by exerting *different* selective pressures on males and females, would impel the two sexes to diverge more and more in their appearance. Thus sexual reproduction provides the pressure to select mates with advantageous genes. In some insect species the sexes are so dimorphic that zoologists originally classified them as different species. Of course, there is a limit to the influence of sexual selection, because other selective pressures also apply. A male who is overly ornamented (Figure 12.13), for example, may be unable to find food or evade predators (R. Brooks, 2000)—activities that are crucial for survival.

In sexual selection, individuals that demand that potential partners display certain characteristics or perform certain behaviors benefit by passing good genes to their offspring. At one level, the ornamentation or extravagant behavior indicates a generally healthy mate, likely to have pretty good genes. But once a particular species begins showing such partiality—for manes on male lions, elaborate tails on birds, balding in men, and so on—the prejudice tends to be self-perpetuating. For example, once a population of females comes to favor mating with maned lions, a female who mates with a male without a mane leaves her offspring (especially her sons) at a distinct disadvantage. Natural selection thus favors the maintenance of such mating preferences. There is considerable debate about the extent to which sexual selection has shaped human reproduction (Box 12.1).

One interesting way in which females of several species enforce these demands is in the control of ovulation (the physical release of an egg from the ovary so that it can be fertilized). In frogs, for example, exposure to courting males facilitates ovulation in the female; the more such behavior the males display, the more eggs are released and made available for fertilization. We saw earlier that a male rat must provide the female with several intromissions before ejaculation or she will not become pregnant; thus female rats exert selective pressure on males to copulate a while before ejaculating. In other species, courtship and/or copulation is *required* for ovulation. In lions, only very vigorous copulation over several days induces the female to ovulate. The reproductive physiology of lionesses enforces strict evolutionary pressure on male behavior.

In the parthenogenetic whiptail lizards and Amazon mollies discussed earlier, closely related species reproduce sexually, and in these sexual species courtship and mating behaviors facilitate ovulation. Some remnant of this courtship-facilitated ovulation must remain in the parthenogenetic females because they, too, release more eggs if they are courted and go through mating behavior. But with whom do you mate when there are only females of your species? With whiptail lizards, females take turns mating with one another. A given female may play the role of a male one moment—wrapping her body around the other female, pressing their cloacae together, biting her neck, and so on—and play the role of a female later (see Figure 12.9a). Two females in a cage alone literally take turns. Such mock mating increases the number of eggs released and laid.

The Amazon mollies "mate" not with one another, but with males of the closely related sailfin molly species. A male sailfin molly courts Amazon females, inserts his modified fin into the female, and deposits sperm. The sperm do not fertilize the eggs, but the Amazon releases more eggs and later gives birth to more daughters for having gone through the mock mating. Why should the male sailfins bother? Perhaps the cost to the male is very low, and perhaps the rehearsal improves later mating with a sailfin female. But another reason that has been suggested is that sailfin females, seeing the male mate with another female (of either species), may regard him as more attractive and may thus be more likely to mate with him (Schlupp et al., 1994).

BOX 12.1 *Evolutionary Psychology*

Speculation about selective pressure on reproductive behavior in various animals leads inevitably to questions about the extent to which our own behaviors have been affected by the difference between male and female reproductive strategies. Are women inherently more selective than men about choosing mating partners? Such a difference could be a result of the tremendous investment in time, energy, and resources that a female mammal must make in each offspring. Are men more promiscuous than women? It's easy to imagine that the low cost of producing sperm (and the potential for a man to expend no energy on child rearing) might favor such behavior. Do romantic relationships tend to sour after about 7 years? If so, is the reason for this tendency the fact that in earlier evolutionary times, it took about that

long to rear a child and thus when that period ended it would be time to find a new mate in case the first mate had some genetic deficits that might be passed on to the offspring? Is there an "ideal" waist-to-hip ratio that indicates maximal fertility in women? Do men in all cultures regard such a ratio as most attractive? Are women attracted to power, and men to youth, because natural selection favored these preferences?

Such speculations have given rise to a lively and controversial field called **evolutionary psychology** (Barkow et al., 1992; Buss, 2000). It's easy to spin plausible tales about how evolution might have shaped our behavior, but the challenge for these theorists is to come up with ways to test (and potentially disprove) these hypotheses. Such an enterprise is especially daunting when ethical considerations mean that

the investigator can never manipulate the variables ("Let's see, I'd like you to marry that person over there and then I'll ask you some questions 7 years from now"), but must rely on correlations and surveys.

Geoffrey Miller (2000) proposes that sexual selection was crucial for evolution of the human brain. If, among early hominids, people came to favor mates who sang, made jokes, or produced artistic works, then such high-order functioning would rapidly evolve in an arms race, as the ever more discriminating brains of one sex demanded ever more impressive performances from the brains of the other sex. Did humor, song, and art originate from the drive to be sexually attractive? And does this account for the large size of the human brain, as hypothesized by Miller (see Chapter 6)?

Sexual Differentiation

For species such as our own, in which the only kind of reproduction is sexual reproduction (so far), and in which sexual selection has generated sexual dimorphism, each individual must become either a male or a female to reproduce. **Sexual differentiation** is the process by which individuals develop either male or female bodies and behavior. In mammals this process begins before birth and continues until the individual becomes capable of reproducing.

The Sex of an Individual Is Determined Early in Life

For mammals sex is determined at the time of conception, when a sperm penetrates the egg and contributes either a Y chromosome or an X chromosome. From that point on, the path of sexual differentiation is set. We will describe that path and its occasional exceptions shortly. Mammals that receive an X chromosome from the father will become females; those that receive a Y chromosome will become males. (The mother always contributes an X chromosome.)

Males are said to be the **heterogametic** sex because they have two different **sex chromosomes** (XY); females are **homogametic** (XX). Female birds are heterogametic. The sex of some reptiles is determined by sex chromosomes; in other reptile species the factor determining whether an individual develops as a male or female is the temperature at which the egg is incubated.

No matter what the mechanisms, the developmentally early event that normally decides whether the individual will become a male or female is known as **sexual determination.** In vertebrates the first visible consequence of sexual determination is in the gonads. Very early in development each individual has a pair of **indifferent gonads,** glands that vaguely resemble both testes and ovaries. During the first month of gestation in humans, the indifferent gonads begin changing into either ovaries or testes.

**GENES AND
BEHAVIOR**

Sex Chromosomes Direct Sexual Differentiation of the Gonads

In mammals the Y chromosome contains a gene called the **SRY gene** (for *sex-determining region* on the *Y* chromosome) that is responsible for the development of testes. If an individual has a Y chromosome, the cells of the indifferent gonad begin making the Sry protein. The Sry protein causes the cells in the core of the indifferent gonad (the medulla) to proliferate at the expense of the outer layers (the cortex), and the indifferent gonad develops into a testis.

If the individual has no Y chromosome (or if it has a Y chromosome but the *SRY* gene is defective), no Sry protein is produced, and the indifferent gonad takes a different course: Cells of the cortical layers proliferate more than those of the medullary layers, and an ovary forms. (In reptiles that lack sex chromosomes, the temperature at which the egg is incubated appears to determine whether or not an Sry-like gene product is made.) For all vertebrates, this early decision of whether to form testes or ovaries has a domino effect, setting off a chain of events that usually results in either a male or a female.

Gonadal Hormones Direct Sexual Differentiation of the Rest of the Body

The most important way the gonads influence sexual differentiation is through their hormonal output. Developing testes produce several hormones, while early ovaries produce very little hormone. If other cells of the embryo receive the testicular hormones, they begin developing masculine characters; if the cells are not exposed to testicular hormones, they develop feminine characters.

We can chart masculine or feminine development by examining the structures that connect the gonads to the outside of the body. The conduits between the gametes and exterior are quite different in males and females (see Figure 12.7), so the proper development of these structures is crucial for sexual reproduction. At the embryonic stage, all individuals have the precursor tissues that could form either the female or the male apparatus.

For example, the early fetus has a genital tubercle that can form either a clitoris or a penis, as well as two sets of ducts that connect the indifferent gonads to the outer body wall: the **wolffian ducts** and the **müllerian ducts** (Figure 12.14*a*). The early fetus has both sets of ducts, but in females the müllerian ducts develop into the fallopian tubes, uterus, and inner vagina (Figure 12.14*c* and *e*), and only a remnant of the wolffian ducts remains. In males, hormones secreted by the testes orchestrate the converse outcome: The wolffian ducts develop into epididymis, vas deferens, and seminal vesicles (Figure 12.14*b* and *d*), while the müllerian ducts shrink to mere remnants.

The development of the wolffian ducts is promoted by the steroidal androgen testosterone; the shrinkage of the müllerian ducts is caused by the protein hormone known as müllerian regression hormone or **anti-müllerian hormone** (**AMH**). If there is no testis to produce testosterone and AMH, the wolffian ducts fail to develop and the müllerian ducts develop as a result of a cascade of gene expression (Vainio et al., 1999).

Testosterone also masculinizes other, non-wolffian-derived structures. Testosterone causes tissues around the urethra to form the prostate gland. Furthermore, testosterone acts on the epithelial tissues around the urethra to form a scrotum and penis. These effects are aided by the local conversion of testosterone into another steroidal androgen, **dihydrotestosterone** (**DHT**). The epithelial cells have the enzyme **5α-reductase** to convert testosterone to DHT, and the DHT binds the androgen receptors even more readily than does testosterone, resulting in greater gene activation and further masculine development. So 5α-reductase serves to locally amplify androgen influence. Without steroidal androgens, the prostate fails to form and the external skin grows into the female labia and clitoris.

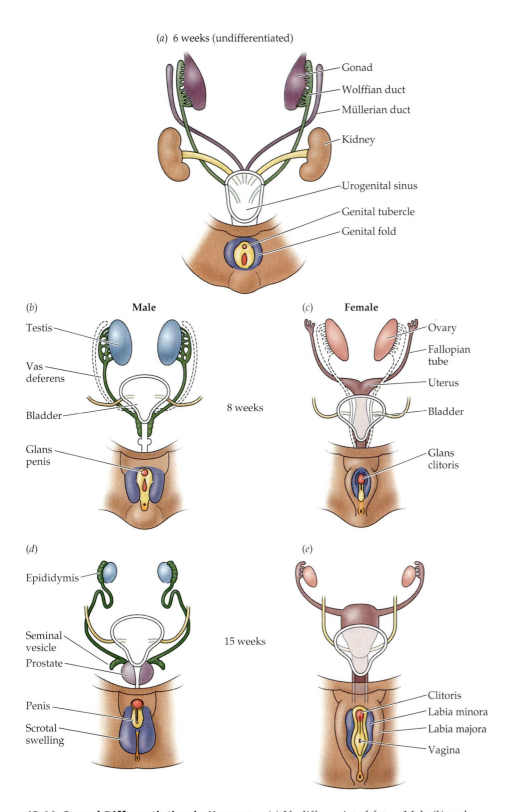

(a) 6 weeks (undifferentiated)

Gonad
Wolffian duct
Müllerian duct
Kidney
Urogenital sinus
Genital tubercle
Genital fold

(b) **Male**

Testis
Vas deferens
Bladder
Glans penis

8 weeks

(c) **Female**

Ovary
Fallopian tube
Uterus
Bladder
Glans clitoris

(d)

Epididymis
Seminal vesicle
Prostate
Penis
Scrotal swelling

15 weeks

(e)

Clitoris
Labia minora
Labia majora
Vagina

12.14 Sexual Differentiation in Humans *(a)* Undifferentiated fetus. Male *(b)* and female *(c)* fetuses at 8 weeks of gestation. Male *(d)* and female *(e)* at 15 weeks of gestation.

12.15 Genetic and Hormonal Mechanisms of Embryonic Sexual Differentiation

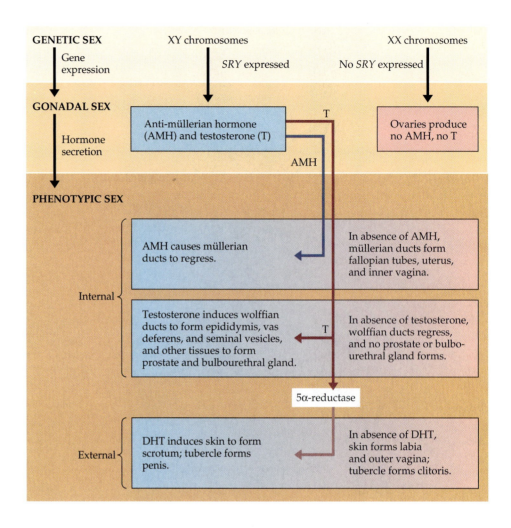

Departures from the Orderly Sequence of Sexual Differentiation Result in Predictable Changes in Development

Some people have only one sex chromosome: a single X. Such genetic makeup (referred to as XO) results in **Turner's syndrome:** an apparent female with poorly developed but recognizable ovaries, as you would expect because no *SRY* gene is available. So the role of the sex chromosomes is to determine the sex of the gonad; gonadal hormones then drive sexual differentiation of the rest of the body (Figure 12.15). Later in life, both hormones and experience guide sexual differentiation (Figure 12.16).

Sometimes XX individuals with well-formed ovaries are exposed to androgens in utero, and depending on the degree of exposure, they may be masculinized. For example, most fetal rats develop in the uterus sandwiched between two siblings. If a female is surrounded by brothers, some of the androgen from the siblings must reach the female because, although her gross appearance will be feminine at birth, her anogenital distance (the distance from the tip of the phallus to the anus) will be slightly greater (i.e., more malelike) than that of a female developing between two sisters (Clemens et al., 1978). In Chapter 9 we saw an example of a similar phenomenon in humans: Females who have a male twin produce otoacoustic emissions that are slightly more typical of males than of females.

In humans several genetic mutations can result in a female who is exposed to androgens in utero. What these various conditions, known as **congenital adrenal hyperplasia (CAH)**, have in common is that the adrenal glands fail to produce sufficient corticosteroids, producing instead considerable amounts of androgens. (The condi-

12.16 Steps toward Adult Gender Identity in Humans

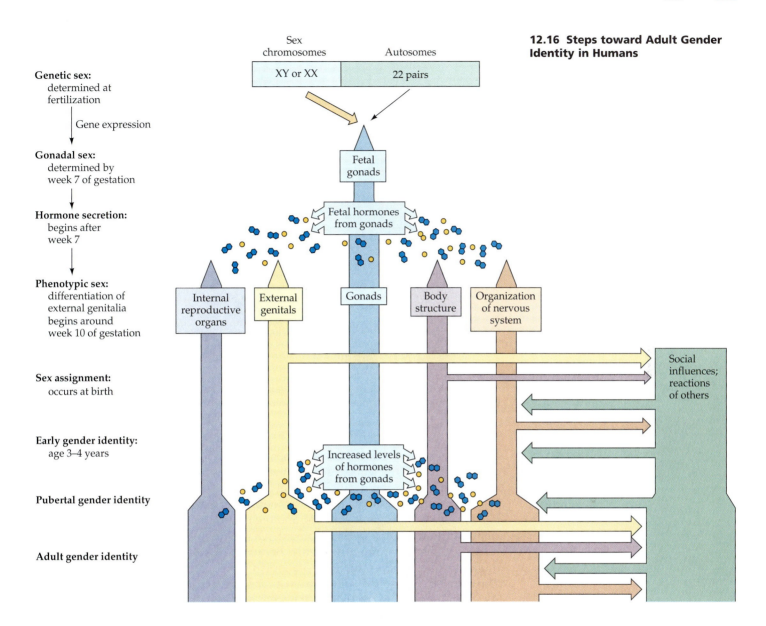

Genetic sex: determined at fertilization

Gene expression

Gonadal sex: determined by week 7 of gestation

Hormone secretion: begins after week 7

Phenotypic sex: differentiation of external genitalia begins around week 10 of gestation

Sex assignment: occurs at birth

Early gender identity: age 3–4 years

Pubertal gender identity

Adult gender identity

Sex chromosomes — Autosomes

XY or XX — 22 pairs

Fetal gonads

Fetal hormones from gonads

Internal reproductive organs — External genitals — Gonads — Body structure — Organization of nervous system

Social influences; reactions of others

Increased levels of hormones from gonads

tion is called *adrenal hyperplasia* because at birth the adrenal glands are swollen from excessive cell division. The word *congenital* means "present at birth.")

In XX individuals with this condition, the androgen levels produced are usually intermediate between those of normal females and males, and the newborn has an **intersex** appearance: a phallus that is intermediate in size between a normal clitoris and a normal penis, and skin folds that resemble both labia and scrotum (Figure 12.17). Sometimes the opening of the vagina fails to form (although the internal portion of the vagina is present), and sometimes the urethra opens somewhere along the base or length of the phallus (rather than below the clitoris as in other females). Such individuals are readily recognizable at birth because, even in severe cases in which penis and scrotum are well formed, no testes are present in the "scrotum." The ovaries of such individuals, as you would expect, are normal and remain in the abdomen. The müllerian duct structures are fully developed.

The controversial treatment for such individuals is surgical correction of the external appearance and administration of medication to inhibit androgen production by the adrenals. But there is a growing view that surgery should be postponed until the individuals reach adulthood so that they can make informed decisions about whether to have surgery and what gender role to follow. CAH females are much more likely

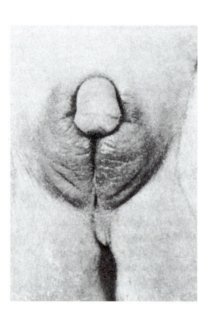
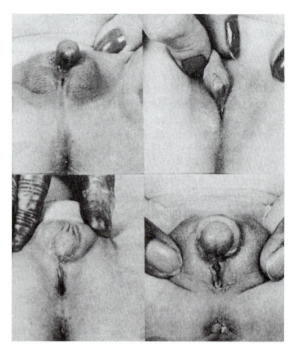

12.17 An Intersex Phenotype These genitalia are characteristic of newborn girls with congenital adrenal hyperplasia (CAH). (Courtesy of John Money.)

to be described by their parents (and themselves) as tomboys than are other girls. In adulthood, most CAH females describe themselves as heterosexual, but they are somewhat more likely to report a homosexual orientation than are other women.

In rats and other mammals, experimenters have deliberately exposed developing females to androgenic steroids, and the results are quite uniform: Given sufficient testosterone during development, XX individuals form wolffian duct structures: prostate, scrotum, and penis. Because the testosterone has no effect on müllerian ducts, these structures—fallopian tubes, uterus, and (internal) vagina—also develop. The gonads develop as ovaries, apparently ignoring the androgens. As we will see later in the chapter, the adult behavior of such androgenized females provided the first clues that early androgens could masculinize the brain as well as the body.

A Defective Androgen Receptor Can Block the Masculinization of Males

An interesting demonstration of the influence of androgens on sexual differentiation is provided by the condition known as **androgen insensitivity.** The gene for the androgen receptor is found on the X chromosome. An XY individual whose X chromosome has a defective androgen receptor gene is incapable of producing the androgen receptor and is therefore unable to respond to androgenic hormones. The gonads of such people develop as normal testes, and the testes produce AMH (which inhibits müllerian duct structures) and plenty of testosterone.

In the absence of working androgen receptors, however, the wolffian ducts fail to develop and the external epithelia form labia and a clitoris. Such individuals look like normal females at birth, and at puberty they develop breasts. (Breast development in humans appears to depend on the ratio of estrogenic to androgenic stimulation at puberty, and since androgen-insensitive individuals receive little androgenic *stimulation,* the functional estrogen-to-androgen ratio is high.)

Androgen-insensitive individuals may be recognized when their menstrual cycles fail to commence because neither ovaries nor uterus are present to produce menstruation. Such women are infertile and, lacking a müllerian contribution, have a shallow vagina, but otherwise they look like other women (Figure 12.18) and, as we'll see in the next section, behave like other women. At the end of this chapter we will describe another mutation that causes some people to appear to change their sex (without surgery) at adolescence.

How Should We Define Gender—by Genes, Gonads, Genitals, or the Brain?

Most humans are either male or female, and whether we examine their chromosomes, gonads, external genitalia, or internal structures, we see a consistent pattern: Each one is either feminine or masculine in character. Behavior is much more difficult than physical features to define as feminine or masculine. The only behavior displayed *exclusively* by one sex is childbirth. Even behaviors that are very rarely displayed by members of one sex or the other (e.g., sexual assault by women or breast-feeding by men) occur sometimes in the unexpected sex. As for behaviors that can be measured and made amenable to experimental study in humans or other animals, we have to resort to group means and statistical tests to see the differences. A given individual almost always displays some behaviors that are more common in the opposite sex.

Androgen-insensitive individuals show us that even morphological features can be confusing criteria by which to judge sex (see Figure 12.18). Androgen-insensitive humans have a male chromosome and testes. Like most males, they do not have fallopian tubes or a uterus, but they do have a vagina and breasts, and in many respects they behave like most females: They dress like females, they are attracted to and marry males, and perhaps most importantly, even after they learn the details of their condition, they continue to call themselves women (Money and Ehrhardt, 1972).

As we will see next, parts of the brain are also typically different between the sexes in humans and other animals. In androgen-insensitive rats, some brain regions are masculine and others are feminine. Thus, from a scientific standpoint we cannot regard an animal, especially a human, as simply masculine or feminine. Rather we must specify which structure or behavior we mean when we say it is typical of females or of males.

Gonadal Hormones Direct Sexual Differentiation of the Brain and Behavior

As scientists began discovering that testicular hormones direct masculine development of the body, behavioral researchers found evidence for a similar influence on the brain. In 1959, Phoenix, Goy, Gerall, and Young described the effect of fetal hormones on the sexual behavior of guinea pigs. Recall that a female guinea pig, like most rodents, normally displays the lordosis posture in response to male mounting for only a short period around the time of ovulation, when her fertility is highest. If a male mounts her at other times, she does not show lordosis. An experimenter can induce the female to display lordosis by injecting ovarian steroids in the sequence they normally follow during ovulation—giving her estrogens for a few days and then progesterone. A few hours after the progesterone injection, the female will display lordosis in response to male mounting.

Phoenix and collaborators knew that when the same regimen of steroids was given to an adult *male* guinea pig, whether or not he was allowed to keep his testes, he almost never showed lordosis in response to mounting males. In the 1959 study, the experimenters exposed female guinea pigs to testosterone in utero. As adults, these females did not show lordosis. Even if their ovaries were removed and they were given the steroidal regimen that reliably activated lordosis in normal females, these fetally androgenized females did not show lordosis.

On the basis of these data, William C. Young and his colleagues proposed the **organizational hypothesis:** The same testicular steroids that masculinize the genitalia

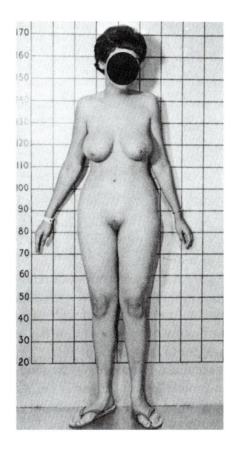

12.18 An Androgen-Insensitive Person   Although this person has the male XY chromosome pattern and therefore testes (undescended), she also has complete androgen insensitivity. Therefore her body has developed in a feminine fashion. (Courtesy of John Money.)

William C. Young
(1899–1965)

also masculinize the developing brain and thereby permanently alter behavior. This **organizational effect** of steroid hormones stood in contrast with the activational effects we mentioned earlier (e.g., the activation of lordosis in adult females in response to estrogens and progesterone).

Whereas steroids have an organizational influence only during early development and the effect is permanent, in adulthood they exert an activational effect, temporarily influencing behavior. Steroids have an organizational effect only when present during a **sensitive period.** The exact boundaries of the sensitive period of development depend on which behavior and which species is being studied. For rats, which are **altricial** (born in an immature state), androgens given just after birth (the **neonatal** period) can affect later behavior. Guinea pigs, which are **precocial** (born in a relatively mature state), must be exposed to androgens **prenatally** (before birth) for adult behavior to be affected.

Early Testicular Secretions Result in Masculine Behavior in Adulthood

The organizational hypothesis provides a unitary explanation for sexual differentiation: The same steroid signal that masculinizes the body (androgens) also masculinizes parts of the brain, ensuring that an individual's behavior usually is appropriate for its sex. From this point of view the nervous system is just another type of tissue listening for the androgenic signal that will instruct it to organize itself in a masculine fashion. If the nervous system does not detect androgens, it will organize itself in a feminine fashion. In fact, outside of the gonads and müllerian ducts, all tissues that develop differently in males and females have been shown to do so under the influence of androgenic steroids. This is one of the functions that steroid hormones, with their capacity to infiltrate the entire body, can fulfill: sending a single message to disparate parts of the body to coordinate an integrated response.

What was demonstrated originally for the lordosis behavior of guinea pigs has been observed in a variety of vertebrate species and for a variety of behaviors. Female rats must also display lordosis for mating to take place; experiments have shown that exposing female rat pups to testosterone either just before birth or during the first 10 days after birth greatly reduces their lordosis responsiveness as adults. Such results explain the previous findings that adult male rats show very little lordosis even when given estrogens and progesterone. Male rats that are castrated during the first week of life, however, display very good lordosis responses after a treatment of estradiol plus progesterone in adulthood. In rats, many behaviors were shown to be consistent with the organizational hypothesis: Animals exposed to either endogenous or exogenous androgens early in life behaved like males, while animals not exposed to androgens early in life behaved like females.

Some sex differences in behavior seem indifferent to early exposure to androgens. For example, male rhesus monkeys yawn more often than females, but this behavior seems to be the result of adult exposure to androgens. If rhesus males are castrated in adulthood, they yawn about as often as normal females, and treating adult females with androgens activates yawning. Exposure to androgens during development has no effect on later yawning behavior, so this sex difference in behavior seems to respond solely to activational rather than to organizational effects of androgens.

In other cases, androgens seem to be needed both in development (to organize the nervous system to enable the later behavior) and in adulthood (to activate that behavior). For example, as we learned earlier, the copulatory behavior of male rats can be quantified in terms of how often they mount a receptive female and how often such mounting results in intromission. Androgens must be present in adulthood to activate this behavior: Adult males that have been castrated stop mounting in a few weeks; injecting them with testosterone eventually restores masculine copulatory behavior. Such androgen treatment has some effect on adult female rats as well, causing them to mount other females more often, but they rarely manage intromission of their phallus (the clitoris) into the stimulus female's vagina.

To see the full range of masculine copulatory behavior in a female rat, you must treat her with androgens just before birth, just after birth, and in adulthood. Such females not only mount receptive females, but they even achieve intromissions regularly and ejaculate a (spermless) fluid (Ward, 1969). Conversely, castrating a male rat at birth results in very few intromissions later, no matter how much androgen it receives in adulthood.

Thus masculine copulatory behavior in rats and several other rodent species seems to depend on both organizational and activational influences of androgens. An early criticism of this conclusion was offered by Frank Beach (1971), who pointed out that the failure of females and neonatally castrated male rats to achieve intromission could well be due to the small size of the phallus rather than any differences in the nervous system. Indeed, there is remarkable correlation between the size of the penis and intromission success in male rats castrated at various ages (Beach and Holz, 1946). Thus although there is excellent evidence that steroids present at birth masculinize the body, Beach found no proof that they masculinize the brain. However, an unexpected development soon made it clear that steroids do indeed organize the developing nervous system of rodents to display male copulatory behavior, as we will see next.

**Frank Beach
(1911–1988)**

The Estrogenic Metabolites of Testosterone Masculinize the Nervous System and Behavior of Rodents

Soon after the organizational hypothesis was published, some researchers reported a paradoxical finding: When newborn female rats were treated with small doses of estrogens, they failed to show lordosis behavior in adulthood (Feder and Whalen, 1965). In fact, a very small dose of estrogens, as little as 10 mg, could permanently masculinize these behaviors, whereas achieving the same effect with testosterone required a higher dose (100 to 1000 mg). The fact that a steroid such as estradiol, regarded as a *female* hormone, could have such a profoundly masculinizing influence on later behavior was very puzzling. The results were especially strange because during development all rat fetuses are exposed to high levels of estrogens that originate in the mother and cross the placenta. If estrogens masculinize the developing brain, why aren't all females masculinized by maternal estrogens?

**COMPETING
HYPOTHESES**

A closer look at the synthesis of steroid hormones reveals the explanation. The major androgen (testosterone) and the major estrogen (estradiol) differ by only one molecule. In fact, testosterone is often used as a precursor for the manufacture of estradiol in the ovary. In a single chemical reaction, called aromatization, the enzyme **aromatase** converts testosterone to estradiol and other androgens to other estrogens. The ovaries normally contain a great deal of aromatase, and the brain was found to have high levels of aromatase as well. From this evidence arose the **aromatization hypothesis,** which suggested that testicular androgens enter the brain and are converted there into estrogens, and that these estrogens are what masculinize the developing nervous system.

Why, then, aren't the brains of females masculinized by maternal estrogens? A protein found in the plasma of rat fetuses, called **α-fetoprotein,** binds estrogens and prevents them from entering the brain. Although both male and female fetuses produce α-fetoprotein, this protein does not bind androgens. The male rat is masculinized when his testes produce testosterone, which traverses the bloodstream (unimpeded by α-fetoprotein), and enters the brain, where aromatase converts the testosterone to an estrogen, the estrogen binds to estrogen receptors, and the steroid–receptor complex regulates gene expression to cause the brain to develop in a masculine fashion (Figure 12.19). If no androgens are present, no estrogens reach the brain, and the fetus develops in a feminine fashion. A lack of aromatase seems to play a role in the unusual sexual differentiation of the spotted hyena (see Box 12.2).

The aromatization hypothesis, as proposed by Frederick Naftolin and further investigated by Bruce McEwen and their colleagues, was soon shown to apply even

Bruce McEwen

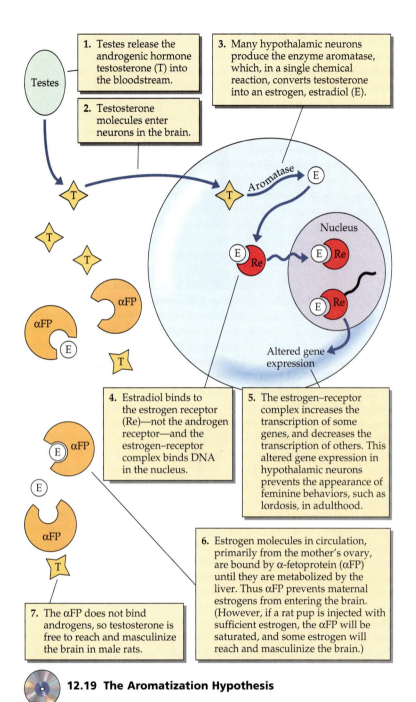

1. Testes release the androgenic hormone testosterone (T) into the bloodstream.

2. Testosterone molecules enter neurons in the brain.

3. Many hypothalamic neurons produce the enzyme aromatase, which, in a single chemical reaction, converts testosterone into an estrogen, estradiol (E).

4. Estradiol binds to the estrogen receptor (Re)—not the androgen receptor—and the estrogen–receptor complex binds DNA in the nucleus.

5. The estrogen–receptor complex increases the transcription of some genes, and decreases the transcription of others. This altered gene expression in hypothalamic neurons prevents the appearance of feminine behaviors, such as lordosis, in adulthood.

6. Estrogen molecules in circulation, primarily from the mother's ovary, are bound by α-fetoprotein (αFP) until they are metabolized by the liver. Thus αFP prevents maternal estrogens from entering the brain. (However, if a rat pup is injected with sufficient estrogen, the αFP will be saturated, and some estrogen will reach and masculinize the brain.)

7. The αFP does not bind androgens, so testosterone is free to reach and masculinize the brain in male rats.

12.19 The Aromatization Hypothesis

to masculine copulatory behavior in rats. If male rats were castrated at birth, they grew up to have a small penis and to show few intromissions even when given testosterone in adulthood. If the males were castrated at birth and given the androgen dihydrotestosterone (DHT), which cannot be converted into an estrogen, as adults they had a penis of normal size but still showed few or no intromission behaviors when given androgens. On the other hand, males castrated as newborns and treated with estrogens achieved intromission regularly when treated with androgens as adults, despite having a very small penis (no larger than in untreated castrated males).

Thus Frank Beach's playful explanation of why female rats achieve few intromissions—"you can't be a carpenter if you don't have a hammer"—was disproved. Rather, early testicular secretions seemed to organize the developing nervous system to masculinize later behavior. This idea was amply confirmed later, when sex differences in the structure of the nervous system were found.

Several Regions of the Nervous System Display Prominent Sexual Dimorphism

Because male and female rats behave differently, researchers assumed that their brains were different, and the organizational hypothesis asserted that early androgens masculinize the developing brain. But these neural differences can be very subtle; the same basic circuit of neurons connected together will produce very different behavior if the strength of the myriad synapses varies. However, sex differences in the number of synapses were identified in the preoptic area (POA) of the hypothalamus as early as 1971 (Raisman and Field, 1971). Later demonstrations of sexual dimorphism in the nervous system would include differences in the number, size, and shape of neurons, as well as the number of synapses.

Song control regions in male songbirds. Fernando Nottebohm and Arthur Arnold were studying the brain regions that control singing in canaries and zebra finches when they noticed something unexpected: Brain sections from males and females showed that the nuclei that control song are *much* larger in males than in females (Nottebohm and Arnold, 1976). Measuring the sections revealed that the nuclei are five to six times larger in volume in males (which produce elaborate songs) than in females (which produce only simple calls). Let's briefly discuss these brain nuclei and their sexual dimorphism.

Birds produce song through a specialized muscular organ called the **syrinx,** which is wrapped around the air passage. The muscles of the syrinx control the frequency of sounds produced by changing the tension of membranes around the air passage. These muscles are controlled by motoneurons of the twelfth cranial nerve (the cranial nerve that controls the tongue in mammals). The corresponding nucleus receives most of its innervation from a brain nucleus called the robustus archistriatum (RA).

The RA receives most of its innervation from a nucleus that is both literally and organizationally higher: the higher vocal center (HVC). Lesions of the HVC abolish

BOX 12.2 *The Paradoxical Sexual Differentiation of the Spotted Hyena*

Scientists of antiquity believed that spotted hyenas were hermaphrodites. The mistake is understandable because the female hyena has a clitoris that is as large as the penis of males (as the figure shows), and like males, she urinates through her phallus. What's more, she appears to have no vagina; during mating the male puts his penis inside the tip of her clitoris and later the pups come into the world through the clitoris.

A group of scientists in Berkeley, California, has begun to understand how this remarkable situation could come about. Because hyenas are born with this sexually monomorphic exterior (although females tend to have larger bodies than do males), either both sexes are exposed to prenatal androgens, or their epithelial tissues develop in the masculine fashion whether or not androgens are present.

Studies of steroid metabolism in the hyena placenta suggest the former situation. In other mammals the placenta rapidly aromatizes androgens into estrogens; this conversion may be a way to protect the mother and fetal females from androgens produced by fetal males. (Remember that in rodents a plasma protein prevents circulating estrogens from masculinizing the brain.) But the spotted hyena placenta is remarkably deficient in the aromatase enzyme (Licht et al., 1992).

Because the hyena mother produces large amounts of the androgen androstenedione (Glickman et al., 1987), and the placenta fails to convert the androstenedione to estrogens, all the fetuses receive considerable amounts of androgens, which may account for their masculine appearance. One test of this hypothesis would be to see whether the placenta of the striped hyena (in which females do not have a masculine appearance) has enzymatic activities more like those of other mammals than like those of the spotted hyena.

Is the spotted hyena brain affected by these early androgens? The fact that female hyenas grow faster than males and are more aggressive than males suggests that it might be. The social lives of hyenas center around the adult females. All adult females are dominant over all males, which means that females always get to eat first and, except during the breeding season, do not tolerate males coming close to them. There is also a dominance hierarchy among the females: The daughters of high-ranking females tend to get first access to food and other resources. Thus there is considerable selective pressure for females to be aggressive, especially with other females.

One remarkable finding from captive-bred hyenas is that female pups begin fighting immediately after birth. They are born with teeth and use them to attack their siblings. Female pups are very aggressive, especially toward a sister. At Berkeley, investigators intervene to prevent serious injury, but field studies indicate that in the wild it is very common for one pup to kill its sibling (Frank et al., 1991), at least during periods when food is scarce (Smale et al., 1999). It remains to be seen whether this extreme aggression is due to prenatal stimulation of the brain with androgens.

Even if the extreme aggressiveness of the female hyena is due to fetal androgens, females do mate with males, so their brains have not been made permanently unreceptive (as would happen in prenatally androgenized rats). Indeed, female hyenas seem to have a typically feminine SDN-POA (see the text) (Fenstemaker et al., 1999) and SNB (see the text) (Forger et al., 1996). Just the same, mating in the spotted hyena is a tense affair: The female seems to just barely tolerate the male's proximity, and the male alternates between approaching and retreating from his more powerful mate. (Photograph courtesy of Stephen Glickman.)

complex song in canaries and zebra finches, and electrical stimulation of the nucleus elicits song snippets. Lesions of the RA also severely disrupt song, as you would expect from the circuitry we've described.

As the organizational hypothesis would suggest, the early action of steroid hormone masculinizes the brains of zebra finches: Exposing a hatchling female to either testosterone or estradiol causes the HVC and the RA to be larger in adulthood. If such a female is also given testosterone as an adult, the nuclei become larger still, and she sings much like a male zebra finch does (Gurney and Konishi, 1979).

Female zebra finches treated with androgens only in adulthood do not sing. Thus in zebra finches, early hormone organizes a masculine song system, and adult hormone activates the system to produce song. Some research suggests that young male zebra finches produce the estrogen locally, in the brain, to masculinize their own birdsong regions (Holloway and Clayton, 2001).

The song of canaries is also affected by androgens, but in this species early steroids seem unimportant. A female canary begins singing after a few weeks of androgen treatment in adulthood. Androgens also cause the HVC and the RA to become larger in volume and the dendrites of neurons in those regions to grow, making new synaptic connections. This difference in hormonal control of song in zebra finches and canaries may relate to the ecological niche occupied by each.

Zebra finches, originally from the Australian desert, are opportunistic breeders; they are ready to breed at any time of the year, awaiting rainfall that will provide additional food. Canaries are seasonal breeders; their reproductive apparatus (including the testes) shuts down in the fall. Therefore, male canaries have high androgen levels in spring and summer and low androgen levels in fall and winter. With this ebb and flow of androgens, singing and the volume of the HVC and the RA also vary: The nuclei grow in the spring as the animal resumes courtship singing and shrink in the fall as singing declines.

Unlike zebra finches, which have only a single, relatively simple song, male canaries produce many, highly elaborate songs, learning additional songs each spring. Thus we can think of male canaries as having brains that remain sensitive to the organizational influences of androgens even in adulthood, and this continual reorganization may help them produce large repertoires to gain a mate.

The preoptic area of rats. The discovery that the brains of songbirds display such obvious sexual dimorphism inspired researchers to look for other neural sex differences. The laboratory of Roger Gorski examined the preoptic area (POA) of the hypothalamus in rats because of an earlier report that the number of synapses in this region was different in males and females and because lesions of the POA disrupt ovulatory cycles in female rats and reduce copulatory behavior in males. Sure enough, there was an easily identifiable nucleus within the POA, and this nucleus was three to five times larger in volume in males than in females (Gorski et al., 1978).

This nucleus, dubbed the **sexually dimorphic nucleus of the POA** (**SDN-POA**), was so much more prominent in male rats that Gorski and colleagues could tell male from female brain sections just by glancing at the slides without a microscope (Figure 12.20). Yet despite intense anatomical study of this brain region for almost a century, no one had noticed the SDN-POA until the birdsong work inspired a search.

Like the song control nuclei in zebra finches, the SDN-POA conformed beautifully to the organizational hypothesis: Males castrated at birth had much smaller SDN-POAs in adulthood, while females androgenized at birth had large, malelike SDN-POAs as adults. Castrating male rats in *adulthood,* however, did not alter the size of the SDN-POA, and neither did treating adult females with androgens. Thus testicular androgens somehow alter the development of the SDN-POA, resulting in a nucleus permanently larger in males than in females.

The function of the SDN-POA is still not completely understood. Lesions of the SDN portion of the POA in rats cause only a slight, temporary decline in male copulatory behavior. A similarly obvious sexually dimorphic nucleus has been described and studied in gerbils (Yahr and Gregory, 1993), and lesions of this SDN-POA significantly reduce the typical scent-marking behavior of male gerbils.

EVOLUTION AT WORK

NEURAL PLASTICITY

12.20 A Sex Difference in the Hypothalamus The sexually dimorphic nucleus of the preoptic area (SDN-POA) is much larger in male rats than in females. (Courtesy of Roger Gorski.)

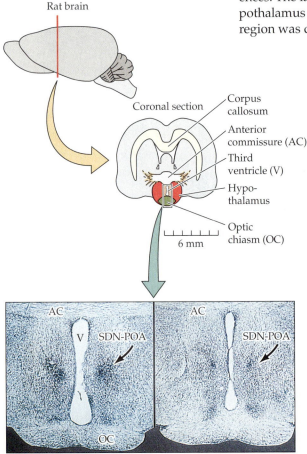

Rat brain

Coronal section

Corpus callosum

Anterior commissure (AC)

Third ventricle (V)

Hypo-thalamus

Optic chiasm (OC)

6 mm

AC

V SDN-POA

AC

SDN-POA

OC

Male

Female

In addition to fitting the organizational hypothesis, the SDN-POA conforms to the aromatization hypothesis: Testosterone is converted to an estrogen in the brain and binds estrogen receptors to masculinize the nucleus. For example, XY rats that are androgen insensitive, like the androgen-insensitive person we discussed earlier (see Figure 12.18), have testes but a feminine exterior. These rats have a masculine SDN-POA because their estrogen receptors are normal. Androgen-insensitive rats also do not display lordosis in response to estrogens and progesterone because the testosterone they secreted early in life was converted to an estrogen in the brain and masculinized their behavior (Olsen, 1979).

Interestingly, the aromatization of androgens to estrogens does not seem to play a role in masculinizing primate behavior. For example, XY humans who are androgen insensitive display very feminine behavior, even though they produce ample levels of androgen and have functional estrogen receptors. So in humans, stimulating estrogen receptors in the developing brain appears to have no masculinizing effect.

Roger Gorski

The spinal cord in mammals.   The birdsong work inspired a search for sexual dimorphism in the spinal cord, where neural elements controlling sexual response should be different for males and females. In rats, for example, the striated bulbocavernosus (BC) muscles (absent in females) that surround the base of the penis are innervated by motoneurons in the **spinal nucleus of the bulbocavernosus (SNB)** (Figure 12.21). Male rats have about 200 SNB cells, but females have far fewer motoneurons in this region of the spinal cord.

There has been considerable progress in understanding how sexual dimorphism in the SNB system develops. On the day before birth, female rats have BC muscles attached to the base of the clitoris that are nearly as large as those of males and that are innervated by motoneurons in the SNB region (Rand and Breedlove, 1987). In fact, a few days before birth, females have as many SNB cells as males do (Nordeen et al., 1985). In the days just before and after birth, however, many SNB cells die, especially in females, and the BC muscles of females die.

A single injection of androgens delivered to a newborn female rat permanently spares some SNB motoneurons and their muscles. Castration of newborn males, accompanied by prenatal blockade of androgen receptors, causes the BC muscles and SNB motoneurons to die as in females. Similarly, androgen-insensitive rats have very few SNB cells and no BC muscle, so aromatization seems to be unimportant for masculine development of this system.

Androgens act on the BC muscles to prevent their demise, and this sparing of the muscles causes the innervating SNB motoneurons to survive (Fishman et al., 1990; C. L. Jordan et al., 1991). Recall from Chapter 7 that about half of all the spinal motoneurons produced early in development normally die, that the death of the mo-

(*a*) Male rat

(*b*) Female rat

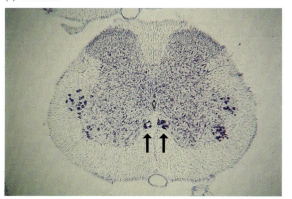
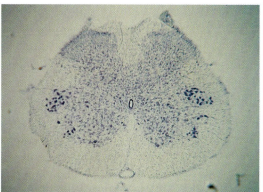

12.21 Sexual Dimorphism in the Spinal Cord   The spinal nucleus of the bulbocavernosus (SNB) consists of large, multipolar motoneurons. Male rats (*a*) have more SNB cells (arrows) than do females (*b*).

toneurons can be prevented if they are provided with enough muscle target, and that the muscles are thought to provide a neurotrophic factor to keep the appropriate number of motoneurons alive into adulthood. For SNB motoneurons the neurotrophic factor may resemble ciliary neurotrophic factor (CNTF) because in mice with the receptor for CNTF knocked out, SNB motoneurons die in males, despite the presence of androgens (Forger et al., 1997).

All male mammals have BC muscles, but in nonrodents their motoneurons are found in a slightly different spinal location and are known as **Onuf's nucleus.** The rat studies suggest that Onuf's nucleus should be sexually dimorphic—that males should have more Onuf's motoneurons than females do. Surprisingly, most female mammals retain a BC muscle into adulthood. For example, in women the BC surrounds the opening of the vagina, and contractions of the BC slightly constrict the opening (hence in women the muscle is sometimes referred to as the *constrictor vestibule*). Nevertheless, the BC is larger in men than in women, and men have more Onuf's motoneurons than women have (Forger and Breedlove, 1986).

The rat studies suggest that the sexual dimorphism in Onuf's nucleus is the result of androgenic action on the muscles that rescues motoneurons from death. Motoneuron counts in the human spinal cord indicate that we all normally lose some of these motoneurons before the twenty-sixth week of gestation (see Figure 7.12) (Forger and Breedlove, 1987), a time during which male fetuses produce androgens.

Social Influences Affect Sexual Differentiation of the Nervous System

The SNB system offers an illuminating example of how social factors can mediate the masculinization produced by steroids. Newborn rat pups can neither urinate nor defecate on their own; the mother (dam) must lick the anogenital region of each pup to elicit a spinal reflex to empty the bladder and colon. (Incidentally, the dam ingests at least some of the wastes and thereby receives pheromones from the pups that affect the composition of her milk as the pups mature. Another reason not to be a rat!)

Celia Moore and colleagues (1992) noticed that dams spend more time licking the anogenital region of male pups than of females. If the dam is made temporarily anosmic (unable to smell) by chemical treatment of the olfactory epithelium (see Chapter 9), she licks all the pups less and does not distinguish between males and females. Males raised by anosmic mothers thus receive less anogenital licking, and remarkably, fewer of their SNB cells survive the period around birth. The dam's stimulation of a male's anogenital region helps to masculinize his spinal cord.

On the one hand, this masculinization is still an effect of androgens because the dam detects male pups by smelling androgen metabolites in their urine. On the other hand, this effect is clearly the result of a social influence: The dam treats a pup differently because he's a male and thereby masculinizes his developing nervous system. Perhaps this example illustrates the futility of trying to distinguish "biological" and "social" influences.

What about humans? Humans are at least as sensitive to social influences as rats are. In every culture most people treat boys and girls differently, even when they are infants. Such differential treatment undoubtedly has some effect on the developing human brain and contributes to later sex differences in behavior. Of course, this is a social influence, but testosterone instigated the influence when it induced formation of a penis.

If prenatal androgens have even a very subtle effect on the fetal brain, then older humans interacting with the baby might detect such differences and treat the baby differently. Thus, originally subtle differences might be magnified by early social experience. Such interactions of steroidal and social influences are probably the norm in the sexual differentiation of human behavior. Much controversy surrounds the debate over whether hormones or social influences determine sexual orientation (see Box 12.3).

Do Early Gonadal Hormones Masculinize Human Behaviors in Adulthood?

Since men and women behave differently, something about them, probably something about their brains, must be different. The only remaining question is whether men and women behave differently because they are raised in a culture that treats them differentially or because they develop with different biological processes, which might be immune to cultural influences. These are not mutually exclusive hypotheses. In fact, because sex roles vary in different societies (and have changed dramatically in our own society in the past few decades), there seems little doubt that society affects sexual differentiation of the brain and behavior. But do prenatal steroids alter the adult behavior of humans?

Answering this question is difficult. Prenatal androgens may or may not act on the brain, but they certainly act on the periphery. If we expose a female fetus to enough androgen, she will look entirely male on the outside at birth and will be treated by family and society as a male. If she (?) behaves as a male in adulthood, we won't know whether that behavior is due to what androgens did to the outside of the body or to the brain. We saw earlier that CAH females, exposed prenatally to androgens, play more like boys than normal females do. Is the reason for this difference in behavior the fact that androgens directly masculinized their brains or that, with their ambiguous genitalia, they or their parents have some doubts about their "real" gender?

COMPETING HYPOTHESES

Some People Seem to Change Sex at Puberty

We close this chapter with a discussion of a fascinating phenomenon that demonstrates again the difficulty of distinguishing prenatal from social influences.

A rare genetic mutation affects the enzyme (5α-reductase) that converts testosterone to dihydrotestosterone (DHT). If an XY individual cannot produce this enzyme, the internal structures still develop in a masculine fashion. Testes develop, müllerian ducts regress, and wolffian duct structures, under the influence of testosterone, are masculinized. The genital epithelium, however, which normally possesses 5α-reductase, is unable to amplify the androgenic signal by converting the testosterone to the more active DHT. Consequently, the phallus is only slightly masculinized and resembles a large clitoris, and the genital folds resemble labia, although they contain the testes. Usually there is no vaginal opening.

Babies in a particular village in the Dominican Republic occasionally are born with this type of appearance (Figure 12.22). These children seem to be regarded as girls in the way they are dressed and raised (Imperato-McGinley et al., 1974). At pu-

(*a*) Newborn

(*b*) Adolescent

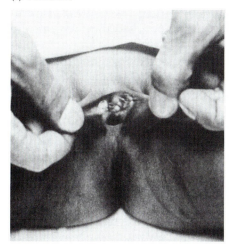

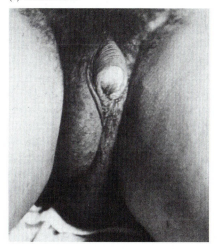

12.22 *Guevedoces* In the Dominican Republic some individuals, called *guevedoces*, are born with ambiguous genitalia (*a*) and are raised as girls. At puberty, however, the phallus grows into a recognizable penis (*b*), and the individuals begin acting like young men. (Courtesy of Julianne Imperato-McGinley.)

BOX 12.3 *What Determines a Person's Sexual Orientation?*

Some people develop romantic attachments to and yearn to have sex with a person of the same sex. Some researchers suggest that this sexual orientation is based on infants observing the adults around them and modeling their behavior on the behavior of the opposite sex, rather than their own. Others believe that something happens to the fetal brain to determine later orientation ("some people are born gay").

For this second group it is tempting to explain homosexual behavior as an example of the organizational action of early steroids that has been demonstrated in animals. If we deprive a male rat of androgens at birth, we can be sure that (with adult steroid treatment) he will display lordosis (a female behavior) in response to another male in adulthood. Superficially, the behavior of the male rat deprived of androgens at birth resembles homosexual behavior, but all we have measured is which sexual motor pattern the animal will display.

A neonatally androgenized animal mounts any rat—male or female. A female rat given estrogens and progesterone displays the lordosis posture in response to mounting by any rat—or even in response to the investigator's hand. In other words, the animals show these behaviors regardless of who or what their partner is. In contrast, we humans are more concerned about what sort of partner we have than about the particular sexual behavior we perform.

It is possible to measure what sort of rat companion a given rat prefers, but such studies paint a more complicated picture. There is more variability in steroid effects on a rat's partner preference than on lordosis or mounting behaviors. Instances of homosexual behavior in wild species are not amenable to laboratory analysis (Bagemihl, 1999).

Simon LeVay (1991) performed postmortem examinations on the brains of homosexual men, heterosexual men, and women, and found that the POA (preoptic area) contains a nucleus (the third interstitial nucleus of the anterior hypothalamus, or INAH-3, see Figure A) that is larger in men than in women and larger in heterosexual men than in homosexual men (Figure B). All but one of the gay men in the study had died of AIDS, and their sexual orientation was documented in their medical records. But the brain differences could not be due to AIDS pathology, because the straight men with AIDS had a significantly larger INAH-3 than did the gay men. To the press and the public, this sounded like strong evidence that sexual orientation is "built in."

It's possible, however, that early social experience affects the development of INAH-3 to determine later sexual orientation. Furthermore, sexual experiences as an adult could affect INAH-3 structure, so the smaller nucleus in some homosexual men may be the result of their homosexuality, rather than the cause. LeVay himself was careful to point out these alternatives, but most journalists never quite caught on. Michael Gorman (1994) suggested that the popular media also focused on LeVay's findings because they could be interpreted as conforming to a popular but very much oversimplified view of gay men—that they are like women.

For women, there are purported markers of fetal androgen exposure—otoacoustic emissions (McFadden and Pasanen, 1998) and finger-length patterns (T. J. Williams et al., 2000)—that suggest that lesbians, as a group, may have been exposed to slightly more fetal androgen than were heterosexual women. But these studies suggest considerable overlap between the two groups, indicating that fetal androgens cannot account fully for adult sexual orientation. Likewise, the finding that homosexual men and women are more likely to be left-handed than heterosexual men and women (Lalumiere et al., 2000) suggests that androgens cannot

berty, however, the testes increase androgen production and the external genitalia become more fully masculinized. The phallus grows into a recognizable penis, the body develops narrow hips and a muscular build, without breasts, and the individuals begin acting like young men. The villagers have nicknamed such individuals **guevedoces,** meaning "eggs (testes) at 12 (years)." These men never develop facial beards, but they usually have girlfriends, indicating that they are sexually interested in women.

There are two possible explanations for why these people raised as girls later behave as men. First, prenatal testosterone may have masculinized their brains; thus despite being raised as girls, when they reach puberty, their brains lead them to seek out females for mates. This explanation suggests that the social influences of growing up—assigning oneself to a gender and mimicking role models of that gender, as well as gender-specific playing and dressing—are unimportant for later behavior and sexual orientation. An alternative explanation is that early hormones have no effect—that this culture simply recognizes and teaches children that some people can start out as girls and change to boys later. If so, then the social influences on gender role development might be completely different in this society from those in ours, and it is not possible to state with certainty whether prenatal hormonal influences or early social influences are more important for sexual differentiation of human behavior.

COMPETING HYPOTHESES

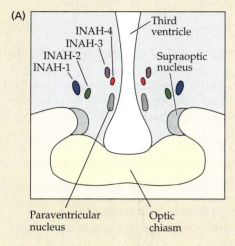

(A) Third ventricle
INAH-4
INAH-3
INAH-2
INAH-1
Supraoptic nucleus
Paraventricular nucleus
Optic chiasm

(B) Size of INAH-3 (mm³)
● = AIDS victims
Females   Males   Homosexual males

to have inherited the same region of their X chromosome from their mother (Hamer et al., 1993). But even in this subpopulation there are exceptions; that is, some of the homosexual brothers received from their mother different genes from that region of the X, so co-inheritance of those genes could not account for their being alike. Finally, monozygotic twins, who have exactly the same genes, do not always have the same sexual orientation (Buhrich et al., 1991).

From a political viewpoint, the controversy—whether sexual orientation is determined before birth or determined by early social influences—is irrelevant. Many religions practiced in Western culture regard homosexuality as a sin that some people choose to commit, and this view forms the prime basis for laws and prejudices against homosexuality. But scientists representing each viewpoint agree that sexual orientation, especially in males, is set very early in life—by age 4 or so. Almost all homosexual and heterosexual men report that from the beginning their interests and romantic attachments matched their adult orientation. Furthermore, despite extensive efforts, no one has come up with a reliable way to change a man's sexual orientation (LeVay, 1996).

be the whole story, because there is no known effect of early androgens on handedness. On the other hand, handedness does seem to be established early in life, so this correlation, too, indicates that early events influence adult orientation.

The reports that sexual orientation is heritable (J. M. Bailey and Bell, 1993) also do little to resolve the controversy. Estimates are that about half the variability in sexual orientation is due to differences in the genome, which leaves ample room for early social influences.

Indeed, this evidence strongly indicates that both genetic and environmental influences affect sexual orientation in humans. Each member of a very select subpopulation of homosexual men—pairs of homosexual brothers—is likely

The reports of sexual dimorphism in the adult human brain, often touted as proof of the predominance of "biological" influences, do not really address the issue. Despite the absence of any airtight demonstrations that prenatal hormones directly affect human brain and behavior, it seems likely that hormones have at least some effect on the developing brain and that society reinforces and accentuates sex differences in humans.

Summary

Sexual Behavior

1. Reproductive behaviors are divided into four stages: sexual attraction, appetitive behaviors, copulation, and postcopulatory behaviors, including parental behaviors in some species.

2. The brain governs the time at which the organism should reproduce and uses protein hormones to induce the gonads to produce gametes. The gonads in turn produce steroid hormones that activate the brain to increase the probability of reproductive behaviors.

3. In humans, very low levels of testosterone are required for either men or women to display a full interest in mating, but additional testosterone has no additional effect. Therefore there is no correlation between circulating androgen levels and reproductive behaviors in men. Nor is there any strong correlation between copulatory behavior and stage of the menstrual cycle in women.

Refer to the *Learning Biological Psychology* CD for the following study aids for this chapter:

10 Objectives

82 Study Questions

2 Activities

1 Animated Tutorial

4. Human copulatory behavior is remarkably varied. Attempts at classification of the stages of copulation in humans suggest that most men show a single pattern, while most women display one of three basic patterns of sexual response. For both sexes, the four basic stages of the sexual response pattern are (1) increasing excitement, (2) plateau, (3) orgasm, and (4) resolution.

Why Are There Two Sexes?

1. Sexual reproduction brings together in a single individual the beneficial mutations that have arisen in separate individuals.

2. In some species, sexual reproduction has led to the evolution of individuals specialized to reproduce as either a male or a female. Sexual differentiation during development then allows males and females to develop different bodies and brains.

3. Male and female vertebrates make different investments in their offspring; consequently, most males of most species are promiscuous, and most females of most species are very discriminating in choosing mates. This situation leads to sexual selection pressures that, over time, can exaggerate sexual dimorphism.

4. There are four different types of mating systems: (1) promiscuity (both sexes mate with multiple partners), (2) polygyny (each male mates with multiple females), (3) polyandry (each female mates with multiple males), and (4) monogamy (a single male and a single female form a lasting bond).

Sexual Differentiation

1. In vertebrates, genetic sex (determined by the presence or absence of a Y chromosome in mammals) determines whether testes or ovaries develop, and hormonal secretions from the gonads determine whether the rest of the body, including the brain, develops in a feminine or masculine fashion. In the presence of testicular secretions a male develops; in the absence of testicular secretions a female develops.

2. The brains of vertebrates are masculinized by the presence of testicular steroids during early development. Such organizational effects of steroids permanently alter the structure and function of the brain and therefore permanently alter the behavior of the individual.

3. Among the prominent sexual dimorphisms in the nervous system (including the song system of birds, the sexually dimorphic nucleus of the preoptic area in rats, and the spinal nucleus of the bulbocavernosus in mammals), gonadal steroids have been shown to alter characteristics such as neuronal size, neuronal survival, dendritic growth, and synapse elimination to engender sex differences in neural structure and in behavior.

4. Several regions of the human brain are sexually dimorphic. However, we do not know whether these dimorphisms are generated by fetal steroid levels or by sex differences in the early social environment. Neither do we know whether any of the identified sex differences in neural structure are responsible for any sex differences in human behavior.

5. There seems to be no reliable animal model of sexual orientation, which is such a salient aspect of human experience. However, all research indicates that sexual orientation is determined early in life and, especially in men, is not a matter of individual choice.

Recommended Reading

Becker, J. B., Breedlove, S. M., and Crews, D. (in press). *Behavioral endocrinology* (2nd ed.). Cambridge, MA: MIT Press.

Blum, D. (1997). *Sex on the brain.* New York: Viking Penguin.

Fausto-Sterling, A. (2000). *Sexing the body.* New York: Basic Books.

LeVay, S. (1996). *Queer science.* Cambridge, MA: MIT Press.

Miller, G. (2000). *The mating mind: How sexual choice shaped the evolution of human nature.* New York: Doubleday.

Nelson, R. J. (2000). *An introduction to behavioral endocrinology* (2nd ed.). Sunderland, MA: Sinauer.

13

Homeostasis:
Active Regulation of Internal States

I n 1998 a California woman was sentenced
to 2 years probation because her daughter, at age 13 and weighing 680 pounds,
had died of complications from obesity. Authorities charged the mother with child endan-
germent because for the last year of her life, the
daughter had not seen a physician and
had lain on the floor, unable to reach
the bathroom or keep herself clean.
Some onlookers complained that the
mother's punishment was too le-
nient; others felt she should never
have been charged at all. Everyone
agreed that the daughter's refusal to attend school or leave the
house at all was due to the shame
she felt about her weight. Clearly,

Salvador Dali, *Couple with their Heads Full of Clouds*, 1936

then, this young girl fervently wished not to be fat. The daughter had tried many diets, yet she steadily gained weight throughout her too-short life.

In a related tragedy, some college wrestlers who were trying to lose weight
quickly just before a tournament followed the traditional route of warming themselves to sweat and lose fluid, but they went too far and died of heart failure. In this
chapter we'll learn that our body temperature, weight, and fluid balance are carefully regulated by a web of internal processes. We are not normally even aware of
these processes, yet the nervous system is intimately involved in every stage.

Homeostasis Maintains Internal States within a Critical Range

Because warmth, water, and food are vital and scarce, elaborate physiological systems have evolved in the body to monitor and maintain them. One hallmark of all three systems is **redundancy:** There are several different means of monitoring our stores, of conserving remaining supplies, and of shedding excesses. Therefore the loss of function of one part of the system can be compensated for by the remaining portions. This redundancy helps keep us alive, but it also makes it difficult for us to figure out how the body regulates temperature, water balance, and food intake. Another hallmark of these three regulatory systems is that each one exploits the organism's behavior to regulate and to acquire more heat, water, or food. This chapter will show that all three regulatory systems—for body temperature, water balance, and food intake—are **homeostatic;** that is, they maintain relatively constant values.

The nervous system coordinates these regulatory systems. The brain closely monitors temperature, water supply, and nutrient supply, and uses a variety of neural and hormonal mechanisms to keep them within the critical range. If we have a surplus of any of the three, our bodies have ways to shed the excess, usually without our being aware of it. But when supplies are running out, we must display active behaviors to gain more; the nervous system initiates these behaviors.

If we are losing body heat, our nervous system directs us to seek warmth. When our internal water supplies are low we seek water, and when our internal nutrient supplies are low we seek food. Our conscious experience is that we feel cold, thirsty, or hungry, respectively. Other animals are unable to use words to tell us how they feel, so for the rest of this chapter we will assume that an animal seeking water is thirsty, and that an animal seeking food is hungry. Probably such animals feel much the same way we do when we say we are thirsty or hungry, but we will not be addressing that issue. Without making any assumptions about the animal's experience, we will say that an animal seeking shelter has an internal drive to conserve heat, an animal seeking water has an internal drive (thirst) for water, and an animal seeking food has an internal drive (hunger) for food. In each case the animal is showing **motivated behavior**—behavior designed to achieve a particular goal. The particular behaviors displayed may vary depending on the circumstances, but each one nevertheless serves the goal of gaining warmth, water, or food.

The homeostatic mechanisms that regulate temperature, body fluids, and metabolism are primarily **negative feedback** systems. That is, in each case there is a desired value or zone called the **set point,** by analogy with the setting of a thermostat (Figure 13.1). (We already discussed negative feedback systems in connection with neural circuits in Chapter 3, and with the regulation of hormone secretion in Chapter 5.) A drop in temperature below the set point activates the thermostat, which turns on the heating system. When the thermostat registers a sufficient rise in temperature, it turns off the heating system. (Note that there is a small range of temperature between the "turn on" and "turn off" signals; otherwise the heating system would be going on and off very frequently. Thus there is really a **set zone** rather than a set point.)

The setting of the thermostat can be changed; for example, it can be turned down at night to save energy. The body temperature for most mammals and birds is usually held within a narrow range—about 36 to 38°C (97 to 100°F)—though the set zone can be altered depending on overall conditions. For example, most mammals reduce their temperature during sleep (rather like turning the thermostat down at night). Our bodies also integrate the demands for nutrients and water to

13.1 Negative Feedback   The thermostatically controlled heating system found in homes is an example of a negative feedback system. All such systems have a sensor (in this example a thermometer) to monitor the variable (in this case temperature) and a device (in this example the furnace) to change the variable (e.g., by heating the room). The device sends a negative feedback signal to the sensor, turning it (heat) off.

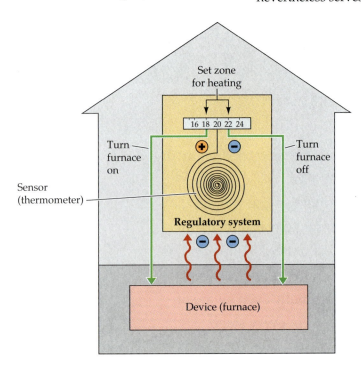

result in a set range of body weight that is often remarkably narrow. Later in the chapter we will see examples of animals vigorously defending their body weight—maintaining a particular weight in the face of physiological challenges.

Unavoidable Losses Require Us to Gain Heat, Water, and Food

The regulation of internal resources is complicated by the fact that staying alive requires us to give up some of them. Because external temperatures rarely hover at 37°C (98.6°F) for long, we must actively heat or cool our bodies. We lose water vapor with each breath, as well as through sweating and, because various biochemical processes produce waste chemicals that can be eliminated only with a little water, through urination. Food provides us with energy and nutrients (chemicals needed for growth, maintenance, and repair of the body), but our behavior uses up energy and incurs wear and tear on the body, so more energy and nutrients are continuously needed. Our homeostatic mechanisms are constantly challenged by these unavoidable losses (sometimes called *obligatory losses*), which require us to gain and conserve heat, water, and food constantly.

Temperature Regulation

Why do we feel so uncomfortable when we're cold? That's nature's way of telling us that body temperature is a vital concern.

Body Temperature Is a Critical Condition for All Biological Processes

As the interior of a cell cools, chemical reactions slow down. The enzyme systems of mammals and birds are most efficient within a narrow range around 37°C. At lower temperatures, reactions slow down, and some stop altogether. At higher temperatures, protein molecules fold together improperly and thus do not function as they should. At very high temperatures, the amino acids that form proteins begin to break apart and fuse together more or less at random, and we say that the tissue is *fixed* (or if it is edible tissue, we say it is *cooked*). Brain cells are especially sensitive to high temperatures. A very prolonged, high fever can cause brain centers that regulate heart rate and breathing to die, thus killing the patient.

At very low temperatures, the bilipid layers that make up cellular membranes become so disrupted by the formation of ice molecules that they cannot re-form even when thawed. Some animals that cannot avoid subfreezing temperatures (Figure 13.2) produce "antifreeze" consisting of special protein molecules that disrupt the formation of ice crystals and prevent damage to membranes (Ahlgren et al., 1988; Barnes, 1989; Liou et al., 2000).

(a)

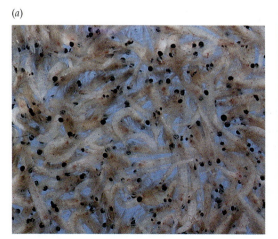

(b)

13.2 Braving the Cold Arctic krill (*a*) and golden-mantled ground squirrels (*b*) are two species that sometimes have body temperatures below 0°C. The krill produce an "antifreeze" in body fluids to prevent ice crystals from forming in cell membranes.

Some Animals Generate Heat; Others Must Obtain Heat from the Environment

For centuries it has been recognized that mammals and birds differ from other animals in the way they regulate body temperature. Our ways of characterizing the difference have become more accurate and meaningful over time, but popular terminology still reflects the old division: Mammals and birds are called *warm-blooded;* all other creatures are called *cold-blooded.* But this classification is misleading. Fence lizards and desert iguanas—both of which are "cold-blooded"—usually have body temperatures only a degree or two below ours, so they are not really "cold."

The set of terminology that next came into vogue distinguished animals that maintain a constant body temperature, called *homeotherms* (from the Greek *homos,* "same," and *therme,* "heat"), from those whose body temperature varies with their environment, called *poikilotherms* (from the Greek *poikilos,* "varied"). This classification also proved inadequate because some mammals (homeotherms) vary their body temperatures during hibernation. Furthermore, many invertebrates in the depths of the ocean (poikilotherms) never experience a change in the chill of the deep waters, so their body temperatures remain quite constant.

In contemporary terms we distinguish between endotherms and ectotherms. **Endotherms** (from the Greek *endon,* "within") regulate their body temperature chiefly by internal metabolic processes. **Ectotherms** (from the Greek *ektos,* "outside") get most of their heat from the environment. Most ectotherms do regulate their body temperature, but through behavioral means, such as by moving to favorable sites or changing their exposure to external sources of heat. Endotherms (mainly mammals and birds) also choose favorable environments, but primarily they regulate body temperature by making internal adjustments. Whether an animal is an ectotherm or an endotherm, if it is placed in a laboratory situation in which there is a gradient of temperature from warm to cold, it will spend most of its time at its preferred environmental temperature. The preferred temperature differs from species to species.

The Advantages of Endothermy Come at a Cost

EVOLUTION AT WORK

No one knows whether endothermy arose in a common ancestor of the birds and mammals or arose separately in these two lines. What we do know is that endotherms pay substantial costs for maintaining a high body temperature and keeping it within narrow limits. Much food must be obtained and metabolized, elaborate regulatory systems are required, and departures of body temperature of a few degrees in either direction impair functioning. What benefits led to the evolution of such a complicated and costly system in comparison with that of ectotherms, which get along with somewhat lower mean body temperatures and have more tolerance for changes in body temperature?

An increased capacity to sustain a high level of muscular activity over prolonged periods may have been the principal gain in the evolution of endothermy (A. F. Bennett and Ruben, 1979). A person's metabolic rate (or heat production) can rise almost tenfold between resting and very strenuous exercise.

Ectotherms are capable of such bursts of high activity for only a few minutes; in this case anaerobic metabolism—metabolism consisting of chemical reactions that do not require oxygen—contributes most of the energy. A high level of anaerobic metabolism can be maintained for only a few minutes; then the animal must rest and repay the oxygen debt. Ectotherms can escape from and sometimes even pursue endotherms over short distances, but in a long-distance race the endotherm will win. Probably the capacity for internal thermoregulation evolved along with an increasing capacity to sustain a high level of muscular activity through aerobic metabolism.

Endotherms Generate Heat through Metabolism

The utilization of stored food in the body is known as **metabolism.** Because the breaking of chemical bonds releases energy as heat, all living (and thus metabolizing) tissues produce heat. The unit of heat is a kilocalorie (kcal); 1 kcal is enough heat to raise the temperature of a liter of water 1°C. An adult human may generate 600 kcal per hour when exercising strenuously, but only 60 kcal per hour when resting.

When the body is at rest, about a third of the heat it generates is produced by the brain. As body activity increases, the heat production of the brain does not rise much, but that of the muscles can increase nearly tenfold, so when we are active our bodies produce a much higher percentage of the heat we generate. Like mechanical devices, muscles produce a good deal of heat while they are accomplishing work. Muscles and gasoline engines have about the same efficiency; each produces about four or five times as much heat as mechanical work. Some of the main ways the human body gains, conserves, and dissipates heat are shown in Figure 13.3.

The rate of heat production can be adjusted to suit conditions, particularly in certain organs. Deposits of brown adipose tissue (also called **brown fat**) are found especially around vital organs in the trunk and around the cervical and thoracic levels of the spinal cord. These fat cells look brown because they are full of mitochondria that break down molecules and produce heat. Under cold conditions the sympathetic nervous system stimulates metabolism within the brown-fat cells, producing heat.

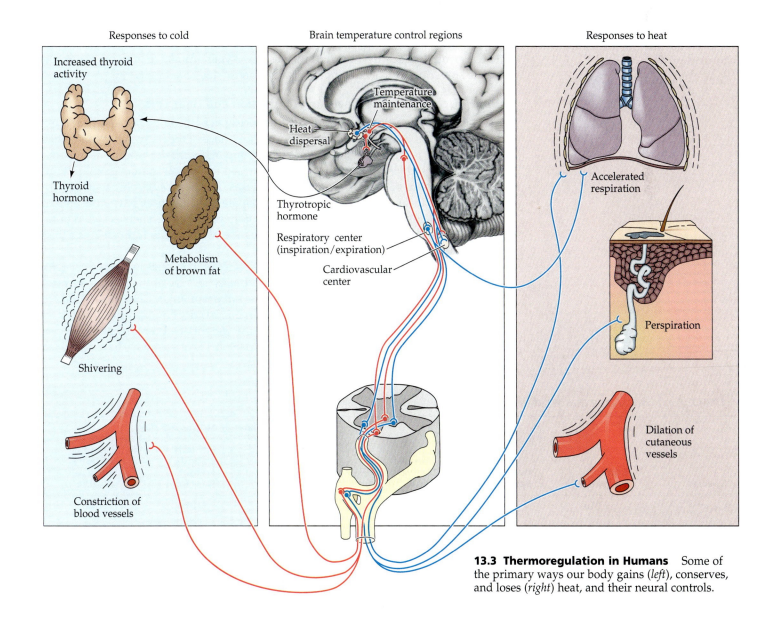

Responses to cold

Increased thyroid activity

Thyroid hormone

Metabolism of brown fat

Shivering

Constriction of blood vessels

Brain temperature control regions

Temperature maintenance

Heat dispersal

Thyrotropic hormone

Respiratory center (inspiration/expiration)

Cardiovascular center

Responses to heat

Accelerated respiration

Perspiration

Dilation of cutaneous vessels

13.3 Thermoregulation in Humans Some of the primary ways our body gains (*left*), conserves, and loses (*right*) heat, and their neural controls.

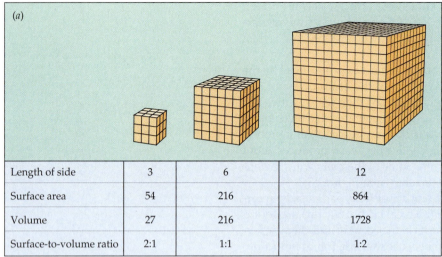

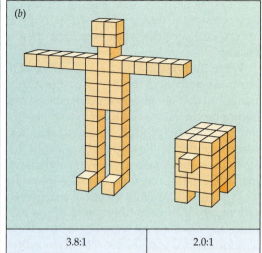

(a)			
Length of side	3	6	12
Surface area	54	216	864
Volume	27	216	1728
Surface-to-volume ratio	2:1	1:1	1:2

(b)	
3.8:1	2.0:1

13.4 Surface-to-Volume Ratio
(a) For a given shape, the ratio of surface to volume of a solid decreases as the volume increases. (b) However, forms with different shapes can have very different surface areas, even if the volume is the same, as it is for the two figures shown here.

A more conspicuous way to generate heat is through muscular activity. At low temperatures, nerve impulses cause muscle cells to contract out of synchrony, producing shivering rather than coordinated movements. Humans start to shiver when the body temperature approaches 36.5°C. This response spreads from facial muscles to the arms and legs. The fivefold increase in oxygen uptake that accompanies extreme shivering shows how metabolically intense this response is.

Body Size and Shape Affect Heat Production and Heat Loss

Heat production is closely related to the surface area of the body because heat is exchanged with the environment primarily at the surface of the body. A big animal like an elephant has relatively little skin surface compared with the volume of its body; a small animal like a canary has a large surface-to-volume ratio. As volume increases, the ratio of surface to volume decreases (Figure 13.4a). A high surface-to-volume ratio means a greater capacity to dissipate heat. You may have noticed that small food items such as peas cool off faster than large objects such as baked potatoes. The reason is that the surface-to-volume ratio of the potato is much lower than that of the pea.

Table 13.1 shows the body sizes of several species of mammals in terms of weight, surface area, and heat production. Smaller animals, because of their larger surface-to-volume ratio, lose heat more rapidly to the environment, so they must produce more heat in relation to body size than larger animals do. For example, the data in Table 13.1 show that it takes 20 cats to equal the weight of a human, but the 20 cats together produce twice the heat of the single person. (That's why we have to buy so

TABLE 13.1 *Body Size and Heat Production of Some Birds and Mammals*

Species	Body weight (kg)	Body Surface (m²)	Surface-to-weight ratio (m²/kg)	Energy output per day		
				Total (kcal)	Per unit of body weight (kcal/kg)	Per unit of body surface (kcal/m²)
Canary	0.016	0.006	0.375	5	310	760
Rat	0.2	0.03	0.15	25	130	830
Pigeon	0.3	0.04	0.13	30	100	670
Cat	3.0	0.2	0.07	150	50	750
Human	60	1.7	0.03	1500	25	850
Elephant	3600	24	0.007	47,000	13	2000

(a)

13.5 Adaptations to Extreme Climates
Adaptations to climates include changes in behavior, physiology, and anatomy. Compare, for example, an Eskimo from arctic Alaska (*a*) with a Nilotic inhabitant of tropical Africa (*b*).

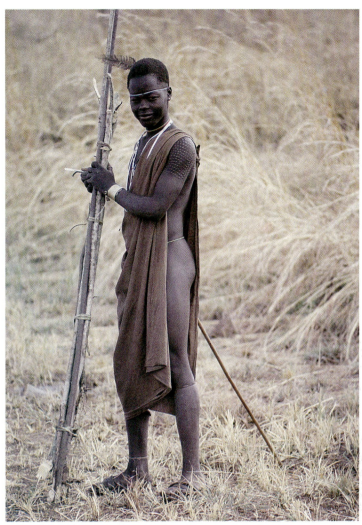

(b)

much cat food!) Small mammals also tend to maintain body temperatures slightly higher than those of large mammals, and they lose heat more easily than larger mammals do. Large animals, on the other hand, lose heat more slowly and thus have lower metabolic rates per gram of body weight.

The effect of surface-to-volume ratio on heat conservation is evident in the distribution of species across environments. Within a group of closely related mammals or birds, for example, those living in cold climates are larger than those in warm environments. Even in a temperate zone, though, a very small mammal like the shrew has to eat almost incessantly to meet its metabolic needs.

Shape also affects the conservation of heat and therefore energy. The humanoid form in Figure 13.4*b* has exactly the same volume as the squat figure beside it, but the more slender form has almost twice as much surface area as the compact form. Because of its lower surface-to-volume ratio, the more compact body conserves heat better and therefore is better able to protect its internal temperature in a cold climate.

Among human groups, taller, more slender body forms have evolved in the Tropics, and shorter, stockier physiques are more typical of colder regions (Figure 13.5). Migrations and the intermingling of human groups blur this tendency, and of course other factors also influence stature, as the pygmies of tropical Africa illustrate. Among many animal groups, body appendages such as the ears are smaller in arctic species than in related tropical species (Figure 13.6). Smaller appendages mean a lower surface-to-volume ratio and thus less heat loss.

Fur of mammals and feathers of birds are special adaptations of the skin that insulate the body from the environment. In cold environments large mammals usu-

EVOLUTION AT WORK

13.6 Adaptations of Appendages to Climate   The external ears in foxes from tropical (*a*), temperate (*b*), and arctic (*c*) climates vary in size.

ally have a thick coat of fur, but thick fur on small animals would interfere with their locomotion. To insulate properly, fur or feathers must be kept in good condition—one reason why many mammals and birds spend a great deal of time grooming and preening. For an animal like the sea otter, which spends its life in cold water, insulation is vital; even a small area of matted fur allowing heat loss could be fatal. Most species of birds have a preen gland or oil gland near the base of the tail; the bird uses its beak to distribute oil from the gland to dress the feathers and waterproof them. Of course, sometimes an animal needs to lose heat, and different species have different adaptations for doing so (Figure 13.7).

Which Behaviors Can Adjust Body Temperature?

Ectotherms generate little heat through metabolism and therefore must rely heavily on behavioral methods to regulate body temperature. The marine iguana of the Galápagos Islands eats seaweed underwater for an hour or more at a time (occasionally coming up for air) in water that is 10 to 15°C cooler than its preferred body temperature. After feeding, the iguana emerges and lies on a warm rock to restore its temperature. While warming up, it lies broadside to the sun to absorb as much heat as possible (Figure 13.8*a*). When its temperature reaches 37°C, the iguana turns to face the sun and thus absorb less heat, and it may extend its legs to keep its body away from warm surfaces (Figure 13.8*b*).

Many other ectotherms regulate their temperature in similar ways. Some snakes, for example, adjust their coils to expose more or less surface to the sun and thus keep their internal temperature relatively constant during the day. Bees regulate the temperature inside the hive by their behavior, keeping the temperature in the brood area at 35 to 36°C. When the air temperature is low, the bees crowd into the brood area and shiver, thus generating heat. When the air temperature is high, the bees reduce the temperature in the brood area by fanning with their wings and by evaporative cooling.

Even endotherms such as mammals and birds control their exposure to the sun and to hot or cold surfaces to avoid making excessive demands on their internal regulatory mechanisms. In hot desert regions many small mammals, such as the kangaroo rat, remain in underground burrows during the day and appear above ground only at night, when the environment is relatively cool. Humans have devised many cultural practices to adapt to conditions of cold or heat. For example, Eskimo learned to design clothing that insulates well but permits the dissipation of heat through vents. Other Eskimo cultural adaptations include the design of efficient shelters, sharing of body heat, choice of diet, and use of seal oil lamps (E. F. Moran, 1981).

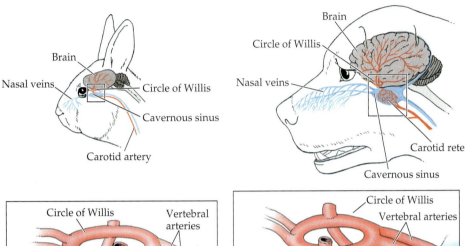

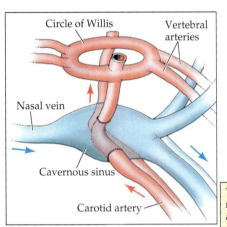

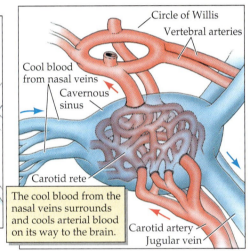

The cool blood from the nasal veins surrounds and cools arterial blood on its way to the brain.

13.7 Variation in Overheating from Exertion Exercise produces heat, but some species, such as the dog, have a special heat exchange system to prevent the brain from overheating (*bottom right*). Human anatomy is more like that of the rabbit (*bottom left*). (After Karasawa et al., 1997.)

13.8   Behavioral Control of Body Temperature (*a*) A Galápagos marine iguana, upon emerging from the cold sea, raises its body temperature by hugging a warm rock and lying broadside to the sun. (*b*) Once its temperature is sufficiently high, the iguana reduces its surface contact with the rock and faces the sun to minimize its exposure. These behaviors afford considerable control over body temperature. (Photographs by Mark R. Rosenzweig.)

(*a*)

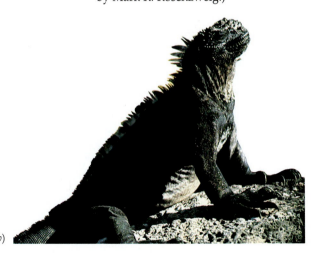

(*b*)

The behavioral thermoregulatory responses of ectotherms and endotherms can be divided into three categories:

1. *Changing exposure of the body surface*—for example, by huddling or extending limbs
2. *Changing external insulation*—for example, by using clothing or nests
3. *Selecting a surrounding that is less thermally stressful*—for example, by moving to the shade or into a burrow

Humans seldom wait for the body to get cold before putting on a coat. We anticipate homeostatic signals on the basis of experience. As any parent will tell you, shivering reflects a lapse of intelligent behavior.

Young Birds and Mammals Need Help to Regulate Body Temperature

Fetuses maintained in the mother's body rely on her to provide warmth and regulate temperature. Most birds keep their eggs warm by using a specially vascularized area of skin (the brood patch), which transfers heat efficiently to the eggs. Even after hatching or birth, the young of many species cannot regulate their temperature very well, mostly because they are small (and lose heat quickly) and have limited energy resources. So they must continue to be protected by their parents.

Because rat pups are born without hair, they have a hard time maintaining body temperature when exposed to cold. The rat mother keeps her pups protected in a warm nest, and this response of the mother is related to her own thermoregulation. As shown in Figure 13.9*a*, newborn rat pups are able to generate heat by using brown-fat deposits like the one between the shoulder blades (Blumberg et al., 1997).

Nonetheless, one problem for newborn rats is insulating their hairless bodies to conserve the heat they generate. They huddle together and vary their positions in the huddle in accordance with changes in temperature (Figure 13.9*b*). Rectal temperatures and oxygen consumption were measured in pups of different ages placed in a cool chamber (23–24°C), either singly or in a group of four. In 5-day-old rats, the temperature of the isolated pups fell below 30°C in less than an hour; those in the group maintained their temperatures above 30°C for 4 hours (Alberts, 1978).

Huddling also significantly reduced oxygen consumption. The form of the huddle changes according to ambient temperatures; it is loose in warm temperatures but tightly cohesive in the cold. Each pup frequently changes positions in the clump, sometimes positioned inside and at other times at the periphery, effectively regulating its temperature. In effect, pups share the costs and benefits of this group activity. Thus, early in the rat's development its thermoregulation benefits from social interaction.

13.9 Physiological and Social Thermoregulation (*a*) This infrared thermograph shows the dorsal surface of a week-old rat pup oriented as shown in the inset. Areas of highest heat production are coded in orange and yellow, and the prominent yellow "hot spot" between the shoulder blades overlies a depot of brown fat, a thermogenic (i.e., heat-producing) organ found in the young of nearly all mammals studied thus far (it is also found in adults, especially in hibernators such as ground squirrels). When rat pups are placed in a cold environment, they begin producing heat by using brown fat. (*b*) Rat pups also use behavioral mechanisms to conserve heat. Animals push to the center of a litter to gain heat and move to the periphery to cool off. Thus an anesthetized pup will be left in the center during high temperatures and pushed to the periphery when temperatures are low. (Part *a* courtesy of Mark S. Blumberg; *b* after Alberts, 1978.)

(*a*)

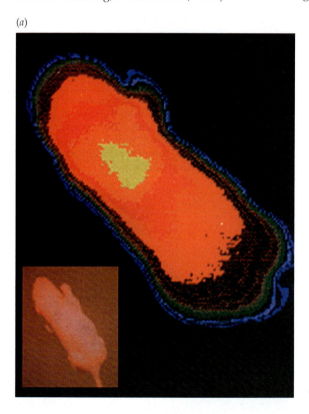

(*b*) High temperature

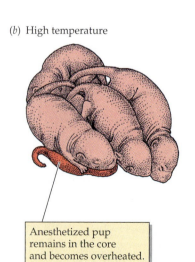

Anesthetized pup remains in the core and becomes overheated.

Low temperature

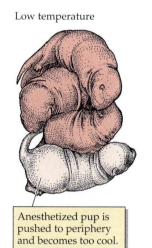

Anesthetized pup is pushed to periphery and becomes too cool.

Some Endotherms Survive by Letting Their Body Temperature Plummet

All endotherms show some variation in body temperature. There's usually a daily fluctuation in body temperature that constitutes a circadian rhythm, which we'll discuss in Chapter 14. When we are ill we may have a fever. This fever is brought on by the body to help fight off infection.

But some endotherms occupy habitats with extreme seasonal variations in temperature. For example, golden-mantled ground squirrels in the far north survive long, cold winters by staying in their burrows, curling up in a tight ball, and allowing their body temperature to plummet. An animal in this state, called **torpor,** is cold to the touch and appears not to breathe, but it does take a breath every few moments or so. Its heart still beats, but only very slowly.

No one knows how these animals evolved the ability to survive this drop in body temperature, which would certainly kill a human, but it seems clear that they save a great deal of energy while in torpor. The state does not last the entire winter; once a week or so the animals arouse from torpor by raising their body temperature, move about the burrow, check on outside conditions, and if things look grim, reenter torpor. The arousal episode requires energy but lasts less than an hour, so the animals save a good deal of energy over the winter (Heldmaier and Ruf, 1992). Reduced glucose availability, which indicates a shortage of available energy, can trigger an episode of torpor (Dark et al., 1994).

The Brain Monitors and Regulates Body Temperature

The nervous system controls and regulates all the processes of heat production and heat loss, sometimes with assistance from the endocrine system. What parts of the nervous system are active in these processes?

In the 1880s physiologists found that small lesions in the hypothalamus of dogs elevated body temperature. Barbour (1912) manipulated the temperature of the hypothalamus in dogs by implanting silver wires. When the wires were heated, body temperature fell; when the wires were cooled, body temperature rose. These results suggested that body temperature is monitored in the hypothalamus and that when temperature there departs in either direction from the desired level, compensatory actions are triggered. In the 1950s, electrical recording from single cells revealed that some of them change their discharge rate in response to small increases or decreases of brain temperature; these cells are scattered throughout the preoptic area (POA) and the anterior hypothalamus.

Lesion experiments in mammals indicate that there are different sites for two kinds of regulation: (1) regulation by locomotor and other behaviors common to both endotherms and ectotherms, and (2) physiological regulation characteristic of endotherms. Lesions in the lateral hypothalamus of rats abolished behavioral regulation of temperature but did not affect the autonomic thermoregulatory responses such as shivering and vasoconstriction (Satinoff and Shan, 1971; van Zoeren and Stricker, 1977). On the other hand, lesions in the POA of rats impaired the autonomic responses but did not interfere with such behaviors as pressing levers to turn heating lamps or cooling fans on or off (Satinoff and Rutstein, 1970; van Zoeren and Stricker, 1977). This is a clear example of parallel circuits for two different ways of regulating the same variable.

Receptors at the surface of the body also monitor temperature. If you enter a cold room, you soon begin to shiver—long before your core temperature falls. If you enter a hot greenhouse or a sauna, you begin to sweat before your hypothalamic temperature rises. The skin provides information to central circuits, which promptly initiate corrective action in *anticipation* of a change in core temperature.

Does the Body Have a Single Master Thermostat?

It would be simple to think that a single integrating center accounts for thermoregulation. However, evidence has accumulated to suggest that a single thermostat is inadequate to account for all the facets of thermoregulation. For one thing, as we saw

(a) Hypothalamus

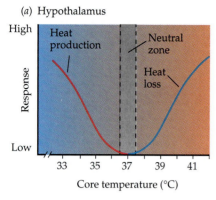

(b) Brainstem

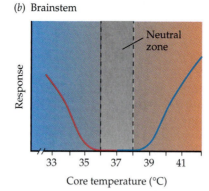

(c) Spinal cord

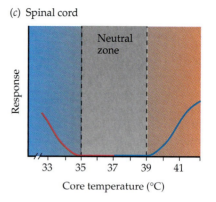

13.10 Multiple Thermostats in the Nervous System Thermoneutral zones of thermoregulatory systems are narrower at higher levels of the nervous system than at lower levels. (After Satinoff, 1978.)

in the previous section, there appear to be different brain sites for behavioral and autonomic regulation of temperature. Even two thermoregulatory circuits may not be sufficient.

For example, W. W. Roberts and Mooney (1974) warmed small sites in the diencephalon and mesencephalon of rats. Normally a rat exposed to increasing heat shows successive potentiation of three different responses: First it grooms, then it moves about actively, and finally it lies quietly in a sprawled-out position. Grooming allows the rat to lose heat by evaporation of saliva from the skin, activity normally helps the rat locate a cooler spot, and sprawling out helps the rat dissipate heat without generating more heat through activity. Local heating of the brain does not produce this sequence; instead, each of these behaviors tends to be elicited by the heating of a different brain region. These observations are not consistent with the hypothesis of a single thermostat.

In addition, there seems to be a hierarchy of thermoregulatory circuits, some located at the spinal level, some centered in the midbrain, and others in the hypothalamus, including the POA. For example, spinal animals (in which the brain is disconnected from the spinal cord) can regulate body temperature somewhat, indicating that a temperature monitor is available to the spinal cord and/or the body. Such animals die in extended cold or heat, however, because they do not respond until body temperature deviates 2 to 3°C from normal values.

Evelyn Satinoff (1978) suggested that the thermal set zones are broader in "lower" regions of the nervous system (Figure 13.10). The thermoregulatory systems at the "highest" level—the hypothalamus—have the narrowest neutral zones, and they normally coordinate and adjust the activity of the other systems. This arrangement can give the impression of a single system, although in reality there are multiple interlinked systems.

Figure 13.11 summarizes the basic thermoregulatory system: Receptors in the skin, body core, and hypothalamus detect temperature and transmit that information to three neural regions (spinal cord, brainstem, and hypothalamus). If body temperature moves outside the set zone, each of these neural regions can initiate autonomic and behavioral responses to return body temperature to the set zone.

Evelyn Satinoff

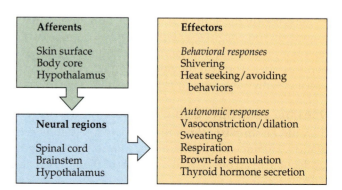

13.11 Basic Elements of Mammalian Thermoregulatory Systems

Fluid Regulation

The water that you drink on a hot day is carefully measured and partitioned by the nervous system to keep every living cell at work.

Our Cells Evolved to Function in Seawater

The first living creatures on Earth were single-celled organisms that arose in the sea. In this setting—a large body of water with fairly uniform concentrations of salts and minerals—most basic cellular reactions evolved, including DNA production and replication, the manufacture of proteins from amino acids, and the storing and harnessing of chemical energy from ATP. These various reactions evolved by natural selection to proceed efficiently only in a particular concentration of salt water. For these creatures, maintaining the proper concentration of salts in the water was effortless: They simply let seawater inside the cell membrane and let it out again. But when multicellular animals began coming out of the water onto land, they either had to evolve all new cellular processes to work without water or they had to bring the water with them. Only the latter solution (no pun intended) was feasible.

EVOLUTION AT WORK

Land animals had to prevent dehydration (excessive loss of water) so that their cells would work properly. Thus they needed a more or less watertight outer layer of cells, and they had to maintain the proper concentration of salts and other molecules in body fluids. The composition of the fluid inside your body, once proteins and the like have been removed, is still similar to that of seawater. During evolution, diversity has arisen across species in the concentration of salt in plasma. For example, in closely related fish species, those that inhabit fresh water have a lower salt concentration in the plasma than those that inhabit seawater. For a given species, if the concentration of molecules is altered even a small amount, the most basic cellular functions cease working properly and the animal dies. A very few species, such as salmon, have adaptations that allow them to live in fresh water at hatching, to grow up in salt water, and to return again to fresh water to breed.

We cannot seal ourselves from the outside world, hoarding our "precious bodily fluids" without alteration. For one thing, completely watertight outer layers are difficult to make and cumbersome. More importantly, many body functions require that we use up some water (and some salt molecules), as, for example, when we produce urine to rid ourselves of waste molecules. Furthermore, giving up some water molecules can be a very good way to shed excess body heat, as we saw in the discussion of temperature regulation. We are obliged to lose some water molecules, and therefore we are obliged to get some more (Table 13.2). Once we begin relinquishing and replacing the body's water, we must monitor and regulate the composition of body fluid to maintain basic cellular processes in order to live.

TABLE 13.2 *Average Daily Water Balance of an Adult Human*	
Source	**Quantity (liters)**
Approximate intake	
Fluid water	1.2
Water content of food	1.0
Water from oxidation of food	0.3
Total	**2.5**
Approximate output	
Urine	1.4
Evaporative loss	0.9
Feces	0.2
Total	**2.5**

Water in the Human Body Moves Back and Forth between Two Major Compartments

Most of our water is contained within the billions of cells that make up the body; this is the *intracellular compartment*. But some fluid is outside of our cells, in the *extracellular compartment*. The extracellular compartment can be subdivided into interstitial fluid (the fluid between cells) and blood plasma (the protein-rich fluid that carries red and white blood cells).

By convention, water in the stomach or elsewhere in the gastrointestinal tract is considered to be outside the body—in neither of these compartments. Water must leave the gastrointestinal tract and enter the body before we can make use of it. Similarly, water that has reached the bladder cannot be returned to the body and so is effectively outside the body as well. Figure 13.12 presents a simplified version of the basic systems that regulate fluid intake. Water continually migrates between the intracellular and extracellular compartments. To understand the forces driving this migration, we must understand osmosis.

Osmosis is the passive movement of molecules from one place to another. The motive force behind osmosis is the constant vibration and movement of molecules. If we put a drop of food coloring in a beaker of water, the molecules of dye meander about because of this jiggling until they are more or less uniformly distributed throughout the beaker. If the water is hot, the dye molecules spread out more quickly.

If we divide the beaker of water in half with a solid barrier that is impermeable to water and dye and we put the dye in the water on one side, the molecules distribute themselves only within that half. If we divide the beaker with a barrier that impedes dye molecules only a little, then the dye first distributes itself within the initial half and then slowly invades and distributes itself across both halves. In this case we say that the barrier is permeable to the dye. A barrier such as a cell membrane that is permeable to some molecules but not others is referred to as **semipermeable.**

Before we look at what happens with semipermeable membranes, let's review a few terms. The liquid in our discussion of membranes is referred to as a **solvent.** The solid (e.g., salt) dissolved in the solvent is called a **solute.** A semipermeable membrane that allows water to pass through it but prevents the passage of salt (NaCl) molecules demonstrates the principles of osmosis. If salty water on one side of a semipermeable membrane is diluted, the motion of the salt molecules pulls in water from the more dilute compartment (Figure 13.13*a*). The tendency to equalize salt concentrations across the membrane can even cause some of the water molecules to overcome gravity, raising the level of the liquid on the saltier side (see Figure 13.13*b*).

Put another way, molecules have a tendency to spread out—to move *down* concentration gradients (from an area of higher concentration to an area of lower concentration). We mentioned this tendency in Chapter 3 in order to explain the move-

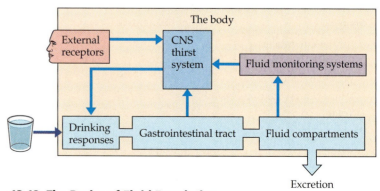

13.12 The Basics of Fluid Regulation

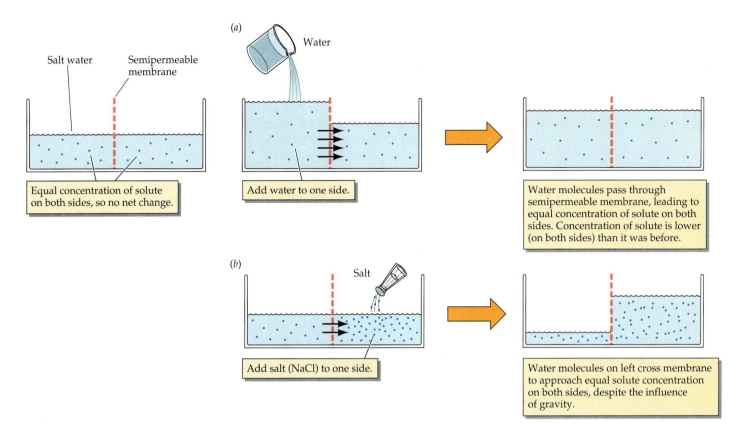

Equal concentration of solute on both sides, so no net change.

Add water to one side.

Water molecules pass through semipermeable membrane, leading to equal concentration of solute on both sides. Concentration of solute is lower (on both sides) than it was before.

Add salt (NaCl) to one side.

Water molecules on left cross membrane to approach equal solute concentration on both sides, despite the influence of gravity.

ment of ions during generation of action potential. In the case we have examined here, in which the semipermeable membrane blocks the passage of salt molecules, the water molecules are moving into the compartment where they are less concentrated (because the salt molecules are there). The force that pushes or pulls water across the membrane (the force that the solutes exert on the membrane that is impermeable to them) is called **osmotic pressure.**

Cell membranes are not as passive as you might think; they strongly resist the passage of some molecules and allow other molecules to pass freely. Recall from Chapter 3, for example, that neurons normally allow very few sodium ions (Na^+) to pass through their membrane unless the voltage-sensitive Na^+ channels are opened, beginning the action potential. We refer to the concentration of solute in a solution as **osmolality.** Normally the concentration of NaCl in the extracellular fluid of mammals is about 0.9% (weight to volume, which means there's about 0.9 g of NaCl for every 100 ml of water). A solution with this concentration of salt is called *physiological saline* and is described as **isotonic,** having the same concentration of salt as mammalian fluids have. A solution with more salt is **hypertonic;** a solution lower in salt is **hypotonic.**

Drugs injected into the extracellular space of muscles are usually mixed in isotonic solution rather than in pure water because if pure water were injected, it would be pulled inside muscle cells (which are filled with ions) by osmotic pressure and would rupture them. At the other extreme, if hypertonic saline were injected, water would be pulled out of the cells, and that too could damage them. These fates could befall any cells exposed to water of the wrong tonicity, so it is crucial that we prevent the fluid surrounding our cells from becoming either too concentrated or too dilute.

The Extracellular Fluid Compartment Serves as a Buffer

The volume of a cell probably can change slightly as proteins are made or degraded, or as new membrane is added. At any one time, however, each cell has a particular volume and is filled with enzymes and other proteins. Because these proteins cannot pass through the cell's external membrane, the cell needs to take in enough

13.13 Osmosis (*a*) Water passes through a semipermeable membrane in whichever direction is necessary to maintain an equal solute concentration on both sides, even against gravity (*b*). Water moves in the same way between compartments in the human body.

water molecules to keep the internal concentrations of salts and proteins within the range at which biochemical reactions run smoothly.

Normally water molecules can pass out of the cell freely, but if a process such as osmotic pressure forces water into the cell too quickly, it will rupture and die. Viewed in this way, the extracellular fluid is a *buffer*—a reservoir that provides and accepts water molecules so that cells can maintain proper internal conditions. The nervous system is responsible for ensuring that the extracellular compartment has about the right amount of water and solute to allow cells to absorb or shed water molecules readily, as conditions dictate.

Two Internal Cues Trigger Thirst

In addition to acting as a buffer, the extracellular fluid is an indicator of conditions in the intracellular compartment. In fact, the nervous system carefully monitors the extracellular compartment to determine whether we should seek water. Two cues indicate that more water may be needed: low extracellular volume (**hypovolemic thirst**) and high extracellular solute concentration (**osmotic thirst**). We'll consider each in turn.

Hypovolemic Thirst Is Triggered by a Loss of Water Volume

The example of hypovolemic thirst that is most easily understood is one we hope you never experience: serious blood loss (hemorrhage). Any animal that loses a significant amount of blood has a lowered total blood volume. Thus blood vessels that would normally be full and slightly stretched no longer contain their full capacity. Blood pressure drops, and the individual (unless unconscious) becomes thirsty.

Note that losing water from blood loss (or from diarrhea or vomiting) does not change the concentration of the extracellular fluid because salts and other ions are lost with the fluid. Rather, only the *volume* of the extracellular fluid is affected in these instances (Figure 13.14*a*). However, continued loss in the extracellular compartment leads to fluid passing out of the intracellular compartment. So when the brain is informed of the initial drop in extracellular volume (by pressure receptors in major blood vessels and the heart known as **baroreceptors**), it initiates thirst to replace the water and salt hunger to replace salts.

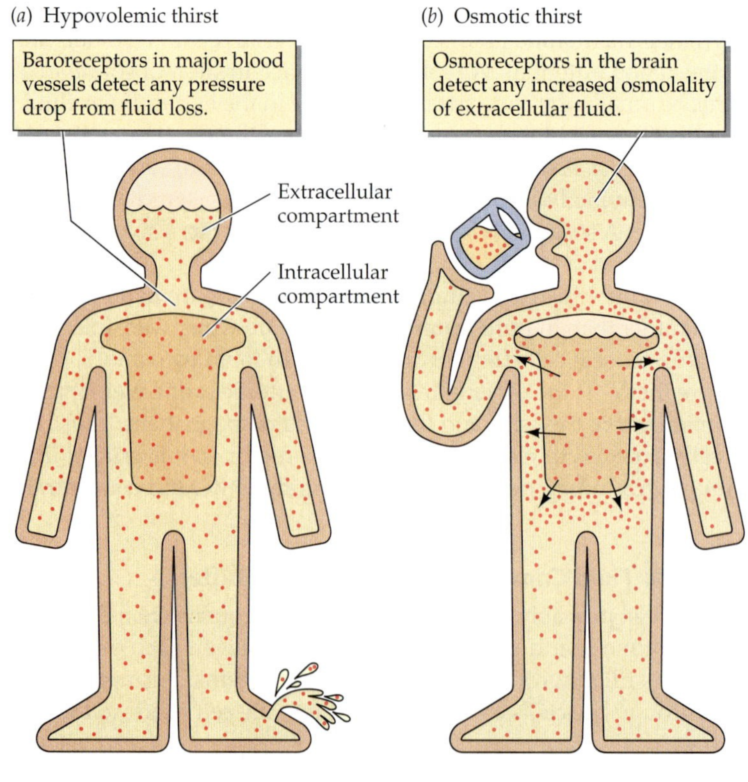

13.14 Two Kinds of Thirst
(*a*) Hypovolemic thirst is triggered by the loss of blood or other body fluids (such as through diarrhea or vomiting) that contain both solutes and water. In this case, extracellular fluid is depleted without the solute concentration being changed in either the intracellular or the extracellular compartments, so there is no osmotic pressure to push water from one compartment to the other. (*b*) Osmotic thirst is triggered when the total volume of water is constant, but a sudden increase in the amount of solute in the extracellular compartment (as after a very salty meal) exerts osmotic pressure that pulls water out of the intracellular compartment.

(*a*) Hypovolemic thirst

Baroreceptors in major blood vessels detect any pressure drop from fluid loss.

Extracellular compartment

Intracellular compartment

(*b*) Osmotic thirst

Osmoreceptors in the brain detect any increased osmolality of extracellular fluid.

The role of vasopressin. When baroreceptors detect a drop in blood pressure (probably by detecting change in the tension in artery walls), they communicate that information through the autonomic nervous system. Selective potentiation of certain autonomic responses counteracts that drop in pressure. The sympathetic portion of the autonomic nervous system stimulates muscles in the artery walls to constrict, which reduces the size of the vessels, compensating for the reduced volume. The brain also receives information from the autonomic nervous system and in response releases the peptide hormone vasopressin from the posterior pituitary gland. The vasopressin further constricts blood vessel walls and instructs the kidneys to reduce the flow of water to the bladder. The latter function explains why this hormone is sometimes called antidiuretic hormone (ADH), as we saw in Chapter 5. (A *diuretic* is a substance that causes excessive urination.)

In the disease **diabetes insipidus,** the production of vasopressin ceases, and the kidneys retain less water; they send more urine to the bladder, and that urine is very pale and dilute (insipid). A consequence of all this urination is that the person is chronically thirsty and must drink a lot of water. Treatment with vasopressin relieves the symptoms. Some rats have a mutation that keeps them from producing functional vasopressin. These Brattleboro rats (so called because they were first isolated in Brattleboro, Vermont) show the symptoms of diabetes insipidus (Figure 13.15). (Note that when people talk about diabetes, they usually do not mean diabetes insipidus, but are referring to diabetes mellitus, which we'll discuss later in this chapter).

13.15 Inherited Diabetes Insipidus in Rats Unable to produce vasopressin (ADH), Brattleboro rats urinate profusely and so must drink a lot of water. Treatment with ADH corrects this condition, which is known as diabetes insipidus.

The renin–angiotensin system. The kidneys also detect the reduced blood flow accompanying hypovolemia and release a hormone called **renin** into the circulation, triggering a cascade of hormones (Figure 13.16). The renin reacts with a protein called angiotensinogen to form the protein angiotensin I. Angiotensin I is converted to **angiotensin II,** which seems to be the active product. (The first demonstrated effect of this protein was to increase blood pressure, which is how it got its name: from the Greek *angeion,* "blood vessel," and the Latin *tensio,* "tension or pressure.")

Angiotensin II has several water-conserving actions. In addition to constricting blood vessels, angiotensin II triggers the release of two hormones: vasopressin, discussed earlier, and aldosterone, to be discussed shortly. In addition, very low doses of angiotensin II injected into the preoptic area are extremely effective in eliciting drinking, even in animals that are not deprived of water (A. N. Epstein et al., 1970). When administered to rats that had been deprived of food but not water, angiotensin II caused them to stop eating and start drinking; thus its effect is highly specific. It appears, then, that angiotensin II can also act on the brain to trigger the sensation of thirst, prompting the animal to drink.

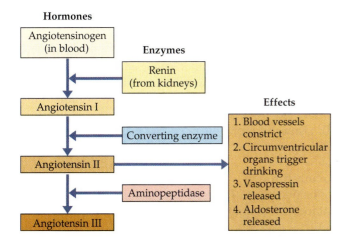

13.16 The Angiotensin Cascade A drop in blood volume is detected by the kidneys. The kidneys then release renin, which catalyzes the conversion of angiotensinogen (already present in blood) to angiotensin I. Angiotensin I is converted to angiotensin II (the most biologically active of the angiotensins).

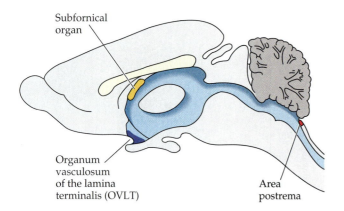

Subfornical organ

Organum vasculosum of the lamina terminalis (OVLT)

Area postrema

13.17 Circumventricular Organs
The circumventricular organs, here seen in a midsagittal view of the rat brain, mediate between the brain and the cerebrospinal fluid (blue). The blood–brain barrier is weak in the subfornical organ and the OVLT, so neurons there can monitor the osmolality of blood.

Where in the brain does angiotensin II act? Although the original work found the preoptic area to be the most sensitive site, it was difficult to see how angiotensin II could reach receptors in this region because the protein does not penetrate the blood–brain barrier. Attention then focused on the **circumventricular organs.** As their name suggests, these organs lie in the walls of the cerebral ventricles (Figure 13.17). The blood–brain barrier is somewhat "leaky" in these regions, so the neurons here have access to blood proteins that other brain regions never see. The circumventricular organs also contain receptor sites that can be affected by substances in the cerebrospinal fluid, and information about stimulation of these sites is carried by axons of the circumventricular cells into other parts of the nervous system.

The neurons in one of these regions, the **subfornical organ,** rapidly respond to intravenous injections of angiotensin II by showing increased metabolic activity (Kadekaro et al., 1989) and expressing IEG (immediate early gene) products (Lebrun et al., 1995). Thus the subfornical organ may be one of the brain sites responding to angiotensin II by triggering thirst. There is some doubt about whether angiotensin II regulates thirst in normal situations because reductions in blood volume that induce thirst do not always produce a measurable change in the concentration of angiotensin II in the blood (S. F. Abraham et al., 1975; Stricker, 1977). Of course, there may be more subtle changes in the concentration or distribution of angiotensin II that are not detected by blood measures.

Osmotic Thirst Is Triggered by a Change in the Concentration of Extracellular Fluid

A more common way to trigger thirst than by loss of blood is by loss of water—through respiration, perspiration, or urination. Although some salt is lost along with the water, generally more water is lost. Thus in addition to the reduction in volume of the extracellular fluid, which triggers the responses described in the previous section, the solute concentration of the extracellular fluid increases. The result is that water is pulled out of cells to balance the concentrations of the intracellular and extracellular compartments.

The solute concentration can be increased without an accompanying increase in volume—for example, by intake of salty food. Such an increase in solute concentration triggers a thirst that is independent of extracellular volume: osmotic thirst (see Figure 13.14b). Osmotic thirst causes us to seek water to protect the intracellular compartment from becoming so depleted of water that its cells are damaged.

In the 1950s it was shown that injecting a small amount of hypertonic (salty) solution into regions of the hypothalamus causes animals to start drinking. This observation suggested that some hypothalamic cells might be **osmoreceptors**—that is, cells that respond to changes in osmotic pressure. Electrical recordings from single nerve cells have revealed osmotically responsive neurons spread widely throughout the preoptic area, the anterior hypothalamus, the supraoptic nucleus, and the organum vasculosum of the lamina terminalis (OVLT), a circumventricular organ (see Figure 13.17).

Perhaps these cells themselves detect the change in osmolality and are themselves osmoreceptors, or perhaps they are informed by other, true osmoreceptors. If there are neuronal osmoreceptors, they may be more "elastic" than other cells and change their rate of firing on the basis of whether they are full (when the extracellular fluid concentration is normal) or "deflated" (when more concentrated extracellular fluid draws water out of the cell). Osmoreceptor cells may also reside among the circumventricular organs, including the OVLT and the subfornical organ, where the blood–brain barrier is weak.

In any case the neural circuits through which osmoreceptors trigger drinking have yet to be fully defined. The two types of thirst (hypovolemic and osmotic), the two fluid compartments (extracellular and intracellular), and the multiple methods to conserve water make for a fairly complicated system for the regulation of water (Figure 13.18).

We Don't Stop Drinking Just Because Our Throat and Mouth Are Wet

Although plausible, the most obvious explanation of why we stop drinking—that our previously dry throat and mouth are now wet—is quite wrong. In one test of this hypothesis, thirsty animals were allowed to drink water but had the water diverted out of the esophagus through a small tube. They remained thirsty and continued drinking. Thus we conclude that moistening the mouth is not sufficient to stop the behavior of drinking or the sensation of thirst.

Furthermore, we stop drinking before water has left the gastrointestinal tract and entered the extracellular compartment. Somehow we monitor how much water we have ingested and stop in anticipation of correcting the extracellular volume and/or osmolality. Experience may teach us and other animals how to gauge accurately whether we've ingested enough to counteract our thirst (hypovolemic or osmotic). Normally all the signals—blood volume, osmolality, moisture in the mouth, estimates of the amount of water we've ingested that's "on the way"—register agreement, but the cessation of one signal alone will not stop thirst; in this way animals ensure against dehydration.

Homeostatic Regulation of Salt Is Required for Effective Regulation of Water

Animals may travel great distances to eat salt and the sodium ion (Na^+) is particularly important to fluid balance. The reason is that we cannot maintain water in the extracellular compartment without solutes; if the extracellular compartment contained pure water, osmotic pressure would drive it into the cells, killing them. The number of Na^+ ions we possess primarily determines how much water we can retain. Thus thirsty animals may prefer slightly salty water (as long as it's hypotonic) over pure water, and this preference may be adaptive for conserving water. Some Na^+ loss is inevitable, as during urination. But when water is at a premium, the body tries to conserve Na^+ in order to retain water.

As noted earlier, low blood volume causes the kidneys to release renin, which makes angiotensin II available in circulation. Angiotensin II then acts on the adrenal glands to release the mineralocorticoid, steroid hormone **aldosterone**. Aldosterone is crucial to Na^+ conservation. Like vasopressin, aldosterone acts directly on the kidneys, but aldosterone induces the kidneys to conserve Na^+ (while vasopressin acts to conserve water). Aldosterone conserves some sodium to aid water retention, but animals must find salt in their diets to survive.

Because some Na^+ aids water retention, you might think that seawater would quench thirst—but it doesn't. Seawater is hypertonic; it has too much Na^+. We lose some water each day without Na^+ (through our skin, with our breathing) and that sodium-free water must be replaced. Adding isotonic water will not help restore the water-to-sodium ratio. If we could excrete lots of sodium ions in our urine, we could drink seawater, use some of the water molecules to replace the day's loss, and excrete the excess salt. But our kidneys cannot excrete enough additional Na^+ in the urine to allow this.

Marine mammals have found a means of excreting excess salt, via kidneys that can produce very concentrated urine. Some desert rodents can also produce highly concentrated urine to help conserve water. Some seabirds, including gulls and pe-

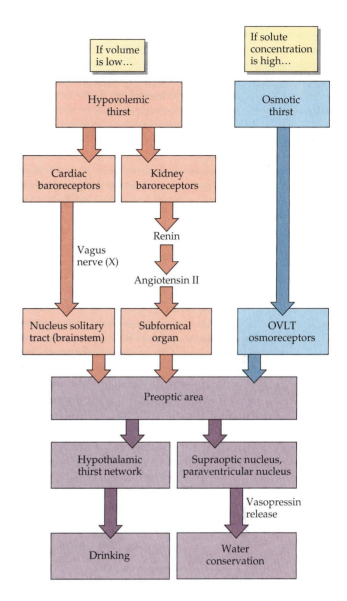

13.18 A More Complete View of Fluid Regulation This more detailed version of Figure 13.12 depicts the thirst signals and brain regions regulating body fluids.

13.19 Secretion of Excess Salt Marine birds, such as this giant petrel, have only seawater to drink for long peroids of time. To compensate, they have salt glands that pull salt out of plasma, sending tiny salt pellets out the nostrils. Note the salt pellet at the tip of the petrel's beak.

trels, have specialized salt glands near the nostrils that can excrete highly concentrated salt solutions (Figure 13.19; Schmidt-Nielsen, 1960) so they can drink seawater.

Food and Energy Regulation

Feast or famine—these are poles of human experience. We are so dependent on food for energy and for building and maintaining our bodies that hunger is a compelling motive and flavors are powerful reinforcements. The need to eat shapes our daily schedules and molds our activities. Our newspapers are full of food-related information: news of successes or failures of food crops; famines and droughts; laws and treaties governing the import and export of foods; hunger strikes; recipes and articles about food; advertisements for restaurants and kitchen appliances; effects of diet and obesity on health; clinics to treat weight problems.

Our basic reliance on food for energy and nutrition is shared with all other animals. In the remainder of this chapter we will look at the general needs and physiological regulation of feeding and energy expenditure, as well as some species-specific aspects of food-related behavior and regulation.

Nutrient Regulation Requires the Anticipation of Future Needs

The regulation of eating and of body energy is intimately related to the regulation of body temperature and water, which we have already considered, but it is more complicated. One reason for the greater complexity is that food is needed not only to supply energy but also to supply nutrients. **Nutrients,** in the technical meaning of the term, are chemicals that are not used as sources of energy but are required for the effective functioning of the body; for example, they are needed for the growth, maintenance, and repair of body structures.

We do not know all the nutritional requirements of the body—even for humans. Of the 20 amino acids found in our bodies, 9 are difficult or impossible for us to manufacture, so we must find them in our diet. These 9 are thus called *essential amino acids*. Similarly, we must obtain a few fatty acids from food. Other nutritional requirements include about 15 vitamins and several minerals.

One reason that eating and nutrient regulation are complicated is that no animal can afford to run out of energy or nutrients; there must be a reserve on hand at all times. If the reserves are too large, though, mobility (for avoiding predators or securing prey) will be compromised. Thus the neurobiology of feeding requires us to understand how the organism *anticipates* the need for energy and nutrients, as well as how these resources are moved in and out of various body reservoirs. For the cells of the body to receive and use vital nutrients, ingested food must be converted into simpler chemicals. These simpler substances are the products of **digestion,** a series of mechanical and chemical processes that take place in the digestive tract.

Most of Our Food Is Used to Provide Us with Energy

All the energy we need to move, think, breathe, and maintain body temperature is derived in the same way: It is released as the chemical bonds of complex molecules are broken to form smaller, simpler compounds. In a sense we "burn" food just as a car burns gasoline for energy. To raise body temperature we release the bond energy as heat. For other bodily processes, such as those in the brain, the energy is utilized by more sophisticated biochemical processes. In either case we assess the amount of energy used in terms of calories. (Recall that in physics, a calorie is the amount of energy it takes to raise the temperature of 1 ml of water by 1°C.)

When nutritionists talk about calories in food, they are describing the potential energy available. Unfortunately, what a nutritionist calls a calorie is actually 1000 calories (a kilocalorie) as defined by physicists. By convention, nutritionists simply leave off the *kilo-* prefix. To avoid confusion, we will use *kilocalories* (kcal) as defined in physics. We can gauge metabolic rate, the amount of energy we use during a given period, in terms of kilocalories per day (kcal/day).

Some of the energy in food cannot be converted to metabolizable form and is instead excreted. In a study of metabolism in the laboratory rat, about 75% of the ingested energy became available for use in body functions (Corbett and Keesey, 1982). The available energy is used in one of three activities:

1. *Processing of newly ingested food.* Typically both metabolic rate and heat production rise just after a meal, and this increase has been interpreted as reflecting energy used to process food. The energy utilization for processing food amounts to about 8%.
2. *Basal metabolism.* The greatest part of the energy—about 55%—is used for maintaining body heat and other resting functions, such as neural potentials.
3. *Active behavioral processes.* Only about 12 to 13% of the energy is spent on this function. In an environment more conducive to activity than the small metabolic chamber used to take these measurements in the laboratory, the percentage of energy spent on active behavioral processes probably would be larger.

It used to be thought that only the expenditure of energy for active behavioral processes showed much elasticity and that basal metabolism and heat production caused by feeding were fixed. In fact, however, the rate of basal metabolism is known to follow a rule, devised by Max Kleiber (1947), that relates energy expenditure to body weight:

$$\text{kcal/day} = 70 \times \text{weight}^{0.75}$$

where weight is expressed in kilograms. This rule has been shown to apply from the largest mammals to mice—a range in size greater than 3000 to 1 (Figure 13.20). Interestingly, this rule holds across species but not within species, which warns us that body weight is only one factor affecting metabolic rate.

Within a species, an animal's basal metabolic rate may depart significantly from the value predicted by Kleiber's equation. For example, food-deprived people have lower basal metabolism, as well as a lower weight. In fact, severe restriction of caloric intake affects metabolic rate much more than it affects body weight (Keesey and Corbett, 1984). Such adjustments in the rate of energy expenditure play a significant role in maintaining energy balance and in keeping an individual's body weight relatively constant (Keesey and Powley, 1986).

Because people and animals adjust their energy expenditures in response to under- or overnutrition, they tend to resist either los-

13.20 The Relation between Body Size and Metabolism Over a wide range of body weights, basal metabolic rate increases in a very regular, predictable fashion. However, endotherms have a higher metabolic rate than ectotherms of a similar body weight. (After Hemmingsen, 1960.)

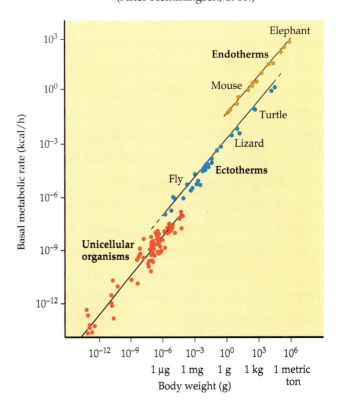

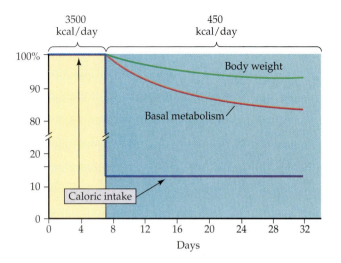

13.21 Why Losing Weight Is So Difficult After 7 days on a diet of 3500 kcal/day, the intake of six obese subjects was restricted to a measly 450 kcal/day—a drop of 87%. However, basal metabolism also declined, by 15%, so after 3 weeks, body weight had declined by only 6%. (After Bray, 1969.)

ing or gaining weight. This tendency helps explain why it is so difficult for some people to lose weight and for others to gain (Figure 13.21). People who hold their weight down by dieting may remain hypometabolic as long as their weight stays below the level that they used to maintain, and thus they must continue dieting to maintain a body weight that would be normal for someone else of similar stature. Mice whose basal metabolic rate has been increased (by a transgenic increase in the energy used by mitochondria) eat more and weigh less than normal mice, without increased locomotor activity (Clapham et al., 2000). Perhaps, someday a drug will be developed to exert this effect on human mitochondria, and produce such wonderful results.

However difficult dieting might be, the only known way to cause animals to live longer is to reduce their calorie intake to levels about 50 to 75% of what they would eat if food were always available (Weindruch and Walford, 1988), which may be related to the resulting decrease in basal metabolism. Both the body (C.-K. Lee et al., 1999) and the brain (C.-K. Lee et al., 2000) give evidence of slower aging with such caloric restriction.

Carbohydrates Provide Energy for Body and Brain

What molecules provide energy to the body, and how does the body regulate that energy? Large carbohydrate molecules can be broken down into simple carbohydrates, including sugars. The most important sugar used by our body is **glucose.** In fact, the brain is quite dependent on glucose for energy, while the rest of the body can use both glucose and more complicated molecules, such as fatty acids, for energy. Because a readily available supply of glucose is crucial for brain function and for survival, the liver stores glucose by combining excess glucose molecules to form a more complex carbohydrate called **glycogen.**

When the concentration of glucose molecules in circulation falls, the liver can convert the glycogen back into glucose molecules and release them into circulation as needed. This shuttling of energy supplies back and forth is controlled by two protein hormones from the pancreas: **Glucagon** promotes the breakdown of glycogen to glucose; **insulin** promotes the conversion of glucose to glycogen (Figure 13.22). Thus the pancreatic hormones determine the balance of ready energy (glucose) from a short-term energy source (glycogen). (Recall from Chapter 5 that glucagon and insulin are secreted from the alpha and beta cells, respectively, of the islets of Langerhans within the pancreas.)

For long-term energy storage we use fat, maintained in fat cells; these fat cells form what is known as **adipose tissue.** Fat molecules are large and complicated. You may think of them as the result of the joining together of many different sugars and other small molecules into a large molecule that is not soluble in water. Fat either comes directly from our food or is manufactured in the body from glucose and other nutrients. If the glycogen store becomes depleted, the body can convert fat into fatty acids to supply energy to itself, and into glucose to provide energy to the brain.

When a human or any other animal is deprived of food, little or no energy is stored in fat deposits. When an animal eats liberally, some of the energy is laid down in fat supplies so that it will be

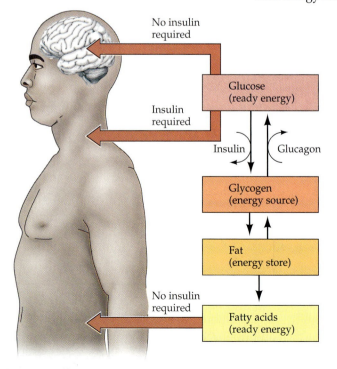

13.22 The Role of Insulin in Energy Utilization The body can make use of either fatty acids or glucose for energy, while the brain can make ready use of only glucose. So the brain requires a constant supply of glucose, which it can use without the aid of insulin. On the other hand, the body can make use of glucose only with the aid of insulin, so in the absence of insulin the body must use fatty acids for energy.

available in the future. As we will see later, considerable evidence suggests that the body maintains its level of fat in the face of all but the most extreme diet restrictions and regains fat after the surgical removal of fat stores.

Insulin Is Crucial for the Regulation of Body Metabolism

We've already mentioned the importance of insulin for converting glucose into glycogen. Another important role of insulin is enabling the body to use glucose. Most cells regulate the import of glucose molecules via **glucose transporters** that span the cell's external membrane and bring glucose molecules from outside the cell into the cell for use. The glucose transporters must interact with insulin in order to function. (Brain cells are an important exception; they can use glucose without the aid of insulin.) Each time you eat a meal, the foods are broken down and glucose is released into the bloodstream. Most of your body requires insulin to make use of that glucose, so three different, sequential mechanisms stimulate insulin release.

1. The stimuli from food (sight, smell, and taste) evoke a conditioned release of insulin in anticipation of glucose arrival in the blood. This release, because it is mediated by the brain, is called the *cephalic phase* of insulin release.
2. During the *digestive phase*, food entering the stomach and intestines causes them to release gut hormones, some of which stimulate the pancreas to release insulin.
3. During the *absorptive phase*, glucose enters the bloodstream, and special cells in the liver, called **glucodetectors** (or *glucostats*), detect this circulating glucose and signal the pancreas to release insulin.

The newly released insulin allows the body to make use of some of the glucose immediately, and other glucose is converted into glycogen. The liver and the pancreas communicate via the nervous system. Autonomic afferents from the liver deliver nerve impulses up the **vagus nerve** to synapse in the **nucleus of the solitary tract** (**NST**) in the brainstem—so information from glucodetectors in the liver travels up the vagus nerve to the NST. Terry Powley and colleagues have mapped these vagal afferents to other brain regions, such as the hypothalamus, informing the brain of circulating glucose levels and contributing to hunger, as we'll discuss later. Efferent fibers carry signals from the brainstem back out the vagus nerve to the pancreas. These efferent fibers modulate insulin secretions from the pancreas.

Terry Powley

Lack of insulin causes the disease **diabetes mellitus.** In *Type I* (or *juvenile-onset*) *diabetes mellitus,* the pancreas stops producing insulin. Although the brain can still make use of glucose from the diet, the rest of the body cannot and is forced to use energy from fatty acids. The result is that lots of glucose is left in the bloodstream because the brain cannot use it all, and the lack of insulin means there is no way to put it into glycogen storage. Some of the glucose is secreted into the urine, making the urine sweet, which is how we get the name *diabetes mellitus* (literally "honey-sweet passing [of water]"). In contrast, *diabetes insipidus* (literally "bland passing"), which we discussed earlier in the chapter, gets its name from the dilute, uncolored urine that it produces.

Untreated Diabetics Eat Ravenously yet Lose Weight

The body did not evolve to gather all its energy efficiently from fatty acids, so an untreated Type I diabetic is chronically undernourished. Although untreated diabetics eat a great deal, because their bodies cannot make much use of the food, they lose weight anyway. Tissues begin showing signs of degradation as a result of such a heavy reliance on the less efficient fatty acids for energy. The urine, in addition to being sweet, is copious as the kidneys try to dump the excess glucose; consequently, untreated diabetics are also chronically thirsty. Finally, the excess glucose in circulation may itself damage some tissues, including the retina, as mentioned in Chapter 10.

The treatment is obvious: provide exogenous insulin by injection. Unfortunately, insulin normally is not secreted just once during the day. The pattern of secretion across the day is complex and varies depending on what is eaten, when it is eaten,

CLINICAL ISSUE

and what other behaviors are displayed. Thus, exogenously providing the proper amount of insulin at the proper time is tricky.

There has long been evidence that Type I diabetes has a genetic component, and recent research indicates that many different genes affect the probability of developing diabetes. One hypothesis suggests that diabetes is an autoimmune disorder—that diabetics produce antibodies that attack their own pancreatic cells, stopping the insulin supply. Why would this happen? After all, the immune system is supposed to help us.

Scientists have found that some viruses that cause upper respiratory infections have a protein that resembles glutamic acid decarboxylase (GAD). When this viral protein is injected into mice, some of the mice produce antibodies that recognize both the viral protein and their own GAD. Because GAD is found on the surface of the pancreatic cells, the antibodies attack and destroy the cells, leading to a loss of insulin and the development of diabetes. Some strains of mice are much more likely to suffer these effects of viral exposure than others (Atkinson et al., 1994; Yoon et al., 1999). Some people exposed to this virus may produce antibodies to defeat the virus that also destroy their own insulin source.

GENES AND BEHAVIOR

Supporting this theory are experimental results showing that some people in the early stages of diabetes have circulating antibodies that recognize GAD (Atkinson and Maclaren, 1994). Many different genes could influence whether a person makes these particular antibodies. If this hypothesis proves correct, it may be possible to inoculate children with other proteins from these viruses so that when they are exposed to the virus, they already have antibodies to defeat the infection without making the harmful antibodies.

Another, more common type of diabetes mellitus is called *Type II,* or *adult-onset, diabetes.* This milder version can be caused either by a gradually decreasing sensitivity to insulin or by gradually decreasing production of the hormone. This condition is far more common in obese people, and because the individuals still produce some insulin, it can usually be treated by reduction of the amount of glucose in the diet and by administration of a drug that stimulates the pancreas to produce more insulin, without the need to resort to insulin injections.

Despite Its Importance, Insulin Is Not the Sole Signal for Either Hunger or Satiety

Given the crucial role of insulin in mobilizing and distributing food energy, you might think that the brain monitors circulating insulin levels to decide when it is time to eat and when it is time to stop eating. For example, if the insulin level is high, there must be food in the pipeline and the fat stores will be increased, so the brain might produce the sensation of satiety so that we stop eating. If insulin levels are low, the brain might signal hunger to impel us to find food and eat. Experiments have shown that lowering an animal's blood insulin levels causes it to become hungry and eat a large meal. If moderate levels of insulin are injected, the animal eats much less. These results suggest that insulin is a satiety signal.

COMPETING HYPOTHESES

Investigators tested this simple hypothesis by injecting a large amount of insulin into animals. But rather than appearing satiated, the animals responded by eating a large meal. High insulin levels direct much of the glucose into fat storage, which means that there is effectively less glucose in circulation for the brain. The brain learns of this functional glucose deficit from glucodetectors in the brain (probably in one or more of the circumventricular organs; see Figure 13.17) and the liver (which communicates to the NST via the vagus nerve). Is circulating glucose signaling satiety and hunger to the brain? Certainly this information plays a role normally, but it can't be the only source of information because untreated diabetics have very high levels of circulating glucose, yet they are chronically hungry.

Studies of diabetic rats provide more evidence that insulin is not the only satiety signal. Like untreated human diabetics, these rats eat a great deal. But if the rats are fed a high-fat diet, they eat normal amounts (M. I. Friedman, 1978), probably because their bodies can make immediate use of the fatty acids without the aid of insulin. Thus, circulating levels of insulin and glucose contribute to hunger and satiety, but they are not sufficient to explain those states entirely. Somehow the brain integrates insulin and glucose levels with other sources of information to decide whether to initiate eating. This seems to be the theme of hunger research—that the brain integrates many different signals rather than relying exclusively on any single signal to trigger hunger. Experience also tempers the brain's regulation of hunger, as discussed next.

Experience Protects Us from Toxins in Food

Learning has a profound effect on the feeding behavior of animals. We've already mentioned the cephalic phase of feeding, during which the stimuli of food evoke a conditioned release of insulin so that we will make quick use of the food. Another example of conditioning is the preference that many species show for foods to which they were exposed during development. Normally such a preference would be adaptive. Some moths prefer to lay their eggs on the leaves of whichever plant they ate as a caterpillar. This choice seems sensible: If it was good enough to enable me to survive to adulthood, it should do for my offspring.

One can influence the food preferences of adult rats by exposing them to the food as nursing pups. Rats normally prefer plain water over garlic-flavored water, but if a rat mother has only garlic-flavored water to drink, she will drink it. Her offspring, nursing for the first 21 days of life, will grow up to prefer garlic water over plain. This preference is strengthened if the pups also are exposed to such water just after weaning (Capretta et al., 1975). Similarly, many adult humans prefer the cuisine they were fed by their parents while growing up.

Another important means by which experience shapes feeding is conditioned **taste aversion.** A young, inexperienced blue jay will readily snap up and eat a monarch butterfly. Score one for the blue jay. A few minutes later, however, the bird will vomit up the butterfly and wipe its bill repeatedly as if to remove any traces (Figure 13.23). That bird will eat other butterflies, but it will not eat another monarch (Wiklund and Sillén-Tullberg, 1985), even when hundreds are available. Score several hundred for the monarchs.

Why does the blue jay vomit up the monarch? The monarch, as a caterpillar, fed on milkweed and gathered from that plant toxins that offend other caterpillars, but that monarch caterpillars tolerate. The toxins remain in the adult's body and also offend birds, making them nauseated. The bird quickly learns to associate the monarch with illness, and to avoid becoming ill again it avoids that food from that point forward.

Investigated by John Garcia, conditioned taste aversion is sometimes referred to as the Garcia effect. The results of Garcia's original work, which involved making rats sick by using X-rays (Garcia et al., 1955), were only very slowly accepted by scientists in the 1960s because learning psychologists then believed that any stimu-

John Garcia

13.23 Taste Aversion A blue jay immediately before (*a*) and a few minutes after (*b*) eating a monarch butterfly and becoming sick from the toxins these butterflies contain. The animal regurgitates the butterfly, wipes its beak repeatedly, and will in the future avoid eating other monarchs. (Courtesy of Lincoln Brower.)

lus could be paired with any other stimulus equally well, and that repeated trials would be necessary for the animal to associate one stimulus with the other. The assertion that animals could learn with a single trial to avoid food associated with illness, but would require many trials to avoid food associated with foot shock, was a heresy. Another reason for the skepticism was the common belief that the interval between presentation of the stimuli could not exceed seconds if the association were to be made (see Chapter 17), but the illness effects in Garcia's studies appeared minutes to hours after ingestion.

We now know that animals from snails to humans readily associate food with illness that occurs even hours later and use this learning ability to avoid poisons. The selective advantage of this propensity seems obvious. A related phenomenon is **neophobia,** the avoidance of new things—in this case new foods. Rats are quite reluctant to eat any new food, and when they do, they tend to eat a small amount and wait a period before eating more. If they become ill after the first sample, conditioned taste aversion diverts them from taking more.

Do Peptide Hormones in the Gut Signal Satiety?

We mentioned earlier that when food arrives in the stomach and intestines, these organs release several peptide hormones. Among them is **cholecystokinin** (**CCK**). The release of CCK is especially pronounced if the food has a high content of fat and/or proteins. CCK seems to have widespread effects, including stimulating the pancreas to release insulin, a function we alluded to earlier. Thus CCK meets the first criterion for a circulating satiety signal: Levels are high when food is already in the intestines and low when the intestines are empty (J. Gibbs and Smith, 1986).

**COMPETING
HYPOTHESES**

CCK also acts as a neurotransmitter in the brain, so we know that some neurons respond to CCK and that circulating CCK could communicate satiety to the brain. When CCK is administered to humans, however, they report experiencing nausea and even vomiting (Miaskiewicz et al., 1989). Apparently exogenous CCK acts on the intestines themselves, increasing muscular contractions and thus producing cramping and nausea.

Does CCK make rats nauseated? It's difficult to know because, for one thing, rats cannot vomit, even when they are very sick. But one indication that exogenous CCK may make rats nauseated is that pairing a new food with CCK treatment causes rats to avoid the food in the future (D. Y. Chen et al., 1993). This result indicates that CCK induces taste aversion.

We must interpret the effects of exogenous CCK on food intake with some suspicion: CCK may make rats feel nauseated rather than satiated, but of course the normally secreted CCK triggered by a meal does not cause us to feel nauseated. Therefore the amount of CCK and/or the co-release of presently unidentified compounds must prevent the production of nausea by endogenous CCK.

There Is Apparently No Single Satiety Center or Single Hunger Center in the Brain

Just as no single molecule in the bloodstream always triggers hunger or satiety, it appears that no single brain region has exclusive control of these sensations. Many findings demonstrate that the hypothalamus regulates metabolic rate, food intake, and body weight. For example, functional MRI shows that drinking glucose after fasting affects the activity of the human medial hypothalamus (Y. Liu et al., 2000).

An early theory of hypothalamic involvement, the *dual-center hypothesis* of eating, offered an overly simple model. According to this theory, the hypothalamus contained two control centers: A hunger center in the **lateral hypothalamus** (**LH**), and a satiety center in the **ventromedial hypothalamus** (**VMH**). Information from all the other brain regions, and from other factors (such as circulating hormones) that influence eating, was presumed to funnel into and act through these hypothalamic control centers. Further research soon dethroned these hypothalamic centers from their exclusive status, as we will see.

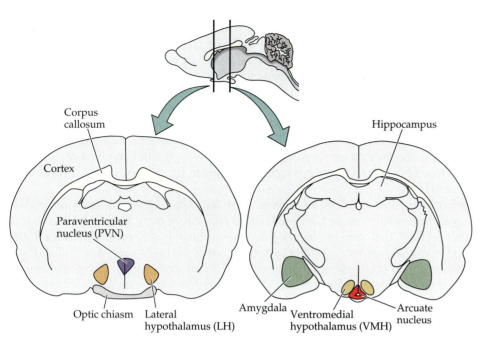

13.24 Brain Regions Implicated in the Regulation of Eating

The Ventromedial Hypothalamus Appeared for a Time to Be the Satiety Center

Occasionally a person develops a pathologically voracious appetite and rapidly becomes obese. In the nineteenth century, physicians found that some such patients had tumors at the base of the brain. In 1940, Hetherington and Ranson reported that bilateral lesions of the ventromedial hypothalamus (Figure 13.24) cause rats to become obese. VMH lesions produced obesity in all the species that were tested—monkeys, dogs and cats, several species of rodents, and some species of birds.

The VMH was promptly called a satiety center because destroying it seemed to prevent animals from ever being satiated with food, but this characterization was soon seen to be inadequate. Destruction of the VMH does not simply cause the rats to become feeding machines. Rather, the eating habits of VMH-lesioned rats are still controlled both by the palatability of food and by body weight, but these controls are no longer exerted in normal ways. If palatable food of high caloric content is available, VMH-lesioned rats typically show two phases of weight gain.

At first they show an amazing increase in consumption, eating two or three times as much as normal; this condition is called **hyperphagia** (from the Greek, *hyper,* "over," and *phagein,* "to eat"). Body weight shoots up—a stage called the *dynamic phase of weight gain* (Figure 13.25). But after a few weeks, weight stabilizes at an obese

COMPETING HYPOTHESES

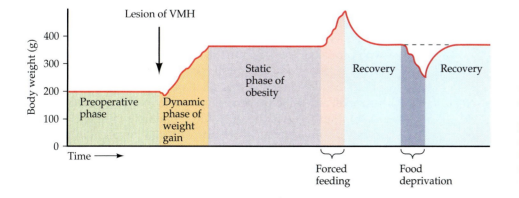

13.25 Lesion-Induced Obesity Rats in which the ventromedial hypothalamus (VMH) has been lesioned overeat and gain weight until they reach a new, higher body weight, which they defend in the face of either forced feeding or food deprivation. Thus they continue to regulate body weight, but at a higher set point. (After Sclafani et al., 1976.)

level, and food intake is not much above normal; this stage is called the *static phase of obesity*. Once animals have reached this new weight, they seem to display normal satiety in response to their food. Because the VMH is gone from these animals, it cannot be responsible for their satiety; therefore it seems likely that other brain regions normally contribute to satiety.

Some observations indicate that the obese VMH-lesioned rat regulates its weight at a new target value. If an obese rat in the static phase is force-fed, its weight rises above the plateau level; but when it is again allowed to eat on its own, body weight returns to the plateau level (see Figure 13.25). Similarly, after an obese rat has been deprived of food and has lost weight, when given free access to food it regains its plateau level.

Furthermore, the plateau body weight also depends on the palatability of the diet. If VMH-lesioned rats are kept on a diet of laboratory chow pellets (rather than a high-fat diet), their weight does not rise much above that of control animals. If the food is adulterated with quinine to make it bitter, the body weight of the VMH-lesioned rats may fall below that of controls (Sclafani et al., 1976). These results suggest that VMH-lesioned rats are finicky and therefore show exaggerated reactions to palatability.

There are several hypotheses about how VMH lesions exert these effects. The VMH-lesioned animals release more insulin than control animals do (Weingarten et al., 1985), so the hyperphagia may be caused by, or at least augmented by, the increased insulin, which, as mentioned earlier, tends to induce eating. Furthermore, the main effect of VMH lesions may be caused by the disruption of axons coming from the **paraventricular nucleus** (**PVN**). These PVN axons normally synapse on brainstem nuclei that regulate the parasympathetic vagus nerve. Because the vagus innervates and receives afferents from both the pancreas and the liver, it seems increasingly likely that "VMH lesions" are disrupting parasympathetic regulation.

The Lateral Hypothalamus Appeared for a Time to Be the Hunger Center

In 1951, Anand and Brobeck announced that bilateral destruction of the lateral hypothalamus (LH) causes rats or cats to stop eating. This refusal to eat, known as *aphagia*, was so severe in some cases that animals died of starvation even when their usual food was present. The investigators proposed that the LH contains a feeding center and that the VMH normally acts as a brake on feeding by inhibiting the LH.

Two important features of the effects of LH damage soon emerged: Phillip Teitelbaum and Eliot Stellar (1954) found that the rats refused not only to eat but also to drink (they showed *adipsia* as well as aphagia). If the experimenters placed a bit of food or a drop of water on the lips or in the mouth of the rat, it spat out the food or water as if it were distasteful. Second, the aphagia and adipsia were not necessarily permanent. A few rats began to eat and drink spontaneously after about a week. Most rats would eventually eat spontaneously if they were kept alive meanwhile by having food and water pumped through a tube directly into the stomach.

Thus just as VMH destruction does not abolish all inhibition of eating, LH destruction does not permanently prevent eating and drinking. Therefore, another brain region must be able to monitor feeding and signal satiety in LH-lesioned rats. Presumably this other region contributes to satiety in normal animals.

Recovered LH-lesioned rats regulate their new body weight with precision. The larger the size of the LH lesion, the lower the target level of body weight. If food is restricted, the weights of LH-lesioned and control rats fall in parallel, and the predeprivation level is regained when free access to food is restored (Figure 13.26). Similarly, if the only food available is eggnog (year-round!), both lesioned and control rats gain weight in parallel; and when the usual diet is restored, both groups fall to their previous levels. When food is adulterated with quinine, the LH-lesioned rats again show changes in parallel with normal controls (Keesey and Boyle, 1973). (Recall that VMH-lesioned rats dis-

Phillip Teitelbaum

Eliot Stellar

13.26 Lesion-Induced Weight Loss
Both normal rats and rats that have recovered from lesions of the lateral hypothalamus (LH) regulate body weight quite well. The LH-lesioned rats regulate around a lowered target weight, but in parallel with normal rats. (After Keesey and Boyle, 1973.)

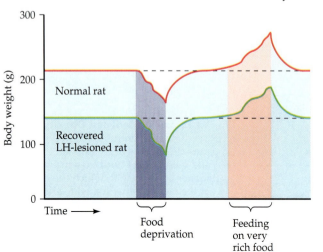

played an exaggerated reaction to quinine.) Thus the LH-lesioned rats are said to defend a lowered weight target or set point (Keesey, 1980).

Human beings may become emaciated if they suffer from lesions or tumors of the lateral hypothalamus. Bilateral damage to the LH through accident or disease is rare, but even unilateral damage to the LH sometimes produces aphagia and adipsia. Cases of *anorexia* (absence of appetite) induced by LH lesions in humans are about one-fourth as frequent as cases of hypothalamic obesity (L. E. White and Hain, 1959).

Satiety and Hunger Functions Are Spread across Several Brain Regions

The dual-center hypothesis was challenged by many observations. As we have seen, animals exhibited some capacity for hunger and satiety despite losing the LH or the VMH, respectively. Controversies arose about the reason that these lesions were effective: Was it that they destroyed integrative centers, as originally believed, or that they interrupted fiber tracts passing through these regions (Marshall et al., 1974)? In addition, many brain regions outside the hypothalamus have been found to be involved in the regulation of feeding behavior, and they do not contribute solely by their connections to the hypothalamus. Among the regions whose destruction impairs the regulation of feeding are the amygdaloid nuclei, the frontal cortex, and the substantia nigra. Taken together, these data suggest that hunger and satiety are not centered in any single brain region, but that a network of cells distributed across the brain is responsible for these functions.

Scientists have become increasingly aware that peripheral structures, notably the liver, also play a crucial role in monitoring energy and nutrient balance and signaling the brain to activate or inhibit eating. We saw earlier that the liver detects glucose levels, and experiments indicate that the liver also detects circulating levels of fatty acids and communicates both kinds of information through the vagus nerve to the NST. For example, cutting the vagus nerve disrupts feeding responses to manipulations of circulating glucose and fatty acids (e.g., Tordoff et al., 1991). From the brainstem NST, this information reaches the hypothalamic nuclei and enters the brain's hunger system.

Leptin Helps Regulate Body Weight

Mice that receive two copies of the gene called *obese* (abbreviated *ob*) regulate their body weight at a high level (Figure 13.27*a*), as you might have guessed from the gene's name. These mice have larger and more numerous fat cells than their heterozygous littermates (*ob/+*; the plus sign indicates the wild-type, normal allele). The fat mice (*ob/ob*) maintain their obesity even when given a diet strongly adulterated with quinine or when required to work hard to obtain food (Cruce et al., 1974).

GENES AND BEHAVIOR

13.27 Inherited Obesity   Both of these mice have two copies of the *obese* gene, which impairs the production of leptin by fat cells. The mouse on the left weighs about 67 grams; a normal (wild-type) mouse at this age weighs about 25 grams. The mouse on the right has been treated with leptin, and weighs about 35 grams.

Jeffrey Friedman

**CLINICAL
ISSUE**

Jeffrey Friedman and coworkers found that *ob/ob* mice have defective genes for the peptide **leptin** (from the Greek *leptos,* "thin"). Fat cells produce leptin and then secrete the protein into the bloodstream (Y. Zhang et al., 1994). Leptin receptors (known as **ObR** because they are receptors to the *obese* gene product, leptin) have been identified in the choroid plexus, the cortex, and several hypothalamic nuclei (Hakansson et al., 1998), to be discussed shortly. Animals with defects in the *ObR* gene, such as Zucker rats (L. M. Zucker and Zucker, 1961; al-Barazanji et al., 1997) and *diabetic* mice (Coleman and Hummel, 1973) also become obese. Thus the brain seems to monitor circulating leptin levels to measure and regulate total body fat. Defects in leptin production or leptin sensitivity caused a false underreporting of body fat, leading the animals to overeat, especially high-fat or sugary foods.

Injecting *ob/ob* mice with normal leptin causes them to lose weight dramatically (Halaas et al., 1995), and injections directly to the hypothalamus are even more effective (Campfield et al., 1995). Behavioral genetic analyses indicate a strong genetic contribution to obesity in humans (representing the effect of many genes, not just one) (R. A. Price and Gottesman, 1991), but variation in the leptin protein does not appear to play a role in human obesity.

Examination of the leptin gene from thousands of obese people detected only two people with mutant leptin—a 64-pound, 2-year-old boy and his cousin, a 190-pound, 8-year-old girl (Montague et al., 1997). Furthermore, obese people, on average, secrete *more* leptin than do thin people. So perhaps what distinguishes obese people from others is a relative insensitivity to leptin rather than an insufficiency of the protein. Nevertheless, injecting leptin also caused normal mice to lose weight, so such treatment may alleviate human obesity no matter what the cause.

Brain Peptides, in Response to Leptin, Mediate Some of the Signals for Hunger

Once leptin reaches the hypothalamic **arcuate nucleus,** a series of peptides is affected. Leptin suppresses the production and release of several peptide neurotransmitters known to induce eating, including **neuropeptide Y** (**NPY**) and **agouti-related peptide** (**AGRP**) (Sahu, 1998; M. W. Schwartz et al., 2000; Seeley and Schwartz, 1997), while enhancing the release of peptides that inhibit eating, including α**-melanocyte stimulating hormone** (α**-MSH**). These arcuate neurons in turn project to the paraventricular nucleus (PVN) and lateral hypothalamus (LH).

Sarah Leibowitz (1991) found that in these regions, NPY infusions cause rats that seemed satiated to begin eating again (Stanley et al., 1989). When animals are deprived of food, NPY levels increase in the PVN (Sahu et al., 1988). So leptin suppresses NPY-producing arcuate neurons, reducing NPY release in the PVN and reducing the signal for hunger. When leptin levels fall, NPY release in the PVN rises and the animal begins eating (Figure 13.28).

What about the other two peptides found in the arcuate that are affected by leptin? Recall that leptin suppresses AGRP release and facilitates α-MSH release. These two peptides have antagonistic effects on the same receptor, the **melanocortin receptor** (**MCR**). α-MSH activates the MCR; AGRP is an endogenous antagonist for the receptor. When leptin stimulates arcuate neurons to release α-MSH in the PVN, the MCR-containing neurons there are activated, inhibiting hunger. Furthermore, because leptin suppresses the release of AGRP (the MCR antagonist) in the PVN, α-MSH has an even greater effect on MCR-responsive neurons there. Two MCRs are expressed in the brain, and mice with either MCR gene knocked out become obese, further suggesting that MCR-responsive neurons suppress hunger.

Two other neuropeptides may also be involved in hunger. Named **orexins** (from the Greek *oregein,* "to desire"), these peptides are normally produced only in the lateral hypothalamic area (Figure 13.29). When orexins are injected into the hypothalamus of rats, the animals eat four to six times more food than control rats eat (Sakurai et al., 1998). Conversely, depriving rats of food increases the production of orexins in the hypothalamus. Whether orexins are affected by circulating leptin levels is under investigation. Orexins also seem to be involved in the sleep disorder narcolepsy (see Chapter 14), but how that function relates to hunger is unknown.

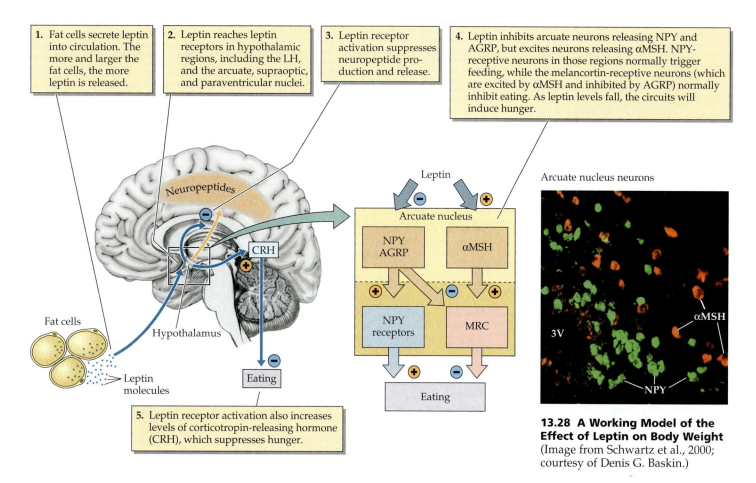

1. Fat cells secrete leptin into circulation. The more and larger the fat cells, the more leptin is released.

2. Leptin reaches leptin receptors in hypothalamic regions, including the LH, and the arcuate, supraoptic, and paraventricular nuclei.

3. Leptin receptor activation suppresses neuropeptide production and release.

4. Leptin inhibits arcuate neurons releasing NPY and AGRP, but excites neurons releasing αMSH. NPY-receptive neurons in those regions normally trigger feeding, while the melancortin-receptive neurons (which are excited by αMSH and inhibited by AGRP) normally inhibit eating. As leptin levels fall, the circuits will induce hunger.

5. Leptin receptor activation also increases levels of corticotropin-releasing hormone (CRH), which suppresses hunger.

13.28 A Working Model of the Effect of Leptin on Body Weight (Image from Schwartz et al., 2000; courtesy of Denis G. Baskin.)

Unfortunately, none of the present dietary, surgical (Box 13.1), or pharmacological interventions reliably reverse obesity for long periods of time. A few individuals improve; many others do not. Furthermore, some of the most effective synthetic drugs for the treatment of obesity in the past have been found to have serious, life-threatening side effects (Cannistra et al., 1997; McCann et al., 1997).

Anorexia Nervosa and Bulimia Are Life-Threatening Eating Disorders

Some young people become obsessed with their body weight and become extremely thin—usually by eating very little and sometimes also regurgitating food, taking laxatives, or drinking large amounts of water to suppress appetite. This condition, which is more common in adolescent girls and women than in males, is called **anorexia nervosa.** Usually the menstrual cycle of females who suffer from anorexia is disrupted or stops altogether. The name of the disorder indicates (1) that the patients have no appetite (*anorexia*) and (2) that the disorder originates in the nervous system (*nervosa*). But the disorder is so poorly understood that both of these assumptions could be mistaken.

For example, people who suffer from anorexia nervosa sometimes think about food a good deal, and physiological evidence suggests that they respond even more than normal subjects to the presentation of food (Broberg and Bernstein, 1989), so their appetite may be normal or even exaggerated. Yet they deny themselves food. The idea that anorexia is primarily a nervous disorder stems from the distorted body image of the patients (they may consider themselves fat when others see them as emaciated) and from the fact that their diet is self-imposed.

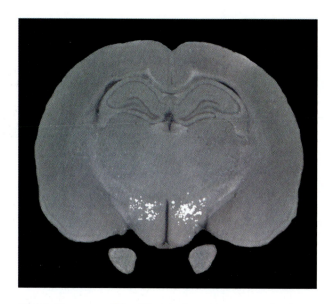

13.29 Neuropeptides That Induce Hunger? In situ hybridization indicates that orexin mRNA (bright spots) is made only in the lateral hypothalamus. Infusion of orexin into this region causes rats to eat more food. (Courtesy of Masashi Yanagisawa.)

BOX 13.1 *Body Fat Stores Are Tightly Regulated, Even after Surgical Removal of Fat*

We've seen that animals maintain a fairly constant body weight, even when given more food than they can eat, and that various lesions may change the body weight the animal defends, but they do not abolish weight regulation completely. Certainly most of us who have tried dieting can attest that the body seems to know how much it wants to weigh, despite our efforts.

Ample evidence suggests that body fat is carefully regulated. Perhaps the most striking demonstration is in golden-mantled ground squirrels. In the wild, these animals show a seasonal variation in body weight. Every spring, as the food supply increases, the animals fatten up considerably. You might think that this extreme seasonal variation in body weight is simply the result of having food available at some times but not others. But when these squirrels are brought into the labora-

tory, they continue to show an annual rhythm in body weight, even when food is always available (Figure A) (I. Zucker, 1988). (We'll discuss annual cycles in more detail in Chapter 14.)

Experimenters can increase or decrease the squirrels' body weight either by force-feeding the animals or by restricting their food. When food is abundant, the squirrels eat just enough to achieve not the body weight they had before the manipulation, but the body weight that is appropriate for the present point in their annual cycle. The return to their normal body composition is not simply a matter of altering diet. The way the squirrels partition what they eat—how much goes into fat, how much goes into glycogen, how much is defecated—also returns to normal. For example, they lower their metabolic rate during the fattening phase so that more food can be shuttled into fat (Dark, 1984).

Golden-mantled ground squirrels show a seasonal cycle also for body fat. Although some of the fat can be surgically removed, after the surgery, just as with body weight, the animals eat until they regain—with remarkable precision—the amount of fat they would have had at that season without surgery (Figure B) (Dark et al., 1984). Interestingly, some of the body fat depots from which fat was removed cannot regenerate new fat cells, but when such a nonregenerating depot is removed, other fat depots increase production in compensation, restoring the animal's total body fat. Needless to say, these results are not encouraging to humans considering liposuction. Usually the fat simply returns after the procedure, which itself is not without risks. The brain of humans, and certainly that of ground squirrels, appears able to measure body fat and alter appetite to maintain a particular amount of fat.

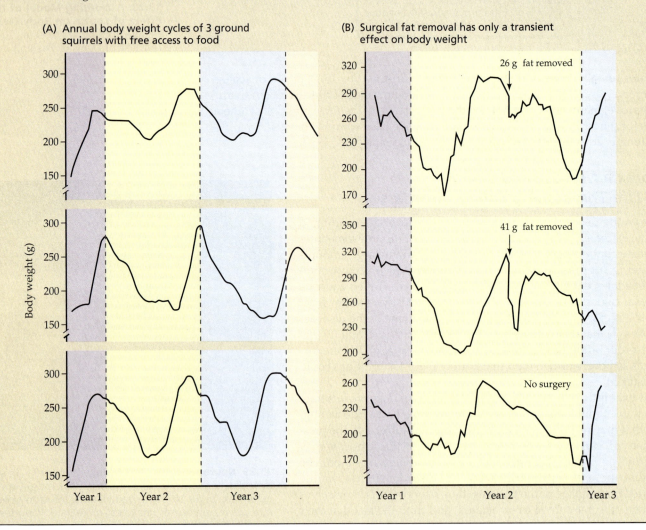

(A) Annual body weight cycles of 3 ground squirrels with free access to food

(B) Surgical fat removal has only a transient effect on body weight

Bulimia (or *bulimia nervosa*, from the Greek *boulimia*, "great hunger") is a related disorder. Like those who suffer from anorexia, people who are bulimic may believe themselves fatter than they are, but they periodically gorge themselves, usually with "junk food," and then either vomit the food or take laxatives to avoid weight gain. Also like sufferers of anorexia, people with bulimia may be obsessed with food and body weight, but not all of them become emaciated. Both anorexia and bulimia can be fatal because in each case the patient's lack of nutrient reserves damages various organ systems and/or leaves the body unable to battle otherwise mild diseases.

Our present culture emphasizes that women, especially young women, must be thin to be attractive. It has been suggested that people who suffer from anorexia and bulimia are the victims of a mismatch between what their biological makeup wants them to weigh (see Box 13.1) and what society expects them to weigh (Figure 13.30*a*). In earlier times, however, when plump women were considered the most beautiful (witness Renaissance paintings, such as the one shown in Figure 13.30*b*), some women still fasted severely and may have been anorexics. The origins of these disorders are still elusive, and to date, the available therapies cure only a minority of patients.

(a)

(b)

13.30 Changing Ideals of Female Beauty Actress Lara Flynn Boyle (*a*) and Helena Fourment, the Flemish painter Paul Rubens's wife, in *Helena Fourment as Aphrodite* (circa 1630) (*b*) exemplify ideal feminine forms of their respective eras. Some people have suggested that our modern weight-conscious notions of female beauty are responsible for some cases of anorexia nervosa and bulimia.

Summary

1. The nervous system plays a crucial role in maintaining the homeostasis that the body requires for proper functioning. Temperature, fluid concentration, chemical energy, and nutrients must all be maintained within a critical range.

2. Several mechanisms that normally act in synchrony can be dissociated experimentally, revealing a redundancy of physiological methods that ensure homeostasis.

Temperature Regulation

1. Endotherms generate most of their body heat through the metabolism of food; ectotherms obtain most of their body heat from the environment. Both endotherms and ectotherms regulate body temperature, but ectotherms depend more on behaviors to capture heat than on internal heat-generating mechanisms.

2. Endotherms can remain active longer than ectotherms can, but endotherms are also obliged to gather more food than ectotherms do to generate their body warmth.

3. Body size and shape drastically affect the rate of heat loss. Small endotherms have a higher metabolic rate, using more energy (per gram of body weight) than large endotherms use.

4. Several regions of the nervous system monitor and help regulate body temperature, including the preoptic area of the hypothalamus, the brainstem, and the spinal cord.

Fluid Regulation

1. Our cells function properly only when the concentration of salts and other ions (the osmolality) of the intracellular compartment of the body is within a critical range. The ex-

Refer to the *Learning Biological Psychology* CD for the following study aids for this chapter:

11 Objectives

78 Study Questions

tracellular compartment is a source of replacement water and a buffer between the intracellular compartment and the outside world.

2. Thirst can be triggered either by a drop in the volume of the extracellular compartment (hypovolemic thirst) or by an increase in the osmolality of the extracellular compartment (osmotic thirst). Either signal indicates that the volume or osmolality of the intracellular compartment may fall outside the critical range. Because of the importance of osmolality, we must regulate salt intake in order to regulate water balance effectively.

3. A drop in blood volume triggers at least three responses: (1) Baroreceptors in the major blood vessels detect any volume drop and signal the brain via the autonomic nervous system. (2) The brain in turn releases vasopressin from the posterior pituitary, and the vasopressin reduces blood vessel volume and the amount of water lost through urination. (3) The kidneys release renin, providing circulating angiotensin II, which reduces blood vessel volume to maintain blood pressure and may also signal the brain that the blood volume has dropped.

Food and Energy Regulation

1. Our digestive system breaks down food and uses most of it for energy, especially because we are endotherms. The brain must have glucose for energy; the body can use either glucose or fatty acids as fuel.

2. Although brain cells can use glucose directly, body cells can import glucose only with the assistance of insulin secreted by the pancreas. Insulin also promotes the storage of glucose in fat. Another pancreatic hormone, glucagon, mobilizes fats to release glucose.

3. Manipulations of either glucose or insulin can affect whether an animal experiences hunger, but experimental studies have indicated that neither glucose nor insulin alone can be the single indicator of hunger or satiety. The nervous system integrates information about these compounds and others, such as the fat indicator leptin, to determine whether an animal should eat.

4. Within the nervous system are several regions that seem to contribute to the sensations of hunger or satiety, but an animal can regulate body weight reasonably well even when it lacks one of these regions. Thus there seems to be no single brain center for either satiety or hunger.

5. The hormone leptin, secreted from fat cells, binds to neurons in the arcuate nucleus to suppress the release of peptides NPY and AGRP while augmenting the release of α-MSH in the paraventricular nucleus. These changes in brain peptides converge to suppress feeding. As leptin levels fall, NPY and AGRP stimulation of the paraventricular nucleus increases while α-MSH stimulation declines, inducing hunger.

6. Powerful genetic and seasonal factors influence body weight, and body weight is very tightly regulated around a set zone, despite extensive dietary, behavioral, or surgical interventions.

Recommended Reading

Blatteis, C. M. (Ed.). (1998). *Physiology and pathophysiology of temperature regulation.* Singapore: World Scientific.

Bray, G. A., and Ryan, D. H. (Eds.). (1999). *Nutrition, genetics, and obesity.* Baton Rouge, LA: Louisiana State University Press.

Cassell, D., and Gleaves, H. (2000). *The encyclopedia of obesity and eating disorders* (2nd ed.). New York: Facts On File.

Ramsay, D. J., and Booth, D. (Eds.). (1991). *Thirst: Physiological and psychological aspects.* London: Springer.

14

Biological Rhythms, Sleep, and Dreaming

He made the moon for the seasons;
The sun knows the place of its setting.
Thou dost appoint darkness and it becomes night
In which all the beasts of the forest crawl about.
The young lions roar after their prey
And seek their food from God.
When the sun rises they withdraw
And lie down in their dens.

— Psalm 104:19–23

Brett Bigbee, *Two Women*, 1990–1992

Courtesy of Alexandre Gallery, New York.

All living systems show repeating, predictable changes over time. The frequency of these oscillations varies from rapid, such as brain potentials, to slow, such as annual changes like hibernation. Daily rhythms, the first topic of this chapter, have an intriguing clocklike regularity. Other rhythms range from minutes to seconds, and some extend from a month to years. One familiar daily rhythm is the sleep–waking cycle: By age 60, most humans have spent 20 years asleep. (Some, alas, on one side or the other of the classroom podium.)

Because sleep accounts for so large a slice of our lives, it is surprising that the behavioral and biological features of sleep remained unstudied for so long. Since the early 1960s, however, sleep has been a major focus of investigation. Sleep is not just nonwaking, but rather the interlocking of elaborate cyclical processes, an alternation of several different states. The behavioral correlates of these different sleep states range from tiny finger twitches to a galaxy of images and dreams. We'll discuss biological rhythms and patterns of sleep in humans and other animals, and the physiological events of sleep.

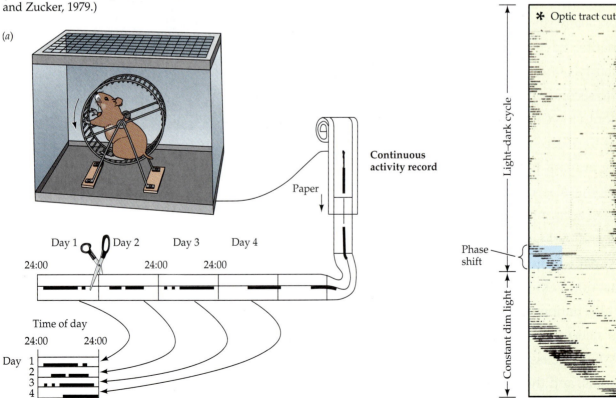

14.1 How Activity Rhythms Are Measured   (*a*) In this traditional setup for studying activity rhythms, a running wheel in a hamster's cage is monitored by an event recorder. Each revolution of the wheel produces a brief pen deflection, which forms a dark mark on a slowly moving roll of paper. The paper strips are cut apart, and each subsequent day's activity is aligned underneath. Computers have now replaced the moving-paper apparatus depicted here, but we have included it to explain the principles clearly. (*b*) A hamster's activity record shows that, normally, a hamster becomes active shortly after the start of the dark phase of the daily cycle and remains active during the dark period (*top*). After several weeks the optic tract in such a hamster was severed (asterisk), but fibers from the eye to the hypothalamus were spared. The hamster was subsequently active earlier each day, but still in synchrony with the light–dark cycle, even if it was shifted. When placed in constant dim light (*bottom*), the hamster became active a few minutes later each day. This *free-running* activity rhythm indicates that the hamster has an endogenous clock that has a period slightly greater than 24 hours. (After I. Zucker, 1976; based on Rusak and Zucker, 1979.)

Biological Rhythms

Biological rhythms range from minutes to seconds, and some extend from months to years. Best studied are daily rhythms, which we discuss first.

Many Animals Show Daily Rhythms in Activity and Physiological Measures

Most functions of any living system display a rhythm of approximately 24 hours. Because these rhythms last about a day, they are called **circadian rhythms** (from the Latin *circa*, "about," and *dies*, "day"). By now circadian rhythms have been studied in a host of creatures at behavioral, physiological, and biochemical levels.

One favorite way to study circadian rhythms in the laboratory takes advantage of the penchant of rodents to run in activity wheels (Figure 14.1*a*). A switch attached to the wheel connects to a microcomputer that registers each revolution. The activity rhythm of a hamster in a running wheel is displayed in Figure 14.1*b*. Like most other rodents, hamsters are **nocturnal**—active during the dark periods. Humans and most other primates are **diurnal**—active during the day. Almost all physiological measures—hormone levels, body temperature, drug sensitivity—change across the course of the day.

These circadian activities show extraordinary precision: The beginning of activity may vary only a few minutes from one day to another. For humans who attend to watches and clocks, this regularity may seem uninteresting, but other animals also display remarkable regularity. They are attending to a *biological clock.*

Circadian Rhythms Are Generated by an Endogenous Clock

If a hamster is placed in a dimly lit environment, it continues to show a daily rhythm in wheel running and other measures, despite the absence of a light–dark cycle, suggesting that the animal has an internal clock to regulate these activities. On the other hand, even though the low level of light is constant, the animal may detect other external cues (e.g., outside noises, temperature, barometric pressure) that signal the time of day. Arguing for the internal clock, however, is the fact that the hamster shows a bit of imprecision in its cycle: Activity starts a few minutes later each day, so eventually the hamster is active while it is daytime outside (see Figure 14.1*b, bottom*). The animal is said to be **free-running,** maintaining its own cycle, which in the absence of external cues, is not exactly 24 hours long.

The free-running period is the animal's natural rhythm. (A **period** is the time between two similar points of successive cycles, such as sunset to sunset.) Because this free-running period does not quite match the period of Earth's rotation, it cannot simply be reflecting an external cue but must be generated inside the animal. So the animal has some sort of endogenous oscillator, which we can call a clock, and in the hamster this clock runs a bit slow.

The internal clock can be set by light. If we expose a free-running nocturnal animal to periodic light and dark, the onset of activity soon becomes synchronized to the beginning of the dark period. The shift of activity produced by a synchronizing stimulus is referred to as a **phase shift** (see Figure 14.1*b, middle*), and the process of shifting the rhythm is called **entrainment.** Any cue that an animal uses to synchronize its activity with the environment is called a **zeitgeber** (German for "time giver"). In the laboratory, light acts as a powerful zeitgeber. Because light stimuli can entrain circadian rhythms, the endogenous oscillatory circuit must have inputs from the visual system, as we'll discuss shortly. In humans, circadian rhythms probably are also entrained by social stimuli.

Circadian Rhythms Allow Animals to Anticipate Changes in the Environment

Why are circadian rhythms valuable to an organism? The major significance of circadian rhythms is that they synchronize behavior and body states to changes in the environment. The cycle of light and dark during the day has great significance for survival. For example, picture the small nocturnal rodent who can avoid many predators during the day by remaining hidden, and who moves about hurriedly in the dark.

An endogenous clock also allows animals to *anticipate* periodic events, such as the appearance of darkness, and to engage in appropriate behavior before conditions change. A snack in the den at the end of the day may prepare the animal for a long night of foraging. In other words, circadian rhythms provide the temporal organization of an animal's behavior. Biological clocks allow for resource partitioning: Diurnal animals are adapted for obtaining food during the daytime, and thus do not compete with nocturnal animals, whose adaptations favor an active life during dark periods.

An Endogenous Circadian Clock Is Located in the Hypothalamus

Where in the body is the clock that drives circadian rhythms, and how does it work? One way to establish the locus of circadian oscillators is to remove different organs and examine behavioral or physiological systems for any changes in circadian organization. A pioneer in the field, Curt Richter, suggested that the brain is the site of the relevant oscillators because removing various endocrine glands had little effect on the free-running rhythm of blinded rats (Richter, 1967). Although Richter did show that gross hypothalamic lesions appeared to interfere with circadian rhythms, he did not pursue this work anatomically.

It was subsequently discovered that a small region of the hypothalamus—the **suprachiasmatic nucleus** (**SCN**), named for its location above the optic chiasm— serves as a circadian oscillator. Lesions confined to the SCN interfere with circadian rhythms of drinking and locomotor behavior (Figure 14.2) (F. K. Stephan and Zucker, 1972), and daily rhythms of adrenal steroid secretion (R. Y. Moore and Eichler, 1972).

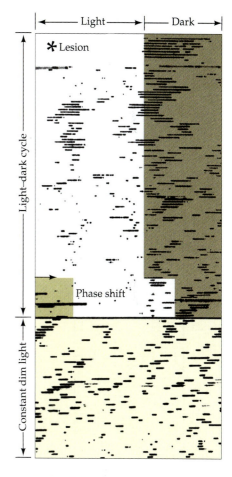

14.2 The Effects of Lesions in the SCN Circadian rhythms in the animal whose activity is plotted here were normal and synchronized to the light–dark period before an SCN lesion was made (asterisk). After the lesion the animal showed some daily rhythms in activity that were synchronous to the light–dark cycle, but when placed in continuous (dim) light, the animal's activity became completely random, indicating that the lesion had eliminated the endogenous rhythm. Note that the lesioned animal does not show a free-running rhythm of activity, but is arrhythmic, running at very different times each day. (From I. Zucker, 1976; based on Rusak and Zucker, 1979.)

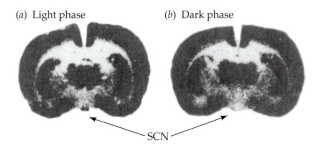

(*a*) Light phase   (*b*) Dark phase

SCN

14.3 The Circadian Rhythm of Metabolic Activity of the SCN   These autoradiograms are from coronal sections of rat brains. (*a*) In a section taken from an animal during a light phase, greater metabolic activity in the SCN is represented by the darkly stained regions at the base of the brain. (*b*) This dark staining is not evident in a section taken from an animal during a dark phase. (From W. J. Schwartz et al., 1979.)

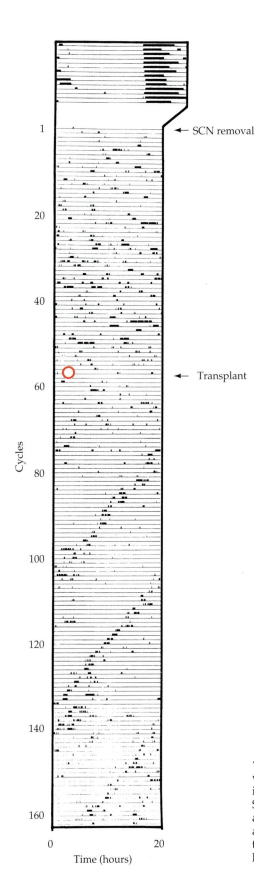

← SCN removal

← Transplant

Cycles

Time (hours)

The clocklike activity of the SCN was also revealed in metabolic studies using autoradiographic mapping of neural activity (Figure 14.3; see also Box 2.1). This circadian rhythm in metabolism can even be seen in SCN cells in a dish (Earnest et al., 1999; Yamazaki et al., 2000). Studies of **brain explants**—small pieces of brain tissue isolated from the body—have offered additional evidence of the endogenous nature of SCN rhythms. Brain slices containing the SCN were placed in a dish with fluids resembling the extracellular environment of the brain and provided with a mixture of oxygen and carbon dioxide gases to permit approximately normal metabolic activities. Electrical recordings from these slices indicate that cells of the SCN show discharge rates that are synchronized to the light–dark cycle the animal had previously experienced. This is striking evidence for the endogenous character of the circadian oscillators in the SCN.

Circadian oscillations are also evident in the neural activity of the isolated SCN—an SCN still inside an animal, but isolated from other brain areas by knife cuts (a hypothalamic "island") (S. T. Inouye, cited in Turek, 1985). However, as we'll see next, transplants of the SCN from one animal to another conclusively prove that the SCN generates a circadian rhythm.

Transplants Prove That the SCN Produces a Circadian Rhythm

Ralph and Menaker (1988) found a male hamster that exhibited an unusually short free-running activity rhythm in constant conditions. As we have seen, normally hamsters free-run at a period slightly longer than 24 hours, but this male showed a period of 22 hours that was stable for 3 weeks. The researchers bred this male and, by studying his offspring, concluded that he possessed a mutation affecting the endogenous circadian rhythm. Animals with two copies of the mutation had an even shorter period: 20 hours. The mutation was named *tau*, after the Greek symbol used by scientists to represent the period of a rhythm. All these animals could be entrained to a normal 24-hour light–dark period; only in constant conditions was their endogenous circadian periodicity revealed.

14.4 Brain Transplants Prove That the SCN Contains a Clock   A wild-type hamster, when kept in constant dim light, displayed an endogenous circadian rhythm, 24.05 hours in duration (*top*). After the SCN was lesioned, the animal became arrhythmic. Later, an SCN from a fetal hamster with two copies of the *tau* mutation was transplanted into the adult hamster (circle). Soon thereafter the adult hamster began showing a free-running activity rhythm of 19.5 hours, matching the SCN of the donor animal. This response to the transplant showed that the period of the clock is determined within the SCN. (From Ralph et al., 1990.)

Dramatic evidence that this endogenous period is contained within the SCN was provided by transplant experiments. Hamsters with a lesioned SCN were placed in constant conditions; as expected, they showed arrhythmicity in activity (Figure 14.4, *upper middle*) (Ralph et al., 1990). Then the investigators transplanted into the hamsters an SCN taken from a fetal hamster with two copies of the mutant *tau* gene. About a week later the hamsters that had received the transplants began showing a free-running activity rhythm again, but the new rhythm matched that of the donor SCN: It was 19.5 hours rather than the original 24.05.

Reciprocal transplants gave comparable results: The endogenous rhythm always matched the genotype of the *donor* SCN, further demonstrating that the circuitry that produces this circadian rhythmicity is within the SCN. The SCN may enforce circadian periodicity through hormone secretion, since a transplanted SCN can restore circadian rhythms even if the tissue is encapsulated to prevent nerve connections but allow hormone release (Silver et al., 1996).

In Mammals, Light Information from the Eyes Reaches the SCN Directly

What pathways entrain circadian rhythms to light–dark cycles? The pathway varies depending on the species (Rusak and Zucker, 1979). Some vertebrates have photoreceptors outside the eye that are part of the mechanism of light entrainment. For example, the **pineal gland** of some amphibians is itself sensitive to light (Jamieson and Roberts, 2000) and helps entrain circadian rhythms to light. Because the skull over the pineal is especially thin in some amphibian species, we can think of them as having a primitive "third eye" in the back of the head.

In some birds, circadian rhythms can be entrained by light even if the eyes are removed, so other photosensitive receptors must be involved in entrainment. In birds too, the pineal possesses these receptors, which detect daylight through the skull. In mammals, however, retinal pathways clearly mediate photoentrainment, because severing the optic nerves prevents entrainment by light of circadian rhythms of all varieties.

In early experiments with rodents, lesions of the primary visual cortex and accessory pathways did not alter entrainment to a light–dark cycle, although these animals appeared "blind" and showed no indication of visually guided orientation or discrimination behavior. Robert Y. Moore (1983) established the existence of a direct **retinohypothalamic pathway**—retinal ganglion cells that project out of the optic chiasm to synapse within the SCN (Figure 14.5).

Robert Y. Moore

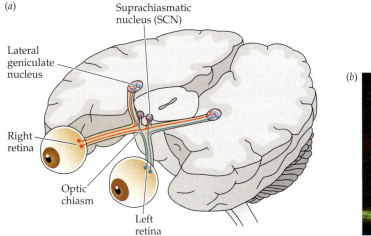

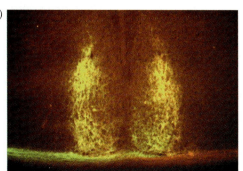

14.5 The Retinohypothalamic Pathway in Mammals (*a*) This pathway carries information about the light–dark cycle in the environment to the SCN. For clarity of synaptic connections, the SCN is shown proportionately larger than other features. (*b*) Axons (seen at the bottom of the image) from the left eye are labeled red, while those from the right are green. Both eyes project so diffusely to the two overlying SCN that they are outlined in yellow. (Photograph courtesy of Andrew Lieberman.)

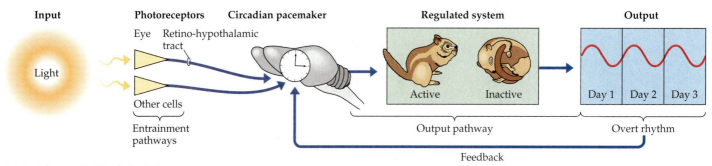

14.6 Schematic Model of the Components of a Circadian System

Lesions of this tiny pathway interfere with photic (light-induced) entrainment. Interestingly, the rod and cone photoreceptors used for form vision (see Chapter 10) do not signal photoperiod information; knockout mice lacking rods and cones still entrain to photoperiod (Freedman et al., 1999). Surgically removing the eyes of these knockout mice causes them to ignore photoperiod, so some other photoreceptor population within the eye must detect the light, perhaps relying on a specialized photopigment called **cryptochrome** ("hidden pigment"; van der Horst et al., 1999).

Light information may also reach the brain without passing through the eyes. S. S. Campbell and Murphy (1998) applied light to the back of the knees of some human subjects and were able to shift the circadian rhythm in body temperature and melatonin secretion. Which cells in this region detect the light, and how they convey that information to the brain, are questions that remain unanswered. Cryptochrome-containing photoreceptor cells distributed throughout the body of the fruit fly display a circadian rhythm in gene expression, and light can shift that rhythm independently in each cell (Plautz et al., 1997).

Figure 14.6 provides a schematic outline of the mammalian circadian system, including entrainment components.

Circadian Rhythms Have Been Genetically Dissected in Flies and Mice

The fruit fly *Drosophila melanogaster* displays circadian rhythms in activity (they are diurnal) and in the time at which they emerge from their pupal skins as adults (morning). Screening of mutant flies revealed occasional animals that, when transferred to constant dim light, failed to free-run in either locomotor activity or emergence as adults. Subtle mutations of the same gene could, depending on the exact change in the gene, cause the animals to have a free-run period that was longer or shorter than normal; thus the gene was dubbed *per,* for *period* (Konopka and Benzer, 1971).

The protein normally produced by the *per* gene regulates the transcription of other genes, including the *per* gene itself! When a cell produces Per protein, it cuts off further transcription of the *per* gene. In the course of hours, the Per protein degrades until transcription resumes. Thus there is a circadian rhythm in the appearance of Per protein in the brain and eyes: More of the protein is present at night rather than in the daytime. Of course, when the *per* gene is deleted, there is no Per protein and the flies are arrhythmic, as mentioned earlier. But when the gene is slightly altered to produce animals with either shorter or longer circadian periods, the circadian rhythm in Per protein production is also correspondingly shorter or longer, so the circadian rhythmicity in *per* gene expression is responsible for the circadian rhythm in behavior.

The Per protein does not act alone, but is part of a cascade of proteins that interact to produce a molecular clock (Figure 14.7). A Per protein molecule can work only if it is coupled with a molecule of Tim (for *timeless,* because flies lacking the *tim* gene show no endogenous circadian rhythm; Sehgal et al., 1994). When Per and Tim bind together, forming a **dimer** (a pair of proteins briefly binding each other), they inhibit the transcription of another gene, called *Clock* (for *circadian locomotor output cycles*

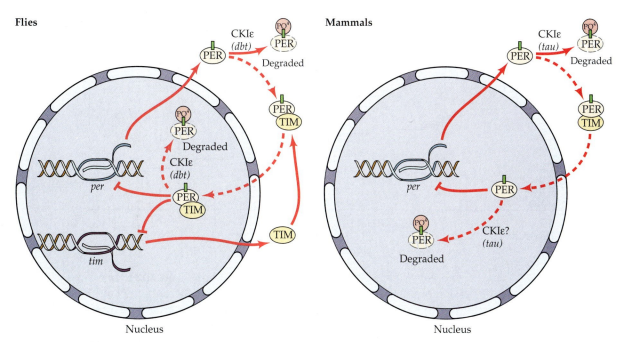

14.7 A Molecular Clock in Flies and Mice The molecular mechanisms underlying the circadian clock are similar in *Drosophila* and the mouse. In both cases, the *per* and *tim* genes code for the Per and Tim proteins, respectively. The *dbt* gene in flies and the *tau* gene in mice code for an enzyme (CKIε) that acts to degrade Per. However, at peak times of Per production, CKIε cannot degrade all the Per, and it is available to bind with Tim to form dimers; in this form CKIε cannot degrade Per. In a negative feedback loop, these Per–Tim dimers inhibit the production of both Per and Tim. Eventually, the Per–Tim dimers begin to degrade, and the *per* and *tim* genes are reactivated. (In addition, in flies, light activates the crypotchrome pigment, which in turn degrades Tim, so that fewer Per–Tim dimers can form.) This cycle of interacting genes, proteins, and enzymes lasts about 24 hours.

*k*aput; Vitaterna et al., 1994). Clock protein promotes the transcription of *per* and *tim*. So as the Per–Tim dimers degrade, Clock production increases to begin another day's transcription of *per* and *tim*. The degradation rates and production rates of these proteins are such that it takes about 24 hours to complete a cycle.

Much of this molecular machinery that was worked out in flies appears to be at work in mammals too (King and Takahashi, 2000; Shearman et al., 2000). Mice with both copies of their *Clock* gene disrupted show severe arrhythmicity in constant conditions (Figure 14.8). If only one copy of the gene is disrupted, the animals free-run for a few days but then suddenly stop showing any circadian rhythmicity.

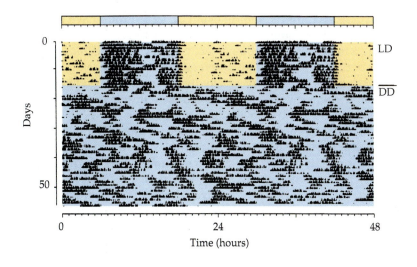

14.8 When the Endogenous Clock Goes Kaput This homozygous *Clock/Clock* mouse showed a normal circadian rhythm when given normal light cues (LD). When put in constant dim light conditions (DD), it maintained an activity period of 27.1 hours for the first 10 days but then lost circadian rhythmicity. Note, however, that an ultradian rhythm (i.e., a rhythm that has a frequency of more than once a day) with a period of just over 5 hours remains. (From J. S. Takahashi, 1995.)

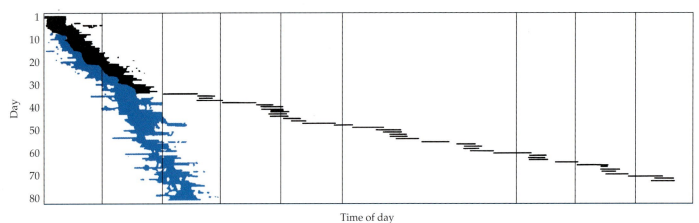

Time of day

14.9 Evidence That Humans Have at Least Two Clocks   In this human subject, bed-rest episodes (black) and body temperature (blue) were entrained to a 24-hour day–night cycle on days 1 to 5. When the person was placed in temporal isolation, both rhythms free-ran and maintained synchrony. But on day 35, they spontaneously desynchronized. The body temperature rhythm shortened, and that of the rest–activity cycle lengthened, indicating that these two rhythms rely on different clocks. (From Czeisler et al., 1980.)

People who feel energetic in the morning ("larks") are likely to carry a different version of the *Clock* gene than "nightowls" have (Katzenberg et al., 1998). In flies, light activates cryptochrome to degrade Tim protein, thus synchronizing the molecular clock with exogenous light. The mammalian version of cryptochrome may play a similar role, since mice lacking either of the two genes for cryptochrome show no endogenous rhythm (Okamura et al., 1999).

The SCN Is Not the Only Endogenous Oscillator

Research shows that at least one major circadian oscillator in the brain governs multiple circadian systems, especially motor activity. But is the SCN the only master oscillator? No. Examination of measures other than wheel running reveals some free-running and entrained rhythms even after SCN lesions.

Moore-Ede (1982) suggested that the circadian timing system of mammals consists of two master pacemakers that drive many other secondary, passive oscillators. This suggestion was based on the desynchronization of various circadian rhythms that occurs in humans when they live (temporarily) in isolation without time cues such as daily light–dark cycles (Figure 14.9). Such desynchronization suggests a spontaneous uncoupling of internal clocks. Nowadays the knowledge that fruitflies have a circadian clock in almost every cell, and that mammals use the same basic molecular machinery as the flies, suggests that humans may have many "clocks" throughout the body and brain (Yamazaki et al., 2000), with the SCN serving as the conductor that normally keeps them synchronized.

Many Biological Events Display Rhythms Shorter than a Day

Among the many diverse rhythmic biological events, a large group have periods that are shorter than those of circadian rhythms. Such rhythms are referred to as **ultradian** (designating a frequency greater than once per day; the Latin *ultra* means "beyond"), and their periods are usually from several minutes to hours. Ultradian rhythms are seen in such behaviors as bouts of activity, feeding, sleep, and hormone release. These ultradian rhythms may be superimposed on a circadian rhythm. Some more complex human behaviors also display ultradian rhythms.

Human subjects isolated from cues about time of day, or some in their normal environment, show a 90-minute cycle of daydreaming that is characterized by vivid sensory imagery (Lavie and Kripke, 1981). Ultradian rhythms in the performance of various tasks may reflect fluctuations in alertness, which may account for the ultradian rhythm in the performance of poorly motivated subjects (Broughton, 1985). One indication of an ultradian rhythm in alertness is that EEG indices of alertness (as defined later in this chapter) vary in an ultradian rhythm. The periods of ultradian rhythms seem to be correlated with measures such as brain and body size: More rapid cycles are typical of smaller animals (Gerkema and Daan, 1985).

Destruction of the SCN in voles, which destroys the circadian timing of their activity, does not affect their ultradian feeding rhythms. However, lesions to other hypothalamic areas disrupt ultradian rhythmicity. These areas include parts of the rostral and basal hypothalamus. Interestingly, an ultradian periodicity remains after loss of the circadian rhythm in a *Clock/Clock* mouse (see Figure 14.8). These findings indicate that separate clocks control circadian and ultradian rhythms. We still do not know whether all ultradian rhythms reflect the operation of a single clock, or many different oscillators separately control a variety of ultradian events. Sleep cycles show an ultradian character, as we'll see later in the chapter.

Animals Use Circannual Rhythms to Anticipate Seasonal Changes

Recall that many animals display a seasonal cycle in body weight (see Box 13.1). Many other behaviors of animals are also characterized by annual rhythms. Some of these rhythms are driven by exogenous factors, such as food availability and temperature. In the laboratory, however, many annual rhythms, including body weight, persist under constant conditions. As with circadian rhythms in constant light, animals in isolation show free-running annual rhythms of a period not quite equal to 365 days. Thus there also seems to be an endogenous **circannual** oscillator.

This realm of research obviously requires considerable patience. Such rhythms are sometimes called **infradian** because their frequency is less than once per day (the Latin *infra* means "below"). A familiar infradian rhythm is the 28-day human menstrual cycle. The relevance of annual rhythms to human behavior is becoming evident in striking seasonal disorders of behavior (see Chapter 16).

The possibility that the SCN controls circannual rhythms of ground squirrels maintained in constant conditions of photoperiod and temperature was assessed by I. Zucker et al. (1983). These researchers measured activity rhythms, reproductive cycles, and body weight cycles of animals that were free-running in both their circadian and their circannual rhythms. SCN lesions clearly disrupted circadian activity cycles, but in at least some animals these lesions did not affect circannual changes in body weight and reproductive status.

Circannual cycles, then, do not arise from a transformation of circadian rhythms (e.g., simply counting 365 circadian cycles), and they seem to involve an oscillatory mechanism that is separate from the SCN. In the laboratory, animals born into summerlike photoperiod (long days) reach puberty sooner than animals born into winterlike short days (Dark et al., 1990), indicating that the season of birth can affect development. Perhaps a similar mechanism is responsible for the greater risk of schizophrenia in people born in February or March (Mortensen et al., 1999).

Irving Zucker

Sleeping and Waking

Most of us enjoy a single period of sleep starting late in the evening and lasting until morning. The onset and termination of sleep seem synchronized to many external events, including light and dark periods. What happens to sleep when all the customary synchronizing or entraining stimuli are removed? Volunteers spent weeks in a dark cave with all cues to external time removed. Their circadian rhythm of the sleep–waking cycle was evident, but slowly shifted from 24 to 25 hours. In other words, people have free-running periods just as a hamster does in constant dim light (Figure 14.10) (R. A. Wever, 1979).

The free-running period of a little more than 24 hours (Czeisler et al., 1999) indicates that humans have an endogenous circadian clock shaped by evolutionary forces that is very similar to the customary 24-hour rhythm. External cues then entrain this endogenous rhythm to 24 hours. We already mentioned that the *Clock* gene participating in the production of a circadian rhythm in the SCN varies in people who like to wake early compared to nightowls, so it is clear that the circadian clock entrains our sleep patterns.

14.10 Humans Free-Run Too These sleep–waking patterns were recorded in a subject who, after 5 days, was isolated from cues about the time of day for the next 77 days. During this period the subject drifted away from a 24-hour daily cycle, getting the equivalent of 74 "nights" of sleep. (From Weitzman et al., 1981.)

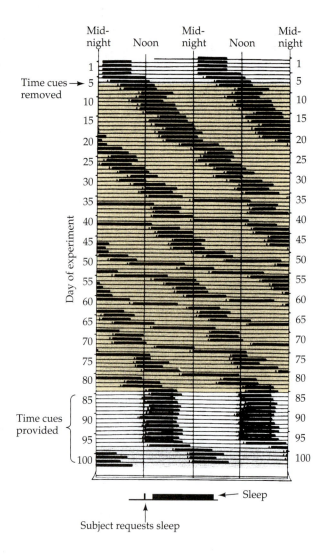

You may think of sleep as a simple event in your life, but for biological psychologists sleep is a remarkably complex, multifaceted set of behaviors. For this reason we will devote the remainder of the chapter to this fascinating phenomenon.

Human Sleep Exhibits Different Stages

Sleep seems to be characterized by the absence of behavior—a period of inactivity with raised thresholds to arousal by external stimuli. Sleep research gained momentum in the 1930s when experimenters found that brain potentials recorded from electrodes on the human scalp (by **electroencephalography,** or **EEG;** see Figure 3.19*a*) provided a way to define, describe, and classify levels of arousal and states of sleep. This measure of brain activity is usually supplemented with recordings of eye movements (**electro-oculography,** or **EOG**) and of muscle tension (**electromyography,** or **EMG**). These methods have revealed two main classes of sleep: **slow-wave sleep** (**SWS**) and **rapid-eye-movement sleep,** or **REM sleep** (*REM* rhymes with *gem*) (Aserinsky and Kleitman, 1953). In humans, slow-wave sleep can be divided further into four distinct stages, which we'll discuss in the next section.

What are the electrophysiological distinctions that define different sleep states? To begin, the pattern of electrical activity in a fully awake, vigilant person is a mixture of many frequencies dominated by waves of relatively fast frequencies (greater than 15 to 20 cycles per second, or hertz [Hz]) and low amplitude, sometimes referred to as *beta activity.*

When you relax and close your eyes, a distinctive rhythm appears, consisting of a regular oscillation at a frequency of 9 to 12 Hz, known as the **alpha rhythm.** As

Nathaniel Kleitman
(1895–1999)

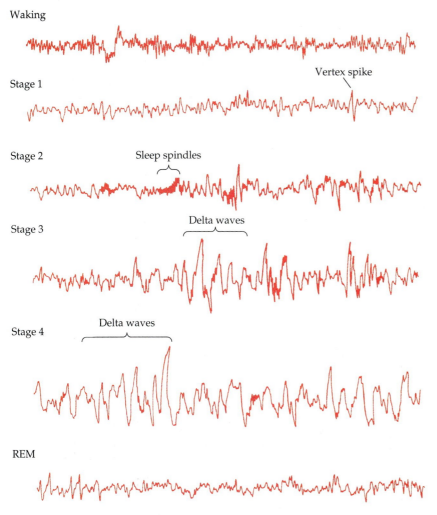

Waking

Stage 1

Vertex spike

Stage 2

Sleep spindles

Stage 3

Delta waves

Stage 4

Delta waves

REM

14.11 Electrophysiological Correlates of Waking and Sleep   These are the characteristic EEG patterns seen during different stages of sleep in humans. The sharp wave called a vertex spike appears during stage 1 sleep. Brief periods of sleep spindles are characteristic of stage 2 sleep. Deeper stages of slow-wave sleep show progressively more of the large, slow delta waves. Note the similarity of activity during waking, stage 1 sleep, and REM sleep. (After Rechtschaffen and Kales, 1968.)

drowsiness sets in, the duration of the alpha rhythm decreases, and the EEG shows events of much smaller amplitude and irregular frequency, as well as vertex spikes (Figure 14.11). This is stage 1 sleep, which is accompanied by a slowing of heart rate and a reduction of muscle tension; in addition, under the closed eyelids the eyes may roll about slowly. This period usually lasts several minutes and gives way to stage 2 sleep, which is defined by 12 to 14 Hz waves called **sleep spindles** that occur in periodic bursts (see Figure 14.11). Many subjects awakened during these first two stages do not acknowledge that they have been asleep, even though they failed to respond to instructions or signals while in those stages.

Someone in stage 2 sleep is quite unresponsive to the external environment. In the early part of a night of sleep, this stage leads to stage 3 sleep, which is defined by the appearance of large-amplitude, very slow waves (so-called **delta waves,** about one per second). Stage 4 sleep, which follows, is defined by the presence of delta waves at least half the time.

After about an hour—the time usually required for progression through these stages, with a brief return to stage 2—something totally different occurs. Quite abruptly, scalp recordings display a pattern of small-amplitude, high-frequency activity similar in many ways to the pattern of an awake individual (see Figure 14.11, *bottom*), but tension in the postural neck muscles has disappeared. If you see a cat sleeping in the sitting, *sphinx* position, it cannot be in REM sleep; in REM it will be sprawled limply on the floor. As we'll see later, this flaccid muscle state appears despite intense activity in brain motor centers because during this stage of sleep, brainstem regions are profoundly inhibiting motoneurons. Because of this seeming contradiction—the brain waves look awake, but the musculature is flaccid and unresponsive—another name for this state is *paradoxical sleep.*

Breathing and pulse rates become fast and irregular. The eyes now show rapid movements under the closed lids, giving this stage its most used name: *REM, or rapid-eye-movement, sleep.* Once you've entered REM sleep, many distinctive physiological changes occur while you remain recumbent and, in terms of common behavioral descriptions, decidedly asleep. It is during REM sleep that we experience vivid dreams.

Thus the EEG portrait shows that sleep consists of a sequence of states instead of just an "inactive" period. Table 14.1 compares the properties of slow-wave sleep and REM sleep.

Sleep Stages Appear in a Pattern during the Night's Sleep

Many people have exposed their sleep life to researchers in sleep laboratories. The bedroom in the experimental setup differs little from the usual sleep environment except for the presence of many wires. These wires lead to an adjacent room, where machines record brain waves and experimenters observe. The subject goes to sleep in a usual way, except that electrodes are pasted in position on the person's scalp. In addition, electrodes near the eye record eye movements, and the tension of muscles is noted by electrical recordings from the skin surface above muscles. Although the on-

TABLE 14.1 *Properties of Slow-Wave and REM Sleep*

Property	Slow-wave sleep	REM sleep
AUTONOMIC ACTIVITIES		
Heart rate	Slow decline	Variable with high bursts
Respiration	Slow decline	Variable with high bursts
Thermoregulation	Maintained	Impaired
Brain temperature	Decreased	Increased
Cerebral blood flow	Reduced	High
SKELETAL MUSCULAR SYSTEM		
Postural tension	Progressively reduced	Eliminated
Knee jerk reflex	Normal	Suppressed
Phasic twitches	Reduced	Increased
Eye movements	Infrequent, slow, uncoordinated	Rapid, coordinated
COGNITIVE STATE	Vague thoughts	Vivid dreams, well organized
HORMONE SECRETION		
Growth hormone secretion	High	Low
NEURAL FIRING RATES		
Cerebral cortex	Many cells reduced and more phasic	Increased firing rates; tonic (sustained) activity
EVENT-RELATED POTENTIALS		
Sensory-evoked	Large	Reduced

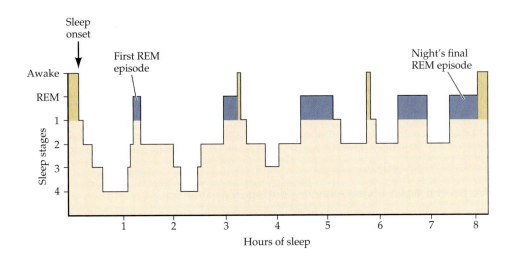

14.12 A Typical Night of Sleep in a Young Adult Note the progressive lengthening of REM episodes (blue) and the loss of stages 3 and 4 sleep as the night goes on. (After Kales and Kales, 1970.)

set, pattern, duration, and termination of sleep are affected by many variables, a certain regularity allows a portrait to be drawn of the typical sleep pattern of adults.

The total sleep time of young adults usually ranges from 7 to 8 hours, and 45 to 50% of sleep is stage 2 sleep. REM sleep accounts for about 20% of total sleep. A typical night of adult human sleep shows repeating cycles about 90 to 110 minutes long, recurring four or five times in a night (Figure 14.12). These cycles change in a subtle but regular manner through the night. Cycles early in the night are characterized by greater amounts of stages 3 and 4 SWS. The latter half of a typical night of sleep is bereft of stages 3 and 4. In contrast, REM sleep is typically more prominent in the later cycles of sleep. The first REM period is the shortest, sometimes lasting only 5 to 10 minutes; the last REM period, just before waking, may last up to 40 minutes.

REM sleep is normally preceded by stage 2 SWS (except in infants and in narcolepsy, a disorder that we will describe at the end of the chapter). Brief arousals (yellow bars in Figure 14.12) occasionally occur immediately after a REM period, and you may shift your posture at this transition (Aaronson et al., 1982). The sleep cycle of 90 to 110 minutes has been viewed by some researchers as the manifestation of a basic ultradian rest–activity cycle (Kleitman, 1969); cycles of similar duration occur during waking periods. (Recall that cycles of daydreaming during waking have an interval of approximately 90 minutes [Lavie and Kripke, 1981].) Many other psychological and physiological properties show a 90- to 110-minute cycle, including eating and drinking, play behavior of children, and changes in heart rate (D. B. Cohen, 1979).

Some Humans Sleep Remarkably Little, yet Function Normally

The portrait of human sleep shows many variations. Some differences can be clearly related to maturational status, functional states like stress, the effects of drugs, and many other external and internal states. Some departures from the "normal" state of human sleep can be quite marked, including unusual people who hardly sleep at all. These cases are more than just folktales. William Dement (1974) described a Stanford University professor who slept only 3 to 4 hours a night for more than 50 years and died at age 80.

Reports of nonsleeping humans verified by scientific observations are quite rare. After searching for that exotic type of person and about to give up the quest, sleep researcher Ray Meddis (1977) finally found a cheerful 70-year-old retired nurse who said she had slept little since childhood. She was a busy person who easily filled up her 23 hours of daily wakefulness. During the night she sat on her bed reading or writing, and at about 2:00 A.M. she fell asleep for an hour or so, after which she readily awakened.

For her first 2 days in Meddis's laboratory, she did not sleep at all because it was all so interesting to her. On the third night she slept a total of 99 minutes, and her sleep contained both SWS and REM sleep periods. Later her sleep was recorded for

5 days. On the first night she did not sleep at all, but on subsequent nights she slept an average of 67 minutes. She never complained about not sleeping more, and she did not feel drowsy during either the day or the night. Meddis described several other people who sleep either not at all or for about 1 hour per night. Some of these people report having parents who slept little.

Other people sleep longer than the normal 7 to 8 hours per night. Such "long sleepers" exhibit more REM and stage 2 sleep, resulting from extra sleep cycles. In some human cultures a nap in the late afternoon is common—the siesta. Modern industrial societies may inhibit a natural tendency (shared with many other primates) to nap during the day.

We Do Our Most Vivid Dreaming during REM Sleep

One exciting aspect of the psychobiology of sleep is the thinking and imagery that accompany sleep. We can record the EEGs of subjects, awaken them at a particular stage—1, 2, 3, 4, or REM—and question them about thoughts or perceptions immediately prior to awakening. Early data from such studies strongly indicated that dreams were restricted largely to REM sleep. Subjects reported dreams 70 to 90% of the time when they were awakened in this stage—in contrast to an incidence of 10 to 15% for non-REM sleep periods.

COMPETING HYPOTHESES

At first, the rapid eye movements characteristic of this period were even thought to be related to "viewing" dream scenes. In other words, if you were dreaming of watching a Ping-Pong match, your eyes would reflect the rapid to-and-fro movement of real-life observations of such a match. This scanning theory of eye movements during REM dreams now seems unlikely because there are many differences between the characteristics of eye movements during actual viewing of scenes and those of REM sleep.

Although all studies report a large percentage of dream reports upon waking from REM sleep, some investigators have increasingly questioned whether REM is the sole sleep state associated with dreams. In response to careful, more persistent questioning, subjects can report dreams upon waking from non-REM sleep, especially stage 2 sleep. Dream reports of REM sleep are characterized by visual imagery, whereas dream reports of non-REM sleep are of a more "thinking" type. REM dreams are apt to include a story that involves odd perceptions and the sense that "you are there" experiencing sights, sounds, smells, and acts. Subjects awakened from non-REM sleep report thinking about problems rather than seeing themselves in a stage presentation.

Cartwright (1979) has shown that the dreams of these two states are so different that judges reading a dream description can indicate the sleep state from which it arose with 90% accuracy. REM sleep dreams during the first half of the night are oriented toward reality. The dreams incorporate the day's experience, and the sequence of events is ordinary. Dreams during the second half of sleep are more unusual and less readily connected with the day's events, becoming more emotionally intense and bizarre. Dreams of depressed patients are emotionally bland, with very reduced activity and mood.

Terrifying dreams have become the subject of close scrutiny (Hartmann, 1984). **Nightmares** are defined as long, frightening dreams that awaken the sleeper from REM sleep. They are occasionally confused with **night terror,** which is a sudden arousal from stage 3 or 4 SWS marked by intense fear and autonomic activation. In night terror the sleeper does not recall a vivid dream but may remember a sense of a crushing feeling on the chest, as though being suffocated (Figure 14.13). Night terrors, common in children during the early part of an evening's sleep, seem to be a disorder of arousal.

Nightmares are quite prevalent, and some people are especially plagued by them. At least 25% of college students report having at least one nightmare per month. (A common one, shared with Freud, is suddenly remembering a final exam that is already in progress.) Medications that enhance the activity of dopamine systems, such as L-dopa, also make nightmares more frequent. Individuals who experience fre-

14.13 Night Terror Although this 1791 painting by Henry Fuseli is called *The Nightmare,* it more aptly illustrates night terror, as the demon crushes the breath from his victim.

quent nightmares may be a more creative group, with "loose" personal boundaries (Hartmann, 1984). Perhaps these people are prone to either a greater or a more rapid activation of dopamine systems.

The Sleep of Different Species Provides Clues about the Evolution of Sleep

Behavioral and EEG descriptions of sleep states let us make precise comparisons of different sleep stages in a variety of animals. As a result, investigators have been able to describe sleep in a wide assortment of mammals and to a lesser extent in reptiles, birds, and amphibians (S. S. Campbell and Tobler, 1984). Species differ widely in various measures of sleep, such as timing and periodic properties. In the sections that follow, we'll look at some of these factors.

REM Sleep Is Evolutionarily Ancient

The amount of daily life occupied by sleep and the percentage of sleep devoted to REM sleep for a variety of animals are shown in Figure 14.14. We can make several generalizations. All the mammals that have been investigated thus far, with the exception of the dolphin, display both REM and SWS. The echidna (spiny anteater) is an egg-laying mammal, a **monotreme,** that shows prolonged SWS but no forebrain activation during sleep, so it is unclear whether it has REM sleep. The only other monotreme is the platypus (see Box 6.1), which does display REM sleep (J. M. Siegel et al., 1999).

A near rival for antiquity among existing mammals is the opossum—a **marsupial** (i.e., an animal that is born at a very early developmental stage and spends a period of its development in a pouch). The other mammals, including humans, are so-called **placental mammals.** Marsupials such as the opossum display both SWS and REM sleep with EEG characteristics that are not distinguishable from those of placental mammals. Among the other vertebrates, only birds display clear signs of both SWS and REM sleep. These comparisons suggest that SWS and REM sleep developed more

EVOLUTION AT WORK

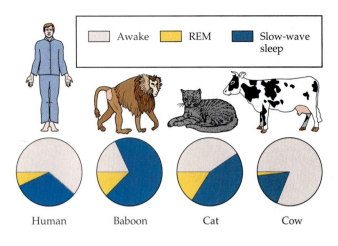

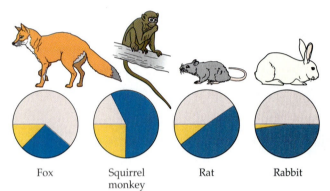

14.14 Amounts of Different Sleep States in Various Mammals

than 150 million years ago in an ancestor common to birds and mammals. Reports that reptiles may display a REM-like sleep support this hypothesis.

Sleep in marine mammals (dolphins, whales, and seals) is especially intriguing because these animals must continually emerge at the surface of the water to breathe. Sleep in dolphins and porpoises is characterized by the complete absence of REM sleep periods, and SWS on only one side of the brain at a time (Mukhametov, 1984). It's as if one whole hemisphere is asleep while the other is awake (Figure 14.15). During these periods of "unilateral sleep," the animals continue to come up to the surface to breathe; hence their sleep is not characterized by relative motor immobilization. Birds can also display unilateral sleep—one hemisphere sleeping while the other hemisphere watches for predators (Rattenborg et al., 1999).

Vertebrate Species Differ in Their Patterns and Types of Sleep

A **sleep cycle** is a period of one episode of SWS followed by an episode of REM sleep. For laboratory rats, one sleep cycle lasts an average of 10 to 11 minutes; for humans, one cycle lasts 90 to 110 minutes (as discussed earlier). Across species, cycle duration is inversely related to metabolic rate; that is, small animals, which tend to have high metabolic rates (see Chapter 13), have short sleep cycles, and large species have long sleep cycles.

Demands other than high metabolic rate can also cause short cycles. Some birds, such as swifts and sooty terns, sleep briefly while gliding. The swift spends almost all its time in the air, except during nesting season, and the sooty tern spends months flying or gliding above water, never alighting, catching fish at the surface. Of necessity, sleep cycles must be short in such birds, if they sleep at all.

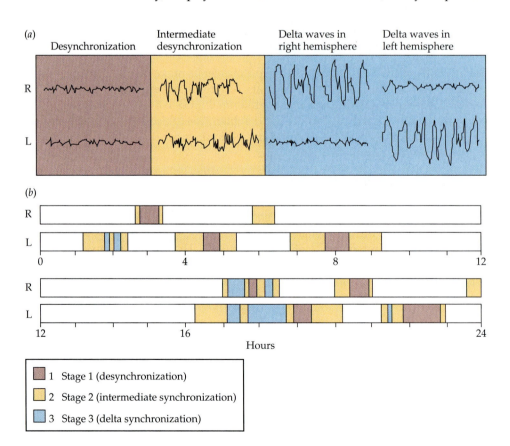

14.15 Sleep in Marine Mammals
(a) EEG patterns in right (R) and left (L) brain hemispheres in a porpoise from recording of roughly symmetrical areas of the parietal cortex. (b) Diagrams of EEG stages in right (R) and left (L) brain hemispheres of a bottle-nosed dolphin during a 24-hour session. The two cerebral hemispheres seem to take turns sleeping. (From Mukhametov, 1984.)

Except for some such seabirds, all vertebrates appear to show (1) a circadian distribution of activity, (2) a prolonged phase of inactivity with (3) raised thresholds to external stimuli, and (4) a characteristic posture during inactivity. Many invertebrates also have clear periods of behavioral quiescence that include heightened arousal thresholds and distinctive postures (Shaw et al., 2000).

Our Sleep Patterns Change across the Life Span

In any mammal the characteristics of sleep–waking cycles change during the course of life. These changes are most evident during early development. In fact, in humans the characteristic EEG picture of different stages of SWS is not evident until 5 or 6 years of age. After this age, EEG data can be classified into stages just as adult EEG data are. Even infant sleep, however, can be generally classified into SWS and REM sleep.

Mammals Sleep More during Infancy Than in Adulthood

A clear cycle of sleeping and waking takes several weeks to become established in human infants (Figure 14.16). A 24-hour rhythm is generally evident by 16 weeks of age. Infant sleep is characterized by shorter sleep cycles than those of adulthood. These features of the sleep of infants seem to be due to the relative immaturity of the brain. For example, premature infants have even shorter cycles than do full-term children. Some animals born in an advanced state of development (precocial animals), such as the guinea pig, show a more mature sleep pattern at birth. The sleep patterns of mentally retarded children are different from those of normal children, with fewer eye movements during sleep and reduced amounts of REM sleep (Petre-Quadens, 1972).

Infant mammals show a large percentage of REM sleep. For example, Figure 14.17 shows that in humans within the first 2 weeks of life, 50% of sleep is REM sleep. The percentage of REM sleep is even greater in premature infants: About 80% of the sleep of infants born after only 30 weeks of gestation is REM sleep.

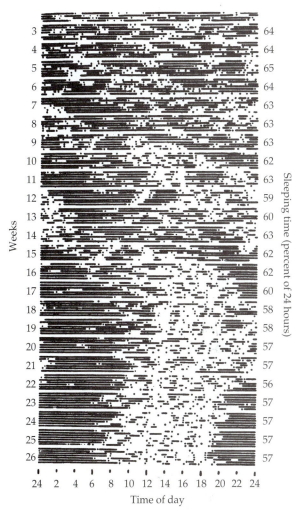

14.16 The Trouble with Babies
A stable pattern of sleep consolidated at night does not appear until about 16 weeks of age. The dark portions indicate time asleep, the blank portions time awake. (From Kleitman and Engelmann, 1953.)

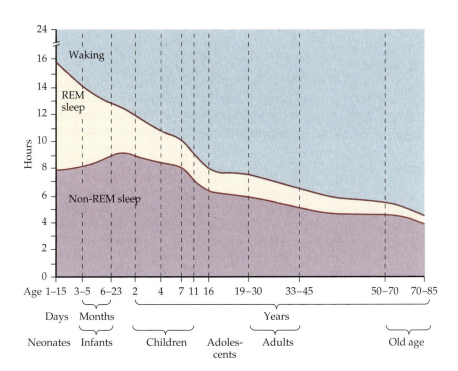

14.17 Human Sleep Patterns Change with Age Early in life we sleep a great deal, and about half of sleep time is spent in REM sleep. By adulthood, we average about 8 hours of sleep a night, 20% of which is REM sleep. (After Roffwarg et al., 1966.)

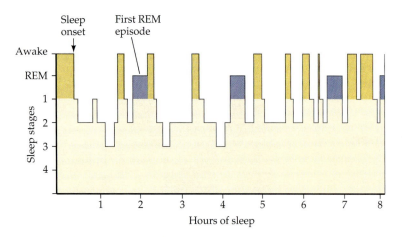

14.18 Typical Pattern of Sleep in an Elderly Person   Recordings of sleep in the elderly are characterized by frequent awakenings (yellow bars), absence of stage 4 sleep, and a reduction of stage 3 sleep. Compare this recording with the young-adult sleep pattern shown in Figure 14.12. (After Kales and Kales, 1974.)

Unlike normal adults, human infants can move directly from an awake state to REM sleep. By about 4 months of age, REM sleep is entered through a period of SWS. REM sleep of infants is quite active, accompanied by muscle twitching, smiles, grimaces, and vocalizations. Perhaps the increased movement during infant REM is due to an inability to inhibit motoneurons and mask activation of brain motor centers. These behaviors during REM do not seem to be related to the events of the day; rather they seem to be endogenously generated (Challamel et al., 1985).

The preponderance of REM sleep early in life suggests that this state provides stimulation that is essential to maturation of the nervous system, but this hypothesis has not been developed in any detail. A hypothesis we'll consider shortly is that REM sleep is important for the consolidation of long-term memories. Because infancy is a time of much learning, this hypothesis may account for the large amount of REM sleep early in life.

Most People Sleep Appreciably Less As They Age

The parameters of sleep change more slowly in old age than in early development. Figure 14.18 shows the pattern of a typical night of sleep in an elderly person. A decline in the total amount of sleep is evident, as is an increase in the number of awakenings during a night (compare with Figure 14.12). Lack of sleep, or insomnia (which we will discuss at the end of this chapter), is a common complaint of the very elderly (Miles and Dement, 1980), although daytime naps may contribute to nighttime sleep difficulties.

The most dramatic progressive decline is in stages 3 and 4 sleep; amounts of these stages in persons of age 60 are only 55% of what they are at age 20. The decline of stages 3 and 4 SWS starts quite early in life, perhaps as early as the third decade (Bliwise, 1989). By age 90, all sleep of stages 3 and 4 has disappeared. This decline in stages 3 and 4 sleep in the aged may be related to diminished cognitive capabilities, since an especially marked reduction of stages 3 and 4 characterizes the sleep of aged humans who suffer from senile dementia. An age-associated decrease in stages 3 and 4 SWS is also seen in other mammals.

Are the changes in the sleep patterns of the elderly directly related to the aging process? A study by Reynolds et al. (1985) examining healthy seniors showed REM features comparable to those of young adults. Wilse B. Webb (1992) emphasized the wide range of variability in the sleep of aged individuals, although a central difference between the young and the old is the older person's inability to maintain sleep, causing sleep "dissatisfaction." In Chapter 18 we'll see that there are also individual differences among rats and humans in brain anatomy and chemistry with aging and that some of these differences are correlated with declines in learning ability.

Manipulating Sleep Reveals an Underlying Structure

Sleep is affected by many environmental, social, and biological influences. From one viewpoint, though, sleep is an amazingly stable state: Major changes in our waking behavior have only a minor impact on subsequent sleep. But some conditions do produce major shifts in sleep measures. The effects of sleep deprivation on sleep are especially interesting because they give insight into the underlying mechanisms of sleep.

Sleep Deprivation Drastically Alters Sleep Patterns

Most of us at one time or another have been willing or not-so-willing participants in informal **sleep deprivation** experiments. Thus most of us are aware of the effect of partial or total sleep deprivation: It makes us sleepy. The study of sleep deprivation is also a way to explore the potential regulatory mechanisms of sleeping and waking. Most of the studies concern **sleep recovery,** asking questions such as, Does a sleep-deprived organism somehow keep track of the amounts and types of lost sleep? When the organism is given the opportunity to compensate, is recovery partial or complete? Can you pay off sleep debts?

The results of sleep deprivation suggest that our bodies need sleep. Our later discussion of the function of sleep will reinforce the idea that we need sleep to remain healthy and to learn.

The effects of sleep deprivation.   Early reports from sleep deprivation studies emphasized a similarity between instances of "bizarre" behavior provoked by sleep deprivation and features of psychosis, particularly schizophrenia. Partial or total sleep deprivation has been examined in the hope that it might illuminate some aspects of the genesis of psychotic behavior. A frequent theme in this work has been the functional role of dreams as a "guardian of sanity." But examination of schizophrenic patients does not seem to confirm this view. For example, these patients can show sleep–waking cycles similar to those of normal adults, and sleep deprivation does not exacerbate their symptoms.

The behavioral effects of prolonged, total sleep deprivation vary appreciably and may depend on some general personality factors and on age. In several studies employing prolonged total deprivation—205 hours (8.5 days)—some subjects showed occasional episodes of hallucinations. But the most common behavior changes noted in these experiments are increases in irritability, difficulty in concentrating, and episodes of disorientation. During each deprivation day, the effects are more prominent in the morning; by late afternoon and early evening, the subjects seem much less affected by the accumulating sleep loss.

The subject's ability to perform tasks is best described by L. C. Johnson (1969): "His performance is like a motor that after much use misfires, runs normally for a while, then falters again" (p. 216). Tasks that elicit strong motivation and are brief in duration may show almost no impairment, even with prolonged sleep deprivation.

Sleep recovery.   Figure 14.19 provides data on sleep recovery in a young man following 11 days of sleep deprivation. No evidence of a psychotic state was noted, and the incentive for this unusually long act of not sleeping was simply the young man's curiosity. Researchers got into the act only after the subject had started his deprivation schedule, which is the reason for the absence of predeprivation sleep data.

In the first night of sleep recovery, stage 4 sleep shows the greatest relative difference from normal. This increase in stage 4 sleep is usually at the expense of stage 2 sleep. However, the rise in stage 4 sleep during recovery never completely makes up for the deficit accumulated over the deprivation period. In fact, the amount is no greater than for deprivation periods half as long. REM sleep after prolonged sleep deprivation shows its greatest recovery during the second postdeprivation night. Eventually, the REM debt comes closer to being paid off.

Experiments of the early 1970s dealing with the "repayment of sleep debts" involved short-term deprivation effects—either total sleep deprivation or, more usually, REM deprivation. Investigators achieved the latter condition by forcefully waking a subject whenever EEG signs of REM sleep appeared. These early, short-term REM deprivation studies showed generally that in postdeprivation recovery sessions subjects made up for the loss of REM sleep in the form of REM episodes of longer-than-normal duration. With more prolonged REM deprivation, the debt is paid off somewhat differently. Recovery of the number of hours of REM sleep is not complete. REM recovery may also involve another form of compensation—greater intensity: REM sleep in recovery nights is more "intense" than normal, with more rapid eye movements per period of time.

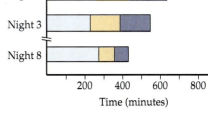

Stages of sleep during recovery

14.19 **Sleep Recovery after 11 Days Awake**   (After Gulevich et al., 1966.)

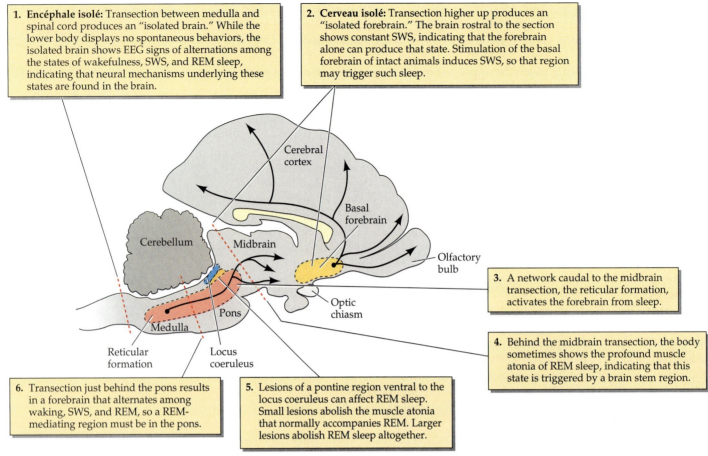

1. **Encéphale isolé:** Transection between medulla and spinal cord produces an "isolated brain." While the lower body displays no spontaneous behaviors, the isolated brain shows EEG signs of alternations among the states of wakefulness, SWS, and REM sleep, indicating that neural mechanisms underlying these states are found in the brain.

2. **Cerveau isolé:** Transection higher up produces an "isolated forebrain." The brain rostral to the section shows constant SWS, indicating that the forebrain alone can produce that state. Stimulation of the basal forebrain of intact animals induces SWS, so that region may trigger such sleep.

3. A network caudal to the midbrain transection, the reticular formation, activates the forebrain from sleep.

4. Behind the midbrain transection, the body sometimes shows the profound muscle atonia of REM sleep, indicating that this state is triggered by a brain stem region.

5. Lesions of a pontine region ventral to the locus coeruleus can affect REM sleep. Small lesions abolish the muscle atonia that normally accompanies REM. Larger lesions abolish REM sleep altogether.

6. Transection just behind the pons results in a forebrain that alternates among waking, SWS, and REM, so a REM-mediating region must be in the pons.

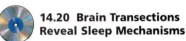

14.20 Brain Transections Reveal Sleep Mechanisms

At Least Three Interacting Neural Systems Underlie Sleep

At one time sleep was regarded as a passive state, as though most of the brain simply stopped working while we slept, leaving us unaware of events around us. We now know that sleep is an active state mediated by at least three interacting neural systems: (1) a forebrain system that by itself can display SWS, (2) a brainstem system that activates the forebrain into wakefulness, and (3) a pontine system that triggers REM sleep.

The Forebrain Generates Short-Wave Sleep

The most straightforward evidence for the three sleep systems comes from experiments in which the brain is transected—literally cut into two parts, an upper part and a lower part. The entire brain can be isolated from the body by an incision between the medulla and the spinal cord. This preparation was first studied by the Belgian physiologist Frédéric Brémer (1935), who called it the *isolated brain,* or **encéphale isolé.**

The EEGs of such animals showed signs of waking that alternated with signs of sleeping (Figure 14.20). During EEG-defined wakeful periods, the pupils were dilated and the eyes followed moving objects. During EEG-defined sleep, the pupils were small, as is characteristic of normal sleep. (Brémer did not distinguish between SWS and REM sleep; this distinction was not discovered until the 1950s. But we now know that REM sleep can also be detected in the isolated brain.) Where are the centers that mediate wakefulness and sleep in the encéphale isolé?

If in other animals the transection is made higher along the brainstem, in the midbrain, a very different result is achieved. Brémer referred to such preparations as an *isolated forebrain,* or **cerveau isolé,** and he found that the EEG from the brain in front

Frédéric Brémer

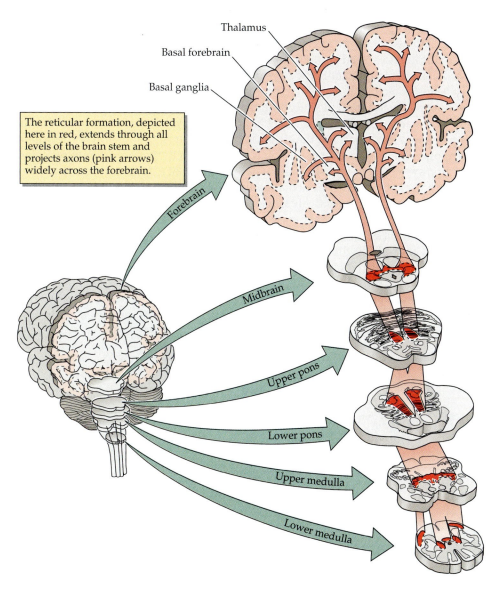

Thalamus

Basal forebrain

Basal ganglia

The reticular formation, depicted here in red, extends through all levels of the brain stem and projects axons (pink arrows) widely across the forebrain.

Forebrain

Midbrain

Upper pons

Lower pons

Upper medulla

Lower medulla

14.21 The Brainstem Reticular Formation The reticular formation is thought to activate the rest of the brain.

of the cut displayed constant SWS (see Figure 14.20). We now know that the isolated forebrain does not show REM sleep, so it appears that the forebrain alone can generate SWS with no contributions from the lower brain regions.

The **basal forebrain,** in the ventral frontal lobe and anterior hypothalamus, appears to be crucial for SWS. Lesions in that region can abolish SWS, and electrical stimulation of the basal forebrain can induce SWS activity (Clemente and Sterman, 1963). Neurons in this region become active at sleep onset, are inhibited by noradrenergic stimulation, and probably use GABA for a neurotransmitter (Gallopin et al., 2000), inhibiting widespread target regions.

The region between these two transections—consisting of the medulla, pons, and lower midbrain—contains the other two sleep–waking centers: one for pushing the forebrain from sleep into wakefulness, and another for triggering REM sleep. We'll look at each of these centers in the two sections that follow.

The Reticular Formation Wakes Up the Forebrain

In the late 1940s, Brémer's experiments were reinterpreted on the basis of experiments in which the extensive region of the brainstem known as the **reticular formation** (Figure 14.21) was stimulated electrically. The reticular formation consists of a diffuse group of cells whose axons and dendrites course in many directions, extending from the medulla through the thalamus. Giuseppe Moruzzi and Horace Magoun (1949), pioneers in the study of the reticular formation, found that they

Giuseppe Moruzzi

Horace Magoun

could wake sleeping animals by electrically stimulating the reticular formation; the animals showed rapid awakening. Lesions of these regions produced persistent sleep in the animals (see Figure 14.20), although this phenomenon was not observed if the lesions interrupted only the sensory pathways in the brainstem.

The effects noted by Brémer were now interpreted as arising not from loss of sensory input alone, but from the interruption of an activating system within the brainstem. This mechanism remained intact in the encéphale isolé animal, but its output was precluded from reaching the cortex in the cerveau isolé animal. The "reticular formation" school argued that waking results from activity of brainstem reticular formation systems and that sleep is the passive result of a decline in activity in the reticular formation. As mentioned already, however, good evidence suggests that the basal forebrain region actively imposes SWS on the brain. The reticular formation seems to activate the basal ganglia, thalamus, and basal forebrain.

Michel Jouvet (1967), a major sleep researcher, particularly emphasized a system of neurons coursing in the midline of the brainstem called the **raphe** (pronounced "ruh-FAY") **nucleus** (Figure 14.22). These neurons use the neurotransmitter serotonin, and Jouvet proposed that serotonin release throughout the brain inhibits the reticular formation, therefore promoting sleep, especially SWS. For example, the drug parachlorophenylalanine (PCPA) blocks the synthesis of serotonin, producing

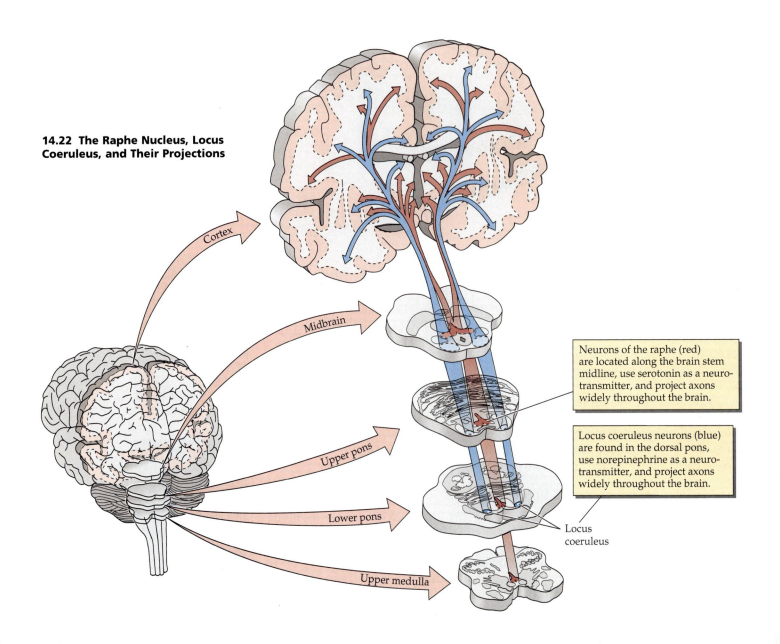

14.22 The Raphe Nucleus, Locus Coeruleus, and Their Projections

Cortex

Midbrain

Upper pons

Lower pons

Upper medulla

Neurons of the raphe (red) are located along the brain stem midline, use serotonin as a neurotransmitter, and project axons widely throughout the brain.

Locus coeruleus neurons (blue) are found in the dorsal pons, use norepinephrine as a neurotransmitter, and project axons widely throughout the brain.

Locus coeruleus

TABLE 14.2 *Neurotransmitter Alterations That Affect Sleep and Arousal*

Neurotransmitter	Site of cell bodies	Manipulation	Effects on sleep
Serotonin	Raphe nuclei	Increase	Promotes sleep
		Decrease	Reduces sleep
Norepinephrine	Locus coeruleus	Increase	Promotes waking, inhibits REM sleep
		Lesions	Abolish loss of muscle tone in REM sleep
Dopamine	Basal ganglia	Increase	Promotes waking
		Decrease	Has variable effects
Acetylcholine	Basal forebrain	Increase	Induces REM
		Decrease	Suppresses REM

a decrease in transmitter levels and a reduction in sleep. Likewise, mice with the serotonin 1B receptor knocked out display less SWS than control mice (Boutrel et al., 1999).

Pharmacological enhancement of serotonin activity frequently prolongs sleep. Serotonin activity can be enhanced by direct injection of the transmitter into the cerebral ventricles or by the use of drugs that enhance serotonin concentrations—for example, by administration of the precursor tryptophan. However, the broad controlling role once attributed to serotonin in neurochemical models of sleep must now be tempered by the recognition that other transmitters also seem to be part of the sleep story (Table 14.2).

The Pons Triggers REM Sleep

Different cuts through the brainstem that are intermediate to the cerveau isolé and encéphale isolé make it clear that the pons is crucial for REM sleep. If a cut is made below the pons, the rostral brain (still connected to the pons) displays REM sleep alternating with SWS (see Figure 14.20). Conversely, if the cut is made just rostral to the pons, leaving the pons attached to the caudal nervous system (medulla and spinal cord), then the caudal half of the animal shows REM sleep (J. M. Siegel, 1994).

You might wonder how we can recognize REM sleep in animals with a transected brainstem. We can monitor REM sleep caudal to the transection by monitoring muscle tone. The profound muscle relaxation (atonia) seen during REM sleep is never seen outside that state. Alternating periods of such atonia are good evidence that REM sleep is being induced. For monitoring REM sleep rostral to the transection, researchers rely on a specific EEG phenomenon that is seen only in REM. During that state, **PGO waves** (*PGO* stands for *pons, geniculate,* and *occipital cortex*) arise from the pons and reach the occipital cortex (Figure 14.23).

Other methods have pinpointed the region of the pons that is important for REM sleep. Lesions of a small region just ventral to the locus coeruleus abolish REM sleep (see Figure 14.20) (L. Friedman and Jones, 1984). Electrical stimulation of the same region, or pharmacological stimulation of this region with cholinergic agonists, can induce or prolong REM sleep. Finally, monitoring of neuronal activity in this region reveals some neurons that seem to be active only during REM sleep (J. M. Siegel, 1994). So the pons seems to have a REM sleep center.

Small lesions that destroy only a part of this pontine REM center indicate that part of this region is specialized to produce the profound muscle atonia of REM. This motor inhibition depends on influences descending from the brain to the spinal cord because reflexes during sleep are not depressed if the spinal cord has been disconnected from the brain. Recordings from spinal motoneurons during REM sleep reveal powerful inhibitory postsynaptic poten-

14.23 PGO Waves Associated with REM Sleep in Cats Bursts of PGO waves or spikes are especially prominent in recordings from the lateral geniculate such as these, but only during REM sleep (*b*).

(*a*) Slow-wave sleep

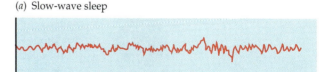

(*b*) REM sleep

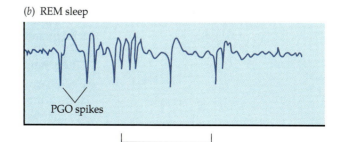

PGO spikes

2 s

tials (IPSPs) that prevent the motoneurons from reaching threshold and producing an action potential. Thus the subject's muscles are not just relaxed, but flaccid. This loss of muscle tone during REM sleep can be abolished by small lesions ventral to the locus coeruleus, suggesting that this region plays a role in uncoupling the motor system during sleep (A. R. Morrison, 1983).

Cats with such lesions seem to act out their dreams. After a bout of SWS, EEGs of these cats become desynchronized as they do during waking and REM sleep, and the animals stagger to their feet. Are they awake or in REM sleep? They move their heads as though visually tracking moving objects (that aren't there), bat with their forepaws at nothing, and ignore objects that are present. This behavior is also accompanied by PGO waves, as already mentioned, that occur only during REM sleep in intact animals. In addition, the cat's *inner eyelid*, the translucent nictitating membrane, partially covers the eyes. Thus although a cat may appear to be in REM sleep, motor activity is not inhibited by the brain. Many cells in this region, like the cells of the locus coeruleus itself, use norepinephrine as a neurotransmitter.

What Are the Biological Functions of Sleep?

Why do most of us spend one-third of our lifetime asleep? Furthermore, why is sleep divided into two dissimilar states with distinct physiological attributes? The functions of sleep are a subject of great debate; our discussion here emphasizes only the major ideas. Keep in mind that the proposed functions or biological roles of sleep are not mutually exclusive; sleep may play many roles. As with other processes, sleep may have acquired more than one function during evolution. The four functions most often ascribed to sleep are

1. Energy conservation
2. Predator avoidance
3. Body restoration
4. Memory consolidation

None of these four proposed functions have yet been proved, and no theory has been proposed to explain why some people who sleep very little show apparently normal intellect and personality.

Sleep Conserves Energy

We consume less energy when we sleep. For example, SWS is marked by reduced muscular tension, lowered heart rate, reduced blood pressure, and slower respiration. Reduced metabolic processes are also related to the characteristic lowered body temperature of sleep. This diminished metabolic activity during sleep suggests that one role of sleep is to conserve energy. From this perspective sleep enforces the cessation of ongoing activities and thus ensures rest.

COMPETING HYPOTHESES

We can see the importance of this function by looking at the world from the perspective of small animals. Small animals have very high metabolic rates, so activity for them is metabolically expensive. Demand can easily outstrip supply. Periods of reduced activity can be especially valuable if they occur when food is scarce.

Some support for the view that sleep conserves energy can be seen in comparative sleep data, which reveal a high correlation between total amount of sleep per day and waking metabolic rate: Small animals sleep more than large species (see Figure 14.14). The energy savings may not be as great as you might think, however, because at least part of sleep, such as the phasic events of REM sleep, is characterized by intense metabolic expenditure.

Sleep Helps Animals Avoid Predators

Intense evolutionary pressures have generated a variety of tactics for avoiding predators. Diurnal animals are well adapted to survive in the daytime; nocturnal animals are adapted for surviving at night. Meddis (1975) suggested that sleep helps animals stay out of harm's way during the part of the day when each is most vulnerable to predation. In this manner, sleep can enable effective sharing of an ecological niche—survival without becoming a meal. From a similar perspective, F. Snyder (1969) suggested that REM sleep is a periodic quasi-awakening to make sure the sleep site is still safe.

Sleep Restores the Body

If someone asked you why you sleep, chances are you would answer that you sleep because you're tired. Indeed, one of the proposed functions of sleep is simply the rebuilding or restoration of materials used during waking, such as proteins (Moruzzi, 1972). The release of growth hormone during SWS supports a restorative hypothesis. Hartmann (1973) suggested that there are two types of restorative needs that sleep deals with differently: physical tiredness and the tiredness associated with emotional activation.

Surprisingly, the restorative perspective is only weakly supported by research. A simple way to test this idea is to look at the effects of changes in presleep activity on the duration or cycle of sleep. Can intense metabolic expenditure during the day influence sleep duration? For most people, exercise may cause them to fall asleep more quickly, but not to sleep longer. On the other hand, prolonged and total sleep deprivation, either forced on rats or as a result of inherited pathology in humans, interferes with the immune system and leads to death (Box 14.1). So the widespread belief that sleep helps us recover from illness is well supported by animal research.

BOX 14.1 *Sleep Deprivation Can Be Fatal*

"Sleep that knits up the ravell'd sleave of care"

—William Shakespeare, *Macbeth,* Act II, Scene 2

Although some people seem to need very little sleep, most of us feel the need to sleep 7 to 8 hours a night. In fact, sustained sleep deprivation in rats causes them to increase their metabolic rate, lose weight, and within an average of 19 days, die (Everson et al., 1989). Allowing them to sleep prevents their death.

After the fatal effect of sleep deprivation had been shown, researchers undertook studies in which they terminated the sleep deprivation before the fatal end point and looked for pathological changes in different organ systems (Rechtschaffen and Bergmann, 1995). No single organ system seems affected in chronically sleep-deprived animals, but early in the deprivation they develop sores on their bodies. These sores seem to be the beginning of the end; shortly thereafter the rats' plasma reveals infections from a host of bacteria, which probably enter through the sores (Everson, 1993).

These bacteria are not normally fatal for rats because the rat's immune system and body defenses keep the bacteria in check, but severely sleep-deprived rats fail to develop a fever in response to these infections. (Fever helps the body to fight infections.) In fact, the animals show a drop in body temperature, which probably speeds bacterial infections, which in turn leads to diffuse organ damage.

The decline of these severely sleep-deprived rats is complicated, but if the sequence of events we have described is responsible for their death, then we should ask why the skin develops the sores that permit bacteria to enter. One observation is that the skin of these rats fails to show an inflammatory response to the infections. Inflammation is the local dilation of blood vessels, which enables greater blood flow and thus allows more immune cells to reach and attack an infection. Signs of inflammation include a reddening of the skin, a rise in local temperature, and swelling. We have no idea how sleep deprivation impairs the inflammatory response, but such response is crucial for maintaining the integrity of our skin. So perhaps Shakespeare's folk theory of the function of sleep, quoted above, isn't so far from the truth.

What about the rare humans who sleep only 1 or 2 hours a night? Why aren't their immune systems and inflammatory responses compromised? We don't know, but since the distinguishing trait of these people is that they don't need much sleep, perhaps their immune system and inflammatory response don't need much sleep either. Or perhaps the small amount of sleep they have almost every night is more efficient at doing whatever sleep does.

Some unfortunate humans inherit a defect in the gene for the prion protein (which can transmit mad cow disease, discussed in Chapter 16), and although they sleep normally at the beginning of life, in midlife they simply stop sleeping—with fatal effect. People with this disease, called *fatal familial insomnia,* die 7 to 24 months after the insomnia begins (Medori et al., 1992). In other people, the gene seems to mutate spontaneously, with the same fatal insomnia (Mastrianni et al., 1999). Autopsy reveals degeneration of the thalamus; this lesion may be responsible for the insomnia (Manetto et al., 1992). (Recall that electrical stimulation of the thalamus can induce sleep in animals.) As in sleep-deprived rats, sleep-deprived humans seem not to have obvious damage to any single organ system. Perhaps these patients die because they are chronically sleep-deprived. Research with rats certainly supports the idea that prolonged insomnia is fatal.

Sleep Appears to Aid Memory Consolidation

Every now and then we are confronted with newspaper reports and advertisements that herald a new technique or gadget that will enable us to learn during sleep. The appeal of such possibilities is overwhelming to some people, including those who begrudgingly accept sleep as a necessary interference with the pursuit of knowledge and those who sport the fantasy that information can be transmitted by the deep embrace of a book.

More seriously, sleep is a state in which many neurons are active. Can we learn during this state? Apparently not. But even if we can't learn during sleep, can sleep help us consolidate what we learned in the preceding period of wakefulness? If so, then sleep deprivation may interfere with learning. Students participating in the ritual of overnight cramming for exams would want to know.

Only simple learning occurs during sleep.   The idea that we can learn while sleeping is a controversial area beset with many conflicting claims (Aarons, 1976). The only overall conclusion one can confidently draw from a large range of studies is that if you are relying on acquiring and retaining complex information during sleep, you should find a backup system (Druckman and Bjork, 1994). Although nonhumans can acquire simple conditioned responses during various sleep stages, experiments that carefully monitor whether a person is truly asleep indicate that neither explicit nor implicit memories (see Chapter 17) for verbal material form during sleep (Wood et al., 1992).

A peculiar property of dreams is that unless we tell them to someone or write them down soon after waking, we tend to forget them (Dement, 1974), as though the brain refuses to consolidate information presented during REM sleep. It is probably beneficial that most dreams are not stored in long-term memory because it would be counterproductive to permanently store events that never happened.

Consolidation of material learned while awake.   Even if we don't acquire new information presented during sleep, we do seem to use sleep to consolidate information we acquired while awake. Jenkins and Dallenbach (1924) reported an experiment that continues to provoke research. They trained some subjects in a verbal learning task at bedtime and tested them 8 hours later on arising from sleep, and they trained other subjects early in the day and tested them 8 hours later (with no intervening sleep). The results showed better retention when a period of sleep intervened between a learning period and tests of recall. What accounts for such an effect?

Several differing psychological explanations have been offered. One suggests that during the waking period between learning and recall, diverse experiences interfere with accurate recall. Sleep during this interval appreciably reduces interfering stimulation. A second explanation notes that memory tends to decay and that this relentless process is simply slower during sleep. These two explanations posit sleep as a passive process in consolidating memory. A third explanation emphasizes an active, functional contribution of sleep to learning. This view says that sleep includes processes that consolidate the learning of waking periods (Kavanu, 1997). Sleep is then seen as providing the conditions to allow a firm "printing" of enduring memory traces.

Ekstrand et al. (1977) compared the magnitude of memory loss in three groups, all of whom had learned lists of paired associates:

**COMPETING
HYPOTHESES**

- Group 1 learned a list in the evening and was tested for retention after an interval of 8 hours of no sleep.
- Group 2 slept for half the night, was then awakened and learned the list, and had 4 more hours of sleep before retention testing.
- Group 3 learned the list, slept 4 hours, and was then awakened and tested for retention.

Group 2 showed the best recall. The experimenters interpreted these results to mean that SWS favors retention, but other interpretations are possible. Idzikowski (1984) showed that 8 hours of sleep (16 hours after learning) leads to better verbal retention than no sleep does.

Many animal studies have explored the notion that sleep is important for learning and retention (C. Smith, 1985). One approach has been to examine the qualitative and quantitative character of sleep following training experiences. The most consistent finding in this type of study is that the amount of REM sleep increases considerably after learning. In several studies the increased REM sleep occurred immediately at the onset of sleep following training. Increases in the amount of REM sleep result either from longer REM episodes or from more frequent REM episodes.

In a few experiments studying exposure to enriched environment, not only REM but also SWS was enhanced. If learning extends over several days, the increase in REM sleep is largest during the steepest part of the learning curve (Bloch, 1976). Perhaps the extended REM permits some sort of practice. Humans learning a reaction time task that activated certain brain regions showed, in a subsequent REM period, increased activation of exactly those brain regions that had been exercised (Maquet et al., 2000), as if the regions used during the task were reviewing the task. Similarly, the patterned activity of neurons in birdsong nuclei while male zebra finches are learning to sing appears to be repeated during subsequent bouts of sleep (Dave and Margoliash, 2000).

The functional significance of REM sleep following learning has been explored by REM sleep deprivation. Subjects in these studies are deprived of REM sleep during the period in which REM increments are normally seen after learning. As short a period as 3 hours of such deprivation retards the rate of learning in some cases (C. Smith, 1995).

In humans certain "perceptual" learning tasks, such as learning to discriminate different textures visually, show little improvement in a single training session but show considerable improvement 8 to 10 hours after the session. Karni et al. (1994) found that if people were deprived of REM sleep after a session, they failed to show improvement the next day. Gais et al. (2000) found that depriving subjects of SWS was more effective than REM deprivation, but the two groups agreed that sleep was necessary for consolidating this procedural memory (see Chapter 17). A person with a brainstem injury that seemed to eliminate REM, but did not prevent him from completing his education (Lavie, 1996), further challenges the idea that REM sleep is absolutely necessary for learning.

Sleep Disorders Can Be Serious, Even Life-Threatening

The peace and comfort of regular, uninterrupted sleep each day may occasionally be disturbed by occurrences such as inability to fall asleep, prolonged sleep, or unusual awakenings. The assessment of sleep is a major focus of sleep disorder clinics, which have become common in major medical centers. The Association for Sleep Disorder Clinics provides a forum for analysis of research needs and accomplishments. Table 14.3 lists the main diagnostic classes of sleep disorders and gives examples of each (Weitzman, 1981).

CLINICAL ISSUE

Some Minor Dysfunctions Are Associated with Sleep

Among the dysfunctions associated with sleep are several events that are more common in children than in adults. **Somnambulism** (sleepwalking) can consist of getting out of bed, walking around the room, and appearing awake. In most children these episodes last a few seconds to minutes, and the child usually does not remember the experience. Because such episodes occur during stages 3 and 4 SWS, they are more common in the first half of the night (when those stages predominate).

The belief that sleepwalkers are acting out a dream is not supported by data (Parkes, 1985). The main problem is the inability of sleepwalkers to wake into full

TABLE 14.3 *A Classification of Sleep Disorders*

1. DISORDERS OF INITIATING AND MAINTAINING SLEEP (INSOMNIA)

   Ordinary, uncomplicated insomnia

   Transient

   Persistent

   Drug-related insomnia

   Use of stimulants

   Withdrawal of depressants

   Chronic alcoholism

   Insomnia associated with psychiatric disorders

   Insomnia associated with sleep-induced respiratory impairment

   Sleep apnea

2. DISORDERS OF EXCESSIVE DROWSINESS

   Narcolepsy

   Drowsiness associated with psychiatric problems

   Drug-related drowsiness

   Drowsiness associated with sleep-induced respiratory impairment

3. DISORDERS OF SLEEP–WAKING SCHEDULE

   Transient disruption

   Time zone change by airplane flight (jet lag)

   Work shift, especially night work

   Persistent disruption

   Irregular rhythm

4. DYSFUNCTIONS ASSOCIATED WITH SLEEP, SLEEP STAGES, OR PARTIAL AROUSALS

   Sleepwalking (somnambulism)

   Sleep enuresis (bed-wetting)

   Night terror

   Nightmares

   Sleep-related seizures

   Teeth grinding

   Sleep-related activation of cardiac and gastrointestinal symptoms

Source: After Weitzman, 1981.

contact with their surroundings. At least one person was acquitted of murder after suggesting that he had suffered from "homicidal somnambulism," but such claims are difficult to evaluate (Broughton et al., 1994).

SWS is also related to two other common sleep disorders in children: night terrors (described earlier) and **sleep enuresis** (bed-wetting). Most people grow out of somnambulism, night terrors, or sleep enuresis without intervention, but pharmacological approaches can be used to reduce the amount of stages 3 and 4 sleep (as well as REM time) while increasing stage 2 sleep. For sleep enuresis, some doctors prescribe a nasal spray of the hormone vasopressin (antidiuretic hormone) before bedtime, which decreases the amount of urine collecting in the bladder.

REM sleep can aggravate some health problems. Intense activation of autonomically innervated visceral organs during REM sleep can increase the severity of impairments. Gastric-ulcer patients secrete 3 to 20 times more acid during REM episodes than do normal subjects, and many ulcer patients report intense pain that awakens them from sleep. Cardiovascular patients experience similar attacks of illness. Hospital reports show that cardiac patients are most likely to die between the hours of 4:00 and 6:00 A.M., the period of most intense and prolonged REM episodes.

Kales (1973) found that 32 out of 39 episodes of angina (chest pain caused by artery disease) occurred during REM episodes. Appropriate medical care for some patients thus might include measures intended to reduce REM sleep.

Insomniacs Have Trouble Falling Asleep or Staying Asleep

Almost all of us experience an occasional inability to fall asleep, and a very few individuals die apparently because they stop sleeping altogether (see Box 14.1). But many people persistently find it difficult to fall asleep and/or stay asleep as long as they would like. Estimates of the prevalence of **insomnia** from surveys range from 15% of the adult population of Scotland to one-third of the people in Los Angeles (Parkes, 1985).

Insomnia is commonly reported by people who are older, female, or users of drugs like tobacco, coffee, and alcohol. Insomnia seems to be the final common outcome for various situational, neurological, psychiatric, and medical conditions. It is not a trivial disorder; adults who regularly sleep for short periods show a higher mortality rate than those who regularly sleep 7 to 8 hours each night (Wingard and Berkman, 1983).

Sometimes there is a discrepancy between a person's reported failure to sleep and EEG indicators of sleep. This discrepancy has been labeled sleep state misperception (McCall and Edinger, 1992). People with this condition report that they did not sleep even when they showed EEG signs of sleep and failed to respond to stimuli during the EEG-defined sleep state. Other insomniacs show less REM sleep and more stage 2 sleep than normal sleepers. No differences are evident in the amounts of stages 3 and 4 sleep.

Situational factors that contribute to insomnia include shift work, time zone changes, and environmental conditions such as novelty (that hard motel bed). Usually these conditions produce transient **sleep-onset insomnia**—a difficulty in falling asleep. Drugs and neurological and psychiatric factors seem to cause **sleep-maintenance insomnia**—a difficulty in remaining asleep. In this type of insomnia, sleep is punctuated by frequent nighttime arousals. This form of insomnia is especially evident in disorders of the respiratory system.

In some people, respiration becomes unreliable during sleep. Respiration in such people can cease or slow to dangerous levels; blood levels of oxygen show a marked drop. This syndrome, called **sleep apnea,** arises from either the progressive relaxation of muscles of the chest, diaphragm, and throat cavity or changes in the pacemaker respiratory neurons of the brainstem. In the former instance, relaxation of the throat obstructs the airway—a kind of self-choking. This mode of sleep apnea is common in very obese people, but it also occurs, often undiagnosed, in non-obese people.

Each episode of apnea arouses the person enough to restore breathing, but the frequent nighttime arousals make such people sleepy in the daytime. Insertion of a removable tube in the throat can restore a normal sleep pattern and eliminate excess daytime sleepiness. For others, breathing through a special machine maintains air pressure in their airways and prevents the collapse.

Investigators have speculated that **sudden infant death syndrome** (**SIDS,** or *crib death*) arises from sleep apnea as a result of a reduction in the brainstem neural activity that normally paces respiration. Continuous monitoring of the sleep of infants at risk for crib death can save the lives of some children.

Although Many Drugs Affect Sleep, There Is No Perfect Sleeping Pill

Throughout recorded history humans have reached for substances to enhance the prospects of sleep. Early civilizations discovered substances in the plant world that induce sleep (Hartmann, 1978). Ancient Greeks used the juice of the poppy to obtain opium and used products of the mandrake plant that we recognize today as scopolamine and atropine. The preparation of barbituric acid in the mid-nineteenth century by the discoverer of aspirin, Adolph von Bayer, began the development of an enormous number of substances—barbiturates—that continue to be used for sleep dysfunctions. Unfortunately, none of these substances can provide a completely normal night of sleep in terms of time spent in various sleep states such as REM sleep, and none of them remain effective when used repeatedly.

Most modern sleeping pills seem to activate GABA receptors, inhibiting broad regions of the brain. But reliance on sleeping pills, including the currently popular benzodiazepine triazolam (Halcion), poses many problems (Rothschild, 1992). Viewed solely as a way to deal with sleep problems, current drugs fall far short of being a suitable remedy for several reasons.

First, continual use of sleep medication causes these substances to lose their sleep-inducing properties, and this declining ability to induce sleep frequently leads to increased self-prescribed dosages that pose a health hazard.

A second major drawback in the use of sleeping pills is that they produce marked changes in the pattern of sleep, both during the period of drug use and for a period following drug use that may last for days. Most commonly, during the initial phase of drug use REM sleep is reduced, especially during the first half of a night of sleep. A gradual adaptation to drug use is evident in the return of REM sleep with continued use of sleeping pills. Sudden withdrawal of sleeping pills results in a period of REM rebound with an intensity that many people experience as unpleasant and that may lead to a return to reliance on sleeping pills.

A final major problem in the frequent use of sleeping pills is their impact on waking behavior. A persistent "sleep drunkenness" coupled with drowsiness, despite intense efforts at maintaining vigilance, may impair productive activity during waking hours.

These problems have led to the development of other biochemical approaches to the treatment of sleep disorders. Because the hormone melatonin is normally released from the pineal at night (see Figure 5.19b), the administration of exogenous melatonin has been suggested to aid the onset of sleep. In fact, melatonin does have a weak hypnotic effect soon after administration (Chase and Gidal, 1997), perhaps because it causes a lowering of body temperature, reducing arousal and causing drowsiness (Dawson and Encel, 1993).

Mendelson (1997) remains unconvinced that melatonin really helps insomnia, but it does seem to reduce the effects of jet lag (Arendt et al., 1997). There are at least two different melatonin receptors, and only one of them seems to mediate the effects of melatonin on circadian rhythms (D. Liu et al., 1997), so drugs that can selectively activate that particular melatonin receptor will probably be developed.

Another approach to treating sleep disorders is to promote increases in the concentration and release of neurotransmitters that may be involved in sleep induction. Hartmann (1978) emphasized serotonin as an important transmitter in this process. Serotonin levels in the brain can be strongly influenced by the administration of tryptophan, which is a precursor in the synthesis of serotonin. Low doses of the precursor under double-blind conditions (in which neither experimenters nor subjects know which subjects receive the drug and which take the control until after the study is over) reduced sleep latency without changing the basic pattern of sleep in humans (Hartmann, 1978). Larger doses, however, can lead to other health problems. Meanwhile, grandmother's suggestion to drink a glass of warm milk before bed may be sound, since milk is a source of tryptophan.

People Who Suffer from Narcolepsy Are Always Sleepy

Although some of us might find it difficult to consider excessive sleeping an affliction, many people are either drowsy all the time or suffer sudden attacks of sleep. In these cases sleep is not viewed as welcome rest, but rather as an encumbrance that endangers and compromises the quality of life.

CLINICAL ISSUE

One of the largest groups of patients found at sleep disorder clinics consists of people who suffer from narcolepsy. **Narcolepsy** is an unusual disorder in which the patient is afflicted by frequent, intense attacks of sleep, which last 5 to 30 minutes and can occur at any time during usual waking hours. Uncontrollable attacks of

(a) (b)

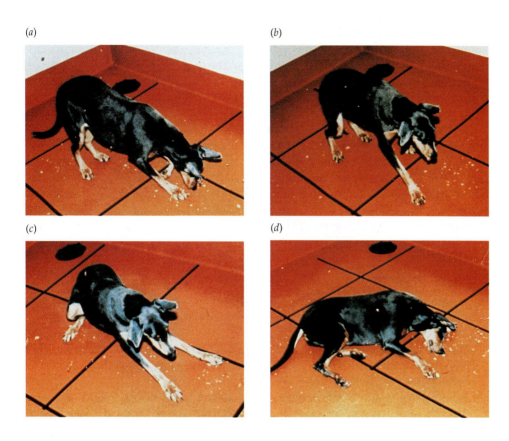

(c) (d)

14.24 Narcolepsy in Dogs
A narcoleptic dog that suffers cataplexy when excited is offered a food treat (*a*), becomes wobbly (*b*), lies down (*c*), and finally falls limply to the floor (*d*). (Courtesy of Seiji Nishino.)

sleep occur several times a day—usually about every 90 minutes (Dantz et al., 1994). People suffering from narcolepsy feel drowsy most of the time.

Individuals with this sleep disorder are distinguished by the appearance of REM sleep at the onset of sleep. In fact, the duration of a narcoleptic attack is similar to the usual period of a REM sleep episode. At night, however, these individuals exhibit a relatively normal sleep pattern. Some investigators consider this disorder to be the result of a brainstem dysfunction in which a waking mechanism fails to suppress the brainstem centers that control REM sleep.

Many people with narcolepsy also show **cataplexy,** a sudden loss of muscle tone, leading to collapse of the body without loss of consciousness. These episodes, like narcoleptic attacks, are triggered by sudden, intense emotional stimuli, including both laughter and anger. Just before sleep onset, some such patients report **sleep paralysis,** which includes the (temporary) inability to move or talk; in this state they may experience sudden sensory hallucinations. This disorder usually manifests itself between the ages of 15 and 25 years and continues throughout life. One human narcolepsy susceptibility gene has been identified (Mignot et al., 1993), and animal models have offered remarkable insights.

Several strains of dogs have been shown to exhibit narcolepsy (Aldrich, 1993): sudden motor inhibition (cataplexy) and very short latencies to sleep onset (Figure 14.24). Many instances of sleep-onset REM episodes are evident, just as in human sufferers of narcolepsy. Cataplexy in these animals is suppressed by the same drugs that are used to treat human cataplexy. These narcoleptic dogs have abnormally high acetylcholine receptor levels in the pons (Aldrich, 1993). Moreover, inducing cataplexy in these animals (by offering very desirable food) causes an increase in the release of acetylcholine in the pontine reticular formation (Reid et al., 1994).

The mutant gene at work in one of these narcoleptic strains of dogs was named *canarc* but was later found to be a receptor for the neuropeptide orexin (we discussed the possible role of orexin in hunger in Chapter 13) (L. Lin et al., 1999). Mice with

Normal

Narcoleptic

14.25 Neural Degeneration in the Amygdala of Narcoleptic Dogs
Gaps in degenerating axons can be detected only when the dogs are 1 to 2 months of age, about the time narcoleptic symptoms begin. (Courtesy of Jerome Siegel.)

Refer to the *Learning Biological Psychology* CD for the following study aids for this chapter:

11 Objectives

81 Study Questions

2 Activities

1 Animated Tutorial

1 Video

the *orexin* gene knocked out also display narcolepsy (Chemelli et al., 1999). No one knows why interfering with orexin signaling leads to narcolepsy, but the narcoleptic dogs show signs of neural degeneration in the amygdala and nearby forebrain structures (Figure 14.25) (J. M. Siegel et al., 1999). Perhaps this degeneration causes inappropriate activation of the cataplexy pathway that is normally at work during REM.

People who suffer from narcolepsy aren't the only ones to experience sleep paralysis on occasion. It seems that the immobilization of the skeletal musculature doesn't always coincide exactly with REM sleep. A person may feel that he or she can't move, either just before dropping off to sleep, or, more often, just after waking. About 40% of both Canadian and Japanese university students have experienced this feeling (Fukuda et al., 1998), although other studies have found considerably lower prevalence (e.g., Ohayon et al., 1999).

Summary

Biological Rhythms

1. Many living systems show circadian rhythms that can be entrained by environmental stimuli, especially light. These rhythms synchronize behavior and body states to changes in the environment.

2. Neural pacemakers in the suprachiasmatic nucleus (SCN) of the hypothalamus are the basis of many (but not all) circadian rhythms. The basis of light entrainment in many cases is a pathway from the retina to the SCN.

3. Rhythms shorter than 24 hours (ultradian rhythms) or longer than 24 hours (infradian rhythms) are evident in both behavior and biological processes. The underlying mechanism does not involve clocks in the SCN.

Sleep and Waking

1. During sleep, almost all mammals alternate between two main states: slow-wave sleep (SWS) and rapid-eye-movement (REM) sleep.

2. Human SWS shows four stages defined by EEG criteria that include bursts of spindles and persistent trains of large, slow waves. During SWS, muscle tension, heart rate, respiratory rate, and temperature decline progressively.

3. REM sleep is characterized by a rapid EEG of low amplitude—almost like the EEG during active waking behavior—and intense autonomic activation, but the postural muscles are flaccid because of profound inhibition of motoneurons.

4. In adult humans, SWS and REM sleep alternate every 90 to 110 minutes. Smaller animals have shorter sleep cycles and spend more overall time asleep.

5. Mental activity does not cease during sleep. Vivid perceptual experiences (dreams) are frequently reported by subjects awakened from REM sleep; reports of ideas or thinking are often given by subjects awakened from SWS.

6. The characteristics of sleep–waking cycles change during the course of life. Mature animals sleep less than the young, and REM sleep accounts for a smaller fraction of their sleep.

7. The prominence of REM sleep in infants suggests that REM sleep contributes to development of the brain and to learning.

8. Deprivation of sleep for a few nights in a row leads to impairment in tasks that require sustained vigilance. During recovery nights following deprivation, the lost SWS and REM sleep are partially restored over several nights.

9. Many brain structures are involved in the initiation and maintenance of sleep. Particular emphasis has been placed on brainstem structures, including the reticular formation, the raphe nucleus, and the locus coeruleus.

10. Researchers have suggested several biological roles for sleep, including conservation of energy, avoidance of predators, restoration of depleted resources, and consolidation of memory.

11. Because memory formation is impaired when sleep deprivation—particularly REM sleep deprivation—follows learning sessions, sleep may aid the consolidation of memory. Little or no new learning, however, can take place during sleep.

12. Sleep appears to promote health because prolonged sleep deprivation or insomnia fatally compromises the ability of an individual to combat infection.

13. Many drugs used to induce sleep inhibit REM sleep during the first few nights. When the drug is withdrawn, there is a rebound increase of REM sleep on the following nights. No pill repeatedly provides a normal night of sleep.

14. Sleep disorders fall into four major categories: (1) disorders of initiation and maintenance of sleep (e.g., insomnia); (2) disorders of excessive drowsiness (e.g., narcolepsy); (3) disorders of the sleep–waking schedule; and (4) dysfunctions associated with sleep, sleep stages, or partial arousals (e.g., sleepwalking).

Recommended Reading

Chokroverty, S. (Ed.). (1999). *Sleep disorders medicine: Basic science, technical considerations, and clinical aspects* (2nd ed.). Boston: Butterworth-Heinemann.

Dement, W. C., and Vaughan, C. (1999). *The promise of sleep.* New York: Delacorte.

Flanagan, O. J. (2000). *Dreaming souls: Sleep, dreams, and the evolution of the conscious mind.* New York: Oxford University Press.

Jouvet, M. (1999). *The paradox of sleep: The story of dreaming.* Cambridge, MA: MIT Press.

King, D. P., and Takahashi, J. S. (2000). Molecular genetics of circadian rhythms in mammals. *Annual Review of Neuroscience, 23,* 713–742.

Kryger, M. K., Roth, T., and Dement, W. C. (Eds.). (2000). *Principles and practice of sleep medicine* (3rd ed.). New York: Saunders.

Pressman, M. R., and Orr, W. C. (Eds.). (1997). *Understanding sleep: The evaluation and treatment of sleep disorders.* Washington, DC: American Psychological Association.

Shneerson, J. M. (2000). *Handbook of sleep medicine.* Malden, MA: Blackwell Science.

PART FIVE

Emotions and Mental Disorders

So far in this text we have discussed a wide variety of behaviors that individuals display in particular circumstances, and in each case it has seemed rather straightforward that these behaviors are adaptive. It is clearly adaptive to be able to detect stimuli that surround us, to make coordinated movements, to drink when body fluids are low, to eat when energy supplies are low—or even to anticipate these needs—and to sleep at night (when moving about may be dangerous). It has been more difficult to understand in biological terms how it is that we are sometimes angry, terrified, or joyful, even though these emotions are clearly an important part of our experience.

Chapter 15 takes up research that attempts to determine the roles that emotions play and the biological mechanisms of emotions. Just as other body systems may malfunction—we have seen examples in the cases of sensory, motor, and regulatory systems—so, too, may emotional systems. Hearing voices that are not present, persistently reliving dreadful memories, or being driven to suicide by depression do not help us survive and reproduce. Chapter 16 deals with dysfunctions that lead to mental illness and the still modest but growing means we have to combat them.

15

Emotions, Aggression, and Stress

The sound of unexpected footsteps in the eerie quiet of the night brings fear to many of us. But the sound of music we enjoy and the voice of someone we love summon feelings of warmth. For some of us, feelings and emotions can become vastly exaggerated; fears, for example, can become paralyzing attacks of anxiety and panic. No story about our behavior is complete without consideration of the many events in a single day that involve feelings.

The psychobiological study of emotions has progressed in several directions. One traditional area focuses on bodily responses during emotional states, especially changes in facial expression, and visceral responses such as changes in heart rate. The study of brain mechanisms related to emotional states has especially emphasized fear and aggression because both are important for human existence, so a special section of this chapter is devoted to aggression.

Leonard Koscianski, *The Way It Is*, 1998

Another topic of research related to emotion is stress, such as the stress that accompanies some health impairments. Stress involves and affects not only the nervous and endocrine systems but also the immune system, so we also discuss the immune system in this chapter. In addition, the chapter emphasizes interrelations among the nervous, endocrine, and immune systems.

What Are Emotions?

The complicated world of emotions includes a wide range of observable behaviors, expressed feelings, and changes in body state. This diversity—that is, the many meanings of the word *emotion*—has made the subject hard to study. For many of us emotions are very personal states, difficult to define or identify except in the most obvious instances. Is the hissing cat frightened, angry, or perhaps enjoying tormenting its solicitous but apprehensive owner? Moreover, many aspects of our emotions seem unconscious even to us. For these reasons, emotions were neglected as a field of study for many years, but there has been a significant renaissance of interest in this fascinating topic.

Emotions Have Four Different Aspects

There are at least four aspects to emotion:

1. *Feelings.* In many cases, emotions are feelings that are private and subjective. Humans can report an extraordinary range of states that they say they feel or experience. These reports of subjective experience may or may not be accompanied by overt indicators.
2. *Actions.* Emotions can be actions commonly deemed "emotional," such as defending or attacking in response to a threat. This aspect of emotion is especially relevant to Darwin's view of the functional roles of emotion. He suggested that some emotions evolved because they aid in generating appropriate reactions to "emergency" events in the environment, such as the sudden appearance of a predator. Darwin (1872) also suggested that facial expression of emotion communicates information to others.
3. *Physiological arousal.* Emotions are states of physiological arousal—expressions or displays of distinctive somatic and autonomic responses. This emphasis suggests that emotional states can be defined by particular constellations of bodily responses. The physiological arousal that accompanies emotion allows us to examine emotion in nonhuman animals as well as in human beings.
4. *Motivational programs.* Emotions are superordinate motivational programs that coordinate responses to solve specific adaptive problems; they are generated by distinct brain systems.

Psychologists Have Defined Different Categories of Emotion

An ongoing discussion about the study of human emotions focuses on whether a basic core set of emotions underlies the more varied and delicate nuances of our world of feelings. From a biological perspective, one reason for interest in this question is the possibility that distinctly separate brain systems are related to different parts of this core set. Plutchik (1994) suggests that there are eight basic emotions, grouped in four pairs of opposites: (1) joy/sadness, (2) affection/disgust, (3) anger/fear, and (4) expectation/surprise. In Plutchik's view, all other emotions are derived from combinations of this basic array, which he believes is quite similar across all human societies.

Figure 15.1 presents this classification of emotions in an arrangement similar to that of the color solid (see Figure 10.5). As we will see, investigators do not yet agree about the number of emotions, how discrete they are, and their relation to cognitive activities. In general, a biological approach to emotions emphasizes a group of discrete, core emotions for which there seems to be a basis for comparisons both across human cultures and between humans and other animals.

Broad Theories of Emotion Emphasize Bodily Responses

In many emotional states we can sense our heart beating fast, our hands and face feeling warm, our palms sweating, and a queasy feeling in our stomach. Strong emotions are nearly inseparable from activation of the skeletal-muscle and/or autonomic

Levels of Intensity

15.1 Basic Emotions In this proposed organizational scheme, the eight basic emotions appear across from their opposites at the middle level. Lower and higher intensity forms of each basic emotion appear at the bottom and top levels, respectively. (Modified from Plutchik, 1994.)

nervous systems. Common expressions capture this association: "with all my heart," "hair standing on end," "a sinking feeling in the stomach."

Several theories have tried to explain the close ties between the subjective psychological phenomena we know as emotions and the activity of visceral organs controlled by the autonomic nervous system, which we described in Chapter 2 (see Figure 2.10). Folk psychology suggests that the autonomic reactions are caused by the emotion: "I was so angry my stomach was churning," as though the anger produced the churning.

The James–Lange Theory Considers Emotions to Be the Perception of Bodily Changes

William James, the leading figure in American psychology at about the start of the twentieth century, turned the folk psychology idea on its head, suggesting that the emotions we experience are caused by the bodily changes. From this perspective, we experience fear because we perceive the body activity triggered by particular stimuli.

About the same time that James was developing his theories of emotion, Danish physician Carl Lange proposed a similar view, which he boldly stated as follows:

> We owe all the emotional side of our mental life, our joys and sorrows, our happy and unhappy hours, to our vasomotor system. If the impressions which fall upon our senses did not possess the power of stimulating it, we would wander through life, unsympathetic and passionless, all impressions of the outer world would only enrich our experience, increase our knowledge, but would give us neither care nor fear (Lange, 1887).

The James–Lange theory thus emphasizes peripheral physiological events in emotion. Different emotions feel different because they are generated by a different constellation of physiological responses. The theory initiated many studies that attempted to link emotions to bodily responses, a focus of lasting interest in the field. Questions such as "What are the responses of the heart in love, anger, fear?" continue to form a prominent part of the biological study of emotions. Although the James–Lange theory initiated this research, it has not survived critical assessment.

COMPETING HYPOTHESES

The Cannon–Bard Theory Emphasizes Central Processes

The simplicity of the James–Lange theory presented ready opportunity for experimental assessment. Physiologists Walter Cannon and Philip Bard studied relations between emotion and the autonomic nervous system. They offered strong criticism of the James–Lange theory, claiming that the experience of emotion starts before the autonomic changes, which are relatively slow. In addition, autonomic changes accompanying strong emotions seemed very much the same, whether the emotion experienced was anger, fear, or great surprise. Cannon (1929) emphasized that these bodily reactions (increased heart rate, glucose mobilization, and other effects) are an emergency response of an organism to a sudden threatening condition, producing maximal activation of the sympathetic nervous system, readying the organism for fight or flight. So the function of emotion is to help us deal with a changing environment.

In Cannon and Bard's view, however, it is the brain's job to decide what particular emotion is an appropriate response to the stimuli. According to this view, the cerebral cortex simultaneously decides on the appropriate emotional response and activates the sympathetic system so that the body is ready for appropriate action, as the brain decides. The Cannon–Bard theory provoked many studies of the effects of brain lesions and electrical stimulation on emotion.

Stanley Schachter Proposed a Cognitive Interpretation of Stimuli and Visceral States

Like Cannon and Bard, Stanley Schachter (1975) also emphasized cognitive mechanisms in emotion, suggesting that individuals interpret visceral activation in terms of the eliciting stimuli, the surrounding situation, their cognitive states, and experi-

15.2 Different Views of the Chain of Events in Emotional Responses (*a*) Folk psychology suggests that emotions cause the body to react. (*b*) James and Lange suggested that the bodily response evokes the emotional experience. (*c*) Cannon and Bard insisted that the brain must interpret the situation to decide which emotion is appropriate. (*d*) Schachter attempted to reconcile these views by suggesting that the intensity of emotion can be affected by the bodily responses and that the brain continuously assesses the situation.

(*a*) Folk psychology

(*b*) James–Lange theory

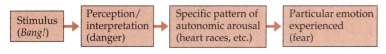

(*c*) Cannon–Bard theory

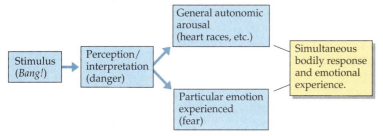

(*d*) Schachter's cognitive theory

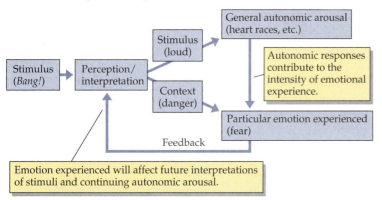

ence. According to Schachter, emotional labels (e.g., anger, fear, joy) depend on the interpretations of a situation—interpretations that are controlled by internal cognitive systems.

In a famous experiment (Schachter and Singer, 1962), people were injected with epinephrine (adrenaline) and told either that there would be no effect or that the heart would race. People who were warned of the reaction reported no emotional experience, but some people who were not forewarned experienced an emotion when their bodies responded to the drug, as would be predicted by the James–Lange theory (bodily reactions are experienced as emotion) but not the Cannon–Bard theory (the cortex separately activates emotion and the bodily reaction).

However, the particular emotion experienced could be affected by whether a confederate in the room acted angry or happy. The unsuspecting subjects injected with epinephrine were much more likely to report feeling angry when in the presence of an "angry" confederate, and more likely to report feeling elated when with a "happy" confederate. These findings contradict the James–Lange prediction that a different constellation of autonomic reactions would instigate feelings of anger or euphoria. Subjects injected with placebo were much less likely to report an emotional experience, no matter how the confederate behaved.

Thus an emotional state is the result of an interaction between physiological activation and cognitive interpretation of that arousal. According to this view, emotion depends not only on the interaction of arousal and cognitive appraisal but also on the perception that a causal connection exists between physiological arousal and emotional cognition (Reisenzein, 1983). Figure 15.2 compares these different theories of emotion.

Schachter's theory has not been without critics. For example, the theory asserts that physiological arousal is *nonspecific*, affecting only the intensity of a perceived emotion but not its quality, yet each different emotion has been claimed to exhibit a specific pattern of autonomic arousal (Cacioppo et al., 1993). When subjects were asked to pose facial expressions distinctive for particular emotions, autonomic patterns of the subjects were different for several emotions, such as fear and sadness (Levenson et al., 1990).

Facial Expressions Reveal Emotional States

Our bodies indicate emotions in many ways. Overt expressions of emotion are evident in posture, gesture, and facial expression; all these dimensions are well cultivated by actors and actresses. The human face, which is hard to hide from view, is a ready source of information. Its elaborate and finely controlled musculature provides for an enormous range of expressions.

Facial Expressions Have Complex Functions in Communication

In his book *The Expression of the Emotions in Man and Animals* (1872), Charles Darwin cataloged the facial expressions of humans and other animals and emphasized the universal nature of these expressions. He noted especially that facial expressions are connected to distinctive emotional states both in humans and in nonhuman primates. In part he viewed facial expressions as information communicated to other animals.

Anger

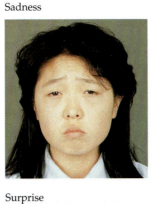

Sadness

Happiness

Fear

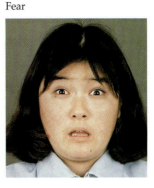

Disgust

Surprise

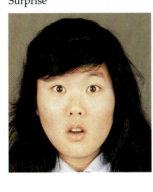

Contempt

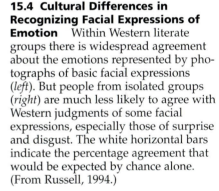

15.3 Universal Facial Expressions of Emotion According to Paul Ekman and colleagues, the seven basic emotional facial expressions shown here are displayed in all cultures. Embarrassment has recently been proposed to be an eighth basic emotion. (Courtesy of David Matsumoto.)

Paul Ekman has provided rich insight into the properties of facial expressions. He and his collaborators have developed an array of analytical tools that enable objective description and measurement of facial expressions among humans of different cultures (Keltner and Ekman, 2000). Analyses of facial expressions reveal that both static features and rapidly changing features of the face provide information.

How many different emotions can be detected in facial expressions? According to Keltner and Ekman (2000), there are distinctive expressions for anger, sadness, happiness, fear, disgust, surprise, contempt, and embarrassment (Figure 15.3). Facial expressions of these emotions are interpreted similarly across many cultures without explicit training.

Cross-cultural similarity is also noted in the *production* of expressions specific to particular emotions. For example, people in a preliterate New Guinea society, when displaying particular emotions, show facial expressions like those of people in industrialized societies. This *universality* hypothesis of facial expression has come under criticism. Fridlund (1994) suggests that universal expressions do not account for the full complement of human facial expressions. Cultural differences may emerge in culture-specific display rules, which stipulate social contexts for facial expression. For example, Russell (1994) found significant differences across cultures in the recognition of some emotional states from facial expressions (Figure 15.4), although all groups performed above the chance level.

15.4 Cultural Differences in Recognizing Facial Expressions of Emotion Within Western literate groups there is widespread agreement about the emotions represented by photographs of basic facial expressions (*left*). But people from isolated groups (*right*) are much less likely to agree with Western judgments of some facial expressions, especially those of surprise and disgust. The white horizontal bars indicate the percentage agreement that would be expected by chance alone. (From Russell, 1994.)

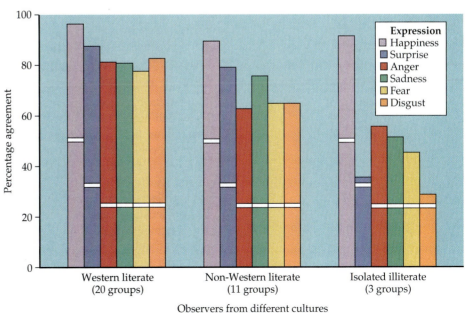

Observers from different cultures

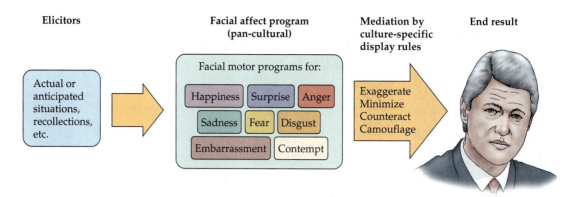

15.5 A Model for Emotional Facial Expressions across Cultures

Paul Ekman

Some anthropologists have suggested that cultures that prescribe rules for facial expression and control and enforce those rules by cultural conditioning might mask the universal property of facial expressions. A model of this process is presented in Figure 15.5. The remaining controversy focuses on the extent to which culture affects the facial display of emotion.

According to Fridlund (1994), a major role of facial expression is *paralinguistic*; that is, the face is accessory to verbal communication, perhaps providing emphasis and direction in conversation. For example, Gilbert et al. (1986) showed that subjects display few facial responses to odor when smelling alone, but significantly more in a social setting. Similarly, bowlers seldom smile when making a strike, but they frequently smile when they turn around to meet the faces of others watching them (Kraut and Johnston, 1979).

Facial Expressions Are Mediated by Muscles, Cranial Nerves, and CNS Pathways

How are facial expressions produced? Within the human face is an elaborate network of finely innervated muscles whose functional roles in addition to facial expression include production of speech, eating, and respiration, among others. Facial muscles can be divided into two categories:

1. *Superficial facial muscles* attach to facial skin (Figure 15.6). They act as sphincters, changing the shape of the mouth, eyes, or nose, for example, or they pull on their attachment to the skin. One such muscle, the frontalis, wrinkles the forehead and raises the eyebrow.
2. *Deep facial muscles* attach to skeletal structures of the head. These muscles enable movements such as chewing. An example of a deep muscle is the masseter, a powerful jaw muscle.

Human facial muscles are innervated by two cranial nerves: (1) the facial nerve (VII), which innervates the superficial muscles of facial expression; and (2) the trigeminal nerve (V), which innervates muscles that move the jaw. Studies of the facial nerve reveal that the right and left sides are completely independent. As Figure 15.6 shows, the main trunk of the facial nerve divides into upper and lower divisions shortly after entering the face. These nerve fibers originate in the brainstem in a region called the nucleus of the facial nerve. Distinct subgroups of neurons within this nucleus form specific branches of the facial nerve, which in turn connect to distinct segments of the face. Within the facial-nerve nucleus, cells that control the muscles of the lower face are clearly separated from those that control the muscles of the upper face.

The face is represented extensively in the human motor cortex (see Figure 11.12). The cerebral cortex innervates the facial nucleus both bilaterally and unilaterally:

The lower two-thirds of the face receives input from the opposite side of the cortex; the upper third receives input from both sides. This pattern of innervation is evident in our ability to produce one-sided movements of the lips (the unilateral movement of an eyebrow is a more exotic talent shared by few).

Some investigators suggest that the brain control of voluntary facial movements is very different from that of facial movements induced by emotion (Rinn, 1984). Whereas voluntary activation of the facial-nerve nucleus is achieved through the corticospinal system, emotional activation of the face is presumed to involve subcortical systems. Support for this view comes from studies of patients who have sustained unilateral damage to the motor cortex. Such patients are unable to retract the corner of the mouth opposite to the damaged hemisphere when asked to do so, but both corners retract during a period of spontaneous, happy laughter or amusement. The reverse syndrome results from damage to subcortical regions such as the basal ganglia, as in Parkinson's disease. Patients who exhibit this reverse syndrome are able to move the facial muscles voluntarily, but they lose spontaneous emotional expression of the face.

Facial muscles

Branches of the facial nerve

Frontalis

Orbicularis oculi

Levator labii superioris

Temporal

Zygomatic

Buccal

Mandibular

15.6 Superficial Facial Muscles and Their Neural Control

In Some Conditions, Facial Musculature Is Inhibited Selectively

Chronic selective inhibition of the facial musculature occurs in Parkinson's disease, and recently it has been reported for patients with schizophrenia (Kring, 1999). Compared with nonpatients, patients with schizophrenia exhibit few outward signs of emotion, although recordings from facial muscles reveal very small, subtle facial activity characteristic of different emotions. In response to emotional stimuli, patients with schizophrenia report experiencing as much emotion as nonpatients. The social interactions of the patients are impaired by their lack of normal facial responses.

Emotions from the Comparative/Evolutionary Viewpoint

In his 1872 book on emotions, mentioned earlier, Charles Darwin presented evidence that expressions of emotions are universal among people of all regions of the world. To reach this conclusion, he obtained data from informants in different countries and analyzed observers' responses to different expressions. These were forerunners of the studies of facial expressions that we reviewed earlier. But Darwin went further and attempted to determine whether humans and other animals share expressions of some emotions. He investigated whether these expressions and emotional mechanisms may have originated among earlier species from which both modern humans and other current species are descended.

EVOLUTION AT WORK

Darwin not only reviewed reports of apparent expressions of emotion in various species of mammals, but he also considered information about the facial musculature and the nerves that innervate these muscles. Before Darwin, most investigators believed that the facial muscles were given uniquely to humans so that they could express their feelings. Darwin emphasized that nonhuman primates have the same facial muscles as humans. Redican (1982) described distinctive primate expressions labeled as (1) *grimace,* perhaps analogous to human expressions of fear or surprise; (2) *tense mouth,* akin to human expressions of anger; and (3) *play face,* similar in form to the human smile.

The facial musculature was as far as Darwin could go in considering the mechanisms of emotional expression, but later in this chapter we will take up brain regions and circuits, as well as endocrine mechanisms, involved in emotions. Much of this research is being done with nonhuman animals, including not only primates but also laboratory rodents. Finding similar brain circuits and endocrine mechanisms for certain emotions in different mammalian orders would support Darwin's hypothesis that these emotions and their mechanisms originated in our distant ancestors.

How May Emotion and Emotional Displays Have Evolved?

How do emotions help individuals survive and reproduce? Several benefits of emotions and their expression have been suggested. Darwin (1872) wrote about their benefits for communication:

> The movements of expression in the face and body . . . are . . . of much importance for our welfare. They serve as the first means of communication between the mother and her infant; she smiles approval, and thus encourages her child on the right path, or frowns disapproval. We readily perceive sympathy in others by their expression; our sufferings are thus mitigated and our pleasure increased; and mutual good feeling is thus strengthened. The movements of expression give vividness and energy to our spoken words. They reveal the thoughts and intentions of others more truly than do words, which may be falsified.

Current proponents of the approach that is called **evolutionary psychology** point to additional ways in which emotions are adaptive and could have developed through natural selection (Cosmides and Tooby, 2000). They suggest that emotions are superordinate motivational programs that coordinate various responses to solve specific adaptive problems, including foraging for food, maintaining cooperative relations with members of one's group, choosing a mate, avoiding predators, and so forth.

For example, an ancestrally common situation that still recurs is that of being alone at night and perceiving cues indicating that you are being stalked by a human or animal predator. As with most kinds of behavior, individuals differ in their responses to this life-threatening situation. Some individuals make poor choices and are therefore less likely to survive and reproduce. Others make more effective choices and, to the extent that this behavior is heritable, their descendants are also more likely to survive in similar situations. Thus through natural selection an effective program for dealing with this situation evolves. In the face of an imminent threat to life, it is better to be able to call on a recipe for action developed and tested over ages of evolution than to have to work out the response from scratch.

The emotion of fear in this situation calls forth shifts in perception, attention, cognition, and action that focus on avoidance of danger and seeking safety, as well as physiological changes that prepare us for either flight or immobility. Other options, such as seeking food, going to sleep, or seeking a mate, are suppressed. The organization and concentration on a cluster of adaptive changes for avoiding danger allowed this problem to be solved with a high probability of success, on the average, over evolutionary time.

Later in this chapter we will see that a stimulus that evokes fear activates a specific brain circuit that projects to three different brain regions, each of which produces a different component of the fear response: motor behavior, autonomic responses, and hormonal responses. Fear has been the emotion most frequently studied, but it seems likely that natural selection has also shaped other emotions.

Emotions from the Developmental Viewpoint

Children show some emotions from the time of birth, and during the first 3 years of life they become capable of showing most of the emotions that adults display (M. Lewis, 2000). At birth, infants show both general distress and contentment or pleasure; interest or attention is classified by some as a third emotion present at birth. By the age of 3 months, infants also show evidence of joy; they start to smile and appear to show excitement and/or happiness in response to familiar faces. Sadness also emerges at this time, especially caused by the withdrawal of positive events. Disgust also appears, in the primitive form of spitting out distasteful objects placed in the mouth. Anger has been reported to appear between 4 and 6 months when babies are frustrated or restrained. Surprise first appears at about 6 months in response to violation of an expectation or to a discovery. Fearfulness first emerges at about 7 or 8 months. Thus what some have called the primary or basic emotions are all present by 8 to 9 months after birth.

Between 18 and 24 months, the emergence of self-consciousness or self-awareness allows an additional group of emotions to develop, including embarrassment, empathy, and envy. Another milestone occurs sometime between 2 and 3 years of age when children become capable of evaluating their behavior against a standard. This ability allows the emergence of "self-conscious evaluative emotions," which Darwin (1872) characterized as unique to our species, including pride, shame, guilt, and regret. By this time children are able to name some of the emotions they experience or that they perceive in others.

Individuals Differ in Their Emotional Responsiveness

Even newborns show individual differences in emotional responsiveness. Responses of various body systems reveal distinct patterns that are characteristic of the individual. John and Beatrice Lacey (1970) referred to this characteristic as **individual response stereotypy.** Their work involved longitudinal (extending over many years) studies of people, from early childhood to adulthood. The stimuli they used to provoke autonomic responses included stress conditions such as immersion of the hand in ice-cold water, performance of rapidly paced arithmetic calculations, and exposure to intense stimuli on the skin. Across these conditions the investigators observed an individual profile of response that is evident even in newborns. For example, some newborns respond vigorously with heart rate changes, others with gastric contractions, and still others with blood pressure responses.

The response patterns are remarkably consistent throughout life. Jerome Kagan and colleagues have classified newborns on the basis of their behavioral responses to cues such as an alcohol-soaked cotton swab. About 20% of the infants were termed *high reactives* because they gave especially strong reactions to the stimuli. Later, many of these high reactives became extremely shy, and by the time they were old enough for school, about a third of them displayed extreme phobias (compared to fewer than 10% of the other children). Kagan (1997) suspects that these consistent patterns of reactivity as children grow up reflect inborn differences in temperament that may relate to individual differences in response to stress, which we will discuss at the end of this chapter.

Jerome Kagan

Autonomic Responses Are Elicited by Emotion-Provoking Stimuli

Although the changing expressions of the face are easy to see, the detection of visceral changes requires electronic gadgets. A subject who is connected to devices that measure heart rate, blood pressure, stomach contractions, dilation or constriction of blood vessels, skin resistance, or sweating of the palms or soles exhibits many changes in response to emotional states. One device that measures several of these bodily responses is called a **polygraph,** popularly known as a *lie detector.* The use of polygraphs to try to detect lying in individuals who are accused of crimes is controversial; most psychophysiologists argue against such use (Box 15.1).

After reviewing a large array of data from studies from the 1950s to the present, Cacioppo et al. (2000) state that most of the evidence on autonomic differentiation of emotions remains inconclusive. Distinct emotional stimuli do not invariably elicit a distinct pattern of autonomic responses. Autonomic differentiation is clearer when positive emotions are contrasted with negative emotions rather than when discrete emotions are compared.

BOX 15.1 *Lie Detector?*

One of the most controversial attempts to apply biomedical science is the so-called lie detector test. This test attempts to detect lying by measuring physiological responses during an interview. A new panel of experts was formed recently by the National Academy of Sciences to examine the issue, at the request of U.S. government agencies (Holden, 2001). This is the first major government-sponsored study of the question since the Office of Technology Assessment (OTA) concluded in 1983 that lie detector (polygraph) tests are not an effective scientific method to check for breaches of security. In 1986 the American Psychological Association stated great reservations about the use of polygraph tests to detect deception because scientific evidence for the validity of these procedures is unsatisfactory.

Lie detector tests are based on the assumption that people have emotional responses when lying because they fear detection and/or feel guilt about lying. Emotions are usually accompanied by bodily responses that are difficult for a person to control, such as changes in heart rate, respiration, and skin conductance (related to sweating). Lie detector tests get the name polygraph (from the Greek *polys*, "many," and *graphein*, "to write") because they employ several physiological measures. The modern form of the polygraph was introduced in 1917 by experimental psychologist William Marston, who coined the term *lie detector*.

Some proponents of polygraph examinations claim that they are accurate in 95% of tests, but the estimate from impartial research is an overall accuracy of about 65% (Nietzel, 2000). Even if the higher figure were correct, the fact that these tests are widely used means that thousands of truthful people could be branded as liars and fired, disciplined, or not hired. On the other hand, many criminals and spies have been able to pass the tests without detection. For example, long-time CIA agent Aldrich Ames, who was sentenced in 1995 to life in prison for espionage, successfully passed polygraph tests after becoming a spy.

It is difficult to do convincing research on lie detection because most studies involve only trivial attempts at deception that do not necessarily involve subjects emotionally. The U.S. Department of Defense has started a study with 120 volunteers, some trained to pretend that they have committed espionage. But Paul Ekman, a member of the National Academy of Sciences panel, said in a written statement that such research won't yield solid results unless the subjects are playing for "high stakes," such as loss of a job (Holden, 2001).

"Because of the controversies that surround the polygraph, most [American] courts do not allow testimony about it in trials. However, it is widely used in the initial stages of criminal investigations, often to convince suspects that they should confess" (Nietzel,

2000, p. 225). Polygraph testing was also widely used in U.S. businesses in the 1970s and 1980s, but in 1988, Congress passed the Employee Polygraph Protection Act, which, with some exceptions, prohibits the use of lie detectors by private businesses involved in interstate commerce. Even where such tests are permitted, employees are granted several rights, such as seeing the questions in advance, and the results of the lie detector test cannot be the sole basis for action against the employee.

Some scientists believe that modern neuroscientific techniques may provide new methods of lie detection that did not exist at the time of the 1983 OTA report. For example, psychologist Richard Davidson points to research on brain mechanisms of fear in the last decade. Fear results in activation of the amygdala that is visible with functional MRI (see Chapter 2), and such a response could be studied in the case of deception. Andrew Ryan, chief of research at the Department of Defense Polygraph Institute, points out that deception probably requires more cognitive effort than truth, and this difference might be detected in brain imaging (Holden, 2001). Detection of deception may become a new focus of brain imaging research, but successful applications would make lie detectors more costly and less widely available. However, no results are yet available, and such research does not support present attempts at lie detection.

Distinct Brain Circuits Mediate or Control Emotions

Are particular neural circuits for emotions localized in particular regions of the brain? This question has been explored in studies involving either localized brain lesions or electrical stimulation. Brain lesion studies, which focus on clinical observations of humans or on experimentally produced lesions in nonhuman animals, have investigated some dramatic syndromes of emotional change, such as the taming of monkeys following lesions of the temporal lobe. Brain stimulation studies have generated brain maps for various emotional responses, especially those involving aggression.

Brain Lesions Affect Emotions

How does the destruction of brain regions affect the behavior of both humans and animal subjects? In the sections that follow, we will explore this question in some detail.

Decorticate rage. Surgical removal of the neocortex provided the oldest experimental demonstration of brain mechanisms and emotion. Early in the twentieth century, decorticate dogs (dogs from which the cortex has been removed) were shown to respond to routine handling with sudden intense rage—sometimes referred to as *sham rage* because it lacked well-directed attack. Snarling, barking, and growling were provoked by ordinary handling, and this behavior included strong visceral responses. Clearly, emotional behaviors of this type are organized at a subcortical level. These observations suggested that the cerebral cortex helps inhibit emotional responsiveness.

Papez's neural circuit. In 1937, James W. Papez, a neuropathologist, proposed a neural circuit of emotion. Papez (which rhymes with "capes") reached his conclusions from brain autopsies of humans with emotional disorders, including psychiatric patients. He also studied the brains of animal subjects such as rabid dogs. He noted the sites of brain destruction in these cases and concluded that the destruction necessary for impairment of emotional feelings had to do with a set of interconnected pathways involved in function of the visceral system.

According to Papez's model, emotional expressions involve hypothalamic control of visceral organs via a circuit that includes the mammillary bodies of the hypothalamus, the anterior thalamus, the cingulate cortex, the hippocampus, and the fornix. This circuit is schematically depicted with arrows in Figure 15.7. As we'll see later, strong evidence suggests that the amygdala is important for both the experience and the recognition of emotions, especially fear, so the modern notion of emotional circuitry has been expanded to include the amygdala and other regions shown in Figure 15.7. The "visceral brain" structures in this expansion of Papez's original model were collectively named the **limbic system** by Paul MacLean (1949).

Klüver–Bucy syndrome. Neurophysiologists Heinrich Klüver and neurosurgeon Paul Bucy (1938) described an unusual syndrome in primates following temporal lobe surgery. During studies on the cortical mechanisms of perception, they removed large portions of the temporal lobes of monkeys. The behavior of these animals changed dramatically after surgery; the highlight was an extraordinary taming effect. Animals that had been wild and fearful of humans prior to surgery became tame and showed neither fear nor aggression afterward. In addition, they showed strong oral tendencies, ingesting a variety of objects, including some that were inedible. Frequent mounting behavior was observed and was described as hypersexuality.

Because lesions restricted to the cerebral neocortex did not produce these results, deeper regions of the temporal lobe, including sites within the limbic system (see Figure 15.7), were implicated, and more detailed investigation focused on the amygdala. This syndrome has also been observed in humans following a variety of disorders that damage the temporal lobes, including degenerative hereditary disorders (Lanska and Lanska, 1994) and Alzheimer's disease (Forstl et al., 1993).

In many of the earlier studies, attempts to ablate the amygdala injured adjacent structures and interrupted fibers passing through the region, making it difficult to interpret results. A recent study attempted to destroy the amygdala bilaterally without harming adjacent tis-

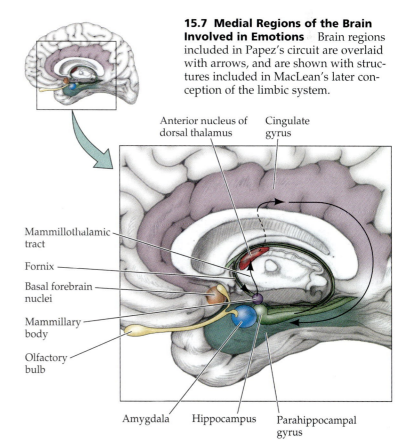

15.7 Medial Regions of the Brain Involved in Emotions Brain regions included in Papez's circuit are overlaid with arrows, and are shown with structures included in MacLean's later conception of the limbic system.

Anterior nucleus of dorsal thalamus

Cingulate gyrus

Mammillothalamic tract

Fornix

Basal forebrain nuclei

Mammillary body

Olfactory bulb

Amygdala   Hippocampus   Parahippocampal gyrus

James Olds
(1922–1976)

Peter Milner

IMPORTANT
METHOD

sue or fibers of passage, and to investigate social interactions in pairs of rhesus monkeys (Emery et al., in press). An individual brain atlas was first prepared for each animal by MRI imaging, and the amygdala was then destroyed by targeted injection of the selective neurotoxin ibotenic acid. Using an established catalog of both social and nonsocial behaviors, the investigators studied the animals both preoperatively and postoperatively. They found that the amygdalectomized monkeys demonstrated increased social affiliation, decreased anxiety, and increased confidence compared to control animals, particularly during early encounters. The amygdala lesions led to a decrease in the usual reluctance of adult monkeys to engage a strange monkey in social behavior.

Electrical Stimulation of the Brain Can Produce Emotional Effects

Another productive approach to understanding the neuroanatomy of emotion is electrical stimulation of sites in the brains of awake, freely moving animals and observation of the effects on behavior. Such stimulation may produce either rewarding or aversive effects or may elicit sequences of emotional behavior.

Positive reinforcement and seeking behavior. In 1954, psychologists James Olds and Peter Milner reported a remarkable experimental finding: Rats could learn to press a lever when the reward or reinforcement was a brief burst of electrical stimulation of the septal area within the limbic system. Another way to describe this phenomenon is **brain self-stimulation.** Heath (1972) reported that patients receiving electrical stimulation in this region feel a sense of pleasure or warmth, and in some instances stimulation in this region provokes sexual excitation.

The report of Olds and Milner (1954) is one of those rare scientific discoveries that starts a new field; many investigators have since employed techniques of brain self-stimulation. Some research has focused on mapping the distribution of brain sites that yield self-stimulation responses (Figure 15.8). Other studies (reviewed by N. M. White and Milner [1992]) have analyzed the similarities and differences between positive responses elicited by brain stimulation and those elicited by other rewarding situations, such as the presentation of food to a hungry animal or water to a thirsty animal. Perhaps electrical stimulation taps into the circuits mediating these more customary rewards.

Research in this area has also moved in a neurochemical direction; many efforts have attempted to identify the relevant transmitters in brain pathways that mediate self-stimulation behavior (P. L. Johnson and Stellar, 1994; Ranaldi and Beninger, 1994; R. A. Wise et al., 1992). As we discussed in Chapter 4, there is a growing belief that drugs of abuse are addictive because they activate these same neural circuits.

Self-stimulation is observed with electrical stimulation of many different subcortical sites and a few frontal cortical regions. Cerebral cortical stimulation in most regions, however, does not have positive reinforcement properties. Positive brain sites are concentrated in the hypothalamus, although these sites also extend into the brainstem. A large tract that ascends from the midbrain to the hypothalamus—the **medial forebrain bundle**—contains many sites that yield strong self-stimulation behavior (see Figure 15.8). This bundle of axons is characterized by widespread origins and an extensive set of brain regions where terminals of these axons can be found. The anatomical arrangements of self-stimulation sites seem similar in different species, although positive sites are spread more extensively in the rat brain than in the cat brain.

Panksepp (2000) has proposed that this system be considered a *seeking system*—a generalized positive appetitive motivation system—because it is activated by various positive incentives, especially when animals are in the early foraging phases of behavior.

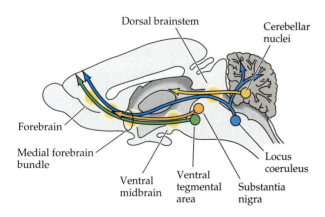

15.8 Self-Stimulation Sites in the Rodent Brain
Animals will work very hard pressing a bar in return for mild electrical stimulation at any of the sites indicated by large, orange circles.

Emotional effects. Electrical stimulation of the brains of alert rats, cats, and monkeys implanted with electrodes has provided maps of the distribution of emotional responses. This work has emphasized limbic system sites and has focused particularly on fear, which we discuss more a little later in the chapter. These maps show that very discrete components of behavioral, autonomic, and hormonal responses are represented at selected sites in the limbic system and the hypothalamic regions. Elicitation of fear responses involves particularly a circuit that includes the central and lateral amygdala, the medial hypothalamus, and the periaqueductal gray.

The Two Cerebral Hemispheres Process Emotion Differently

The fact that the two cerebral hemispheres play different roles in cognitive processes in humans is well established by many experimental and clinical observations (see Chapter 19). Researchers have investigated the possibility that there are hemispheric differences in emotion processing. Differences between the cerebral hemispheres have been explored from several perspectives. One perspective focuses on the special role of the right hemisphere in the perception of emotional states. Another perspective emphasizes the lateralization of emotional expression, especially in facial displays (Fridlund, 1988).

Emotional syndromes. A major theme to emerge from studies of patients who have sustained injury or disease confined to one hemisphere is that the hemispheres differ in emotional tone. Patients who have suffered strokes involving the left anterior cerebral hemisphere have the highest frequency of depressive symptoms; the closer the lesion is to the frontal pole, the more intense is the depressive portrait. In these patients, injury-produced language deficits are not correlated with severity of depression (Starkstein and Robinson, 1994). In contrast, patients with right-hemisphere lesions are described as unduly cheerful and indifferent to their loss. Table 15.1 lists some of the clinical syndromes that include emotional changes following cerebrovascular disorders.

Results of unilateral injections of sodium amytal into a single carotid artery (the Wada test) offer additional data about hemispheric differences in emotion. This procedure, described in Box 19.1, is used to determine the hemisphere that is dominant for language. Generally, injection of sodium amytal into the left hemisphere produces a depressive aftereffect, whereas an identical injection into the carotid artery on the right side elicits smiling and a feeling of euphoria.

Richard J. Davidson (1994) has presented a different view of the role of the cerebral hemispheres in emotion processing. According to this view, anterior regions of the left and right hemispheres are specialized for approach and withdrawal process-

TABLE 15.1 *Some Clinical Syndromes Associated with Cerebrovascular Disease*

Syndrome	Clinical symptoms	Location of associated lesion
Indifference reaction	Undue cheerfulness or joking, denial of illness, loss of interest, and apathy	Right parietal or temporal lobe
Major depression	Depressed mood, daily mood variation, loss of energy, anxiety, restlessness, worry, weight loss, decreased appetite, early morning awakening, delayed sleep onset, social withdrawal, and irritability	Left frontal lobe; left basal ganglia
Pathological laughing and crying	Frequent, usually brief laughing and/or crying; crying that is not caused by sadness, or that is out of proportion to it; social withdrawal secondary to emotional outbursts	Frequently bilateral hemispheric lesions; can occur with almost any lesion location
Mania	Elevated mood, increased energy, increased appetite, decreased sleep, feeling of well-being, pressured speech, flight of ideas, grandiose thoughts	Right basotemporal or right orbitofrontal region

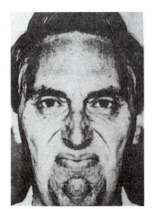

(*a*) Left sides

(*b*) Original

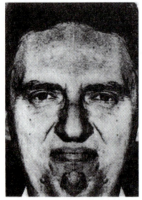

(*c*) Right sides

15.9 Emotions and Facial Asymmetry Composite faces reveal differences between right and left in the level of intensity of emotional expression. Photographs constructed from only the left side of the face (*a*) are judged to be more emotional than either the original face (*b*) or a composite based on just the right side of the face (*c*). (Courtesy of Ruben C. Gur.)

es, respectively. Thus damage to the left frontal region results in a deficit in approach, as evident in the loss of interest and pleasure in other people and the difficulty in initiating behavior. The diminished activation of this area is associated with sadness and depression. In contrast, activation of the right anterior region is associated with withdrawal-related emotions, such as fear and disgust. Deficits in right anterior activation produced by lesions or injury will reduce withdrawal behavior and related negative emotions.

Relevant evidence comes from electrophysiological experiments with humans. For example, in one study by Davidson and colleagues (R. J. Davidson et al., 1990), subjects were presented with film clips while their facial expressions and brain electrical activity were recorded. The film excerpts were intended to produce either disgust or happiness. Disgust was associated with greater electrophysiological activation on the right side; happiness was characterized by similar effects on the left side.

Processing of emotional stimuli. Dichotic listening techniques (see Figure 19.15) have shown that the cerebral hemispheres may function differently in how they recognize emotional stimuli. Ley and Bryden (1982) presented normal subjects with brief sentences spoken in happy, sad, angry, and neutral voices. The sentences were presented through headsets—a different sentence in each ear. Subjects were instructed to attend to one ear and report both the content of the message and its emotional tone.

Subjects showed a distinct left-ear advantage for identifying the *emotional tone* of the voice and a right-ear advantage for understanding the *meaning* of the brief message. Because each ear projects more strongly to the opposite hemisphere (see Chapter 9), these results indicate that the right hemisphere is better than the left in interpreting emotional aspects of vocal messages.

The presentation of different stimuli to each eye has also revealed hemispheric differences in the visual perception of emotional states or stimuli. The stimuli in these studies usually consist of faces displaying different emotional expressions. In a variety of tasks that emphasize either reaction time or identification, the common finding is that emotional stimuli presented to the left visual field (projecting to the right hemisphere) result in faster reaction times and more accurate identification of emotional states (Bryden, 1982). Likewise, in one split-brain patient, in whom the corpus callosum connecting the two hemispheres had been surgically cut (see Chapter 19), the right cerebral hemisphere was much better than the left at discriminating emotional facial expressions (V. E. Stone et al., 1996).

Asymmetry of emotional facial expressions. By cutting a photograph of the face of a person who is displaying an emotion down the exact middle of the face, we can create two new composite photos, one made by combining two left sides (one of which is printed in mirror image) and the other made by combining two right sides of the face. The results reveal that facial expressions are not symmetrical (Figure 15.9). Furthermore, the two photos produced from the same original photo elicit different responses from people looking at them. In several studies, most subjects judged the left-sides photos as more emotional than the right-sides photos.

This composite-photo technique originated in 1902 (Hallervorden, 1902), but the main research has been conducted since the 1970s. A review of 49 experiments on facial asymmetry in emotional expression (Borod et al., 1997) concluded that the right cerebral hemisphere is dominant for the perception of facial expression of emotion, and this is true for both posed and spontaneous faces, for pleasant and unpleasant emotions, and for both sexes and all ages.

The Brain Circuits for Emotions Can Be Traced

We now have findings from a variety of methods used to locate brain regions involved in the emotions and to trace the brain circuits of the emotions. These include electrical stimulation of brain regions, electrical recording, study of the effects of localized brain lesions, noninvasive recording of localized brain activity, localized neuropharmacological stimulation of brain regions, and analysis of neurochemical responses. In many cases these biological techniques are coupled with evocation of emotional responses or reports of emotional experience. Because much research has been done on the emotion of fear, we will treat it in some detail, and then we will briefly summarize similar work done on other emotions.

Fear Is Mediated by Circuitry That Includes the Amygdala

There is nothing subtle about fear. Many animals display similar behavior under conditions that provoke fear, such as danger to one's life posed by either a nonhuman predator or a modern predator that confronts us on a city street. This lack of subtlety and the similarity of fear-related behavior across species may explain why we know much more about the neural circuitry of fear than of any other emotion (LeDoux, 1995). For example, it is very easy to reliably elicit fear by using classical conditioning, in which the person or animal is presented with a stimulus such as light or sound that is paired with a brief aversive stimulus such as mild electrical shock. After several such pairings, the response to the sound or light itself is the typical fear portrait, including freezing and autonomic signs such as cardiac and respiratory changes (Figure 15.10*a*).

NEURAL PLASTICITY

Studies of such fear conditioning have provided a map of the neural circuitry that implicates the **amygdala** as a key structure in the mediation of fear (Figure 15.10). The amygdala is located at the anterior medial portion of each temporal lobe and is composed of about a dozen distinct nuclei, each with a distinctive set of connections. Some of the connections with the rest of the brain include direct projections from sensory cortex. Lesions of the central nucleus of the amygdala prevent blood pressure increases and constrain freezing behavior in response to the conditioned fear stimulus.

Interconnections within the amygdala form an important part of the story. Information about the conditioned stimulus (the sound) reaches the lateral portion of the amygdala first, is then transmitted to two other small subregions of the amygdala (the basolateral and basomedial portions), and then goes to the central nucleus. The central nucleus then transmits information to various brainstem centers to evoke emotional responses (see Figure 15.10*b*): Pathways through the central gray (periaqueductal gray) evoke motor behavior, those through the lateral hypothalamus evoke autonomic responses, and those through the bed nucleus of the stria terminalis evoke hormonal responses.

The data from this type of experiment fit well with observations that humans who experience temporal lobe seizures that include the amygdala commonly report intense fear as a prelude or warning about the immediate prospect of a seizure (J. Engel, 1992). Likewise, stimulation of various sites within the temporal lobe of humans—a procedure performed to identify seizure-provoking sites—elicits fear in some patients (Bancaud et al., 1994). Furthermore, when human subjects are shown a visual cue previously associated with shock, blood flow to the amygdala increases (LaBar et al., 1998). Pictures of fearful faces elicit responses in the amygdala that are visible with functional MRI (see Chapter 2), whereas disgusted faces elicit a different pattern of brain responses that does not include the amygdala (Phillips et al., 1998). Finally, people with bilateral damage to the amygdala rate photos of people showing negative facial expressions to be as trustworthy as photos showing positive emotions (Adolphs et al., 1998), suggesting that the amygdala normally serves to make us wary of people who are in a negative mood.

The role of the amygdala in emotions is more elaborate than mere involvement with fear. Earlier we discussed the Klüver–Bucy syndrome, which is characterized by marked changes in emotional responses. The fact that the change-inducing surgery performed by Klüver and Bucy removed much of the amygdala indicated that this region plays a role in learning the emotional significance of external events, especially social actions (Aggleton, 1993).

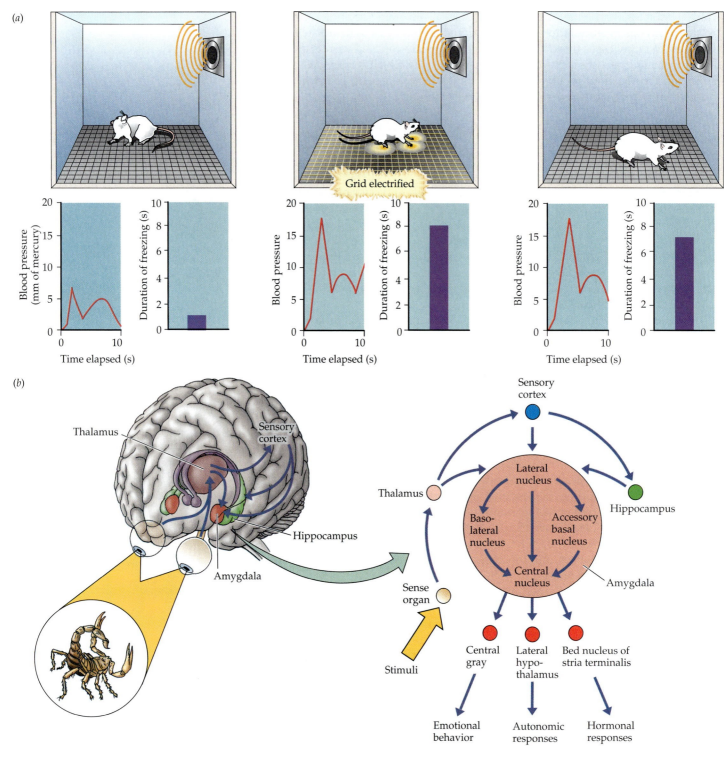

(a)

(b)

15.10 The Circuitry of Fear (*a*) In one classical-conditioning procedure to study fear, a tone is associated with a mild electrical shock, which causes increased blood pressure and "freezing" (*left* and *middle*); eventually the tone alone elicits these responses (*right*). (*b*) Proposed circuitry for the mediation of conditioned fear responses. A fear-inducing stimulus reaches the thalamus and is relayed to the cortex and hippocampus. All three regions project to the lateral nucleus of the amygdala. The information ultimately reaches the amygdala's central nucleus, which projects to three different brain regions, each of which seems to produce a different component of the fear response. (After LeDoux, 1994.)

A case description of a patient without an amygdala illustrates the role of this structure in mediating recognition of emotion in human facial expressions (Adolphs et al., 1994). This patient suffered from a rare medical condition that results in the bilateral loss of the amygdala without damage to the surrounding hippocampus or overlying neocortex. When shown photos of facial expressions that represented six basic emotions—happiness, surprise, fear, disgust, sadness, and anger—she was markedly impaired in the recognition of fear, although she could select faces of people she knew and learn the identity of new faces. In addition, this patient could not appreciate similarities between emotional expressions; for example, she did not evaluate faces showing surprise and happiness as more alike than faces displaying sadness and happiness. Another patient, with partial bilateral removal of the amygdala, showed similar impairments (A. W. Young et al., 1996). The amygdala thus appears important in mediating features of social cognition in which subtle emotional discriminations are significant.

Neural Circuitry Has Also Been Studied for Other Emotions

Considerable progress has been made in identifying the neural circuits of other emotions in addition to fear. Table 15.2 presents some of this information, based on a survey of research on rodent brains (Panksepp, 1998, 2000). Much of this work used well-established techniques such as making localized brain lesions, transecting tracts, electrical stimulation, and electrical recording. Recently some investigators have visualized emotional circuits by seeing where immediate early genes (see Box 2.1) are expressed when an emotion is evoked (e.g., Kollack-Walker et al., 1999; Neophytou et al., 2000). (We saw in Chapter 6 the use of immediate early genes to trace the song circuit in songbirds.) Note in Table 15.2 that there is no one-to-one correspondence between an emotion and a brain region; that is, each emotion involves activity of more than one brain region, and some brain regions are involved in more than one emotion.

**IMPORTANT
METHOD**

Different Emotions Activate Different Regions of the Human Brain

What regions of the human brain are active during different emotions, and what does this information reveal about the emotions? In Chapter 1 we saw that certain regions of the brain are activated when a person looks at a picture of his or her romantic partner (see Figure 1.7) (Bartels and Zeki, 2000). This is one of numerous recent studies of brain responses during emotional experience (e.g., Canli et al., 2001; A. R. Damasio et al., 2000; Lane et al., 1999; Maddock, 1999; Phillips et al., 1998, 2000; Teasdale et al., 1999).

Different techniques have been used both to evoke emotions and to record brain responses. Some investigators evoke emotions by presenting subjects with pictures

---

TABLE 15.2 *Rodent Brain Regions Involved in Some Basic Emotions*

Basic emotion	Key brain areas
Seeking/expectancy	Nucleus accumbens–ventral tegmental area; mesolimbic mesocortical outputs (see Figure 4.3b); lateral hypothalamus–periaqueductal gray
Fear	Central and lateral amygdala to medial hypothalamus and dorsal periaqueductal gray
Panic	Anterior cingulate; bed nucleus of stria terminalis; dorsomedial thalamus; dorsal periaqueductal gray
Happiness/play	Dorsomedial thalamus; parafascicular area; ventral periaqueductal gray

Labeled diagram of a sagittal rodent brain section showing: Anterior cingulate, Nucleus accumbens, Bed nucleus of stria terminalis, Amygdala, Dorsomedial thalamus, Lateral hypothalamus, Ventral tegmental area, Parafascicular area, Periaqueductal gray.

Source: Panksepp, 2000.

or sounds that have been pretested to elicit emotions. Others ask subjects to recall and reexperience episodes from their own lives that involved intense emotion. In some cases, physiological measures as well as ratings are used to quantify the intensity of the emotional experience. Both PET and fMRI recordings have been made. Some studies look at a single emotion, some compare two kinds of emotional responses in the same subjects, but only a few have compared more than two. Here we review the results of a few of these studies.

To determine what brain systems are involved in the overwhelming emotion of romantic love, investigators at University College, London, recruited volunteers who professed to be "truly, deeply, and madly in love" (Bartels and Zeki, 2000). Seventeen subjects were selected by means of written statements and interviews (11 female, 6 male; ages 21–37). Each subject furnished four color photographs, one of his or her boy- or girlfriend and three of friends who were the same sex as the loved partner and were similar in age and length of friendship. Functional MRI brain scans were taken while each subject was shown counterbalanced sequences of the four photographs. Brain activity elicited by viewing of the loved person was compared with that elicited by viewing of friends.

Love, compared with friendship, involved increased activity in the medial insula and anterior cingulate cortex and, subcortically, in the caudate and putamen, all bilaterally (see Figure 1.7). It also led to *reduced* activity in the posterior cingulate and amygdala, and in the right prefrontal, parietal, and middle temporal cortices. This combination of sites differs from those found in previous studies of other emotional states, suggesting that a unique network of brain areas is responsible for the emotion of love. Results were similar for female and male subjects.

A study by Antonio Damasio et al. (2000) seems particularly valuable because it involved a relatively large group of subjects, it attempted to quantify the intensity of emotional experiences, and it compared brain activation during four different kinds of emotion. It started with 53 potential subjects, aged 24 to 42, with no history of neurological or psychiatric disorder. In a screening session, they were asked to recall and attempt to reexperience episodes involving sadness, happiness, anger, and fear, as well as an equally specific but emotionally neutral episode. Measures were taken of skin conductance response (SCR) and heart rate (HR), and subjects rated the intensity of the experience on a scale of 0 to 4. Subjects were retained if they showed, for at least two emotions, at least a 50% increase in SCR, 5% increase in HR, and a rating of at least 3. Each of the 41 retained subjects underwent PET scans for the two emotions for which he or she showed the strongest responses.

IMPORTANT METHOD

During the experimental session, the subject was asked to signal as soon as the desired emotion was experienced. In each case, the physiological responses (SCR and HR) preceded the signal, supporting the idea that at least some physiological responses precede the feeling of emotion. PET images were averaged for all subjects experiencing a given emotion, and activity during the neutral state was subtracted from activity during the emotion.

Each emotion aroused activity in several different brain regions. There was a significant departure from the control level of 43 sites during anger, 42 during sadness, 22 during fear, and 15 during happiness; most sites showed increases in activity, but some showed decreases. The exact numbers of sites are not important because changes at other sites were close to the level of significance, and testing greater numbers of subjects would probably have yielded more sites of significant activity. The four emotions were accompanied by significant differences in patterns of brain activity (Figure 15.11).

Damasio and colleagues note that many, but not all, of their observations are consistent with other studies. One notable exception is the lack of activation of the amygdala during fear and anger, whereas others have reported involvement of the amygdala in these emotions. They note that most other reports show involvement of the amygdala during recognition or induction of an emotion by a visual stimulus, whereas their study emphasized the *feeling* phase. Future work could test whether there is a change from the amygdala to other areas in the transition from induction to feeling of fear or anger.

Antonio Damasio

(a) **Sadness**

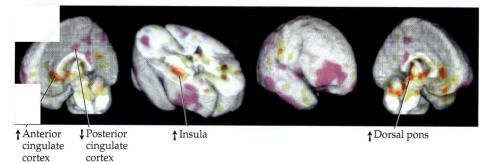

↑Anterior ↓Posterior ↑Insula ↑Dorsal pons
cingulate cingulate
cortex cortex

(b) **Happiness**

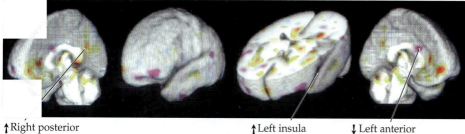

↑Right posterior ↑Left insula ↓Left anterior
cingulate cortex cingulate cortex

(c) **Fear**

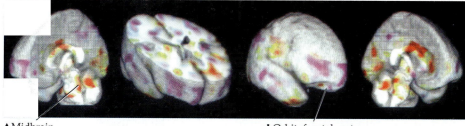

↑Midbrain ↓Orbitofrontal cortex

(d) **Anger**

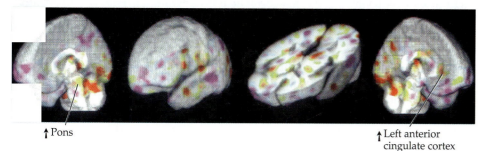

↑Pons ↑Left anterior
cingulate cortex

15.11 Brain Regions Involved in Four Emotions   Red and yellow indicate areas of increased activity; purple indicates areas of decreased activity. For the identified sites, an upward arrow indicates increased activity; a downward arrow, decreased activity. (Courtesy of Antonio Damasio.)

The results of the imaging studies show that there is no simple, one-to-one relation between an emotion and changed activity of a brain region. Each emotion involves altered activity of several brain regions, and the same brain region may participate in more than one emotion. For example, activity of the cingulate cortex is altered in sadness, happiness, and anger; the left secondary somatosensory cortex (S2) is deactivated in both anger and fear. Damasio emphasizes that many of the brain regions activated by emotions are also regions involved in motivational processes and that emotions are part of the mechanisms by which we regulate our lives.

Another group of investigators, noting that findings of brain activity evoked by emotions have not all been consistent, asked whether stable personality traits might modulate brain activation by emotional stimuli (Canli et al., 2001). They studied effects of extraversion and neuroticism on brain responses to emotionally positive and negative pictures. Fourteen healthy female volunteers, 19 to 42 years of age, had fMRI scans taken while they looked at 20 positive and 20 negative pictures from a stan-

15.12 The Effects of Extraversion and Neuroticism on Brain Responses in Emotion (*Upper panels*) Coronal fMRI sections showing regions of activation to positive or negative pictures (*center panels*) in subjects previously tested for extraversion or neuroticism (*bottom panels*). Blue indicates regions where neuroticism scores correlated with brain activation in response to negative pictures. Yellow and red indicate regions where extraversion scores correlated with brain activation in response to positive pictures. (From Canli et al., 2001; courtesy of Turhan Canli.)

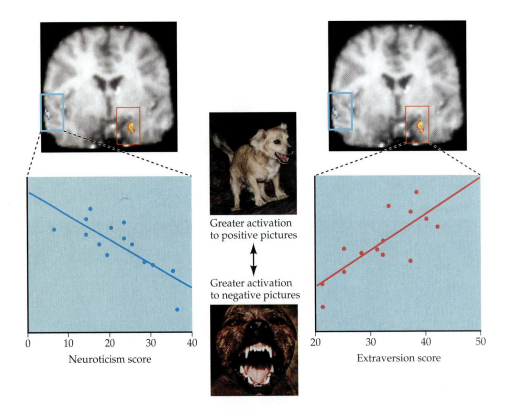

dardized set. They also took a standardized personality questionnaire. Scores for extraversion correlated with the level of brain activation to positive (relative to negative) pictures in several brain regions (Figure 15.12): frontal and temporal cortex, amygdala, caudate, and putamen. Brain activation to negative pictures correlated with neuroticism scores in left frontal and parietal regions; there was a correlation with *decreased* brain activation in the right middle frontal gyrus.

Thus extraversion correlated with level of brain activation in response to positive pictures in several sites but did not correlate with activation in response to negative pictures. In contrast, neuroticism correlated with brain activation in response to negative but not positive pictures. Note that activation in the left frontal cortex is modulated by both extraversion and neuroticism, while activation in other regions is modulated mainly by one or the other personality trait. Thus some of the differences observed among studies of brain responses to emotions may depend on the personalities of the subjects selected.

Although different emotions appear to activate somewhat different patterns of responses, as we saw in Figure 15.11, there is a good deal of overlap among patterns for different emotions. Richard Lane (2000) suggests that four main regions are involved in different aspects of emotional responses:

1. The *rostral anterior cingulate* and *medial prefrontal cortex*, for establishing a representation of the emotional state
2. The *anterior insula*, for processing visceral information
3. The *right temporal pole*, for performing complex sensory discrimination of emotional stimuli and perhaps also retrieving emotion-laden memories
4. The *ventral cingulate cortex*, for regulating autonomic responses

Neural Circuitry, Hormones, and Synaptic Transmitters Mediate Violence and Aggression

Violence, assaults, and homicide exact a high toll in many human societies; for example, homicide is the most prominent cause of death in young adults in the United States. Many different approaches have investigated the psychological, anthropological, and biological dimensions of aggression. These concerted efforts have clarified many aspects of aggression, including its biological bases in hormonal and neurophysiological mechanisms.

What Is Aggression?

Surely we all know aggression. Consideration, however, suggests that this all-too-familiar term has many different meanings. In common usage, the term *aggression* refers to an emotional state that many humans describe as consisting of feelings of hate and a desire to inflict harm. This perspective emphasizes aggression as a powerful inner feeling. However, when we view aggression as an overt response—overt behavior that involves actual or intended destruction of another organism—we see several different forms.

Some investigators view the attack behavior of an animal directed at natural prey as *predatory aggression.* Comparative psychologists such as Stephen Glickman (1977), however, have argued that this behavior is more appropriately designated as *feeding behavior.* Aggression between males of the same species is observed in most vertebrates. The relevance to humans may be the fact that the ratio of males to females arrested on charges of murder in the United States is 5 to 1. Further, aggressive behavior between boys, in contrast to that between girls, is evident early, in the form of vigorous and destructive play behavior.

Some animals display maternal aggression; an extreme form of this behavior is the cannibalism of young by rodent mothers. Animals that are cornered and unable to escape display fear-induced aggression. Finally, one form of aggression is referred to as *irritable aggression;* it can emerge from frustration or pain and frequently has the quality described as uncontrollable rage.

Androgens Seem to Increase Aggression

Male sex hormones play a major role in some forms of aggressive behavior, especially in social encounters between males (Nelson, 1995). One set of data relates levels of circulating androgens to different measures of aggressive behavior. At sexual maturity, intermale aggression markedly increases in many species. T. D. McKinney and Desjardins (1973) have shown changes in aggressiveness in mice that start at puberty, and immature mice treated with androgens display increased aggression. Levels of testosterone change seasonally in many species and seem related to variation in aggression in animals as diverse as birds and primates (Wingfield et al., 1987).

Observations of the behavioral effects of castration give additional evidence for the relation between hormones and aggression. Reductions in the level of circulating androgens produced following castration are commonly associated with a profound reduction in intermale aggressive behavior. Restoring testosterone by injection in castrated animals increases fighting behavior in mice (Figure 15.13).

The aggressive behavior of female mammals can also depend on reproductive hormones. Although the prevailing view among researchers is that males of most mammalian species are typically the more aggressive sex, in some species such dimorphism is not

15.13 The Effects of Androgens on the Aggressive Behavior of Mice
Counts of the number of biting attacks initiated by males before and after castration (*a*) and by females before and after removal of the ovaries (*b*) reveal significantly higher aggression in males before castration. When castrated males are treated with testosterone (*c*), aggressive behavior is reinstated. (From G. C. Wagner et al., 1980.)

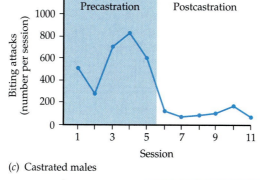

(*a*) Males

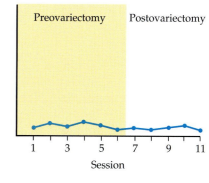

(*b*) Females

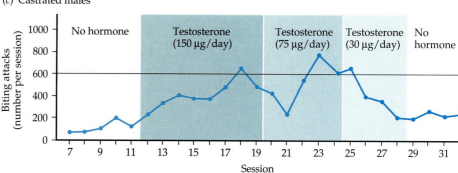

(*c*) Castrated males

evident. For example, female hamsters are generally more aggressive than males, but a female becomes transiently less aggressive when in estrus.

The idea of a relationship between hormones—especially androgens—and human aggression is controversial. Arguments summoned in legal briefs frequently cite the literature on nonhuman animals. Some human studies have shown a positive correlation between testosterone levels and the magnitude of hostility, as measured by behavior rating scales. One study of prisoners (Kreuz and Rose, 1972), however, showed no relation between testosterone levels and several measures of aggressiveness; another study (Ehrenkranz et al., 1974) showed positive relations.

Comprehensive studies of military veterans suggest that testosterone *is* related to antisocial behavior (Dabbs and Morris, 1990). Nonaggressive tendencies in males are associated with satisfaction in family functioning and with low levels of serum testosterone (Julian and McKenry, 1979). Among females, testosterone concentrations are highest in women prisoners convicted of unprovoked violence and lowest among women convicted of defensive violent crimes (Dabbs and Hargrove, 1997; Dabbs et al., 1988).

At least two variables seem to confound the correlations between testosterone and aggression. First is the observation that experience can affect testosterone levels. In mice and monkeys, the loser in aggressive encounters shows reduced androgen levels (Bernstein and Gordon, 1974; Lloyd, 1971), so low levels of testosterone in nonviolent prisoners may be a result, rather than a cause, of their behavior. In men, testosterone levels rise in the winners and fall in the losers after sporting events or chess matches. Even male fans watching a sporting event respond with either an increase or decrease in testosterone levels, depending on whether the team they are rooting for wins or loses, respectively (Bernhardt, 1997).

These observations suggest that a second confounding variable between testosterone and aggression is dominance, since chess players could hardly be said to be aggressive. Robert Sapolsky discusses these and other issues concerning the influence of androgens on aggression in his book *The Trouble with Testosterone* (1997).

Despite the lack of a close relationship between aggression and androgens, people have tried to modify the behavior of male criminals by manipulating sex hormones. Castration studies generally show that violence in sex offenders is reduced by this surgical procedure, especially where "excessive libido" is considered the instigator of sexual assaults (Brain, 1994). The administration of antiandrogen drugs such as cyproterone acetate, which exerts its impact by competing with testosterone for receptor sites, acts as reversible castration.

Several studies on criminals convicted of sexual assault have shown that administration of these substances reduces sexual drive and interest. However, some researchers have suggested that the effects of antiandrogens on aggressive behavior are less predictable than their effects on sexual behavior. Many ethical issues are involved in this approach to the rehabilitation of sex offenders, and the intricacies of such intervention have yet to be worked out.

Serotonin Levels Are Negatively Correlated with Aggression

IMPORTANT METHOD

Aggressive behavior in various animals, including humans, seems especially connected to mechanisms of the synaptic transmitter serotonin. Studies show a negative correlation between brain serotonin activity and aggression. For example, Higley et al. (1992) studied 28 monkeys chosen from more than 4500 monkeys maintained on an island off the coast of South Carolina. These animals roamed freely, and researchers collected observations of aggressive behavior and noted body wounds from fights. Animals were ranked from least to most aggressive by researchers who knew nothing of the animals' neurochemical activity. Data from this study show a significant negative correlation between magnitude of aggression and serotonin activity measured in cerebrospinal fluid.

Many other observations support the view that diminished concentrations of serotonin metabolites, such as 5-HIAA (5-hydroxyindoleacetic acid), are correlated with human aggression and violence. Diminished serotonin activity (as measured by the 5-HIAA concentration in cerebrospinal fluid) is seen in humans who become violent with alcohol use (Virkkunen and Linnoila, 1993), in U.S. Marines expelled for excessive violence (G. L. Brown et al., 1979), in children who torture animals (Kruesi, 1979), and in children whose poor impulse control produces disruptive behavior.

We must caution that serotonin levels are not inflexible quantities that are indifferent to social stimuli and contexts. Quite the contrary. Examining primate groups, Raleigh et al. (1992) showed that low-ranking male primates have low levels of serotonin but that serotonin levels increase with social ascent. When the dominant male loses his high status, his serotonin levels decline.

Further, serotonin is not the "antiaggression" transmitter. Other substances have been implicated in various forms of aggression in both humans and other animals. The list includes noradrenergic and GABA systems, as well as neuropeptides that might act as modulators of aggression. In addition, increased aggression is often seen in knockout mice, no matter which of several genes is deleted (Nelson et al., 1995). Agression must be regulated by many systems.

The Neurology of Human Violence Is a Topic of Controversy

Some forms of human violence are characterized by sudden intense physical assaults. In a controversial book, *Violence and the Brain,* V. H. Mark and Ervin (1970) suggested that some forms of intense human violence are derived from temporal lobe seizure disorders. They offered horrifying examples from newspaper accounts as preliminary evidence. For example, in 1966 Charles Whitman climbed a tower at the University of Texas and murdered, by random shooting, several passing individuals. Earlier he had killed family members, and letters he left behind revealed a portrait of a bewildered young man possessed by an intense need to commit violence. Postmortem analysis of Whitman's brain suggested the presence of a tumor deep in the temporal lobe.

Other, more formal data cited by Mark and Ervin include the occurrence of aggression in temporal lobe seizure patients and the long-controversial claim that a large percentage of habitually aggressive criminals display abnormal EEGs that indicate likely temporal lobe disease. Mark and Ervin argued that temporal lobe disorders may underlie many forms of human violence and produce a disorder they labeled **dyscontrol syndrome.**

They presented several detailed clinical reports of humans with possible temporal lobe seizure disorders who had depth electrodes implanted within the temporal lobe. Electrical stimulation of various sites along the electrode tracks resulted in seizures typical of the patient. Intense assaultive behavior was directly related to elicitation of temporal lobe seizure. In some patients, neurosurgical intervention—the removal of some temporal lobe regions, especially the region of the amygdala—profoundly reduced both seizure activity and reports of assaultive behavior.

Much of the controversy surrounding Mark and Ervin's book has to do with the claim that a large proportion of human violence has this neuropathological origin (Valenstein, 1973). Vigorous controversy is also promoted by the claim that neurosurgery can alleviate forms of violent behavior that many people feel are more readily understood as products of social distress and developmental impairment.

Many other studies have linked violence in humans with some forms of seizure disorders or other clinical neurological pathology (D. O. Lewis, 1990). A high percentage of both juveniles and adults arrested for violent crimes have abnormal EEGs (D. O. Lewis et al., 1979; D. Williams, 1969). Devinsky and Bear (1984) examined a group of patients with seizures involving the limbic system. These patients showed aggressive behavior that occurred after an epileptic focus developed within this system. None of these patients had a history that included traditional sociological factors linked to aggression, such as parental abuse, poverty, or use of drugs. In these patients aggression is an event between seizures; directed aggression is seldom seen during an actual seizure involving the limbic system (Delgado-Escueta et al., 1981).

COMPETING HYPOTHESES

Although the relation of violence and aggression to epilepsy remains controversial, a growing set of clinical observations supports this association in some individuals. Some of these observations are case histories that show an unequivocal link between a seizure and a violent act. For example, studies conducted on a babysitter who had killed the child in her charge in a most violent manner showed that her violent response to the child was elicited during a temporal lobe seizure provoked by the child's laughter—a specific seizure-eliciting stimulus for this person (J. Engel, 1992).

Undoubtedly human violence and aggression stem from many sources. In recent years biological studies of aggression have been vigorously criticized by both politicians and social scientists. These critics argue that emphasizing biological factors such as genetics or brain mechanisms could lead to a failure to focus on the most evident origins of human violence and aggression, as well as to odious forms of biological controls of social dysfunction.

However, violence envelops the behavior of relatively few individuals. Furthermore, it is important to understand the possible roles of biological factors, especially because the quality of life of some violent persons might be significantly improved if biological problems such as diminished serotonin activity are addressed. Treatments that enhance serotonin activity in the brain may be an important addition to a social–environmental or psychotherapeutic intervention (Coccaro and Siever, 1995).

Stress Activates Many Bodily Responses

Hans Selye
(1907–1982)

We all experience stress, but what is it? Attempts to define *stress* have not overcome a certain vagueness implicit in this term. Some researchers emphasize that **stress** is a multidimensional concept that includes the stress stimuli, the processing system including the cognitive assessment of the stimuli, and the stress responses. The early use of the concept *stress* is closely identified with the work of Hans Selye, who popularized the term and defined it in a broad way as "the rate of all the wear and tear caused by life" (Selye, 1956).

In many studies over almost 40 years, Selye described the impact of "stressors" on the responses of different organ systems of the body. He emphasized the connection between stress and disease in his "general adaptation syndrome." According to this scheme, the initial response to stress—called the **alarm reaction**—is followed by a second stage—the **adaptation stage**—which includes the successful activation of the appropriate response systems and the reestablishment of homeostatic balance. If stress is prolonged or frequently repeated, the **exhaustion phase** sets in, and it is characterized by increased susceptibility to disease.

In contemporary studies, this concept of stress and disease has been modified; some investigators note that the common ingredient to stressful stimuli is uncertainty or unpredictability about how to gain positive outcomes in response to these stimuli (S. Levine and Ursin, 1980). This model, which considers a broad array of factors relevant to stress and disease, including the roles of coping strategies and learning, emphasizes that stress per se does not inevitably lead to dysfunction or illness, and it helps account for the variability in health histories of humans exposed to similar stressful life experiences.

Laboratory studies of human stress have used painful stimuli, such as exposure to electrical shock or immersion of the hand in ice-cold water, to induce stress. Researchers have frequently criticized the artificiality of such laboratory studies. Placing a hand in a bucket of ice cubes certainly pales in comparison to dangerous situations that threaten life or produce psychological trauma. Some researchers have sought to explore the biology of stress by studying real-life stress situations in military training, especially aviation training and parachute training, in which stress involves fear of bodily harm and fear of failure.

Ursin et al. (1978) studied a group of young recruits in the Norwegian military both before and during the early phase of parachute training, using a variety of psychological and physiological measures. In the training period, subjects were propelled down a long sloping wire suspended from a tower 12 m high. This parachute training evokes an experience somewhat like that of free fall. Initial apprehension is high, and at first the sense of danger is acute, although recruits know that they are not likely to lose their lives in this part of the training.

On each jump day in this study, samples of blood revealed activation of tropic hormones from the anterior pituitary and of both the sympathetic and parasympathetic systems (Figure 15.14). Under stressful conditions the hypothalamus produces corticotropin-releasing hormone (CRH), which, as we saw in Chapter 5 (see Table 5.3), causes the release of adrenocorticotropic hormone (ACTH) from the anterior pituitary. ACTH causes the release of corticosteroid hormones such as cortisol from the adrenal cortex.

Initially, cortisol levels were elevated in the blood, but successful jumps during training quickly led to a decrease in the pituitary–adrenal response. On the first jump, testosterone levels in the plasma fell below those of controls, but these levels returned to normal with subsequent jumps. Other substances that showed marked

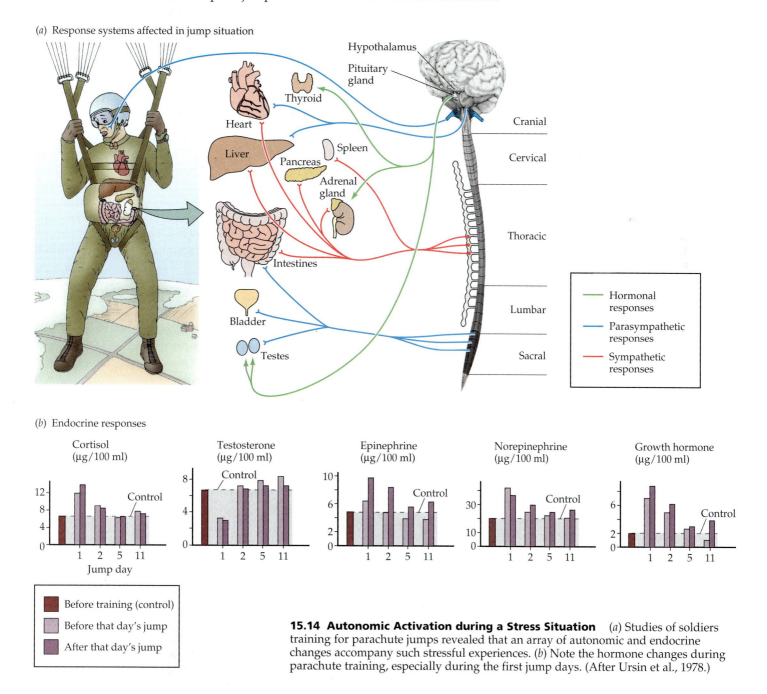

(a) Response systems affected in jump situation

(b) Endocrine responses

Jump day

Before training (control)

Before that day's jump

After that day's jump

15.14 Autonomic Activation during a Stress Situation   (a) Studies of soldiers training for parachute jumps revealed that an array of autonomic and endocrine changes accompany such stressful experiences. (b) Note the hormone changes during parachute training, especially during the first jump days. (After Ursin et al., 1978.)

(a)

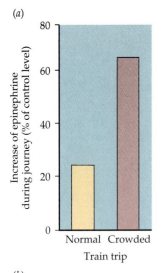

(b)

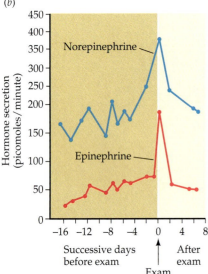

15.15 Hormone Changes in Humans in Response to Social Stresses
(a) Small changes in crowding on a morning commuter train ride affect hormone levels in humans. A 10% increase in the number of passengers during a period of gasoline rationing (*right*) resulted in a much higher increase in epinephrine secretion. (b) Levels of epinephrine and norepinephrine in a graduate student during a 2-week period before, during, and after a thesis exam reflect levels of stress. (After Frankenhaeuser, 1978.)

increases in concentration at the initial jump included growth hormone, which is also controlled by a tropic hormone from the anterior pituitary, and epinephrine and norepinephrine from the adrenal medulla (see Figure 15.14b), whose release is mediated by the sympathetic nervous system.

Less dramatic real-life situations also evoke clear endocrine responses, as shown by the research of Frankenhaeuser (1978). For example, riding in a commuter train was found to provoke the release of epinephrine; the longer the ride and the more crowded the train, the greater the hormonal response (Figure 15.15a). Factory work also leads to the release of epinephrine; the shorter the work cycle—that is, the more frequently the person has to repeat the same operations—the higher the levels of epinephrine. The stress of a Ph.D. oral exam was shown to lead to a dramatic increase in both epinephrine and norepinephrine (Figure 15.15b).

Stress experienced by animals in the wild has become an interesting area of study for investigators who are trying to understand the stress response of humans. Robert Sapolsky (2001) studied baboons living freely in a natural reserve in Kenya. At first appearance, these animals seem to have a good life; food is abundant, predators are rare. The stresses they experience are the impacts they exert on each other. For males, this stress is the vigorous competition that surrounds courtship and the establishment of dominance hierarchies. An animal's place in the dominance hierarchy influences the physiology of the stress response, as seen in the animal's response to anesthesia produced by a dart gun syringe. In general, the testosterone levels of dominant males recover more rapidly after a stressful event than do those of subordinate males. Likewise, the subordinates display a more prolonged increase in levels of circulating cortisol.

Why do individuals differ in their response to stress? One hypothesis focused on early experience. Rat pups clearly find it stressful to have a human experimenter pick them up and handle them. Yet Seymour Levine et al. (1967) found that rats that had been handled as pups were less susceptible to adult stress than rats that had been left alone as pups. For example, the previously handled rats secreted less corticosteroid in response to a wide variety of adult stressors. This effect was termed **stress immunization** because a little stress early in life seemed to make the animals more resilient to later stress.

A follow-up study has suggested that there is more to the story. When pups are returned to their mother after a separation, she spends considerable time licking and grooming them. In fact, she will lick the pups much longer if they were handled by humans during the separation. Michael Meaney and colleagues suggest that this gentle tactile stimulation is crucial for the stress immunization effect. They found that, even among undisturbed litters, the offspring of mother rats that exhibited more licking and grooming behavior were more resilient in their response to adult stress than other rats were (D. Liu et al., 1997).

Stress and Emotions Are Related to Some Human Diseases

During the past 50 years, many psychiatrists and psychologists have strongly emphasized the role of psychological factors in disease. The field that developed out of this interest came to be known as **psychosomatic medicine** after an eminent psychoanalyst, Thomas French, suggested that particular diseases arise from distinctive sets of psychological characteristics or personality conflicts.

From this perspective, ulcers are related to frustration of oral needs and the development of oral dependency, hypertension is seen as arising from hostile competitive activities, and migraine headaches represent repressed hostile needs or impulses. Each disease state or illness is thought to be associated with a specific set of psychological characteristics—those that generate some form of unresolved conflict. Although these ideas were prominent in the early development of psychosomatic medicine, current views make fewer claims for highly particular associations. Instead they emphasize that emotional responsiveness is only one factor among many that determine the onset, maintenance, and treatment of body disorders.

Emotional stimuli activate a diversity of neural and hormonal changes that influence pathological processes of body organs. Studies in psychosomatic medicine have broadened in scope and now range from evaluating emotions, stress, and sickness on a global scale to unraveling particular relations between emotions and bodily responses or conditions. A field called **health psychology** (or behavioral medicine) has developed from this interest (Baum and Posluszny, 1999; Schwartzer and Gutiérrez-Doña, 2000). Figure 15.16 shows how several factors that affect human health and disease interact.

One global approach to linking stress and human disease is to study the covariation between precisely defined stressful life events and the incidence of particular diseases over a long period of time. Although many methodological problems complicate this approach, some consistent relations between stressful events and illness have been found (Adler and Matthews, 1994). For example, men who report frequent and severe stress in a period of 1 to 5 years prior to interviews are more likely to experience heart disease during a 12-year period following the interview than those who report little stress (Rosengren et al., 1991).

A study of naval shipboard personnel by Rahe et al. (1972) provides another example. Navy personnel were asked to report major life events associated with stress (such as death of family members or divorce) and a history of illness for a 10-year period. Results showed that subjects who reported few stressful events for a particular period had had few episodes of illness in the following year. In contrast, subjects who had experienced many stressful events reported a much higher level of illness in the following year. However, some other studies fail to find this association between stressful life events and subsequent disease (Hollis et al., 1990). The social network within which stress occurs may be a more important determinant of disease outcome than is stress itself (Adler and Matthews, 1994).

Mere frequency of stressful life events may be less related to serious illness than was emphasized in earlier studies. In a study of stressful events and heart attack, Byrne and Whyte (1980) compared a group of coronary patients with a control group of people who were admitted to emergency rooms with suspected heart difficulties but who were rapidly diagnosed as not being heart attack cases. Patients who had had heart attacks reported neither a higher frequency nor a greater intensity of stressful events than did the controls. However, these patients were significantly more *distressed* by stressful life events and tended to be more anxious. The emotional impact of stress thus appears to have greater significance for future serious illness than does the mere occurrence of stressful events.

As well as retrospective studies, investigators are now conducting experiments on relations among stress, the immune system, and health. For example, one experiment considered the effects of university examinations on wound healing in dental students (Marucha et al., 1998). Two small wounds were placed on the hard palate of 11 dental students. The first was timed during summer vacation; the second was placed on the contralateral side 3 days before the first major examination of the term. Two independent daily measures showed that no student healed as rapidly during the exam period, and overall the healing took 40% longer. A measure of immunological response declined 68% during the exam period. The experimenters conclude that even something as transient, predictable, and relatively benign as examination stress (do students agree with this description?) can have significant consequences for wound healing.

Emotions and Stress Influence the Immune System

For a long while, researchers viewed the immune system as an automatic mechanism: A pathogen, such as a virus, arrived on the scene, and soon the defense mech-

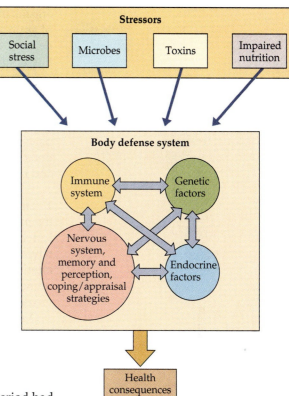

15.16 Factors That Interact during the Development and Progression of Disease

IMPORTANT METHOD

anisms of the immune system went to work, usually prevailing with their armory of antibodies and other immunological devices. Few investigators thought of the nervous system as having an important role in this process, although the notion that the mind can influence well-being has been a persistent theme in human history.

In the 1980s a new field, **psychoneuroimmunology,** appeared; its existence signals a new awareness that the immune system—with its collection of cells that recognize intruders—interacts with other organs, especially hormone systems and the nervous system. Studies of both human and nonhuman subjects now clearly show psychological and neurological influences on the immune system. These interactions go in both directions: The brain influences responses of the immune system, and immune cells and their products affect brain activities.

The immune system.   To understand this intriguing story, we need to note some of the main features of the immune system. There are two basic types of immunological responses, mediated by two different classes of cells called *lymphocytes.* **B lymphocytes** (or B cells), which form in the bone marrow, mediate **humoral immunity**—a reponse in which these cells produce proteins called antibodies, or immunoglobulins, that either directly neutralize antigens (foreign molecules) such as viruses or bacteria or enhance destruction of antigens by other cells.

A second type of immunological response, **cell-mediated immunity,** is mediated by **T lymphocytes** (T cells), so called because they form in the thymus gland. These cells directly attack various antigens. They act as *killer cells,* forming a strong part of the body's attack against substances that can cause tumors. T cells are also involved in the rejection of organ transplants. In addition, T cells interact with humoral reactions mediated by B cells. In some of these interactions antibody reactions are enhanced, and this response requires special T lymphocytes called *helper T cells.* Other T lymphocytes suppress humoral reactions and are referred to as *suppressor T cells.*

These basic components of the immune system also interact with other body substances and cells in defending the body against disease and harmful substances. The organs of the body where these immune system cells form and reside include the thymus gland, bone marrow, spleen, and lymph nodes (Figure 15.17).

Communication among the nervous, immune, and endocrine systems.   The potential for interactions between the brain and the immune system is revealed in many anatomical and physiological studies (e.g., Ader and Cohen, 1993; Ader et al., 1990; Felten et al., 1993). The nervous system influences the immune system either through the autonomic nervous system or through the hypothalamic–pituitary–neuroendocrine system. Anatomical studies have noted the presence of nerve fibers from the autonomic nervous system in immune system organs such as the spleen and thymus gland. Within these organs, nerve endings are found among groups of lymphocytes. These fibers are usually noradrenergic, sympathetic postganglionic axons, but the potential impact of their activity is still mysterious.

Other transmitters are also found in immune system tissues, including various neuropeptides. Receptors for neurotransmitters have been found on lymphocytes; these substances probably exert their effects via a second-messenger system. Noradrenergic innervation is claimed to affect antibody production and immune cell proliferation, as well as other aspects of the immune system (D. L. Bellinger et al., 1992). The same cells are also affected by the hormones released through the hypothalamic–pituitary–neuroendocrine system, by either enhancement or depression of various immune cell functions (Haas and Schauenstein, 1997).

The reciprocal character of relations between the immune system and the brain is also seen in other studies that show the effects of antibodies on the firing rates of brain neurons, especially in regions within the hypothalamus (Besedovsky and del Rey, 1992; Besedovsky et al., 1985). Other immune system products, such as the hormones interferon and the interleukins, also affect brain activity. For example, a local painful inflammation causes an increase in a type of interleukin in the cere-

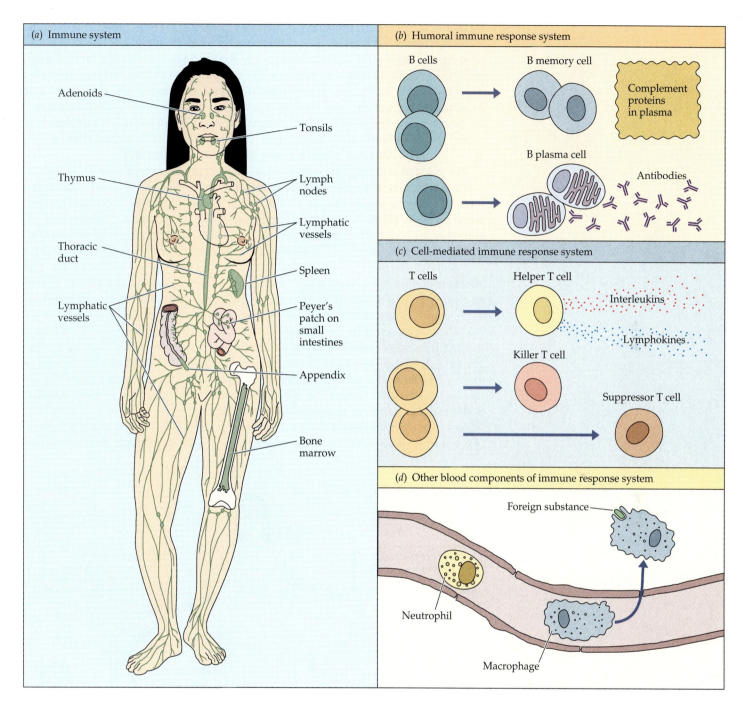

(a) Immune system

Adenoids

Tonsils

Thymus

Lymph nodes

Thoracic duct

Lymphatic vessels

Spleen

Lymphatic vessels

Peyer's patch on small intestines

Appendix

Bone marrow

(b) Humoral immune response system

B cells

B memory cell

Complement proteins in plasma

B plasma cell

Antibodies

(c) Cell-mediated immune response system

T cells

Helper T cell

Interleukins

Lymphokines

Killer T cell

Suppressor T cell

(d) Other blood components of immune response system

Foreign substance

Neutrophil

Macrophage

brospinal fluid; this in turn causes release of a prostaglandin into the brain, causing hypersensitivity to pain elsewhere in the body (Bartfai, 2001; Samad et al., 2001).

Thus the brain seems to be directly informed about the actions of the immune system. In fact, it has been suggested that "the immune system serves as a sensory organ for stimuli not recognized by the classical sensory system" (Blalock, 1984) or as a kind of sensory receptor system (Besedovsky and del Rey, 1992).

Another way to show the role of the brain in immune system responsiveness is to examine the effects of brain lesions on immune responses. Lesions of the hypothalamus in experimental animals can influence immune processes such as antibody production (M. Stein et al., 1981). Some of these effects are quite specialized, involving responses to some antigens but not others. Furthermore, the specific hypothalamic site of the lesion also determines the character of immune effects. Some

15.17 Main Components of the Human Immune System (a) The various components of the immune system protect us via three classes of cells: B lymphocytes (b) produce antibodies to attack invading microbes. T lymphocytes (c) release hormones to stimulate B cells to divide. T cells also form killer cells that, together with macrophages (d), directly attack foreign tissues or microbes. (Neutrophils are a type of white blood cell.)

ways in which the hypothalamus influences immune system processes involve neuroendocrine mechanisms mediated through the pituitary gland.

Reciprocal communication holds true also for the relations between the endocrine and the nervous and immune systems. Some examples of these relationships are shown in Figure 15.18. Not only do these three systems interact, but they may share a common origin. It has long been proposed that the endocrine system originated from neurosecretory cells (Turner and Bagnara, 1976). More recently it has been suggested that immune system messengers are similar to hormones and that the two systems share a common origin (Ottaviani and Franceschi, 1997).

One piece of evidence that suggests this connection is that mollusks produce cells that engulf and remove foreign substances, and these cells contain both ACTH and interleukins—molecules that are characteristic of the vertebrate endocrine and immune systems, respectively. Such observations make it hard to maintain distinctions among neurotransmitters, hormones, and lymphokines (messenger molecules such as the interleukins used by the immune system) (Ottavani and Franceschi, 1997).

Immunosuppression as a defense mechanism. Under stressful conditions, as noted earlier, a chain of processes starting with the production of corticotropin-releasing hormone causes the release of corticosteroid hormones from the adrenal cortex. One effect of these hormones is to suppress immunological responses by inhibiting the proliferation of some lymphocytes and triggering the death of others. You might ask why, during times of stress, the brain causes adrenal steroids to be released, if these steroids suppress the immune system. In a delightful book entitled *Why Zebras Don't Get Ulcers,* Robert Sapolsky (1994) considers a variety of evolutionary hypotheses about why immunity is suppressed during stress.

To the extent that stress might be a sudden emergency, the temporary suppression of immune responses makes some sense because the stress response demands a rap-

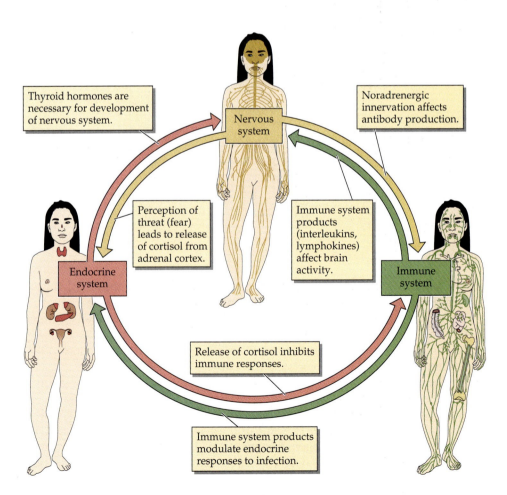

15.18 Examples of Reciprocal Relations among the Nervous, Endocrine, and Immune Systems

Thyroid hormones are necessary for development of nervous system.

Noradrenergic innervation affects antibody production.

Perception of threat (fear) leads to release of cortisol from adrenal cortex.

Immune system products (interleukins, lymphokines) affect brain activity.

Release of cortisol inhibits immune responses.

Immune system products modulate endocrine responses to infection.

Nervous system

Endocrine system

Immune system

id mobilization of energy; immune responses extend longer than the immediacy of a demanding situation would require. A zebra wounded by a lion must first escape and hide, and only then does infection of the wound pose a threat. So the stress of the encounter first suppresses the immune system, saving resources until a safe haven is found. Later the animal can afford to mobilize the immune system to heal the wound. The adrenal steroids also suppress swelling (inflammation) of injuries, especially of joints, to help the animal remain mobile long enough to find refuge.

Robert Sapolsky

In the wild, animals are under stress for only a short while; an animal stressed for a prolonged period dies. So natural selection favored stress reactions as a drastic effort to deal with a short-term problem. What makes humans unique is that, with our highly social lives and keen analytical minds, we are capable of experiencing stress for prolonged periods—months or even years. The bodily reactions to stress, which evolved to deal with short-term problems, become a handicap when extended too long (Sapolsky, 1994). For example, only long-term stress, lasting over a month, affects the probability that a person will catch a cold (S. Cohen et al., 1998). Sapolsky has compiled a list of stress responses that are beneficial in the short term but detrimental in the long term (Table 15.3).

Psychological stress and immunity. The anatomical and physiological data described in the previous section suggest some bases for the role of psychological factors in immune system responses. How can we determine whether psychological factors such as emotions and stress affect either susceptibility or responses to infectious diseases? One approach is to examine unusual immunological responses or disease history in emotionally disturbed populations. For example, several lines of evidence suggest that the competence of the immune system is decreased during depression (M. Stein et al., 1991). Such a compromise of the immune system would increase susceptibility to infectious diseases, cancer, and autoimmune disorders. Altered immune function is also observed in people who are grieving the death of a relative, especially a spouse (M. Stein and Miller, 1993).

**CLINICAL
ISSUE**

Psychological factors have been related to the susceptibility to and progression of many infectious diseases (Kiecolt-Glaser and Glaser, 1995). For example, the relation between academic stress and immunological functioning has been examined in several studies of medical or dental students during exam periods (which presumably are accompanied by high levels of stress) and in subsequent periods of no exams or low levels of stress.

Stressful exam periods usually produce a decline in natural killer cell activity (Glaser et al., 1986) and γ-interferon, a glycoprotein that helps regulate the immune system. Of most importance, some studies have noted that the student's *perception* of the stress of the academic program is a predictor of the level of circulating anti-

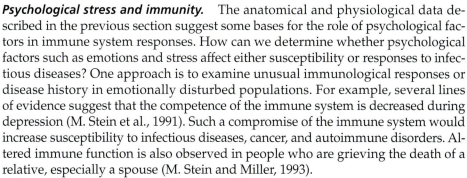

TABLE 15.3 *The Stress Response and Consequences of Prolonged Stress*

Principal components of the stress response	Common pathological consequences of prolonged stress
Mobilization of energy at the cost of energy storage	Fatigue, muscle wasting, steroid diabetes
Increased cardiovascular and cardiopulmonary tone	Hypertension (high blood pressure)
Suppression of digestion	Ulcers
Suppression of growth	Psychogenic dwarfism, bone decalcification
Suppression of reproduction	Suppression of ovulation, impotency, loss of libido
Suppression of immunity and of inflammatory response Analgesia	Impaired disease resistance
Neural responses, including altered cognition and sensory thresholds	Accelerated neural degeneration during aging

Source: Sapolsky, 1992.

body: Those who perceived the program as stressful showed the lowest levels. Observations of immune function during marital disruption, such as separation and divorce, show decreases in immune function, as well as increased mortality rates (Kielcolt-Glaser and Glaser, 1995).

Studies of nonhumans allow more precise intervention and yield intriguing data. For example, Ader (1987) was able to condition immunosuppression in rats. This result was demonstrated in studies in which saccharin solution was paired with administration of a chemical immunosuppressive drug. Continued pairings of this type led to the ability of saccharin alone to reduce the response to pathogens.

In complementary experiments, Spector (1987) found that classical-conditioning techniques can enhance the activity of natural killer cells. He exposed mice to the odor of camphor for several hours. This treatment by itself had no impact on the immune system. Some mice were then injected with a chemical that increased the activity of natural killer cells, and this injection was paired with presentation of the camphor odor. After the tenth session of pairings of odor and chemical, mice presented with the odor of camphor alone showed a large increase in natural killer cell activity. These studies indicate that the brain can learn to associate certain conditions with infection and can mobilize the immune system in anticipation.

Another connection between the nervous and immune systems was described in Chapter 14, where we learned that sleep deprivation impairs the responsiveness of the immune system.

Emotions and Stress Influence Cardiac Disease

Each day several thousand Americans suffer heart attacks, and many more suffer from other vascular disorders. About one-half of all cardiac-related deaths occur within a few minutes of the onset of symptoms. For many of these individuals, death appears to be caused by the influence of the nervous system on mechanisms that control rhythms of the heart. Common views of causes of heart attacks emphasize the role of emotions. Many an excited person has heard the admonition, "Calm down before you blow a fuse!"

CLINICAL ISSUE

M. Friedman and Rosenman (1974) focused on differences between two behavior patterns—type A and type B—in the development and maintenance of heart disease. Type A behavior is characterized by excessive competitive drive, impatience, hostility, and accelerated speech and movements; in short, life is hectic and demanding for such individuals. In contrast, type B behavior patterns are more relaxed, with little evidence of aggressive drive or emphasis on getting things done fast. Of course, this is a crude dichotomy; many individuals have some of each pattern in their characteristic style. For many years research seemed to indicate that type A individuals show a substantially higher incidence and prevalence of coronary heart disease than do type B individuals. However, studies since 1985 have cast doubt on this association, and some researchers have suggested that the type A concept is too broad (Steptoe, 1993).

A strong association between hostility and heart disease has been noted in these studies (Almada et al., 1991). Excessive expression of hostility may also be related to social isolation, which has been implicated as a risk factor for heart disease in several studies. For example, men who are socially isolated and have experienced significant recent life stress, such as family separation, have a much higher mortality rate than do socially integrated controls (Ruberman et al., 1984). In normal young subjects, the presence of a friend during a demanding task lessens the magnitude of cardiovascular responses to this type of stress.

Comparing two different primate species, Hennessy et al. (1995) showed a possible relation between species-characteristic response patterns and disease. They noted that squirrel monkeys are excitable, restless, and frequently on the move. In contrast, titi monkeys are more low-key. At rest, the squirrel monkey shows a much higher heart rate and higher levels of the hormone cortisol in blood than does the titi monkey. Long-term studies of these animals have revealed that squirrel monkeys are susceptible to heart disease, while titi monkeys, in contrast, are more prone to disorders of the immune system. These and other studies show the role of CNS influences and hormones on cardiac arrhythmias (Bohus and Koolhaas, 1993).

Summary

1. The term *emotion* includes private subjective feelings, as well as expressions or displays of particular somatic and autonomic responses. The four main aspects of emotions are feelings, actions, physiological arousal, and motivational programs. Psychologists have generated different categorization systems to account for the varieties of emotions.

2. Whereas the James–Lange theory considered emotions to be the perceptions of stimulus-induced bodily changes, the Cannon–Bard theory emphasized the integration of emotional experiences and responses in the brain. A cognitive theory of emotions argues that activity in a physiological system is not enough to provoke an emotion; rather, the key feature in emotion is the interpretation of visceral activities.

3. Distinct facial expressions represent anger, contempt, happiness, sadness, disgust, fear, surprise, and embarrassment, and these expressions are interpreted similarly across many cultures. Facial expressions are controlled by distinct sets of facial muscles that in turn are controlled by the facial and trigeminal nerves.

4. Studies of brain lesions have revealed that particular brain circuits and interconnected regions mediate and control emotions. Relevant regions include limbic system sites described in Papez's neural circuit and other related regions, including the amygdala.

5. Emotions may have evolved as coordinated motivational programs that are useful in solving specific adaptive problems.

6. Electrical stimulation of some brain regions is rewarding.

7. The left and right cerebral hemispheres process emotions differently. In normal people, the right hemisphere is better at interpreting emotional states or stimuli.

8. Fear is mediated by circuitry that involves the amygdala, which is directly connected to cortical sensory regions.

9. Aggressive behavior is increased by androgens. Brain regions of the limbic system and related sites differ in their relationship to aggressive behavior; stimulation of some regions elicits a full, species-typical pattern of aggression. Serotonin levels are negatively correlated with aggression.

10. Assessment of stress in real-life situations shows that stress elevates the levels of several hormones, including cortisol, epinephrine, and norepinephrine, and suppresses other hormones, such as testosterone.

11. Stress affects human health and influences the outcome of disease. Incidence of illness tends to be higher in people who sustain prolonged stress, although constitutional factors, as well as strategies for coping with stress, are also important. The nervous system and immune system interact to monitor and maintain health.

12. Reciprocal relations are found among the nervous, endocrine, and immune systems.

 Refer to the *Learning Biological Psychology* CD for the following study aids for this chapter:

6 Objectives

68 Study Questions

2 Activities

Recommended Reading

Frijda, N. H. (2000). Emotions. In K. Pawlik and M. R. Rosenzweig (Eds.), *International handbook of psychology* (pp. 207–222). London: Sage.

LeDoux, J. (1995). *The emotional brain.* New York: Simon and Schuster.

Lewis, M., and Haviland-Jones, J. M. (Eds.). (2000). *Handbook of emotions* (2nd ed.). New York: Guilford.

Panksepp, J. (1998). *Affective neuroscience.* New York: Oxford University Press.

Russell, J. A., and Fernandez-Dols, J. M. (Eds.). (1997). *The psychology of facial expression.* Cambridge, England: Cambridge University Press.

Sapolsky R. (1997). *The trouble with testosterone: And other essays on the biology of the human predicament.* New York: Scribner.

Stanford, S. C., and Gray, J. A. (Eds.). (1993). *Stress—From synapse to syndrome.* San Diego, CA: Academic Press.

Stoff, D. M., and Cairns, R. B. (Eds.). (1996). *Aggression and violence: Genetic, neurobiological, and biosocial perspectives.* Mahwah, NJ: Erlbaum.

16

Psychopathology: Biological Bases of Behavior Disorders

The need to find out more about neurological and psychiatric disorders is urgent because they are responsible for some of the more poignant aspects of human debility. They frequently envelop all aspects of an person's existence, and in some instances they rob an individual of the precious sense of personal identity. Most importantly, people afflicted with these disorders are not an exotic few. Surveys show that at least 50 million to 75 million persons in the United States alone suffer from neurological and psychiatric diseases.

On the optimistic side, in a relatively short time the marriage of neurosciences and psychiatry has yielded new insights into disorders such as schizophrenia, anxiety, epilepsy, and other afflictions that have traveled along with human history. We have had an explosion of information about the "broken brain" that gives us the hope that some long-standing mysteries, such as the nature of schizophrenia, are going to be solved and that effective treatments will be based on genuine psychobiological understanding of causes, processes, and mechanisms.

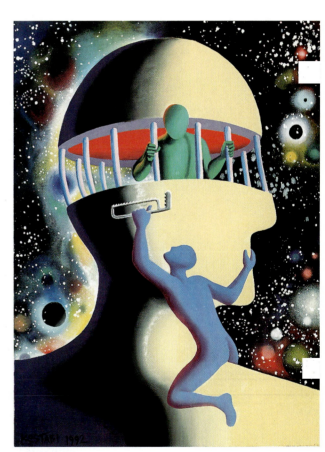

Mark Kostabi, *Mindscape*, 1992

Our aim in this chapter is to focus on some of the advances in this field that promise successful understanding of psychiatric disorders and the ability to treat them. Although no single remedy has been found that cures all who suffer from any of these disorders, recent discoveries have restored millions of people to normal life.

The Toll of Psychiatric Disorders Is Huge

Since the beginning of the twentieth century, the mental health movement has supported large-scale studies that try to determine the number and distribution of psychiatric cases. How many and who among us are or have been psychiatrically ill? All epidemiological studies depend on the clarity of a diagnosis. In psychiatric epidemiology these problems become particularly pressing because there has been much argument about the definition of different psychiatric disorders.

The prevalence of various disorders for the average 6-month period and lifetime, as estimated by one large study sponsored by the National Institutes of Mental Health (NIH) (Robins and Regier, 1991), is given in Table 16.1. About one-third of the U.S. population at some point in life reports symptoms that match the defining features of a major psychiatric disorder. Total rates for mental disorders in men and women are comparable, although the proportions of disorders are slightly different for the two sexes. Depression is far more prevalent in females, and drug dependency and alcoholism are more frequent in males. Certain psychiatric disorders—for example, drug abuse and schizophrenia—tend to appear relatively early in life. The age range 25 to 44 shows peaks for depression and antisocial personality, whereas cognitive impairment occurs especially in people older than 65.

Another study (Kessler et al., 1994) offers an even graver portrait: Almost half the population in this study reported at least one lifetime psychiatric disorder; 30% reported at least one disorder in the previous 12-month period.

Clearly, mental disorders exact an enormous toll on our lives. Efforts to understand these disorders depend on research in diverse areas ranging from cell biology to sociology. Some seeds for a biological perspective in psychiatry were sown at about the beginning of the twentieth century. At that time, one widely prevalent psychosis accounted for 20 to 25% of the patient population in mental hospitals. Descriptions of these patients emphasized profound delusions, grandiosity and euphoria, poor judgment, impulsive and capricious behavior, and profound changes in thought structure. This disorder was known in all societies of the world and had been noted for centuries. Many people regarded it as a psychosis derived from the stresses and strains of personal and social interactions.

TABLE 16.1 *Standardized Six-Month and Lifetime Prevalence of DIS[a]/DSM-IV Disorders in Persons 18 Years and Older*

Disorders	Rate (%)	
	Previous 6 months	Lifetime
Any psychiatric disorder covered	19.1	32.2
Substance use disorders	6.0	16.4
Alcohol abuse or dependence	4.7	13.3
Drug abuse or dependence	2.0	5.9
Schizophrenia	0.9	1.5
Affective disorders	5.8	8.3
Manic episode	0.5	0.8
Major depressive episode	3.0	5.8
Minor depression	—	3.3
Anxiety disorders	8.9	14.6
Phobia	7.7	12.5
Panic	0.8	1.6
Obsessive–compulsive disorder	1.5	2.5

Note: The rates are standardized to the age, sex, and race distribution of the 1980 noninstitutionalized population of the United States aged 18 years and older.

[a]Diagnostic Interview Schedule

Then, in 1911, the microbiologist Hideyo Noguchi discovered the cause of this profound psychosis. Examining the brains of patients during autopsy, he established that extensive brain changes were wrought by *Treponema pallidum*, a bacterium of the class Spirochaeta. This psychosis was produced by syphilis, a venereal infection that has journeyed through history with humans and has appeared in almost all cultures. The later discovery of antibiotics that would cure syphilis and prevent this type of psychosis encouraged the development of biological psychiatry and the attempt to find drugs to combat other forms of psychopathology.

Schizophrenia Is the Major Neurobiological Challenge in Psychiatry

Throughout the world, some persons are recognized as unusual because they hear voices that others don't, feel intensely frightened, sense persecution from unseen enemies, and act strangely. People with *schizophrenia* seem to have been a part of all the cultures of the world since the dawn of civilization, although the antiquity of this condition is debated (Bark, 1988; Hare, 1988). For many, this state lasts a lifetime; for others, it appears and disappears unpredictably. Of all the psychiatric disorders, schizophrenia has summoned the most intense public interest because it seems such a cruel exaggeration of the human condition. It is also a "public" disorder because many people who suffer from schizophrenia become homeless on our streets.

Epidemiological surveys of schizophrenia reveal a prevalence of 1 to 2% of the population. But this disorder has commanded a huge portion of community health resources because of its chronic and overwhelming character.

Schizophrenia Is Characterized by an Unusual Array of Symptoms

The modern story of schizophrenia starts with Emil Kraepelin, a distinguished German psychiatrist whose book *Dementia Praecox and Paraphrenia* (1919) became the cornerstone of this field. Kraepelin searched for coherent patterns in the many symptoms of psychiatric disorders. His descriptions were rich with details, and he argued that the elements of schizophrenia fit into several distinct clinical forms.

CLINICAL ISSUE

Features common to the varied forms of schizophrenia included bizarre disturbances in thought, paranoid and grandiose delusions, auditory hallucinations, and an odd array of emotional changes. Kraepelin's use of the term *dementia praecox* embodies his view that this disorder begins during adolescence (*praecox* comes from the Latin for "early") and moves relentlessly to a chronic state of cognitive impairment (*dementia* comes from the Latin *de*, "away from," and *mens*, "mind"). According to Kraepelin, the cause must be partly genetic, although the relationship to inheritance is not simple.

In the early twentieth century another important work introduced the term **schizophrenia** (from the Greek *schizein*, "to split," and *phren*, "mind"). In 1911, Eugen Bleuler's monograph *Dementia Praecox; or, The Group of Schizophrenias* (Bleuler, 1952) examined more closely the underlying psychological processes of schizophrenia. Bleuler identified the key symptom as **dissociative thinking,** a major impairment in the logical structure of thought. Bleuler also distinguished between primary (fundamental) and secondary (accessory) symptoms. Fundamental symptoms, according to Bleuler, included the four *A*s: loosening of associations, autism (unmindfulness of reality), affective disturbance, and ambivalence. Accessory symptoms included delusions and hallucinations.

Emil Kraepelin
(1856–1926)

The qualitative, subjective descriptions offered by Kraepelin and Bleuler left much room for controversy. German psychiatrist Kurt Schneider (1959) emphasized a more pragmatic orientation, giving primacy to a few major "first-rank" symptoms of schizophrenia. These first-rank symptoms included (1) auditory hallucinations, (2) highly personalized delusions, and (3) changes in affect. During the 1980s and 1990s researchers continued to refine diagnostic and descriptive categories so that both convey a common understanding of the basic features and withstand the rigors of

Eugen Bleuler
(1857–1939)

Irving Gottesman

reliability assessments (Gottesman, 1991). This symptom-oriented approach led to efforts to delineate the highly discriminating signs for clear diagnosis. The 1994 *Diagnostic and Statistical Manual of Mental Disorders: DSM-IV* of the American Psychiatric Association incorporates this view.

Some investigators have proposed a major division of schizophrenic symptoms into two separate groups: positive and negative (Andreasen, 1991). **Positive symptoms** refer to abnormal states such as hallucinations, delusions, and excited motor behavior. **Negative symptoms** reflect insufficient functioning—for example, slow and impoverished thought and speech, emotional and social withdrawal, blunted affect.

The blunted emotions of those who suffer from schizophrenia may be apparent only in how well they *express* themselves in facial and body signals because they report experiencing very strong emotions (Kring, 1999). Researchers continue to question whether schizophrenia is a single entity or a family of related disorders. Still, defined according to modern criteria, schizophrenia is not distinctive to any particular society; it is a universal disorder found throughout the world (Jablensky et al., 1992).

A Genetic Component Contributes to the Development of Schizophrenia

For many years genetic studies of schizophrenia were controversial, although the notion of inheritance of mental illness is quite old. Data and speculations in this research area sparked vigorous interchanges, some related to the failure of early researchers to appreciate that environments are major modifiers of gene actions. For any genotype there is often a large range of alternative outcomes that are determined by both developmental and environmental factors.

The basic aim of studies in this area is to understand the role of genetic factors in causing and maintaining schizophrenic states. If a genetic contribution is established as a significant ingredient in the genesis of schizophrenia, then it will be important to establish programs to aid the population at risk.

**GENES AND
BEHAVIOR**

Family studies. If schizophrenia is inherited, relatives of patients with schizophrenia should show a higher incidence of the disorder than is found in the general population. In addition, the risk of schizophrenia among relatives should increase with the closeness of the relationship because close relatives share a greater number of genes. In general, parents and siblings of patients with schizophrenia have a higher risk of being or becoming schizophrenic than do individuals in the general population (Figure 16.1). The risk is greater in cases of closer biological relatedness. However, the mode of inheritance of schizophrenia is not simple; that is, it does not involve a single recessive or dominant gene (Tamminga and Schulz, 1991). Most likely, multiple genes play a role in the emergence of schizophrenia.

It is easy to find fault with family studies. First, they confuse hereditary and experiential factors because members of a family share both. Second, the data usually depend on the recollections of relatives whose memories are likely to be clouded by zealous efforts to attribute blame for the disorder. "Funny," departed aunts and uncles are easily designated as the agents responsible for the mental disorder.

Twin studies. In twins, nature provides researchers with what seem to be the perfect conditions for a genetic experiment. Human twins from the same fertilized egg—called **monozygotic** (*identical*) twins—share an identical set of genes. Twins from two different eggs—**dizygotic** (*fraternal*) twins—like other full siblings, have only half of their genes in common.

When both individuals of a twin pair suffer from schizophrenia, they are described as being **concordant** for this trait. If only one member of the pair exhibits the disorder, the pair is described as **discordant.** Whereas about 50% of monozygotic twin pairs who show schizophrenia are concordant for the disorder, the rate of concordance for dizygotic twins is only about 17%. The significantly higher concordance rate among monozygotic twins (who are twice as closely related genetically as dizygotic twins are) is strong evidence of a genetic factor. It is assumed that any influ-

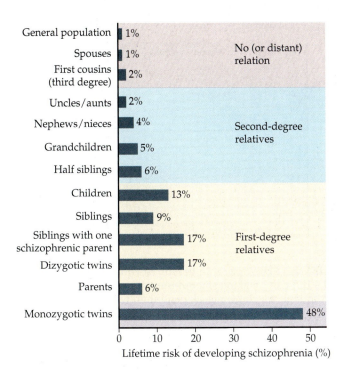

General population 1%
Spouses 1%
First cousins (third degree) 2%

No (or distant) relation

Uncles/aunts 2%
Nephews/nieces 4%
Grandchildren 5%
Half siblings 6%

Second-degree relatives

Children 13%
Siblings 9%
Siblings with one schizophrenic parent 17%
Dizygotic twins 17%
Parents 6%

First-degree relatives

Monozygotic twins 48%

0   10   20   30   40   50
Lifetime risk of developing schizophrenia (%)

16.1 The Heritability of Schizophrenia The more closely related a person is to a patient with schizophrenia, the greater are his or her chances of also developing schizophrenia. (After Gottesman, 1991.)

ence of family structure, socioeconomic stresses, and other environmental factors would have an equal effect on monozygotic versus dizygotic twins.

Studies of schizophrenia in twins have been criticized on several grounds. For example, some data indicate that twins are unusual from a developmental perspective in that they usually show lower birth weights and different developmental progress than nontwins. In addition, parental treatment of fraternal twins differs considerably from their interaction with identical twins, thus generating a confounding environmental variable.

Even with identical twins, however, the concordance rate for schizophrenia is far less than 100%. Although identical twins have the same genetic constitution, one member of the identical-twin pair may suffer from schizophrenia while the other one is normal.

Studies of identical twins who are discordant for schizophrenia can provide useful information about the possible factors that lead to schizophrenia and those that protect against its emergence. E. Fuller Torrey noted that the twin who developed schizophrenia in such cases tended to be the one who was more abnormal throughout life. The symptomatic twin frequently weighed less at birth and had an early developmental history that included more instances of physiological distress (Torrey et al., 1994; Wahl, 1976). This developmental history is connected with the parents' view of the symptomatic twin as more vulnerable. During development this twin was more submissive, tearful, and sensitive than the identical sibling. This type of study, showing that a genetic tendency does not mean that schizophrenia is inevitable, may someday suggest how to prevent the disorder.

During childhood the developmental difficulties of twins who later suffer from schizophrenia are accompanied by behavioral, cognitive, and other neurological signs, such as impairments in motor coordination (Torrey et al., 1994). For example, Elaine Walker showed that observers watching home films of children can pick out the child who went on to suffer from schizophrenia in adulthood with uncanny accuracy (Walker, 1991).

The distinctions between those who suffer from schizophrenia and those who don't include several neuropsychological characteristics, such as eye tracking. Eye-tracking measurements record eye movements as they follow a moving target on a screen. Many studies show abnormal eye tracking in patients with schizophrenia (Levy et al.,

E. Fuller Torrey

Elaine Walker

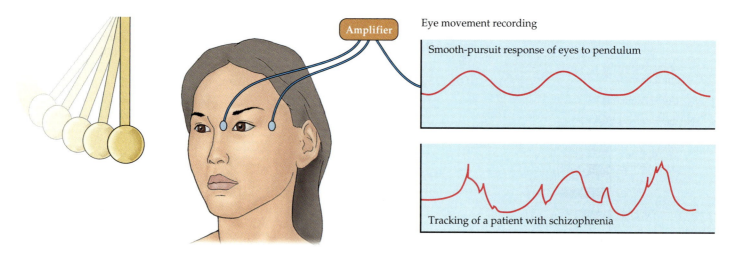

Eye movement recording

Amplifier

Smooth-pursuit response of eyes to pendulum

Tracking of a patient with schizophrenia

16.2 Eye Tracking in Patients with Schizophrenia versus Normal People   Patients with schizophrenia have greater difficulty making smooth-pursuit movements with their eyes than normal people do. Although watching a clock pendulum works as a test, modern researchers have their subjects view a moving cursor on a computer screen.

1993; Stuve et al., 1997). In smooth-pursuit movements, such as those we perform as we follow the slow to-and-fro movements of the pendulum of an old clock, patients with schizophrenia are unable to keep up with the moving object and show the intrusion of the rapid, jerky eye movements called saccades (see Chapter 11). Figure 16.2 compares the eye tracking of normal people to that of people with schizophrenia.

Adoption studies.   Criticisms of twin studies led to adoption studies, which have produced substantial support for the significance of genetic factors in many psychiatric disorders. The biological parents of adoptees who suffer from schizophrenia are far more likely to have suffered from this disorder than are the adopting parents (Kety et al., 1975, 1994).

Studies of families, twins, and adoptees provide consistent evidence that genetics contributes to the incidence of schizophrenia. But many questions remain unanswered: (1) How is the disorder transmitted? (2) What is being inherited? (3) What genes are related to this disorder, and what processes do they control? It is clear that no single gene causes schizophrenia (Faraone and Tsuang, 1985), but certain single genes may greatly increase susceptibility to this disorder (Brzustowicz et al., 2000), perhaps in response to stress (as we discuss shortly). A better understanding of the environmental and biological factors that increase the risk of schizophrenia will aid the genetic counseling of individuals who are at risk because of their close relationship to a patient with schizophrenia.

The Brains of Some Patients with Schizophrenia Show Structural Changes

Because in many patients the symptoms of schizophrenia are so marked and persistent, some investigators have hypothesized that the brains of people with this illness would show distinctive and measurable structural anomalies (Trimble, 1991). During the past century, postmortem studies have occasionally yielded exciting findings along these lines, but the brains used were usually from patients who had died at an advanced age, or who had been hospitalized and medicated for many years, so it was difficult to establish that any structural differences observed were exclusively due to the illness, rather than the result of normal aging or side effects of medication. The advent of CT and MRI scans has made it possible to study brain anatomy in living patients at all stages of their illness (Hyde and Weinberger, 1990), and significant, consistent differences in brain structure have indeed been found in the brains of schizophrenic patients, particularly in the size of the cerebral ventricles.

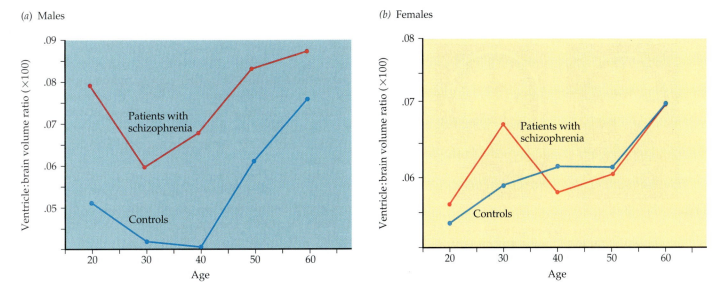

(a) Males

(b) Females

16.3 Ventricular Enlargement in Schizophrenia (a) The volume of the cerebral ventricles, relative to overall brain volume, is greater in male patients with schizophrenia than in control subjects. (b) This difference is also seen in some female patients. (After Hyde and Weinberger, 1990.)

Ventricular abnormalities. Studies of patients with schizophrenia have consistently revealed an enlargement of cerebral ventricles, especially the lateral ventricles (Figure 16.3) (Hyde and Weinberger, 1990). Ventricular enlargement is not related to length of illness or to duration of hospitalization. D. R. Weinberger et al. (1980) found that the degree of ventricular enlargement predicts the patient's response to antipsychotic drugs. Patients with more enlarged ventricles show poorer response to these drugs.

Although many studies have confirmed that patients with schizophrenia have enlarged lateral ventricles, the findings must be qualified: Patients with this anatomical characteristic form a distinct subgroup of people who suffer from this disorder (Kemali et al., 1985). Attempts to characterize the patients with enlarged ventricles have revealed other general features, some of them controversial (Gooding and Iacono, 1995).

Neuropsychiatrist Nancy Andreasen found in MRI studies that enlargement of the ventricles is a static trait in patients, remaining for many years after the initial onset of the disease (Andreasen, 1994). A study of identical twins discordant for schizophrenia yielded startlingly clear results: The twin with schizophrenia had decidedly enlarged lateral ventricles, but the ventricles of the well twin were of normal size (Figure 16.4) (Torrey et al., 1994).

Limbic system abnormalities. This twin study also revealed that more than 75% of discordant pairs show a marked difference in the size of the hippocampus and the amygdala: These structures are smaller in the twin with schizophrenia. This observation suggests that the ventricular enlargement in patients with schizophrenia arises from atrophy or destruction of adjacent neural tissue. When brain cells in the regions adjacent to the cerebral ventricles shrink or die, the ventricles expand to fill those regions. Some of these changes might arise early in development, even in the prenatal period (Mednick et al., 1994).

Neuropathological studies of the limbic systems of patients with schizophrenia have revealed differences between patients and controls in several areas, including the hippocampus, amygdala, and parahippocampal regions. Kovelman and Scheibel (1984), comparing the brains of chronic sufferers of schizophrenia with those of medical patients of the same age that did not exhibit brain pathology, noted changes in the hippocampus of the former.

Nancy Andreasen

(a) MRI brain images of twins discordant for schizophrenia

35-year-old female identical twins

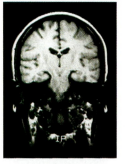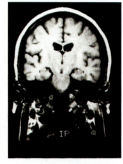

Well   Affected

28-year-old male identical twins

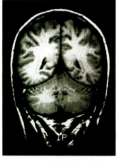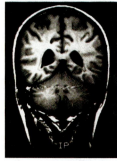

Well   Affected

(b) Differences in ventricular volumes

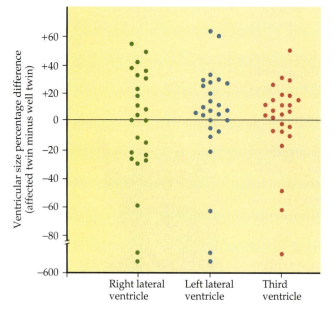

16.4 Identical Genes, Different Fates (a) Although each member of these pairs of monozygotic twins has the same genes, only one of each set of twins (the twin with larger ventricles) developed schizophrenia. (b) Measurements of ventricles of many discordant identical twins. (After Torrey et al., 1994; MRIs courtesy of E. Fuller Torrey.)

Figure 16.5 shows an example of cellular differences. The pyramidal cells of chronic sufferers of schizophrenia were disoriented, in a type of cellular disarray (see Figure 16.5e). Presumably the lack of normal cellular polarity is related to abnormal synaptic linkages, including both inputs and outputs of these cells. The degree of disorientation was positively related to the severity of the disorder. Conrad et al. (1991) extended the earlier work and established that disorientation of hippocampal pyramidal cells is evident in both the right and the left hippocampus.

This cellular derangement probably arises during early cell development and might reflect maternal exposure to an influenza infection during the second trimester of pregnancy (Machón et al., 1997). These abnormalities of cellular arrangement in the hippocampus are said to resemble those of mutant mice that show disordered neurogenesis in the hippocampus (A. B. Scheibel and Conrad, 1993). Other studies have noted differences between patients and controls in the entorhinal cortex, parahippocampal cortex, and cingulate cortex (Shapiro, 1993).

Regional and cellular abnormalities. At one time there were very few reliable findings of brain structural pathology in schizophrenia. Now an overabundance of positive findings overwhelms the effort toward an integrative portrait of the regional and cellular pathology of schizophrenia.

Several studies have noted marked shrinkage of the cerebellar vermis in chronic patients and have shown that this abnormality is not related to prolonged use of antipsychotic drugs (Heath et al., 1979; Snider, 1982). Chronic sufferers of schizophrenia whose disorder started early in life have thicker regions in the corpus callosum, both in anatomical preparations and in some CT scans (Bigelow et al., 1983). One study, examining postmortem materials, found evidence that neuronal migration during the fetal period had been abnormal in the frontal cortex of patients with schizophrenia (Akbarian et al., 1996).

Deficits shown by patients with schizophrenia in tests that are sensitive to frontal cortical lesions have also drawn attention to possible frontal cortical abnormalities. Although some studies show reduced frontal cortical volume in patients, others have failed to show major abnormalities of the frontal cortex (Wible et al., 1995). So if the frontal lobes of people suffering from schizophrenia have a normal structure, what about the *activity* of the frontal cortex?

Functional Maps Reveal Differences in Schizophrenic Brains

Positron emission tomography (PET), functional magnetic resonance imaging (fMRI), and single-photon emission computerized tomography (SPECT) offer windows for viewing the schizophrenic brain. (PET, fMRI, and CT were introduced in Chapter 2; SPECT is much like PET, but it images only a single plane.)

In schizophrenia, the functional lateralization of the cerebral hemispheres may be altered, according to some blood flow imaging studies. The left hemisphere is more active than the right during resting states (Gur et al., 1987), at least in the frontal lobe (K. F. Berman and Weinberger, 1990).

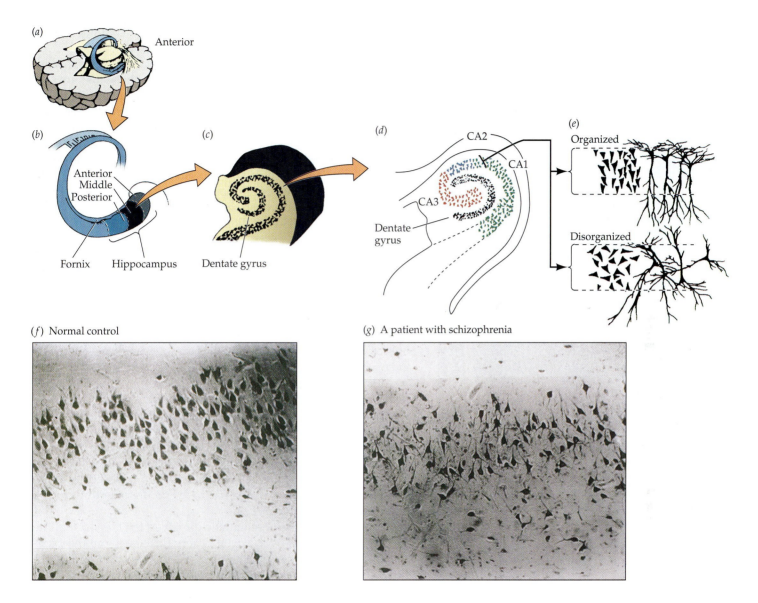

(a) Anterior

(b) Anterior / Middle / Posterior
Fornix   Hippocampus

(c) Dentate gyrus

(d) CA2 / CA1 / CA3
Dentate gyrus

(e) Organized / Disorganized

(f) Normal control

(g) A patient with schizophrenia

16.5 Cellular Disarray of the Hippocampus in Chronic Schizophrenia
(a) This horizontal section of the cerebral hemispheres shows the location of the hippocampus. (b) Enlargements of the hippocampus and fornix show the location of anterior, middle, and posterior hippocampal segments. (c) The hippocampus and dentate gyrus are enlarged in this cross section. (d) The hippocampus is subdivided into three regions: CA1, CA2, and CA3. (e) Orientations of the pyramidal cells of a control subject (*upper*) and a patient with schizophrenia (*lower*) are compared in these hippocampal cross sections. (f, g) Histological cross sections show differences in tissue between a normal control (f) and a patient with schizophrenia (g). (After Kovelman and Scheibel, 1984; f and g courtesy of Arnold Scheibel.)

Early observations using PET indicated that patients with schizophrenia show relatively less metabolic activity in the frontal lobes (compared with their posterior lobes) than do normal subjects (Buchsbaum et al., 1984). This observation, referred to as the **hypofrontality hypothesis,** generated controversy and fueled interest in the role of the frontal lobes in schizophrenia (D. R. Weinberger et al., 1994). In discordant identical twins, frontal blood flow levels are low only in the twin who suffers from schizophrenia (Andreasen et al., 1986; Morihisa and McAnulty, 1985).

Some experiments show this effect only during difficult cognitive tasks that particularly activate the frontal area (Figure 16.6) and at which frontally damaged patients often fail. Unlike control subjects, patients with schizophrenia show no increase in their prefrontal activation above basal levels during the task (D. R. Weinberger et al., 1994). Drugs that alleviate symptoms of schizophrenia, discussed in the next section, also increase activation of frontal cortex (Honey et al., 1999). Neurons in the frontal cortex of patients with schizophrenia have dendrites with a reduced density of synaptic spines compared to control subjects (L. A. Glantz and Lewis, 2000), which may contribute to a less active frontal cortex

The Brains of Patients with Schizophrenia Show Neurochemical Changes

As knowledge about the neurochemistry of the brain has grown, hypotheses about the bases of schizophrenia have become more precise. Although exciting ideas and

(a) At rest

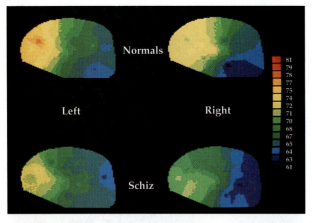

(b) During card sort test

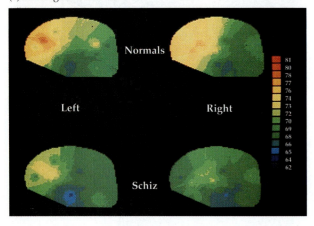

16.6 Hypofrontality in Schizophrenia   The frontal cortex is less activated in patients with schizophrenia ("Schiz") compared to their twins who don't have schizophrenia ("Normals") either at rest (a) or during the Wisconsin Card Sort task (b), a task that is very difficult for people with damage to the frontal lobes. Areas of high activation are shown in red and yellow. (Courtesy of Karen Berman.)

data are apparent in the research, several problems continue to frustrate major progress in our study of schizophrenia.

First, it is very hard to separate the neurochemical events that are primary causes of a psychiatric disorder from those that are secondary effects. Some secondary effects arise from the profound impairments of social behavior and may range from dietary limitations to prolonged stress. Treatment variables, especially the long-term use of traditional antipsychotic substances, can mask or distort primary causes because they frequently produce marked changes in the physiology and biochemistry of brain and body.

Another major problem in neurochemical research of schizophrenia is the definition of schizophrenia itself. Is it a single disorder, or many disorders with different origins and outcomes?

The dopamine hypothesis.   Many clinical and basic experimental findings have suggested that abnormally high levels of dopamine receptor stimulation form the basis of schizophrenia. In Chapter 4 we learned that dopamine is a synaptic transmitter in the brain; its role in brain positive-reinforcement circuits is discussed further in Chapter 15. The first clues suggesting that dopamine plays a role in schizophrenia came from observations of (1) amphetamine psychosis, (2) the effects of antipsychotic drugs, and (3) Parkinson's disease.

Although many drugs, such as LSD and mescaline, produce profound perceptual, cognitive, and emotional changes, some of which resemble aspects of psychoses, several features of the behavioral effects of these drugs are quite dissimilar from symptoms of schizophrenia. Most drug-induced psychoses are characterized by confusion, disorientation, and outright delirium; these are not typical symptoms of schizophrenia. Hallucinations produced by these drugs are usually visual, in contrast to the predominantly auditory hallucinations of schizophrenia.

Patients with schizophrenia who are given LSD report that the experience produced by the drug is very different from the experiences of their disorder. Furthermore, psychiatrists can readily distinguish taped conversations of people suffering from schizophrenia from those of subjects given hallucinogenic agents. But one drug state—*amphetamine psychosis*—comes close to replicating the schizophrenic state.

Some individuals use amphetamine on an everyday basis as a stimulant. Because tolerance (see Chapter 4) develops, maintaining the same level of euphoria requires that the self-administered dose be progressively increased, potentially reaching as much as 3000 mg per day. (Contrast this level with the usual 5 mg taken to control appetite or prolong wakefulness.) Many individuals taking these large doses of amphetamine develop symptoms of paranoia, often involving delusions of persecution with auditory hallucinations, and exhibit suspiciousness and bizarre postures.

The similarity of amphetamine psychosis to schizophrenia is also supported by the finding that amphetamine exacerbates symptoms of schizophrenia. Neurochemically, amphetamine promotes the release of catecholamines, particularly dopamine, and prolongs the action of the released transmitter by blocking reuptake. Rapid relief from amphetamine psychosis is provided by injection of the dopamine antagonist **chlorpromazine**—a substance that brings us to the second part of the story of the dopamine hypothesis.

Chlorpromazine has had much wider use than merely as an antidote to amphetamine psychosis. In the early 1950s, about half a million people were patients in psychiatric hospitals in the United States. This number has decreased dramatically. Several factors contributed to this reduction, of which the most significant was the introduction of chlorpromazine in the treatment of schizophrenia.

In the search for a substance to produce muscle relaxation for surgery, French surgeon Henri Laborit discovered in the 1940s that chlorpromazine not only achieves this effect, but also reduces worry and preoperative tension. An insightful investigator, Laborit collaborated with psychiatrists in trying this substance on psychiatric patients; they found remarkable antipsychotic effects. Chlorpromazine was then introduced on a large scale in psychiatric hospitals around the world, with a profound impact.

By now, a massive number of well-controlled studies point to the fact that chlorpromazine and many other substances related to it (called **phenothiazines**) have a specific antipsychotic effect. These substances act in the brain by blocking postsynaptic receptor sites for dopamine, specifically the D_2 type.

As noted in Chapter 4, there are several major dopamine-containing pathways. Investigators believe that dopamine terminals in the limbic system constitute a major site of action of antipsychotic drugs (also called **neuroleptics** or *major tranquilizers*). These cells originate in the brainstem, near the substantia nigra (see Figure 4.3). The clinical effectiveness of antipsychotic agents is directly related to the magnitude of postsynaptic receptor blockade of dopamine sites. This result suggests that schizophrenia may be produced either by excessive levels of available dopamine or by excessive postsynaptic sensitivity to dopamine, which might involve a large population of postsynaptic dopamine receptor sites.

Another trail leading to the dopamine hypothesis of schizophrenia is the study of Parkinson's disease (see Chapter 11). Parkinson's disease is caused by the degeneration of nerve cells located in the brainstem (in the substantia nigra). These cells contain dopamine, and administering the substance L-dopa, a precursor for the synthesis of dopamine, increases the amount of released dopamine, which thus provides some relief of parkinsonian symptoms.

Two observations of patients with Parkinson's connect this disease with schizophrenia and the dopamine hypothesis. First, some patients given L-dopa to relieve parkinsonian symptoms become psychotic. Second, some patients with schizophrenia receiving chlorpromazine develop parkinsonian symptoms. In fact, treatment with traditional antipsychotic drugs can result in permanent movement disorders (Box 16.1). Furthermore, patients with schizophrenia who have enlarged ventricles show a marked reduction in levels of dopamine β-hydroxylase, an enzyme that catalyzes the conversion of dopamine into norepinephrine (see Box 4.1) (D. E. Sternberg et al., 1982).

The earliest, simplest dopamine model of schizophrenia argued that this disorder arises from the hyperfunctioning of dopamine circuits. This hyperfunctioning could develop from excessive release of dopamine (a presynaptic effect) or an excess of dopamine receptors (a postsynaptic effect). For years, the strongest evidence for this simple hypothesis was the remarkable clinical success of dopamine blockers in treating schizophrenia. Indeed, the clinical effectiveness of the many neuroleptic drugs introduced in the past 40 years has been directly related to their effectiveness in blocking or antagonizing dopamine (Figure 16.7). Drugs that have the opposite effect—increasing dopamine activity—worsen schizophrenic symptoms.

Criticisms of a dopamine model of schizophrenia began to emerge in the 1980s (Alpert and Friedhoff, 1980). Clinical observations revealed that some patients with schizophrenia show no changes when treated with drugs that affect dopamine. Another problem for the dopamine hypothesis is a new generation of neuroleptics called *atypical* because unlike "conventional" neuroleptics, they don't affect just dopamine receptors.

Introduced during the 1990s, atypical antipsychotic drugs such as **clozapine** block serotonin receptors ($5-HT_{2A}$) as well as D_2 dopamine receptors (see Figure 16.7). Atypical neuroleptics are just as effective as the older generation of drugs, but they are less likely to induce motor side effects (see Box 16.1) and more effective at treating negative symptoms than traditional neuroleptics are. Even more troubling for the dopamine hypothesis is the report that clozapine can *increase* dopamine release in frontal cortex (Hertel et al., 1999).

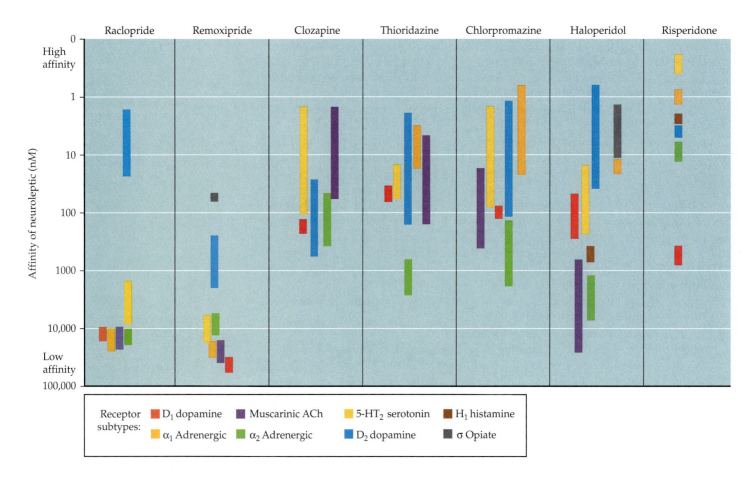

16.7 Antipsychotic Drugs That Affect Dopamine Receptors Drugs vary widely in the affinity with which they bind to various neurotransmitter receptors. Drugs that block dopamine receptors, specifically the D_2 variety (blue), are more effective at combating symptoms of schizophrenia. Atypical neuroleptics such as clozapine block 5-HT_2 receptors (yellow) more effectively than D_2 receptors. (After Seeman, 1990.)

Studies of dopamine metabolites in blood, cerebrospinal fluid, and urine have provided inconsistent results regarding the possible hyperfunctioning of dopamine terminals. For example, many patients with schizophrenia have normal levels of dopamine metabolites in cerebrospinal fluid. Some postmortem and PET studies of schizophrenic brains reveal an increase in dopamine receptors, especially the D_2 type (Breier et al., 1997; K. L. Davis et al., 1991), even in patients who have been off of neuroleptic drugs for some time (Okubo et al., 1997). But PET studies of D_2 receptor density in people who suffer from schizophrenia are inconsistent, as are efforts to relate a D_2 receptor gene to schizophrenia.

Another problem with the dopamine hypothesis is the lack of correspondence between the time at which drugs block dopamine (quite rapidly) and the behavior changes that signal the clinical effectiveness of the drug (usually on the order of weeks). Thus the relation of dopamine to schizophrenia may be more complex than that envisioned in the simple model of hyperactive dopamine synapses.

The psychotogen hypothesis. Several proposals have suggested that schizophrenia develops from faulty metabolic processes in the brain that produce abnormal substances that generate psychotic behavior. Such hypothetical substances, called **psychotogens,** might be similar in some ways to hallucinogenic agents. The chemical structure of some manufactured hallucinogens resembles that of some neurotransmitters. Metabolic faults in particular pathways might cause the brain to convert an innocuous molecule into a behaviorally maladaptive substance capable of producing schizophrenic symptoms.

The **transmethylation hypothesis** suggests that the addition of a methyl group (CH_3) to some naturally occurring brain compounds can convert the substances into known hallucinogenic agents. This hypothesis was offered in the 1950s by Humphry Osmond and John R. Smythies, who showed hallucinogenic properties for a sub-

BOX 16.1 *Long-Term Effects of Antipsychotic Drugs*

Few people would deny that drugs like chlorpromazine have had a revolutionary impact on the treatment of schizophrenia. With such treatment, many people who might otherwise have been in mental hospitals their whole lives can take care of themselves in nonhospital settings. Drugs of this class can justly be regarded as antipsychotic.

Traditional antipsychotic drugs often have other effects that bring their use into question. Soon after beginning to take these drugs, some users develop maladaptive motor symptoms (**dyskinesia**, from the Greek *dys*, "bad" and *kinesis*, "motion"). Although many of these symptoms are transient and disappear when the dosage of drug is reduced, some drug-induced motor changes emerge only after prolonged drug treatment—after months, sometimes years. This condition is called **tardive dyskinesia** (the Latin *tardus* means "slow").

The motor effects of tardive dyskinesia include many involuntary movements, especially involving the face, mouth, lips, and tongue. Elaborate uncontrollable movements of the tongue are particularly prominent, including incessant rolling movements and sucking or smacking of the lips. Some patients show twisting and sudden jerking movements of the arms or legs (D. E. Casey, 1989).

Traditional antipsychotic substances affect a large percentage of patients—as much as one-third—in this way. The drugs usually affect females more severely than they do males (J. M. Smith et al., 1979). The relationship between drug parameters and the likelihood of such side effects is complex (Toenniessen et al., 1985). What is alarming is that this motor impairment frequently becomes permanent, even if drug treatment is halted.

The underlying mechanism for tardive dyskinesia continues to be a puzzle. Some researchers claim that it arises from the chronic blocking of dopamine receptors, which results in receptor site supersensitivity. Critics of this view, however, point out that tardive dyskinesia frequently takes a long time to develop and may be irreversible—a time course that is different from dopamine receptor supersensitivity. In addition, there is no difference in D_1 or D_2 receptor binding between patients with tardive dyskinesia and those without these symptoms.

A GABA deficiency hypothesis of tardive dyskinesia was offered by Fibiger and Lloyd (1984). They believed that tardive dyskinesia is the result of drug-induced destruction of GABA neurons in the corpus striatum. Neuroleptic-induced changes in enzymes related to GABA have been observed in experimental animals. A noradrenergic hypothesis of this disorder has also been presented, on the basis of evidence that the concentration of norepinephrine in the cerebrospinal fluid is correlated with tardive dyskinesia (Kaufmann et al., 1986).

Long-term treatment with traditional antipsychotic drugs has another unusual effect: Prolonged blockage of dopamine receptors seems to increase the number of dopamine receptors and lead to receptor supersensitivity. In some patients, discontinuation of the drugs or a lowering of dosage results in a sudden, marked increase in positive symptoms of schizophrenia, such as delusions or hallucinations. This **supersensitivity psychosis** can often be reversed by administration of increased dosages of dopamine receptor–blocking agents. A newer generation of antipsychotic drugs has fewer side effects, which may make schizophrenia patients more likely to continue self-medication.

---

stance called *adrenochrome*. This substance was viewed as a possible metabolic product of the neurotransmitter norepinephrine. But administering substances that should increase methylation did not reliably exacerbate the symptoms. This inconsistency, coupled with problems in understanding how the mechanism could account for the effects of antipsychotic drugs, limits the current credibility of the proposal.

Can the body produce amphetamine-like substances by metabolizing norepinephrine? The amphetamine molecule resembles the molecules of catecholamine transmitters. Because amphetamine psychosis resembles paranoid schizophrenia, an endogenous amphetamine-like substance would be a very interesting discovery. Several investigators have argued that phenylethylamine (PEA)—a substance with amphetamine-like properties—is produced in small quantities by the metabolism of norepinephrine in patients with schizophrenia.

One powerful psychotogen comes close to producing a schizophrenia-like state. Initially developed to produce a *dissociative* anesthetic state (one in which an animal is insensitive to pain but shows some types of arousal or responsiveness), this substance, called **phencyclidine** (**PCP**), produces auditory hallucinations, strange depersonalization, disorientation, and intense assaultive behavior. In some cases, prolonged psychotic states can develop from the use of this substance.

Treating monkeys with PCP for 2 weeks produced a schizophrenia-like syndrome, including poor performance on a test that is sensitive to prefrontal damage (Jentsch et al., 1997). This deficit was reversed by treatment with a dopamine-blocking

COMPETING HYPOTHESES

(a) Effects of PCP on various receptors

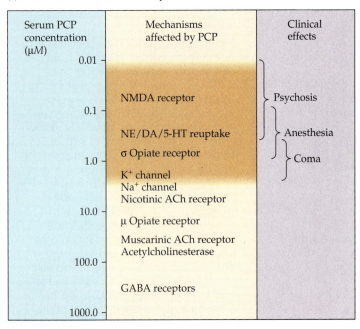

(b) A model of PCP action on the NMDA receptor

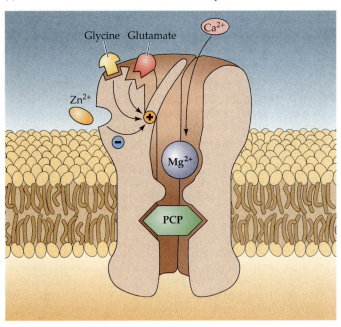

16.8 The Effects of PCP on the NMDA Receptor   (a) The serum concentrations of PCP that elicit clinical effects are the same concentrations that result in PCP binding of the NMDA receptor. (b) This model describes PCP action at the NMDA receptor.

antipsychotic drug—further evidence that this drug-induced state is similar to schizophrenia. The mechanism of action of PCP involves the NMDA-type glutamate receptor (see Box 4.2), as illustrated in Figure 16.8. Thus a glutamate hypothesis of schizophrenia has also been advanced (Moghaddam and Adams, 1998).

An Integrative Psychobiological Model of Schizophrenia Emphasizes the Interaction of Multiple Factors

At times, research on schizophrenia seems to have given us many pieces of a large puzzle whose overall appearance is still unknown. Some efforts at integrating the many psychological and biological findings in the field have resulted in important views about the origins of schizophrenia. One such model, presented by Mirsky and Duncan (1986), views schizophrenia as an outcome of the interaction of genetic, developmental, and stress factors. According to this model, at each life stage specific features contribute to an enhanced vulnerability to schizophrenia.

Genetic influences leading to "brain abnormalities" may provide the basic neurological substrate for schizophrenia. Birth complications that deprive the baby of oxygen—often evident in patients with schizophrenia (Rosso et al., 2000)—may exaggerate such abnormalities. Mirsky and Duncan suggested that through childhood and adolescence, neurological deficits are manifested by behaviors such as impaired cognitive skills, attention deficits, irritability, and delayed gross motor development.

According to this model, the emergence of schizophrenia and related disorders depends on whether the compromised brain is subjected to environmental stressors (Figure 16.9). City life is considered more stressful than rural life, and people raised in a city are more likely to develop schizophrenia than rural dwellers (Mortensen et al., 1999). The magnitude of brain abnormalities in vulnerable individuals determines how much stress is needed to produce a schizophrenic disorder. Schizophrenia emerges when the combination of stress and brain abnormalities exceeds a threshold value. People with many schizophrenic brain abnormalities may become symptomatic with relatively minor environmental stresses.

Models like this one suggest the possibility of strategies for decreasing the likelihood of schizophrenia for a child at risk (Häfner, 1998). New biological aids, such as PET scans and genetic tools, might help us identify and understand the at-risk child at a stage early in life, when interventions to reduce stress might avert schizophrenia later in life.

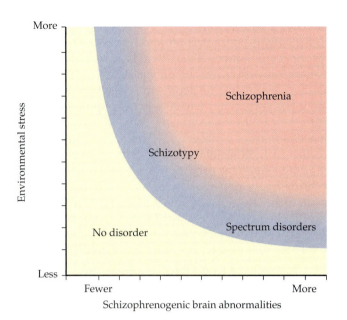

16.9 A Model of the Interaction of Stress and Brain Abnormalities in Schizophrenia Environmental stress and certain brain abnormalities may combine to produce a schizophrenic disorder. Disorders ranging from more mild to more severe are called, respectively, *spectrum disorders, schizotypy,* and *schizophrenia.* (After Mirsky and Duncan, 1986.)

Autism Is a Disorder of Social Competence

Autism is a life-long developmental disorder characterized by impaired social interactions and language, and a narrow range of interests and activities. Children with autism may or may not appear mentally deficient, but they tend to perseverate (such as by continually nodding the head or making stereotyped finger movements), and they seem to have a difficult time judging other people's thoughts or feelings. Autism seems to represent a profound disorder in the ability to form and develop social relations. When shown photos of the faces of family members, autistic individuals reveal a pattern of brain activation quite different from controls (Figure 16.10), suggesting a very different brain organization for the fundamental social skill of recognizing others. Autism is a heartbreaking disorder in which apparently normal toddlers begin regressing, losing language skills, and withdrawing from family interaction.

The disorder is found in about one to two children per thousand, is much more common in males than females, and has a strong heritability (Rapin and Katzman, 1998). One study has implicated a particular allele of the *Hox* gene as more common in autism (Rodier, 2000). Unfortunately, at one time psychiatrist Bruno Bettelheim blamed autism on improper parental behavior, such as a "cold, distant" mother, but that idea has been almost universally discounted.

Several structural differences between the brains of people with autism and controls have been reported, including a reduction in the size of the corpus callosum and certain cerebellar regions (Egaas et al., 1995). There is no cure, but many children with autism are helped a great deal by highly structured training in language and behavior. A report on TV that a mother had helped her autistic son by treating him with a gastrointestinal hormone, secretin, was not supported by placebo-controlled studies (Sandler et al., 1999).

Depression Is a Major Psychiatric Disorder

It seems as though no person now alive nor any one of our forebears has been a stranger to depression. Many of us experience periods of unhappiness that we commonly describe as depression. In some people, however, a depressive state is more than a passing malaise and occurs over and over with cyclical regularity. Such people are usually over 40 years old, and women are two to three times more likely than men to suffer from depression.

Control

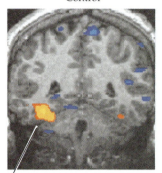

Fusiform gyrus

Patient with autism

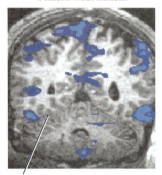

Fusiform gyrus

16.10 A Face-Recognition Deficit in Autism Control subjects display an activation (yellow) of the fusiform gyrus when viewing photos of family members. Autistic individuals display a different pattern of brain response, which may contribute to their reduced social skills. (After Pierce et al., 2001; courtesy of Karen Pierce.)

Depression is characterized not by sadness, but by an unhappy mood; loss of interests, energy, and appetite; difficulty in concentration; and restless agitation. Pessimism seems to seep into every act (Solomon, 2001). Periods of such *unipolar depression* (i.e., depression that alternates with normal emotional states) can occur with no readily apparent stress. Without treatment, the depression often lasts for several months. Depressive illnesses of this sort afflict 13 to 20% of the population at any one time (Cassens et al., 1990).

Some individuals experience periods of depression alternating with periods of excessively expansive moods that include sustained overactivity, talkativeness, increased energy, and strange grandiosity. This condition is called **bipolar disorder** (also known as *manic–depressive psychosis*). Men and women are equally affected, and the age of onset is usually much earlier than that of unipolar depression. Most people suffering from bipolar disorder benefit from treatment with the element **lithium** (Kingsbury and Garver, 1998). No one knows why this metal helps bipolar disorder, and care must be taken to avoid toxic side effects of an overdose. Lithium treatment has been reported to increase the volume of gray matter in the human brain (G. J. Moore et al., 2000). Perhaps the fact that the manic phases blocked by lithium are so exhilarating is the reason that some bipolar clients stop taking the medication. Unfortunately, doing so means that the depressive episodes return as well.

Depression can be lethal; it often leads to suicide. Most estimates indicate that about 80% of all suicide victims are profoundly depressed. Unlike the incidence of schizophrenia, suicide rates show great variability across time, age, and places in the world. Although the trend during the twentieth century in the United States and western Europe showed an overall progressive decline in the incidence of suicide, there is a disturbing trend toward an increase in suicide in younger populations. Several studies have associated the younger age of suicide victims with the frequent use of drugs in this age group (Rich et al., 1986; Sigurdson et al., 1994).

Inheritance Is an Important Determinant of Depression

Genetic studies of unipolar and bipolar disorders reveal strong hereditary contributions (Moldin et al., 1991). Concordance is much higher for monozygotic (identical) than for dizygotic (fraternal) twins (Kendler et al., 1999). The concordance rates for monozygotic twins are similar whether the twins are reared apart or together. Adoption studies show high rates of affective illness in the biological parents in comparison to foster parents. Although several early studies implicated specific chromosomes, subsequent linkage studies have failed to identify the locus of any relevant gene. There probably is no single gene for depression.

Some Affective Disorders Are Associated with Medical Conditions

**CLINICAL
ISSUE**

In some individuals, depression develops secondarily to other body disorders, especially endocrine and brain disorders. For example, **Cushing's syndrome** is characterized by high levels of serum cortisol, which arise from pituitary tumors that produce excessive amounts of ACTH (adrenocorticotropic hormone), from adrenal tumors, or from deliberate therapy involving corticosteroids. In more than 85% of patients with Cushing's syndrome, depression appears quite early in the disorder, even before other signs, such as obesity or unusual growth and distribution of body hair (Haskett, 1985; Krystal et al., 1990).

Depression also accompanies brain disorders such as Parkinson's disease (see Chapter 11). Earlier in the chapter we noted that most researchers attribute Parkinson's disease to insufficient production of dopamine. But some investigators argue that patients with Parkinson's develop depression in reaction to the motor disabilities of the disorder; others assert that depression accompanies this disorder because Parkinson's disease affects emotional circuitry and associated transmitters (Sano et al., 1990).

About 50% of patients who suffer from Parkinson's are in a state of depression that is unrelated to either the duration or the severity of the motor disability. Research suggests that serotonin plays a strong role in their depression. The levels of serotonin metabolites in the cerebrospinal fluid are lower in patients with Parkinson's than in controls of the same age (Sano et al., 1990). Administering the precursor for serotonin synthesis alleviates depression in these patients. Some of the effects of serotonin in this disorder might arise from a common anatomical lesion in such patients—the loss of large neurons in the dorsal raphe nucleus, which contain large amounts of serotonin.

Functional Maps of the Brain Show Changes with Depression

PET scans of depressed patients show increases in blood flow in the frontal cortex and the amygdala compared with controls (Figure 16.11) (Drevets, 1998). In addition to increasing in the frontal cortex, blood flow decreases in the parietal and posterior temporal cortex—systems that have been implicated in attentional networks and language. The increase in blood flow in the amygdala—a structure involved in mediating fear (see Chapter 15)—persists even after the alleviation of depression over time. Patients treated with antidepressants, however, show normal blood flow in the amygdala.

Several Neurochemical Theories Attempt to Explain Depression

Work on the psychobiology of affective illness has been greatly influenced since the 1960s by a theory offered by Joseph Schildkraut and Seymour Kety (1967): the *monoamine hypothesis of depression.* According to this view, depressive illness is associated with a decrease in synaptic activity of connections that employ the monoamine transmitters norepinephrine and serotonin. This decrease is especially characteristic of hypothalamic and associated limbic system circuitry.

Support for this hypothesis comes from the clinical effectiveness of two forms of treatment: antidepressant drugs and electroconvulsive shock therapy. Some antidepressant drugs inhibit **monoamine oxidase**—the enzyme that inactivates norepinephrine, dopamine, and serotonin—thus raising the level of available monoamines. In contrast, the drug **reserpine,** which depletes norepinephrine and serotonin in the brain (by releasing intraneuronal monoamine oxidase, thereby breaking down these transmitters), can cause profound depression. Electroconvulsive shock treatment is effective in many depressed patients, and the seizures produced by this treatment have a strong impact on biogenic amines.

The most recent class of antidepressants consists of the selective serotonin reuptake inhibitors (SSRIs), such as Prozac (Table 16.2). In rats, such drugs increase neurogenesis in the hippocampus (Malberg et al., 2000). SSRI treatment also increases the production of brain steroids (Griffin and Mellon, 1999), such as allopregnanolone (see Chapter 4), that stimulate GABA receptors, which may contribute to the effectiveness of SSRIs. Interestingly, psychotherapy and SSRI treatment together are more effective in combating depression than either one is alone (Keller et al., 2000).

Studies of suicide victims show lower concentrations of serotonin or its metabolites in the brain (Asberg et al., 1986). Low levels of the metabolites of serotonin are

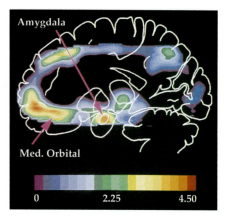

16.11 Brain Activity Patterns in Depression This PET scan reveals increased activity in the frontal cortex (*Med. Orbital*) and the amygdala of depressed patients. This image is the result of the subtraction of brain scans of control subjects from those of depressed subjects. Areas of highest activation are shown in red and orange. (Courtesy of Wayne C. Drevets.)

TABLE 16.2 *Drugs Used to Treat Depression*

Drug class	Mechanism of action	Examples[a]
Monoamine oxidase inhibitors (MAOIs)	Inhibit the enzyme monoamine oxidase, which breaks down serotonin, norepinephrine, and dopamine	Marplan, Nardil, Parnate
Tricyclics and heterocyclics	Inhibit the reuptake of norepinephrine, serotonin, and/or dopamine	Elavil, Wellbutrin, Aventyl, Ludiomil, Norpramin
Selective serotonin reuptake inhibitors (SSRIs)	Block the reuptake of serotonin, having little effect on norepinephrine or dopamine synapses	Prozac, Paxil, Zoloft

[a]We give here the more commonly used trade names rather than chemical names.

also found in the cerebrospinal fluid of people who attempt suicide. Furthermore, suicide attempters who show lower levels of serotonin metabolites are ten times more likely to die of suicide later in their lives than are suicide attempters who show higher levels. In addition, a variant version of the gene for the $5\text{-}HT_{2A}$ receptor is more common in suicide victims than in controls (Du et al., 2000).

Why Do More Females than Males Suffer from Depression?

Studies all over the world show that more women than men suffer from major depression. The NIH epidemiological survey mentioned at the start of this chapter documents this sex difference (Robins and Regier, 1991). All the U.S. sites revealed a twofold difference for major depression. Similar findings have been noted in Sweden. What accounts for these sex differences? The answer to this question is especially important for achieving an understanding of the causes of depression.

Several hypotheses have been advanced. Some researchers argue that the sex differential arises from differences in how males and females seek help—notably, that women use health facilities more than men do. But even though the NIH survey was a door-to-door survey, not an assessment of appearance at health centers, significant sex differences were apparent. This fact appears to rule out the hypothesis that the sex difference in the incidence of depression is caused by sex differences in help-seeking patterns.

Several psychosocial explanations have been advanced. One view emphasizes that depression in women arises from the social discrimination that prevents them from achieving mastery by self-assertion. According to this view, inequities lead to dependency, low self-esteem, and depression. Another psychosocial focus leans on the learned-helplessness model (which we will discuss shortly). According to this view, stereotypical images of men and women produce in women a cognitive set of classic feminine values, reinforced by societal expectations, of which helplessness is one dimension.

A genetic interpretation of the gender difference in depression is that depression is an inherited disorder linked to the X chromosome. But relatives of male and female sufferers of depression show no differences in depression rates (which would be expected with X linking). Thus although there is a strong genetic determinant for depression in general, there does not seem to be a genetic basis for sex differences in depression.

Some researchers have emphasized gender differences in endocrine physiology. The occurrence of clinical depression often is related to events in the female reproductive cycle—for example, before menstruation, during use of contraceptive pills, following childbirth, and during menopause. Although several hormones have been linked to depression, there is little relation between circulating levels of hormones related to female reproductive physiology and measures of depression.

Epidemiological studies of Amish communities (Egeland and Hostetter, 1983) provide a different slant on the mystery of gender differences in depression. An exhaustive survey of this religious community, which prohibits the use of alcohol and shuns modernity, reveals no sex difference in major depression. This finding suggests that in the general population, heavy use of alcohol masks depression in many males, making it appear as if fewer males than females suffer from depression. (Alcoholism is more common in males than in females.)

The Hypothalamic–Pituitary–Adrenal Axis Is Involved in Depression

For many years researchers have sought easily measurable biochemical, physiological, or anatomical indicators of various mental disorders. These indicators, called **biological markers,** may reflect factors relevant to the causes of a disorder or its current state. The development of laboratory tests designed to reveal such factors is important especially because some behavioral assessments may not provide clues to genetic mechanisms or differential responses to drugs. Thus two patients might present a similar portrait of depression but respond differently to antidepressant drugs.

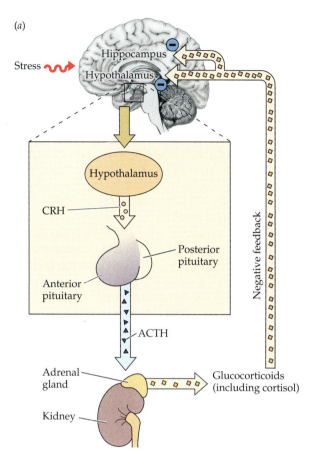

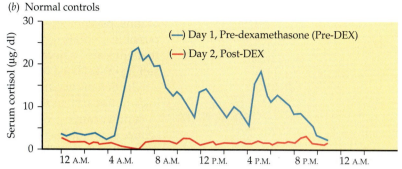

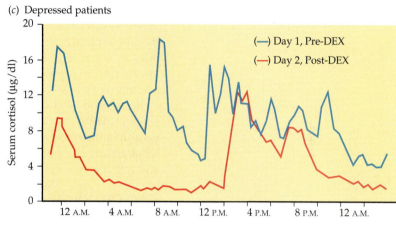

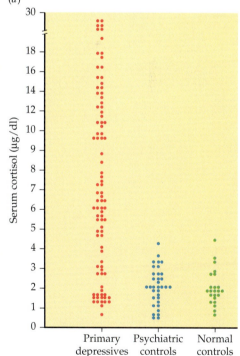

16.12 The Hypothalamic–Pituitary–Adrenal Axis in Depression (*a*) Evidence shows that the hypothalamic–pituitary–adrenal system is involved in depression. (*b*) The normal circadian rhythm in the secretion of cortisol (day 1) is abolished by treatment with the synthetic glucocorticoid dexamethasone (day 2). (*c*) The same dose of dexamethasone is far less effective in depressed patients. (*d*) Circulating cortisol levels are usually higher in depressed subjects than in psychiatric or normal controls.

An appropriate biological marker could suggest what drug to use for a particular patient.

Of the various mental disorders, research on depression has been especially productive in generating potential biological markers, in particular several that are linked to hormonal responses to stress that involve the hypothalamic–pituitary–adrenal system (Figure 16.12*a*). Another reason that investigators studying depression are interested in the hypothalamic–pituitary–adrenal system is that it is activated by stress, which is also believed to activate depression in susceptible individuals (Heit et al., 1997).

Suicide victims show very high levels of circulating cortisol, which suggests hyperfunction of the hypothalamic–pituitary–adrenal axis in depression (Roy, 1992). Early work in this area focused on the hypothalamic–pituitary–adrenal system because hospitalized patients with depression showed elevated cortisol levels. This finding suggested that ACTH (adrenocorticotropic hormone) is released in excessive amounts by the anterior pituitary. One method for analyzing the pituitary–adrenal function is the **dexamethasone suppression test.**

Dexamethasone is a potent synthetic corticoid that ordinarily suppresses the typical early-morning rise in ACTH. Generally given late at night, dexamethasone seems to "fool" the hypothalamus into believing that there is a high level of circulating cortisol. In normal individuals, dexamethasone clearly suppresses cortisol levels (Figure 16.12*b*), but in many depressed individuals it fails to have this effect (Figure 16.12*c*). As depression is relieved, dexamethasone again suppresses cortisol normally.

The normalization is claimed to occur no matter what the cause of relief—lapse of time, psychotherapy, pharmacotherapy, or electroconvulsive shock therapy. One possible mediating mechanism is that in depressed people the cells of the hypothalamus are subject to abnormal excitatory drive from limbic system regions, resulting in sustained release of ACTH. Some evidence suggests that depression causes a reduction of cellular corticosteroid receptors, resulting in subnormal negative feedback in this system (Barden et al., 1995).

A provocative proposal is that stress and the attendant release of glucocorticoids reduce brain production of neurotrophic factors, such as brain-derived neurotrophic factor (BDNF; see Chapter 7), leading to neuronal atrophy and therefore depression (Duman et al., 1997). According to this hypothesis, drugs that increase the stimulation of serotonin and/or norepinephrine cause an increase in cyclic AMP in the brain, which causes an increase in the production of cAMP responsive element–binding protein (CREB, discussed in Chapter 18) and therefore an increase in BDNF release. The BDNF then maintains other brain neurons to alleviate depression. Favoring this theory is evidence that stress reduces BDNF production in the rat hippocampus and that SSRI drugs block this effect.

Both hypo- and hyperthyroid conditions have been associated with affective changes. Thyroid hormone supplementation can enhance the responsiveness of patients to antidepressant drugs. However, additional studies are needed to determine whether any components of the hypothalamic–pituitary–thyroid axis are sensitive and reliable markers of depression.

Sleep Characteristics Change in Affective Disorders

The disturbance of sleep that accompanies depression is not news, but the character of the change and the fact that induced changes in sleep might influence depression are new pieces in the puzzle. Difficulty in falling asleep and inability to maintain sleep are common in major depression. In addition, EEG sleep studies of depressed patients show certain abnormalities that go beyond difficulty in falling asleep.

The sleep of patients with major depressive disorders is marked by a striking reduction in stages 3 and 4 of slow-wave sleep (SWS) and a corresponding increase in stages 1 and 2 (Figure 16.13a). Changes in REM sleep include a shortened time from sleep onset to the first REM episode (Figure 16.13b). Furthermore, the temporal distribution of REM sleep is altered; an increased amount of REM sleep occurs during the first half of sleep, as though REM sleep were displaced toward an earlier period in the night (Wehr et al., 1985). REM sleep in people suffering from depression is also more vigorous, marked by very frequent rapid eye movements.

Are these sleep abnormalities specific to depression? This question remains steeped in controversy. Some of the abnormalities are seen in other psychiatric states, and most likely some are nonspecific. However, alterations of REM sleep seem to have a special connection to depression; shortened REM sleep latency correlates significantly with the severity of depression. The role of REM sleep in depression is also supported by the clinical effectiveness of various types of sleep therapy. Vogel et al. (1980) focused on the fact that REM sleep seems misplaced and extended in the sleep of patients with depression, who almost seem to start sleep where normal people leave off. This analysis inspired studies on the effect of selective REM sleep deprivation on the symptoms of depression.

A marked antidepressant effect of REM sleep deprivation has been noted in several studies of patients suffering from major affective disorders. Patients were awakened as they entered REM sleep, which reduced the overall amounts of REM sleep; the procedure was continued for 2 to 3 weeks. A control group of patients suffering from depression were awakened from non-REM sleep. Depression was evaluated on the basis of a clinical rating scale. At the end of 3 weeks, the REM sleep–deprived group showed a significantly lower depression score than the non-REM sleep–deprived group. Three weeks later the treatments were reversed, and by the end of another 3 weeks, the effect had also switched. Several antidepressant drugs, such as monoamine oxidase inhibitors, suppress REM sleep for extended periods. Vogel as-

(*a*) Sleep pattern of a patient with depression

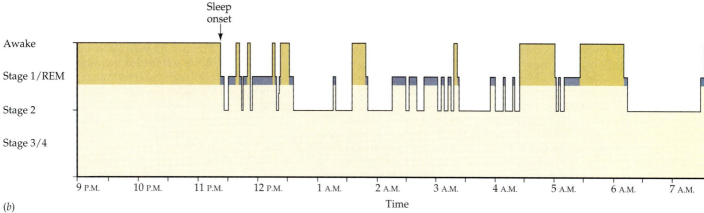

(*b*)

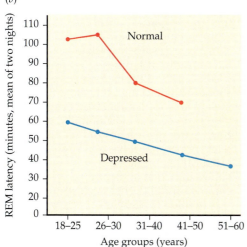

16.13 Sleep and Depression
(*a*) Depressed subjects spend little or no time in sleep stages 3 and 4. (Compare with Figure 14.12.) (*b*) Patients suffering from depression also enter their first REM period earlier in the night. Thus REM sleep seems to be distributed differently in people with depression.

serted that REM sleep deprivation improves severe depression to the extent that it modifies REM sleep abnormalities.

Another sleep therapy approach has emerged from the analysis of circadian rhythms of sleep in patients with depression. Wehr et al. (1983) found that these patients show abnormal phase relationships in some body rhythms, in addition to alterations in REM sleep cycles. This analysis generated a type of circadian treatment for depression. Wehr et al. (1982) had patients go to bed 6 hours before their usual time and reported that several patients showed a rapid improvement in their depression. In addition to these links between daily rhythms and depression, seasonal rhythms have been implicated in a particular depressive condition known as *seasonal affective disorder (SAD)*, which is described in Box 16.2.

Seizures Can Relieve Depression in Some Patients

About 50 years ago treatments in psychiatry were few, yet the needs were enormous. The title of a book by Elliot Valenstein (1986)—*Great and Desperate Cures*—captures the general thinking: try anything in the face of an overwhelming absence of knowledge about the brain. During this period several desperate cures were introduced with little rationale. One of them was the induction of seizures to treat schizophrenia.

Initially, convulsions were produced chemically, by use of the convulsant drug Metrazol. Beginning in the late 1930s, convulsions were produced by electricity delivered through two large electrodes placed on the skin over the skull (electroconvulsive shock therapy). Although this treatment had no clinical impact on schizophrenia, frequent use of this technique showed that such induced seizures could rapidly reverse severe depression.

Eliot Valenstein

BOX 16.2 *The Season to Be Depressed*

Seasonal rhythms characterize the behavior and physiology of many animals, including humans. For some unfortunate people, winter brings a low period, which may become a profound depression. For many such people the winter depression alternates with summer mania (Blehar and Rosenthal, 1989). In wintertime, affected people feel depressed, slow down, generally sleep a lot, and overeat. Come summer they are elated, energetic, and active, and they become thinner. This syndrome—called **seasonal affective disorder** (**SAD**)—appears predominantly in women and generally starts in early adulthood.

Some studies have reported a positive correlation between latitude and the frequency of SAD: The farther from the Equator, the more cases of SAD. But a study in a country at a far northern latitude—Iceland—where a relatively high rate of SAD would be expected, failed to confirm this relationship (Magnusson and Stefansson, 1993). On the contrary, this study revealed a much lower rate for SAD in Iceland. Perhaps population selection over centuries has tended to diminish the reproductive prominence of individuals susceptible to SAD in Iceland and has led to greater tolerance in this population of prolonged periods of winter darkness.

Some support for this idea comes from studies of SAD in descendants of Icelandic emigrants in Canada. In this population, SAD is lower than in other populations at the same latitude (Magnusson and Axelsson, 1993).

In nonhuman animals, many seasonal rhythms are controlled by the length of the day. For example, migration or hibernation may be triggered by changes in the duration of daylight. Some researchers have suggested that SAD in humans shows a similar dependence. To examine that prospect, researchers have explored whether exposure to light that simulates sunlight can act as an antidepressant.

In one investigation (Rosenthal et al., 1985), a group of patients was secured by a newspaper advertisement that described the typical features of SAD. The patients who were selected for the study had at least two winter episodes of depression. Experimental treatment consisted of two 1-week exposures to additional light separated by 1 week of no additional light. During the treatment periods, patients were exposed to bright light twice during the day: from 5:00 A.M. to 8:00 A.M., and from 5:30 P.M. to 8:30 P.M. This distribution extended normal daylight and thus tended to simulate the long daylight period that is characteristic of summer.

The results indicated that bright light has a significant antidepressant effect that is reversed upon withdrawal of the light. No significant effects were noted following exposure to dim light. The improvement in mood appeared after a few days and generally persisted through the week of treatment. Removal of the light quickly produced relapse (Wehr et al., 1986).

One important biological effect of light is that it suppresses melatonin, a hormone found in the pineal gland that affects gonadotropins and may be of importance in controlling sleep. Whereas exposure to darkness stimulates melatonin synthesis, light suppresses it. People with SAD have been shown to have a high threshold for melatonin suppression. However, oral administration of melatonin did not influence this disorder. Serotonin may be relevant because it has a marked seasonal rhythm in humans, with lower values in winter and spring than in summer or fall (Egrise et al., 1986).

Attention to seasonal affective disorder arose primarily because of animal research dealing with photoperiodic behavior and circadian control systems—another example of basic research leading to alleviation of the distresses and diseases of humans.

The advent of antidepressant drugs led to the temporary retirement of this clinical tool. For some patients, however, antidepressant drugs are relatively ineffective. Furthermore, patients in imminent danger of committing suicide need a treatment that works faster to relieve depression than do most antidepressant drugs (although new types are constantly being developed and made available for clinical trials).

Starting in the 1980s, electroconvulsive shock treatment was resumed to treat suicidal patients who failed to respond to antidepressant drugs. Although somewhat different from its original form, this treatment still elicits a large-scale seizure (R. D. Weiner, 1994). The mechanisms that make electroconvulsive shock therapy an effective treatment of depression remain elusive, although recently developed imaging techniques are being used to gain insight into possible mediating changes in brain function (Nobler et al., 1994).

Animal Models Aid Research on Depression

Because it is difficult to ask a monkey or a cat or a rat if it has delusions of persecution or if it hears voices urging it to commit awful crimes, animal models of schizophrenia are limited. But many of the signs of depression are behaviorally overt—such as decreased social contact, problems with eating, and changes in activity. An animal model for the study of depression can provide the ability to evaluate proposed neurobiological mechanisms, a convenient way to screen potential treatments,

TABLE 16.3 *Characteristics of Animal Models of Depression*

Model	Activity change	Sensitivity to antidepressants	Decreased social contact
Stress models			
Learned helplessness	+	+	−
Chronic mild stress	−	+	−
Behavorial despair separation models (e.g., primate separations)	+	+	+
Pharmacological models (e.g., reserpine reversal)	+	+	−
Anatomical models (e.g., olfactory bulbectomy)	+	+	−
Genetic models (e.g., Flinders-sensitive line)	+	+	−

and the ability to explore possible causes experimentally (Lachman et al., 1993). Table 16.3 lists the characteristics of animal models used in studies of depression.

In one type of stress model—**learned helplessness**—an animal is exposed to a repetitive stressful stimulus, such as an electrical shock, that it cannot escape. Like depression, learned helplessness has been linked to a decrease in serotonin function (Petty et al., 1994). Removing the olfactory bulb from rodents creates a model of depression: The animals display irritability, hyperactivity, preferences for alcohol, elevated levels of corticosteroids, and deficiency in passive avoidance conditioning—all of which are reversed by many antidepressants. A genetically developed line of rats—the Flinders-sensitive line—has been proposed as a model of depression because these animals show reduced locomotor activity, reduced body weight, increased REM sleep, learning difficulties, and exaggerated immobility in response to chronic stress (Overstreet, 1993). These varied animal models may be useful in finding the essential paths that cause and maintain depression (Lachman et al., 1993).

There Are Several Types of Anxiety Disorders

All of us have at times felt apprehensive and fearful. Some people experience this state with an intensity that is overwhelming and includes irrational fears, a sense of terror, unusual body sensations such as dizziness, difficulty breathing, trembling, shaking, and a feeling of loss of control. For some, anxiety comes in sudden attacks of panic that are unpredictable and last for minutes or hours. And anxiety can be lethal: A follow-up of patients with panic disorder revealed an increased mortality in men with this disorder resulting from cardiovascular disease and suicide (Coryell et al., 1986).

The American Psychiatric Association distinguishes two major groupings of anxiety disorders: phobic disorders and anxiety states. **Phobic disorders** are intense, irrational fears that become centered on a specific object, activity, or situation that the person feels he or she must avoid. **Anxiety states** include recurrent panic states; generalized, persistent anxiety disorders; and posttraumatic stress disorders.

Panic Can Be Provoked Chemically

Several decades ago psychiatrists observed that some patients experience intense anxiety attacks during or after vigorous physical exercise. This effect was thought to be caused by a buildup of lactate in the blood. This observation inspired Pitts and McClure (1967) to administer sodium lactate to patients with anxiety. In some patients the infusions produced immediate panic attacks that resembled the naturally occurring episodes; this chemical treatment did not produce panic attacks in other people.

Margraf and Roth (1986) contested the study on the grounds that it failed to exclude confounding psychological factors: Patients showed a certain level of panic even when infused with placebo. However, PET scans (which we will discuss in the next section) do support the lactate induction effect. In an attempt to account for chemically induced panic, Liebowitz et al. (1986) suggested that the lactate-induced panic stimulates central noradrenergic mechanisms of the locus coeruleus and its outputs. This suggestion is partially supported by the observation that another locus coeruleus stimulant—inhaled 5% carbon dioxide—produces panic in clinically vulnerable individuals.

Anxiety and Panic Disorders Are Characterized by Structural and Functional Changes in the Temporal Lobes

Many patients who suffer from recurrent panic attacks have temporal lobe abnormalities, according to MRI studies. Ontiveros et al. (1989) found temporal lobe abnormalities—including small lesions in white matter and dilation of the lateral ventricles—in 40% of patients with panic disorder. The magnitude of neuroanatomical anomalies correlated significantly with the total number of spontaneous attacks and the age of onset of panic (patients whose episodes of panic begin at an earlier age have more anomalies).

Intriguing PET scan observations have provided a portrait of the anatomy of anxiety. Studies by Reiman et al. (1986) revealed abnormalities in the resting, nonpanic state. They compared patients whose panic disorder could be induced by injection of sodium lactate, patients who were not vulnerable to lactate-induced panic, and normal controls. Those who were vulnerable to lactate-induced panic showed a markedly abnormal increase in blood flow in the right parahippocampus. This region contains the major input and output pathways of the hippocampus. Gloor et al. (1982) found that electrical stimulation of this region in awake patients commonly elicits sensations of strong fear and apprehension. In addition to this regional effect, lactate-vulnerable panic patients had abnormally high oxygen metabolism in the brain.

The work of Reiman and collaborators raises the possibility that a biological indicant—PET scan data—can distinguish two major anxiety groups: those vulnerable to lactate-induced panic and those not vulnerable to this form of induced attack. This distinction might reflect a fundamental difference in underlying biological mechanisms. Although these PET observations were criticized because of the possible confounding factor of temporal muscle activity (Posner and Raichle, 1994), other metabolic studies also point to the role of temporal lobe structures in the elicitation and maintenance of anxiety states (Rauch et al., 1995).

Drug Treatment of Anxiety Provides Clues to the Mechanisms of This Disorder

Throughout history people have consumed all sorts of substances in the hopes of controlling anxiety. The list includes alcohol, bromides, scopolamine, opiates, and barbiturates. But not until 1960 was a drug introduced that would forever change the treatment of anxiety. Molecular changes in an antibacterial substance produced the drug meprobamate, which, under the trade name Miltown, became famous as a tranquilizing agent.

Competition among drug companies led to the development of a class of substances called **benzodiazepines,** which have become the most common drugs used in the treatment of anxiety. One type of benzodiazepine—diazepam (trade name Valium)—is one of the most prescribed drugs in history. These drugs are commonly described as **anxiolytic** ("anxiety relieving"), although at high doses they also have anticonvulsant and sleep-inducing properties.

Early behavioral and electrophysiological data established that the benzodiazepines are associated in some way with the action of GABA synapses (see Chapter 4) (recall from Chapter 3 that GABA is the most common inhibitory transmitter in the brain). This interaction with GABA receptors results in enhancement of the action at inhibitory synapses in the brain that use GABA. Thus GABA-mediated postsynaptic inhibition is facilitated by benzodiazepines. Benzodiazepine receptors are widely distributed throughout the brain and are especially concentrated in the cerebral cortex and some subcortical areas, such as the hippocampus and the amygdala (Figure 16.14).

The ultimate function of the benzodiazepine–GABA receptor complex is to regulate the permeability of neural membranes to chloride ions. When GABA, upon release from a presynaptic terminal, activates its receptor, chloride ions are allowed to move from the outside to the inside of the nerve cell, hyperpolarizing and therefore inhibiting the neuron from firing. Benzodiazepines alone do little to chloride conductance, but in the presence of GABA, they markedly enhance GABA-provoked increases in chloride permeability. Research also suggests that specific anxiety peptides occur naturally in the brain and act in association with the benzodiazepine receptor (Marx, 1985).

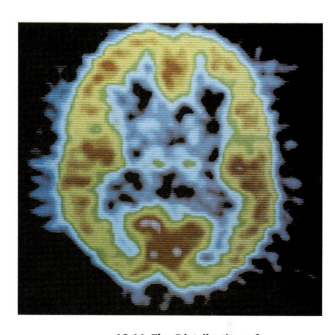

16.14 The Distribution of Benzodiazepine Receptors in the Human Brain This PET scan of benzodiazepine receptors shows their wide distribution in the brain. Highest concentrations are shown in orange and red. (Courtesy of Goran Sedvall.)

In Posttraumatic Stress Disorder, Horrible Memories Won't Go Away

Some people experience some especially awful moments in life that seem indelible, resulting in vivid impressions that persist through the remainder of life. Persons exposed to sustained periods of unrelieved horrors, such as the "killing fields" of war, may find it intensely difficult to shut out these events even long after they have passed. The kind of event that seems particularly likely to produce subsequent stress disorders is one that is intense and usually associated with witnessing abusive violence and/or death. Other such events may be the sudden loss of a close friend, torture, kidnapping, and profound social dislocation, such as in forced migration.

In these cases, memories of horrible events intrude into consciousness and produce the same intense visceral arousal—the fear and trembling—that the original event caused. These traumatic memories are easily reawakened by stressful circumstances and even by innocuous stimuli. An ever watchful and fearful stance becomes the portrait of individuals afflicted with what is called **posttraumatic stress disorder** (**PTSD,** once called *combat fatigue, war neurosis,* or *shell shock*).

Studies on risk factors associated with PTSD in Vietnam War veterans have clarified the interaction of genetic and environmental factors in this disorder. The disorder is particularly prevalent among those who served in the most intense combat areas (True et al., 1993). Familial factors also affect vulnerability, as shown in twin studies of Vietnam era veterans. Researchers compared twins—both monozygotic and dizygotic—who had served in combat zones with other veterans who had not served in Southeast Asia. Monozygotic twins were more similar than dizygotic twins, and the specific contribution of inheritance to PTSD is claimed to account for one-third of the variance.

A comprehensive psychobiological model of the development of PTSD draws connections between the symptoms and the neural mechanisms of fear conditioning, extinction, and behavioral sensitization (Charney et al., 1993). The investigators argue that patients learn to avoid a large range of stimuli associated with the original trauma. A kind of emotional numbing is the consequence of this avoidance, which can also be seen as a type of conditioned emotional response. Work in animals has revealed that this type of memory—*fear conditioning*—is very persistent and involves the amygdala and some brainstem pathways that are part of a circuit of startle response behavior (see chapter 15). NMDA receptor–mediated mechanisms in the amygdala are important for the development of fear conditioning.

The persistence of memory and fear in PTSD may also depend on the failure or fragility of extinction mechanisms. In experimental animals, NMDA antagonists delivered to the amygdala prevent the extinction of fear-mediated startle. Sites pro-

16.15 A Neural Model of Posttraumatic Stress Disorder The original trauma activates two systems: one in the brainstem, which sensitizes the subject to related stimuli in the future, and another in the amygdala, which conditions a long-lasting fearful reaction.

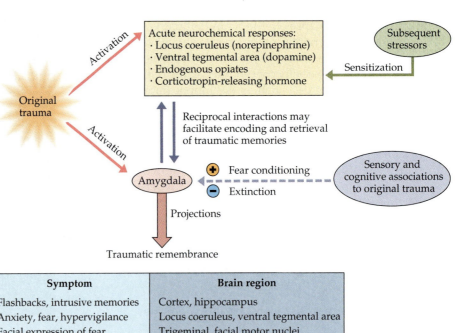

Symptom	Brain region
Flashbacks, intrusive memories	Cortex, hippocampus
Anxiety, fear, hypervigilance	Locus coeruleus, ventral tegmental area
Facial expression of fear	Trigeminal, facial motor nuclei
Anhedonia, depression	Nucleus accumbens
Startle	Reticular formation
Hyperventilation	Medullary respiratory center
Sympathetic activation: rapid heart rate, increased blood pressure	Lateral hypothalamus
Parasympathetic activation: diarrhea, increased urination	Vagal nerve nucleus

jecting to the amygdala, such as the hippocampus and prefrontal cortex, may also lose their effectiveness in suppressing learned fear responses.

Another element of this model—behavioral sensitization mechanisms—enhances response magnitude after exposure to a stimulus. The neural mechanisms probably involve dopamine because repeated stressors increase dopamine function in the forebrain. Figure 16.15 presents this intriguing neural model. One important implication of this model is that it might direct clinical intervention. For example, it suggests a potentially important use for drugs that block conditioned responses.

Exposure to stress leads to high levels of circulating glucocorticoids, which some researchers have suggested might lead to cell loss in the hippocampus (Sapolsky et al., 1990) or might prevent normal cell gain in the hippocampus (E. Gould et al., 1998). Patients who display combat-related PTSD show (1) memory changes such as amnesia for some war experiences, (2) flashbacks, and (3) deficits in short-term memory (Bremner et al., 1993). Reports of such psychological changes have led to MRI studies of the brains of combat veterans with PTSD. Measurements of the right hippocampus reveal an 8% reduction in the volume of this structure, with no changes in other brain regions (Bremner et al., 1995). Chapter 17 will discuss two research-based methods that have been proposed to prevent or alleviate posttraumatic stress disorder.

In Obsessive–Compulsive Disorders, Thoughts and Acts Keep Repeating

Neatness, orderliness, and similar traits are attributes we tend to admire, especially during those chaotic moments when we realize we have created another tottering pile of papers, bills, or the like. What, then, constitutes what we call **obsessive–compulsive disorder (OCD)**? In her book *The Boy Who Couldn't Stop Washing* (1989b), Judith Rapoport, a psychiatrist at the National Institutes of Health with extensive experience in researching and treating people afflicted with OCD, described a remarkable group of people whose lives are riddled with repetitive acts that are carried out without rhyme, reason, or the ability to stop.

In OCD patients, routine acts that we all engage in, such as checking whether the door is locked when we leave our home, are repeated over and over. Recurrent thoughts, such as fears of germs or other potential harms in the world, invade the consciousness. Table 16.4 summarizes the symptoms of OCD. These symptoms progressively isolate a person from ordinary social engagement with the world. For many patients, hours of each day are consumed by compulsive acts such as repetitive hand washing.

Determining the number of persons afflicted with OCD is difficult, especially because many people with this disorder tend to hide their symptoms. It is estimated that more than 4 million people are affected by OCD in the United States (Rapoport, 1989a). In many cases, the initial symptoms of this disorder appear in childhood; the peak age group, however, is 25 to 44 years.

For a long time this disorder was thought of as a psychiatric dysfunction associated with psychological conflict. More recently, evidence has accumulated that this disorder is rooted in the neurobiology of the brain. Rapoport (1989a) suggested that the features of this disorder reflect "subroutines" associated with grooming and territoriality that have evolved gradually. Symptoms arise when brain malfunction causes these programs to be executed without the usual provoking stimuli—such as cleaning something that is already clean.

TABLE 16.4 *Symptoms of Obsessive-Compulsive Disorders*

Symptoms	Percent of patients
OBSESSIONS	
Dirt, germs, or environmental toxins	40
Something terrible happening (fire, death or illness of self or loved one)	24
Symmetry, order, or exactness	17
Religious obsessions	13
Body wastes or secretions (urine, stool, saliva)	8
Lucky or unlucky numbers	8
Forbidden, aggressive, or perverse sexual thoughts, images, or impulses	4
Fear of harming self or others	4
Household items	3
Intrusive nonsense sounds, words, or music	1
COMPULSIONS	
Performing excessive or ritualized hand washing, showering, bathing, tooth brushing, or grooming	85
Repeating rituals (going in or out of a door, getting up from or sitting down on a chair)	51
Checking (doors, locks, stove, appliances, emergency brake on car, paper route, homework)	46
Removing contaminants from contacts	23
Touching	20
Preventing harm to self or others	16
Ordering or arranging	17
Counting	18
Hoarding or collecting	11
Cleaning household or inanimate objects	6
Engaging in miscellaneous rituals (such as writing, moving, speaking)	26

The basal ganglia, frontal cortex, and OCD. PET scan studies of patients with OCD show significantly higher metabolic rates in the left orbital gyrus and bilaterally in the caudate nucleus. The basal ganglia have also been implicated in other disorders related to OCD, such as Tourette's syndrome (Box 16.3). Studies of regional cerebral blood flow in patients in whom OCD symptoms have been provoked support this finding.

In a recent study, investigators provoked a symptomatic state by using stimuli that patients reported provoked OCD symptoms (Rauch et al., 1994). Brain images obtained in response to an innocuous stimulus were subtracted from those obtained when symptoms were provoked. Statistically significant increases in regional blood flow were seen in the right caudate nucleus, left anterior cingulate cortex, and bilateral orbitofrontal cortex. This pattern of enhanced blood flow supports an anatomical model of obsessive–compulsive disorders proposed by Insel (1992) that emphasizes a circuit involving a loop among frontal, striatal, and thalamic structures.

Serotonin and OCD. The basic observation behind the serotonin hypothesis of obsessive–compulsive disorders is that clomipramine, a tricyclic antidepressant (see Table 16.2), markedly reduces the symptoms of this disorder. Although OCD is classified as an anxiety disorder, some clinicians have long believed that this disorder is related to depression. For example, studies of the incidence of OCD and depres-

---

BOX 16.3 *Tics, Twitches, and Snorts: The Unusual Character of Tourette's Syndrome*

Their faces twitch in an insistent way, and every now and then, out of nowhere, they blurt out an odd sound or, quite suddenly, an obscene word. At times they fling their arms, kick their legs, or make violent shoulder movements. Sufferers of **Tourette's syndrome** also exhibit heightened sensitivity to tactile, auditory, and visual stimuli (A. J. Cohen and Leckman, 1992). Many patients also sense the buildup of an urge to emit verbal or phonic tics; they report that these acts relieve this powerfully felt need. Professionals have long argued about whether this collection of symptoms forms a psychiatric disturbance derived from the stresses of life or emerges from a disturbance in brain structures and/or function.

Tourette's syndrome begins early in life; the mean age of diagnosis is 6 to 7 years (de Groot et al., 1995). Figure A draws a portrait of the chronology of symptoms. Associated behavioral disturbances include attention deficit hyperactivity disorder (ADHD), problems in school, and obsessive–compulsive disorder (Park et al., 1993).

Genetics appears to play a potent role in this disorder. The contemporary view is that Tourette's syndrome is me-

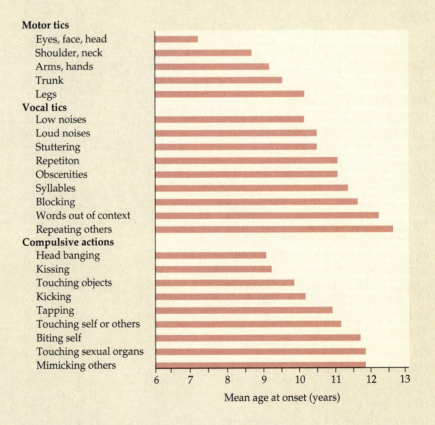

(A) The chronology of Tourette's symptoms

sion show some overlap between them. Like patients with depression, patients who suffer from OCD exhibit decreased REM sleep latency.

Comparisons of antidepressants used to treat OCD generally show that clomipramine has greater antiobsessional effects than most other antidepressants have. What sets clomipramine apart? One significant difference between clomipramine and other antidepressants is the potency of its ability to block serotonin uptake. Blocking the reuptake of serotonin has significant antiobsessional effects.

Neurosurgery Has Been Used to Treat Psychiatric Disorders

Through the ages the mentally disabled have been treated by methods limited only by the human imagination. Some methods have been gruesome, inspired by views that people with mental disorders are controlled by demonic forces. Although psychiatry was purged of such moralistic views in the twentieth century, until recently treatment was a trial-and-error affair.

In the 1930s, experiments on frontal lobe lesions in chimpanzees inspired psychiatrist Egas Moniz to attempt similar operations in patients. Moniz was intrigued by the report of a calming influence in nonhuman primates, and when he tried frontal surgery, little else was available. His observations led to the beginning of **psychosurgery,** defined as the use of surgically produced brain lesions to modify

COMPETING HYPOTHESES

---

diated by a single gene inherited in a dominant manner (Eapen et al., 1993). Twin studies of the disorder reveal a concordance rate among monozygotic twins of 53 to 77%, contrasted with a concordance rate among dizygotic twins of 8 to 23% (Hyde et al., 1992; R. A. Price et al., 1985).

An unusual view of genetic factors in Tourette's is provided by a study of a set of triplets who were reared apart after the age of 2 months (Segal et al., 1990). The triplets consisted of a pair of monozygotic female twins and a dizygotic male. They were reunited when they were 47 years old. The male had a history of eye blinking, facial tics, and repetitive arm and finger movements that had begun at age 4. Eye blinking persisted into adulthood. The female twins showed a more severe set of symptoms: frequent motor and phonic tics, head jerks, shoulder jerks, and kicking leg movements.

The symptoms of patients with Tourette's resemble some of those seen in patients with basal ganglia disease. MRI studies show subtle changes in basal ganglia structure in these patients. For example, normal subjects usually show asymmetry in the volumes of left and right basal ganglia structures, but patients with Tourette's

syndrome fail to show this asymmetry, and they show lower overall volumes of basal ganglia such as the caudate nucleus and globus pallidus (B. Peterson et al., 1993).

More persuasive are PET studies of dopamine receptors in monozygotic twins. The twin with more severe symptoms almost always showed significantly higher binding of the D_2 dopamine receptor in the caudate—a correlation of +0.99. In the MRI scan at the bottom of Figure B, the locations of the caudate nuclei are indicated by ovals, which match the areas of highest binding shown in the PET scan above (Wolf et al., 1996). This finding may explain why drugs that affect dopamine functioning can reduce the frequency of some of the motor features of Tourette's syndrome (A. L. Peterson and Azrin, 1992).

Administration of haloperidol, a dopamine antagonist, significantly reduces tic frequency and is the primary treatment of this disorder. Unfortunately, side effects limit the duration of this treatment. Behavior modification techniques that aim at reducing the frequency of some symptoms, especially tics, are claimed to help some patients (A. L. Peterson and Azrin, 1992). (Figure B courtesy of Steven Wolf.)

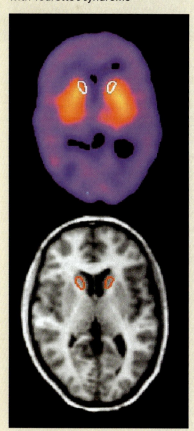

(B) D_2 binding in the brain of a twin with Tourette's syndrome

(a) Horizontal view

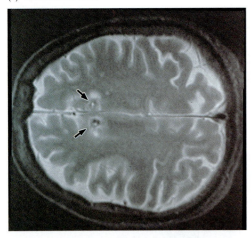

(b) Sagittal view

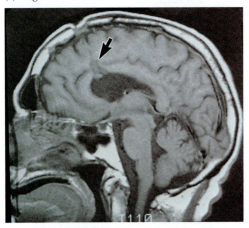

16.16 Neurosurgery to Treat Obsessive–Compulsive Disorder
These horizontal (a) and sagittal (b) MRIs show the brain of a patient who underwent a cingulotomy—the disruption of cingulate cortex connections (arrows)—in an attempt to treat OCD. (From Martuza et al., 1990; courtesy of Robert L. Martuza.)

severe psychiatric disorders. Psychosurgery has provoked vigorous debate since the inception of its use, which continues to the present (Valenstein, 1980, 1986).

During the 1940s, **lobotomy** (disconnecting parts of the frontal lobes from the rest of the brain) was forcefully advocated by several neurosurgeons and psychiatrists. A presidential commission on psychosurgery estimated that during this period, 10,000 to 50,000 U.S. patients underwent this surgery (National Commission for the Protection of Human Subjects in Biomedical and Behavioral Research, 1978). During the most intense period of enthusiasm, patients of all diagnostic types were operated on, and different varieties of surgery were employed.

Interest in psychosurgery arose from the saddening sight of many people in mental hospitals living empty, disturbed lives without hope of change. Today frontal surgery is rare and generally limited to treatment of intense pain. Its use in psychiatry has practically ended, although the commission on psychosurgery urged further consideration of the role of surgery in psychiatry. (Recall from Chapter 15 that temporal lobe surgery has also been used to treat violent behavior attributed to seizures.)

Assessments of the value of frontal lobe surgery in psychiatric treatment are steeped in controversy. William Sweet (1973) argued that more localized brain lesions might significantly relieve particular psychiatric disorders. Strong support for this view was offered by Ballantine et al. (1987), who reported on the treatment of depression and anxiety disorders by stereotaxic cingulotomy (lesions that interrupt pathways in the cingulate cortex).

Clinical evaluations reported positive outcomes of this procedure in many chronically depressed patients who were not aided by other treatments. For example, a follow-up study on a group of severely disabled OCD patients (Jenike et al., 1991) indicated that one-third of patients who underwent cingulotomy (Figure 16.16) benefited substantially from this intervention (Martuza et al., 1990). A long-term follow-up study of OCD patients who received ventromedial frontal lesions as a last-resort therapy for OCD indicated significant improvement in obsessive–compulsive symptoms (Irle et al., 1998). This clinical improvement was sustained in some patients for 20 years. However, the use of drugs has overshadowed psychosurgery, especially because neurosurgical interventions are not reversible.

Prions, Mad Cows, and Creutzfeldt–Jakob Disease

Over two centuries ago shepherds in Europe recognized a fatal disease in sheep called *scrapie* because the animals "scraped" their skin, presumably in an attempt to relieve itching. The shepherds learned that the only way they could stop an outbreak was to kill all the sheep, burn the carcasses and the fields they had used, and keep new sheep away from those fields for years.

These drastic measures were needed because the disease is not transmitted by a virus or bacteria, which would rely on relatively fragile DNA or RNA for reproduction. Rather, scrapie is caused when a particular endogenous protein that normally takes one shape takes on a new, abnormal shape. Once one protein molecule does this, it induces the other molecules of that protein to also fold abnormally. The accumulation of abnormally folded proteins leads to brain degeneration. These infectious protein particles were named **prions** by their discoverer, Stanley Prusiner, who was awarded a Nobel Prize in 1999 for this research.

Unfortunately, at some point meat from sheep suffering from scrapie was fed to some cows in England and caused the cow version of the prion protein to fold abnormally (Figure 16.17). Eventually this produced a bovine version of scrapie called **bovine spongiform encephalopathy** (**BSE,** or *mad cow disease*) because of massive brain degeneration, leaving the brain "spongy."

Unfortunately, before BSE was detected, infected cows provided beef for Britons and caused a similar disorder called **Creutzfeldt–Jakob disease** (**CJD**) in humans.

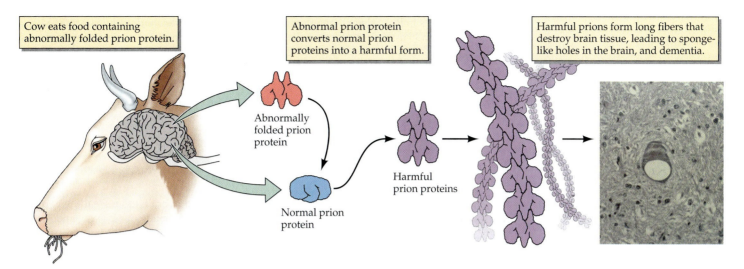

Cow eats food containing abnormally folded prion protein.

Abnormal prion protein converts normal prion proteins into a harmful form.

Harmful prions form long fibers that destroy brain tissue, leading to sponge-like holes in the brain, and dementia.

Abnormally folded prion protein

Normal prion protein

Harmful prion proteins

16.17 Prions Are Proteins that Transmit Disease

CJD is fatal, causing widespread brain degeneration and therefore dementia, sleep disorders (see Chapter 14), schizophrenia-like symptoms, and death.

Before "mad cows" introduced it in humans, CJD was a very rare disease, and it cannot readily spread among humans because we aren't normally exposed to each other's brain tissue. Neurosurgeons learned that instruments used on the brain of a CJD patient must be destroyed because no sterilization procedure prevents them from infecting subsequent patients. It will be difficult to stop the spread of CJD because BSE symptoms arise years after prion infection, making it difficult to spot infected cows.

Summary

1. Biological approaches have enabled better distinctions within large classes of mental disorders, such as schizophrenia and anxiety.

2. There is strong evidence for a genetic factor in the origin of schizophrenia. Consistent evidence comes from studies of the incidence of schizophrenia in families, twins, and adoptees.

3. Structural changes in the brains of patients with schizophrenia—including enlarged ventricles, limbic system abnormalities, and abnormalities of other brain regions—may arise from early developmental problems.

4. Biological theories of schizophrenia include two general classes of ideas: (1) the view that schizophrenia comes about because of failure at a particular level in the operation of neurotransmitters at synapses, and (2) the view that schizophrenia develops from a metabolic fault that results in the production of a toxic substance, a psychotogen with properties similar to known hallucinogenic agents.

5. The dopamine hypothesis attributes schizophrenia to excessive release of or sensitivity to dopamine. Supporting evidence comes from studies on the effects of antipsychotic drugs, amphetamine psychosis, and Parkinson's disease.

6. According to an integrative psychobiological model, the emergence of schizophrenia depends on the interaction of a vulnerable biological substrate and environmental stressors. The greater the biological vulnerability of an individual, the less stress is needed to precipitate a schizophrenic disorder.

7. Biological studies of affective disorders such as depression reveal a strong genetic factor and the importance of levels of various neurotransmitters, including serotonin.

8. People suffering from depression show increased blood flow in the frontal cortex and the amygdala, and decreased blood flow in the parietal and posterior temporal cortex.

9. In the general population, females are more likely than males to suffer from depression. Various hypotheses have been proposed to explain this sex difference, but all of them remain inconclusive.

Refer to the *Learning Biological Psychology* CD for the following study aids for this chapter:

8 Objectives

73 Study Questions

1 Activity

10. Changes in REM sleep that accompany depression include shortened onset to REM sleep and larger percentages of REM sleep in overall amounts of sleep. Some sleep treatments appear to act as antidepressants.

11. Anxiety states are characterized by functional changes in the temporal lobes that can be revealed by PET scans.

12. Antianxiety drugs (benzodiazepines) affect receptors for the transmitter GABA. These drugs enhance the inhibitory influence of this neurotransmitter.

13. Obsessive–compulsive disorder is characterized by changes in basal ganglia and frontal structures and strongly linked to serotonin activities.

14. Neurosurgery continues to be used as a form of psychiatric treatment in a limited number of instances.

15. Infectious proteins, called prions, become concentrated in brain tissues leading to damage and dementia in bovine spongiform encephalopathy (mad-cow disease) and Creutzfeldt–Jakob disease.

Recommended Reading

Bloom, F. E., and Kupfer, D. J. (Eds.). (1995). *Psychopharmacology: The fourth generation of progress.* New York: Raven.

Fogel, B. S., and Schiffer, R. B. (1996). *Neuropsychiatry: A comprehensive textbook.* New York: Williams and Wilkins.

Gottesman, I. I. (1995). *Schizophrenia genesis: The origins of madness.* New York: Freeman.

Nathan, P. E., and Gorman, J. M. (Eds.). (1998). *A guide to treatments that work.* New York: Oxford University Press.

Solomon, A. (2001). *The noonday demon: An atlas of depression*, New York: Scribner.

Torrey, E. F., Bowler, A. E., Taylor, E. H., and Gottesman, I. I. (1994). *Schizophrenia and manic depressive disorder.* New York: Basic Books.

Whybrow, P. C. (1997). *A mood apart.* New York: Basic Books.

PART SIX

Cognitive Neuroscience

*L*earning and memory, language, and cognition are the fascinating focal points of much current research. We start Part 6 with a top-down approach in Chapter 17, describing learning and memory in whole organisms and identifying the associated neural regions and systems. In Chapter 18 we investigate the neuronal and synaptic mechanisms and the neural networks that may underlie learning and memory. Chapter 19 focuses on the most elaborate products of brain function: the biology of language and cognitive states that are so distinctively human.

Striking cases of impaired memory start our discussion. We can discover a great deal about learning and memory by examining how they fail. Clinical cases show that memory can fail in quite different ways, and these observations demonstrate that there are different kinds of learning and memory. The clinical cases also provide clues about the brain regions that are especially involved in memory. Carefully designed animal research has delved deeper into this question. Noninvasive brain imaging is helping investigators acquire new evidence about the brain mechanisms of learning and memory. Together these and other approaches are providing converging evidence to yield a comprehensive picture of the brain mechanisms.

17

Learning and Memory: Biological Perspectives

Investigating learning and memory and their biological mechanisms is one of the most active and exciting areas of biological psychology. All the distinctively human aspects of our behavior are learned: the languages we speak, how we dress, the foods we eat and how we eat them, and so on. Much of our own individuality depends on learning and memory. Research on learning and memory gives us a better understanding of almost all the topics we have taken up so far because almost every aspect of behavior and cognition requires learning: how we perceive, the skilled acts we perform, our motivations, and the ways we achieve our goals. Conditions that impair memory are particularly frightening; they make it impossible to take part in normal social life and can rob us of our identity.

Rex Stevens, *Betsy (for Roy)*, 1997

Valuable research on learning and memory is being done at all the levels of organization of the nervous system, from the intact organism to subcellular mechanisms. A major theme in this chapter is the search for the neural regions involved in learning and memory. In this search, investigators use a variety of techniques: studying people with impaired memory; examining the effects of precise, experimental brain lesions in animals on learning and memory; and making noninvasive brain scans of people with normal abilities while they learn or remember tasks that are carefully designed to bring out particular aspects of learning or remembering.

Many Kinds of Brain Damage Can Impair Memory

Many kinds of brain damage, caused by disease or accident, impair learning and memory, and study of such cases is continuing to provide powerful lessons. We'll start by looking at some of these cases before progressing to newer brain-imaging techniques that provide novel information about the involvement of brain regions in learning and memory. Study of different types of memory impairment has revealed the existence of different classes of learning and memory, which we will discuss later in the chapter. First let's look at a few cases of memory impairment that have posed puzzles and have stimulated a great deal of controversy.

For Patient H.M., the Present Vanishes into Oblivion

CLINICAL ISSUE

Henry, known in the literature as *patient H.M.,* had suffered from epileptic seizures since the age of 16. His condition became steadily worse and could not be controlled by medication; he had to stop work at the age of 27. His symptoms indicated that the seizures began in the medial basal regions of both temporal lobes, so in 1953 a neurologist removed this tissue, including much of the amygdala and hippocampus on both sides, as confirmed in a recent MRI study (Figure 17.1) (Corkin et al., 1997; Hilts, 1995; Scoville and Milner, 1957).

Similar operations had been performed earlier without harmful effects, although in those cases less tissue had been removed. After H.M. recovered from the operation, his seizures were milder, and they could be controlled by medication. But this relief came at a terrible, unforeseen price: H.M. now suffered a peculiar kind of amnesia. **Amnesia** (Greek for "forgetfulness") is a severe impairment of memory.

Most of H.M.'s old memories remained intact, but he had difficulty retrieving memories that had formed during the 10 years before the operation. Such memory loss is called **retrograde amnesia** (from the Latin *retro-*, "backward," and *gradi,* "to go"). Retrograde amnesia is not rare. What was striking about H.M. was an unusual symptom: his apparent inability to retain *new* material for more than a brief period. When he met someone new, almost as soon as that person left the room H.M. was unable to recall the person's name or even that he had met someone. The inability to form new memories after the onset of an illness is called **anterograde amnesia** (from the Latin *antero-*, "forward," and *gradi,* "to go").

Even now, years after the operation, H.M. retains a new fact only briefly; as soon as he is distracted, the newly acquired information vanishes. He doesn't know his age or the current date, and he doesn't know that his parents (with whom he lived) died years ago. But he converses easily, and his IQ remains a little above average (Corkin et al., 1997). The observation of impaired memory, coupled with normal perception and general intellectual functions, shows that memory can be separated from other cognitive functions. Studies to characterize H.M.'s capacities continue (e.g., Hood et al., 1999; MacKay et al., 1998).

There are a few indications that H.M. has formed some bits of long-term memory in the years since his operation. For example, when asked where he is, he sometimes guesses the Massachusetts Institute of Technology, the place where he has been

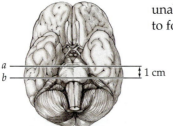

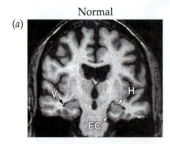

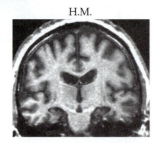

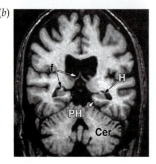

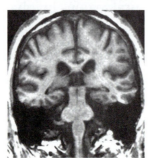

17.1 Brain Tissue Removed from Patient H.M. (*a*) Approximately corresponding MRI scans of a normal subject (*left*) and patient H.M. (*right*) show that the hippocampus (H) and entorhinal cortex (EC), which are prominent in the normal scan, are absent bilaterally in H.M. (*b*) A more caudal scan (see drawing at top for planes of section) shows some of the hippocampal formation intact (H) in H.M., but the parahippocampus (PH) is absent, and H.M.'s cerebellum (Cer) is markedly atrophied. f, fornix; V, lateral ventricle. (From Corkin et al., 1997; courtesy of Suzanne Corkin.)

interviewed and tested many times in the last 40 years. He recognizes that something is wrong with him because he has no memories of the past several years or even of what he did earlier in the same day. His description of this isolation from his past is poignant (B. Milner, 1970):

> Every day is alone in itself, whatever enjoyment I've had, and whatever sorrow I've had. . . . Right now, I'm wondering, have I done or said anything amiss? You see, at this moment everything looks clear to me, but what happened just before? That's what worries me. It's like waking from a dream. I just don't remember. (p. 37)

H.M.'s short-term memory is normal. For example, if he is given a series of digits and is asked to repeat the list immediately, like most people he can usually repeat a list of seven digits without error. But if he is given a list of words to study and is tested on them after other tasks have intervened, he cannot repeat the list; in fact, he does not even remember having studied the list. Thus H.M. provides clear evidence that *short-term memory (STM)* differs from *long-term memory (LTM)*.

Psychologists have recognized the distinction between STM and LTM on behavioral and cognitive grounds since the time of William James (1890). Short-term memory is usually considered to last only about 30 s, or as long as a person rehearses the material; it holds only a limited number of items (J. Brown, 1958; L. R. Peterson and Peterson, 1959). Long-term memory is an enduring form that lasts for hours, days, weeks, or more; it has very large capacity. We will discuss long- and short-term memory in more depth later in this chapter.

After publication of H.M.'s case, similar cases were reported that resulted not from brain surgery but from disease. On rare occasions, herpes simplex virus destroys tissue in the medial temporal lobe. This destruction can produce a severe failure to form new long-term memories, although acquisition of short-term memories is normal (A. R. Damasio, Eslinger, et al., 1985). An episode of reduced blood supply to the brain (**ischemia**), such as can be produced by a heart attack, can also damage the medial temporal lobe and memory formation. Within this general region of the brain, can we pinpoint a specific site as the cause of these memory problems?

At first, H.M.'s memory deficit was ascribed to bilateral destruction of much of the hippocampus because other surgery patients who had received the same type of damage to more anterior structures, including the amygdala, but less damage to the hippocampus, did not exhibit memory impairment. To test this hypothesis, investigators began to remove the hippocampus from experimental animals to reproduce H.M.'s deficit. But after a decade of research, brain scientists had to confess failure: Neither in rats nor in monkeys did widespread failure of memory consolidation follow bilateral destruction of the hippocampus; the effects that were observed could not be distinguished from possible effects of motivational or perceptual factors (Isaacson, 1972).

Different investigators attempted to account for this puzzling discrepancy between human and animal results in different ways. Some investigated the roles of various structures in the medial temporal lobe and the diencephalon; others looked more carefully into the behavioral tests used to measure memory. This broadened research produced major gains in knowledge—about amnesia in people and ways to test memory, about functions of the hippocampus and neighboring structures, and about brain mechanisms of memory. Later in this chapter we will review research with both human and animal subjects that reveals more precisely the structures in the medial temporal lobe where damage causes symptoms like those of H.M. Before such research could yield useful results, however, it was necessary to define more exactly what was impaired and what was spared in H.M.'s memory.

**COMPETING
HYPOTHESES**

An early, incorrect hypothesis to explain why human results differed from those in other animals was that the impairment caused by damage to the medial temporal lobe in humans involves chiefly verbal material and that animals, of course, cannot be tested for such deficits. An interesting finding suggested that H.M.'s memory deficit was restricted mainly to verbal material and might not hold for motor learning.

(*a*) The mirror-tracing task

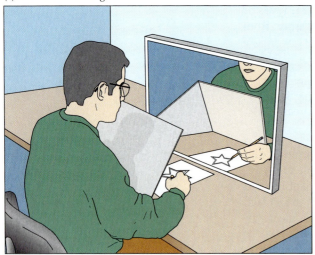

(*b*) Performance of H.M. on mirror-tracing task

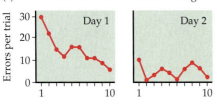

17.2 H.M.'s Performance on a Mirror-Tracing Task (*a*) H.M. was given this mirror-tracing task to test motor memory. (*b*) His performance at this task on three successive days showed progressive improvement and thus long-term memory. (After B. Milner, 1965.)

Brenda Milner

CLINICAL ISSUE

Brenda Milner (1965) presented a mirror-tracing task to H.M. (Figure 17.2*a*), and he showed considerable improvement over ten trials. The next day the test was presented again. When asked if he remembered it, he said no, yet his performance was better than at the start of the first day (Figure 17.2*b*). Over three successive days, H.M. never recognized the problem, but his improved tracings showed memory. If an animal subject with the same type of brain damage showed similar proof of memory, we would have no doubt that the animal had normal memory because we do not ask animal subjects whether they *recognize* the test.

Two other types of findings, however, indicated that the memory problems of H.M. and similar patients could not be attributed solely to difficulties with verbal material. First, such patients also have difficulty in reproducing or recognizing pictures and spatial designs that are not recalled in verbal terms. Second, although the patients have difficulty with the specific content of verbal material, they can learn some kinds of information *about* verbal material (N. J. Cohen and Squire, 1980).

For example, they can learn to read words printed mirror-reversed. The requirement for this task is not motor skill, but rather the ability to deal with abstract rules or procedures. If some words are used repeatedly, normal subjects come to recognize them and to read them easily. Patients of several kinds—those with temporal lobe amnesia, those who suffer from Korsakoff's syndrome (which we will describe shortly), and those who have recently received electroconvulsive shock therapy—learn the skill of mirror reading well but show impaired learning of the specific words.

Thus the important distinction is probably not between motor and verbal performances but between two kinds of memory: (1) **Declarative memory** is what we usually think of as memory: facts and information acquired through learning. It is memory we are aware of accessing. (2) **Nondeclarative memory** is shown by performance rather than by conscious recollection. It is sometimes called **procedural memory.** Examples of nondeclarative memory are memory for the mirror-tracing task and for the skill of mirror reading, as we just described. The two kinds of memory can be distinguished as follows: Declarative memory deals with *what*; nondeclarative memory deals with *how.* Thus an animal's inability to speak is probably not what accounts for its apparent immunity to the effects of medial temporal lesions on memory storage. Rather, the culprit is the difficulty in measuring declarative memory in animals.

Different types of tests measure declarative and nondeclarative memories. Direct (explicit) tests of memory refer to a specific prior episode. Examples of direct tests include requests for information such as "Repeat the list of words you studied 10 minutes ago" or "What did you eat for dinner yesterday?" They also have been defined as requiring conscious recognition of the material. Indirect (or implicit) tests of memory do not refer to a specific prior episode and do not require conscious recognition; the memory is inferred from performance. For example, memory for the recent presentation of certain words may be inferred from ease of recognizing them versus control words in blurred or very rapid presentation or from the probability of using them in a word completion test.

Damage to the Medial Diencephalon Can Also Prevent Formation of New Memories

The medial temporal lobe is not the only brain region involved in the formation of declarative memories. For example, the case of *patient N.A.* indicates that damage to the dorsomedial thalamus can also impair memory formation (Squire and Moore, 1979; Teuber et al., 1968). N.A. became amnesic as a result of a bizarre accident in which a miniature fencing foil injured his brain after entering through his nostril. N.A. is markedly amnesic, primarily for verbal material, and he can give little information about events since his accident in 1960, but he shows almost normal recall for events of the 1940s and 1950s (Kaushall et al., 1981).

An MRI study of N.A. (Figure 17.3) shows damage to the left dorsal thalamus, bilateral damage to the mammillary nuclei, and probable damage to the mammillothalamic tract (Squire et al., 1989). Like H.M., N.A. shows normal short-term memory but is impaired in forming declarative, but not nondeclarative, long-term memories. The similarity in symptoms raises the question of whether the medial temporal region and the midline diencephalic region are parts of a larger system. We will return to this question in Chapter 18.

Patients with Korsakoff's Syndrome Show Damage to Midline Diencephalic Structures and to the Frontal Cortex

In 1887 Russian neurologist S. S. Korsakoff published a paper about a syndrome in which impaired memory was a major feature. This paper became a classic, and the syndrome was subsequently named after him: **Korsakoff's syndrome.** Sufferers of Korsakoff's syndrome fail to recall many items or events of the past; if such an item is presented again or if it happens to be recalled, the patient does not feel familiar with it. These patients frequently deny that anything is wrong with them. They often show disorientation to time and place, and they may **confabulate**—that is, fill a gap in memory with a falsification that they seem to accept as true.

The main cause of Korsakoff's syndrome is lack of the vitamin thiamine. Alcoholics who obtain most of their calories from alcohol and neglect their diet often exhibit this deficiency. Treating such a person with thiamine can prevent further deterioration of memory functions. Animal models of Korsakoff's syndrome are created through either drug-induced thiamine deficiency (Langlais et al., 1992) or surgical lesions.

Mair et al. (1979) examined two Korsakoff's patients for several years, using a battery of behavioral tests; later they examined the brains of these patients in detail. Both brains showed shrunken, diseased mammillary bodies, as well as some damage in the dorsomedial thalamus. Temporal lobe structures, including the hippocampus and the temporal stem, were normal. Thus these cases confirm the less precise, earlier studies. Mair et al. (1979) characterize the mammillary bodies as "a narrow funnel through which connections from the midbrain as well as the temporal lobe neocortex and limbic system gain access to the frontal lobes" (p. 778). Damage to the basal frontal lobes, also found in patients suffering from Korsakoff's syndrome, is probably what differentiates them from other patients who have amnesia, such as H.M.

Patient K.C. Shows that Brain Damage Can Destroy Autobiographical Memories While Sparing General Memories

One striking case of brain damage shows profound effects on memory and supports an important distinction between two kinds of declarative memory that cognitive psychologist Endel Tulving (1972) has defined: semantic memory and episodic memory. **Semantic memory** is generalized memory, such as knowing the meaning of a word without knowing where or when you learned that word. **Episodic memory** is autobiographical memory that pertains to a person's particular history; you show episodic memory when you recall a specific episode or relate an event to a particular time and place (such as remembering where and when you last saw a certain friend).

Evidence for the distinction between semantic and episodic memory appeared in studies of *patient K.C.*, who had sustained brain injuries in a traffic accident. The original description of his case noted only extensive damage to the left frontal-parietal and the right parietal-occipital cerebral cortex (Tulving, 1989), but recent brain scans also show severely reduced volume of the hippocampus and shrinkage of the parahippocampal cortex (R. S. Rosenbaum et al., 2000). K.C. can no longer retrieve

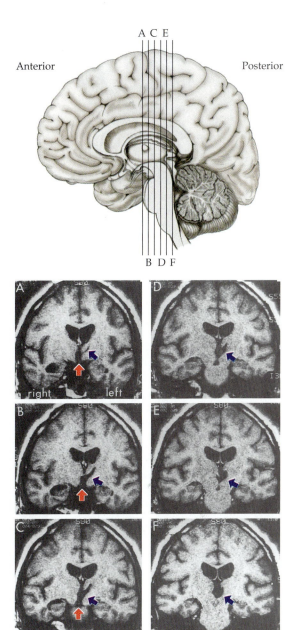

17.3 The Brain Damage in Patient N.A. Successive MRI scans were made through the diencephalic region (*top*); note that right and left are reversed in these scans, as if you were face-to-face with the patient. A prominent lesion on the left side of the brain is indicated by the purple arrows. The floor of the third ventricle also appears to be missing throughout much of the caudal two-thirds of the hypothalamus, as indicated by the red arrows in scans A through C. Where the mammillary nuclei should be present in B and C, there is no indication of intact tissue. (From Squire et al., 1989; MRI scans courtesy of Larry Squire.)

Endel Tulving

any personal memory of his past, although his general knowledge remains good. He converses easily and plays a good game of chess, but he cannot remember where he learned to play chess or from whom. K.C. has difficulty acquiring new semantic knowledge, but he can acquire some, if care is taken to space out the trials to prevent interference among items (Tulving et al., 1991). But even with this method he cannot acquire new episodic knowledge.

The neocortical damage, rather than impairment of the hippocampal region, appears to be responsible for the loss of episodic memory because other patients with hippocampal damage do not show this symptom. Studies of normal human subjects indicate increased blood flow in the anterior regions of the cortex during recall of episodic memories, and increases in posterior regions during recall of semantic materials, so the anterior cortical damage may be what robs K.C. of episodic memory (Tulving, 1989).

There Are Several Kinds of Memory and Learning

We have already mentioned the distinctions between declarative and nondeclarative memories and between semantic and episodic memories. We will also be discussing some other kinds of memories and seeking to find the brain regions that are especially involved in them. As a basis for this discussion, Figure 17.4 presents a classification of some of the main kinds of long-term memory and gives an example of each. In addition, Box 17.1 reviews some basic definitions of learning.

In **skill learning,** subjects perform a challenging task on repeated trials in one or more sessions. The mirror-tracing task performed by H.M. (see Figure 17.2) is an example. Learning to read mirror-reversed text, also mentioned earlier, is a kind of perceptual skill learning.

Priming, also called *repetition priming,* is a change in the processing of a stimulus, usually a word or a picture, as a result of prior exposure to the same stimulus or related stimuli. For example, if a person is shown the word *stamp* in a list and later is asked to complete the word stem *STA-,* he or she is more likely to reply *stamp* than is a person who was not exposed to that word. Even patients like H.M., who do not recall being shown the list of words, nevertheless show the effect of prior presentation, or priming.

Conditioning, shown at lower right in Figure 17.4, is defined in Box 17.1. Different brain areas are responsible for conditioning depending on the complexity of the conditioning situation.

Even "Simple" Learning May Be Complex

It is important to keep in mind that even relatively simple learning situations may be rather complex, as a few examples will illustrate.

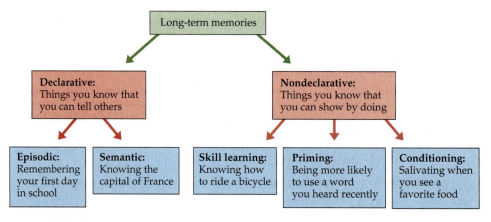

17.4 Kinds of Long-Term Memory

BOX 17.1 *Learning and Memory: Some Basic Concepts and Definitions*

Because you have probably studied learning and memory in one or more psychology courses, here we only briefly review some of the basic concepts and definitions. Basic experiments on learning and memory, as described for neuroscientists by Rescorla (1988), examine the organism's experience and behavior at two separate times. At the first time (t_1), the organism is exposed to a particular experience—a sensory stimulus or another opportunity to learn. At a later time (t_2), the investigator assesses the organism to determine whether the t_1 experience has modified its behavior.

The aim is to determine whether a particular t_1 experience produces an outcome at t_2 that would be absent without the t_1 experience. Therefore, studies of learning usually compare two organisms (or two groups of organisms) at t_2: those that were exposed to the t_1 experience and those that did not have that experience but instead had a "control" experience at t_1. The basic learning paradigms can be organized in terms of the different types of experience provided at t_1 and the different techniques of assessment used at t_2.

There are three main experimental paradigms:

1. A single stimulus (S_1), without any other event or constraint, is presented to the organism. The result may be habituation, dishabituation, or sensitization (defined below).
2. One stimulus (S_1) is presented in relation with another stimulus (S_2). This paradigm (called *Pavlovian*, or *classical*, *conditioning*; see below) allows us to study how the organism learns about the structure of its environment and the relations among stimuli in its world.
3. A single stimulus (S_1) is delivered in such a way that it reinforces a certain behavior. Called *instrumental*, or *operant*, *conditioning* (see below), this paradigm allows us to study how an organism learns about the impact of its own actions on the world.

Nonassociative learning involves only a single stimulus at t_1. Three kinds of nonassociative learning are habituation, dishabituation, and sensitization. **Habituation** is a decrease in response to a stimulus as the stimulus is repeated (when the decrement cannot be attrib-

uted to sensory adaptation or motor fatigue). When the response to a stimulus has become habituated, a strong stimulus (of the same sort or even in another sensory modality) will often cause the response to the habituated stimulus to increase sharply in amplitude; it may become even larger than the original response. The increase in response amplitude over the baseline level is called **dishabituation** (the habituation has been removed). Even a response that has not been habituated may increase in amplitude after a strong stimulus. This effect is known as **sensitization:** The response is greater than the baseline level because of prior stimulation.

Chicks develop an attachment to any conspicuous object—normally, the mother hen—exposed to them shortly after hatching. This kind of learning is called **imprinting,** and its neural basis has been studied. Some newly born mammals, such as lambs, also show imprinting.

Learning that involves relations between events—for example, between two or more stimuli, between a stimulus and a response, or between a response and its consequence—is called **associative learning.** In one form, **classical conditioning** (also called *Pavlovian conditioning*), an initially neutral stimulus comes to predict an event. At the end of the nineteenth century, Ivan Pavlov (Figure A) found that a dog would salivate when presented with an auditory or visual stimulus if the stimulus came to predict an event that normally caused salivation. If the experi-

menter rang a bell just before putting meat powder in the dog's mouth, repeating this sequence a few times would cause the dog to respond to the bell itself by salivating.

In this case the sound is called the *conditioned stimulus* (*CS*) and the meat powder in the mouth is the *unconditioned stimulus* (*US*); the meat powder already evokes an unconditioned response (UR), and the acquired response to the CS (salivation in response to the bell in this example) is called the conditioned response (CR). Another form of classical conditioning is **sensory–sensory conditioning:** When two stimuli occur in conjunction, one stimulus comes to predict the occurrence of the other.

In **instrumental conditioning** (also called **operant conditioning**), an association is formed between the animal's behavior and its consequence(s). The first investigation of instrumental learning was Edward L. Thorndike's report (1898) of cats learning to escape from a puzzle box (Figure B). When placed in a small box with a latch inside, a cat would initially engage in a variety of behaviors and take quite a bit of time to free itself. But after several trial-and-error sequences, the cat learned to perform skillfully and economically the specific response (the conditioned instrumental response) that permitted escape (the reward). A modern example of an apparatus designed to study instrumental learning is an operant conditioning apparatus, often called a *Skinner box* after its originator, B. F. Skinner

(A) Pavlov and spectators in his laboratory

BOX 17.1 *(continued)*

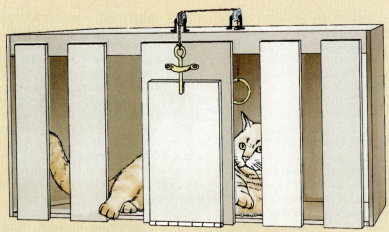

(B) Thorndike's puzzle box

(C) A Skinner box

(Figure C). Here the conditioned instrumental response is pressing a bar to gain the reward of a food pellet.

Typical learning events have multiple dimensions or attributes. For example, Pavlov's dogs learned not only the relation between the conditioned auditory stimulus (the bell) and the meat powder, but also many other aspects of the situation. They learned the location of the test apparatus and the rewarding features of the test situation, so when the dogs came into the test room they would eagerly leap onto the test stand. They also learned when in the day to expect to be tested. Thorndike's cats learned sensory aspects of the test situation, as well as the correct motor responses.

Different brain regions may process different dimensions or attributes of a learning or memory situation: space, time, sensory dimensions, response, and emotional aspects (Kesner et al., 1993; R. J. McDonald and White, 1993). Later in the chapter we will consider some experiments performed to test this so-called attribute model of memory.

Conditional Learning Depends on Context

Typical examples of learning have multiple dimensions, as conditional learning reveals. In **conditional learning** the subject learns that a particular response to a particular stimulus is appropriate in one setting but not in another. More formally, the conditioned stimulus (CS) or unconditioned stimulus (US) becomes associated with the context in which it occurs. A CS evokes a conditioned response (CR) in one context but evokes no response (or not as strong a response) in another. For example, if you are playing a game and a ball flies toward your face, you catch it if you are playing on a basketball court, but you give it a header if you are playing on a soccer field. Conditional learning does not require a big brain, or any brain at all; even the relatively simple mollusk *Aplysia* can do it (Colwill et al., 1988).

Close Temporal Pairing of Stimuli Is Not Necessary for Conditioning

Neuroscientists have often assumed that close temporal proximity of CS and US is required for conditioning, but several experiments during the 1960s demonstrated that such pairing is neither necessary nor sufficient. Although proximity is important in some experiments, such as the eye-blink conditioning of mammals that we will describe shortly, it would be wrong to overgeneralize from these examples. Proximity does not guarantee conditioning, and conditioning does not necessarily require proximity, as experiments going back to Pavlov (1927) demonstrate. In order for conditioning to occur, the CS must be a reliable predictor of the US—in fact, the most reliable predictor available (Rescorla, 1988).

Several kinds of conditioning have an optimal CS–US interval, but the optimum varies considerably depending on the task. For conditioning the eye-blink reflex in mammals, the interval is about 200 ms; for the siphon- or gill-withdrawal reflex in *Aplysia,* about 0.5 s; for operant-conditioned bar pressing in rats, about 2 s; and for taste aversion in rats (see Chapter 13), an hour or more. This wide variation in optimal CS–US interval raises the question of whether temporal pairing of stimuli is a general requirement for conditioning.

Conditioned Responses Have Many Dimensions

In conditioning, both the response and the stimulus tend to have multiple dimensions. Consider the example of eye-blink conditioning, which is studied in both human and animal subjects. In these experiments a tone or buzzer (the conditioned stimulus) precedes a puff of air to the eye (the unconditioned stimulus) that causes the subject to blink. After a few trials, the subject begins to blink in response to the CS, before the puff of air is delivered. Blinking early protects the eye from the mildly unpleasant air puff. But even before subjects develop the specific conditioned response (CR) of blinking to the CS, they show some nonspecific CRs that may include increases in heart rate and blood pressure, changes in respiration, and changes in electrical resistance of the skin. These nonspecific autonomic responses develop earlier than the appearance of the specific CR in many situations, especially if the US is aversive; perhaps they help prepare the subject to respond to a novel or threatening situation.

Do Animals Learn Stimulus–Response Chains or Form Cognitive Maps?

Many psychologists in the 1930s and 1940s were searching for the laws that govern all learning. Psychologists such as Clark L. Hull held that animals form stimulus–response associations reinforced by rewards or punishments, and they applied this to behavior such as that of rats in runways or mazes (Hull, 1943). An opposing position was that of Edward C. Tolman (1949b), who held that when rats explore a maze, they do not learn a series of turns, but instead form a **cognitive map.** For example, after rats had run a maze several times, the experimenters removed a section of wall, thus opening up a shortcut to the goal area. Most rats took the shortcut as soon as it became available, thus showing their knowledge of the overall layout of the maze.

Edward C. Tolman
(1886–1959)

Tolman and his students also demonstrated that rats' performance may not reveal all they know unless the test situation is appropriate to reveal the knowledge. One kind of evidence for this is the phenomenon called **latent learning,** described in the following experiment (Blodgett, 1929; Tolman and Honzik, 1930).

Rats were divided into two groups and were allowed to gain experience in a maze. One group received food when they reached the goal area of the maze; they ran to that area more and more quickly in successive daily trials. Animals of the other group were allowed to explore the maze for a few daily sessions without receiving any reward. Then, in one session, they found food in the goal area. In the next trial they raced to the goal, reaching it just as rapidly as the rats that had been rewarded on every trial. If the experimenter hadn't offered the reward, he would not have realized that the previously unrewarded group had learned the maze as well as the uniformly rewarded rats; until the reward was introduced, the learning was latent, just as an image on photographic film is latent until the film is developed.

IMPORTANT
METHOD

Later, from his surveys of research on learning, Tolman accepted, at least provisionally, the observations of a variety of researchers; he proposed that there are different kinds of learning and that each may have its own laws. He stated these views in an article entitled "There Is More than One Kind of Learning" (Tolman, 1949a). A quarter century passed before many workers began to follow the suggestion to look for separate laws for different kinds of learning.

Memory Has Temporal Stages: Short, Intermediate, and Long

The terms *learning* and *memory* are so often paired that it sometimes seems as if one necessarily implies the other. We cannot be sure that learning has occurred unless a

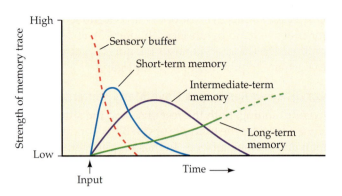

17.5 Multiple-Trace Hypothesis of Memory   According to this hypothesis, an initial brief iconic memory (stored in a sensory buffer) is followed by a short-term memory trace, which may be followed by an intermediate-term memory trace. If the learning is sufficiently strong, a long-term memory trace may also result. (After McGaugh, 1968.)

memory can be elicited later. (Here we are using *memory* in the common meaning of anything that shows that learning has occurred.) Even demonstrating that *something* has been learned, however, does not guarantee that the memory for the learned material will be retrievable again in the future. A memory may later be absent for a variety of reasons: It may never have adequately formed, it may have decayed with time, it may have been impaired by injury to the brain, or it may be temporarily unretrievable because of the particular state of the subject.

Investigators often contrast short-term and long-term memories, but like many twofold distinctions, this differentiation is probably too simple. The multiple-trace hypothesis of memory classifies different types of memory by duration (Figure 17.5). The briefest memories are called **iconic memories** (from the Greek *eikon,* "image"). An example would be impressions of a scene that is illuminated for only an instant. You may be able to grasp one part of the display, but the rest vanishes from your memory in seconds. (A very brief auditory memory is called *echoic,* as if you could still hear it ringing in your ears.) These brief memories are thought to reflect the continuation of sensory neural activity, the so-called sensory buffers (see Figure 17.5).

Somewhat longer than iconic memories are **short-term memories (STMs)**. For example, suppose you want to telephone a person whose number you have never dialed before. You look up the number, and if nothing distracts or interrupts you, you call the number successfully, displaying an STM of the telephone number. If the line is busy, however, and you want to call back a minute later, you may have to look up the number again. If you rehearse or use the number, then it can remain in STM until you turn to another activity.

Unfortunately, the label *STM* is not used consistently among investigators from different fields. Cognitive psychologists, who first used the term, found that if subjects are not allowed to rehearse, STM lasts only about 30 s (J. Brown, 1958; L. R. Peterson and Peterson, 1959). Many biologists define STM as memory that is not permanent but that lasts for minutes or hours, even up to a day. For example, Kandel et al. (1987) wrote that in the sea slug *Aplysia,* "a single training trial produces short-term sensitization that lasts from minutes to hours" (p. 17), and long-term memory is "memory that lasts more than one day" (p. 35). The lack of agreement on the duration of short-term and long-term memory undermines attempts to find biological mechanisms of the stages of memory.

Some memories last beyond the short term but fall short of long-term memories. For example, suppose you drive to school or work and park your car in a different place each day. If things go well, you remember each afternoon where you parked your car that morning, but you may not recall where you parked your car yesterday or a week ago. You are also likely to recall today's weather forecast, but not that of a few days ago. These are examples of what is sometimes called **intermediate-term** memory (**ITM**)—that is, a memory that outlasts STM but that is far from being permanent (McGaugh, 1966; Rosenzweig et al., 1993).

Memories that last for days to years are called **long-term memories** (**LTMs**). Because many memories that last for days or weeks do, however, become weaker and may even fade out completely with time, some investigators use the term **permanent memory** to designate memories that appear to continue without decline for the rest of the life of an organism, or at least as long as the organism remains in good health.

The fact that some memories last only for seconds and others for months is not proof that short-term memories are based on cognitive or biological mechanisms that differ from those of long-term memories. The scientist's task is to find out whether these memories are based on the same or different processes and mechanisms. As we will see, there are good reasons—both clinical and experimental—to conclude that the cognitive processes and biological mechanisms that underlie STM storage are different from those that underlie LTM storage.

Early behavioral evidence for differences between short-term and long-term memory stores came from the performance of subjects who learned lists of words or numbers. If you see or hear a list of ten words presented one at a time, and then 30 s later you try to repeat the list, you will probably remember best the first and the last items of the list. Figure 17.6 shows typical results from such an experiment: a U-shaped serial position curve. The superior performance for the start of the list is called the **primacy effect.** The superior performance for the end of the list is called the **recency effect.** If subjects try to recall the list a few minutes after having seen or heard the items, there is no recency effect; that is, it is short-lived and thus attributed to STM. The primacy effect, however, lasts longer and is usually attributed to LTM.

Experimental animals also show U-shaped serial position functions. These results provide one type of behavioral evidence to separate STM from a longer-lasting memory store (or stores) in animal subjects, and they offer the possibility of relating behavioral and biological mechanisms of memory stages in the same subjects. Wright et al. (1985) gave similar recognition memory tests to pigeons, monkeys, and humans. For each test the material consisted of four sequentially presented color slides. Each slide was presented for 1 s to monkeys and humans and 2 s to pigeons, with a 1 s interval between items for all groups. After a delay, a probe item was presented; on half the trials the probe item matched one of the four test patterns. Subjects demonstrated their memory by making one response if the probe matched a test item and another response if it was new.

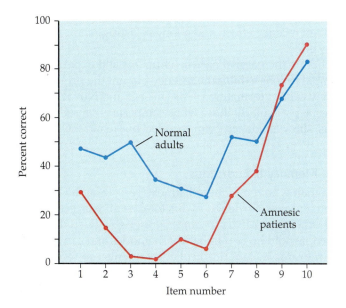

17.6 Serial Position Curves from Immediate-Recall Experiments These curves show the percentage of correct responses for immediate recall of a list of ten words. The patients with amnesia performed as well on the most recent items (8 through 10) as the normal adults, but they performed significantly worse on earlier items. (After Baddeley and Warrington, 1970.)

17.7 Recognition Memory Curves for Humans, Monkeys, and Pigeons These curves show the percentage of correct responses to a probe item for four positions in the stimulus series, for humans (*a*), monkeys (*b*), and pigeons (*c*). (After Wright et al., 1985.)

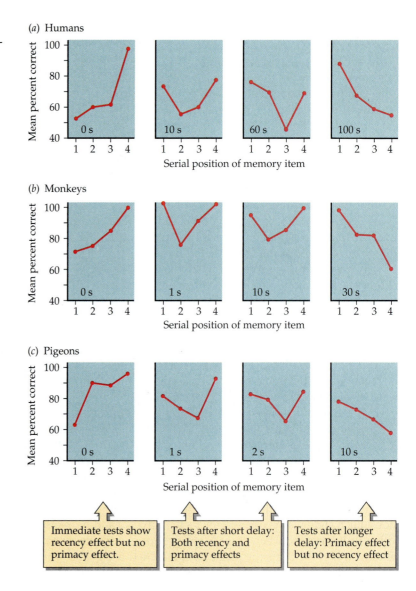

(*a*) Humans

(*b*) Monkeys

(*c*) Pigeons

Immediate tests show recency effect but no primacy effect.

Tests after short delay: Both recency and primacy effects

Tests after longer delay: Primacy effect but no recency effect

All three species showed primacy and recency effects in their serial position curves, differing only in the delays that reveal each (Figure 17.7). Thus results for all three species provide evidence of two distinct memory processes: a transient STM that accounts for the short-lived recency effect, and a longer-lasting memory store that accounts for the primacy effect.

Brain lesion studies corroborate the parallel between humans and experimental animals: Rats with hippocampal lesions exhibit the recency but not the primacy effect, as though, like H.M., they cannot form new LTMs (Kesner and Novak, 1982). Similarly, patients with amnesia, particularly those whose amnesia is caused by impairment of the hippocampus, show a reduced primacy effect but retain the recency effect (see Figure 17.6).

The Capacity of Long-Term Memory Is Enormous

A fascinating case study of a man who remembered almost everything he had experienced from childhood on and was burdened by his total recall was presented by psychologist Alexander Luria in *The Mind of a Mnemonist* (1987). Even the fallible memory stores of most people hold huge numbers of memories and can acquire enormous amounts more. For example, American college students can recognize, on the average, about 50,000 different words. Many people who master several languages readily acquire even vaster vocabularies. Beyond the words, a language has grammar and grammatical forms, idioms, and familiar phrases; it is estimated that learning a language means acquiring on the order of 100,000 items of knowledge. Most of us recognize hundreds or thousands of faces and countless visual scenes and objects, hundreds of voices and many other familiar sounds, and hundreds of different odors. Depending on our interests, we may be able to recognize and sing or play many tunes and identify and supply information about a great many athletes, actors, or historical characters.

Such memories can be acquired rapidly and retained well. For example, psychologist Lionel Standing presented color slides to subjects for 5 s each in blocks of 20 to 1000 or more slides. A few days later he tested recognition memory by presenting pairs of slides, one previously seen and one new, and requiring subjects to indicate which of the pair they had seen before. After an early study showed 90% recognition for 2560 items, Standing increased the number of items to 10,000 and found little decrease in scores. He concluded that, for all practical purposes, "there is no upper bound to memory capacity" (Standing, 1973).

Of course, these results do not mean that the subjects learned all the details of the pictures; the two-alternative, forced-choice procedure guarantees only that *something* about the picture makes it more familiar than the paired item. Nevertheless, the amount of information acquired and the rapidity of acquisition are impressive. And it doesn't require a human brain to accomplish such a task; pigeons readily learned 320 slides in a picture recognition test with no indication that this amount approached their memory capacity, and they retained many of the discriminations for 2 years (Vaughan and Greene, 1984). An example of such memory retention in nature is displayed by Clark's nutcracker, a bird that can locate several thousand cache sites months after hiding food in them (Vander Wall, 1982). What kind of memory mechanisms provide for the enormous capacity of long-term memory?

Can Memories Be Lost or Distorted?

Although the capacity of long-term memory is enormous, we all experience instances of forgetting and inaccurate memory. Early in the twentieth century, investigators supposed that the **memory trace** (the record laid down in memory, presumably in the central nervous system, by a learning experience) decays or fragments with time. But then other workers studied how memories suffer interference from events before or after their formation, and many concluded that memories do not deteriorate with disuse.

Further research showed that each time a memory trace is activated during recall, it is subject to changes and fluctuations, so with successive activations it may deviate more and more from its original form. Furthermore, new information that is provided at the time of recall can add new aspects to the memory trace, so a later evocation of the memory is likely to reactivate the newer traces along with the older, and produce distorted or false memories. (See Estes, 1997, for a review of research on memory loss, recovery, and distortion.) Later in this chapter we will see that certain drugs given at the time of recall can significantly weaken a memory, although given at another time they do not affect memory.

Different Regions of the Brain Process Different Aspects of Memory

We will consider first the roles of different parts of the medial temporal lobe in the formation of declarative memory and then take up how other parts of the brain are involved in the formation of memories for specific aspects of experience.

The Medial Temporal Lobe and Declarative Memory

As we saw earlier, the brain damage suffered by H.M. involved several parts of the medial temporal lobe. Investigators attempted to determine which parts were chiefly responsible for H.M.'s inability to form new declarative memories. Some answers came from other clinical cases and postmortem examination of their brains, and,

(a) Sample

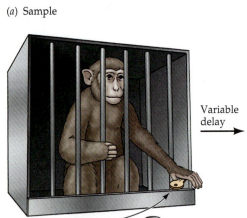

Variable delay →

| The monkey is originally presented with a sample object. When he displaces it, he finds a pellet of food beneath. |

(b) Test

| After a variable delay (seconds to minutes) the monkey is presented with the original object and another object. |

(c) Food found under the nonmatching object

| Over a series of trials with different pairs of objects, the monkey learns that food is present under the object that differs from the sample. |

17.8 The Delayed Non-Matching-to-Sample Task

IMPORTANT METHOD

more recently, from brain scans of patients. Study of monkeys with experimental lesions of parts of the medial temporal region allowed the roles of the different structures to be examined systematically.

An important advance came when psychologists Brenda Spiegler and Mortimer Mishkin (1981) adopted a method for testing memory in monkeys that involved declarative memory—the kind of memory impaired in H.M. This is a test of object recognition memory known as the **delayed non-matching-to-sample** (**DNMS**) task (Figure 17.8). This method tested the ability to recognize which of two objects had been seen, after delays ranging from 8 seconds to 2 minutes. Monkeys with extensive damage to the medial temporal lobe were severely impaired on this task, especially with the longer delays.

Other tests have also proved useful, for example, the **visual paired comparison** (**VPC**) task. This task, originally devised for testing human infants, measures an individual's tendency to look at a novel object in comparison with a familiar object. Normal subjects prefer to inspect a novel object. Patients with amnesia are impaired on this task (McKee and Squire, 1993), and so are monkeys with medial temporal lobe lesions (Bachevalier et al., 1993).

Using these and other tasks, investigators made lesions in various parts of the medial temporal region of monkeys and tested their behavior. The amygdala, which was lesioned in H.M., was found not to be important for the formation of declarative memories, although it is important in fear learning. A retrospective analysis of several studies, employing four different tests of memory with behavioral measures combined to provide composite scores, and lesions varying in size, yielded the results shown in Figure 17.9 (Zola-Morgan et al., 1994): Significant impairment was produced by lesions that included the hippocampus proper, the dentate gyrus, and the subiculum; increased impairment was caused by lesions that included not only these regions but also the adjacent entorhinal cortex and the parahippocampal cortex; finally, the greatest impairment was caused by lesions that also included the anterior entorhinal and perihippocampal cortices.

In human patients, too, damage restricted to the hippocampus produces memory impairments similar to but not as severe as those seen with the more extensive damage in H.M. (Rempel-Clower et al., 1996; Zola-Morgan and Squire, 1986). The memory impairment involves all sensory modalities and types of material. Zola and Squire (2000) concluded that the hippocampus is the final stage of convergence within the medial temporal lobe, combining operations of the adjacent, more specialized regions of cortex; even in the absence of the hippocampus, some mem-

(a) Ventral view of monkey brain showing
   areas of different medial temporal lesions

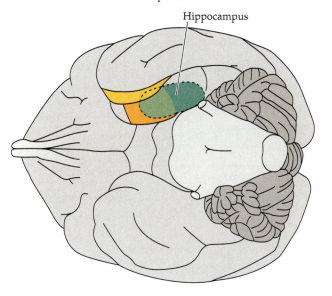

(b) Scores of groups with different lesions

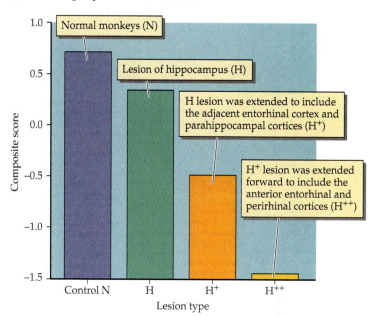

17.9 Behavioral Scores as a Function of Medial Temporal Lobe Lesions (a) In this ventral view of a monkey brain, the hippocampus is dorsal to the cross-hatched area. Green, parahippocampal cortex; orange, entorhinal cortex; yellow, perirhinal cortex. (After Squire and Zola-Morgan, 1991). (b) Different bilateral lesions of the medial temporal lobe yielded different results in tests of memory. N, control animals; H: lesions restricted to hippocampus and subiculum; H+: H lesion extended to include the adjacent entorhinal and parahippocampal cortices; H++: H+ lesion extended forward to include anterior entorhinal and perirhinal cortices.

ory function can be supported by the cortical components of the medial temporal system.

Different Brain Regions Are Involved in Different Attributes of Memory

Any particular memory is composed of features or aspects that are specific and unique to that learning experience, as investigators of human memory noted decades ago (Spear, 1976; Underwood, 1969). Some of the main features (or attributes) of memories are *space, time, sensory perception, response,* and *affect* (i.e., emotional tone or content). For example, as you look at this book, you are aware of spatial aspects of your experience—where the book is in relation to you and where you are; you know the approximate or even the exact time; you perceive the color, shape, and other aspects of the book; you are aware of making certain responses, such as holding the book, turning the page, and writing notes; and you are experiencing a particular affect or emotional state—feeling content, eager, and happy (we hope).

Biological psychologists have tested the hypothesis that the different attributes of memory are processed by different regions of the brain. For example, Raymond Kesner (1980, 1991, 1998), drawing on the reports of many other investigators, designed a program of experiments with rats, as well as experimental and observational studies of people with various kinds of brain damage. Figure 17.10 shows some basic attributes of memory and the brain regions that are believed to process them.

In all of Kesner's tasks, only working, short-term memory was tested. Thus for a *spatial recognition task,* Kesner et al. (1993) used the well-known eight-arm radial maze (Figure 17.11a). Appropriate pretraining taught the rat to expect to find a bit of food at the end of each arm of the maze. For this spatial recognition task, each trial consisted of a study phase and a test phase. In the study phase the rat was allowed to run down any arm. When it returned to the central platform, all doors to the arms were closed, confining the rat for a period of 1 to 30 s.

Next, two doors were opened, allowing the rat a choice between the arm it had recently entered and another arm; the rat found food only if it chose the arm it had entered in the study phase of the trial. In each of the four daily trials, different arms

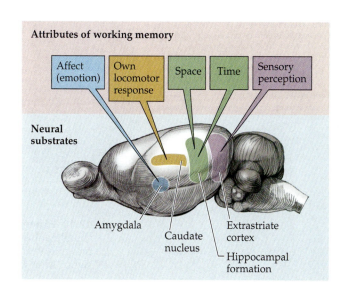

17.10 Basic Attributes of Memory and the Region of the Rat Brain Thought to Process Each (After Kesner, 1980.)

(*a*) Spatial location recognition memory

In the study phase of each trial, the rat can choose any of the eight arms. In the test phase, doors block all but two arms: the arm entered on the study phase and one other. The rat obtains food only if it chooses the arm it entered on the study phase.

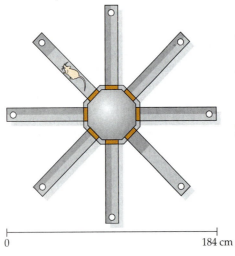

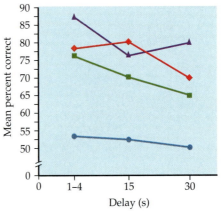

Only rats with hippocampal lesions make significantly more errors than controls.

(*b*) Response recognition memory

In the first part of each trial, the rat is placed in the middle compartment on one side (2), and it finds food if it enters the compartment either to its right (1) or left (3). In the second part of the trial, it is placed in the middle compartment on the other side (5), and it finds food only if it turns to the same side as it had in the first part.

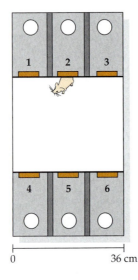

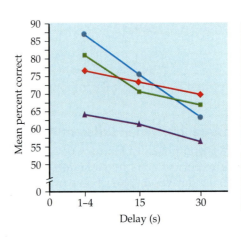

Only rats with caudate nucleus lesions make significantly more errors than controls.

(*c*) Object recognition memory (nonmatching-to-sample)

In the study phase of each trial, the rat obtains food by displacing a sample object over a small food well (top). In the test phase (bottom), the rat chooses between two objects and obtains food only if it chooses the object that does *not* match the sample.

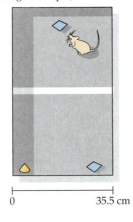

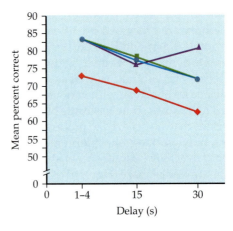

Only rats with lesions of the extrastriate visual cortex make significantly more errors than controls.

17.11 Experiments to Test Specific Attributes of Animals' Memory Brain lesion experiments testing spatial location recognition (*a*), response recognition (*b*), and object recognition (*c*)—using the setups shown on the left—yielded the results shown on the right. (After Kesner et al., 1993.)

were used. Different groups of animals were tested after having received a sham lesion or a lesion in the hippocampus, the caudate nucleus, or the extrastriate cortex (visual cortex outside the primary visual area). The results of this experiment showed that only the animals with hippocampal lesions made more mistakes than the controls (the animals with sham lesions) on this predominantly spatial task.

To emphasize memory for the animal's own locomotor *response*, the investigators ran trials in a different apparatus (Figure 17.11*b*). In the study phase of a trial, the rat was placed in the middle arm on one side (e.g., 2), where it could make an initial turn to its left (3) or right (1). Then it was placed in a different starting location (5) and was rewarded only if it made a turn to the same side of its body as before, not to the same direction in space. Performance on this task, which depends on memory of the previous response, was impaired by lesions of the caudate nucleus but not by lesions of the other brain regions tested.

A task that emphasizes *sensory perception* is the object recognition (or non-matching-to-sample) test. In the study phase the rat was first rewarded each time it pushed aside the sample object. In the test phase the rat was presented with two objects—one like the sample object that had been presented during the study phase and one novel object; the rat was rewarded only if it chose the object that did not match the sample. Only lesions of the extrastriate visual cortex significantly impaired performance on this visual memory task. Thus Kesner et al. (1993) found a triple **dissociation** among brain regions and the tests. That is, lesions of each of three brain regions affected memory performance on only one of the three tests, and performance on each test was affected by lesions in only one of the three brain regions. This dissociation is good evidence that these different aspects of working memory are processed separately and, in part at least, by the brain regions indicated. Of course, an even more complete set of brain regions remains to be tested, if only to try to exclude them as important in processing these aspects of memory.

IMPORTANT METHOD

Further work by Kesner and Williams (1995) on memory involving *affect* indicated that this attribute of memory is impaired by lesions of the amygdala, but not by lesions in the hippocampal formation or in the cerebral cortex dorsal to the hippocampus.

A similar research project in another laboratory found similar results. R. J. McDonald and White (1993) used three different problems, all run in the radial maze. They also found a triple dissociation of three neural memory systems: (1) a system that includes the hippocampus, which acquires information about relationships among stimuli and events (declarative memories); (2) a different system that includes the dorsal striatum, which mediates the formation of reinforced stimulus–response associations (habits, or nondeclarative memories); and (3) another system that includes the amygdala, which mediates rapid acquisition of behaviors on the basis of biologically significant events with affective properties.

Place Cells in the Hippocampus Process Spatial Memory

One of the clues that led investigators to test for the processing of spatial memory in the hippocampus was the discovery that some cells in the rat hippocampus seem to encode spatial location (O'Keefe and Dostrovsky, 1971). That is, these neurons produce action potentials preferentially when the rat is in a particular location or is moving toward that location, so they have been called **place cells.** This discovery led to a great deal of research to understand the properties of place cells and how they form.

The monkey hippocampus also contains some place cells that respond like those of rats, but monkeys have relatively fewer of these cells than rats have (Rolls and O'Mara, 1995). More cells in the monkey hippocampus respond to the part of the environment the monkey is looking at, so investigators researching them refer to them as *spatial view cells* and suggest that they reflect the importance of vision for monkeys. Perhaps there are place or spatial cells in the hippocampus of bird species that cache and retrieve food, since they have larger hippocampal formations than species that do not cache, as we reported in Chapter 6.

17.12 Hypothesized Memory Processes: Encoding, Consolidation, and Retrieval

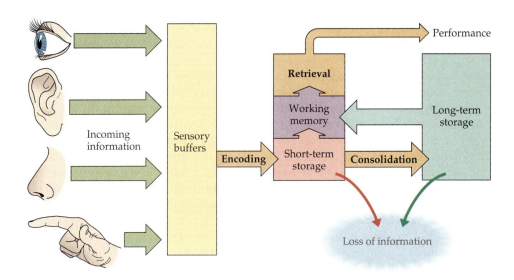

Memory Processes Extend from Acquisition to Retrieval

Psychologists who study learning and memory suggest that several successive processes are necessary to guarantee recall of a past event: **encoding, consolidation, and retrieval** (Figure 17.12). The original information must enter sensory channels and then be *encoded* rapidly into a form that passes into short-term memory. Some of this information may then be *consolidated* in long-term storage. The final stage of processing is *retrieval*—that is, the use of information that was stored earlier.

Most cognitive psychologists believe that the neural processes for short-term and long-term memory storage differ; there is both neurological and neurochemical evidence for this hypothesis. For example, patients with brain damage like that of H.M. retain new items in short-term storage but show no long-term memory for them. With the three stages outlined here in mind, investigators have tried to determine whether particular examples of "forgetting" in normal subjects involve failure of encoding, of consolidation, or of retrieval, and whether pathological impairments of memory selectively involve one or another of these main processes. Performance on a memory test can be either enhanced or impaired, depending on the conditions of acquisition, of consolidation, or of retrieval.

Brain regions involved in encoding. Evidence that activation of particular brain regions underlies the encoding of declarative memories comes from research in which separate activations are recorded for each stimulus in a series. When memory for the stimuli is tested later, the activations can be analyzed separately for stimuli remembered (and thus encoded successfully) and for stimuli forgotten (not encoded).

Beginning in the late 1990s, advances in functional MRI permitted the measurement of event-related brain responses to individual brief stimuli, such as a picture or a word presented for as little as 1 s (Buckner et al., 1996; B. R. Rosen et al., 1998). In one experiment, subjects looked at a series of photographs and classified each scene as indoors or outdoors; they were not told that they would be asked later to remember the pictures (Brewer et al., 1998). Thirty minutes later they were shown these pictures mixed with novel ones and were asked to identify which they had seen previously and which they had not. In a similar experiment, subjects saw words one at a time and were asked to classify them as abstract or concrete (A. D. Wagner et al., 1998).

When the activations elicited by individual stimuli were classified according to later success or failure of recognition, it was found that although the stimuli activated many brain areas, only a few areas predicted success of recognition. In the case of the pictures, the critical areas showing greater activation to correctly recalled stimuli were the right prefrontal cortex and the parahippocampal cortex in both hemispheres. In the case of the words, the critical areas were the *left* prefrontal cortex and

IMPORTANT METHOD

the *left* parahippocampal cortex. These findings are compatible with results we will discuss in Chapter 19 showing that the right hemisphere is more involved in spatial perception, while the left hemisphere is mainly responsible for language.

Consolidating declarative information. Studies of patients with brain injury suggest that consolidation of declarative long-term memories takes considerable time and involves the hippocampus. To study this problem, four groups of investigators independently designed experiments in which animals learned equivalent material at various times before they sustained lesions of the hippocampal formation. These studies were done with rats (J. J. Kim and Fanselow, 1992; Winocur, 1990), mice (Cho et al., 1993), and monkeys (Zola-Morgan and Squire, 1990). Psychologist-neuroscientist Larry Squire has studied this problem and many other aspects of memory with both human and nonhuman subjects.

In the monkey experiment, animals learned to discriminate between two objects in 20 different pairs at each of 5 periods (16, 12, 8, 4, and 2 weeks before surgery)—a total of 100 pairs. Eleven of the monkeys were then given bilateral lesions of the hippocampal formation, including the subicular complex and the entorhinal cortex; seven monkeys formed the control group, receiving no lesions.

Two weeks after surgery the investigators showed the animals each of the 100 previously presented pairs in a mixed order. The control monkeys remembered more of what they had learned most recently than of what they had learned earlier (Figure 17.13). The lesioned monkeys, however, performed significantly worse than the controls on the object pairs they had learned 2 and 4 weeks before surgery; they did not differ from the controls for pairs learned earlier. Note also that the lesioned monkeys performed worse on items learned 2 and 4 weeks before surgery than on the items learned earlier. Experiments with rodents yielded similar results, except that the time course is measured in days rather than weeks.

These results show that the hippocampal system is *not* a repository of long-term memory. In each of the animal experiments it was possible to identify a time after learning when damage to this system had no effect on memory. Thus the information that initially depends on the medial temporal system for processing does not depend on it for long-term (or permanent) storage. Permanent storage is thought to occur in regions of the neocortex where the information is first processed and held in short-term memory; after further processing that involves the medial temporal region (and probably the midline diencephalic region as well), the permanent memory storage becomes independent of the medial temporal–diencephalic region.

The fact that memories require consolidation for long-term storage may help explain the retrograde amnesia that is common with injury to the brain. Memories that have not yet been completely consolidated in the cortex may be seriously impaired by interruption of processing. Conditions that follow learning can also modulate the strength of memory, as we will see in the next section.

Emotion Can Modulate Memory Formation

Most of us would agree that emotionally arousing experiences tend to be well remembered—sometimes too well. Descartes (1662) wrote, "The usefulness of all the passions [emotions] consists in their strengthening in the soul thoughts which are good for it to conserve. . . . And all the harm they can do consists in their strengthening and prolonging these thoughts more than is necessary." Similarly, William James (1890) wrote, "An experience may be so exciting emotionally as almost to leave a scar on the cerebral tissues" (p. 670).

Recently investigators have found evidence that emotions can modulate memory formation in several ways. For example, emotions often enhance memory for aspects of an event or story that are closely tied to the emotional aspects, but they can also weaken memories that are not central to the emotional theme (Reisberg and

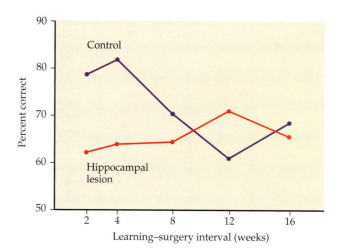

17.13 Retention by Monkeys of Object Discrimination Problems An equal number of items was learned 2, 4, 8, 12, and 16 weeks before the experimental animals underwent hippocampal surgery. For the control animals memory was best for the most recently learned items; for the lesioned animals memory was significantly worse for the items learned 2 and 4 weeks prior to surgery. (After Zola-Morgan and Squire, 1990.)

Larry Squire

Heuer, 1995). Animal research (e.g., McGaugh, 1992; McGaugh et al., 1993) has attempted to find the neural mechanisms involved in emotional modulation of memory, and it has been extended to include human memory (Pitman and Orr, 1995).

An emotionally arousing story is remembered significantly better than a closely matched but more emotionally neutral story; this emotional enhancement of memory may be caused by activation of beta-adrenergic stress hormones (Cahill et al., 1994). In an experiment designed to test the relation between emotion and memory, some subjects were given an emotional version of a story, and some were given a neutral version; both versions were accompanied by the same 12 slides. The first four items of both stories were identical, with four slides showing a mother and son going to visit the father's workplace in a hospital. In the second phase the two narratives differed, but the same five slides were shown: In the neutral version, the boy saw wrecked cars in a junkyard and then witnessed a disaster drill at the hospital; in the emotional version, the boy was badly injured in a traffic accident and was treated in the emergency room and in surgery. In the third phase (three slides), the mother went to pick up her other child at preschool.

The subjects heard the narratives and saw the slides while connected to heart rate and blood pressure monitors and were told that the study concerned physiological responses to different types of stimuli. One hour before the story presentation, all subjects received injections; some received a control injection of physiological saline solution; the others received propranolol, a beta-adrenergic receptor antagonist. (Propranolol and other so-called beta-blockers are used to combat high blood pressure.) A week later, without expecting any further contact with the stories, the subjects were asked to recall as many of the slides as possible and then took an 80-item multiple choice recognition memory test that assessed memory for both visual and narrative story elements.

Subjects who had received the control injection remembered the second, emotionally arousing phase of the story significantly better than the first or third phases. But subjects who had received the propranolol injection did not show better memory for the second, "emotional" phase than for the first and third phases. Control and propranolol-treated subjects scored about the same on the first and third phases of the story. Thus the drug did not affect memory in general but blocked only the enhancement related to emotional arousal.

Did the propranolol affect memory strength by preventing the subjects from having an emotional reaction to the stories? To test this question, the investigators had each subject rate his or her degree of emotion in response to the story just after it was presented. The "emotional" version was rated significantly more arousing than the neutral version by subjects given the beta-blocker as well as by subjects given the control injection, so it was not the failure of emotional experience that prevented enhancement of memory.

Another hypothesis was that propranolol acted after training to block enhancement of the processes of memory formation. This hypothesis is supported by animal research that we will review in Chapter 18. In fact, the human experiment just described was based directly on earlier animal research.

Can Modulation of Learning Help in Understanding, Alleviating, or Preventing Posttraumatic Stress Disorder?

When some people are exposed to life-threatening events or other catastrophic experiences, they develop a syndrome known as **posttraumatic stress disorder** (**PTSD**), as discussed in Chapter 16 (Figure 16.14). One set of symptoms is "reliving experiences such as intrusive thoughts, nightmares, dissociative flashbacks to elements of the original traumatic event, and . . . preoccupation with that event" (Keane, 1998, p. 398).

A hypothesis to help explain this phenomenon is that patients with PTSD are caught in a positive feedback loop in which each episode of reexperiencing (intrusive memory, flashback) produces a stress hormone response, especially involving adrenergic hormones. This hormonal response then acts to strengthen the memory that produced it, thereby increasing the likelihood of reexperiencing the memory (Pitman, 1989). On the basis of this hypothesis, Cahill (1997) proposed a strategy to prevent PTSD formation by suppressing adrenergic activity with drugs either shortly before a traumatic experience or as quickly as possible after it. For example, rescue workers could take an appropriate drug on their way to the scene of a disaster, and rape victims could be given an antiadrenergic drug such as propranolol as part of their treatment as soon as possible after the attack. This treatment would not delete memories of the event but would diminish the traumatic aspects.

It may be possible also to diminish some of the impact of already established traumatic memories, according to results of animal experiments. As noted earlier, a variety of treatments are amnestic (memory-impairing) if they are given shortly before or shortly after original learning; such treatments include electroconvulsive shock and drugs, such as inhibitors of protein synthesis or NMDA receptor antagonists.

A recent study with rats has shown that when a previously formed memory is reactivated, it can be weakened by administration of propranolol up to 2 hours after reactivation of the memory (Przybyslawski et al., 1999; Sara, 2000). Przybyslawski and colleagues suggested that "adrenoreceptor antagonists may be promising pharmacological agents for attenuating debilitating memories"; that is, the drug could be given when the memory is recalled, and it might weaken the strength of the memory. Similarly, a study of fear conditioning in rats showed that when a consolidated fear memory was reactivated, it returned to a labile state that required protein synthesis for reconsolidation, just as new memories require protein synthesis for consolidation into long-term memories (Nader et al., 2000).

**CLINICAL
ISSUE**

Brain Imaging Provides New Insights about Regions Involved in Different Kinds of Memories

Studies of brain lesions, both naturally occurring and experimentally induced, yield a great deal of information about the brain regions involved in different kinds of memories, as we have seen. But examination of brain-injured patients and animals with experimental lesions does not reveal what functions are served by the injured or missing tissue. Rather the behavior shows what the surviving brain regions can accomplish after the lesion. Brain-imaging techniques are providing evidence about memory processes in the healthy brain.

Before examining some results of imaging studies, we should note that imaging techniques, as powerful as they are, have their limitations. Gabrieli (1998) points out that a great deal of psychological interpretation is involved in trying to understand the mental process that is signified by activation of a particular brain region. Most reports state the *differences* in the activations caused by two tasks, as noted in Box 2.3. Such differences are open to a variety of interpretations, and they are often affected by variables such as task difficulty or trial duration. In addition, the tasks must be designed around limitations of the imaging techniques: At present a homogeneous behavioral condition must be maintained for about 2 minutes in PET and for 1 second in fMRI recordings.

**IMPORTANT
METHOD**

The combination of lesion and neuroimaging studies helps overcome the limitations of each of these sources of evidence, and each provides constraints on data from the other source. For example, a memory task may activate several different brain regions, but some of these regions can be injured without affecting performance on that task. So some of the activations may represent correlated processes that are not required for the form of memory being measured. The lesion evidence makes it possible to discriminate between activations that are essential or nonessential for a specific form of memory. In the sections that follow, we will take up the kinds of memory shown in Figure 17.4.

Imaging Studies of Declarative Memory

Imaging studies confirm and extend the conclusions from lesion studies that implicated the medial temporal and diencephalic systems in the formation of new de-

17.14 Encoding and Retrieval Activate Different Medial Temporal Regions of the Brain (*a*) This reference figure shows the position of a sagittal slice 25 mm from the midline. (*b*) Indicated here are the locations of peak activities in the hippocampal formation in 22 experiments on encoding (red) and 34 experiments on retrieval (blue). (Part *a* after Talairach and Tournoux, 1988; *b* after Lepage et al., 1998.)

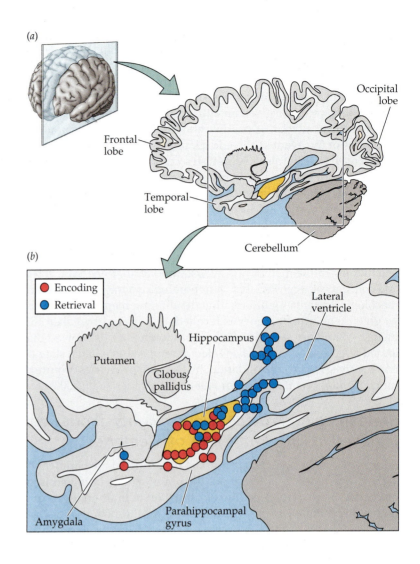

clarative long-term memories. Imaging studies show activation of these regions during both encoding of new material (e.g., C. E. Stern et al., 1996; Tulving et al., 1996) and retrieval (e.g., Schacter et al., 1996). A recent survey of 53 PET studies of memory revealed that encoding and retrieval activations are focused in somewhat different medial temporal brain regions (Figure 17.14) (Lepage et al., 1998).

Activations in the hippocampal region associated with *encoding* episodic memories are located primarily in the rostral portions of the region. Activations associated with *retrieving* episodic memories are located primarily in the caudal portions. The figure shows only the peak of activity in each study. Both retrieval and encoding activated both regions, but encoding activated the subiculum significantly more than retrieval did, and retrieval activated the parahippocampal cortex significantly more than encoding did. These results were unexpected. Thus the imaging studies are beginning to provide information about the specific contributions of different components of the medial temporal region to declarative memory.

Whereas the medial temporal region is necessary for processing information for long-term storage, the neocortex has been considered to be the site of storage of long-term declarative memories. Patients like H.M., who no longer have a hippocampus, nevertheless retain memories that were stored before brain lesion. On the other hand, some patients with lesions of the neocortex can no longer retrieve the names of specific categories of objects—for example, living things such as animals, manufactured things such as tools, or even more specific categories such as flowers or motor vehicles.

Neuroimaging studies of normal subjects provide data consistent with specific localizations for such categories. For example, asking subjects to name tools or animals yields cortical activations that overlap in some areas but differ in others (A. Martin et al., 1996). These results with normal subjects indicate that the surprising regional specificity of representations of knowledge in patients reflects the localized cortical geography of the normal brain.

Gabrieli (1998) pointed out two principles that emerge from the neuroimaging studies of cortical locations of declarative memory:

> First, knowledge in any domain (e.g., for pictures or words, living or manufactured objects) is distributed over a specific, but extensive, neural network that often extends over several lobes. Injury to any component of that network could affect performance in that domain, with the specific effect reflecting what aspect of that knowledge is represented in that component of the network. Second, some localization appears to be a consequence of how various classes of knowledge interact with different perceptual and motor systems (p. 94).

For example, naming tools causes activation in the left prefrontal regions near motor cortex.

Several imaging studies (Nyberg et al., 1996; Tulving, 1998; Tulving and Markowitsch, 1997) have shown relatively greater activation in the left hemisphere during encoding of information and in the right hemisphere during retrieval (Figure 17.15). Note that this is an asymmetry but not an absolute difference; the frontal and temporal regions of both hemispheres are active during both encoding and retrieval. Tulving (1998) suggested that this effect—known as the **hemispheric encoding retrieval asymmetry** (**HERA**) effect—can be used to answer the question, Are encoding and retrieval processes basically similar or basically different?

One current point of view is that encoding and retrieval are distinct processes, as indicated in Figure 17.12. On the other hand, many investigators hypothesize that retrieval involves reactivation of the same patterns of mental or neural activity that occurred in the original experience. Tulving (1998) concluded that the HERA effect points to basic differences in the neuroanatomy of the encoding and retrieval systems, thereby confirming that they are distinct processes.

Buckner (1996) pointed out that while a model like HERA attempts to find a unifying principle for activity across multiple areas of the frontal lobes, it is also important to investigate the specific functions of the different cortical regions in learning and memory. Further research (reviewed by Lepage et al., 2000) suggests a

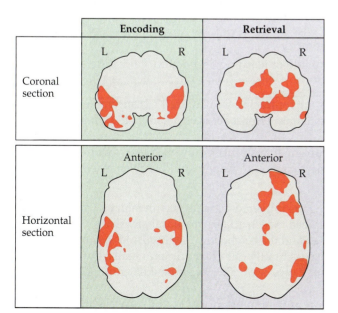

17.15 Hemispheric Asymmetry in Encoding and Retrieval
These representations of the brain, based on data from four different experiments, show that encoding evokes greater activity in the left temporal lobe, whereas retrieval evokes greater activity in the right frontal lobe. (After Tulving and Markowitsch, 1997.)

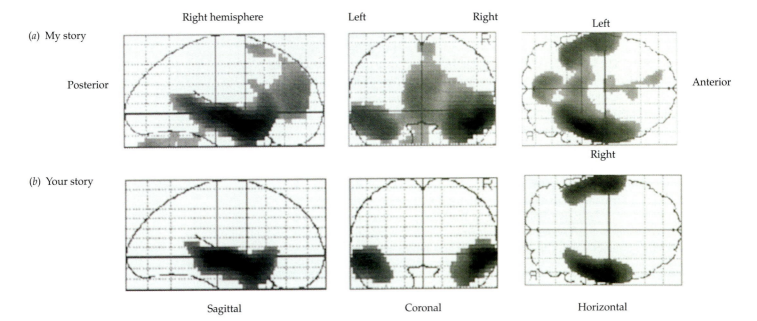

(a) My story

Right hemisphere

Left

Right

Left

Posterior

Anterior

Right

(b) Your story

Sagittal

Coronal

Horizontal

17.16 My Story versus Your Story
Autobiographical passages (*a*) caused greater activation of the right frontal and temporal lobes than nonautobiographical passages (*b*). (After Fink et al., 1996; courtesy of Gereon Fink.)

reformulation of the HERA model. When subjects adopt a neurocognitive set or mode favoring recall of episodic events, three specific sites in right prefrontal cortex and two in left prefrontal cortex are activated; the right hemisphere sites are activated more strongly than the left hemisphere sites. These sites are activated whether or not recall of items is correct. Thus the *set* to recall activates sites in both hemispheres, but with greater activity in the right. Further research confirms that encoding involves the left hemisphere more strongly than the right.

The distinction between semantic (general) memory and episodic (autobiographical) memory is supported by the case of patient K.C., discussed earlier, who can no longer access any memories about his life, although he retains much general knowledge. But, as in many cases of brain lesions caused by accident or disease, the damage to K.C.'s brain was widespread and did not offer much information about the site(s) of episodic memories. In an attempt to localize episodic memory processes better, experimenters had subjects listen to autobiographical passages and to passages written by others (Fink et al., 1996). The autobiographical passages, relative to the others, caused greater activation of right frontal and temporal lobe regions, as Figure 17.16 shows. So autobiographical memories and semantic memories appear to be processed in different locations.

Imaging Studies of Skill Memory

Imaging studies have been made of learning and memory for different kinds of skills:

- *Sensorimotor skills,* such as mirror tracing (see Figure 17.2) and rotary pursuit, in which the subject tries to maintain contact between a handheld stylus and a small target on a rotating disc
- *Perceptual skills,* such as learning to read mirror-reversed text (mentioned earlier)
- *Cognitive skills,* such as tasks that require planning and problem solving (e. g., the Tower of Hanoi problem)

All three kinds of skill learning are impaired in patients with injury to the basal ganglia or with Huntington's disease, which attacks the basal ganglia. Other brain regions, such as the motor cortex and the cerebellum, are involved in some examples of skill learning. Here we discuss briefly only sensorimotor skills, the variety that has been studied the most. For a review of other kinds of skill learning, see Gabrieli (1998).

Neuroimaging studies support the importance of both the basal ganglia and the cerebellum, as well as of motor neocortex, for sensorimotor skill learning. Rotary pursuit learning, in which subjects use a wand to track a spot on a rotating disk, activated the primary and secondary motor cortices (Grafton et al., 1992). Learning of specific sequences of finger movements activated the primary and secondary motor cortices and the basal ganglia (Doyon et al., 1996; Hazeltine et al., 1997). Some studies also show activation of the cerebellum, which appears to be related to the correction of errors in finger movements (Flament et al., 1996). Often the activations shift among brain regions as performance changes during the course of learning, so learning appears to involve a complex set of interacting neural networks.

Imaging Studies of Repetition Priming

Repetition priming (or simply *priming*) is a change in processing of a stimulus due to prior exposure to the same or a related stimulus. Priming does not require declarative memory of the stimulus—H.M. and other patients with amnesia show priming for words they don't remember having seen—so priming does not require the medial temporal or diencephalic regions. In addition, patients who suffer from Huntington's disease show normal priming, so intact basal ganglia are not required.

Priming tasks can be distinguished as perceptual or conceptual. *Perceptual* priming reflects prior processing of the *form* of the stimulus; *conceptual* priming reflects the *meaning* of the stimulus. Perceptual priming, such as priming on word stem completion tasks, is related to *reduced* activity, relative to baseline activity during word stem completion, in bilateral occipitotemporal cortex (Schacter et al., 1996). Presumably the activity is reduced for the primed words because responding to them requires less effort than responding to nonprimed words does. Conceptual priming is related to reduced activity in left frontal neocortex (Blaxton et al., 1996; Gabrieli et al., 1996; A. D. Wagner, Desmond, et al., 1997).

Imaging Studies of Conditioning

Research on brain circuits involved in classical conditioning will be taken up in Chapter 18. That work shows that cerebellar circuits are responsible for simple delay conditioning (in which there is no time gap between the conditioned stimulus and the unconditioned stimulus). Delay conditioning occurs normally even if the hippocampus has been lesioned, but for trace conditioning (in which the CS ends before the US starts), the hippocampus is required, as it is also for discrimination reversal conditioning (in which the stimulus that signals reward [CS+] and the stimulus that does not signal reward [CS–] are reversed).

A PET study of human delay eye-blink conditioning used both behavioral intervention and the correlational approach (Logan and Grafton, 1995). During the first (control) session of the experiment, PET scans were made while subjects received an unpaired tone and puff of air to the right eye. In the second session, 1 to 6 days later, the stimuli were paired. In the third session, 2 to 7 days after the first, PET scans were made while the subjects received paired stimuli. Comparison of the scans from this third session with those from the first showed increased activity in several regions of the brain (Figure 17.17*a*). Activity in some of these regions correlated significantly with conditioning behavior (Figure 17.17*b*).

Thus the neural network activated during human delay eye-blink conditioning includes not only the cerebellar and brainstem regions found in animal research, but also the hippocampus, the ventral striatum, and regions of the cerebral cortex. But activity in these other areas may not be *essential* for eye-blink conditioning. For example, patients with hippocampal damage can acquire the conditioned eye-blink response, whereas patients with unilateral cerebellar damage can acquire a conditioned eye-blink response only on the side where the cerebellum is intact (Papka et al., 1994).

NEURAL PLASTICITY

Brain Regions Involved in Different Kinds of Learning and Memory: A Summary

Figure 17.18 summarizes the findings we have reviewed about brain regions involved in different kinds of learning and memory. This is not a complete picture of the subject—there are other kinds of learning and other brain areas involved—but it underscores some major points:

(a) Areas showing increased activity with conditioning

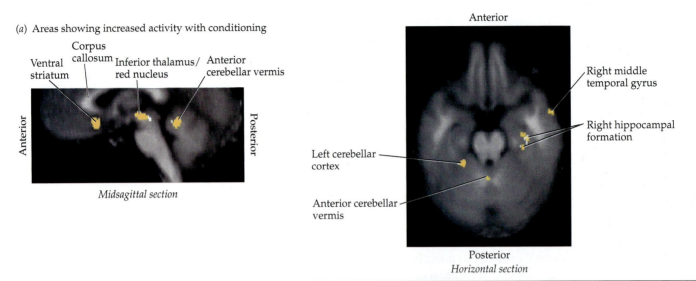

Midsagittal section

Horizontal section

(b) Areas showing correlations with learning performance

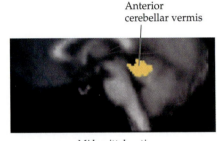

Midsagittal section

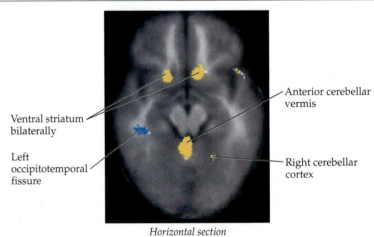

Horizontal section

17.17 A PET Study of Human Eye-Blink Conditioning (a) The yellow areas shown here reflect increased metabolic activity in conditioning versus the control condition. (b) Areas where metabolic change during conditioning is significantly correlated with learning performance; positive correlations are shown in yellow. Note the negative correlation (blue) in the left occipitotemporal fissure. (From Logan and Grafton, 1995.)

- Many regions of the brain are involved in learning and memory.
- The kinds of learning and memory that have been distinguished from each other on cognitive grounds—such as declarative versus nondeclarative, or semantic versus episodic—are mediated by different, or at least partially different, brain structures and regions.
- The same brain structure may be involved in different kinds of learning and memory; for example, the cerebellum is involved in both sensorimotor learning and delay conditioning.
- A given kind of learning may require activity of a circuit involving several different brain regions.
- Some kinds of learning that appear rather similar, such as delay and trace conditioning, may nevertheless involve different structures.

Comparative Approaches Yield Insights about the Evolution of Learning and Memory

Learning and memory exist throughout the animal kingdom, and some forms of short-term learning appear in single-celled organisms. Although there has been a good deal of speculation about the early evolution of abilities to learn and remember, we cannot research this subject directly because we cannot measure the behavior of extinct animals.

The fact that learning is so widespread suggests that it was an early evolutionary development, with changes occurring as organisms evolved to occupy new niches

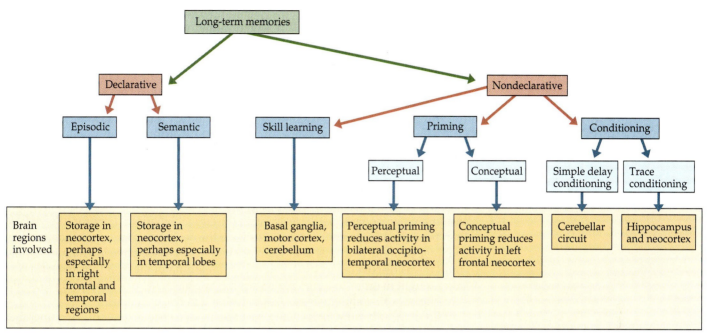

   17.18 Brain Regions Involved in Different Kinds of Learning and Memory

and meet new challenges. A fruitful approach is to compare the learning and memory of related species in which differences in ecological niche and lifestyle have caused different selection pressures for specific kinds of learning and therefore changes in brain structure.

As we consider attempts at comparing learning ability among existing species, we will see that it is not a simple matter. Just as it is difficult, perhaps impossible, to devise a "culture-free" intelligence test for human beings, so has it been difficult to devise tests for animals that do not favor the sensory and/or motor capacities of some species and work against those of others. The problem has become even more complicated now that research has shown that relatively simple animals are capable of a greater variety of learning than was suspected only a few years ago (Carew and Sahley, 1986; Krasne and Glanzman, 1995).

Learning Abilities Are Widely Distributed

Nonassociative learning appears to be very widespread among organisms. Simple animals with small nervous systems readily habituate to repeated mild stimuli and become sensitized to strong stimuli. Furthermore, the time courses and other features of habituation and sensitization are similar, whether studied in an earthworm, a mollusk, or a mammal. Some investigators have reported nonassociative learning even in paramecia and bacteria, single-celled organisms that do not have a nervous system.

The fact that learning and memory are so widespread has led to attempts to study basic mechanisms of learning and memory in organisms without nervous systems or with relatively simple nervous systems. It is tempting to suppose that all animals share some basic processes of learning and memory storage, in which case relatively simple animals could be taken as models to study processes that all animals use. However, learning may have arisen separately in some of these diverse animal forms; similar learning behaviors may represent convergent evolution in the face of common demands of the environment, but perhaps not all animals use the same mechanisms to accomplish learning and memory storage. We will have to critically examine claims that findings with relatively simple animals can be extrapolated directly to other forms.

Neuroscientist Seymour Kety (1976) urged the search for varieties of mechanisms in learning and memory:

> So profound and powerful an adaptation as learning and memory is not apt to rest upon a single modality. Rather, I suspect that advantage is taken of every opportunity provided by evolution. There were forms of memory before organisms developed nervous systems, and after that remarkable leap forward it is likely that every new pathway and neural complexity, every new neurotransmitter, hormone, or metabolic process that played upon the nervous system and subserved a learning process was preserved and incorporated. (p. 321)

Until recently, associative learning was believed to have a more restricted distribution than nonassociative learning in the animal kingdom. For example, *Aplysia* had been used for many years to investigate the neural mechanisms of habituation, but investigators had sought in vain for evidence of associative learning in *Aplysia* until it was discovered in 1980. Evidence for learning in the fruit fly *Drosophila* was long sought in order to try to relate learning to genetic factors, but only in 1974 did investigators first announce successful training in these animals.

Part of the difficulty in assessing the capacity of a species to learn and remember is that these capacities may be highly specific. Certain species can learn particular associations well even though they are very poor at other tasks that do not seem more difficult to us. Evidence for specificity has accumulated since the 1960s and has led to two successive and quite different concepts.

First came the concept of **genetic constraints on learning,** which became prominent in the 1960s. This formulation held that species-typical genetic factors restrict the kinds of learning that a species can accomplish, or at least accomplish readily. For example, bees readily learn to come to a particular station to feed on a 24-hour schedule, which of course occurs in nature, but they cannot learn to come on an 8- or 12-hour schedule. Birds of some species do not learn the pattern of markings or even the color of their eggs even though they turn the eggs over frequently, yet they learn to recognize their young individually within 3 days after they hatch, just the time when the chicks begin to wander about.

COMPETING HYPOTHESES

The interpretation of such observations changed in the 1980s. Rather than supposing that the genes of certain species constrain their general ability to learn and thus make them selectively stupid, investigators now believe it more likely that **specific abilities to learn and remember** evolve in response to selective pressures in particular ecological niches (J. L. Gould, 1986; Sherry and Schacter, 1987). Let's consider an example of a specific learning ability.

Selection for Spatial Memory Is Associated with Increased Hippocampal Size in Mammals and Birds

A notable research program has used both naturalistic observations and experimental studies with birds and rodents to determine the effects that selection for spatial ability may have on brain measures: "If a particular neuroanatomical feature occurs in different species exposed to the same selective pressure, and is better accounted for by this selective pressure than by the phylogenetic relations among the species, then it is reasonable to conclude that the feature is indeed an adaptation—the result of convergent evolution in response to natural selection" (Sherry et al., 1992, p. 298).

EVOLUTION AT WORK

We saw one example of this research in Chapter 6: Species of birds that store or cache food for retrieval days or weeks later have hippocampal regions larger than those of related species that do not cache food (see Figure 6.4). The differences in size of hippocampus among these species could not be accounted for by other factors, including migratory behavior, social organization, diet, mode of development, nest dispersion, and habitat (Krebs et al., 1989; Sherry et al., 1989). Furthermore, surgical removal of the hippocampus in a food-storing species disrupts the birds' ability to retrieve cached food and to solve other spatial problems, without obvious effects on other behaviors (Sherry and Vaccarino, 1989). Thus the larger hippocampus in food-storing species of birds seems to be an adaptive modification that makes it possible for them to retrieve cached food.

Interestingly, the greater hippocampal size that is typical in food-storing species develops only if individual birds use spatial memory to retrieve stored food. Clayton and Krebs (1994) found this when they raised crows in the laboratory, giving some birds the chance to store and retrieve food while other birds ate ftom feeders and had no opportunity to store food. The birds who stored and retrieved food developed hippocampal formations that were larger than those of the birds that ate from feeders.

Comparison of two related species of kangaroo rats provided an independent test of this hypothesis. Both species are small, nocturnal, seed-eating, desert rodents from the same genus. One species, Merriam's kangaroo rat (*Dipodomys merriami*) hoards food in scattered locations and requires spatial memory to relocate its caches. In contrast, the bannertail kangaroo rat (*Dipodomys spectabilis*) hoards seeds in its burrow and thus needs no specialized spatial memory to retrieve them. As with food-storing versus non-food-storing birds, *D. merriami* has a significantly larger hippocampus than that of *D. spectabilis* (L. F. Jacobs and Spencer, 1994).

People have long bred animals selectively to enhance certain traits; such artificial selection can produce results similar to those of natural selection, and more rapidly. For example, pigeons have been bred for their ability to fly rapidly and accurately to their home lofts. Pigeons of these strains have larger hippocampi than breeds of pigeons not selected for homing ability (Rehkamper et al., 1988).

Investigators who test the spatial learning and memory of laboratory rats and mice have often observed that males perform better than females, and human males perform better than human females on many spatial tasks (D. F. Halpern, 1986). Some researchers have suggested that males in general are superior in spatial learning and memory, but others have hypothesized that the behavioral roles of the two sexes determine whether a sex difference in spatial memory exists in a given species and, if it does, which sex is superior in this behavior.

An instructive comparison has been made between two species of North American voles (Figure 17.19). Pine voles (*Microtus pinetorum*) are monogamous, and field observations show that the males and females travel over ranges that are equal in size. In contrast, meadow voles (*Microtus pennsylvanicus*) are highly polygynous (i.e., a male mates with several females), and the ranges of males are several times larger than those of females. In this polygynous mating system, males compete in order to include within their home range as many female ranges as possible.

The polygynous male meadow voles, in comparison with females of the same species, have significantly better scores on laboratory tests of spatial learning and memory. The monogamous pine voles show no sex differences on these tests. Furthermore, the polygynous male meadow voles have a significantly larger hippocampus than do the females, whereas among the monogamous pine voles, there is no significant difference in hippocampal size between the sexes (L. F. Jacobs et al., 1990).

When the size of the hippocampus differs between the sexes of a species, it is not invariably the male that shows the larger size. For example, the hippocampus of the female brown-headed cowbird (*Molothrus ater*) is significantly larger than that of the male, as investigators predicted on the basis of the breeding behavior of this species (Sherry et al., 1993). The female cowbird is parasitic: She lays her eggs in the nests of other species, which then do the work of hatching and feeding the cowbird chick. In order to do this, the female cowbird has to find and keep track of nests so that she can slip in and lay an egg when the other birds are away. The male cowbird does not

(*a*) Sizes of home range

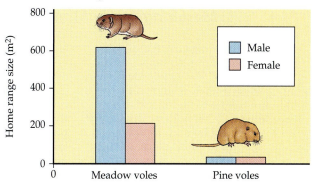

(*b*) Ranking in spatial learning

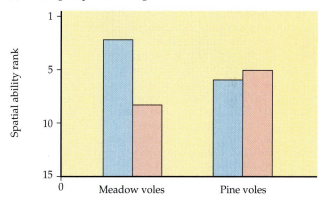

(*c*) Relative hippocampal size

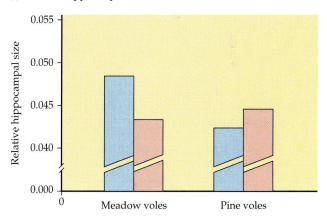

17.19 Sex, Memory, and Hippocampal Size Males and females of two species of voles were compared on three variables: (*a*) size of home range, (*b*) score on a spatial learning task, (*c*) hippocampal size divided by brain size. (After L. F. Jacobs et al., 1990.)

BOX 17.2 *Mastering London Topography Changes Hippocampal Structure in Taxi Drivers*

Can spatial training alter the anatomy of the hippocampus in humans as it does in animals? To test this idea, a group of investigators studied the brains of licensed London taxi drivers (Maguire et al., 2000). These drivers are very well suited for such a study because in order to obtain a license, they must undergo intensive training about London streets and locations (called colloquially "being on The Knowledge"). This training requires 2 years, on the average, and it is followed by a stringent set of police examinations.

In an earlier study using positron emission tomography (PET), the same investigators had found that having London taxi drivers recall complex routes around the city caused activation of a network of brain regions that included the right hippocampus; recall of landmarks for which the subjects had no knowledge of their location within a spatial framework activated similar brain regions except for the right hippocampus (Maguire et al., 1997).

In the new study the experimental subjects were 16 right-handed men whose careers as licensed drivers ranged from 1.5 to 42 years; all had healthy general medical, neurological, and psychiatric profiles. Structural MRI scans of their brains were obtained and measured. For comparison, the investigators studied MRI scans of 50 healthy right-handed males with a similar age range and who did not drive taxis. The only brain regions that showed structural differences between the taxi driv-

ers and control subjects were the right and left hippocampi. The posterior part of the hippocampus was significantly larger in taxi drivers than in controls in both the right and the left hemispheres. In contrast, the anterior part of the hippocampus was significantly smaller in taxi drivers than in controls. There was no significant difference between taxi drivers and controls in either the midportion (body) or the overall size of the hippocampi.

Could these differences reflect an innate predisposition to learn to navigate the streets of London? To test this possibility, the investigators plotted the volume of the anterior and the posterior hippocampus against the number of months each person had spent as a taxi driver. The volume of the anterior right hippocampus correlated significantly negatively with duration of taxi experience ($r = -0.6$, $p < 0.05$), and the volume of the posterior right hippocampus correlated significantly positively with duration of taxi experience ($r = 0.6$, $p < 0.05$). Thus the greater the duration of taxi experience, the greater the anatomical effect in the right hippocampus. These correlations indicate strongly that experience alters the hippocampus, rather than initial hippocampal differences reflecting an innate disposition to acquire spatial knowledge. The left hippocampus did not show significant changes with duration of experience, suggesting that the left and right hippocampus participate differently in spatial navigation and memory.

Although this report offers surprising new information, like much innovative research it also raises many new questions. For example, is there a behavioral correlate to the reduction of size of the anterior hippocampus in taxi drivers? A report of this research in *The Economist* ("Neuroscience," 2000) comments ironically,

Whether the loss of frontal [hippocampal] tissue has any relationship with the robust political opinions for which London cabbies are renowned is an area that remains mercifully uninvestigated (p. 83).

In a commentary on this study, Terrazas and McNaughton (2000) pointed out some surprises and some paths for future work. For example, they expressed surprise that changes in the brain with experience appear to accumulate for as long as 20 years; rather they expected the greatest changes to occur earlier, when knowledge acquisition was greatest. MRI measures can be done repeatedly in the same subjects, so these investigators would like to see longitudinal studies of some taxi drivers. To test whether it is only acquisition of spatial knowledge that produces localized effects in the hippocampus, they suggested comparable studies with groups that have similarly high demands of nonspatial learning, such as years of legal training and legal practice or medical studies and practice. Clearly the research by Maguire et al. has raised as many questions as it has solved.

---

participate in this spatial sleuthing and gets along with a smaller hippocampus. No sex difference in hippocampal size was found in two closely related species that are not parasitic. This example is one of the few indications that spatial ability can influence the size of the hippocampus when other factors—such as sex, breeding system, or foraging behavior—have been ruled out.

Recent research indicates that spatial learning can change the anatomy of the hippocampus in adult humans as well (Box 17.2).

Learning and Memory Change throughout Life

It is easier for us to form some kinds of new memories when we are in the middle of our lives, as young or mature adults, than when we are infants or elderly. Can these changes in ability over the life span be explained in neural terms? Do they provide clues about the neural mechanisms of learning and memory?

Many kinds of animals must be ready to learn as soon as they are born or hatched. For example, newly hatched chicks eagerly sample objects in their environment to find what is edible. Their yolk sacs provide nourishment, so they can sample small bits without having to ingest much. By the time the yolk sac is used up 3 to 4 days after hatching, the chicks need to have learned what is safe and good to eat. Thus chicks are good subjects for some kinds of learning experiments.

Chicks are precocial—able to locomote and care for themselves from the time they emerge—but even altricial animals (those that are helpless at birth) must learn to adapt to their environment. For example, even though rat pups' eyes and ears are closed for about the first 2 weeks after birth, each pup in a litter learns which of the mother's nipples is "its own."

In laboratory experiments, young rat pups learn rapidly which of two artificial nipples provides milk; they can use cues of texture or odor to learn this distinction (Woo and Leon, 1987). Human infants learn quickly to distinguish the faces of their main caregivers from those of others. And human infants can be conditioned in the first days after birth to turn their heads to one side or the other at the sound of a tone in order to find the nipple of a nursing bottle (Papousek, 1992). Conditioning can thus be studied in newly born or newly hatched animals without the complicating effects of prior learning. In primates, conditioning requires the cerebellum and related structures, and the anatomy and neurophysiology of the cerebellum are rather mature at birth.

Working Memory Requires Brain Development

A classic test of cognitive development devised by Swiss psychologist Jean Piaget now appears to require development of the dorsolateral prefrontal cortex. This "A not B" test requires an infant to uncover a toy that she sees hidden in one of two possible locations (A or B); both locations are used in a series of trials. After the toy is hidden, the infant's visual fixation is broken so that she cannot look at the location during the delay.

Human infants will not reliably reach for a hidden object until they are 7 to 8 months old. Before this age an infant will reach correctly to either location only if there is no delay (except for breaking visual fixation) between the hiding and the reaching. But with a delay of only 1 to 5 s during which the infant is prevented from reaching, she tends to reach for the object in the last location where she reached successfully, even if that is not the location where she just saw the toy hidden.

These observations suggest that with a short delay, the habit of successful reaching is stronger than the representational memory of the hidden object. No long-term memory is required in either case; only short-term working memories are involved. Testing of infants every 2 weeks shows a steady rise in their ability to perform successfully at longer delays. This improvement is due to maturation, not experience, because infants of a given age test equally well whether or not they were given prior tests. By age 8 to 12 months, most infants perform successfully with a delay of 10 s between seeing the object hidden and reaching for it. In the next section we'll see that some adult patients with amnesia fail the "A not B" test.

Adele Diamond and Patricia Goldman-Rakic (1989) confirmed these observations with human infants and also studied monkeys, using a similar test. Monkeys perform the test well by 2 to 4 months. The investigators used both intact monkeys and monkeys with lesions of dorsolateral prefrontal cortex or control lesions of inferior parietal cortex (Figure 17.20). Normal monkeys performed well on the test at delays of 10 s and more, as did monkeys with lesions of parietal cortex, but monkeys with lesions of prefrontal cortex made errors similar to those of 7- to 8-month-old human infants. Thus a normal, relatively mature dorsolateral prefrontal cortex appears to be required for representational memory of the hidden object to be retained as long as 10 s. Further research on the roles of prefrontal cortex in memory will be discussed in Chapter 18.

Patricia Goldman-Rakic

Aging Impairs Some Aspects of Learning and Memory

The capacity of older people to learn and remember has become a topic of heightened interest in recent years. This awareness stems in part from the growing proportion of elderly people in the population of developed countries and the recog-

17.20 Cortical Regions Tested for Roles in Representational Memory
The brain sites of monkeys shown here were lesioned for experiments on dorsolateral prefrontal cortex and inferior parietal cortex, regions known to be involved in representational memory. (After A. Diamond and Goldman-Rakic, 1989.)

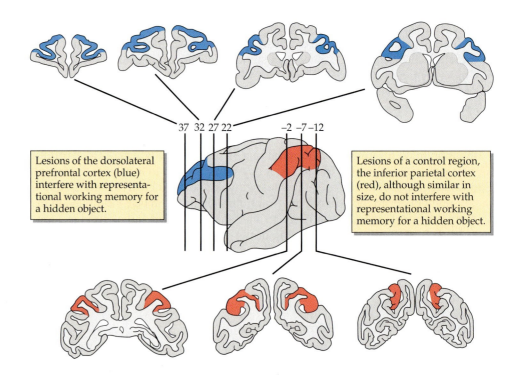

Lesions of the dorsolateral prefrontal cortex (blue) interfere with representational working memory for a hidden object.

Lesions of a control region, the inferior parietal cortex (red), although similar in size, do not interfere with representational working memory for a hidden object.

nition that some reductions in performance accompany normal aging. It also reflects attention to pathological forms of cognitive impairment that are more likely to affect older people, such as Alzheimer's disease (see Chapter 7).

Older people and animals in normal health show some decrements in abilities to learn and remember (N. D. Anderson and Craik, 2000; Balota et al., 2000; Gallagher and Rapp, 1997; Gallagher et al., 1995; Kubanis and Zornetzer, 1981). Accurate comparisons of learning and memory in people of different ages are difficult because of confounding factors. For example, differences in learning ability may be caused not by age alone, but by other factors, such as educational level, how recently the subjects have experienced formal learning, or motivation. After experimenters correct for such factors, differences related to age usually accompany only some tasks, not all.

What kinds of tasks usually show decrements in performance with aging? Normal elderly people tend to show some memory impairment in tasks of conscious recollection that require effort (Hasher and Zacks, 1979) and that rely primarily on internal generation of the memory rather than on external cues (Craik, 1985). Giving elderly subjects easily organized task structures, or cues, can often raise their performance to the level of the young. Thus the type of task helps determine whether impairment is observed. Recent neuroimaging studies have shown impairment in both the encoding and the retrieval of information in old subjects compared with young. There is greater variability among old subjects than among young, and for many tasks some elderly subjects perform as well or almost as well as the young.

In cases of pathological forms of aging, such as Alzheimer's disease, some memory systems deteriorate, and it has been suggested that what remains are memory processes similar to those of infants. In fact, testing the implications of this idea led Morris Moscovitch (1985) to discover a cognitive disability in patients with amnesia similar to the failure on the "A not B" test that Piaget had described for 8-month-old infants. Most patients suffering from amnesia, shown a familiar object in a new location, B, continue to search for it at A, even passing by the object in plain sight in order to search for it at A. They appear to remember the search procedure and not the object being sought.

We will see in Chapter 18 that certain neurochemical and neuroanatomical changes correlate closely with the impairments in behavior. Further research may suggest effective therapeutic measures.

Summary

1. The abilities to learn and remember affect all behaviors that are characteristically human. Because every animal species appears capable of some learning and memory, the ability to learn must be required for survival. Whereas evolution by natural selection brings about adaptation over successive generations, learning permits prompt adaptation within the lifetime of the individual.

2. Individuals whose learning or memory capacities are impaired as a result of brain damage may provide valuable information about how different regions of the brain are involved in these processes.

3. Patients with Korsakoff's syndrome show gaps in memory, which they may attempt to fill by confabulation; this syndrome involves severe retrograde and anterograde amnesia, as well as impairment in encoding new information. Patients show damage to the mammillary nuclei, midline thalamus, and frontal cortex.

4. Some learning results in the formation of habits (gaining nondeclarative knowledge, or learning *how*); other learning results in the formation of representational memories (gaining declarative knowledge, or learning *what*). Abilities to form habits and memories appear to depend on different brain circuits.

5. Declarative memory tends to be flexible—accessible to many response systems. Nondeclarative memory tends to be inflexible: The information is not readily expressed by response systems that were not involved in the original learning.

6. Learning includes both nonassociative forms, such as habituation, dishabituation, and sensitization, and associative forms, such as classical (Pavlovian) conditioning and instrumental conditioning.

7. Conditioning involves learning relations and predictability among events. Close temporal pairing of stimuli is neither necessary nor sufficient for successful conditioning.

8. Memories are often classified by how long they last. Frequently used classifications include iconic, short-term, intermediate-term, and long-term. Some disorders prevent the formation of long-term declarative memory while not impairing short-term memory.

9. Studies of people with brain damage in different locations and experimented with animals show that different attributes of memory are processed by different brain regions.

10. Although the capacity of long-term memory is huge, most of what we experience is not remembered. Attention, reinforcement, and emotional responses help determine what is held in memory beyond the short term.

11. Recall of a past event requires three memory processes: encoding, consolidation, and retrieval.

12. Memory strength can be modulated by emotional state and other conditions in the period following learning.

13. It may be possible to weaken traumatic memories by giving treatments that impair consolidation of memory. This can be done either shortly after the original experience or when the memory is reactivated.

14. Some patients with damage to the medial temporal lobe or medial diencephalon show particular impairment in consolidation of long-term representational memories. Recent research has focused both on the type of memory test and on the sites of brain damage. Hippocampal lesions in people and animals impair the formation of representational long-term memories but spare the formation of habits (nondeclarative, or procedural, memories).

15. The hippocampal region is required for processing but not for storage of long-term declarative memory. Long-term (or permanent) memory is probably stored in the neocortex.

16. Brain imaging is helping to identify brain regions involved in various aspects of learning and remembering. Encoding of information evokes greater activity in the left frontal region; to retrieve information evokes greater activity in the right frontal region. Sensorimotor skill learning is accompanied by activation in the basal ganglia, the cerebellum, and the motor cortex. Delay conditioning is accomplished by a cerebellar circuit, but trace conditioning requires the hippocampus.

Refer to the ***Learning Biological Psychology*** CD for the following study aids for this chapter:

7 Objectives

69 Study Questions

1 Activity

1 Video (six parts)

17. The capacities for associative as well as nonassociative learning are very widespread among animal species. The evolution of powerful and flexible brain mechanisms of learning and memory may have resulted from the earlier development of precise and elaborate systems to handle specific sensorimotor adjustments and then from the extension of these systems for more general use.

18. Abilities to learn and remember change throughout life. For some aspects of these changes, biological correlates have been found; other aspects continue to pose questions.

Recommended Reading

Baddeley, A. (1990). *Human memory: Theory and practice.* Needham Heights, MA: Allyn and Bacon.

Baudry, M., and Zola, S. (Eds.). (1998). Brain and memory: From genes to behavior. Proceedings of the Sixth Conference on the Neurobiology of Learning and Memory. *Neurobiology of Learning and Memory, 70,* 1–103.

Cohen, N. J., and Eichenbaum, H. (1993). Memory, amnesia, and the hippocampal system. Cambridge, MA: MIT Press.

Gabrieli, J. D. E. (1998). Cognitive neuroscience of human memory. *Annual Review of Psychology, 49,* 87–115.

Luria, A. R. (1987). *The mind of a mnemonist.* Cambridge, MA: Harvard University Press.

Squire, L. R., Knowlton, B., and Musen, G. (1993). The structure and organization of memory. *Annual Review of Psychology, 44,* 453–495.

Tulving, E., and Craik, F. I. M. (Eds.). (2000). *The Oxford handbook of memory.* Oxford, England: Oxford University Press.

Zola-Morgan, S., and Squire, L. R. (1993). Neuroanatomy of memory. *Annual Review of Neuroscience, 16,* 547–563.

18

Learning and Memory: Neural Mechanisms

W hereas Chapter 17 stressed behavioral aspects of learning and memory and the general regions of the nervous system where plastic changes that underlie learning and memory occur, in Chapter 18 we take up detailed sites and neural mechanisms. We will focus on three main topics:

1. What are the basic biological mechanisms—at the molecular, synaptic, and cellular levels—for long-term storage of information in the nervous system?
2. At the level of neural circuits, how do the formation and modification of circuits function in memory?
3. What sequence of neurochemical events underlies the storage of long-term memory?

In reviewing neural mechanisms of learning and memory, we must be careful not to overgeneralize. Some investigators have been so happy to find a specific site or precise mechanism of change for one kind of memory that they have erroneously proposed that their finding accounts for many or all other kinds of memory too. Careful work is needed to determine which mechanisms may be common among different forms of learning and which mechanisms are specific to particular forms of learning.

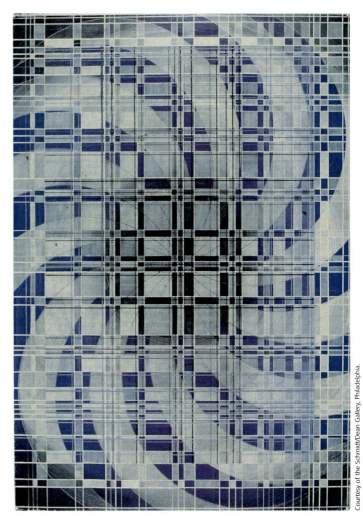

Robert Straight, *D-260*, 2000

New Experimental Techniques Enable Rapid Progress in Research on Mechanisms of Memory

Only in the last few decades have investigators discovered how to use behavioral intervention, coupled with biological measures, to study the mechanisms of learning and memory—that is, to study changes in the nervous system as a result of training (see Figure 1.3 for definitions of somatic and behavioral intervention). A variety of techniques, with a steady increase in their spatial and temporal resolution, have become available.

Now the combined use of somatic and behavioral interventions is yielding rapid progress in our understanding of the neural mechanisms of learning and memory. This approach is revealing how a brief experience can lead to a cascade of neurochemical events that may, in some cases, include protein synthesis and structural changes at synapses. Newer methods are also enabling investigators to determine how neural circuits are established or altered to serve memories.

Changes in Synapses May Be Mechanisms of Memory Storage

Soon after experiments on memory began in the 1880s, and as information accumulated on the physiology and anatomy of the nervous system, investigators began to speculate that changes in synapses could be a mechanism to store memories. British neurophysiologist Charles S. Sherrington (1897), in the same publication in which he proposed the term *synapse,* stated that changes in neural connections were likely to be important for learning:

> Shut off from all opportunity of reproducing itself and adding to its number by mitosis or otherwise, the nerve cell directs its pent-up energy towards amplifying its connections with its fellows, in response to the events which stir it up. Hence, it is capable of an education unknown to other tissues. (p. 1117)

The great Spanish neuroanatomist Santiago Ramón y Cajal (1894) also suggested that neurons extend their axons and dendrites to make new connections with other neurons in both development and learning.

Early in the twentieth century, when Ivan Pavlov sought to explain conditioning in neural terms, it was natural to think that neurons in the sensory cortex, representing the conditioned stimulus (CS), developed or strengthened their connections to neurons in the motor cortex, where the unconditioned response (UR) is represented; thus CS–UR linkages would develop. These linkages would form or strengthen neural chains, such as we saw in Figure 3.18.

Later, however, it was discovered that cortical lesions that should have interrupted such cross-cortical connections did not abolish conditioned responses or memories for other kinds of learning. This finding appeared to invalidate the hypothesis that memories depend on direct neural chains, or at least cross-cortical chains. Investigators then began to consider other kinds of neural circuits and even to speculate about other mechanisms, such as the interaction of electrical fields in the brain.

Different Kinds of Neural Circuits May Underlie Memories

It will be helpful for us to organize the varied research on neural mechanisms of learning and memory according to the kinds of neural circuits that investigators consider, which range from simple neural chains to parallel distributed circuits. We will define each kind of circuit briefly here; these definitions will become more meaningful as we discuss research related to them. Most theorizing about circuits locates the site(s) of memory storage in one or more plastic synapses (shown in Figure 18.1 in orange).

The neural chain (see Figure 18.1*a*), at its simplest, can be a monosynaptic reflex arc, as in the knee jerk reflex (see Figure 3.16). Some studies indicate that even the

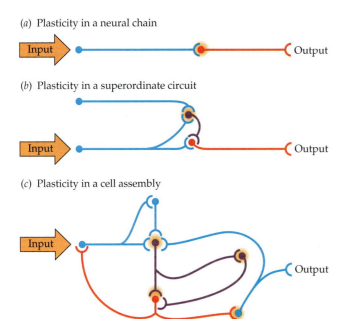

(a) Plasticity in a neural chain

Input → ● ———————— ● ——— (Output

(b) Plasticity in a superordinate circuit

Input →

Output

(c) Plasticity in a cell assembly

Input →

Output

18.1 Sites of Synaptic Plasticity in Neural Networks Changes at sites of synaptic plasticity—such as the sites shown here (highlighted in orange) in a neural chain (*a*), a higher-order segment of a circuit (*b*), and a cell assembly (*c*)—may underlie memory storage.

simplest variety—a monosynaptic neural circuit—can show some learning, as we will see a little later. In this case, learning is said to cause intrinsic change in the circuit.

Many simple neural circuits also receive input from superordinate circuits (see Figure 18.1*b*), also called *modulatory circuits.* We saw an example in the case of the motor system, where the activity of spinal reflex circuits is modulated by higher-order circuits at the level of the brainstem, basal ganglia, and motor cortex (see Chapter 11). In this chapter we will see an example (eye-blink conditioning) of plasticity in a superordinate modulatory circuit; the basic reflex circuit itself, however, shows no change during training.

Many kinds of learning may require the establishment of relatively complex networks of neurons—**cell assemblies,** as psychologist Donald O. Hebb called them in his influential book, *The Organization of Behavior* (1949). In Figure 18.1*c*, several plastic synapses help form a neural network.

Many current hypotheses suggest that a single group or ensemble of neurons can encode many different memories—each neuron participating to a greater or lesser extent in a particular memory, just as a person may belong to several different clubs or groups. In this case, each unit change may be too small to affect behavior significantly by itself, but the aggregate of changes in many neurons can produce large effects. The encoding of memories in an ensemble of neurons also depends on the plasticity of the synapses involved.

Before we look at the research on different kinds of neural circuits, we will consider two important background topics: First we will examine the ways in which synapses can change and thereby store information. Then we will discuss technological developments beginning in the 1940s that encouraged research on the neural mechanisms of memory: the ability to measure changes in electrical activity, in neurochemistry, and in neuroanatomy in response to training. Finding such changes encouraged research on the neural mechanisms of memory.

The Nervous System May Form and Store Memories in Various Ways

As knowledge of synaptic anatomy and chemistry increased, hypotheses about plastic synaptic changes became more numerous and precise. Changes in existing synapses and changes in numbers of synapses have been proposed as mechanisms of information storage (see Figure 18.2).

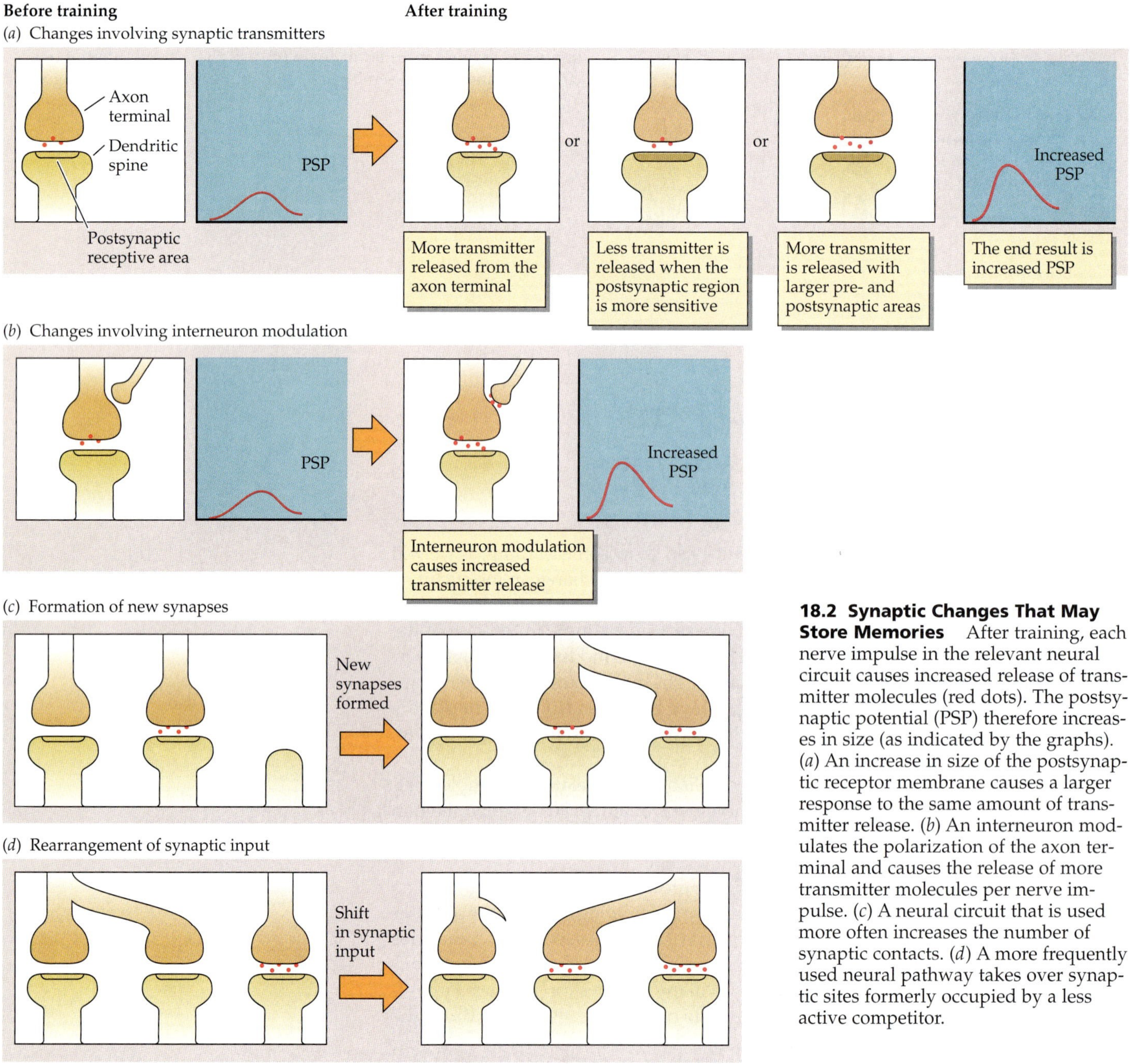

Before training

(a) Changes involving synaptic transmitters

After training

Axon terminal

Dendritic spine

Postsynaptic receptive area

PSP

or

or

More transmitter released from the axon terminal

Less transmitter is released when the postsynaptic region is more sensitive

More transmitter is released with larger pre- and postsynaptic areas

Increased PSP

The end result is increased PSP

(b) Changes involving interneuron modulation

PSP

Increased PSP

Interneuron modulation causes increased transmitter release

(c) Formation of new synapses

New synapses formed

(d) Rearrangement of synaptic input

Shift in synaptic input

18.2 Synaptic Changes That May Store Memories After training, each nerve impulse in the relevant neural circuit causes increased release of transmitter molecules (red dots). The postsynaptic potential (PSP) therefore increases in size (as indicated by the graphs). (a) An increase in size of the postsynaptic receptor membrane causes a larger response to the same amount of transmitter release. (b) An interneuron modulates the polarization of the axon terminal and causes the release of more transmitter molecules per nerve impulse. (c) A neural circuit that is used more often increases the number of synaptic contacts. (d) A more frequently used neural pathway takes over synaptic sites formerly occupied by a less active competitor.

Physiological Changes at Synapses May Store Information

Some of the changes that may store information can be measured physiologically. The changes could be presynaptic, postsynaptic, or both. Certain possibilities concern the release of synaptic transmitters and their effects on postsynaptic receptor molecules (Figure 18.2a). These include greater release of neurotransmitter molecules and/or greater effects when the receptor molecules become more numerous or more sensitive. The result of such changes would be an increase in the size of the postsynaptic potential (PSP). Changes in the rate of *inactivation* of the transmitter could produce a similar effect.

The amount of neurotransmitter released could also be affected by the influence of terminals from other neurons on the end boutons (Figure 18.2b). That is, impulses from other neurons could alter the polarization of the boutons and thus affect the amount of neurotransmitter released.

Structural Changes at Synapses May Provide Long-Term Storage

Many investigators believe that long-term memories require changes in the nervous system so dramatic that they can be seen by microscopic techniques. Structural changes resulting from use are apparent in other parts of the body. For example, exercise changes the mass and/or shape of muscles and bone. In a similar way, new synapses could form or synapses could be eliminated as a function of training (Figure 18.2*c*).

Training could also lead to reorganization of synaptic connections. For example, it could cause a more used pathway to take over endings formerly occupied by a less active competitor (Figure 18.2*d*).

What Conditions Are Required to Induce Memory-Related Changes at Synapses?

Psychologist Donald O. Hebb suggested conditions that could account for the development of the nervous system and for learning. Hebb (1949) proposed that the functional relationship between a presynaptic neuron (A) and a postsynaptic neuron (B) could change if A frequently took part in exciting B:

> When an axon of cell A is near enough to excite a cell B and repeatedly or persistently takes part in firing it, some growth process or metabolic change takes place in one or both cells such that A's efficacy, as one of the cells firing B, is increased. (p. 62)

Donald O. Hebb
(1904–1985)

Investigators have sought to determine whether Hebb's hypothesis is correct, and positive examples have been found. For example, Kelso and Brown (1986) followed the pattern of differential conditioning in slices of rat hippocampus. They placed three stimulating electrodes in a tract running to the CA1 region. (We will discuss specific regions of the hippocampus later in the chapter.) One electrode was set to deliver a strong, suprathreshold shock, and the other two delivered weak, subthreshold shocks. Stimulation of one weak electrode was paired with the strong electrode, occurring just before stimulation of the strong electrode; the other weak electrode was not paired with the strong stimulus. After a few minutes of such stimulation, the response to the paired weak stimulus was significantly increased in amplitude, whereas the response to the unpaired weak stimulus was unchanged.

Thus in the absence of a complex circuit, hippocampal synapses show the kinds of conditional changes that could mediate aspects of associative learning. Synapses that show such properties are called **Hebbian synapses.** Hebb later expressed some amusement that his formulation had attracted so much attention because he thought it was only a formal expression of ideas that many theorists had held for many years and that other aspects of his theory were more original (P. M. Milner, 1993).

Hebb (1949) also restated what he called the old idea "that any two cells or systems of cells that are repeatedly active at the same time will tend to become 'associated,' so that activity in one facilitates activity in the other" (p. 70). Thus two cells, C and D, that send impulses simultaneously to the same region will tend to make connections to intermediate cells in common, and then no longer act independently of each other. This is an extension of the preceding hypothesis, and it can be used to explain phenomena such as sensory–sensory conditioning and conditional learning (see Chapter 17). Both of these mechanisms can be summed up by the expression "Neurons that fire together wire together" (Löwell and Singer, 1992, p. 211).

To explain how neural activity could lead to the formation of new synaptic connections as a result of experience, Hebb proposed the dual-trace hypothesis. According to this hypothesis, formation of a memory involves first a relatively brief transient process: Learning experience sets up activity that tends to reverberate through the activated neural circuits. This activity holds the memory for a short period. If sufficient, the activity helps build up a stable change in the nervous system— a long-lasting memory trace.

Negative Changes May Also Store Information in the Nervous System

We have mentioned only increases in synaptic effects with training, and Hebb wrote only about strengthening synaptic connections, never about weakening them. Changes in the opposite direction, however, could just as well mediate learning and memory, since both making and breaking contacts alter circuits. Later theorists added *weakening connections* to Hebb's formulations, thus greatly increasing their power to account for features of learning and memory. Thus our list of the ways of increasing synaptic activity or numbers (see Figure 18.2) should be considered short-hand notation for *increasing or decreasing.*

Computing What to Remember Requires Circuits of Neurons

For many aspects of learning and memory it may not be possible to find correlates in the responses of individual neurons or synapses; it may be necessary to study the activities of sets or ensembles of neurons. Consider, for example, the cards that a cheering section at a football game holds up: Looking at one or a few cards cannot reveal the pattern made by all the cards. Hebb therefore proposed the concept of cell assemblies—that is, large groups of cells that tend to be active at the same time because they have been activated simultaneously or in close succession in the past.

Such groups would include cells that are widely dispersed in the brain and that do not necessarily show any orderly spatial arrangement. Excitation of cells in one part of the assembly would tend to activate other cells in the assembly and so to excite the whole assembly. Such cell assemblies could represent "perceptual elements" that could be grouped into more complex ensembles to give rise to perceptions. Certainly the behavior of neural ensembles depends on unit activity, but it may not be entirely reducible to the activity of individual units.

In Chapter 17 we found that various kinds of learning require specialized circuits to compute particular features of what is to be remembered. For example, some experiments have demonstrated that different regions of the brain are necessary to process and store different attributes of memory. Each of these brain regions possesses its own particular anatomy of circuits, which differs from that of the other regions, and each region processes an aspect of information that the other regions do not.

Several experiments revealed that close temporal pairing of stimuli is neither necessary nor sufficient for conditioning to occur; here, too, complex networks are necessary to process the information, and monosynaptic circuits do not suffice. The distinction between computation by neural networks and storage of information was stressed by Gallistel (1990), who noted that neuroscientists have been much more concerned with storage than with neural computation.

Cerebral Changes Result from Training

Training and Experience Cause the Brain to Change Chemically and Anatomically

NEURAL PLASTICITY

In the early 1960s two experimental programs showed that the brain can be altered by training or differential experience. First was the demonstration by an interdisciplinary team (Figure 18.3) that either formal training or informal experience in varied environments leads to measurable changes in the neurochemistry and neuroanatomy of the rodent brain (E. L. Bennett et al., 1964; Renner and Rosenzweig, 1987; Rosenzweig, 1984; Rosenzweig et al., 1961).

Soon thereafter came the announcement by Hubel and Wiesel that depriving one eye of light in a young kitten, starting at the age at which the eyes open, reduces the number of cortical cells responding to that eye (see Chapter 7) (Hubel and Wiesel, 1965; Wiesel and Hubel, 1963, 1965). Although depriving an eye of light is a severe condition, whereas giving animals training or different degrees of experience without depriving them of any sensory modality is a mild and natural treatment, both approaches lead to measurable changes in the nervous system.

18.3 Pioneer Investigators of the Effects of Training and Differential Experience on Brain Chemistry and Anatomy Pictured from left to right are Edward L. Bennett, neurochemist; Marian C. Diamond, neuroanatomist; David Krech, biological psychologist; and Mark R. Rosenzweig, biological psychologist. (Photograph taken around 1965.)

In some experiments, animals have differential opportunities for informal learning. In several experiments, for example, littermates of the same sex were assigned by a random procedure to various laboratory environments. The following three environments were the most common:

1. The **standard condition** (**SC**). Three animals were kept in a standard laboratory cage and provided with food and water (Figure 18.4*a*). This is the typical environment for laboratory animals.
2. The **impoverished** (or *isolated*) **condition** (**IC**). A single animal was housed in an SC-sized cage (Figure 18.4*b*).
3. The **enriched condition** (**EC**). A group of 10 to 12 animals was kept in a large cage containing a variety of stimulus objects, which were changed daily (Figure 18.4*c*).

(*a*) Standard condition

(*b*) Impoverished condition

(*c*) Enriched condition

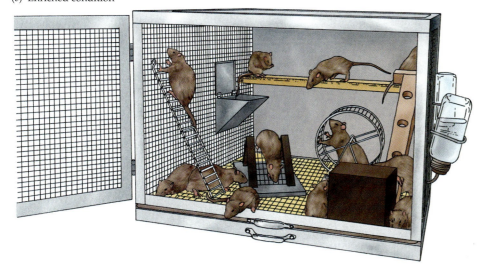

18.4 Experimental Environments to Test Effects of Enrichment on Learning and Brain Measures Interaction with an enriched environment has measurable effects on brain measures, on stress reactions, and on learning.

This environment is considered enriched because it provides greater opportunities for informal learning than does the SC.

In the initial experiments of this series, rats were assigned to the different conditions at weaning (about 25 days after birth), and they were kept in these conditions for 80 days.

At the end of the period of differential experience, each brain was dissected into standard samples for chemical analysis. In the initial experiments, animals in the enriched condition (EC) were found to have developed significantly greater activity of the enzyme acetylcholinesterase (AChE) in the cerebral cortex than their IC littermates had. (Recall that AChE breaks down the synaptic transmitter ACh and clears the synapse for renewed stimulation.) Control experiments showed that this effect could not be attributed to either greater handling of the EC animals or greater locomotor activity in the EC situation (Rosenzweig et al., 1961). Scrutiny of the data then revealed that the experimental groups differed not only in total enzymatic activity but also in weight of the cortical samples: The EC animals had developed a significantly heavier cerebral cortex than their IC littermates had (Rosenzweig et al., 1962).

This result was a real surprise because since the beginning of the twentieth century, brain weight had been considered a very stable characteristic and not subject to environmental influences. The differences in brain weight were extremely reliable, although small. Moreover, these differences were not distributed uniformly throughout the cerebral cortex. They were largest in the occipital cortex and smallest in the adjacent somesthetic cortex. Later experiments demonstrated that shorter periods could produce cerebral changes and that brains of adult rats also responded to differential experience.

The differences in cortical weights among groups were caused by differences in cortical thickness: Animals exposed to the EC environment developed slightly but significantly thicker cerebral cortices than their SC or IC littermates (M. C. Diamond, 1967; M. C. Diamond et al., 1964). More refined neuroanatomical measurements were soon undertaken on pyramidal cells in the occipital cortex, including sizes of cell bodies, counts of dendritic spines, measurements of dendritic branching, and measurements of the size of synaptic contacts (Rosenzweig et al., 1972). Each of these measurements showed significant effects of differential experience, as we will see shortly.

Enriched Experience Has Beneficial Effects on Brain Anatomy, Neurochemistry, and Behavior

Experience in the EC environment promotes better learning and problem solving in a variety of tests. An enriched environment alters the expression of a large number of genes, many of which can be related to neuronal structure, synaptic plasticity, and transmission; a number of these genes may play important roles in learning and memory (Rampon, Tang, et al., 2000). Enriched experience also aids recovery from or compensation for a variety of conditions, including malnutrition, thyroid insufficiency, and brain damage (Galani et al., 1997; Hamm et al., 1996; Johansson and Ohlsson, 1996; Rampon, Tang et al., 2000; Will et al., 1977). In some cases a combination of transplanting fetal cells and giving enriched experience is significantly more effective in restoring function after brain damage than either treatment is alone (Kelche et al., 1995). As we will see later in this chapter, enriched experience also appears to protect against age-related declines in memory, both in laboratory animals and in humans.

Because enriched experience has such widespread effects on brain anatomy, neurochemistry, and behavior, it appears that most experiments done with animals raised in standard, restricted laboratory environments are actually using animals with stunted brains, so the possibility of generalizing from such results may be limited.

Learning Can Produce New Synaptic Connections

The idea that learning and memory can be mediated by the formation of new synaptic contacts has had its ups and downs during the last century. Proposed as early as

NEURAL PLASTICITY

the 1870s by Alexander Bain, this idea was supported by such eminent neurobiologists as Ramón y Cajal (1894) and Sherrington (1897). Because no concrete evidence was produced to back it up, however, support for the hypothesis waned. Hebb (1949) helped revive the synaptic hypothesis of learning, but in 1965 John C. Eccles (the neurophysiologist who shared the 1963 Nobel Prize in physiology or medicine) remained firm in his belief that learning and memory storage involve "growth just of bigger and better synapses that are already there, not growth of new connections" (Eccles, 1965, p. 97). Not until the 1970s did experiments with laboratory rats assigned to enriched or impoverished environments provide evidence that learning can produce new synaptic connections.

We saw in Chapters 2 and 7 that growth of dendritic spines is a late aspect of the development of neurons and is affected by experience. When dendritic spines were counted in experiments testing EC versus IC, the number of spines per unit of length of dendrite was found to be significantly greater in EC than in IC animals (Globus et al., 1973). This effect was not uniform over the dendritic tree; it was most pronounced for basal dendrites. Different aspects of the dendritic tree receive inputs from different sources, and the basal dendrites of pyramidal cells receive input especially from adjacent neurons in the same region. Thus enriched experience appears to lead to the development of increased numbers of synaptic contacts and richer, more complex intracortical networks.

Psychologist William Greenough also placed laboratory rats in SC, EC, and IC environments, and he quantified dendritic branching by the methods shown in Figure 18.5. The dendritic branching developed by EC animals was significantly greater than that of IC animals (Greenough and Volkmar, 1973; Volkmar and Greenough, 1972). The SC values fell between the IC and EC values and tended to be closer to the IC values. With enriched experience, each cell did not send its dendrites out farther, but instead tended to fill its allotted volume more densely with branches. These

NEURAL PLASTICITY

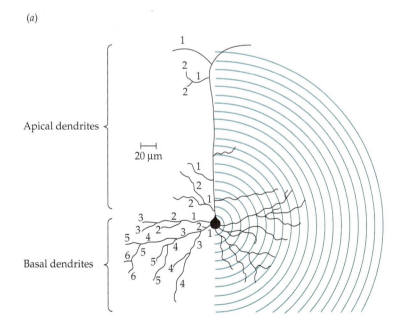

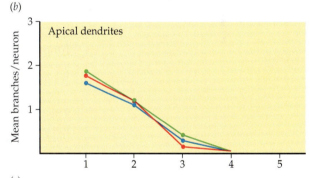

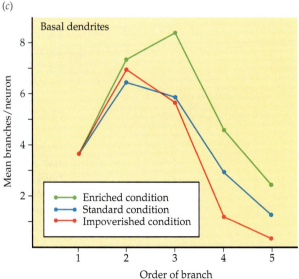

18.5 Measurement of Dendritic Branching (*a*) An enlarged photograph of a neuron is used to quantify branching either by counts of the number of branches of different orders (*left*), or by counts of the number of intersections with concentric rings (*right*). (*b, c*) These results were obtained by counts of the number of branches on apical dendrites (*b*) and basal dendrites (*c*). There are significant differences in branching, especially in the basal dendrites, among rats kept for 30 days in enriched, standard, or impoverished environments. (From Greenough, 1976.)

results, together with the dendritic spine counts, indicate that EC animals develop new synapses and more elaborate information-processing circuits.

More refined measures showed that in layers I to IV of the occipital cortex, the EC rats had about 9400 synapses per neuron, versus about 7600 for the IC rats—a difference of more than 20% (Turner and Greenough, 1985). The value for SC rats was intermediate, but closer to the IC level. A period of 4 days in EC cages was enough to produce significant increases in dendritic lengths compared to those of rats kept in individual cages (Wallace et al., 1992).

Greenough and collaborators have also studied effects of formal training on brain measures. One experiment used split-brain rats, administering training to only one eye so that it involved only a single cerebral hemisphere; effects of training on dendritic branching appeared mainly in the trained hemisphere (Chang and Greenough, 1982).

**IMPORTANT
METHOD**

Another study compared effects of four conditions on adult rats: an acrobatic condition (AC) in which rats learned to traverse an increasingly difficult series of obstacles (e.g., narrow platforms, rope ladders, and seesaws); a forced-exercise (FX) condition in which the rats ran on a treadmill for as much as 60 minutes daily; a voluntary exercise condition in which rats had free access to a running wheel; and isolated housing in a small cage (IC). An area of rat cerebellar cortex related to movements of the limbs and head showed a significantly increased number of synaptic contacts in the AC group, whereas increased locomotion in the FX group increased capillaries in the cerebellar cortex but not neural measures (Isaacs et al., 1992). In a similar study, AC rats developed more synapses in the motor cortex (Kleim et al., 1996). These results provide strong support for the view that new synaptic contacts form in specific brain regions in response to learning and the formation of long-term memory.

Several neuroanatomical studies confirm that dendritic morphology is dynamic. Electrical activity of neurons promotes growth of fine extensions from dendrites. These extensions, called **filopodia,** occur not only during development, as mentioned in Chapter 7, but throughout the life span. They may become dendritic spines if they make contact with an axon (Maletic-Savatic et al., 1999; S. J. Smith, 1999). Other filopodia retract and disappear. Activation of either AMPA or NMDA receptors causes spine morphology to become more stable and more regular (M. Fischer et al., 2000).

The *size* of synaptic contacts also changes as a result of differential experience. The mean length of the postsynaptic thickening in synapses of the occipital cortex is significantly greater in EC rats than in their IC littermates (M. C. Diamond et al., 1975; Greenough and Volkmar, 1973). Such increases in the size and number of synaptic contacts may increase the certainty of synaptic transmission in the circuits where changes occur. The fact that these changes, related to long-term memory, are found in the cerebral cortex is consistent with the hypothesis that much long-term memory is *stored* in the cortex, whereas information is *processed* for memory storage in other brain regions, such as the hippocampus, depending on the attributes of the particular memory (see Chapter 17).

Experiments with several strains of rats showed similar effects of EC and IC environments on both brain values and problem-solving behavior. Similar effects on brain measurements have been found in several species of mammals: mice, gerbils, ground squirrels, cats, and monkeys (Renner and Rosenzweig, 1987,); effects of differential experience on brain measurements have also been found in birds and in fish. Recent reviews take up the effects of differential experiences on brain and behavior in a variety of vertebrate species (Rampon and Tsien, 2000: van Praag et al., 2000).

Insects too show effects of differential environments on their nervous systems. The fruit fly *Drosophila* shows greater branching of neuronal processes when placed in an enriched environment with leafy branches and with other *Drosophila,* in comparison with *Drosophila* kept in isolation in small vials (Heisenberg et al., 1995; Technau, 1984). Heisenberg et al. (1995) concluded that most regions of the *Drosophila* brain that show extensive neuronal branching "are continuously reorganized throughout life in response to specific living conditions" (p. 1951). Insect brain regions known as the mushroom bodies function similarly to the avian and mammalian hippocampus, and these regions enlarge in the bee when it gains spatial experience (Capaldi et al., 1999). Adult crickets placed in an enriched environment produce more new neurons in their mushroom bodies than do crickets in an impoverished environment (Lamossese et al., 2000).

A few studies indicate similar plasticity of the human brain to differential experience. For example, we saw in Chapter 11 that the hand area of the motor cortex becomes larger in musicians, presumably due to their extensive practice. Also, the occipital cortex of blind persons becomes sensitive to auditory stimuli, and transcranial magnetic stimulation of the occipital cortex can disrupt Braille reading, indicating that cross-modal neural reorganization can take place in the mature human brain (Kujala et al., 2000). A recent study assigned 100 children to a two-year enriched nursery school program at ages 3–5 while others received normal educational experience (Raine et al., 2001). When the children were tested at age 11, using skin conductance and electroencephalographic measures of arousal and attention, the children with early environmental enrichment showed increases in orienting and arousal.

Thus, the cerebral effects of experience that were surprising when first reported for rats in the early 1960s are now seen to occur widely in the animal kingdom–from flies to philosophers (Mohammed, 2001).

The finding that measurable changes can be induced in the brain by experience, even in adult animals, was one of several factors that led increasing numbers of investigators to ask in more detail how the nervous system reacts to training and how new information can be stored by the nervous system.

Invertebrate Nervous Systems Show Plasticity

The relative simplicity of the central nervous systems of some invertebrates led several investigators to try to find in them the neural circuits necessary and sufficient for learning, with the goal of studying plastic synaptic changes in these circuits. Invertebrate preparations, such as the large sea slug *Aplysia* (Figure 18.6), appeared to offer certain advantages for this research, although some of these advantages were overestimated:

- The number of nerve cells in an *Aplysia* ganglion is relatively small (though still on the order of a thousand) compared to that in a mammalian brain.
- As we saw in Chapter 6, many individual cells in invertebrate ganglia can be recognized, both because of their shapes and sizes and because the cellular structure of the ganglion is uniform from individual to individual. Thus it is possible to identify certain cells and to trace their sensory and motor connections. The neurotransmitters in some of these large, identifiable cells are also known.

A well-known program of research on neural plasticity in invertebrates was initiated by Eric R. Kandel, who was awarded the Nobel Prize in physiology or medicine in 2000 for research on neural mechanisms of learning and memory. Kandel investigated sites and mechanisms of plasticity for both nonassociative and associative learning in *Aplysia* (Kandel et al., 1987). Much of Kandel's research indicated that learning takes place within a simple sensorimotor chain that controls the behavior being studied. Many interesting results have been reported from this program, but since the mid-1980s some investigators have voiced reserva-

NEURAL PLASTICITY

18.6 Characteristic Behaviors of *Aplysia* (*a*) Locomotion. (*b*) In the usual posture, the siphon is extended and the gill is spread out on the back. Ordinarily only the tip of the siphon would be visible in a lateral view; here the rest of the siphon and the gill are shown as if the animal were transparent. (*c*) The siphon and the gill retract in response to light touch. (*d*) The head retracts and the animal releases ink in response to a strong stimulus. (After Kandel, 1976.)

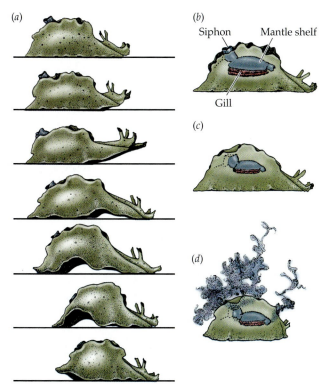

tions about its methods and findings. For example, if the ganglia of *Aplysia* are inactivated or removed, *Aplysia* can still show some learning, using small peripheral neurons that are difficult to study (Lukowiak and Colebrook, 1988–1989). And neurons in the ganglia do not behave like isolated parallel channels; rather they behave like members of a large distributed network (Wu et al., 1994).

Both the number and the size of synaptic junctions have been found to vary with training in *Aplysia* (C. H. Bailey and Chen, 1983). This finding is similar to previous findings with mammals (M. C. Diamond et al., 1975; West and Greenough, 1972). It refutes the earlier claim of some investigators that neurochemical events at existing synapses are sufficient to account for learning and long-term memory.

**NEURAL
PLASTICITY**

The similarity of results obtained with *Aplysia* and with rats indicates that over a wide range of species, information can be stored in the nervous system by changes in both size and number of synaptic contacts. These findings confirm the hypotheses diagrammed in Figure 18.2. Thus even in a relatively simple animal like *Aplysia*, the structural remodeling of the nervous system that we considered early in development (see Chapter 7) probably continues to some extent throughout life and can be driven by experience. Kandel and his associates have also studied the cascade of neurochemical events that accompany learning in *Aplysia*, as we will note later in this chapter.

Reviewing research on learning in invertebrates, Krasne and Glanzman (1995) pointed to evidence for a variety of circuits. Although several studies focus on changes intrinsic to simple circuits, these authors pointed out that the role of higher-level control circuits may be underestimated in these studies because the circuits are likely to be impaired in restrained or partially dissected animals. In both *Aplysia* and crayfish, there is evidence of modulation by higher-level circuitry in freely behaving animals. Furthermore, evidence suggests that learned changes in defensive behavior of these two animals are due to changes in synaptic efficacy distributed over large numbers of synaptic sites; in other words, there appears to be parallel distributed processing.

Could Long-Term Potentiation Be a Model for Studying Mechanisms of Learning and Memory?

Investigators have long sought a way of isolating a vertebrate brain circuit in which learning occurs in order to study the mechanisms in detail, much as invertebrate "reduced preparations" are being studied. Long-term potentiation in the mammalian brain may be the answer. **Long-term potentiation (LTP)** is a stable and enduring increase in the magnitude of the response of neurons after afferent cells to the region have been stimulated with bursts of electrical stimuli of moderately high frequency (Figure 18.7a).

Timothy Bliss

LTP was first discovered in 1973 in the hippocampus of the intact rabbit by British neurophysiologist Timothy Bliss and Norwegian Terje Lømo, then a psychology student. The surprising aspect of their finding was the long-lasting nature of the increase in response magnitude. A shorter-term effect of this sort had long been known under the name of posttetanic potentiation (PTP), which occurs at neuromuscular junctions.

The 1973 report of Bliss and Lømo has become one of the most frequently cited papers on brain mechanisms of memory. Soon after this report, other investigators demonstrated that LTP could also be studied in slices of rat hippocampus maintained in a tissue chamber (Schwartzkroin and Wester, 1975). LTP can be observed in awake and freely moving animals, in anesthetized animals, or in tissue slices, which is the focus of most current research. Although most of the work on LTP has been done in the hippocampus of the rat (Figure 18.7b), LTP has been observed in many other brain areas in several species of mammals, and even in fishes. LTP can also be studied in sensorimotor synapses of the sea slug *Aplysia* in a cell culture (X. Y. Lin and Glanzman, 1994).

Terje Lømo

Bliss and Lømo (1973) were cautious as to whether LTP bears any relation to normal behavior. However, LTP does resemble memory in several ways: LTP can be induced within seconds, it may last for days or weeks (Bliss and Gardner-Medwin, 1973), and it shows a labile consolidation period that lasts for several minutes after induction (Barrionuevo et al., 1980). Such properties have attracted many investigators to the study of LTP. After reviewing some other findings about LTP, we will consider more critically how well LTP may serve as a mechanism of memory. We'll follow our discussion of LTP by looking at an opposite phenomenon, the weakening of synaptic responses, which may also be important as a mechanism of learning.

Different Kinds of LTP Occur at Different Sites in the Hippocampal Formation

Even within the hippocampal formation, there is more than one kind of LTP, although for some time LTP was assumed to be a unitary phenomenon. The hippocampal formation (see Figure 18.7b) consists of two interlocking C-shaped regions—the hippocampus and the **dentate gyrus**—and includes the adjacent **subiculum** (also called the *subicular complex* or *hippocampal gyrus*).

The strange shapes of the structures in the hippocampal formation earned them picturesque names: *Hippocampus* itself comes from the Greek *hippokampos,* "seahorse," as we noted in Chapter 2. But other neuroanatomists called it by the Latin name *cornu ammonis* ("Ammon's horn"), referring to the horn of the ram that represented the Egyptian deity Ammon. One region where LTP is investigated is known as CA1 (cornu ammonis 1), another as CA3. The dentate gyrus got its name from its toothlike projections (the Latin *dens* means "tooth"). The subiculum (from the Latin *subicere,* meaning "to raise or lift") can be seen as a support for the rest of the hippocampal formation.

Main inputs to the hippocampal formation come from the nearby entorhinal cortex via the axons of the perforant pathway that push through ("perforate") the subiculum (see Figure 18.7b). The site at which LTP was originally demonstrated consists of synapses from the perforant path to the dentate gyrus. From the dentate gyrus, so-called mossy fibers run to the hippocampus, where they synapse in area CA3. Until recently, LTP was not much studied at these CA3 synapses, possibly because this projection has relatively few synapses, and induction of LTP there requires special conditions, as we will see later. Neurons in CA3 send their axons, called *Schaffer collaterals,* to area CA1; LTP has been studied intensively at these synapses. The CA1 and CA3 regions also receive inputs from the corresponding regions of the hippocampus in the other hemisphere of the brain via commissural fibers (fibers that cross over through the corpus callosum).

The discovery of selective agonists for different kinds of glutamate receptors in the 1980s allowed investigators to characterize the pharmacology of synaptic transmission in the hippocampus and to study the neurochemistry of hippocampal LTP. LTP in area CA1 was found to require the kind of glutamate receptors that respond to the glutamate agonist *N*-methyl-D-aspartate (the NMDA receptors that we introduced in Box 4.2; see also Figure 18.8). Blocking of these receptors by antagonists of NMDA made it impossible to induce LTP in CA1, even though the NMDA antagonists did not affect other glutamate receptors, the AMPA receptors.

Although NMDA antagonists prevent the induction of LTP, they do not affect LTP that has already been established. For a time it appeared that induction of all hippocampal LTP and many kinds of learning might depend on NMDA receptors, but then NMDA antagonists were found not to prevent induction of LTP in some afferents of the dentate gyrus or CA3. Both of these regions obtain their inputs from the lateral perforant path, whereas the NMDA receptor–dependent form of LTP receives its input via the medial perforant path.

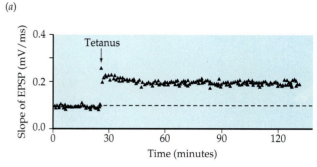

(a)

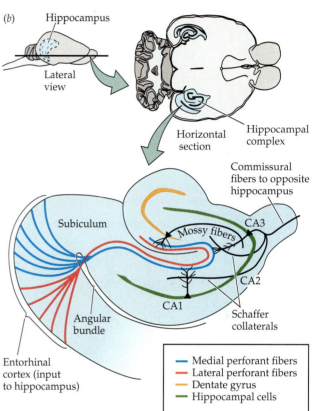

(b)

18.7 Long-Term Potentiation in the Hippocampus (a) In LTP, as this example shows, after brief tetanic stimulation the slope of excitatory postsynaptic potential (EPSP) responses increases markedly and remains high throughout the recording period. (b, top) This diagram shows location of the hippocampal formation in whole rat brain and in a horizontal section. (b, bottom) This diagram of the right hippocampal formation shows input fibers from the entorhinal cortex via the perforant pathway.

NMDA Receptors and AMPA Receptors Play Separate Roles in the Induction of LTP in the CA1 Region

When the neurotransmitter glutamate is released at a synapse that has both AMPA receptors and NMDA receptors, a moderate level of stimulation activates only the AMPA receptors, which handle most of the normal traffic of messages at these synapses. The NMDA receptors do not respond because magnesium ions (Mg^{2+}) block the NMDA receptor channel (Figure 18.8*a*), so few Ca^{2+} ions can enter the neuron. Sufficient activation of AMPA receptors or other excitatory receptors in the same neuron can partially depolarize the membrane to less than –35 mV. This partial depolarization removes the Mg^{2+} block (Figure 18.8*b*); the NMDA receptors now respond actively to glutamate and admit large amounts of Ca^{2+} through their channels. Thus the NMDA receptors are fully active only when they are gated by a combination of voltage and the ligand.

The large influx of Ca^{2+} can lead to the next steps in the induction of LTP by activating some **protein kinases** (enzymes that catalyze phosphorylation, the addition of phosphate groups [PO_4] to protein molecules). Phosphorylation changes the properties of many protein molecules. Several protein kinases are present in relatively large amounts in neurons, including protein kinase A (PKA), protein kinase C (PKC), calcium–calmodulin kinase (CaM kinase, or CaMK), and tyrosine kinase (TK). Blockage of any of these kinases can prevent the induction of LTP. CaM kinase has the interesting property of remaining activated once it is put into that state by Ca^{2+}, even

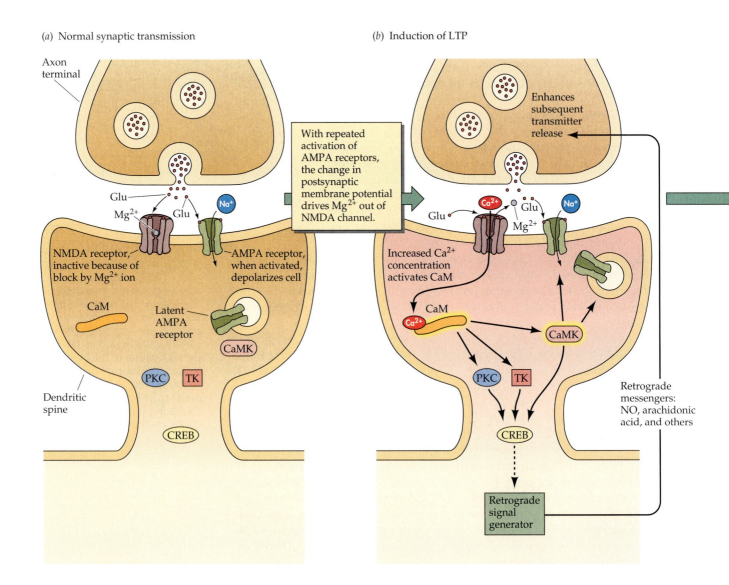

(*a*) Normal synaptic transmission

(*b*) Induction of LTP

if the level of Ca^{2+} subsequently falls; only a specific enzyme can cause CaM kinase to revert to its inactive state. Thus CaM kinase could play a role in maintaining LTP.

CaM kinase affects AMPA receptors in two ways (Figure 18.8c) (Malenka and Nicoll, 1999). It phosphorylates AMPA receptors already present in the dendritic spine membrane, thus increasing their conductance to Na^+ and K^+ ions. It also promotes the movement of AMPA receptors from the interior of the spine into the membrane, making more receptors available to stimulate the spine. Additional steps in the neurochemical cascade underlying LTP will be described shortly.

In an attempt to test the importance of the NMDA receptor (NR) for LTP, Joe Z. Tsien and colleagues (Rampon, Jiang, et al., 2000) prepared genetically modified mice in which a major subunit of NR, the NR1 subunit, was prevented from expression in the brain. These knockout mice grew normally and appeared normal, but investigators were unable to induce LTP in their hippocampal slices. The knockout mice were also inferior to wild-type mice in several behavior tests known to involve the hippocampus. These results clearly supported the hypothesized importance of the NMDA receptors.

GENES AND BEHAVIOR

But then the researchers tried giving the knockout mice experience in an enriched environment like that shown in Figure 18.4c. To their surprise, they found that the enriched experience significantly improved the performance of the knockout mice, making them as good as the wild-type mice on some tests. Tsien and colleagues plan to test whether enriched experience will also restore LTP in knockout mice, but they have not yet done so. At least for some types of learning and memory that are de-

(c) Enhanced synapse, after induction of LTP

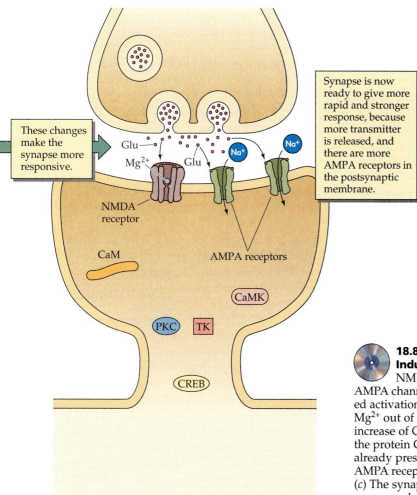

18.8 Roles of the AMPA and NMDA Receptors in the Induction of LTP in the CA1 Region (a) Normally the NMDA channel is blocked by a Mg^{2+} molecule, and only the AMPA channel functions in excitation of the neuron. (b) With repeated activation of AMPA receptors, depolarization of the neuron drives Mg^{2+} out of the NMDA channel, and Ca^{2+} ions enter. The rapid increase of Ca^{2+} ions triggers processes that lead to LTP. Activation of the protein CaM kinase increases the conductance of AMPA receptors already present in the membrane and promotes the movement of AMPA receptors from the interior of the spine into the membrane. (c) The synapse is enhanced after induction of LTP. CREB, cAMP response element–binding protein; Glu, glutamate; TK, tyrosine kinase.

pendent on the hippocampus, NR mechanisms are not essential. As Box 18.1 describes, enhancing NR activity by altering NR2 subunits improves LTP and some kinds of learning and memory.

Opioid Peptides Modulate the Induction of LTP in the CA3 Region

Although much research focuses on the role of the NMDA receptor in LTP, at the synapses between mossy fibers and CA3 neurons (see Figure 18.7*b*), LTP can be induced even in the presence of an NMDA antagonist, so NMDA receptors are not needed here (E. W. Harris and Cotman, 1986). On the other hand, the induction of LTP in region CA3 can be blocked by the presence of the opioid antagonist naloxone (Derrick and Martinez, 1994).

The opioid-dependent form of LTP may be the predominant form of LTP in fibers that convey information from cortex to hippocampus (Derrick, 1993). In other parts of the brain, too, LTP can be induced without NMDA receptors being activated. For example, in the visual cortex of adult rats, LTP can be induced in the presence of a strong antagonist of NMDA (Aroniadou et al., 1993). But administering blockers of other Ca^{2+} channels prevents the induction of LTP. Aroniadou et al. (1993) concluded that with maturity, the role of the NMDA receptors becomes less important, whereas voltage-gated Ca^{2+} channels assume increasing importance in maintaining synaptic plasticity.

LTP Is Induced via a Cascade of Neurochemical Steps

Several neurochemical steps have been identified in the induction of LTP, and we will see that some of these steps have also been implicated in other kinds of memory formation. In fact, many of these steps are seen whenever a signal leads cells to change the kinds of compounds they synthesize or the rate of synthesis. We have already seen that the entry of Ca^{2+} ions into neurons activates some protein kinases, which are essential for induction and maintenance of LTP. These include PKA, PKC, and CaM kinase (Figure 18.9).

Research on learning in vertebrates shows that inhibitors of CaM kinase inhibit the formation of intermediate-term memory (ITM), whereas inhibitors of PKC prevent the formation of long-term memory (LTM) (Rosenzweig et al., 1992, 1993; Serrano et al., 1994). Huang and Kandel (1994) reported a similar finding concerning LTP in the CA1 region of the hippocampus: One train of 100 Hz stimuli induces a form of LTP that lasts 1 to 3 hours and is blocked by an inhibitor of CaM kinase, but not by an inhibitor of PKA or of protein synthesis; three trains of 100 Hz stimuli induce LTP that lasts 6 to 10 hours and is blocked by inhibitors of PKA or of protein synthesis. Thus what Huang and Kandel (1994) called two kinds of LTP resemble, respectively, ITM and LTM (see Chapter 17 to review the definitions of the different types of memory).

The activated protein kinases, in turn, not only catalyze the phosphorylation of proteins but also trigger the synthesis of proteins. First they activate cAMP responsive element–binding protein (CREB), a compound we will discuss later in this chapter that occupies a strategic position in the neurochemical cascade underlying memory formation. Mutant mice that lack the main forms of CREB show an intermediate-term potentiation but lack LTP (Bourtchuladze et al., 1994). The activation of CREB recruits transcription factors and leads to increases in the expression of **immediate early genes** (**IEGs**), a class of genes that are rapidly but transiently expressed in response to extracellular signals such as neurotransmitters and growth factors. Many IEGs code for transcription factors that govern the growth and differentiation of cell types by regulating the expression of other genes.

It is clear that the induction of LTP involves protein synthesis. The earlier stages of LTP, lasting an hour or so, appear not to require protein synthesis, but thereafter inhibition of protein synthesis prevents longer-lasting LTP (Frey et al., 1993; Krug et al., 1984). Three hours after the induction of LTP, certain proteins increase while others decrease, indicating a complex pattern of changes in proteins (Fazeli et al., 1993). Some of these changes may be involved in structural changes in synapses.

Evidence has accumulated that induction of LTP requires a retrograde signal,

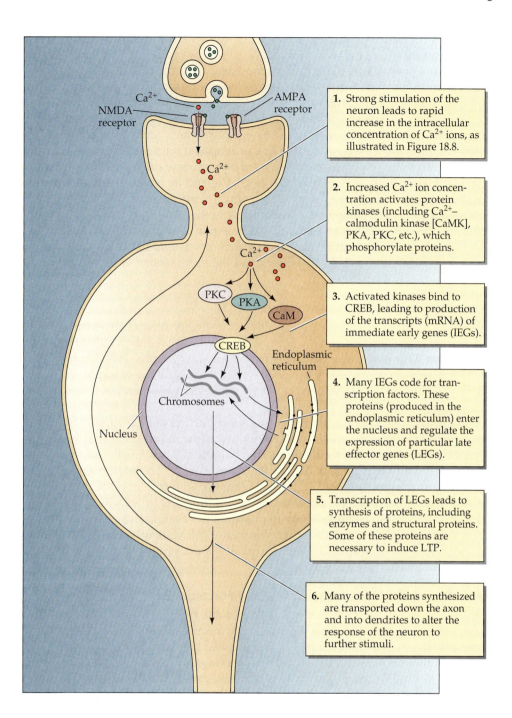

18.9 Steps in the Neurochemical Cascade during the Induction of LTP This illustration is based on LTP induction in the CA1 region of the hippocampus.

1. Strong stimulation of the neuron leads to rapid increase in the intracellular concentration of Ca²⁺ ions, as illustrated in Figure 18.8.

2. Increased Ca²⁺ ion concentration activates protein kinases (including Ca²⁺–calmodulin kinase [CaMK], PKA, PKC, etc.), which phosphorylate proteins.

3. Activated kinases bind to CREB, leading to production of the transcripts (mRNA) of immediate early genes (IEGs).

4. Many IEGs code for transcription factors. These proteins (produced in the endoplasmic reticulum) enter the nucleus and regulate the expression of particular late effector genes (LEGs).

5. Transcription of LEGs leads to synthesis of proteins, including enzymes and structural proteins. Some of these proteins are necessary to induce LTP.

6. Many of the proteins synthesized are transported down the axon and into dendrites to alter the response of the neuron to further stimuli.

from the postsynaptic neuron to the presynaptic neuron (see Figure 18.8*b*). The postsynaptic site is thought to release the signal when conditions of LTP are met, and the presynaptic neuron responds to the signal by increasing transmitter release. Thus Colley and Routtenberg (1993) speak of the pre- and postsynaptic neurons as being engaged in a "synaptic dialogue" in forming LTP. Nitric oxide (NO), arachidonic acid, and nerve growth factor are among the 17 candidates proposed by different investigators as possible retrograde messengers in LTP (J. R. Sanes and Lichtman, 1999). The latter reviewers also point out that well over a hundred different molecules have been implicated in hippocampal LTP, suggesting that investigators have not yet pinpointed the essential processes in LTP.

Changes in synapse morphology have also been reported when LTP is induced both in intact animals (K. S. Lee et al., 1980) and in slice preparations (Engert and Bonhoeffer, 1999; Toni et al., 1999). Use of refined imaging that allowed inspection of specific regions of a dendrite in CA1 showed that induction of LTP, but not short-lived enhancement, caused new spines to appear, whereas in control regions of the same dendrite where LTP was blocked, no significant spine growth occurred (Engert and Bonhoeffer, 1999). This result is consistent with studies suggesting that long-term memory, but not short-term or intermediate-term memory, depends on the synthesis of proteins in the brain, a topic we will consider later in this chapter.

Some of the complexity of and discrepancies in the results of experiments on LTP may come from the fact that several different phenomena seem to be involved. Reviews of the evidence suggest four or five overlapping but separable effects of prior stimulation on the amplitude of responses of hippocampal cells (W. C. Abraham and Goddard, 1985; Bliss and Collingridge, 1993). Depending on how and when the experimenter measures the responses and on which treatments are used to affect them, one or another phenomenon may predominate in the results. We have also seen significant differences between LTP induced in region CA1 and LTP in CA3. Further work is needed to sort out these complex phenomena and to decide the extent to which any of them can help us understand the mechanisms of various kinds of learning.

Long-Term Depression Is the Converse of LTP

We noted early in this chapter that negative as well as positive changes can store information in the nervous system. Several investigators have shown that **long-term depression (LTD)** may play a role in memory (Bear and Malenka, 1994; Linden, 1994). LTD is the converse of LTP: a lasting decrease in the magnitude of responses of neurons after afferent cells have been activated with electrical stimuli of relatively low frequency.

In the CA1 region of the hippocampus, the induction of LTD appears to require the entry of Ca^{2+} through NMDA receptors, just as the induction of LTP does. How can the entry of Ca^{2+} call for the induction of both LTP and LTD? The critical factor is the amount of change of Ca^{2+}. A large surge of Ca^{2+} in the postsynaptic neuron triggers the induction of LTP by activating Ca^{2+}-dependent protein kinases. In contrast, small increases of postsynaptic Ca^{2+} induce LTD by selectively activating the opposite kind of enzyme—protein phosphatases that catalyze dephosphorylation, the removal of phosphate groups (Lisman, 1989; Mulkey et al., 1993). Different sites on the AMPA receptor are phosphorylated or dephosphorylated in LTP and LTD, respectively (H.-K. Lee et al., 2000).

Are LTP and LTD Mechanisms of Memory Formation?

Several reviewers (e.g., G. Lynch et al., 1991; Staubli, 1995; Teyler and DiScenna, 1986) support the claim that LTP is a mechanism of memory formation because of similarities between LTP and examples of learning and memory. As we have noted, LTP can be induced within seconds, it may last for days or weeks, and it shows a labile consolidation period that lasts for several minutes after induction. These properties of LTP have suggested to some investigators that LTP is a kind of synaptic plasticity that underlies certain forms of learning and memory. They have therefore sought to test this hypothesis by examining (1) whether other properties of LTP are reflected in properties of learning and memory, and vice versa, and (2) whether various treatments (e.g., drugs) have similar effects on LTP and on learning and memory.

Some scientists study both LTP and conditioning in the same neural circuit. One study recorded LTP while an *Aplysia* preparation was being conditioned (G. G. Murphy and Glanzman, 1999). The strength of responses was studied in the abdominal ganglion at a synapse between a sensory neuron from the siphon and a siphon motor neuron. For a cellular analog to sensory–sensory classical conditioning, the conditioned stimulus (CS) was brief intracellular stimulation of the sensory siphon neuron, and the unconditioned stimulus (US) was extracellular stimulation of the nerve from the tail to the abdominal ganglion. Some preparations received a series of paired stimuli: CS followed immediately by US. Then, 60 minutes later, a test shock to the sensory neuron evoked a larger response in the motor neuron than a test shock before the pairing had. The larger response was evidence that LTP had been induced.

The same preparations also received a series of unpaired presentations of CS and US in another siphon neuron, and no enhancement occurred. In addition, if the pairing occurred when the NMDA antagonist aminophosphonovalerate (APV) was added to the solution bathing the preparation, no enhancement occurred, although synaptic transmission was not blocked (presumably because AMPA receptors continued to respond to the glutamate). It has not yet been shown whether APV blocks behavioral conditioning in *Aplysia*, and this demonstration will be an obvious next step to test further whether conditioning is mediated, in part at least, by LTP involving activation of NMDA receptors.

Studies involving fear conditioning in rats (e.g., Rogan et al., 1997) have shown than training causes not only conditioning but also LTP. In a study by McKernan and Shinnick-Gallagher (1997), rats received bursts of noise as the CS, and a startle response was the CR. Twenty-four hours later, coronal slices through the amygdala were prepared from the brains. Slices were also prepared from animals given unpaired CS and US or given only noise stimuli. LTP was found in the slices from animals that had received paired training but not in slices from rats in the other conditions. Thus the experimenters were able to study and analyze the synaptic effects of whole-animal fear learning in an in vitro slice, employing the techniques traditionally used in the study of LTP. Potentiation was found only in synapses in the fear-conditioning circuit and not in other nearby synapses, providing additional evidence that LTP serves as a substrate for this kind of learning.

Other evidence for a similarity between LTP and learning comes from experiments in which a particular gene is disrupted to produce so-called knockout mice—mice in which one gene has been made nonfunctional (see Box 7.3). Some laboratories have produced knockout mice lacking one of the enzymes crucial to the LTP cascade, then studied the animals to assess their ability to learn a maze. Kandel's group (Grant et al., 1992) disrupted four different kinases in four different groups of mice. They found that hippocampal LTP was reduced only in the mice missing the kinase gene *fyn,* and that these were the only mice that showed a deficit in maze learning.

This result strongly suggests that the fyn protein is important in both LTP and maze learning, and that the electrophysiological phenomenon of LTP is related to learning. Another group of investigators (A. J. Silva et al., 1992) produced knockout mice lacking the CaM kinase II gene; these mice were also slower at learning spatial relations. Interestingly, all of the knockout mice were able to learn the task eventually, indicating that none of these genes is absolutely necessary for learning.

Such findings support the idea that LTP is a kind of synaptic plasticity that underlies or is similar to certain forms of learning and memory and that it can therefore be used to investigate the mechanisms of those forms of learning and memory. The variety of forms of LTP, however, shows that it cannot serve as a general model for learning and memory; rather, certain kinds of LTP may be important for certain kinds of learning and memory, but even this supposition has yet to be proved. Thus some investigators maintain the prudent doubt expressed by Bliss and Lømo in their initial paper that LTP has anything to do with normal behavior.

A recent review concluded, "Although definitive proof that LTP and LTD are involved with learning has defied research efforts, . . . LTP and LTD remain the best candidates for a cellular process that underlies learning and memory in the vertebrate brain" (J. L. Martinez et al., 1998, p. 239). On the other hand, A. J. Silva, Giese, et al. (1998) cautioned that while LTP may be a key contributor to the synaptic changes that encode memories in hippocampal circuits, other cellular mechanisms complement and interact with LTP, and LTP may be necessary but not sufficient for processing and encoding information in the hippocampus.

COMPETING HYPOTHESES

Glial Cells May Participate in Learning and Memory

Although most research on mechanisms of learning and memory concentrates on neurons, some investigators (e.g., Laming et al., 2000) are pointing to interactions of glial cells with neurons in learning and memory. Here are a few examples: (1) Transgenic mice that overexpress an astrocytic calcium-binding protein were impaired in the Morris water maze, although they performed normally in nonspatial tasks (Gerlai et al., 1995). (2) One-trial aversive learning in chicks was impaired by an astrocyte-specific inhibitor of cellular reaccumulation of potassium ions (Hertz et al., 1996). (3) Experience in an enriched environment, which improves learning and memory formation, increases gliogenesis as well as neurogenesis (Nilsson et al., 1999) and increases glial-derived neurotrophic factor as well as brain-derived neurotrophic factor (D. Young et al., 1999). (4) Alcohol abuse, which is often accompanied by cognitive impairment, leads to significant loss of glial cells but not of neural cells in the hippocampus (Korbo, 1999).

The Mammalian Cerebellum Houses the Brain Circuit for a Simple Conditioned Reflex

While many investigators studied learning in the apparently simpler nervous systems of invertebrates and others probed the phenomenon of LTP, some tried to define a circuit for learning in intact mammals. Psychologist Richard F. Thompson and his colleagues have been studying the neural circuitry of eye-blink conditioning in the rabbit since the 1970s (Lavond et al., 1993; R. F. Thompson, 1990; R. F. Thompson et al., 1998). Their research has produced a great deal of knowledge about how the eye-blink reflex of the rabbit becomes conditioned and has encouraged other neuroscientists to investigate the neural circuits involved in other kinds of learning.

When a puff of air to the cornea (US) follows an acoustic tone (CS), a stable conditioned response (CR) develops rapidly: The rabbit comes to blink when the tone is sounded. The basic circuit of the eye-blink reflex is simple, involving two cranial nerves and some interneurons that connect their nuclei (shown in black on Figure 18.10). Sensory fibers from the cornea run along cranial nerve V (the trigeminal nerve) to its nucleus in the brainstem. From there some interneurons go to the nucleus of cranial nerve VII (the facial nerve), which is also in the brainstem. Motor fibers in nerves VI and VII activate the muscle fibers that cause the eyelids to close.

Early in their work, Thompson and colleagues found that during conditioning, the hippocampus develops neural responses whose temporal patterns closely resemble those of the eye-blink responses. Although the hippocampal activity closely parallels the course of conditioning, this result does not prove that the hippocampus is required for conditioning. In fact, destruction of the hippocampus has little effect on the acquisition or retention of the conditioned eye-blink response in rabbits (Lockhart and Moore, 1975). Therefore the hippocampus is *not* required for this conditioning. It may, however, participate in the conditioning, as indicated by the finding that abnormal hippocampal activity can disrupt the acquisition of conditioning.

Thompson and his coworkers then searched further, mapping in detail the brain structures where neurons are electrically active during conditioning. They found that learning-related increases in the activity of individual neurons are prominent in the cerebellum, in both its cortex and deep nuclei, and in certain nuclei in the pons (see Figure 18.10).

Deep Cerebellar Nuclei Are Necessary for Eye-Blink Conditioning

In the cerebellum there are only negligible responses to the CS and the US before the stimuli are paired, but a neuronal replica of the learned behavioral response emerges during conditioning. These responses, which precede the behavioral eye-blink responses by 50 ms or more, are found in the deep cerebellar nuclei on the same side as the eye that is trained. The cerebellar response predicts and corresponds with the form of the CR (McCormick and Thompson, 1984).

Lesion experiments were undertaken to determine whether the cerebellar responses are required for conditioning or whether, like the hippocampal responses, they only correlate with the CR. In an animal that had already been conditioned, destruction of the interpositus nucleus on the side that had been trained abolished the

CR. (Whereas the cerebral cortex and the basal ganglia govern activity on the opposite side, each hemisphere of the cerebellum governs motor activity on the same side of the body.) The CR could not be relearned on the same side, but the opposite eye could be conditioned normally. In a naive animal, prior destruction of the interpositus nucleus on one side prevented conditioning on that side. The effect of the cerebellar lesions could not be attributed to interference with sensory or motor tracts because the animal still showed a normal unconditioned blink when a puff of air was delivered to its eye.

The circuit of the conditioned reflex was mapped in further detail by a combination of methods: electrophysiological recording, localized lesions, localized stimulation of neurons, localized infusion of small amounts of drugs, and tracing of fiber pathways. For example, prior work showed that the inhibitory synaptic transmitter GABA (γ-aminobutyric acid) is the main transmitter in the deep cerebellar nuclei. Using well-conditioned rabbits, the investigators injected a small amount of a blocking agent for GABA into the deep cerebellar nuclei on the side of the CR. The injection resulted in the disappearance of the behavioral CR and of its electrophysiological neuronal replica. This effect was reversible: As the blocking agent wore off, the CR returned.

On the basis of these and other experiments, Thompson proposed a simplified schematic circuit for the conditioned eye-blink response (Figure 18.10). This circuit includes the input and output parts of the eye-blink reflex circuit, shown with black arrows at the lower left of Figure 18.10. This pathway ensures the eye-blink reflex, but additional pathways are required to bring together information about the US and the CS.

The pathway that carries information about the corneal stimulation (the US) goes to the inferior olivary nucleus of the brainstem, from where it is carried into the cerebellum by way of axons called climbing fibers, which go to the deep cerebellar nuclei and to cells of the cerebellar cortex, including granule cells and Purkinje cells. The same cerebellar cells also receive information about the auditory CS by a pathway through the auditory nuclei in the brainstem and the pontine nuclei (orange arrows in Figure 18.10); the latter send axons called mossy fibers into the cerebellum. Efferent information controlling the CR travels along another pathway (blue arrows in Figure 18.10), which runs from the interpositus nucleus of the cerebellum to the red nucleus. From there it goes to the cranial motor nucleus of nerves VI and VII, which control the eye-blink response.

IMPORTANT METHOD

18.10 Sites in the Neural Circuit for Conditioning of the Eye-Blink Reflex (*a*) The pathway for the unconditioned eye-blink reflex is shown at the left (black arrows). When a tone (CS) regularly precedes a puff of air delivered to the cornea (US), the inputs from the CS and US converge at the cerebellar cortex and the interpositus nucleus of the cerebellum (top), where new connections are formed. (*b*) After lesions of the interpositus nucleus of the cerebellum, the unconditioned reflex is preserved, but the CR cannot be learned. (After R. F. Thompson and Krupa, 1994.)

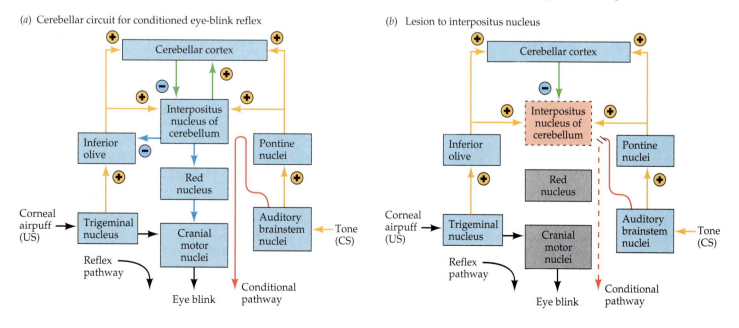

Studies on human subjects are consistent with the animal research on eye-blink conditioning, as we noted in Chapter 17 (see Figure 17.16).

The role of the cerebellum in conditioning is not restricted to eye-blink conditioning. The cerebellum is also needed for the conditioning of leg flexion; in this task an animal learns to withdraw its leg when a tone sounds in order to avoid a shock to the paw (Donegan et al., 1983; Voneida, 1990). On the other hand, the cerebellum is not required for all forms of conditioning of skeletal muscular responses; cerebellar lesions do not prevent operant conditioning of a treadle-press response in the rabbit (L. Holt, M. D. Mauk, and R. F. Thompson, unpublished, cited in Lavond et al., 1993, p. 328).

The Hippocampus Is Required for Some Kinds of Eye-Blink Conditioning

The hippocampus is not required for animals to acquire a simple form of eye-blink conditioning—specifically, *delay conditioning*—when little or no time passes between the end of the CS and the US. When the time intervals are longer (in what is called *trace conditioning*), however, animals from which the hippocampus has been removed are not able to form conditioned eye-blink responses (Moyer et al., 1990). Removal of the hippocampus also prevents the formation of *discrimination reversal conditioning*—that is, as stated in Chapter 17, conditioning in which the stimulus that previously served as CS+ is now CS–, and vice versa (Berger and Orr, 1983).

Features of the Investigation of Brain Substrates of Classical Conditioning

Richard F. Thompson

Richard Thompson and colleagues stress three points about investigations of mammalian brain substrates of classical conditioning (Lavond et al., 1993), to which we'll add two more:

1. The investigations were deliberately restricted to a relatively simple form of conditioning, in the hope that a good understanding of simple conditioning would aid in the study of more complex forms of learning.
2. Learning involves regions of the brain other than just the cerebellum. At the least, the hippocampus and the cerebral cortex are important in more complex learning, and the amygdala appears to be involved in the learning of fear; all three regions probably are involved in aversive classical conditioning.
3. The evidence for localization of plasticity in aversive classical conditioning relies not on a single technique, but on converging results from various techniques.
4. Research using electrophysiological recording demonstrates that brain circuits involved in learning *can* be identified even in the complex mammalian brain.
5. In this case at least, plasticity does not occur in the circuit of the unconditioned reflex; the reflex circuit remains unaffected, but the response can be conditioned through a somewhat complex circuit, a superordinate circuit imposed on the unconditioned reflex (see Figures 18.1*b* and 18.10).

IMPORTANT METHOD

Are New Neurons Required for Some Kinds of Learning?

As we saw in Chapter 7, evidence since the 1990s has convinced neuroscientists that new nerve cells are generated in the adult brain, especially in the hippocampus. Adult mice living in an enriched environment produce additional cells in the hippocampus, compared to mice housed in standard cages (Kempermann et al., 1997). The production of new neurons in the hippocampus declines with age in the mouse, but even in senescent (20-month-old) mice, experience in an enriched environment resulted in a threefold increase in new neurons, as compared with animals in standard housing. New neurons also appear in the hippocampus of adult monkeys (E. Gould et al., 1998) and adult humans (Eriksson et al., 1998).

Now some of the investigators who have studied neurogenesis claim that new neurons in the hippocampus are required for trace conditioning (conditioning in which a time interval separates the CS from the US, a kind of conditioning known to be dependent on the hippocampus, as we have just seen) of the eye-blink response (Shors et al., 2001). To test their hypothesis, Shors et al. injected rats with an agent, methylazoxymethanol (MAM), that kills proliferating cells. The agent was injected over 2 weeks at a carefully controlled dose that killed about 80% of new neurons in the hippocampus and impaired trace conditioning but had no apparent effect on overall health. A stronger dose led to weight loss and illness; a weaker dose had no effect on conditioning.

Rats given the effective treatment with MAM were still capable of delay conditioning, which does not depend on the hippocampus. This is one of several indications that the deficit caused by MAM is specific to hippocampus-dependent learning. Although this is an important first step in testing the function(s) of newly generated neurons, it is not conclusive. Thus Macklis (2001) points out that trace conditioning is more difficult than delay conditioning, so a level of stress that does not affect delay conditioning might nevertheless impair trace conditioning. We might also note that MAM kills proliferating glial cells as well as neurons, and this may play a role in the impairment caused by the drug treatment.

**COMPETING
HYPOTHESES**

Memories of Different Durations Form by Different Neurochemical Mechanisms

Memories differ markedly in how long they last, from iconic and short-term memories to long-term and permanent memories, as we saw in Chapter 17. Behavioral evidence suggests that memories of different lengths reflect the operation of different neural processes. For example, individuals like H.M. (see Chapter 17), who have no trouble forming short-term memories, may have an impaired ability to form long-term memories. With habituation and sensitization, the formation of relatively short-term memories in *Aplysia* involves mainly neurochemical changes at existing synapses, whereas the formation of long-term memories also involves structural changes in existing synapses and changes in the number of synapses.

Since the 1950s, drugs have been used extensively to study memory formation; this approach has led to many interesting discoveries and to new concepts. Unlike brain lesions or other permanent interventions, many chemical treatments are advantageous for this research because they are reversible. Drugs can produce relatively brief, accurately timed effects, and subjects can be tested in their normal state both before and after treatment. Chemical agents can be given systemically or locally. Systemic administration permits the study of a whole system of widely separated neurons, such as neurons that employ a particular synaptic transmitter. Local injection into a specific brain site can be used to investigate localized processes.

**IMPORTANT
METHOD**

Different agents appear to affect different stages of memory formation. This result has given rise to the concept of sequential neurochemical processes in memory formation. Since about 1960, much research on the formation of long-term memory (e.g., H. P. Davis and Squire, 1984; Flood et al., 1977; Rosenzweig, 1984) has centered on the hypothesis that long-term memory cannot form without increased protein synthesis during the minutes (perhaps hours) that follow training. More recently investigators have studied the neurochemical processes involved in earlier stages of memory formation—short-term and intermediate-term memories (M. E. Gibbs and Ng, 1977; Mizumori et al., 1985; Rosenzweig et al., 1992).

Australian psychologists Marie Gibbs and Kim Ng (1977) found evidence that short-term, intermediate-term, and long-term memory in chicks reflect three sequentially linked neurochemical processes. Their experiments studied chicks trained with a single-trial peck avoidance response: The chicks pecked at a small, shiny bead coated with an aversive liquid; after making a single peck, the chicks usually avoided a similar bead whether it was presented minutes, hours, or days later. (Some investigators refer to the aversive bead as *bitter*, but bitter taste alone is not enough to cause chicks to form a strong LTM [P. J. Colombo, personal communication].)

The formation of memory for the unpleasant experience could be impaired if an amnestic (amnesia-causing) agent was administered close to the time of training. Gibbs and Ng reported that different families of amnestic agents caused memory to

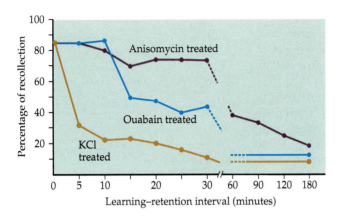

18.11 Timing of the Effects of Different Amnestic Agents Different amnestic agents are thought to impair different stages of memory. They therefore provide a means of observing the duration of each stage. (After M. E. Gibbs and Ng, 1977.)

fail at different times after training (Figure 18.11). The agents that caused memory failure by about 5 minutes after training were considered to prevent the formation of STM, those that caused failure about 15 minutes after training were thought to prevent the formation of ITM, and those that caused memory to fail by about 60 minutes after training were thought to be affecting LTM.

Here are some examples of effects caused by different agents: Both the NMDA receptor antagonist APV and lanthanum chloride, which inhibits the influx of Ca^{2+} ions, prevent the formation of STM (and therefore of the succeeding ITM and LTM stages). Ouabain, which inhibits $Na^+–K^+$ ATPase, prevents the formation of ITM (and therefore also LTM). Protein synthesis inhibitors, such as anisomycin, prevent the formation of only LTM.

Protein kinase inhibitors were known to be amnestic, but at first it was not known which stage(s) of memory formation they affected. Peter Serrano found that two classes of protein kinase inhibitors affect two different stages of memory formation (Rosenzweig et al., 1993; Serrano et al., 1994): Those that act on calcium–calmodulin kinase (CaM kinase) but not on protein kinase C (PKC) impair the formation of ITM; those that act on PKC but not on CaM kinase impair the formation of LTM. (As noted earlier, these two kinds of protein kinase inhibitors have a similar differential effect on long-term potentiation in the hippocampus [Huang and Kandel, 1994].)

Not all effects of amnestic agents conform to the three predicted times of the onset of amnesia or to the stage they would be expected to affect (Rosenzweig et al., 1993). For example, the opioid leu-enkephalin causes amnesia beginning more than 4 hours after training, which is later than the LTM stage as defined by other findings. MK801, an inhibitor of NMDA receptors, causes amnesia 3 to 4 hours after training, in contrast to the almost immediate effect of the NMDA receptor antagonist APV. Thus unsettled issues remain, but most of the data confirm at least three stages of memory formation.

The Formation of Long-Term Memory Requires Protein Synthesis

Experiments to test the hypothesis that the formation of long-term memory (LTM) requires protein synthesis have employed both behavioral intervention (in the form of training) and somatic intervention (in the form of agents that inhibit protein synthesis). Training increases the branching of dendrites and the number of synaptic contacts (Black and Greenough, 1998). The enlarged outgrowths of the neurons are made, in part, of proteins. Furthermore, direct measures of protein in the cerebral cortex of rats show a significant increase with enriched experience (E. L. Bennett et al., 1969). Experiments in the laboratory of neurochemist Steven Rose (Schliebs et al., 1985) have shown that after a chick is trained briefly, parts of its brain can be removed and the training-induced increase in protein synthesis can be followed within a tissue chamber; brain samples from control (untrained) chicks show a significantly lower rate of protein synthesis.

The other side of the story is that inhibiting the synthesis of proteins in the brain at the time of training can prevent the formation of LTM, even though this inhibition does not interfere with acquisition or retrieval during tests of STM or ITM. This field of investigation is a good example of the rigorous testing and elimination of alternatives that characterize an advancing area of research.

Of the many new antibiotic drugs that are created each year, some have been found to inhibit the formation of memory by inhibiting protein synthesis, but many have been abandoned for memory research because of toxic side effects. Furthermore, even strong inhibition of protein synthesis seemed to prevent memory only for rather weak training, so investigators wondered whether there was a real effect of inhibition on memory formation. Use of the protein synthesis inhibitor anisomycin helped overcome previous problems.

Anisomycin was first used in memory experiments when J. H. Schwartz et al. (1971), studying *Aplysia,* showed that inhibiting more than 95% of protein synthesis did not affect either neuronal functioning or short-term neural correlates of habituation or sensitization. Then anisomycin was found to prevent LTM storage in mice, although it did not affect STM (E. L. Bennett et al., 1972; Flood et al., 1973). This inhibitor is an effective amnestic agent at low doses; 25 times the effective amnestic dose is nonlethal. Because anisomycin is safe, it can be given in repeated doses; administering it every 2 hours keeps cerebral protein synthesis at about 10% of normal.

It may seem strange that the brain can get along with protein synthesis almost completely blocked for hours, but cells contain large supplies of proteins; existing enzymes, for example, can continue directing the cell's metabolism. With repeated administration of anisomycin, Flood et al. (1975, 1977) demonstrated that even relatively strong training could be overcome by inhibition of protein synthesis; the stronger the training, the longer the inhibition had to be maintained to cause amnesia.

Protein synthesis involved in the formation of LTM appears to occur in two successive waves—the first about 1 hour after training, the second about 5 to 8 hours after training (reviewed by Matthies, 1989). Administering inhibitors of protein synthesis so that they were effective at either of these periods prevented the formation of LTM. Among the proteins synthesized at these two time periods are synaptic glycoproteins—neural cell adhesion molecules (NCAMs) that are involved in synaptic remodeling. Administration of an antiserum prepared against chick brain glycoprotein prevented LTM formation, not only in chicks but also in rats, and for tasks using either positive or negative reinforcements (Roullet et al., 1997). Thus in general, at least part of the necessity of protein synthesis for establishing LTM seems to involve changes in synaptic membranes.

Additional Evidence Supports the Idea That Memory Forms in Stages

M. E. Gibbs and Ng (1979) reported that chicks, untreated by any drug, showed dips in the strength of memory at about 15 minutes and 55 minutes after training. They suggested that the dips marked the times of transition between STM and ITM, and between ITM and LTM, respectively. They also found that preventing the formation of one stage of memory inhibited the formation of the following stage(s). These results support the concepts that memory forms in stages and that each stage of memory depends on the preceding one(s).

Further evidence for successive stages of memory formation comes from experiments by Diane Lee using relatively weak training. After weak training, achieved by use of a weak solution of the aversive substance, the retention function for control chicks (with no drug treatment) shows four components (Figure 18.12), which may reflect, successively, the sensory buffer (the immediate continuation of sensory input; see Figure 17.5), STM, ITM, and LTM (Rosenzweig et al., 1993).

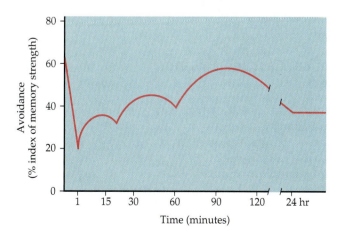

18.12 Four Components of Retention Strength after Weak Training in Chicks The components of this smoothed curve may reflect, successively, the sensory buffer, STM, ITM, and LTM. (After Rosenzweig et al., 1993.)

If these components do represent successive stages, it should be possible to inhibit each of them with specific agents. The final rise in memory strength, beginning about 60 minutes after training and hypothesized to reflect LTM, was abolished by inhibitors of protein synthesis, in conformity with the hypothesis. Inhibitors of STM abolished all stages after the initial descending limb of the function (the presumptive sensory buffer), thus supporting the hypothesis that the stages are sequentially dependent. So far, it has not been possible with an amnestic agent to inhibit the formation of the presumptive ITM stage after weak training.

In *Drosophila*, Each Stage in Memory Formation Depends on a Different Gene

Because much is known about its genetics, the fruit fly *Drosophila* brings distinct advantages to the study of mechanisms of learning and memory, even though its central nervous system (which has about 100,000 very small neurons) is more complex than that of the mollusk *Aplysia*. Research with *Drosophila* has corroborated findings obtained with *Aplysia*, and it has added new information about stages of memory formation and the genetics of these stages.

IMPORTANT METHOD

Research on mechanisms of memory in *Drosophila* began when geneticist William Quinn et al. (1974) developed a method to condition groups of *Drosophila*. They put about 40 flies in a glass tube and let them move upward toward one of two odors that normally are equally attractive. Reaching the upper part of one tube brought an electrical shock; the other odor was not associated with shock. The group could then be tested after various time intervals for approach to each of the odors. As the procedure was refined, about 90% of the flies avoided the odor associated with shock (Jellies, 1981). The geneticists then tested mutant strains of *Drosophila*. In 1976 they announced the isolation of the first mutant that failed to learn to discriminate the odors, and they named it *dunce* (Dudai et al., 1976).

Tests showed that *dunce* had a real problem with learning; its deficiency was not in olfaction, locomotion, or general activity. Three more learning mutants were isolated and named *cabbage, turnip,* and *rutabaga*; another mutant, *amnesiac*, learned normally but forgot more rapidly than normal flies (Quinn et al., 1979). Mutants found in other laboratories were also deficient in learning. Tests with other procedures showed that the failures of these mutants were not restricted to odor–shock training but occurred as well in other tests of associative learning, although the mutants appeared normal in nonlearning behaviors.

Further research showed that memory in *Drosophila* has four stages, which the investigators called *short-term memory, middle-term memory, anesthesia-resistant memory* (*ARM*), and *long-term memory* (Dubnau and Tully, 1998). Each stage can be canceled by deficiency in one or more genes specific to that stage. Thus this genetic research provides independent support for the existence of separate stages of memory. Although ARM has not been reported in other animals, Dubnau and Tully (1998) suggested that, given the many similarities between learning in *Drosophila* and other animals, "it seems likely that ARM and LTM will be shown to exist as parallel forms of long-lasting memory in vertebrates as well" (p. 438).

The Basic Neurochemical Cascade Extends from Stimulus to LTM

A cascade of neurochemical processes extends all the way from the initial stimulation of a neuron, through conduction of nerve impulses, to short-term changes in responsiveness, and in some cases to intermediate-term changes or even long-term storage of information. Here we will review some of the processes we have already discussed, adding some additional information.

In Chapter 3 we discussed the steps in the activation of membrane ion channels and the flow of ions in conduction of the nerve impulse (see Figure 3.10), as well as the sequence of events in chemical transmission at synapses (see Figure 3.13). More recently we noted the roles of the AMPA and NMDA receptors in the first steps of LTP induction (see Figure 18.8), and then later steps (see Figure 18.9). Figures 18.8 and 18.9 showed that several protein kinases are activated, including PKA, PKC, and calcium–calmodulin kinase (CaM kinase).

Recent research has concentrated on steps that intervene between activation of the protein kinases, in some cases by cyclic AMP (cAMP), and production of the transcripts (mRNA) of immediate early genes (IEGs). A large family of transcription factors bind to cAMP responsive element (CRE) promoter sites (i.e., lengths of DNA adjacent to various genes). When transcription factors bind to such sites, they can increase or decrease the expression of the adjacent genes. One of the best-known factors binding to CRE sites is cAMP responsive element–binding protein (CREB). Several studies have now indicated that CREB is necessary for the formation of long-term memory in both invertebrates and mammals (see the review by A. J. Silva, Kogan, et al., 1998).

In *Drosophila*, genetic studies implicated the cAMP–PKA pathway because mutant *Drosophila* strains with disruptions in these compounds showed impaired memory (Tully, 1991). To see whether CREB is required, experimenters inserted a repressor of CREB activity that could be turned on when they wished, by an increase in temperature. Induction of the CREB repressor 3 hours before behavioral training prevented the formation of LTM without affecting the formation of other memory stages (Yin et al., 1994).

GENES AND BEHAVIOR

In mice, genetic deletion of the main forms of CREB impaired LTM but not STM for training involving both reward (Kogan et al., 1997) and punishment (Bourtchuladze et al., 1994). Thus mutation of CREB has rather general effects on memory. The possible significance of CREB for human memory is indicated by the fact that a mutation of CREB results in a syndrome characterized by mental retardation (Petrij et al., 1995).

As research continues, we can expect to see the emphasis shift to other steps of the neurochemical cascade. But even though some steps may be easier to investigate or manipulate, it is important to realize that the entire cascade is normally activated to form long-term memory.

Neurochemical Effects of Learning Can Be Used to Trace Changes in Neural Circuits

As well as helping to reveal the processes that lead to the storage of information in the nervous system, neurochemical compounds produced after training trials can serve as tracers for new or altered neural circuits. Here we will briefly mention two examples of such research.

An article by Christine Gall et al. (1998) entitled "Mapping Brain Networks Engaged by, and Changed by, Learning" reports how changes in expression of the immediate early gene *c-fos* are differentially activated in the amygdala and the hippocampus in successive stages of learning of an odor discrimination task by rats. The balance of activity shifts during the course of learning, both within and between these structures, and the investigators are seeking to relate the shifts to the behavioral output.

Other investigators are studying the regional distribution of a later product of training—neural cell adhesion molecules (NCAMs) (K. J. Murphy and Regan, 1998), as mentioned earlier in the chapter. NCAMs are produced both during development of the nervous system and beginning about 6 to 8 hours after learning trials in both chicks and rats. NCAM production is associated with the appearance or stabilization of new dendritic spines. The distribution of NCAMs can be traced within hippocampal–neocortical pathways, suggesting that they play a role in reciprocal connections that underlie the eventual storage of information in the cortex (Figure 18.13).

NEURAL PLASTICITY

18.13 Increases in the Expression of Neural Cell Adhesion Molecules in Response to Training   Ten to 12 hours after rats are trained in either spatial or nonspatial problems, increased expression of neural cell adhesion molecules (NCAMs) is seen transiently in the dentate gyrus of the hippocampus (*a*) and in the temporal cortex (*b*). The NCAMs appear, stained green, in the dendrites; the cell nuclei are stained red. (From K. J. Murphy and Regan, 1998; courtesy of Ciaran Regan.)

(*a*) Dentate gyrus

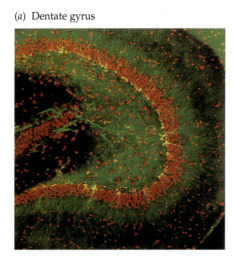

(*b*) Temporal cortex

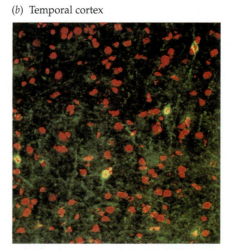

Several Models for the Study of Learning and Memory Show Similar Cascades of Neurochemical and Anatomical Processes

Several other models have been proposed for studying the mechanisms of neural plasticity, including (1) changed responsiveness to drugs, including both tolerance and sensitization (Nestler and Duman, 1995); (2) increased susceptibility to epileptic seizures (*kindling*) (Post and Weiss, 1989); and (3) change in the timing of circadian rhythms by exposure to a brief light (Taylor, 1990).

Without going into detail about research on these models, we should note here that the resulting findings about cellular mechanisms of plasticity show some of the same neurochemical processes as those obtained from research on conditioning in invertebrate systems, on the formation of memory in vertebrates, and on LTP (see Figure 18.9).

Memory Formation Can Be Modulated

Many agents and conditions in addition to those we have already discussed also affect the formation of memory. For example, the general state of arousal of an organism affects its ability to form memories; a moderate state of arousal is optimal (Bloch, 1976). Rapid-eye-movement (REM) sleep in the hours following learning has long been known to improve the formation of LTM in animals (Bloch, 1976), and investigators have demonstrated a similar effect in human perceptual learning (Karni et al., 1994). The emotional state immediately following the learning experience also affects the formation of memory for that experience.

Specific agents that affect memory formation include stimulants (such as amphetamine and caffeine), depressants (such as phenobarbital and chloral hydrate), neuropeptides, so-called neuromodulators that affect the activity or "gain" of neurons (including agents that elsewhere serve as neurotransmitters, such as acetylcholine and norepinephrine), drugs that affect the cholinergic transmitter system or the catecholamine transmitters, opioid peptides, and hormones.

Thus many conditions or agents can either enhance or impair memory formation, depending on the time or strength of treatment or other conditions. This variation implies that some biological processes are essential in the formation of memories and that others are modulatory, superimposed on the basic processes. The fact that many treatments that follow training affect memory formation supports other evidence that the cascade of events underlying memory formation takes considerable time.

Emotions Can Affect Memory Storage

Emotion appears to enhance the formation of memory, as we saw in Chapter 17. In research with humans, however, it is difficult to separate effects on memory formation from effects on attention at the time of learning or on rehearsal after the learning session. Research with animal subjects has clarified these effects and has investigated the neurochemical systems and the brain regions involved in the emotional enhancement of memory formation (see reviews by McGaugh et al., 1993, 1995). Substances effective in modulating memory storage include neurotransmitters and hormones such as acetylcholine, epinephrine, norepinephrine, vasopressin, the opioids, and GABA, as well as agonists and antagonists of these agents.

Several lines of evidence suggest that epinephrine affects memory formation by influencing the amygdala. Posttraining electrical stimulation of the amygdala can enhance or impair memory formation, depending on the experimental conditions. Lesions of the amygdala block the memory-enhancing effects of systemic injections of epinephrine (Cahill and McGaugh, 1991). Injection of epinephrine into the amygdala enhances memory formation at doses too small to be effective elsewhere in the brain. This treatment appears to cause the release of norepinephrine within the amygdala, as do emotional experiences. Injections of propranolol, a blocker of β-adrenergic receptors, into the amygdala block the memory-enhancing effects. Opioid peptides also block the release of norepinephrine in the amygdala and elsewhere in the brain.

On the basis of a variety of experimental findings on the effects and interactions of several families of agents—adrenergic, opioid, GABA-ergic, and cholinergic—on memory storage, McGaugh et al. (1993) propose the following model (Figure 18.14): The amygdala influences memory formation in certain brain regions to which it sends axons, including the hippocampus and the caudate nucleus. The amygdala integrates the influences of several neuromodulatory systems that act on it, including adrenergic, opioid, GABA-ergic, and cholinergic systems.

Because several different neurotransmitter systems are involved in this model, multiple agents can affect the influences of emotion on memory formation; some of these agents and their synaptic sites of activity are shown in Figure 18.14. An intact amygdala is not required for either the acquisition or the long-term storage of memory, although it may be a temporary locus of memory storage for a few days after training. Long-term memory may be stored in brain regions influenced by amygdala activity.

The amygdala appears to play more than one role in memory formation. We saw in Chapter 15 evidence that the amygdala is required for fear conditioning and that the amygdala appears to play a special role in learning about rewards and punishments. In addition to having these direct roles in some kinds of learning, the amygdala can modulate learning in which other brain regions play more direct roles. It can enhance declarative learning mediated by the hippocampus, and it can enhance nondeclarative learning mediated by the caudate nucleus.

It is possible that the amygdala can be modulated, reciprocally, in its memory-forming activity by regions such as the hippocampus (Izquierdo and Medina, 1997). Earlier we saw indications that the hippocampus, as well as playing a direct role in the formation of declarative memories, can modulate the activity of the cerebellum in eye-blink conditioning.

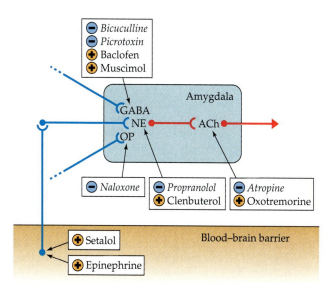

18.14 A Model of Neuromodulatory Interactions in the Regulation of Memory Storage This diagram shows sites of activity of drugs that affect different neuromodulatory and neurotransmitter systems in the amygdala. Antagonists of the transmitters are italicized; agonists are not. ACh, acetylcholine; GABA, γ-aminobutyric acid; NE, norepinephrine; OP, opioids. (After McGaugh, 1992.)

James L. McGaugh

Some Brain Measures Correlate with Age-Related Impairments of Memory

In Chapter 17 we saw that, even in apparently healthy older humans and animals, some measures of learning and memory decline with age while others remain intact. Investigators are trying to find changes in the nervous system that may explain age-related declines in learning and memory. As we discussed in Chapter 7, the *ApoE4* gene predisposes individuals to Alzheimer's disease (Raber et al., 2000;

BOX 18.1 *Modifying Brains for Better Learning and Memory*

Now that investigators have found out quite a bit about both direct and modulatory processes involved in learning and memory, attempts are being made to improve some of these processes. Many changes *impair* learning and memory—for example, blockage of protein kinases, reduction in CREB, or inhibition of protein synthesis. Can other changes *improve* learning and memory? We'll consider an example of a change in the NMDA receptor that is implicated in some kinds of learning.

The NMDA receptor (NR) consists of the core NR1 subunit and NR2 subunits. The NR2 subunits determine the length of time the NR channel is open to Ca^{2+} and thus the size of the excitatory postsynaptic potential (EPSP). Young animals express predominantly NR2B subunits, which allow longer Ca^{2+} conduction and thus larger EPSPs. The number of these subunits is downregulated in the transition from juvenile to adult, and shorter-acting NR2A units come to predominate.

Joe Z. Tsien and coworkers (Y. P. Tang et al., 1999) prepared transgenic mice in which larger-than-normal numbers of juvenile NR2B subunits are expressed, especially in the cerebral cortex and the hippocampus. These animals showed normal growth and body weights and mated normally. Analysis of hippocampal neurons in transgenic versus wild-type mice revealed that the

transgenic mice had greater numbers of NR2B per synapse and about four-fold greater flow of Ca^{2+} during activation. Hippocampal slices from transgenic mice showed enhanced LTP but no difference in LTD compared to wild-type mice.

At 3 to 6 months of age, two lines of transgenic mice were compared with wild-type mice in a variety of behavioral tasks. In examining a novel object rather than a familiar object (see the figure)—a test that requires the hippocampus—all three lines showed equal amounts of initial exploration of the objects and all showed equal preference for the novel object 1 hour later. When tested 1 day or 3 days later, however, both transgenic lines exhibited significantly stronger preference for the novel object than did the wild-type mice, thus showing stronger long-term memory.

In two forms of associative emotional memory, the two transgenic lines learned more strongly than the wild-type mice. The lines were tested for extinction of the fear response by repeated exposure to a neutral environment without shock. Although the transgenic mice showed greater fear responses early in the tests, they extinguished the fear responses more rapidly than the wild-type mice. In the Morris hidden-platform water maze, a test known to require activation of

NMDA receptors in the hippocampus, both the transgenic and wild-type mice learned, but the transgenic mice learned faster.

The investigators propose that their research indicates a potential new direction for treatment of disorders of learning and memory and "a promising strategy for creation of other genetically modified mammals with enhanced intelligence and memory" (Y. P. Tang et al., 1999, p. 69). They showed their enthusiasm by naming their transgenic mice *Doogies* after the teenage genius in the television show *Doogie Howser, M.D.*

These findings certainly indicate that the NMDA receptor is involved in several kinds of learning. Whether the findings will help treat disorders of learning and memory is less sure. Humans have an NR2B gene nearly identical to that in mice, but some neuroscientists worry that a drug that increases NMDA receptor activation could increase the risk of epilepsy or stroke, and drug companies are already investigating the manipulation of NR2B levels to treat strokes.

Others wonder whether general enhancement of learning and intelligence is a good idea socially. Tim Tully, a member of a group that in 1995 announced genetic improvement of long-term memory of *Drosophila* by inducing activation of a form of CREB (J. C. Yin

Strittmatter and Roses, 1996). This gene also makes people more vulnerable to other conditions that damage the nervous system and impair learning and memory.

IMPORTANT METHOD

Other work is being done with laboratory animals, in which both behavioral measures and brain measures can be obtained from the same individuals (Gallagher and Rapp, 1997). This method is more powerful than obtaining behavioral and brain measures in separate groups and trying to draw inferences from group means, as earlier studies had done. The animal research on aging also benefits from the shorter life spans of animals, compared to the life span of humans.

Various Mechanisms Have Been Investigated to Explain the Decline of Learning and Memory with Aging

In Chapter 17 we saw that, while many types of learning and memory remain rather stable during aging, impairments are seen especially in declarative memories that require organizational effort on the part of the person, as well as in eye-blink conditioning. Many investigators have attempted to account for these age-related impairments, as recent reviews show (e.g., Prull et al., 2000; Raz, 2000). A variety of mechanisms have been examined as potential causes of declines in learning and memory during aging. They include loss of neurons and/or neural connections, im-et al., 1995), suggested that we may have evolved to learn less rapidly in maturity to prevent overloading of the brain's memory capacity. Joe Tsien prefers to think that the decrease in learning with age is evolutionarily adaptive for the population because it reduces the possibility that older individuals—who may have already reproduced—will compete successfully against younger ones for resources such as food. This debate shows no prospects of early resolution.

Investigators have also genetically altered the expression of nerve growth factor (NGF) to improve learning and memory. We saw in Chapter 7 that NGF is important in the development of the nervous system. It is also important in the maintenance and plasticity of the CNS later in life, but the production of NGF typically declines with age. CNS-derived stem cells, genetically engineered to secrete NGF, were grafted into the basal forebrain of senescent rats (Martinez-Serrano et al., 1996). Testing in the Morris water maze showed that the treated rats recovered their cognitive ability.

The mechanism by which NGF restores cognitive ability is not clear. A recent study, however, reports that when the decline of cortical innervation by cholinergic systems in aged monkeys was reversed by the placement of NGF-secreting cells in the

A Mouse Investigates the Novel Object of a Pair

basal forebrain, the age-related decline in number and complexity of cholinergic axon terminals in the cortex was also reversed (Conner et al., 2001).

Even without genetic intervention, giving rats enriched experience (like that illustrated in Figure 18.4*c*) significantly increases the cerebral levels of NGF and other neurotrophins (Ickes et al., 2000). And in another study, combining genetic engineering to increase NGF in rats with experience in complex mazes led to increases in the size of neurons in the basal forebrain and

to superior problem solving (A. I. Brooks et al., 2000). It is clear that modulatory factors such as NGF and complex experience can enhance learning and counteract some of the effects of aging. In clinical tests derived from this research, investigators have begun transplanting, into the brains of patients with Alzheimer's disease, cells taken from the patient's skin and modified to produce NGF. It is hoped that this treatment may slow and perhaps even reverse the decline of memory.

pairment of the cholinergic system, and impaired representation of information by neural circuits. We'll consider each of these possible mechanisms in turn. Box 18.1 considers how age-related changes in NMDA receptors and in nerve growth factor affect learning.

Impairment of the formation and retrieval of declarative memories. In brain-imaging studies, older subjects show less cortical activation, especially when encoding or retrieval require self-initiated efforts. Thus in Figure 18.15, the older subjects show less activation of frontal and temporal regions during learning of new faces (Grady et al., 1995), a task in which encoding requires the subjects to organize the stimuli. The age difference is less noticeable for recognizing faces in this study because here the stimuli provide the organization. In fact, brain-imaging studies of recall yield a variety of effects, with older subjects showing less frontal activation in some studies but more in others.

**CLINICAL
ISSUE**

Reviewing these reports, Grady and Craik (2000) note that it is still unclear whether increased activation in elderly subjects represents recruitment of neurons to compensate for difficulty or just more diffuse or nondifferentiated activity. Clearly, this topic needs more study.

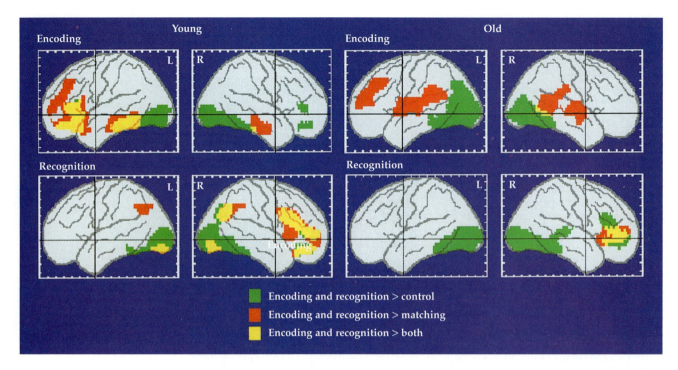

18.15 Active Brain Regions during Encoding and Recognition Tasks in Young and Old People Lateral views of the cerebral hemispheres show regions of enhanced cerebral blood flow caused by encoding (*top*) and retrieving (*bottom*) information. (From Grady et al., 1995; courtesy of Cheryl Grady.)

Loss of neurons and/or neural connections. Loss of neurons and/or neural connections with aging has been offered as a reason for impairment of learning and memory. The brain as a whole shows a gradual loss of weight after the age of 30 (see Figure 7.1), and some parts of the brain lose a larger proportion of weight or volume than other parts. We saw in Chapter 7 that shrinkage of the hippocampus in older people correlates significantly with impairment of memory (see Figure 7.24) (Golomb et al., 1994). Although not all investigators agree, most reports show age-related declines in both neuronal numbers (Simic et al., 1997) and synapses (Geinisman et al., 1995) in the hippocampus. Brain volume declines with age especially in the frontal regions (Raz, 2000).

Decline in the acetylcholine system. Some studies of age-related changes focus on brain regions that provide inputs to the hippocampal formation. One such region is the **septal complex,** which provides input from subcortical structures to the hippocampus. The neurons of the septal complex are located in the medial septal nucleus and the vertical limb of the diagonal band (Figure 18.16). Many of these neurons use acetylcholine (ACh) as their transmitter. These regions of the septohippocampal pathway, along with neurons of the nucleus basalis, appear to be involved in the neuropathology of Alzheimer's disease (McGeer et al., 1984; Rossor et al., 1982), and they have also been implicated in declines of memory associated with normal aging (Drachman and Leavitt, 1972).

Frontal section through
the septal complex

Corpus
callosum

Cerebral
cortex

Caudate–
putamen

Septal
complex

Diagonal
band

Optic
nerve

18.16 The Septal Complex in the Rat The septal complex is a site at which changes related to defects in memory that occur with aging are studied.

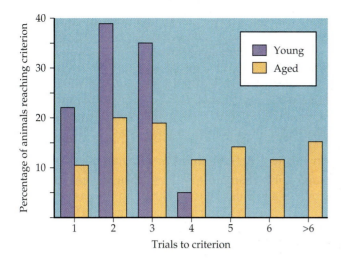

18.17 Performance of Young and Aged Rats in a Water Maze
All young rats reached criterion by the fourth test trial; many aged rats required more trials to reach criterion, but some were as quick to learn as the young rats. (After Gallagher et al., 1995.)

Michela Gallagher

Michela Gallagher et al. (1995) compared brain measures in two groups of aged rats: (1) those that perform about as well as young rats on tests of learning and memory, and (2) those that show impairment on these tests. Rats of three age groups—young (4–7 months), middle-aged (16–18 months), and aged (25–29 months)—were trained on a water maze. Special measures of performance taken on every fifth trial showed the number of animals that had reached a designated level of performance (the criterion) by that trial (Figure 18.17).

Most young rats reached criterion by the second trial, most middle-aged rats by the third trial, and most aged rats by the fourth trial. No young rat required more than four trials, but some aged rats did not reach criterion even by the sixth trial. However, more than one-fourth of the aged rats reached criterion by the second trial and thus performed as well as the young rats. So the aged rats showed much greater variability in their scores than did the young rats, as has been found in many other studies.

The investigators then measured the activity of the enzyme choline acetyltransferase (ChAT) in the septal complex; this enzyme catalyzes the synthesis of ACh. Any rats that showed pathology in the gross anatomy of the nervous system were eliminated from the study. ChAT activity in the septal complex was as high in aged rats that performed well as it was in young rats, but the aged rats that performed poorly showed significantly lower ChAT activity than the unimpaired aged rats or the young rats. ChAT activity did not decrease automatically with age, but only when aging was associated with impaired performance. This study thus suggests (but does not prove) that the decrease in ChAT causes impaired performance with age. Further research may reveal more conclusively the factors that lead to impairment and may suggest interventions that can preserve cognitive functions during aging.

Impairment in eye-blink conditioning with age. We saw earlier in this chapter that cerebellar circuits account for eye-blink conditioning when there is little or no delay between CS and US (delay conditioning) but that the hippocampus is required for trace conditioning (when a time interval separates CS and US). Acquiring both kinds of eye-blink conditioning takes increasing numbers of trials with age. We saw a little earlier in this chapter that both numbers of neurons and numbers of synapses in the hippocampus decline with age. Postmortem studies in humans show age-related losses of cerebellar Purkinje cells (Torvik et al., 1986). Thus both the hippocampus and the cerebellum show age-related losses that may account for the decreased ability to acquire eye-blink conditioning with age.

Impaired coding by place cells. Experiments on so-called place cells in the hippocampus (cells that respond when the animal is in a particular location in its environment) show differences in the encoding of information related to aging in rats.

In aged rats that showed poorer spatial learning in behavioral tests, the number of hippocampal neurons that responded to spatial cues did not appear to be different from that in young rats, but the neurons encoded a smaller amount of spatial information (Tanila, Shapiro, et al., 1997). When the visual cues surrounding a radial maze were changed, the spatial selectivity of place cells decreased considerably in memory-impaired aged rats, compared with that of young rats and that of aged rats with intact memory (Tanila, Sipila, et al., 1997). As noted earlier, the aged rats showed greater interindividual variability than the younger rats.

Can the Effects of Aging on Memory Be Prevented or Alleviated?

The hippocampus is more susceptible than most brain regions to some kinds of pathology. It can be attacked by certain kinds of encephalitis, and it is easily injured by hypoxia (lack of oxygen), which may occur during major surgery. In Chapter 16 we saw that glucocorticoids—adrenal hormones secreted during stress—can damage the hippocampus, which is particularly rich in glucocorticoid receptors.

Experiments with rats show that early handling, as opposed to isolation, lowers the concentration of glucocorticoids in adults and retards signs of aging of the hippocampus (Sapolsky, 1993). Rats raised in an enriched condition (EC), as opposed to those in an impoverished (isolated) condition (IC), have lower basal levels of corticosterone and, when challenged by a stressful situation, show a more rapid return of glucocorticoids to low basal levels (Mohammed et al., 1993). Thus adequate early experience may help protect the hippocampus.

Rats with enriched experience show greater expression of nerve growth factor (NGF) in the hippocampus than do IC rats (Mohammed et al., 1993; Ottoson et al., 1995). On the basis of these results, investigators in some clinical studies are infusing NGF into the brains of Alzheimer's patients (Nordberg, 1996; Seiger et al., 1993) in an attempt to prevent or alleviate impairment to the hippocampus and thus preserve memory (see also Box 18.1).

CLINICAL ISSUE

Longitudinal research on humans indicates that enriched experience throughout life can help reduce the risk of cognitive decline in old age. Schaie (1994), summarizing a 35-year-long study of more than 5000 individuals, listed the following among seven factors that reduce the risk of "normal" cognitive decline:

- Living in favorable environmental circumstances (e.g., having received above-average education, pursuing occupations that involve high complexity and low routine, earning above-average income, and maintaining intact families).
- Being involved in activities typical of complex and intellectually stimulating environments (e.g., extensive reading, travel, attendance at cultural events, continuing-education activities, and participation in clubs and professional associations).
- "Being married to a spouse with high cognitive status" (Schaie, 1994, p. 310).

Enriched experience may also cushion the brain and intellectual function against decline in old age. Masliah et al. (1991) report that loss of synapses correlates strongly with the severity of symptoms in Alzheimer's disease. Enriched experience produces richer neural networks in the brains of all species that have been studied in this regard, as noted earlier in this chapter. If humans experience similar effects, as seems likely, then enriched experience may set up reserves of connections that help protect intellectual function from Alzheimer's.

Summary

Refer to the *Learning Biological Psychology* CD for the following study aids for this chapter:

17 Objectives

80 Study Questions

1 Activity

1 Animated Tutorial

1 Video

1. Memory storage has long been hypothesized to involve changes in neural circuits. Research since the 1960s has demonstrated both functional and structural synaptic changes related to learning.

2. Much current research on neural changes related to learning and memory is based on two hypotheses stated by D. O. Hebb in 1949: (1) The functional relationship between two neurons changes when one frequently takes part in exciting the other. (2) Any two

neurons or systems of neurons that are repeatedly active at the same time tend to become "associated"; that is, activity in one facilitates activity in the other.

3. An early indication that training affects brain measures was the finding that formal training or enriched experience in rats leads to structural changes in the cerebral cortex, including alterations in the number and size of synaptic contacts and in the branching of dendrites.

4. Research on the mollusk *Aplysia* and other invertebrates has demonstrated the existence of plasticity in invertebrate nervous systems.

5. Long-term potentiation (LTP) of neural responses is a lasting increase in amplitude of the response of neurons caused by brief high-frequency stimulation of their afferents. It can be studied in intact animals or in isolated slices of brain tissue. Some of the many different forms of LTP may be components of or models for various kinds of learning. Long-term depression (LTD) may be a reversal of LTP.

6. Conditioning of the eye-blink response in the rabbit is crucially dependent on the cerebellum on the same side of the head; the hippocampus may facilitate acquisition of this response. Eye-blink conditioning in humans involves not only cerebellar and brainstem regions, but also the hippocampus and regions of the cerebral cortex.

7. Neurochemical mechanisms are being investigated for successive stages of memory formation: short-term memory (STM), intermediate-term memory (ITM), and long-term memory (LTM). Each stage appears to be linked to a different part of the cascade of neurochemical events that underlie memory formation. LTM appears to require protein synthesis in the posttraining period: Training induces increased synthesis of protein in certain brain regions, and blocking protein synthesis prevents the formation of LTM, although it does not prevent learning or the formation of STM or ITM.

8. STM and ITM formation may depend on two different mechanisms of polarization of neurons. Different drugs that affect these mechanisms can cause specific failure at one or the other time period. The stages of memory formation appear to be sequentially linked because failure of one stage causes failure of the succeeding stage(s).

9. Findings suggest that numerous neural structures and mechanisms are involved in learning and memory. Different brain circuits and different neurochemical mechanisms may be found for different stages of memory formation. Among the species in which neural mechanisms of memory storage have been studied, the mechanisms have been found to be similar, though not identical. This similarity suggests that learning and memory formation use parts of the basic cascade of neurochemical events that extends from initial stimulation of neurons to protein synthesis.

10. Memory formation can be modulated (facilitated or impaired) by neural states and by a variety of agents, including stimulants, depressants, certain neurotransmitters, opioid peptides, hormones, and sensory stimulation.

11. Some neurochemical and neuroanatomical measures correlate with specific declines in learning and memory that occur in most elderly subjects. Some biological changes occur only in those subjects who show behavioral decline. The incidence of memory impairments in old age can be reduced by adequate early environment and continuing enriched experience.

Recommended Reading

Baudry, M., and Zola, S. (Eds.). (1998). Brain and memory: From genes to behavior. Proceedings of the Sixth Conference on the Neurobiology of Learning and Memory. *Neurobiology of Learning and Memory, 70*, 1–303.

Gallagher, M., and Rapp, P. R. (1997). The use of animal models to study effects of aging on cognition. *Annual Review of Psychology, 48*, 339–370.

Martinez, J. L., and Kesner, R. P. (Eds.). (1998). *Learning and memory: A biological view* (3rd ed.). New York: Academic Press.

McGaugh, J. L., Weinberger, N. M., and Lynch, G. (Eds.). (1995). *Brain and memory: Modulation and mediation of neuroplasticity.* New York: Oxford University Press.

Prull, M. W., Gabrieli, J. D. E., and Bunge, S. A. (2000). Age-related changes in memory: A cognitive neuroscience perspective. In F. I. M. Craik and T. A. Salthouse (Eds.), *The handbook of aging and cognition* (pp. 91–153). Mahwah, NJ: Erlbaum.

Silva, A. J., Kogan, J. H., Frankland, P. W., and Kida, S. (1998). CREB and memory. *Annual Review of Neuroscience, 21*, 127–148.

19

Language and Cognition

Inspection of the week's best-seller list confirms the impression that only humans write books, though chimps may dabble in paint and rats may occasionally eat books. By this and many other measures, human mental life is distinctive in the animal world, although it's increasingly clear that members of other species also communicate effectively with one another. Clues to the relation between the brain and human cognition come from individuals with brain disorders and from hemispheric differences in the brain function of normal people. Imaging techniques such as PET and functional MRI provide confirmation and further insight into cognition in clinically normal individuals.

Jesper Christiansen, *Meteorpainting*, 1995, acrylic on canvas, 71" × 71"

Courtesy of the artist and DCA Gallery, New York.

In the mid-nineteenth century, the neurologist Paul Broca discovered that lesions in the left hemisphere impair speech and language. One of the most fascinating conclusions from this point, and those that followed, is that the left and right sides of the brain may perform different but complementary functions. The advent of structural and functional brain imaging has expanded our understanding of brain processes and structures involved in human mental life.

The Development and Evolution of Speech and Language Are Remarkable and Mysterious

There are an estimated 7000 languages in the world today, about a thousand of which have been studied by linguists (Wuethrich, 2000). All these languages have similar basic elements, and each is composed of a set of sounds and symbols that have distinct meanings. These elements are arranged in distinct orders according to rules characteristic of the particular language. Thus anyone who knows the sounds (**phonemes**), symbols, and rules (**grammar**) of a particular language can generate sentences that convey information to others who have similar knowledge of the language.

Children's acquisition of language is an incredible accomplishment because they do not need formal instruction, yet they discern the phonemes, vocabulary, and grammar rapidly. At birth, a baby can distinguish between sounds from Dutch and sounds from Japanese. Because adult monkeys can also make this discrimination (Ramus et al., 2000), this ability may reflect a basic property of the primate auditory system.

But by attending to these sounds, the human baby, which began life babbling nearly all the phonemes found in any human language, soon comes to use only the subset of phonemes in use around her. By 7 months of age, infants pay more attention to sentences with unfamiliar structure than to sentences with familiar structure (Marcus et al., 1999), indicating that they have already acquired a sense of the rules of language and are actively looking out for exceptions. The rare children who are profoundly isolated during early development develop little or no language, pointing to the importance of experience during sensitive periods early in life. Restoration of hearing in one adult who had been deaf most of her life also supports this hypothesis because even with her hearing restored, did not learn to speak (Curtiss, 1989).

NEURAL PLASTICITY

The notion of a sensitive period for language acquisition is also supported by the difficulty that postadolescents experience in learning a second language. Imaging studies indicate that people who learn a second language early in life activate the same brain region when using either language. But people learning a second language later than age 11 seem to use different brain regions for each language (K. H. Kim et al., 1997). This difference in brain organization may be related to the greater fluency of people who learn another language by the age of 6 or 7 (J. S. Johnson and Newport, 1989).

Over the centuries, scholars have speculated about the evolution of language, but data are scarce. The oldest written records available are clay tablets only about 6000 years old. The absence of older records has promoted a sense of mystery and the creation of elaborate tales about the beginnings of language. For many years, scholars suggested that speech and language originally developed from gestures, especially those involving facial movements. Anthropologist Gordon Hewes (1973) suggested that gestures came under voluntary control early in human history and became an easy mode of communication before the emergence of speech.

Even today, hand movements seem to facilitate speech because if you prevent people from gesturing, they make more slips and have more pauses in their speech (Krauss, 1998). Furthermore, people who have been blind from birth, and so have never seen the hand gestures of others, make hand gestures while they speak (Iverson and Goldin-Meadow, 1998). Later we'll see that deaf people who communicate exclusively with gestures use the same part of the brain that hearing people use while speaking and listening, further indication of a close link between gestures and speech. Many ideas about the evolution of the human brain focus on the development of language (Corballis, 1998; Deacon, 1997), arguing, for example, about whether Neanderthals could talk (Lieberman, 1998).

In the sections that follow we'll examine communication in other species for clues to the evolution of language, then discuss the various human brain regions involved in different language processes.

Some Nonhumans Engage in Elaborate Vocal Behavior

Chirps, barks, meows, songs, and other sounds are among the many vocalizations produced by nonhuman animals. Many of these sounds seem to distinguish species, signal readiness to mate, or alert the group to danger. Whales sing and may imitate songs they hear from distant oceans (Noad et al., 2000), and some seal mothers recognize their pup's vocalizations even after 4 years of separation (Insley, 2000). Could the vocal behavior of nonhuman animals be related to the evolution of human language? Are some attributes of nonhuman vocal behavior akin to human speech? We'll explore these questions by focusing on the vocalizations of birds and nonhuman primates.

Birdsong.   Many birds sing pleasant tunes, and these songs offer some intriguing analogies to human speech. Birdsongs vary in complexity: Some repeat a simple basic unit; others are more elaborate (Figure 19.1). The principal roles of birdsong are territory defense and mate selection (Ball and Hulse, 1998). The intricate patterning of some songs suggests a connection to human speech. Although no investigator believes that birdsong is an evolutionary precursor to human speech, Peter Marler (1970) and other scientists have shown that birdsong can provide an interesting analogy and experimental tool.

Although some birds, such as chickens and ringdoves, have simple vocal behavior that is not affected by early deafening or by rearing in isolation (Baptista, 1996), many birds must learn the appropriate song. For example, the songs of canaries, zebra finches, and white-crowned sparrows depend on exposure to sounds at particular developmental stages—much as human speech does (DeVoogd, 1994). In these songbirds, only males of the species sing, and song is acquired in several distinct stages:

1. Initial exposure to the song of a tutor, usually the father
2. A period of successive approximation of the produced song to the stored model
3. Fixing, or **crystallization,** of the song in a permanent form

Peter Marler

19.1 Songs of Three Bird Species
For each species, the top trace shows the exact sound pattern detected by a sensitive microphone. The bottom trace shows the same pattern analyzed by a sound spectrograph, which reveals the amount of energy in different sound frequencies at each moment. (After Greenewalt, 1968.)

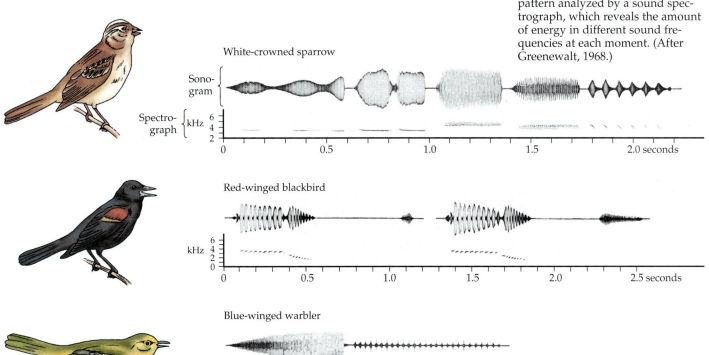

19.2 Effects of Isolation on Birdsong Development (*a*) These sonograms show the typical adult song patterns of two sparrow species. The songs illustrated in part *b* were produced by males reared in isolation; those in part *c,* by males deafened in infancy. Both early auditory isolation and deafening result in abnormal song, but the two species still produce different patterns. Deafening has a more profound effect because the animal is prevented from hearing its own song production, as well as that of other males. (After Marler and Sherman, 1983, 1985.)

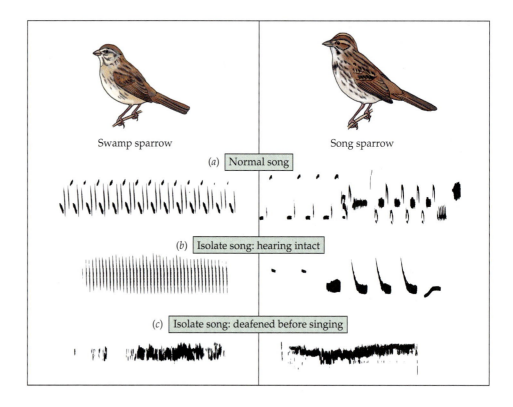

Swamp sparrow   Song sparrow

(*a*) Normal song

(*b*) Isolate song: hearing intact

(*c*) Isolate song: deafened before singing

Masakazu Konishi

Normally, song learning is complete by sexual maturity (90 days). Male songbirds raised in acoustic isolation fail to develop normal song (Figure 19.2). However, if such isolated birds are exposed to tape recordings of species-typical vocalizations during an early **sensitive period,** they acquire normal song; if the birds are exposed to taped songs only later in life, the song acquired is abnormal. Interestingly, an adult male raised in auditory isolation *can* learn to sing if, instead of being exposed only to a recording of the song, he is exposed to a living, singing male tutor (R. G. Morrison and Nottebohm, 1993), suggesting that social stimuli can extend the sensitive period (Eales, 1985).

Masakazu Konishi (1985) demonstrated that songbirds show quite abnormal song if they are deafened during the second stage before they have learned how to produce the final song. So the male must first hear himself sing and compare his chirps with the memory of the tutor's song until he has replicated it. Deafening after the song has crystallized has very little effect on song production, as if the song has become fixed. However, if instead of deafening the bird, you purposely distort the auditory feedback he hears while singing, the song deteriorates (Leonardo and Konishi, 1999), indicating that males normally listen to their song and that the neural circuits retain enough plasticity to correct any errors that arise.

When a bird is exposed to synthetic songs, composed of notes of both the same species and another species, it prefers to copy the song of its own species (Baptista, 1996; Marler, 1991; Marler and Peters, 1982), indicating a predisposition to learn the appropriate song. Here again, a bird is more likely to learn the song of another species if its tutor is a live bird rather than a recording, suggesting to Luis Baptista and Lou Petrinovich (1986) that social stimuli direct the attention of developing birds to an appropriate "mentor," whose song they copy.

The brain birdsong system has been well described as a series of brain nuclei and their connections that control the neural output to the vocal production organ, the **syrinx** (Figure 19.3) (Arnold and Schlinger, 1993; DeVoogd, 1994). A direct pathway, extending from the higher vocal center (HVC) to the nucleus robustus of the archistriatum (RA) to the brainstem twelfth nerve nucleus, seems to control the vocal organ. Lesions along this direct pathway at any stage of development will disrupt

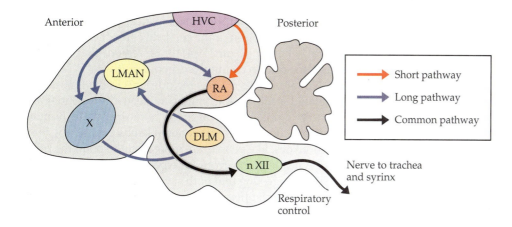

19.3 Vocal Control Centers of the Songbird Brain   Two neural pathways control birdsong. A direct route from the higher vocal center (HVC) to the nucleus robustus of the archistriatum (RA) to the nucleus of the twelfth cranial nerve (n XII) is crucial for song; lesions of any of these areas will disrupt song. The indirect path that includes the lateral magnocellular nucleus of the anterior neostriatum (LMAN) may play a role in song learning: Lesions of the LMAN halt the development of song in young birds, but lesions of the LMAN in adult zebra finches do not affect singing. X, area X of the locus parolfactorium. (After Arnold, 1980.)

song. A less direct pathway extends from the HVC to the brainstem, and lesions of one of its components, the lateral magnocellular nucleus of the anterior neostriatum (LMAN), will stop song development, but similar lesions during adulthood do not affect song performance (Bottjer et al., 1984).

These results suggest that components of the indirect pathway help sculpt the direct pathway so that it alone can mediate singing. Song development is paralleled by changes in the size and organization of these nuclei. Regions of the brain that control song are larger in individual canaries that have more elaborate songs. Furthermore, comparisons of different species of songbirds reveal that larger song repertoires are related to larger control regions in the brain (Brenowitz and Arnold, 1986). Song learning is also accompanied by the generation in adulthood of new neurons (neurogenesis; see Chapter 7) in at least some birdsong regions (Scharff et al., 2000).

Some birds show a striking similarity to humans in the neurology of vocal control. Changes in membranes of the syrinx are produced by adjacent muscles innervated by the right and left twelfth nerves, cranial nerves that control the musculature of the neck. When these nerves are cut, the effects on song differ markedly depending on whether the right or the left nerve is cut. Cutting the right twelfth nerve produces almost no change in song. Cutting the left twelfth nerve produces an almost entirely silent bird; such birds "look like actors in silent cinema film" (Nottebohm, 1987). All the correct body movements are made, but no sound comes out.

This observation indicates left dominance of vocal control mechanisms in these birds. Peripheral dominance is matched by differences in brain hemispheres. Fernando Nottebohm (1980) has mapped the vocal control centers of the canary brain (see Figure 19.3), showing that lesions of the direct vocal control pathway (HVC to RA to twelfth nerve nucleus) in the left hemisphere markedly impair the production of song; singing becomes unstable and monotonous. But minimal changes are seen following lesions in right hemisphere structures. We don't yet know any anatomical differences between the two sides to explain why only the left hemisphere seems to control birdsong (Ball and Hulse, 1998); we'll see that human language is also normally controlled by the left cerebral hemisphere.

Fernando Nottebohm

Vocalization in nonhuman primates.   The calls of nonhuman primates have been examined intensively in both field and laboratory studies (Seyfarth and Cheney, 1997). Many nonhuman primate vocalizations seem preprogrammed, including infant crying and the emotional vocalizations of adults, such as shrieking in pain and moaning. Ploog and his collaborators (Ploog, 1992) cataloged the calls that squirrel monkeys make and the communication properties of those sounds in a social context. The monkeys' calls include shrieking, quacking, chirping, growling, and yapping sounds. Many of these calls can penetrate a forest for some distance, communicating alarm, territoriality, and other emotional statements.

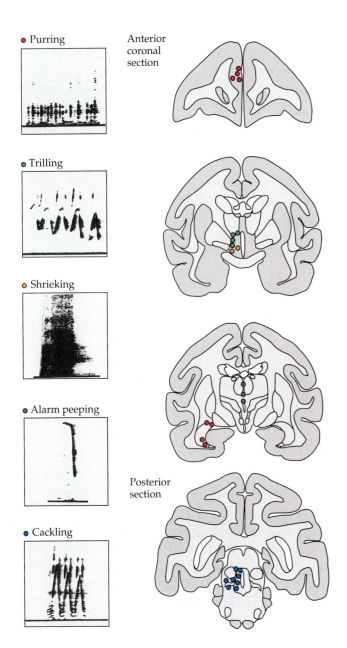

19.4 Elicitation of Vocalizations by Electrical Stimulation of the Monkey Brain Stimulation at different sites in the monkey brain results in different, species-typical vocalizations. The left column shows spectrograms of different vocalizations, and the coronal sections in the right column show brain sites at which the different vocalizations are elicited. (After Ploog, 1992; spectrograms courtesy of Uwe Jürgens.)

Direct electrical stimulation of subcortical regions can elicit some calls, but stimulation of the cerebral cortex generally fails to elicit vocal behavior (Figure 19.4). Brain regions that elicit vocalizations also seem to be involved in defense, attack, feeding, and sex behaviors. These regions include sites in the limbic system and related structures. Changes in electrical potential are recorded from monkey cortical areas homologous to human speech areas prior to actual vocalization (Gemba et al., 1995). Furthermore, monkeys, like people, are more likely to point the right ear toward vocalizations from conspecifics (Ghazanfar and Hauser, 1999), suggesting that both species rely more heavily on the left cerebral hemisphere to decode communication, an idea that has been amply confirmed in humans, as we'll see shortly.

Can Nonhuman Primates Acquire Language with Training?

Throughout history people have tried to teach animals to talk. In most cases, however, any communication between animal and human resulted because the person learned to meow, grunt, or bark rather than because the animal learned to produce human speech. Since both the vocal tracts and the vocal repertoires of nonhuman primates are different from those of humans, scientists have given up attempting to train animals to produce human speech. Can nonhuman primates be taught other forms of communication that have features similar to human language, including the ability to represent objects with symbols and to manipulate these symbols according to rules of order? Can animals other than humans generate a novel string of symbols, such as a new sentence?

R. Allen Gardner and Beatrice Gardner (1969, 1984) taught chimpanzees American Sign Language (ASL), the sign language used by people who are deaf in the United States. The chimps mastered many signs and appeared to be able to use them spontaneously and to generate new sequences of signs. F. G. Patterson (1981) claimed to have taught a gorilla a vocabulary of several hundred ASL words. David Premack (1971) used another approach. He taught chimpanzees a system based on an assortment of colored chips (symbols) that could adhere to a magnetic board. After extensive training, the chimpanzees could manipulate the chips in ways that may reflect an acquired ability to form short sentences and to note various logical classifications.

At the Yerkes Regional Primate Research Center at Emory University, Project Lana has focused on teaching *Yerkish* to chimpanzees (Rumbaugh, 1977). Yerkish is a computer-based language in which different keys on a console represent words. Apes are quite good at acquiring many words in this language, and they appear to string together novel, meaningful chains. On the basis of studies such as these, Sue Savage-Rumbaugh et al. (1993) claimed that the ability to comprehend language preceded the appearance of speech by several million years. Although nonhuman primates do not have a vocal system that permits speech, those as intelligent as the chimpanzee appear to have a capacity for learning at least some components of language (Figure 19.5).

Debate about the extent to which chimpanzees learn language has been vigorous, including both methodological and theoretical issues. One of the main critics of the conclusion that chimps can acquire language is Herbert Terrace (1979), who raised a young chimp and taught it many signs. Terrace tested carefully to see whether his chimp or others could construct sentences.

According to linguists, grammar is the essence of language, so investigators look for the ability of sign-using chimps to generate meaningful and novel sequences

19.5 Chimpanzee Using Symbols   Although there is no doubt that chimpanzees can learn to use arbitrary signs and/or symbols to communicate, some researchers still question whether this usage is equivalent to human language. (Courtesy of Sue Savage-Rumbaugh.)

of signs. As we have noted, the studies by Gardner and Gardner suggested that sign-using chimps made distinctive series of signs, just as though they were using words in a sentence. Terrace, however, argued that strings of signs were explicitly presented to the chimps and that the animals merely imitated rather than generating new combinations. He suggested that the imitation was quite subtle and might involve cuing practices of which the experimenter was unaware.

Savage-Rumbaugh et al. (1998) opened a broader debate emphasizing the nature of language. True symbolization, they argued, is something more than the representation of objects or action. True symbolization involves an intention to communicate an internal representational process akin to thought. This process may not be a component of language learning in chimpanzees, although of course questioning the animals about this feature of language use is difficult.

Savage-Rumbaugh (1993) has argued that apes can comprehend spoken words, produce novel combinations of words, and respond appropriately to sentences arranged according to a syntactic rule. She believes that the ape's linguistic capacity has been underestimated. We'll learn later about a brain asymmetry in humans (the planum temporale) that has been related to language; a similar asymmetry is seen in chimpanzee brains (Gannon et al., 1998).

This debate is far from settled, but the accomplishments of the trained chimpanzees have at least forced investigators to sharpen their criteria of what constitutes language. Pinker (1994) asserts, "Even putting aside vocabulary, phonology, morphology, and syntax, what impresses one the most about chimpanzee signing is that fundamentally, deep down, chimps just don't get it."

Language Disorders Result from Region-Specific Brain Injuries

Much of our early understanding of the relationship between brain mechanisms and language was derived from observation of language impairments following brain injury resulting from accidents, diseases, or strokes.

Several Defining Signs Characterize Aphasia

Early Egyptian medical records, written at least 3000 years ago, describe people who became speechless after blows to the temporal bone (Finger, 1994). In 1861, French neurologist Paul Broca examined a man who had lost the ability to speak. Postmortem study of this patient revealed damage to the left inferior frontal region—a region now known as **Broca's area** (Figure 19.6). In approximately 90 to 95% of the cases of language impairment due to brain injury—called **aphasia**—the damage is to the left cere-

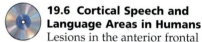

19.6 Cortical Speech and Language Areas in Humans   Lesions in the anterior frontal region called *Broca's area* interfere with speech production; injury to an area of temporoparietal cortex called *Wernicke's area* interferes with language comprehension; injury to the supramarginal gyrus interferes with repetition of heard speech. For most individuals, these functional regions are found only in the left hemisphere.

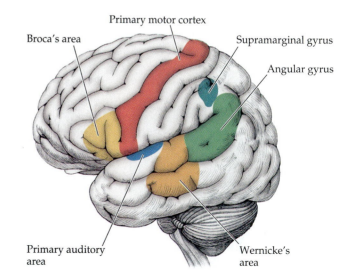

bral hemisphere. Damage to the right hemisphere is responsible for the remaining 5 to 10% of the cases of aphasia. Techniques such as the Wada test (Box 19.1) confirm that most of us use our left cerebral hemisphere to control language.

The most prominent sign of aphasia is the substitution of a word by a sound, an incorrect word, or an unintended word. This characteristic is called **paraphasia.** At times an entirely novel word—called a **neologism**—may be generated by the substitution of a phoneme. Paraphasic speech in aphasic patients is evident both in spontaneous conversation and in attempts to read aloud from a text.

Conversational speech reveals another important aspect of speech: its fluency or ease of production. **Nonfluent speech** is talking with considerable effort, in short sentences, and without the usual melodic character of conversational speech. In some cases of aphasia, speech is even more fluent than normal, and it shows other abnormalities as well. Many patients with aphasic syndromes also show disturbances in the ability to repeat words or sentences. There seems to be one advantage to aphasia: Patients who suffer from this disorder are better than controls at detecting when someone is lying (Etcoff et al., 2000), presumably because they focus on facial features and are not distracted by the words being spoken.

Almost all patients with aphasia show some impairment in writing (**agraphia**) and disturbances in reading (**alexia**). Finally, the brain impairments or disorders that produce aphasia also produce a distinctive motor impairment called *apraxia* (see Chapter 11). Apraxia is characterized by impairment in the execution of learned movements that is unrelated to paralysis, coordination problems, sensory impairments, or the comprehension of instructions. Patients suffering from apraxia are unable to imitate some common gestures, such as sticking out the tongue or waving goodbye, although these acts might appear in their spontaneous behavior.

Three Major Types of Aphasia Result from Injury to Particular Brain Regions

Among the neurologists and researchers who have sought to classify the many different types of aphasia, a prime concern has been the relation between the particular form of language disorder and the region of brain destruction or impairment. Figure 19.6 shows the main brain regions of the left hemisphere that are related to language abilities. Table 19.1 summarizes the main features of various types of aphasia that we'll cover in this chapter.

Broca's aphasia. As noted earlier, lesions in the left inferior frontal region (Broca's area) produce a type of aphasia known as **Broca's aphasia;** it is also described as a *nonfluent aphasia.* Patients with Broca's aphasia have considerable difficulty producing speech, talking only in a labored and hesitant manner. Frequently they have lost the ability of readily naming persons or objects—an impairment referred to as

Paul Broca
(1824–1880)

TABLE 19.1 *Language Symptomatology in Aphasia*

Type of aphasia	Brain area affected	Spontaneous speech	Comprehension	Paraphasia	Repetition	Naming
Broca's aphasia		Nonfluent	Good	Uncommon	Poor	Poor
Wernicke's aphasia		Fluent	Poor	Common	Poor	Poor
Global aphasia		Nonfluent	Poor	Variable	Poor	Poor
Conduction aphasia		Fluent	Good	Common	Poor	Poor
Subcortical aphasia	L R	Variable	Variable	Common	Good	Variable

anomia. Reading and writing are also impaired. However, the ability to utter automatic speech is often preserved. Such speech includes greetings (*hello*); short, common expressions (*oh, my God*); and swear words. Although these patients have difficulty *expressing* themselves verbally or in writing, their *comprehension* remains relatively intact. Most Broca's aphasics have **hemiplegia**—partial paralysis involving one side of the body—on the right side because the lesion often extends to nearby motor cortex.

The composite CT scans in Figure 19.7*c* reveal lesion sites in patients with Broca's aphasia. Seven years after a stroke, one Broca's patient (Figure 19.7*b*) still spoke slowly, used mainly nouns and very few verbs or function words, and spoke only with great effort. When asked to repeat the phrase *go ahead and do it if possible,* she could say only, "Go to do it," with pauses between each word. Broca's patients with brain lesions as extensive as hers show little recovery of speech with the passing of time.

Wernicke's aphasia.   German neurologist Carl Wernicke described several syndromes of aphasia following brain lesions. The syndrome now known as **Wernicke's aphasia** includes a complex array of signs. Patients with this syndrome have very fluent verbal output, but what they say contains many paraphasias that often make their speech unintelligible. Sound substitutions (e.g., "girl" becomes "curl") and word substitutions (e.g., *bread* becomes *cake*) are common, as are neologisms.

Word substitutions and speech errors occur in a context that preserves syntactical structure, although sentences seem empty of content. The ability to repeat words and sentences is impaired. Furthermore, patients are unable to *understand* what they read or hear. In some cases reading comprehension is more impaired than comprehension of spoken speech; in other cases the reverse is true. Unlike patients with Broca's aphasia, patients with Wernicke's aphasia usually do not display partial paralysis.

In Wernicke's aphasia the most prominent brain lesions are in posterior regions of the left superior temporal gyrus and extend partially into adjacent parietal cortex, including the supramarginal and angular gyri (see Figure 19.7*d*) (H. Damasio, 1995). When *word deafness* (inability to understand spoken words) is more evident than reading impairment, patients show greater involvement of the first temporal gyrus, especially tracts from the auditory cortex. In contrast, when *word blindness*

Carl Wernicke
(1848–1905)

19.7 Brain Lesions That Produce Aphasia

(a) This diagram shows the levels of the CT scan slices in parts *b* through *e*. Each level is labeled according to brain language regions shown by that slice: B, Broca's area; SM, supramarginal gyrus; W, Wernicke's area. (b) CT scans for a patient with Broca's aphasia, aged 51, 7 years after stroke. (c–e) Composite CT scan lesion sites for four cases of Broca's aphasia (c), four cases of Wernicke's aphasia (d), and five cases of global aphasia (e). In c, large lesions (blue) were located in Broca's area on slices B and B/W, and the peak amount of tissue damage occurred in the frontoparietal areas on slices SM and SM + 1. In d, lesions were located in Wernicke's area on slice W and in the supramarginal gyrus area on slice SM. In e, large lesions were present in every language area. (After Naeser and Hayward, 1978; CT scans courtesy of Margaret Naeser.)

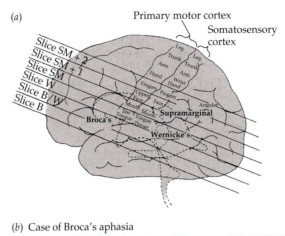

(a)

(b) Case of Broca's aphasia

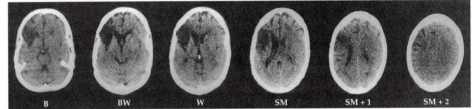

(c) Broca's aphasia

   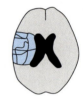

(d) Wernicke's aphasia

  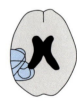

(e) Global aphasia

Slice B   Slice B/W   Slice W   Slice SM   Slice SM + 1   Slice SM + 2

(inability to understand written words) predominates, greater destruction of the angular gyrus is evident.

Global aphasia. In some patients brain injury or disease results in total loss of the ability to understand language or to speak, read, or write. This syndrome is called **global aphasia.** Patients suffering from global aphasia retain some ability for automatic speech, especially emotional exclamations. They can utter very few words, and no semblance of syntax is evident in their speech. The area of abnormality in the brain is broad, encompassing large realms of frontal, temporal, and parietal cortex, including Broca's area, Wernicke's area, and the supramarginal gyrus (see Figure 19.7e). The prognosis for language recovery in these patients is quite poor.

The Wernicke–Geschwind Model of Aphasia Represents Some Features of Speech and Language Anatomically

One traditional approach to understanding aphasic disturbances, begun by Wernicke in the early twentieth century, uses a *connectionist* perspective. According to this view, deficits can be understood as breaks in an interconnected network of components, each of which is involved with a particular feature of language analysis or production.

Norman Geschwind (1972) developed such a theory, often referred to as *disconnection theory* to emphasize the symptoms of language impairment following the loss of *connections* among brain regions in a network. According to this perspective, when a word or sentence is heard, the auditory cortex transmits information about the sounds to Wernicke's area, where the sounds are analyzed to decode what they mean. For the word to be spoken, Wernicke's area must transmit this information to Broca's area, where a speech plan is activated. Broca's area then transmits this plan to adjacent motor cortex, which controls the relevant articulatory muscles (Figure 19.8*a*).

The axons transmitting information from Wernicke's area to Broca's area form a bundle of nerve fibers called the **arcuate fasciculus** (from the Latin *arcuatus*, "bow-shaped," and *fasciculus*, "small bundle"). Patients with lesions of these axons have relatively fluent speech and comprehension of spoken words because Broca's and Wernicke's areas are intact. But they display **conduction aphasia,** a major impair-

19.8 The Wernicke–Geschwind Connectionist Model of Aphasia (After Geschwind, 1976.)

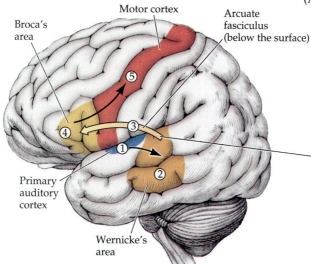

(a) Speaking a heard word

1. Information about the sound is analyzed by primary auditory cortex and transmitted to Wernicke's area.

2. Wernicke's area analyzes the sound information to determine the word that was said.

3. This information from Wernicke's area is transmitted through the arcuate fasciculus to Broca's area.

4. Broca's area forms a motor plan to repeat the word and sends that information to motor cortex.

5. Motor cortex implements the plan, manipulating the larynx and related structures to say the word.

Lesions of the arcuate fasciculus disrupt the transfer from Wernicke's area to Broca's area, so the patient has difficulty repeating spoken words, but may retain comprehension of spoken language (because of intact Wernicke's area) and may still be able to speak spontaneously (because of intact Broca's area).

Motor cortex · Broca's area · Arcuate fasciculus (below the surface) · Primary auditory cortex · Wernicke's area

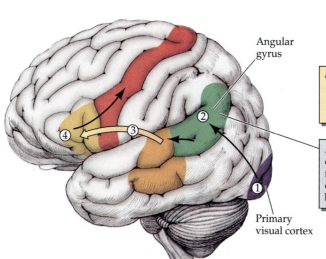

(b) Speaking a written word

1. Visual cortex analyzes the image and transmits the information about the image to the angular gyrus.

2. The angular gyrus decodes the image information to recognize the word and associate this visual form with the spoken form in Wernicke's area.

3. Information about the word is transmitted via the arcuate fasciculus to Broca's area.

4. Broca's area formulates a motor plan to say the appropriate word and transmits that plan to motor cortex for implementation.

A lesion of the angular gyrus disrupts the flow of information from visual cortex, so the person has difficulty saying words he has seen but not words he has heard.

Angular gyrus · Primary visual cortex

ment in the *repetition* of words and sentences. When these patients attempt to repeat words, they offer **phonemic paraphasias**—words with incorrect phonemes substituting for correct sounds. Sometimes conduction aphasia can result from damage to auditory cortex, as well as the insula and supramarginal gyrus.

According to the Wernicke–Geschwind model, saying the name of a seen object or word involves the transfer of visual information to the angular gyrus, which then arouses the auditory pattern in Wernicke's area. From Wernicke's area the auditory form is transmitted via the arcuate fasciculus to Broca's area. There the model for the spoken form is activated and transmitted to the face area of the motor cortex, and the word is then spoken (Figure 19.8b).

Thus lesions involving the angular gyrus disconnect the systems involved in visual and auditory language. So patients with lesions in this region have difficulty reading aloud, but they are able to speak and understand speech. The Wernicke–Geschwind model is known to be something of an oversimplification, since not all patients with injury to a particular region show the predicted behavioral deficit (Howard, 1997).

Users of Sign Language Show Aphasia following Brain Injury

We've already noted how human hands and arms gesture during speech, and how spoken language may have evolved from such gestures. Formal hand and arm gestures with specific rules of arrangement form the basis of nonvocal languages of the deaf, such as American Sign Language (ASL). ASL consists of an elaborate code and grammar; Figure 19.9 shows some examples of ASL signs.

An exhaustive analysis of ASL by two linguists (Klima and Bellugi, 1979) clearly establishes this gesture-based set of symbols as a language that is as elaborate as its vocal counterparts. In fact, sign languages show features as subtle as dialect. Adding to the complexity of ASL is its heavy reliance on visuospatial differences to convey differences in meaning (Poizner et al., 1990).

Given the unique features of sign language, investigators have been interested in determining whether it is similar to spoken language in its neural organization. Is there hemispheric specialization for a language system based on hand signals, most of which are formed by the right hand, although some involve both hands?

Meckler et al. (1979) described a young man who was raised by deaf–mute parents and who began to suffer from aphasia after an accident. Previously he had used both spoken and sign language for communication. After the accident, impairments in his spoken language and sign language were equally severe, as though the damaged brain region had subserved both languages. Chiarello et al. (1982) analyzed sign language deficits in an older deaf–mute person. She had well-developed sign language skills until, following a stroke in the left temporal cortex (including Wernicke's area), she became unable to generate hand signals with either hand.

19.9 American Sign Language
Patients with aphasia who are deaf show deficits in understanding and/or producing sign language that are analogous to language deficits in hearing patients.

Feeling

Be quiet

Secret

Bellugi et al. (1983) described aphasia in three deaf signers who had damage to the left hemisphere. In these patients, differential damage in the left hemisphere impaired different components of sign language. Damage in one region affected grammatical features; damage elsewhere affected word production.

These cases indicate that the neural mechanisms of spoken and sign languages are similar. Cerebral injury in these cases affects a mechanism that controls rules for the ordering of symbolic information, whether conveyed by speech or by hand. Deaf patients with damage to the right hemisphere are like hearing patients with the same type of injury: They show impairments in various visuospatial tasks (described later in the chapter), but their signing is appropriate and includes all linguistic categories of expression.

Functional-imaging work shows that both hearing and deaf people activate the same areas of the left hemisphere during language tasks (Neville et al., 1998; Petitto et al., 2000). However, signers also show extensive activation of homologous areas of the right hemisphere. What contribution the right hemisphere makes to sign language, and why damage there does not obviously impair ASL fluency, are questions that remain unanswered.

Dyslexia Is Characterized by Difficulty with Reading

Some students seem to take forever to learn to read. Their efforts are laden with frustration, and prolonged practice produces only small improvements. The inability to read is called **dyslexia** (from the Greek *dys*, "bad," and *lexis*, "word"). Some dyslexic children have a high IQ, sugggesting a specific problem with language rather than a general cognitive deficit. The diagnosis of dyslexia is more common in boys and left-handed people. Some controversy surrounds this syndrome, and its characteristics are probably broader than a reading disorder and encompass other aspects of language dysfunction. Clearly, dyslexia is a fuzzy clinical category, but it has been connected to interesting anatomical and physiological findings (Tallal et al., 1993).

Galaburda (1994) summarized various pathological features in the brains of patients with dyslexia. These postmortem observations analyzed four patients who had died from acute disease or trauma associated with injury that did not involve the brain. All the brains showed striking anomalies in the arrangement of cortical cells, especially in areas of the frontal and temporal cortical regions.

These anomalies consisted of unusual groupings of cells in outer layers of the cerebral cortex that distorted the normal layered arrangements and columnar organization (Figure 19.10). Some cells were disoriented, and excessive cortical folding (**micropolygyria**) was observed. Nests of extra cells, **ectopias,** were seen. The researchers argued that these anomalies of cerebral cortical cell arrangements probably arose quite early, perhaps during the middle of gestation, a period during which active cell migration occurs in cerebral cortex. The result of these deficits might be the production of unusual patterns of connectivity in language-related regions of the temporal cortex.

Atypical asymmetries of a specific region near the Sylvian sulcus within the temporal lobes has been described in boys with impairments of language skills (Plante et al., 1991). Although the anatomical asymmetry of brain language areas is clear (as

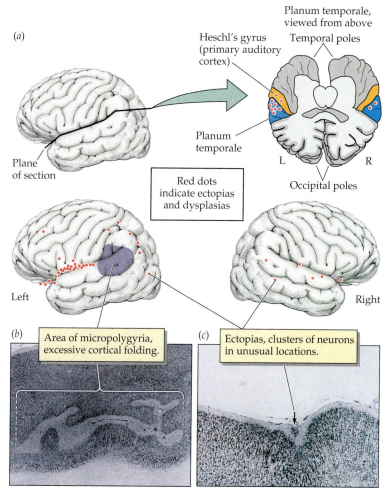

19.10 Neural Disorganization in the Brain of a Patient with Dyslexia

(*a, top*) Drawings of the left and right planum temporale (see Figure 19.16) from the brain of a person suffering from dyslexia show these regions as nearly symmetrical; in most people the left planum temporale is considerably larger. The dots and the shaded area represent regions where microscopic anomalies called *ectopias, dysplasias,* and *micropolygyrias* have been found in the brains of dyslexic individuals. (*a,bottom*) Anomalies in patients with dyslexia are much more common in the left hemisphere, which is primarily responsible for language function. (*b, c*) These micrographs show (*b*) micropolygyria (literally, "many tiny gyri") and (*c*) ectopias, clusters of neurons in unusual locations, such as this cluster in cortical layer I (arrow), which is normally devoid of neuronal cell bodies. (After Galaburda, 1994; micrographs courtesy of Albert Galaburda.)

we'll see later in this chapter), the presence or absence of asymmetry in dyslexic brains (G. D. Rosen et al., 1993) is controversial.

Schultz et al. (1994) caution that age and sex have a potent impact on these data, suggesting that behavioral differences found between those who suffer from dyslexia and those who don't might be due to small age differences in various studies between control and patient populations. The investigators failed to see anatomical distinctions between patients with dyslexia and controls when differences in overall brain size, age, and sex were controlled.

Shaywitz et al. (1998), using fMRI, found that the pattern of brain activation during a reading task was different between patients with dyslexia and controls. Subjects suffering from dyslexia showed relatively little activation of the posterior regions, including Wernicke's area, while showing a relative overactivation of anterior regions. Compared to controls, dyslexics also show less activation of visual cortex (Demb et al., 1998) and a disruption of the spread of activation across the angular gyrus (K. R. sPugh et al., 2000) in response to written words. Perhaps such differences in brain activation will offer a less ambiguous diagnosis of dyslexia. Three different genes, found on three different chromosomes, have been proposed to affect the probability of developmental dyslexia (Fagerheim et al., 1999).

Sometimes people who have not displayed developmental dyslexia suffer from the disorder in adulthood as a result of disease or injury, usually to the left hemisphere. This **acquired dyslexia** (or *alexia*) also tells us about how the brain processes language. One type, known as **deep dyslexia,** is characterized by errors in which patients read a word as another word that is related in meaning; for example, the printed word *cow* is read as *horse.* These patients are also unable to read aloud words that are abstract as opposed to concrete, and they make frequent errors in which they seem to fail to see small differences in words. It's as though they grasp words whole, without noting the details of the letters, so they have a hard time reading nonsense words.

In another acquired dyslexia, **surface dyslexia,** the patient makes different types of errors when reading. These patients can read nonsense words just fine, indicating that they know the rules of which letters make which sounds. But they find it difficult to recognize words where the letter-to-sound rules are irregular; *The Tough Coughs As He Ploughs the Dough* by Dr. Seuss (1987), for example, would confound them. In contrast to patients with deep dyslexia, those with surface dyslexia seem restricted to the details and sounds of letters.

These two syndromes suggest that we have two different brain systems for reading: one focused on the sounds of letters, the other on the meanings of whole words (McCarthy and Warrington, 1990).

Electrical Stimulation Provides Information about the Organization of Language in the Brain

Electrical stimulation of the brain is used to explore language functions of the human cerebral cortex. Subjects in these studies are patients undergoing surgery for the relief of seizures. Electrical stimulation helps neurosurgeons locate—and thus avoid damaging—language-related cortical regions. By observing language interference produced by the electrical stimuli, the surgeon can identify these regions. Patients are given only local anesthesia, so that they can continue to communicate verbally.

Pioneering work by Penfield and Roberts (1959) provided a map of language-related zones of the left hemisphere (Figure 19.11*a*). Pooled data from many patients showed that stimulation anywhere within a large anterior zone stops speech. Other forms of language interference, such as misnaming or impaired repetition of words, were evident from stimulation of both this region and more posterior temporoparietal cortex regions. Electrical stimulation of Broca's area adds other features to the list of effects: Patients were unable to comprehend auditory or visual semantic material. The impairment included the inability to follow oral commands, point to objects, or understand written questions (Schaffler et al., 1993).

George Ojemann and collaborators (summarized in Calvin and Ojemann, 1994) examined the effects of electrical stimulation within a wide extent of cerebral cortex, focusing on the possible compartmentalization of linguistic systems such as naming, reading, speech production, and verbal memory. An interesting example of the effects of cortical stimulation on naming is shown in Figure 19.11*b*, which shows the different loci of naming errors in English and Spanish in a bilingual subject.

Ojemann and Mateer (1979) presented more detailed cortical maps, which reveal several different systems. Stimulation of one system arrests speech and impairs all facial movements. This system, located in the inferior premotor frontal cortex, was regarded as the cortical, final motor pathway for speech. Stimulation of a second system alters sequential facial movements and impairs phoneme identification. This system includes sites in the inferior frontal, temporal, and parietal cortex. A third system is defined by stimulation-induced memory errors: It surrounds the sites of the systems that impair phoneme identification. Reading errors are elicited by stimulation of yet other cortical positions.

Ojemann also noted that stimulation of the thalamus at the time of verbal input increases the accuracy of subsequent recall (as late as 1 week after stimulation). He suggests that a thalamic mechanism specifically modulates the recall of verbal information. This conclusion fits with the description of patient N.A. in Chapter 17, in whom damage to the thalamus impaired verbal memory.

Functional Neuroimaging Portrays the Organization of the Brain for Speech and Language

A series of PET studies, summarized by Posner and Raichle (1994), examined brain activation during different levels of the processing of words. These levels include (1) passive exposure to visually presented words, (2) passive exposure to spoken words, (3) oral repetition of words, and (4) generation of a semantic association to a presented word. The successive levels of these experiments and the accompanying PET scans are presented in Figure 19.12.

Passive viewing of words activates a posterior area within the left hemisphere (Figure 19.12*a*). Passive hearing of words shifts the focus of maximum brain activation to the temporal lobes (Figure 19.12*b*). Repeating the words orally activates the motor cortex of both sides, the supplementary motor cortex, and a portion of the cerebellum and insular cortex (Figure 19.12*c*). During word repetition or reading aloud, activity was relatively absent in Broca's area. But when subjects were required to present a verb that was an appropriate semantic association for a presented noun, language-related regions in the left hemisphere, including Broca's area, were markedly activated (Figure 19.12*d*).

Interestingly, slightly different brain regions are activated when native speakers are reading Italian versus English (Paulesu et al., 2000). Perhaps the reason for this difference is that the sound associated with each letter is very regular in Italian, while in English, a given letter may have a very different sound in one word from the sound it has in another (to repeat the earlier example, compare the sounds of "ough" in *tough, cough,* and *dough*).

Functional brain imaging also suggests that different parts of the brain are used to store the names of different types of objects. Hanna Damasio et al. (1996), using PET scans in neurologically normal people, found that different regions of the left hemisphere (other than Broca's or Wernicke's areas) were activated differentially depending on whether the subjects were asked to name tools, animals, or unique per-

(*a*) Sites where stimulation interferes with speech in monolingual patients

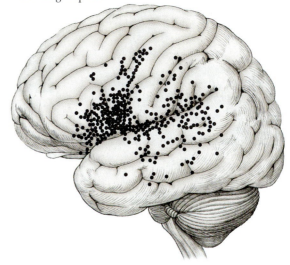

(*b*) Sites where stimulation affects speech in a bilingual patient

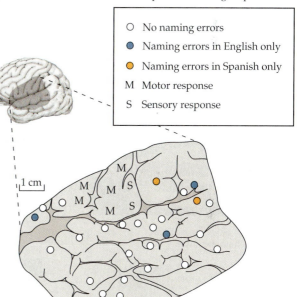

○	No naming errors
●	Naming errors in English only
●	Naming errors in Spanish only
M	Motor response
S	Sensory response

19.11 Electrical Stimulation of Some Brain Sites Can Interfere with Language (*a*) This summary of data obtained from many patients shows the brain sites where stimulation interferes with speech production. (*b*) This map shows stimulation sites that affected the speech of a patient who was bilingual—fluent in Spanish and English. Different regions interfere with either one language or the other, but not both. (Part *a* after Penfield and Roberts, 1959; *b* after Ojemann and Mateer, 1979.)

(*a*) Passively viewing words

(*b*) Listening to words

(*c*) Speaking words

(*d*) Generating a verb associated
with each noun shown

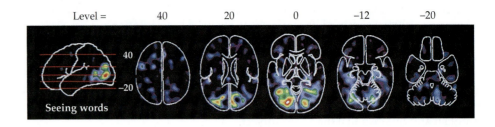

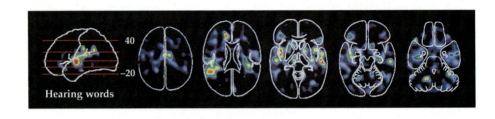

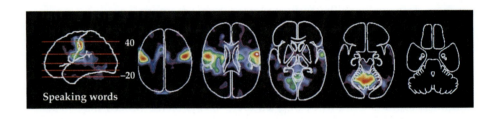

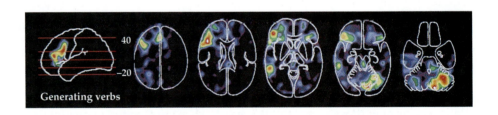

19.12 Subtractive PET Scans of Brain Activation in Progressively More Complex Language Tasks (*Left*) For clarity concerning the tasks, we depict the subjects at a desk, but when the PET scans were made, the subjects reclined with their heads in a PET scanner and viewed a specially mounted display. (*Right*) These PET scans correspond to the tasks at left; see text for details of these results. (After Posner and Raichle, 1994; PET scans courtesy of Marcus Raichle.)

sons. Close scrutiny of stroke patients confirmed the idea: Damage in one area affected recognition of animals but not of tools or people, damage to another area affected recognition of tools but not of the other categories, and so on (Tranel et al., 1997). Later studies in neurologically normal people indicated that word retrieval in these three different categories (tools, animals, people) also activates three different regions in the frontal lobes (Grabowski et al., 1998).

Finally, event-related potentials (ERPs; see Chapter 3) also confirm the activation of different brain regions depending on which aspect of language is being performed. Subjects are asked to read a sentence in which they encounter a word that is grammatically correct but, because of its meaning, doesn't fit. "The man started the car engine and stepped on the pancake." About 400 ms after the patient reads the word "pancake," a negative wave is detected on the scalp (Kutas and Hillyard,

19.13 Children with Williams Syndrome Children with Williams syndrome often have a characteristic facial shape, caused by the loss of a copy of the *elastin* gene. The loss of copies of other nearby genes is thought to cause the mild mental retardation paired with verbal fluency. (Courtesy of the Williams Syndrome Association.)

1980). Such "N400" responses (*N* denotes "negative," and the number represents the response time in milliseconds) to word meanings seem to be centered over the temporal lobe (Neville et al., 1992) and therefore may originate from Wernicke's area. But *grammatically* inappropriate words elicit a positive potential about 600 ms after they are encountered (a P600 response), as though it takes the brain 200 ms longer to detect this level of error (Osterhout et al., 1997).

Williams Syndrome Offers Clues about Language

Williams syndrome, which occurs in approximately 1 out of 20,000 births (Bower, 2000), offers a fascinating dissociation between what we normally regard as intelligence and language. Individuals with **Williams syndrome** speak freely and fluently with a large vocabulary yet may be unable to draw simple images, to arrange colored blocks to match an example, or to tie shoelaces. The individuals are very sociable, ready to strike up conversation and smile. They may also display strong musical talent, either singing or playing an instrument.

The syndrome seems to be caused by the deletion of more than a dozen genes from one of the two chromosomes numbered 7 (de Luis et al., 2000). No one understands why the remaining copies of these genes, on the other chromosome 7, do not compensate for the lost copies. The absence of one copy of the gene called *elastin* (which encodes a protein important for connective tissue in skin and ligaments), leads to elflike facial features (Figure 19.13). Several of the other missing genes are thought to lead to changes in brain development and to the behavioral features of the syndrome.

The psychological development of such individuals is complicated because as infants they may display a greater understanding of numerosity than other infants but show poor grasp of numbers in adulthood. Conversely, their language performance is poor in infancy but greatly improved by adulthood (Paterson et al., 1999). These findings suggest that it is the developmental process that is distinctively altered in Williams syndrome.

The Left Brain Is Different from the Right Brain

By the early twentieth century it was firmly established that the cerebral hemispheres are not equivalent in mediating language functions (Finger, 1994). The left hemisphere seemed to control this function and was commonly described as the dominant hemisphere. However, the right hemisphere does not just sit within the skull awaiting the call to duty when the left side of the brain is injured. In fact, many researchers have slowly drifted from notions of cerebral *dominance* to ideas of hemispheric *specialization,* or **lateralization.** This emphasis implies that some functional systems are connected more to one side of the brain than the other—that is, that functions become lateralized—and that each hemisphere is specialized for particular ways of working.

Lateralization of function is not a surprising idea; a broad look at the distribution of body organs shows considerable asymmetry between the right and left sides. For example, the heart is slightly to the left of the midline and the liver is on the right. This basic asymmetry in body plan is shared by all vertebrates and is genetically programmed. Sometimes a person with a defect in one of the genes involved will develop the reverse pattern (B. Casey and Hackett, 2000). Almost all vertebrates, even toads (Vallortigara et al., 1999), also show preferences for using one limb or the other for particular behaviors.

Nevertheless, at the level of brain processing in normal individuals, the interconnections of the hemispheres ordinarily mask evidence of hemisphere specialization. But by studying patients whose interhemispheric pathways have been disconnected—**split-brain individuals**—researchers have been able to see cerebral hemispheric specialization in cognitive, perceptual, emotional, and motor activities.

Are There Two Minds in One Head?

Starting in the 1930s, a small group of human patients underwent a surgical procedure designed to provide relief from frequent, disabling epileptic seizures (Bogen et al., 1988). In these patients epileptic activity that was initiated in one hemisphere spread to the other hemisphere via the corpus callosum, the large bundle of fibers that connect the two hemispheres. Surgically cutting the corpus callosum appreciably reduces the frequency and severity of such seizures.

Studies at that time seemed to show that this remedy for seizures caused no apparent changes in brain function, as assessed by general behavior tests such as IQ tests. But the human corpus callosum is a huge bundle of more than a million axons, and it seemed strange that the principal connection between the cerebral hemispheres could be cut without producing detectable changes in behavior. The eminent physiological psychologist Karl Lashley, with characteristic sardonic humor, suggested that perhaps the only function of the corpus callosum was to keep the two hemispheres from floating apart in the cerebrospinal fluid. However, subsequent animal research with careful testing revealed deficits in behavior as consequences of hemispheric disconnection.

For example, in one study on cats, both the corpus callosum and the optic chiasm were sectioned, so that each eye was connected only to the hemisphere on its own side. Such cats learned with the left eye that a particular symbol stood for reward but that the inverted symbol did not, while with the right eye they were able to learn the opposite—that the inverted symbol was rewarded rather than the upright symbol. Thus each hemisphere was ignorant of what the other had learned (Sperry et al., 1956).

Beginning in the 1960s, split-brain humans were studied extensively, both pre- and postoperatively, through a series of psychological tests devised by Roger Sperry and colleagues at the California Institute of Technology. In this group of patients, stimuli can be directed to either hemisphere by being presented to different places on the surface of the body. For example, objects the patient feels with the left hand result in activity in nerve cells of the sensory regions in the right hemisphere. Because the corpus callosum is cut in these patients, most of the information sent to one half of the brain cannot travel to the other half. By controlling stimuli in this fashion—selectively presenting them to one hemisphere or the other—the experimenter can test the capabilities of each hemisphere.

In some of Sperry's studies, words were projected to either the left or the right hemisphere; that is, visual stimuli were presented in either the right or the left side

(*a*) Normal individual

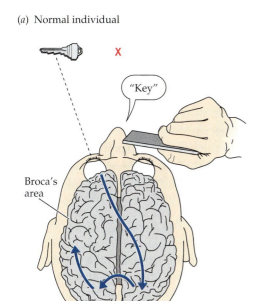

(*b*) Split-brain individual; object in left visual field

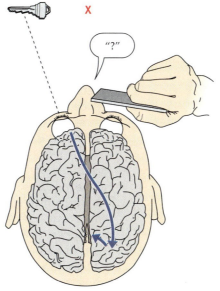

Split-brain individual; object in right visual field

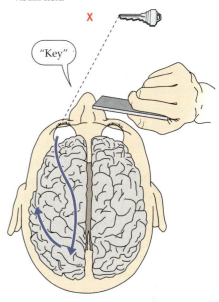

19.14 Testing of a Split-Brain Individual Words or pictures projected to the left visual field activate the right visual cortex. (*a*) In normal individuals, activation of the right visual cortex excites corpus callosum fibers, which transmit verbal information to the left hemisphere, where the information is analyzed and language is produced. (*b*) In split-brain patients, the severing of callosal connections prevents language production in response to stimuli in the left visual field (*left*). However, split-brain individuals are able to respond verbally to stimuli in the right visual field (*right*).

of the visual field. Split-brain subjects can easily read and verbally communicate words projected to the left hemisphere, but no such linguistic capabilities were evident when the information was directed to the right hemisphere (Figure 19.14). Zaidel (1976) showed that the right hemisphere has a small amount of linguistic ability; for example, it can recognize simple words. In general, however, the vocabulary and grammatical capabilities of the right hemisphere are far less developed than they are in the left hemisphere.

Sperry's findings not only confirmed the animal research, but they were more dramatic because they showed that only the processes taking place in the left hemisphere could be described verbally by the patients. Thus in most people the left hemisphere possesses language and speech mechanisms. For our discussion here, the important result is that each hemisphere by itself can process and store information without any participation by the other hemisphere.

The ability of the "mute" right hemisphere was tested by nonverbal means. For example, a picture of a key might be projected to the left visual field and so reach only the right visual cortex. The subject would then be asked to touch several different objects that she could not see and hold up the correct one. Such a task could be performed correctly by the left hand (controlled by the right hemisphere) but not by the right hand (controlled by the left hemisphere). In such a patient, the left hemisphere literally does not know what the left hand is doing.

Whereas the left hemisphere controls speech, the right hemisphere seems to be somewhat better at processing spatial information, especially if the response is manual rather than simple recognition of a correct visual pattern.

The Two Hemispheres Process Information Differently in Normal Humans

Almost all the research concerning differences between the hemispheres in the processing of information has concentrated on two modalities: hearing and vision. In each modality, psychologists can detect differences in behavioral response to confirm that, in most people, the left cerebral hemisphere has specialized to process language.

The right-ear advantage. Through earphones, we can present different sounds to each ear at the same time; this process is called the **dichotic listening technique.** The subject hears a particular speech sound in one ear and, at the same time, a different vowel, consonant, or word in the other ear. The task for the subject is to identify or recall these sounds.

Although this technique may seem to be a program designed to produce confusion, in general, data from dichotic listening experiments indicate that right-handed persons identify verbal stimuli delivered to the right ear more accurately than stimuli presented simultaneously to the left ear. This result is described as a right-ear "advantage" for verbal information. In contrast, about 50% of left-handed individuals reveal a reverse pattern, showing a left-ear advantage—more accurate performance for verbal stimuli delivered to the left ear.

Doreen Kimura argues that auditory information exerts stronger neural effects on the opposite side than on the same side (Figure 19.15). That is, auditory stimuli presented to the right ear produce stronger effects on the left auditory cortex than on the right auditory cortex, and vice versa. Thus whereas sounds presented to the right ear exert stronger control over language mechanisms in the left hemisphere, speech sounds presented to the left ear are less potent in activating language-processing regions in the left cerebral hemisphere (Kimura, 1973). Several studies have shown that the right-ear advantage for speech sounds in right-handed individuals is restricted to particular kinds of speech sounds (Tallal and Schwartz, 1980). The right-ear advantage is evident with simultaneously presented consonants such as *b, d, t,* and *k,* but not with vowel sounds.

Visual perception of linguistic stimuli. We can study hemispheric specialization in normal humans by briefly exposing visual half-fields to stimuli (see Figures 10.13 and 19.14). If the stimulus exposure lasts less than 100 to 150 ms, input can be restricted to one hemisphere because this amount of time is not sufficient for the eyes to shift their direction. Of course, in intact humans further processing may involve the transmission of information through the corpus callosum to the other hemisphere.

Most studies show that verbal stimuli (words and letters) presented to the right visual field (going to the left hemisphere) are better recognized than the same input presented to the left visual field (going to the right hemisphere). On the other hand, nonverbal visual stimuli (such as faces) presented to the left visual field are better recognized than the same stimuli presented to the right visual field. Simpler visual processing, such as detection of light, hue, or simple patterns, is equivalent in the two hemispheres. But for more complex materials, in vision as well as audition, most verbal stimuli are processed better in the left hemisphere of most individuals.

Does the Left Hemisphere Hear Words and the Right Hemisphere Hear Music?

The left and right auditory cortical areas appear to play somewhat different roles in human perception of speech and music. An early clue to this difference came from a study of the anatomy of the temporal lobes in adults (Geschwind and Levitsky, 1968); in 65% of the brains examined, the upper surface of the lobe—a region known

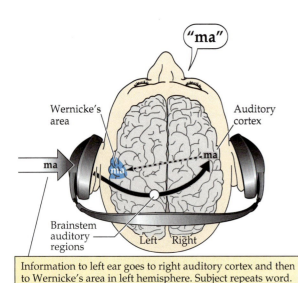

Information to left ear goes to right auditory cortex and then to Wernicke's area in left hemisphere. Subject repeats word.

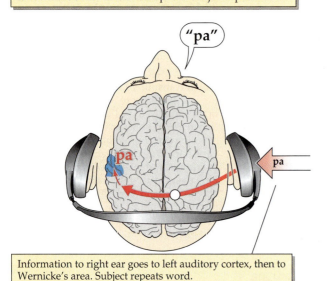

Information to right ear goes to left auditory cortex, then to Wernicke's area. Subject repeats word.

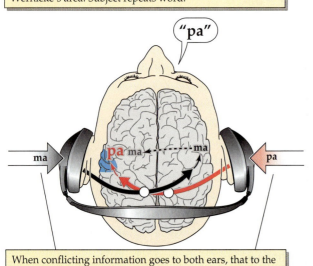

When conflicting information goes to both ears, that to the right ear reaches Wernicke's area first. Subject repeats only the right ear information.

19.15 Kimura's Model of the Right-Ear Advantage (*a*) A word delivered to the left ear results in stronger stimulation of the right auditory cortex. (*b*) A word delivered to the right ear results in stronger input to the left hemisphere. (*c*) When words are delivered to both ears simultaneously, the one to the right ear is the one usually perceived because the right ear has more direct connections to the left hemisphere. (After Kimura, 1973.)

as the **planum temporale**—was larger in the left hemisphere than in the right (Figure 19.16b). In only 11% of adults was the right side larger. The region examined includes part of the area known as *Wernicke's area*; damage to this area impairs the perception of speech. Perhaps the difference in size of this region between the two hemispheres reflects the left hemisphere dominance.

We saw earlier that left hemisphere dominance for speech is less common in left-handed people than in right-handed people, and MRI studies show that the asymmetry of the planum temporale is also reduced in left-handed people (Steinmetz et al., 1991), reinforcing the idea that the planum temporale is involved in speech. The difference in size of the planum temporale is even more evident in newborns than in adults; it appeared in 86% of the infant brains examined. This size difference develops in about the thirtieth week of gestation (Witelson and Pallie, 1973).

This evidence suggests an innate basis for cerebral specialization for language and speech perception because the asymmetry is established before any experience with speech. The planum temporale of chimpanzees also tends to be larger on the left (Gannon et al., 1998), suggesting that either the asymmetry of this region preceded its involvement in language, or chimpanzees already possess a precursor to language, as we discussed at the start of this chapter.

In the case of music, studies indicate a major role for the auditory areas of the right hemisphere. These studies show that musical perception is impaired particularly by damage to the right hemisphere (Samson and Zatorre, 1994) and that music activates the right hemisphere more than the left (Zatorre et al., 1994). But perfect pitch (the ability to identify any musical note without comparing it to a reference note) seems to involve the left rather than the right hemisphere.

Schlaug et al. (1995) made MRI measurements of the planum temporale in three kinds of subjects, all right-handed (because the larger size of the left planum temporale is seen especially in right-handed individuals): (1) musicians with perfect pitch, (2) musicians without perfect pitch, and (3) nonmusicians. The size of the left planum temporale was twice as large in musicians with perfect pitch than in nonmusicians (see Figure 9.16c). The size of the left planum temporale in musicians without perfect pitch was intermediate, but closer to that of nonmusicians. Because perfect pitch requires both verbal ability (to name the pitch) and musical ability, perhaps it is not surprising to find that, like language, it is associated with the left hemisphere.

Despite these data, we cannot assign the perception of speech and pitch entirely to the left hemisphere and the perception of music entirely to the right hemisphere. We have seen that the right hemisphere can play a role in speech perception even in people in whom the left hemisphere is speech-dominant. Furthermore, although damage to the right hemisphere

Doreen Kimura

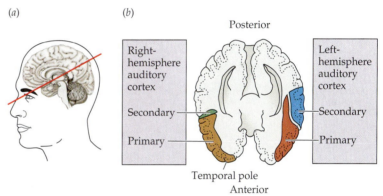

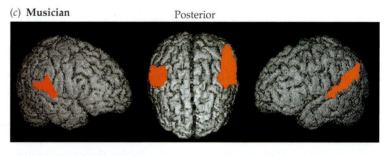

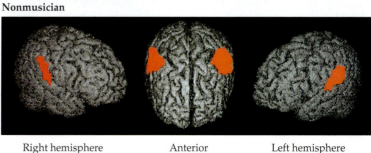

19.16 Structural Asymmetry of the Human Planum Temporale (a) This diagram shows the orientation of the brain section in part b. (b) The planum temporale (green and blue) is on the upper surface of the human temporal lobe. (c) MRI images from the brain of a musician with perfect pitch (*top*) and the brain of a nonmusician (*bottom*) show some difference: In the musician, the left planum temporale is larger. (After Schlaug et al., 1995; c courtesy of Gottfried Schlaug.)

can impair the perception of music, it does not abolish it. Damage to *both* sides of the brain can completely wipe out musical perception (Samson and Zatorre, 1991). Thus even though each hemisphere plays a greater role than the other in different kinds of auditory perception, the two hemispheres appear to collaborate in these as well as in many other functions.

Are Left-Handed People Different?

Anthropologists speculate that the predominance of right-handedness goes back a long time into prehistory. People portrayed in cave paintings held things in their right hand, and Stone Age tools seem to be shaped for the right hand. Skull fractures of animals preyed on by ancient humans are usually on the animal's left side, so anthropologists conclude that most attackers held an implement in the right hand.

Throughout history many unusual attributes have been ascribed to the left-handed person—from an evil personality to an "abnormal" cortical organization of language. (Indeed, the term *sinistral*, which means "left-handed," comes from the same Latin root as the word *sinister*.) Left-handed people make up a small percentage of human populations. A figure of around 10% is commonly reported, although this percentage may be lower in parts of the world where teachers actively discourage left-handedness. For example, there is a higher percentage of left-handed Chinese-Americans in U.S. schools, which are generally more tolerant of left-handedness, than among Chinese in China. Surveys of left-handed writing in American college populations reveal an incidence of 13.8% (Spiegler and Yeni-Komshian, 1983). This percentage is viewed as a dramatic increase over prior generations, perhaps reflecting a continuing decline in the social pressures toward right-handedness and an increase in the acceptability of left-handedness. Interestingly, other primates also show a preference for using the right hand (Westergaard et al., 1998).

Hardyck et al. (1976) examined more than 7000 children in grades 1 through 6 for school achievement, intellectual ability, motivation, socioeconomic level, and the like. A detailed analysis showed that left-handed children do not differ from right-handed children on any measure of cognitive performance. However, the idea that left-handed people are "damaged" humans has been common in the past and has even found occasional support in research.

D. A. Silva and Satz (1979) note that several studies show a higher incidence of left-handedness in clinical populations than in the general population. They examined handedness in more than 1400 patients in a school for the mentally retarded and showed an incidence of 17.8% left-handedness, nearly twice the level in the general population. In this population, more left-handers than right-handers had abnormal EEGs. Investigators have suggested that brain injury explains the high rate of left-handedness in this population. Early brain injury, these investigators argue, can cause a shift in handedness. Because most people are right-handed, early one-sided brain injury is more likely to effect a change from right-handedness to left-handedness than the reverse.

Many Theories Attempt to Explain the Evolutionary Origins of Hemispheric Asymmetry and Specialization

Some scientists believe that hemispheric specialization originated in the differential use of the limbs for many routine tasks. Picture early humans hunting. One hand holds the weapon and provides power; the other is used in more delicate guidance or body balance. In time the evolutionary successes offered by handedness might have been used in the emergence of language and speech.

Some theories about the emergence of speech and language focus on the motor aspects of speech, others on the cognitive properties of language. The speech motor apparatus involves many delicate muscle systems situated in the midline of the body, such as the tip of the tongue. Sensitivity and precision of stimulus analysis on the body surface are reduced in the exact midline. Perhaps this result reflects the mutual antagonism of right and left axon terminals in the skin. For speech this pe-

TABLE 19.2 *Proposed Cognitive Modes of the Two Cerebral Hemispheres in Humans*

Left hemisphere	Right hemisphere
Phonetic	Nonlinguistic
Sequential	Holistic
Analytical	Synthetic
Propositional	Gestalt
Discrete temporal analysis	Form perception
Language	Spatial

culiarity of the midline would be catastrophic for precise control. Asymmetry of motor control of speech production might then offer unchallenged control of relevant parts of the speech apparatus. Such sidedness in the motor production of sound is seen even in the control of singing in birds, as we discussed earlier.

Arguments that propose a fundamental difference in cognitive style between the hemispheres suggest other connections to language and evolutionary advantages of cerebral specialization. According to this view, the left hemisphere provides processing that is analytical, and the right hemisphere offers a more holistic or general analysis of information (Table 19.2). Some theorists suggest that hemisphere specialization allows for separate cognitive modes that are mutually incompatible (Ivry and Robertson, 1998). But the notion, now common among the public, that the two hemispheres are so different that they need separate instruction, is not supported by the data. For example, although the left hand draws better than the right hand after commissurotomy, neither hand draws as well as before the surgery.

EVOLUTION AT WORK

The Frontal Lobes of Humans Are Related to Higher-Order Aspects of Cognitive and Emotional Functions

Because the complexity of human beings far exceeds that of other animals, researchers have sought characteristics of the brain that might account for human preeminence. As we noted in Chapter 6, among the most striking differences is the comparatively large size of the human prefrontal cortex. In part because of its size, the frontal region has been regarded as the seat of intelligence and abstract thinking. Adding to the mystery of frontal lobe function is the unusual assortment of behavioral changes that follows surgical or accidental lesions of this region.

The boundaries of the frontal lobes are not precisely defined, but the human frontal cortex occupies almost one-third of the entire cerebral cortical surface. At the posterior portion the frontal cortex includes motor and premotor regions (see Chapter 11). The anterior part is often referred to as **prefrontal cortex,** which is a critical component of a widespread neuronal network, with extensive linkages throughout the brain (Fuster, 1990; Mega and Cummings, 1994). The prefrontal cortex is further subdivided into a *dorsolateral* region and an *orbitofrontal* region (Figure 19.17a). In other animals the frontal cortex, especially prefrontal regions, is a smaller portion of the cerebral cortex (Figure 19.17b).

The study of prefrontal cortical function in animals began with the work of Carlyle Jacobsen in the 1930s. In his experiments with chimpanzees, Jacobsen employed delayed-response learning. The animals were shown where food was hidden, but they had to wait before being allowed to reach for it. This simple test situation revealed a remarkable impairment in chimpanzees with prefrontal lesions: These animals performed this task very poorly, in contrast with animals that sustained lesions in other brain regions. In interpreting this phenomenon, Jacobsen emphasized the memory function of the frontal cortex. However, in light of the effects of prefrontal damage in humans, which we take up next, it seems more likely that the

(a) The prefrontal cortex in humans

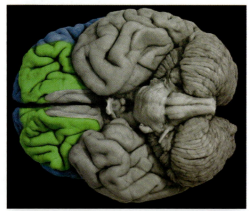

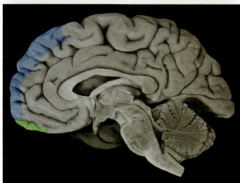

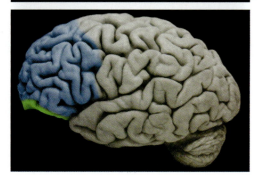

(b) Relative prefrontal cortex size in several mammals

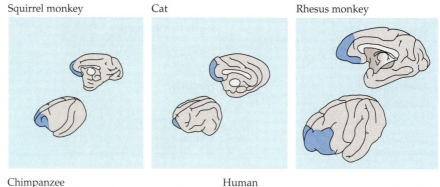

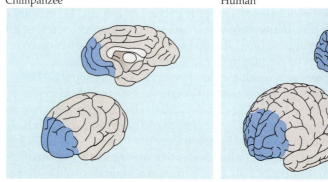

19.17 The Prefrontal Cortex (a) The human prefrontal cortex can be subdivided into a dorsolateral region (blue) and an orbitofrontal region (green). Lesions in these different areas of prefrontal cortex have different effects on behavior. (b) The relative percentage of prefrontal cortex is greatest in humans and decreases successively in other primates, carnivores, and rodents (not shown). The brains here are drawn to different scales. (Photographs courtesy of S. Mark Williams and Dale Purves, Duke University Medical Center.)

chimpanzees were unable to direct their attention properly and/or to formulate a plan of which hiding place to examine when the time came.

Frontal Lobe Injury in Humans Leads to Emotional, Motor, and Cognitive Changes

The complexity of change following prefrontal damage is epitomized by the classic case of Phineas Gage. In 1848, Mr. Gage accidentally exploded gunpowder that sent an iron rod through his skull, producing a massive lesion of the prefrontal cortex. Sober and reliable before his accident, Gage became moody and uninhibited afterward, unconcerned about other people's reactions or the future consequences of his behavior.

The last sentence of the physician's report reads, "His mind was radically changed, so decidedly that his friends and acquaintances said that he was 'no longer Gage.'" Attempts to account for Gage's syndrome in neurological terms have undergone successive changes. In the latter part of the nineteenth century, neurologists began to realize that the bases of speech and motor behavior are localized in specific brain regions, but they were still reluctant to believe that moral reasoning and social behavior have localized neural mechanisms. We'll soon see, however, that Gage's symptoms are indeed related to damage to specific brain regions.

Now, a century and a half after Phineas Gage's accident, measurement of his skull and modern imaging techniques indicate that his injury was probably confined to the orbitofrontal region of both frontal lobes, sparing the dorsolateral region (Figure

19.18). Having made these measurements, Hanna Damasio and Antonio Damasio and colleagues searched their extensive roster of neurological cases and found that Gage's syndrome matches that of several other patients with known brain damage in the region of Gage's probable injury (H. Damasio et al., 1994).

The clinical portrait of humans with frontal lesions reveals an unusual collection of emotional, motor, and cognitive changes. The emotional reactivity of these patients shows a persistent strange apathy, broken by bouts of euphoria (an exalted sense of well-being). Ordinary social conventions are readily cast aside by impulsive activity. Concern for the past or the future is rarely evident (J. D. Duffy and Campbell, 1994; Petrides and Milner, 1982). Frontal patients show shallow emotions, even including reduced responsiveness to pain. Frequently, though, they exhibit episodes in which this apathy is replaced by boastfulness and silliness and, sometimes, unbridled sexual activity. Standard IQ test performance shows only slight changes after injury or stroke. Forgetfulness is shown in many tasks requiring sustained attention. In fact, some of these patients even forget their own warnings to "remember."

Clinical examination of patients with frontal lesions also reveals an array of strange impairments in motor activities, especially in the realm of "plans" for action. The patients seem to **perseverate** (continue beyond a reasonable degree) in any activity. For example, if the patient is asked to open and then close the fist, once the activity has begun—and it is difficult to initiate such acts in patients with frontal lesions—the patient continues a persistent sequence of fist opening and closing. The overall level of motor activity—especially ordinary, spontaneous movements—is quite diminished in these patients. For example, facial expression becomes blank, and head and eye movements are markedly reduced. Some reflexes that are evident only very early in life, such as the infantile grasp reflex of the hand, reappear in frontal cases.

Many clinical assessments of these patients have emphasized an impairment in goal-directed behavior, especially an inability to plan acts and use foresight. Daily activities of these patients seem disorganized and without a clear program for successive activities. Table 19.3 lists the main clinical features of patients with lesions of various portions of the frontal lobes.

Lhermitte et al. (1986) described an unusual phenomenon in patients with damaged frontal lobes—a syndrome characterized by spontaneous imitation of the gestures and behavior of the examiner. Lhermitte et al. saw this syndrome as related to one they identified as *utilization behavior,* defined as an exaggerated dependence on the environment for behavioral cues. The syndrome was observed during clinical exams in which the examiner made body gestures or engaged in writing or handling of objects. All patients with disease involving the frontal lobes spontaneously imitated the gestures of the examiner in detail. Patients were aware of their imitative behavior.

The extraordinary environmental dependency of the behavior of patients with damaged frontal lobes was also evident in complex social situations. In a doctor's office, one patient saw a blood pressure gauge and immediately took the physician's blood pressure. After eyeing a tongue depressor, she placed it in front of the doctor's mouth. Upon walking into a bedroom, one patient proceeded to get undressed and go to bed. He hurried out of bed when the examiner picked up a piece of his clothing. In these acts there is a certain mechanical character; Lhermitte describes these patients as powerless in the face of influences from the outside world. The loss

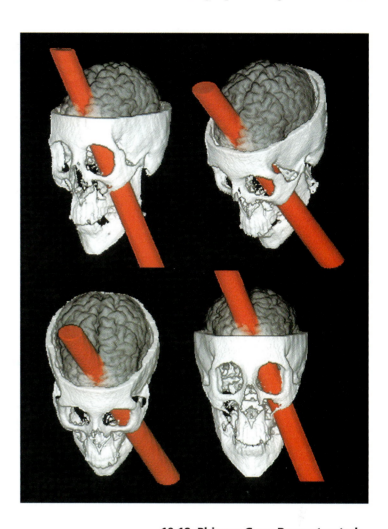

19.18 Phineas Gage Reconstructed
This computer reconstruction, based on measurements of Phineas Gage's skull, shows, from several different perspectives, the brain areas that are most likely to have been damaged in his famous accident. The red cylinder shows the path of the tamping iron, which entered the skull below the left eye and exited through the top of the head, severely damaging both frontal lobes. (From H. Damasio et al., 1994; courtesy of Hanna Damasio.)

Hanna Damasio

TABLE 19.3 *Core Characteristics of the Regional Prefrontal Syndromes*

Dysexecutive type (dorsolateral)	Disinhibited type (orbitofrontal)	Apathetic type (mediofrontal)
Diminished judgment, planning, insight, and temporal organization	Stimulus-driven behavior	Diminished spontaneity
Cognitive impersistence	Diminished social insight	Diminished verbal output (including mutism)
Motor programming deficits (possibly including aphasia and apraxia)	Distractibility	Diminished motor behavior (including akinesis)
Diminished self-care	Emotional lability	Urinary incontinence
		Lower-extremity weakness and sensory loss
		Diminished spontaneous prosody
		Increased response latency

of self-criticism is another aspect of the behavior of these patients, as is evident in the act of calmly urinating against a public building in plain view.

Deficits in Spatial Perception Follow Some Types of Brain Injury

CLINICAL ISSUE

Injury to the parietal lobe produces impairments such as these: Faces cannot be recognized from photographs. Spatial orientation can become severely disturbed. Objects placed in the hand cannot be recognized by touch alone. One side of the body may be completely neglected, even to the point of being rejected as one's own.

The diversity of behavioral changes following injury to the parietal lobe is related partly to its large expanse and its critical position adjacent to occipital, temporal, and frontal regions. The anterior end of the parietal region includes the postcentral gyrus, which is the primary cortical receiving area for somatic sensation. Brain injury in this area does not produce numbness; rather, it produces sensory deficits on the opposite side that seem to involve complex sensory processing. For example, objects placed in the hand opposite the injured somatosensory area can be felt but cannot be identified by touch and active manipulation. This deficit is called **astereognosis** (from the Greek *a-*, "not"; *stereos*, "solid"; and *gnosis*, "knowledge").

More extensive injuries in the parietal cortex, not restricted to the somatosensory cortex, affect interactions between or among sensory modalities, such as visual or tactile matching tasks, which require the subject to identify visually an object that is touched or to reach for an object that is identified visually.

In Prosopagnosia, a Face Is No Longer a Face

Suppose one day you look in the mirror and you see someone who is not familiar to you. As incredible as this scenario might seem, some individuals do suffer this fate after brain damage. This rare syndrome is called **prosopagnosia** (from the Greek *prosop-*, "face"; *a-*, "not"; and *gnosis*, "knowledge"). Such patients fail to recognize not only their own faces but also the faces of relatives and friends. No amount of remedial training restores their ability to recognize anyone's face. In contrast, the ability to recognize *objects* may be retained, and the patient readily identifies familiar people by the sounds of their voices.

Faces simply lack meaning in the patient's life. No disorientation or confusion accompanies this condition. There is no evidence of diminished intellectual abilities. Visual acuity is maintained, although most patients have a small visual-field defect—that is, an area of the visual field where they are "blind." Most research indicates that lesions of the right hemisphere cause prosopagnosia. For example, using the Wada test (see Box 19.1) to anesthetize the right hemisphere causes patients to mistake famous faces for their own, while anesthetizing the left hemisphere has

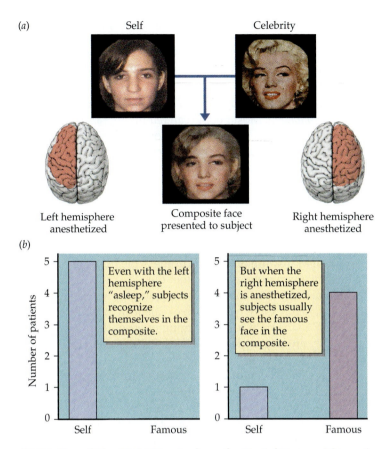

(a)

Self   Celebrity

Left hemisphere anesthetized   Composite face presented to subject   Right hemisphere anesthetized

(b)

Even with the left hemisphere "asleep," subjects recognize themselves in the composite.

But when the right hemisphere is anesthetized, subjects usually see the famous face in the composite.

Number of patients

Self   Famous   Self   Famous

19.19 Use of the Right Hemisphere for Facial Recognition Anesthetizing the left hemisphere in a Wada test does not interfere with a subject's ability to recognize his own face in a picture "morphed" from his face and that of a celebrity. But when the right hemisphere is anesthetized, the subject interprets the morphed face as that of the celebrity. (From Keenan et al., 2001; courtesy of Julian Keenan.)

no effect on facial recognition (Figure 19.19). Still, Tranel and Damasio (1985) suggest that *bilateral* lesions, usually at the junction of the parietal, temporal, and occipital lobes, are necessary for the full syndrome to appear.

Prosopagnosia often involves other perceptual categories besides faces (Gauthier et al., 1999). Some patients suffering from prosopagnosia cannot recognize their own cars and do not recognize common makes of cars in general, although they can distinguish between cars and trucks. Bird-watchers are no longer able to recognize distinctive birds. Thus the deficit seems to be in identifying a particular instance from a large category where all cases have many things in common.

PET studies indicate that different patterns of brain activation are seen in normal subjects depending on whether they are distinguishing the gender of a face, recognizing a new face, or recognizing a familiar face (Andreasen et al., 1996), which suggests that there are three different systems subserving these different attributes.

Neglect of One Side of the Body and Space Can Result from Parietal Lobe Injury

Brain damage involving the right inferior parietal cortex produces an unusual set of behavioral changes (Rafal, 1994). The key feature is neglect of the left side of both the body and space. A patient may fail to dress the left side of her body and may even disclaim "ownership" of her left arm or leg.

In some instances familiar people presented on the left side of the patient are completely neglected, although no visual-field defect is apparent. This phenomenon, called

Model   Patient's copy

19.20 Diagnostic Test for Hemispatial Neglect When asked to duplicate drawings of common, symmetrical objects, patients suffering from hemispatial neglect ignore the left side of the model they are copying. (From Kolb and Whishaw, 1990.)

hemispatial neglect, can also be seen in simple test situations. A common test requires the patient to copy drawings of familiar objects. In a typical result, a patient who is asked to draw the face of a clock, for example, draws numbers only on the right side of the clock face (Figure 19.20) (Schenkerberg et al., 1980).

Associated with this dramatic change is a feature called *extinction of simultaneous double stimulation.* Most people can readily report the presence of two stimuli when presented simultaneously on both sides of the body. Patients with right inferior parietal lesions, however, are unable to note the double nature of the stimulation and usually report only the stimulus presented to the right side. This syndrome extends to visual imagery as well; when dreaming, for example, these patients scan only one side of dream scenes (Doricchi et al., 1991). Although many patients with injury to this region show recovery from unilateral neglect, the feature of extinction is quite persistent.

Yet another dramatic feature of this syndrome is the frequent denial of illness. Patients may adamantly maintain that they are capable of engaging in their customary activities and do not recognize the impressive signs of unilateral neglect. Remarkably, having these patients wear prisms to shift their visual field 10° to the right for a few minutes eases their symptoms: For a few hours they are less neglectful of the left visual field (Rossetti et al., 1998).

Many hypotheses have been offered to account for these symptoms. Some investigators have regarded the disorder as a consequence of loss of the ability to analyze spatial patterns; this hypothesis is consistent with the fact that unilateral neglect occurs with lesions of the right hemisphere but not with lesions of the left hemisphere. Others regard the syndrome as an attentional deficit. The neurologist Marek-Marsel Mesulam (1985) noted that recordings of single cells from posterior parietal cortex in monkeys show firing patterns that are sensitive to manipulations of attention. For example, some nerve cells in this area increase their discharge rates when the animal's eyes follow or track a meaningful object—frequently one that has been associated with reward.

Following Some Injuries, the Brain Can Recover Function

The course of behavior following brain injury often reveals conspicuous changes. Striking examples of language recovery following stroke have been observed in many adults. Amazing examples of language recovery have been described in children following the removal of a diseased cerebral hemisphere. Many theories are offered to describe the mechanisms mediating the **recovery of function** after lesions.

CLINICAL ISSUE

In spite of these encouraging developments, prevention is clearly better than the cure. Motor vehicle accidents, horseback riding, diving, and contact sports such as boxing are major causes of injuries to the brain and spinal cord. Box 19.2 describes the devastating effects of boxing on the brain.

Different Strategies Aim to Reduce Brain Damage Following Injury or Stroke

Most strokes are caused by a blood clot that blocks a blood vessel, cutting off the supply of oxygen and glucose to a brain region. In a minority of cases, the loss of blood flow to a brain region is caused by the rupture of a blood vessel. In either case, brain cells begin to die. At present, we don't know how to induce the adult brain to produce new neurons to replace those that die, so an important consideration in the management of stroke is to try to prevent as much neuronal death as possible.

One obvious strategy is to try to unblock the blood vessel as soon as possible, and various thrombolytics (literally "clot dissolvers"; from the Greek *thrombos,* "clot," and *lytikos,* "able to loosen") have been shown to be effective in restoring circulation. There is a growing consensus that part of the neuronal death following stroke

BOX 19.2 *A Sport That Destroys the Mind*

Boxing has a long history, much of it unpleasant. In ancient Greece and Rome, some boxers were admired for their courage and strength, but others, wearing leather wrappings studded with metal nuggets, bludgeoned each other to death for the entertainment of spectators. Although rules were developed during the eighteenth century in England, including the use of padded gloves, the goal of prizefighting has always been not to display grace and agility, but to knock the opponent out. A bout usually ends when one fighter has sustained a brief loss of consciousness.

To achieve that goal, boxers aim relentlessly at the head, which sustains blow after blow. The result of so many blows to the head has been called **dementia pugilistica** (the Latin *pugil* means "boxer"), a fancy term for the mental state commonly known as *punch-drunk* (Erlanger et al., 1999). Punch-drunk boxers have markedly impaired cognitive abilities. Even a boxer as formerly loquacious (and tal-

ented at dodging blows) as Muhammad Ali is, today, unable to utter more than a word or two at a time. Deaths in the ring are usually due to brain injuries, especially brain hemorrhage (Ryan, 1998). Several professional societies, as well as various medical and neurological societies, have urged the banning of this sport.

Brain scans indicate that very few boxers escape unscathed. Casson et al. (1982) studied ten active professional boxers who had been knocked out. The group included those of championship caliber, as well as mediocre or poor boxers. None of the knockouts sustained by the fighters involved a loss of consciousness lasting more than 10 s. Yet at least five of the group had definitely abnormal CT scans. The abnormalities included mild generalized cortical atrophy, which in some cases included ventricular dilation. Only one boxer had a clearly normal brain picture. The age of the boxers was not related to the degree of cortical atrophy.

The most successful boxers were the ones with the most profound cortical atrophy. In fact, the total number of professional fights correlated directly with the magnitude of brain changes. During a career of boxing, a fighter accumulates many blows to the head; the most "successful" boxers thus frequently sustain the most punishment (A. H. Roberts, 1969) because they participate in more matches. A Parkinson's-like syndrome of tremors or paralysis may result from boxing. A large-scale CT study of 338 active boxers showed that scans were abnormal in 7% (brain atrophy) and borderline in 12% (B. D. Jordan et al., 1992).

Amateur soccer players may also suffer mild concussions, in their case from hitting the ball with their head, because they show slightly impaired memory and planning ability (Matser et al., 1999). But only in boxing is head trauma an explicit goal—no small reason that many believe boxing is a sport whose time has passed.

---

is caused by neurons being overly excited, producing too many action potentials, leading to death (J.-M. Lee et al., 1999; Rossi et al., 2000). Thus new treatment strategies are being developed to suppress this excitotoxicity (Figure 19.21).

Some Recovery from Brain Injury Follows Relief from Generalized Physiological Abnormalities

Any brain injury destroys particular collections of nerve cells and produces more generalized disturbances that temporarily affect the responsiveness of other nerve cells. In the region of a brain injury, for example, frequently the properties of the blood–brain barrier change. Some researchers have suggested that the time course of functional deficits following structural damage to nerve cells reflects the inhibitory impact of blood-borne substances that ordinarily are prevented from reaching the environment of nerve cells (Seil et al., 1976). In time, the changes in the blood vessels around a site of injury reestablish the blood–brain barrier and increase blood flow to transiently distressed but intact tissue.

In addition, the brain tissue around the site of the stroke usually swells, as a result of **edema,** the buildup of intracellular fluid. The pressure from this swelling can mechanically damage nearby brain tissue, so physicians may administer drugs, such as glucocorticoids, to inhibit swelling. In cases of brain injury, a neurosurgeon may need to open the skull to relieve the brain from damaging pressure buildup within the skull. As recovery proceeds, the edema subsides and neurons that had been inhibited (but not killed) by the swelling resume function.

The anatomist Constantin von Monakow (1914) coined the term **diaschisis** to describe the distant inhibitory effects of brain lesions that seemed to be reversible. With time, usage of this term has expanded to include a host of potentially reversible, nonspecific effects that make the immediate consequences of a brain lesion more intense than the persistent deficits.

Constantin von Monakow (1853–1930)

Sequence of damaging events with stroke:

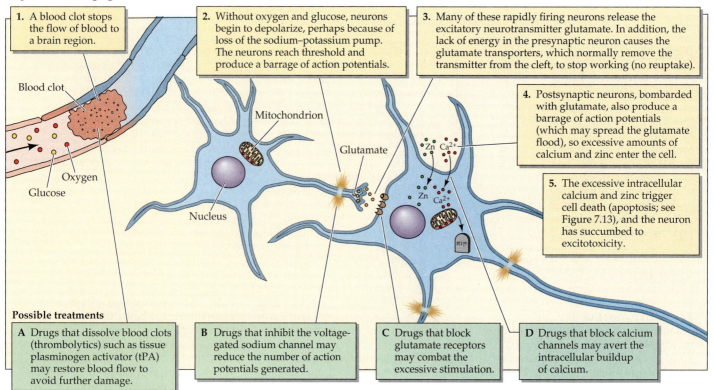

1. A blood clot stops the flow of blood to a brain region.

2. Without oxygen and glucose, neurons begin to depolarize, perhaps because of loss of the sodium–potassium pump. The neurons reach threshold and produce a barrage of action potentials.

3. Many of these rapidly firing neurons release the excitatory neurotransmitter glutamate. In addition, the lack of energy in the presynaptic neuron causes the glutamate transporters, which normally remove the transmitter from the cleft, to stop working (no reuptake).

4. Postsynaptic neurons, bombarded with glutamate, also produce a barrage of action potentials (which may spread the glutamate flood), so excessive amounts of calcium and zinc enter the cell.

5. The excessive intracellular calcium and zinc trigger cell death (apoptosis; see Figure 7.13), and the neuron has succumbed to excitotoxicity.

Blood clot

Oxygen

Glucose

Mitochondrion

Nucleus

Glutamate

Zn Ca^{2+}

Zn Ca^{2+}

Possible treatments

A Drugs that dissolve blood clots (thrombolytics) such as tissue plasminogen activator (tPA) may restore blood flow to avoid further damage.

B Drugs that inhibit the voltage-gated sodium channel may reduce the number of action potentials generated.

C Drugs that block glutamate receptors may combat the excessive stimulation.

D Drugs that block calcium channels may avert the intracellular buildup of calcium.

19.21 Strategies for Minimizing Brain Damage following Stroke or Injury

Slowly Developing and Rapidly Developing Brain Lesions Have Different Effects

The impairment caused by a brain lesion increases with the rate at which the lesion develops. Some investigators refer to this phenomenon as **lesion momentum,** or mass × velocity (Finger, 1978). A lesion in the brainstem that incapacitates animals when made all at one time may have only slight effect if done in two successive stages. The partial lesion may stimulate regrowth or relearning or both, so that some compensation has already been achieved by the time the rest of the tissue is removed.

Experimental findings suggest a mechanism for the staged-lesion effect: A lesion that causes loss of synaptic connections may result in the release of chemical signals that facilitate the sprouting of terminals. When a small lesion precedes a larger lesion by 4 days to 2 weeks, the recovery from the second lesion is significantly faster and more extensive than if the earlier lesion had not occurred. Thus the earlier lesion seems to prime the system to respond to the subsequent lesion (Scheff et al., 1978).

In a clinical example, an adult patient with a brain tumor encroaching on the speech areas of his left hemisphere underwent several operations, spaced many months apart (Geschwind, 1976). Each time the tumor regrew, it was necessary to remove more of the cortical speech areas, and each time the patient recovered his speech. In the end he was still speaking, even though only a fragment of the speech areas remained. Aging can also be thought of as a slowly developing condition, which probably helps mitigate its effects on the brain.

Many Aphasic Patients Show Some Recovery

Many people with brain disorders that produce aphasia recover some language abilities. For some people language recovery depends on specific forms of speech therapy. The relative extent of recovery from aphasia can be predicted from several factors. For example, recovery is better in survivors of brain damage due to trauma, such as a blow to the head, than in those whose brain damage is caused by stroke. Patients with more severe language loss recover less. Left-handed people show better recovery than those who are right-handed.

Kertesz (1979) reported that the largest amount of recovery usually occurs during the initial 3 months following brain damage (Figure 19.22). In many instances, little further improvement is noted after 1 year, although this result may reflect impoverished therapeutic tools rather than a property of neural plasticity. In general, patients suffering from Broca's aphasia have the highest rate of recovery.

Improvement in language abilities following stroke might involve a shift to right hemisphere control of language. A case presented by Cummings et al. (1979) lends some support to the hypothesis of a change from left hemisphere to right hemisphere control of language in an adult.

One unusual innovation, called *melodic intonation therapy,* draws attention to the differences between song and speech. Individuals suffering from aphasia can frequently sing words and phrases even though they show major handicaps in the ability to speak words. Melodic intonation therapy attempts to enhance communication by having patients sing sentences they would ordinarily attempt to deliver in conversational form. Therapists have experienced some success in slowly transforming the communication of such subjects from a song mode to a nonmelodic speech pattern.

Damage to the left hemisphere in children can also produce aphasia, but they often recover language. Language recovery is possible even after removal of the entire left hemisphere (Box 19.3). These observations show that the right hemisphere *can* take over the language functions of the left hemisphere if impairment occurs early in life. But as we grow older, the brain slowly loses the ability to compensate for injury.

NEURAL PLASTICITY

(a)

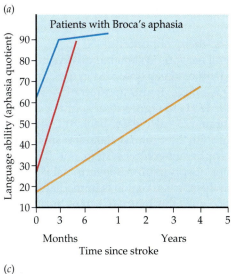

(b)

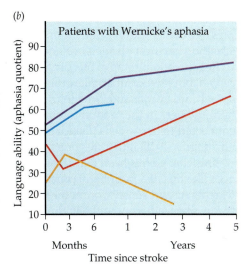

(c)

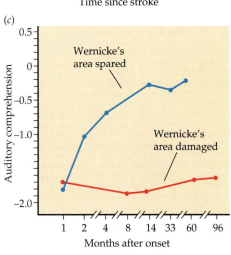

19.22 Courses of Recovery of Patients with Aphasia (a, b) The course of recovery from Broca's aphasia (a) differs from the course of recovery from Wernicke's aphasia (b). These graphs depict the aphasia quotient (AQ), a score derived from a clinical test battery. Higher scores indicate better language performance. (c) Here the course of recovery of auditory comprehension of speech after a stroke in which Wernicke's area was damaged is compared with the course of recovery after a stroke in which Wernicke's area was spared. (Parts a and b after Kertesz, 1979; c after Naeser et al., 1990.)

BOX 19.3 *The Comparatively Minor Effects of Childhood Loss of One Hemisphere*

During early development the brain is a vulnerable organ—a fact that is especially apparent when we look at the effect of a prolonged, difficult birth involving a period of oxygen loss: Some children born under such circumstances sustain lateralized brain injury involving a single cerebral hemisphere. Early in development such a child may show paralysis on one side of the body and frequent seizures. These seizures can be difficult to control with medication, and they may occur so often that they endanger life.

Surgical removal of the malfunctioning hemisphere reduces seizures. Although at first some severe effects of

the surgery are evident, over a long period of time the restoration of behavior is practically complete. This result is strikingly illustrated in a case presented by A. Smith and Sugar (1975). The boy they described showed paralysis on his right side as an infant, and by 5 years of age he was experiencing 10 to 12 seizures a day. Although the boy's verbal comprehension was normal, his speech was hard to understand. To treat the problem, doctors removed all the cerebral cortex of the left hemisphere. At first, his language capacity worsened, but then improved rapidly.

Long-term follow-up studies extended to age 26, when the patient had

almost completed college. Tests revealed an above-normal IQ and superior language abilities; thus the early loss of most of the left hemisphere had not precluded language development. This patient also had remarkable development of nonverbal functions, including visuospatial tasks and manual tasks.

Whereas adult hemispherectomy of the left side usually results in drastic impairment of language, affecting both speech and writing, this case shows that childhood hemispherectomy can be followed by extensive functional recovery, demonstrating the additional plasticity of the young brain.

The Brain Regrows and Reorganizes Anatomically after Being Injured

Anatomical dogma for many years declared that changes in the adult central nervous system are solely destructive. The intricate structure and connections of nerve cells were considered to be structurally fixed once adulthood was reached. Injury, it was thought, could lead only to the shrinkage or death of nerve cells. Many impressive contemporary demonstrations to the contrary have now led us to emphasize the structural plasticity of nerve cells and their connections.

Regeneration of the axons of the peripheral nervous system has always been accepted, but now comparable structural regrowth has been observed in the brain and spinal cord (Veraa and Grafstein, 1981). For example, injury to catecholamine-containing fibers in the medial forebrain bundle leads to regrowth of axonal portions connected to nerve cells. Dendrites in the brain may also grow back following injury. Figure 19.23 illustrates one form of regrowth after injury: **collateral sprouting**.

This change has been described in the peripheral nervous system, and the story goes like this: If a peripheral sensory or motor fiber is injured, the terminal portions degenerate and sensory or motor function in the affected region is immediately lost. Nerve fibers adjacent to the injured fibers recognize this injury (perhaps by a chemical signal delivered from the injured site), and they respond by developing sprouts or branches from intact axons. In time, usually weeks, these sprouts connect to denervated skin or muscle and acquire functional control of these regions on the periphery of the body (J. Diamond et al., 1976).

This mechanism seems to result in functional compensation for a loss of neuronal connections. Incidentally, the injured nerve fiber (axon) slowly regrows, and as it approaches the skin or muscles to which it had been connected, the sprouts retract. Again, chemical signals from the regrowing original fiber probably produce this change.

Demonstrations of collateral sprouting in the brain and spinal cord, once rarely observed, are now reported with regularity. A growing view is that injury of the nervous system might release nerve growth factors. One group of researchers has reported that chemicals in the area of tissue surrounding brain injury contain a growth-promoting substance (Nieto-Sampedro and Cotman, 1985). Grafting specialized glial cells from the olfactory bulb can aid regeneration in the rat spinal cord (Y. Li et al., 1997).

Perhaps the most exciting prospect for brain repair following stroke or injury is the use of **embryonic stem cells.** These are cells, derived from embryos, that have

(*a*) Normal connections of fimbria and medial forebrain bundle to a septal nucleus cell

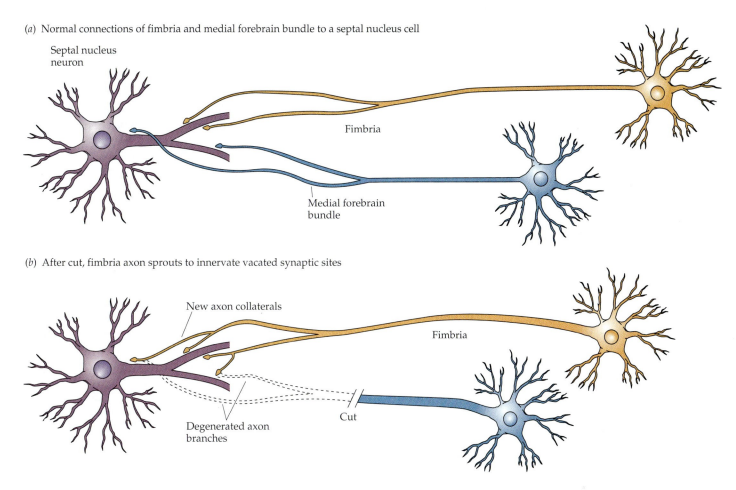

Septal nucleus
neuron

Fimbria

Medial forebrain
bundle

(*b*) After cut, fimbria axon sprouts to innervate vacated synaptic sites

New axon collaterals

Fimbria

Degenerated axon
branches

Cut

not yet differentiated into specific roles and therefore seem to be able to develop, under local chemical cues, into the type of neuron needed. The finding that a limited number of new neurons are produced by the adult brain, which we have mentioned several times before, demonstrates that neurons can become integrated into functional brain circuits. Such cells even seem to migrate to the site of injury to take on their new roles (Björklund and Lindvall, 2000).

Although not all studies report encouraging results (Freed et al., 2001), in several studies implants of embryonic stem cells have been shown to reduce symptoms of Parkinson's disease (see Chapter 11) and stroke (Kondziolka et al., 2000). But great controversy surrounds the ethical issue of exploiting human embryos for such purposes. A limited number of embryonic stem cells can be harvested from the blood in the umbilical cord without harming the newborn or the mother, but another possible source of stem cells is genetic engineering. One goal is to harvest from a patient some cells—say, white blood cells—and induce them to revert to the state of embryonic stem cells. This approach might avoid problems of tissue rejection because the implanted cells would be genetically identical to the patient.

Rehabilitation and Retraining Can Help Recovery from Brain and Spinal Cord Injury

Training can restore some functions after brain or spinal cord injury. The range of restorative opportunities following damage to the nervous system broadens with new research reports about neural plasticity that are more encouraging than ever. For example, although we have long been led to believe that paralysis produced by injury to the spinal cord is untreatable, some new reports offer cautious optimism about the prospects that training can restore some walking ability in such patients (Wickelgren, 1998). Contemporary work with humans follows in the path of research on animals and shows some restoration of walking in spinal cord–injured humans following training (Barbeau et al., 1998).

19.23 Collateral Sprouting of a Brain Neuron (*a*) The septal nucleus is normally innervated by the fimbria and the medial forebrain bundle. (*b*) After the medial forebrain bundle has been severed, a fimbria axon develops sprouts that occupy synaptic sites formerly occupied by axon terminals from the medial forebrain bundle. (After Raisman, 1978.)

Cognitive and/or perceptual handicaps that develop from brain impairments can also be modified by training. It is important at this point to distinguish between the role of experience in compensating for brain injury and its role in restoring behavior lost after injury. It is well known that experiences significantly reduce the impact of brain injury by fostering compensatory behavior. For example, vigorous eye movements can make up for large scotomata (blind spots in the visual field) that result from injury to the visual pathways. Behavior strategies can be changed after a brain injury to enable successful performance on a variety of tests.

The role of experience in the possible reorganization of pathways following a lesion was noted in Chapter 11, where we described how an individual whose arm afferents have been cut can recover control of the limbs. D. Berman et al. (1978) described a striking phenomenon of recovery that involves a change in feedback signals governing behavior. Several studies performed with brain-lesioned rats have demonstrated that postlesion experience in a complex environment can improve subsequent problem-solving behavior (Will et al., 1977).

Animals were placed in impoverished or enriched environments of the same kinds that had been shown to lead to changes in brain measures (see Chapter 18). Although the brain-injured animals still made more errors than did intact rats, those in the enriched environments made significantly fewer errors than those in the impoverished environments. Simply placing a group of animals together in a large cage had a measurable beneficial effect; giving the animals access to varied stimuli was even more helpful (Rosenzweig, 1980). Thus even an injured brain can profit from experience.

In the case of human patients, some rehabilitation experts have questioned the wisdom of placing certain patients in sensory isolation (patients in coma, or patients kept in fixed positions in isolated rooms for intravenous therapy). Such patients, even if they cannot respond, might be aided by visitors, music, and changing visual stimuli. Some current programs of rehabilitation are putting these insights into effect.

Previous generations may have been too pessimistic about recovery from stroke, for now there's increasing evidence that people can regain considerable use of limbs affected by stroke if they are forced to. **Constraint-induced-movement therapy** persuades stroke patients to use the affected arm by simply tying the "good" arm to a splint for up to 90% of waking hours. But immobilizing the good arm isn't enough; such patients are subjected to rehabilitation therapy 6 hours a day to practice repetitively moving the affected limb. Most patients who received this treatment regained 75% of normal use of the paralyzed arm after only 2 weeks of this therapy, and there was evidence of a remapping of the motor cortex (Liepert et al., 2000).

Another surprising use of experience for rehabilitation involves a simple mirror. Altschuler et al. (1999) treated stroke patients who had reduced use of one arm by placing them before a mirror with only their "good" arm visible. To the patients, it looked as though they were seeing the entire body, but now both arms were the good arm. The patient was told to make symmetrical fluid motions with both arms. In the mirror, the motions looked perfectly symmetrical, of course, but surprisingly, most of the patients soon learned to use the "weak" arm more extensively. It was as though the visible feedback, indicating that the weak arm was moving perfectly, overcame the brain's reluctance to use that arm.

Brain Structures That Remain Intact after Injury Can Substitute for Damaged Structures

Recovery following brain injury demonstrates that remaining neural tissue can mediate required behaviors. One perspective suggests that neural systems contain appreciable redundancy and that recovery involves the use of redundant pathways. However, what appears to be redundancy may arise from the complexity of the neural substrates of behavior and the simple ways in which recovery is assessed. Thus if the neural substrate for some behavior is broadly represented in the brain, behavior may be reinstated because of the extensiveness of neural controls rather than because of redundant or repeated systems.

Functional-imaging studies of patients who have suffered a stroke suggest that intact regions, which had not played a role in the behavior before injury, are now pitching in. PET studies on patients with hemiplegia show that whereas movement of the unaffected hand activates motor cortex only on the opposite side of the body, attempted movement of the affected hand activates motor cortex on *both* sides (Chollet and Weiller, 1994). Such results indicate that cortex on the side opposite the injury mediates recovered movements (H. J. Rosen et al., 2000). Perhaps the most important message to convey to victims of stroke is the encouragement that with effort and perseverance, their remarkably plastic brains can recover much of the lost behavioral capacity.

NEURAL PLASTICITY

Summary

1. Humans are distinct in the animal kingdom for their language and associated cognitive abilities. Possible evolutionary origins of human speech may be seen in aspects of gestures.

2. Studies of communication among nonhumans provide analogies to human speech. For example, the control of birdsong is lateralized in the brains of some species of songbirds. Further, in some of these species early experience is essential for proper song development.

3. Limitations of the vocal tract in nonhumans are proposed as one reason that they do not have speech, but nonhuman primates like the chimpanzee can learn to use signs of the American Sign Language. However, controversy surrounds claims that these animals can arrange signs in novel orders to create new sentences.

4. Ninety to 95% of human language impairments involve injuries of the left hemisphere. Left anterior lesions produce an impairment in speech production called Broca's aphasia. More posterior lesions, involving the temporoparietal cortex, affect speech comprehension, as seen in Wernicke's aphasia.

5. Left hemisphere lesions in users of sign language produce impairments in the use of sign language that are similar to impairments in spoken language shown by nondeaf individuals suffering from aphasia.

6. Split-brain individuals show striking examples of hemispheric specialization. Most words projected only to the right hemisphere, for example, cannot be read, while the same stimuli directed to the left hemisphere can be read. Verbal abilities of the right hemisphere are also reduced; however, spatial-relation tasks are performed better by the right hemisphere than by the left.

7. Normal humans show many forms of cognitive specialization of the cerebral hemispheres, although these specializations are not as striking as those shown by split-brain individuals. For example, most normal humans show a right-ear advantage and greater accuracy for verbal stimuli in the right visual field.

8. Anatomical asymmetry of the hemispheres is seen in some structures in the human brain. Especially striking is the large size difference in the planum temporale (which is larger in the left hemisphere than in the right hemisphere of most right-handed individuals).

9. Broad theoretical statements about different cognitive modes of the two hemispheres exceed confirmations from current experimental and clinical data. In most cases mental activity depends on interactions between the cerebral hemispheres.

10. The frontal lobes of humans are quite large compared with those of other animals. Injury in parts of this region produces an unusual syndrome of profound emotional changes, including reduced responsiveness to many stimuli. Tasks that require sustained attention show drastic impairment after frontal lesions.

11. In most patients, parietal cortex injuries produce many perceptual changes. A dramatic example after bilateral damage is the inability to recognize familiar objects and the faces of familiar people. Some patients with right parietal injury neglect or ignore the left side of both the body and space.

12. Many functional losses following brain injury show at least partial recovery. Most recovery from aphasia occurs in the year following stroke, with fewer changes evident after that. Mechanisms of functional recovery may involve structural regrowth of cell extensions—dendrites and axons—and the formation of new synapses.

Refer to the *Learning Biological Psychology* CD for the following study aids for this chapter:

7 Objectives

66 Study Questions

1 Activity

13. Retraining is a significant part of functional recovery and may involve both compensation, by establishing new solutions to adaptive demands, and reorganization of surviving networks. Greater recovery is evident in young individuals. Less impairment occurs when lesions are produced over a period of time—that is, when lesion momentum is reduced.

Recommended Reading

Bradbury, J. W., and Vehrencamp, S. L. (1998). *Principles of animal communication*. Sunderland, MA: Sinauer.

Gazzaniga, M. S. (Ed.). (2000). *The new cognitive neurosciences* (2nd ed.). Cambridge, MA: MIT Press.

Hauser, M. (Ed.). (1999). *The design of animal communication*. Cambridge, MA: MIT Press.

Ivry, R. B., and Robertson, L. C. (1998). *The two sides of perception*. Cambridge, MA: MIT Press.

Lieberman, P. (1998). *Eve spoke: Human language and human evolution*. New York: Norton.

Ogden, J. A. (1996). *Fractured minds*. New York: Oxford University Press.

Pinker, S. (1999). *Words and rules: The ingredients of language*. New York: Basic Books.

Rapp, B. (Ed.). (2001). *The handbook of cognitive neuropsychology: What deficits reveal about the human mind*. Philadelphia: Psychology Press.

Savage-Rumbaugh, S., Shanker, S., and Talbot, T. (1998). *Apes, language and the human mind*. New York: Oxford University Press.

Schacter, D. L. (1999). *The cognitive neuropsychology of false memories*. Hove, England: Psychology Press.

Afterword

The Ever-Changing Brain

As a student, you are of course relieved to reach, at last, the final pages of a textbook. As authors, we too were relieved to arrive here. But we feel moved to have a final word with you to emphasize an overall theme that runs throughout the book and to discuss the importance of that theme explicitly before you go.

Plasticity Is a Defining Feature of the Brain

Sometimes in this book we have likened the brain to a machine, and that analogy is useful up to a point: The brain is a physical object whose parts must obey the laws of a material world. For example, in the early chapters we described how the various parts of the brain communicate using physical media such as neurotransmitters, hormones, and action potentials. However, we have also described a nervous system that is remarkably plastic, and in a constant state of flux.

When we described psychological phenomena such as learning, perception, and cognition, it was implicit that these aspects of the mind are a product of the physical machine called the brain. But this machine is unlike any human-made machine because it is continually remodeling itself—rearranging the relationships between its parts—in a manner that (normally) improves its function. As you undoubtedly know from bitter experience, all human-made machines reach their peak performance once they are assembled and simply tumble downhill after that. Computer scientists struggle and yearn to develop systems that can truly learn from experience—something that is accomplished quite easily when an egg and a sperm combine.

The study of behavior is psychologists' special domain, and their research has illuminated how behavior may change. Since the nineteenth century it has been assumed that changes in behavior must be reflections of physical changes in the brain. (The only alternative would have been a regression to nonphysical explanations—spirits or demons—to explain why people or other animals change their behavior.) But the complexity of the brain is so daunting that, until recently, few researchers even attempted to find out what part of the brain had been altered when behavior changed.

During the past few decades, however, psychologists and other neuroscientists have produced many concrete demonstrations that changes in behavior are due to brain changes. Indeed, it is now clear that constant change is one of the brain's defining features. Just as important is the now abundant evidence that the relationship between changes in the brain and changes in behavior is bidirectional: Experience also can alter neural structure.

Brain-imaging techniques such as PET and fMRI are now enabling us to see changes in the responses of the brain that take place during the course of a single experiment, as examples in the learning research described in Chapters 17 and 18 demonstrate. Here we will briefly recap some of the topics discussed in the book where plasticity plays a particularly dramatic role, and we will add a few more striking examples.

Plasticity Is Prominent in Neural Development

The nervous systems of developing individuals are even more plastic than those of adults. That's why infants learn new languages and recover from brain injuries so much more readily than we adults do. In Chapter 7 we reviewed the many processes that occur as the brain puts itself together and showed how cell–cell interactions play a crucial role in all of those processes: The notochord induces cells to become motoneurons; targets secrete neurotrophic factors to attract and maintain neurons; radial glial cells guide migrating cells to their final destination. On the basis of what their neighboring cells are doing, developing cells take on an assigned role and make the appropriate connections to fulfill that role.

Thus the cells of the developing nervous system are in constant communication with one another, and they direct and constrain each other's fate. Because some of the neurons communicating these directions are sensory neurons that respond to stimuli in the environment, experience itself shapes the brain. The best-studied example of environmental effects on crucial aspects of development is in the visual system. As you will recall, early experience is crucial for maintaining the connections between the eye and brain that are needed to detect exactly the stimuli that surround us as adults.

Plasticity Occurs at the Molecular Level

Even at the molecular level, plasticity and change are the norm. Remember from Chapter 3 that the number of neurotransmitter receptors in the postsynaptic region of a given synapse can increase or decrease depending on the amount of activity at that synapse. Usually this activity serves to regulate the activity of a particular pathway: Cells in the basal ganglia that receive too little dopamine stimulation start making more receptors to compensate, until they become supersensitive. Conversely, overstimulation leads to "down-regulation" of the receptors so that the signal is attenuated. Since experience can clearly affect which of our brain cells are firing, it must also indirectly affect the number and distribution of neurotransmitter receptors.

Endocrine Regulation Shows Plasticity

Chapter 5 presented many examples of the complicated feedback systems in the endocrine system that regulate secretion to maintain relatively steady hormone levels. But experience also modulates patterns of hormone secretion: Losing an aggressive encounter can lower testosterone levels, stress can augment ACTH secretion and kill hippocampal cells, and exposure to pheromones can accelerate or delay puberty. Although there are no data to indicate that pheromones play a role in human puberty, during the past century the average age at which individuals undergo puberty in our society has declined markedly, indicating that some environmental factors—perhaps better nutrition or greater exposure to sexual stimuli—have affected our reproductive systems too.

Sensory Systems Show Plasticity

As noted already, research on sensory systems has been especially fruitful in demonstrating experiential effects on brain development and structure. In Chapter 8 we learned that changes in tactile stimulation, even in adulthood, can alter the projection patterns of information from the skin to the brain. This was first demonstrated in monkeys, and new, noninvasive techniques are now confirming that these same effects occur in humans.

For example, Yang et al. (1994) examined people who had lost a hand in an accident. On the side of the brain receiving information from the remaining hand, stimulation of that hand excited a region of the somatosensory cortex sandwiched between brain regions responding to the face and upper arm; as the map of primary somatosensory cortex in Figure 8.18 shows, this is normal. However, on the side of the brain that was no longer receiving information because of the lost hand, regions sensitive to the face and upper arm were found to be immediately adjacent to each other. Connections from the face and upper arm had shifted on that side of the brain to take over the region that had formerly been excited by stimuli from the hand (see Figure 8.12).

These data suggest that sensory information is constantly competing not only for our attention, but for space in the brain—space to analyze and process the information that is most relevant to the business of surviving and reproducing. We also saw in Chapter 9 that even in an adult animal the receptive fields of auditory cortical neurons could be changed by conditioning.

Plasticity and Psychopathology

Our bodies and brains constantly make adjustments for the time of day and time of year, as detailed in Chapter 14. In nonhuman animals, body weight and many other parameters are affected by whether an individual is exposed to summerlike long days or winterlike short days. Similarly, in humans the short days of winter exacerbate some bouts of depression, so it seems that our nervous systems may also be carefully measuring the seasons.

In Chapter 16 we saw that even severe psychopathologies such as schizophrenia are not entirely concordant in identical twins, so something other than genes can influence these disorders, and the best candidate for that "something" is differences in experience.

Hopes are blossoming that recovery from brain accidents may be accomplished with grafts of genetically manipulated cells. These procedures clearly work in some cases, and may be feasible one day in others. But to the extent that these transplants work at all, the success is due to the fact that the rest of the brain is capable of changing to integrate these new cells into an existing network. Thus the underlying plasticity of the brain will prove to be of vital practical importance in this arena.

Plasticity, Learning, and Memory

In Chapters 17 and 18 we dealt with the phenomena that most explicitly depend on structural alterations in the adult nervous system: learning and memory. If our adult brains could not change, we would not be able to learn anything, and this college course and all others would be a waste of time. (Please save opinions on this matter for course evaluation forms!) But we *can* learn, and scientists have made remarkable progress in finding structural changes that may underlie learning and memory.

Again we find that even the number or kind of neurotransmitter receptors can be altered by experience, as one of the foremost models of learning, long-term potentiation (LTP), illustrates. Recall that in a synapse that is activated in a particular way, the NMDA receptor allows ions to enter the postsynaptic cell; these ions then change the synapse so that it will transmit its signal more forcefully in the future. In other words, "neurons that fire together wire together." LTP is a very active research area, and the details of the process are still being worked out, but on the basis of inferences from behavior and what was known of neuroscience, psychologist Donald Hebb predicted in 1949 that strengthening of synaptic action is the foundation of learning ("the Hebbian synapse").

As work with model systems proceeds, we continue to find evidence corroborating Hebb's basic idea that both the strength of existing synapses and the number and pattern of synaptic connections can be altered by the learning experience. This area of work also illuminates the reciprocal relationship between experience and brain structure that we discussed earlier and described in Chapter 1: Experience alters the brain, and the brain seeks out particular experiences.

Prostheses Require and May Foster Plasticity

Because the nervous system is very plastic, sometimes artificial devices—prostheses—can be integrated by the brain to improve functioning in cases of sensory or motor disabilities. For example, in Chapter 9 we discussed cochlear implants that afford partial hearing to many deaf people. In Chapter 11 we discussed a robotic arm governed by brain activity; such devices may, in the future, help paralyzed people to move their limbs under control of brain circuits. These and many other recent and experimental sensory and motor prostheses are described in a book by Gregory Benford (2001).

Here we want to emphasize that most prostheses require learning to be used successfully. Cochlear implants are limited in the number of auditory frequencies to which they respond, and users have to learn how to interpret this information and to integrate it with other sensory input. The robotic arm controlled by brain activity similarly requires learning for successful use. So behavioral plasticity and underlying neural processes are necessary parts of any prosthetic program.

Furthermore, use of a prosthetic device may foster neural plasticity. An example comes from research on a strain of cats in which the organ of Corti degenerates before the onset of hearing, leaving the auditory nerve fibers intact (Klinke et al., 1999). When kittens were given cochlear implants with only a single channel, they could learn to get food when a signal sounded. Although cortical responses were abnormal in deaf kittens, after months of use of the implant, the cortical responses became larger and covered a larger area of the cortex than in control deaf animals without an implant. Thus there is reciprocal interplay between the prosthetic device and neural plasticity: Plasticity is needed to use the device, and the prosthesis causes plastic changes in the nervous system.

Plasticity Occurs over the Life Span

Currently, much attention is being given to changes in the brain during early development and the importance of early experience for children's later development. These aspects of plasticity are certainly important, but we shouldn't forget that learning occurs over the whole life span, which makes the study of adult plasticity an equally valuable endeavor.

In Chapter 18 we saw that two major models of neural plasticity were discovered in the 1960s: (1) The work of Hubel and Wiesel (1965; Wiesel and Hubel, 1963) showed that preventing a kitten's eye from receiving light during early development reduced the number of cortical cells that respond to that eye later in life. If a kitten is a few months old, however, depriving an eye of light does not affect its adult cortical representation, so the kind of plasticity necessary for "wiring" of the visual cortex occurs only during an early critical period. (2) As discussed in Chapter 17, Rosenzweig and colleagues (1961; E. L. Bennett et al., 1964) found that exposing rats to enriched environments alters neurochemical and neuroanatomical aspects of the cortex. In contrast to Hubel and Wiesel's findings, successive extensions of the initial work showed that such effects could be induced not only in young rats but also in juveniles (Zolman and Morimoto, 1962), in young adults (Rosenzweig et al., 1964; E. L. Bennett et al., 1964), and in old rats (Riege, 1971), although the size of the effects was greatest in the young animals. Thus this research demonstrated that some forms of neural plasticity persist throughout the life span.

Temporal Constraints on Plasticity Are Diverse

The many examples of neural plasticity that we have presented and discussed in this book are not limited to the two contrasting possibilities mentioned in the previous section. Several different models are needed to encompass them all. Furthermore, even kinds of learning and/or neural plasticity that seem to be similar may in fact follow different time courses over the life span. For example, LTP can be evoked in the supragranular visual cortex of rats only to day 30, whereas it can be evoked in the infragranular layers into adulthood (Perkins and Teyler, 1988). Recall from Chapter 17 that a person who can no longer form certain kinds of memories because of brain damage or disease can still form other kinds perfectly well.

Plasticity Can Be Limited to an Early Critical or Sensitive Period

Ocular dominance columns in the visual cortex form early and do not change later in life (Wiesel and Hubel, 1963). In cats, plasticity appears to be maximal at about 1 month of age and then declines over the next 3 months, after which time the visual pathways are virtually immutable (Figure 1a). During this plastic period, every major response property of cortical cells (ocular dominance, orientation selectivity, direction selectivity, disparity sensitivity) can be modified by manipulation of the visual environment (Mower et al., 1983, p. 178). It is not clear what normally termi-

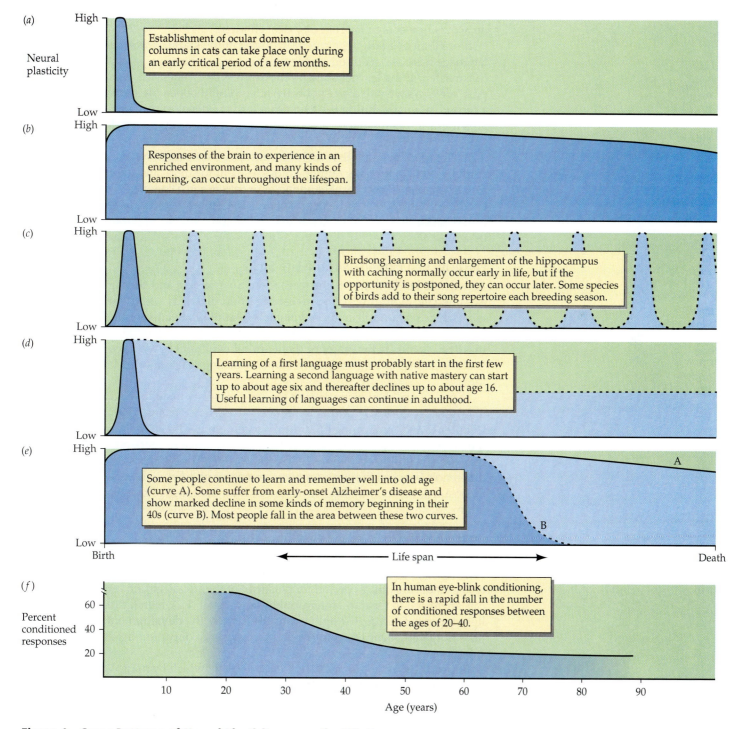

Figure 1   Some Patterns of Neural Plasticity across the Life Span

nates plasticity in these aspects of the visual system. Bear and Singer (1986) suggested one possibility: They reported that they could restore plasticity in the visual cortex of adult cats by perfusing the area with acetylcholine and noradrenaline, so perhaps localized developmental decreases in synthesis of these transmitters are responsible for the decline in plasticity.

Another example of learning that seems to be limited to an early critical period is learning of a first language with complete mastery. Investigators are not in complete agreement about the age limits, but such learning appears to be possible up to about 3 years of age, with a gradual fall-off thereafter (Morford and Mayberry, 1999). Fortunately, very few children with normal hearing are deprived of the possibility of acquiring speech in their first years, so most of the research in this area is based on acquisition of sign language by deaf children.

More than one language can be acquired at the start in infancy. Or, after a first language has been acquired, a second language can be acquired with complete native mastery if the learner starts at the age of 6 or 7 years (J. S. Johnson and Newport, 1989). As we will discuss shortly, it has recently been discovered that learning a second language during the teen years leads to development of a second Broca's area in the left hemisphere, adjacent to the original Broca's area (K. H. Kim et al., 1997).

In Chapter 7 we saw that early handling by experimenters and early maternal stimulation help to make rat pups more resilient to stress later in life. Similarly, we saw in Chapter 18 that early handling or experience in a complex environment lowers the concentration of glucocorticoids in the rat brain and causes more rapid return of glucocorticoids to the basal level, which protects the hippocampus from signs of aging.

Plasticity Can Extend over the Life Span

As we noted in Chapter 18, the research of Rosenzweig and colleagues at Berkeley extended early findings of postweaning brain plasticity using enriched environments in juvenile, adult, and aged animals (Figure 1b). Related results with aged rats were reported by Cummins et al. (1973) and by Greenough et al. (1986). Life-long plasticity accounts for many of the learning experiences we have in life, such as learning a musical instrument as an adult, learning to use another language, and so forth.

Experimental demonstrations of life-long plasticity include remapping of the somatosensory cortex in adults by altering experience (Kaas, 1991), mentioned in Chapter 8, and remapping of auditory receptive fields (N. M. Weinberger, 1998), mentioned in Chapter 9. Sexual behavior can also leave its mark on the nervous system, even in adulthood (Figure 2; Breedlove, 1997). Thus it is possible that structural differences between the sexes (or between people of differing sexual orientation) are the result of behavioral differences rather than the cause of them, as we discussed in Box 12.3.

Plasticity Can Occur at the First Opportunity

Some kinds of plasticity occur as soon as the opportunity occurs. The limit is not a matter of age or maturity but of opportunity. For example, despite the comments already made, the critical period for plasticity of the visual system can be extended if cats are reared in the dark. Interestingly, however, if dark-reared cats are exposed to light for only 6 hours, the light exposure triggers the developmental process, and once triggered, it runs to completion in the absence of further input (Mower et al., 1983).

Birdsong learning provides another example in which learning occurs at the first opportunity, as mentioned in Chapter 19. Normally a male bird learns its song from its father, but if a bird is prevented from hearing song at the usual age, it can still learn later, provided it is given an accurate model (Eales, 1985). For many years it was believed that it is not possible for a bird to acquire a normal song after a criti-

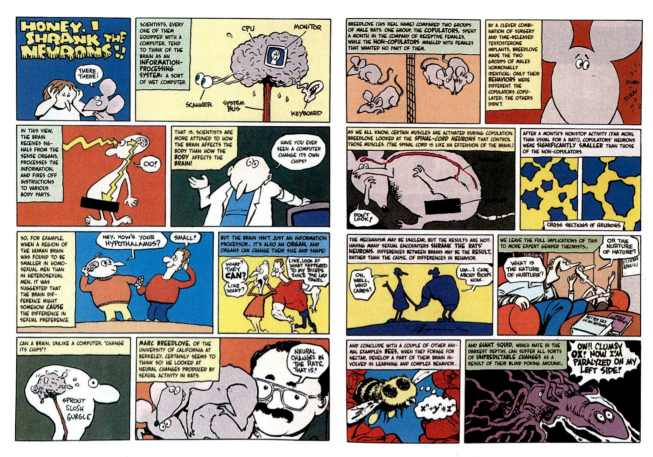

Figure 2 Sex on the Brain?
(From "Science Classics" by Larry Gonick; courtesy of Larry Gonick and *Discover* magazine.)

cal period has passed—a conclusion that was based on experiments with a taped song tutor. However, when live tutors or naturalistic taped tutors are used, later acquisition of song can take place. This finding fits in well with the observation that some species of songbirds add to their repertoire during each breeding season, which requires recurring periods of neural plasticity (Figure 1*c*).

In species of birds that cache food, such as nutcrackers, the hippocampus is larger than in related species that do not cache. If one of these birds is denied the opportunity to cache, the hippocampus does not show this size difference. The opportunity to cache can be postponed well beyond the usual age in laboratory-raised birds, but once the birds have the opportunity to cache, they do so promptly, and the hippocampus reflects this experience by enlarging (Clayton, 1995), as we mentioned in Chapter 17.

Some Forms of Plasticity Are Greatest at an Early Age but Remain in Later Life in Some Form

Aligning the two eyes to prevent amblyopia (or "lazy eye") is usually thought to be effective only for the first 5 to 6 years of life. But considerable improvement in amblyopia can be shown even by adults, if the condition is not too severe and if they exercise the weak eye sufficiently. As we mentioned in Chapter 10, one study reported considerable recovery from long-standing amblyopia after the normal eye was lost or severely damaged (Romero-Apis et al., 1982).

Chow and Stewart (1972) deprived cats of pattern vision in one eye for about 20 months after birth. When the kittens were tested for pattern perception with the previously deprived eye, they showed almost no discrimination on formal tests and were not able to guide locomotion with the previously deprived eye, although they performed well with the other eye. As we described in Chapter 10, the investigators then undertook an intensive program of rehabilitation with some of the cats, and over time the cats developed some pattern discrimination in the previously deprived eye, and they could use it to guide their locomotion. Furthermore, the cats' recovery was accompanied by morphological changes in the lateral geniculate nucleus, and electrophysiological recording showed increased numbers of binocular cells in the visual cortex. Here again, learning to see and plasticity of the visual system occurred after the usual developmental period had ended.

The literature on human recovery from congenital blindness is mixed, but it has been studied in people born with dense cataracts that were removed in adulthood. Gregory (1987) notes that "often the eye takes a long time to settle down after a cataract operation," which may partially explain why many of the historical cases show slow development of vision. A patient studied by Gregory and Wallace (1963) received corneal grafts that provided good retinal images immediately after the operation, and the patient could quickly recognize objects he already knew by touch, but his vision never became fully normal. Learning to see is slow in adults, as it is in infants, but it appears to be possible to learn to see as an adult. The question is complicated by the fact that a person who has not seen until adulthood has learned other ways to adjust to the environment, and it may be difficult to abandon these compensatory behaviors.

In Some Cases, Later Plasticity Depends on Early Training

Eric Knudsen has found that the development of auditory–visual neurons in the optic tectum of the barn owl can be finely manipulated in the young bird. In Chapter 9 we saw that a young owl equipped with prismatic lenses that displace the visual image learns to adapt to the lenses and locate objects accurately. If the prisms are fitted to an adult bird, the range of adjustment is normally quite restricted. Recent work (Knudsen, 1998), however, has shown that if an owl learns an abnormal auditory–visual adjustment as a juvenile and is then returned to the normal condition, it can easily reacquire the abnormal adjustment as an adult. It appears that the early learning leaves a neural trace that, even if not used for an extended period, can be reestablished later, when needed.

The ability to learn a second language with native mastery is possible if the learner starts the second language by the age of 6 or 7, provided the first language was begun during the first year or two (Figure 1*d*). Mastery of the second language shows increasing departures from full native skill as the starting age increases from 7 to 16. Furthermore, people who started their second language in their teens form a second Broca's area adjacent to the Broca's area for their first language (K. H. Kim et al., 1997). Nevertheless, even people who start to learn a second (or third or fourth) language as an adult can gain conversational fluency, provided they work hard enough at it.

The Decline in Plasticity in the Latter Part of the Life Span Takes Many Forms

As we noted in Chapters 7 and 18, abilities to learn and remember decline on the average in the latter part of the life span, but this varies with the kinds of learning. Let's consider the example of eye-blink conditioning, shown as a function of age in Figure 1*f*. Whereas panels *a* through *e* in Figure 1 are schematic, each summarizing a number of studies, in contrast Figure 1*f* is based on a single experiment that involved 150 healthy participants with ages ranging from 20 to 89 years (Woodruff-Pak and Jaeger, 1998).

The subjects were trained in delayed eye-blink conditioning and were given some other tests. Figure 1*f* shows the percentage of conditioned responses (CRs) during 72 trials when a tone (the conditioned stimulus) was paired with an air puff to the eye. Note the rapid fall in the number of CRs over the first three decades (twenties through forties). After age 40, there was no further significant decline with age. The investigators found that the decline in conditioning with age paralleled a decline in accurately timed tapping and estimates of elapsed time, both of which, like eye-blink conditioning, are known to depend on cerebellar function.

On many other kinds of learning, some older people and animals perform as well as younger conspecifics (Figure 1*e*, curve A). On the other hand, some individuals suffer from early-onset Alzheimer's disease and show a marked decline in the formation of declarative memories in their forties (curve B). Most people fall into the area between these two curves as they age. In those older individuals who show declines in ability with age, some studies show changes in neuroanatomy (such as shrinkage of the hippocampus) or in neurochemistry that may explain the decline. The *ApoE4* gene, which intensifies the effects of conditions that impair the brain, also shows its influence mainly in older individuals. Thus all the observed declines in ability shown in Figure 1*e* may be pathological rather than normal, and it may become possible to counteract or prevent them.

It has been proposed that the decline of abilities to learn and remember in the latter part of the life span occurs because there has been no evolutionary pressure to maintain these abilities after the reproductive period (Baltes, 1997), which may indicate why special interventions are required to prevent them. In Chapter 18 we saw that enriched experience early in life and continued throughout the life span helps to reduce the risk of cognitive decline in old age. At an international symposium on cognitive decline in old age, the research was summarized as follows (Rosenzweig and Bennett, 1996):

> It's a fortunate person whose brain
> Is trained early, again and again,
> And who continues to use it
> To be sure not to lose it,
> So the brain, in old age, may not wane. (p. 63)

Future Directions

To the extent that certain types of neural plasticity are limited to parts of the life span, it will be important to find the mechanisms that enable plasticity and those that inhibit it. Factors that inhibit continuing plasticity include declines in production of neurotransmitters and nerve growth factors, age-related shrinkage of neural structures such as the hippocampus, and changes in receptor molecules. Other mechanisms remain to be identified, but identifying such mechanisms may allow us to improve our capacity for learning and memory in the future and to extend some kinds of learning further over the life span.

The perspective we hope to have imparted to you concerning the neurosciences is that the brain is indeed dynamic—changing, malleable, and adaptable. Of course this emphasis reflects our biases because we are both psychologists and neuroscientists. But it also reflects a central problem in understanding the nervous system: the control of behavior. What is most impressive about the behavior of both humans and other animals is its variety: Individuals of a given species use many behavioral routes to accomplish the same goals; they display diverse behaviors across the span of their lifetimes; they develop many strategies to solve life's basic problems of survival and reproduction.

We hope that you already had an appreciation for the diversity of behaviors within and across species, but few people on the street understand that this diversity of behaviors requires a plastic brain and that the changes to the brain that underlie this plasticity must be physical—such as changes in receptor or type, neurotransmitter levels, cell numbers, or neuronal connections. The remaining challenge—and it is a formidable one—is to try to understand exactly how experience molds the nervous system and exactly how neural changes alter later behaviors. We and the more than other 20,000 or so other neuroscientists at work around the world, hope to tell you more about these issues in the future.

Appendix

Molecular Biology: Basic Concepts and Important Techniques

Genes Carry Information That Encodes the Synthesis of Proteins

The most important thing about **genes** is that they are pieces of information, inherited from parents, that affect the development and function of our cells. The information carried by the genes is a very specific sort: Each gene codes for the construction of a specific string of amino acids to form a **protein** molecule. The various proteins, each encoded by its own gene, make up the physical structure and most of the constituents of cells, including enzymes.

Enzymes are molecules that allow particular chemical reactions to occur in our cells. For example, only cells that have liver-typical proteins will look like a liver cell and be able to perform liver functions. Neurons are cells that make neuron-typical proteins so that they can look and act like neurons. The genetic information for making these sorts of proteins is crucial for an animal to live and for a nervous system to work properly.

One thing we hope this book will help you understand is that everyday experience can affect whether and when particular genetic recipes for making various proteins are used. But first let's review how genetic information is stored and how proteins are made. Our discussion will be brief because we assume that you've been exposed to this material before in an introductory biology course.

Genetic Information Is Stored in Molecules of DNA

The information for making all of our proteins could, in theory, be stored in any sort of format—on sheets of paper, magnetic tape, a CD-ROM—but all living creatures on this planet store their genetic information in a chemical called **deoxyribonucleic acid,** or **DNA.** Each molecule of DNA consists of a long strand of chemicals called **nucleotides** strung one after the other. There are only four nucleotides: guanine, cytosine, thymine, and adenine (abbreviated G, C, T, and A). The particular sequence of nucleotides (for example, GCTTACC or TGGTCC or TGA) holds the information that will eventually make a protein. Because many millions of these nucleotides can be joined one after the other, a tremendous amount of information can be stored in very little space—on a single molecule of DNA.

A set of nucleotides that has been strung together can snuggle tightly against another string of nucleotides if it has the proper sequence: T nucleotides can fit across from A nucleotides, and G nucleotides can fit across from C nucleotides. Thus T nucleotides are said to be complementary to A nucleotides, and C nucleotides are complementary to G nucleotides. In fact, most of the time our DNA consists not of a single strand of nucleotides, but of two complementary strands of nucleotides wrapped around one another.

The two strands of nucleotides are said to **hybridize** with one another, coiling slightly to form the famous double helix (Figure A.1). The double-stranded DNA twists and coils further, becoming visible in microscopes as **chromosomes,** which resemble twisted lengths of yarn. We and many other organisms are known as **eukaryotes** because we store our chromosomes in a membranous sphere called a **nucleus** inside each cell. You may remember that the ability of DNA to exist as two complementary strands of nucleotides is crucial for the duplication of the chromosomes, but that story will not concern us here. Just remember that, with very few exceptions, every cell in your body has a faithful copy of all the DNA you received from your parents.

A.1 Duplication of DNA   Such duplication of the genome must take place before cell division so that each daughter cell has the full complement of genetic information.

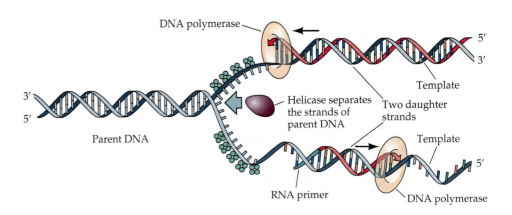

DNA Is Transcribed to Produce Messenger RNA

The information from DNA is used to assemble another molecule—**ribonucleic acid, or RNA**—that serves as a template or guide for later steps. Like DNA, RNA is made up of a long string of four different nucleotides. For RNA, those nucleotides are G and C (which, you recall, are complementary to each other), and A and U (uracil), which are also complementary to each other. Note that the T nucleotide is found only in DNA, and the U nucleotide is found only in RNA.

When a particular gene becomes active, the double strand of DNA unwinds enough so that one strand becomes free of the other and becomes available to special cellular machinery (including an enzyme called transcriptase) that begins **transcription**—the construction of a specific string of RNA nucleotides that are complementary to the exposed strand of DNA (Figure A.2). This length of RNA, sometimes called the message, or messenger RNA (mRNA), is also sometimes called a **transcript** because it contains a faithful transcript of the information in the DNA. Each DNA nucleotide encodes a specific RNA nucleotide (an RNA G for every DNA C, an RNA C for every DNA G, an RNA U for every DNA A, and an RNA A for every DNA T). This transcript is made in the nucleus where the DNA resides; then the mRNA molecule moves to the cytoplasm, where protein molecules are assembled.

RNA Molecules Direct the Formation of Protein Molecules

In the cytoplasm are special organelles, called **ribosomes,** that attach themselves to a molecule of RNA, "read" the sequence of RNA nucleotides, and using that information, begin linking together amino acids to form a protein molecule. The structure and function of a protein molecule depend on which particular amino acids are put together and in what order. The decoding of an RNA transcript to manufacture a particular protein is called **translation** (see Figure A.2), as distinct from transcription, the construction of the mRNA molecule.

Each trio (or "triplet") of RNA nucleotides encodes for one of about 20 different amino acids. Special molecules associated with the ribosome recognize the trio of RNA nucleotides and bring the appropriate amino acid so that the ribosome can fuse that amino acid to the previous one. If the resulting string of amino acids is short (say, 50 amino acids or so), it is called a **peptide;** if it is long, it is called a *protein*. Thus the ribosome assembles a very particular sequence of amino acids at the behest of a very particular sequence of RNA nucleotides, which were themselves encoded in the DNA inherited from our parents. In short, the secret of life is that DNA makes RNA, and RNA makes protein.

There are fascinating amendments to this short story. Often the information from separate stretches of DNA is spliced together to make a single transcript; so-called alternate splicing can create different transcripts from the same gene. Sometimes a transcript is modified extensively before translation begins; special chemical processes can cleave long proteins to create one or several active peptides. But we will not consider those processes in this book.

Keep in mind that each cell has the complete library of genetic information (collectively known as the **genome**) but makes only a fraction of all the proteins encoded in that DNA. In modern biology we say that each cell **expresses** only some genes; that is, the cell transcribes certain genes and makes the corresponding gene products (protein molecules). Thus each cell must come to express all the genes needed to perform its function. Modern biologists refer to the expression of a particular subset of the genome as cell differentiation: The process differentiates the appearance and function of different types of cells. During development, individual cells appear to become more and more specialized, expressing progressively fewer genes. Many molecular biologists are striving to understand which cellular and molecular mechanisms "turn on" or "turn off" gene expression in order to understand development and pathologies such as cancer.

Molecular Biologists Have Craftily Enslaved Microorganisms and Enzymes

Many basic methods of molecular biology are not explicitly discussed in the text, so we will not describe them in detail here. However, you should understand what some of the terms *mean*, even if you don't know exactly how the methods are performed.

Molecular biologists have found ways to incorporate foreign DNA from other species into the DNA of microorganisms such as bacteria and viruses. After incorporating the foreign DNA, the microorganisms are allowed to reproduce rapidly, producing more and more copies of the (foreign) gene of interest. At this point the gene is said to be **cloned** because the researcher can make as many copies as she likes. To ensure that the right gene is being cloned, the researcher generally clones many, many different genes, each into different bacteria, and then "screens" the bacteria rapidly to find the rare one that has incorporated the gene of interest.

When enough copies of the DNA have been made, the microorganisms are ground up and the DNA extracted. If sufficient DNA has been generated, chemical steps can then determine the exact sequence of nucleotides found in that stretch of DNA—a process known as **sequencing.** Once the sequence of nucleotides has been determined, the sequence of complementary nucleotides in the messenger RNA for that gene can be inferred. The sequence of mRNA nucleotides tells the investigator the sequence of amino acids that will be made from that transcript because biologists know which amino acid is encoded by each triplet of DNA nucleotides. In this manner scientists have discovered the amino acid sequence of neurotransmitter receptors, including the structure of photoreceptors that allows us to see.

The business of obtaining many copies of DNA has been boosted by a technique called the **polymerase chain reaction,** or **PCR.** This technique exploits a special type of polymerase enzyme that, like other such enzymes, induces the formation of a DNA molecule that is complementary to an existing single strand of DNA. Because this particular polymerase enzyme evolved in bacteria that inhabit geothermal hot springs, it can function in a broad range of temperatures. By heating double-stranded DNA, we can cause the two strands to separate, making each strand available to polymerase enzymes that, when the temperature is cooled enough, construct a new "mate" for each strand so that they are double-stranded again. The first PCR yields only double the number of DNA molecules you began with; repeating the process results in four times as many molecules as at first. Repeatedly heating and

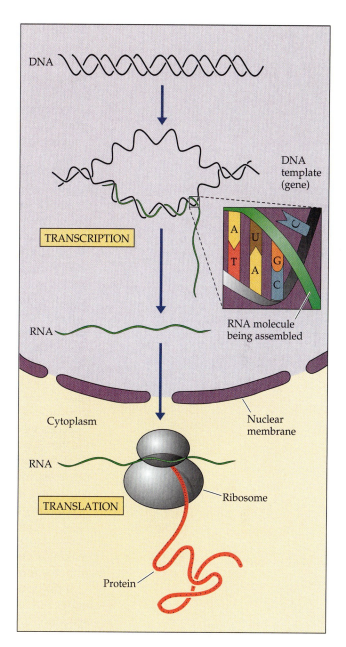

A.2 DNA Makes RNA, and RNA Makes Protein

cooling the DNA of interest in the presence of this heat-resistant polymerase enzyme soon yields millions of copies of the original DNA molecule.

Thus PCR amplifies even tiny amounts of DNA into amounts large enough for chemical analysis or other manipulations, such as introducing DNA into cells. For example, you might inject some of the DNA encoding a protein of interest into a fertilized mouse egg (a zygote) and then return the zygote to a pregnant mouse to grow. Occasionally the injected DNA becomes incorporated into the zygote's genome, so the **transgenic** mouse that results carries and uses this foreign gene.

Southern Blots Identify Particular Genes

Because all cells contain a complete copy of the genome, if we want to know whether a particular individual or a particular species carries a certain gene, we can gather DNA from just about any cell population (for humans, blood is drawn; for rodents, the tip of the tail may be used). Then we can grind up the cells and use chemical extraction procedures to isolate the DNA (discarding the RNA and protein). Finding a particular gene in that DNA really boils down to finding *a particular sequence of DNA nucleotides.* To do that, we can exploit the tendency of nucleic acids to hybridize with one another.

If we were looking for the DNA sequence GCT, for example, we could manufacture the sequence CGA (there are machines to do that readily), which would then stick to (hybridize with) any DNA sequence of GCT. The manufactured sequence CGA is called a **probe** because it is made to include some radioactive molecules so that we can follow the radioactivity to find out where the sequence goes. Of course, such a short length of nucleotides will be found in many genes. In order for a probe to recognize one particular gene, it has to be at least 15 nucleotides long.

When we extract DNA from an individual, it's convenient to let enzymes cut up the very long stretches of DNA into more manageable pieces of 1000 to 20,000 nucleotides each. A process called **gel electrophoresis** uses electrical current to separate those millions of pieces more or less by size. Large pieces move slowly through a tube of gelatin-like material, and small pieces move rapidly. The tube of gel is then sliced and placed on top of a sheet of paperlike material called *nitrocellulose.* When fluid is allowed to flow through the gel and nitrocellulose, DNA molecules are pulled out of the gel and deposited on the waiting nitrocellulose. This process of making a "sandwich" of gel and nitrocellulose and using fluid to move molecules from the former to the latter is called **blotting** (Figure A.3).

If the gene we are looking for is among those millions of DNA fragments sitting on the nitrocellulose, our radiolabeled probe should recognize and hybridize to the sequence. The nitrocellulose sheet is soaked in a solution containing our radiolabeled probe; we wait for the probe to find and hybridize with the gene of interest (if it is present), and rinse the sheet to remove probe molecules that did not find the gene. Then photographic film is placed next to the nitrocellulose. The particles emitted by the radioactive probe molecule will expose the film just as light does. If the radiolabeled probe found the gene, the film will be dark at one particular place, corresponding to the size of DNA fragment that contained the gene (see Figure A.3).

This process of looking for a particular sequence of DNA is called **Southern blotting,** named after the man who developed the technique, Edward Southern, and the final film is often called a *Southern blot.* Southern blots are useful for determining whether related individuals share a particular gene or for assessing the evolutionary relatedness of different species.

Northern Blots Identify Particular RNA Transcripts

A more relevant method for our discussions is the **Northern blot** (whimsically named as the opposite of a Southern blot). A Northern blot can identify which tissues make use of a particular gene. If liver cells are making a particular protein, for example, then some transcripts for the gene that encodes that protein should be pres-

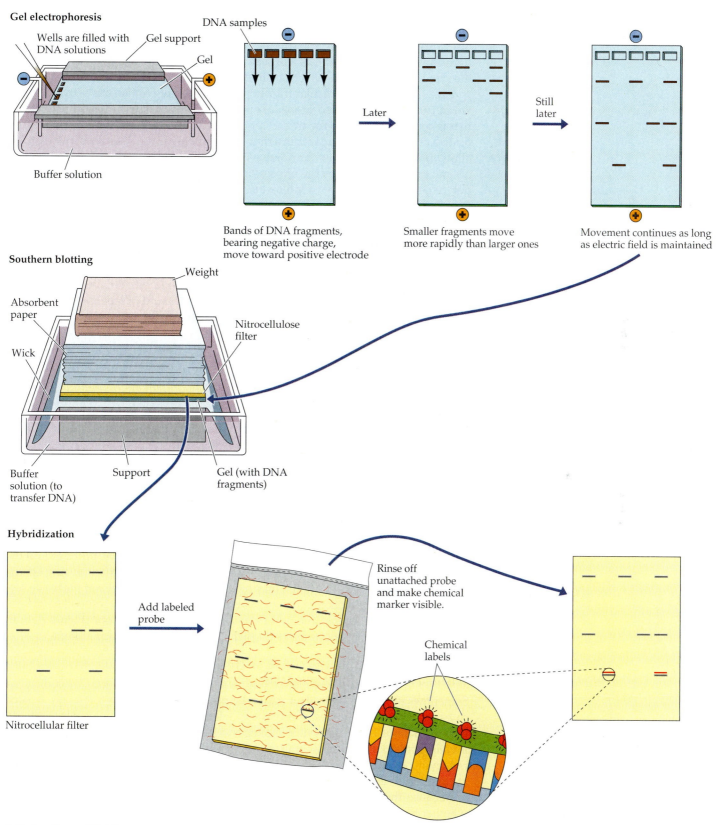

Gel electrophoresis

Wells are filled with DNA solutions
Gel support
DNA samples
Gel

Buffer solution

Bands of DNA fragments, bearing negative charge, move toward positive electrode

Later

Smaller fragments move more rapidly than larger ones

Still later

Movement continues as long as electric field is maintained

Southern blotting

Weight
Absorbent paper
Wick
Nitrocellulose filter
Buffer solution (to transfer DNA)
Support
Gel (with DNA fragments)

Hybridization

Nitrocellular filter

Add labeled probe

Rinse off unattached probe and make chemical marker visible.

Chemical labels

A.3 Southern Blotting

ent. So we can take the liver, grind it up, and use chemical processes to isolate most of the RNA (throwing the DNA and protein away). Unlike purified DNA, this mixture consists of RNA molecules of many different sizes—long, medium, and short transcripts. Gel electrophoresis will separate the transcripts by size, and we can blot the size-sorted mRNAs onto nitrocellulose sheets.

To see whether the particular transcript we are looking for is among the mRNAs, we construct a radiolabeled probe (of either DNA nucleotides or RNA nucleotides) that is complementary to the transcript of interest and long enough that it will hybridize only to that particular transcript. We incubate the nitrocellulose in the probe, allow time for the probe to hybridize with the targeted transcript (if present), rinse off any unused probes, lay the nitrocellulose next to photographic film, and wait a day or so. If the transcript of interest is present, we should see a band on the film (see Figure A.3). The presence of several bands indicates that the probe has hybridized to more than one transcript and we need to make a more specific probe or alter chemical conditions to make the probe less likely to bind similar transcripts.

Because different gene transcripts are of different lengths, the transcript of interest should have reached a particular point in the gel electrophoresis; small transcripts should have moved far; large transcripts should have moved only a little. If our probe has found the right transcript, the single band of labeling should be at the point that is appropriate for a transcript of that length.

In Situ Hybridization Identifies Cells That Possess a Particular Transcript

Northern blots can tell us whether a particular *organ* has transcripts for a particular gene product. For example, Northern blot analyses have indicated that thousands of genes are transcribed only in the brain. Presumably the proteins encoded by these genes are used exclusively in the brain. But such results alone are not very informative because the brain consists of so many different kinds of glial and neuronal cells. We can refine Northern blot analyses somewhat by dissecting out a particular part of the brain—say, the hippocampus—to isolate mRNAs. Sometimes, though, it is important to know *exactly which cells* are making the transcript. In that case we use **in situ hybridization.**

With in situ hybridization we use the same sort of labeled probe, constructed of nucleotides that are complementary to (and will therefore hybridize with) the targeted transcript, as in Northern blots. Instead of using the probe to find and hybridize with the transcript on a sheet of nitrocellulose, however, we use the probe to find the transcripts "in place" (in situ)—that is, on a section of tissue. After rinsing off the probe molecules that didn't find a match, we can look for the probe in the tissue section. Any cells in the section that were transcribing the gene of interest will have transcripts in the cytoplasm and should have some of our labeled probe (Figure A.4). In situ hybridization can tell us exactly which cells are using a particular gene.

Western Blots Identify the Organ or Tissue Region Where a Particular Protein Is Made

Sometimes we wish to identify a particular protein rather than its transcript. In such cases we can use antibodies. **Antibodies** are large, complicated molecules (proteins, in fact) that our immune system makes and releases into the bloodstream to fight invading microbes, thereby arresting and preventing disease (see Figure 15.16). Injection of a rabbit or mouse with the protein of interest can induce the animal to create antibodies that recognize and attach to that particular protein.

Because there are ways to label such antibodies, they can be used to tell us whether the targeted protein is present. We grind up an organ, isolate the proteins (throwing the DNA and RNA away), and separate them via gel electrophoresis. Then we blot these proteins out of the gel and onto nitrocellulose. Next we use the antibodies to tell us whether the targeted protein is among those made by that organ. If the antibodies identify only the protein we care about, there should be a single band of labeling (if there are two, then the antibodies recognize more than one

A.4 In Situ Hybridization

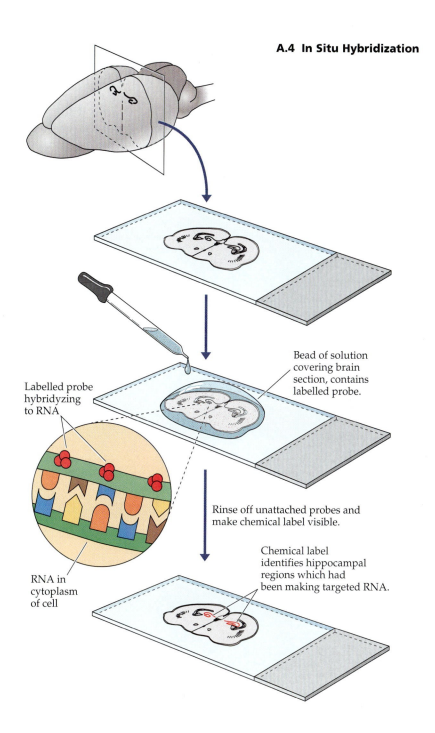

Bead of solution covering brain section, contains labelled probe.

Labelled probe hybridyzing to RNA

RNA in cytoplasm of cell

Rinse off unattached probes and make chemical label visible.

Chemical label identifies hippocampal regions which had been making targeted RNA.

protein). Because proteins come in different sizes, the single band of label should be at the position corresponding to the size of the protein we are studying. Such blots are called **Western blots.**

To review, Southern blots identify particular DNA pieces (genes), Northern blots identify particular RNA pieces (transcripts), and Western blots identify particular proteins (sometimes called *products*).

Antibodies Can Also Tell Us Which Cells Possess a Particular Protein

If we need to know which particular cells within an organ such as the brain are making a particular protein, we can use the same sorts of antibodies that we use in Western blots, but in this case directed at that protein in tissue sections. We slice up the brain, expose the sections to the antibodies, allow time for them to find and attach to the protein, rinse off unattached antibodies, and use chemical treatments to visualize the antibodies. Cells that were making the protein will be labeled from the chemical treatments (see Box 2.1).

Because antibodies from the *immune* system are used to identify *cells* with the aid of *chemical* treatment, this method is called **immunocytochemistry,** or **ICC.** This technique can even tell us where, within the cell, the protein is found. Such information can provide important clues about the function of the protein. For example, if the protein is found in axon terminals, it may be a neurotransmitter.

Glossary

2-deoxyglucose (2-DG) A molecule that resembles glucose. When injected into an animal, 2-DG accumulates more readily in active neurons than in inactive neurons, so it can indicate which parts of the brain are active during a given task.

5α-reductase An enzyme that converts testosterone into dihydrotestosterone (DHT).

5-HT See *serotonin*.

Aδ fiber A moderately large, myelinated, and therefore fast-conducting axon, usually transmitting pain information. See Table 8.2. Contrast with *C fiber*.

absolute refractory phase See *refractory phase*.

accommodation The process of focusing by the ciliary muscles and the lens to form a sharp image on the retina.

acetylcholine (ACh) One of the best-known synaptic transmitters. Acetylcholine acts as an excitatory transmitter at synapses between motor nerves and skeletal muscles but as an inhibitory transmitter between the vagus nerve and the heart muscle.

acetylcholinesterase (AChE) An enzyme that inactivates the transmitter acetylcholine both at synaptic sites and elsewhere in the nervous system.

ACh See *acetycholine*.

AChE See *acetylcholinesterase*.

acquired dyslexia Dyslexia that occurs as a result of injury or disease. See also *alexia*.

acquired immune deficiency syndrome (AIDS) A disease characterized by the loss of immune function that is spread by the human immunodeficiency virus (HIV).

act Complex behavior, as distinct from a simple movement. Also called *action pattern*.

ACTH See *adrenocorticotropic hormone*.

actin A protein that, along with myosin, mediates the contraction of muscle fibers. See Figure 11.7.

action pattern See *act*.

action potential The propagated electrical message of a neuron that travels along the axon to adjacent neurons. Also called *nerve impulse*. See Figures 3.5, 3.7.

activational effect A temporary change in behavior resulting from the administration of a hormone to an adult animal. Contrast with *organizational effect*.

acupuncture The insertion of needles at designated points on the skin to alleviate pain.

adaptation The progressive loss of receptor sensitivity as stimulation is maintained. See Figure 8.7.

adaptation stage The second stage in the stress response; it includes successful activation of the appropriate response systems and the reestablishment of homeostatic balance.

adenohypophysis See *anterior pituitary*.

adequate stimulus The type of stimulus for which a given sensory organ is particularly adapted. Light energy, for example, is the adequate stimulus for photoreceptors.

ADH See *antidiuretic hormone*.

adipose tissue Tissue made up of fat cells.

adipsia A condition in which an individual refuses to drink.

adrenal cortex The outer covering of the adrenal gland. Each of the three cellular layers of the adrenal cortex produces different hormones. See Figures 5.1, 5.15, Table 5.2.

adrenal gland An endocrine gland adjacent to the kidney. See Figures 5.1, 5.16.

adrenal medulla The inner core of the adrenal gland. The adrenal medulla secretes epinephrine and norepinephrine. See Figures 5.1, 5.16.

adrenaline See *epinephrine*.

adrenocorticoids A class of steroid hormones that are secreted by the adrenal cortex. Also called *adrenosteroids*.

adrenocorticotropic hormone (ACTH) A tropic hormone secreted by the anterior pituitary gland that controls the production and release of hormones of the adrenal cortex. See Table 5.2, Figure 5.15.

adrenosteroids See *adrenocorticoids*.

afferent fiber An axon that carries nerve impulses from a sensory organ to the central nervous system, or from one region to another region of interest. Contrast with *efferent fiber*.

affinity See *binding affinity*.

afterpotential The positive or negative change in membrane potential that may follow a nerve impulse.

agnosia The inability to recognize objects, despite being able to describe them in terms of form and color; may occur after localized brain damage.

agonist **1.** A molecule, usually a drug, that binds a receptor and initiates a response like that of another molecule, usually a neurotransmitter. Contrast with *antagonist* (definition 1). **2.** A muscle that moves a body part in the same general way as the muscle of interest; a synergistic muscle. Contrast with *antagonist* (definition 2).

agouti-related peptide (AGRP) A peptide that is a naturally occurring antagonist to α-melanocyte stimulating hormone at melanocortin receptors.

agraphia The inability to write.

AGRP See *agouti-related peptide*.

AIDS See *acquired immune deficiency syndrome*.

alarm reaction The initial response to stress.

aldosterone A mineralocorticoid hormone, secreted by the adrenal cortex, that helps maintain homeostasis in the concentrations of ions in blood and extracellular fluid by inducing the kidneys to conserve sodium.

alexia The inability to read.

alkaloids A class of chemicals, found in plants, that includes many psychoactive agents, such as curare, the opium alkaloids (morphine and codeine), and lysergic acid (to which LSD is related).

all-or-none Referring to the fact that the amplitude of the nerve impulse is independent of the magnitude of the stimulus. Stimuli above a certain threshold produce nerve impulses of identical magnitude (although they may vary in frequency); stimuli below this threshold produce no nerve impulses. See Figure 3.5. Contrast with *graded potential*.

allele Any particular version of a gene.

allomone   A chemical signal that is released outside the body by one species and affects the behavior of other species. See Figure 5.4. Contrast with *pheromone*.

allopregnanolone   A naturally occurring steroid that modulates GABA receptor activity in much the same way that benzodiazepine anxiolytics do.

α-fetoprotein   A protein found in the plasma of fetuses. In rodents α-fetoprotein binds estrogens and prevents them from entering the brain.

α-melanocyte stimulating hormone (α-MSH)   A peptide that binds the melanocortin receptor.

alpha motoneuron   A motoneuron that controls the main contractile fibers (extrafusal fibers) of a muscle. See Figure 11.9.

α-MSH   See *α-melanocyte stimulating hormone*.

alpha rhythm   A brain potential that occurs during relaxed wakefulness, especially at the back of the head; its frequency is 8 to 12 Hz. See Figure 14.11.

ALS   See *amyotrophic lateral sclerosis*.

altricial   Referring to animals that are born in an undeveloped state and depend on maternal care, as human infants do. Contrast with *precocial*.

Alzheimer's disease   A form of dementia that may appear in middle age but is more frequent among the aged.

amacrine cells   A class of cells in the retina that contact both the bipolar cells and the ganglion cells, and are especially significant in inhibitory interactions within the retina.

amblyopia   Reduced visual acuity that is not caused by optical or retinal impairments.

AMH   See *anti-müllerian hormone*.

amine hormones   A class of compounds, each composed of a single amino acid that has been modified into a related molecule, such as melatonin or epinephrine. Also called *monoamine hormones*.

amnesia   Severe impairment of memory.

amnestic   An amnesia-causing agent.

AMPA receptor   A glutamate receptor that also binds the glutamate agonist AMPA (α-amino-3-hydroxy-5-methyl-4-isoxazole-propionic acid). The AMPA receptor is responsible for most of the activity at glutaminergic synapses. See Box 4.2, Figure 18.8.

amphetamine   A molecule that resembles the structure of the catecholamine transmitters and that enhances their activity.

amplitude   Here, the distance of particle movement in a defined period of time, usually measured as dynes per square centimeter. See Box 9.1.

ampulla (pl. ampullae)   An enlarged region of each semicircular canal that contains the receptor cells (hair cells) of the vestibular system. See Figure 9.15.

amygdala   A group of nuclei in the medial anterior part of the temporal lobe. See Figure 2.15.

amyloid precursor protein (APP)   A protein that, when cleaved by several enzymes, produces β-amyloid. Buildup of β-amyloid is thought to cause Alzheimer's disease.

amyotrophic lateral sclerosis (ALS)   A disease in which motoneurons and their target muscles waste away.

analgesia   Absence of or reduction in pain.

analgesic   Referring to painkilling properties.

analogy   Similarity of function, although the structures of interest may look different (e.g., the hand of a human and the trunk of an elephant).

anandamide   An endogenous substance that binds the cannabinoid receptor.

androgen insensitivity   The inability to respond to androgenic hormones; caused by a defect in the gene for the androgen receptor.

androgens   A class of hormones that includes testosterone and other male hormones. See Table 5.2, Figure 5.17.

androstenedione   The chief sex hormone secreted by the human adrenal cortex. This hormone is responsible for the adult pattern of body hair in men and women.

angiography   A noninvasive technique for examining brain structure in humans by taking X-rays after special dyes are injected into cerebral blood vessels. Inferences about adjacent tissue can be made from examination of the outline of the principal blood vessels.

angiotensin II   A substance that is produced in the blood by the action of renin and that may be involved in control of thirst.

angular gyrus   A brain region in which strokes can lead to word blindness.

anion   A negatively charged ion, such as a protein or chloride ion. Contrast with *cation*.

anomia   The inability to name persons or objects readily.

anorexia   Absence of appetite.

anorexia nervosa   A syndrome in which individuals severely deprive themselves of food.

anosmia   The inability to smell.

antagonist   **1.** A molecule, usually a drug, that interferes with or prevents the action of a transmitter. Contrast with *agonist* (definition 1). **2.** A muscle that counteracts the effect of another muscle. Contrast with *synergist* or *agonist* (definition 2).

anterior   Toward the front or head of an animal. Contrast with *posterior*.

anterior pituitary   The front lobe of the pituitary gland; secretes tropic hormones. Also called *adenohypophysis*. See Figures 5.1, 5.14, Table 5.2.

anterograde amnesia   The inability to form new memories beginning with the onset of a disorder. Contrast with *retrograde amnesia*.

anterograde degeneration   The loss of the distal portion of an axon resulting from injury to the axon. Also called *wallerian degeneration*. See Box 7.1. Contrast with *retrograde degeneration*.

anterolateral system   A somatosensory system that carries most of the pain information from the body to the brain. Also called *spinothalamic system*. See Figures 8.23, 8.24.

antibody   A large protein that recognizes and permanently binds to particular shapes, normally as part of the immune system attack on foreign particles.

antidiuretic hormone (ADH)   See *vasopressin*.

antigen   A substance that stimulates the production of antibodies.

anti-müllerian hormone (AMH)   A protein hormone secreted by the fetal testis that inhibits müllerian duct development. Also called *müllerian regression hormone*.

antipsychotics   A class of drugs that alleviate schizophrenia.

anxiety states   A class of psychological disorders that include recurrent panic states, generalized persistent anxiety disorders, and posttraumatic stress disorders.

anxiolytics   A class of substances that are used to combat anxiety; examples include alcohol, opiates, barbiturates, and the benzodiazepines.

aphagia   The refusal to eat; often related to damage to the lateral hypothalamus.

aphasia   An impairment in language understanding and/or production that is caused by brain injury.

apical dendrite   The dendrite that extends from a pyramidal cell to the outermost surface of the cortex. Contrast with *basal dendrite*.

ApoE   Apolipoprotein E, a protein that may help break down amyloid. Individuals carrying the *ApoE4* allele are more likely to develop Alzheimer's disease.

apoptosis   See *cell death*.

APP   See *amyloid precursor protein*.

appetitive behavior   The second stage of mating behavior; helps establish or maintain sexual interaction. See Figure 12.2.

apraxia   An impairment in the ability to begin and execute skilled voluntary movements, even though there is no muscle paralysis.

arachnoid   The thin covering (one of the three meninges) of the brain that lies between the dura mater and pia mater.

arcuate fasciculus   A tract connecting Wernicke's speech area to Broca's speech area. See Figure 19.8.

arcuate nucleus   An arc-shaped hypothalamic nucleus.

area 17   See *primary visual cortex.*

area postrema   One of the circumventricular nuclei that have weak blood–brain barriers. See Figure 13.17.

arginine vasopressin   See *vasopressin.*

aromatase   An enzyme that converts many androgens into estrogens.

aromatization   The chemical reaction that converts testosterone to estradiol, and other androgens to other estrogens.

aromatization hypothesis   The hypothesis that testicular androgens enter the brain and are converted there into estrogens to masculinize the developing nervous system of some rodents.

aspartate   An amino acid transmitter that is excitatory at many synapses.

associative learning   A type of learning in which an association is formed between two stimuli or between a stimulus and a response; includes both classical and instrumental conditioning. Contrast with *nonassociative learning.*

astereognosis   The inability to recognize objects by touching and feeling them.

astrocyte   A star-shaped glial cell with numerous processes (extensions) that run in all directions. The extensions of astrocytes provide structural support for the brain and may isolate receptive surfaces. See Figure 2.6.

ataxia   An impairment in the direction, extent, and rate of muscular movement; often caused by cerebellar pathology.

attention   A state or condition of selective awareness or perceptual receptivity, possibly involving activation of certain brain regions. See Figure 8.13.

attribute model of memory   A model in which different brain regions process different dimensions or attributes of a learning or memory situation—space, time, sensory dimensions, response, and emotional aspects.

audiologist   A person who measures hearing abilities.

auditory cortex   A region of the temporal lobe that receives input from the medial geniculate nucleus. See Figure 9.6.

auditory-evoked potential   A change in EEG potential that follows presentation of an auditory stimulus. See Figure 3.19.

auditory nerve   Cranial nerve VIII, which runs from the cochlea to the brainstem auditory nuclei. Also called *vestibulocochlear nerve.* See Figures 2.8, 9.1.

autism   A disorder arising during childhood, characterized by social withdrawal and stereotypy.

autocrine   Referring to a signal that is secreted by a cell into its environment and that feeds back to the same cell. See Figure 5.4.

autonomic ganglia   One of the three main divisions of the peripheral nervous system; includes the two chains of sympathetic ganglia and the more peripheral parasympathetic ganglia.

autonomic nervous system   The part of the peripheral nervous system that supplies neural connections to glands and to smooth muscles of internal organs. Its two divisions (sympathetic and parasympathetic) act in opposite fashion. See Figure 2.10.

autonomic response specificity   Patterns of bodily response governed by the autonomic nervous system that are characteristic of an individual.

autoradiography   A histological technique that shows the distribution of radioactive chemicals in tissues.

autoreceptor   A receptor for a synaptic transmitter that is located in the presynaptic membrane. Autoreceptors tell the axon terminal how much transmitter has been released.

autosome   One of a pair of chromosomes that are identical. All chromosomes except the sex chromosomes are autosomes.

axon   A single extension from the nerve cell that carries nerve impulses from the cell body to other neurons. See Figures 2.3, 2.5.

axon collateral   A branch of an axon from a single neuron.

axon hillock   A cone-shaped area from which the axon originates out of the cell body. Depolarization must reach a critical threshold at the axon hillock for the neuron to transmit a nerve impulse. See Figure 2.4.

axon terminal   The end of an axon or axon collateral, which forms a synapse on a neuron or other target.

axonal transport   The transportation of materials from the neuron cell body to distant regions in the dendrites and axons, and from the axon terminals back to the cell body.

B cell   See *B lymphocyte.*

B lymphocyte   An immune system cell that mediates humoral immunity. Also called *B cell.* See Figure 15.17.

ballistic movement   A rapid muscular movement that is thought to be organized or programmed by the cerebellum. Contrast with *ramp movement.*

barbiturates

baroreceptor   A pressure receptor in the heart or a major artery that detects a fall in blood pressure and communicates that information to the brain via the autonomic nervous system.

basal dendrite   One of several dendrites on a pyramidal cell that extend horizontally from the cell body. Contrast with *apical dendrite.*

basal forebrain   A ventral region in the forebrain that has been implicated in sleep and Alzheimer's disease. See Figure 4.2.

basal ganglia   A group of forebrain nuclei found deep within the cerebral hemispheres. See Figures 2.13, 2.15, 11.12.

basal metabolism   The rate of metabolism when a body is at rest.

basal nucleus of Meynert   See *magnocellular nucleus of the basal forebrain.*

base   A component of a DNA or RNA molecule. DNA contains four bases (adenine, thymine, cytosine, and guanine), a pair of which forms each rung of the molecule. The order of these bases determines the genetic information of a DNA molecule.

basic rest–activity cycle   A cycle of repeating periods of rest and activity that occur both in waking hours and during sleep.

basilar artery   An artery formed by the fusion of the vertebral arteries; its branches supply blood to the brainstem and to posterior portions of the cerebral hemispheres. See Figure 2.20.

basilar membrane   A membrane in the cochlea that contains the principal structures involved in auditory transduction. See Figures 9.1, 9.3.

Bcl-2   A family of genes, the protein products of which regulate apoptosis.

BDNF   See *brain-derived neurotrophic factor.*

BEAM   See *brain electrical activity mapping.*

behavioral intervention   An approach to finding relations between bodily variables and behavioral variables that involves intervening in the behavior of an organism and looking for resultant changes in body structure or function. See Figure 1.3. Contrast with *somatic intervention.*

behavioral teratology   The study of impairments in behavior that are produced by embryonic or fetal exposure to toxic substances.

benzodiazepines   A class of antianxiety drugs that bind with high affinity to receptors in the central nervous system; one example is diazepam (Valium).

β-amyloid   A protein that accumulates in senile plaques in Alzheimer's disease.

β-secretase   An enzyme that cleaves amyloid precursor protein (APP), forming amyloid that can lead to Alzheimer's disease.

bigamy A mating system in which an individual has two mates or spouses. Contrast with *monogamy* and *polygamy*.

binaural detection The detection of sound using two ears. See Figure 9.10. Contrast with *monaural detection*.

binaural interaction The interaction of signals from two ears; especially important for localizing auditory stimuli.

binding affinity Theoretically, the length of time a transmitter or drug molecule binds to a receptor molecule. Practically, the concentration of transmitter or drug molecule that is required to bind half of the receptors at equilibrium.

binocular deprivation Depriving both eyes of form vision, as by sealing the eyelids. Contrast with *monocular deprivation*.

binocular disparity The slight difference between the views from the two eyes; important in depth perception.

biological marker A biological variable that accompanies a psychological disorder, irrespective of whether it directly causes the disorder.

biological rhythm Any change in a biological measure that repeats periodically.

bipolar cells A class of interneurons of the retina that receive information from rods and cones and pass the information to retinal ganglion cells. See Figures 10.7, 10.25.

bipolar disorder A psychiatric disorder characterized by periods of depression that alternate with excessive, expansive moods. Also called *manic–depressive psychosis*. Contrast with *unipolar depression*.

bipolar neuron A nerve cell that has a single dendrite at one end and a single axon at the other end; found in some vertebrate sensory systems. See Figure 2.3. Contrast with *multipolar neuron* and *monopolar neuron*.

blind spot The place through which blood vessels enter the retina. Because there are no receptors in this region, light striking it cannot be seen. See Figure 10.1.

blood–brain barrier The mechanisms that make the movement of substances from capillaries into brain cells more difficult than exchanges in other body organs, thus affording the brain greater protection from exposure to some substances found in the blood.

bouton See *synaptic bouton*.

bovine spongiform encephalopathy (BSE) Mad cow disease; a disorder caused by improperly formed prion proteins, leading to dementia and death.

brain-derived neurotrophic factor (BDNF) A protein purified from the brains of many animals that can keep some classes of neurons alive; resembles nerve growth factor.

brain electrical activity mapping (BEAM) A system of analysis and display of electrical brain signals. See Figure 3.19.

brain explant A small piece of brain tissue isolated from the body.

brain self-stimulation The process in which animals will work to provide electrical stimulation to particular brain sites, presumably because the experience is very rewarding.

brainstem The region of the brain that consists of the midbrain, the pons, and the medulla.

Brattleboro rat A rat that has a mutation in the gene for vasopressin that keeps the animal from producing functional hormone. Brattleboro rats show symptoms of diabetes insipidus.

brightness One of the basic dimensions of light perception; varies from dark to light. See Figure 10.5.

Broca's aphasia An impairment in speech production; related to damage in Broca's area. See Figure 19.7.

Broca's area An area in the frontal region of the left hemisphere of the brain that is involved in the production of speech. See Figures 19.6, 19.7, 19.8.

Brodmann's areas A classification of cortical regions based on subtle variations in the relative appearance of the six layers of neocortex. See Figure 2.17.

brown fat Tissue made up of fat cells that is found especially around vital organs in the trunk and around the cervical and thoracic levels of the spinal cord. Because it is capable of intense metabolism, brown fat can generate heat. Also called *brown adipose tissue*.

BSE See *bovine spongiform encephalopathy*.

bulimia A syndrome in which individuals believe themselves fatter than they are and periodically gorge themselves, usually with "junk food," and then either vomit or take laxatives to avoid weight gain. Also called *bulimia nervosa*.

C fiber A small, unmyelinated axon that conducts pain information slowly and adapts slowly. See Table 8.2. Contrast with *A δ fiber*.

caffeine A stimulant compound found in coffee, cacao, and other plants that may have evolved to protect plants against insect predators. Caffeine stimulates and causes uncoordinated behavior in insects and inhibits their growth and reproduction.

CAH See *congenital adrenal hyperplasia*.

calcitonin A hormone released by the thyroid gland. See Table 5.2.

calorie The amount of energy required to raise the temperature of 1 ml of water by 1°C.

CAM See *cell adhesion molecule*.

cAMP See *cyclic adenosine monophosphate*.

cannabinoids A class of substances that bind the same endogenous receptors that are bound by the active ingredient in marijuana, tetrahydrocannabinol (THC).

capsaicin A compound synthesized by various plants, to deter predators, that mimics the experience of burning. Capsaicin is responsible for the burning sensation in chili peppers.

carotid arteries The major arteries that ascend the left and right sides of the neck to the brain. The branch that enters the brain is called the internal carotid artery. See Figure 2.20.

CART See *cocaine- and amphetamine-related peptide*.

caspases A family of proteins that regulate cell death (apoptosis).

castration Removal of the gonads, usually the testes.

CAT See *computerized axial tomography*.

cataplexy The sudden loss of muscle tone, leading to collapse of the body without loss of consciousness.

catecholamines A class of monoamines that serve as neurotransmitters, including dopamine and norepinephrine. See Table 4.1.

cation A positively charged ion, such as a potassium or sodium ion. Contrast with *anion*.

caudal An anatomical term referring to structures toward the tail end of an organism. Contrast with *rostral*.

caudate nucleus One of the basal ganglia; it has a long extension or tail. See Figure 2.15.

CCK See *cholecystokinin*.

cell adhesion molecule (CAM) A protein found on the surface of a cell that guides cell migration and/or axonal pathfinding.

cell assembly A large group of cells that tend to be active at the same time because they have been activated simultaneously or in close succession in the past.

cell-autonomous Referring to cell processes that are directed by the cell itself rather than under the influence of other cells.

cell body The region of a neuron that is defined by the presence of the nucleus. See Figures 2.1, 2.3.

cell–cell interactions The general process during development in which one cell affects the differentiation of other, usually neighboring, cells.

cell death The developmental process during which "surplus" nerve cells die. Also called *apoptosis*. See Figure 7.3.

cell differentiation The developmental stage in which cells acquire distinctive characteristics, such as those of neurons, as the result of expressing particular genes. See Figure 7.3.

cell-mediated immunity   An immunological response that involves T lymphocytes. See also *immune system*. See Figure 15.17.

cell migration   The movement of cells from site of origin to final location. See Figures 7.3, 7.4.

cell proliferation   The production of cells by mitotic division. See Figure 7.4.

cellular fluid   See *intracellular fluid*.

central deafness   A hearing impairment that is related to lesions in auditory pathways or centers, including sites in the brainstem, thalamus, or cortex.

central nervous system (CNS)   The portion of the nervous system that includes the brain and the spinal cord. See Figures 2.7, 2.13.

central pattern generator   Neural circuitry that is responsible for generating a rhythmic pattern of behavior, such as walking.

central sulcus   A major groove that divides the frontal lobe from the parietal lobe. See Figure 2.11.

cephalic   See *rostral*.

cerebellar cortex   The outer surface of the cerebellum. See Figure 2.16.

cerebellum (pl. cerebellums or cerebella)   A structure located at the back of the brain, dorsal to the pons, that is involved in the central regulation of movement. See Figures 2.11, 2.13, 2.16.

cerebral cortex   The outer covering of the cerebral hemispheres, which consists largely of nerve cell bodies and their branches. See Figure 2.17.

cerebral hemispheres   The right and left halves of the forebrain. See Figure 2.11.

cerebral ventricle   A cavity in the brain that contains cerebrospinal fluid. See Figure 2.19.

cerebrospinal fluid (CSF)   The fluid that fills the cerebral ventricles. See Figure 2.19.

cerveau isolé   An experimental preparation in which an animal's nervous system has been cut in the upper midbrain, dividing the brain from the brainstem. See Figure 14.20. Contrast with *encéphale isolé*.

cervical   Referring to the neck region. See Figures 2.9, 2.10.

cGMP   See *cyclic guanosine monophosphate*.

chemical transmitter   See *synaptic transmitter*.

chemoaffinity hypothesis   The notion that each cell has a chemical identity that directs it to synapse on the proper target cell during development. See Box 7.2.

chemoattractants   Compounds that attract particular classes of growth cones. Contrast *chemorepellents*.

chemorepellents   Compounds that repel particular classes of growth cones. Contrast *chemoattractants*.

chlorpromazine   An antipsychotic drug, one of the class of phenothiazines.

cholecystokinin (CCK)   A hormone that is released from the lining of the duodenum and that may be involved in the satiation of hunger. See Table 5.2.

cholinergic   Referring to cells that use acetylcholine as their synaptic transmitter.

choreic movement   An uncontrollable, brief, and forceful muscular movement that is related to basal ganglia dysfunction.

choroid plexus   A highly vascular portion of the lining of the ventricles that secretes cerebrospinal fluid.

chromosome   A complex of condensed strands of DNA and associated protein molecules; found in the nucleus of cells.

ciliary muscle   One of the muscles that controls the shape of the lens inside the eye, focusing an image on the retina. See Figure 10.2.

cilium (pl. cilia)   A hairlike extension; the extensions in the hair cells of the cochlea, for example, are cilia. See Figure 9.1.

cingulate cortex   A region of medial cerebral cortex that lies dorsal to the corpus callosum. Also called *cingulum*. See Figures 2.15, 16.15.

cingulate gyrus   A cortical portion of the limbic system, found in the frontal and parietal midline. See Figures 2.11, 2.15.

cingulum   See *cingulate cortex*.

circadian oscillator   A theoretical circuit with an output that repeats about once per day.

circadian rhythm   A pattern of behavioral, biochemical, and physiological fluctuation that has a 24-hour period.

circannual   Occurring on a roughly annual basis.

circle of Willis   A structure at the base of the brain that is formed by the joining of the carotid and basilar arteries. See Figure 2.20.

circuit   An assemblage that includes an arrangement of neurons and their interconnections. Circuits often perform a particular limited function. In a local circuit, all the neurons are contained within a level of brain organization of a particular region. Contrast with *system*.

circumvallate papillae   One of three types of small structures on the tongue that contain taste receptors. See Figure 9.17.

circumventricular organ   An organ that lies in the wall of a cerebral ventricle. Circumventricular organs contain receptor sites that can be affected by substances in the cerebrospinal fluid. See Figure 13.17.

CJD   See *Creutzfeldt–Jakob disease*.

classical conditioning   A type of associative learning in which an originally neutral stimulus (the conditioned stimulus, or CS)—through pairing with another stimulus that elicits a particular response (the unconditioned stimulus, or US)—acquires the power to elicit that response when presented alone. A response elicited by the US is called an unconditioned response (UR); a response elicited by the CS alone is called a conditioned response (CR). Also called *Pavlovian conditioning*.

clitoris (pl. clitorides)   A small mound of tissue just anterior to the vaginal opening. Stimulation of the clitoris produces orgasm in most women. See Figures 12.7, 12.14.

cloaca (pl. cloacae)   The sex organ in many birds, through which sperm are discharged (in the male) and eggs are laid (in the female). This is the same passage through which wastes are eliminated.

clones   Asexually produced organisms that are genetically identical.

closed-loop control mechanism   A control mechanism that provides a flow of information from whatever is being controlled to the device that controls it. See Figure 11.3. Contrast with *open-loop control mechanism*.

clozapine   An antipsychotic drug.

CNS   See *central nervous system*.

CNV   See *contingent negative variation*.

cocaine   A drug of abuse, derived from the coca plant, that acts by potentiating catecholamine stimulation.

cocaine- and amphetamine-related peptide (CART)   A peptide produced in the brain when an animal is injected with either cocaine or amphetamine.

coccygeal   Referring to the last, caudalmost, class of vertebrae in the spinal column. See Figure 2.10.

cochlea   A snail-shaped structure in the inner ear that contains the primary receptors for hearing. See Figure 9.1.

cochlear amplifier   The mechanism by which the cochlea is physically distorted by outer hair cells in order to "tune" the cochlea to be particularly sensitive to some frequencies more than others.

cochlear implant   An electromechanical device that detects sounds and selectively stimulates nerves in different regions of the cochlea via surgically implanted electrodes.

cochlear nuclei   Brainstem nuclei that receive input from auditory hair cells and send output to the superior olivary complex. See Figure 9.6.

coding   The rules by which action potentials in a sensory system reflect a physical stimulus.

cognitive map A mental representation of a spatial relationship.

coitus The sexual act. Also called *copulation*.

colliculus (pl. colliculi) A small elevation. Two pairs of colliculi are found on the dorsal surface of the midbrain. See Figure 2.11. The rostral pair (the superior colliculi) receive visual information (see Figure 10.13); the caudal pair (the inferior colliculi) receive auditory information (see Figure 9.6).

colloid A large, gluelike molecule that cannot pass through the cell membrane. When injected into the peritoneum, colloids attract and retain water by osmotic pressure.

co-localization Here, the appearance of more than one neurotransmitter in a given presynaptic terminal.

commissural fiber An axon that crosses the sagittal midline.

complex cortical cell A cell in the visual cortex that responds best to a bar of a particular size and orientation anywhere within a particular area of the visual field. See Figure 10.16. Contrast with *simple cortical cell*.

complex environment See *enriched condition*.

computerized axial tomography (CAT) A noninvasive technique for examining brain structure in humans through computer analysis of X-ray absorption at several positions around the head; affords a virtual direct view of the brain. The resulting images are referred to as CAT scans or CT scans. See Figure 2.21.

concentration gradient Variation of concentration of a substance within a region. See Figure 3.2.

concordant Referring to any trait that is seen in both individuals of identical twins. Contrast with *discordant*.

conditional learning A type of learning that teaches that a particular response to a particular stimulus is appropriate in one setting but not another.

conditioned response (CR) See *classical conditioning*.

conditioned stimulus (CS) See *classical conditioning*.

conditioned taste aversion The behavior in which an animal refuses to eat a food if it previously has become ill after eating that food.

conditioning A form of learning in which an organism comes to associate two stimuli, or a stimulus and a response. See Box 17.1. See also *classical conditioning, instrumental conditioning*.

condom A rubber sheath that is fitted over the penis to trap semen during sexual intercourse in order to prevent pregnancy and the transmission of disease.

conduction aphasia A language disorder in which comprehension remains intact but repetition of spoken language is impaired; related to damage of the pathways connecting Wernicke's area and Broca's area.

conduction deafness A hearing impairment that is associated with pathology of the external-ear or middle-ear cavities.

cone One of the receptor cells in the retina that are responsible for color vision. The three types of cones have somewhat different sensitivities to light of different wavelengths. See Figure 10.7. Contrast with *rod*.

confabulate To fill in a gap in memory with a falsification; often seen in Korsakoff's syndrome.

congenital Present at birth.

congenital adrenal hyperplasia (CAH) Any of several genetic mutations that can result in exposure of a female fetus to androgens, which results in a clitoris that is larger than normal at birth.

congenital insensitivity to pain A syndrome of being born without pain perception.

consolidation A stage of memory formation in which information in short-term or intermediate-term memory is transferred to long-term memory. See Figure 17.12.

consolidation hypothesis See *perseveration-consolidation hypothesis*.

constraint-induced-movement therapy A therapy for recovery of movement after stroke or injury, in which the person's unaffected limb is constrained while he is required to perform tasks with the affected limb.

contingent negative variation (CNV) A slow, event-related potential that is recorded from the scalp. A CNV arises in the interval between a warning signal and a signal that directs action.

convergence The phenomenon of neural connections in which many cells send signals to a single cell. See Figure 3.17. Contrast with *divergence*.

convergent evolution The evolutionary process by which responses to similar ecological features bring about similarities in behavior or structure among animals that are only distantly related (i.e., that differ in genetic heritage).

Coolidge effect The propensity of an animal that has appeared sexually satiated with a present partner to resume sexual activity when provided with a novel partner.

copulation See *coitus*.

copulatory behavior Coitus.

copulatory lock Reproductive behavior in which the male's penis swells after ejaculation so that the male and female are forced to remain joined for 5 to 10 minutes; occurs in dogs and some rodents, but not in humans.

cornea The transparent outer layer of the eye, whose curvature is fixed, bends light rays, and is primarily responsible for forming the image on the retina. See Figure 10.2.

coronal plane The plane that divides the body or brain into front and back parts. Also called *frontal plane* or *transverse plane*. See Box 2.2.

corpus callosum The band of axons that connects the two cerebral hemispheres. See Figures 2.11, 2.18.

correlation The covariation of two measures.

correlational approach An approach to finding relations between bodily variables and behavioral variables that involves finding the extent to which a particular body measure co-varies with a particular behavioral measure. See Figure 1.3.

cortex (pl. cortices) Outer layers. **1.** The cerebral cortex consists of the outer layers (gray matter) of the cerebral hemispheres. See Figure 2.12. **2.** The cerebellar cortex consists of the outer layers of the cerebellum. See Figure 2.16. **3.** The adrenal cortex consists of the outer layers of the adrenal gland. See Figure 5.15.

cortical barrel A barrel-shaped portion of somatosensory cortex. Each barrel receives input from receptors of an individual whisker. See Figure 7.21.

cortical column One of the vertical columns that constitute the basic organization of the neocortex. See Figure 8.19.

cortical deafness A hearing impairment that is caused by a fault or defect in the cortex.

cortical plate A structure arising from the early proliferation of cells at the rostral end of the neural tube; the beginnings of the cerebral cortex.

corticospinal system See *pyramidal system*.

corticosteroids A class of steroid hormones secreted from the adrenal cortex, including glucocorticoids and mineralocorticoids.

corticotropin-releasing hormone (CRH) A releasing hormone, produced by the hypothalamus, that controls the daily rhythm of adrenocorticotropic hormone release.

cortisol A glucocorticoid hormone of the adrenal cortex.

courtship The period during which two potential sexual partners increase their attractiveness toward each other.

CR See *classical conditioning*.

cranial Referring to the skull (cranium).

cranial nerves One of the three main subdivisions of the peripheral nervous system, composed of a set of pathways concerned mainly with sensory and motor systems associated with the head. See Figure 2.8.

cretinism   Reduced stature and mental retardation caused by thyroid deficiency.

Creutzfeldt–Jakob disease (CJD)   A brain disorder, leading to dementia and death, that is caused by improperly folded prion proteins.

CRH   See *corticotropin-releasing hormone.*

crib death   See *sudden infant death syndrome.*

critical range   The range within which a particular biological measure must remain to ensure good health.

cross-tolerance   A condition in which the development of tolerance for an administered drug causes an individual to develop tolerance for another drug.

cryptochrome   A protein that promotes the degradation of tim protein in the molecular circadian clock.

crystallization   The final stage of birdsong formation, in which fully formed adult song is achieved.

CS   See *classical conditioning.*

CSF   See *cerebrospinal fluid.*

CT scan   See *computerized axial tomography.*

cupula (pl. cupulae)   A small gelatinous column that forms part of the lateral-line system of aquatic animals and occurs within the vestibular system of mammals. See Figure 9.15.

Cushing's syndrome   A condition in which levels of adrenal glucocorticoids are high, often arising from pituitary tumors, adrenal tumors, or deliberate therapy involving corticosteroids.

cyclic adenosine monophosphate (cyclic AMP, or cAMP)   A second messenger that is involved in the synaptic activities of dopamine, norepinephrine, and serotonin.

cyclic AMP   See *cyclic adenosine monophosphate.*

cyclic GMP   See *cyclic guanosine monophosphate.*

cyclic guanosine monophosphate (cyclic GMP, or cGMP)   A second messenger that is common in postsynaptic cells.

cytoarchitectonics   The study of anatomical divisions of the brain based on the kinds and spacing of cells and the distribution of axons.

cytokine   A protein that induces the proliferation of other cells, as in the immune system. Examples include interleukins and interferons.

DA   See *dopamine.*

dB   See *decibel.*

deafferentation   The removal of sensory (afferent) input.

death gene   A gene that is expressed only when a cell becomes committed to natural cell death (apoptosis).

decibel (dB)   A measure of sound intensity. See Box 9.1.

declarative memory   A memory that can be stated or described. Contrast with *nondeclarative memory.*

decomposition of movement   Difficulty of movement in which gestures are broken up into individual segments instead of being executed smoothly; a symptom of cerebellar lesions.

deep dyslexia   Dyslexia in which the patient reads a word as another word that is semantically related. Contrast with *surface dyslexia.*

degradation   Here, the process by which neurotransmitter molecules are broken down into inactive metabolites.

dehydration   Excessive loss of water.

delayed non-matching-to-sample (DNMS)   A test in which the subject must respond to the unfamiliar stimulus of a pair. See Figure 17.8.

delta wave   The slowest type of EEG wave, characteristic of stage 3 and 4 slow-wave sleep. See Figure 14.11.

dementia   Drastic failure of cognitive ability, including memory failure and loss of orientation.

dementia pugilistica   The dementia that develops in boxers; it is especially prominent in successful boxers because they participate in more bouts.

dendrite   One of the extensions of the cell body that are the receptive surfaces of the neuron. See Figures 2.1, 2.3.

dendrite thorn   See *dendritic spine.*

dendritic branching   The pattern and quantity of branching of dendrites. See Figure 18.5.

dendritic knob   A portion of olfactory receptor cells present in the olfactory epithelium. See Figure 9.19.

dendritic spine   An outgrowth along the dendrite of a neuron. Also called *dendrite thorn.* See Figures 2.1, 2.4.

dendritic tree   The full arrangement of dendrites of a single cell.

denervation supersensitivity   A condition in which target cells, upon losing neural input, produce more than the normal number of receptors, resulting in an exaggerated response when synaptic transmitter is applied.

dentate gyrus   A strip of gray matter in the hippocampal formation.

deoxyribonucleic acid (DNA)   A nucleic acid that is present in the chromosomes of cells and codes hereditary information.

dependence   Here, the strong desire to self-administer a drug of abuse.

depolarization   A reduction in membrane potential (the inner membrane surface becomes less negative in relation to the outer surface); caused by excitatory neural messages. See Figure 3.5. Contrast with *hyperpolarization.*

depression   A psychiatric condition characterized by such symptoms as an unhappy mood; loss of interests, energy, and appetite; and difficulty in concentration. See also *bipolar disorder, unipolar depression.*

dermatome   A strip of skin innervated by a particular spinal root. See Figure 8.17.

dermis   The layer of skin beneath the outermost layer (the epidermis). See Figure 8.3.

dexamethasone suppression test   A test of pituitary–adrenal function in which the subject is given dexamethasone, a synthetic glucocorticoid hormone, which should cause a decline in the production of adrenal corticosteroids.

diabetes insipidus   Excessive urination, caused by the failure of vasopressin to induce the kidneys to conserve water.

diabetes mellitus   Excessive glucose in the urine, caused by the failure of insulin to induce glucose absorption by the body.

Diablo   A protein released by mitochondria, in response to high calcium levels, that activates apoptosis.

diaschisis   A temporary period of generalized impairment following brain injury.

dichotic listening technique   A test in which different sounds are presented to each ear at the same time; used to determine hemispheric differences in processing auditory information. See Figure 19.15.

dichotic stimuli   Stimuli that differ at the two ears.

dichromat   An organism that has only two classes of wavelength-sensitive light receptor cells.

diencephalon   The posterior part of the forebrain, including the thalamus and hypothalamus. See Figure 2.13.

differential classical conditioning   Classical conditioning in which two conditioned stimuli are used in the same animal; one (CS+) is paired with the unconditioned stimulus, and the other (CS–) is unpaired and has no consequence for the animal.

differentiation   See *cell differentiation.*

diffuse bipolar cell   A retinal bipolar cell that receives input from several receptors. Contrast with *midget bipolar cell.*

digestion   The process by which food is broken down to provide energy and nutrients.

dimer   A complex of two proteins that have bound together.

discordant   Referring to any trait that is seen in only one individual of identical twins. Contrast with *concordant.*

dishabituation   The restoration of response amplitude following habituation.

dissociation   Here, the loss of one function with damage to brain region A but not B, and the loss of a different function with damage to brain region B but not A.

dissociative thinking   A condition, seen in schizophrenia, that is characterized by disturbances of thought and difficulty relating events properly.

distal   An anatomical term referring to structures toward the periphery or toward the end of a limb. See Box 2.2. Contrast with *proximal*.

diurnal   Active during the day. Contrast with *nocturnal*.

divergence   The phenomenon of neural connections in which one cell sends signals to many other cells. See Figure 3.17. Contrast with *convergence*.

dizygotic   Referring to twins derived from separate eggs. Such twins are no more closely related genetically than are other full siblings. Contrast with *monozygotic*.

DNA   See *deoxyribonucleic acid*.

DNMS   See *delayed non-matching-to-sample*.

dopamine (DA)   A synaptic transmitter produced mainly in the basal forebrain and diencephalon that is active in the basal ganglia, the olfactory system, and limited parts of the cerebral cortex. See Table 4.1, Figure 4.3.

dopaminergic   Referring to cells that use dopamine as their synaptic transmitter.

dorsal   An anatomical term referring to structures toward the back of the body or the top of the brain. See Box 2.2. Contrast with *ventral*.

dorsal column system   A somatosensory system that delivers most touch stimuli via the dorsal columns of spinal white matter to the brain. See Figure 8.16.

dorsal root   See *roots*.

double-blind test   A test of a drug or treatment in which neither the subjects nor the attending researchers know which subjects are receiving the drug or treatment and which are receiving the placebo or control.

double dissociation   The phenomenon in which condition or treatment A causes impairment on behavioral test X but no impairment on test Y, whereas condition B causes impairment on test Y but not on test X.

Down syndrome   Mental retardation that is associated with an extra copy of chromosome 21.

dual-trace hypothesis   The hypothesis that the formation of a memory involves first a relatively brief transient memory storage process followed by a stable change in the nervous system, which is a long-lasting memory trace.

dualism   The notion, promoted by Descartes, that the mind is subject only to spiritual interactions while the body is subject only to material interactions.

ductus deferens   See *vas deferens*.

duplex theory   A theory of pitch perception that combines place theory and volley theory.

dura mater   The outermost of the three coverings (meninges) that embrace the brain and spinal cord. See also *pia mater* and *arachnoid*.

dynamic phase of weight gain   The initial period following destruction of the ventromedial hypothalamus, during which the animal's body weight increases rapidly. See Figure 13.25. Contrast with *static phase of obesity*.

dynorphins   One of three kinds of endogenous opioids. See Table 4.1.

dyscontrol syndrome   A condition consisting of temporal lobe disorders that may underlie some forms of human violence.

dyskinesia   See *tardive dyskinesia*.

dyslexia   A reading disorder attributed to brain impairment.

dystrophin   A gene product that is needed for normal muscle function. Dystrophin is defective in some forms of muscular dystrophy.

eardrum   See *tympanic membrane*.

EC   See *enriched condition*.

ecstasy   See *MDMA*.

ectoderm   The outer cellular layer of the developing fetus. The ectoderm gives rise to the skin and the nervous system.

ectopia   Something out of place—for example, clusters of neurons seen in unusual positions in the cortex of people who suffer from dyslexia. See Figure 19.10.

ectotherm   An animal whose body temperature is regulated by, and that gets most of its heat from, the environment. Examples include snakes and bees. Contrast with *endotherm*.

edema   The swelling of tissue, especially in the brain, in response to injury.

EEG   See *electroencephalography*.

efferent fiber   An axon that carries information from the nervous system to the periphery. Contrast with *afferent fiber*.

egg   See *ovum*.

ejaculation   The forceful expulsion of semen from the penis.

electrical force   Here, the tendency of like-charged particles to repel each other and opposite-charged particles to attract each other.

electrical synapse   The region between neurons where the presynaptic and postsynaptic membranes are so close that the nerve impulse can jump to the postsynaptic membrane without first being translated into a chemical message. See Box 3.1.

electroencephalography (EEG)   The recording and study of gross electrical activity of the brain recorded from large electrodes placed on the scalp. See Figures 3.19, 14.11.

electromyography (EMG)   The electrical recording of muscle activity. See Figure 11.2.

electro-oculography (EOG)   The electrical recording of eye movements, useful in determining sleep stages.

electroretinography (ERG)   The electrical recording of responses of the retina to flashes of different stimuli.

embryo   The earliest stage in a developing animal; humans are considered embryos until 8 to 10 weeks after conception.

embryonic stem cell   A cell, derived from an embryo, that has the capacity to form any type of tissue the donor might produce.

EMG   See *electromyography*.

encéphale isolé   An experimental preparation in which an animal's brainstem has been separated from the spinal cord by a cut below the medulla. See Figure 14.20. Contrast with *cerveau isolé*.

encephalization factor   A measure of brain size relative to body size.

encoding   A stage of memory formation in which the information entering sensory channels is passed into short-term memory. See Figure 17.12.

end-plate potential   The action potential that is induced at the neuromuscular junction when the axon terminal releases its neurotransmitter, which in vertebrates is acetylcholine.

endocast   A cast of the cranial cavity of a skull, especially useful for studying fossils of extinct species.

endocrine   Referring to glands that release chemicals to the interior of the body. These glands secrete the principal hormones. See Figure 5.4.

endocrine gland   A gland that secretes products into the bloodstream to act on distant targets. See Figure 5.1. Contrast with *exocrine gland*.

endogenous   Produced inside the body. Contrast with *exogenous*.

endogenous opioids   A family of peptide transmitters that have been called the body's own narcotics. The three kinds of endogenous opioids are enkephalins, endorphins, and dynorphins. See Table 4.1.

endogenous oscillator   A circuit that generates regularly repeating sequences of neural activity or behavior.

endorphins   One of three kinds of endogenous opioids. See Table 4.1.

endotherm   An animal whose body temperature is regulated chiefly by internal metabolic processes. Examples include mammals and birds. Contrast with *ectotherm*.

enkephalins   One of three kinds of endogenous opioids. See Table 4.1.

enriched condition (EC)   A condition in which laboratory rodents are house in a large cage with several conspecifics and a variety of stimulus objects. Also called *complex environment*. See Figure 18.4. Contrast with *impoverished condition* and *standard condition*.

entrainment   The process of synchronizing a biological rhythm to an environmental stimulus. See Figure 14.1.

enzyme   A complicated protein whose action increases the probability of a specific chemical reaction.

EOAE   See *evoked otoacoustic emission*.

EOG   See *electro-oculography*.

ependymal layer   See *ventricular zone*.

epidermis   The outermost layer of skin, over the dermis. See Figure 8.3.

epididymis   A crescent-shaped structure next to the testis in which sperm are stored. See Figures 12.7, 12.15.

epilepsy   A brain disorder marked by major sudden changes in the electrophysiological state of the brain that are referred to as seizures. See Box 3.2.

epinephrine   A compound that acts both as a hormone (secreted by the adrenal medulla) and as a synaptic transmitter. Also called *adrenaline*. See Table 4.1.

episodic memory   Memory of a particular incident or a particular time and place.

EPSP   See *excitatory postsynaptic potential*.

equilibrium potential   The state in which the tendency of ions to flow from regions of high concentration is exactly balanced by the opposing potential difference across the membrane.

ERG   See *electroretinography*.

estradiol   The primary type of estrogen that is secreted by the ovary. See Table 5.2.

estrogens   A class of steroid hormones produced by female gonads. See Table 5.2, Figures 5.15, 5.17.

estrus   The period during which female animals are sexually receptive.

event-related potential   A large change in electrical potential in the brain that is elicited by a discrete sensory or motor event. Also called *evoked potential*. See Figure 3.19.

evoked otoacoustic emission (EOAE)   A sound produced by the cochlea in response to acoustic stimulation. Contrast with *spontaneous otoacoustic emission*.

evoked potential   See *event-related potential*.

evolution by natural selection   The Darwinian theory that evolution proceeds by differential success in reproduction.

evolutionary psychology   A field devoted to asking how natural selection has shaped behavior, especially reproductive behaviors in humans and other animals.

excitatory postsynaptic potential (EPSP)   A depolarizing potential in the postsynaptic neuron that is caused by excitatory presynaptic impulses. EPSPs increase the probability that the postsynaptic neuron will fire a nerve impulse. See Figure 3.11. Contrast with *inhibitory postsynaptic potential*.

excitotoxicity   The property by which neurons die when overstimulated, as with large amounts of glutamate.

exhaustion phase   A stage in the response to stress that is caused by prolonged or frequently repeated stress and is characterized by increased susceptibility to disease.

exocrine gland   A gland that secretes products through ducts to the site of action. Contrast with *endocrine gland*.

exogenous   Arising from outside the body. Contrast with *endogenous*.

external capsule   A light-colored band of fibers lateral to the putamen.

external ear   The part of the ear that we readily see (the pinna) and the canal that leads to the eardrum. See Figure 9.1.

external fertilization   The process by which eggs are fertilized outside of the female's body, as in many fishes and amphibians. Contrast with *internal fertilization*.

extinction   In conditioning, a feature in which the learned response wanes when not reinforced.

extracellular fluid   The fluid in the spaces between cells (interstitial fluid) and in the vascular system.

extracellular space   The space between cells.

extrafusal fiber   One of the ordinary muscle fibers that lie outside the spindles and provide most of the force for muscle contraction. See Figure 11.9. Contrast with *intrafusal fiber*.

extraocular muscle   One of the muscles attached to the eyeball that control its position and movements.

extrapyramidal system   A motor system that includes the basal ganglia and some closely related brainstem structures.

extrastriate cortex   Visual cortex outside of area 17 (which is primary visual cortex, or striate cortex). See Figure 10.13.

facial nerve   Cranial nerve VII, which innervates facial musculature and some sensory receptors. See Figures 2.8, 15.6.

fallopian tube   The structure between the ovary and the uterus where fertilization takes place in humans. Also called *oviduct* or *uterine tube*. See Figures 12.7, 12.15.

fast muscle fiber   A type of striated muscle that contracts rapidly but fatigues readily. Contrast with *slow muscle fiber*.

fat   A large, complex carbohydrate that provides long-term energy storage. A lipid.

fatal familial insomnia   An inherited disorder in which humans sleep normally at the beginning of their life, but in midlife stop sleeping, and 7 to 24 months later die.

feature detector model   A model of visual pattern analysis that emphasizes linear and angular components of the stimulus array. Contrast with *spatial-frequency filter model*.

feedback circuit   A circuit in which output information is used to modulate the input of that same circuit.

fertilization   The fusion of sperm and egg to produce a zygote.

fetal alcohol syndrome   A disorder, including mental retardation and characteristic facial anomalies, that affects children exposed to alcohol (through maternal ingestion) during fetal development.

fetus   A developing individual after the embryo stage. Humans are considered to be fetuses from 10 weeks after fertilization until birth.

filopodium (pl. filopodia)   A very fine, tubular outgrowth from the growth cone.

final common pathway   The motoneurons, because they direct all the activity of the spinal cord and brain to the muscles.

fission   The process of splitting in two. Some unicellular organisms reproduce by fisson; that is, they simply split into two daughter cells.

fixed action pattern   Complex preprogrammed, species-specific behavior that is triggered by particular stimuli and carried out without sensory feedback.

flaccid paralysis   A loss of reflexes below the level of transection of the spinal cord.

flexion reflex   The abrupt withdrawal of a limb in response to intense stimulation of the foot.

fMRI   See *functional MRI*.

foliate papillae   One of three types of small structures on the tongue that contain taste receptors. See Figure 9.17.

follicle-stimulating hormone (FSH)   A tropic hormone, released by the anterior pituitary, that controls the production of estrogens and progesterone. See Table 5.2, Figures 5.15, 5.17.

forebrain   The frontal division of the neural tube, containing the cerebral hemispheres, the thalamus, and the hypothalamus. Also called *prosencephalon*. See Figure 2.13.

fornix (pl. fornices)   A fiber tract that extends from the hippocampus to the mammillary body. See Figures 2.11, 2.15.

Fourier analysis   The analysis of a complex pattern into the sum of sine waves. See Box 9.1.

fourth ventricle   The passageway within the pons that receives cerebrospinal fluid from the third ventricle and releases it to surround the brain and spinal cord. See Figure 2.19.

fovea (pl. foveae)   A small depression in the center of the retina that has a dense concentration of cones and maximal visual acuity. See Figure 10.2.

fragile X syndrome   A condition that is a frequent cause of inherited mental retardation; produced by a fragile site on the X chromosome that seems prone to breaking because the DNA there is unstable.

free-running period   The natural period of a behavior that is displayed if external stimuli do not provide entrainment.

frequency   The number of cycles per second in a sound wave; measured in hertz (Hz). See Box 9.1.

frontal lobe   The most anterior portion of the cerebral cortex. See Figure 2.11.

frontal plane   See *coronal plane.*

FSH   See *follicle-stimulating hormone.*

functional MRI (fMRI)   Magnetic resonance imaging that detects changes in blood flow and therefore identifies regions of the brain that are particularly active during a given task.

fundamental   Here, the predominant frequency of an auditory tone or a visual scene. Harmonics are multiples of the fundamental. See Box 9.1.

fungiform papillae   One of three types of small structures on the tongue that contain taste receptors. See Figure 9.17.

G proteins   A class of proteins that reside next to the intracellular portion of a receptor and that are activated when the receptor binds an appropriate ligand on the extracellular surface.

GABA   See *γ-aminobutyric acid.*

gamete   A sex cell (sperm or egg) that contains only unpaired chromosomes and therefore has only half the total number of autosomal chromosomes.

γ-aminobutyric acid (GABA)   Probably the major inhibitory transmitter in the mammalian nervous system; widely distributed in both invertebrate and vertebrate nervous systems. See Table 4.1.

gamma efferent   A motor neuron that controls muscle spindle sensitivity. See Figure 11.9.

ganglion (pl. ganglia)   A collection of nerve cell bodies outside the central nervous system. Contrast with *nucleus.*

ganglion cells   A class of cells in the retina whose axons form the optic nerve. See Figures 10.7, 10.25.

gel electrophoresis   A method of separating molecules of differing size or electrical charge by forcing them to flow through a gel. See Figure A.3 in the Appendix.

gender identity   The way that one identifies oneself, and is identified by others, as a male or a female.

gene   A length of DNA that encodes the information for constructing a particular protein.

generalized seizure   An epileptic seizure that arises from pathology at brain sites and projects to widespread regions of the brain. Generalized seizures include loss of consciousness and symmetrical involvement of body musculature. See Box 3.2. See also *grand mal seizure* and *petit mal seizure.*

generator potential   A local change in the resting potential of a receptor cell that mediates between the impact of stimuli and the initiation of nerve impulses.

genetic constraints on learning   The concept, prominent from the 1960s to the early 1980s, that species-typical factors restrict the kinds of learning that a species can accomplish readily. Contrast with *specific abilities to learn and remember.*

genetics   The study of inheritance, including the genes encoded in DNA.

genome   The sum of all the genetic information an individual has inherited.

genotype   The sum of all the genetic information an individual has inherited. Contrast with *phenotype.*

GH   See *growth hormone.*

giant axon   A large-diameter axon; found in some invertebrates. The size of giant axons facilitates research on the properties of neural membrane structure and function. See Figure 3.9.

glia   See *glial cells.*

glial cells   Nonneural brain cells that provide structural, nutritional, and other types of support to the brain. Also called *glia* or *neuroglia.* See Figure 2.6.

glioma (pl. gliomas or gliomata)   A brain tumor resulting from the aberrant production of glial cells.

global aphasia   The total loss of ability to understand language, or to speak, read, or write. See Figure 19.7.

globus pallidus   One of the basal ganglia. See Figure 2.15.

glomerulus (pl. glomeruli)   A complex arbor of dendrites from a group of olfactory cells.

glossopharyngeal nerve   Cranial nerve IX, which serves taste receptors in the tongue. See Figure 2.8.

glucagon   A hormone, released by alpha cells in the islets of Langerhans, that increases blood glucose. See Table 5.2, Figure 5.19.

glucocorticoids   A class of steroid hormones, released by the adrenal cortex, that affect carbohydrate metabolism.

glucodetector   A cell that detects and informs the nervous system about levels of circulating glucose. Also called *glucostat.*

glucose   An important sugar molecule used by the body and brain for energy.

glucose transporter   A molecule that spans the external membrane of a cell and transports glucose molecules from outside the cell to inside for use.

glucostat   See *glucodetector.*

glutamate   An amino acid transmitter, the most common excitatory transmitter. See Table 4.1.

glutaminergic   Referring to cells that use glutamate as their synaptic transmitter.

glycine   An amino acid transmitter, often inhibitory. See Table 4.1.

glycogen   A complex carbohydrate made by the combining of glucose molecules for a short-term store of energy.

GnRH   See *gonadotropin-releasing hormone.*

goiter   A swelling of the thyroid gland caused by iodide deficiency.

Golgi stain   A histological stain that fills a small proportion of neurons with a dark, silver-based precipitate. See Box 2.1.

Golgi tendon organ   One of the receptors located in tendons that send impulses to the central nervous system when a muscle contracts. See Figure 11.9.

Golgi type I cell   A type of large nerve cell. See Figure 2.16.

gonadotropin-releasing hormone (GnRH)   A hypothalamic hormone that controls the release of luteinizing hormone and follicle-stimulating hormone from the pituitary. See Figure 5.17.

gonads   The sexual organs (ovaries in females, testes in males), which produce gametes for reproduction. See Figure 5.1, Table 5.2.

graded potential   An electrical potential that is initiated at a postsynaptic site and can vary continuously in size. Also called *local potential* or *postsynaptic potential.* See Figure 3.5. Contrast with *all-or-none.*

grammar   The rules for usage of a particular language.

grand mal seizure   A type of generalized epileptic seizure in which nerve cells fire in high-frequency bursts. Grand mal seizures cause loss of consciousness and sudden muscle contraction. See Box 3.2. Contrast with *petit mal seizure.*

grandmother cell An extrapolation of the feature detector model suggesting that if there were enough levels of analysis, a unit could be constructed that would enable a person to recognize his or her grandmother.

granule cell A type of small nerve cell. See Figure 2.16.

gray matter Areas of the brain that are dominated by cell bodies and are devoid of myelin. See Figure 2.12. Contrast with *white matter.*

growth cone The growing tip of an axon or a dendrite. See Figure 7.10.

growth hormone (GH) A tropic hormone, secreted by the anterior pituitary, that influences the growth of cells and tissues. Also called *somatotropic hormone.* See Table 5.2, Figure 5.15.

guevedoces Literally "eggs at 12," a nickname for individuals who are raised as girls but at puberty change appearance and begin behaving as boys.

gustatory system The taste system. See Figure 9.18.

gut hormone A hormone that is released by the stomach or intestines, sometimes in response to food.

gyrus (pl. gyri) A ridged or raised portion of a convoluted brain surface. See Figure 2.11. Contrast with *sulcus.*

habituation A form of nonassociative learning in which an organism becomes less responsive following repeated presentations of a stimulus. See Box 17.1. Contrast with *sensitization* (definition 1).

hair cell One of the receptor cells for hearing in the cochlea. Displacement of hair cells by sound waves generates nerve impulses that travel to the brain. See Figure 9.1.

hallucinogens A class of drugs that alter sensory perception and produce peculiar experiences. See also *psychedelic.*

harmonics Multiples of a particular frequency. See Box 9.1.

health psychology A field that studies psychological influences on health-related processes, such as why people become ill or how they remain healthy.

Hebbian synapse A synapse that is strengthened when it successfully drives the postsynaptic cell.

hemiplegia Partial paralysis involving one side of the body.

hemispatial neglect A syndrome in which the patient ignores objects presented to one side and may even deny connection with that side of the body.

hemispheric encoding retrieval asymmetry (HERA) The hypothesis that one hemisphere is especially active during the encoding of a memory while the other hemisphere is especially active during the retrieval of the memory.

HERA See *hemispheric encoding retrieval asymmetry.*

hermaphrodite An individual that can reproduce as either a male or a female.

heroin Diacetylmorphine, an artificially modified, very potent form of morphine.

hertz (Hz) Cycles per second, as of an auditory stimulus.

heterogametic Referring to the sex that has two different sex chromosomes. Male mammals and female birds are heterogametic. Contrast with *homogametic.*

hindbrain The rear division of the brain; in the mature vertebrate, the hindbrain contains the cerebellum, pons, and medulla. Also called *rhombencephalon.* See Figure 2.13.

hippocampal gyrus See *subiculum.*

hippocampus (pl. hippocampi) A portion of the cerebral hemispheres found curled in the basal medial part of the temporal lobe that is thought to be important for learning and memory. See Figures 2.15, 17.1, 18.7.

histology The study of tissue structure.

HIV See *human immunodeficiency virus.*

homeostasis The tendency for the internal environment to remain constant.

homeotherm An older term, now considered inadequate, for an animal that maintains a relatively constant body temperature. Examples include birds and mammals. A more accepted term is *endotherm.* Contrast with *poikilotherm.*

hominid A primate of the family Hominidae, of which humans are the only living species.

homogametic Referring to the sex that has two similar types of sex chromosomes. Female mammals and male birds are homogametic. Contrast with *heterogametic.*

homology A resemblance based on common ancestry, such as the similarities in forelimb structures of mammals. See Figure 6.3.

homoplasy The similar appearance of features (e.g., the body forms of a tuna and a dolphin), often due to convergent evolution.

horizontal cells Specialized retinal cells that contact both the receptor cells and the bipolar cells.

horizontal plane The plane that divides the body or brain into upper and lower parts. See Box 2.2.

hormone A chemical secreted by an endocrine gland that is conveyed by the bloodstream and regulates target organs or tissues. See Table 5.2.

horseradish peroxidase (HRP) An enzyme found in horseradish and other plants that is used to determine the cells of origin of a particular set of axons. See Box 2.1.

HRP See *horseradish peroxidase.*

hue One of the basic dimensions of light perception. Hue varies around the color circle through blue, green, yellow, orange, and red. See Figure 10.5.

human immunodeficiency virus (HIV) The virus that can be passed through genital, anal, or oral sex and causes acquired immune deficiency syndrome (AIDS).

humoral immunity An immunological response in which B lymphocytes produce antibodies that either directly destroy antigens, such as viruses or bacteria, or enhance the destruction of antigens by other cells. See also *immune system.* See Figure 15.17.

hunger The internal state of an animal seeking food. Contrast with *satiety.*

huntingtin A protein produced by a gene (called *HD*) that, when containing too many trinucleotide repeats, results in Huntington's disease in a carrier.

Huntington's disease A progressive genetic disorder characterized by choreic movements and profound changes in mental functioning. Also called *Huntington's chorea.*

hyperphagia A condition involving increasing food intake, often related to damage to the ventromedial hypothalamus.

hyperpolarization An increase in membrane potential (the inner surface of the membrane becomes more negative in relation to the outer surface); caused by inhibitory neural messages. See Figure 3.5. Contrast with *depolarization.*

hypertonic Referring to a solution with a higher concentration of salt than that found in interstitial fluid and blood plasma (more than about 0.9% salt). Contrast with *hypotonic* and *isotonic.*

hypofrontality hypothesis The hypothesis that schizophrenia may reflect underactivation of the frontal lobes.

hypothalamic–pituitary portal system A system of capillaries that transport releasing hormones from the hypothalamus to the anterior pituitary.

hypothalamus Part of the diencephalon, lying ventral to the thalamus. See Figures 2.11, 2.13, Table 5.2.

hypotonic Referring to a solution with a lower concentration of salt than that found in interstitial fluid and blood plasma (less than about 0.9% salt). Contrast with *hypertonic* and *isotonic.*

hypovolemic thirst The response to a reduced volume of extracellular fluid. Contrast with *osmotic thirst.*

hypoxia A transient lack of oxygen.

Hz See *hertz.*

IAPs See *inhibitors of apoptosis.*

IC See *impoverished condition.*

iconic memory A very brief type of memory that stores the sensory impression of a scene. Contrast with *short-term memory.*

ideational apraxia An impairment in the ability to carry out a sequence of actions, even though each element or step can be done correctly.

identifiable neurons Neurons that are large and similar from one individual to the next, enabling investigators to recognize them and give them code names.

ideomotor apraxia The inability to carry out a simple motor activity in response to a verbal command, even though this same activity is readily performed spontaneously.

IEGs See *immediate early genes.*

IHC See *inner hair cell.*

immediate early genes (IEGs) A class of genes that show rapid but transient increases in response to extracellular signals such as neurotransmitters and growth factors. Examples include *c-fos* and *c-jun.*

immune system The system that defends an organism from harmful foreign biological substances introduced into the body. It includes both cell-mediated immunity and humoral immunity. See Figures 15.17, 15.18.

immunocytochemistry A method for detecting a particular protein in tissues in which (1) an antibody recognizes and binds to the protein, and (2) chemical methods are then used to leave a visible reaction product around each antibody. See Box 5.1.

impermeable Referring to a barrier that does not allow a substance of interest to pass through.

impoverished condition(IC) A condition in which laboratory rodents are housed singly in a small cage with adequate food and water but no complex stimulation. Also called *isolated condition.* See Figure 18.4. Contrast with *standard condition* and *enriched condition.*

imprinting A form of learning in which young animals learn to follow the first relatively large moving object they see, usually their mother.

in estrus Referring to a female animal that is receptive to copulation, usually as a result of steroid hormone exposure. Also called *in heat.*

in heat See *in estrus.*

in situ hybridization A method for detecting particular RNA transcripts in tissue sections by providing a nucleotide probe that is complementary to, and will therefore hybridize with, the transcript of interest. See Figure A.4 in the Appendix.

in vitro Literally "in glass," usually a laboratory dish; outside the body.

in vivo Literally "in life"; within a living body.

incus (pl. incudes) A middle-ear bone situated between the malleus (attached to the tympanic membrane) and the stapes (attached to the cochlea); one of the three ossicles that conduct sound across the middle ear. See Figure 9.1.

individual response stereotypy The tendency of individuals to show the same response pattern to particular situations throughout their life span.

indoleamines A class of monoamines that serve as neurotransmitters, including serotonin and melatonin. See Table 4.1.

induction The process by which one set of cells influences the fate of neighboring cells, usually by secreting a chemical factor that changes gene expression in the target cells.

inferior colliculi See *colliculus.*

infradian Referring to a rhythmic biological event whose period is longer than that of a circadian rhythm—i.e., longer than a day. Contrast with *ultradian.*

infundibulum (pl. infundibula) The stalk of the pituitary gland.

inhibitors of apopotosis (IAPs) A family of proteins that inhibit caspases and thereby stave off apoptosis.

inhibitory postsynaptic potential (IPSP) A hyperpolarizing potential in the postsynaptic neuron that is caused by inhibitory connections. IPSPs decrease the probability that the postsynaptic neuron will fire a nerve impulse. See Figure 3.11. Contrast with *excitatory postsynaptic potential.*

inner ear The cochlea and vestibular canals. See Figure 9.1.

inner hair cell (IHC) One of the two types of receptor cells for hearing in the cochlea. See Figure 9.1.

innervate To provide neural input.

innervation The supply of neural input to an organ or a region of the nervous system.

innervation ratio The ratio expressing the number of muscle fibers innervated by a single motor axon. The fewer muscle fibers an axon innervates (i.e., the lower the ratio), the finer the control of movements.

insomnia Lack of sleep or of sufficient sleep.

instrumental conditioning A form of associative learning in which the likelihood that an act (instrumental response) will be performed depends on the consequences (reinforcing stimuli) that follow it. Also called *operant conditioning.*

instrumental response See *instrumental conditioning.*

insulin A hormone, released by beta cells in the islets of Langerhans, that lowers blood glucose. See Table 5.2, Figure 5.20.

intermediate-term memory (ITM) A form of memory that lasts longer than short-term memory, but does not last as long as long-term memory.

internal capsule The fiber band that extends between the caudate nucleus on its medial side and the globus pallidus and putamen on its lateral side.

internal carotid artery See *carotid arteries.*

internal fertilization The process by which sperm fertilize eggs inside of the female's body. All mammals, birds, and reptiles have internal fertilization. Contrast with *external fertilization.*

interneuron A neuron that is neither a sensory neuron nor a motoneuron.

intracellular fluid Water within cells. Also called *cellular fluid.*

intrafusal fiber One of the small muscle fibers that lie within each muscle spindle. See Figure 11.9. Contrast with *extrafusal fiber.*

intromission Insertion of the erect penis into the vagina during copulatory behavior.

inverse agonist A substance that binds to a receptor and causes it to do the opposite of the naturally occurring transmitter.

ion An atom or molecule that has acquired an electrical charge by gaining or losing one or more electrons.

ion channel A pore in the cell membrane that permits the passage of certain ions through the membrane when the channels are open. See Figures 3.6, 3.7.

ionotropic receptor A receptor protein that includes an ion channel that is opened when the receptor is bound by an agonist. See Figure 3.15. Contrast with *metabotropic receptor.*

IPSP See *inhibitory postsynaptic potential.*

iris (pl. irides) The circular structure of the eye that provides an opening to form the pupil. See Figure 10.2.

ischemia The loss or reduction of blood circulation.

islets of Langerhans Clusters of cells in the pancreas that release two hormones (insulin and glucagon) with opposite effects on glucose utilization. See Figure 5.20.

isolated condition See *impoverished condition.*

isotonic Referring to a solution with a concentration of salt that is the same as that found in interstitial fluid and blood plasma (about 0.9% salt). Contrast with *hypertonic* and *hypotonic.*

ITM See *intermediate-term memory.*

kinases A class of enzymes that catalyze the addition of a phosphate group to certain proteins.

kindling A method of experimentally inducing an epileptic seizure by repeatedly stimulating a brain region. See Box 3.2.

knee jerk reflex   A variant of the stretch reflex, in which stretching of the tendon beneath the knee leads to an upward kick of the leg. See Figure 3.16.

knockout organism   An individual in which a particular gene has been disabled by an experimenter. See Box 7.3.

Korsakoff's syndrome   A memory disorder, related to a thiamine deficiency, that is generally associated with chronic alcoholism.

Krause's end bulb   A skin receptor cell type.

L-dopa   The immediate precursor of the transmitter dopamine.

labeled lines   The concept that each nerve input to the brain reports only a particular type of information.

labia (sing. labium)   The folds of skin that surround the opening of the human vagina. See Figures 12.7, 12.15.

labile memory   An early stage of memory formation during which the formation of a memory can be easily disrupted by conditions that influence brain activity.

lamellipodium (pl. lamellipodia)   A sheetlike extension of a growth cone.

laminar organization   The horizontal layering of cells found in some brain regions. See Figures 2.17, 8.19.

latency   The time delay before a subject displays a behavior of interest.

latent learning   Learning that has taken place but has not (yet) been demonstrated by performance.

lateral   An anatomical term referring to structures toward the side of the body. See Box 2.2. Contrast with *medial*.

lateral geniculate nucleus (LGN)   The part of the thalamus that receives information from the optic tract and sends it to visual areas in the occipital cortex. See Figure 10.15.

lateral hypothalamus (LH)   A hypothalamic region that may be involved in eating. Lesions of the LH result in fasting and weight loss. See Figures 13.24, 13.29.

lateral inhibition   The phenomenon by which interconnected neurons inhibit their neighbors, producing contrast at the edges of regions. See Figure 10.6.

lateral-line system   A sensory system, found in many kinds of fish and some amphibians, that informs the animal of water motion in relation to the body surface.

lateral ventricle   A complexly shaped lateral portion of the ventricular system within each hemisphere of the brain. See Figure 2.19.

lateralization   The tendency for the right and left halves of a system to differ from one another.

learned helplessness   A learning paradigm in which individuals are subjected to inescapable, unpleasant conditions.

lens   A structure in the eye that helps form an image on the retina. The shape of the lens is controlled by the ciliary muscles inside the eye. See Figure 10.2.

lentiform nucleus   The lens-shaped region in the basal ganglia that encompasses the globus pallidus and the putamen. Also called *lenticular nucleus*. See Figure 2.15.

leptin   A protein, manufactured and secreted by fat cells, that may communicate to the brain the amount of body fat stored. Leptin is defective in obese mice.

lesion   Damage, as to a brain region, caused by disease or experimental design.

lesion momentum   The phenomenon in which the brain is impaired more by a lesion that develops quickly than by a lesion that develops slowly.

LGN   See *lateral geniculate nucleus*.

LH   See *lateral hypothalamus* or *luteinizing hormone*.

lie detector   See *polygraph*.

ligand   A substance that binds to receptor molecules, such as those at the surface of the cell.

ligand-gated ion channel   An ion channel that opens or closes in response to the presence of a particular chemical; an example is the ionotropic neurotransmitter receptor. Contrast with *voltage-gated ion channel*.

limbic system   A loosely defined, widespread group of brain nuclei that innervate each other to form a network; involved in mechanisms of emotion and learning. See Figure 2.15.

lithium   An element that often relieves the symptoms of bipolar depression.

lobotomy   The detachment of a portion of the frontal lobe from the rest of the brain. Now largely discredited, lobotomy was once a treatment for schizophrenia and many other ailments.

local circuit   See *circuit*.

local potential   See *graded potential*.

local potential change   A change in potential that is initiated at a postsynaptic site.

localization of function   The concept that specific brain regions are responsible for various types of experience, behavior, and psychological processes.

locus coeruleus   A small nucleus in the brainstem whose neurons produce norepinephrine and modulate large areas of the forebrain. See Figure 14.22.

long-term depression (LTD)   A lasting decrease in the magnitude of responses of neurons after afferent cells have been stimulated with electrical stimuli of relatively low frequency. Contrast with *long-term potentiation*.

long-term memory (LTM)   An enduring form of memory that lasts for days, weeks, months, or years and has a very large capacity. Contrast with *permanent memory*.

long-term potentiation (LTP)   A stable and enduring increase in the magnitude of responses of neurons after afferent cells have been stimulated with electrical stimuli of moderately high frequency. See Figures 18.7, 18.9. Contrast with *long-term depression*.

lordosis   A female receptive posture in quadrupeds in which the hindquarter is raised and the tail is turned to one side, facilitating intromission by the male. See Figures 12.3, 12.6.

LSD (lysergic acid diethylamide)   A hallucinogenic drug.

LTD   See *long-term depression*.

LTM   See *long-term memory*.

LTP   See *long-term potentiation*.

lumbar   Referring to the lower part of the spinal cord or back. See Figures 2.9, 2.10.

luteinizing hormone (LH)   A tropic hormone, released by the anterior pituitary, that influences the hormonal activities of the gonads. See Table 5.2, Figures 5.15, 5.17.

lymphocytes   Immune system cells. Two different classes of lymphocytes (B and T) mediate two types of immunological responses. See Figure 15.17.

lymphokine   A secreted protein that induces immune system cells to divide.

lysergic acid diethylamide   See *LSD*.

mad cow disease   See *bovine spongiform encephalopathy*.

magnetic resonance imaging (MRI)   A noninvasive technique that uses magnetic energy to generate images that reveal some of structural details in the living brain. See Figures 1.7, 2.21.

magnocellular layers   The two ventral or inner layers of the lateral geniculate nucleus, so called because their cells are large. See Figures 10.15, 10.26. Contrast with *parvocellular layers*.

magnocellular nucleus of the basal forebrain   A collection of neurons in the basal forebrain that modulates the activity of many areas of the neocortex by providing cholinergic innervation and that is implicated in Alzheimer's disease. Also called *Meynert's nucleus, basal nucleus of Meynert*, or *nucleus basalis of Meynert*. See Figure 7.26.

magnocellular system   The division of primate visual pathways that appears to be mainly responsible for the perception of depth and movement. See Figures 10.26. Contrast with *parvocellular system*.

malleus (pl. mallei)   A middle-ear bone that is connected to the tympanic membrane; one of the three ossicles that conduct sound across the middle ear. See Figure 9.1.

mammillary body   One of a pair of nuclei at the base of the brain that are slightly posterior to the pituitary stalk; a component of the limbic system. See Figure 2.11.

mammillothalamic tract   The fiber bundle that connects the mammillary bodies to the thalamus.

manic–depressive psychosis   See *bipolar disorder.*

MAO   See *monoamine oxidase.*

MAO inhibitor   An antidepressant drug that inhibits the enzyme monoamine oxidase, thus prolonging the action of catecholamine transmitters.

marijuana   A drug of abuse, usually smoked. The active ingredient is the chemical tetrahydrocannabinol (THC).

marsupial   An animal that is born at a very early developmental stage and that spends a period of its development in the maternal pouch.

MCR   See *melanocortin receptor.*

MDMA   A drug of abuse, 3,4-methylenedioxymethamphetamine, also known as *ecstasy.*

medial   An anatomical term referring to structures toward the middle of an organ or organism. See Box 2.2. Contrast with *lateral.*

medial amygdala   A portion of the amygdala that receives olfactory and pheromonal information.

medial forebrain bundle   A collection of axonal tracts traveling in the midline region of the forebrain. See Figure 4.3.

medial geniculate nucleus   A nucleus in the thalamus that receives input from the inferior colliculus and sends output to the auditory cortex. See Figure 9.6.

medial preoptic area (mPOA)   A region of the anterior hypothalamus implicated in the regulation of many behaviors, including thermoregulation, sexual behavior, and gonadotropin secretion.

medulla (pl. medullas or medullae)   The caudal part of the hindbrain. Also called *myelencephalon.* See Figures 2.11, 2.13.

medullary reticular formation   The hindmost portion of the brainstem reticular formation, implicated in motor control and copulatory behavior. See Figure 12.6.

Meissner's corpuscle   A skin receptor cell type. See Figures 8.3, 8.14.

melanocortin receptor (MCR)   A receptor that is activated by α-melanocyte stimulating hormone (α-MSH) peptide.

melatonin   An amine hormone that is released by the pineal gland. See Tables 4.1, 5.2.

membrane potential   A difference in electrical potential across the membrane of a nerve cell during an inactive period. Also called *resting potential.* See Figures 3.1, 3.4.

memory   A cognitive representation that is often acquired rapidly and that may last a long time.

memory trace   A persistent change in the brain that reflects the storage of memory.

meninges (sing. meninx)   The three protective sheets of tissue that surround the brain and spinal cord, called the dura mater, pia mater, and arachnoid.

menstruation   A visible flow of cells and blood that exits through the vagina between ovulations in some mammals, including humans and dogs.

Merkel's disc   A skin receptor cell type. See Figures 8.3, 8.14.

mesencephalon   See *midbrain.*

mesolimbocortical system   A set of dopaminergic axons arising in the midbrain and innervating the limbic system and cortex. See Figure 4.3.

mesostriatal system   A set of dopaminergic axons arising from the midbrain and innervating the basal ganglia, including those from the substantia nigra to the striatum. See Figure 4.3.

messenger RNA (mRNA)   A strand of RNA that carries the code of a section of a DNA strand to the cytoplasm. See the Appendix.

metabolic rate   The rate of the use of energy during a given period; measured in terms of kilocalories per day.

metabolism   The breakdown of complex molecules into smaller molecules.

metabotropic receptor   A type of transmitter receptor that does not contain an ion channel but may, when activated, use a G protein system to open a nearby ion channel. See Figure 3.15. Contrast with *ionotropic receptor.*

metencephalon   A subdivision of the hindbrain that includes the cerebellum and the pons. See Figure 2.13.

Meynert's nucleus   See *magnocellular nucleus of the basal forebrain.*

microelectrode   An especially small electrode, such as the fine, fluid-filled glass electrodes used to record the membrane potential of neurons.

microfilament   A very small filament (7 nm in diameter) found within all cells. Microfilaments determine cell shape.

microglial cells   Extremely small glial cells that remove cellular debris from injured or dead cells. Also called *microglia.*

micropolygyria   A condition of the brain in which small regions are characterized by more gyri than usual. See Figure 19.10.

microtubule   A small hollow cylindrical structure (20–26 nm in diameter) in axons that is involved in axonal transport. See Figure 2.5.

midbrain   The middle division of the brain. Also called *mesencephalon.* See Figures 2.11, 2.13.

middle canal   The central of the three spiraling canals inside the cochlea, situated between the vestibular canal and the tympanic canal. See Figure 9.1.

middle ear   The cavity between the tympanic membrane and the cochlea. See Figure 9.1.

midget bipolar cell   A retinal bipolar cell that connects to just one cone. Contrast with *diffuse bipolar cell.*

milk letdown reflex   The reflexive release of maternal oxytocin in response to suckling, or to stimuli associated with suckling. See Figure 5.12.

millivolt (mV)   A thousandth of a volt.

mineralocorticoids   A class of steroid hormones, released by the adrenal cortex, that affect ion concentrations in body tissues.

minimal discriminable frequency difference   The smallest change in frequency that can be detected reliably between two tones.

mitosis (pl. mitoses)   The process of division of somatic cells that involves duplication of DNA.

modulation of memory formation   Facilitation or inhibition of memory formation by factors other than those directly involved in memory formation.

modulatory role   The role that some hormones play in maintaining the sensitivity of neural circuits and other structures to hormonal influences.

modulatory site   A portion of a receptor that, when bound by a compound, alters the receptor's response to its transmitter.

monaural detection   The detection of sound using only one ear. Contrast with *binaural detection.*

monoamine hormones   See *amine hormones.*

monoamine hypothesis of depression   The hypothesis that depressive illness is associated with a decrease in the synaptic activity of connections that employ monoamine synaptic transmitters.

monoamine oxidase (MAO)   An enzyme that breaks down and thereby inactivates monoamine transmitters.

monoamines   A class of synaptic transmitters that contain a single amino group, NH_2. Examples include the catecholamines and indoleamines. See Table 4.1.

monocular deprivation   The deprivation of light to one eye. Contrast with *binocular deprivation.*

monogamy   A mating system in which a female and a male form a breeding pair that may last for one breeding period or for a lifetime. A durable and exclusive relation between a male and a female is called a pair bond. Contrast with *bigamy* and *polygamy*.

monopolar neuron   A nerve cell with a single branch that leaves the cell body and then extends in two directions: One end is the receptive pole, the other end the output zone. See Figure 2.3. Contrast with *multipolar neuron* and *bipolar neuron*.

monotreme   An egg-laying mammal belonging to an order that contains only two species: the echidna and the platypus.

monozygotic   Referring to twins derived from a single fertilized eggs. Such individuals have the same genotype. Contrast with *dizygotic*.

morphine   An opiate compound derived from the poppy flower.

mossy fiber   One of the fibers that extend from the dentate gyrus to the hippocampus, where they synapse in area CA3. See Figures 2.16, 18.7.

motion sickness   The experience of nausea from unnatural passive movement, as in a car or boat.

motivated behavior   Behavior that an organism displays even in the face of barriers or contingencies.

motoneuron   A nerve cell in the spinal cord that transmits motor messages from the spinal cord to muscles. Also called *motor neuron*. See Figure 11.8.

motor cortex   A region of cerebral cortex that sends impulses to motoneurons. See Figures 11.13, 11.16.

motor neuron   See *motoneuron*.

motor plan   A plan for action in the nervous system.

motor unit   A single motor axon and all the muscle fibers that it innervates.

movement   A brief, unitary activity of a muscle or body part; less complex than an act.

mPOA   See *medial preoptic area*.

MRH   See *müllerian regression hormone*.

MRI   See *magnetic resonance imaging*.

mRNA   See *messenger RNA*.

müllerian duct   A primitive duct system in the embryo that will develop into female reproductive structures (fallopian tubes, uterus, and upper vagina) if testes are not present in the embryo. See Figure 12.15. Contrast with *wolffian duct*.

müllerian regression hormone (MRH)   The hormone that causes shrinkage of the müllerian ducts during development.See *anti-müllerian hormone*.

multiple sclerosis   Literally "many scars"; a disorder characterized by widespread degeneration of the white matter.

multipolar neuron   A nerve cell that has many dendrites and a single axon. See Figure 2.3. Contrast with *bipolar neuron* and *monopolar neuron*.

muscarinic   Referring to cholinergic receptors that respond to the chemical muscarine as well as to acetylcholine. Muscarinic receptors mediate chiefly the inhibitory activities of acetylcholine. Contrast with *nicotinic*.

muscle fiber   A large, cylindrical cell, making up most of a muscle, which can contract in response to neurotransmitter released from a motoneuron. See Figure 11.7. See also *extrafusal fiber* and *intrafusal fiber*.

muscle spindle   A muscle receptor that lies parallel to a muscle and sends impulses to the central nervous system when the muscle is stretched. See Figure 11.9.

muscular dystrophy   A disease that leads to degeneration and functional changes in muscles.

mutation   A change in the nucleotide sequence of a gene as a result of unfaithful replication.

mV   See *millivolt*.

myasthenia gravis   A disorder characterized by a profound weakness of skeletal muscles; caused by a loss of acetylcholine receptors.

myelencephalon   See *medulla*.

myelin   The fatty insulation around an axon, formed by accessory cells. This myelin sheath improves the speed of conduction of nerve impulses. See Figures 2.6, 3.10.

myelination   The process of myelin formation. See Figures 2.6, 7.16.

myopia   "Nearsightedness"; the inability to focus the retinal image of objects that are far away.

myosin   A protein that, along with actin, mediates the contraction of muscle fibers. See Figure 11.7.

naloxone   A potent antagonist of opiates that is often administered to people who have taken drug overdoses. Naloxone binds to receptors for endogenous opioids.

narcolepsy   A disorder that involves frequent, intense episodes of sleep, which last from 5 to 30 minutes and can occur anytime during the usual waking hours.

natural selection   See *evolution by natural selection*.

NE   See *norepinephrine*.

negative feedback   The property by which some of the output of a system feeds back to reduce the effect of input signals. See Figure 3.18. Contrast with *positive feedback*.

negative symptom   In psychiatry, a symptom that reflects insufficient functioning. Examples include emotional and social withdrawal, blunted affect, and slowness and impoverishment of thought and speech. Contrast with *positive symptom*.

neocortex   The relatively recently evolved portions of the cerebral cortex. All of the cortex seen at the surface of the human brain is neocortex.

neologism   An entirely novel word, sometimes produced by patients with aphasia.

neonatal   Referring to newborns.

neophobia   The avoidance of new things.

Nernst equation   An equation used to calculate the equilibrium potential at a membrane.

nerve   A collection of axons bundled together outside the central nervous system. See Figures 2.7, 2.8. Contrast with *tract*.

nerve cell   See *neuron*.

nerve ending   In the periphery, an ending of a nerve thought to detect damage and transmit pain information.

nerve growth factor (NGF)   A substance that markedly affects the growth of neurons in spinal ganglia and in the ganglia of the sympathetic nervous system. See Figure 7.14.

nerve impulse   See *action potential*.

neural chain   A simple kind of neural circuit in which neurons are attached linearly, end to end. See Figure 3.17.

neural folds   In the developing embryo, ridges of ectoderm that form around the neural groove and come together to form the neural tube in the embryo. These neural folds will give rise to the entire nervous system. See Figure 7.2.

neural groove   In the developing embryo, the groove between the neural folds. See Figure 7.2.

neural plasticity   The ability of the nervous system to change in response to experience or the environment.

neural tube   An embryonic structure with subdivisions that correspond to the future forebrain, midbrain, and hindbrain. The cavity of this tube will include the cerebral ventricles and the passages that connect them. See Figure 7.2.

neurocrine   Referring to synaptic transmitter function. See Figure 5.4.

neuroendocrine cell   A neuron that releases hormones into local or systemic circulation. Also called *neurosecretory cell*.

neurofibrillary tangle   An abnormal whorl of neurofilaments within nerve cells. Neurofibrillary tangles are especially apparent in people suffering from dementia. See Figure 7.26.

neurofilament   A small rodlike structure found in axons. Neurofilaments are involved in the transport of materials. See Figure 2.5.

neurogenesis   The mitotic division of nonneuronal cells to produce neurons. See Figure 7.4.

neuroglia   See *glial cells.*

neurohypophysis   See *posterior pituitary.*

neuroleptics   A class of antipsychotic drugs, traditionally dopamine receptor blockers.

neuromodulator   A substance that influences the activity of synaptic transmitters.

neuromuscular junction   The region where the motoneuron terminal and the adjoining muscle fiber meet; where the nerve transmits its message to the muscle fiber.

neuromuscular synapse elimination   In postnatal development, the withdrawal by motoneurons of some of their terminal branches until every muscle fiber is innervated by only a single motoneuron.

neuron   The basic unit of the nervous system. Each neuron is composed of a cell body, receptive extension(s) (dendrites), and a transmitting extension (axon). Also called *nerve cell.* See Figures 2.2, 2.3.

neuron doctrine   The hypothesis that the brain is composed of separate cells that are distinct structurally, metabolically, and functionally.

neuronal cell death   The selective death (apoptosis) of many nerve cells.

neuropathic pain   Pain caused by damage to peripheral nerves; often difficult to treat.

neuropeptide   A peptide that is used by neurons for signaling.

neuropeptide Y   A peptide neurotransmitter that may carry some of the signals for feeding.

neuropil   The conglomeration of dendrites and the synapses upon them.

neurosecretory cell   See *neuroendocrine cell.*

neurotoxicology   The study of the effects of toxins and poisons on the nervous system.

neurotransmitter   See *synaptic transmitter.*

neurotrophic factor   A target-derived chemical that acts as if it "feeds" certain neurons to help them survive.

NGF   See *nerve growth factor.*

nicotine   A compound found in plants, including tobacco, that acts as an agonist on a large class of cholinergic receptors.

nicotinic   Referring to cholinergic receptors that respond to nicotine. Nicotinic receptors mediate chiefly the excitatory activities of acetylcholine, including at the neuromuscular junction. Contrast with *muscarinic.*

night terror   A sudden arousal from stage 3 or stage 4 slow-wave sleep that is marked by intense fear and autonomic activation. Contrast with *nightmare.*

nightmare   A long, frightening dream that awakens the sleeper from REM sleep. Contrast with *night terror.*

nigrostriatal bundle (NSB)   A dopaminergic tract that extends from the substantia nigra of the midbrain to the lateral hypothalamus, the globus pallidus, and the caudate putamen.

Nissl stain   A histological stain that outlines all cell bodies because the dyes are attracted to RNA, which encircles the nucleus.

NMDA receptor   A glutamate receptor that also binds the glutamate agonist NMDA (*N*-methyl-D-aspartate). The NMDA receptor is both ligand gated and voltage sensitive, which enables it to participate in a wide variety of information processing. See Box 4.2, Figure 18.8.

nociceptor   A receptor that responds to stimuli that produce tissue damage or pose the threat of damage.

nocturnal   Active during the dark periods of the daily cycle. Contrast with *diurnal.*

node of Ranvier   A gap between successive segments of the myelin sheath where the axon membrane is exposed. See Figures 2.6, 3.10.

nonassociative learning   A type of learning in which presentation of a particular stimulus alters the strength or probability of a response according to the strength and temporal spacing of that stimulus; includes habituation and sensitization. Contrast with *associative learning.*

noncompetitive   Referring to a drug that affects a transmitter receptor while binding at a site other than that bound by the endogenous ligand.

nondeclarative memory   A memory that is shown by performance rather than by conscious recollection. Also called *procedural memory.* Contrast with *declarative memory.*

nonfluent speech   Talking with considerable effort, short sentences, and the absence of the usual melodic character of conversational speech.

nonprimary motor cortex   Frontal lobe regions adjacent to primary motor cortex that contribute to motor control and modulate the activity of the primary motor cortex. See Figure 11.16.

nonprimary sensory cortex   See *secondary sensory cortex.*

noradrenaline   See *norepinephrine.*

noradrenergic   Referring to systems using norepinephrine (noradrenaline) as a transmitter.

norepinephrine (NE)   A synaptic transmitter that is produced mainly in brainstem nuclei and in the adrenal medulla. Also called *noradrenaline.* See Table 4.1.

Northern blot   A method of detecting a particular RNA transcript in a tissue or organ, by separating RNA from that source with gel electrophoresis, blotting the separated RNAs onto nitrocellulose, then using a nucleotide probe to hybridize with, and highlight, the transcript of interest.

notochord   A midline structure arising early in the embryonic development of vertebrates. See Figure 7.2.

NSB   See *nigrostriatal bundle.*

NST   See *nucleus of the solitary tract.*

nucleotide   A portion of a DNA or RNA molecule that is composed of a single base and the adjoining sugar–phosphate unit of the strand. See Figure A.2 in the Appendix.

nucleus (pl. nuclei)   Here, an anatomical collection of neurons within the central nervous system (e.g., the caudate nucleus). Contrast with *ganglion.*

nucleus accumbens   A region of the forebrain that receives dopaminergic innervation from the ventral tegmental area. Dopamine release in this region may mediate the reinforcing qualities of many activities, including drug abuse.

nucleus basalis of Meynert   See *magnocellular nucleus of the basal forebrain.*

nucleus of the solitary tract (NST)   A brainstem nucleus that receives information from the parasympathetic vagus (tenth) cranial nerve. See Figure 13.18.

nucleus ruber   See *red nucleus.*

nutrient   A chemical that is needed for growth, maintenance, and repair of the body but is not used as a source of energy.

nystagmus   An abnormal to-and-fro movement of the eye during attempts to fixate gaze.

ObR   The receptor that binds leptin, the protein product of the *obese* (*ob*) gene.

obsessive–compulsive disorder (OCD)   A syndrome in which the affected individual engages in recurring, repetitive acts that are carried out without rhyme, reason, or the ability to stop.

occipital cortex   The cortex of the occipital lobe of the brain. Also called *visual cortex.* See Figure 10.13.

occipital lobe   The posterior lobe of the brain. See Figure 2.11

OCD   See *obsessive–compulsive disorder.*

ocular dominance histogram   A graph that portrays the strength of response of a brain neuron to stimuli presented to either the left eye or the right eye. Used to determine the effects of manipulating visual experience. See Figure 7.19.

ocular dominance slab   A slab of visual cortex, about 0.5 mm wide, in which the neurons of all layers respond preferentially to stimulation of one eye. See Figure 10.22.

odorant   A molecule that elicits a perceived odor.

off-center bipolar cell   A retinal bipolar cell that is inhibited by light in the center of its receptive field and excited by light in the surround. See Figure 10.14. Contrast with *on-center bipolar cell*.

off-center ganglion cell   Retinal ganglion cell that is activated when light is presented to the periphery, rather than the center, of the cell's receptive field. See Figure 10.14. Contrast with *on-center ganglion cell*.

off-center/on-surround   Referring to a concentric receptive field in which the center inhibits the cell of interest while the surround excites it. See Figure 10.14. Contrast with *on-center/off-surround*.

OHC   See *outer hair cell*.

olfactory bulb   An anterior projection of the brain that terminates in the upper nasal passages and, through small openings in the skull, provides receptors for smell. See Figures 2.11, 9.19.

olfactory cilium   Hairlike structure arising from the olfactory receptor cells. See Figure 9.19.

olfactory epithelium (pl. epithelia)   A sheet of cells, including olfactory receptors, that lines the dorsal portion of the nasal cavities and adjacent regions, including the septum that separates the left and right nasal cavities. See Figure 9.19.

oligodendrocyte   A type of glial cell that is commonly associated with nerve cell bodies. Some oligodendrocytes form myelin sheaths. See Figure 2.6.

on-center bipolar cell   A retinal bipolar cell that is excited by light in the center of its receptive field and inhibited by light in the surround. See Figure 10.14. Contrast with *off-center bipolar cell*.

on-center ganglion cell   A retinal ganglion cell that is activated when light is presented to the center, rather than the periphery, of the cell's receptive field. See Figure 10.14. Contrast with *off-center ganglion cell*.

on-center/off-surround   Referring to a concentric receptive field in which the center excites the cell of interest while the surround inhibits it. See Figure 10.14. Contrast with *off-center/on-surround*.

ontogeny   The process by which an individual changes in the course of its lifetime—that is, grows up and grows old.

Onuf's nucleus   The human homolog of the spinal nucleus of the bulbocavernosus (SNB) in rats.

open-loop control mechanism   A control mechanism in which feedback from the output of the system is not provided to the input control. Contrast with *closed-loop control mechanism*.

operant conditioning   See *instrumental conditioning*.

opiate receptor   A receptor that responds to endogenous and/or exogenous opiates.

opiates   A class of compounds that exert an effect like that of opium, including reduced pain sensitivity. See Table 4.1 under "opioids."

opioids   A class of peptides produced in various regions of the brain that bind to opiate receptors and act like opiates. See Table 4.1.

opium   A heterogeneous extract of the seedpod juice of the opium poppy, *Papaver somniferum*.

opponent-process hypothesis   The theory that color vision depends on systems that produce opposite responses to light of different wavelengths. See Figures 10.24, 10.25.

opsin   One of the two components of photopigments in the retina. The other component is RETINAL.

optic chiasm   The point at which the two optic nerves meet. See Figures 2.11, 10.13.

optic disc   The region of the retina devoid of receptor cells because ganglion cell axons and blood vessels exit the eyeball there. See Figure 10.2.

optic nerve   Cranial nerve II; the collection of ganglion cell axons that extend from the retina to the optic chiasm. See Figure 2.8.

optic radiation   Axons from the lateral geniculate nucleus that terminate in the primary visual areas of the occipital cortex. See Figure 10.13.

optic tectum (pl. tecta)   The optical center of the midbrain. See Box 7.2.

optic tract   The axons of retinal ganglion cells after they have passed the optic chiasm; most terminate in the lateral geniculate nucleus. See Figure 10.13.

orexins   A group of proteins expressed in the lateral hypothalamus that trigger feeding; they have also been implicated in narcolepsy

organ of Corti   A structure in the inner ear that lies on the basilar membrane of the cochlea. It contains the hair cells and terminations of the auditory nerve. See Figure 9.1.

organizational effect   A permanent alteration of the nervous system, and thus permanent change in behavior, resulting from the action of a steroid hormone on an animal early in its development. Contrast with *activational effect*.

organizational hypothesis   The hypothesis that early testicular steroids masculinize the developing brain to alter behavior permanently.

organum vasculosum of the lamina terminalis (OVLT)   One of the circumventricular organs. See Figure 13.17.

orgasm   The climax of sexual experience, marked by extremely pleasurable sensations.

orientation column   A column of visual cortex that responds to rod-shaped stimuli of a particular orientation. See Figure 10.22.

oscillator circuit   A neural circuit that produces a recurring, repeating pattern of output. See Figure 3.18.

osmolality   The number of solute particles per unit volume of solvent.

osmoreceptor   One of the cells in the hypothalamus that are hypothesized to respond to changes in osmotic pressure.

osmosis   The passive movement of molecules from one place to another. The motive force behind osmosis is the constant vibration and movement of molecules.

osmotic pressure   The force produced by osmosis.

osmotic thirst   The response to increased osmotic pressure in brain cells. Contrast with *hypovolemic thirst*.

ossicles   Three small bones (incus, malleus, and stapes) that transmit sound across the middle ear, from the tympanic membrane to the oval window. See Figure 9.1.

otolith   A small bony crystal on the gelatinous membrane in the vestibular system. See Figure 9.15.

otologist   A person who studies the outer, middle, and inner ear.

ototoxic   Toxic to the ears, especially the middle or inner ear.

outer hair cell (OHC)   One of the two types of receptor cells of the cochlea. See Figure 9.1.

oval window   The opening from the middle ear to the inner ear. See Figure 9.1.

ovaries   The female gonads, which produce eggs for reproduction. See Figures 5.1, 12.7, 12.15, Table 5.2.

overshoot   Here, the portion of the action potential during which the cell is transiently positive with relation to the extracellular medium. See Figure 3.7. Contrast with *undershoot*.

oviduct   See *fallopian tube*.

oviparity   Reproduction through egg laying. Contrast with *viviparity*.

OVLT   See *organum vasculosum of the lamina terminalis*.

ovulation   The production and release of an egg (ovum).

ovulatory cycle   The periodic occurrence of ovulation. See Figure 12.5.

ovum (pl. ova)   An egg, the female gamete.

oxytocin   A hormone, released from the posterior pituitary, that triggers milk letdown in the nursing female. See Table 5.2, Figures 5.11, 5.12.

pacinian corpuscle   A skin receptor cell type. See Figures 8.3, 8.4, 8.14.

pain   The discomfort normally associated with tissue damage.

pair bond See *monogamy*.

pancreas An endocrine gland, located near the posterior wall of the abdominal cavity, that secretes insulin and glucagon. See Figures 5.1, 5.19, Table 5.2.

papilla (pl. papillae) A small bump that projects from the surface of the tongue. Papillae contain most of the taste receptor cells. See Figure 9.17.

paracrine Referring to cellular communication in which a chemical signal diffuses to nearby target cells through the intermediate extracellular space. See Figure 5.4.

paradoxical sleep See *rapid-eye-movement sleep*.

paragigantocellular nucleus (PGN) A region of the brainstem reticular formation implicated in sleep.

parallel fiber One of the axons of the granule cells that form the outermost layer of the cerebellar cortex. See Figure 2.16.

parallel processing The use of several different circuits at the same time to process the same stimuli; a novelty in computers, but an ancient property of nervous systems.

paraphasia A symptom of aphasia that is distinguished by the substitution of a word by a sound, an incorrect word, an unintended word, or a neologism (a meaningless word).

parasympathetic nervous system One of the two systems that compose the autonomic nervous system. The parasympathetic division arises from both the cranial nerves and the sacral spinal cord. The other system is the sympathetic nervous system. See Figures 2.10, 2.13.

paraventricular nucleus (PVN) A nucleus of the hypothalamus. See Figures 5.11, 13.24.

paresis (pl. pareses) Partial paralysis.

parietal lobe A major sector of the cerebral hemispheres. See Figure 2.11.

Parkinson's disease A degenerative neurological disorder, characterized by tremors at rest, muscular rigidity, and reduction in voluntary movement, that involves dopaminergic neurons of the substantia nigra.

parthenogenesis Literally "virgin birth"; the production of offspring without the contribution of a male or sperm.

parvocellular layers The four dorsal or outer layers of the primate lateral geniculate nucleus, so called because their cells are relatively small. See Figures 10.15, 10.26. Contrast with *magnocellular layers*.

parvocellular system The division of primate visual pathways that appears to be mainly responsible for analysis of color and form and for recognition of objects. See Figure 10.26. Contrast with *magnocellular system*.

passive avoidance response A response that an organism has learned not to make (e.g., learning not to enter a compartment where it has been given a shock).

patch clamp technique The use of very narrow pipette microelectrodes, clamped by suction onto tiny patches of the neural membrane, to record the electrical activity of a single square micrometer of membrane, including single ion channels.

pattern coding Coding of information in sensory systems based on the temporal pattern of action potentials.

Pavlovian conditioning See *classical conditioning*.

PCP See *phencyclidine*.

PCR See *polymerase chain reaction*.

penis The male genital organ, which enters the female's vagina to deliver semen. See Figures 12.4, 12.7.

peptide A short string of amino acids. Longer strings of amino acids are called proteins.

perforant path The route of axons that "perforate" the subiculum to provide the main inputs to the hippocampal formation.

periaqueductal gray The neuronal body–rich region of the midbrain surrounding the cerebral aqueduct that connects the third and fourth ventricles.

period The interval of time between two similar points of successive cycles, such as sunset to sunset.

peripheral nervous system The portion of the nervous system that includes all the nerves and neurons outside the brain and spinal cord. See Figure 2.13.

permanent memory A type of memory that lasts without decline for the life of an organism. Contrast with *long-term memory*.

perseverate To continue to show a behavior repeatedly.

Perseveration-consolidation hypothesis The hypothesis that information passes through two stages in memory formation. During the first stage the memory is held by perseveration (repetition) of neural activity and is easily disrupted. During the second stage the memory becomes fixed, or consolidated, and is no longer easily disrupted.

PET See *positron emission tomography*.

petit mal seizure A type of generalized epileptic seizure that is characterized by a spike-and-wave electrical pattern. A person having a petit mal seizure is unaware of the environment and later cannot recall what happened. See Box 3.2. Contrast with *grand mal seizure*.

PGN See *paragigantocellular nucleus*.

PGO wave An EEG wave of activity from the pons to the lateral geniculate and on to the occipital cortex, usually seen only during REM sleep in cats.

phallus (pl. phalli or phalluses) The clitoris or penis.

phantom limb The experience of sensory messages that are attributed to an amputated limb.

phase shift A shift in the activity of a biological rhythm, typically provided by a synchronizing environmental stimulus.

phasic receptor A receptor that shows a rapid fall in nerve impulse discharge as stimulation is maintained.

phencyclidine (PCP) An anesthetic agent that is also a psychedelic drug. Phencyclidine makes many people feel dissociated from themselves and their environment.

phenothiazines A class of antipsychotic drugs that reduce the positive symptoms of schizophrenia.

phenotype The sum of an individual's physical characteristics at one particular time. Contrast with *genotype*.

phenylketonuria (PKU) An inherited disorder of protein metabolism in which the absence of an enzyme leads to a toxic buildup of certain compounds, causing mental retardation.

pheromone A chemical signal that is released outside the body of an animal and affects other members of the same species. See Figure 5.4. Contrast with *allomone*.

phobic disorder An intense, irrational fear that becomes centered on a specific object, activity, or situation that a person feels he or she must avoid.

phoneme A sound that is produced for language.

phonemic paraphasia A symptom of aphasia in which incorrect phonemes are substituted for correct sounds.

phosphoinositides A class of common second messenger compounds in postsynaptic cells.

phosphorylation The addition of phosphate groups (PO_4) to proteins.

photon A quantum of light energy.

photopic system A system in the retina that operates at high levels of light, shows sensitivity to color, and involves the cones. See Table 10.1. Contrast with *scotopic system*.

phrenology The belief that bumps on the skull reflect enlargements of brain regions responsible for certain behavioral faculties. See Figure 1.12.

phylogeny The evolutionary history of a particular group of organisms. See Figure 6.1.

physical dependence The state of an individual that has frequently taken high doses of a drug and will encounter unpleasant withdrawal symptoms if he or she stops.

physiological nystagmus Small, rapid movement of the eyes that prevents retinal adaptation and permits sustained viewing of a scene.

physiological saline A mixture of water and salt in which the concentration of salt is 0.9%, approximately equal in osmolarity to mammalian extracellular fluid.

pia mater The innermost of the three coverings (meninges) that embrace the brain and spinal cord. See also *dura mater* and *arachnoid.*

pineal gland A secretory gland in the brain midline; the source of melatonin release. See Figures 2.11, 5.1, Table 5.2.

pinna (pl. pinnae) See *external ear.*

pitch A dimension of auditory experience in which sounds vary from low to high.

pituitary gland A small, complex endocrine gland located in a socket at the base of the skull. The anterior pituitary and posterior pituitary are separate in function. See Figures 2.11, 5.11, 5.14.

PKU See *phenylketonuria.*

place cell A neuron within the hippocampus that selectively fires when the animal is in a particular location.

place theory A theory of frequency discrimination stating that pitch perception depends on the place of maximal displacement of the basilar membrane produced by a sound. Contrast with *volley theory.*

placebo A substance, given to a patient, that is known to be ineffective or inert but that sometimes brings relief.

placebo effect A response to an inert substance (a placebo) that mimics the effects of an actual drug. For example, people suffering pain frequently experience relief from sugar tablets presented as medicine.

placenta (pl. placentas or placentae) The specialized organ produced by the mammalian embryo that attaches to the walls of the uterus to provide nutrients, energy, and gas exchange to the fetus.

placental mammal A mammal that produces a highly specialized placenta. All mammals except marsupials and monotremes are placental mammals.

planum temporale A region of superior temporal cortex adjacent to the primary auditory area. See Figure 19.16.

plasticity Malleability. See specifically *neural plasticity.*

poikilotherm An older term, now considered inadequate, for an animal whose body temperature varies with the environment. Examples include reptiles. A more accepted term is *ectotherm.* Contrast with *homeotherm.*

polyandry A mating system in which one female mates with more than one male. Contrast with *polygyny.*

polygamy A mating system in which an individual mates with more than one other animal. Contrast with *monogamy* and *bigamy.*

polygraph A device that measures several bodily responses, such as heart rate and blood pressure; popularly known as a *lie detector.*

polygyny A mating system in which one male mates with more than one female. Contrast with *polyandry.*

polymerase chain reaction (PCR) A method for reproducing a particular RNA or DNA sequence manyfold, allowing amplification for sequencing or manipulating the sequence.

polymodal Involving several sensory modalities.

pons (pl. pontes) A portion of the metencephalon. See Figures 2.11, 2.13.

positive feedback The property by which the output of a system feeds back to increase the input. A rarity in biological systems. Contrast with *negative feedback.*

positive reward model A model of addictive behavior that emphasizes the rewarding attributes of drug ingestion.

positive symptom In psychiatry, an abnormal state. Examples include hallucinations, delusions, and excited motor behavior. Contrast with *negative symptom.*

positron emission tomography (PET) A technique for examining brain function in intact humans by combining tomography with injections of radioactive substances used by the brain. Analysis of the metabolism of these substances reflects regional differences in brain activity. See Figure 2.21.

postcentral gyrus The strip of parietal cortex, just behind the central sulcus, that receives somatosensory information from the entire body. See Figure 2.11.

postcopulatory behavior The final stage in mating behavior. Species-specific postcopulatory behaviors include rolling (in the cat) and grooming (in the rat). See Figure 12.2.

posterior Toward the back or tail of an animal. Contrast with *anterior.*

posterior pituitary The rear division of the pituitary gland. Also called *neurohypophysis.* See Figures 5.1, 5.11, Table 5.2.

postganglionic cell A cell in the autonomic nervous system that resides in the peripheral ganglia and sends its axons to innervate target organs. See Figure 2.10.

postsynaptic Referring to the region of a synapse that receives and responds to neurotransmitter. See Figure 2.4. Contrast with *presynaptic.*

postsynaptic potential See *graded potential.*

posttetanic potentiation A well-known example of neural plasticity in which a rapid series of action potentials (a tetanus) is induced in a nerve, with the result that subsequent single action potentials cause a stronger postsynaptic potential in the target.

posttraumatic stress disorder (PTSD) A disorder in which memories of an unpleasant episode repeatedly plague the victim.

potassium equilibrium potential See *equilibrium potential.*

precentral gyrus The strip of frontal cortex, just in front of the central sulcus, that is crucial for motor control. See Figure 2.11.

precocial Referring to animals that are born in a relatively developed state and that are able to survive without maternal care. Contrast with *altricial.*

preferred temperature The environmental temperature at which an animal chooses to spend most of its time.

prefrontal cortex The anteriormost region of the frontal lobe.

preganglionic cell A cell of the autonomic nervous system that resides in the CNS and sends its axons to innervate autonomic ganglia. See Figure 2.10.

premotor cortex A region of nonprimary motor cortex just anterior to the primary motor cortex. See Figure 11.16.

prenatal Before birth.

preoptic area A region of the hypothalamus just anterior to the level of the optic chiasm.

presenilin An enzyme that cleaves amyloid precursor protein (APP) to form amyloid, which can lead to Alzheimer's disease.

presynaptic Referring to the region of a synapse that releases neurotransmitter. See Figure 2.4. Contrast with *postsynaptic.*

primacy effect The superior performance seen in a memory task for items at the start of a list; usually attributed to long-term memory. Contrast with *recency effect.*

primary motor cortex The apparent executive region for initiation of movement; primarily the precentral gyrus.

primary sensory cortex For a given sensory modality, the region of cortex that receives most of the information about that modality from the thalamus or, in the case of olfaction, directly from the secondary sensory neurons.

primary sensory ending The axon that transmits information from the central portion of a muscle spindle. See Figure 11.9.

primary somatosensory cortex (S1) The gyrus just posterior to the central sulcus where sensory receptors on the body surface are mapped. See Figures 8.16 and 8.18.

primary visual cortex (V1) The region of the occipital cortex where most visual information first arrives. Also called *striate cortex, area 17,* or *V1.* See Figures 10.12, 10.13, 10.18.

priming 1. In pheromones, the ability of a pheromone to slowly alter the physiology of a conspecific. 2. In memory, the phenomenon by which exposure to a stimulus facilitates subsequent responses to the same or a similar stimulus.

prion A protein that canbecome improperly folded and thereby can induce other proteins to follow suit, leading to long protein chains that impair neural function.

procedural memory See *nondeclarative memory*.

proceptive behavior A behavior displayed by an animal that prompts its partner to initiate mating behaviors.

progesterone The primary type of progestin secreted by the ovary. See Table 5.2, Figure 5.17.

progestins A major class of steroid hormones that are produced by the ovary, including progesterone. See Table 5.2, Figure 5.15.

prolactin A protein hormone, produced by the anterior pituitary, that promotes mammary development for lactation in female mammals. See Table 5.2, Figure 5.15.

promiscuity A mating system in which animals mate with several members of the opposite sex and do not establish durable associations with sex partners.

proprioceptive Referring to information from the periphery about the body's position and movement.

prosencephalon See *forebrain*.

prosopagnosia A condition characterized by the inability to recognize faces.

prostate gland A male secondary sexual gland that contributes fluid to semen. See Figures 12.7, 12.15.

prosthetic device An artificial replacement for a body part lost by accident or disease.

protein A long string of amino acids. The basic building material of organisms on this planet. See also *peptide*.

protein hormone A class of hormones that consists of protein molecules.

protein kinase An enzyme that adds phosphate groups (PO_4) to protein molecules.

proximal An anatomical term referring to structures near the trunk or center of an organism. See Box 2.2. Contrast with *distal*.

psychedelic Referring to a mental state with intensified sensory perception and distortions or hallucinations. Psychedelic drugs (also called *hallucinogens*) produce such states.

psychoneuroimmunology The study of the immune system and its interaction with the nervous system and behavior.

psychopharmacology The study of the effects of drugs on the nervous system and behavior.

psychosocial dwarfism Reduced stature caused by stress early in life that inhibits deep sleep. See Box 5.2.

psychosomatic medicine A field of study that emphasizes the role of psychological factors in disease.

psychosurgery Surgery in which brain lesions are produced to modify severe psychiatric disorders.

psychotogen A substance that generates psychotic behavior.

PTSD See *posttraumatic stress disorder*.

pupil The aperture, formed by the iris, that allows light to enter the eye. See Figure 10.2.

pure tone A tone with a single frequency of vibration. See Box 9.1.

Purkinje cell A type of large nerve cell in the cerebellar cortex. See Figure 2.16.

pursuit movement A type of eye movement in which the gaze smoothly and continuously follows a moving object.

putamen One of the basal ganglia. See Figure 2.15.

PVN See *paraventricular nucleus*.

pyramidal cell A type of large nerve cell that has a roughly pyramid-shaped cell body; found in the cerebral cortex. See Figure 2.17.

pyramidal system The motor system that includes neurons within the cerebral cortex and their axons, which form the pyramidal tract. Also called *corticospinal system*. See Figure 11.11.

pyramidal tract The path of axons arising from the motor cortex and terminating in the spinal cord.

quantum (pl. quanta) A unit of radiant energy.

radial glial cells Glial cells that form early in development, spanning the width of the emerging cerebral hemispheres, and guide migrating neurons. See Figure 7.6.

radioimmunoassay (RIA) A technique that uses antibodies to measure the concentration of a substance, such as a hormone in blood. See Box 5.1.

ramp movement A slow, sustained motion that is thought to be generated in the basal ganglia. Also called *smooth movement*. Contrast with *ballistic movement*.

range fractionation A hypothesis of stimulus intensity perception stating that a wide range of intensity values can be encoded by a group of cells, each of which is a specialist for a particular range of stimulus intensities. See Figure 8.5.

raphe nucleus A group of neurons in the midline of the brainstem that contains serotonin and is involved in sleep mechanisms. See Figure 14.22.

rapid-eye-movement (REM) sleep A stage of sleep characterized by small-amplitude, fast-EEG waves, no postural tension, and rapid eye movements. Also called *paradoxical sleep*. See Figure 14.11. Contrast with *slow-wave sleep*.

recency effect The superior performance seen in a memory task for items at the end of a list; attributed to short-term memory. Contrast with *primacy effect*.

receptive field The stimulus region and features that cause the maximal response of a cell in a sensory system. See Figures 8.10, 10.14, 10.16.

receptivity The state of readiness in the female to show responses that are necessary for the male to achieve intromission.

receptor The initial element in a sensory system, responsible for stimulus transduction. Examples include the hair cells in the cochlea, and the rods and cones in the retina. See also *receptor molecule*.

receptor cell A specialized cell that responds to a particular energy or substance in the internal or external environment. The receptor cell converts this energy into a change in the electrical potential across its membrane.

receptor molecule A protein that captures and reacts to molecules of the transmitter or hormone. Also called *receptor*.

receptor site A region of specialized membrane that contains receptor molecules located on the postsynaptic surface of a synapse. Receptor sites receive and react with chemical transmitters.

recovery of function The recovery of behavioral capacity following brain damage from stroke or injury.

red nucleus A brainstem structure related to the basal ganglia. Also called *nucleus ruber*.

reductionism The scientific strategy of breaking a system down into increasingly smaller parts in order to understand it completely.

redundancy The property of having a particular process, usually an important one, monitored and regulated by more than one mechanism.

reflex A simple, highly stereotyped, and unlearned response to a particular stimulus (e.g., an eye blink in response to a puff of air). See Figures 3.16, 11.10.

refraction The bending of light rays by a change in the density of a medium, such as the cornea and the lens of the eyes.

refractory phase 1. A period during and after a nerve impulse in which the responsiveness of the axon membrane is reduced. A brief period of complete insensitivity to stimuli (absolute refractory phase) is followed by a longer period of reduced sensitivity (relative refractory phase) during which only strong stimulation produces a nerve impulse. 2. A period following copulation during which an individual cannot recommence copulation. The absolute refractory phase of the male sexual response is illustrated in Figure 12.8.

regulation   An adaptive response to early injury, as when developing individuals compensate for missing or injured cells.

reinforcing stimulus   See *instrumental conditioning.*

relative refractory phase   See *refractory phase.*

releasing hormones   A class of hormones, produced in the hypothalamus, that traverse the hypothalamic–pituitary portal system to control the pituitary's release of tropic hormones. See Figure 5.15.

REM sleep   See *rapid-eye-movement sleep.*

renin   A hormone released by the kidneys when they detect reduced blood flow.

reserpine   A drug that causes the depletion of monoamines and can lead to depression.

resting potential   See *membrane potential.*

reticular formation   An extensive region of the brainstem (extending from the medulla through the thalamus) that is involved in arousal. See Figure 14.21.

reticulospinal tract   A tract of axons arising from the brainstem reticular formation and descending to the spinal cord to modulate movement. See Figure 11.12.

retina   The receptive surface inside the eye that contains the rods and cones. See Figures 10.2, 10.7.

retinal   One of the two components of the photopigment found in the eye. The other component is opsin.

retinohypothalamic pathway   The projection of retinal ganglion cells to the suprachiasmatic nuclei.

retrieval   A process in memory during which a stored memory is used by an organism. See Figure 17.12.

retroactive amnesia   A type of memory loss in which events immediately preceding a head injury are not recalled. See *retrograde amnesia.*

retrograde amnesia   Difficulty in retrieving memories formed before the onset of amnesia. Contrast with *anterograde amnesia.*

retrograde degeneration   Destruction of the nerve cell body following injury to its axon. See Box 7.1. Contrast with *anterograde degeneration.*

retrograde signal   A signal that is thought to be released by the postsynaptic region that instructs the presynaptic neuron to increase subsequent transmitter release.

reuptake   The process by which released synaptic transmitter molecules are taken up and reused by the presynaptic neuron, thus stopping synaptic activity.

rhodopsin   The photopigment in rods that responds to light.

rhombencephalon   See *hindbrain.*

RIA   See *radioimmunoassay.*

ribonucleic acid (RNA)   A nucleic acid that implements information found in DNA. Two forms of RNA are transfer RNA and messenger RNA.

ribosomes   Structures in the cell body where the translation of genetic information (the production of proteins) takes place.

RNA   See *ribonucleic acid.*

rod   One of the light-sensitive receptor cells in the retina that are most active at low levels of light. See Figure 10.7. Contrast with *cone.*

roots   The two distinct branches of a spinal nerve, each of which serves a separate function. The dorsal root carries sensory information from the peripheral nervous system to the spinal cord. The ventral root carries motor messages from the spinal cord to the peripheral nervous system. See Figure 2.9.

rostral   An anatomical term referring to structures toward the head end of an organism. Also called *cephalic.* See Box 2.2. Contrast with *caudal.*

round window   A membrane separating the cochlear duct from the middle-ear cavity. See Figure 9.1.

rubrospinal tract   Axons arising from the red nucleus in the midbrain and innervating neurons of the spinal cord. See Figure 11.12.

Ruffini's ending   A skin receptor cell type. See Figures 8.3, 8.14.

S1   See *somatosensory I.*

S2   See *somatosensory II.*

saccade   A series of rapid movements of the eyes that occur regularly during normal viewing. Also called *saccadic movement.*

saccule   A small, fluid-filled sac under the utricle that responds to static positions of the head. See Figure 9.15.

sacral   Referring to the lower part of the spinal cord or back. See Figures 2.9, 2.10.

sagittal plane   The plane that bisects the body or brain into right and left portions. See Box 2.2.

saltatory conduction   The form of conduction characteristic of myelinated axons, in which the nerve impulse jumps from one node of Ranvier to the next.

satiety   A feeling of fulfillment or satisfaction. Contrast with *hunger.*

saturation   One of the basic dimensions of light perception. Saturation varies from rich to pale (e.g., from red to pink to gray in the color solid of Figure 10.5).

saxitoxin (STX)   An animal toxin that blocks sodium channels when applied to the outer surface of the cell membrane.

SC   See *standard condition.*

Schaffer collateral   An axon branch from a neuron in area CA3 that projects to area CA1 in the hippocampus. See Figure 18.7.

schema (pl. schemata or schemas)   In terms of actions, a high-level program for movement.

schizophrenia   A severe psychopathology characterized by negative symptoms such as emotional withdrawal and impoverished thought, and by positive symptoms such as hallucinations and delusions.

Schwann cell   The accessory cell that forms myelin in the peripheral nervous system.

SCN   See *suprachiasmatic nucleus.*

scotoma (pl. scotomas or scotomata)   A region of blindness caused by injury to the visual pathway or brain.

scotopic system   A system in the retina that operates at low levels of light and involves the rods. See Table 10.1. Contrast with *photopic system.*

SDN-POA   See *sexually dimorphic nucleus of the preoptic area.*

seasonal affective disorder   A putative depression brought about by the short days of winter.

second messenger   A slow-acting substance in the postsynaptic cell that amplifies the effects of nerve impulses and can initiate processes that lead to changes in electrical potential at the membrane.

secondary sensory cortex   For a given sensory modality, the cortical regions receiving direct projections from primary sensory cortex for that modality. Also called *nonprimary sensory cortex.*

secondary sensory ending   The axon transmitting information from the ends of a muscle spindle.

secondary somatosensory cortex (S2)   The region of cortex that receives direct projections from primary somatosensory cortex. See Figure 8.18.

secretin   A hormone that is released from the small intestine during digestion. See Table 5.2.

seizure   An epileptic episode. See Box 3.2.

selective permeability   The property of a membrane to allow some substances to pass through, but not others.

selective potentiation   The enhancement of the sensitivity or activity of certain neural circuits.

semantic memory   Generalized memory—for instance, knowing the meaning of a word without knowing where or when you learned that word.

semen   A mixture of fluid, including sperm, that is released during ejaculation.

semicircular canal   One of the three fluid-filled tubes in the inner ear that are part of the vestibular system. Each of the tubes, which are at right angles to each other, detects angular acceleration. See Figure 9.15.

seminal vesicle   A gland that stores fluid to contribute to semen. See Figures 12.7, 12.15.

semipermeable membrane   A membrane that allows some but not all molecules to pass through.

senile dementia   A neurological disorder of the aged that is characterized by progressive behavioral deterioration, including personality change and profound intellectual decline. It includes, but is not limited to, Alzheimer's disease.

senile plaques   A neuroanatomical change that correlates with senile dementia. Senile plaques are small areas of the brain that have abnormal cellular and chemical patterns. See Figure 7.25*a*.

sensitive period   The period during development in which an organism can be permanently altered by a particular experience or treatment.

sensitization   **1.** A form of nonassociative learning in which an organism becomes more responsive to most stimuli after being exposed to unusually strong or painful stimulation. See Box 17.1. Contrast with *habituation*. **2.** A process in which the body shows an enhanced response to a given drug after repeated doses. Contrast with *tolerance*.

sensorineural deafness   A hearing impairment that originates from cochlear or auditory nerve lesions.

sensory conflict theory   A theory of motion sickness suggesting that discrepancies between vestibular information and visual information may simulate food poisoning and therefore trigger nausea.

sensory neuron   A neuron that is directly affected by changes in the environment, such as light, an odor, or a touch.

sensory pathway   The chain of neural connections from sensory receptor cells to the cortex.

sensory receptor organ   An organ specialized to receive particular stimuli; examples include the eye and the ear.

sensory–sensory conditioning   A form of learning in which two stimuli are presented in conjunction, and one stimulus comes to predict the occurrence of the other.

sensory transduction   The process in which a receptor cell converts the energy in a stimulus into a change in the electrical potential across its membrane.

septal complex   A brain region that provides subcortical input to the hippocampal formation.

serotonergic   Referring to neurons that use serotonin as their synaptic transmitter.

serotonin (5-HT)   A synaptic transmitter that is produced in the raphe nuclei and is active in structures throughout the cerebral hemispheres. See Table 4.1, Figures 4.5, 14.22.

set point   The point of reference in a feedback system. An example is the setting of a thermostat.

set zone   The range of a variable that a feedback system tries to maintain.

sex chromosome   One of a pair of chromosomes that in female mammals are identical (XX) but in males are different (XY). Contrast with *autosome*.

sex-determining region on the Y chromosome gene   See *SRY gene*.

sex steroids   Steroid hormones secreted by the gonads: androgens, estrogens, and progestins.

sexual attraction   The first step in the mating behavior of many animals, in which animals emit stimuli that attract members of the opposite sex. See Figure 12.2.

sexual determination   The developmentally early event that normally decides whether the individual will become a male or a female.

sexual differentiation   The process by which individuals develop either malelike or femalelike bodies and behavior.

sexual dimorphism   A structural difference between the sexes.

sexual receptivity   See *receptivity*.

sexual selection   Darwin's theoretical mechanism for the evolution of anatomical and behavioral differences between males and females.

sexually dimorphic nucleus of the preoptic area (SDN-POA)   A region of the preoptic area that is five to six times larger in volume in male rats than in females. See Figure 12.20.

short-term memory (STM)   A form of memory that usually lasts only for seconds or as long as rehearsal continues. Contrast with *iconic memory*.

SIDS   See *sudden infant death syndrome*.

simple cortical cell   A cell in the visual cortex that responds best to an edge or a bar of a particular width and with a particular direction and location in the visual field. See Figure 10.16. Contrast with *complex cortical cell*.

sinistral   Left-handed.

size principle   The idea that as increasing numbers of motor neurons are recruited to produce muscle responses of increasing strength, small, low-threshold neurons are recruited first and then large, high-threshold neurons.

skill learning   Learning to perform a task that requires motor coordination.

sleep apnea   A sleep disorder that involves the slowing or cessation of respiration during sleep, which wakens the patient. Excessive daytime somnolence results from the frequent nocturnal awakening.

sleep cycle   A period of slow-wave sleep followed by a period of REM sleep. In humans, a sleep cycle lasts approximately 90 minutes.

sleep deprivation   The partial or total prevention of sleep.

sleep enuresis   Bed-wetting.

sleep-maintenance insomnia   Difficulty in staying asleep. Contrast with *sleep-onset insomnia*.

sleep-onset insomnia   Difficulty in getting to sleep. Contrast with *sleep-maintenance insomnia*.

sleep paralysis   A state during the transition to or from sleep, in which the ability to move or talk is temporarily lost.

sleep recovery   The process of sleeping more than normally after a period of sleep deprivation, as though in compensation.

sleep spindle   A characteristic 14- to 18-Hz wave in the EEG of a person said to be in stage 2 sleep. See Figure 14.11.

slow muscle fiber   A type of striated muscle fiber that contracts slowly but does not fatigue readily. Contrast with *fast muscle fiber*.

slow-wave sleep (SWS)   Sleep, divided into stages 1 through 4, that is defined by the presence of slow-wave EEG activity. See Figure 14.11. Contrast with *rapid-eye-movement (REM) sleep*.

SMA   See *supplementary motor area*.

smooth movement   See *ramp movement*.

smooth muscle   A type of muscle fiber that is controlled by the autonomic nervous system rather than by voluntary control. Contrast with *striated muscle*.

SNB   See *spinal nucleus of the bulbocavernosus*.

SOAE   See *spontaneous otoacoustic emission*.

sodium equilibrium potential   See *equilibrium potential*.

sodium–potassium pump   The energetically expensive mechanism that pushes sodium ions out of a cell, and potassium ions in.

solute   The solid compound that is dissolved in a liquid. Contrast with *solvent*.

solvent   The liquid (often water) in which a compound is dissolved. Contrast with *solute*.

somatic intervention   An approach to finding relations between bodily variables and behavioral variables that involves manipulating body structure or function and looking for resultant changes in behavior. See Figure 1.3. Contrast with *behavioral intervention*.

somatomedins   A group of proteins, released from the liver in response to growth hormone, that aid body growth and maintenance.

somatosensory   Referring to touch and pain sensation.

somatosensory cortex   The portion of parietal cortex that receives tactile stimuli from the body.

somatotropic hormone   See *growth hormone.*

somnambulism   Sleepwalking.

Southern blot   A method of detecting a particular DNA sequence in the genome of an organism, by separating DNA with gel electrophoresis, blotting the separated DNAs onto nitrocellulose, then using a nucleotide probe to hybridize with, and highlight, the gene of interest. See Figure A.3 in the Appendix.

spasticity   Markedly increased rigidity in response to forced movement of the limbs.

spatial-frequency filter model   A model of pattern analysis that emphasizes Fourier analysis of visual stimuli. Contrast with *feature detector model.*

spatial summation   The summation at the axon hillock of postsynaptic potentials from across the cell body. If this summation reaches threshold, a nerve impulse is triggered. See Figure 3.12. Contrast with *temporal summation.*

specific abilities to learn and remember   The concept that specific abilities to learn and remember evolve where needed. Contrast with *genetic constraints on learning.*

specific nerve energies   The doctrine that the receptors and neural channels for the different senses are independent and operate in their own special ways, and can produce only one particular sensation each.

specific-pathway hypothesis   The idea that each auditory input to the brain transmits information about only a narrow range of frequencies.

spectrally opponent cell   A visual receptor cell that has opposite firing responses to different regions of the spectrum. See Figures 10.24, 10.25.

sperm (pl. sperm)   The gamete produced by males for fertilization of eggs (ova).

spinal animal   An animal whose spinal cord has been surgically disconnected from the brain to enable the study of behaviors that do not require brain control.

spinal nerve   A nerve that emerges from the spinal cord. There are 31 pairs of spinal nerves. See Figure 2.9.

spinal nucleus of the bulbocavernosus (SNB)   A group of motoneurons in the spinal cord of rats that innervate striated muscles controlling the penis. See Figure 12.21. See also *Onuf's nucleus.*

spinal root   See *roots.*

spinal shock   A period of decreased synaptic excitability in the neurons of the spinal cord after it has been isolated surgically from the brain.

spindle cell   A type of small, rod-shaped nerve cell.

spinothalamic system   See *anterolateral system.*

split-brain individual   An individual whose corpus callosum has been severed, halting communication between the right and left hemispheres.

spontaneous otoacoustic emission (SOAE)   A sound produced by the ears of many normal people. Contrast with *evoked otoacoustic emission.*

***SRY* gene**   A gene on the Y chromosome that directs the developing gonads to become testes. The name *SRY* stands for *sex-determining region on the Y chromosome.*

stage 1 sleep   The initial stage of slow-wave sleep, which is characterized by small-amplitude EEG waves of irregular frequency, slow heart rate, and reduced muscle tension. See Figure 14.11.

stage 2 sleep   A stage of slow-wave sleep that is defined by bursts of regular 14- to 18-Hz EEG waves (called sleep spindles) that progressively increase and then decrease in amplitude. See Figure 14.11.

stage 3 sleep   A stage of slow-wave sleep that is defined by the spindles seen in stage 2 sleep, mixed with larger-amplitude slow waves. See Figure 14.11.

stage 4 sleep   A stage of slow-wave sleep that is defined by the presence of high-amplitude slow waves of 1 to 4 Hz. See Figure 14.11.

standard condition (SC)   The usual environment for laboratory rodents, with a few animals in a cage and adequate food and water, but no complex stimulation. See Figure 18.4. Contrast with *enriched condition* and *impoverished condition.*

stapedius   A middle-ear muscle that is attached to the stapes. See Figure 9.1.

stapes (pl. stapes or stapedes)   A middle-ear bone that is connected to the oval window; one of the three ossicles that conduct sounds across the middle ear. See Figure 9.1.

static phase of obesity   A later period following destruction of the ventromedial hypothalamus, during which an animal's weight stabilizes at an obese level and food intake is not much above normal. See Figure 13.25. Contrast with *dynamic phase of weight gain.*

stellate cell   A type of small nerve cell that has many branches. See Figure 2.16.

stem cell   A cell that is undifferentiated and therefore can take on the fate of any cell the donor organism can produce.

stereocilium (pl. stereocilia)   A relatively stiff hair that protrudes from a hair cell in the auditory or vestibular system. See Figure 9.1.

stereopsis   The ability to perceive depth using the slight difference in visual information from the two eyes. See Figure 10.26.

steroid hormones   A class of hormones, each of which is composed of four interconnected rings of carbon atoms.

steroid receptor cofactors   Proteins that affect the cell's response when a steroid hormone binds its receptor.

stimulation-elicited behavior   A motivational behavior, such as eating, drinking, or fearful escape, that is elicited by electrical stimulation of sites in the brain.

STM   See *short-term memory.*

stress   Any circumstance that upsets homeostatic balance. Examples include exposure to extreme cold or heat or an array of threatening psychological states.

stress immunization   The concept that mild stress early in life makes an individual better able to handle stress later in life.

stretch reflex   The contraction of a muscle in response to stretch of that muscle. See Figure 11.10.

striate cortex   See *primary visual cortex.*

striated muscle   A type of muscle with a striped appearance, generally under voluntary control. Contrast with *smooth muscle.*

striatum   The caudate nucleus and putamen together.

stroke   A disorder of blood vessels—either a block or a rupture of a vessel—that destroys or cripples particular brain regions.

STX   See *saxitoxin.*

subcutaneous   Beneath the skin.

subfornical organ   One of the circumventricular organs. See Figure 13.17.

subiculum (pl. subicula)   A region adjacent to the hippocampus that contributes to the hippocampal formation. Also called *hippocampal gyrus.* See Figure 18.7.

substance P   A peptide transmitter implicated in pain transmission.

substance-related disorder   Drug addiction, either the abuse of drugs or the more serious dependence on drugs.

substantia nigra   A brainstem structure in humans that is related to the basal ganglia and named for its dark pigmentation. Depletion of dopaminergic cells in this region has been implicated in Parkinson's disease.

sudden infant death syndrome (SIDS)   The sudden, unexpected death of an apparently healthy human infant who simply stops breathing, usually during sleep. SIDS is not well understood. Also called *crib death.*

sulcus (pl. sulci)   A furrow of convoluted brain surface. See Figure 2.11. Contrast with *gyrus.*

superior colliculi   See *colliculus.*

superior olivary nuclei A brainstem structure that receives input from both right and left cochlear nuclei, and provides the first binaural analysis of auditory information. See Figure 9.6.

superordinate circuit A neural circuit that is hierarchically superior to other, simple circuits.

supplementary motor area (SMA) A region of nonprimary motor cortex that receives input from the basal ganglia and modulates the activity of the primary motor cortex. See Figure 11.16.

suprachiasmatic nucleus (SCN) A small region of the hypothalamus above the optic chiasm that is the location of a circadian oscillator. See Figure 14.5.

supraoptic nucleus A nucleus of the hypothalamus. See Figure 5.11.

surface dyslexia A form of acquired dyslexia in which the patient seems to attend only to the fine details of reading. Contrast with *deep dyslexia*.

SWS See *slow-wave sleep*.

Sylvian fissure A deep fissure that demarcates the temporal lobe. See Figure 2.11.

sympathetic chain A chain of ganglia that runs along each side of the spinal column; part of the sympathetic nervous system. See Figure 2.10.

sympathetic nervous system One of two systems that compose the autonomic nervous system. The sympathetic nervous system arises from the thoracic and lumbar spinal cord. The other system is the parasympathetic nervous system. See Figure 2.10.

synapse An area composed of the presynaptic (axonal) terminal, the postsynaptic (usually dendritic) membrane, and the space (or cleft) between them. The synapse is the site at which neural messages travel from one neuron to another. Also called *synaptic region*. See Figure 2.4.

synapse rearrangement The loss of some synapses and development of others; a refinement of synaptic connections that is often seen in development. See Figure 7.3.

synaptic bouton The presynaptic swelling of the axon terminal from which neural messages travel across the synaptic cleft to other neurons.

synaptic cleft The space between the presynaptic and postsynaptic elements. This gap measures about 20 to 40 nm. See Figures 2.4, 3.13.

synaptic region See *synapse*.

synaptic transmitter The chemical in the presynaptic bouton that serves as the basis of communication between neurons. The transmitter travels across the synaptic cleft and reacts with the postsynaptic membrane when triggered by a nerve impulse. Also called *neurotransmitter* or *chemical transmitter*. See Figure 3.13, Table 4.1.

synaptic vesicle A small, spherical structure that contains molecules of synaptic transmitter. See Figure 2.4.

synaptogenesis The establishment of synaptic connections as axons and dendrites grow. See Figure 7.3.

synergist A muscle that acts together with another muscle. See also *agonist* (definition 2). Contrast with *antagonist* (definition 2).

synthetic Here, a chemical that is human-made.

syrinx (pl. syringes or syrinxes) The vocal organ in birds.

system A high level of brain organization that includes specialized circuits (e.g., the visual system). Contrast with *circuit*.

T cell See *T lymphocyte.*

T lymphocyte An immune system cell that attacks foreign microbes or tissue; "killer cell." Also called *T cell*. See Figure 15.17.

tardive dyskinesia A disorder characterized by involuntary movements, especially involving the face, mouth, lips, and tongue; related to prolonged use of antipsychotic drugs, such as chlorpromazine. See Box 16.1.

tastant A substance that can be tasted.

taste aversion See *conditioned taste aversion*.

taste bud A cluster of 50 to 150 cells that detects tastes. Taste buds are found in papillae on the tongue. See Figure 9.17.

tau 1. A protein associated with neurofibrillary tangles in Alzheimer's disease. 2. A mutation in hamsters that causes a shorter circadian period in free-running conditions.

taxonomy The classification of organisms. See Table 6.1 and Figure 6.2.

tectorial membrane A structure in the cochlear duct. See Figure 9.1.

tectum (pl. tecta) The dorsal portion of the midbrain, including the inferior and superior colliculi.

telencephalon The frontal subdivision of the forebrain that includes the cerebral hemispheres when fully developed. See Figure 2.13.

temporal lobe A major sector of the cerebral hemispheres. See Figure 2.11.

temporal summation The summation of postsynaptic potentials that reach the axon hillock at different times. The closer together the potentials are, the more complete the summation. See Figure 3.12. Contrast with *spatial summation*.

tendon Strong tissue that connects muscles to bone.

TENS See *transcutaneous electrical nerve stimulation*.

tensor tympani The muscle attached to the malleus and the tympanic membrane that modulates mechanical linkage to protect the delicate receptor cells of the inner ear from damaging sounds. See Figure 9.1.

testes (sing. testis) The male gonads, which produce sperm and androgenic steroid hormones. See Figures 5.1, 12.7, 12.14, Table 5.2.

testosterone A hormone, produced by male gonads, that controls a variety of bodily changes that become visible at puberty. See Figures 5.15, 5.17, Table 5.2.

tetrahydrocannabinol (THC) The psychoactive ingredient in marijuana.

tetrodotoxin (TTX) A toxin from puffer fish ovaries that blocks the voltage-gated sodium channel, preventing action potential conduction.

thalamus (pl. thalami) The brain regions that surround the third ventricle. See Figures 2.11, 2.13.

THC See *tetrahydrocannabinol*.

third ventricle The midline ventricle that conducts cerebrospinal fluid from the lateral ventricles to the fourth ventricle. See Figure 2.19.

thirst The internal state of an animal seeking water.

thoracic Referring to the level of the chest—here, the vertebrae that have ribs attached and the spinal cord segments originating from those vertebrae. See Figures 2.9, 2.10.

threshold The stimulus intensity that is just adequate to trigger a nerve impulse at the axon hillock.

thyroid gland An endocrine gland located below the vocal apparatus in the throat that regulates metabolic processes, especially carbohydrate use and body growth. See Figure 5.1, Table 5.2.

thyroid-stimulating hormone (TSH) A tropic hormone, released by the anterior pituitary gland, that increases the release of thyroxine and the uptake of iodide by the thyroid gland. See Figures 5.10, 5.15.

thyrotropin-releasing hormone (TRH) A hypothalamic hormone that regulates the release of thyroid-stimulating hormone. See Figure 5.10.

thyroxine A hormone released by the thyroid gland. See Table 5.2.

timbre The relative intensities of the various harmonics, which gives each instrument its characteristic sound quality.

tinnitus A sensation of noises or ringing in the ears.

tip link A fine, threadlike fiber that runs along and connects the tips of stereocilia. See Figure 9.4.

TMS See *transcranial magnetic stimulation*.

tolerance   A condition in which, with repeated exposure to a drug, an individual becomes less responsive to a constant dose. Contrast with *sensitization* (definition 2).

tomography   A technique for revealing the detailed structure of a particular tissue using radiation. Examples include computerized axial tomography (CAT or CT) and positron emission tomography (PET).

tonic receptor   A receptor in which the frequency of nerve impulse discharge declines slowly or not at all as stimulation is maintained.

tonotopic organization   A major organizational feature in auditory systems in which neurons are arranged as an orderly map of stimulus frequency, with cells responsive to high frequencies located at a distance from those responsive to low frequencies.

torpor   The condition in which animals allow body temperature to fall drastically. During torpor, animals are unresponsive to most stimuli.

Tourette's syndrome   A heightened sensitivity to tactile, auditory, and visual stimuli that may be accompanied by the buildup of an urge to emit verbal or phonic tics.

toxin   A poisonous substance, especially one that is produced by living organisms.

tract   A bundle of axons found within the central nervous system. Contrast with *nerve*.

transcranial magnetic stimulation (TMS)   Localized electrical stimulation of the brain through the skull caused by changes in the magnetic field in coils of wire around the head. Depending on the parameters, TMS may elicit a response or disrupt functioning in the region for a brief time. Also known as repetitive TMS or rTMS.

transcription   The process during which mRNA forms bases complementary to a strand of DNA. The resulting message (called a transcript) is then used to translate the DNA code into protein molecules. See Figure A.2 in the AppendixAppendix.

transcutaneous electrical nerve stimulation (TENS)   The delivery of electrical pulses through electrodes attached to the skin, which excite nerves that supply the region to which pain is referred. TENS can relieve the pain in some instances.

transducer   A device that converts energy from one form to another. Sensory receptor cells are one example.

transduction   The conversion of one form of energy to another.

transgenic   Referring to animals in which a new or altered gene has been deliberately introduced into the genome. See Box 7.3.

translation   The process by which amino acids are linked together (directed by an mRNA molecule) to form protein molecules. See Figure A.2 in the Appendix.

transmethylation hypothesis   A hypothesized explanation of schizophrenia suggesting that the addition of a methyl group to some naturally occurring brain compounds can convert them to hallucinogenic agents, or psychotogens.

transmitter   See *synaptic transmitter*.

transneuronal degeneration   The degeneration of neurons that formed synapses on, or received synapses from, a recently departed neuron.

transporters   Specialized receptors in the presynaptic membrane that recognize transmitter molecules and return them to the presynaptic neuron for reuse.

transverse plane   See *coronal plane*.

tremor   A rhythmic, repetitive movement caused by brain pathology.

tremor at rest   A tremor that occurs when the affected region, such as a limb, is fully supported; a symptom of Parkinson's disease.

TRH   See *thyrotropin-releasing hormone*.

trichromatic hypothesis   A hypothesis of color perception that there are three different types of cones, each excited by a different region of the spectrum and each having a separate pathway to the brain.

tricyclic antidepressants   A class of compounds whose structure resembles that of chlorpromazine and of related antipsychotic drugs. Tricyclic antidepressants may relieve depression, but only after 2 to 3 weeks of daily administration.

trigger mechanism   A particular stimulus characteristic that is most effective in evoking responses from a particular cell.

triiodothyronine   A thyroid hormone. See Table 5.2.

trinucleotide repeat   A repetition of the same three nucleotides within a gene, which can lead to dysfunction, as in the cases of Huntington's disease and fragile X syndrome.

triplet code   A code for an amino acid specified by three successive bases of a DNA molecule.

tropic hormones   A class of anterior pituitary hormones that affect the secretion of other endocrine glands. See Figure 5.15.

TSH   See *thyroid-stimulating hormone*.

TTX   See *tetrodotoxin*.

tuning curve   A graph of the responses of a single auditory nerve fiber or neuron to sounds that vary in frequency and intensity.

turbinates   Complex shapes underlying the olfactory mucosa that direct inspired air over receptor cells. See Figures 9.19, 9.21.

Turner's syndrome   A condition seen in individuals carrying a single X chromosome but no other sex chromosome.

tympanic canal   One of three principal canals running along the length of the cochlea. See Figure 9.1.

tympanic membrane   The partition between the external ear and the middle ear. Also called *eardrum*. See Figure 9.1.

ultradian   Referring to a rhythmic biological event whose period is shorter than that of a circadian rhythm, usually from several minutes to several hours. Contrast with *infradian*.

umami   A putative basic taste, probably mediated by the amino acid glutamate in foods.

umyelinated axon   A fine-diameter axon that lacks a myelin sheath.

unconditioned response (UR)   See *classical conditioning*.

unconditioned stimulus (US)   See *classical conditioning*.

undershoot   Here, the portion of the action potential when the membrane potential is transiently hyperpolarized relative to the resting potential. See Figure 3.7. Contrast with *overshoot*.

unipolar depression   Depression that alternates with normal emotional states. Contrast with *bipolar disorder*.

UR   See *classical conditioning*.

urethra (pl. urethras or urethrae)   The duct that carries urine from the bladder to outside the body.

US   See *classical conditioning*.

uterine tube   See *fallopian tube*.

uterus (pl. uteri)   The organ in which the fertilized egg implants and develops in mammals. See Figures 12.7, 12.14.

utricle   A small, fluid-filled sac in the vestibular system that responds to static positions of the head. See Figure 9.15.

V1   See *primary visual cortex*.

vagina   The opening in female genitalia that permits entry of the penis during copulation and later releases the fetus or egg. See Figures 12.7, 12.14.

vagus nerve   Cranial nerve X, which fulfills many functions, including innervation of many parasympathetic ganglia throughout the body and transmittal of information from various body organs to the brain. See Figures 2.8, 13.28.

vanilloid receptor 1 (VR1)   A receptor that binds capsaicin to transmit the burning sensation from chili peppers. It may be the receptor for detecting sudden increases in temperature.

vas deferens (pl. vasa deferentia)   A duct that connects the epididymis to the seminal vesicles. Also called *ductus deferens*. See Figures 12.7, 12.14.

vasopressin A peptide hormone from the posterior pituitary that promotes water conservation and increases blood pressure, controlling the removal of water from blood by the kidneys. Also called *arginine vasopressin* or *antidiuretic hormone*. See Table 5.2.

ventral An anatomical term referring to structures toward the belly or front of the body, or the bottom of the brain. See Box 2.2. Contrast with *dorsal*.

ventral root See *roots*.

ventral tegmental area A portion of the midbrain that projects dopaminergic fibers to the nucleus accumbens.

ventricle See *cerebral ventricle*.

ventricular system A system of fluid-filled cavities inside the brain. See Figure 2.19.

ventricular zone A region lining the cerebral ventricles that displays mitosis, providing neurons mainly early in development and glial cells throughout life. See Figure 7.6.

ventromedial hypothalamus (VMH) A hypothalamic region involved in inhibiting eating, among other functions. See Figures 12.6, 13.24.

vertebral arteries Arteries that ascend the vertebrae, enter the base of the skull, and join together to form the basilar artery. See Figure 2.20.

vestibular canal One of three principal canals running along the length of the cochlea. See Figure 9.1.

vestibular nuclei Brainstem nuclei that receive information from the vestibular organs through cranial nerve VIII.

vestibular system A receptor system in the inner ear that responds to mechanical forces, such as gravity and acceleration. See Figure 9.15.

vestibulocochlear nerve See *auditory nerve*.

vestibulospinal tract The group of axons originating from the vestibular nuclei in the brainstem, which innervates neurons in the spinal cord. See Figure 11.12.

visual acuity Sharpness of vision.

visual cortex See *occipital cortex*.

visual field The whole area that you can see without moving your head or eyes.

visual paired comparison (VPC) A task, originally devised for testing human infants, that measures an individual's tendency to look at a novel object in comparison with a familiar one.

viviparity Literally "live birth"; reproduction in which the zygote develops extensively within the female until a well-formed individual emerges. Contrast with *oviparity*.

VMH See *ventromedial hypothalamus*.

VNO See *vomeronasal organ*.

volley theory A theory of frequency discrimination that emphasizes the relation between sound frequency and the firing pattern of nerve cells. For example, a 500-Hz tone would produce 500 neural discharges per second by a nerve cell or group of nerve cells. Contrast with *place theory*.

voltage-gated ion channel An ion channel that opens or closes in response to the voltage difference across the membrane—for example, the voltage-gated Na^+ channel that mediates the action potential. Contrast with *ligand-gated ion channel*.

volt A measure of the electrical potential difference between two regions.

vomeronasal organ (VNO) A collection of specialized receptor cells near but separate from the olfactory epithelium. These sensory cells detect pheromones and send electrical signals to the accessory olfactory bulb in the brain.

vomeronasal system A specialized chemical detection system that detects pheromones and transmits information to the brain.

VPC See *visual paired comparison*.

VR1 See *vanilloid receptor 1*.

vulva (pl. vulvae) The region around the opening of the vagina.

Wada test A test in which a short-lasting anesthetic is delivered into one carotid artery to determine which cerebral hemisphere mediates language. See Box 19.1.

wallerian degeneration See *anterograde degeneration*.

wavelength Here, the length between two peaks in a repeated stimulus such as a wave, light, or sound. See Box 9.1.

Wernicke's aphasia A language impairment that is characterized by fluent, meaningless speech and little language comprehension; related to damage to Wernicke's area. See Figure 19.7.

Wernicke's area A region of the left hemisphere that is involved in language comprehension. See Figures 19.6, 19.7, 19.8.

Western blot A method of detecting a particular protein molecule in a tissue or organ, by separating proteins from that source with gel electrophoresis, blotting the separated proteins onto nitrocellulose, then using an antibody that binds, and highlights, the protein of interest.

whisker barrel A barrel-shaped column of somatosensory cortex that receives information from a particular whisker. See Figure 7.21.

white matter A shiny layer underneath the cortex that consists largely of axons with white myelin sheaths. See Figures 2.11, 2.12. Contrast with *gray matter*.

Williams syndrome A disorder characterized by largely intact, even fluent linguistic function, but clear mental retardation on standard IQ tests. Individuals suffering from this syndrome have great difficulty in copying a pattern of blocks, or assembling a picture from its parts. See Figure 19.13.

withdrawal symptom An uncomfortable symptom that arises when a person stops taking a drug that he or she has used frequently, especially at high doses.

wolffian duct A primitive duct system in the embryo that will develop into male structures (the epididymis, vas deferens, and seminal vesicles) if testes are present in the embryo. See Figure 12.14. Contrast with *müllerian duct*.

word blindness The inability to recognize written words.

word deafness The specific inability to hear words, although other sounds can be detected.

zeitgeber Literally "time-giver"; the stimulus (usually the light–dark cycle) that entrains circadian rhythms.

Zucker strain A strain of rats that display obesity.

zygote The fertilized egg.

References

Aarons, L. (1976). Sleep-assisted instruction. *Psychological Bulletin, 83,* 1–40.

Aaronson, S. T., Rashed, S., Biber, M. P., and Hobson, J. A. (1982). Brain state and body position. A time-lapse video study of sleep. *Archives of General Psychiatry, 39,* 330–335.

Abdullaev, Y. G., and Posner, M. I. (1998). Event-related brain potential imaging of semantic encoding during processing single words. *Neuroimage, 7,* 1–13.

Abel, E. L. (1982). Consumption of alcohol during pregnancy: A review of effects on growth and development of offspring. *Human Biology, 54,* 421–453.

Abel, E. L. (1984). Prenatal effects of alcohol. *Drug and Alcohol Dependence, 14,* 1–10.

Abraham, S. F., Baker, R. M., Blaine, E. H., Denton, D. A., et al. (1975). Water drinking induced in sheep by angiotensin—A physiological or pharmacological effect? *Journal of Comparative and Physiological Psychology, 88,* 503–518.

Abraham, W. C., Dragunow, M., and Tate, W. P. (1991). The role of immediate early genes in the stabilization of long-term potentiation. *Molecular Neurobiology, 5,* 297–314.

Abraham, W. C., and Goddard, G. V. (1985). Multiple traces of neural activity in the hippocampus. In N. M. Weinberger, J. L. McGaugh, and G. Lynch (Eds.), *Memory systems of the brain* (pp. 62–76). New York: Guilford.

Adelson, E. H. (1993). Perceptual organization and the judgment of brightness. *Science, 262,* 2042–2044.

Ader, R. (1981). A historical account of conditioned immunobiologic responses. In R. Ader (Ed.), *Psychoneuroimmunology* (pp. 321–354). New York: Academic Press.

Ader, R. (1985). Conditioned immunopharmacological effects in animals: Implications for a conditioning model of pharmacotherapy. In L. White, B. Tursky, and G. E. Schwartz (Eds.), *Placebo* (pp. 306–332). New York: Guilford.

Ader, R., and Cohen, N. (1993). Psychoneuroimmunology: Conditioning and stress. *Annual Review of Psychology, 44,* 53–85.

Ader, R., Felten, D., and Cohen, N. (1990). Interactions between the brain and the immune system. *Annual Review of Pharmacology and Toxicology, 30,* 561–602.

Adler, N., and Matthews, K. (1994). Health psychology: Why do some people get sick and some stay well? *Annual Review of Psychology, 45,* 229–259.

Adolphs, R., Tranel, D., and Damasio, A. R. (1998). The human amygdala in social judgment. *Nature, 393,* 470–474.

Adolphs, R., Tranel, D., Damasio, H., and Damasio, A. (1994). Impaired recognition of emotion in facial expressions following bilateral damage to the human amygdala. *Nature, 372,* 669–672.

Aggleton, J. P. (1993). The contribution of the amygdala to normal and abnormal emotional states. *Trends in Neurosciences, 16,* 328–333.

Agmon-Snir, H., Carr, C. E., and Rinzel, J. (1998). The role of dendrites in auditory coincidence detection. *Nature, 393,* 268–272.

Ahlgren, J. A., Cheng, C. C., Schrag, J. D., and DeVries, A. L. (1988). Freezing avoidance and the distribution of antifreeze glycopeptides in body fluids and tissues of Antarctic fish. *Journal of Experimental Biology, 137,* 549–563.

Akbarian, S., Kim, J. J., Potkin, S. G., Hagman, J. O., et al. (1995). Gene expression for glutamic acid decarboxylase is reduced without loss of neurons in prefrontal cortex of schizophrenics. *Archives of General Psychiatry, 52,* 267–278.

Akbarian, S., Kim, J. J., Potkin, S. G., Hetrick, W. P., et al. (1996). Maldistribution of interstitial neurons in prefrontal white matter of the brains of schizophrenic patients. *Archives of General Psychiatry, 53,* 425–436.

al-Barazanji, K. A., Buckingham, R. E., Arch, J. R., Haynes, A., et al. (1997). Effects of intracerebroventricular infusion of leptin in obese Zucker rats. *Obesity Research, 5,* 387–394.

Albert, S. M., Gurland, B., Maestre, G., Jacobs, D. M., et al. (1995). APOE genotype influences functional status among elderly without dementia. *American Journal of Medical Genetics, 60,* 583–587.

Alberts, J. R. (1978). Huddling by rat pups: Multisensory control of contact behavior. *Journal of Comparative and Physiological Psychology, 92,* 220–230.

Alberts, J. R., and Brunjes, P. C. (1978). Ontogeny of thermal and olfactory determinants of huddling in the rat. *Journal of Comparative and Physiological Psychology, 92,* 89–906.

Aldrich, M. A. (1993). The neurobiology of narcolepsy-cataplexy. *Progress in Neurobiology, 41,* 533–541.

Alexander, B. K., and Hadaway, P. F. (1982). Opiate addiction: The case for an adaptive orientation. *Psychological Bulletin, 92,* 367–381.

Alho, H., Varga, V., and Krueger, K. E. (1994). Expression of mitochondrial benzodiazepine receptor and its putative endogenous ligand diazepam binding inhibitor in cultured primary astrocytes and C-6 cells: Relation to cell growth. *Cell Growth and Differentiation, 5,* 1005–1014.

Almada, S. J., Zonderman, A. B., Shekelle, R. B., Dyer, A. R., et al. (1991). Neuroticism and cynicism and risk of death in middle-aged men: The Western Electric Study. *Psychosomatic Medicine, 53,* 165–175.

Alpert, M., and Friedhoff, A. J. (1980). An un-dopamine hypothesis of schizophrenia. *Schizophrenia Bulletin, 6,* 387–390.

Altman, J. (1969). Autoradiographic and histological studies of postnatal neurogenesis. IV. Cell proliferation and migration in the anterior forebrain, with special reference to persisting neurogenesis in the olfactory bulb. *Journal of Comparative Neurology, 137,* 433–457.

Altschuler, E. L., Wisdom, S. B., Stone, L., Foster, C., Galasko, D., et al. (1999). Rehabilitation of hemiparesis after stroke with a mirror. *Lancet, 353,* 2035–2036.

American Academy of Ophthalmology. (1994). Amblyopia: Etiology, diagnosis, and treatment. *Journal of Ophthalmic Nursing and Technology, 13,* 273–275.

American Psychiatric Association. (1994). *Diagnostic and statistical manual of mental disorders: DSM-IV* (4th ed.). Washington, DC: American Psychiatric Association.

Amos, L. A., and Cross, R. A. (1997). Structure and dynamics of molecular motors. *Current Opinion in Structural Biology, 7,* 239–246.

Amunts, K., Schlaug, G., Jaencke, L., Steinmetz, H., et al. (1997). Motor cortex and hand motor skills: Structural compliance in the human brain. *Human Brain Mapping, 5,* 206–215.

Anand, B. K., and Brobeck, J. R. (1951). Localization of a "feeding center" in the hypothalamus of the rat. *Proceedings of the Society for Experimental Biology and Medicine, 77,* 323–324.

Andersen, P. M., Nilsson, P., Ala-Hurula, V., Keranen, M. L., et al. (1995). Amyotrophic lateral sclerosis associated with homozygosity for an Asp90Ala mutation in CuZn-superoxide dismutase. *Nature Genetics, 10,* 61–66.

Anderson, N. D., and Craik, F. I. M. (2000). Memory in the aging brain. In E. Tulving and F. I. M. Craik (Eds.), *The Oxford handbook of memory* (pp. 411–425). Oxford, England: Oxford University Press.

Anderson, S. A., Eisenstat, D. D., Shi, L., and Rubenstein, J. L. (1997). Interneuron migration from basal forebrain to neocortex: Dependence on Dlx genes. *Science, 278,* 474–476.

Andreasen, N. C. (1984). *The broken brain: The biological revolution in psychiatry.* New York: Harper & Row.

Andreasen, N. C. (1989). Neural mechanisms of negative symptoms. *British Journal of Psychiatry. Supplement, 7,* 93–99.

Andreasen, N. C. (1991). Assessment issues and the cost of schizophrenia. *Schizophrenia Bulletin, 17,* 475–481.

Andreasen, N. C. (1994). Changing concepts of schizophrenia and the ahistorical fallacy. *American Journal of Psychiatry, 151,* 1405–1407.

Andreasen, N. C., Flaum, M., Swayze, V. O. D. S., Alliger, R., et al. (1993). Intelligence and brain structure in normal individuals. *American Journal of Psychiatry, 150,* 130–134.

Andreasen, N., Nassrallah, H. A., Dunn, V., Olson, S. C., et al. (1986). Structural abnormalities in the frontal system in schizophrenia. *Archives of General Psychiatry, 43,* 136–144.

Andreasen, N. C., O'Leary, D. S., Arndt, S., Cizadlo, T., et al. (1996). Neural substrates of facial recognition. *Journal of Neuropsychiatry and Clinical Neurosciences, 8,* 139–146.

Andreasen, N. C., Rezai, K., Alliger, R., Swayze, V. W., et al. (1992). Hypofrontality in neuroleptic-naive patients and in patients with chronic schizophrenia. Assessment with xenon 133 single-photon emission computed tomography and the Tower of London. *Archives of General Psychiatry, 49,* 943–958.

Angier, N. (1992). A potent peptide prompts an urge to cuddle. *New York Times.*

Anholt, R. R. (1993). Molecular neurobiology of olfaction. *Critical Reviews in Neurobiology, 7,* 1–22.

Arbas, E. A., Meinertzhagen, I. A., and Shaw, S. R. (1991). Evolution in nervous systems. *Annual Review of Neuroscience, 14,* 9–38.

Arendt, J., Skene, D. J., Middleton, B., Lockley, S. W., et al. (1997). Efficacy of melatonin treatment in jet lag, shift work, and blindness. *Journal of Biological Rhythms, 12,* 604–617.

Arnold, A. P. (1980). Sexual differences in the brain. *American Scientist, 68,* 165–173.

Arnold, A. P., and Schlinger, B. A. (1993). Sexual differentiation of brain and behavior: The zebra finch is not just a flying rat. *Brain, Behavior and Evolution, 42,* 231–241.

Aroniadou, V. A., Maillis, A., and Stefanis, C. C. (1993). Dihydropyridine-sensitive calcium channels are involved in the induction of N-methyl-D-aspartate receptor-independent long-term potentiation in visual cortex of adult rats. *Neuroscience Letters, 151,* 77–80.

Asberg, M., Nordstrom, P., and Traskman-Bendz, L. (1986). Cerebrospinal fluid studies in suicide. An overview. *Annals of the New York Academy of Sciences, 487,* 243–255.

Aserinsky, E., and Kleitman, N. (1953). Regularly occurring periods of eye motility, and concomitant phenomena, during sleep. *Science, 118,* 273–274.

Ashmore, J. F. (1994). The cellular machinery of the cochlea. *Experimental Physiology, 79,* 113–134.

Atkinson, M. A., Bowman, M. A., Campbell, L., Darrow, B. L., et al. (1994). Cellular immunity to a determinant common to glutamate decarboxylase and Coxsackie virus in insulin-dependent diabetes. *Journal of Clinical Investigation, 94,* 2125–2129.

Atkinson, M. A., and Maclaren N. K. (1994). The pathogenesis of insulin-dependent diabetes mellitus. *New England Journal of Medicine, 331,* 1428–1436.

Avan, P., Loth, D., Menguy, C., and Teyssou, M. (1992). Hypothetical roles of middle ear muscles in the guinea-pig. *Hearing Research, 59,* 59–69.

Azar, B. (1995). NIAAA: 25 years of alcohol research. *American Psychological Association Monitor, 26,* 5, 23.

Azar, B. (1998). Why can't this man feel whether or not he's standing up? *American Psychological Association Monitor,* 18–20.

Bachevalier, J., Brickson, M., and Hagger, C. (1993). Limbic-dependent recognition memory in monkeys develops early in infancy. *Neuroreport, 4,* 77–80.

Bach-y-Rita, P. (1992). Recovery from brain damage. *Journal of Neurologic Rehabilitation, 6,* 191–199.

Baddeley, A. D., and Warrington, E. K. (1970). Amnesia and the distinction between long- and short-term memory. *Journal of Verbal Learning and Verbal Behavior, 9,* 176–189.

Bagemihl, B. (1999). *Biological exuberance: Animal homosexuality and natural diversity.* New York: St. Martin's.

Bailey, C. H., and Chen, M. (1983). Morphological basis of long-term habituation and sensitization in *Aplysia. Science, 220,* 91–93.

Bailey, J. M., and Bell, A. P. (1993). Familiality of female and male homosexuality. *Behavior Genetics, 23,* 313–322.

Ball, G. F., and Hulse, S. H. (1998). Birdsong. *American Psychologist, 53,* 37–58.

Ballantine, H. T., Bouckoms, A. J., Thomas, E. K., and Giriunas, I. E. (1987). Treatment of psychiatric illness by stereotactic cingulotomy. *Biological Psychiatry, 22,* 807–820.

Balota, D. A., Dolan, P. O., and Duchek, J. M. (2000). Memory changes in healthy older adults. In E. Tulving and F. I. M. Craik (Eds.), *The Oxford handbook of memory* (pp. 395–409). Oxford, England: Oxford University Press.

Baltes, P. B. (1997). On the incomplete architecture of human ontogeny: Selection, optimization, and compensation as foundation of developmental theory. *American Psychologist, 52,* 366–380.

Bancaud, J., Brunet-Bourgin, F., Chauvel, P., and Halgren, E. (1994). Anatomical origin of deja vu and vivid "memories" in human temporal lobe. *Brain, 117,* 71–90.

Bannon, A. W., Decker, M. W., Holladay, M. W., Curzon, P., et al. (1998). Broad-spectrum, non-opioid analgesic activity by selective modulation of neuronal nicotinic acetylcholine receptors. *Science, 279,* 77–81.

Baptista, L. F. (1996). Nature and its nurturing in avian vocal development. In D. E. Kroodsma and E. H. Miller (Eds.), *Ecology and evolution of acoustic communication in birds* (pp. 39–60). Ithaca, NY: Cornell University Press.

Baptista, L., and Petrinovich, L. (1986). Song development in the white-crowned sparrow: Social factors and sex differences. *Animal Behaviour, 34,* 1359–1371.

Barasa, A. 1960. Forma, grandezza e densita dei neuroni della corteccia cerebrale in mammiferi di grandezza corporea differente. *Zeitschrift für Zellforschung, 53,* 69–89.

Barbeau, H., Norman, K., Fung, J., Visintin, M., et al. (1998). Does neurorehabilitation play a role in the recovery of walking in neurological populations? *Annals of the New York Academy of Sciences, 860,* 377–392.

Barbour, H. G. (1912). Die Wirkung unmittelbarer Erwärmung und Abkühlung der Warmenzentren auf die Korpertemperatur. *Archiv für Experimentalle Pathologie und Pharmakologie, 70,* 1–26.

Bard, F., Cannon, C., Barbour, R., Burke, R. L., et al. (2000). Peripherally administered antibodies against amyloid beta-peptide enter the central nervous system and reduce pathology in a mouse model of Alzheimer disease. *Nature Medicine, 6,* 916–919.

Barden, N., Reul, J. M., and Holsboer, F. (1995). Do antidepressants stabilize mood through actions on the hypothalamic-pituitary-adrenocortical system? *Trends in Neurosciences, 18,* 6–11.

Baringara, M. (1999). Shedding light on visual imagination. *Science, 284,* 22.

Bark, N. M. (1988). On the history of schizophrenia. Evidence of its existence before 1800. *New York State Journal of Medicine, 88,* 374–383.

Barkow, J. H., Cosmides, L., and Tooby, J. (1992). *The adapted mind: Evolutionary psychology and the generation of culture.* New York: Oxford University Press.

Barlow, H. B. (1953). Summation and inhibition in the frog's retina. *Journal of Physiology (London), 119,* 69–88.

Barlow, H. B., and Levick, W. R. (1965). The mechanism of directionally selective units in rabbit's retina. *Journal of Physiology, 178,* 477–504.

Barnes, B. M. (1989). Freeze avoidance in a mammal: Body temperatures below 0° C in an Arctic hibernator. *Science, 244,* 1593–1595.

Barnett, S. A. (1975). *The rat: A study in behavior.* Chicago: University of Chicago Press.

Barr, E., and Leiden, J. M. (1991). Systemic delivery of recombinant proteins by genetically modified myoblasts. *Science, 254,* 1507–1509.

Barrionuevo, G., Schottler, F., and Lynch, G. (1980). The effects of repetitive low frequency stimulation on control and "potentiated" synaptic responses in the hippocampus. *Life Sciences, 27,* 2385–2391.

Bartels, A., and Zeki, S. (2000). The neural basis of romantic love. *Neuroreport, 11,* 3829–3834.

Bartfai, T. (2001). Telling the brain about pain. *Nature, 410,* 425–426.

Bartoshuk, L. M. (1993). Genetic and pathological taste variation: What can we learn from animal models and human disease? In D. Chadwick, J. Marsh, and J. Goode (Eds.), *The molecular basis of smell and taste transduction* (pp. 251–267). New York: Wiley.

Bartoshuk, L. M., and Beauchamp, G. K. (1994). Chemical senses. *Annual Review of Psychology, 45,* 419–449.

Bartoshuk, L. M., Fast, K., Karrer, T. A., Marino, S., et al. (1992). PROP supertasters and the perception of sweetness and bitterness. *Chemical Senses, 17,* 594.

Basbaum, A., and Fields, H. L. (1978). Endogenous pain control mechanisms: Review and hypothesis. *Annals of Neurology, 4,* 451–462.

Basbaum, A., and Fields, H. L. (1984). Endogenous pain control systems: Brainstem spinal pathways and endorphin circuitry. *Annual Review of Neuroscience, 7,* 309–339.

Basil, J. A., Kamil, A. C., Balda, R. P., and Fite, K. V. (1996). Differences in hippocampal volume among food storing corvids. *Brain, Behavior and Evolution, 47,* 156–164.

Baskerville, K. A., Schweitzer, J. B., and Herron, P. (1997). Effects of cholinergic depletion on experience-dependent plasticity in the cortex of the rat. *Neuroscience, 80,* 1159–1169.

Baulieu, E. E. (1998). Neurosteroids: A novel function of the brain. *Psychoneuroendocrinology, 23,* 963–987.

Baum, A., and Posluszny, D. M. (1999). Health psychology: Mapping biobehavioral contributions to health and illness. *Annual Review of Psychology, 50,* 137–163.

Baumgardner, T. L., Green, K. E., and Reiss, A. L. (1994). A behavioral neurogenetics approach to developmental disabilities: Gene-brain-behavior associations. *Current Opinion in Neurology, 7,* 172–178.

Bavelier, D., Corina, D., Jezzard, P., Padmanabhan, S., et al. (1997). Sentence reading: A functional MRI study at 4 tesla. *Journal of Cognitive Neuroscience, 9,* 664–686.

Beach, F. A. (1971). Hormonal factors controlling the differentiation, development, and display of copulatory behavior in the ramstergig and related species. In E. Tobach, L. R. Aronson, and E. Shaw (Eds.), *The Biopsychology of Development* (pp. 249–296). New York: Academic Press.

Beach, F. A. (1977). *Human sexuality in four perspectives.* Baltimore: Johns Hopkins University Press.

Beach, F. A., and Holz, A. M. (1946). Mating behavior in male rats castrated at various ages and injected with androgen. *Journal of Experimental Zoology, 101,* 91–142.

Bear, M. F., and Malenka, R. C. (1994). Synaptic plasticity. *Current Opinion in Neurobiology, 4,* 389–399.

Beauchamp, G. K., Cowart, B. J., Mennella, J. A., and Marsh, R. R. (1994). Infant salt taste: Developmental, methodological, and contextual factors. *Developmental Psychobiology, 27,* 353–365.

Beggs, W. D., and Foreman, D. L. (1980). Sound localization and early binaural experience in the deaf. *British Journal of Audiology, 14,* 41–48.

Bellinger, D. L., Ackerman, K. D., Felten, S. Y., and Felten, D. L. (1992). A longitudinal study of age-related loss of noradrenergic nerves and lymphoid cells in the rat spleen. *Experimental Neurology, 116,* 295–311.

Bellugi, U., Poizner, H., and Klima, E. S. (1983). Brain organization for language: Clues from sign aphasia. *Human Neurobiology, 2,* 155–171.

Belluscio, L., Gold, G. H., Nemes, A., and Axel, R. (1998). Mice deficient in G(olf) are anosmic. *Neuron, 20,* 69–81.

Benford, G. (2001). *Beyond human: The new world of cyborgs and androids.* New York: TV Books.

Bennett, A. F., and Ruben, J. A. (1979). Endothermy and activity in vertebrates. *Science, 206,* 649–654.

Bennett, E. L., Diamond, M. L., Krech, D., and Rosenzweig, M. R. (1964). Chemical and anatomical plasticity of brain. *Science, 146,* 610–619.

Bennett, E. L., Orme, A. E., and Hebert, M. (1972). Cerebral protein synthesis inhibition and amnesia produced by scopolamine, cycloheximide, streptovitacin A, anisomycin, and emetine in rat. *Federation Proceedings, 31,* 838.

Bennett, E. L., Rosenzweig, M. R., and Diamond, M. C. (1969). Rat brain: Effects of environmental enrichment on wet and dry weights. *Science, 163,* 825–826.

Bennett, M. V. (2000). Electrical synapses, a personal perspective (or history). *Brain Research Reviews, 32,* 16–28.

Bennett, W. (1983). The nicotine fix. *Rhode Island Medical Journal, 66,* 455–458.

Benson, A. J. (1990). Sensory functions and limitations of the vestibular system. In R. Warren and A. H. Wertheim (Eds.), *Perception and control of self-motion* (pp. 145–170). Hillsdale, NJ: Erlbaum.

Berger, T. W., and Orr, W. B. (1983). Hippocampectomy selectively disrupts discrimination reversal conditioning of the rabbit nictitating membrane response. *Behavioural Brain Research, 8,* 49–68.

Berman, D., Derasmo, M. J., Marti, A., and Berman, A. J. (1978). Unilateral forelimb deafferentation in the monkey: Purposive movement. *Journal of Medical Primatology, 7,* 106–113.

Berman, K. F., and Weinberger, D. R. (1990). The prefrontal cortex in schizophrenia and other neuropsychiatric diseases: *In vivo* physiological correlates of cognitive deficits. *Progress in Brain Research, 85,* 521–536.

Bernhardt, P. C. (1997). Influences of serotonin and testosterone in aggression and dominance: Convergence with social psychology. *Current Directions in Psychological Science, 2*(6), 44–48.

Bernhardt, P. C., Dabbs, J. M., Jr., Fielden, J. A., and Lutter, C. D. (1998). Testosterone changes during vicarious experiences of winning and losing among fans at sporting events. *Physiology & Behavior, 65,* 59–62.

Bernstein, I. S., and Gordon, T. P. (1974). The function of aggression in primate societies. *American Scientist, 62,* 304–311.

Bernstein-Goral, H., and Bregman, B. S. (1993). Spinal cord transplants support the regeneration of axotomized neurons after spinal cord lesions at birth: A quantitative double-labeling study. *Experimental Neurology, 123,* 118–132.

Besedovsky, H. O., and del Rey, A. (1992). Immune-neuroendocrine circuits: Integrative role of cytokines. *Frontiers of Neuroendocrinology, 13,* 61–94.

Besedovsky, H. O., del Rey, A. E., and Sorkin, E. (1985). Immune-neuroendocrine interactions. *Journal of Immunology, 135,* 750s–754s.

Betarbet, R., Sherer, T. B., MacKenzie, G., Garcia-Osuna, M., et al. (2000). Chronic systemic pesticide exposure reproduces features of Parkinson's disease. *Nature Neuroscience, 3,* 1301–1306.

Bigelow, L., Nasrallah, H. A., and Rauscher, F. P. (1983). Corpus callosum thickness in chronic schizophrenia. *British Journal of Psychiatry, 142,* 284–287.

Binder, J. R., Rao, S. M., Hammeke, T. A., Yetkin, F. Z., et al. et al. (1994). Functional magnetic resonance imaging of human auditory cortex. *Annals of Neurology, 35,* 662–672.

Birnbaumer, L., Abramowitz, J., and Brown, A. M. (1990). Receptor-effector coupling by G proteins. *Biochimica et Biophysica Acta, 1031,* 163–224.

Björklund, A., and Lindvall, O. (2000). Cell replacement therapies for central nervous system disorders. *Nature Neuroscience, 3,* 537–544.

Björklund, A., Hokfelt, T., and Kuhar, M. J. (1992). *Neuropeptide receptors in the CNS.* Amsterdam: Elsevier.

Black, J. E., and Greenough, W. T. (1998). Developmental approaches to the memory process. In J. L. Martinez, Jr., and R. P. Kesner (Eds.), *Neurobiology of learning and memory* (pp. 55–88). San Diego, CA: Academic Press.

Blakemore, C. (1976). The conditions required for the maintenance of binocularity in the kitten's visual cortex. *Journal of Physiology (London), 261,* 423–444.

Blakemore, C., and Campbell, F. W. (1969). On the existence of neurones in the human visual system selectively sensitive to the orientation and size of retinal images. *Journal of Physiology (London), 203,* 237–260.

Blalock, J. E. (1984). The immune system as a sensory organ. *Journal of Immunology, 132,* 1067–1070.

Blaxton, T. A., Bookheimer, S. Y., Zeffiro, T. A., Figlozzi, C. M., et al. (1996). Functional mapping of human memory using PET: Comparisons of conceptual perceptual tasks. *Canadian Journal of Experimental Psychology, 50,* 42–56.

Blehar, M. C., and Rosenthal, N. E. (1989). Seasonal affective disorders and phototherapy. Report of a National Institute of Mental Health-sponsored workshop. *Archives of General Psychiatry, 46,* 469–474.

Bleuler, E. (1952). *Dementia praecox; or, The group of schizophrenias.* New York: International Universities Press.

Bliss, T. V. P., and Collingridge, G. L. (1993). A synaptic model of memory: Long-term potentiation in the hippocampus. *Nature, 361,* 31–39.

Bliss, T. V. P., and Gardner-Medwin, A. R. (1973). Long-lasting potentiation of synaptic transmission in the dentate area of the unanaesthetized rabbit following stimulation of the perforant path. *Journal of Physiology (London), 232,* 357–374.

Bliss, T. V. P., and Lømo, T. (1973). Long-lasting potentiation of synaptic transmission in the dentate area of the anaesthetized rabbit following stimulation of the perforant path. *Journal of Physiology (London), 232,* 331–356.

Bliwise, D. L. (1989). Neuropsychological function and sleep. *Clinics in Geriatric Medicine, 5,* 381–394.

Bloch, V. (1976). Brain activation and memory consolidation. In M. R. Rosenzweig and E. L. Bennett (Eds.), *Neural mechanisms of learning and memory* (pp. 583-590). Cambridge, MA: MIT Press.

Blodgett, H. C. (1929). The effect of the introduction of reward upon the maze performance of rats. *University of California Publications in Psychology, 4,* 113–134.

Blue, M. E., and Parnavelas, J. G. (1983). The formation and maturation of synapses in the visual cortex of the rat. II. Quantitative analysis. *Journal of Neurocytology, 12,* 697–712.

Blumberg, M. S., Sokoloff, G., and Kirby, R. F. (1997). Brown fat thermogenesis and cardiac rate regulation during cold challenge in infant rats. *American Journal of Physiology, 272,* R1308–R1313.

Blumenfeld, H. (2002). *Neuroanatomy through Clinical Cases.* Sunderland, MA: Sinauer Associates.

Bodnar, R. J., Kelly, D. D., Brutus, M., and Glusman, M. (1980). Stress-induced analgesia: Neural and hormonal determinants. *Neuroscience and Biobehavioral Reviews, 4,* 87–100.

Bogen, J. E., Schultz, D. H., and Vogel, P. J. (1988). Completeness of callostomy shown by magnetic resonance imaging in the long term. *Archives of Neurology, 45,* 1203–1205.

Bohus, B., and Koolhaas, J. M. (1993). Stress and the cardiovascular system: Central and peripheral physiological mechanisms. In S. C. Stanford and P. Salmon (Eds.), *Stress: From synapse to syndrome* (pp. 75–117). London: Academic Press.

Bonese, K. F., Wainer, B. H., Fitch, F. W., Rothberg, R. M., et al. (1974). Changes in heroin self-administration by a rhesus monkey after morphine immunisation. *Nature, 252,* 708–710.

Bonhoeffer, F., and Huf, J. (1985). Position-dependent properties of retinal axons and their growth cones. *Nature, 315,* 409–410.

Bonhoeffer, T., and Grinvald, A. (1991). Iso-orientation domains in cat visual cortex are arranged in pinwheel-like patterns. *Nature, 353,* 429–431.

Brooks, R. (2000). Negative genetic correlation between male sexual attractiveness and survival. *Nature, 406,* 67–70.

Brenowitz, E. A. (1991). Evolution of the vocal control system in the avian brain. *Seminars in the Neurosciences, 3,* 399–407.

Brenowitz, E. A., & Arnold, A. (1986). Interspecific comparisons of the size of neural song control regions and song complexity in dueting birds: Evolutionary implications. *Journal of Neuroscience, 6,* 2875–2879.

Brooks, V. B. (1984). Cerebellar function in motor control. *Human Neurobiology, 2,* 251–260.

Brose, K., Bland, K. S., Wang, K. H., Arnott, D., et al. (1999). Slit proteins bind Robo receptors and have an evolutionarily conserved role in repulsive axon guidance. *Cell, 96,* 795–806.

Broughton, R. (1985). Slow-wave sleep awakenings in normal and in pathology: A brief review. In W. P. Koella, E. Ruther, and H. Schulz (Eds.), *Sleep '84* (pp. 164–167). Stuttgart, Germany: Gustav Fischer.

Broughton, R., Billings, R., Cartwright, R., Doucette, D., et al. (1994). Homicidal somnambulism: A case report. *Sleep, 17,* 253–264.

Brown, G. L., Goodwin, F. K., Ballenger, J. C., Goyer, P. F., et al. (1979). Aggression in humans correlates with cerebrospinal fluid amine metabolites. *Psychiatry Research, 1,* 131–139.

Brown, J. (1958). Some tests of the decay theory of immediate memory. *Quarterly Journal of Experimental Psychology, 10,* 12–21.

Brown, T. H., Zador, A. M., Mainen, Z. F., and Claiborne, B. J. (1992). Hebbian computations in hippocampal dendrites and spines. In T. M. McKenna, J. Davis, and S. F. Zornetzer (Eds.), *Neural nets: Foundations to applications: [unnumbered series]. Single neuron computation* (pp. 81–116). Boston: Academic Press.

Brown, W. A. (1998). The placebo effect. *Scientific American, 278*(1), 90–95.

Brown, W. L. (1968). An hypothesis concerning the function of the metapleural gland in ants. *American Naturalist, 102,* 188–191.

Brownell, W. E., Bader, C. R., Bertrand, D., and de Ribaupierre, Y. (1985). Evoked mechanical responses of isolated cochlear outer hair cells. *Science, 227,* 194–196.

Brownlee, S., and Schrof, J. M. (1997). The quality of mercy. Effective pain treatments already exist. Why aren't doctors using them? *U.S. News & World Report, 122,* 54–67.

Brunet, L. J., Gold, G. H., and Ngai, J. (1996). General anosmia caused by a targeted disruption of the mouse olfactory cyclic nucleotide-gated cation channel. *Neuron, 17,* 681–693.

Brunjes, P. C. (1994). Unilateral naris closure and olfactory system development. *Brain Research. Brain Research Reviews, 19,* 146–160.

Bryden, M. P. (1982). *Laterality: Functional asymmetry in the intact brain.* New York: Academic Press.

Brzustowicz, L. M., Hodgkinson, K. A., Chow, E. W., Honer, W. G., et al. (2000). Location of a major susceptibility locus for familial schizophrenia on chromosome 1q21-q22. *Science, 288,* 678–682.

Buchsbaum, M., Mirsky, A., DeLisi, L. E., Morihisa, J., et al. (1984). The Genain quadruplets: Electrophysiological, positron emission and X-ray tomographic studies. *Psychiatry Research, 13,* 95–108.

Buck, L. B. (1996). Information coding in the mammalian olfactory system. *Cold Spring Harbor Symposia on Quantitative Biology, 61,* 147–155.

Buck, L., and Axel, R. (1991). A novel multigene family may encode odorant receptors: A molecular basis for odor recognition. *Cell, 65,* 175–187.

Buckner, R. L. (1996). Beyond HERA: Contributions of specific prefrontal brain areas to long-term memory retrieval. *Psychonomic Bulletin & Review, 3,* 149–158.

Buckner, R. L., Bandettini, P. A., O'Craven, K. M., Savoy, R. L., et al. (1996). Detection of cortical activation during averaged single trials of a cognitive task using functional magnetic resonance imaging. *Proceedings of the National Academy of Sciences, USA, 93,* 14878–14883.

Buhrich, N., Bailey, J. M., and Martin, N. G. (1991). Sexual orientation, sexual identity, and sex-dimorphic behaviors in male twins. *Behavior Genetics, 21,* 75–96.

Buldyrev, S. V., Cruz, L., Gomez-Isla, T., Gomez-Tortosa, E., et al. (2000). Description of microcolumnar ensembles in association cortex and their disruption in Alzheimer and Lewy body dementias. *Proceedings of the National Academy of Sciences, USA, 97,* 5039–5043.

Bullock, T. H. (1984). Comparative neuroscience holds promise for quiet revolutions. *Science, 225,* 473–478.

Bullock, T. H. (1986). Some principles in the brain analysis of important signals: Mapping and stimulus recognition. *Brain, Behavior and Evolution, 28,* 145–156.

Buss, D. M. (2000). *The dangerous passion: Why jealousy is as necessary as love and sex.* New York: Free Press.

Buss, D. M., and Malamuth, N. M. (1996). *Sex, power, conflict: Evolutionary and feminist perspectives.* New York: Oxford University Press.

Busse, E. W., and Silverman, A. J. (1952). Electroencephalographic changes in professional boxers. *Journal of the American Medical Association, 149,* 1522–1525.

Butcher, L. L., and Woolf, N. J. (1986). Central cholinergic systems: Synopsis of anatomy and overview of physiology and pathology. In A. B. Scheibel, A. F. Wechsler, and A. B. Brazier (Eds.), *The biological substrates of Alzheimer's disease.* Orlando, FL: Academic Press.

Butler, R. A., Diamond, I. T., and Neff, W. D. (1957). Role of auditory cortex in discrimination of changes in frequency. *Journal of Neurophysiology, 20,* 108–120.

Byrne, D. G., and Whyte, H. M. (1980). Life events and myocardial infarction revisited. *Psychosomatic Medicine, 42,* 1–10.

Cabelli, R. J., Hohn, A., and Shatz, C. J. (1995). Inhibition of ocular dominance column formation by infusion of NT-4/5 or BDNF. *Science, 267,* 1662–1666.

Cacioppo, J. T., Berntson, G. G., Larsen, J. T., Poehlmann, K. M., et al. (2000). The psychophysiology of emotion. In M. Lewis and J. M. Haviland-Jones (Eds.), *Handbook of emotions* (2nd ed., pp. 173–191). New York: Guilford.

Cacioppo, J. T., Klein, D. J., Berntson, G. G., and Hatfield, E. (1993). The psychophysiology of emotion. In M. Lewis and J. M. Haviland (Eds.), *Handbook of emotions* (pp. 119–142). New York: Guilford.

Cadoret, R. J., O'Gorman, T., Troughton, E., and Heywood, E. (1986). An adoption study of genetic and environmental factors in drug abuse. *Archives of General Psychiatry, 43,* 1131–1136.

Cahill, L. (1997). The neurobiology of emotionally influenced memory: Implications for understanding traumatic memory. In R. Yehuda and A. C. McFarlane (Eds.), *Annals of the New York Academy of Sciences: Vol. 41. Psychobiology of traumatic stress disorder* (pp. 238–246). New York: New York Academy of Sciences.

Cahill, L., and McGaugh, J. L. (1991). NMDA-induced lesions of the amygdaloid complex block the retention-enhancing effect of posttraining epinephrine. *Psychobiology, 19,* 206–210.

Cahill, L., Prins, B., Weber, M., and McGaugh, J. L. (1994). Beta-adrenergic activation and memory for emotional events. *Nature, 371,* 702–704.

Calvert, G. A., Bullmore, E. T., Brammer, M. J., Campbell, R., et al. (1997). Activation of auditory cortex during silent lipreading. *Science, 276,* 593–596.

Calvin, W. H., and Ojemann, G. A. (1994). *Conversations with Neil's brain: The neural nature of thought and language.* Reading, MA: Addison-Wesley.

Campbell, F. W., and Robson, J. G. (1968). Application of Fourier analysis to the visibility of gratings. *Journal of Physiology (London), 197,* 551–566.

Campbell, R. (1982). The lateralisation of emotion: A critical review. *International Journal of Psychology, 17,* 211–219.

Campbell, S. S., and Murphy, P. J. (1998). Extraocular circadian phototransduction in humans. *Science, 279,* 396–399.

Campbell, S. S., and Tobler, I. (1984). Animal sleep: A review of sleep duration across phylogeny. *Neuroscience and Biobehavioral Reviews, 8,* 269–301.

Campfield, L. A., Smith, F. J., Guisez, Y., Devos, R., et al. (1995). Recombinant mouse OB protein: Evidence for a peripheral signal linking adiposity and central neural networks. *Science, 269,* 546–549.

Canli, T., Zhao, Z., Kang, E., Gross, J., et al. (2001). An fMRI study of personality influences on brain reactivity to emotional stimuli. *Behavioral Neuroscience, 115,* 33–42.

Cannistra, L. B., Davis, S. M., and Bauman, A. G. (1997). Valvular heart disease associated with dexfenfluramine. *New England Journal of Medicine, 337,* 636.

Cannon, S. C. (1996). Ion-channel defects and aberrant excitability in myotonia and periodic paralysis. *Trends in Neurosciences, 19,* 3–10.

Cannon, W. B. (1929). *Bodily changes in pain, hunger, fear and rage.* New York: Appleton.

Cao, Y. Q., Mantyh, P. W., Carlson, E. J., Gillespie, A. M., et al. (1998). Primary afferent tachykinins are required to experience moderate to intense pain. *Nature, 392,* 390–394.

Capaldi, E. A., Robinson, G. E., and Fahrback, S. E. (1999). Neuroethology of spatial learning: The birds and the bees. *Annual Review of Psychology, 50,* 651–682.

Capretta, P. J., Petersik, J. T., and Stewart, D. J. (1975). Acceptance of novel flavours is increased after early experience of diverse tastes. *Nature, 254,* 689–691.

Carew, T. J. (1989). Development assembly of learning in *Aplysia. Trends in Neurosciences, 12,* 389–394.

Carew, T. J., and Sahley, C. L. (1986). Invertebrate learning and memory: From behavior to molecule. *Annual Review of Neuroscience, 9,* 435–487.

Carlsson, A., Hansson, L. O., Waters, N., and Carlsson, M. L. (1997). Neurotransmitter aberrations in schizophrenia: New perspectives and therapeutic implications. *Life Sciences, 61,* 75–94.

Carlton, P. L., and Manowitz, P. (1984). Dopamine and schizophrenia: An analysis of the theory. *Neuroscience and Biobehavioral Reviews, 8,* 137–153.

Carpenter, A. F., Georgopoulos, A. P., and Pellizzer, G. (1999). Motor cortical encoding of serial order in a context-recall task. *Science, 283,* 1752–1757.

Carroll, J., McMahon, C., Neitz, M., and Neitz, J. (2000). Flicker-photometric electroretinogram estimates of L:M cone photoreceptor ratio in men with photopigment spectra derived from genetics. *Journal of the Optical Society of America. Part A, Optics, Image Science, and Vision, 17,* 499–509.

Carter, C. S. (1992). Oxytocin and sexual behavior. *Neuroscience and Biobehavioral Reviews, 16,* 131–144.

Cartwright, R. D. (1979). The nature and function of repetitive dreams: A survey and speculation. *Psychiatry, 42,* 131–137.

Casey, B., and Hackett, B. P. (2000). Left-right axis malformations in man and mouse. *Current Opinion in Genetics and Development, 10,* 257–261.

Casey, D. E. (1989). Clozapine: Neuroleptic-induced EPS and tardive dyskinesia. *Psychopharmacology, 99,* S47–S53.

Cassens, G., Wolfe, L., and Zola, M. (1990). The neuropsychology of depressions. *Journal of Neuropsychiatry and Clinical Neurosciences, 2,* 202–213.

Casson, I. R., Sham, R., Campbell, E. A., Tarlau, M., et al. (1982). Neurological and CT evaluation of knocked-out boxers. *Journal of Neurology, Neurosurgery and Psychiatry, 45,* 170–174.

Caterina, M. J., Leffler, A., Malmberg, A. B., Martin, W. J., et al. (2000). Impaired nociception and pain sensation in mice lacking the capsaicin receptor. *Science, 288,* 306–313.

Caterina, M. J., Schumacher, M. A., Tominaga, M., Rosen, T. A., et al. (1997). The capsaicin receptor: A heat-activated ion channel in the pain pathway. *Nature, 389,* 816–824.

Caviness, V. S. (1980). The developmental consequences of abnormal cell position in the reeler mouse. *Trends in Neurosciences, 3,* 31–33.

Caza, P. A., and Spear, N. E. (1984). Short-term exposure to an odor increases its subsequent preference in preweaning rats: A descriptive profile of the phenomenon. *Developmental Psychobiology, 17,* 407–422.

Challamel, M. J., Lahlou, S., and Jouvet, M. (1985). Sleep and smiling in neonate: A new approach. In W. P. Koella, E. Ruther, and H. Schulz (Eds.), *Sleep '84.* Stuttgart, Germany: Gustav Fischer.

Chang, F.-L., and Greenough, W. T. (1982). Lateralized effects of monocular training on dendritic branching in adult split-brain rats. *Brain Research, 232,* 283–292.

Chapin, J. K., Moxon, K. A., Markowitz, R. S., and Nicolelis, M. A. (1999). Real-time control of a robot arm using simultaneously recorded neurons in the motor cortex. *Nature Neuroscience, 2,* 664–670.

Chapman, C. R., Casey, K. L., Dubner, R., Foley, K. M., et al. (1985). Pain measurement: An overview. *Pain, 22,* 1–31.

Charney, D. S., Deutch, A. Y., Krystal, J. H., Southwick, S. M., et al. (1993). Psychobiologic mechanisms of posttraumatic stress disorder. *Archives of General Psychiatry, 50,* 295–305.

Chase, J. E., and Gidal, B. E. (1997). Melatonin: Therapeutic use in sleep disorders. *Annals of Pharmacotherapy, 31,* 1218–1226.

Chaudhari, N., Landin, A. M., and Roper, S. D. (2000). A metabotropic glutamate receptor variant functions as a taste receptor. *Nature Neuroscience, 3,* 113–119.

Chemelli, R. M., Willie, J. T., Sinton, C. M., Elmquist, J. K., et al. (1999). Narcolepsy in orexin knockout mice: Molecular genetics of sleep regulation. *Cell, 98,* 437–451.

Chen, D. Y., Deutsch, J. A., Gonzalez, M. F., and Gu, Y. (1993). The induction and suppression of c-fos expression in the rat brain by cholecystokinin and its antagonist L364,718. *Neuroscience Letters, 149,* 91–94.

Chen, M. S., Huber, A. B., Van Der Haar M. E., Frank, M., et al. (2000). Nogo-A is a myelin-associated neurite outgrowth inhibitor and an antigen for monoclonal antibody IN-1. *Nature, 403,* 434–439.

Cheng, H., Cao, Y., and Olson, L. (1996). Spinal cord repair in adult paraplegic rats: Partial restoration of hind limb function. *Science, 273,* 510–513.

Chiarello, C., Knight, R., and Mundel, M. (1982). Aphasia in a prelingually deaf woman. *Brain, 105,* 29–52.

Cho, Y. H., Berachochea, D., and Jaffard, R. (1993). Extended temporal gradient for the retrograde and anterograde amnesia produced by ibotenate entorhinal cortex lesions in mice. *Journal of Neuroscience, 13,* 1759–1766.

Chollet, F., and Weiller, C. (1994). Imaging recovery of function following brain injury. *Current Opinion in Neurobiology, 4,* 226–230.

Chow, K. L., and Stewart, D. L. (1972). Reversal of structural and functional effects of long-term visual deprivation in cats. *Experimental Neurology, 34,* 409–433.

Christensen, D. (1999). Designer estrogens: Getting all the benefits, few of the risks. *Science News, 156,* 252–254.

Clapham, J. C., Arch, J. R. S., Chapman, H., Haynes, A., et al. (2000). Mice overexpressing human uncoupling protein-3 in skeletal muscle are hyperphagic and lean. *Nature, 406,* 415–418.

Clark, W. W. (1991). Noise exposure from leisure activities: A review. *Journal of the Acoustical Society of America, 90,* 175–181.

Classen, J., Liepert, J., Wise, S. P., Hallett, M., et al. (1998). Rapid plasticity of human cortical movement representation induced by practice. *Journal of Neurophysiology, 79,* 1117–1123.

Clayton, N. S. (1995). The neuroethological development of food-storing memory: A case of use it, or lose it. *Behavioural Brain Research, 70,* 95–102.

Clayton, N. S., and Krebs, J. R. (1994). Hippocampal growth and attrition in birds affected by experience. *Proceedings of the National Academy of Sciences, USA, 91,* 7410–7414.

Clemens, L. G., Gladue, B. A., and Coniglio, L. P. (1978). Prenatal endogenous androgenic influences on masculine sexual behavior and genital morphology in male and female rats. *Hormones and Behavior, 10,* 40–53.

Clemente, C. D., and Sterman, M. B. (1963). Cortical synchronization and sleep patterns in acute restrained and chronic behaving cats induced by basal forebrain stimulation. *Electroencephalography and Clinical Neurophysiology, Suppl. 24,* 172+.

Cloninger, C. (1987). Neurogenetic adaptive mechanisms in alcoholism. *Science, 236,* 410–416.

Clutton-Brock, T. H., and Harvey, P. H. (1980). Primates, brains and ecology. *Journal of Zoology, 190,* 309–323.

Coccaro, E. F., and Siever, L. J. (1995). Personality disorders. In F. E. Bloom and D. J. Kupfer (Eds.), *Psychopharmacology: The fourth generation of progress* (pp. 1567–1679). New York: Raven.

Cohen, A. H., Baker, M. T., and Dobrov, T. A. (1989). Evidence for functional regeneration in the adult lamprey spinal cord following transection. *Brain Research, 496,* 368–372.

Cohen, A. J., and Leckman, J. F. (1992). Sensory phenomena associated with Gilles de la Tourette's syndrome. *Journal of Clinical Psychiatry, 53,* 319–323.

Cohen, D. B. (1979). *Sleep and dreaming: Origin, nature and functions.* Oxford, England: Pergamon.

Cohen, N. J., and Squire, L. R. (1980). Preserved learning and retention of pattern-analyzing skill in amnesia: Dissociation of knowing how and knowing what. *Science, 210,* 207–210.

Cohen, S., Frank, E., Doyle, W. J., Skoner, D. P., et al. (1998). Types of stressors that increase susceptibility to the common cold in healthy adults. *Health Psychology, 17,* 214–223.

Cohen, S., Lichtenstein, E., Prochaska, J. O., Rossi, J. S., et al. (1989). Debunking myths about quitting: Evidence from 10 perspective studies of persons who attempt to quit smoking by themselves. *American Psychologist, 44,* 1355–1365.

Colangelo, W., and Jones, D. G. (1982). The fetal alcohol syndrome: A review and assessment of the syndrome and its neurological sequelae. *Progress in Neurobiology, 19,* 271–314.

Coleman, D. L., and Hummel, K. P. (1973). The influence of genetic background on the expression of the obese (Ob) gene in the mouse. *Diabetologia, 9,* 287–293.

Colley, P. A., and Routtenberg, A. (1993). Long-term potentiation as synaptic dialogue. *Brain Research Review, 18,* 115–122.

Collings, V. B. (1974). Human taste response as a function of locus of stimulation on the tongue and soft palate. *Perception and Psychophysics, 16,* 169–174.

Colwill, R. M., Absher, R. A., and Roberts, M. L. (1988). Conditional discrimination learning in *Aplysia californica. Journal of Neuroscience, 8,* 4440–4444.

Conel, J. L. (1939). *The postnatal development of the human cerebral cortex: Vol. 1. The cortex of the newborn.* Cambridge, MA: Harvard University Press.

Conel, J. L. (1947). *The postnatal development of the human cerebral cortex: Vol. 3. The cortex of the three-month infant.* Cambridge, MA: Harvard University Press.

Conel, J. L. (1959). *The postnatal development of the human cerebral cortex: Vol. 6. The cortex of the twenty-four-month infant.* Cambridge, MA: Harvard University Press.

Conner, J. M., Darracq, M. A., Roberts, J., and Tuszynski, M. H. (2001). Nontropic actions of neurotrophins: Subcortical nerve growth factor gene delivery reverses age-related degeneration of primate cortical cholinergic innervation. *Proceedings of the National Academy of Sciences, USA, 98,* 1941–1946.

Conrad, A. J., Abebe, T., Austin, R., Forsythe, S., et al. (1991). Hippocampal pyramidal cell disarray in schizophrenia as a bilateral phenomenon. *Archives of General Psychiatry, 48,* 413–417.

Constantine-Paton, M., Cline, H. T., and Debski, E. (1990). Patterned activity, synaptic convergence, and the NMDA receptor in developing visual pathways. *Annual Review of Neuroscience, 13,* 129–154.

Convit, A., de Leon, M. J., Golomb, J., George, A. E., et al. (1993). Hippocampal atrophy in early Alzheimer's disease: Anatomic specificity and validation. *Psychiatric Quarterly, 64,* 371–387.

Cooke, B. M., Chowanadisai, W., and Breedlove, S. M. (2000). Post-weaning social isolation of male rats reduces the volume of the medial amygdala and leads to deficits in adult sexual behavior. *Behavioural Brain Research, 117,* 107–113.

Corballis, M. C. (1998). Evolution of the human mind. In M. Sabourin, F. Craik, and M. Robert (Eds.), *Advances in psychological science: Vol. 2. Biological and cognitive aspects* (pp. 31–62). East Sussex, England: Psychology Press.

Corbett, S. W., and Keesey, R. E. (1982). Energy balance of rats with lateral hypothalamic lesions. *American Journal of Physiology, 242,* E273–E279.

Corkin, S., Amaral, D. G., Gonzalez, R. G., Johnson, K. A., et al. (1997). H.M.'s medial temporal lobe lesion: Findings from magnetic resonance imaging. *Journal of Neuroscience, 17,* 3964–3979.

Corkin, S., Milner, B., and Rasmussen, T. (1970). Somatosensory thresholds: Contrasting effects of postcentral-gyrus and posterior parietal-lobe excisions. *Archives of Neurology, 23,* 41–58.

Corwin, J. T., and Oberholtzer, J. C. (1997). Fish n' chicks: Model recipes for hair-cell regeneration? *Neuron, 19,* 951–954.

Coryell, W., Noyes, R., Jr., and House, J. D. (1986). Mortality among outpatients with anxiety disorders. *American Journal of Psychiatry, 143,* 508–510.

Cosmides, L., and Tooby, J. (2000). Evolutionary psychology and the emotions. In M. Lewis and J. M. Haviland-Jones (Eds.), *Handbook of emotions* (2nd ed., pp. 91–115). New York: Guilford.

Costanzo, R. M. (1991). Regeneration of olfactory receptor cells. *CIBA Foundation Symposium, 160,* 233–242.

Cotanche, D. A. (1987). Regeneration of hair cell stereociliary bundles in the chick cochlea following severe acoustic trauma. *Hearing Research, 30,* 181–195.

Courtney, S., Ungerleider, L., Keil, K., and Haxby, J. (1996). Object and spatial visual working memory activate separate neural systems in human cortex. *Cerebral Cortex, 6,* 39–49.

Cowan, W. M. (1979). The development of the brain. *Scientific American, 241*(3), 112–133.

Crabbe, J. C., Wahlsten, D., and Dudek, B. C. (1999). Genetics of mouse behavior: Interactions with laboratory environment. *Science, 284,* 1670–1672.

Cragg, B. G. (1975). The development of synapses in the visual system of the cat. *Journal of Comparative Neurology, 160,* 147–166.

Craig, A. D., Reiman, E. M., Evans, A., and Bushnell, M. C. (1996). Functional imaging of an illusion of pain. *Nature, 384,* 258–260.

Craik, F. I. M. (1985). Paradigms in human memory research. In L.-G. Nilsson and T. Archer (Eds.), *Perspectives on learning and memory* (pp. 197–221). Hillsdale, NJ: Erlbaum.

Craik, F. I. M. (1986). A functional account of age differences in memory. In F. Klix and H. Hogendorf (Eds.), *Human memory and cognitive capabilities* (Vol. A, pp. 409–422). Amsterdam: North-Holland.

Crews, D. (1994). Temperature, steroids and sex determination. *Journal of Endocrinology, 142,* 1–8.

Crick, F., and Mitchison, G. (1983). The function of dream sleep. *Nature, 304,* 111–114.

Crouch, R. (1997). Letting the deaf be deaf. Reconsidering the use of cochlear implants in prelingually deaf children. *Hastings Center Report, 27*(4), 14–21.

Cruce, J. A. F., Greenwood, M. R. C., Johnson, P. R., and Quartermain, D. (1974). Genetic versus hypothalamic obesity: Studies of intake and dietary manipulation in rats. *Journal of Comparative and Physiological Psychology, 87,* 295–301.

Cummings, J. L. (1995). Dementia: The failing brain. *Lancet, 345,* 1481–1484.

Cummings, J. L., Benson, D. F., Walsh, M. J., and Levine, H. L. (1979). Left-to-right transfer of language dominance: A case study. *Neurology, 29,* 1547–1550.

Cummins, R. A., Walsh, R. N., Budtz-Olsen, O. E., Reidel, J. C., et al. (1973). Environmentally-induced changes in the brains of elderly rats. *Nature, 243,* 516–518.

Curcio, C. A., Sloan, K. R., Packer, O., Hendrickson, A. E., et al. (1987). Distribution of cones in human and monkey retina: Individual variability and radial asymmetry. *Science, 236,* 579–582.

Curtiss, S. (1989). The independence and task-specificity of language. In M. H. Bornstein and J. S. Bruner (Eds.), *Interaction in human development* (pp. 105–137). Hillsdale, NJ: Erlbaum.

Czeisler, C. A., Duffy, J. F., Shanahan, T. L., Brown, E. N., et al. (1999). Stability, precision, and near-24-hour period of the human circadian pacemaker. *Science, 284,* 2177–2181.

Czeisler, C. A., Zimmerman, J. C., Ronda, J. M., Moore-Ede, M. C., et al. (1980). Timing of REM sleep is coupled to the circadian rhythm of body temperature in man. *Sleep, 2,* 329–346.

Dabbs, J. M., Jr., and Hargrove, M. F. (1997). Age, testosterone, and behavior among female prison inmates. *Psychosomatic Medicine, 59,* 477–480.

Dabbs, J. M., and Morris, R. (1990). Testosterone, social class, and antisocial behavior in a sample of 4,462 men. *Psychological Science, 1 (3),* 209–211.

Dabbs, J. M., Ruback, R. B., Frady, R. L., Hopper, C. H., et al. (1988). Saliva testosterone and criminal violence among women. *Personality and Individual Differences, 9,* 269–275.

Dalton, P., Doolittle, N., Nagata, H., and Breslin, P. A. (2000). The merging of the senses: Integration of subthreshold taste and smell. *Nature Neuroscience, 3,* 431–432.

Daly, M., and Wilson, M. (1978). *Sex, evolution and behavior.* North Scituate, MA: Duxbury Press.

Damasio, A. R., Chui, H. C., Corbett, J., and Kassell, N. (1980). Posterior callosal section in a non-epileptic patient. *Journal of Neurology, Neurosurgery and Psychiatry, 43,* 351–356.

Damasio, A. R., Eslinger, P. J., Damasio, H., Van Hoesen, G. W., et al. (1985). Multimodal amnesic syndrome following bilateral temporal and basal forebrain damage. *Archives of Neurology, 42,* 252–259.

Damasio, A. R., Grabowski, T. J., Bechara, A., Damasio, H., et al. (2000). Subcortical and cortical brain activity during the feeling of self-generated emotions. *Nature Neuroscience, 3,* 1049–1056.

Damasio, A. R., Graff-Radford, N. R., Eslinger, P. J., Damasio, H., et al. (1985). Amnesia following basal forebrain lesions. *Archives of Neurology, 42,* 263–271.

Damasio, H. (1995). *Human brain anatomy in computerized images.* New York: Oxford University Press.

Damasio, H., Grabowski, T., Frank, R., Galaburda, A. M., et al. (1994). The return of Phineas Gage: Clues about the brain from the skull of a famous patient. *Science, 264,* 1102–1105.

Damasio, H., Grabowski, T. J., Tranel, D., Hichwa, R. D., et al. (1996). A neural basis for lexical retrieval. *Nature, 380,* 499–505. [Published erratum appears in *Nature, 381,* 810 (1996).]

Damasio, H., Tranel, D., Spradling, J., and Alliger, R. (1989). In A. M. Galaburda (Ed.), *From reading to neurons: Conference, Florence, Italy, June 8–12, 1987* (pp. 307–330). Cambridge, MA: MIT Press.

D'Amato, R. J., Alexander, G. M., Schwartzman, R. J., Kitt, C. A., et al. (1987). Evidence for neuromelanin involvement in MPTP-induced neurotoxicity. *Nature, 327,* 324–326.

Dantz, B., Edgar, D. M., and Dement, W. C. (1994). Circadian rhythms in narcolepsy: Studies on a 90 minute day. *Electroencephalography and Clinical Neurophysiology, 90,* 24–35.

Darian-Smith, I., Davidson, I., and Johnson, K. O. (1980). Peripheral neural representations of the two spatial dimensions of a textured surface moving over the monkey's finger pad. *Journal of Physiology (London), 309,* 135–146.

Dark, J. (1984). Seasonal weight gain is attenuated in food-restricted ground squirrels with lesions of the suprachiasmatic nuclei. *Behavioral Neuroscience, 98,* 830–835.

Dark, J., Miller, D. R., and Zucker, I. (1994). Reduced glucose availability induced torpor in Siberian hamsters. *American Journal of Physiology, 267,* R496–R501.

Dark, J., Spears, N., Whaling, C. S., Wade, G. N., Meyer, J. S., and Zucker, I. (1990). Long day lengths promote brain growth in meadow voles. *Developmental Brain Research, 53,* 264–269.

Darwin, C. (1859). *On the origin of species by means of natural selection, or, The preservation of favoured races in the struggle for life.* London: J. Murray.

Darwin, C. (1871). The descent of man, and selection in relation to sex. London: J. Murray.

Darwin, C. (1872). *The expression of the emotions in man and animals.* London: J. Murray.

Darwin, F. (1888). *Life and letters of Charles Darwin: Vol. 3.* London: J. Murray.

Dave, A. S., and Margoliash, D. (2000). Song replay during sleep and computational rules for sensorimotor vocal learning. *Science, 290,* 812–816.

Davenport, J. W. (1976). Environmental therapy in hypothyroid and other disadvantaged animal populations. In R. N. Walsh and W. T. Greenough (Eds.), *Environments as therapy for brain dysfunction* (pp. 71-114). New York: Plenum.

Davey-Smith, G., Frankel, S., and Yarnell, J. (1997). Sex and death: Are they related? Findings from the Caerphilly Cohort Study. *British Medical Journal (Clinical Research Edition), 315,* 1641–1644.

Davidson, J. M., Camargo, C. A., and Smith, E. R. (1979). Effects of androgen on sexual behavior in hypogonadal men. *Journal of Clinical Endocrinology and Metabolism, 48,* 955–958.

Davidson, R. J. (1994). Asymmetric brain function, affective style, and psychopathology: The role of early experience and plasticity. *Development and Psychopathology, 6,* 741–758.

Davidson, R. J., Ekman, P., Saron, C. D., Senulis, J. A., et al. (1990). Approach-withdrawal and cerebral asymmetry: Emotional expression and brain physiology: I. *Journal of Personality and Social Psychology, 58,* 330–341.

Davis, H. P., and Squire, L. R. (1984). Protein synthesis and memory: A review. *Psychological Bulletin, 96,* 518–559.

Davis, K. L., Kahn, R. S., Ko, G., and Davidson, M. (1991). Dopamine in schizophrenia: A review and reconceptualization. *American Journal of Psychiatry, 148,* 1474–1486.

Daw, N. W., Brunken, W. J., and Parkinson, D. (1989). The function of synaptic transmitters in the retina. *Annual Review of Neuroscience, 12,* 205–225.

Daw, N. W., Stein, P. S., and Fox, K. (1993). The role of NMDA receptors in information processing. *Annual Review of Neuroscience, 16,* 207–222.

Dawson, D., and Encel, N. (1993). Melatonin and sleep in humans. *Journal of Pineal Research, 15,* 1–12.

Deacon, T. W. (1997). What makes the human brain different? In W. H. Durham (Ed.), *Annual Review of Anthropology: Vol. 26* (pp. 337–357). Palo Alto, CA: Annual Reviews Inc.

Dearborn, G. V. N. (1932). A case of congenital general pure analgesia. *Journal of Nervous and Mental Disease, 75,* 612–615.

DeArmond, S., Fusco, M., and Dewey, M. (1989). *Structure of the human brain: A photographic atlas.* New York: Oxford University Press.

De Felipe, C., Herrero, J. F., O'Brien, J. A., Palmer, J. A., et al. (1998). Altered nociception, analgesia and aggression in mice lacking the receptor for substance P. *Nature, 392,* 394–397.

de Groot, C. M., Janus, M. D., and Bornstein, R. A. (1995). Clinical predictors of psychopathology in children and adolescents with Tourette syndrome. *Journal of Psychiatric Research, 29,* 59–70.

Dekaban, A. S., and Sadowsky, D. (1978). Changes in brain weights during the span of human life: Relation of brain weights to body heights and body weights. *Annals of Neurology, 4,* 345–356.

de Leon, M. J., Golomb, J., George, A. E., Convit, A., et al. (1993). The radiologic prediction of Alzheimer disease: The atrophic hippocampal formation. *American Journal of Neuroradiology, 14,* 897–906.

Delgado-Escueta, A. V., Mattson, R. H., King, L., Goldensohn, E. S., et al. (1981). The nature of aggression during epileptic seizures. *New England Journal of Medicine, 305,* 711–716.

DeLong, M. R., Georgopoulos, A. P., Crutcher, M. D., Mitchell, S. J., et al. (1984). Functional organization of the basal ganglia: Contributions of single-cell recording studies. *CIBA Foundation Symposium, 107,* 64–82.

de Luis, O., Valero, M. C., and Jurado, L. A. (2000). WBSCR14, a putative transcription factor gene deleted in Williams-Beuren syndrome: Complete characterisation of the human gene and the mouse ortholog. *European Journal of Human Genetics, 8,* 215–222.

Demb, J. B., Boynton, G. M., and Heeger, D. J. (1998). Functional magnetic resonance imaging of early visual pathways in dyslexia. *Journal of Neuroscience, 18,* 6939–6951.

Dement, W. C. (1974). *Some must watch while some must sleep.* San Francisco: Freeman.

Demmer, J., Dragunow, M., Lawlor, P. A., Mason, S. E., et al. (1993). Differential expression of immediate early genes after hippocampal long-term potentiation in awake rats. *Brain Research, 17,* 279–286.

Dennis, S. G., and Melzack, R. (1983). Perspectives on phylogenetic evolution of pain expression. In R. L. Kitchell, H. H. Erickson, E. Carstens, and L. E. Davis (Eds.), *Animal pain* (pp. 151–161). Bethesda, MD: American Physiological Society.

Denti, A., McGaugh, J. L., Landfield, P. W., and Shinkman, P. (1970). Effects of posttrial electrical stimulation of the mesencephalic reticular formation on avoidance learning in rats. *Physiology & Behavior, 5,* 659–662.

Denton, D. A. (1982). *The hunger for salt: An anthropological, physiological, and medical analysis.* Berlin: Springer.

Deol, M. S., and Gluecksohn-Waelsch, S. (1979). The role of inner hair cells in hearing. *Nature, 278,* 250–252.

de Paiva, A., Poulain, B., Lawrence, G. W., Shone, C. C., et al. (1993). A role for the interchain disulfide or its participating thiols in the internalization of botulinum neurotoxin A revealed by a toxin derivative that binds to ecto-acceptors and inhibits transmitter release intracellularly. *Journal of Biological Chemistry, 268,* 20838–20844.

Derrick, B. (1993). *Opioid receptor-dependent long-term potentiation.* Unpublished doctoral dissertation, University of California, Berkeley.

Derrick, B. E., and Martinez, J. L. (1994). Frequency-dependent associative long-term potentiation at the hippocampal mossy fiber-CA3 synapse. *Proceedings of the National Academy of Sciences, USA, 91,* 10290–10294.

Descartes, R. (1662). *De homine.* Paris: Petrvm Leffen & Franciscvm Moyardvm.

Desimone, R., Albright, T. D., Gross, C. G., and Bruce, C. (1984). Stimulus-selective properties of inferior temporal neurons in the macaque. *Journal of Neuroscience, 4,* 2051–2062.

Desimone, R., and Schein, S. J. (1987). Visual properties of neurons in area V4 of the macaque: Sensitivity to stimulus form. *Journal of Neurophysiology, 57,* 835–868.

Deutschlander, M. E., Borland, S. C., and Phillips, J. B. (1999). Extraocular magnetic compass in newts. *Nature, 400,* 324–325.

De Valois, K. K., De Valois, R. L., and Yund, E. W. (1979). Responses of striate cortex cells to grating and checkerboard patterns. *Journal of Physiology (London), 291,* 483–505.

De Valois, R. L., Albrecht, D. G., and Thorell, L. G. (1977). Spatial tuning of LGN and cortical cells in the monkey visual system. In H. Spekreijse and H. van der Tweel (Eds.), *Spatial contrast* (pp. 60–63). Amsterdam: Elsevier.

De Valois, R. L., and De Valois, K. K. (1980). Spatial vision. *Annual Review of Psychology, 31,* 309–341.

De Valois, R. L., and De Valois, K. K. (1988). *Spatial vision.* New York: Oxford University Press.

De Valois, R. L., and De Valois, K. K. (1993). A multi-stage color model. *Vision Research, 33,* 1053–1065.

Devane, W. A., Dysarz, F. A., Johnson, M. R., Melvin, L. S., et al. (1988). Determination and characterization of a cannabinoid receptor in rat brain. *Molecular Pharmacology, 34,* 605–613.

Devane, W. A., Hanus, L., Breuer, A., Pertwee, R. G., et al. (1992). Isolation and structure of a brain constituent that binds the cannabinoid receptor. *Science, 258,* 1946–1949.

Devinsky, O., and Bear, D. (1984). Varieties of aggressive behavior in temporal lobe epilepsy. *American Journal of Psychiatry, 141,* 651–656.

DeVoogd, T. J. (1994). Interactions between endocrinology and learning in the avian song system. *Annals of the New York Academy of Sciences, 743,* 19–41.

DeVoogd, T. J., Krebs, J. R., Healy, S. D., and Purvis, A. (1993). Relations between song repertoire size and the volume of brain nuclei related to song: Comparative evolutionary analyses amongst oscine birds. *Proceedings of the Royal Society of London. Series B: Biological Sciences, 254,* 75–82.

de Vries, H. (1901). *Die Mutationen und die Mutationsperioden bei der Entstehung der Arten: Vortrag, gehalten in der allgemeinen Sitzung der*

Naturwissenschaftlichen Hauptgruppe der Versammlung Deutscher Naturforscher und Aerzte in Hamburg am 26. September 1901. Leipzig, Germany: Veit.

de Waal, F. B. M. (1999). Cultural primatology comes of age. *Nature, 399,* 635–636.

De Weerd, P., Peralta, M. R., Desimone, R., and Ungerleider, L. G. (1999). Loss of attentional stimulus selection after extrastriate cortical lesions in macaques. *Nature Neuroscience, 2,* 753–758.

Dewsbury, D. A. (1972). Patterns of copulatory behavior in male mammals. *Quarterly Review of Biology, 47,* 1–33.

Diamond, A., and Goldman-Rakic, P. S. (1989). Comparison of human infants and rhesus monkeys on Piaget's AB task: Evidence for dependence on dorsolateral prefrontal cortex. *Experimental Brain Research, 74,* 24–40.

Diamond, J., Cooper, E., Turner, C., and Macintyre, L. (1976). Trophic regulation of nerve sprouting. *Science, 193,* 371–377.

Diamond, M. C. (1967). Extensive cortical depth measurements and neuron size increases in the cortex of environmentally enriched rats. *Journal of Comparative Neurology, 131,* 357–364.

Diamond, M. C., Krech, D., and Rosenzweig, M. R. (1964). The effects of an enriched environment on the histology of the rat cerebral cortex. *Journal of Comparative Neurology, 123,* 111–119.

Diamond, M. C., Lindner, B., Johnson, R., Bennett, E. L., et al. (1975). Differences in occipital cortical synapses from environmentally enriched, impoverished, and standard colony rats. *Journal of Neuroscience Research, 1,* 109–119.

Dichgans, J. (1984). Clinical symptoms of cerebellar dysfunction and their topodiagnostical significance. *Human Neurobiology, 2,* 269–279.

Di Chiara, G., Tanda, G., Bassareo, V., Pontieri, F., et al. (1999). Drug addiction as a disorder of associative learning. Role of nucleus accumbens shell/extended amygdala dopamine. *Annals of the New York Academy of Sciences, 877,* 461–485.

Diebel, C. E., Proksch, R., Green, C. R., Neilson, P., et al. (2000). Magnetite defines a vertebrate magnetoreceptor. *Nature, 406,* 299–302.

Dlugos, C., and Pentney, R. (1997). Morphometric evidence that the total number of synapses on Purkinje neurons of old f344 rats is reduced after long-term ethanol treatment and restored to control levels after recovery. *Alcohol and Alcoholism, 32(2),* 161–172.

Dolphin, A. C., Errington, M. L., and Bliss, T. V. P. (1982). Long-term potentiation of the perforant path in vivo is associated with increased glutamate release. *Nature, 297,* 496–498.

Domjan, M., and Purdy, J. E. (1995). Animal research in psychology: More than meets the eye of the general psychology student. *American Psychologist, 50,* 496–503.

Donegan, N. H., Lowery, R. W., and Thompson, R. F. (1983). Effects of lesioning cerebellar nuclei on conditioned leg-flexion responses. *Society for Neuroscience Abstracts, 9,* 331.

Doricchi, F., Guariglia, C., Paolucci, S., and Pizzamiglio, L. (1991). Disappearance of leftward rapid eye movements during sleep in left visual hemi-inattention. *Neuroreport, 2,* 285–288.

Doyle, K., Burggraaff, B., Fujikawa, S., Kim, J., et al. (1997). Neonatal hearing screening with otoscopy, auditory brain stem response, and otoacoustic emissions. *Otolaryngology and Head and Neck Surgery, 116,* 597–603.

Doyon, J., Owen, A. M., Petrides, M., Sziklas, V., et al. (1996). Functional anatomy of visuomotor skill learning in human subjects examined with positron emission tomography. *European Journal of Neuroscience, 8,* 637–648.

Drachman, D. A., and Leavitt, J. (1972). Memory impairment in the aged: Storage versus retrieval deficit. *Journal of Experimental Psychology, 93,* 302–308.

Drevets, W. C. (1998). Functional neuroimaging studies of depression: The anatomy of melancholia. *Annual Review of Medicine, 49,* 341–361.

Drickamer, L. C. (1992). Behavioral selection of odor cues by young female mice affects age of puberty. *Developmental Psychobiology, 25,* 461–470.

Dronkers, N. F., Redfern, B., and Shapiro, J. K. (1993). Neuroanatomic correlates of production deficits in severe broca's aphasia. *Journal of Clinical and Experimental Neuropsychology, 15,* 59–60.

Druckman, D., and Bjork, R. A. (1994). *Learning, remembering, believing: Enhancing human performance.* Washington, DC: National Academy Press.

Du, L., Bakish, D., Lapierre, Y. D., Ravindran, A. V., et al. (2000). Association of polymorphism of serotonin 2A receptor gene with suicidal ideation in major depressive disorder. *American Journal of Medical Genetics, 96,* 56–60.

Dubnau, J., and Tully, T. (1998). Gene discovery in *Drosophila:* New insights for learning and memory. *Annual Review of Neuroscience, 21,* 407–444.

Duchamp-Viret, P., Chaput, M. A., and Duchamp, A. (1999). Odor response properties of rat olfactory receptor neurons. *Science, 284,* 2171–2174.

Dudai, Y. (1988). Neurogenic dissection of learning and short term memory in *Drosophila. Annual Review of Neuroscience, 11,* 537–563.

Dudai, Y., Jan, Y.-N., Byers, D., Quinn, W. G., et al. (1976). Dunce, a mutant of *Drosophila* deficient in learning. *Proceedings of the National Academy of Sciences, USA, 73,* 1684–1688.

Duffy, F. H., Burchfiel, J. L., and Lombroso, C. T. (1979). Brain electrical activity mapping (BEAM): A method for extending the clinical utility of EEG and evoked potential data. *Annals of Neurology, 5,* 309–321.

Duffy, F. H., Jones, K., Bartels, P., McAnulty, G., et al. (1992). Unrestricted principal components analysis of brain electrical activity: Issues of data dimensionality, artifact, and utility. *Brain Tomography, 4,* 291–307.

Duffy, J. D., and Campbell, J. J. (1994). The regional prefrontal syndromes: A theoretical and clinical overview. *Journal of Neuropsychiatry and Clinical Neurosciences, 6,* 379–387.

Duman, R. S., Heninger, G. R., and Nestler, E. J. (1997). A molecular and cellular theory of depression. *Archives of General Psychiatry, 54,* 597–606.

Durand, S. E., Heaton, J. T., Amateau, S. K., and Brauth, S. E. (1997). Vocal control pathways through the anterior forebrain of a parrot (*Melopsittacus undulatus*). *Journal of Comparative Neurology, 377,* 179–206.

Durand, S. E., Liang, W., and Brauth, S. E. (1998). Methionine enkephalin immunoreactivity in the brain of the budgerigar (*Melopsittacus undulatus*): Similarities and differences with respect to oscine songbirds. *Journal of Comparative Neurology, 393,* 145–168.

During, M. J., Symes, C. W., Lawlor, P. A., Lin, J., et al. (2000). An oral vaccine against NMDAR1 with efficacy in experimental stroke and epilepsy. *Science, 287,* 1453–1460.

Eales, L. A. (1985). Song learning in zebra finches (*Taeniopygia gyttata*): Some effects of song model availability on what is learnt and when. *Animal Behaviour, 33,* 1293–1300.

Eapen, V., Pauls, D. L., and Robertson, M. M. (1993). Evidence for autosomal dominant transmission in Tourette's syndrome. United Kingdom cohort study. *British Journal of Psychiatry, 162,* 593–596.

Earnest, D. J., Liang, F. Q., Ratcliff, M., and Cassone, V. M. (1999). Immortal time: Circadian clock properties of rat suprachiasmatic cell lines. *Science, 283,* 693–695.

Earnshaw, W. C., Martins, L. M., and Kaufmann, S. H. (1999). Mammalian caspases: Structure, activation, substrates, and functions during apoptosis. *Annual Review of Biochemistry, 68,* 383–424.

Eccles, J. C. (1965). Possible ways in which synaptic mechanisms participate in learning, remembering and forgetting. In D. P. Kimble (Ed.), *The anatomy of memory* (pp. 12–87). Palo Alto, CA: Science and Behavior Books.

Edwards, J. S., and Palka, J. (1991). Insect neural evolution—A fugue or an opera? *Seminars in the Neurosciences, 3,* 391–398.

Egaas, B., Courchesne, E., and Saitoh, O. (1995). Reduced size of corpus callosum in autism. *Archives of Neurology, 52,* 794–801.

Egeland, J. A., and Hostetter, A. M. (1983). Amish study, 1: Affective disorders among the Amish, 1976–1980. *American Journal of Psychiatry, 140,* 56–71.

Egrise, D., Rubinstein, M., Schoutens, A., Cantraine, F., and Mendlewicz, J. (1986). Seasonal variation of platelet serotonin uptake and 3H-imipramine binding in normal and depressed subjects. *Biological Psychiatry, 21,* 283–292.

Ehrenkranz, J., Bliss, E., and Sheard, M. H. (1974). Plasma testosterone: Correlation with aggressive behavior and social dominance in man. *Psychosomatic Medicine, 36,* 469–475.

Elbert, T., Pantev, C., Wienbruch, C., Rockstroh, B., and Taub, E. (1995). Increased cortical representation of the fingers of the left hand in string players. *Science, 270,* 305–307.

Emery, N. J., Capitanio, J. P., Mason, W. A., Machado, C. J., et al. (In press). The effects of bilateral lesions of the amygdala on dyadic social interactions in rhesus monkeys (*Macaca mulatta*). *Behavioral Neuroscience.*

Engel, A. G. (1984). Myasthenia gravis and myasthenic syndromes. *Annals of Neurology, 16,* 519–535.

Engel, J., Jr. (1992). Recent advances in surgical treatment of temporal lobe epilepsy. *Acta Neurologica Scandinavica. Supplementum, 140,* 71–80.

Engert, F., and Bonhoeffer, T. (1999). Dendritic spine changes associated with hippocampal long-term synaptic plasticity. *Nature, 399,* 66–70.

Epelbaum, M., Milleret, C., Buisseret, P., and Dufier, J. L. (1993). The sensitive period for strabismic amblyopia in humans. *Ophthalmology, 100,* 323–327.

Epstein, A. N., Fitzsimons, J. T., and Rolls, B. J. (1970). Drinking induced by injection of angiotensin into the brain of the rat. *Journal of Physiology (London), 210,* 457–474.

Epstein, C. J. (1986). Developmental genetics. *Experientia, 42,* 1117–1128.

Erhardt, V. R., and Goldman, M. B. (1992). Adverse endocrine effects. In M. S. Keshavan and J. S. Kennedy (Eds.), *Drug-induced dysfunction in psychiatry.* New York: Hemisphere.

Erickson, C. J. (1978). Sexual affiliation in animals: Pair bonds and reproductive strategies. In J. B. Hutchison (Ed.), *Biological determinants of sexual behavior* (pp. 697–725). New York: Wiley.

Erickson, J. T., Conover, J. C., Borday, V., Champagnat, J., et al. (1996). Mice lacking brain-derived neurotrophic factor exhibit visceral sensory neuron losses distinct from mice lacking NT4 and display a severe developmental deficit in control of breathing. *Journal of Neuroscience, 16,* 5361–5371.

Eriksson, P. S., Perfilieva, E., Bjork-Eriksson, T., Alborn, A. M., et al. (1998). Neurogenesis in the adult human hippocampus. *Nature Medicine, 4,* 1313–1317.

Erlanger, D. M., Kutner, K. C., Barth, J. T., and Barnes, R. (1999). Neuropsychology of sports-related head injury: Dementia pugilistica to post concussion syndrome. *Clinical Neuropsychologist, 13,* 193–209.

Ernst, T., Chang, L., Leonido-Yee, M., and Speck, O. (2000). Evidence for long-term neurotoxicity associated with methamphetamine abuse: A 1H MRS study. *Neurology, 54,* 1344–1349.

Estes, W. K. (1997). Processes of memory loss, recovery, and distortion. *Psychological Review, 104,* 148–169.

Etcoff, N. L., Ekman, P., Magee, J. J., and Frank, M. G. (2000). Lie detection and language comprehension. *Nature, 405,* 139.

Evans, C. J., Keith, D. E., Morrison, H., Magendzo, K., et al. (1992). Cloning of a delta opioid receptor by functional expression. *Science, 258,* 1952–1955.

Evarts, E. V., Shinoda, Y., and Wise, S. P. (1984). *Neurophysiological approaches to higher brain functions.* New York: Wiley.

Everson, C. A. (1993). Sustained sleep deprivation impairs host defense. *American Journal of Physiology, 265,* R1148–R1154.

Everson, C. A., Bergmann, B. M., and Rechtschaffen A. (1989). Sleep deprivation in the rat: III. Total sleep deprivation. *Sleep, 12,* 13–21.

Eybalin, M. (1993). Neurotransmitters and neuromodulators of the mammalian cochlea. *Physiological Reviews, 73,* 309–373.

Fagerheim, T., Raeymaekers, P., Tonnessen, F. E., Pedersen, M., et al. (1999). A new gene (DYX3) for dyslexia is located on chromosome 2. *Journal of Medical Genetics, 36,* 664–669.

Falk, D. (1993). Sex differences in visuospatial skills: Implications for hominid evolution. In K. R. Gibson and T. Ingold (Eds.), *Tools, language and cognition in human evolution* (pp. 216–229). Cambridge, England: Cambridge University Press.

Faraone, S. V., and Tsuang, M. T. (1985). Quantitative models of the genetic transmission of schizophrenia. *Psychological Bulletin, 98,* 41–66.

Farbman, A. I. (1994). The cellular basis of olfaction. *Endeavour, 18,* 2–8.

Fazeli, M. S., Corbet, J., Dunn, M. J., Dolphin, A. C., et al. (1993). Changes in protein synthesis accompanying long-term potentiation in the dentate gyrus *in vivo. Journal of Neuroscience, 13,* 1346–1353.

Feany, M. B., and Bender, W. W. (2000). A *Drosophila* model of Parkinson's disease. *Nature, 404,* 394–398.

Feder, H. H., and Whalen, R. E. (1965). Feminine behavior in neonatally castrated and estrogen-treated male rats. *Science, 147,* 306–307.

Feinberg, I. (1982). Schizophrenia: Caused by a fault in programmed synaptic elimination during adolescence. *Journal of Psychiatry Research, 17,* 319–334.

Feldman, R. S., Meyer, J. S., and Quenzer, L. F. (1997). *Principles of neuropsychopharmacology.* Sunderland, MA: Sinauer Associates.

Felten, D. L., Felten, S. Y., Bellinger, D. L., and Madden, K. S. (1993). Fundamental aspects of neural-immune signaling. *Psychotherapy and Psychosomatics, 60,* 46–56.

Fenstemaker, S. B., Zup, S. L., Frank, L. G., Glickman, S. E., et al. (1999). A sex difference in the hypothalamus of the spotted hyena. *Nature Neuroscience, 2,* 943–945.

Ferguson, J. N., Young, L. J., Hearn, E. F., Matzuk, M. M., et al. (2000). Social amnesia in mice lacking the oxytocin gene. *Nature Genetics, 25,* 284–288.

Fernald, R. D. (1995). Social control of cell size: Males and females are different. *Progress in Brain Research, 105,* 171–177.

Fernald, R. D. (2000). Evolution of eyes. *Current Opinion in Neurobiology, 10,* 444–450.

Ferrer, A., Wells, K. E., and Wells, D. J. (2000). Immune responses to dystropin: Implications for gene therapy of Duchenne muscular dystrophy. *Gene Therapy, 7,* 1439–1446.

Ferster, D. (1998). A sense of direction. *Nature, 392,* 433–434.

Ferster, D., Chung, S., and Wheat, H. (1996). Orientation selectivity of thalamic input to simple cells of cat visual cortex. *Nature, 380,* 249–252.

Fibiger, H. C., and Lloyd, K. G. (1984). The neurobiological substrates of tardive dyskinesia: The GABA hypothesis. *Trends in Neurosciences, 8,* 462.

Fields, S. (1990). Pheromone response in yeast. *Trends in Biochemical Sciences, 15,* 270–273.

Fifkova, E., Anderson, C. L., Young, S. J., and Van Harreveld, A. (1982). Effect of anisomycin on stimulation-induced changes in dendritic spines of the dentate granule cells. *Journal of Neurocytology, 11,* 183–210.

Finch, C. E., and Kirkwood, T. B. L. (2000). *Chance, development, and aging.* New York: Oxford University Press.

Finger, S. (Ed.). (1978). *Recovery from brain damage: Research and theory.* New York: Plenum.

Finger, S. (1994). *Origins of neuroscience: A history of explorations into brain function.* New York: Oxford University Press.

Fink, G. R., Markowitsch, H. J., Reinkemeier, M., Bruckbauer, T., et al. (1996). Cerebral representation of one's own past: Neural networks involved in autobiographical memory. *Journal of Neuroscience, 16,* 4275–4282.

Finlay, B. L., and Darlington, R. B. (1995). Linked regularities in the development and evolution of mammalian brains. *Science, 268,* 1578–1584.

Firestein, S. (2000). The good taste of genomics. *Nature, 404,* 552–553.

Fischer, C., Hatzidimitriou, G., Wlos, J., Katz, J., et al. (1995). Reorganization of ascending 5-HT axon projections in animals previously exposed to the recreational drug (+/-)3,4-methylenedioxymethamphetamine (MDMA, "ecstasy"). *Journal of Neuroscience, 15,* 5476–5485.

Fischer, M., Kaech, S., Knutti, D., and Matus, A. (1998). Rapid actin-based plasticity in dendritic spines. *Neuron, 20,* 847–854.

Fischer, M., Kaech, S., Wagner, U., Brinkhaus, H., et al. (2000). Glutamate receptors regulate actin-based plasticity in dendritic spines. *Nature Neuroscience, 3,* 887–894.

Fishman, R. B., Chism, L., Firestone, G. L., and Breedlove, S. M. (1990). Evidence for androgen receptors in sexually dimorphic perineal muscles of neonatal male rats. Absence of androgen accumulation by the perineal motoneurons. *Journal of Neurobiology, 21,* 694–704.

Fitts, P. M., and Posner, M. I. (1967). *Human performance.* Belmont, CA: Brooks/Cole.

Flament, D., Ellermann, J. M., Kim, S. G., Ugurbil, K., et al. (1996). Functional magnetic resonance imaging of cerebellar activation during the learning of a visuomotor dissociation task. *Human Brain Map, 4,* 210–226.

Flood, J. F., Bennett, E. L., Orme, A. E., and Rosenzweig, M. R. (1975). Relation of memory formation to controlled amounts of brain protein synthesis. *Physiology & Behavior, 15,* 97–102.

Flood, J. F., Bennett, E. L., Rosenzweig, M. R., and Orme, A. E. (1973). The influence of duration of protein synthesis inhibition on memory. *Physiology & Behavior, 10,* 555–562.

Flood, J. F., Jarvik, M. E., Bennett, E. L., Orme, A. E., et al. (1977). The effect of stimulants, depressants and protein synthesis inhibition on retention. *Behavioral Biology, 20,* 168–183.

Florence, S. L., Taub, H. B., and Kaas, J. H. (1998). Large-scale sprouting of cortical connections after peripheral injury in adult macaque monkeys. *Science, 282,* 1117–1121.

Forger, N. G., and Breedlove, S. M. (1986). Sexual dimorphism in human and canine spinal cord: Role of early androgen. *Proceedings of the National Academy of Sciences, USA, 83,* 7527–7531.

Forger, N. G., and Breedlove, S. M. (1987). Seasonal variation in mammalian striated muscle mass and motoneuron morphology. *Journal of Neurobiology, 18,* 155–165.

Forger, N. G., Frank, L. G., Breedlove, S. M., and Glickman, S. E. (1996). Sexual dimorphism of perineal muscles and motoneurons in spotted hyenas. *Journal of Comparative Neurology, 375,* 333–343.

Forger, N. G., Howell, M., Bengston, L., Mackenzie, L., et al. (1997). Sexual dimorphism in the spinal cord is absent in mice lacking the ciliary neurotrophic factor receptor. *Journal of Neuroscience, 17,* 9605–9612.

Forger, N. G., Roberts, S. L., Wong, V., and Breedlove, S. M. (1993). Ciliary neurotrophic factor maintains motoneurons and their target muscles in developing rats. *Journal of Neuroscience, 13,* 4720–4726.

Forstl, H., Burns, A., Levy, R., Cairns, N., et al. (1993). Neuropathological correlates of behavioural disturbance in confirmed Alzheimer's disease. *British Journal of Psychiatry, 163,* 364–368.

Foster, N. L., Cahse, T. N., Mansi, L., Brooks, R., et al. (1984). Cortical abnormalities in Alzheimer's disease. *Annals of Neurology, 16,* 649–654.

Fox, H. E., White, S. A., Kao, M. H., and Fernald, R. D. (1997). Stress and dominance in a social fish. *Journal of Neuroscience, 17,* 6463–6469.

Francis, R. C. (1992). Sexual lability in teleosts developmental factors. *Quarterly Review of Biology, 67,* 1–18.

Frank, L. G., Glickman, S. E., and Licht, P. (1991). Fatal sibling aggression, precocial development, and androgens in neonatal spotted hyenas. *Science, 252,* 702–704.

Frankenhaeuser, M. (1978). Psychoneuroendocrine approaches to the study of emotion as related to stress and coping. *Nebraska Symposium on Motivation, 26,* 123–162.

Franz, S. I. (1902). On the functions of the cerebrum: I. The frontal lobes in relation to the production and retention of simple sensory-motor habits. *American Journal of Physiology, 8,* 1–22.

Frazier, W. T., Kandel, E. R., Kupfermann, l., Waziri, R., et al. (1967). Morphological and functional properties of identified neurons in the abdominal ganglion of *Aplysia californica. Journal of Neurophysiology, 30,* 1288–1351.

Freed, C. R., Greene, P. E., Breeze, R. E., Tsai, W.-Y., et al. (2001). Transplantation of embryonic dopamine neurons for severe Parkinson's disease. *New England Journal of Medicine, 344,* 710–719.

Freedman, M. S., Lucas, R. J., Soni, B., von Schantz, M., et al. (1999). Regulation of mammalian circadian behavior by non-rod, non-cone, ocular photoreceptors. *Science, 284,* 502–504.

Freund, H.-J. (1984). Premotor areas in man. *Trends in Neurosciences, 7,* 481–483.

Frey, U., Huang, Y.-Y., and Kandel, E. R. (1993). Effects of cAMP simulate a late stage of LTP in hippocampal CA1 neurons. *Science, 260,* 1661–1664.

Fridlund, A. (1988). What can asymmetry and laterality in EMG tell us about the face and brain? *International Journal of Neuroscience, 39,* 53–69.

Fridlund, A. J. (1994). *Human facial expression: An evolutionary view.* San Diego, CA: Academic Press.

Fried, I., Wilson, C. L., MacDonald, K. A., and Behnke, E. J. (1998). Electric current stimulates laughter. *Nature, 391,* 650.

Friedland, R. P., Koss, E., Lerner, A., Hedera, P., et al. (1993). Functional imaging, the frontal lobes, and dementia. *Dementia, 4,* 192–203.

Friedman, L., and Jones, B. E. (1984). Study of sleep-wakefulness states by computer graphics and cluster analysis before and after lesions of the pontine tegmentum in the cat. *Electroencephalography and Clinical Neurophysiology, 57,* 43–56.

Friedman, M., and Rosenman, R. H. (1974). *Type A behavior and your heart.* New York: Knopf.

Friedman, M. B. (1977). Interactions between visual and vocal courtship stimuli in the neuroendocrine response of female doves. *Journal of Comparative and Physiological Psychology, 91,* 1408–1416.

Friedman, M. I. (1978). Hyperphagia in rats with experimental diabetes mellitus: A response to a decreased supply of utilizable fuels. *Journal of Comparative and Physiological Psychology, 92,* 109–117.

Froehlich, J., Harts, J., Lumeng, L., and Li, T. (1990). Naloxone attenuates voluntary ethanol intake in rats selectively bred for high ethanol preference. *Pharmacology, Biochemistry and Behavior, 35,* 385–390.

Fukuda, K., Ogilvie, R. D., Chilcott, L., Vendittelli, A.-M., et al. (1998). The prevalence of sleep paralysis among Canadian and Japanese college students. *Dreaming: Journal of the Association for the Study of Dreams, 8*(2), 59–66.

Fulton, S., Woodside, B., and Shizgal, P. (2000). Modulation of brain reward circuitry by leptin. *Science, 287,* 125–128.

Furukawa, S., Xu, L., and Middlebrooks, J. C. (2000). Coding of sound-source location by ensembles of cortical neurons. *Journal of Neuroscience, 20,* 1216–1228.

Fuster, J. M. (1990). Prefrontal cortex and the bridging of temporal gaps in the perception-action cycle. *Annals of the New York Academy of Sciences, 608,* 318–336.

Fuster, J. M., Bodner, M., and Kroger, J. K. (2000). Cross-modal and cross-temporal association in neurons of frontal cortex. *Nature, 405,* 347–351.

Gabrieli, J. D. E. (1998). Cognitive neuroscience of human memory. *Annual Review of Psychology, 49,* 87–115.

Gabrieli, J. D. E., Sullivan, E. V., Desmond, J. E., Stebbins, G. T., et al. (1996). Behavioral and functional neuroimaging evidence for pre-

served conceptual implicit memory in global amnesia. *Society for Neuroscience, 22,* 1449.

Gais, S., Plihal, W., Wagner, U., and Born, J. (2000). Early sleep triggers memory for early visual discrimination skills. *Nature Neuroscience, 3,* 1335–1339.

Galaburda, A. M. (1994). Developmental dyslexia and animal studies: At the interface between cognition and neurology. *Cognition, 56,* 833–839.

Galaburda, A. M., Wang, P. P., Bellugi, U., and Rossen, M. (1994). Cytoarchitectonic anomalies in a genetically based disorder: Williams syndrome. *Neuroreport, 5,* 753–757.

Galani, R., Jarrard, L. E., Will, B. E., and Kelche, C. (1997). Effects of post-operative housing conditions on functional recovery in rats with lesions of the hippocampus, subiculum, or entorhinal cortex. *Neurobiology of Learning and Memory, 67,* 43–56.

Gall, C. M., Hess, U. S., and Lynch, G. (1998). Mapping brain networks engaged by, and changed by, learning. *Neurobiology of Learning and Memory, 70,* 14–36.

Gallagher, M., Nagahara, A. H., and Burwell, R. D. (1995). Cognition and hippocampal systems in aging: Animal models. In J. L. McGaugh, N. M. Weinberger, and G. Lynch (Eds.), *Brain and memory: Modulation and mediation of neuroplasticity* (pp. 103–126). New York: Oxford University Press.

Gallagher, M., and Rapp, P. R. (1997). The use of animal models to study the effects of aging on cognition. *Annual Review of Psychology, 48,* 339–370.

Gallant, J. L., Braun, J., and Van Essen, D. C. (1993). Selectivity for polar, hyperbolic, and Cartesian gratings in macaque visual cortex. *Science, 259,* 100–103.

Gallistel, C. R. (1990). *The organization of learning.* Cambridge, MA: MIT Press.

Gallistel, C. R., Gomita, Y., Yadin, E., and Campbell, K. A. (1985). Forebrain origins and terminations of the medial forebrain bundle metabolically activated by rewarding stimulation or by reward-blocking doses of pimozide. *Journal of Neuroscience, 5,* 1246–1261.

Gallopin, T., Fort, P., Eggermann, E., Cauli, B., et al. (2000). Identification of sleep-promoting neurons *in vitro. Nature, 404,* 992–995.

Gannon, P. J., Holloway, R. L., Broadfield, D. C., and Braun, A. R. (1998). Asymmetry of chimpanzee planum temporale: Humanlike pattern of brain language area homolog. *Science, 279,* 220–222.

Gaoni, Y., and Mechoulam, R. (1964). *Journal of the American Chemical Society, 86,* 1646.

Garavan, H., Morgan, R. E., Mactutus, C. F., Levitsky, D. A., et al. (2000). Prenatal cocaine exposure impairs selective attention: Evidence from serial reversal and extradimensional shift tasks. *Behavioral Neuroscience, 114,* 725–738.

Garcia, J., Kimmeldorf, D. J., and Koelling, R. A. (1955). Conditioned aversion to saccharin resulting from exposure to gamma radiation. *Science, 122,* 157–158.

Gardner, L. I. (1972). Deprivation dwarfism. *Scientific American, 227*(1), 76–82.

Gardner, R. A., and Gardner, B. T. (1969). Teaching sign language to a chimpanzee. *Science, 165,* 664–672.

Gardner, R. A., and Gardner, B. T. (1984). A vocabulary test for chimpanzees (*Pan troglodytes*). *Journal of Comparative Psychology, 98,* 381–404.

Gauthier, I., Behrmann, M., and Tarr, M. J. (1999). Can face recognition really be dissociated from object recognition? *Journal of Cognitive Neuroscience, 11,* 349–370.

Gazzaniga, M. S. (1992). *Nature's mind: The biological roots of thinking, emotions, sexuality, language, and intelligence.* New York: Basic Books.

Geinisman, Y., Detoledo-Morrell, L., Morrell, F., and Heller, R. E. (1995). Hippocampal markers of age-related memory dysfunction: Behavioral, electrophysiological and morphological perspectives. *Progress in Neurobiology, 45,* 223–252.

Gemba, H., Miki, N., and Sasaki, K. (1995). Cortical field potentials preceding vocalization and influences of cerebellar hemispherectomy upon them in monkeys. *Brain Research, 697,* 143–151.

Georgopoulos, A. P., Kalaska, J. F., Caminiti, R., and Massey, J. T. (1982). On the relations between the direction of two-dimensional arm movements and cell discharge in primate motor cortex. *Journal of Neuroscience, 2,* 1527–1537.

Georgopoulos, A. P., Taira, M., and Lukashin, A. (1993). Cognitive neurophysiology of the motor cortex. *Science, 260,* 47–52.

Gerard, C. M., Mollereau, C., Vassart, G., and Parmentier, M. (1991). Molecular cloning of a human cannabinoid receptor which is also expressed in testis. *Biochemical Journal, 279,* 129–134.

Gerkema, M. P., and Daan, S. (1985). Ultradian rhythms in behavior: The case of the common vole (*Microtus arvalis*). In H. Schulz and P. Lavie (Eds.), *Ultradian rhythms in physiology and behavior* (pp. 11–32). Berlin: Springer.

Gerlai, R., Wojtowicz, J. M., Marks, A., and Roder, J. (1995). Overexpression of a calcium-binding protein, S100 beta, in astrocytes alters synaptic plasticity and impairs spatial learning in transgenic mice. *Learning and Memory, 2*, 26–39.

Geschwind, N. (1972). Language and the brain. *Scientific American, 226*(4), 76–83.

Geschwind, N. (1976). Language and cerebral dominance. In T. N. Chase (Ed.), *Nervous system: Vol. 2. The clinical neurosciences* (pp. 433–439). New York: Raven.

Geschwind, N., and Levitsky, W. (1968). Human brain: Left-right asymmetries in temporal speech region. *Science, 161*, 186–187.

Geyer, M. A., and Markou, A. (1995). Animal models of psychiatric disorders. In F. E. Bloom and D. J. Kupfer (Eds.), *Psychopharmacology: The fourth generation of progress* (pp. 787–798). New York: Raven.

Ghazanfar, A. A., and Hauser, M. D. (1999). The neuroethology of primate vocal communication: Substrates for the evolution of speech. *Trends in Cognitive Sciences, 3*, 377–384.

Ghez, C., Hening, W., and Gordon, J. (1991). Organization of voluntary movement. *Current Opinion in Neurobiology, 1*, 664–671.

Gibbs, J., and Smith, G. P. (1986). Satiety: The roles of peptides from the stomach and the intestine. *Federation Proceedings, 45*, 1391–1395.

Gibbs, M. E., and Ng, K. T. (1977). Psychobiology of memory: Towards a model of memory formation. *Biobehavioral Reviews, 1*, 113–136.

Gibbs, M. E., and Ng, K. T. (1979). Neuronal depolarization and the inhibition of short-term memory formation. *Physiology & Behavior, 23*, 369–375.

Gibson, J. R., Beierlein, M., and Connors, B. W. (1999). Two networks of electrically coupled inhibitory neurons in neocortex. *Nature, 402*, 75–79.

Gilbert, A. N., and Wysocki, C. J. (1987). The smell survey results. *National Geographic, 172*, 514–525.

Gilbert, A. N., Yamazaki, K., Beauchamp, G. K., and Thomas, L. (1986). Olfactory discrimination of mouse strains (*Mus musculus*) and major histocompatibility types by humans (*Homo sapiens*). *Journal of Comparative Psychology, 100*, 262–265.

Gilchrist, I. D., Brown, V., and Findlay, J. M. (1997). Saccades without eye movements. *Nature, 390*, 130–131.

Gillingham, J. C., and Clark, D. L. (1981). An analysis of prey-searching behavior in the western diamondback rattlesnake *Crotalus atrox*. *Behavioral and Neural Biology, 32*, 235–240.

Gitelman, D. R., Alpert, N. M., Kosslyn, S., Daffner, K., et al. (1996). Functional imaging of human right hemispheric activation for exploratory movements. *Annals of Neurology, 39*, 174–179.

Giusberti, F., Cornoldi, C., De Beni, R., and Massironi, M. (1998). Perceptual illusions in imagery. *European Psychologist, 3*, 281–288.

Glantz, L. A., and Lewis, D. A. (2000). Decreased dendritic spine density on prefrontal cortical pyramidal neurons in schizophrenia. *Archives of General Psychiatry, 57*, 65–73.

Glantz, M. D. (1992). A developmental psychopathology model of drug abuse vulnerability. In M. D. Glantz and R. W. Pickens (Eds.), *Vulnerability to drug abuse* (pp. 389–418). Washington, DC: American Psychological Association.

Glantz, M., and Pickens, R. (1992). *Vulnerability to drug abuse*. Washington, DC: American Psychological Association.

Glaser, R., Rice, J., Speicher, C. E., Stout, J. C., et al. (1986). Stress depresses interferon production by leukocytes concomitant with a decrease in natural killer cell activity. *Behavioral Neuroscience, 100*, 675–678.

Glavin, G. B. (1991). Dopamine and gastroprotection. The brain-gut axis. *Digestive Diseases and Sciences, 36*, 1670–1672.

Glickman, S. E. (1977). Comparative psychology. In P. Mussen and M. R. Rosenzweig (Eds.), *Psychology: An introduction* (2nd ed., pp. 625-703). Lexington, MA: Heath.

Glickman, S. E., Frank, L. G., Davidson, J. M., Smith, E. R., et al. (1987). Androstenedione may organize or activate sex-reversed traits in female spotted hyenas. *Proceedings of the National Academy of Sciences, USA, 84*, 344–347.

Globus, A., Rosenzweig, M. R., Bennett, E. L., and Diamond, M. C. (1973). Effects of differential experience on dendritic spine counts in rat cerebral cortex. *Journal of Comparative and Physiological Psychology, 82*, 175–181.

Gloor, P., Olivier, A., Quesney, L. F., Andermann, F., et al. (1982). The role of the limbic system in experiential phenomena of temporal lobe epilepsy. *Annals of Neurology, 12*, 129–144.

Goldsmith, T. H. (1986). Interpreting trans-retinal recordings of spectral sensitivity. *Journal of Comparative Physiology. A, Sensory, Neural, and Behavioral Physiology, 159*, 481–487.

Golomb, J., de Leon, M. J., George, A. E., Kluger, A., et al. (1994). Hippocampal atrophy correlates with severe cognitive impairment in elderly patients with suspected normal pressure hydrocephalus. *Journal of Neurology, Neurosurgery and Psychiatry, 57*, 590–593.

Goodale, M. A., and Haffenden, A. (1998). Frames of reference for perception and action in the human visual system. *Neuroscience and Biobehavioral Reviews, 22*, 161–172.

Gooding, D., and Iacono, W. (1995). Schizophrenia through the lens of a developmental psychopathology perspective. In D. Cichetti and D. J. Cohen (Eds.), *Developmental Psychopathology: Vol. 2. Risk, Disorder, and Adaptation* (pp. 535–580). New York: Wiley.

Goodman, C. (1979). Isogenic grasshoppers: Genetic variability and development of identified neurons. In X. O. Breakefeld (Ed.), *Neurogenetics*. New York: Elsevier.

Goodman, C. S. (1996). Mechanisms and molecules that control growth cone guidance. *Annual Review of Neuroscience, 19*, 341–377.

Goodman, M., Tagle, D. A., Fitch, D. H., Bailey, W., et al. (1990). Primate evolution at the DNA level and a classification of hominoids. *Journal of Molecular Evolution, 30*, 260–266.

Gorelick, D. A., and Balster, R. L. (1995). Phencyclidine. In F. E. Bloom and D. J. Kupfer (Eds.), *Psychopharmacology: The fourth generation of progress* (pp. 1767–1776). New York: Raven.

Gorman, M. R. (1994). Male homosexual desire: Neurological investigations and scientific bias. *Perspectives in Biology and Medicine, 38*, 61–81.

Gorski, R. A., Gordon, J. H., Shryne, J. E., and Southam, A. M. (1978). Evidence for a morphological sex difference within the medial preoptic area of the rat brain. *Brain Research, 148*, 333–346.

Gottesman, I. I. (1991). *Schizophrenia genesis: The origins of madness*. New York: Freeman.

Gottlieb, G. (1976). The roles of experience in the development of behavior and the nervous system. In G. Gottlieb (Ed.), *Studies on the development of behavior and the nervous system: Vol. 3. Neural and behavioral specificity*. New York: Academic Press.

Gould, E., Beylin, A., Tanapat, P., Reeves, A., et al. (1999). Learning enhances adult neurogenesis in the hippocampal formation. *Nature Neuroscience, 2*, 260–265.

Gould, E., Reeves, A. J., Graziano, M. S., and Gross, C. G. (1999). Neurogenesis in the neocortex of adult primates. *Science, 286*, 548–552.

Gould, E., Tanapat, P., McEwen, B. S., Flugge, G., et al. (1998). Proliferation of granule cell precursors in the dentate gyrus of adult monkeys is diminished by stress. *Proceedings of the National Academy of Sciences, USA, 95*, 3168–3171.

Gould, J. L. (1986). The biology of learning. *Annual Review of Psychology, 37*, 163–192.

Gould, S. J. (1981). *The mismeasure of man*. New York: Norton.

Grabowski, T. J., Damasio, H., and Damasio, A. R. (1998). Premotor and prefrontal correlates of category-related lexical retrieval. *Neuroimage, 7*, 232–243.

Grady, C. L., and Craik, F. I. M. (2000). Changes in memory processing with age. *Current Opinion in Neurobiology, 10*, 224–231.

Grady, C. L., McIntosh, A. R., Horowitz, B., Maisog, J. M., et al. (1995). Age-related reductions in human recognition memory due to impaired encoding. *Science, 269*, 218–221.

Grafton, S. T., Mazziotta, J. C., Presty, S., Friston, K. J., et al. (1992). Functional anatomy of human procedural learning determined with regional cerebral blood flow and PET. *Journal of Neuroscience, 12*, 2542–2548.

Grant, S. G., O'Dell, T. J., Karl, K. A., Stein, P. L., et al. (1992). Impaired long-term potentiation, spatial learning, and hippocampal development in fyn mutant mice. *Science, 256*, 1903–1910.

Gratton, G., Fabiani, M., Goodman-Wood, M. R., and Desoto, M. C. (1998). Memory-driven processing in human medial occipital cortex: An event-related optical signal (EROS) study. *Psychophysiology, 35*, 348–351.

Graybiel, A. M. (1995). The basal ganglia. *Trends in Neurosciences, 18*, 60–62.

Graybiel, A. M., Aosaki, T., Flaherty, A. W., and Kimura, M. (1994). The basal ganglia and adaptive motor control. *Science, 265*, 1826–1831.

Graziano, M. S., Hu, X. T., and Gross, C. G. (1997). Coding the locations of objects in the dark. *Science, 277*, 239–241.

Green, W. H., Campbell, M., and David, R. (1984). Psychosocial dwarfism: A critical review of the evidence. *Journal of the American Academy of Child Psychiatry, 23,* 39–48.

Greenewalt, CH. (1968). *Bird song: Acoustics and physiology.* Washington, DC: Smithsonian Institution Press.

Greenough, W. T., McDonald, J. W., Parnisari, R. M., and Camel, J. E. (1986). Environmental conditions modulate degeneration and new dendrite growth in cerebellum of senescent rats. *Brain Research, 380,* 136–143.

Greenough, W. T. (1976). Enduring brain effects of differential experience and training. In M. R. Rosenzweig and E. L. Bennett (Eds.), *Neural mechanisms of learning and memory* (pp. 255–278). Cambridge, MA: MIT Press.

Greenough, W. T., and Volkmar, F. R. (1973). Pattern of dendritic branching in occipital cortex of rats reared in complex environments. *Experimental Neurology, 40,* 491–504.

Greenspan, R. J., Finn, J. A., Jr., and Hall, J. C. (1980). Acetylcholinesterase mutants in *Drosophila* and their effects on the structure and function of the central nervous system. *Journal of Comparative Neurology, 189,* 741–774.

Greer, S. (1983). Cancer and the mind. *British Journal of Psychiatry, 143,* 535–543.

Greer, S., Morris, T., and Pettingale, K. W. (1979). Psychological response to breast cancer: Effect on outcome. *Lancet, 2,* 785–787.

Gregory, R. L. (1987). Blindness, recovery from. In R. L. Gregory (Ed.), *The Oxford companion to the mind* (pp. 94–96). Oxford, England: Oxford University Press.

Gregory, R. L., and Wallace, J. G. (1963). *Recovery from early blindness: A case study.* Cambridge, England: Cambridge University Press.

Grevert, P., Albert, L. H., and Goldstein, A. (1983). Partial antagonism of placebo analgesia by naloxone. *Pain, 16,* 129–143.

Grevert, P., and Goldstein, A. (1985). Placebo analgesia, naloxone, and the role of endogenous opioids. In L. White, B. Tursky, and G. E. Schwartz (Eds.), *Placebo* (pp. 332–351). New York: Guilford.

Griffin, L. D., and Mellon, S. H. (1999). Selective serotonin reuptake inhibitors directly alter activity of neurosteroidogenic enzymes. *Proceedings of the National Academy of Sciences, USA, 96,* 13512–13517.

Grill, R., Murai, K., Blesch, A., Gage, F. H., et al. (1997). Cellular delivery of neurotrophin-3 promotes corticospinal axonal growth and partial functional recovery after spinal cord injury. *Journal of Neuroscience, 17,* 5560–5572.

Grillner, P., Hill, R., and Grillner, S. (1991). 7-Chlorokynurenic acid blocks NMDA receptor-induced fictive locomotion in lamprey—Evidence for a physiological role of the glycine site. *Acta Physiologica Scandinavica, 141,* 131–132.

Grillner, S. (1985). Neurobiological bases of rhythmic motor acts in vertebrates. *Science, 228,* 143–149.

Grosof, D. H., Shapley, R. M., and Hawken, M. J. (1993). Macaque V1 neurons can signal "illusory" contours. *Nature, 365,* 550–552.

Grunt, J. A., and Young, W. C. (1953). Consistency of sexual behavior patterns in individual male guinea pigs following castration and androgen therapy. *Journal of Comparative and Physiological Psychology, 46,* 138–144.

Gudermann, T., Schoneberg, T., and Schultz, G. (1997). Functional and structural complexity of signal transduction via G-protein-coupled receptors. *Annual Review of Neuroscience, 20,* 399–427.

Gulevich, G., Dement, W., and Johnson, L. (1966). Psychiatric and EEG observations on a case of prolonged (264 hours) wakefulness. *Archives of General Psychiatry, 15,* 29–35.

Gur, R. E., Resnick, S. M., Alavi, A., Gur, R. C., et al. (1987). Regional brain function in schizophrenia. I. A positron emission tomography study. *Archives of General Psychiatry, 44,* 119–125.

Gurney, M. E., and Konishi, M. (1979). Hormone induced sexual differentiation of brain and behavior in zebra finches. *Science, 208,* 1380–1382.

Gurney, M. E., Pu, H., Chiu, A. Y., Dal Canto, M. C., et al. (1994). Motor neuron degeneration in mice that express a human Cu,Zn superoxide dismutase mutation. *Science, 264,* 1772–1775.

Gusella, J. F., and MacDonald, M. E. (1993). Hunting for Huntington's disease. *Molecular Genetic Medicine, 3,* 139–158.

Haas, H. S., and Schauenstein, K. (1997). Neuroimmunomodulation via limbic structures—The neuroanatomy of psychoimmunology. *Progress in Neurobiology, 51,* 195–222.

Haass, C., and Kahle, P. J. (2000). Parkinson's pathology in a fly. *Nature, 404,* 341–343.

Hadley, M. E. (2000). *Endocrinology* (5th ed.). Englewood Cliffs, NJ: Prentice-Hall.

Häfner, H. (1998). Neurodevelopmental disorder and psychosis: One disease or major risk factor? *Current Opinion in Psychiatry, 11,* 17–18.

Hagstrom, S. A., Neitz, J., and Neitz, M. (1998). Variations in cone populations for red-green color vision examined by analysis of mRNA. *Neuroreport, 9,* 1963–1967.

Hakansson, M. L., Brown, H., Ghilardi, N., Skoda, R. C., et al. (1998). Leptin receptor immunoreactivity in chemically defined target neurons of the hypothalamus. *Journal of Neuroscience, 18,* 559–572.

Halaas, J. L., Gajiwala, K. S., Maffei, M., Cohen, S. L., et al. (1995). Weight-reducing effects of the plasma protein encoded by the obese gene. *Science, 269,* 543–546.

Hall, J. C., and Greenspan, R. J. (1979). Genetic analysis of *Drosophila* neurobiology. *Annual Review of Genetics, 13,* 127–195.

Hall, W. G., and Oppenheim, R. W. (1987). Developmental psychobiology: Prenatal, perinatal, and early postnatal aspects of behavioral development. *Annual Review of Psychology, 38,* 91–128.

Hallervorden, J. (1902). Eine neue Methode experimenteller Physiognomik. *Psychiatrisch-Neurologische Wochenschrift, 28,* 309–311.

Halpern, D. F. (1986). A different answer to the question, "Do sex-related differences in spatial abilities exist?" *American Psychologist, 41,* 1014–1015.

Halpern, M. (1987). The organization and function of the vomeronasal system. *Annual Review of Neuroscience, 10,* 325–362.

Halpern, M., Halpern, J., Erichsen, E., and Borghjid, S. (1997). The role of nasal chemical senses in garter snake response to airborne odor cues from prey. *Journal of Comparative Psychology, 111,* 251–260.

Halsband, U., Matsuzaka, Y., and Tanji, J. (1994). Neuronal activity in the primate supplementary, pre-supplementary and premotor cortex during externally and internally instructed sequential movements. *Neuroscience Research, 20,* 149–155.

Hamburger, V. (1958). Regression versus peripheral control of differentiation in motor hypoplasia. *American Journal of Anatomy, 102,* 365–410.

Hamburger, V. (1975). Cell death in the development of the lateral motor column of the chick embryo. *Journal of Comparative Neurology, 160,* 535–546.

Hamer, D. H., Hu, S., Magnuson, V. L., Hu, N., et al. (1993). A linkage between DNA markers on the X chromosome and male sexual orientation. *Science, 261,* 321–327.

Hamm, R. J., Temple, M. D., O'Dell, D. M., Pike, B. R., et al. (1996). Exposure to environmental complexity promotes recovery of cognitive function after traumatic brain injury. *Journal of Neurotrauma, 13,* 41–47.

Hammond, P. (1974). Cat retinal ganglion cells: Size and shape of receptive field centres. *Journal of Physiology (London), 242,* 99–118.

Hampton, R. R., Sherry, D. F., Shettleworth, S. J., Khurgel, M., et al. (1995). Hippocampal volume and food-storing behavior are related in parids. *Brain, Behavior and Evolution, 45,* 54–61.

Hanaway, J., Woolsey, T. A., Gado, M. H., and Roberts, M. P. (1998). *The brain atlas.* Bethesda, MD: Fitzgerald Science.

Hardyck C., Petrinovich, L., and Goldman R. (1976). Left-handedness and cognitive deficit. *Cortex, 12,* 226–279.

Hare, E. (1988). Schizophrenia as a recent disease. *British Journal of Psychiatry, 153,* 521–531.

Hari, R., Forss, N., Avikainen, S., Kirveskari, E., et al. (1998). Activation of human primary motor cortex during action observation: A neuromagnetic study. *Proceedings of the National Academy of Sciences, USA, 95,* 15061–15065.

Harris, E. W., and Cotman, C. W. (1986). Long-term potentiation of guinea pig mossy fiber responses is not blocked by N-methyl D-aspartate antagonists. *Neuroscience Letters, 70,* 132–137.

Harris, R. M., and Woolsey, T. A. (1983). Computer-assisted analyses of barrel neuron axons and their putative synaptic contacts. *Journal of Comparative Neurology, 220,* 63–79.

Hartmann, E. (1973). Sleep requirement: Long sleepers, short sleepers, variable sleepers, and insomniacs. *Psychosomatics, 14,* 95–103.

Hartmann, E. (1978). *The sleeping pill.* New Haven, CT: Yale University Press.

Hartmann, E. (1984). *The nightmare: The psychology and biology of terrifying dreams.* New York: Basic Books.

Hartse, K., Zorick, F., Sicklesteel, J., and Roth, T. (1988). Isolated cataplexy: A familial study. *Henry Ford Hospital Medical Journal, 36*(1), 24–27.

Harvey, P. H., and Krebs, J. R. (1990). Comparing brains. *Science, 249,* 140–146.

Harvey, P. H., and Pagel, M. D. (1991). *The comparative method in evolutionary biology.* New York: Oxford University Press.

Hasher, L., and Zacks, R. T. (1979). Automatic and effortful processes in memory. *Journal of Experimental Psychology: General, 108,* 356-358 .

Haskett, R. F. (1985). Diagnostic categorization of psychiatric disturbance in Cushing's syndrome. *American Journal of Psychiatry, 142,* 911–916.

Hatten, M. E. (1990). Riding the glial monorail: A common mechanism for glial-guided neuronal migration in different regions of the developing mammalian brain. *Trends in Neurosciences, 13,* 179–184.

Hauser, P., Zametkin, A. J., Martinez, P., Vitiello, B., et al. (1993). Attention deficit-hyperactivity disorder in people with generalized resistance to thyroid hormone. *New England Journal of Medicine, 328,* 997–1001.

Hazeltine, E., Grafton, S. T., and Ivry, R. (1997). Attention and stimulus characteristics determine the locus of motor-sequence encoding. A PET study. *Brain, 120,* 123–140.

Healy, S. D., and Krebs, J. R. (1993). Development of hippocampal specialisation in a food-storing bird. *Behavioural Brain Research, 53,* 127–130.

Heath, R. G. (1972). Pleasure and brain activity in man. *Journal of Nervous and Mental Diseases, 154,* 3–18.

Heath, R. G., Franklin, D. E., and Shraberg, D. (1979). Gross pathology of the cerebellum in patients diagnosed and treated as functional psychiatric disorders. *Journal of Nervous and Mental Disorders, 167,* 585–592.

Hebb, D. O. (1949). *The organization of behavior.* New York: Wiley.

Heffner, H. E., and Heffner, R. S. (1989). Unilateral auditory cortex ablation in macaques results in a contralateral hearing loss. *Journal of Neurophysiology, 62,* 789–801.

Hefti, F., and Mash, D. C. (1989). Localization of nerve growth factor receptors in the normal human brain and in Alzheimer's disease. *Neurobiology of Aging, 10,* 75–87.

Heisenberg, M., Heusipp, M., and Wanke, C. (1995). Structural plasticity in the *Drosophila* brain. *Journal of Neuroscience, 15,* 1951–1960.

Heit, S., Owens, M. J., Plotsky, P., and Nemeroff, C. B. (1997). Corticotropin-releasing factor, stress, and depression. *Neuroscientist, 3,* 186–194.

Held, R. (1993). Binocular vision—Behavioral and neuronal development. In M. H. Johnson (Ed.), *Brain development and cognition: A reader* (pp. 152–166). Oxford, England: Blackwell.

Heldmaier, G., and Ruf, T. (1992). Body temperature and metabolic rate during natural hypothermia in endotherms. *Journal of Comparative Physiology. B, Biochemical, Systemic, and Environmental Physiology, 162,* 696–706.

Hemmingsen, A. M. (1960). Energy metabolism as related to body size and respiratory surfaces, and its evolution. *Reports of Steno Memorial Hospital, Copenhagen, 9,* 1–110.

Hendrickson, A. (1985). Dots, stripes and columns in monkey visual cortex. *Trends in NeuroSciences, 8,* 406–410.

Henneman, E. (1991). The size principle and its relation to transmission failure in Ia projections to spinal motoneurons. *Annals of the New York Academy of Sciences, 627,* 165–168.

Hennessy, M. B., Mendoza, S. P., Mason, W. A., Moberg, G. P., et al. (1995). Endocrine sensitivity to novelty in squirrel monkeys and titi monkeys: Species differences in characteristic modes of responding to the environment. *Physiology & Behavior, 57,* 331–338.

Hertel, P., Fagerquist, M. V., and Svensson, T. H. (1999). Enhanced cortical dopamine output and antipsychotic-like effects of raclopride by alpha-2 adrenoceptor blockade. *Science, 286,* 105–107.

Hertz, L., Gibbs, M. E., O'Dowd, B. S., Sedman, G. L., et al. (1996). Astrocyte-neuron interaction during one-trial aversive learning in the neonate chick. *Neuroscience and Biobehavioral Reviews, 20,* 537–551.

Hetherington, A. W., and Ranson, S. W. (1940). Hypothalamic lesions and adiposity in the rat. *Anatomical Record, 78,* 149–172.

Hewes, G. (1973). Primate communication and the gestural origin of language. *Current Anthropology, 14,* 5–24.

Higley, J. D., Mehlman, P. T., Taub, D. M., Higley, S. B., et al. (1992). Cerebrospinal fluid monoamine and adrenal correlates of aggression in free-ranging rhesus monkeys. *Archives of General Psychiatry, 49,* 436–441.

Hille, B. (2001). *Ion channels of excitable membranes* (3rd ed.). Sunderland, MA: Sinauer Associates.

Hillis, D. M., Moritz, C., and Mable, B. K. (eds.). (1996). *Molecular systematics* (2nd ed.). Sunderland, MA: Sinauer Associates.

Hilts, P. J. (1995). *Memory's ghost: The strange tale of Mr. M. and the nature of memory.* New York: Simon & Schuster.

Hindler, C. G. (1989). Epilepsy and violence. *British Journal of Psychiatry, 155,* 246–249.

Hingson, R., Alpert, J., Day, N., Dooling, E., et al. (1982). Effects of maternal drinking and marijuana use on fetal growth and development. *Pediatrics, 70,* 539–546.

Hippocrates. (1991). *On the sacred disease* (F. Adams, Trans.) [On-line, at www.soli.com]. (Library of the Future Series, 3rd ed., Version 4.5.) World Library. (Original work written in 400 B.C.E.)

Hiramoto, M., Hiromi, Y., Giniger, E., and Hotta, Y. (2000). The *Drosophila* Netrin receptor Frazzled guides axons by controlling Netrin distribution. *Nature, 406,* 886–889.

Hirsch, E., Moye, D., and Dimon, J. H. (1995). Congenital indifference to pain: Long-term follow-up of two cases. *Southern Medical Journal, 88,* 851–857.

Hirsch, H. V. B., and Spinelli, D. N. (1971). Modification of the distribution of receptive field orientation in cats by selective visual exposure during development. *Experimental Brain Research, 12,* 509–527.

Hobson, J. A., and McCarley, R. W. (1977). The brain as a dream state generator: An activation-synthesis hypothesis of the dream process. *American Journal of Psychiatry, 134,* 1335–1348.

Hochstein, S., and Shapley, R. M. (1976). Quantitative analysis of retinal ganglion cell classifications. *Journal of Physiology (London), 252,* 237–264.

Hodgkin, A. L., and Huxley, A. F. (1952). A quantitative description of membrane current and its application to conduction and excitation in nerve. *Journal of Physiology (London), 117,* 500–544.

Hodgkin, A. L., and Katz, B. (1949). The effect of sodium ions on the electrical activity of the giant axon of the squid. *Journal of Physiology (London), 108,* 37–77.

Holcomb, H. H., Links, J., Smith, C., and Wong, D. (1989). Positron emission tomography: Measuring the metabolic and neurochemical characteristics of the living human nervous system. In N. C. Andreasen (Ed.), *Brain imaging: Applications in psychiatry* (pp. 235–370). Washington, DC: American Psychiatric Press.

Holden, C. (2001). Panel seeks truth in lie detector debate. *Science, 291,* 967.

Hollis, J. R., Connett, J. E., Stevens, V. J., and Greenlick, M. R. (1990). Stressful life events, Type A behavior, and the prediction of cardiovascular and total mortality over six years. MRFIT Group. *Journal of Behavioral Medicine, 13,* 263–280.

Holloway, C. C., and Clayton, D. F. (2001). Estrogen synthesis in the male brain triggers development of the avian song control pathway in vitro. *Nature Neuroscience, 4,* 170–175.

Holman, B. L., Mendelson, J., Garada, B., Teoh, S. K., et al. (1993). Regional cerebral blood flow improves with treatment in chronic cocaine polydrug users. *Journal of Nuclear Medicine, 34,* 723–727.

Honey, G. D., Bullmore, E. T., Soni, W., Varatheesan, M., et al. (1999). Differences in frontal cortical activation by a working memory task after substitution of risperidone for typical antipsychotic drugs in patients with schizophrenia. *Proceedings of the National Academy of Sciences, USA, 96,* 13432–13437.

Hood, K. L., Postle, B. R., and Corkin, S. (1999). An evaluation of the concurrent discrimination task as a measure of habit learning: Performance of amnesic subjects. *Neuropsychologia, 37,* 1375–1386.

Horai, S., Hayasaka, K., Kondo, R., Tsugane, K., et al. (1995). Recent African origin of modern humans revealed by complete sequences of hominoid mitochondrial DNAs. *Proceedings of the National Academy of Sciences, USA, 92,* 532–536.

Horne, J. A. (1985). Sleep function, with particular reference to sleep deprivation. *Annals of Clinical Research, 17,* 199–208.

Howard, D. (1997). Language in the human brain. In M. D. Rugg (Ed.), *Cognitive neuroscience* (pp. 277–304). Cambridge, MA: MIT Press.

Huang, Y. Y., and Kandel, E. R. (1994). Recruitment of long-lasting and protein kinase A-dependent long-term potentiations in the CA1 region of the hippocampus requires repeated tetanization. *Learning and Memory, 1,* 74–82.

Hubbard, A. (1993). A traveling-wave amplifier model of the cochlea. *Science, 259,* 68–71.

Hubel, D. H., and Wiesel, T. N. (1959). Receptive fields of single neurones in the cat's striate cortex. *Journal of Physiology (London), 148,* 573–591.

Hubel, D. H., and Wiesel, T. N. (1965). Binocular interaction in striate cortex kittens reared with artificial squint. *Journal of Neurophysiology, 28,* 1041–1059.

Hubel, D. H., Wiesel, T. N., and LeVay, S. (1977). Plasticity of ocular dominance in monkey striate cortex. *Philosophical Transactions of the Royal Society of London. Series B: Biological Sciences, 278,* 377–409.

Hudspeth, A. J. (1989). How the ear's works work. *Nature, 341,* 397–404.

Hudspeth, A. J. (1992). Hair-bundle mechanics and a model for mechano-electrical transduction by hair cells. *Society of General Physiologists Series, 47,* 357–370.

Hudspeth, A. J. (1997). How hearing happens. *Neuron, 19,* 947–950.

Huffman, K. J., Nelson, J., Clarey, J., and Krubitzer, L. (1999). Organization of somatosensory cortex in three species of marsupials, *Dasyurus hallucatus, Dactylopsila trivirgata,* and *Monodelphis domestica:* Neural correlates of morphological specializations. *Journal of Comparative Neurology, 403,* 5–32.

Hughes, J., Smith, T. W., Kosterlitz, H. W., Fothergill, L. A., et al. (1975). Identification of two related pentapeptides from the brain with potent opiate agonist activity. *Nature, 258,* 577–580.

Hull, C. L. (1943). *Principles of behavior.* New York: Appleton-Century.

Huntington, G. (1872). On chorea. *Medical and Surgical Reporter, 26,* 317–321.

Huttenlocher, P. R., and Dabholkar, A. S. (1997). Regional differences in synaptogenesis in human cerebral cortex. *Journal of Comparative Neurology, 387,* 167–178.

Huttenlocher, P. R., deCourten, C., Garey, L. J., and Van der Loos, H. (1982). Synaptogenesis in the human visual cortex-evidence for synapse elimination during normal development. *Neuroscience Letters, 33,* 247–252.

Hyde, T. M., and Weinberger, D. R. (1990). The brain in schizophrenia. *Seminars in Neurology, 10,* 276–286.

Hyde, T. M., Aaronson, B. A., Randolph, C., Rickler, K. C., et al. (1992). Relationship of birth weight to the phenotypic expression of Gilles de la Tourette's syndrome in monozygotic twins. *Neurology, 42,* 652–658.

Ickes, B. R., Pham, T. M., Sanders, L. A., Albeck, D. S., et al. (2000). Long-term environmental enrichment leads to regional increases in neurotrophin levels in rat brain. *Experimental Neurology, 164,* 45–52.

Idzikowski, C. (1984). Sleep and memory. *British Journal of Psychology, 75,* 439–449.

Ignarro, L. J. (1991). Signal transduction mechanisms involving nitric oxide. *Biochemical Pharmacology, 41,* 485–490.

Imperato-McGinley, J., Guerrero, L., Gautier, T., and Peterson, R. E. (1974). Steroid 5 α-reductase deficiency in man: An inherited form of male pseudohermaphroditism. *Science, 86,* 1213–1215.

Indo, Y., Tsuruta, M., Hayashida, Y., Karim Ma, et al. (1996). Mutations in the trka/ngf receptor gene in patients with congenital insensitivity to pain with anhidrosis. *Nature Genetics, 13,* 485–488.

Ingram, D. K. (1985). Analysis of age-related impairments in learning and memory in rodent models. *Annals of the New York Academy of Sciences, 444,* 312–331.

Insel, T. R. (1992). Toward a neuroanatomy of obsessive-compulsive disorder. *Archives of General Psychiatry, 49,* 739–744.

Insley, S. J. (2000). Long-term vocal recognition in the northern fur seal. *Nature, 406,* 404–405.

Institute for Health Policy, Brandeis University. (1993). *Substance abuse: The nation's number one health problem: Key indicators for policy.* Princeton, NJ: Robert Wood Johnson Foundation.

Institute of Medicine. (1990). *Broadening the base of treatment for alcohol problems.* Washington, DC: National Academy Press.

Irle, E., Exner, C., Thielen, K., Weniger, G., et al. (1998). Obsessive-compulsive disorder and ventromedial frontal lesions: Clinical and neuropsychological findings. *American Journal of Psychiatry, 155,* 255–263.

Isaacs, K. R., Anderson, B. J., Alcantara, A. A., Black, J. E., et al. (1992). Exercise and the brain: Angiogenesis in the adult rat cerebellum after vigorous physical activity and motor skill learning. *Journal of Cerebral Blood Flow and Metabolism, 12,* 110–119. [Published erratum appears in *Journal of Cerebral Blood Flow and Meatbolism, 12,* 533 (1992).]

Isaacson, R. L. (1972). Hippocampal destruction in man and other animals. *Neuropsychologia, 10,* 47–64.

Isles, A. R., Baum, M. J., Ma, D., Keverne, E. B., et al. (2001). Urinary odour preferences in mice. *Nature, 409,* 783–784.

Ito, J., Sakakibara, J., Iwasaki, Y., and Yonekura, Y. (1993). Positron emission tomography of auditory sensation in deaf patients and patients with cochlear implants. *Annals of Otology, Rhinology & Laryngology, 102,* 797–801.

Ito, M. (1987). Cerebellar adaptive function in altered vestibular and visual environments. *Physiologist, 30,* S81.

Iverson, J. M., and Goldin-Meadow, S. (1998). Why people gesture when they speak. *Nature, 396,* 228.

Ivry, R. (1993). Cerebellar involvement in the explicit representation of temporal information. *Annals of the New York Academy of Sciences, 682,* 214–230.

Ivry, R. B., and Robertson, L. C. (1998). *The two sides of perception.* Cambridge, MA: MIT Press.

Iwamura, Y., and Tanaka, M. (1978). Postcentral neurons in hand region of area 2: Their possible role in the form discrimination of tactile objects. *Brain Research, 150,* 662–666.

Iwasato, T., Datwani, A., Wolf, A. M., Nishiyama, H., et al. (2000). Cortex-restricted disruption of NMDAR1 impairs neuronal patterns in the barrel cortex. *Nature, 406,* 726–731.

Izquierdo, I., and Medina, J. H. (1997). Memory formation: The sequence of biochemical events in the hippocampus and its connection to activity in other brain structures. *Neurobiology of Learning and Memory, 68,* 285–316.

Jablensky, A., Sartorius, N., Ernberg, G., Anker, M., et al. (1992). Schizophrenia: Manifestations, incidence and course in different cultures. *Psychological Medicine, Monograph Supplement, 20.*

Jackson, H., and Parks, T. N. (1982). Functional synapse elimination in the developing avian cochlear nucleus with simultaneous reduction in cochlear nerve axon branching. *Journal of Neuroscience, 2,* 1736–1743.

Jacobs, G. H. (1984). Within-species variations in visual capacity among squirrel monkeys (*Saimiri sciureus*): Color vision. *Vision Research, 24,* 1267–1277.

Jacobs, G. H. (1993). The distribution and nature of colour vision among the mammals. *Biological Reviews of the Cambridge Philosophical Society, 68,* 413–471.

Jacobs, G. H., Neitz, J., and Neitz, M. (1993). Genetic basis of polymorphism in the color vision of platyrrhine monkeys. *Vision Research, 33,* 269–274.

Jacobs, L. F., Gaulin, S. J., Sherry, D. F., and Hoffman, G. E. (1990). Evolution of spatial cognition: Sex-specific patterns of spatial behavior predict hippocampal size. *Proceedings of the National Academy of Sciences, USA, 87,* 6349–6352.

Jacobs, L. F., and Spencer, W. D. (1994). Natural space-use patterns and hippocampal size in kangaroo rats. *Brain, Behavior and Evolution, 44,* 125–132.

Jacobson, M. (1991). *Developmental neurobiology.* New York: Plenum.

James, W. (1890). *Principles of psychology.* New York: Holt.

Jamieson, D., and Roberts, A. (2000). Responses of young *Xenopus laevis* tadpoles to light dimming: Possible roles for the pineal eye. *Journal of Experimental Biology, 203,* 1857–1867.

Jarvis, E. D., and Mello, C. V. (2000). Molecular mapping of brain areas involved in parrot vocal communication. *Journal of Comparative Neurology, 419,* 1–31.

Jarvis, E. D., Ribeiro, S., da Silva, M. L., Ventura, D., et al. (2000). Behaviourally driven gene expression reveals song nuclei in hummingbird brain. *Nature, 406,* 628–632.

Jellies, J. A. (1981). *Associative olfactory conditioning in* Drosophila melanogaster *and memory retention through metamorphosis.* Unpublished doctoral dissertation, Illinois State University, Normal, IL.

Jenike, M. A., Baer, L., Ballantine, T., Martuza, R. L., et al. (1991). Cingulotomy for refractory obsessive-compulsive disorder. A long-term follow-up of 33 patients. *Archives of General Psychiatry, 48,* 548–555.

Jenkins, J., and Dallenbach, K. (1924). Oblivescence during sleep and waking. *American Journal of Psychology, 35,* 605–612.

Jentsch, J. D., Redmond, D. E., Jr., Elsworth, J. D., Taylor, J. R., et al. (1997). Enduring cognitive deficits and cortical dopamine dysfunction in monkeys after long-term administration of phencyclidine. *Science, 277,* 953–955.

Jerison, H. J. (1991). *Brain size and the evolution of mind.* New York: American Museum of Natural History.

Jernigan, T. L., Bellugi, U., Sowell, E., Doherty, S., et al. (1993). Cerebral morphologic distinctions between Williams and Down syndromes. *Archives of Neurology, 50,* 186–191.

Johansson, B. B., and Ohlsson, A. L. (1996). Environment, social interaction, and physical activity as determinants of functional outcome after cerebral infarction in the rat. *Experimental Neurology, 139,* 322–327.

Johnsen, A., Andersen, V., Sunding, C., and Lifjeld, J. T. (2000). Female bluethroats enhance offspring immunocompetence through extra-pair copulations. *Nature, 406,* 296–299.

Johnson, E. M., Jr., and Deckwerth, T. L. (1993). Molecular mechanisms of developmental neuronal death. *Annual Review of Neuroscience, 16,* 31–46.

Johnson, J. S., and Newport, E. L. (1989). Critical period effects in second language learning: The influence of maturational state on the acquisition of English as a second language. *Cognitive Psychology, 21,* 60–99.

Johnson, K. O., and Hsiao, S. S. (1992). Neural mechanisms of tactual form and texture perception. *Annual Review of Neuroscience, 15,* 227–250.

Johnson, L. C. (1969). Psychological and physiological changes following total sleep deprivation. In A. Kales (Ed.), *Sleep: Physiology and pathology.* Philadelphia: Lippincott.

Johnson, P. L., and Stellar, J. R. (1994). Effects of accumbens DALA microinjections on brain stimulation reward and behavioral activation in intact and 6-OHDA treated rats. *Psychopharmacology, 114,* 665–671.

Johnson-Greene, D., Adams, K., Gilman, S., Koeppe, R., et al. (1997). Effects of abstinence and relapse upon neuropsychological function and cerebral glucose metabolism in severe chronic alcoholism. *Journal of Clinical and Experimental Neuropsychology, 19,* 378–385.

Jones, K. E., Lyons, M., Bawa, P., and Lemon, R. N. (1994). Recruitment order of motoneurons during functional tasks. *Experimental Brain Research, 100,* 503–508.

Jordan, B. D., Jahre, C., Hauser, W. A., Zimmerman, R. D., et al. (1992). CT of 338 active professional boxers. *Radiology, 185,* 509–512.

Jordan, B., Relkin, N., Ravdin, L., Jacobs, A., et al. (1997). Apolipoprotein E epsilon4 associated with chronic traumatic brain injury in boxing. *JAMA, 278,* 136–140.

Jordan, C. L., Breedlove, S. M., and Arnold, A. P. (1991). Ontogeny of steroid accumulation in spinal lumbar motoneurons of the rat: Implications for androgen's site of action during synapse elimination. *Journal of Comparative Neurology, 313,* 441–448.

Jordan, C. L., Letinsky, M. S., and Arnold, A. P. (1988). Synapse elimination occurs late in the hormone-sensitive levator ani muscle of the rat. *Journal of Neurobiology, 19,* 335–356.

Jouvet, M. (1967). Neurophysiology of the states of sleep. In G. C. Quarton, T. Melnechuk, and F. O. Schmitt (Eds.), *The neurosciences* (pp. 529–544). New York: Rockefeller University.

Julian, T., and McKenry, P. C. (1979). Relationship of testosterone to men's family functioning at mid-life: A research note. *Aggressive Behavior, 15,* 281–289.

Julien, R. J. (1992). *A primer of drug action* (6th ed.). New York: Freeman.

Kaada, B. (1967). Brain mechanisms related to aggressive behavior. In C. D. Clemente and D. B. Lindsley (Eds.), *Aggression and defense.* Berkeley: University of California.

Kaas, J. H. (1991). Plasticity of sensory and motor maps in adult mammals. *Annual Review of Neuroscience, 14,* 137–167.

Kaas, J. H. (2000). The reorganization of sensory and motor maps after injury in adult mammals. In M. S. Gazzaniga (Ed.), *The new cognitive neurosciences* (pp. 223–236). Cambridge, MA: MIT Press.

Kaas, J. H., and Hackett, T. A. (1999). "What" and "where" processing in auditory cortex. *Nature Neuroscience, 2,* 1045–1047.

Kaas, J. H., Nelson, R. J., Sur, M., Lin, C. S., et al. (1979). Multiple representations of the body within the primary somatosensory cortex of primates. *Science, 204,* 521–523.

Kadekaro, M., Cohen, S., Terrell, M. L., Lekan, H., et al. (1989). Independent activation of subfornical organ and hypothalamo-neuro-hypophysial system during administration of angiotensin II. *Peptides, 10,* 423–429.

Kafitz, K. W., Rose, C. R., Thoenen, H., and Konnerth, A. (1999). Neurotrophin-evoked rapid excitation through TrkB receptors. *Nature, 401,* 918–921.

Kagan, J. (1997). Temperament and the reactions to unfamiliarity. *Child Development, 68,* 139–143.

Kakei, S., Hoffman, D. S., and Strick, P. L. (1999). Muscle and movement representations in the primary motor cortex. *Science, 285,* 2136–2139.

Kales, A. (1973). Treating sleep disorders. *American Family Physician, 8,* 158–168.

Kales, A., and Kales, J. (1970). Evaluation, diagnosis and treatment of clinical conditions related to sleep. *JAMA, 213,* 2229–2235.

Kales, A., and Kales, J. D. (1974). Sleep disorders. Recent findings in the diagnosis and treatment of disturbed sleep. *New England Journal of Medicine, 290,* 487–499.

Kalin, N. H., Dawson, G., Tariot, P., Shelton, S., et al. (1987). Function of the adrenal cortex in patients with major depression. *Psychiatry Research, 22,* 117–125.

Kandel, E. R. (1976). *Cellular basis of behavior.* San Francisco: Freeman.

Kandel, E. R., Castellucci, V. F., Goelet, P., and Schacher, S. (1987). 1987 cell-biological interrelationships between short-term and long-term memory. *Research Publications—Association for Research in Nervous and Mental Disease, 65,* 111–132.

Kandel, E. R., Schacher, S., Castellucci, V. F., and Goelet, P. (1986). The long and short of memory in *Aplysia*: A molecular perspective. *Fidia Research Foundation Neuroscience Award Lectures, 2,* 7–47.

Karasawa, J., Touho, H., Ohnishi, H., and Kawaguchi, M. (1997). Rete mirabile in humans—Case report. *Neurologia Medico-Chirurgica, 37,* 188–192.

Karni, A., Tanne, D., Rubenstein, B. S., Askenasy, J. J., et al. (1994). Dependence on REM sleep of overnight improvement of a perceptual skill. *Science, 265,* 679–682.

Karp, L. E. (1976). *Genetic engineering, threat or promise?* Chicago: Nelson-Hall.

Kastner, S., De Weerd, P., Desimone, R., and Ungerleider, L. G. (1998). Mechanisms of directed attention in the human extrastriate cortex as revealed by functional MRI. *Science, 282,* 108–111.

Katz, L. C., and Shatz, C. J. (1996). Synaptic activity and the construction of cortical circuits. *Science, 274,* 1133–1138.

Katzenberg, D., Young, T., Finn, L., Lin, L., et al. (1998). A CLOCK polymorphism associated with human diurnal preference. *Sleep, 21,* 569–576.

Kaufmann, C. A., Jeste, D. V., Shelton, R. C., Linnoila, M., et al. (1986). Noradrenergic and neuroradiological abnormalities in tardive dyskinesia. *Biological Psychiatry, 21,* 799–812.

Kaushall, P. I., Zetin, M., and Squire, L. R. (1981). A psychosocial study of chronic, circumscribed amnesia. *Journal of Nervous and Mental Disease, 169,* 383–389.

Kavanau, J. L. (1997). Memory, sleep and the evolution of mechanisms of synaptic efficacy maintenance. *Neuroscience, 79,* 7–44.

Kawai, N., and Matsuzawa, T. (2000). Numerical memory span in a chimpanzee. *Nature, 403,* 39–40.

Keane, T. M. (1998). Psychological and behavioral treatments of post-traumatic stress disorder. In P. E. Nathan, and J. M. Gorman (Eds.), *A guide to treatments that work* (pp. 398–407). New York: Oxford University Press.

Keele, S. W., and Summers, J. J. (1976). The structure of motor programs. In G. E. Stelmach (Ed.), *Motor control: Issues and trends.* New York: Academic Press.

Keenan, J. P., Nelson, A., O'Connor, M., and Pascual-Leone, A. (2001). Self-recognition and the right hemisphere. *Nature, 409,* 305.

Keesey, R. E. (1980). A set-point analysis of the regulation of body weight. In A. J. Stunkard (Ed.), *Obesity.* Philadelphia: Saunders.

Keesey, R. E., and Boyle, P. C. (1973). Effects of quinine adulteration upon body weight of LH-lesioned and intact male rats. *Journal of Comparative and Physiological Psychology, 84,* 38–46.

Keesey, R. E., and Corbett, S. W. (1984). Metabolic defense of the body weight set-point. *Research Publications—Association for Research in Nervous and Mental Disease, 62,* 87–96.

Keesey, R. E., and Powley, T. L. (1986). The regulation of body weight. *Annual Review of Psychology, 37,* 109–133.

Kelche, C., Roeser, C., Jeltsch, H., Cassel, J. C., et al. (1995). The effects of intrahippocampal grafts, training, and postoperative housing on behavioral recovery after septohippocampal damage in the rat. *Neurobiology of Learning and Memory, 63,* 155–166.

Keller, M. B., McCullough, J. P., Klein, D. N., Arnow, B., et al. (2000). A comparison of nefazodone, the cognitive behavioral-analysis system of psychotherapy, and their combination for the treatment of chronic depression. *New England Journal of Medicine, 342,* 1462–1470.

Kelso, S. R., and Brown, T. H. (1986). Differential conditioning of associative synaptic enhancement in hippocampal brain slices. *Science, 232,* 85–87.

Keltner, D., and Buswell, B. N. (1996). Evidence for the distinctness of embarrassment, shame, and guilt: A study of recalled antecedents and facial expressions of emotion. *Cognition & Emotion, 10,* 155–171.

Keltner, D., and Ekman, P. (2000). Facial expression of emotion. In M. Lewis and J. M. Haviland-Jones (Eds.), *Handbook of emotions* (2nd ed., pp. 236–250). New York: Guilford.

Kemali, D., Galderisi, M. S., Ariano, M. G., Cesarelli, M., et al. (1985). Clinical and neuropsychological correlates of cerebral ventricular enlargement in schizophrenia. *Journal of Psychiatric Research, 19,* 587–596.

Kemp, D. T. (1979). The evoked cochlear mechanical responses and the auditory microstructure—Evidence for a new element in cochlear mechanics. *Scandinavian Audiology. Supplementum, 9,* 35–47.

Kemp, M. (2001). The harmonious hand. Marin Mersenne and the science of memorized music. *Nature, 409,* 666.

Kempermann, G., Kuhn, H. G., and Gage, F. H. (1997). More hippocampal neurons in adult mice living in an enriched environment. *Nature, 386,* 493–495.

Kendler, K. S., Gardner, C. O., and Prescott, C. A. (1999). Clinical characteristics of major depression that predict risk of depression in relatives. *Archives of General Psychiatry, 56,* 322–327.

Kertesz, A. (1993). Recovery and treatment. In K. M. Heilman and E. Valenstein (Eds.), *Clinical neuropsychology*, 3rd. ed. New York: Oxford University Press.

Kesner, R. P. (1980). An attribute analysis of memory: The role of the hippocampus. *Physiological Psychology, 8*, 189–197.

Kesner, R. P. (1991). Neurobiological views of memory. In J. L. Martinez and R. P. Kesner (Eds.), *Learning and memory: A biological view* (2nd ed., pp. 499–547). New York: Academic Press.

Kesner, R. P. (1998). Neurobiological views of memory. In J. L. Martinez, Jr., and R. P. Kesner (Eds.), *Neurobiology of learning and memory* (3rd ed., pp. 361–416). San Diego, CA: Harcourt Brace.

Kesner, R. P., Bolland, B. L., and Dakis, M. (1993). Memory for spatial locations, motor responses, and objects: Triple dissociation among the hippocampus, caudate nucleus, and extrastriate visual cortex. *Experimental Brain Research, 93*, 462–470.

Kesner, R. P., and Novak, J. M. (1982). Serial position curve in rats: Role of the dorsal hippocampus. *Science, 218*, 173–175.

Kesner, R. P., and Williams, J. M. 1995. Memory for magnitude of reinforcement: Dissociation between the amygdala and hippocampus. *Neurobiology of Learning and Memory, 64*, 237–244.

Kessler, R. C., McGonagle, K. A., Zhao, S., Nelson, C. B., et al. (1994). Lifetime and 12-month prevalence of DSM-III-R psychiatric disorders in the United States. Results from the National Comorbidity Survey. *Archives of General Psychiatry, 51*, 8–19.

Kety, S. (1976). Biological concomitants of affective states and their possible role in memory processes. In M. R. Rosenzweig and E. L. Bennett (Eds.), *Neural mechanisms of learning and memory* (pp. 321–326). Cambridge, MA: MIT Press.

Kety, S., Rosenthal, D., Wender, P. H., Schulsinger, F., et al. (1975). Mental illness in the biological and adoptive families of adopted individuals who have become schizophrenic. A preliminary report based on psychiatric interviews. In R. R. Fieve, D. Rosenthal, and H. Brill (Eds.), *Genetic research in psychiatry*. Baltimore: Johns Hopkins University.

Kety, S. S., Wender, P. H., Jacobsen, B., Ingraham, L. J., et al. (1994). Mental illness in the biological and adoptive relatives of schizophrenic adoptees. Replication of the Copenhagen Study in the rest of Denmark. *Archives of General Psychiatry, 51*, 442–455.

Keverne, E. B. (1999). The vomeronasal organ. *Science, 286*, 716–720.

Keynes, R. J., and Cook, G. M. (1992). Repellent cues in axon guidance. *Current Opinion in Neurobiology, 2*, 55–59.

Kiang, N. Y. S. (1965). *Discharge patterns of single fibers in the cat's auditory nerve*. Cambridge, MA: MIT Press.

Kiecolt-Glaser, J. K., and Glaser, R. (1995). Psychoneuroimmunology and health consequences: Data and shared mechanisms. *Psychosomatic Medicine, 57*, 269–274.

Killiany, R. J., Moss, M. B., Albert, M. S., Sandor, T., et al. (1993). Temporal lobe regions on magnetic resonance imaging identify patients with early Alzheimer's disease. *Archives of Neurology, 50*, 949–954.

Kim, D.-S., Duong, T. Q., and Kim, S.-G. (2000). High-resolution mapping of iso-orientation columns by fMRI. *Nature Neuroscience, 3*, 164–169.

Kim, J. J., and Fanselow, M. S. (1992). Modality-specific retrograde amnesia of fear. *Science, 256*, 675–677.

Kim, K. H., Relkin, N. R., Lee, K. M., and Hirsch, J. (1997). Distinct cortical areas associated with native and second languages. *Nature, 388*, 171–174.

Kimmel, H. L., Gong, W., Vechia, S. D., Hunter, R. G., et al. (2000). Intraventral tegmental area injection of rat cocaine and amphetamine-regulated transcript peptide 55-102 induces locomotor activity and promotes conditioned place preference. *Journal of Pharmacology and Experimental Therapeutics, 294*, 784–792.

Kimura, D. (1973). The asymmetry of the human brain. *Scientific American, 228* (3),, 70-78.

King, D. P., and Takahashi, J. S. (2000). Molecular genetics of circadian rhythms in mammals. *Annual Review of Neuroscience, 23*, 713–742.

Kingsbury, S. J., and Garver, D. L. (1998). Lithium and psychosis revisited. *Progress in Neuro-psychopharmacology & Biological Psychiatry, 22*, 249–263.

Kinnamon, S. C., and Cummings, T. A. (1992). Chemosensory transduction mechanisms in taste. *Annual Review of Physiology, 54*, 715–731.

Kinsey, A. C., Pomeroy, W. B., and Martin, C. E. (1948). *Sexual behavior in the human male*. Philadelphia: Saunders.

Kinsey, A. C., Pomeroy, W. B., Martin, C. E., and Gebhard, P. H. (1953). *Sexual behavior in the human female*. Philadelphia: Saunders.

Kleiber, M. (1947). Body size and metabolic rate. *Physiological Reviews, 15*, 511–541.

Kleim, J. A., Barbay, S., and Nudo, R. J. (1998). Functional reorganization of the rat motor cortex following motor skill learning. *Journal of Neurophysiology, 80*, 3321–3325.

Kleim, J. A., Lussnig, E., Schwartz, E. R., Comery, T. A., et al. (1996). Synaptogenesis and FOS expression in the motor cortex of the adult rat after motor skill learning. *Journal of Neuroscience, 16*, 4529–4535.

Kleitman, N. (1969). Basic rest-activity cycle in relation to sleep and wakefulness. In A. Kales (Ed.), *Sleep: Physiology and pathology*. Philadelphia: Lippincott.

Kleitman, N., and Engelmann, T. (1953). Sleep characteristics of infants. *Journal of Applied Physiology, 6*, 269–282.

Klima, E. S., and Bellugi, U. (1979). *The signs of language*. Cambridge, MA: Harvard University Press.

Klinke, R., Kral, A., Heid, S., Tillein, J., et al. (1999). Recruitment of the auditory cortex in congenitally deaf cats by long-term cochlear electrostimulation. *Science, 285*, 1729–1733.

Kluckhohn, C. (1949). *Mirror for man*. New York: Whittlesey House.

Klüver, H., and Bucy, P. C. (1938). An analysis of certain effects of bilateral temporal lobectomy in the rhesus monkey, with special reference to "psychic blindness." *Journal of Psychology, 5*, 33–54.

Knibestol, M., and Valbo, A. B. (1970). Single unit analysis of mechanoreceptor activity from the human glabrous skin. *Acta Physiologica Scandinavica, 80*, 178–195.

Knudsen, E. I. (1982). Auditory and visual maps of space in the optic tectum of the owl. *Journal of Neuroscience, 2*, 1177–1194.

Knudsen, E. I. (1984). The role of auditory experience in the development and maintenance of sound localization. *Trends in Neurosciences, 7*, 326–330.

Knudsen, E. I. (1985). Experience alters the spatial tuning of auditory units in the optic tectum during a sensitive period in the barn owl. *Journal of Neuroscience, 5*, 3094–3109.

Knudsen, E. I. (1998). Capacity for plasticity in the adult owl auditory system expanded by juvenile experience. *Science, 279*, 1531–1533.

Knudsen, E., and Knudsen, P. (1985). Vision guides adjustment of auditory localization in young barn owls. *Science, 230*, 545–548.

Knudsen, E. I., Knudsen, P. F., and Esterly, S. D. (1984). A critical period for the recovery of sound localization accuracy following monaural occlusion in the barn owl. *Journal of Neuroscience, 4*, 1012–1020.

Knudsen, E. I., and Konishi, M. (1978). A neural map of auditory space in the owl. *Science, 200*, 795–797.

Kobatake, E., and Tanaka, K. (1994). Neuronal selectivities to complex object features in the ventral visual pathway of the macaque cerebral cortex. *Journal of Neurophysiology, 71*, 856–867.

Kobilka, B. (1992). Adrenergic receptors as models for G protein-coupled receptors. *Annual Review of Neuroscience, 15*, 87–114.

Kogan, J. H., Frankland, P. W., Blendy, J. A., Coblentz, J., et al. (1997). Spaced training induces normal long-term memory in CREB mutant mice. *Current Biology, 7*, 1–11.

Kojima, M., Hosoda, H., Date, Y., Nakazato, M., et al. (1999). Ghrelin is a growth hormone releasing acylated peptide from stomach. *Nature, 402*, 656–660.

Kolb, B., and Whishaw, I. Q. (1990). *Fundamentals of human neuropsychology*. San Francisco: Freeman.

Kollack-Walker, S., Don, C., Watson, S. J., and Akil, H. (1999). Differential expression of c-fos mRNA within neurocircuits of male hamsters exposed to acute or chronic defeat. *Journal of Neuroendocrinology, 11*, 547–559.

Kölmel, H. W. (1988). Pure homonymous hemiachromatopsia. Findings with neuro-ophthalmologic examination and imaging procedures. *European Archives of Psychiatry and Neurological Sciences, 237*, 237–243.

Kolodny, E. H., and Cable, W. J. L. (1982). Inborn errors of metabolism. *Annals of Neurology, 11*, 221–232.

Kondo, Y., Sachs, B. D., and Sakuma, Y. (1997). Importance of the medial amygdala in rat penile erection evoked by remote stimuli from estrous females. *Behavioural Brain Research, 88*, 153–160.

Kondziolka, D., Wechsler, L., Goldstein, S., Meltzer, C., et al. (2000). Transplantation of cultured human neuronal cells for patients with stroke. *Neurology, 55*, 565–569.

Konishi, M. (1985). Birdsong: From behavior to neuron. *Annual Review of Neuroscience, 8*, 125–170.

Konopka, R. J., and Benzer, S. (1971). Clock mutants of *Drosophila melanogaster*. *Proceedings of the National Academy of Sciences, USA, 68*, 2112–2116.

Koob, G. F. (1995). Animal models of drug addiction. In F. E. Bloom and D. J. Kupfer (Eds.), *Psychopharmacology: The fourth generation of progress* (pp. 759–772). New York: Raven.

Koob, G. F., Sandman, C. A., and Strand, F. L. (1990). *A decade of neuropeptides: Past, present, and future.* New York: New York Academy of Sciences.

Kopin, I. J., and Markey, S. P. (1988). MPTP toxicity: Implications for research in Parkinson's disease. *Annual Review of Neuroscience, 11,* 81–96.

Korbo, L. (1999). Glial cell loss in the hippocampus of alcoholics. *Alcoholism, Clinical and Experimental Research, 23,* 164–168.

Korenman, S. G., and Barchas, J. D. (1993). *Biological basis of substance abuse.* New York: Oxford University Press.

Kosslyn, S. M. (1994). *Image and brain: The resolution of the imagery debate.* Cambridge, MA: MIT Press.

Kosslyn, S. M., Alpert, N. M., Thompson, W. L., Maljkovic, V., et al. (1993). Visual mental imagery activates topographically organized visual cortex. *Journal of Cognitive Neuroscience, 5,* 263–287.

Kosslyn, S. M., Chabris, C. F., Marsolek, C. J., and Koenig, O. (1992). Categorical versus coordinate spatial relations: Computational analyses and computer simulations. *Journal of Experimental Psychology: Human Perception and Performance, 18,* 562–577.

Kosslyn, S. M., Pascual-Leone, A., Felician, O., Camposano, S., et al. (1999). The role of Area 17 in visual imagery: Convergent evidence from PET and RTMS. *Science, 208,* 167–170.

Kovelman, J. A., and Scheibel, A. B. (1984). A neurohistological correlate of schizophrenia. *Biological Psychiatry, 19,* 1601.

Kraepelin, E. (1919). *Dementia praecox and paraphrenia.* Edinburgh, Scotland: Livingstone.

Kramer, M. S., Cutler, N., Feighner, J., Shrivastava, R., et al. (1998). Distinct mechanism for antidepressant activity by blockade of central substance P receptors. *Science, 281,* 1640–1645.

Krasne, F. B., and Glanzman, D. L. (1995). What we can learn from invertebrate learning. *Annual Review of Psychology, 45,* 585–624.

Krauss, R. M. (1998). Why do we gesture when we speak? *Current Directions in Psychological Science, 7*(2), 54–60.

Kraut, R. E., and Johnston, R. E. (1979). Social and emotional messages of smiling: An ethological approach. *Journal of Personality and Social Psychology, 37,* 1539–1553.

Krebs, J. R., Sherry, D. F., Healy, S. D., Perry, V. H., et al. (1989). Hippocampal specialisation of food-storing birds. *Proceedings of the National Academy of Sciences, USA, 86,* 1388–1392.

Kreuz, L. E., and Rose, R. M. (1972). Assessment of aggressive behavior and plasma testosterone in a young criminal population. *Psychosomatic Medicine, 34,* 321–332.

Kril, J., Halliday, G., Svoboda, M., and Cartwright, H. (1997). The cerebral cortex is damaged in chronic alcoholics. *Neuroscience, 79,* 983–998.

Kring, A. M. (1999). Emotion in schizophrenia: Old mystery, new understanding. *Current Directions in Psychological Science, 8*(5), 160–163.

Kristensen, P., Judge, M. E., Thim, L., Ribel, U., et al. (1998). Hypothalamic CART is a new anorectic peptide regulated by leptin. *Nature, 393,* 72–76.

Krubitzer, L. A., Manger, P., Pettigrew, J. D., and Calford, M. B. (1995). The organization of neocortex in monotremes: In search of the prototypical plan. *Journal of Comparative Neurology 348,* 1–45.

Kruesi, M. J. (1979). Cruelty to animals and CSF 5HIAA. *Psychiatry Research, 28,* 115–116.

Krug, M., Lössner, B., and Ott, T. (1984). Anisomycin blocks the late phase of long-term potentiation in the dentate gyrus of freely moving rat. *Brain Research Bulletin, 13,* 39–42.

Krystal, F. B., Krishnan, K. R., Raitiere, M., Poland, R., et al. (1990). Differential diagnosis and pathophysiology of Cushing's syndrome and primary affective disorder. *Journal of Neuropsychiatry and Clinical Neurosciences, 2,* 34–43.

Kubanis, P., and Zornetzer, S. F. (1981). Age-related behavioral and neurobiological changes: A review with emphasis on memory. *Behavioral and Neural Biology, 31,* 115–172.

Kuffler, S. W. (1953). Discharge patterns and functional organization of mammalian retina. *Journal of Neurophysiology, 16,* 37–68.

Kujala, T., Alho, K., and Naatanen, R. (2000). Cross-modal reorganization of human cortical functions. *Trends in Neurosciences, 23,* 115–120.

Kuljis, R. O., and Rakic, P. (1990). Hypercolumns in primate visual cortex can develop in the absence of cues from photoreceptors. *Proceedings of the National Academy of Sciences, USA, 87,* 5303–5306.

Kulkarni, A., and Colburn, H. S. (1998). Role of spectral detail in sound-source localization. *Nature, 396,* 747–749.

Kutas, M., and Hillyard, S. A. (1980). Reading senseless sentences: Brain potentials reflect semantic incongruity. *Science, 207,* 203–205.

LaBar, K. S., Gatenby, J. C., Gore, J. C., Ledoux, J. E., et al. (1998). Human amygdala activation during conditioned fear acquisition and extinction: A mixed-trial fMRI study. *Neuron, 20,* 937–945.

Lacey, J. I., and Lacey, B. C. (1970). Some autonomic-central nervous system interrelationships. In P. Black (Ed.), *Physiological correlates of emotion.* New York: Academic Press.

Lachman, H. M., Papolos, D. F., Boyle, A., Sheftel, G., et al. (1993). Alterations in glucorticoid inducible RNAs in the limbic system of learned helpless rats. *Brain Research, 609,* 110–116.

Lack, D. (1968). *Ecological adaptations for breeding in birds.* London: Methuen.

Lajoie, Y., Teasdale, N., Cole, J. D., Burnett, M., et al. (1996). Gait of a deaf-ferented subject without large myelinated sensory fibers below the neck. *Neurology, 47,* 109–115.

Lalumiere, M. L., Blanchard, R., and Zucker, K. J. (2000). Sexual orientation and handedness in men and women: A meta-analysis. *Psychological Bulletin, 126,* 575–5s92.

Laming, P. R., Kimelberg, H., Robinson, S., Salm, A., et al. (2000). Neuronal-glial interactions and behaviour. *Neuroscience and Biobehavioral Reviews, 24,* 295–340.

Land, M. F., and Fernald, R. D. (1992). The evolution of eyes. *Annual Review of Neuroscience, 15,* 1–29.

Landau, B., and Levy, R. M. (1993). Neuromodulation techniques for medically refractory chronic pain. *Annual Review of Medicine, 44,* 279–287.

Lane, R. D. (2000). Neural correlates of conscious emotional experience. In R. D. Lane (Ed.), *Cognitive neuroscience of emotion* (pp. 345–370). New York: Oxford University Press.

Lane, R. D., Chua, P. M., and Dolan, R. J. (1999). Common effects of emotional valence, arousal, and attention on neural activation during visual processing of picutres. *Neuropsychologia, 37,* 989–997.

Lange, C. S. (1887). Ueber Gemuthsbewegungen. In W. James and C. G. Lange (Eds.), *The emotions* (pp. 33–90). Baltimore: Williams & Wilkins.

Langlais, P. J., Mandel, R. J., and Mair, R. G. (1992). Diencephalic lesions, learning impairments, and intact retrograde memory following acute thiamine deficiency in the rat. *Behavioural Brain Research, 48,* 177–185.

Langston, J. W. (1985). MPTP and Parkinson's disease. *Trends in Neurosciences, 8,* 79–83.

Lanska, D. J., and Lanska, M. J. (1994). Kluver-Bucy syndrome in juvenile neuronal ceroid lipofuscinosis. *Journal of Child Neurology, 9,* 67–69.

Larkin, J. E., Freeman, D. A., and Zucker, I. (2001). Low ambient temperature accelerates short-day responses in Siberian hamsters by altering responsiveness to melatonin. *Journal of Biological Rhythms, 16,* 76–86.

Larroche, J.-C. (1977). *Developmental pathology of the neonate.* Amsterdam: Excerpta Medica.

Larsson, J., Gulyas, B., and Roland, P. E. (1996). Cortical representation of self-paced finger movement. *Neuroreport, 7,* 463–468.

Laufer, R., and Changeux, J. P. (1989). Activity-dependent regulation of gene expression in muscle and neuronal cells. *Molecular Neurobiology, 3,* 1–53.

Lavie, P. (1996). *The enchanted world of sleep* (A. Berris, Trans.). New Haven, CT: Yale University Press.

Lavie, P., and Kripke, D. F. (1981). Ultradian circa 1 1/2 hour rhythms: A multioscillatory system. *Life Sciences, 29,* 2445–2450.

Lavond, D. G., Kim, J. J., and Thompson, R. F. (1993). Mammalian brain substrates of aversive classical conditioning. *Annual Review of Psychology, 44,* 317–342.

Laxova, R. (1994). Fragile X syndrome. *Advances in Pediatrics, 41,* 305–342.

Leber, S. M., Breedlove, S. M., and Sanes, J. R. (1990). Lineage, arrangement, and death of clonally related motoneurons in chick spinal cord. *Journal of Neuroscience, 10,* 2451–2462.

Lebrun, C. J., Blume, A., Herdegen, T., Seifert, K., et al. (1995). Angiotensin II induces a complex activation of transcription factors in the rat brain: Expression of Fos, Jun and Krox proteins. *Neuroscience, 65,* 93–99.

Ledent, C., Valverde, O., Cossu, G., Petitet, F., et al. (1999). Unresponsiveness to cannabinoids and reduced addictive effects of opiates in CB₁ receptor knockout mice. *Science, 283,* 401–404.

LeDoux, J. E. (1994). Emotion, memory and the brain. *Scientific American, 270*(6), 50–57.

LeDoux, J. E. (1995). Emotion: Clues from the brain. *Annual Review of Psychology, 46,* 209–235.

Lee, C.-K., Klopp, R. G., Weindruch, R., and Prolla, T. A. (1999). Gene expression profile of aging and its retardation by caloric restriction. *Science, 285,* 1390–1393.

Lee, C.-K., Weindruch, R., and Prolla, T. A. (2000). Gene-expression profile of the ageing brain in mice. *Nature Genetics, 25,* 294–297.

Lee, H.-K., Barbarosie, M., Kameyama, K., Bear, M. F., et al. (2000). Regulation of distinct AMPA receptor phosphorylation sites during bidirectional synaptic plasticity. *Nature, 405,* 955–959.

Lee, J.-M., Zipfel, G. J., and Choi, D. W. (1999). The changing landscape of ischaemic brain injury mechanisms. *Nature, 399*(6738 Suppl.), A7–A14.

Lee, K. S., Schottler, F., Oliver, M., and Lynch, G. (1980). Brief bursts of high-frequency stimulation produce two types of structural change in rat hippocampus. *Journal of Neurophysiology, 44,* 247–258.

Lee, P. H., Helms, M. C., Augustine, C. J., and Hall, W. C. (1997). Role of intrinsic synaptic circuitry in collicular sensorimotor integration. *Proceedings of the National Academy of Sciences, USA, 94,* 13299–13304.

Lefebvre, L., Whittle, P., Lascaris, E., and Finkelstein, A. (1997). Feeding innovations and forebrain size in birds. *Animal Behavior, 53,* 549–560.

Lefebvre, P. P., Malgrange, B., Staecker, H., Moonen, G., et al. (1993). Retinoic acid stimulates regeneration of mammalian auditory hair cells. *Science, 260,* 692–695.

Leibowitz, S. F. (1991). Brain neuropeptide Y: An integrator of endocrine, metabolic and behavioral processes. *Brain Research Bulletin, 27,* 333–337.

Leinders-Zufall, T., Lane, A. P., Puche, A. C., Ma, W., et al. (2000). Ultrasensitive pheromone detection by mammalian vomeronasal neurons. *Nature, 405,* 792–796.

LeMay, M. (1977). Asymmetries of the skull and handedness. *Journal of the Neurological Sciences, 32,* 243–253.

Lendvai, B., Stern, E. A., Chen, B., and Svoboda, K. (2000). Experience-dependent plasticity of dendritic spines in the developing rat barrel cortex *in vivo. Nature, 404,* 876–881.

Lenhoff, H. M., Wang, P. P., Greenberg, F., and Bellugi, U. (1997). Williams syndrome and the brain. *Scientific American, 277* (6), 68–73.

Lennie, P., Krauskopf, J., and Sclar, G. (1990). Chromatic mechanisms in striate cortex of macaque. *Journal of Neuroscience, 10,* 649–669.

Leon, M., Croskerry, P. G., and Smith, G. K. (1978). Thermal control of mother-young contact in rats. *Physiology & Behavior, 21,* 790–811.

Leonard, B. E. (1992). *Fundamentals of psychopharmacology.* New York: Wiley.

Leonardo, A., and Konishi, M. (1999). Decrystallization of adult birdsong by perturbation of auditory feedback. *Nature, 399,* 466–470.

Lepage, M., Ghaffar, O., Nyberg, L., and Tulving, E. (2000). Prefrontal cortex and episodic memory retrieval mode. *Proceedings of the National Academy of Sciences, USA, 97,* 506–511.

Lepage, M., Habib, R., and Tulving, E. (1998). Hippocampal PET activations of memory encoding and retrieval: The HIPER model. *Hippocampus, 8,* 313–322.

LeRoith, D., Shemer, J., and Roberts, C. T., Jr. (1992). Evolutionary origins of intercellular communication systems: Implications for mammalian biology. *Hormone Research, 38,* 1–6.

Lessard, N., Pare, M., Lepore, F., and Lassonde, M. (1998). Early-blind human subjects localize sound sources better than sighted subjects. *Nature, 395,* 278–280.

LeVay, S. (1991). A difference in hypothalamic structure between heterosexual and homosexual men. *Science, 253,* 1034–1037.

LeVay, S. (1996). *Queer science: The use and abuse of research into homosexuality.* Cambridge, MA: MIT Press.

Levenson, R. W., Ekman, P., and Friesen, W. V. (1990). Voluntary facial action generates emotion-specific autonomic nervous system activity. *Psychophysiology, 27,* 363–384.

Leventhal, A. G. (1979). Evidence that the different classes of relay cells of the cat's lateral geniculate nucleus terminate in different layers of the striate cortex. *Experimental Brain Research, 37,* 349–372.

Leventhal, A. G., Thompson, K. G., Liu, D., Zhou, Y., et al. (1995). Concomitant sensitivity to orientation, direction, and color of cells in layers 2, 3, and 4 of monkey striate cortex. *Journal of Neuroscience, 15,* 1808–1818.

Levi-Montalcini, R. (1963). In J. Allen (Ed.), *The nature of biological diversity.* New York: McGraw-Hill.

Levi-Montalcini, R. (1982). Developmental neurobiology and the natural history of nerve growth factor. *Annual Review of Neuroscience, 5,* 341–362.

Levine, J. D., Gordon, N. C., and Fields, H. L. (1978). The mechanism of placebo analgesia. *Lancet, 2,* 654–657.

Levine, J. S., and MacNichol, E. F. (1982). Color vision in fishes. *Scientific American, 246*(2), 140–149.

Levine, S., Haltmeyer, G. C., and Karas, G. G. (1967). Physiological and behavioral effects of infantile stimulation. *Physiology & Behavior, 2,* 55–59.

Levine, S., and Ursin, H. (1980). *Coping and health.* New York: Plenum.

Levinthal, F., Macagno, E., and Levinthal, C. (1976). Anatomy and development of identified cells in isogenic organisms. *Cold Spring Harbor Symposium on Quantitative Biology, 40,* 321–331.

Levitt, P., Harvey, J., Friedman, E., Simansky, K., et al. (1997). New evidence for neurotransmitter influences on brain development. *Trends in Neurosciences, 20,* 269–274.

Levy, D. L., Holzman, P. S., Matthysse, S., and Mendell, N. R. (1993). Eye tracking dysfunction and schizophrenia: A critical perspective. *Schizophrenia Bulletin, 19,* 461–536.

Lewin, G. R., and Barde, Y. A. (1996). Physiology of the neurotrophins. *Annual Review of Neuroscience, 19,* 289–317.

Lewis, D. O. (1990). Neuropsychiatric and experiential correlates of violent juvenile delinquency. *Neuropsychology Review, 1,* 125–136.

Lewis, D. O., Shankok, S. S., and Pincus, J. (1979). Juvenile male sexual assaulters. *American Journal of Psychiatry, 136,* 1194–1195.

Lewis, M. (2000). The emergence of human emotions. In M. Lewis and J. M. Haviland-Jones (Eds.), *Handbook of emotions* (2nd ed., pp. 265–280). New York: Guilford.

Lewis, R. (1998). Flies invade human genetics. *Scientist, 12,* 1, 4–5.

Lewy, A. J., Ahmed, S., Jackson, J. M., and Sack, R. L. (1992). Melatonin shifts human circadian rhythms according to a phase-response curve. *Chronobiology International, 9,* 380–392.

Ley, R. G., and Bryden, M. P. (1982). A dissociation of right and left hemispheric effects for recognizing emotional tone and verbal content. *Brain and Cognition, 1,* 3–9.

Lhermitte, F., Pillon, B., and Serdaru, M. (1986). Human autonomy and the frontal lobes. Part 1. Imitation and utilization behavior: A neuropsychological study of 75 patients. *Annals of Neurology, 19,* 326–335.

Li, P., Wilding, T. J., Kim, S. J., Calejesan, A. A., et al. (1999). Kainate-receptor-mediated sensory synaptic transmission in mammalian spinal cord. *Nature, 397,* 161–164.

Li, S., and Tator, C. H. (2000). Action of locally administered NMDA and AMPA/kainate receptor antagonists in spinal cord injury. *Neurological Research, 22,* 171–180.

Li, X. J., Li, S. H., Sharp, A. H., Nucifora, F. C., Jr., et al. (1995). A Huntingtin-associated protein enriched in brain with implications for pathology. *Nature, 378,* 398–402.

Li, X. J., Sharp, A. H., Li, S. H., Dawson, T. M., et al. (1996). Huntingtin-associated protein (HAP1): Discrete neuronal localizations in the brain resemble those of neuronal nitric oxide synthase. *Proceedings of the National Academy of Sciences, USA, 93,* 4839–4844.

Li, Y., Field, P. M., and Raisman, G. (1997). Repair of adult rat corticospinal tract by transplants of olfactory ensheathing cells. *Science, 277,* 2000–2002.

Licht, P., Frank, L. G., Pavgi, S., Yalcinkaya, T. M., et al. (1992). Hormonal correlates of "masculinization" in female spotted hyenas (*Crocuta crocuta*). 2. Maternal and fetal steroids. *Journal of Reproduction and Fertility, 95,* 463–474.

Lichtman, J. W., and Purves, D. (1980). The elimination of redundant preganglionic innervation to hamster sympathetic ganglion cells in early post-natal life. *Journal of Physiology (London), 301,* 213–228.

Lieberman, P. (1998). *Eve spoke: Human language and human evolution.* New York: Norton.

Liebowitz, M. R., Gorman, J. M., Fryer, A., Dillon, D., et al. (1986). Possible mechanisms for lactate's induction of panic. *American Journal of Psychiatry, 143,* 495–502.

Liepert, J., Bauder, H., Wolfgang, H. R., Miltner, W. H., et al. (2000). Treatment-induced cortical reorganization after stroke in humans. *Stroke, 31,* 1210–1216.

Lin, L., Faraco, J., Li, R., Kadotani, H., et al. (1999). The sleep disorder canine narcolepsy is caused by a mutation in the hypocretin (orexin) receptor 2 gene. *Cell, 98,* 365–376.

Lin, X. Y., and Glanzman, D. L. (1994). Long-term potentiation of *Aplysia* sensorimotor synapses in cell culture: Regulation by postsynaptic voltage. *Proceedings of the Royal Society of London. Series B: Biological Sciences, 255,* 113–118.

Lindemann, B. (1995). Sweet and salty: Transduction in taste. *News in Physiological Sciences, 10,* 166–170.

Linden, D. J. (1994). Long-term synaptic depression in the mammalian brain. *Neuron, 12,* 457–472.

Lindvall, O., Sawle, G., Widner, H., Rothwell, J. C., et al. (1994). Evidence for long-term survival and function of dopaminergic grafts in progressive Parkinson's disease. *Annals of Neurology, 35,* 172–180.

Liou, Y.-C., Tocilj, A., Davies, P., and Jia, Z. (2000). Mimicry of ice structure by surface hydroxyls and water of a beta-helix antifreeze protein. *Nature, 406,* 322–324.

Lisk, R. D. (1962). Diencephalic placement of estradiol and sexual receptivity in the female rat. *American Journal of Physiology, 203,* 493–496.

Lisman, J. (1989). A mechanism for the Hebb and the anti-Hebb processes underlying learning and memory. *Proceedings of the National Academy of Sciences, USA, 86,* 9574–9578.

Littlewood, E. A., and Muller, U. (2000). Stereocilia defects in the sensory hair cells of the inner ear in mice deficient in integrin alpha8beta1. *Nature Genetics, 24,* 424–428.

Liu, C. N., and Chambers, W. W. (1958). Intraspinal sprouting of dorsal root axons. *Archives of Neurology and Psychiatry, 79,* 46–61.

Liu, D., Diorio, J., Tannenbaum, B., Caldji, C., et al. (1997). Maternal care, hippocampal glucocorticoid receptors, and hypothalamic-pituitary-adrenal responses to stress. *Science, 277,* 1659–1662.

Liu, S., Qu, Y., Stewart, T. J., Howard, M. J., et al. (2000). Embryonic stem cells differentiate into oligodendrocytes and myelinate in culture and after spinal cord transplantation. *Proceedings of the National Academy of Sciences, USA, 97,* 6126–6131.

Liu, Y., Gao, J. H., Liotti, M., Pu, Y., et al. (1999). Temporal dissociation of parallel processing in the human subcortical outputs. *Nature, 400,* 364–367.

Liu, Y., Gao, J.-H., Liu, H.-L., and Fox, P. T. (2000). The temporal response of the brain after eating revealed by functional MRI. *Nature, 405,* 1058–1062.

Livingstone, M. S. (1998). Mechanisms of direction selectivity in macaque V1. *Neuron, 20,* 509–526.

Livingstone, M. S., and Hubel, D. (1984). Anatomy and physiology of a color system in the primate visual cortex. *Journal of Neuroscience, 4,* 309–356.

Livingstone, M. S., and Hubel, D. (1988). Segregation of form, color, movement, and depth: Anatomy, physiology, and perception. *Science, 240,* 740–749.

Lloyd, J. A. (1971). Weights of testes, thymi, and accessory reproductive glands in relation to rank in paired and grouped house mice (*Mus musculus*). *Proceedings of the Society for Experimental Biology and Medicine, 137,* 19–22.

Lockhart, M., and Moore, J. W. (1975). Classical differential and operant conditioning in rabbits (*Orycytolagus cuniculus*) with septal lesions. *Journal of Comparative and Physiological Psychology, 88,* 147–154.

Loeb, G. E. (1990). Cochlear prosthetics. *Annual Review of Neuroscience, 13,* 357–371.

Loewenstein, W. R. (1971). Mechano-electric transduction in the Pacinian corpuscle. Initiation of sensory impulses in mechanoreception. In *Handbook of sensory physiology: Vol. 1. Principles of receptor physiology* (pp. 269–290). Berlin: Springer.

Logan, C. G., and Grafton, S. T. (1995). Functional anatomy of human eye-blink conditioning determined with regional cerebral glucose metabolism and positron emission tomography. *Proceedings of the National Academy of Sciences, USA, 92,* 7500–7504.

Logothetis, N. K., Guggenberger, H., Peled, S., and Pauls, J. (1999). Functional imaging of the monkey brain. *Nature Neuroscience, 2,* 555–562.

Lomassese, S. S., Strambi, C., Strambi, A., Charpin, P., et al. (2000). Influence of environmental stimulation on neurogenesis in the adult insect brain. *Journal of Neurobiology, 45,* 162–171.

Löwel, S., and Singer, W. (1992). Selection of intrinsic horizontal connections in the visual cortex by correlated neuronal activity. *Science, 255,* 209–212.

Lukowiak, K., and Colebrook, E. (1988–1989). Neuronal mechanisms of learning in an in vitro *Aplysia* preparation: Sites other than the sensory-motor neuron synapse are involved. *Journal de Physiologie, 83,* 198–206.

Luria, A. R. (1987). *The mind of a mnemonist.* Cambridge, MA: Harvard University Press.

Lush, I. E. (1989). The genetics of tasting in mice. VI. Saccharin, acesulfame, dulcin and sucrose. *Genetical Research, 53,* 95–99.

Lynch, E. D., Lee, M. K., Morrow, J. E., Welcsh, P. L., et al. (1997). Nonsyndromic deafness DFNA1 associated with mutation of a human homolog of the *Drosophila* gene *diaphanous. Science, 278,* 1315–1318.

Lynch, G., and Baudry, M. (1984). The biochemistry of memory: A new and specific hypothesis. *Science, 224,* 1057–1063.

Lynch, G., Larson, J., Staubli, U., and Granger, R. (1991). Variants of synaptic potentiation and different types of memory operations in hippocampus and related structures. In L. R. Squire, N. M. Weinberger, G. Lynch, and J. L. McGaugh (Eds.), *Memory: Organization and locus of change* (pp. 330–363). New York: Oxford University Press.

Macagno, E., Lopresti, U., and Levinthal, C. (1973). Structural development of neuronal connections in isogenic organisms: Variations and similarities in the optic system of *Daphnia magna. Proceedings of the National Academy of Sciences, USA, 70,* 57–61.

Mace, G. M., Harvey, P. H., and Clutton-Brock, T. H. (1981). Brain size and ecology in small mammals. *Journal of Zoology, 193,* 333–354.

Machón, R. A., Mednick, S. A., and Huttunen, M. O. (1997). Adult major affective disorder after prenatal exposure to an influenza epidemic. *Archives of General Psychiatry, 54,* 322–328.

MacKay, D. G., Stewart, R., and Burke, D. M. (1998). H.M. revisited: Relations between language comprehension, memory, and the hippocampal system. *Journal of Cognitive Neuroscience, 10,* 377–394.

Macklis, J. D. (2001). New memories from new neurons. *Nature, 410,* 314–316.

MacLean, P. D. (1949). Psychosomatic disease and the "visceral brain": Recent developments bearing on the Papez theory of emotion. *Psychosomatic Medicine, 11,* 338–353.

MacLean, P. D. (1970). The triune brain, emotion, and scientific bias. In F. O. Schmitt (Ed.), *The neurosciences* (pp. 336–348). New York: Rockefeller University.

Madden, J. (2001). Sex, bowers and brains. *Proceedings of the Royal Society of London Series B-Biological Sciences,* 268 (1469), 833–838.

Maddock, R. J. (1999). The retrosplenial cortex and emotion: New insights from functional imaging in the human brain. *Trends in Neurosciences, 22,* 310–316.

Madrazo, I., Franco-Bourland, R., Ostrosky-Solis, F., Aguilera, M., et al. (1990). Fetal homotransplants (ventral mesencephalon and adrenal tissue) to the striatum of parkinsonian subjects. *Archives of Neurology, 47,* 1281–1285.

Maffei, L., and Fiorentini, A. (1973). The visual cortex as a spatial frequency analyser. *Vision Research, 13,* 1255–1267.

Magavi, S. S., Leavitt, B. R., and Macklis, J. D. (2000). Induction of neurogenesis in the neocortex of adult mice. *Nature, 405,* 951–955.

Magee, J. C., and Cook, E. P. (2000). Somatic EPSP amplitude is independent of synapse location in hippocampal pyramidal neurons. *Nature Neuroscience, 3,* 895–903.

Magnusson, A., and Axelsson, J. (1993). The prevalence of seasonal affective disorder is low among descendants of Icelandic emigrants in Canada. *Archives of General Psychiatry, 50,* 947–951.

Magnusson, A., and Stefansson, J. G. (1993). Prevalence of seasonal affective disorder in Iceland. *Archives of General Psychiatry, 50,* 941–946.

Maguire, E. A., Frackowiak, R. S. J., and Frith, C. D. (1997). Recalling routes around London: Activation of the right hippocampus in taxi drivers. *Journal of Neuroscience, 17,* 7103–7110.

Maguire, E. A., Gadian, D. G., Johnsrude, I. S., Good, C. D., Ashburner, J., Frackowiak, R. S., and Frith, C. D. (2000). Navigation-related structural change in the hippocampi of taxi drivers. *Proceedings of the National Academy of Sciences, USA, 97,* 4398–4403.

Mainen, Z. F., Malinow, R., and Svoboda, K. (1999). Synaptic calcium transients in single spines indicate that NMDA receptors are not saturated. *Nature, 399,* 151–155.

Mair, W. G. P., Warrington, E. K., and Wieskrantz, L. (1979). Memory disorder in Korsakoff's psychosis. *Brain, 102,* 749–783.

Maki, P. M., and Resnick, S. M. (2000). Longitudinal effects of estrogen replacement therapy on pet cerebral blood flow and cognition. *Neurobiology of Aging, 21,* 373–383.

Malberg, J. E., Eisch, A. J., Nestler, E. J., and Duman, R. S. (2000). Chronic antidepressant treatment increases neurogenesis in adult rat hippocampus. *Journal of Neuroscience, 20,* 9104–9110.

Malenka, R. C., and Nicoll, R. A. (1999). Long-term potentiation—A decade of progress? *Science, 285,* 1870–1874.

Maletic-Savatic, M., Malinow, R., and Svoboda, K. (1999). Rapid dendritic morphogenesis in CA1 hippocampal dendrites induced by synaptic activity. *Science, 283,* 1923–1927.

Malinow, R., and Tsien, R. W. (1990). Presynaptic enhancement shown by whole-cell recordings of long-term potentiation in hippocampal slices. *Nature, 346,* 177–180.

Manetto, V., Medori, R., Cortelli, P., Montagna, P., et al. (1992). Fatal familial insomnia: Clinical and pathologic study of five new cases. *Neurology, 42,* 312–319.

Manfredi, M., Bini, G., Cruccu, G., Accornero, N., et al. (1981). Congenital absence of pain. *Archives of Neurology, 38,* 507–511.

Manger, P. R., Collins, R., and Pettigrew, J. D. (1998). The development of the electroreceptors of the platypus (*Ornithorhynchus anatinus*). *Philosophical Transactions of the Royal Society of London. Series B: Biological Sciences, 353,* 1171–1186.

Mangiarini, L., Sathasivam, K., Seller, M., Cozens, B., et al. (1996). Exon 1 of the HD gene with an expanded CAG repeat is sufficient to cause a progressive neurological phenotype in transgenic mice. *Cell, 87,* 493–506.

Mani, S. K., Fienberg, A. A., O'Callaghan, J. P., Snyder, G. L., et al. (2000). Requirement for DARPP-32 in progesterone-facilitated sexual receptivity in female rats and mice. *Science, 287,* 1053–1056.

Manova, M. G., and Kostadinova, I. I. (2000). Some aspects of the immunotherapy of multiple sclerosis. *Folia Medica, 42*(1), 5–9.

Mantyh, P. W., Demaster, E., Malhotra, A., Ghilardi, J. R., et al. (1995). Receptor endocytosis and dendrite reshaping in spinal neurons after somatosensory stimulation. *Science, 268,* 1629–1632.

Mantyh, P. W., Rogers, S. D., Honore, P., Allen, B. J., et al. (1997). Inhibition of hyperalgesia by ablation of lamina I spinal neurons expressing the substance P receptor. *Science, 278,* 275–279.

Maquet, P., Laureys, S., Peigneux, P., Fuchs, S., et al. (2000). Experience-dependent changes in cerebral activation during human REM sleep. *Nature Neuroscience, 3,* 831–836.

Marcus, G. F., Vijayan, S., Bandi Rao, S., and Vishton, P. M. (1999). Rule learning by seven-month-old infants. *Science, 283,* 77–80.

Margoliash, D. (1986). Preference for autogenous song by auditory neurons in a song system of the white-crowned sparrow. *Journal of Neuroscience, 6,* 1643–1661.

Margoliash, D., and Fortune, E. S. (1992). Temporal and harmonic combination-sensitive neurons in the zebra finch's HVc. *Journal of Neuroscience, 12,* 4309–4326.

Margraf, J., and Roth, W. T. (1986). Sodium lactate infusions and panic attacks: A review and critique. *Psychosomatic Medicine, 48,* 23–50.

Mariani, J., and Changeaux, J.-P. (1981). Ontogenesis of olivocerebellar relationships. I. Studies by intracellular recordings of the multiple innervation of Purkinje cells by climbing fibers in the developing rat cerebellum. *Journal of Neuroscience, 1,* 696–702.

Mark, R. F. (1980). Synaptic repression at neuromuscular junctions. *Physiological Reviews, 60,* 355–395.

Mark, V. H., and Ervin, F. R. (1970). *Violence and the brain.* New York: Harper & Row.

Marlatt, G. A. (1992). Substance abuse: Implications of a biopsychological model for prevention, treatment, and relapse prevention. In J. Grabowski and G. R. VandenBos (Eds.), *Psychopharmacology: Basic mechanisms and applied interventions* (pp. 131–162). Washington, DC: American Psychological Association.

Marler, P. (1970). Birdsong and speech development: Could there be parallels? *American Scientist, 58,* 669–673.

Marler, P. (1991). Song-learning behavior: The interface with neuroethology. *Trends in Neurosciences, 14,* 199–206.

Marler, P., and Peters, S. (1982). Developmental overproduction and selective attrition: New processes in the epigenesis of birdsong. *Developmental Psychobiology, 15,* 369–378.

Marler, P., and Sherman, V. (1983). Song structure without auditory feedback: Emendations of the auditory template hypothesis. *Journal of Neuroscience, 3,* 517–531.

Marler, P., and Sherman, V. (1985). Innate differences in singing behaviour of sparrows reared in isolation from adult conspecific song. *Animal Behavior, 33,* 57–71.

Marsden, C. D., Rothwell, J. C., and Day, B. L. (1984). The use of peripheral feedback in the control of movement. *Trends in Neurosciences, 7,* 253–257.

Marshall, J. F., Richardson, J. S., and Teitelbaum, P. (1974). Nigrostriatal bundle damage and the lateral hypothalamic syndrome. *Journal of Comparative and Physiological Psychology, 87,* 800–830.

Martin, A., Wiggs, C. L., Ungerleider, L. G., and Haxby, J. V. (1996). Neural correlates of category-specific knowledge. *Nature, 379,* 649–652.

Martin, J. V., Wyatt, R. J., and Mendelson, W. B. (1985). Growth hormone secretion in sleep and waking. In W. P. Koella, E. Ruther, and H. Schulz (Eds.), *Sleep '84* (pp. 185–188). Stuttgart, Germany: Gustav Fischer.

Martin, W. R., and Hayden, M. R. (1987). Cerebral glucose and dopa metabolism in movement disorders. *Canadian Journal of Neurological Sciences, 14,* 448–451.

Martina, M., Vida, I., and Jonas, P. (2000). Distal initiation and active propagation of action potentials in interneuron dendrites. *Science, 287,* 295–300.

Martinez, A., Anllo-Vento, L., Sereno, M. I., Frank, L. R., et al. (1999). Involvement of striate and exttrastriate visual cortical areas in spatial attention. *Nature Neuroscience, 2,* 364–369.

Martinez, J. L., Jr., Barea-Rodriguez, E. J., and Derrick, B. E. (1998). Long-term potentiation, long-term depression, and learning. In J. L. Martinez, Jr., and R. P. Kesner (Eds.), *Neurobiology of learning and memory* (pp. 211–246). San Diego, CA: Academic Press.

Martinez, J. L., and Derrick, B. E. (1996). Long-term potentiation and learning. *Annual Review of Psychology, 47,* 33.

Martinez-Serrano, A., Fischer, W., Soderstrom, S., Ebendal, T., et al. (1996). Long-term functional recovery from age-induced spatial memory impairments by nerve growth factor gene transfer to the rat basal forebrain. *Proceedings of the National Academy of Sciences, USA, 93,* 6355–6360.

Martuza, R. L., Chiocca, E. A., Jenike, M. A., Giriunas, I. E., et al. (1990). Stereotactic radiofrequency thermal cingulotomy for obsessive compulsive disorder. *Journal of Neuropsychiatry and Clinical Neurosciences, 2,* 331–336.

Marucha, P. T., Kiecolt-Glaser, J. K., and Favagehi, M. (1998). Mucosal wound healing is impaired by examination stress. *Psychosomatic Medicine, 60,* 362–365.

Marx, J. L. (1985). "Anxiety peptide" found in brain. *Science, 227,* 934.

Marzani, D., and Wallman, J. (1997). Growth of the two layers of the chick sclera is modulated reciprocally by visual conditions. *Investigative Ophthalmology and Visual Science, 38,* 1726–1739.

Masliah, E., Salmon, D. P., Butters, N., DeTeresa, R., et al. (1991). Physical basis of cognitive alterations in Alzheimer's disease: Synapse loss is the major correlate of cognitive impairment. *Annals of Neurology, 30,* 572–580.

Masters, W. H., and Johnson, V. E. (1966). *Human sexual response.* Boston: Little, Brown.

Masters, W. H., and Johnson, V. E. (1970). *Human sexual inadequacy.* Boston: Little, Brown.

Masters, W. H., Johnson, V. E., and Kolodny, R. C. (1994). *Heterosexuality.* New York: HarperCollins.

Masterton, R. B. (1993). Central auditory system. *ORL; Journal of Oto-Rhino-Laryngology and Its Related Specialties, 55,* 159–163.

Masterton, R. B., and Imig, T. J. (1984). Neural mechanisms for sound localization. *Annual Review of Physiology, 46,* 275–287.

Mastrianni, J. A., Nixon, R., Layzer, R., Telling, G. C., et al. (1999). Prion protein conformation in a patient with sporadic fatal insomnia. *New England Journal of Medicine, 340,* 1630–1638.

Mateo, J. M., and Johnston, R. E. (2000). Kin recognition and the "armpit effect": Evidence of self-referent phenotype matching. *Proceedings of the Royal Society of London. Series B: Biological Sciences, 267,* 695–700.

Mathias, R. (1994). NIDA, the FDA, and nicotine regulation. *NIDA Notes, 9,* 5, 7.

Matser, E. J., Kessels, A. G., Lezak, M. D., Jordan, B. D., et al. (1999). Neuropsychological impairment in amateur soccer players. *JAMA, 282,* 971–973.

Matsuda, L. A., Lolait, S. J., Brownstein, M. J., Young, A. C., et al. (1990). Structure of a cannabinoid receptor and functional expression of the cloned cDNA. *Nature, 346,* 561.

Matsunami, H., Montmayeur, J. P., and Buck, L. B. (2000). A family of candidate taste receptors in human and mouse. *Nature, 404,* 601–604.

Matthews, G. (1996). Synaptic exocytosis and endocytosis: Capacitance measurements. *Current Opinion in Neurobiology, 6,* 358–364.

Matthies, H. (1989). Neurobiological aspects of learning and memory. *Annual Review of Psychology, 40,* 381–404.

Mattson, S. N., Riley, E. P., Gramling, L., Delis, D. C., et al. (1998). Neuropsychological comparison of alcohol-exposed children with or without physical features of fetal alcohol syndrome. *Neuropsychology, 12,* 146–153.

McAllister, A. K., Katz, L. C., and Lo, D. C. (1997). Opposing roles for endogenous BDNF and NT-3 in regulating cortical dendritic growth. *Neuron, 18,* 767–778.

McBurney, D. H., Smith, D. V., and Shick, T. R. (1972). Gustatory cross adaptation: Sourness and bitterness. *Perception & Psychophysics, 11,* 2228–2232.

McCall, W. V., and Edinger, J. D. (1992). Subjective total insomnia: An example of sleep state misperception. *Sleep, 15,* 71–73.

McCann, U. D., Seiden, L. S., Rubin, L. J., and Ricaurte, G. A. (1997). Brain serotonin neurotoxicity and primary pulmonary hypertension from fenfluramine and dexfenfluramine. A systematic review of the evidence. *JAMA, 278,* 666–672.

McCarthy, R. A., and Warrington, E. K. (1990). *Cognitive neuropsychology: A clinical introduction.* San Diego, CA: Academic Press.

McClintock, M. K. (1971). Menstrual synchrony and suppression. *Nature, 229,* 244–245.

McComb, K., Moss, C., Sayialel, S., and Baker, L. (2000). Unusually extensive networks of vocal recognition in African elephants. *Animal Behavior, 59*, 1103–1109.

McCormick, D. A., and Thompson, R. F. (1984). Cerebellum: Essential involvement in the classically conditioned eyelid response. *Science, 223*, 296–299.

McDonald, J. J., Teder-Sälejärvi, W. A., and Hillyard, S. A. (2000). Involuntary orienting to sound improves visual perception. *Nature, 407*, 906–908.

McDonald, R. J., and White, N. M. (1993). A triple dissociation of memory systems: Hippocampus, amygdala and dorsal striatum. *Behavioral Neuroscience, 107*, 3–22.

McFadden, D. (1993a). A masculinizing effect on the auditory systems of human females having male co-twins. *Proceedings of the National Academy of Sciences, USA, 90*, 11900–11904.

McFadden, D. (1993b). A speculation about the parallel ear asymmetries and sex differences in hearing sensitivity and otoacoustic emissions. *Hearing Research, 68*, 143–151.

McFadden, D., and Champlin, C. A. (1990). Reductions in overshoot during aspirin use. *Journal of the Acoustical Society of America, 87*, 2634–2642.

McFadden, D., and Pasanen, E. (1998). Comparison of the auditory systems of heterosexuals and homosexuals: Click-evoked otoacoustic emissions. *Proceedings of the National Academy of Sciences, USA, 95*, 2709–2713.

McGaugh, J. L. (1966). Time-dependent processes in memory storage. *Science, 153*, 1351–1358.

McGaugh, J. L. (1968). A multi-trace view of memory storage processes. In D. Bovet (Ed.), *Attuali orientamenti della ricerca sull' apprendimento e la memoria* (pp. 13-24). Rome: Academia Nazionale dei Lincei.

McGaugh, J. L. (1992). Neuromodulatory systems and the regulation of memory storage. In L. R. Squire and N. Butters (Eds.), *Neuropsychology of memory* (2nd ed., pp. 386–401). New York: Guilford.

McGaugh, J. L. (1995). Emotional activation, neuromodulatory systems, and memory. In D. L. Schacter (Ed.), *Memory distortions: How minds, brains, and societies reconstruct the past* (pp. 255–273). Cambridge, MA: Harvard University Press.

McGaugh, J. L., and Herz, M. J. (1972). *Memory consolidation.* San Francisco: Albion.

McGaugh, J. L., Introini-Collison, I. B., Cahill, L. F., Castellano, C., et al. (1993). Neuromodulatory systems and memory storage: Role of the amygdala. *Behavioural Brain Research, 58*, 81–90.

McGaugh, J. L., Weinberger, N. M., and Lynch, G. (Eds.). (1995). Brain and memory: Modulation and mediation of neuroplasticity. New York: Oxford University Press.

McGeer, P., McGeer, E., Suzuki, J., Dolman, C., et al. (1984). Aging, Alzheimer's disease, and the cholinergic system of the basal forebrain. *Neurology, 34*, 741–745.

McGue, M. (1999). The behavioral genetics of alcoholism. *Current Trends in Psychological Science, 8*(4), 109–115.

McKee, R. D., and Squire, L. R. (1993). On the development of declarative memory. *Journal of Experimental Psychology: Learning, Memory, and Cognition, 19*, 397–404.

McKenna, K. (1999). The brain is the master organ in sexual function: Central nervous system control of male and female sexual function. *International Journal of Impotence Research, 11*(Suppl. 1), S48–S55.

McKernan, M. G., and Shinnick-Gallagher, P. (1997). Fear conditioning induces a lasting potentiation of synaptic currents in vitro. *Nature, 390*, 607–611.

McKim, W. A. (1991). *Drugs and behavior: An introduction to behavioral pharmacology* (2nd ed.). Englewood Cliffs, NJ: Prentice Hall.

McKinney, T. D., and Desjardins, C. (1973). Postnatal development of the testis, fighting behavior, and fertility in house mice. *Biology of Reproduction, 9*, 279–294.

McKinney, W. T. (1988). *Models of mental disorders: A new comparative psychiatry.* New York: Plenum.

McLaughlin, S. K., McKinnon, P. J., Spickofsky, N., Danho, W., et al. (1994). Molecular cloning of G proteins and phosphodiesterases from rat taste cells. *Physiology & Behavior, 56*, 1157–1164.

McMahon, H. T., Foran, P., Dolly, J. O., Verhage, M., et al. (1992). Tetanus toxin and botulinum toxins type A and B inhibit glutamate, gamma-aminobutyric acid, aspartate, and met-enkephalin release from synaptosomes. Clues to the locus of action. *Journal of Biological Chemistry, 267*, 21338–21343.

McNamara, J. O. (1984). Role of neurotransmitters in seizure mechanisms in the kindling model of epilepsy. *Federation Proceedings, 43*, 2516–2520.

McNamara, J. O. (1999). Emerging insights into the genesis of epilepsy. *Nature, 399*(6738 Suppl.), A15–A22.

Meckler, R. J., Mack, J. L., and Bennett, R. (1979). Sign language aphasia in a non-deaf mute. *Neurology, 29*, 1037–1040.

Meddis, R. (1975). On the function of sleep. *Animal Behavior, 23*, 676–691.

Meddis, R. (1977). *The sleep instinct.* London: Routledge & Kegan Paul.

Meddis, R. (1979). The evolution and function of sleep. In D. A. Oakley and H. C. Plotkin (Eds.), *Brain, behavior and evolution.* London: Methuen.

Mednick, S. A., Huttunen, M. O., and Machon, R. A. (1994). Prenatal influenza infections and adult schizophrenia. *Schizophrenia Bulletin, 20*, 263–267.

Medori, R., Montagna, P., Tritschler, H. J., LeBlanc, A., Cortelli, P., Tinuper, P., Lugaresi, E., and Gambetti, P. (1992). Fatal familial insomnia: A second kindred with mutation of prion protein gene at codon 178. *Neurology, 42*, 669–670.

Mega, M. S., and Cummings, J. L. (1994). Frontal-subcortical circuits and neuropsychiatric disorders. *Journal of Neuropsychiatry and Clinical Neurosciences, 6*, 358–370.

Meisel, R. L., and Luttrell, V. R. (1990). Estradiol increases the dendritic length of ventromedial hypothalamic neurons in female Syrian hamsters. *Brain Research Bulletin, 25*, 165–168.

Meisel, R. L., and Sachs, B. D. (1994). The physiology of male sexual behavior. In E. Knobil and J. D. Neill (Eds.), *The physiology of reproduction* (2nd ed., Vol. 1, pp. 3–105). New York: Raven.

Mello, C. V., and Clayton, D. F. (1994). Song-induced ZENK gene expression in auditory pathways of songbird brain and its relation to the song control system. *Journal of Neuroscience, 14*, 6652–6666.

Melzack, R. (1984). Neuropsychological basis of pain measurement. *Advances in Pain Research, 323*–341.

Melzack, R. (1990). The tragedy of needless pain. *Scientific American, 262*(2), 27–33.

Melzack, R., and Wall, P. D. (1965). Pain mechanisms: A new history. *Science, 150*, 971–979.

Mendel, G. (1967). *Experiments in plant hybridisation* [Royal Horticultural Society of London, Trans.]. Cambridge, MA: Harvard University Press.

Mendelson, W. B. (1997). Efficacy of melatonin as a hypnotic agent. *Journal of Biological Rhythms, 12*, 651–656.

Meredith, M. A., and Stein, B. E. (1983). Interactions among converging sensory inputs in the superior colliculus. *Science, 221*, 389–391.

Merigan, W. H., and Maunsell, J. H. (1993). How parallel are the primate visual pathways? *Annual Review of Neuroscience, 16*, 369–402.

Merzenich, M. M., and Jenkins, W. M. (1993). Reorganization of cortical representations of the hand following alterations of skin inputs induced by nerve injury, skin island transfers, and experience. *Journal of Hand Therapy, 6*, 89–104.

Merzenich, M. M., and Kaas, J. H. (1980). Principles of organization of sensory-perceptual systems in mammals. *Progress in Psychobiology and Physiological Psychology, 9*.

Merzenich, M. M., Schreiner, C., Jenkins, W., and Wang, X. (1993). Neural mechanisms underlying temporal integration, segmentation, and input sequence representation: Some implications for the origin of learning disabilities. *Annals of the New York Academy of Sciences, 682*, 1–22.

Mesulam, M.-M. (1985). Attention, confusional states and neglect. In M.-M. Mesulam (Ed.), *Principles of behavioral neurology.* Philadelphia: Davis.

Mesulam, M. M. (1989). Behavioral neuroanatomy of cholinergic innervation in the primate cerebral cortex. *EXS, 57*, 1–11.

Miaskiewicz, S. L., Stricker, E. M., and Verbalis, J. G. (1989). Neurohypophyseal secretion in response to cholecystokinin but not meal-induced gastric distention in humans. *Journal of Clinical Endocrinology and Metabolism, 68*, 837–843.

Micheva, K., and Beaulieu, C. (1996). Quantitative aspects of synaptogenesis in the rat barrel field cortex with special reference to GABA circuitry. *Journal of Comparative Neurology, 373*, 340–354.

Middlebrooks, J. C., and Pettigrew, J. D. (1981). Functional classes of neurons in primary auditory cortex of the cat distinguished by sensitivity to sound location. *Journal of Neuroscience, 1*, 107–120.

Mignot, E., Nishino, S., Sharp, L. H., Arrigoni, J., et al. (1993). Heterozygosity at the canarc-1 locus can confer susceptibility for narcolepsy: Induction of cataplexy in heterozygous asymptomatic dogs after administration of a combination of drugs acting on monoaminergic and cholinergic systems. *Journal of Neuroscience, 13*, 1057–1064.

Mignot, E., Wang, C., Rattazzi, C., Gaiser, C., et al. (1991). Genetic linkage of autosomal recessive canine narcolepsy with a mu immunoglobulin heavy-chain switch-like segment. *Proceedings of the National Academy of Sciences, USA, 88*, 3475–3478.

Miles, L. E., and Dement, W. C. (1980). Sleep and aging. *Sleep, 3,* 1220.

Miller, G. F. (2000). *The mating mind: How sexual choice shaped the evolution of human nature.* New York: Doubleday.

Miller, J. M., and Spelman, F. A. (1990). *Cochlear implants: Models of the electrically stimulated ear.* New York: Springer.

Milner, B. (1965). Memory disturbance after bilateral hippocampal lesions. In P. M. Milner and S. E. Glickman (Eds.), *Cognitive processes and the brain; An enduring problem in psychology.* Princeton, NJ: Van Nostrand.

Milner, B. (1970). Memory and the medial temporal regions of the brain. In D. H. Pribram and D. E. Broadbent (Eds.), *Biology of memory.* New York: Academic Press.

Milner, P. M. (1992). The functional nature of neuronal oscillations. *Trends in Neurosciences, 15,* 387–388.

Milner, P. M. (1993). The mind and Donald O. Hebb. *Scientific American, 268*(1), 124–129.

Mirsky, A. F., and Duncan, C. C. (1986). Etiology and expression of schizophrenia: Neurobiological and psychosocial factors. *Annual Review of Psychology, 37,* 291–321.

Mishina, M., Kurosaki, T., Tobimatsu, T., Morimoto, Y., et al. (1984). Expression of functional acetylcholine receptor from cloned cDNAs. *Nature, 307,* 604–608.

Mishkin, M., and Ungerleider, L. (1982). Contribution of striate inputs to the visuospatial functions of parieto-preoccipital cortex in monkeys. *Behavioural Brain Research, 6,* 57–77.

Miyashita, Y. (1993). Inferior temporal cortex: Where visual perception meets memory. *Annual Review of Neuroscience, 16,* 245–263.

Mizumori, S. J. Y., Rosenzweig, M. R., and Bennett, E. L. (1985). Long-term working memory in the rat: Effects of hippocampally applied anisomycin. *Behavioral Neuroscience, 99,* 220–232.

Moghaddam, B., and Adams, B. W. (1998). Reversal of phencyclidine effects by a group II metabotropic glutamate receptor agonist in rats. *Science, 281,* 1349–1352.

Mohammed, A. (2001). *Enrichment and the brain. Plasticity in the adult brain: From genes to neurotherapy.* 22nd International Summer School of Brain Research, Amsterdam, Netherlands.

Mohammed, A., Henriksson, B. G., Soderstrom, S., Ebendal, T., et al. (1993). Environmental influences on the central nervous system and their implications for the aging rat. *Behavioural Brain Research, 23,* 182–191.

Moldin, S. O., Reich, T., and Rice, J. P. (1991). Current perspectives on the genetics of unipolar depression. *Behavior Genetics, 21,* 211–242.

Mombaerts, P. (1999). Seven-transmembrane proteins as odorant and chemosensory receptors. *Science, 286,* 707–711.

Monakow, C. von. (1914). *Die Lokalisation im Grosshirn und der Abbau der Funktion durch kortikale Herde.* Wiesbaden, Germany: Bergmann.

Moncada, S., Palmer, R. M., and Higgs, E. A. (1991). Nitric oxide: Physiology, pathophysiology, and pharmacology. *Pharmacological Reviews, 43,* 109–142.

Money, J., and Ehrhardt, A. A. (1972). *Man and woman, boy and girl.* Baltimore: Johns Hopkins University Press.

Montague, C. T., Farooqi, I. S., Whitehead, J. P., Soos, M. A., et al. (1997). Congenital leptin deficiency is associated with severe early-onset obesity in humans. *Nature, 387,* 903–908.

Monti-Bloch, L., Jennings-White, C., Dolberg, D. S., and Berliner, D. L. (1994). The human vomeronasal system. *Psychoneuroendocrinology, 19,* 673–686.

Moore, C. L., Dou, H., and Juraska, J. M. (1992). Maternal stimulation affects the number of motor neurons in a sexually dimorphic nucleus of the lumbar spinal cord. *Brain Research, 572,* 52–56.

Moore, G. J., Bebchuk, J. M., Wilds, I. B., Chen, G., et al. (2000). Lithium-induced increase in human brain grey matter. *Lancet, 356,* 241-242.

Moore, R. Y. (1983). Organization and function of a central nervous system circadian oscillator: The suprachiasmatic nucleus. *Federation Proceedings, 42,* 2783–2789.

Moore, R. Y., and Eichler, V. B. (1972). Loss of circadian adrenal corticosterone rhythm following suprachiasmatic lesions in the rat. *Brain Research, 42,* 201–206.

Moore-Ede, M. C. (1982). *The clocks that time us: Physiology of the circadian timing system.* Cambridge, MA: Harvard University Press.

Moran, D. T., Jafek, B. W., and Rowley, J. C. (1991). The vomeronasal (Jacobson's) organ in man: Ultrastructure and frequency of occurrence. *Journal of Steroid Biochemistry and Molecular Biology, 39,* 545–552.

Moran, E. F. (1981). Human adaptation to arctic zones. *Annual Review of Anthropology, 10,* 1–25.

Morford, J. P., and Mayberry, R. I. (2000). A reexamination of "early exposure" and its implications for language acquisition by eye. In C.

Chamberlain, J. P. Morford, and R. I. Mayberry (Eds.), *Language acquisition by eye* (pp. 111-127). Mahwah, NJ: Erlbaum.

Mori, E., Hirono, N., Yamashita, H., Imamura, T., et al. (1997). Premorbid brain size as a determinant of reserve capacity against intellectual decline in Alzheimer's disease. *American Journal of Psychiatry, 154,* 18–24.

Mori, K., Nagao, H., and Yoshihara, Y. (1999). The olfactory bulb: Coding and processing of odor molecule information. *Science, 286,* 711–715.

Morihisa, J., and McAnulty, G. B. (1985). Structure and function: Brain electrical activity mapping and computed tomography in schizophrenia. *Biological Psychiatry, 20,* 3–19.

Morrell, F. (1991). The role of secondary epileptogenesis in human epilepsy [Editorial]. *Archives of Neurology, 48,* 1221–1224.

Morrison, A. R. (1983). A window on the sleeping brain. *Scientific American, 248*(4), 94–102.

Morrison, R. G., and Nottebohm, F. (1993). Role of a telencephalic nucleus in the delayed song learning of socially isolated zebra finches. *Journal of Neurobiology, 24,* 1045–1064.

Mortensen, P. B., Pedersen, C. B., Westergaard, T., Wohlfahrt, J., et al. (1999). Effects of family history and place and season of birth on the risk of schizophrenia. *New England Journal of Medicine, 340,* 603–608.

Moruzzi, G. (1972). The sleep-waking cycle. *Ergebnisse der Physiologie, biologischen Chemie und experimentellen Pharmakologie, 64,* 1–165.

Moruzzi, G., and Magoun, H. W. (1995). Brain stem reticular formation and activation of the EEG. *Journal of Neuropsychiatry and Clinical Neurosciences, 7,* 251–267.

Moscovitch, M. (1985). Memory from infancy to old age: Implications for theories of normal and pathological memory. *Annals of the New York Academy of Sciences, 444,* 78–96.

Moscovitch, M., and Olds, J. (1982). Asymmetries in spontaneous facial expressions and their possible relation to hemispheric specialization. *Neuropsychologia, 20,* 71–81.

Mott, F. W. (1895). Experimental inquiry upon the afferent tracts of the central nervous system of the monkey. *Brain, 18,* 1–20.

Mountcastle, V. B. (1979). An organizing principle for cerebral function: The unit module and the distributed system. In F. O. Schmitt and F. G. Worden (Eds.), *The neurosciences: Fourth study program* (pp. 21-24). Cambridge, MA: MIT Press.

Mountcastle, V. B. (1984). Central nervous mechanisms in mechanoreceptive sensibility. In I. Darian-Smith (Ed.), *Handbook of physiology, Section 1: Vol. 3. Sensory processes* (pp. 789–878). Bethesda, MD: American Physiological Society.

Mountcastle, V. B., Andersen, R. A., and Motter, B. C. (1981). The influence of attentive fixation upon the excitability of the light-sensitive neurons of the posterior parietal cortex. *Journal of Neuroscience, 1,* 1218–1235.

Movshon, J. A., and van Sluyters, R. C. (1981). Visual neural development. *Annual Review of Psychology, 32,* 477–522.

Mower, G. D., Christen, W. G., and Caplan, C. J. (1983). Very brief visual experience eliminates plasticity in the cat visual cortex. *Science, 221,* 178–180.

Moyer, J. R., Jr., Deyo, R. A., and Disterhoft, J. F. (1990). Hippocampectomy disrupts trace eye-blink conditioning in rabbits. *Behavioral Neuroscience, 104,* 243–252.

Mukhametov, L. M. (1984). Sleep in marine mammals. In A. Borbely and J. L. Valatx (Eds.), *Experimental Brain Research. Supplementum: 8. Sleep mechanisms.* Berlin: Springer.

Mulkey, R. M., Herron, C. E., and Malenka, R. C. (1993). An essential role for protein phosphatases in hippocampal long-term depression. *Science, 261,* 1051–1055.

Münte, T. F., Kohlmetz, C., Nager, W., and Altenmüller, E. (2001). Superior auditory spatial tuning in conductors. *Nature, 409,* 580.

Murasugi, C. M., Salzman, C. D., and Newsome, W. T. (1993). Microstimulation in visual area MT: Effects of varying pulse amplitude and frequency. *Journal of Neuroscience, 13,* 1719–1729.

Murphy, G. G., and Glanzman, D. L. (1999). Cellular analog of differential classical conditioning in *Aplysia*: Disruption by the NMDA receptor antagonist DL-2-amino-5-phosphonovalerate. *Journal of Neuroscience, 19,* 10595–10602.

Murphy, K. J., and Regan, C. M. (1998). Contributions of cell adhesion molecules to altered synaptic weightings during memory consolidation. *Neurobiology of Learning and Memory, 70,* 73–81.

Murtra, P., Sheasby, A. M., Hunt, S. P., and De Felipe, C. (2000). Rewarding effects of opiates are absent in mice lacking the receptor for substance P. *Nature, 405,* 180–183.

Mussa-Ivaldi, S. (2000). Real brains for real robots. *Nature, 408,* 305–306.

Nader, K., Bechara, A., and Van Der Kooy, D. (1997). Neurobiological constraints on behavioral models of motivation. *Annual Review of Psychology, 48,* 85–114.

Nader, K., Schafe, G. E., and Le Doux, J. E. (2000). Fear memories require protein synthesis in the amygdala for reconsolidation after retrieval. *Nature, 406,* 722–726.

Naeser, M., Gaddie, A., Palumbo, C., and Stiassny-Eder, D. (1990). Late recovery of auditory comprehension in global aphasia. Improved recovery observed with subcortical temporal isthmus lesion vs. Wernicke's cortical area lesion. *Archives of Neurology, 47,* 425–432.

Naeser, M., and Hayward, R. (1978). Lesion localization in aphasia with cranial computed tomography and the Boston Diagnostic Aphasia Exam. *Neurology, 28,* 545–551.

Nastiuk, K. L., Mello, C. V., George, J. M., and Clayton, D. F. (1994). Immediate-early gene responses in the avian song control system: Cloning and expression analysis of the canary c-jun DNA. *Brain Research. Molecular Brain Research, 27,* 299–309.

Natelson, B. H. (1985). Neurocardiology: An interdisciplinary area for the 80s. *Archives of Neurology, 42,* 178–184.

Nathan, P. E., and Gorman, J. M. (1998). *A guide to treatments that work.* New York: Oxford University Press.

Nathans, J. (1987). Molecular biology of visual pigments. *Annual Review of Neuroscience, 10,* 163–194.

Nathanson, J. A. (1984). Caffeine and related methylxanthines: Possible naturally occurring pesticides. *Science, 226,* 184–187.

National Commission for the Protection of Human Subjects of Biomedical and Behavioral Research. (1978). *Special study, implications of advances in biomedical and behavioral research: Report and recommendations of the National Commission for the Protection of Human Subjects of Biomedical and Behavioral Research* (DHEW Publication No. OS 78-0015). Washington, DC: U.S. Department of Health, Education, and Welfare.

National Research Council, Commission on Life Science. (1988). *Use of laboratory animals in biomedical and behavioral research.* Washington, DC: National Academy Press.

National Research Council, Committee on Animals as Monitors of Environmental Hazards. (1991). *Animals as sentinels of environmental health hazards.* Washington, DC: National Academy Press.

Neff, W. D., and Casseday, J. H. (1977). Effects of unilateral ablation of auditory cortex on monaural cat's ability to localize sound. *Journal of Neurophysiology, 40,* 44–52.

Neitz, J., Geist, T., and Jacobs, G. H. (1989). Color vision in the dog. *Visual Neuroscience, 3,* 119–125.

Neitz, J., and Jacobs, G. H. (1984). Electroretinogram measurements of cone spectral sensitivity in dichromatic monkeys. *Journal of the Optical Society of America. Part A, Optics and Image Science, 1,* 1175–1180.

Nelson, R. J. (1995). *Introduction to behavioral endocrinology.* Sunderland, MA: Sinauer Associates.

Nelson, R. J., Demas, G. E., Huang, P. L., Fishman, M. C., et al. (1995). Behavioural abnormalities in male mice lacking neuronal nitric oxide synthase. *Nature, 378,* 383–386.

Neophytou, S. I., Graham, M., Williams, J., Aspley, S., et al. (2000). Strain differences to the effects of aversive frequency ultrasound on behaviour and brain topography of c-fos expression in the rat. *Brain Research, 854,* 158–164.

Nestler, E. J., and Duman, R. S. (1995). Intracellular messenger pathways as mediators of neural plasticity. In F. E. Bloom and D. J. Kupfer (Eds.), *Psychopharmacology: The fourth generation of progress* (pp. 695–704). New York: Raven.

Neuroscience: Taxicology. (2000). *Economist, 353,* 8162, 125.

Neville, H. J., Bavelier, D., Corina, D., Rauschecker, J., et al. (1998). Cerebral organization for language in deaf and hearing subjects: Biological constraints and effects of experience. *Proceedings of the National Academy of Sciences, USA, 95,* 922–929.

Neville, H. J., Mills, D. L., and Lawson, D. S. (1992). Fractionating language: Different neural subsystems with different sensitive periods. *Cerebral Cortex, 2,* 244–258.

Newsome, W. T., Wurtz, R. H., Dursteler, M. R., and Mikami, A. (1985). Deficits in visual motion processing following ibotenic acid lesions of the middle temporal visual area of the macaque monkey. *Journal of Neuroscience, 5,* 825–840.

Nicolelis, M. A. (2001). Actions from thoughts. *Nature, 409,* 403–407.

Nicoll, J. A., Burnett, C., Love, S., Graham, D. I., et al. (1997). High frequency of apolipoprotein E epsilon 2 allele in hemorrhage due to cerebral amyloid angiopathy. *Annals of Neurology, 41,* 716–721.

Nicoll, J. A., Roberts, G. W., and Graham, D. I. (1996). Amyloid beta-protein, APOE genotype and head injury. *Annals of the New York Academy of Sciences, 777,* 271–275.

Nieto-Sampedro, M., and Cotman, C. W. (1985). Growth factor induction and temporal order in central nervous system repair. In C. W. Cotman (Ed.), *Synaptic plasticity* (pp. 407–457). New York: Guilford.

Nietzel, M. T. (2000). Police psychology. In A. E. Kazdin (Ed.), *Encyclopedia of psychology* (Vol. 6, pp. 224–226). Washington, DC: American Psychological Association.

Nilsson, M., Perfilieva, E., Johansson, U., Orwar, O., et al. (1999). Enriched environment increases neurogenesis in the adult rat dentate gyrus and improves spatial memory. *Journal of Neurobiology, 39,* 569–578.

Noad, M. J., Cato, D. H., Bryden, M. M., Jenner, M.-N., et al. (2000). Cultural revolution in whale songs. *Nature, 408,* 537–538.

Nobler, M. S., Sackeim, H. A., Prohovnik, I., Moeller, J. R., et al. (1994). Regional cerebral blood flow in mood disorders. III. Treatment and clinical response. *Archives of General Psychiatry, 51,* 884–897.

Nobre, A. C., Sebestyen, G. N., Gitelman, D. R., Mesulam, M. M., et al. (1997). Functional localization of the system for visuospatial attention using positron emission tomography. *Brain, 120,* 515–533.

Noguchi, H. (1911). *Serum diagnosis of syphilis and the butyric acid test for syphilis.* Philadelphia: Lippincott.

Nordberg, A. (1996). Functional studies of new drugs for the treatment of Alzheimer's disease. *Acta Neurologica Scandinavica. Supplementum, 165,* 137–144.

Nordeen, E. J., Nordeen, K. W., Sengelaub, D. R., and Arnold, A. P. (1985). Androgens prevent normally occurring cell death in a sexually dimorphic spinal nucleus. *Science, 229,* 671–673.

Norman, A. W., and Litwack, G. (1987). *Hormones.* Orlando, FL: Academic Press.

Norsell, U. (1980). Behavioral studies of the somatosensory system. *Physiological Reviews, 60,* 327–354.

Noseworthy, J. H. (1999). Progress in determining the causes and treatment of multiple sclerosis. *Nature, 399*(6738 Suppl.), A40–A47.

Nottebohm, F. (1980). Brain pathways for vocal learning in birds: A review of the first 10 years. *Progress in Psychobiology and Physiological Psychology, 9.*

Nottebohm, F. (1981). A brain for all seasons: Cyclical anatomical changes in song control nuclei of the canary brain. *Science, 214,* 1368–1370.

Nottebohm, F. (1987). Plasticity in adult avian central nervous system: Possible relations between hormones, learning, and brain repair. In F. Plum (Ed.), *Handbook of physiology, Section 1: Vol. 5, Higher functions of the nervous system.* Washington, DC: American Physiological Society.

Nottebohm, F. (1991). Reassessing the mechanisms and origins of vocal learning in birds. *Trends in Neurosciences, 14,* 297–304.

Nottebohm, F., and Arnold, A. P. (1976). Sexual dimorphism in vocal control areas of the songbird brain. *Science, 194,* 211–213.

Nottebohm, F., Stokes, T. M., and Leonard, C. M. (1976). Central control of song in the canary, *Serinus canarius. Journal of Comparative Neurology, 165,* 457–486.

Nougier, V., Bard, C., Fleury, M., Teasdale, N., et al. (1996). Control of single-joint movements in deafferented patients: Evidence for amplitude coding rather than position control. *Experimental Brain Research, 109,* 473–482.

Novikov, S. N. (1993). The genetics of pheromonally mediated intermale aggression in mice: Current status and prospects of the model. *Behavior Genetics, 23,* 505–508.

Nozza, R., Sabo, D., and Mandel, E. (1997). A role for otoacoustic emissions in screening for hearing impairment and middle ear disorders in school-age children. *Ear and Hearing, 18,* 227–239.

Nudo, R. J., Milliken, G. W., Jenkins, W. M., and Merzenich, M. M. (1996). Use-dependent alterations of movement representations in primary motor cortex of adult squirrel monkeys. *Journal of Neuroscience, 16,* 785–807.

Nyberg, L., Cabeza, R., and Tulving, E. (1996). PET studies of encoding and retrieval: The HERA model. *Psychonomic Bulletin & Review, 3,* 135–148.

Ohayon, M. M., Zulley, J., Guilleminault, C., and Smirne, S. (1999). Prevalence and pathologic associations of sleep paralysis in the general population. *Neurology, 52,* 1194–1200.

Ojemann, G., and Mateer, C. (1979). Human language cortex: Localization of memory, syntax, and sequential motor-phoneme identification systems. *Science, 205,* 1401–1403.

Okamura, H., Miyake, S., Sumi, Y., Yamaguchi, S., et al. (1999). Photic induction of *mPer1* and *mPer2* in *Cry*-deficient mice lacking a biological clock. *Science, 286,* 2531–2534.s

O'Keefe, J., and Dostrovsky, J. (1971). The hippocampus as a spatial map. Preliminary evidence from unit activity in the freely-moving rat. *Brain Research, 34,* 171–175.

Okubo, Y., Suhara, T., Suzuki, K., Kobayashi, K., et al. (1997). Decreased prefrontal dopamine D1 receptors in schizophrenia revealed by PET. *Nature, 385,* 634–636.

Olds, J., and Milner, P. (1954). Positive reinforcement produced by electrical stimulation of septal area and other regions of the rat brain. *Journal of Comparative and Physiological Psychology, 47,* 419–427.

Olsen, K. L. (1979). Androgen-insensitive rats are defeminised by their testes. *Nature, 279,* 238–239.

Ona, V. O., Li, M., Vonsattel, J. P., Andrews, L. J., Khan, S. Q., Chung, W. M., Frey, A. S., Menon, A. S., Li, X. J., Stieg, P. E., et al. (1999). Inhibition of caspase-1 slows disease progression in a mouse model of Huntington's disease. *Nature, 399,* 263–267.

Ontiveros, A., Fontaine, R., Breton, G., Elie, R., et al. (1989). Correlation of severity of panic disorder and neuroanatomical changes on magnetic resonance imaging. *Journal of Neuropsychiatry and Clinical Neurosciences, 1,* 404–408.

Oppenheim, R. W. (1991). Cell death during development of the nervous system. *Annual Review of Neuroscience, 14,* 453–501.

Orban, G., Dupont, P., Vogels, R., De, B. B., et al. (1996). Task dependency of visual processing in the human visual system. *Behavioural Brain Research, 76,* 215–223.

Østerberg, G. (1935). Topography of the rods and cones in the human retina. *Acta Ophthalmologica. Supplementum, 6.*

Osterhout, L. (1997). On the brain response to syntactic anomalies: Manipulations of word position and word class reveal individual differences. *Brain and Language, 59,* 494–522.

Ott, A., Slooter, A. J., Hofman, A., Van Harskamp, F., et al. (1998). Smoking and risk of dementia and Alzheimer's disease in a population-based cohort study: The Rotterdam study. *Lancet, 351,* 1840–1843.

Ottaviani, E., and Franceschi, C. (1997). The invertebrate phagocytic immunocyte: Clues to a common evolution of immune and neuroendocrine systems. *Immunology Today, 18,* 169–174.

Ottoson, D., Bartfai, T., Hokfelt, T., and Fuxe, K. (Eds.). (1995). *Wenner-Gren international series: Vol. 66. Challenges and perspectives in neuroscience.* Amsterdam: Elsevier.

Overstreet, D. H. (1993). The Flinders sensitive line rats: A genetic animal model of depression. *Neuroscience and Biobehavioral Reviews, 17,* 51–68.

Oyster, C. W. (1999). *The human eye: Structure and function.* Sunderland, MA: Sinauer Associates.

Panksepp, J. (1998). *Affective neuroscience.* New York: Oxford University Press.

Panksepp, J. (2000). Emotions as natural kinds within the mammalian brain. In M. Lewis and J. M. Haviland-Jones (Eds.), *Handbook of emotions* (2nd ed., pp. 137–156). New York: Guilford.

Pantev, C., Oostenveld, R., Engelien, A., Ross, B., et al. (1998). Increased auditory cortical representation in musicians. *Nature, 392,* 811–814.

Pantle, A., and Sekuler, R. (1968). Size detecting mechanisms in human vision. *Science, 162,* 1146–1148.

Papez, J. W. (1937). A proposed mechanism of emotion. *Archives of Neurology and Psychiatry, 38,* 725–745.

Papka, M., Ivry, R., and Woodruff-Pak, D. S. (1994). Eyeblink classical conditioning and time production in patients with cerebellar damage. *Society of Neuroscience Abstracts, 20,* 360.

Papousek, H. (1992). Experimental studies of appetitional behavior in human newborns and infants. *Advances in Infancy Studies, 7,* xix–liii.

Park, S., Como, P. G., Cui, L., and Kurlan, R. (1993). The early course of the Tourette's syndrome clinical spectrum. *Neurology, 43,* 1712–1715.

Parkes, J. D. (1985). *Sleep and its disorders.* Philadelphia: Saunders.

Parr, B. A., and McMahon, A. P. (1998). Sexually dimorphic development of mammalian reproductive tract requires *Wnt-7a. Nature, 395,* 707–710.

Pascual-Leone, A., Bartres-Faz, D., and Keenan, J. P. (1999). Transcranial magnetic stimulation: Studying brain-behaviour relationship by induction of "virtual lesions." *Philosophical Transactions of the Royal Society of London. Series B: Biological Sciences, 354,* 1–10.

Paterson, S. J., Brown, J. H., Gsödl, M. K., Johnson, M. H., et al. (1999). Cognitive modularity and genetic disorders. *Science, 286,* 2355–2358.

Patterson, F. G. (1978). The gestures of a gorilla: Language acquisition in another pongid. *Brain and Language, 5,* 72–97.

Patterson, F. (1981). *The education of Koko.* New York: Holt, Rinehart, and Winston.

Patterson, T. A., Rosenzweig, M. R., and Bennett, E. L. (1987). Amnesia produced by anisomycin in an appetitive task is not due to conditioned aversion. *Behavioral and Neural Biology, 47,* 17–26.

Paulesu, E., McCrory, E., Fazio, F., Menoncello, L., et al. (2000). A cultural effect on brain function. *Nature Neuroscience, 3,* 91–96.

Paulson, H. L., and Fischbeck, K. H. (1996). Trinucleotide repeats in neurogenetic disorders. *Annual Review of Neuroscience, 19,* 79–107.

Pavlov, I. P. (1927). *Conditioned reflexes.* Oxford, England: Oxford University Press.

Pearson, K. G. (1993). Common principles of motor control in vertebrates and invertebrates. *Annual Review of Neuroscience, 16,* 265–297.

Pechura, C. M., and Martin, J. B. (Eds.). (1991). *Mapping the brain and its functions: Integrating enabling technologies into neuroscience research.* Washington, DC: National Academy Press.

Peck, J. R., and Waxman, D. (2000). Mutation and sex in a competitive world. *Nature, 406,* 399–404.

Peele, S., and Brodsky, A. (1991). *The truth about addiction and recovery.* New York: Simon & Schuster.

Pena, J. L., and Konishi, M. (2000). Cellular mechanisms for resolving phase ambiguity in the owl's inferior colliculus. *Proceedings of the National Academy of Sciences, USA, 97,* 11787–11792.

Penfield, W., and Roberts, L. (1959). *Speech and brain-mechanisms.* Princeton, NJ: Princeton University Press.

Pennisi, E. (1997). The architecture of hearing. *Science, 278,* 1223–1224.

Peris, J., Boyson, S. J., Cass, W. A., Curella, P., et al. (1990). Persistence of neurochemical changes in dopamine systems after repeated cocaine administration. *Journal of Pharmacology and Experimental Therapeutics, 253,* 38–44.

Perkins, A. T., and Teyler, T. J. (1988). A critical period for long-term potentiation in the developing rat visual cortex. *Brain Research, 439,* 222–229.

Perl, E. R. (1980). Afferent basis of nociception and pain: Evidence from the characteristics of sensory receptors and their projections to the spinal dorsal horn. *Research Publications—Association for Research in Nervous and Mental Disease, 58,* 19–45.

Perry, V. H. O. R., and Cowey, A. (1984). Retinal ganglion cells that project to the dorsal lateral geniculate nucleus in the macaque monkey. *Neuroscience, 12,* 1101–1123.

Pert, C. B., and Snyder, S. H. (1993). Properties of opiate-receptor binding in rat brain. *Proceedings of the National Academy of Sciences, USA, 70,* 2243–2247.

Pertwee, R. G. (1997). Pharmacology of cannabinoid CB1 and CB2 receptors. *Pharmacology and Therapeutics, 74(2),* 129–180.

Peschanski, M., Defer, G., N'Guyen, J. P., Ricolfi, F., et al. et al. (1994). Bilateral motor improvement and alteration of L-dopa effect in two patients with Parkinson's disease following intrastriatal transplantation of foetal ventral mesencephalon. *Brain, 117,* 487–499.

Peter, M. E., Medema, J. P., and Krammer, P. H. (1997). Does the *Caenorhabditis elegans* protein CED-4 contain a region of homology to the mammalian death effector domain? *Cell Death and Differentiation, 4,* 51–134.

Peterhans, E., and von der Heydt, R. (1989). Mechanisms of contour perception in monkey visual cortex. II. Contours bridging gaps. *Journal of Neuroscience, 9,* 1749–1763.

Peters, A., Palay, S. L., and Webster, H. deF. (1991). *The fine structure of the nervous system: Neurons and their supporting cells* (3rd ed.). New York: Oxford University Press.

Peterson, A. L., and Azrin, N. H. (1992). An evaluation of behavioral treatments for Tourette syndrome. *Behaviour Research and Therapy, 30,* 167–174.

Peterson, B., Riddle, M. A., Cohen, D. J., Katz, L. D., et al. (1993). Reduced basal ganglia volumes in Tourette's syndrome using three-dimensional reconstruction techniques from magnetic resonance images. *Neurology, 43,* 941–949.

Peterson, L. R., and Peterson, M. J. (1959). Short-term retention of individual verbal items. *Journal of Experimental Psychology, 58,* 193–198.

Petitto, L. A., Zatorre, R. J., Gauna, K., Nikelski, E. J., et al. (2000). Speech-like cerebral activity in profoundly deaf people processing signed languages: Implications for the neural basis of human language. *Proceedings of the National Academy of Sciences, USA, 97,* 13961–13966.

Petre-Quadens, O. (1972). Sleep in mental retardation. In C. D. Clemente, D. R. Purpura, and F. E. Mayer (Eds.), *Sleep and the maturing nervous system* (pp. 1–2). New York: Academic Press.

Petrides, M., and Milner, B. (1982). Deficits on subject-ordered tasks after frontal- and temporal-lobe lesions in man. *Neuropsychologia, 20,* 249–262.

Petrie, K., Dawson, A. G., Thompson, L., and Brook, R. (1993). A double-blind trial of melatonin as a treatment for jet lag in international cabin crew. *Biological Psychiatry, 33,* 526–530.

Petrij, F., Giles, R., Dauwerse, H., Saris, J., et al. (1995). Rubinstein-taybi syndrome caused by mutations in the transcriptional co-activator cbp. *Nature, 376,* 348–351.

Pettigrew, J. D., and Freeman, R. D. (1973). Visual experience without lines: Effect on developing cortical neurons. *Science, 182,* 599–601.

Petty, F., Kramer, G., Wilson, L., and Jordan, S. (1994). In vivo serotonin release and learned helplessness. *Psychiatry Research, 52,* 285–293.

Pfaff, D. W. (1980). *Estrogens and brain function: Neural analysis of a hormone-controlled mammalian reproductive behavior.* New York: Springer.

Pfaff, D. W. (1997). Hormones, genes, and behavior. *Proceedings of the National Academy of Sciences, USA, 94,* 14213–14216.

Pfaffmann, C., Frank, M., and Norgren, R. (1979). Neural mechanisms and behavioral aspects of taste. *Annual Review of Psychology, 30,* 283–325.

Pfefferbaum, A., Sullivan, E. V., Mathalon, D. H., Shear, P. K., et al. (1995). Longitudinal changes in magnetic resonance imaging brain volumes in abstinent and relapsed alcoholics. *Alcoholism: Clinical and Experimental Research, 19,* 1177–1191.

Pfrieger, F. W., and Barres, B. A. (1997). Synaptic efficacy enhanced by glial cells in vitro. *Science, 277,* 1684–1687.

Phillips, M. L., Young, A. W., Scott, S. K., Calder, A. J., et al. (1998). Neural responses to facial and vocal expressions of fear and disgust. *Proceedings of the Royal Society of London. Series B: Biological Sciences, 265,* 1809–1817.

Phoenix, C. H., Goy, R. W., Gerall, A. A., and Young, W. C. (1959). Organizing action of prenatally administered testosterone propionate on the tissues mediating mating behavior in the female guinea pig. *Endocrinology, 65,* 369–382.

Pickens, R., and Thompson, T. (1968). Drug use by U.S. Army enlisted men in Vietnam: A followup on their return home. *Journal of Pharmacology and Experimental Therapeutics, 161,* 122–129.

Pierce, K., Müller, R.-A., Ambrose, J., Allen, G., et al. (In press). People with autism process faces ouside the "fusiform face area": Evidence from fMRI. *Brain, 124.*

Pilla, M., Perachon, S., Sautel, F., Garrido, F., et al. (1999). Selective inhibition of cocaine-seeking behaviour by a partial dopamine D$_3$ receptor agonist. *Nature, 400,* 371–375.

Pines, J. (1992). Cell proliferation and control. *Current Opinion in Cell Biology, 4*(2), 144–148.

Pinker, S. (1994). *The language instinct.* New York: Morrow.

Pitman, R. K. (1989). Post-traumatic stress disorder, hormones, and memory. *Biological Psychiatry, 26,* 221–223.

Pitman, R. K., and Orr, S. P. (1995). Psychophysiology of emotional memory networks in posttraumatic stress disorder. In J. L. McGaugh, N. M. Weinberger, and G. Lynch (Eds.), *Brain and memory: Modulation and mediation of neuroplasticity* (pp. 75–83). New York: Oxford University Press.

Pitts, J. W., and McClure, J. N. (1967). Lactate metabolism in anxiety neurosis. *New England Journal of Medicine, 277,* 1329–1336.

Plante, E. (1991). MRI findings in the parents and siblings of specifically language-impaired boys. *Brain and Language, 41,* 67–80.

Plante, E., Swisher, L., Vance, R., and Rapcsak, S. (1991). MRI findings in boys with specific language impairment. *Brain and Language, 41,* 52–66.

Plautz, J. D., Kaneko, M., Hall, J. C., and Kay, S. A. (1997). Independent photoreceptive circadian clocks throughout *Drosophila. Science, 278,* 1632–1635.

Pleim, E. T., and Barfield, R. J. (1988). Progesterone versus estrogen facilitation of female sexual behavior by intracranial administration to female rats. *Hormones and Behavior, 22,* 150–159.

Ploog, D. W. (1992). Neuroethological perspectives on the human brain: From the expression of emotions to intentional signing and speech. In A. Harrington (Ed.), *So human a brain: Knowledge and values in the neurosciences* (pp. 3–13). Boston: Birkhauser.

Plutchik, R. (1994). *The psychology and biology of emotion.* New York: HarperCollins.

Poinar, G. O., Jr. (1994). The range of life in amber: Significance and implications in DNA studies. *Experientia, 50,* 536–542.

Poizner, H., Bellugi, U., and Klima, E. S. (1990). Biological foundations of language: Clues from sign language. *Annual Review of Neuroscience, 13,* 283–307.

Polleux, F., Morrow, T., and Ghosh, A. (2000). Semaphorin 3A is a chemoattractant for cortical apical dendrites. *Nature, 404,* 567–573.

Polymeropoulos, M. H., Lavedan, C., Leroy, E., Ide, S. E., et al. (1997). Mutation in the alpha-synuclein gene identified in families with Parkinson's disease. *Science, 276,* 2045–2047.

Poritsky, R. (1969). Two and three dimensional ultrastructure of boutons and glial cells on the motoneuronal surface in the cat spinal cord. *Journal of Comparative Neurology, 135,* 423–452.

Posner, M. I., and Raichle, M. E. (1994). *Images of mind.* New York: Scientific American Library.

Post, R. M., and Weiss, S. R. B. (1989). Non-homologous animal models of affective disorders: Clinical relevance of sensitization and kindling. In G. F. Koob, C. L. Ehlers, and D. J. Kupfers (Eds.), *Animal models of depression* (pp. 30–54). Cambridge, MA: Birkhauser.

Post, R., Weiss, S., Smith, M., Rosen, J., et al. (1995). Stress, conditioning, and the temporal aspects of affective disorders. *Annals of the New York Academy of Sciences, 771,* 677–696.

Premack, D. (1971). Language in a chimpanzee? *Science, 172,* 808–822.

Price, M. A., and Vandenbergh, J. G. (1992). Analysis of puberty-accelerating pheromones. *Journal of Experimental Zoology, 264,* 42–45.

Price, M. P., Lewin, G. R., McIlwrath, S. L., Cheng, C., et al. (2000). The mammalian sodium channel BNC1 is required for normal touch sensation. *Nature, 407,* 1007–1011.

Price, R. A., and Gottesman, I. I. (1991). Body fat in identical twins reared apart: Roles for genes and environment. *Behavior Genetics, 21,* 1–7.

Price, R. A., Kidd, K. K., Cohen, D. J., Pauls, D. L., et al. (1985). A twin study of Tourette syndrome. *Archives of General Psychiatry, 42,* 815–820.

Proksch, J. W., Gentry, W. B., and Owens, S. M. (2000). Anti-phencyclidine monoclonal antibodies provide long-term reductions in brain phencyclidine concentrations during chronic phencyclidine administration in rats. *Journal of Pharmacology and Experimental Therapeutics, 292,* 831–837.

Prull, M. W., Gabrieli, J. D. E., and Bunge, S. A. (2000). Age-related changes in memory: A cognitive neuroscience perspective. In F. I. M. Craik and T. A. Salthouse (Eds.), *The handbook of aging and cognition* (pp. 91-153). Mahwah, NJ: Erlbaum.

Przybyslawski, J., Roullet, P., and Sara, S. J. (1999). Attenuation of emotional and nonemotional memories after their reactivation: Role of beta adrenergic receptors. *Journal of Neuroscience, 19,* 6623–6628.

Pugh, E. N., Jr., and Lamb, T. D. (1990). Cyclic GMP and calcium: The internal messengers of excitation and adaptation in vertebrate photoreceptors. *Vision Research, 30,* 1923–1948.

Pugh, E. N., Jr., and Lamb, T. D. (1993). Amplification and kinetics of the activation steps in phototransduction. *Biochimica et Biophysica Acta, 1141,* 111–149.

Pugh, K. R., Mencl, W. E., Shaywitz, B. A., Shaywitz, S. E., et al. (2000). The angular gyrus in developmental dyslexia: Task-specific differences in functional connectivity within posterior cortex. *Psychological Science, 11*(1), 51–56.

Purdy, R. H., Moore, P. H., Jr., Morrow, A. L., and Paul, S. M. (1992). Neurosteroids and GABA receptor function. *Advances in Biochemical Psychopharmacology, 47,* 87–92.

Purves, D. (1988). *Body and brain: A trophic theory of neural connections.* Cambridge, MA: Harvard University Press.

Purves, D., Augustine, G. J., Fitzpatrick, D., Katz, L., et al. (Eds.). (2001). *Neuroscience* (2nd ed.). Sunderland, MA: Sinauer.

Purves, W. K. Orians, G. H., Sadava, D., and Heller, H. C., (2001). *Life, the science of biology* (6th ed.). Sunderland, MA: Sinauer Associates.

Quinn, W. G., Harris, W. A., and Benzer, S. (1974). Conditioned behavior in *Drosophila melanogaster. Proceedings of the National Academy of Sciences, USA, 71,* 708–712.

Quinn, W. G., Sziber, P. P., and Booker, R. (1979). The *Drosophila* memory mutant amnesiac. *Nature, 277,* 212–214.

Raab, D. H., and Ades, H. W. (1946). Cortical and midbrain mediation of a conditioned discrimination of acoustic intensities. *American Journal of Psychology, 59,* 59–83.

Raber, J., Wong, D., Yu, G. Q., Buttini, M., et al. (2000). Apolipoprotein E and cognitive performance. *Nature, 404,* 352–354.

Rafal, R. D. (1994). Neglect. *Current Opinion in Neurobiology, 4,* 231–236.

Rahe, R. H., Biersner, R. J., Ryman, D. H., and Arthur, R. J. (1972). Psychosocial predictors of illness behavior and failure in stressful training. *Journal of Health and Social Behavior, 13,* 393–397.

Raine, A., Venables, P. H., Dalais, C., Mellingen, K., et al. (2001). Early educational and health enrichment at age 3-5 years is associated with increased autonomic and central nervous system arousal and orienting at age 11 years: Evidence from the Mauritius Child Health Project. *Psychophysiology, 38,* 254–266.

Rainville, P., Duncan, G. H., Price, D. D., Carrier, B., et al. (1997). Pain affect encoded in human anterior cingulate but not somatosensory cortex. *Science, 277,* 968–971.

Raisman, G. (1978). What hope for repair of the brain? *Annals of Neurology, 3,* 101–106.

Raisman, G., and Field, P. M. (1971). Sexual dimorphism in the preoptic area of the rat. *Science, 173,* 731–733.

Rajendra, S., Lynch, J. W., Pierce, K. D., French, C. R., et al. (1994). Startle disease mutations reduce the agonist sensitivity of the human inhibitory glycine receptor. *Journal of Biological Chemistry, 269,* 18739–18742.

Rakic, P. (1971). Guidance of neurons migrating to the fetal monkey neo-cortex. *Brain Research, 33,* 471–476.

Rakic, P. (1985). Mechanisms of neuronal migration in developing cerebellar cortex. In G. M. Edelman, W. M. Cowan, and E. Gull (Eds.), *Molecular basis of neural development.* New York: Wiley.

Rakic, P., Bourgeois, J.-P., Eckenhoff, M. F., Zecevic, N., et al. (1986). Concurrent overproduction of synapses in diverse regions of the primate cerebral cortex. *Science, 232,* 232–235.

Raleigh, M. J., Brammer, G. L., McGuire, M. T., Pollack, D. B., et al. (1992). Individual differences in basal cisternal cerebrospinal fluid 5-HIAA and HVA in monkeys. The effects of gender, age, physical characteristics, and matrilineal influences. *Neuropsychopharmacology, 7,* 295–304.

Ralph, M. R., Foster, R. G., Davis, F. C., and Menaker, M. (1990). Transplanted suprachiasmatic nucleus determines circadian period. *Science, 247,* 975–978.

Ralph, M. R., and Lehman, M. N. (1991). Transplantation: A new tool in the analysis of the mammalian hypothalamic circadian pacemaker. *Trends in Neurosciences, 14,* 362–366.

Ralph, M. R., and Menaker, M. (1988). A mutation of the circadian system in golden hamsters. *Science, 241,* 1225–1227.

Ramachandran, V. S., and Rogers-Ramachandran D. (2000). Phantom limbs and neural plasticity. *Archives of Neurology, 57,* 317–320.

Ramey, C. T., Campbell, F. A., Burchinal, M., Skinner, M. L., et al. (2000). Persistent effects of early childhood education on high-risk children and their mothers. *Applied Developmental Science, 4*(1), 2–14.

Ramón y Cajal, S. (1894). La fine structure des centres nervous. *Proceedings of the Royal Society of London. Series B: Biological Sciences, 55,* 444–468.

Rampon, C., Jiang, C. H., Dong, H., Tang, Y. P., et al. (2000). Effects of environmental enrichment on gene expression in the brain. *Proceedings of the National Academy of Sciences, USA, 97,* 12880–12884.

Rampon, C., Tang, Y. P., Goodhouse, J., Shimizu, E., et al. (2000). Enrichment induces structural changes and recovery from nonspatial memory deficits in CA1 NMDAR1-knockout mice. *Nature Neuroscience, 3,* 238–244.

Rampon, C., and Tsien, J. Z. (2000). Genetic analysis of learning behavior-induced structural plasticity. *Hippocampus, 10,* 605–609.

Ramsay, D. J., and Booth, D. A. (1991). *Thirst: Physiological and psychological aspects.* New York: Springer.

Ramus, F., Hauser, M. D., Miller, C., Morris, D., et al. (2000). Language discrimination by human newborns and by cotton-top tamarin monkeys. *Science, 288,* 349–351.

Ranaldi, R., and Beninger, R. J. (1994). The effects of systemic and intracerebral injections of D1 and D2 agonists on brain stimulation reward. *Brain Research, 651,* 283–292.

Rand, M. N., and Breedlove, S. M. (1987). Ontogeny of functional innervation of bulbocavernosus muscles in male and female rats. *Brain Research, 430,* 150–152.

Randolph, M., and Semmes, J. (1974). Behavioral consequences of selective subtotal ablations in the postcentral gyrus of *Macaca mulatta. Brain Research, 70,* 55–70.

Rao, P. D. P., and Finger, T. E. (1984). Asymmetry of the olfactory system in the brain of the winter flounder *Pseudopleuronectes americanus. Journal of Comparative Neurology, 225,* 492–510.

Rapin, I., and Katzman, R. (1998). Neurobiology of autism. *Annals of Neurology, 43,* 7–14.

Rapoport, J. L. (1989a). The biology of obsessions and compulsions. *Scientific American, 260*(6), 82–89.

Rapoport, J. L. (1989b). *The boy who couldn't stop washing: The experience & treatment of obsessive-compulsive disorder.* New York: Dutton.

Rasmussen, P. (1996). The congenital insensitivity-to-pain syndrome (analgesia congenita): Report of a case. *International Journal of Paediatric Dentistry, 6,* 117–122.

Rattenborg, N. C., Lima, S. L., and Amlaner, C. J. (1999). Half-awake to the risk of predation. *Nature, 397,* 397–398.

Rauch, S. L., Jenike, M. A., Alpert, N. M., Baer, L., et al. (1994). Regional cerebral blood flow measured during symptom provocation in obsessive-compulsive disorder using oxygen 15-labeled carbon dioxide and positron emission tomography. *Archives of General Psychiatry, 51,* 62–70.

Rauch, S. L., Savage, C. R., Alpert, N. M., Miguel, E. C., et al. (1995). A positron emission tomographic study of simple phobic symptom provocation. *Archives of General Psychiatry, 52,* 20–28.

Rauschecker, J. P. (1999). Making brain circuits listen. *Science, 285,* 1686–1687.

Raz, N. (2000). Aging of the brain and its impact on cognitive performance: Integration of structural and functional findings. In F. I. M. Craik and T. A. Salthouse (Eds.), *The handbook of aging and cognition* (2nd ed., pp. 1–90). Mahwah, NJ: Erlbaum.

Recanzone, G. H., Schreiner, D. E., and Merzenich, M. M. (1993). Plasticity in the frequency representation of primary auditory cortex following discrimination training in adult owl monkeys. *Journal of Neuroscience, 13,* 87–103.

Rechtschaffen, A., and Bergmann, B. M. (1995). Sleep deprivation in the rat by the disk-over-water method. *Behavioural Brain Research, 69,* 55–63.

Rechtschaffen, A., and Kales, A. (1968). *A manual of standardized terminology, techniques and scoring system for sleep stages of human subjects.* Bethesda, MD: U.S. National Institute of Neurological Diseases and Blindness, Neurological Information Network.

Redfern, P. A. (1970). Neuromuscular transmission in new-born rats. *Journal of Physiology (London), 109,* 701–709.

Redican, W. K. (1982). An evolutionary perspective on human facial displays. In P. Ekman (Ed.), *Emotion in the human face* (2nd ed., pp. 212–280). Elmsford, NY: Pergamon.

Reedy, F. E. J., Bartoshuk, L. M., Miller, I. J. J., Duffy, V. B., et al. (1993). Relationships among papillae, taste pores, and 6-n-propylthiouracil (prop) suprathreshold taste sensitivity. *Chemical Senses, 18,* 618–619.

Rehkamper, G., Haase, E., and Frahm, H. D. (1988). Allometric comparison of brain weight and brain structure volumes in different breeds of the domestic pigeon, *Columba livia* f. d. (fantails, homing pigeons, strassers). *Brain, Behavior and Evolution, 31,* 141–149.

Reichardt, L. F., and Tomaselli, K. J. (1991). Extracellular matrix molecules and their receptors: Functions in neural development. *Annual Review of Neuroscience, 14,* 531–570.

Reid, M. S., Tafti, M., Nishino, S., Siegel, J. M., et al. (1994). Cholinergic regulation of cataplexy in canine narcolepsy in the pontine reticular formation is mediated by M2 muscarinic receptors. *Sleep, 17,* 424–435.

Reiman, E. M., Raichle, M., Robins, E., Butler, F. K., et al. (1986). The application of positron emission tomography to the study of panic disorder. *American Journal of Psychiatry, 143,* 469–477.

Reisberg, D., and Heuer, F. (1995). Emotion's multiple effects on memory. In J. L. McGaugh, N. M. Weinberger, and G. Lynch (Eds.), *Brain and memory: Modulation and mediation of neuroplasticity* (pp. 84–92). New York: Oxford University Press.

Reisenzein, R. (1983). The Schachter theory of emotion: Two decades later. *Psychological Bulletin, 94,* 239–264.

Rempel-Clower, N. L., Zola, S. M., Squire, L. R., and Amaral, D. G. (1996). Three cases of enduring memory impairment after bilateral damage limited to the hippocampal formation. *Journal of Neuroscience, 16,* 5233–5255.

Rende, R., and Plomin, R. (1995). Nature, nurture, and the development of psychopathology. In D. Ciccheti and D. J. Cohen (Eds.), *Developmental psychopathology: Vol. 1. Theory and methods* (pp. 291–314). New York: Wiley.

Renner, M. J., and Rosenzweig, M. R. (1987). *Enriched and impoverished environments: Effects on brain and behavior.* New York: Springer.

Reppert, S. M. (1985). Maternal entrainment of the developing circadian system. *Annals of the New York Academy of Sciences, 453,* 162–169.

Reppert, S. M., Perlow, M. J., Tamarkin, L., and Klein, D. C. (1979). A diurnal melatonin rhythm in primate cerebrospinal fluid. *Endocrinology, 104,* 295–301.

Rescorla, R. A. (1988). Behavioral studies of Pavlovian conditioning. *Annual Review of Neuroscience, 11,* 329–352.

Ressler, K. J., Sullivan, S. L., and Buck, L. B. (1994). A molecular dissection of spatial patterning in the olfactory system. *Current Opinion in Neurobiology, 4,* 588–596.

Reynolds, C. F., Kupfer, D. J., Taska, L. S., Hoch, C. H., et al. (1985). Sleep of healthy seniors: A revisit. *Sleep, 8,* 20–29.

Rhode, W. S. (1984). Cochlear mechanics. *Annual Review of Physiology, 46,* 231–246.

Ribeiro, R. C., Kushner, P. J., and Baxter, J. D. (1995). The nuclear hormone receptor gene superfamily. *Annual Review of Medicine, 46,* 443–453.

Rich, C. L., Young, D., and Fowler, R. C. (1986). San Diego suicide study. I. Young vs. old subjects. *Archives of General Psychiatry, 43,* 577–582.

Richard, F., and Dutrillaux, B. (1998). Origin of human chromosome 21 and its consequences: A 50-million-year-old story. *Chromosome Research, 6*(4), 263–268.

Richter, C. (1967). Sleep and activity: Their relation to the 24-hour clock. *Proceedings of the Association for Research in Nervous and Mental Diseases, 45,* 8–27.

Ridley, R. M., and Baker, H. F. (1991). Can fetal neural transplants restore function in monkeys with lesion-induced behavioural deficits? *Trends in Neurosciences, 14,* 366–370.

Riege, W. H. (1971). Environmental influences on brain and behavior of year-old rats. *Developmental Psychobiology, 4*(2), 157–167.

Riley, V. (1981). Psychoneuroendocrine influences on immunocompetence and neoplasia. *Science, 212,* 1100–1110.

Rinn, W. E. (1984). The neuropsychology of facial expression: A review of the neurological and psychological mechanisms for producing facial expressions. *Psychological Bulletin, 95,* 52–77.

Rizzolatti, G., and Arbib, M. A. (1998). Language within our grasp. *Trends in Neurosciences, 21,* 188–194.

Rizzolatti, G., Fadiga, L., Fogassi, L., and Gallese, V. (1999). Resonance behaviors and mirror neurons. *Archives Italiennes de Biologie, 137,* 85–100.

Rizzolatti, G., Fadiga, L., Gallese, V., and Fogassi, L. (1996). Premotor cortex and the recognition of motor actions. *Brain Research. Cognitive Brain Research, 3,* 131–134.

Roberts, A. H. (1969). *Brain damage in boxers.* London: Pitman.

Roberts, W. W., and Mooney, R. D. (1974). Brain areas controlling thermoregulatory grooming, prone extension, locomotion, and tail vasodilation in rats. *Journal of Comparative and Physiological Psychology, 86,* 470–480.

Robertson, D., and Irvine, D. R. (1989). Plasticity of frequency organization in auditory cortex of guinea pigs with partial unilateral deafness. *Journal of Comparative Neurology, 282,* 456–471.

Robins, L. N., and Regier, D. A. (1991). *Psychiatric disorders in America: The epidemiologic catchment area study.* New York: Free Press.

Rocca, W. A., Hofman, A., Brayne, C., Breteler, M. M., et al. (1991). The prevalence of vascular dementia in Europe: Facts and fragments from 1980–1990 studies. *Annals of Neurology, 30,* 817–824.

Rochlin, M. W., Wickline, K. M., and Bridgman, P. C. (1996). Microtubule stability decreases axon elongation but not axoplasm production. *Journal of Neuroscience, 16,* 3236–3246.

Röder, B., Teder-Sälejärvi, W., Sterr, A., Rösler, F., et al. (1999). Improved auditory spatial tuning in blind humans. *Nature, 400,* 162–166.

Rodier, P. M. (2000). The early origins of autism. *Scientific American, 282*(2), 56–63.

Roelink, H., Augsburger, A., Heemskerk, J., Korzh, V., et al. (1994). Floor plate and motor neuron induction by vhh-1, a vertebrate homolog of hedgehog expressed by the notochord. *Cell, 76,* 761–775.

Roffwarg, H. P., Muzio, J. N., and Dement, W. C. (1966). Ontogenetic development of the human sleep-dream cycle. *Science, 152,* 604–619.

Rogan, M. T., Staubli, U. V., and Ledoux, J. E. (1997). Fear conditioning induces associative long-term potentiation in the amygdala. *Nature, 390,* 604–607.

Roland, E., and Larson, B. (1976). Focal increase of cerebral blood flow during stereognostic testing in man. *Archives of Neurology, 33,* 551–558.

Roland, P. E. (1980). Quantitative assessment of cortical motor dysfunction by measurement of the regional cerebral blood flow. *Scandinavian Journal of Rehabilitation Medicine, 7,* 27–41.

Roland, P. E. (1984). Metabolic measurements of the working frontal cortex in man. *Trends in Neurosciences, 7,* 430–436.

Rolls, E. T., and O'Mara, S. M. (1995). View-responsive neurons in the primate hippocampal complex. *Hippocampus, 5,* 409–424.

Romanski, L. M., Tian, B., Fritz, J., Mishkin, M., et al. (1999). Dual streams of auditory afferents target multiple domains in the primate prefrontal cortex. *Nature Neuroscience, 2,* 1131–1136.

Romero-Apis, D., Babayan-Mena, J. I., Fonte-Vazquez, A., Gutierrez-Perez, D., et al. (1982). Perdida del ojo fijador en adulto con ambliopia estrabica. *Anales Sociedad Mexicana de Oftalmologia, 56,* 445–452.

Roorda, A., and Williams, D. R. (1999). The arrangement of the three cone classes in the living human eye. *Nature, 397,* 520–522.

Rorabaugh, W. J. (1976). Estimated U.S. alcoholic beverage consumption, 1790–1860. *Journal of Studies on Alcohol, 37,* 357–364.

Rosen, B. R., Buckner, R. L., and Dale, A. M. (1998). Event-related functional MRI: Past, present, and future. *Proceedings of the National Academy of Sciences, USA, 95,* 773–780.

Rosen, G. D., Sherman, G. F., and Galaburda, A. M. (1993). Neuronal subtypes and anatomic asymmetry: Changes in neuronal number and cell-packing density. *Neuroscience, 56,* 833–839.

Rosen, H. J., Petersen, S. E., Linenweber, M. R., Snyder, A. Z., et al. (2000). Neural correlates of recovery from aphasia after damage to left inferior frontal cortex. *Neurology, 55,* 1883–1894.

Rosenbaum, D. A. (1991). *Human motor control.* San Diego, CA: Academic Press.

Rosenbaum, R. S., Priselac, S., Köhler, S., Black, S. E., et al. (2000). Remote spatial memory in an amnesic person with extensive bilateral hippocampal lesions. *Nature Neuroscience, 3,* 1044–1048.

Rosenman, R. H., Brand, R. J., Jenkins, C. D., Friedman, M., et al. (1975). Coronary heart disease in the Western Collaborative Group Study: Final follow-up experience of 8 1/2 years. *JAMA, 233,* 872–877.

Rosenthal, N. E., Sack, D. A., Carpenter, C. J., Parry, B. L., et al. (1985). Antidepressant effects of light in seasonal affective disorder. *American Journal of Psychiatry, 142,* 606–608.

Rosenzweig, M. R. (1946). Discrimination of auditory intensities in the cat. *American Journal of Psychology, 59,* 127–136.

Rosenzweig, M. R. (1980). Animal models for effects of brain lesions and for rehabilitation. In P. Bach-y-Rita (Ed.), *Recovery of function: Theoretical considerations for brain injury rehabilitation* (pp. 127-172). Bern, Switzerland: Hans Huber.

Rosenzweig, M. R. (1984). Experience, memory, and the brain. *American Psychologist, 39,* 365–376.

Rosenzweig, M. R., and Bennett, E. L. (1977). Effects of environmental enrichment or impoverishment on learning and on brain values in rodents. In A. Oliveno (Ed.), *Genetics, environment, and intelligence* (pp. 1–2). Amsterdam: Elsevier/North-Holland.

Rosenzweig, M. R., and Bennett, E. L. (1978). Experimental influences on brain anatomy and brain chemistry in rodents. In G. Gottlieb (Ed.), *Studies on the development of behavior and the nervous system: Vol. 4. Early influences* (pp. 289–327). New York: Academic Press.

Rosenzweig, M. R., and Bennett, E. L. (1996). Psychobiology of plasticity: Effects of training and experience on brain and behavior. *Behavioural Brain Research, 78,* 57–65.

Rosenzweig, M. R., Bennett, E. L., Colombo, P. J., Lee, D. W., et al. (1993). Short-term, intermediate-term, and long-term memory. *Behavioural Brain Research, 57,* 193–198.

Rosenzweig, M. R., Bennett, E. L., and Diamond, M. C. (1972). Brain changes in response to experience. *Scientific American, 226*(2), 22–29.

Rosenzweig, M. R., Bennett, E. L., and Krech, D. (1964). Cerebral effects of environmental complexity and training among adult rats. *Journal of Comparative and Physiological Psychology, 57,* 438–439.

Rosenzweig, M. R., Bennett, E. L., Martinez, J. L., Colombo, P. J., et al. (1992). Studying stages of memory formation with chicks. In L. R. Squire and N. Butters (Eds.), *Neuropsychology of memory* (2nd ed., pp. 533–546). New York: Guilford.

Rosenzweig, M. R., Krech, D., and Bennett, E. L. (1961). Heredity, environment, brain biochemistry, and learning. *Current trends in psychological theory* (pp. 87–110). Pittsburgh, PA: University of Pittsburgh Press.

Rosenzweig, M., Krech, D., Bennett, E. L., and Diamond, M. (1962). Effects of environmental complexity and training on brain chemistry and anatomy: A replication and extension. *Journal of Comparative and Physiological Psychology, 55,* 429–437.

Roses, A. D. (1995). On the metabolism of apolipoprotein E and the Alzheimer diseases. *Experimental Neurology, 132,* 149–156.

Rossetti, Y., Rode, G., Pisella, L., Farné, A., et al. (1998). Prism adaptation to a rightward optical deviation rehabilitates left hemispatial neglect. *Nature, 395,* 166–169.

Rossi, D. J., Oshima, T., and Attwell, D. (2000). Glutamate release in severe brain ischaemia is mainly by reversed uptake. *Nature, 403,* 316–321.

Rosso, I. M., Cannon, T. D., Huttunen, T., Huttunen, M. O., et al. (2000). Obstetric risk factors for early-onset schizophrenia in a Finnish birth cohort. *American Journal of Psychiatry, 157,* 801–807.

Rossor, M., Garrett, N., Johnson, A., Mountjoy, C., et al. (1982). A postmortem study of the cholinergic and Gaba systems in senile dementia. *Brain, 105,* 313–330.

Rothschild, A. J. (1992). Disinhibition, amnestic reactions, and other adverse reactions secondary to triazolam: A review of the literature. *Journal of Clinical Psychiatry, 53,* 69–79.

Rothstein, J. D. (2000). Bundling up excitement. *Nature, 407,* 141, 143.

Rothwell, J. (1994). *Control of human voluntary movement* (2nd ed.). London: Chapman and Hall.

Roullet, P., Mileusnic, R., Rose, S. P. R., and Sara, S. J. (1997). Neural cell adhesion molecules play a role in rat memory formation in appetitive as well as aversive tasks. *Neuroreport, 8,* 1907–1911.

Roy, A. (1992). Hypothalamic-pituitary-adrenal axis function and suicidal behavior in depression. *Biological Psychiatry, 32,* 812–816.

Ruberman, W., Weinblatt, E., Goldberg, J. D., and Chaudhary, B. S. (1984). Psychosocial influences on mortality after myocardial infarction. *New England Journal of Medicine, 311,* 552–559.

Ruby, P., and Decety, J. (2001). Effects of subjective perspective taking during simulation of action: A PET investigation of agency. *Nature Neuroscience, 4,* 546–550.

Rumbaugh, D. M. (1977). *Language learning by a chimpanzee: The LANA project.* New York: Academic Press.

Rusak, B., and Boulos, Z. (1981). Pathways for photic entrainment of mammalian circadian rhythms. *Photochemistry and Photobiology, 34,* 267–273.

Rusak, B., and Zucker, I. (1975). Biological rhythms and animal behavior. *Annual Review of Psychology, 26,* 137–171.

Rusak, B., and Zucker, I. (1979). Neural regulation of circadian rhythms. *Physiological Reviews, 59,* 449–526.

Russell, J. A. (1994). Is there universal recognition of emotion from facial expressions? A review of the cross–cultural studies. *Psychological Bulletin, 115,* 102–141.

Ryan, A. J. (1998). Intracranial injuries resulting from boxing. *Clinics in Sports Medicine, 17*(1), 155–168.

Rymer, R. (1993). *Genie: An abused child's flight from silence.* New York: HarperCollins.

Sack, R. L., Blood, M. L., and Lewy, A. J. (1992). Melatonin rhythms in night shift workers. *Sleep, 15,* 434–441.

Sackheim, H., Gur, R. C., and Saucy, M. C. (1978). Emotions are expressed more intensely on the left side of the face. *Science, 202,* 434–436.

Sahu, A. (1998). Evidence suggesting that galanin (GAL), melanin-concentrating hormone (MCH), neurotensin (NT), proopiomelanocortin (POMC) and neuropeptide Y (NPY) are targets of leptin signaling in the hypothalamus. *Endocrinology, 139,* 795–798.

Sahu, A., Kalra, P. S., and Kalra, S. P. (1988). Food deprivation and ingestion induce reciprocal changes in neuropeptide Y concentration in the paraventricular nucleus. *Peptides, 9,* 83–86.

Sakurai, T., Amemiya, A., Ishii, M., Matsuzaki, I., et al. (1998). Orexins and orexin receptors: A family of hypothalamic neuropeptides and G protein-coupled receptors that regulate feeding behavior. *Cell, 92,* 573–585.

Salvini-Plawen, L. V., and Mayr, E. (1977). On the evolution of photoreceptors and eyes. *Evolutionary Biology, 10,* 207–263.

Salzman, C. D., Murasugi, C. M., Britten, K. H., and Newsome, W. T. (1992). Microstimulation in visual area MT: Effects on direction discrimination performance. *Journal of Neuroscience, 12,* 2331–2355.

Samad, T. A., Moore, K. A., Sapirstein, A., Billet, S., et al. (2001). Interleukin-1β-mediated induction of Cox-2 in the CNS contributes to inflammatory pain hypersensitivity. *Nature, 410,* 471–475.

Samson, S., and Zatorre, R. J. (1991). Recognition memory for text and melody of songs after unilateral temporal lobe lesion: Evidence for dual encoding. *Journal of Experimental Psychology; Learning, Memory, and Cognition, 17,* 793–804.

Samson, S., and Zatorre, R. J. (1994). Contribution of the right temporal lobe to musical timbre discrimination. *Neuropsychologia, 32,* 231–240.

Sanacora, G., Kershaw, M., Finkelstein, J. A., and White, J. D. (1990). Increased hypothalamic content of preproneuropeptide Y messenger ribonucleic acid in genetically obese Zucker rats and its regulation by food deprivation. *Endocrinology, 127,* 730–737.

Sandler, A. D., Sutton, K. A., DeWeese, J., Girardi, M. A., et al. (1999). Lack of benefit of a single dose of synthetic human secretin in the treatment of autism and pervasive developmental disorder. *New England Journal of Medicine, 341,* 1801–1806.

Sanes, J. N., and Donoghue, J. P. (2000). Plasticity and primary motor cortex. *Annual Review of Neuroscience, 23,* 393–415.

Sanes, J. R., and Lichtman, J. W. (1999). Development of the vertebrate neuromuscular junction. *Annual Review of Neuroscience, 22,* 389–442.

Sano, M., Stanley, M., Lawton, A., Cote, L., et al. (1991). Tritiated imipramine binding. A peripheral marker for serotonin in Parkinson's disease. *Archives of Neurology, 48,* 1052–1054.

Sano, M., Stern, Y., Cote, L., Williams, J. B., et al. (1990). Depression in Parkinson's disease: A biochemical model. *Journal of Neuropsychiatry and Clinical Neurosciences, 2,* 88–92.

Sapolsky, R. M. (1992a). Neuroendocrinology of the stress-response. In J. B. Becker, S. M. Breedlove, and D. Crews (Eds.), *Behavioral endocrinology,* pp. 287–324. Cambridge, MA: MIT Press.

Sapolsky, R. M. (1992b). *Stress, the aging brain, and the mechanisms of neuron death.* Cambridge, MA: MIT Press.

Sapolsky, R. M. (1993). Potential behavioral modification of glucocorticoid damage to the hippocampus [Special issue: Alzheimer's disease: Animal models and clinical perspectives]. *Behavioural Brain Research, 57,* 175–182.

Sapolsky, R. M. (1994). *Why zebras don't get ulcers.* New York: Freeman.

Sapolsky, R. M. (1997). *The trouble with testosterone: And other essays on the biology of the human predicament.* New York: Scribner.

Sapolsky, R. M. (2001). *A primate's memoir.* New York: Scribner.

Sapolsky, R. M., Uno, H., Rebert, C. S., and Finch, C. E. (1990). Hippocampal damage associated with prolonged glucocorticoid exposure in primates. *Journal of Neuroscience, 10,* 2897–2902.

Sara, S. J. (2000). Retrieval and reconsolidation: Toward a neurobiology of remembering. *Learning and Memory, 7,* 73–84.

Sartorius, N., Jablensky, A., Korten, A., Ernberg, G., et al. (1986). Early manifestations and first-contact incidence of schizophrenia in different cultures. A preliminary report on the initial evaluation phase of the WHO Collaborative Study on determinants of outcome of severe mental disorders. *Psychological Medicine, 16,* 909–928.

Sartucci, F., Bonfiglio, L., Del Seppia, C., Luschi, P., et al. (1997). Changes in pain perception and pain-related somatosensory evoked potentials in humans produced by exposure to oscillating magnetic fields. *Brain Research, 769,* 362–366.

Satinoff, E. (1978). Neural organization and evolution of thermal regulation in mammals. *Science, 201,* 16–22.

Satinoff, E., and Rutstein, J. (1970). Behavioral thermoregulation in rats with anterior hypothalamic lesions. *Journal of Comparative and Physiological Psychology, 71,* 77–82.

Satinoff, E., and Shan, S. Y. (1971). Loss of behavioral thermoregulation after lateral hypothalamic lesions in rats. *Journal of Comparative and Physiological Psychology, 77,* 302–312.

Savage-Rumbaugh, E. S. (1990). Language acquisition in a nonhuman species: Implications for the innateness debate. *Developmental Psychobiology, 23,* 599–620.

Savage-Rumbaugh, E. S. (1993). *Language comprehension in ape and child.* Chicago: University of Chicago Press.

Savage-Rumbaugh, E. S., Murphy, J., Sevcik, R. A., Brakke, K. E., et al. (1993). *Monographs of the Society for Research in Child Development: Vol. 58, No. 3–4. Language comprehension in ape and child.* Chicago: University of Chicago Press.

Savage-Rumbaugh, E. S., Rumbaugh, D. M., and Boysen, S. (1980). Do apes use language? *American Scientist, 68,* 49–61.

Savage-Rumbaugh, [E.] S., Shanker, S., and Talbot, T. (1998). *Apes, language and the human mind.* New York: Oxford University Press.

Scalaidhe, S. P. O., Wilson, F. A. W., and Goldman-Rakic, P. S. (1997). Areal segregation of face-processing neurons in prefrontal cortex. *Science, 278,* 1135–1138.

Schachter, S. (1975). Cognition and peripheralist-centralist controversies in motivation and emotion. In M. S. Gazzaniga and C. Blakemore (Eds.), *Handbook of psychobiology.* New York: Academic Press.

Schachter, S., and Singer, J. (1962). Cognitive, social, and physiological determinants of emotional state. *Psychological Review, 69,* 379–399.

Schacter, D. L., Alpert, N. M., Savage, C. R., Rauch, S. L., et al. (1996). Conscious recollection and the human hippocampal formation: Evidence from positron emission tomography. *Proceedings of the National Academy of Sciences, USA, 93,* 321–325.

Schacter, D. L., and Buckner, R. L. (1998a). On the relations among priming, conscious recollection, and intentional retrieval: Evidence from neuroimaging research. *Neurobiology of Learning and Memory, 70,* 284–303.

Schacter, D., and Buckner, R. (1998b). Priming and the brain. *Neuron, 20,* 185–195.

Schaffler, L., Luders, H. O., Dinner, D. S., Lesser, R. P., et al. (1993). Comprehension deficits elicited by electrical stimulation of Broca's area. *Brain, 116,* 695–715.

Schaie, K. W. (1994). The course of adult intellectual development. *American Psychologist, 49,* 304–313.

Scharff, C., Kirn, J. R., Grossman, M., Macklis, J. D., et al. (2000). Targeted neuronal death affects neuronal replacement and vocal behavior in adult songbirds. *Neuron, 25,* 481–492.

Scheff, S. W., Bernardo, L. S., and Cotman, C. W. (1978). Decrease in adrenergic axon sprouting in the senescent rat. *Science, 202,* 775–778.

Scheibel, A. B. (1982). Age-related changes in the human forebrain. *Neurosciences Research Program Bulletin, 20,* 577–583.

Scheibel, A. B., and Conrad, A. S. (1993). Hippocampal dysgenesis in mutant mouse and schizophrenic man: Is there a relationship? *Schizophrenia Bulletin, 19,* 21–33.

Scheibel, M. E., Tomiyasu, U., and Scheibel, A. B. (1977). The aging human Betz cells. *Experimental Neurology, 56,* 598–609.

Schein, S. J., and Desimone, R. (1990). Spectral properties of V4 neurons in the macaque. *Journal of Neuroscience, 10,* 3369–3389.

Schein, S. J., Marrocco, R. T., and de Monasterio, F. M. (1982). Is there a high concentration of color-selective cells in area V4 of monkey visual cortex? *Journal of Neurophysiology, 47,* 193–213.

Schenkerberg, T., Bradford, D. C., and Ajax, E. T. (1980). Line bisection and unilateral visual neglect in patients with neurologic impairment. *Neurology, 30,* 509–518.

Schiff, B. B., and Lamon, M. (1989). Inducing emotion by unilateral contraction of facial muscles: A new look at hemispheric specialization and the experience of emotion. *Neuropsychologia, 27,* 923–935.

Schiffman, S. S., Simon, S. A., Gill, J. M., and Beeker, T. G. (1986). Bretylium tosylate enhances salt taste. *Physiology & Behavior, 36,* 1129–1137.

Schildkraut, J. J., and Kety, S. S. (1967). Biogenic amines and emotion. *Science, 156,* 21–30.

Schiller, P. H. (1993). The effects of V4 and middle temporal (MT) area lesions on visual performance in the rhesus monkey. *Visual Neuroscience, 10,* 717–746.

Schiller, P. H. (1996). On the specificity of neurons and visual areas. *Behavioural Brain Research, 76,* 21–35.

Schilthuizen, M. (2001). Bowerbirds, brainy birds. *Science online.* http://sciencenow.sciencemag.org/cgi/content/full/2001/410/2.

Schlaug, G., Jancke, L., Huang, Y., and Steinmetz, H. (1995). In vivo evidence of structural brain asymmetry in musicians. *Science, 267,* 699–701.

Schliebs, R., Rose, S. P. R., and Stewart, M. G. (1985). Effect of passive-avoidance training on in vitro protein synthesis in forebrain slices of day-old chicks. *Journal of Neurochemistry, 44,* 1014–1028.

Schlupp, I., Marler, C., and Ryan, M. J. (1994). Benefit to male sailfin mollies of mating with heterospecific females. *Science, 263,* 373–374.

Schmidt-Nielsen, K. (1960). *Animal physiology.* Englewood Cliffs, NJ: Prentice-Hall.

Schmolesky, M. T., Wang, Y., Pu, M., and Leventhal, A. G. (2000). Degradation of stimulus selectivity of visual cortical cells in senescent rhesus monkeys. *Nature Neuroscience, 3,* 384–390.

Schnapf, J. L., and Baylor, D. A. (1987). How photoreceptor cells respond to light. *Scientific American, 256*(4), 40–47.

Schnapp, B. J. (1997). Retroactive motors. *Neuron, 18,* 523–526.

Schneider, G. E. (1969). Two visual systems. *Science, 163,* 895–902.

Schneider, K. (1959). *Clinical psychopathology.* New York: Grune & Stratton.

Schuckit, M. A., and Smith, T. L. (1997). Assessing the risk for alcoholism among sons of alcoholics. *Journal of Studies on Alcohol, 58,* 141–145.

Schulteis, G., and Martinez, J. L., Jr. (1992). Peripheral modulation of learning and memory: Enkephalins as a model system. *Psychopharmacology, 109,* 347–364.

Schultz, R. T., Cho, N. K., Staib, L. H., Kier, L. E., et al. (1994). Brain morphology in normal and dyslexic children: The influence of sex and age. *Annals of Neurology, 35,* 732–742.

Schuman, E. M., and Madison, D. V. (1991). A requirement for the intercellular messenger nitric oxide in long-term potentiation. *Science, 265,* 1503–1506.

Schuster, C. R. (1970). Psychological approaches to opiate dependence and self-administration by laboratory animals. *Federation Proceedings, 29,* 1–5.

Schutz, F. (1965). Sexuelle Pragung bei Anatiden. *Zeitschrift für Tierpsychologie, 22,* 50–103.

Schwartz, J. H., Castellucci, V. F., and Kandel, E. R. (1971). Functioning of identified neurons and synapses in abdominal ganglion of *Aplysia* in absence of protein synthesis. *Journal of Neurophysiology, 34,* 939–963.

Schwartz, L. M. (1992). Insect muscle as a model for programmed cell death. *Journal of Neurobiology, 23,* 1312–1326.

Schwartz, M. W., Woods, S. C., Porte, D., Jr., Seeley, R. J., et al. (2000). Central nervous system control of food intake. *Nature, 404,* 661–671.

Schwartz, W. J., Smith, C. B., Davidsen, L., Savaki, H., et al. (1979). Metabolic mapping of functional activity in the hypothalamo-neurohypophysial system of the rat. *Science, 205,* 723–725.

Schwartzer, R., and Gutierrez-Dona, B. (2000). Health psychology. In K. Pawlik and M. R. Rosenzweig (Eds.), *International handbook of psychology* (pp. 452–465). London: Sage.

Schwartzkroin, P. A., and Wester, K. (1975). Long-lasting facilitation of a synaptic potential following tetanization in the in vitro hippocampal slice. *Brain Research, 89,* 107–119.

Schwenk, K. (1994). Why snakes have forked tongues. *Science, 263,* 1573–1577.

Sclafani, A., Springer, D., and Kluge, L. (1976). Effects of quinine adulteration on the food intake and body weight of obese and nonobese hypothalamic hyperphagic rats. *Physiology & Behavior, 16,* 631–640.

Scoville, W. B., and Milner, B. (1957). Loss of recent memory after bilateral hippocampal lesions. *Journal of Neurology, Neurosurgery and Psychiatry, 20,* 11–21.

Seeley, R. J., and Schwartz, M. W. (1997). The regulation of energy balance: Peripheral hormonal signals and hypothalamic neuropeptides. *Current Directions in Psychological Science, 6*(2), 39–44.

Seeman, P. (1990). Atypical neuroleptics: Role of multiple receptors, endogenous dopamine, and receptor linkage. *Acta Psychiatrica Scandinavica. Supplementum, 358,* 14–20.

Seeman, P., Guan, H. C., and Van Tol, H. H. (1993). Dopamine D4 receptors elevated in schizophrenia. *Nature, 365,* 441–445.

Segal, N. L., Dysken, M. W., Bouchard, T. J., Jr., Pedersen, N. L., et al. (1990). Tourette's disorder in a set of reared-apart triplets: Genetic and environmental influences. *American Journal of Psychiatry, 147,* 196–199.

Sehgal, A., Price, J. L., Man, B., and Young, M. W. (1994). Loss of circadian behavioral rhythms and per RNA oscillations in the *Drosophila* mutant timeless. *Science, 263,* 1603–1606.

Seiger, A., Nordberg, A., von Holst, H., Backman, L., et al. (1993). Intracranial infusion of purified nerve growth factor to an Alzheimer patient: The first attempt of a possible future treatment strategy. *Behavioural Brain Research, 57,* 255–261.

Seil, F. J., Kelly, J. M., and Leiman, A. L. (1974). Anatomical organization of cerebral neocortex in tissue culture. *Experimental Neurology, 45,* 435–450.

Seil, F. J., Leiman, A. L., Herman, M. M., and Fisk, R. A. (1977). Direct effects of ethanol on central nervous system cultures: An electrophysiological and morphological study. *Experimental Neurology, 55,* 390–404.

Seil, F. J., Leiman, A. L., and Kelly, J. (1976). Neuroelectric blocking factors in multiple sclerosis and normal human sera. *Archives of Neurology, 33,* 418–422.

Selkoe, D. J. (1991). Amyloid protein and Alzheimer's disease. *Scientific American, 265*(5), 68–71.

Selkoe, D. J. (1999). Translating cell biology into therapeutic advances in Alzheimer's disease. *Nature, 399*(6738 Suppl.), A23–A31.

Selye, H. (1956). *The stress of life.* New York: McGraw-Hill.

Semendeferi, K., and Damasio, H. (2000). The brain and its main anatomical subdivisions in living hominoids using magnetic resonance imaging. *Journal of Human Evolution, 38,* 317–332.

Semendeferi, K., Damasio, H., Frank, R., and Van Hoesen, G. W. (1997). The evolution of the frontal lobes: A volumetric analysis based on three-dimensional reconstructions of magnetic resonance scans of human and ape brains. *Journal of Human Evolution, 32,* 375–388.

Sendtner, M., Holtmann, B., and Hughes, R. A. (1996). The response of motoneurons to neurotrophins. *Neurochemical Research, 21,* 831–841.

Serrano, P. A., Beniston, D. S., Oxonian, M. G., Rodriguez, W. A., et al. (1994). Differential effects of protein kinase inhibitors and activators on memory formation in the 2-day-old chick. *Behavioral and Neural Biology, 61,* 60–72.

Serviere, J., Webster, W. R., and Calford, M. B. (1984). Isofrequency labelling revealed by a combined [14C]-2-deoxyglucose, electrophysiological, and horseradish peroxidase study of the inferior colliculus of the cat. *Journal of Comparative Neurology, 228,* 463–477.

Seuss, Dr. (1987). *The tough coughs as he ploughs the dough: Early writings and cartoons by Dr. Seuss.* New York: Morrow.

Seyfarth, R. M., and Cheney, D. L. (1997). Behavioral mechanisms underlying vocal communication in nonhuman primates. *Animal Learning & Behavior, 25,* 249–267.

Shapiro, R. M. (1993). Regional neuropathology in schizophrenia: Where are we? Where are we going? *Schizophrenia Research, 10,* 187–239.

Sharma, J., Angelucci, A., and Sur, M. (2000). Induction of visual orientation modules in auditory cortex. *Nature, 404,* 841–847.

Shaw, P. J., Cirelli, C., Greenspan, R. J., and Tononi, G. (2000). Correlates of sleep and waking in *Drosophila melanogaster. Science, 287,* 1834–1837.

Shaywitz, S. E., Shaywitz, B. A., Pugh, K. R., Fulbright, R. K., et al. (1998). Functional disruption in the organization of the brain for reading in dyslexia. *Proceedings of the National Academy of Sciences, USA, 95,* 2636–2641.

Shearman, L. P., Sriram, S., Weaver, D. R., Maywood, E. S., et al. (2000). Interacting molecular loops in the mammalian circadian clock. *Science, 288,* 1013–1019.

Sherrington, C. S. (1897). Part III. The central nervous system. In M. Foster (Ed.), *A textbook of physiology.* London: Macmillan.

Sherrington, C. S. (1898). Experiments in examination of the peripheral distribution of the fibres of the posterior roots of some spinal nerves. *Philosophical Transactions, 190,* 45–186.

Sherry, D. F. (1992). Memory, the hippocampus, and natural selection: Studies of food-storing birds. In L. R. Squire and N. Butters (Eds.), *Neuropsychology of memory* (2nd ed., pp. 521–532). New York: Guilford.

Sherry, D. F., Jacobs, L. F., and Gaulin, S. J. (1992). Spatial memory and adaptive specialization of the hippocampus. *Trends in Neurosciences, 15,* 298–303.

Sherry, D. F., Jacobs, L. F., and Gaulin, S. J. (1993). "The hippocampus and spatial memory": Reply. *Trends in Neurosciences, 16,* 57.

Sherry, D. F., and Schacter, D. L. (1987). The evolution of multiple memory systems. *Psychological Review, 94,* 439–454.

Sherry, D. F., and Vaccarino, A. L. (1989). Hippocampus and memory for food caches in black-capped chickadees. *Behavioral Neuroscience, 103,* 308–318.

Sherry, D. F., Vaccarino, A. L., Buckenham, K., and Herz, R. S. (1989). The hippocampal complex of food-storing birds. *Brain Behavior and Evolution, 34,* 308–317.

Sherwin, B. B. (1998). Use of combined estrogen-androgen preparations in the postmenopause: Evidence from clinical studies. *International Journal of Fertility and Women's Medicine, 43*(2), 98–103.

Shiang, R., Ryan, S. G., Zhu, Y. Z., Hahn, A. F., O'Connell, P., and Wasmuth, J. J. (1993). Mutations in the alpha 1 subunit of the inhibitory glycine receptor cause the dominant neurologic disorder, hyperexplexia. *Nature Genetics, 5,* 351–358.

Shors, T. J., Miesegaes, G., Beylin, A., Zhao, M., et al. (2001). Neurogenesis in the adult is involved in the formation of trace memories. *Nature, 410,* 372–376.

Shoulson, I. (1992). Neuroprotective clinical strategies for Parkinson's disease. *Annals of Neurology, 32,* S143–S145.

Siarey, R. J., Coan, E. J., Rapoport, S. I., and Galdzicki, Z. (1997). Responses to NMDA in cultured hippocampal neurons from trisomy 16 mice. *Neuroscience Letters, 232,* 131–134.

Sibley, C. G., and Ahlquist, J. E. (1987). DNA hybridization evidence of hominoid phylogeny: Results from an expanded data set. *Journal of Molecular Evolution, 26,* 99–121.

Sibley, C. G., and Ahlquist, J. E. (1990). *Phylogeny and classification of birds: A study in molecular evolution.* New Haven, CT: Yale University Press.

Sibley, C. G., Comstock, J. A., and Ahlquist, J. E. (1990). DNA hybridization evidence of hominoid phylogeny: A reanalysis of the data. *Journal of Molecular Evolution, 30,* 202–236.

Siegel, J. M. (1994). Brainstem mechanisms generating REM sleep. In M. H. Kryger, T. Roth, and W. C. Dement (Eds.), *Principles and practice of sleep medicine* (2nd ed., pp. 125–144). Philadelphia: Saunders.

Siegel, J. M., Manger, P. R., Nienhuis, R., Fahringer, H. M., et al. (1999). Sleep in the platypus. *Neuroscience, 91,* 391–400.

Siegel, J. M., Nienhuis, R., Gulyani, S., Ouyang, S., et al. (1999). Neuronal degeneration in canine narcolepsy. *Journal of Neuroscience, 19,* 248–257.

Siegel, R. K. (1989). *Intoxication: Life in pursuit of artificial paradise.* New York: Dutton.

Sierra-Honigmann, M. R., Nath, A. K., Murakami, C., García-Cardeña, G., et al. (1998). Biological action of leptin as an angiogenic factor. *Science, 281,* 1683–1686.

Siever, L. J., and Davis, K. L. (1985). Overview: Toward a dysregulation hypothesis of depression. *American Journal of Psychiatry, 142,* 1017–1031.

Sigurdson, E., Staley, D., Matas, M., Hildahl, K., et al. (1994). A five year review of youth suicide in Manitoba. *Canadian Journal of Psychiatry, 39,* 397–403.

Silberman, E. K., and Weingartner, H. (1986). Hemispheric lateralization of function related to emotion. *Brain and Cognition, 5,* 322–353.

Silva, A. J., Giese, K. P., Fedorov, N. B., Frankland, P. W., et al. (1998). Molecular, cellular, and neuroanatomical substrates of place learning. *Neurobiology of Learning and Memory, 70,* 44–61.

Silva, A. J., Kogan, J. H., Frankland, P. W., and Kida, S. (1998). CREB and memory. *Annual Review of Neuroscience, 21,* 127–148.

Silva, A. J., Paylor, R., Wehner, J. M., and Tonegawa, S. (1992). Impaired spatial learning in alpha-calcium-calmodulin kinase II mutant mice. *Science, 257,* 206–211.

Silva, D. A., and Satz, P. (1979). Pathological left-handedness. Evaluation of a model. *Brain and Language, 7,* 8–16.

Silver, R., Lesauter, J., Tresco, P., and Lehman, M. (1996). A diffusible coupling signal from the transplanted suprachiasmatic nucleus controlling circadian locomotor rhythms. *Nature, 382,* 810–813.

Simic, G., Kostovic, I., Winblad, B., and Bogdanovic, N. (1997). Volume and number of neurons of the human hippocampal formation in normal aging and Alzheimer's disease. *Journal of Comparative Neurology, 379,* 482–494.

Simpson, J. B., Epstein, A. N., and Camardo, J. S., Jr. (1978). Localization of receptors for the dipsogenic action of angiotensin II in the subfornical organ of rat. *Journal of Comparative and Physiological Psychology, 92,* 581–601.

Skinner, M., Holden, L., and Holden, T. (1997). Parameter selection to optimize speech recognition with the nucleus implant. *Otolaryngology and Head and Neck Surgery, 117,* 188–195.

Skrede, K. K., and Malthe-Sorenssen, E. (1981). Increased resting and evoked release of transmitter following repetitive electrical tetanization in hippocampus: A biochemical correlate to long-lasting synaptic potentiation. *Brain Research, 208,* 436–441.

Smale, L., Holekamp, K. E., and White, P. A. (1999). Siblicide revisited in the spotted hyaena: Does it conform to obligate or facultative models? *Animal Behaviour, 58,* 545–551.

Smale, L., Lee, T. M., Nelson, R. J., and Zucker, I. (1990). Prolactin counteracts effects of short day lengths on pelage growth in the meadow vole, *Microtus pennsylvanicus. Journal of Experimental Zoology, 253,* 186–188.

Small, S. L. (1994). Pharmacotherapy of aphasia. A critical review. *Stroke, 25,* 1282–1289.

Smith, A., and Sugar, O. (1975). Development of above normal language and intelligence 21 years after hemispherectomy. *Neurology, 25,* 813–818.

Smith, C. (1985). Sleep states and learning. A review of the animal literature. *Neuroscience and Biobehavioral Reviews, 9,* 157–169.

Smith, C. (1995). Sleep states and memory processes. *Behavioural Brain Research, 69,* 137–145.

Smith, C. M., and Luskin, M. B. (1998). Cell cycle length of olfactory bulb neuronal progenitors in the rostral migratory stream. *Developmental Dynamics, 213,* 220–227.

Smith, D. E., Roberts, J., Gage, F. H., and Tuszynski, M. H. (1999). Age-associated neuronal atrophy occurs in the primate brain and is reversible by growth factor gene therapy. *Proceedings of the National Academy of Sciences, USA, 96,* 10893–10898.

Smith, J. M., Kucharski, L., Oswald, W. T., and Waterman, L. J. (1979). A systematic investigation of tardive dyskinesia in inpatients. *American Journal of Psychiatry, 136,* 918–922.

Smith, M. A., Brandt, J., and Shadmehr, R. (2000). Motor disorder in Huntington's disease begins as a dysfunction in error feedback control. *Nature, 403,* 544–549.

Smith, P. B., Compton, D. R., Welch, S. P., Razdan, R. K., et al. (1994). The pharmacological activity of anandamide, a putative endogenous cannabinoid, in mice. *Journal of Pharmacology and Experimental Therapeutics, 270,* 219–227.

Smith, S. J. (1999). Dissecting dendrite dynamics. *Science, 283,* 1860–1861.

Snider, S. R. (1982). Cerebellar pathology in schizophrenia—Cause or consequence? *Neuroscience and Biobehavioral Reviews, 6,* 47–53.

Snyder, A. Z., Abdullaev, Y. G., Posner, M. I., and Raichle, M. E. (1995). Scalp electrical potentials reflect regional cerebral blood flow responses during processing of written words. *Proceedings of the National Academy of Sciences, USA, 92,* 1689–1693.

Snyder, F. (1969). Sleep and REM as biological enigmas. In A. Kales (Ed.), *Sleep: Physiology and pathology* (pp. 266–280). Philadelphia: Lippincott.

Snyder, S. H., and D'Amato, R. J. (1985). Predicting Parkinson's disease. *Nature, 317,* 198–199.

Snyder, S. H., and D'Amato, R. J. (1986). MPTP: A neurotoxin relevant to the pathophysiology of Parkinson's disease. *Neurology, 36,* 250–258.

Sobel, N., Khan, R. M., Saltman, A., Sullivan, E. V., et al. (1999). The world smells different to each nostril. *Nature, 402,* 35.

Sobel, N., Prabhakaran, V., Desmond, J. E., Glover, G. H., et al. (1998). Sniffing and smelling: Separate subsystems in the human olfactory cortex. *Nature, 392,* 282–286.

Sobel, N., Prabhakaran, V., Zhao, Z., Desmond, J. E., et al. (2000). Time course of odorant-induced activation in the human primary olfactory cortex. *Journal of Neurophysiology, 83,* 537–551.

Solomon, A. (1998). Personal history: Anatomy of melancholy. *The New Yorker, 73,* 46–61.

Song, H.-J., Ming, G.-L., He, Z., Lehmann, M., et al. (1998). Conversion of neuronal growth cone responses from repulsion to attraction by cyclic nucleotides. *Science, 281,* 1515–1518.

Sorensen, P. W., and Goetz, F. W. (1993). Pheromonal and reproductive function of F prostaglandins and their metabolites in teleost fish. *Journal of Lipid Mediators, 6,* 385–393.

Souied, E. H., Benlian, P., Amouyel, P., Feingold, J., et al. (1998). The epsilon4 allele of the apolipoprotein E gene as a potential protective factor for exudative age-related macular degeneration. *American Journal of Ophthalmology, 125*, 353–359.

Spear, N. F. (1976). Retrieval of memories: A psychobiological approach. In W. K. Estes (Ed.), *Handbook of learning and cognitive processes: Vol. 4. Attention and memory.* Hillsdale, NJ: Erlbaum.

Spector, N. H. (1987). Old and new strategies in the conditioning of immune responses. *Annals of the New York Academy of Sciences, 496,* 522–531.

Sperry, R. W. (1974). Lateral specialization in the surgically separated hemispheres. In F. O. Schmitt and F. G. Worden (Eds.), *The neurosciences: Third study program* (pp. 5–16). Cambridge, MA: MIT Press.

Sperry, R. W., Stamm, J., and Miner, N. (1956). Relearning tests for interocular transfer following division of optic chiasma and corpus callosum in cats. *Journal of Comparative and Physiological Psychology, 49,* 529–533.

Spiegler, B. J., and Mishkin, M. (1981). Evidence for the sequential participation of inferior temporal cortex and amygdala in the acquisition of stimulus-reward associations. *Behavioural Brain Research, 3,* 303–317.

Spiegler, B. J., and Yeni-Komshian, G. H. (1983). Incidence of left-handed writing in a college population with reference to family patterns of hand preference. *Neuropsychologia, 21,* 651–659.

Squire, L. R., Amaral, D. G., Zola-Morgan, S., and Kritchevsky, M. P. G. (1989). Description of brain injury in the amnesic patient N.A. based on magnetic resonance imaging. *Experimental Neurology, 105,* 23–35.

Squire, L. R., Knowlton, B., and Musen, G. (1993). The structure and organization of memory. *Annual Review of Psychology, 44,* 453–495.

Squire, L. R., and McKee, R. (1992). Influence of prior events on cognitive judgments in amnesia. *Journal of Experimental Psychology. Learning, Memory, and Cognition, 18,* 106–115.

Squire, L. R., and Moore, R. Y. (1979). Dorsal thalamic lesion in a noted case of chronic memory dysfunction. *Annals of Neurology, 6,* 503–506.

Squire, L. R., and Slater, P. C. (1975). Forgetting in very long-term memory as assessed by an improved questionnaire technique. *Journal of Experimental Psychology: Human Learning and Memory, 104,* 50–54.

Squire, L. R., and Zola-Morgan, S. (1991). The medial temporal lobe memory system. *Science, 253,* 1380–1386.

Standing, L. G. (1973). Learning 10,000 pictures. *Quarterly Journal of Experimental Psychology, 25,* 207–222.

Stanley, B. G., Anderson, K. C., Grayson, M. H., and Leibowitz, S. F. (1989). Repeated hypothalamic stimulation with neuropeptide Y increases daily carbohydrate and fat intake and body weight gain in female rats. *Physiology & Behavior, 46,* 173–177.

Starkstein, S. E., and Robinson, R. G. (1994). Neuropsychiatric aspects of stroke. In C. E. Coffey, J. L. Cummings, M. R. Lovell, and G. D. Pearlson (Eds.), *The American Psychiatric Press textbook of geriatric neuropsychiatry* (pp. 457–477). Washington, DC: American Psychiatric Press.

Starmer, G. A. (1994). *Drugs and traffic safety.* Canberra, Australia: Federal Office of Road Safety.

Staubli, U. V. (1995). Parallel properties of long-term potentiation and memory. In J. L. McGaugh, N. M. Weinberger, and G. Lynch (Eds.), *Brain and memory: Modulation and mediation of neuroplasticity* (pp. 303–318). New York: Oxford University Press.

Staubli, U., Le, T. T., and Lynch, G. (1995). Variants of olfactory memory and their dependencies on the hippocampal formation. *Journal of Neuroscience, 15,* 1162–1171.

Stein, B., and Meredith, M. A. (1993). *The merging of the senses.* Cambridge, MA: MIT Press.

Stein, M., Keller, S., and Schleifer, S. (1981). The hypothalamus and the immune response. In H. Weiner, A. Hofer, and A. J. Stunkard (Eds.), *Brain behavior and bodily disease* (pp. 45–63). New York: Raven.

Stein, M., and Miller, A. H. (1993). Stress, the hypothalamic-pituitary-adrenal axis, and immune function. *Advances in Experimental Medicine and Biology, 335,* 1–5.

Stein, M., Miller, A. H., and Trestman, R. L. (1991). Depression, the immune system, and health and illness. Findings in search of meaning. *Archives of General Psychiatry, 48,* 171–177.

Steinmetz, H., Volkmann, J., Jancke, L., and Freund, H. J. (1991). Anatomical left-right asymmetry of language-related temporal cortex is different in left- and right-handers. *Annals of Neurology, 29,* 315–319.

Stella, N., Schweitzer, P., and Piomelli, D. (1997). A second endogenous cannabinoid that modulates long-term potentiation. *Nature, 388,* 773–778.

Stephan, F. K., and Zucker, I. (1972). Circadian rhythms in drinking behavior and locomotor activity of rats are eliminated by hypothalamic lesions. *Proceedings of the National Academy of Sciences, USA, 69,* 1583–1586.

Stephan, H., Frahm, H., and Baron, G. (1981). New and revised data on volumes of brain structures in insectivores and primates. *Folia Primatologica, 35,* 1–29.

Steptoe, A. (1993). Stress and the cardiovascular system: A psychosocial perspective. In S. C. Stanford and P. Salmon (Eds.), *Stress: From synapse to syndrome* (pp. 119–141). London: Academic Press.

Stern, C. E., Corkin, S., Gonzalez, R. G., Guimaraes, A. R., et al. (1996). The hippocampal formation participates in novel picture encoding: Evidence from functional magnetic resonance imaging. *Proceedings of the National Academy of Sciences, USA, 93,* 8660–8665.

Stern, K., and McClintock, M. (1998). Regulation of ovulation by human pheromones. *Nature, 392,* 177–179.

Sternberg, D. E., VanKammen, D. P., Lerner, P., and Bunney, W. E. (1982). Schizophrenia: Dopamine beta-hydroxylase activity and treatment response. *Science, 216,* 1423–1425.

Sternberg, R. J. (2000). Cognition. The holy grail of general intelligence. *Science, 289,* 399–401.

Stoerig, P., and Cowey, A. (1997). Blindsight in man and monkey. *Brain, 120,* 535–559.

Stone, J., Dreher, G., and Leventhal, A. (1979). Hierarchical and parallel mechanisms in the organization of visual cortex. *Brain Research, 180,* 345–394.

Stone, V. E., Nisenson, L., Eliassen, J. C., and Gazzaniga, M. S. (1996). Left hemisphere representations of emotional facial expressions. *Neuropsychologia, 34,* 23–29.

Stricker, E. M. (1977). The renin-angiotensin system and thirst: A reevaluation. II. Drinking elicited in rats by caval ligation or isoproterenol. *Journal of Comparative and Physiological Psychology, 91,* 1220–1231.

Striedter, G. F. (1997). The telencephalon of tetrapods in evolution. *Brain, Behavior and Evolution, 49,* 179–213.

Strittmatter, W. J., and Roses, A. D. (1996). Apolipoprotein E and Alzheimer's disease. *Annual Review of Neuroscience, 19,* 53–77.

Stromswold, K. (1995). The cognitive and neural bases of language acquisition. In M. S. Gazzaniga (Ed.), *The cognitive neurosciences* (pp. 855–870). Cambridge, MA: MIT Press.

Stroud, R. M., and Finer-Moore, J. (1985). Acetylcholine receptor structure, function, and evolution. *Annual Review of Cell Biology, 1,* 317–351.

Stuve, T. A., Friedman, L., Jesberger, J. A., Gilmore, G. C., et al. (1997). The relationship between smooth pursuit performance, motion perception and sustained visual attention in patients with schizophrenia and normal controls. *Psychological Medicine, 27,* 143–152.

Sullivan, R. M., and Leon, M. (1986). Early olfactory learning induces an enhanced olfactory bulb response in young rats. *Brain Research, 392,* 278–282.

Sweet, W. H. (1973). Treatment of medically intractable mental disease by limited frontal leucotomy—Justifiable? *New England Journal of Medicine, 289,* 1117–1125.

Takagi, S. F. (1989). Standardized olfactometries in Japan—A review over ten years. *Chemical Senses, 14,* 25–46.

Takahashi, J. S. (1995). Molecular neurobiology and genetics of circadian rhythms in mammals. *Annual Review of Neuroscience, 18,* 531–554.

Takahashi, Y. (1979). Growth hormone secretion related to the sleep and waking rhythm. In R. Drucker-Colin, M. Shkurovich, and M. B. Sterman (Eds.), *The functions of sleep.* New York: Academic Press.

Talairach, J., and Tournoux, P. (1988). *Co-planar stereotaxic atlas of the human brain: A 3-dimensional proportional system, an approach to cerebral imaging.* Stuttgart, Germany: Thieme.

Tallal, P., Galaburda, A. M., Llinas, R. R., and von Euler, C. (1993). *Temporal information processing in the nervous system: Special reference to dyslexia and dysphasia.* New York: New York Academy of Sciences.

Tallal, P., and Schwartz, J. (1980). Temporal processing, speech perception and hemispheric asymmetry. *Trends in Neurosciences, 3,* 309–311.

Tamminga, C. A., and Schulz, S. C. (1991). *Schizophrenia research.* New York: Raven.

Tanaka, K. (1993). Neuronal mechanisms of object recognition. *Science, 262,* 685–688.

Tanaka, Y., Kamo, T., Yoshida, M., and Yamadori, A. (1991). "So-called" cortical deafness. Clinical, neurophysiological and radiological observations. *Brain, 114,* 2385–2401.

Tanda, G., Munzar, P., and Goldberg, S. R. (2000). Self-administration behavior is maintained by the psychoactive ingredient of marijuana in squirrel monkeys. *Nature Neuroscience, 3,* 1073–1074.

Tandan, R., and Bradley, W. G. (1985). Amyotrophic lateral sclerosis: Part I. Clinical features, pathology, and ethical issues in management. *Annals of Neurology, 18,* 271–281.

Tang, N. M., Dong, H. W., Wang, X. M., Tsui, Z. C., et al. (1997). Cholecystokinin antisense RNA increases the analgesic effect induced by electroacupuncture or low dose morphine: Conversion of low responder rats into high responders. *Pain, 71,* 71–80.

Tang, Y. P., Shimizu, E., Dube, G. R., Rampon, C., et al. (1999). Genetic enhancement of learning and memory in mice. *Nature, 401,* 63–69.

Tanila, H., Shapiro, M., Gallagher, M., and Eichenbaum, H. (1997). Brain aging: Changes in the nature of information coding by the hippocampus. *Journal of Neuroscience, 17,* 5155–5166.

Tanila, H., Sipila, P., Shapiro, M., and Eichenbaum, H. (1997). Brain aging: Impaired coding of novel environmental cues. *Journal of Neuroscience, 17,* 5167–5174.

Tardiff, B. E., Newman, M. F., Saunders, A. M., Strittmatter, W. J., et al. (1997). Preliminary report of a genetic basis for cognitive decline after cardiac operations. The neurologic outcome research group of the Duke Heart Center. *Annals of Thoracic Surgery, 64,* 715–720.

Taub, E. (1976). Movement in nonhuman primates deprived of somatosensory feedback. *Exercise and Sport Sciences Reviews, 4,* 335–374.

Taylor, R. (1990). Immediate-early genes may offer a new key to the circadian clock. *Journal of NIH Research, 2,* 49–53.

Teasdale, J. D., Howard, R. J., Cox, S. G., Ha, Y., et al. (1999). Functional study of the cognitive generation of affect. *American Journal of Psychiatry, 156,* 209–215.

Technau, G. M. (1984). Fiber number in the mushroom bodies of adult *Drosophila melanogaster* depends on age, sex and experience. *Journal of Neurogenetics, 1,* 113–126.

Teitelbaum, P., and Stellar, E. (1954). Recovery from failure to eat produced by hypothalamic lesions. *Science, 120,* 894–895.

Tenn, W. (1968). *The seven sexes.* New York: Ballantine.

Terman, G. W., Shavit, Y., Lewis, J. W., Cannon, J. T., et al. (1984). Intrinsic mechanisms of pain inhibition: Activation by stress. *Science, 226,* 1270–1277.

Terrace, H. S. (1979). *Nim.* New York: Knopf.

Terrazas, A., and McNaughton, B. L. (2000). Brain growth and the cognitive map. *Proceedings of the National Academy of Sciences, USA, 97,* 4414–4416.

Tessier-Lavigne, M., and Placzek, M. (1991). Target attraction: Are developing axons guided by chemotropism? *Trends in Neurosciences, 14,* 303–310.

Tessier-Lavigne, M., Placzek, M., Lumsden, A. G., Dodd, J., et al. (1988). Chemotropic guidance of developing axons in the mammalian central nervous system. *Nature, 336,* 775–778.

Tetel, M. J. (2000). Nuclear receptor coactivators in neuroendocrine function. *Journal of Neuroendocrinology, 12,* 927–932.

Tetrud, J. W., Langston, J. W., Irwin, I., and Snow, B. (1994). Parkinsonism caused by petroleum waste ingestion. *Neurology, 44,* 1051–1054.

Teuber, H.-L., Milner, B., and Vaughan, H. G. (1968). Persistent anterograde amnesia after stab wound of the basal brain. *Neuropsychologia, 6,* 267–282.

Teyler, T. J., and DiScenna, P. (1986). Long-term potentiation. *Annual Review of Neuroscience, 10,* 131–161.

Thannickal, T. C., Moore, R. Y., Nienhuis, R., Ramanathan, L., et al. (2000). Reduced number of hypocretin neurons in human narcolepsy. *Neuron, 27,* 469–474.

Thaw, A. K., Frankmann, S., and Hill, D. L. (2000). Behavioral taste responses of developmentally NaCl-restricted rats to various concentrations of NaCl. *Behavioral Neuroscience, 114,* 437–441.

Theunissen, F. E., and Doupe, A. J. (1998). Temporal and spectral sensitivity of complex auditory neurons in the nucleus HVc of male zebra finches. *Journal of Neuroscience, 18,* 3786–3802.

Thibos, L. N. L. W. R. (1985). Orientation bias of brisk-transient y-cells of the cat retina for drifting and alternating gratings. *Experimental Brain Research, 58,* 1–10.

Thiruchelvam, M., Richfield, E. K., Baggs, R. B., Tank, A. W., et al. (2000). The nigrostriatal system as a preferential target of repeated exposures to combined parquat and maneb: Implications for Parkinson's disease. *Journal of Neuroscience, 20,* 9207–9214.

Thomas, C. B., Duszynski, K. R., and Shaffer, J. W. (1979). Family attitudes reported in youth as potential predictors of cancer. *Psychosomatic Medicine, 41,* 287–302.

Thompson, G. N., and Halliday, D. (1990). Significant phenylalanine hydroxylation in vivo in patients with classical phenylketonuria. *Journal of Clinical Investigation, 86,* 317–322.

Thompson, P. M., Giedd, J. N., Woods, R. P., MacDonald, D., et al. (2000). Growth patterns in the developing brain detected by using continuum mechanical tensor maps. *Nature, 404,* 190–193.

Thompson, R. F. (1990). Neural mechanisms of classical conditioning in mammals. *Philosophical Transactions of the Royal Society of London. Series B: Biological Sciences, 329,* 161–170.

Thompson, R. F. (1992). Memory. *Current Opinion in Neurobiology, 2,* 203–208.

Thompson, R. F., and Krupa, D. J. (1994). Organization of memory traces in the mammalian brain. *Annual Review of Neuroscience, 17,* 519–549.

Thompson, R. F., Thompson, J. K., Kim, J. J., Krupa, D. J., et al. (1998). The nature of reinforcement in cerebellar learning. *Neurobiology of Learning and Memory, 70,* 150–176.

Thompson, T., and Schuster, C. R. (1964). Morphine self-administration, food reinforced and avoidance behaviour in rhesus monkeys. *Psychopharmacologia, 5,* 87–94.

Thorpe, S.J., and Fabre-Thorpe, M (2001). Seeking categories in the brain. *Science, 291,* 260–263.

Thurber, J., and White, E. B. (1929). *Is sex necessary? or, Why you feel the way you do.* New York: Harper and Bros..

Timberlake, W. (1993). Animal behavior: A continuing synthesis. *Annual Review of Psychology, 44,* 675–708.

Tobias, P. V. (1980). L'evolution du cerveau humain. *La Recherche, 11,* 282–292.

Toenniessen, L. M., Casey, D. E., and McFarland, B. H. (1985). Tardive dyskinesia in the aged. Duration of treatment relationships. *Archives of General Psychiatry, 42,* 278–284.

Tolman, E. C. (1949a). *Purposive behavior in animals and men.* Berkeley: University of California Press.

Tolman, E. C. (1949b). There is more than one kind of learning. *Psychological Review, 56,* 144–155.

Tolman, E. C., and Honzik, C. H. (1930). Introduction and removal of reward, and maze performance in rats. *University of California Publications in Psychology, 4,* 257–275.

Toni, N., Buchs, P. A., Nikonenko, I., Bron, C. R., et al. (1999). LTP promotes formation of multiple spine synapses between a single axon terminal and a dendrite. *Nature, 402,* 421–425.

Tootell, R. B. H., Hadjikhani, N. K., Vanduffel, W., Liu, A. K., et al. (1998). Functional analysis of primary visual cortex (V1) in humans. *Proceedings of the National Academy of Sciences, USA, 95,* 811–817.

Tootell, R. B., Silverman, M. S., Hamilton, S. L., De Valois, R. L., et al. (1988). Functional anatomy of macaque striate cortex. III. Color. *Journal of Neuroscience, 8,* 1569–1593.

Tootell, R. B., Silverman, M. S., Switkes, E., and De Valois, R. L. (1982). Deoxyglucose analysis of retinotopic organization in primate striate cortex. *Science, 218,* 902–904.

Tordoff, M., Rawson, N., and Friedman, M. (1991). 2,5-anhydro-d-mannitol acts in liver to initiate feeding. *American Journal of Physiology, 261,* R283–R288.

Torrey, E. F., Bowler, A. E., Taylor, E. H., and Gottesman, I. I. (1994). *Schizophrenia and manic depressive disorder.* New York: Basic Books.

Torvik, A., Torp, S., and Lindboe, C. F. (1986). Atrophy of the cerebellar vermis in ageing. A morphometric and histologic study. *Journal of the Neurological Sciences, 76,* 283–294.

Trachtenberg, R. E., Jin, S., Patterson, M., Schneider, L. S., et al. (2000). Exceptional familial clustering for extreme longevity in humans. *Journal of the American Geriatrics Society, 48,* 1483–1485.

Tranel, D., and Damasio, A. R. (1985). Knowledge without awareness: An autonomic index of facial recognition by prosopagnosics. *Science, 228,* 1453–1454.

Tranel, D., Damasio, H., and Damasio, A. R. (1997). A neural basis for the retrieval of conceptual knowledge. *Neuropsychologia, 35,* 1319–1327.

Travis, J. (1992). Can "hair cells" unlock deafness? *Science, 257,* 1344–1345.

Treisman, M. (1977). Motion sickness—Evolutionary hypotheses. *Science, 197,* 493–495.

Trimble, M. R. (1991). Interictal psychoses of epilepsy. *Advances in Neurology, 55,* 143–152.

Trivers, R. (1985). *Social evolution.* Menlo Park, CA: Benjamin/Cummings.

True, W. R., Rice, J., Eisen, S. A., Heath, A. C., et al. (1993). A twin study of genetic and environmental contributions to liability for posttraumatic stress symptoms. *Archives of General Psychiatry, 50,* 257–264.

Truman, J. W. (1983). Programmed cell death in the nervous system of an adult insect. *Journal of Comparative Neurology, 216,* 445–452.

Tsen, G., Williams, B., Allaire, P., Zhou, Y.-D., et al. (2000). Receptors with opposing functions are in postsynaptic microdomains under one presynaptic terminal. *Nature Neuroscience, 3,* 126–132.

Ts'o, D. Y., Frostig, R. D., Lieke, E. E., and Grinvald, A. (1990). Functional organization of primate visual cortex revealed by high resolution optical imaging. *Science, 249,* 417–420.

Tully, T. (1987). *Drosophila* learning and memory revisited. *Trends in Neurosciences, 10,* 330–335.

Tully, T. (1991). Physiology of mutations affecting learning and memory in *Drosophila*—The missing link between gene product and behavior. *Trends in Neurosciences, 14,* 163–164.

Tulving, E. (1972). Episodic and semantic memory. In E. Tulving and W. Donaldson (Eds.), *Organization of memory* (pp. 381–403). New York: Academic Press.

Tulving, E. (1989). Memory: Performance, knowledge, and experience. *European Journal of Cognitive Psychology, 1,* 3–26.

Tulving, E. (1998). Brain/mind correlates of human memory. In M. Sabourin, F. Criak, and M. Robert (Eds.), *Advances in psychological science: Vol. 2. Biological and cognitive aspects* (pp. 441–460). Hove, East Sussex, England: Psychology Press.

Tulving, E., Hayman, C. A., and Macdonald, C. A. (1991). Long-lasting perceptual priming and semantic learning in amnesia: A case experiment. *Journal of Experimental Psychology: Learning, Memory, and Cognition, 17,* 595–617.

Tulving, E., and Markowitsch, H. J. (1997). Memory beyond the hippocampus. *Current Opinion in Neurobiology, 7,* 209–216.

Tulving, E., Markowitsch, H. J., Craik, F. E., Habib, R., et al. (1996). Novelty and familiarity activations in PET studies of memory encoding and retrieval. *Cerebral Cortex, 6,* 71–79.

Turek, F. (1985). Circadian neural rhythms in mammals. *Annual Review of Physiology, 47,* 49–64.

Turkewitz, G. (1988). A prenatal source for the development of hemispheric specialization. In D. L. Molfese and S. J. Segalowitz (Eds.), *Brain lateralization in children: Developmental implications* (pp. 73–81). New York: Guilford.

Turner, A. M., and Greenough, W. T. (1985). Differential rearing effects on rat visual cortex synapses. I. Synaptic and neuronal density and synapses per neuron. *Brain Research, 329,* 195–203.

Turner, C. D., and Bagnara, J. T. (1976). *General endocrinology* (6th ed.). New York: Academic Press.

Underwood, B. J. (1969). Attributes of memory. *Psychology Review, 76,* 559–573.

Ungerleider, L. G., Courtney, S. M., and Haxby, J. V. (1998). A neural system for human visual working memory. *Proceedings of the National Academy of Sciences, USA, 95,* 883–890.

Ursin, H., Baade, E., and Levine, S. (1978). *Psychobiology of stress: A study of coping men.* New York: Academic Press.

U.S. Department of Health and Human Services. (1991). *Drug abuse and drug abuse research: The third triennial report to Congress.* Rockville, MD: National Institute on Drug Abuse.

Vainio, S., Heikkila, M., Kispert, A., Chin, N., et al. (1999). Female development in mammals is regulated by Wnt-4 signalling. *Nature, 397,* 405–409.

Valbo, A. B., and Johansson, R. S. (1984). Properties of cutaneous mechanoreceptors in the human hand related to touch sensation. *Human Neurobiology, 3,* 3–15.

Valenstein, E. S. (1973). *Brain control.* New York: Wiley-Interscience.

Valenstein, E. S. (1980). *The psychosurgery debate: Scientific, legal, and ethical perspectives.* San Francisco: Freeman.

Valenstein, E. S. (1986). *Great and desperate cures: The rise and decline of psychosurgery and other radical treatments for mental illness.* New York: Basic Books.

Vallbona, C., Hazlewood, C., and Jurida, G. (1997). Response of pain to static magnetic fields in postpolio patients: A double-blind pilot study. *Archives of Physical Medicine and Rehabilitation, 78,* 1200–1203.

Vallortigara, G., Rogers, L. J., and Bisazza, A. (1999). Possible evolutionary origins of cognitive brain lateralization. *Brain Research. Brain Research Reviews, 30,* 164–175.

van Bergeijk, W. A. (1967). The evolution of vertebrate hearing. In W. D. Neff (Ed.), *Contributions to sensory physiology: Vol. 3.* New York: Academic Press.

van der Horst, G. T., Muijtjens, M., Kobayashi, K., Takano, R., et al. (1999). Mammalian Cry1 and Cry2 are essential for maintenance of circadian rhythms. *Nature, 398,* 627–630.

Vander Wall, S. B. (1982). An experimental analysis of cache recovery in Clark's nutcracker. *Animal Behaviour, 30,* 84–94.

VanDoren, M. J., Matthews, D. B., Janis, G. C., Grobin, A. C., et al. (2000). Neuroactive steroid 3alpha-hydroxy-5alpha-pregnan-20-one modulates electrophysiological and behavioral actions of ethanol. *Journal of Neuroscience, 20,* 1982–1989.

Van Essen, D. C., Anderson, C. H., and Felleman, D. J. (1992). Information processing in the primate visual system: An integrated systems perspective. *Science, 255,* 419–423.

Van Essen, D. C., and Drury, H. A. (1997). Structural and functional analyses of human cerebral cortex using a surface-based atlas. *Journal of Neuroscience, 17,* 7079–7102.

van Praag, H., Kempermann, G., and Gage, F. H. (2000). Neural consequences of environmental enrichment. *Nature Reviews: Neuroscience, 1,* 191–198.

van Valen, L. (1974). Brain size and intelligence in man. *American Journal of Physical Anthropology, 40,* 417–423.

van Zoeren, J. G., and Stricker, E. M. (1977). Effects of preoptic, lateral hypothalamic, or dopamine-depleting lesions on behavioral thermoregulation in rats exposed to the cold. *Journal of Comparative and Physiological Psychology, 91,* 989–999.

Vassar, R., Ngai, J., and Axel, R. (1993). Spatial segregation of odorant receptor expression in the mammalian olfactory epithelium. *Cell, 74,* 309–318.

Vaughan, W., and Greene, S. L. (1984). Pigeon visual memory capacity. *Journal of Experimental Psychology: Animal Behavior Processes, 10,* 256–271.

Veraa, R. P., and Grafstein, B. (1981). Cellular mechanisms for recovery from nervous system injury: A conference report. *Experimental Neurology, 71,* 6–75.

Verhagen, A. M., Ekert, P. G., Pakusch, M., Silke, J., et al. (2000). Identification of DIABLO, a mammalian protein that promotes apoptosis by binding to and antagonizing IAP proteins. *Cell, 102,* 43–53.

Villringer, A., and Chance, B. (1997). Non-invasive optical spectroscopy and imaging of human brain function. *Trends in Neurosciences, 20,* 435–442.

Virkkunen, M., and Linnoila, M. (1993). Brain serotonin, type II alcoholism and impulsive violence. *Journal of Studies on Alcohol (Supplement), 11,* 163–169.

Vitaterna, M. H., King, D. P., Chang, A. M., Kornhauser, J. M., et al. (1994). Mutagenesis and mapping of a mouse gene, Clock, essential for circadian behavior. *Science, 264,* 719–725.

Vogel, G. (1997). Cocaine wreaks subtle damage on developing brains. *Science, 278,* 38–39.

Vogel, G. (1999). Chimps in the wild show stirrings of culture. *Science, 284,* 2070–2073.

Vogel, G. W., Vogel, F., McAbee, R. S., and Thurmond, A. J. (1980). Improvement of depression by REM sleep deprivation: New findings and a theory. *Archives of General Psychiatry, 37,* 247–253.

Volkmar, F. R., and Greenough, W. T. (1972). Rearing complexity affects branching of dendrites in the visual cortex of the rat. *Science, 176,* 1445–1447.

Voneida, T. J. (1990). The effect of rubrospinal tractotomy on a conditioned limb response in the cat. *Society for Neuroscience Abstracts, 16,* 279.

Wada, J. A., and Rasmussen, T. (1960). Intracarotid injection of sodium amytal for the lateralization of cerebral speech dominance: Experimental and clinical observations. *Journal of Neurosurgery, 17,* 266–282.

Wagner, A. D., Desmond, J. E., Demb, J. B., Glover, G. H., et al. (1997). Semantic repetition priming for verbal and pictorial knowledge: A functional MRI study of left inferior prefrontal cortex. *Journal of Cognitive Neuroscience, 9,* 714–726.

Wagner, A. D., Schacter, D. L., Rotte, M., Koutstaal, W., et al. (1998). Building memories: Remembering and forgetting of verbal experiences as predicted by brain activity. *Science, 281,* 1188–1191.

Wagner, G. C., Beuving, L. J., and Hutchinson, R. R. (1980). The effects of gonadal hormone manipulations on aggressive target-biting in mice. *Aggressive Behavior, 6,* 1–7.

Wahl, O. F. (1976). Monozygotic twins discordant for schizophrenia: A review. *Psychological Bulletin, 83,* 91–106.

Wald, G. (1964). The receptors of human color vision. *Science, 145,* 1007–1016.

Walker, E. F. (1991). *Schizophrenia: A life-course developmental perspective.* San Diego, CA: Academic Press.

Wall, P. D. (1980). Mechanisms of plasticity of connection following damage of adult mammalian nervous systems. In P. Bach-y-Rita (Ed.), *Recovery of function: Theoretical considerations for brain injury rehabilitation* (pp. 1–2). Bern, Switzerland: Hans Huber.

Wall, P. D. (1991). *Defeating pain: The war against a silent epidemic.* New York: Plenum.

Wallace, C. S., Kilman, V. L., Withers, G. S., and Greenough, W. T. (1992). Increases in dendritic length in occipital cortex after 4 days of differential housing in weanling rats. *Behavioral & Neural Biology, 58,* 64–68.

Walls, G. L. (1942). *The vertebrate eye: Vol. 1.* Bloomfield Hills, MI: Cranbrook Institute of Science.

Walsh, R. N., Cummins, R. A., and Budtz-Olsen, O. E. (1973). Environmentally induced changes in the dimensions of the rat cerebrum: A replication and extension. *Developmental Psychobiology, 6,* 3–7.

Walters, R. J., Hadley, S. H., Morris, K. D. W., and Amin, J. (2000). Benzodiazepines act on GABA$_A$ receptors via two distinct and separable mechanisms. *Nature Neuroscience, 3,* 1273–1280.

Wang, F., Nemes, A., Mendelsohn, M., and Axel, R. (1998). Odorant receptors govern the formation of a precise topographic map. *Cell, 93,* 47–60.

Wang, J. B., Imai, Y., Eppler, C. M., Gregor, P., et al. (1993). µ Opiate receptor: cDNA cloning and expression. *Proceedings of the National Academy of Sciences, USA, 90,* 10230–10234.

Ward, I. L. (1969). Differential effect of pre- and postnatal androgen on the sexual behavior of intact and spayed female rats. *Hormones and Behavior, 1,* 25–36.

Wareing, M., Fisk, J. E., and Murphy, P. N. (2000). Working memory deficits in current and previous users of MDMA ("ecstasy"). *British Journal of Psychology, 91,* 181–188.

Watkins, J. C., and Collingridge, G. L. (1994). *The NMDA receptor* (2nd ed.). Oxford, England: Oxford University Press.

Waxman, S. G., and Kocsis, J. D. (1997). Spinal cord repair: Progress towards a daunting goal. *Neuroscientist, 3,* 263–269.

Webb, W. B. (1992). *Sleep, the gentle tyrant.* Bolton, MA: Anker.

Weeks, J. C., and Levine, R. B. (1990). Postembryonic neuronal plasticity and its hormonal control during insect metamorphosis. *Annual Review of Neuroscience, 13,* 183–194.

Wehling, M. (1997). Specific, nongenomic actions of steroid hormones. *Annual Review of Physiology, 59,* 365–393.

Wehr, T. A., Goodwin, F. K., Wirz-Justice, A., Breitmaier, J., et al. (1982). 48-hour sleep-wake cycles in manic-depressive illness: Naturalistic observations and sleep deprivation experiments. *Archives of General Psychiatry, 39,* 559–565.

Wehr, T. A., Jacobsen, F. M., Sack, D. A., Arendt, J., et al. (1986). Phototherapy of seasonal affective disorder. *Archives of General Psychiatry, 43,* 870–875.

Wehr, T. A., Sack, D. A., Duncan, W. C., Mendelson, W. B., et al. (1985). Sleep and circadian rhythms in affective patients isolated from external time cues. *Psychiatry Research, 15,* 327–339.

Wehr, T., Sack, D., Rosenthal, N., Duncan, W., et al. (1983). Circadian rhythm disturbances in manic-depressive illness. *Federation Proceedings, 42,* 2809–2814.

Weinberger, D. R. (1985). Clinical-neuropathological correlations in schizophrenia: Theoretical implications. In M. Alpert (Ed.), *Controversies in schizophrenia: Changes and constancies: Proceedings on the 74th Annual Meeting of the American Psychopathological Association, New York City, March 1–3, 1984* (pp. 92–106). New York: Guilford.

Weinberger, D. (1987). Implications of normal brain development for the pathogenesis of schizophrenia. *Archives of General Psychiatry, 44,* 660–669.

Weinberger, D. R., Aloia, M. S., Goldberg, T. E., and Berman, K. F. (1994). The frontal lobes and schizophrenia. *Journal of Neuropsychiatry and Clinical Neurosciences, 6,* 419–427.

Weinberger, D. R., Bigelow, L. B., Kleinman, J. E., Klein, S. T., et al. (1980). Cerebral ventricular enlargement in chronic schizophrenia. An association with poor response to treatment. *Archives of General Psychiatry, 37,* 11–13.

Weinberger, D. R., Zigun, J. R., Bartley, A. J., Jones, D. W., et al. (1992). Anatomical abnormalities in the brains of monozygotic twins discordant and concordant for schizophrenia. *Clinical Neuropharmacology, 15,* 122A–123A.

Weinberger, N. M. (1995). Dynamic regulation of receptive fields and maps in the adult sensory cortex. *Annual Review of Neuroscience, 18,* 129–159.

Weinberger, N. M. (1998). Physiological memory in primary auditory cortex: Characteristics and mechanisms. *Neurobiology of Learning and Memory, 70,* 226–251.

Weindruch, R., and Walford, R. L. (1988). *The retardation of aging and disease by dietary restriction.* Springfield, IL: Thomas.

Weiner, H. (1992). *Perturbing the organism: The biology of stressful experience.* Chicago: University of Chicago Press.

Weiner, R. D. (1994). Treatment optimization with ECT. *Psychopharmacology Bulletin, 30,* 313–320.

Weingarten, H., Chang, P., and Mcdonald, T. (1985). Comparison of the metabolic and behavioral disturbances following paraventricular- and ventromedial-hypothalamic lesions. *Brain Research Bulletin, 14,* 551–559.

Weitzman, E. D. (1981). Sleep and its disorders. *Annual Review of Neurosciences, 4,* 381–417.

Weitzman, E. D., Czeisler, C. A., Zimmerman, J. C., and Moore-Ede, M. C. (1981). Biological rhythms in man: Relationship of sleep-wake, cortisol, growth hormone, and temperature during temporal isolation. In J. B. Martin, S. Reichlin, and K. L. Bick (Eds.), *Neurosecretion and brain peptides.* New York: Raven.

Weller, L., and Weller, A. (1993). Human menstrual synchrony: A critical assessment. *Neuroscience and Biobehavioral Reviews, 17,* 427–439.

Wessberg, J., Stambaugh, C. R., Kralik, J. D., Beck, P. D., et al. (2000). Real-time predictions of hand trajectory by ensembles of cortical neurons in primates. *Nature, 408,* 361–365.

West, R. W., and Greenough, W. T. (1972). Effect of environmental complexity on cortical synapses of rats: Preliminary results. *Behavioral Biology, 7,* 279–284.

Westergaard, G. C., Kuhn, H. E., and Suomi, S. J. (1998). Bipedal posture and hand preference in humans and other primates. *Journal of Comparative Psychology, 112,* 55–64.

Westheimer, G. (1984). Spatial vision. *Annual Review of Psychology, 35,* 201–226.

Wever, E. G. (1974). The evolution of vertebrate hearing. In W. D. Keidel and W. D. Neff (Eds.), Handbook of sensory physiology: Vol. 5. Auditory system. New York: Springer.

Wever, R. A. (1979). Influence of physical workload on freerunning circadian rhythms of man. *Pflugers Archiv. European Journal of Physiology, 381,* 119–126.

Wexler, B. E., and Heninger, G. R. (1979). Alterations in cerebral laterality during acute psychotic illness. *Archives of General Psychiatry, 36,* 278–284.

Wexler, N. S., Rose, E. A., and Housman, D. E. (1991). Molecular approaches to hereditary diseases of the nervous system: Huntington's disease as a paradigm. *Annual Review of Neuroscience, 14,* 503–529.

White, L. E., and Hain, R. F. (1959). Anorexia in association with a destructive lesion of the hypothalamus. *Archives of Pathology, 68,* 275–281.

White, N. M., and Milner, P. M. (1992). The psychobiology of reinforcers. *Annual Review of Psychology, 43,* 443–471.

Whiten, A., Goodall, J., McGrew, W. C., Nishida, T., et al. (1999). Cultures in chimpanzees. *Nature, 399,* 682–685.

Wible, C. G., Shenton, M. E., Hokama, H., Kikinis, R., et al. (1995). Prefrontal cortex and schizophrenia. A quantitative magnetic resonance imaging study. *Archives of General Psychiatry, 52,* 279–288.

Wickelgren, I. (1998). Teaching the spinal cord to walk. *Science, 279,* 319–321.

Wiesel, T. N., and Hubel, D. H. (1963). Single-cell responses in striate cortex of kittens deprived of vision in one eye. *Journal of Neurophsyiology, 26,* 1002–1017.

Wiesel, T. N., and Hubel, D. H. (1965). Extent of recovery from the effects of visual deprivation in kittens. *Journal of Neurophysiology, 28,* 1060–1072.

Wikler, K. C., and Rakic, P. (1990). Distribution of photoreceptor subtypes in the retina of diurnal and nocturnal primates. *Journal of Neuroscience, 10,* 3390–3401.

Wiklund, C., and Sillén-Tullberg, B. (1985). Why distasteful butterflies have aposematic larvae and adults, but cryptic pupae: Evidence from predation experiments on the monarch and the European swallowtail. *Evolution, 39,* 1155–1158.

Will, B. E., Rosenzweig, M. R., Bennett, E. L., Hebert, M., et al. (1977). Relatively brief environmental enrichment aids recovery of learning capacity and alters brain measures after postweaning brain lesions in rats. *Journal of Comparative and Physiological Psychology, 91,* 33–50.

Willerman, L., Schultz, R., Rutledge, J. N., and Bigler, E. D. (1991). In vivo brain size and intelligence. *Intelligence, 15,* 223–228.

Williams, D. (1969). Neural factors related to habitual aggression. *Brain, 92,* 503–520.

Williams, T. J., Pepitone, M. E., Christensen, S. E., Cooke, B. M., et al. Huberman, A. D., Breedlove, N. J., Breedlove, T. J., Jordan, C. L., and Breedlove, S. M. (2000). Finger-length ratios and sexual orientation. *Nature, 404,* 455–456.

Willner, P. (1991). *Behavioural models in psychopharmacology.* New York: Cambridge University Press.

Wilson, M. A., and McNaughton, B. L. (1994). Reactivation of hippocampal ensemble memories during sleep. *Science, 165,* 676–679.

Winberg, S., Winberg, Y., and Fernald, R. D. (1997). Effect of social rank on brain monoaminergic activity in a cichlid fish. *Brain, Behavior and Evolution, 49,* 230–236.

Wingard, D. L., and Berkman, L. F. (1983). Mortality risk associated with sleeping patterns among adults. *Sleep, 6,* 102–107.

Wingfield, J. C., Ball, G. F., Dufty, A. M., Hegner, R. E., et al. (1987). Testosterone and aggression in birds. *American Scientist, 75,* 602–608.

Winocur, G. (1990). Anterograde and retrograde amnesia in rats with dorsal hippocampal or dorsomedial thalamic lesions. *Behavioural Brain Research, 38,* 145–154.

Wise, R. A. (1984). Neural mechanisms of the reinforcing action of cocaine. In J. Grabowski (Ed.), *NIDA Research Monograph: 50. Cocaine: Pharmacology, effects and treatment of abuse* (pp. 15–33). Rockville, MD: National Institute on Drug Abuse.

Wise, R. A. (1996). Neurobiology of addiction. *Current Opinion in Neurobiology, 6,* 243–251.

Wise, R. A. (1997). Drug self-administration viewed as ingestive behaviour. *Appetite, 28,* 1–5.

Wise, R. A., Bauco, P., Carlezon, W. A., Jr., and Trojniar, W. (1992). Self-stimulation and drug reward mechanisms. *Annals of the New York Academy of Sciences, 654,* 192–198.

Wise, S. P., and Strick, P. L. (1984). Anatomical and physiological organization of the non-primary motor cortex. *Trends in Neurosciences, 7,* 442–447.

Witelson, S. F., and Pallie, W. (1973). Left hemisphere specialization for language in the newborn. Neuroanatomical evidence of asymmetry. *Brain, 96,* 641–646.

Wolf, S. S., Jones, D. W., Knable, M. B., Gorey, J. G., et al. (1996). Tourette syndrome: Prediction of phenotypic variation in monozygotic twins by caudate nucleus D2 receptor binding. *Science, 273,* 1225–1227.

Wolinsky, E., and Way, J. (1990). The behavioral genetics of *Caenorhabditis elegans. Behavior Genetics, 20,* 169–189.

Woo, C. C., and Leon, M. (1987). Sensitive period for neural and behavioral response development to learned odors. *Developmental Brain Research, 36,* 309–313.

Wood, J. M., Bootzin, R. R., Kihlstrom, J. F., and Schacter, D. L. (1992). Implicit and explicit memory for verbal information presented during sleep. *Psychological Science, 3(_4),* 236–239.

Woodruff-Pak, D. S., and Jaeger, M. E. (1998). Predictors of eyeblink classical conditioning over the adult age span. *Psychology and Aging, 13,* 193–205.

Woolf, C. J., and Salter, M. W. (2000). Neuronal plasticity: Increasing the gain in pain. *Science, 288,* 1765–1769.

Woolsey, C. N. (1981a). *Cortical sensory organization: Multiple auditory areas.* Crescent Manor, NJ: Humana.

Woolsey, C. N. (1981b). *Cortical sensory organization: Multiple somatic areas.* Crescent Manor, NJ: Humana.

Woolsey, C. N. (1981c). *Cortical sensory organization: Multiple visual areas.* Crescent Manor, NJ: Humana.

Woolsey, T. A., Durham, D., Harris, R. M., Simous, D. T., et al. (1981). Somatosensory development. In R. S. Aslin, J. R. Alberts, and M. R. Peterson (Eds.), *Sensory and perceptual development: Influence of genetic and experiential factors.* New York: Academic Press.

Woolsey, T. A., and Wann, J. R. (1976). Areal changes in mouse cortical barrels following vibrissal damage at different postnatal ages. *Journal of Comparative Neurology, 170,* 53–66.

Wright, A. A., Santiago, H. C., Sands, S. F., Kendrick, D. F., et al. (1985). Memory processing of serial lists by pigeons, monkeys, and people. *Science, 229,* 287–289.

Wu, J. Y., Cohen, L. B., and Falk, C. X. (1994). Neuronal activity during different behaviors in *Aplysia:* A distributed organization? *Science, 263,* 820–823.

Wuethrich, B. (2000). Learning the world's languages—before they vanish. *Science, 288,* 1156–1159.

Xerri, C., Coq, J., Merzenich, M., and Jenkins, W. (1996). Experience-induced plasticity of cutaneous maps in the primary somatosensory cortex of adult monkeys and rats. *Journal de Physiologie, 90,* 277–287.

Xu, L., Furukawa, S., and Middlebrooks, J. C. (1999). Auditory cortical responses in the cat to sounds that produce spatial illusions. *Nature, 399,* 688–691.

Yahr, P., and Gregory, J. E. (1993). The medial and lateral cell groups of the sexually dimorphic area of the gerbil hypothalamus are essential for male sex behavior and act via separate pathways. *Brain Research, 631,* 287–296.

Yamazaki, S., Numano, R., Abe, M., Hida, A., et al. (2000). Resetting central and peripheral circadian oscillators in transgenic rats. *Science, 288,* 682–685.

Yanagisawa, K., Bartoshuk, L. M., Catalanotto, F. A., Karrer, T. A., et al. (1992). Anesthesia of the chorda tympani nerve: Insights into a source of dysgeusia. *Chemical Senses, 17,* 724.

Yang, T. T., Gallen, C. C., Ramachandran, V. S., Cobb, S., et al. (1994). Noninvasive detection of cerebral plasticity in adult human somatosensory cortex. *Neuroreport, 5,* 701–704.

Yasuda, K., Raynor, K., Kong, H., Breder, C., et al. (1993). Cloning and functional comparison of kappa and delta opioid receptors from mouse brain. *Proceedings of the National Academy of Sciences, USA, 90,* 6736–6740.

Yin, J. C., Del Vecchio, M., Zhou, H., and Tully, T. (1995). CREB as a memory modulator: Induced expression of a dCREB2 activator isoform enhances long-term memory in *Drosophila. Cell, 81,* 107–115.

Yin, J. C., Wallach, J. S., Del Vecchio, M., Wilder, E. L., et al. (1994). Induction of a dominant negative CREB transgene specifically blocks long-term memory in *Drosophila. Cell, 79,* 49–58.

Yoon, J.-W., Yoon, C.-S., Lim, H.-W., Huang, Q. Q., et al. (1999). Control of autoimmune diabetes in NOD mice by GAD expression or suppressiosn in β cells. *Science, 284,* 1183–1187.

Yoshinaga-Itano, C. (1999). Benefits of early intervention for children with hearing loss. *Otolaryngologic Clinics of North America, 32,* 1089–1102.

Young, A. B. (1993). Role of excitotoxins in heredito-degenerative neurologic diseases. *Research Publications—Association for Research in Nervous and Mental Disease, 71,* 175–189.

Young, A. W., Hellawell, D. J., Van De Wal, C., and Johnson, M. (1996). Facial expression processing after amygdalotomy. *Neuropsychologia, 34,* 31–39.

Young, D., Lawlor, P. A., Leone, P., Dragunow, M., et al. (1999). Environmental enrichment inhibits spontaneous apoptosis, prevents seizures and is neuroprotective. *Nature Medicine, 5,* 448–453.

Yu, S., Pritchard, M., Kremer, E., Lynch, M., et al. (1991). Fragile X genotype characterized by an unstable region of DNA. *Science, 252,* 1179–1181.

Zaidel, E. (1976). Auditory vocabulary of the right hemisphere following brain bisection or hemidecortication. *Cortex, 12,* 191–211.

Zantua, J. B., Wasserstrom, S. P., Arends, J. J., Jacquin, M. F., et al. (1996). Postnatal development of mouse "whisker" thalamus: Ventroposterior medial nucleus (VPM), barreloids, and their thalamocortical relay neurons. *Somatosensory and Motor Research, 13,* 307–322.

Zatorre, R. J., Evans, A. C., and Meyer, E. (1994). Neural mechanisms underlying melodic perception and memory for pitch. *Journal of Neuroscience, 14,* 1908–1919.

Zecevic, N., and Rakic, P. (1976). Differentiation of Purkinje cells and their relationship to other components of developing cerebellar cortex in man. *Journal of Comparative Neurology, 167,* 27–48.

Zeki, S. (1993). *A vision of the brain.* London: Blackwell.

Zeki, S., Watson, J. D., Lueck, C. J., Friston, K. J., et al. (1991). A direct demonstration of functional specialization in human visual cortex. *Journal of Neuroscience, 11,* 641–649.

Zeng, F. G., and Shannon, R. V. (1999). Psychophysical laws revealed by electric hearing. *Neuroreport, 10,* 1931–1935.

Zhang, L. I., Tao, H. W., Holt, C. E., Harris, W. A., et al. (1998). A critical window for cooperation and competition among developing retinotectal synapses. *Nature, 395,* 37–44.

Zhang, Y., Proenca, R., Maffei, M., Barone, M., et al. (1994). Positional cloning of the mouse obese gene and its human homologue. *Nature, 372,* 425–432.

Zhao, H., Ivic, L., Otaki, J. M., Hashimoto, M., et al. (1998). Functional expression of a mammalian odorant receptor. *Science, 279,* 237–242.

Zheng, J. L., and Gao, W. Q. (2000). Overexpression of Math1 induces robust production of extra hair cells in postnatal rat inner ears. *Nature Neuroscience, 3,* 580–586.

Zheng, J., Shen, W., He, D. Z., Long, K. B., et al. (2000). Prestin is the motor protein of cochlear outer hair cells. *Nature, 405,* 149–155.

Zihl, J., von Cramon, D., and Mai, N. (1983). Selective disturbance of movement vision after bilateral brain damage. *Brain, 106,* 313–340.

Zola, S. M., and Squire, L. R. (2000). The medial temporal lobe and the hippocampus. In E. Tulving and F. I. M. Craik (Eds.), *The Oxford handbook of memory* (pp. 485–500). Oxford, England: Oxford University Press.

Zola-Morgan, S., and Squire, L. R. (1986). Memory impairment in monkeys following lesions of the hippocampus. *Behavioral Neuroscience, 100,* 155–160.

Zola-Morgan, S. M., and Squire, L. R. (1990). The primate hippocampal formation: Evidence for a time-limited role in memory storage. *Science, 250,* 288–290.

Zola-Morgan, S., Squire, L. R., and Ramus, S. J. (1994). Severity of memory impairment in monkeys as a function of locus and extent of damage within the medial temporal lobe memory system. *Hippocampus, 4,* 483–495.

Zolman, J. F., and Morimoto, H. (1962). Effects of age of training on cholinesterase activity in the brain of maze-bright rats. *Journal of Comparative and Physiological Psychology, 55,* 794–800.

Zucker, I. (1976). Light, behavior, and biologic rhythms. *Hospital Practice, 11,* 83–91.

Zucker, I. (1988). Seasonal affective disorders: Animal models non fingo. *Journal of Biological Rhythms, 3,* 209–223.

Zucker, I., Boshes, M., and Dark, J. (1983). Suprachiasmatic nuclei influence circannual and circadian rhythms of ground squirrels. *American Journal of Physiology, 244,* R472–R480.

Zucker, L. M., and Zucker, T. F. (1961). "Fatty," a mutation in the rat. *Journal of Heredity, 52,* 275–278.

Zurek, P. M. (1981). Spontaneous narrowband acoustic signals emitted by human ears. *Journal of the Acoustical Society of America, 69,* 514–523.

Author Index

Subject Index

Illustration Credits

The following figures use elements originally rendered for *Neuroanatomy through Clinical Cases* by Hal Blumenfeld, M.D., Ph.D. (Blumenfeld, 2002): Figures 1.12*b*, 2.8, 2.10, 2.14, 2.15, 2.18, 2.19*a*, 2.20, Box 3.2A, 4.2, 4.3, 4.4, 4.5, 5.10, 5.11, 5.12, 5.16, 5.18, 5.19*a*, 5.21, 6.7, 7.23, 7.25, 8.4, 8.6, 8.8, 8.12, 8.17*a*, 8.18*a*, 8.19, 8.22, 11.13*a*, 11.16, 11.17, 11.21, 13.3, 13.22, 13.28, 15.7, 15.14, 16.12, 17.1, 17.3, 19.6, 19.8, 19.10, 19.11, 19.16*a*, 19.19*a*.

Chapter 1

1.1 "Brainy Dolphins Pass the Human 'Mirror' Test" © 2001 by The New York Times Company; "When the Heart Sings, Part of the Cortex Gets Busy" © 1999 by The New York Times Company; "In Early Experiments, Cells Repair Damaged Brains"© 2000 by The New York Times Company; "The New Science of Alzheimer's Disease" © 2000 by Time Pix.
1.10 Reproduced with gracious permission of Her Majesty Queen Elizabeth II, copyright reserved.
1.11 © Bettmann/CORBIS.
1.12*a* © Bettmann/CORBIS.

Chapter 2

2.4*b* TEM © Dennis Kunkel Microscopy, Inc.
2.7*b* From Gray's Anatomy, 35th ed, Figure 2.9, page 807. Reprinted with permission of the publisher Churchill Livingstone. (Dissection by M. C. E. Hutchinson, photograph by Kevin Fitzpatrick, Guy's Hospital Medical School, London.)
2.21 CT scans © Dan McCoy/Rainbow. MRIs © Hank Morgan, Science Source/Photo Researchers, Inc. PET scans courtesy of Jamie Eberling.

Chapter 3

3.19*a* Courtesy of Neuroscan Labs, a division of Neurosoft, Inc.

Chapter 4

4.6 © Biological Photo Service.
4.11 © Roger Ressmeyer/CORBIS.

Chapter 5

5.17 © J. H. Robinson/Photo Researchers, Inc.

Chapter 8

8.1(*a*) © 1986 Scott Camazine/Photo Researchers Inc.; (*b*) © Art Wolfe; (*c*) © Tom McHugh/Photo Reserachers, Inc.; (*d*) © Art Wolfe.
8.20 Culver Pictures, Inc.

Chapter 12

12.1 Courtesy of James Thurber Literary Properties.
12.9*c* © Mark Smith/Photo Researchers, Inc.
12.11 Yorgos Nikas/Tony Stone Images.
12.13 Doug Wechsler/VIREO.
Box 12.2 Stephen Glickman; © Laurence Frank.

Chapter 13

13.2(*a*) Steinhart Aquarium, © Tom McHugh/Photo Researchers, Inc.; (*b*) © Tim Davis/Photo Researchers, Inc.
13.5(*a*) © Wm. Bacon III/Photo Researchers, Inc.; (*b*) © 1989 G. J. James/Biological Photo Service.
13.6 © Art Wolfe.
13.19 © Rod Planck/Photo Researchers, Inc.
13.27 John Sholtis/The Rockefeller University.
13.30(*a*) AP/Wide World Photos. (*b*) Kunsthistorisches Museum, Vienna.

Chapter 16

16.17 © EURELIOS/Phototake.

Chapter 17

Box 17.1 (A) © Bettmann/CORBIS; (C) © Richard Wood/The Picture Cube.

Chapter 18

Box 18.1 © Princeton University.

Scientist Photographs

Chapter 6: Charles Darwin, Karl Lashley: © Bettmann/CORBIS; Theodore Bullock: Neuroscience History Archives, Brain Research Institute, University of California, Los Angeles.

Chapter 9: Georg von Békésy: courtesy of Harvard University Press.

Chapter 10: Torsten Wiesel: Robert Reichert.

Chapter 11: Sir Charles Sherrington: Neuroscience History Archives, Brain Research Institute, University of California, Los Angeles.

Chapter 12: Alfred Kinsey: The Kinsey Institute for Research in Sex, Gender, and Reproduction. Photograph by William Dellenback; Virginia Johnson and William Masters: Becker Medical Library of Washington University, Saint Louis.

Chapter 13: Jeffrey Friedman: courtesy of Rockefeller University; John Garcia: Neuroscience History Archives, Brain Research Institute, University of California, Los Angeles.

About the Book

Editor: Peter Farley

Project Editor: Kerry Falvey

Copy Editor: Stephanie Hiebert

Production Manager: Christopher Small

Book Production: Janice Holabird, Joan Gemme, and Jefferson Johnson in QuarkXpress on the Macintosh

Art: J/B Woolsey Associates

Photo Researcher: David McIntyre

Fine Art Consultant: Steven Diamond, Inc.

Book and Cover Design: Jefferson Johnson

Cover Manufacturer: Courier Companies, Inc.

Book Manufacturer: Courier Companies, Inc.